NINETY-SIXTH EDITION
SINCE 1912

WHO'S WHO IN BASEBALL 2011

Official Lifetime Records Of Major League Players

Editor
Pete Palmer

Associate Editor
Stuart Shea

Managing Editor
Rory S. Slifkin

EDITOR'S NOTE: *Denotes League Leader throughout the publication.

WHO'S WHO IN BASEBALL is published annually by Who's Who in Baseball Magazine Co., Inc., 1115 Broadway, New York, New York 10010. Single copy price: $9.95. Submissions of manuscripts, illustrations and/or photographs must be accompanied by a stamped, self-addressed envelope. The publisher assumes no responsibility for unsolicited material.

BATTERS

ABREU, BOB KELLY (BOBBY)

Born, Maracay, Venezuela, March 11, 1974.
Bats Left. Throws Right. Height, 6 feet. Weight, 210 pounds.

Year Club	Lea	Pos	G	AB	R	H	2B	3B	HR	RBI	SB	Avg
1991 Astros	Gulf Coast	OF-SS	56	183	21	55	7	3	0	20	10	.301
1992 Asheville...........	So. Atl.	OF	135	480	81	140	21	4	8	48	15	.292
1993 Osceola	Fla. St.	OF	129	474	62	134	21	17	5	55	10	.283
1994 Jackson	Texas	OF	118	400	61	121	25	9	16	73	12	.303
1995 Tucson	P.C.	OF-2B	114	415	72	126	24	17	10	75	16	.304
1996 Tucson	P.C.	OF	132	484	86	138	14	16	13	68	24	.285
1996 Houston	N.L.	OF	15	22	1	5	1	0	0	1	0	.227
1997 Jackson	Texas	OF	3	12	2	2	1	0	0	0	0	.167
1997 New Orleans..........	A.A.	OF	47	194	25	52	9	4	2	22	7	.268
1997 Houston a-b-c	N.L.	OF	59	188	22	47	10	2	3	26	7	.250
1998 Philadelphia	N.L.	OF	151	497	68	155	29	6	17	74	19	.312
1999 Philadelphia	N.L.	OF	152	546	118	183	35	*11	20	93	27	.335
2000 Philadelphia	N.L.	OF	154	576	103	182	42	10	25	79	28	.316
2001 Philadelphia	N.L.	OF	*162	588	118	170	48	4	31	110	36	.289
2002 Philadelphia	N.L.	OF	157	572	102	176	*50	6	20	85	31	.308
2003 Philadelphia	N.L.	OF	158	577	99	173	35	1	20	101	22	.300
2004 Philadelphia	N.L.	OF	159	574	118	173	47	1	30	105	40	.301
2005 Philadelphia	N.L.	OF	*162	588	104	168	37	1	24	102	31	.286
2006 Philadelphia	N.L.	OF	98	339	61	94	25	2	8	65	20	.277
2006 New York d...........	A.L.	OF	58	209	37	69	16	0	7	42	10	.330
2007 New York	A.L.	OF	158	605	123	171	40	5	16	101	25	.283
2008 New York e...........	A.L.	OF	156	609	100	180	39	4	20	100	22	.296
2009 Los Angeles	A.L.	OF	152	563	96	165	29	3	15	103	30	.293
2010 Los Angeles	A.L.	OF	154	573	88	146	41	1	20	78	24	.255
Major League Totals		15 Yrs.	2105	7626	1358	2257	524	57	276	1265	372	.296
Division Series												
1997 Houston	N.L.	PH	3	3	0	1	0	0	0	0	1	.333
2006 New York	A.L.	OF	4	15	2	5	1	0	0	4	0	.333
2007 New York	A.L.	OF	4	15	1	4	1	0	1	2	1	.267
2009 Los Angeles	A.L.	OF	3	9	4	5	2	0	0	1	0	.556
Division Series Totals			14	42	7	15	4	0	1	7	2	.357
Championship Series												
2009 Los Angeles	A.L.	OF	6	25	2	4	2	0	0	2	0	.160

a On disabled list from May 25 to July 1, 1997.
b Selected in expansion draft by Tampa Bay Devil Rays, November 18, 1997.
c Traded to Philadelphia Phillies for infielder Kevin Stocker, November 19, 1997.
d Traded to New York Yankees with pitcher Cory Lidle for infielder C.J. Henry, pitcher Matt Smith, catcher Jesus Sanchez and pitcher Carlos Monasterios, July 30, 2006.
e Filed for free agency, October 30, 2008. Signed with Los Angeles Angels, February 12, 2009.

ABREU, ETANISLAO TONI (TONY)

Born, Puerta Plato, Dominican Republic, November 13, 1984.
Bats Both. Throws Right. Height, 5 feet, 11 inches. Weight, 200 pounds.

Year Club	Lea	Pos	G	AB	R	H	2B	3B	HR	RBI	SB	Avg
2003 Vero Beach..........	Fla.St.	2B	3	10	0	0	0	0	0	0	0	.000
2003 Dodgers	Gulf Coast	2B-SS	44	163	30	48	7	5	0	20	9	.294
2004 Vero Beach..........	Fla.St.	SS	11	43	8	18	3	1	0	3	4	.419
2004 Columbus...........	So.Atl.	2B-SS	104	358	50	108	21	8	8	54	16	.302
2005 Vero Beach..........	Fla.St.	2B-SS	96	394	54	129	23	7	4	43	14	.327
2005 Jacksonville	Southern	2B-SS	24	96	10	24	3	2	0	9	0	.250
2006 Jacksonville	Southern	2B-SS	118	457	66	131	24	3	6	55	8	.287
2007 Las Vegas............	P.C.	2B-SS-3B	54	234	48	83	22	5	2	18	5	.355
2007 Los Angeles	N.L.	3B-2B-SS	59	166	19	45	14	1	2	17	0	.271
2008 Los Angeles a.........	N.L.			INJURED—Did Not Play								
2009 Chattanooga......	Southern	2B-SS	23	89	11	26	4	1	0	5	0	.292
2009 Albuquerque...........	P.C.	2B-3B-SS	54	218	36	77	18	3	11	48	3	.353
2009 Los Angeles b	N.L.	2B-3B	6	8	0	2	0	0	0	1	0	.250
2010 Reno	P.C.	SS-2B-3B	24	94	17	33	7	1	2	21	2	.351
2010 Arizona c	N.L.	3B-SS-2B	81	193	16	45	11	1	1	13	2	.233
Major League Totals		3 Yrs.	146	367	35	92	25	2	3	31	2	.251

a On disabled list from March 26 to November 4, 2008.
b Sent to Arizona Diamondbacks as player to be named later for pitcher Jon Garland, October 9, 2009.
c On disabled list from May 24 to June 15, 2010.

ALLEN, BRANDON DURELL

Born, Conroe, Texas, February 12, 1986.
Bats Left. Throws Right. Height, 6 feet, 2 inches. Weight, 235 pounds.

Year	Club	Lea	Pos	G	AB	R	H	2B	3B	HR	RBI	SB	Avg
2004	Bristol	Appal.	1B-OF	58	185	17	38	9	1	3	23	2	.205
2005	Great Falls	Pioneer	1B	66	231	41	61	11	2	11	42	7	.264
2006	Kannapolis	So.Atl.	1B	109	395	36	84	17	2	15	68	6	.213
2007	Kannapolis	So.Atl.	1B	129	516	84	146	39	5	18	93	7	.283
2008	Winston-Salem	Carolina	1B	89	319	57	89	26	4	15	44	14	.279
2008	Birmingham	Southern	1B	41	153	30	42	6	2	14	31	3	.275
2009	Birmingham	Southern	1B	62	241	39	70	12	3	7	35	1	.290
2009	Reno	P.C.	1B	38	145	33	47	8	1	12	32	6	.324
2009	Charlotte	Int.	1B	15	61	6	16	4	0	1	8	0	.262
2009	Arizona a	N.L.	1B	32	104	13	21	7	0	4	14	0	.202
2010	Reno	P.C.	1B-OF	107	371	72	97	18	3	25	86	14	.261
2010	Arizona	N.L.	OF-1B	22	45	5	12	3	0	1	6	0	.267
Major League Totals			2 Yrs.	54	149	18	33	10	0	5	20	0	.221

a Traded by Chicago White Sox to Arizona Diamondbacks for pitcher Tony Pena, July 7, 2009.

ALVAREZ, PEDRO MANUEL

Born, New York, New York, February 6, 1987.
Bats Left. Throws Right. Height, 6 feet, 3 inches. Weight, 225 pounds.

Year	Club	Lea	Pos	G	AB	R	H	2B	3B	HR	RBI	SB	Avg
2009	Lynchburg	Carolina	3B	66	243	38	60	14	1	14	55	1	.247
2009	Altoona	Eastern	3B	60	222	42	74	18	0	13	40	1	.333
2010	Indianapolis	Int.	3B	66	242	42	67	15	4	13	53	4	.277
2010	Pittsburgh	N.L.	3B	95	347	42	89	21	1	16	64	0	.256

ANDERSON, GARRET JOSEPH

Born, Los Angeles, California, June 30, 1972.
Bats Left. Throws Left. Height, 6 feet, 3 inches. Weight, 225 pounds.

Year	Club	Lea	Pos	G	AB	R	H	2B	3B	HR	RBI	SB	Avg
1990	Mesa Angels	Arizona	OF	32	127	5	27	2	0	0	14	3	.213
1990	Boise	Northwest	OF	25	83	11	21	3	1	1	8	0	.253
1991	Quad City	Midwest	OF	105	392	40	102	22	2	2	42	5	.260
1992	Palm Springs	California	OF	81	322	46	104	15	2	1	62	1	.323
1992	Midland	Texas	OF	39	146	16	40	5	0	2	19	2	.274
1993	Vancouver	P.C.	OF-1B	124	467	57	137	34	4	4	71	3	.293
1994	Vancouver	P.C.	OF-1B	123	505	75	162	42	6	12	102	3	.321
1994	California	A.L.	OF	5	13	0	5	0	0	0	1	0	.385
1995	Vancouver	P.C.	OF	14	61	9	19	7	0	0	12	0	.311
1995	California	A.L.	OF	106	374	50	120	19	1	16	69	6	.321
1996	California	A.L.	OF	150	607	79	173	33	2	12	72	7	.285
1997	Anaheim	A.L.	OF	154	624	76	189	36	3	8	92	10	.303
1998	Anaheim	A.L.	OF	156	622	62	183	41	7	15	79	8	.294
1999	Anaheim	A.L.	OF	157	620	88	188	36	2	21	80	3	.303
2000	Anaheim	A.L.	OF	159	647	92	185	40	3	35	117	7	.286
2001	Anaheim	A.L.	OF	161	672	83	194	39	2	28	123	13	.289
2002	Anaheim	A.L.	OF	158	638	93	195	*56	3	29	123	6	.306
2003	Anaheim	A.L.	OF	159	638	80	201	*49	4	29	116	6	.315
2004	Rancho Cucamonga	Calif.	OF	3	9	1	4	0	0	1	1	0	.444
2004	Anaheim a	A.L.	OF	112	442	57	133	20	1	14	75	2	.301
2005	Los Angeles	A.L.	OF	142	575	68	163	34	1	17	96	1	.283
2006	Los Angeles	A.L.	OF	141	543	63	152	28	2	17	85	1	.280
2007	Rancho Cucamonga	Calif.	OF	6	18	3	4	1	0	0	2	0	.222
2007	Los Angeles b	A.L.	OF	108	417	67	124	31	1	16	80	1	.297
2008	Los Angeles c	A.L.	OF	145	557	66	163	27	3	15	84	7	.293
2009	Atlanta d-e-f	N.L.	OF	135	496	52	133	27	0	13	61	1	.268
2010	Los Angeles f	N.L.	OF	80	155	8	28	6	1	2	12	1	.181
Major League Totals			17 Yrs.	2228	8640	1084	2529	522	36	287	1365	80	.293
	Division Series												
2002	Anaheim	A.L.	OF	4	18	5	7	2	0	1	4	0	.389
2004	Anaheim	A.L.	OF	3	13	1	2	0	0	0	0	0	.154
2005	Los Angeles	A.L.	OF	5	19	2	5	0	1	2	7	0	.263
2007	Los Angeles	A.L.	OF	3	9	0	2	1	0	0	0	0	.222
2008	Los Angeles	A.L.	OF	4	19	1	3	0	0	0	0	0	.158
Division Series Totals				19	78	9	19	3	1	3	11	0	.244

Year Club	Lea	Pos	G	AB	R	H	2B	3B	HR	RBI	SB	Avg
Championship Series												
2002 Anaheim	A.L.	OF	5	20	3	5	1	0	1	3	0	.250
2005 Los Angeles	A.L.	OF	5	17	2	3	0	0	1	2	0	.176
Championship Series Totals			10	37	5	8	1	0	2	5	0	.216
World Series Record												
2002 Anaheim	A.L.	OF	7	32	3	9	1	0	0	6	0	.281

a On disabled list from April 22 to June 10, 2004.
b On disabled list from April 28 to June 3 and June 17 to July 3, 2007.
c Not offered contract, October 28, 2008. Signed with Atlanta Braves, February 24, 2009.
d On disabled list from April 20 to May 5, 2009.
e Filed for free agency, November 5, 2009. Signed with Los Angeles Dodgers organization, March 4, 2010.
f Released by Los Angeles Dodgers, August 9, 2010.

ANDINO, ROBERT LAZARO

Born, Miami, Florida, April 25, 1984.
Bats Right. Throws Right. Height, 6 feet. Weight, 195 pounds.

Year Club	Lea	Pos	G	AB	R	H	2B	3B	HR	RBI	SB	Avg
2002 Marlins	Gulf Coast	SS	9	27	2	7	0	0	0	2	3	.259
2002 Jamestown	N.Y.-Penn.	SS	9	36	2	6	1	1	0	3	1	.167
2003 Greensboro	So.Atl.	SS	119	416	45	78	17	2	2	27	6	.188
2004 Jupiter	Fla.St.	SS-2B	48	196	18	55	7	2	0	15	6	.281
2004 Greensboro	So.Atl.	SS	76	295	27	83	10	1	8	46	9	.281
2005 Carolina	Southern	SS-2B	127	516	63	139	30	0	5	48	22	.269
2005 Florida	N.L.	SS	17	44	4	7	4	0	0	1	1	.159
2006 Albuquerque	P.C.	SS-2B	120	498	70	127	18	6	8	46	13	.255
2006 Florida	N.L.	SS	11	24	0	4	1	0	0	2	1	.167
2007 Albuquerque	P.C.	SS-2B	142	598	85	166	25	13	13	50	21	.278
2007 Florida	N.L.	SS	7	13	0	5	1	0	0	0	0	.385
2008 Albuquerque	P.C.	SS-2B	43	181	28	52	14	3	6	26	9	.287
2008 Florida	N.L.	2B-SS-3B-OF	44	63	7	13	2	0	2	9	0	.206
2009 Baltimore a	A.L.	SS-2B-3B-OF	78	198	31	44	7	0	2	10	3	.222
2010 Norfolk	Int.	SS-2B	132	546	72	144	30	4	13	76	16	.264
2010 Baltimore	A.L.	2B-SS-3B	16	61	6	18	4	0	2	6	1	.295
Major League Totals		6 Yrs.	173	403	48	91	19	0	6	28	6	.226

a Traded to Baltimore Orioles for pitcher Hayden Penn, April 1, 2009.

ANDRUS (TORRES), ELVIS AUGUSTO

Born, Maracay, Venezuela, August 26, 1988.
Bats Right. Throws Right. Height, 6 feet. Weight, 185 pounds.

Year Club	Lea	Pos	G	AB	R	H	2B	3B	HR	RBI	SB	Avg
2005 Danville	Appal.	SS	6	18	3	5	1	0	0	1	1	.278
2005 Braves	Gulf Coast	SS-2B	46	166	26	49	6	1	3	20	7	.295
2006 Rome	So.Atl.	SS	111	437	67	116	25	4	3	50	23	.265
2007 Bakersfield	Calif.	SS	27	110	19	33	2	0	2	12	15	.300
2007 Myrtle Beach a	Carolina	SS	99	385	59	94	20	3	3	37	25	.244
2008 Frisco	Texas	SS	118	482	82	142	19	2	4	65	54	.295
2009 Texas	A.L.	SS	145	480	72	128	17	8	6	40	33	.267
2010 Texas	A.L.	SS	148	588	88	156	15	3	0	35	32	.265
Major League Totals		2 Yrs.	293	1068	160	284	32	11	6	75	65	.266
Division Series												
2010 Texas	A.L.	SS	5	24	2	8	1	0	0	1	3	.333
Championship Series												
2010 Texas	A.L.	SS	6	27	4	9	2	0	0	2	4	.333
World Series Record												
2010 Texas	A.L.	SS	5	17	2	3	0	0	0	1	1	.176

a Traded by Atlanta Braves to Texas Rangers with catcher Jarrod Saltalamacchia, pitcher Neftali Feliz, pitcher Matt Harrison and pitcher Beau James for infielder Mark Teixeira and pitcher Ron Mahay, July 31, 2007.

ANKIEL, RICHARD ALEXANDER (RICK)

Born, Fort Pierce, Florida, July 19, 1979.
Bats Left. Throws Left. Height, 6 feet, 1 inch. Weight, 210 pounds.

Year Club	Lea	Pos	G	AB	R	H	2B	3B	HR	RBI	SB	Avg
1998 Peoria	Midwest	P	3	0	0	0	0	0	0	0	0	.000
1998 Pr William	Carolina	P	9	0	0	0	0	0	0	0	0	.000
1999 Arkansas	Texas	P	8	10	1	4	0	0	1	1	0	.400

Year	Club	Lea	Pos	G	AB	R	H	2B	3B	HR	RBI	SB	Avg
1999	Memphis	P.C.	P	16	21	3	6	2	0	0	4	0	.286
1999	St. Louis	N.L.	P	9	10	0	1	0	0	0	0	0	.100
2000	St. Louis	N.L.	P	35	68	8	17	1	1	2	9	0	.250
2001	Memphis	P.C.	P	3	0	0	0	0	0	0	0	0	.000
2001	Johnson City	Appal.	P	41	105	21	30	7	0	10	35	0	.286
2001	St. Louis	N.L.	P	6	8	1	0	0	0	0	0	0	.000
2002	St. Louis a	N.L.	INJURED—Did Not Play										
2003	Tennessee	Southern	P	30	25	2	6	1	0	1	5	0	.240
2004	Tennessee	Southern	P	2	4	0	0	0	0	0	0	0	.000
2004	St. Louis b	N.L.	P	5	1	0	0	0	0	0	0	0	.000
2005	Quad Cities	Midwest	OF	51	185	33	50	10	1	11	45	0	.270
2005	Springfield	Texas	OF	34	136	18	33	7	0	10	30	0	.243
2006	St. Louis c	N.L.	INJURED—Did Not Play										
2007	Memphis	P.C.	OF	102	389	62	104	15	3	32	89	4	.267
2007	St. Louis	N.L.	OF	47	172	31	49	8	1	11	39	1	.285
2008	St. Louis	N.L.	OF	120	413	65	109	21	2	25	71	2	.264
2009	St. Louis d-e	N.L.	OF	122	372	50	86	21	2	11	38	4	.231
2010	Omaha	P.C.	OF	18	67	8	17	6	0	4	9	0	.254
2010	Kansas City	A.L.	OF	27	92	14	24	7	0	4	15	1	.261
2010	Atlanta f-g-h	N.L.	OF	47	119	17	25	6	1	2	9	2	.210
Major League Totals			8 Yrs.	418	1255	186	311	64	7	55	181	10	.248
	Division Series												
2000	St. Louis	N.L.	P	1	1	0	0	0	0	0	0	0	.000
	Championship Series												
2000	St. Louis	N.L.	P	2	0	0	0	0	0	0	0	0	.000

a On disabled list from March 26 to June 5, 2002.
b On disabled list from March 25 to September 1, 2004.
c On disabled list from March 24 to November 2, 2006.
d On disabled list from May 5 to May 24, 2009.
e Filed for free agency, November 5, 2009. Signed with Kansas City Royals, January 25, 2010.
f On disabled list from May 3 to July 22, 2010.
g Traded to Atlanta Braves with pitcher Kyle Farnsworth and cash for outfielder Gregor Blanco, pitcher Jesse Chavez and pitcher Tim Collins, July 31, 2010.
h Filed for free agency, November 1, 2010. Signed with Washington Nationals, December 21, 2010.

ARIAS, JOAQUIN

Born, Santo Domingo, Dominican Republic, September 21, 1984.
Bats Right. Throws Right. Height, 6 feet, 1 inch. Weight, 170 pounds.

Year	Club	Lea	Pos	G	AB	R	H	2B	3B	HR	RBI	SB	Avg
2002	Yankees	Gulf Coast	2B-SS-3B	57	203	29	61	7	6	0	21	2	.300
2003	Battle Creek	Midwest	SS	130	481	60	128	12	8	3	48	12	.266
2004	Stockton a	Calif.	SS	123	500	77	150	20	8	4	62	30	.300
2005	Frisco	Texas	SS	120	499	65	157	23	8	5	56	20	.315
2006	Oklahoma	P.C.	SS	124	493	56	132	14	10	4	49	26	.268
2006	Texas	A.L.	SS-3B	6	11	4	6	1	0	0	1	0	.545
2007	Rangers	Arizona	SS	2	7	1	2	1	0	0	1	0	.286
2007	Oklahoma b	P.C.	SS	3	11	3	2	0	0	0	1	1	.182
2008	Oklahoma	P.C.	SS-2B	104	432	59	128	15	9	7	49	23	.296
2008	Texas	A.L.	2B	32	110	15	32	7	3	0	9	4	.291
2009	Texas	A.L.	2B-3B	3	8	0	0	0	0	0	0	0	.000
2009	Okla.	P.C.	SS	118	504	63	134	14	3	5	52	24	.266
2010	Frisco	Texas	1B-SS-2B-3B	8	31	4	6	0	0	0	1	0	.194
2010	Texas	A.L.	2B-1B-SS	50	98	18	27	5	1	0	9	1	.276
2010	New York c-d-e	N.L.	2B-SS-OF	22	30	5	6	1	0	0	4	0	.200
Major League Totals			4 Yrs.	113	257	42	71	14	4	0	23	5	.276

a Sent to Texas Rangers as player to be named later for infielder Alex Rodriguez, March 23, 2004.
b On disabled list from March 23 to October 15, 2007.
c On disabled list from April 30 to May 16 and July 31 to August 16, 2010.
d Traded to New York Mets for outfielder Jeff Francoeur, September 1, 2010.
e Claimed on waivers by Kansas City Royals, November 4, 2010.

AVILA, ALEXANDER THOMAS (ALEX)

Born, Hialeah, Florida, January 29, 1987.
Bats Left. Throws Right. Height, 5 feet, 11 inches. Weight, 210 pounds.

Year	Club	Lea	Pos	G	AB	R	H	2B	3B	HR	RBI	SB	Avg
2008	West Michigan	Midwest	C	58	213	21	65	14	0	1	22	0	.305
2009	Erie	Eastern	C-1B	93	329	52	87	23	1	12	55	2	.264

Year	Club	Lea	Pos	G	AB	R	H	2B	3B	HR	RBI	SB	Avg
2009	Detroit	A.L.	C	29	61	9	17	4	0	5	14	0	.279
2010	Detroit	A.L.	C	104	294	28	67	12	0	7	31	2	.228
Major League Totals			2 Yrs.	133	355	37	84	16	0	12	45	2	.237

AVILES, MICHAEL ANTHONY (MIKE)

Born, New York, New York, March 13, 1981.
Bats Right. Throws Right. Height, 5 feet, 9 inches. Weight, 195 pounds.

Year	Club	Lea	Pos	G	AB	R	H	2B	3B	HR	RBI	SB	Avg
2003	Royals 1	Arizona	SS	52	212	51	77	19	5	6	39	11	.363
2004	Wilmington	Carolina	SS	126	463	66	139	40	4	6	68	2	.300
2005	Wichita	Texas	SS-3B-2B	133	521	79	146	33	6	14	80	11	.280
2006	Omaha	P.C.	3B-SS-2B	129	469	52	124	21	3	8	47	14	.264
2007	Omaha	P.C.	SS-3B-2B	133	538	78	159	27	6	17	77	5	.296
2008	Omaha	P.C.	2B-SS	51	214	42	72	21	6	10	42	3	.336
2008	Kansas City	A.L.	SS-2B-3B	102	419	68	136	27	4	10	51	8	.325
2009	Kansas City a	A.L.	SS-3B	36	120	10	22	3	1	1	8	1	.183
2010	Omaha	P.C.	SS-2B	17	70	8	19	3	1	1	8	0	.271
2010	Kansas City	A.L.	2B-SS-3B	110	424	63	129	16	3	8	32	14	.304
Major League Totals			3 Yrs.	248	963	141	287	46	8	19	91	23	.298

a On disabled list from May 24 to November 16, 2009.

AYBAR, ERICK JOHAN

Born, Bani, Dominican Republic, January 14, 1984.
Bats Both. Throws Right. Height, 5 feet, 10 inches. Weight, 170 pounds.

Year	Club	Lea	Pos	G	AB	R	H	2B	3B	HR	RBI	SB	Avg
2002	Provo	Pioneer	SS	67	273	64	89	15	6	4	29	15	.326
2003	Cedar Rapids	Midwest	SS	125	496	83	153	30	10	6	57	32	.308
2004	Rancho Cucamonga	Calif.	SS-2B	136	573	102	189	25	11	14	65	51	.330
2005	Arkansas	Texas	SS	134	535	101	162	29	10	9	54	49	.303
2006	Salt Lake	P.C.	SS	81	339	63	96	20	3	6	45	32	.283
2006	Los Angeles	A.L.	SS-2B	34	40	5	10	1	1	0	2	1	.250
2007	Rancho Cucamonga	Calif.	SS	2	5	3	2	0	0	0	0	3	.400
2007	Salt Lake	P.C.	SS-2B	3	12	2	4	0	0	0	2	2	.333
2007	Los Angeles a	A.L.	2B-SS-OF-3B	79	194	18	46	5	1	1	19	4	.237
2008	Rancho Cucamonga	Calif.	SS	3	10	2	4	1	0	0	3	2	.400
2008	Los Angeles b	A.L.	SS-2B	98	346	53	96	18	5	3	39	7	.277
2009	Los Angeles	A.L.	SS	137	504	70	157	23	9	5	58	14	.312
2010	Los Angeles	A.L.	SS	138	534	69	135	18	4	5	29	22	.253
Major League Totals			5 Yrs.	486	1618	215	444	65	20	14	147	48	.274
	Division Series												
2007	Los Angeles	A.L.	OF	1	1	0	0	0	0	0	0	0	.000
2008	Los Angeles	A.L.	SS	4	18	0	2	0	0	0	1	0	.111
2009	Los Angeles	A.L.	SS	3	11	2	4	1	1	0	2	0	.364
Division Series Totals				8	30	2	6	1	1	0	3	0	.200
	Championship Series												
2009	Los Angeles	A.L.	SS	6	20	2	5	1	0	0	1	3	.250

a On disabled list from July 2 to August 6 and August 20 to September 5, 2007.
b On disabled list from May 21 to June 18, 2008.

AYBAR, WILLY DEL JESUS

Born, Bani, Dominican Republic, March 9, 1983.
Bats Both. Throws Right. Height, 6 feet. Weight, 200 pounds.

Year	Club	Lea	Pos	G	AB	R	H	2B	3B	HR	RBI	SB	Avg
2000	Great Falls	Pioneer	3B	70	266	39	70	15	1	4	49	5	.263
2001	Vero Beach	Fla.St.	3B	2	7	0	2	0	0	0	0	0	.286
2001	Wilmington	So.Atl.	3B	120	431	45	102	25	2	4	48	7	.237
2002	Vero Beach	Fla.St.	3B	108	372	56	80	18	2	11	65	15	.215
2003	Vero Beach	Fla.St.	3B-2B-SS	119	445	47	122	29	3	11	74	9	.274
2004	Jacksonville	Southern	2B	126	482	56	133	27	0	15	77	8	.276
2005	Las Vegas	P.C.	3B-2B	108	401	47	119	26	4	5	60	1	.297
2005	Los Angeles	N.L.	3B-2B	26	86	12	28	8	0	1	10	3	.326
2006	Las Vegas	P.C.	3B-2B	50	197	30	62	12	1	10	41	1	.315
2006	Richmond	Int.	3B-2B	3	10	2	3	1	0	0	1	0	.300
2006	Los Angeles-Atlanta a-b	N.L.	3B-2B	79	243	32	68	18	0	4	30	1	.280
2007	Atlanta c	N.L.	INJURED—Did Not Play										

Year	Club	Lea	Pos	G	AB	R	H	2B	3B	HR	RBI	SB	Avg
2008	Vero Beach	Fla.St.	2B-3B	3	12	1	3	0	0	0	1	0	.250
2008	Durham	Int.	2B-3B-1B	5	20	3	6	3	0	0	3	0	.300
2008	Tampa Bay d-e	A.L.	3B-1B-2B	95	324	33	82	17	2	10	33	2	.253
2009	Tampa Bay	A.L.	1B-2B-3B	105	296	38	75	12	0	12	41	1	.253
2010	Tampa Bay f	A.L.	DH-2B-3B-1B	100	270	22	62	13	0	6	43	0	.230
Major League Totals			5 Yrs.	405	1219	137	315	68	2	33	157	7	.258
	Division Series												
2008	Tampa Bay	N.L.	1B-DH	4	11	2	3	1	0	0	1	0	.273
2010	Tampa Bay	N.L.	DH	3	6	0	1	1	0	0	0	0	.167
Division Series Totals				7	17	2	4	2	0	0	1	0	.235
	Championship Series												
2008	Tampa Bay	N.L.	DH	6	19	3	8	1	0	2	6	0	.421
	World Series Record												
2008	Tampa Bay	N.L.	1B-DH	4	4	0	1	0	0	0	0	0	.250

a Traded to Atlanta Braves with pitcher Danys Baez and cash for outfielder Wilson Betemit, July 28, 2006.
b On disabled list from August 12 to September 1, 2006.
c On disabled list from March 25 to November 13, 2007.
d Traded with infielder Chase Fontaine to Tampa Bay Rays for pitcher Jeff Ridgway, January 8, 2008.
e On disabled list from April 10 to May 29, 2008.
f Filed for free agency, November 3, 2010.

BAKER, JEFFREY GLEN (JEFF)

Born, Bad Kissingen, West Germany, June 21, 1981.
Bats Right. Throws Right. Height, 6 feet, 2 inches. Weight, 210 pounds.

Year	Club	Lea	Pos	G	AB	R	H	2B	3B	HR	RBI	SB	Avg
2003	Asheville	So.Atl.	3B	70	263	44	76	17	0	11	44	4	.289
2004	Visalia	Calif.	3B-SS	73	271	60	88	23	1	11	64	1	.325
2004	Tulsa	Texas	3B	24	91	10	27	5	1	4	20	1	.297
2005	Colorado	N.L.	3B	12	38	6	8	4	0	1	4	0	.211
2005	Colorado Springs	P.C.	3B	61	228	40	69	16	1	10	41	3	.303
2006	Colorado Springs	P.C.	OF-3B	128	482	71	147	30	4	20	108	7	.305
2006	Colorado	N.L.	OF-1B	18	57	13	21	7	2	5	21	2	.368
2007	Colorado Springs	P.C.	1B-OF	7	26	3	6	1	0	1	2	0	.231
2007	Colorado a	N.L.	1B-OF-3B	85	144	17	32	2	2	4	12	0	.222
2008	Colorado	N.L.	2B-1B-3B-OF	104	299	55	80	22	1	12	48	4	.268
2009	Modesto	Calif.	2B-3B	2	5	1	2	1	0	0	1	0	.400
2009	Colorado Springs	P.C.	2B-3B	7	23	3	5	2	0	1	1	0	.217
2009	Colorado-Chicago b-c	N.L.	2B-3B-1B	81	226	27	65	15	2	4	24	1	.288
2010	Chicago	N.L.	3B-2B-1B-OF	79	206	29	56	13	2	4	21	1	.272
Major League Totals			6 Yrs.	379	970	147	262	63	9	30	130	8	.270
	Division Series												
2007	Colorado	N.L.	PH	1	1	0	1	0	0	0	1	0	1.000
	Championship Series												
2007	Colorado	N.L.	PH	2	2	0	1	0	0	0	0	0	.500
	World Series Record												
2007	Colorado	N.L.	PH	1	1	0	0	0	0	0	0	0	.000

a On disabled list from August 12 to September 1, 2007.
b Traded to Chicago Cubs for pitcher Al Alburquerque, July 2, 2009.
c On disabled list from April 27 to July 2, 2009.

BARAJAS, RODRIGO RICHARD (ROD)

Born, Ontario, California, September 5, 1975.
Bats Right. Throws Right. Height, 6 feet, 2 inches. Weight, 245 pounds.

Year	Club	Lea	Pos	G	AB	R	H	2B	3B	HR	RBI	SB	Avg
1996	Visalia	Calif.	C	27	74	6	12	3	0	0	8	0	.162
1996	Lethbridge a	Pioneer	C-1B	51	175	47	59	9	3	10	50	2	.337
1997	High Desert	Calif.	C-1B	57	199	24	53	11	0	7	30	0	.266
1998	High Desert	Calif.	C	113	442	67	134	26	0	23	81	1	.303
1999	El Paso	Texas	C-1B	127	510	77	162	41	2	14	95	2	.318
1999	Arizona	N.L.	C	5	16	3	4	1	0	1	3	0	.250
2000	Tucson	P.C.	C-1B-3B	110	416	43	94	25	0	13	75	4	.226
2000	Arizona	N.L.	C	5	13	1	3	0	0	1	3	0	.231
2001	Arizona	N.L.	C	51	106	9	17	3	0	3	9	0	.160
2001	Tucson	P.C.	1B-C-3B	45	162	23	52	13	0	9	32	3	.321
2002	Arizona	N.L.	C-1B	70	154	12	36	10	0	3	23	1	.234
2002	Tucson	P.C.	C-1B	5	16	2	7	1	0	1	1	0	.438
2003	Tucson	P.C.	C	4	16	3	7	1	0	1	4	0	.438

Year	Club	Lea	Pos	G	AB	R	H	2B	3B	HR	RBI	SB	Avg
2003	Lancaster	Calif.	C	3	12	2	5	0	0	0	3	0	.417
2003	Arizona b-c	N.L.	C	80	220	19	48	15	0	3	28	0	.218
2004	Texas d	A.L.	C-1B	108	358	50	89	26	1	15	58	0	.249
2005	Texas	A.L.	C-1B	120	410	53	104	24	0	21	60	0	.254
2006	Texas e	A.L.	C-1B	97	344	49	88	20	0	11	41	0	.256
2007	Reading	Eastern	C	2	5	0	1	0	0	0	0	0	.200
2007	Lakewood	So.Atl.	C	6	16	0	6	2	0	0	2	0	.375
2007	Philadelphia f-g	N.L.	C-1B	48	122	16	28	8	0	4	10	0	.230
2008	Toronto	A.L.	C-1B	104	349	44	87	23	0	11	49	0	.249
2009	Toronto	A.L.	C	125	429	43	97	19	0	19	71	1	.226
2010	Mets	Gulf Coast	DH	1	4	1	1	0	0	1	3	0	.250
2010	St. Lucie	Fla.St.	C	4	17	1	4	0	0	0	2	0	.235
2010	New York-LA h-i-j-k	N.L.	C	99	313	39	75	14	0	17	47	0	.240
Major League Totals			12 Yrs.	912	2834	338	676	163	1	109	402	2	.239
	Division Series												
2001	Arizona	N.L.	C	1	0	0	0	0	0	0	0	0	.000
2002	Arizona	N.L.	C	2	4	1	1	0	0	1	1	0	.250
Division Series Totals				3	4	1	1	0	0	1	1	0	.250
	World Series Record												
2001	Arizona	N.L.	C	2	5	1	2	0	0	1	1	0	.400

a Loaned to Oakland A's organization, April 5 to June 16, 1996.
b On disabled list from April 7 to April 28, 2003.
c On disabled list from July 5 to July 23, 2003.
d Not offered contract, December 21, 2003. Signed with Texas Rangers organization, January 12, 2004.
e Filed for free agency, October 28, 2006. Signed with Philadelphia Phillies organization, December 21, 2006.
f On disabled list from August 3 to September 1, 2007.
g Filed for free agency, October 30, 2007. Signed with Toronto Blue Jays, January 24, 2008.
h Filed for free agency, November 9, 2009. Signed with New York Mets, February 24, 2010.
i On disabled list from July 25 to August 19, 2010.
j Claimed on waivers by Los Angeles Dodgers, August 22, 2010.
k Filed for free agency, November 1, 2010, re-signed with Los Angeles Dodgers, December 3, 2010.

BARMES, CLINT HAROLD

Born, Vincennes, Indiana, March 6, 1979.
Bats Right. Throws Right. Height, 6 feet. Weight, 210 pounds.

Year	Club	Lea	Pos	G	AB	R	H	2B	3B	HR	RBI	SB	Avg
2000	Portland	Northwest	SS-OF	45	181	37	51	6	4	2	16	12	.282
2000	Asheville	So.Atl.	2B-SS-3B-OF	19	81	11	14	4	0	0	4	4	.173
2001	Salem	Carolina	SS	38	121	17	30	3	3	0	9	4	.248
2001	Asheville	So.Atl.	SS	74	285	40	74	14	1	5	24	21	.260
2002	Carolina	Southern	SS	103	438	62	119	23	2	15	60	15	.272
2003	Colorado Springs	P.C.	SS-2B	136	493	63	136	35	1	7	54	12	.276
2003	Colorado	N.L.	SS	12	25	2	8	2	0	0	2	0	.320
2004	Colorado Springs	P.C.	SS-2B	125	533	104	175	42	2	16	51	20	.328
2004	Colorado	N.L.	2B-SS	20	71	14	20	3	1	2	10	0	.282
2005	Tulsa	Texas	SS	8	34	6	11	1	0	0	0	1	.324
2005	Colorado a	N.L.	SS	81	350	55	101	19	1	10	46	6	.289
2006	Colorado	N.L.	SS-2B	131	478	57	105	26	4	7	56	5	.220
2007	Colorado Springs	P.C.	SS-OF-2B-3B	108	428	68	128	20	6	11	44	8	.299
2007	Colorado	N.L.	SS-2B-OF-3B	27	37	5	8	3	0	0	1	0	.216
2008	Colorado Springs	P.C.	2B-SS	5	18	2	5	0	0	0	3	0	.278
2008	Colorado b	N.L.	2B-SS-3B-OF	107	393	47	114	25	6	11	44	13	.290
2009	Colorado	N.L.	2B-SS	154	550	69	135	32	3	23	76	12	.245
2010	Colorado c	N.L.	2B-SS-3B	133	387	43	91	21	0	8	50	3	.235
Major League Totals			8 Yrs.	665	2291	292	582	131	15	61	285	39	.254
	Division Series												
2009	Colorado	N.L.	2B	4	14	0	0	0	0	0	0	0	.000

a On disabled list from June 6 to September 2, 2005.
b On disabled list from May 24 to June 23, 2008.
c Traded to Houston Astros for pitcher Felipe Paulino, November 18, 2010.

BARTLETT, JASON ALAN

Born, Mountain View, California, October 30, 1979.
Bats Right. Throws Right. Height, 6 feet. Weight, 180 pounds.

Year	Club	Lea	Pos	G	AB	R	H	2B	3B	HR	RBI	SB	Avg
2001	Eugene	Northwest	SS	68	267	49	80	12	4	3	37	12	.300
2002	Lake Elsinore	California	SS	75	308	57	77	14	4	1	33	24	.250

Year	Club	Lea	Pos	G	AB	R	H	2B	3B	HR	RBI	SB	Avg
2002	Fort Myers a	Fla.St.	SS-3B-2B	39	145	24	38	7	0	2	9	11	.262
2003	New Britain	Eastern	SS	139	548	96	162	31	8	8	48	41	.296
2004	Rochester	Int.	SS-2B	67	269	54	89	15	7	3	29	7	.331
2004	Twins	Gulf Coast	SS	5	14	1	5	1	0	0	1	0	.357
2004	Minnesota	A.L.	SS-2B	8	12	2	1	0	0	0	1	2	.083
2005	Rochester	Int.	SS	61	229	41	76	10	2	5	33	2	.332
2005	Minnesota	A.L.	SS	74	224	33	54	10	1	3	16	4	.241
2006	Rochester	Int.	SS	58	235	42	72	23	3	1	20	6	.306
2006	Minnesota	A.L.	SS	99	333	44	103	18	2	2	32	10	.309
2007	Minnesota b	A.L.	SS	140	510	75	135	20	7	5	43	23	.265
2008	Tampa Bay c	A.L.	SS	128	454	48	130	25	3	1	37	20	.286
2009	Charlotte	Fla.St.	SS	3	11	2	5	0	1	0	0	0	.455
2009	Tampa Bay d	A.L.	SS	137	500	90	160	29	7	14	66	30	.320
2010	Durham	Int.	SS	1	3	0	2	1	0	0	0	0	.667
2010	Tampa Bay e-f	A.L.	SS	135	468	71	119	27	3	4	47	11	.254
Major League Totals			7 Yrs.	721	2501	363	702	129	23	29	242	100	.281
	Division Series												
2006	Minnesota	A.L.	SS	3	11	0	3	1	0	0	0	0	.273
2008	Tampa Bay	N.L.	SS	4	14	3	4	1	0	0	0	0	.286
2010	Tampa Bay	N.L.	SS	5	15	0	6	1	0	0	0	0	.400
Division Series Totals				12	40	3	13	3	0	0	0	0	.325
	Championship Series												
2008	Tampa Bay	N.L.	SS	7	23	4	5	0	1	1	1	1	.217
	World Series Record												
2008	Tampa Bay	N.L.	SS	5	14	1	3	0	0	0	2	1	.214

a Traded by San Diego Padres to Minnesota Twins for outfielder Brian Buchanan, July 12, 2002.
b Traded to Tampa Bay Devil Rays with pitcher Matt Garza and pitcher Eduardo Morlan for infielder Brendan Harris, outfielder Jason Pridie and outfielder Delmon Young, November 28, 2007.
c On disabled list from July 3 to July 24, 2008.
d On disabled list from May 25 to June 15, 2009.
e On disabled list from May 30 to June 16, 2010.
f Traded to San Diego Padres with player to be named later for pitcher Adam Russell, pitcher Brandon Gomes, pitcher Cesar Ramos and infielder Cole Figueroa, December 17, 2010.

BARTON, DARIC WILLIAM

Born, Springfield, Vermont, August 16, 1985.
Bats Left. Throws Right. Height, 6 feet. Weight, 215 pounds.

Year	Club	Lea	Pos	G	AB	R	H	2B	3B	HR	RBI	SB	Avg
2003	Johnson City	Appal.	C-3B	54	172	29	50	10	0	4	29	0	.291
2004	Peoria a	Midwest	C	90	313	63	98	23	0	13	77	4	.313
2005	Stockton	Calif.	1B-3B-OF-C	79	292	60	93	16	2	8	52	0	.318
2005	Midland	Texas	1B-OF	56	212	38	67	20	1	5	37	1	.316
2006	Athletics	Arizona	1B	2	5	1	1	1	0	0	2	0	.200
2006	Sacramento	P.C.	1B	43	147	25	38	6	4	2	22	1	.259
2007	Sacramento	P.C.	1B-3B	136	516	84	151	38	5	9	70	3	.293
2007	Oakland	A.L.	1B	18	72	16	25	9	0	4	8	1	.347
2008	Sacramento	P.C.	1B	8	31	4	6	0	0	1	3	0	.194
2008	Oakland b	A.L.	1B-3B	140	446	59	101	17	5	9	47	2	.226
2009	Sacramento	P.C.	1B	70	253	48	66	21	1	9	48	1	.261
2009	Athletics	Arizona	1B	6	18	3	5	1	0	1	3	0	.278
2009	Stockton	Calif.	1B	1	4	0	0	0	0	0	0	0	.000
2009	Oakland c	A.L.	1B	54	160	31	43	12	1	3	24	0	.269
2010	Oakland	A.L.	1B	159	556	79	152	33	5	10	57	7	.273
Major League Totals			4 Yrs.	371	1234	185	321	71	11	26	136	10	.260

a Traded by St. Louis Cardinals to Oakland Athletics with pitcher Danny Haren and pitcher Kiko Calero for pitcher Mark Mulder, December 18, 2004.
b On disabled list from July 14 to August 1, 2008.
c On disabled list from July 27 to August 21, 2009.

BAUTISTA, JOSE ANTONIO

Born, Santo Domingo, Dominican Republic, October 19, 1980.
Bats Right. Throws Right. Height, 6 feet. Weight, 190 pounds.

Year	Club	Lea	Pos	G	AB	R	H	2B	3B	HR	RBI	SB	Avg
2001	Williamsport	N.Y.-Penn.	3B-OF	62	220	43	63	10	3	5	30	8	.286
2002	Hickory	So.Atl.	3B-SS	129	438	72	132	26	3	14	57	3	.301
2003	Lynchburg	Carolina	3B-2B	51	165	28	40	14	2	4	20	1	.242
2003	Pirates a	Gulf Coast	3B	7	23	5	8	1	0	1	3	0	.348

Year	Club	Lea	Pos	G	AB	R	H	2B	3B	HR	RBI	SB	Avg
2004	Pittsburgh	N.L.	OF	23	40	1	8	2	0	0	0	0	.200
2004	Balt.-Tam. Bay-K.C. b-c-d-e.	A.L.	3B-OF	41	48	5	10	1	0	0	2	0	.208
2005	Altoona............	Eastern	3B	117	445	63	126	27	1	23	90	7	.283
2005	Indianapolis...........	Int.	3B	13	51	6	13	3	0	1	4	1	.255
2005	Pittsburgh	N.L.	3B	11	28	3	4	1	0	0	1	1	.143
2006	Indianapolis...........	Int.	3B-OF-2B	29	101	12	28	9	0	2	9	2	.277
2006	Pittsburgh	N.L.	OF-3B-2B	117	400	58	94	20	3	16	51	2	.235
2007	Pirates	Gulf Coast	3B	2	8	1	3	2	0	0	1	0	.375
2007	Pittsburgh f	N.L.	3B-OF	142	532	75	135	36	2	15	63	6	.254
2008	Indianapolis...........	Int.	OF-2B	5	20	6	6	2	0	2	8	1	.300
2008	Pittsburgh	N.L.	3B	107	314	38	76	15	0	12	44	1	.242
2008	Toronto g.............	A.L.	3B-1B-2B	21	56	7	12	2	0	3	10	0	.214
2009	Toronto	A.L.	OF-3B	113	336	54	79	13	3	13	40	4	.235
2010	Toronto	A.L.	OF-3B-1B	161	569	109	148	35	3	*54	124	9	.260
Major League Totals			7 Yrs.	736	2323	350	566	125	11	113	335	23	.244

a Selected by Baltimore Orioles from Pittsburgh in Rule V draft, December 15, 2003.
b Claimed on waivers by Tampa Bay Devil Rays, June 3, 2004.
c Sold to Kansas City Royals, June 28, 2004.
d Traded to New York Mets for catcher Justin Huber, July 30, 2004.
e Traded to Pittsburgh Pirates with infielder Ty Wigginton and pitcher Matt Peterson for pitcher Kris Benson and infielder Jeff Keppinger, July 30, 2004.
f On disabled list from July 15 to August 1, 2007.
g Traded to Toronto Blue Jays for player to be named later, August 21, 2008. Pittsburgh Pirates received infielder Robinzon Diaz to complete trade, August 25, 2008.

BAY, JASON RAYMOND

Born, Trail, British Columbia, Canada, September 20, 1978.
Bats Right. Throws Right. Height, 6 feet, 2 inches. Weight, 205 pounds.

Year	Club	Lea	Pos	G	AB	R	H	2B	3B	HR	RBI	SB	Avg
2000	Vermont........	N.Y.-Penn.	OF	35	135	17	41	5	0	2	12	17	.304
2001	Jupiter	Fla.St.	OF-2B	38	123	12	24	4	1	1	10	10	.195
2001	Clinton	Midwest	OF	87	318	67	115	20	4	13	61	15	.362
2002	St. Lucie...........	Fla.St.	OF	69	261	48	71	12	2	9	54	22	.272
2002	Binghamton........	Eastern	OF	34	107	17	31	4	2	4	19	13	.290
2002	Mobile a-b	Southern	OF	23	81	16	25	5	2	4	12	4	.309
2003	Portland..............	P.C.	OF	91	307	64	93	11	1	20	59	23	.303
2003	San Diego-Pittsburgh c-d-e.	N.L.	OF	30	87	15	25	7	1	4	14	3	.287
2004	Nashville	P.C.	OF	4	10	3	4	2	0	1	3	0	.400
2004	Pittsburgh f-g.........	N.L.	OF	120	411	61	116	24	4	26	82	4	.282
2005	Pittsburgh	N.L.	OF	*162	599	110	183	44	6	32	101	21	.306
2006	Pittsburgh	N.L.	OF	159	570	101	163	29	3	35	109	11	.286
2007	Pittsburgh	N.L.	OF	145	538	78	133	25	2	21	84	4	.247
2008	Pittsburgh	N.L.	OF	106	393	72	111	23	2	22	64	7	.282
2008	Boston h	A.L.	OF	49	184	39	54	12	2	9	37	3	.293
2009	Boston i.............	A.L.	OF	151	531	103	142	29	3	36	119	13	.267
2010	New York j...........	N.L.	OF	95	348	48	90	20	6	6	47	10	.259
Major League Totals			8 Yrs.	1017	3661	627	1017	213	29	191	657	76	.278
	Division Series												
2008	Boston..............	A.L.	OF	4	17	3	7	2	0	2	5	0	.412
2009	Boston..............	A.L.	OF	3	8	0	1	0	0	0	0	0	.125
Division Series Totals				7	25	3	8	2	0	2	5	0	.320
	Championship Series												
2008	Boston..............	A.L.	OF	7	24	3	7	1	0	1	4	0	.292

a Traded by Montreal Expos to New York Mets with pitcher Jim Serrano for infielder Lou Collier, March 26, 2002.
b Traded to San Diego Padres with pitcher Bobby M. Jones and pitcher Josh Reynolds for pitcher Jason Middlebrook and pitcher Steve Reed, July 31, 2002.
c On disabled list from May 26 to July 8, 2003.
d Traded to Pittsburgh Pirates with pitcher Oliver Perez and player to be named later for outfielder Brian Giles, August 26, 2003.
e Pittsburgh Pirates received pitcher Cory Stewart to complete trade, October 2, 2003.
f On disabled list from March 26 to May 7, 2004.
g Selected Rookie of the Year in National League for 2004.
h Traded to Boston Red Sox for outfielder Manny Ramirez, outfielder Brandon Moss and pitcher Craig Hansen, July 31, 2008.
i Filed for free agency, November 5, 2009. Signed with New York Mets, December 29, 2009.
j On disabled list from July 26 to November 2, 2010.

BECKHAM, JAMES GORDON (GORDON)

Born, Atlanta, Georgia, September 16, 1986.
Bats Right. Throws Right. Height, 6 feet. Weight, 190 pounds.

Year Club	Lea	Pos	G	AB	R	H	2B	3B	HR	RBI	SB	Avg
2008 Kannapolis	So.Atl.	SS	14	58	11	18	2	0	3	8	0	.310
2009 Birmingham	Southern	SS-2B-3B	38	147	23	44	17	0	4	22	1	.299
2009 Charlotte	Int.	3B-SS	7	28	6	13	6	0	0	3	1	.464
2009 Chicago	A.L.	3B	103	378	58	102	28	1	14	63	7	.270
2010 Chicago	A.L.	2B	131	444	58	112	25	2	9	49	4	.252
Major League Totals		2 Yrs.	234	822	116	214	53	3	23	112	11	.260

BELL, JOSHUA L. (JOSH)

Born, Rockford, Illinois, November 13, 1986.
Bats Both. Throws Right. Height, 6 feet, 3 inches. Weight, 220 pounds.

Year Club	Lea	Pos	G	AB	R	H	2B	3B	HR	RBI	SB	Avg
2005 Dodgers	Gulf Coast	3B-SS	45	157	26	50	7	1	1	21	5	.318
2006 Ogden	Pioneer	3B-1B	64	250	45	77	17	3	12	53	4	.308
2007 Inland Empire	Calif.	3B	20	75	4	13	2	1	2	9	0	.173
2007 Great Falls	Midwest	3B	108	398	65	115	21	3	15	62	5	.289
2008 Inland Empire	Calif.	3B	51	187	34	51	12	2	6	21	4	.273
2009 Bowie	Eastern	3B	33	114	18	33	5	0	9	24	0	.289
2009 Chattanooga a	Southern	3B	94	334	47	99	30	2	11	52	3	.296
2010 Norfolk	Int.	3B	81	316	43	88	25	0	13	50	2	.278
2010 Baltimore	A.L.	3B	53	159	15	34	5	0	3	12	0	.214

a Traded by Los Angeles Dodgers to Baltimore Orioles with pitcher Steve Johnson for pitcher George Sherrill, July 30, 2009.

BELLIARD, RONALD (RONNIE)

Born, Bronx, New York, April 7, 1975.
Bats Right. Throws Right. Height, 5 feet, 8 inches. Weight, 215 pounds.

Year Club	Lea	Pos	G	AB	R	H	2B	3B	HR	RBI	SB	Avg
1994 Brewers	Arizona	2B-3B-SS	39	143	32	42	7	3	0	27	7	.294
1995 Beloit	Midwest	2B-3B	130	461	76	137	28	5	13	76	16	.297
1996 El Paso	Texas	2B	109	416	73	116	20	8	3	57	26	.279
1997 Tucson	P.C.	2B-SS	118	443	80	125	35	4	4	55	10	.282
1998 Louisville	Int.	2B-SS	133	507	114	163	36	7	14	73	32	.321
1998 Milwaukee	N.L.	2B	8	5	0	1	0	0	0	0	0	.200
1999 Louisville	Int.	2B	29	108	14	26	4	0	1	8	12	.241
1999 Milwaukee	N.L.	2B-3B-SS	124	457	60	135	29	4	8	58	4	.295
2000 Milwaukee	N.L.	2B	152	571	83	150	30	9	8	54	7	.263
2001 Milwaukee a	N.L.	2B	101	364	69	96	30	3	11	36	5	.264
2002 Milwaukee b	N.L.	2B-3B	104	289	30	61	13	0	3	26	2	.211
2003 Colorado Springs	P.C.	2B	6	19	2	5	1	0	0	0	0	.263
2003 Colorado c-d	N.L.	2B	116	447	73	124	31	2	8	50	7	.277
2004 Cleveland	A.L.	2B	152	599	78	169	48	1	12	70	3	.282
2005 Cleveland	A.L.	2B	145	536	71	152	36	1	17	78	2	.284
2006 Cleveland	A.L.	2B-3B	93	350	43	102	21	0	8	44	2	.291
2006 St. Louis e-f	N.L.	2B	54	194	20	46	9	1	5	23	0	.237
2007 Washington	N.L.	2B-1B-SS-3B	147	511	57	148	35	1	11	58	3	.290
2008 Potomac	Carolina	3B	1	3	0	0	0	0	0	0	0	.000
2008 Harrisburg	Eastern	2B-3B	3	12	0	0	0	0	0	0	0	.000
2008 Washington g	N.L.	1B-3B-2B-SS	96	296	37	85	22	0	11	46	3	.287
2009 Washington-LA h-i	N.L.	2B-1B-3B	110	264	39	73	14	1	10	39	3	.277
2010 Los Angeles j	N.L.	2B-3B-1B	82	162	24	35	10	1	2	19	2	.216
Major League Totals		13 Yrs.	1484	5045	685	1377	328	24	114	601	43	.273
Division Series												
2006 St. Louis	N.L.	2B	4	13	2	6	1	0	0	2	1	.462
2009 Los Angeles	N.L.	2B	3	11	2	3	0	0	0	1	0	.273
Division Series Totals			7	24	4	9	1	0	0	3	1	.375
Championship Series												
2006 St. Louis	N.L.	2B	7	25	0	6	0	0	0	2	1	.240
2009 Los Angeles	N.L.	2B	5	19	2	6	0	0	0	0	1	.316
Championship Series Totals			12	44	2	12	0	0	0	2	2	.273
World Series Record												
2006 St. Louis	N.L.	2B	3	12	0	0	0	0	0	0	0	.000

a On disabled list from August 9 to September 30, 2001.
b Not offered 2003 contract, December 21, 2002. Signed with Colorado Rockies organization, January 17, 2003.

c On disabled list from June 2 to June 23, 2003.
d Waived by Colorado Rockies, November 20, 2003. Signed with Cleveland Indians, December 26, 2003.
e Traded to St. Louis Cardinals for infielder Hector Luna, July 30, 2006.
f Filed for free agency, October 30, 2006. Signed with Washington Nationals organization, February 19, 2007.
g On disabled list from May 16 to June 10 and September 15 to October 3, 2008.
h Traded to Los Angeles Dodgers for pitcher Luis Garcia and player to be named later, August 30, 2009. Washington Nationals received pitcher Victor Garate to complete trade, September 2, 2009.
i Filed for free agency, November 5, 2009. re-signed with Los Angeles Dodgers, January 26, 2010.
j Released by Los Angeles Dodgers, September 9, 2010.

BELTRAN, CARLOS IVAN

Born, Manati, Puerto Rico, April 24, 1977.
Bats Both. Throws Right. Height, 6 feet. Weight,200 pounds.

Year	Club	Lea	Pos	G	AB	R	H	2B	3B	HR	RBI	SB	Avg
1995	Royals	Gulf Coast	OF	52	180	29	50	9	0	0	23	5	.278
1996	Lansing	Midwest	OF	11	42	3	6	2	0	0	0	1	.143
1996	Spokane	Northwest	OF	59	215	29	58	8	3	7	29	10	.270
1997	Wilmington	Carolina	OF	120	419	57	96	15	4	11	46	17	.229
1998	Wilmington	Carolina	OF	52	192	32	53	14	0	5	32	11	.276
1998	Wichita	Texas	OF	47	182	50	64	13	3	14	44	7	.352
1998	Kansas City	A.L.	OF	14	58	12	16	5	3	0	7	3	.276
1999	Kansas City a	A.L.	OF	156	663	112	194	27	7	22	108	27	.293
2000	GC Royals	Gulf Coast	PH	1	4	3	2	1	0	1	1	0	.500
2000	Wilmington	Carolina	OF	3	13	2	4	0	1	2	6	0	.308
2000	Omaha	P.C.	OF	5	18	4	6	1	0	2	2	1	.333
2000	Kansas City b	A.L.	OF	98	372	49	92	15	4	7	44	13	.247
2001	Kansas City	A.L.	OF	155	617	106	189	32	12	24	101	31	.306
2002	Kansas City	A.L.	OF	*162	637	114	174	44	7	29	105	35	.273
2003	Wichita	Texas	OF	3	9	3	3	2	0	0	1	1	.333
2003	Kansas City c	A.L.	OF	141	521	102	160	14	10	26	100	41	.307
2004	Kansas City	A.L.	OF	69	266	51	74	19	2	15	51	14	.278
2004	Houston d-e	N.L.	OF	90	333	70	86	17	7	23	53	28	.258
2005	New York	N.L.	OF	151	582	83	155	34	2	16	78	17	.266
2006	New York	N.L.	OF	140	510	127	140	38	1	41	116	18	.275
2007	New York f	N.L.	OF	144	554	93	153	33	3	33	112	23	.276
2008	New York	N.L.	OF	161	606	116	172	40	5	27	112	25	.284
2009	Brooklyn	N.Y.-Penn.	OF	5	18	1	3	0	0	0	2	0	.167
2009	New York g	N.L.	OF	81	308	50	100	22	1	10	48	11	.325
2010	St. Lucie	Fla.St.	OF	14	49	5	18	5	0	0	5	0	.367
2010	New York h	N.L.	OF	64	220	21	56	11	3	7	27	3	.255
Major League Totals			13 Yrs.	1626	6247	1106	1761	351	67	280	1062	289	.282
	Division Series												
2004	Houston	N.L.	OF	5	22	9	10	2	0	4	9	2	.455
2006	New York	N.L.	OF	3	9	2	2	0	0	0	1	1	.222
Division Series Totals				8	31	11	12	2	0	4	10	3	.387
	Championship Series												
2004	Houston	N.L.	OF	7	24	12	10	1	0	4	5	4	.417
2006	New York	N.L.	OF	7	27	8	8	1	0	3	4	1	.296
Championship Series Totals				14	51	20	18	2	0	7	9	5	.353

a Selected Rookie of the Year in American League for 1999.
b On disabled list from July 4 to September 3, 2000.
c On disabled list from March 21 to April 18, 2003.
d Traded to Houston Astros for pitcher Octavio Dotel and catcher John Buck, June 24, 2004.
e Filed for free agency, October 28, 2004. Signed with New York Mets, January 11, 2005.
f On disabled list from July 25 to August 10, 2007.
g On disabled list from June 22 to September 8, 2009.
h On disabled list from March 26 to July 15, 2010.

BELTRE, ADRIAN

Born, Santo Domingo, Dominican Republic, April 7, 1979.
Bats Right. Throws Right. Height, 5 feet, 11 inches. Weight, 220 pounds.

Year	Club	Lea	Pos	G	AB	R	H	2B	3B	HR	RBI	SB	Avg
1995	LA-S.Domingo	Dominican	3B	62	218	56	67	15	3	8	40	2	.307
1996	Savannah	So.Atl.	3B-2B	68	244	48	75	14	3	16	59	4	.307
1996	San Berndno a	California	3B	63	238	40	62	13	1	10	40	3	.261
1997	Vero Beach	Fla.St.	3B-OF	123	435	95	138	24	2	26	104	25	.317
1998	San Antonio	Texas	3B	64	246	49	79	21	2	13	56	20	.321
1998	Los Angeles	N.L.	3B-SS	77	195	18	42	9	0	7	22	3	.215

Year Club	Lea	Pos	G	AB	R	H	2B	3B	HR	RBI	SB	Avg
1999 Los Angeles..........	N.L.	3B	152	538	84	148	27	5	15	67	18	.275
2000 Los Angeles b	N.L.	3B-SS	138	510	71	148	30	2	20	85	12	.290
2001 Vero Beach..........	Fla.St.	3B	3	9	0	4	1	0	0	1	0	.444
2001 Las Vegas.............	P.C.	3B	2	5	2	3	1	0	1	2	0	.600
2001 Los Angeles c.........	N.L.	3B-SS	126	475	59	126	22	4	13	60	13	.265
2002 Los Angeles..........	N.L.	3B	159	587	70	151	26	5	21	75	7	.257
2003 Los Angeles..........	N.L.	3B-SS	158	559	50	134	30	2	23	80	2	.240
2004 Los Angeles d	N.L.	3B-SS	156	598	104	200	32	0	*48	121	7	.334
2005 Seattle	A.L.	3B	156	603	69	154	36	1	19	87	3	.255
2006 Seattle	A.L.	3B-2B	156	620	88	166	39	4	25	89	11	.268
2007 Seattle	A.L.	3B	149	595	87	164	41	2	26	99	14	.276
2008 Seattle	A.L.	3B	143	556	74	148	29	1	25	77	8	.266
2009 Seattle e-f...........	A.L.	3B	111	449	54	119	27	0	8	44	13	.265
2010 Boston g	A.L.	3B	154	589	84	189	*49	2	28	102	2	.321
Major League Totals		13 Yrs.	1835	6874	912	1889	397	28	278	1008	113	.275
Division Series												
2004 Los Angeles..........	N.L.	3B	4	15	1	4	0	0	0	1	0	.267

a On disabled list from June 25 to July 2, 1996.
b On disabled list from May 28 to June 16, 2000.
c On disabled list from March 23 to May 12, 2001.
d Filed for free agency, October 29, 2004. Signed with Seattle Mariners, December 17, 2004.
e On disabled list from June 29 to August 4 and August 13 to September 1, 2009.
f Filed for free agency, November 5, 2009. Signed with Boston Red Sox, January 7, 2010.
g Filed for free agency, November 2, 2010. Signed with Texas Rangers, January 5, 2011.

BERKMAN, WILLIAM LANCE (LANCE)

Born, Waco, Texas, February 10, 1976.
Bats Both. Throws Left. Height, 6 feet, 1 inch. Weight, 220 pounds.

Year Club	Lea	Pos	G	AB	R	H	2B	3B	HR	RBI	SB	Avg
1997 Kissimmee..........	Fla.St.	OF	53	184	31	54	10	0	12	35	2	.293
1998 Jackson	Texas	OF	122	425	82	130	34	0	24	89	6	.306
1998 New Orleans...........	P.C.	OF	17	59	14	16	4	0	6	13	0	.271
1999 New Orleans...........	P.C.	OF	64	226	42	73	20	0	8	49	7	.323
1999 Houston a	N.L.	OF-1B	34	93	10	22	2	0	4	15	5	.237
2000 New Orleans...........	P.C.	OF	31	112	18	37	4	2	6	27	4	.330
2000 Houston.............	N.L.	OF-1B	114	353	76	105	28	1	21	67	6	.297
2001 Houston.............	N.L.	OF	156	577	110	191	*55	5	34	126	7	.331
2002 Houston.............	N.L.	OF	158	578	106	169	35	2	42	*128	8	.292
2003 Houston.............	N.L.	OF	153	538	110	155	35	6	25	93	5	.288
2004 Houston.............	N.L.	OF-1B	160	544	104	172	40	3	30	106	9	.316
2005 Round Rock...........	P.C.	OF	4	14	2	4	1	0	0	1	0	.286
2005 Houston b	N.L.	1B-OF	132	468	76	137	34	1	24	82	4	.293
2006 Houston.............	N.L.	1B-OF	152	536	95	169	29	0	45	136	3	.315
2007 Houston.............	N.L.	1B-OF	153	561	95	156	24	2	34	102	7	.278
2008 Houston.............	N.L.	1B	159	554	114	173	*46	4	29	106	18	.312
2009 Houston c	N.L.	1B	136	460	73	126	31	1	25	80	7	.274
2010 Trenton............	Eastern	DH	2	8	1	2	0	0	0	0	0	.250
2010 Round Rock...........	P.C.	1B	2	6	3	3	2	0	1	3	0	.500
2010 Houston.............	N.L.	1B	85	298	39	73	16	1	13	49	3	.245
2010 New York d-e-f-g	A.L.	DH-1B	37	106	9	27	7	0	1	9	0	.255
Major League Totals		12 Yrs.	1629	5666	1017	1675	382	26	327	1099	82	.296
Division Series												
2001 Houston.............	N.L.	OF	3	12	0	2	0	0	0	0	0	.167
2004 Houston.............	N.L.	OF	5	22	5	9	1	0	1	3	0	.409
2005 Houston.............	N.L.	1B-OF	4	14	4	5	1	0	1	5	0	.357
2010 New York	A.L.	DH	1	4	2	2	1	0	1	2	0	.500
Division Series Totals			13	52	11	18	3	0	3	10	0	.346
Championship Series												
2004 Houston.............	N.L.	OF	7	24	7	7	2	0	3	9	1	.292
2005 Houston.............	N.L.	1B-OF	6	21	2	6	2	0	1	3	0	.286
2010 New York	A.L.	1B-DH	4	12	1	3	0	1	0	2	0	.250
Championship Series Totals			17	57	10	16	4	1	4	14	1	.281
World Series Record												
2005 Houston.............	N.L.	OF-1B	4	13	0	5	2	0	0	6	1	.385

a On disabled list from April 13 to May 14, 1999.
b On disabled list from March 25 to May 6, 2005.
c On disabled list from July 23 to August 12, 2009.

d On disabled list from March 26 to April 20, 2010.
e Traded to New York Yankees with cash for pitcher Mark Melancon and infielder Jimmy Parades, July 31, 2010.
f On disabled list from August 16 to September 1, 2010.
g Filed for free agency, November 1, 2010. Signed with St. Louis Cardinals, December 4, 2010.

BERNADINA, ROGEARVIN ARGELO (ROGER)

Born, Willemstad, Curacao, Netherlands Antilles, June 12, 1984.
Bats Left. Throws Left. Height, 6 feet, 1 inch. Weight, 200 pounds.

Year Club	Lea	Pos	G	AB	R	H	2B	3B	HR	RBI	SB	Avg
2002 Expos	Gulf Coast	OF	57	196	22	54	7	0	3	18	1	.276
2003 Savannah	So.Atl.	OF	77	278	36	66	12	3	4	39	11	.237
2004 Savannah	So.Atl.	OF	129	450	67	107	24	7	7	66	24	.238
2005 Savannah	So.Atl.	OF	122	417	64	97	15	3	12	54	35	.233
2006 Potomac	Carolina	OF	123	434	60	117	19	3	6	42	28	.270
2007 Harrisburg	Eastern	OF	97	371	58	100	15	2	6	36	40	.270
2007 Columbus	Int.	OF	13	42	6	7	3	0	0	1	0	.167
2008 Harrisburg	Eastern	OF	73	266	47	86	11	7	5	38	26	.323
2008 Columbus	Int.	OF	47	191	33	67	13	3	4	16	15	.351
2008 Washington	N.L.	OF	26	76	10	16	1	1	0	2	4	.211
2009 Syracuse	Int.	OF	5	18	1	3	0	0	0	0	1	.167
2009 Washington	N.L.	OF	3	4	1	1	1	0	0	0	1	.250
2009 Nationals a	Gulf Coast	OF	2	4	0	1	0	0	0	0	0	.250
2010 Syracuse	Int.	OF	14	61	8	23	2	1	2	8	7	.377
2010 Washington	N.L.	OF	134	414	52	102	18	3	11	47	16	.246
Major League Totals		3 Yrs.	163	494	63	119	20	4	11	49	21	.241

a On disabled list from April 19 to November 8, 2009.

BETANCOURT (PEREZ), YUNIESKY

Born, Santa Clara, Cuba, January 31, 1982.
Bats Right. Throws Right. Height, 5 feet, 10 inches. Weight, 190 pounds.

Year Club	Lea	Pos	G	AB	R	H	2B	3B	HR	RBI	SB	Avg
2005 San Antonio	Texas	SS-2B	52	227	25	62	10	3	5	20	12	.273
2005 Tacoma	P.C.	SS-2B	49	183	13	54	9	6	2	30	7	.295
2005 Seattle a	A.L.	SS-2B	60	211	24	54	11	5	1	15	1	.256
2006 Seattle	A.L.	SS	157	558	68	161	28	6	8	47	11	.289
2007 Seattle	A.L.	SS	155	536	72	155	38	2	9	67	5	.289
2008 Seattle	A.L.	SS	153	559	66	156	36	3	7	51	4	.279
2009 NW Arkansas	Texas	SS	3	13	2	2	0	0	1	1	0	.154
2009 Tacoma	P.C.	2B	1	2	0	1	1	0	0	1	0	.500
2009 Seattle-Kansas City b	A.L.	SS	134	470	40	115	20	6	6	49	3	.245
2010 Kansas City c	A.L.	SS	151	556	60	144	29	2	16	78	2	.259
Major League Totals		6 Yrs.	810	2890	330	785	162	24	47	307	26	.272

a Played in Cuba 2000-2004. Signed with Seattle Mariners, January 26, 2005.
b Traded to Kansas City Royals with cash for pitcher Dan Cortes and pitcher Derrick Saito, July 10, 2009.
c Traded to Milwaukee Brewers with pitcher Zack Greinke for outfielder Lorenzo Cain, infielder Alcides Escobar, pitcher Jeremy Jeffress and pitcher Jake Odorizzi, December 19, 2010.

BETEMIT, WILSON

Born, Santo Domingo, Dominican Republic, November 2, 1981.
Bats Both. Throws Right. Height, 6 feet, 2 inches. Weight, 220 pounds.

Year Club	Lea	Pos	G	AB	R	H	2B	3B	HR	RBI	SB	Avg
1997 Braves	Gulf Coast	SS	32	113	12	24	6	1	0	15	0	.212
1998 Braves	Gulf Coast	SS	51	173	23	38	8	4	5	16	6	.220
1999 Danville	Appal.	SS	67	259	39	83	18	2	5	53	6	.320
2000 Jamestown	N.Y.-Penn.	SS	69	269	54	89	15	2	5	37	3	.331
2001 Myrtle Beach	Carolina	SS	84	318	38	88	20	1	7	43	8	.277
2001 Greenville	Southern	SS	47	183	22	65	14	0	5	19	6	.355
2001 Atlanta	N.L.	SS	8	3	1	0	0	0	0	0	1	.000
2002 Braves	Gulf Coast	SS	7	19	2	5	4	0	0	2	1	.263
2002 Richmond	Int.	SS	93	343	43	84	17	1	8	34	8	.245
2003 Richmond	Int.	3B-SS	127	478	55	125	23	13	8	65	8	.262
2004 Richmond	Int.	3B-SS	105	356	48	99	24	2	13	59	3	.278
2004 Atlanta	N.L.	SS-3B	22	47	2	8	0	0	0	3	0	.170
2005 Atlanta	N.L.	3B-SS-2B	115	246	36	75	12	4	4	20	1	.305
2006 Atlanta-LA a	N.L.	3B-SS-2B	143	373	49	98	23	0	18	53	3	.263
2007 Los Angeles	N.L.	3B-SS-2B-OF	84	156	22	36	8	0	10	26	0	.231
2007 New York b	A.L.	1B-3B-SS-2B	37	84	11	19	4	0	4	24	0	.226

Year	Club	Lea	Pos	G	AB	R	H	2B	3B	HR	RBI	SB	Avg
2008	Scranton/WB	Int.	1B-3B-2B-SS	8	27	5	9	4	0	1	5	0	.333
2008	New York c-d	A.L.	1B-3B-SS-2B	87	189	24	50	13	0	6	25	0	.265
2009	Chicago	A.L.	1B-3B	20	45	2	9	5	0	0	3	0	.200
2009	Charlotte e	Int.	3B-1B-SS	72	261	36	63	19	0	11	49	2	.241
2010	Omaha	P.C.	SS-1B-3B	29	113	9	30	6	2	2	17	1	.265
2010	Kansas City	A.L.	3B-1B-2B	84	276	36	82	20	0	13	43	0	.297
Major League Totals			8 Yrs.	600	1419	183	377	85	4	55	197	5	.266
Division Series													
2004	Atlanta	N.L.	PH	1	0	0	0	0	0	0	0	0	.000
2005	Atlanta	N.L.	PH	2	2	0	1	0	0	0	0	0	.500
2006	Los Angeles	N.L.	3B	3	8	3	4	1	0	1	1	0	.500
Division Series Totals				6	10	3	5	1	0	1	1	0	.500

a Traded to Los Angeles Dodgers for pitcher Danys Baez, infielder Willy Aybar and cash, July 28, 2006.
b Traded to New York Yankees for pitcher Scott Proctor, July 31, 2007.
c On disabled list from April 14 to May 6 and May 11 to May 26, 2008.
d Traded to Chicago White Sox with pitcher Jeff Marquez and pitcher Jhonny Nunez for infielder Nick Swisher and pitcher Kaneoka Texeira, November 13, 2008.
e Filed for free agency, October 5, 2009. Signed with Kansas City Royals organization, November 12, 2009.

BLAKE, WILLIAM CASEY (CASEY)

Born, Des Moines, Iowa, August 23, 1973.
Bats Right. Throws Right. Height, 6 feet, 2 inches. Weight, 210 pounds.

Year	Club	Lea	Pos	G	AB	R	H	2B	3B	HR	RBI	SB	Avg
1996	Hagerstown	So.Atl.	3B-1B-OF	48	172	29	43	13	1	2	18	5	.250
1997	Dunedin	Fla.St.	3B-SS	129	449	56	107	21	0	7	39	19	.238
1998	Dunedin	Fla.St.	3B	88	340	62	119	28	3	11	65	9	.350
1998	Knoxville	Southern	3B	45	172	41	64	15	4	7	38	10	.372
1999	Syracuse	Int.	3B	110	387	69	95	16	2	22	75	9	.245
1999	St. Catharines	N.Y.-Penn.	3B	1	3	0	2	0	0	0	0	0	.667
1999	Toronto	A.L.	3B	14	39	6	10	2	0	1	1	0	.256
2000	Syracuse	Int.	3B-SS	30	106	10	23	6	1	2	7	0	.217
2000	Salt Lake	P.C.	3B-SS-1B	80	293	59	93	22	2	12	52	7	.317
2000	Minnesota a-b	A.L.	3B-1B	7	16	1	3	2	0	0	1	0	.188
2001	Edmonton	P.C.	3B-1B-2B-SS	94	375	64	116	24	6	10	49	14	.309
2001	Minn.-Baltimore c-d	A.L.	1B-3B	19	37	3	9	1	0	1	4	3	.243
2002	Edmonton	P.C.	3B-2B-1B-OF	126	482	87	149	25	3	19	58	24	.309
2002	Minnesota e	A.L.	3B-1B	9	20	2	4	1	0	0	1	0	.200
2003	Cleveland	A.L.	3B-1B	152	557	80	143	35	0	17	67	7	.257
2004	Cleveland	A.L.	3B-1B	152	587	93	159	36	3	28	88	5	.271
2005	Cleveland	A.L.	OF-3B-1B	147	523	72	126	32	1	23	58	4	.241
2006	Lake County	So.Atl.	OF	1	2	1	1	0	0	1	2	0	.500
2006	Akron	Eastern	OF	1	3	0	1	1	0	0	1	0	.333
2006	Cleveland f	A.L.	OF-1B	109	401	63	113	20	1	19	68	6	.282
2007	Cleveland	A.L.	3B-1B-OF	156	588	81	159	36	4	18	78	4	.270
2008	Cleveland	A.L.	3B-1B-SS	94	325	46	94	24	0	11	58	2	.289
2008	Los Angeles g-h	N.L.	3B-1B-2B	58	211	25	53	12	1	10	23	1	.251
2009	Los Angeles	N.L.	3B-1B-OF	139	485	84	136	25	6	18	79	3	.280
2010	Los Angeles	N.L.	3B-1B	146	509	56	126	28	1	17	64	0	.248
Major League Totals			12 Yrs.	1202	4298	612	1135	254	17	163	590	35	.264
Division Series													
2007	Cleveland	A.L.	3B	4	17	1	2	1	0	0	2	0	.118
2008	Los Angeles	N.L.	3B	3	11	2	3	0	0	0	2	0	.273
2009	Los Angeles	N.L.	3B	3	11	1	3	0	0	0	1	0	.273
Division Series Totals				10	39	4	8	1	0	0	5	0	.205
Championship Series													
2007	Cleveland	A.L.	3B	7	26	4	9	2	0	1	2	0	.346
2008	Los Angeles	N.L.	3B-2B	5	19	2	5	0	0	1	2	0	.263
2009	Los Angeles	N.L.	3B	5	19	0	2	0	0	0	1	1	.105
Championship Series Totals				17	64	6	16	2	0	2	5	1	.250

a Claimed on waivers from Toronto Blue Jays by Minnesota Twins, May 23, 2000.
b On disabled list from June 28 to July 7, 2000.
c Claimed on waivers by Baltimore Orioles, September 21, 2001.
d Claimed on waivers by Minnesota Twins, October 12, 2001.
e Filed for free agency, October 14, 2002. Signed with Cleveland Indians, December 18, 2002.
f On disabled list from June 14 to July 13 and August 6 to August 25, 2006.
g Traded to Los Angeles Dodgers for pitcher Jonathan Meloan and catcher Carlos Santana, July 26, 2008.
h Filed for free agency, October 30, 2008, re-signed with Los Angeles Dodgers, December 9, 2008.

BLANCO (PEREZ), ANDRES ELOY

Born, Urama, Venezuela, April 11, 1984.
Bats Both. Throws Right. Height, 5 feet, 10 inches. Weight, 190 pounds.

Year	Club	Lea	Pos	G	AB	R	H	2B	3B	HR	RBI	SB	Avg
2002	Wilmington	Carolina	SS	5	13	2	4	1	0	0	0	0	.308
2002	Royals	Gulf Coast	SS	52	193	27	48	8	0	0	14	16	.249
2003	Wilmington	Carolina	SS	113	394	61	96	11	3	0	25	13	.244
2004	Wichita	Texas	SS	93	324	34	80	10	2	0	21	7	.247
2004	Kansas City	A.L.	SS	19	60	9	19	2	2	0	5	1	.317
2005	High Desert	Calif.	2B	3	10	0	5	1	0	0	3	1	.500
2005	Royals	Arizona	SS	7	25	6	8	1	0	2	9	1	.320
2005	Wichita	Texas	SS	9	37	5	7	0	0	1	5	0	.189
2005	Omaha	P.C.	SS	35	114	13	29	4	2	1	9	2	.254
2005	Kansas City	A.L.	2B-SS	26	79	6	17	0	1	0	5	0	.215
2006	Omaha	P.C.	SS	88	283	30	67	9	4	2	20	6	.237
2006	Kansas City	A.L.	SS-2B	33	87	9	21	4	1	0	9	0	.241
2007	Royals	Arizona	SS	2	2	0	0	0	0	0	0	0	.000
2007	Omaha a-b	P.C.	SS-2B	28	97	8	19	2	0	0	8	0	.196
2008	Iowa	P.C.	SS-2B-3B	102	298	30	85	8	2	1	36	9	.285
2009	Iowa	P.C.	SS-3B-2B	64	230	30	70	17	2	6	29	6	.304
2009	Chicago c	N.L.	2B-SS	53	123	15	31	8	0	1	12	0	.252
2010	Texas d	A.L.	2B-SS-3B	68	166	17	46	10	1	0	13	0	.277
Major League Totals			5 Yrs.	199	515	56	134	24	5	1	44	1	.260

a Filed for free agency, October 29, 2007. Signed with Chicago Cubs organization, November 20, 2007.
b Filed for free agency, November 3, 2008, re-signed with Chicago Cubs organization, November 20, 2007.
c On disabled list from August 4 to September 1, 2009.
d Sold to Texas Rangers, March 27, 2010.

BLANCO (PEDRAZA), GREGOR MIGUEL

Born, Caracas, Venezuela, December 12, 1983.
Bats Left. Throws Left. Height, 5 feet, 11 inches. Weight, 170 pounds.

Year	Club	Lea	Pos	G	AB	R	H	2B	3B	HR	RBI	SB	Avg
2002	Macon	So.Atl.	OF	132	468	87	127	14	9	7	36	40	.271
2003	Myrtle Beach	Carolina	OF	126	461	66	125	19	7	5	36	34	.271
2004	Myrtle Beach	Carolina	OF	119	435	73	117	17	9	8	41	25	.269
2005	Mississippi	Southern	OF	123	401	64	101	11	12	6	37	28	.252
2006	Richmond	Int.	OF	73	269	43	79	12	1	0	19	14	.294
2006	Mississippi	Southern	OF	66	251	45	72	16	3	0	9	17	.287
2007	Richmond	Int.	OF	124	464	81	131	18	5	3	35	23	.282
2008	Atlanta	N.L.	OF	144	430	52	108	14	4	1	38	13	.251
2009	Atlanta	N.L.	OF	24	43	5	8	0	1	0	1	2	.186
2009	Gwinnett	Int.	OF	90	333	54	76	9	1	2	30	10	.228
2010	Gwinnett	Int.	OF	44	154	26	44	8	0	1	11	9	.286
2010	Atlanta	N.L.	OF	36	58	9	18	1	1	0	3	1	.310
2010	Kansas City a	A.L.	OF	49	179	22	49	8	3	1	11	10	.274
Major League Totals			3 Yrs.	253	710	88	183	23	9	2	53	26	.258

a Traded to Kansas City Royals with pitcher Jesse Chavez and pitcher Tim Collins for outfielder Rick Ankiel, pitcher Kyle Farnsworth and cash, July 31, 2010.

BLOOMQUIST, WILLIAM PAUL (WILLIE)

Born, Bremerton, Washington, November 27, 1977.
Bats Right. Throws Right. Height, 5 feet, 11 inches. Weight, 195 pounds.

Year	Club	Lea	Pos	G	AB	R	H	2B	3B	HR	RBI	SB	Avg
1999	Everett	Northwest	2B	41	178	35	51	10	3	2	27	17	.287
2000	Lancaster	California	2B-SS	64	256	63	97	19	6	2	51	22	.379
2000	Tacoma a	P.C.	2B	51	191	17	43	5	1	1	23	5	.225
2001	San Antonio	Texas	SS-2B	123	491	59	125	23	2	0	28	34	.255
2002	Tacoma	P.C.	OF-2B-3B-SS	104	337	47	91	14	3	6	47	20	.270
2002	Seattle b	A.L.	OF-2B	12	33	11	15	4	0	0	7	3	.455
2003	Seattle	A.L.	3B-SS-OF	89	196	30	49	7	2	1	14	4	.250
2004	Tacoma	P.C.	SS-OF	3	12	2	5	0	0	1	3	1	.417
2004	Seattle c	A.L.	3B-SS-1B-OF	93	188	27	46	10	0	2	18	13	.245
2005	Seattle d	A.L.	2B-SS-OF-3B	82	249	27	64	15	2	0	22	14	.257
2006	Seattle	A.L.	OF-SS-2B-3B	102	251	36	62	6	2	1	15	16	.247
2007	Seattle	A.L.	OF-2B-3B-SS	91	173	28	48	3	0	2	13	7	.277
2008	Seattle e-f	A.L.	OF-SS-2B-3B	71	165	32	46	1	0	0	9	14	.279
2009	Kansas City	A.L.	OF-SS-2B-1B	125	434	52	115	11	8	4	29	25	.265
2010	Kansas City	A.L.	OF-3B-2B	72	170	31	45	10	1	3	17	8	.265

Year	Club	Lea	Pos	G	AB	R	H	2B	3B	HR	RBI	SB	Avg
2010	Cincinnati g-h.........	N.L.	OF-2B	11	17	0	5	0	0	0	0	0	.294
Major League Totals	....		9 Yrs.	748	1876	274	495	67	15	13	144	104	.264

a On disabled list from August 6 to September 29, 2000.
b On disabled list from April 22 to May 3 and June 6 to 18, 2002.
c On disabled list from May 2 to May 21, 2004.
d On disabled list from August 30 to October 31, 2005.
e On disabled list from August 10 to September 29, 2008.
f Filed for free agency, October 30, 2008. Signed with Kansas City Royals, January 9, 2009.
g Sold to Cincinnati Reds, September 13, 2010.
h Filed for free agency, November 1, 2010. Signed with Arizona Diamondbacks, January 18, 2011.

BLUM, GEOFFREY EDWARD (GEOFF)

Born, Redwood City, California, April 26, 1973.
Bats Both. Throws Right. Height, 6 feet, 3 inches. Weight, 205 pounds.

Year	Club	Lea	Pos	G	AB	R	H	2B	3B	HR	RBI	SB	Avg
1994	Vermont.....	N.Y.-Penn.	SS	63	241	48	83	15	1	3	38	5	.344
1995	Wst Plm Bch	Fla.St.	2B-SS-3B	125	457	54	120	20	2	1	62	6	.263
1996	Harrisburg	Eastern	2B-SS-1B-OF	120	396	47	95	22	2	1	41	6	.240
1997	Ottawa	Int.	2B-SS-3B	118	407	59	101	21	2	3	35	14	.248
1998	Ottawa	Int.	2B-SS	8	23	1	4	0	0	0	1	0	.174
1998	Expos.......	Gulf Coast	2B	5	18	0	3	1	1	0	1	0	.167
1998	Jupiter.........	Fla.St.	2B-3B-SS	17	58	13	16	6	0	0	5	1	.276
1998	Harrisburg.....	Eastern	3B-SS-2B	39	139	25	43	12	3	6	21	2	.309
1999	Ottawa	Int.	SS	77	268	43	71	14	1	10	37	6	.265
1999	Montreal a	N.L.	SS-2B	45	133	21	32	7	2	8	18	1	.241
2000	Montreal...........	N.L.	3B-SS-2B-1B	124	343	40	97	20	2	11	45	1	.283
2001	Montreal...........	N.L.	3B-OF-2B-1B	148	453	57	107	25	0	9	50	9	.236
2002	Houston b	N.L.	3B-OF-SS-1B	130	368	45	104	20	4	10	52	2	.283
2003	Houston c	N.L.	3B-2B-SS-1B	123	420	51	110	19	0	10	52	0	.262
2004	Tampa Bay d	A.L.	3B-2B-OF-1B	112	339	38	73	21	0	8	35	2	.215
2005	Lake Elsinore .	California	3B-OF	2	8	3	2	0	0	2	5	0	.250
2005	San Diego	N.L.	3B-2B-SS-1B	78	224	26	54	13	1	5	22	3	.241
2005	Chicago e-f-g......	A.L.	1B-3B-SS-2B	31	95	6	19	2	1	1	3	0	.200
2006	San Diego h.......	N.L.	SS-3B-1B-2B	109	276	27	70	17	1	4	34	0	.254
2007	San Diego i.........	N.L.	2B-3B-SS-OF	122	330	34	83	21	1	5	33	0	.252
2008	Houston...........	N.L.	3B-2B-1B-SS	114	325	36	78	14	1	14	53	1	.240
2009	Round Rock........	P.C.	3B	2	7	0	1	1	0	0	1	0	.143
2009	Houston j..........	N.L.	3B-1B-SS	120	381	34	94	14	1	10	49	0	.247
2010	Corpus Christi ...	Texas	SS	3	9	0	2	2	0	0	1	0	.222
2010	Houston k-l	N.L.	SS-1B-3B-2B	93	202	22	54	10	1	2	22	0	.267
Major League Totals	....		12 Yrs.	1349	3889	437	975	203	15	97	468	19	.251
	Division Series												
2005	Chicago	A.L.	1B	1	1	0	0	0	0	0	0	0	.000
2006	San Diego	N.L.	SS-3B	4	8	0	1	1	0	0	1	0	.125
Division Series Totals	....			5	9	0	1	1	0	0	1	0	.111
	World Series Record												
2005	Chicago	A.L.	2B	1	1	1	1	0	0	1	1	0	1.000

a On disabled list from May 21 to June 15, 1999.
b Traded to Houston Astros for infielder Chris Truby, March 12, 2002.
c Traded to Tampa Bay Devil Rays for pitcher Brandon Backe, December 14, 2003.
d Released by Tampa Bay Devil Rays, November 19, 2004. Signed with San Diego Padres, December 8, 2004.
e On disabled list from April 30 to May 18, 2005.
f Traded to Chicago White Sox for pitcher Ryan Meaux, July 31, 2005.
g Filed for free agency, October 31, 2005. Signed with San Diego Padres, November 16, 2005.
h Filed for free agency, October 28, 2006, re-signed with San Diego Padres, December 1, 2006.
i Filed for free agency, October 30, 2007. Signed with Houston Astros, November 20, 2007.
j On disabled list from June 13 to June 28, 2009.
k On disabled list from July 3 to August 3, 2010.
l Filed for free agency, November 1, 2010. Signed with Arizona Diamondbacks, November 15, 2010.

BOESCH, BRENNAN P.

Born, Santa Monica, California, April 12, 1985.
Bats Left. Throws Left. Height, 6 feet, 4 inches. Weight, 235 pounds.

Year	Club	Lea	Pos	G	AB	R	H	2B	3B	HR	RBI	SB	Avg
2006	Oneonta	N.Y.-Penn.	OF	70	292	27	85	15	6	5	54	3	.291
2007	West Michigan.....	Midwest	OF	126	513	52	137	19	4	10	86	15	.267
2008	Lakeland............	Fla.St.	OF	111	417	46	104	17	8	7	64	3	.249

Year	Club	Lea	Pos	G	AB	R	H	2B	3B	HR	RBI	SB	Avg
2009	Erie	Eastern	OF	131	527	89	145	26	7	28	93	11	.275
2010	Toledo	Int.	OF	15	58	6	22	3	1	3	17	2	.379
2010	Detroit	A.L.	OF	133	464	49	119	26	3	14	67	7	.256

BONIFACIO, EMILIO JOSE

Born, Santo Domingo, Dominican Republic, April 23, 1985.
Bats Both. Throws Right. Height, 5 feet, 11 inches. Weight, 195 pounds.

Year	Club	Lea	Pos	G	AB	R	H	2B	3B	HR	RBI	SB	Avg
2003	Missoula	Pioneer	2B	54	146	20	29	1	1	0	16	15	.199
2004	South Bend	Midwest	2B	120	411	59	107	9	6	1	37	40	.260
2005	South Bend	Midwest	2B	127	522	81	141	14	7	1	44	55	.270
2006	Lancaster	Calif.	2B	130	546	117	175	35	7	7	50	61	.321
2007	Mobile	Southern	2B-SS	132	551	84	157	21	5	2	40	41	.285
2007	Arizona	N.L.	2B	11	23	2	5	1	0	0	2	0	.217
2008	Tucson	P.C.	2B-OF-SS	85	367	49	111	18	5	1	29	17	.302
2008	Columbus	Int.	2B	8	31	9	14	2	0	0	3	4	.452
2008	Arizona-Washington a-b	N.L.	2B-OF	49	169	29	41	6	5	0	14	7	.243
2009	Florida	N.L.	3B-SS-OF-2B	127	461	72	116	11	6	1	27	21	.252
2010	New Orleans	P.C.	OF-2B-SS	40	164	19	45	8	3	0	11	8	.274
2010	Florida	N.L.	OF-SS-3B-2B	73	180	30	47	6	3	0	10	12	.261
Major League Totals			4 Yrs.	260	833	133	209	24	14	1	53	40	.251

a Traded to Washington Nationals for pitcher Jon Rauch, July 22, 2008.
b Traded to Florida Marlins with pitcher P.J. Dean and infielder Jake Smolinski for pitcher Scott Olsen and outfielder Josh Willingham, November 11, 2008.

BORBON, JULIO ALBERTO

Born, Starkville, Mississippi, February 20, 1986.
Bats Left. Throws Left. Height, 6 feet, 1 inch. Weight, 180 pounds.

Year	Club	Lea	Pos	G	AB	R	H	2B	3B	HR	RBI	SB	Avg
2007	Rangers	Arizona	OF	2	8	0	2	1	0	0	0	0	.250
2007	Spokane	Northwest	OF	7	29	1	5	0	0	0	2	3	.172
2008	Bakersfield	Calif.	OF	66	291	47	89	20	0	2	36	36	.306
2008	Frisco	Texas	OF	60	255	40	86	12	2	5	22	17	.337
2009	Okla.	P.C.	OF	96	407	71	125	12	7	2	34	25	.307
2009	Texas	A.L.	DH-OF	46	157	30	49	4	0	4	20	19	.312
2010	Texas	A.L.	OF	137	438	60	121	11	4	3	42	15	.276
Major League Totals			2 Yrs.	183	595	90	170	15	4	7	62	34	.286
	Division Series												
2010	Texas	A.L.	OF	3	6	1	0	0	0	0	0	0	.000
	Championship Series												
2010	Texas	A.L.	PH	3	1	2	0	0	0	0	0	0	.000
	World Series Record												
2010	Texas	A.L.	PH	2	2	1	1	0	0	0	0	0	.500

BOURGEOIS, JASON JERROD

Born, Houston, Texas, January 4, 1982.
Bats Right. Throws Right. Height, 5 feet, 9 inches. Weight, 190 pounds.

Year	Club	Lea	Pos	G	AB	R	H	2B	3B	HR	RBI	SB	Avg
2000	Rangers	Gulf Coast	2B	24	88	18	21	4	0	0	6	9	.239
2001	Pulaski	Appal.	2B	62	251	60	78	12	2	7	34	21	.311
2002	Charlotte	Fla.St.	2B-SS	9	27	5	5	1	0	0	4	1	.185
2002	Savannah	So.Atl.	SS-2B	127	522	72	133	21	5	8	49	22	.255
2003	Stockton	Calif.	2B-SS-3B	69	277	75	91	22	3	4	34	16	.329
2003	Frisco	Texas	2B	55	202	28	51	5	4	4	21	3	.252
2004	Frisco	Texas	2B-SS	138	530	73	135	19	7	2	58	30	.255
2005	Richmond a-b	Int.	2B-OF-SS	119	388	33	93	20	2	2	16	8	.240
2006	San Antonio	Texas	OF-2B-SS	107	411	65	114	22	7	4	38	23	.277
2007	Charlotte	Int.	2B-OF-3B	84	338	51	105	18	3	7	34	23	.311
2007	Birmingham c-d	Southern	OF-2B-3B	43	162	25	48	10	3	2	20	15	.296
2008	Charlotte	Int.	OF-2B	127	510	83	146	23	5	9	48	30	.286
2008	Chicago e	A.L.	2B	6	3	0	1	1	0	0	0	0	.333
2009	Nashville	P.C.	OF	105	424	61	134	18	6	2	41	36	.316
2009	Milwaukee f	N.L.	OF	24	37	6	7	0	0	1	3	3	.189
2010	Round Rock	P.C.	OF	65	235	37	81	10	3	5	28	18	.345
2010	Houston	N.L.	OF-2B	69	123	16	27	4	1	0	3	12	.220
Major League Totals			3 Yrs.	99	163	22	35	5	1	1	6	15	.215

a Claimed on waivers from Texas Rangers by Atlanta Braves, March 24, 2005.
b Selected by Seattle Mariners in Rule V minor league draft, December 8, 2005.
c Filed for free agency, October 15, 2006. Signed with Chicago White Sox organization, January 19, 2007.
d Filed for free agency, October 29, 2007, re-signed with Chicaqo White Sox organization, November 19, 2007.
e Filed for free agency, October 17, 2008. Signed with Milwaukee Brewers organization, November 25, 2008.
f Claimed on waivers by Houston Astros, October 26, 2009.

BOURJOS, PETER CHRISTOPHER

Born, Park Ridge, Illinois, March 31, 1987.
Bats Right. Throws Right. Height, 6 feet, 1 inch. Weight, 180 pounds.

Year	Club	Lea	Pos	G	AB	R	H	2B	3B	HR	RBI	SB	Avg
2006	Orem	Pioneer	OF	65	250	42	73	16	7	5	28	13	.292
2007	Angels	Arizona	OF	4	16	3	5	0	1	0	2	0	.313
2007	Cedar Rapids	Midwest	OF	63	237	37	65	9	6	5	29	19	.274
2008	Rancho Cucamonga	Calif.	OF	121	509	83	150	29	10	9	51	50	.295
2009	Arkansas	Texas	OF	110	437	72	123	16	14	6	51	32	.281
2010	Salt Lake	P.C.	OF	102	414	85	130	13	12	13	52	27	.314
2010	Los Angeles	A.L.	OF	51	181	19	37	6	4	6	15	10	.204

BOURN, MICHAEL RAY

Born, Houston, Texas, December 27, 1982.
Bats Left. Throws Right. Height, 5 feet, 11 inches. Weight, 180 pounds.

Year	Club	Lea	Pos	G	AB	R	H	2B	3B	HR	RBI	SB	Avg
2003	Batavia	N.Y.-Penn.	OF	35	125	12	35	0	1	0	4	23	.280
2004	Lakewood	So.Atl.	OF	109	413	92	130	20	14	5	53	58	.315
2005	Reading	Eastern	OF	135	544	80	146	18	8	6	44	38	.268
2006	Reading	Eastern	OF	80	318	62	87	5	6	4	26	30	.274
2006	Scranton-WB	Int.	OF	38	152	34	43	5	7	1	15	15	.283
2006	Philadelphia	N.L.	OF	17	8	2	1	0	0	0	0	1	.125
2007	Philadelphia a-b	N.L.	OF	105	119	29	33	3	3	1	6	18	.277
2008	Houston	N.L.	OF	138	467	57	107	10	4	5	29	41	.229
2009	Houston	N.L.	OF	157	606	97	173	27	12	3	35	*61	.285
2010	Houston	N.L.	OF	141	535	84	142	25	6	2	38	*52	.265
Major League Totals			5 Yrs.	558	1735	269	456	65	25	11	108	173	.263
Division Series													
2007	Philadelphia	N.L.	PH	2	1	0	0	0	0	0	0	0	.000

a On disabled list from July 31 to September 10, 2007.
b Traded to Houston Astros with pitcher Geoff Geary and infielder Mike Costanzo for infielder Eric Bruntlett and pitcher Brad Lidge, November 12, 2007.

BOWKER, JOHN BRITE

Born, Sacramento, California, July 8, 1983.
Bats Left. Throws Left. Height, 6 feet, 2 inches. Weight, 200 pounds.

Year	Club	Lea	Pos	G	AB	R	H	2B	3B	HR	RBI	SB	Avg
2004	Giants	Arizona	OF	10	43	14	22	7	1	2	11	1	.512
2004	Salem-Keizer	Northwest	OF	31	127	23	41	9	2	4	16	1	.323
2005	San Jose	Calif.	OF	121	464	66	124	27	1	13	67	3	.267
2006	San Jose	Calif.	OF	112	462	61	131	32	6	7	66	6	.284
2006	Fresno	P.C.	OF	2	4	0	2	0	0	0	0	0	.500
2007	Connecticut	Eastern	OF	139	522	79	160	35	6	22	90	3	.307
2008	Fresno	P.C.	1B-OF	23	93	13	22	3	1	2	9	2	.237
2008	San Francisco	N.L.	1B-OF	111	326	31	83	14	3	10	43	1	.255
2009	Fresno	P.C.	OF-1B	104	366	82	125	22	4	21	83	10	.342
2009	San Francisco	N.L.	OF-1B	31	67	7	13	2	2	2	7	1	.194
2010	Fresno	P.C.	OF-1B	51	197	36	61	12	1	14	36	1	.310
2010	Indianapolis	Int.	1B-OF	25	91	10	29	7	2	4	10	0	.319
2010	San Fran.-Pittsburgh a	N.L.	OF-1B	67	151	16	33	8	0	5	21	0	.219
Major League Totals			3 Yrs.	209	544	54	129	24	5	17	71	2	.237

a Traded to Pittsburgh Pirates with pitcher Joe Martinez for pitcher Javier Lopez, July 31, 2010.

BRADLEY, MILTON OBELLE

Born, Harbor City, Florida, April 15, 1978.
Bats Both. Throws Right. Height, 6 feet. Weight, 225 pounds.

Year	Club	Lea	Pos	G	AB	R	H	2B	3B	HR	RBI	SB	Avg
1996	Expos	Gulf Coast	OF	32	112	18	27	7	1	1	12	7	.241
1997	Expos	Gulf Coast	OF	9	25	6	5	2	0	1	2	2	.200

Year Club	Lea	Pos	G	AB	R	H	2B	3B	HR	RBI	SB	Avg
1997 Vermont	N.Y.-Penn.	OF	50	200	29	60	7	5	3	30	7	.300
1998 Jupiter	Fla.St.	OF	67	261	55	75	14	1	5	34	17	.287
1998 Cape Fear	So.Atl.	OF	75	281	54	85	21	4	6	50	13	.302
1999 Harrisburg	Eastern	OF	86	346	62	114	22	5	12	50	14	.329
2000 Ottawa	Int.	OF	88	342	58	104	20	1	6	29	10	.304
2000 Montreal	N.L.	OF	42	154	20	34	8	1	2	15	2	.221
2001 Montreal	N.L.	OF	67	220	19	49	16	3	1	19	7	.223
2001 Ottawa	Int.	OF	35	136	21	37	7	2	2	13	14	.272
2001 Buffalo	Int.	OF	30	114	18	29	3	0	5	15	9	.254
2001 Cleveland a	A.L.	OF	10	18	3	4	1	0	0	0	1	.222
2002 Buffalo	Int.	OF	6	23	3	6	0	0	0	3	2	.261
2002 Akron	Eastern	OF	3	11	1	3	1	0	0	1	0	.273
2002 Cleveland b	A.L.	OF	98	325	48	81	18	3	9	38	6	.249
2003 Cleveland c	A.L.	OF	101	377	61	121	34	2	10	56	17	.321
2004 Los Angeles d-e	N.L.	OF	141	516	72	138	24	0	19	67	15	.267
2005 Las Vegas	P.C.	OF	5	13	2	4	0	0	0	1	1	.308
2005 Los Angeles f-g	N.L.	OF	75	283	49	82	14	1	13	38	6	.290
2006 Stockton	Calif.	OF	2	7	1	1	0	0	0	0	0	.143
2006 Sacramento	P.C.	OF	6	24	3	5	0	0	2	6	1	.208
2006 Oakland h	A.L.	OF	96	351	53	97	14	2	14	52	10	.276
2007 Sacramento	P.C.	OF	2	5	1	0	0	0	0	0	0	.000
2007 Oakland	A.L.	OF	19	65	6	19	4	0	2	7	2	.292
2007 San Diego i-j-k-l	N.L.	OF	42	144	31	45	5	1	11	30	3	.313
2008 Texas m	A.L.	DH-OF	126	414	78	133	32	1	22	77	5	.321
2009 Chicago n	N.L.	OF	124	393	61	101	17	1	12	40	2	.257
2010 Seattle o	A.L.	OF	73	244	28	50	9	1	8	29	8	.205
Major League Totals		11 Yrs.	1014	3504	529	954	196	16	123	468	84	.272
Division Series												
2004 Los Angeles	N.L.	OF	4	11	1	3	1	0	1	1	2	.273
2006 Oakland	A.L.	OF	3	13	1	1	0	0	1	2	0	.077
Division Series Totals			7	24	2	4	1	0	2	3	2	.167
Championship Series												
2006 Oakland	A.L.	OF	4	18	4	9	2	0	2	5	0	.500

a Traded to Cleveland Indians for pitcher Zach Day, July 31, 2001.
b On disabled list from May 2 to June 4 and August 12 to August 30, 2002.
c On disabled list from April 23 to May 8 and August 10 to October 3, 2003.
d Traded to Los Angeles Dodgers for outfielder Franklin Gutierrez and player to be named later, April 4, 2004.
e Cleveland Indians received pitcher Andrew Brown to complete trade, May 19, 2004.
f On disabled list from May 30 to July 23 and August 23 to October 28, 2005.
g Traded to Oakland Athletics with infielder Antonio Perez for outfielder Andre Ethier, December 13, 2005.
h On disabled list from April 27 to June 6 and June 15 to July 14, 2006.
i On disabled list from April 23 to May 11 and May 15 to May 30 and June 3 to June 20, 2007.
j Traded to San Diego Padres for pitcher Andrew Brown, June 29, 2007.
k On disabled list from June 21 to July 7, 2007.
l Filed for free agency, October 29, 2007. Signed with Texas Rangers, December 12, 2007.
m Filed for free agency, October 30, 2008. Signed with Chicago Cubs, January 6, 2009.
n Traded to Seattle Mariners for pitcher Carlos Silva, December 18, 2009.
o On disabled list from July 27 to October 8, 2010.

BRANTLEY, MICHAEL CHARLES JR.

Born, Bellevue, Washington, May 15, 1987.
Bats Left. Throws Left. Height, 6 feet, 2 inches. Weight, 200 pounds.

Year Club	Lea	Pos	G	AB	R	H	2B	3B	HR	RBI	SB	Avg
2005 Brewers	Arizona	OF	44	173	34	60	3	1	0	19	14	.347
2005 Helena	Pioneer	OF	10	34	8	11	2	0	0	3	2	.324
2006 West Virginia	So.Atl.	OF	108	360	47	108	10	2	0	42	24	.300
2007 West Virginia	So.Atl.	1B-OF	56	218	41	73	15	1	2	32	18	.335
2007 Huntsville	Southern	OF-1B	59	187	28	47	6	1	0	21	17	.251
2008 Huntsville a	Southern	OF-1B	106	420	80	134	17	2	4	40	28	.319
2009 Columbus	Int.	OF	116	457	80	122	21	2	6	37	46	.267
2009 Cleveland	A.L.	OF	28	112	10	35	4	0	0	11	4	.313
2010 Columbus	Int.	OF	67	273	54	87	13	2	4	29	13	.319
2010 Cleveland	A.L.	OF	72	297	38	73	9	3	3	22	10	.246
Major League Totals		2 Yrs.	100	409	48	108	13	3	3	33	14	.264

a Sent by Milwaukee Brewers to Cleveland Indians as player to be named later for pitcher C.C. Sabathia, October 3, 2008.

BRANYAN, RUSSELL OLES

Born, Warner Robins, Georgia, December 19, 1975.
Bats Left. Throws Right. Height, 6 feet, 3 inches. Weight, 230 pounds.

Year Club	Lea	Pos	G	AB	R	H	2B	3B	HR	RBI	SB	Avg
1994 Burlington	Appal.	3B	55	171	21	36	10	0	5	13	4	.211
1995 Columbus..........	So.Atl.	3B	76	277	46	71	8	6	19	55	1	.256
1996 Columbus..........	So.Atl.	3B	130	482	102	129	20	4	40	106	7	.268
1997 Kinston...........	Carolina	3B	83	297	59	86	26	2	27	75	3	.290
1997 Akron.............	Eastern	3B	41	137	26	32	4	0	12	30	0	.234
1998 Akron.............	Eastern	3B	43	163	35	48	11	3	16	46	1	.294
1998 Cleveland	A.L.	3B	1	4	0	0	0	0	0	0	0	.000
1999 Buffalo	Int.	3B	109	395	51	82	11	1	30	67	8	.208
1999 Cleveland	A.L.	3B	11	38	4	8	2	0	1	6	0	.211
2000 Buffalo	Int.	3B-OF	64	229	46	56	9	2	21	60	1	.245
2000 Cleveland	A.L.	OF-3B	67	193	32	46	7	2	16	38	0	.238
2001 Cleveland	A.L.	3B-OF	113	315	48	73	16	2	20	54	1	.232
2002 Cleveland	A.L.	OF-3B	50	161	16	33	4	0	8	17	1	.205
2002 Cincinnati a	N.L.	OF-1B-3B	84	217	34	53	9	1	16	39	3	.244
2003 Louisville	Int.	OF-1B-3B	14	49	5	16	5	0	1	3	0	.327
2003 Cincinnati b-c.........	N.L.	3B-OF-1B	74	176	22	38	12	0	9	26	0	.216
2004 Richmond	Int.	OF	11	28	5	5	0	0	1	4	1	.179
2004 Buffalo	Int.	1B-3B-OF	82	313	58	90	16	2	25	75	5	.288
2004 Milwaukee d-e-f.......	N.L.	3B-1B	51	158	21	37	11	1	11	27	1	.234
2005 Nashville	P.C.	OF-3B	6	17	4	5	4	0	1	3	0	.294
2005 Milwaukee g..........	N.L.	3B-1B-OF	85	202	23	52	11	0	12	31	1	.257
2006 Tampa Bay...........	A.L.	OF-3B-1B	64	169	23	34	10	0	12	27	2	.201
2006 San Diego h-i.........	N.L.	3B	27	72	14	21	1	0	6	9	0	.292
2007 San Diego	N.L.	3B-OF	61	122	16	24	5	1	7	19	1	.197
2007 Buffalo	Int.	DH	1	4	0	0	0	0	0	0	0	.000
2007 San Diego-Phil.-St. Louis j-k-l..	N.L.	3B-OF-1B	89	163	22	32	5	1	10	26	1	.196
2008 Nashville	P.C.	3B-1B-OF	45	153	24	55	15	0	12	36	4	.359
2008 Milwaukee m-n-o......	N.L.	3B-1B	50	132	24	33	8	0	12	20	1	.250
2009 Seattle p-q	A.L.	1B	116	431	64	108	21	1	31	76	2	.251
2010 Akron.............	Eastern	1B	2	8	1	2	0	0	0	0	0	.250
2010 Columbus.............	Int.	1B	4	14	1	4	2	0	0	1	0	.286
2010 Cleveland-Seattle r-s-t..	A.L.	DH-1B	109	376	47	89	19	0	25	57	1	.237
Major League Totals		13 Yrs.	991	2807	394	657	136	8	189	453	14	.234
Division Series												
2001 Cleveland	A.L.	OF	2	3	1	1	0	0	0	0	0	.333
2006 San Diego	N.L.	3B	4	13	1	3	1	1	0	3	0	.231
Division Series Totals			6	16	2	4	1	1	0	3	0	.250

a Traded to Cincinnati Reds for infielder Ben Broussard, June 7, 2002.
b On disabled list from March 18 to May 29, 2003.
c On disabled list from August 13 to August 28, 2003.
d Not offered contract, December 21, 2003. Signed with Atlanta Braves organization, January 21, 2004.
e Traded to Cleveland Indians for player to be named later, April 26, 2004. Milwaukee Brewers received pitcher Scott Sturkie to complete trade, May 25. 2004.
f Sold to Milwaukee Brewers, July 26, 2004.
g On disabled list from June 2 to July 4, 2005.
h Released by Milwaukee Brewers, January 17, 2006. Signed with Tampa Bay Devil Rays organization, January 31, 2006.
i Traded to San Diego Padres for pitcher Evan Meek and player to be named later, August 24, 2006. Tampa Bay Devil Rays received pitcher Dale Thayer to complete trade, September 15, 2006.
j Released by San Diego Padres, July 28, 2007. Signed with Cleveland Indians organization, August 7, 2007.
k Sold to Philadelphia Phillies, August 9, 2007.
l Traded to St. Louis Cardinals for player to be named later, August 31, 2007.
m Filed for free agency, October 30, 2007. Signed with Milwaukee Brewers organization, February 20, 2008.
n On disabled list from August 12 to September 23, 2008.
o Filed for free agency, November 1, 2008. Signed with Seattle Mariners, December 3, 2008.
p On disabled list from August 29 to September 29, 2009.
q Filed for free agency, November 9, 2009. Signed with Cleveland Indians, February 24, 2010.
r On disabled list from March 26 to April 20, 2010.
s Traded to Seattle Mariners for infielder Juan Diaz and outfielder Ezequiel Carrera, June 26, 2010.
t Filed for free agency, November 3, 2010.

BRAUN, RYAN JOSEPH

Born, Mission Hills, California, November 17, 1983.
Bats Right. Throws Right. Height, 6 feet, 2 inches. Weight, 200 pounds.

Year Club	Lea	Pos	G	AB	R	H	2B	3B	HR	RBI	SB	Avg
2005 Helena	Pioneer	3B	10	41	6	14	2	1	2	10	2	.341

Year	Club	Lea	Pos	G	AB	R	H	2B	3B	HR	RBI	SB	Avg
2005	West Virginia	So.Atl.	3B	37	152	21	54	16	2	8	35	2	.355
2006	Brevard County	Fla.St.	3B	59	226	34	62	12	2	7	37	14	.274
2006	Huntsville........	Southern	3B	59	231	42	70	19	1	15	40	12	.303
2007	Nashville	P.C.	3B	34	117	28	40	12	0	10	22	4	.342
2007	Milwaukee a..........	N.L.	3B	113	451	91	146	26	6	34	97	15	.324
2008	Milwaukee	N.L.	OF	151	611	92	174	39	7	37	106	14	.285
2009	Milwaukee	N.L.	OF	158	635	113	*203	39	6	32	114	20	.320
2010	Milwaukee	N.L.	OF	157	619	101	188	45	1	25	103	14	.304
Major League Totals			4 Yrs.	579	2316	397	711	149	20	128	420	63	.307
	Division Series												
2008	Milwaukee	N.L.	OF	4	16	0	5	2	0	0	2	0	.313

a Selected Rookie of the Year in National League for 2007.

BRIGNAC, REID MICHAEL

Born, St.Amant, Louisiana, January 16, 1986.
Bats Left. Throws Right. Height, 6 feet, 3 inches. Weight, 195 pounds.

Year	Club	Lea	Pos	G	AB	R	H	2B	3B	HR	RBI	SB	Avg
2004	Princeton...........	Appal.	SS	25	97	16	35	4	2	1	25	2	.361
2004	Charleston.........	So.Atl.	SS	3	14	3	7	1	0	0	5	0	.500
2005	SW Michigan	Midwest	SS	127	512	77	135	29	2	15	61	5	.264
2006	Visalia	Calif.	SS	100	411	82	134	26	3	21	83	12	.326
2006	Montgomery	Southern	SS	28	110	18	33	6	2	3	16	3	.300
2007	Montgomery	Southern	SS	133	527	91	137	30	5	17	81	15	.260
2008	Tampa Bay...........	A.L.	SS	4	10	1	0	0	0	0	0	0	.000
2008	Durham..............	Int.	SS-2B	97	352	43	88	26	2	9	43	5	.250
2009	Durham..............	Int.	SS-2B	96	415	51	117	28	2	8	44	5	.282
2009	Tampa Bay...........	A.L.	SS-2B	31	90	10	25	8	2	1	6	2	.278
2010	Tampa Bay...........	A.L.	2B-SS-OF	113	301	39	77	13	1	8	45	3	.256
Major League Totals			3 Yrs.	148	401	50	102	21	3	9	51	5	.254
	Division Series												
2010	Tampa Bay...........	N.L.	SS	2	3	0	0	0	0	0	0	0	.000

BROWN, DOMONIC LARUN

Born, Lithonia, Georgia, September 3, 1987.
Bats Left. Throws Left. Height, 6 feet, 5 inches. Weight, 200 pounds.

Year	Club	Lea	Pos	G	AB	R	H	2B	3B	HR	RBI	SB	Avg
2006	Phillies.........	Gulf Coast	OF	34	117	13	25	3	0	1	7	13	.214
2007	Clearwater...........	Fla.St.	OF	3	9	2	4	1	0	1	7	0	.444
2007	Williamsport.....	N.Y.-Penn.	OF	74	285	43	84	11	5	3	32	14	.295
2008	Lakewood..........	So.Atl.	OF	114	444	77	129	23	3	9	54	22	.291
2009	Reading	Eastern	OF	37	147	20	41	9	4	3	20	8	.279
2009	Clearwater	Fla.St.	OF	66	238	41	72	12	3	11	44	15	.303
2009	Phillies.........	Gulf Coast	OF	3	10	4	5	0	2	0	0	0	.500
2010	Reading	Eastern	OF	65	236	50	75	16	3	15	47	12	.318
2010	Lehigh Valley..........	Int.	OF	28	107	15	37	6	1	5	21	5	.346
2010	Philadelphia..........	N.L.	OF	35	62	8	13	3	0	2	13	2	.210
	Division Series												
2010	Philadelphia..........	N.L.	PH	1	1	1	0	0	0	0	0	0	.000
	Championship Series												
2010	Philadelphia..........	N.L.	PH	2	2	0	0	0	0	0	0	0	.000

BRUCE, JAY ALLEN

Born, Beaumont, Texas, April 3, 1987.
Bats Left. Throws Left. Height, 6 feet, 3 inches. Weight, 205 pounds.

Year	Club	Lea	Pos	G	AB	R	H	2B	3B	HR	RBI	SB	Avg
2005	Reds...........	Gulf Coast	OF	37	122	29	33	9	2	5	25	4	.270
2005	Billings............	Pioneer	OF	17	70	16	18	2	0	4	13	2	.257
2006	Dayton...........	Midwest	OF	117	444	69	129	42	5	16	81	19	.291
2007	Sarasota............	Fla.St.	OF	67	268	49	87	27	5	11	49	4	.325
2007	Louisville............	Int.	OF	50	187	28	57	12	2	11	25	2	.305
2007	Chattanooga.......	Southern	OF	16	66	10	22	7	1	4	15	2	.333
2008	Louisville............	Int.	OF	49	184	34	67	9	5	10	37	8	.364
2008	Cincinnati............	N.L.	OF	108	413	63	105	17	1	21	52	4	.254
2009	Louisville............	Int.	OF	5	18	3	5	0	0	0	0	2	.278
2009	Cincinnati a	N.L.	OF	101	345	47	77	15	2	22	58	3	.223

Year Club	Lea	Pos	G	AB	R	H	2B	3B	HR	RBI	SB	Avg
2010 Cincinnati	N.L.	OF	148	509	80	143	23	5	25	70	5	.281
Major League Totals		3 Yrs.	357	1267	190	325	55	8	68	180	12	.257
Division Series												
2010 Cincinnati	N.L.	OF	3	8	1	2	0	0	1	1	0	.250

a On disabled list from July 12 to September 14, 2009.

BUCK, JOHNATHAN RICHARD (JOHN)

Born, Kemmerer, Wyoming, July 7, 1980.
Bats Right. Throws Right. Height, 6 feet, 3 inches. Weight, 220 pounds.

Year Club	Lea	Pos	G	AB	R	H	2B	3B	HR	RBI	SB	Avg
1998 Astros	Gulf Coast	C	36	126	24	36	9	0	3	15	2	.286
1999 Auburn	N.Y.-Penn.	C	63	233	36	57	17	0	3	29	7	.245
1999 Michigan	Midwest	C	4	10	1	1	1	0	0	0	0	.100
2000 Michigan	Midwest	C	109	390	57	110	33	0	10	71	2	.282
2001 Lexington	So.Atl.	C	122	443	72	122	24	1	22	73	4	.275
2002 Round Rock	Texas	C	120	448	48	118	29	3	12	89	2	.263
2003 New Orleans	P.C.	C	78	274	32	70	18	2	2	39	1	.255
2004 New Orleans	P.C.	C	65	227	31	68	11	0	12	35	0	.300
2004 Kansas City a	A.L.	C	71	238	36	56	9	0	12	30	1	.235
2005 Kansas City	A.L.	C	118	401	40	97	21	1	12	47	2	.242
2006 Kansas City	A.L.	C	114	371	37	91	21	1	11	50	0	.245
2007 Kansas City	A.L.	C	113	347	41	77	18	0	18	48	0	.222
2008 Kansas City	A.L.	C	109	370	48	83	23	1	9	48	0	.224
2009 Omaha	P.C.	C	7	27	3	7	1	0	2	4	0	.259
2009 Kansas City b-c	A.L.	C	59	186	16	46	12	4	8	36	1	.247
2010 New Hampshire	Eastern	C	3	11	2	3	0	0	2	6	0	.273
2010 Toronto d-e	A.L.	C	118	409	53	115	25	0	20	66	0	.281
Major League Totals		7 Yrs.	702	2322	271	565	129	7	90	325	4	.243

a Traded by Houston Astros to Kansas City Royals with pitcher Octavio Dotel for outfielder Carlos Beltran, June 24, 2004.
b On disabled list from May 31 to July 6, 2009.
c Not offered contract, December 12, 2009. Signed with Toronto Blue Jays, December 16, 2009.
d On disabled list from August 5 to August 20, 2010.
e Filed for free agency, November 1, 2010. Signed with Florida Marlins, November 16, 2010.

BURRELL, PATRICK BRIAN (PAT)

Born, Eureka Springs, Arkansas, October 10, 1976.
Bats Right. Throws Right. Height, 6 feet, 4 inches. Weight, 235 pounds.

Year Club	Lea	Pos	G	AB	R	H	2B	3B	HR	RBI	SB	Avg
1998 Clearwater	Fla.St.	1B	37	132	29	40	7	1	7	30	2	.303
1999 Scranton-WB	Int.	1B	9	33	4	5	0	0	1	4	0	.152
1999 Reading	Eastern	1B	117	417	84	139	28	6	28	90	3	.333
2000 Scranton-WB	Int.	OF	40	143	31	42	15	1	4	25	1	.294
2000 Philadelphia	N.L.	1B-OF	111	408	57	106	27	1	18	79	0	.260
2001 Philadelphia	N.L.	OF	155	539	70	139	29	2	27	89	2	.258
2002 Philadelphia	N.L.	OF	157	586	96	165	39	2	37	116	1	.282
2003 Philadelphia	N.L.	OF	146	522	57	109	31	4	21	64	0	.209
2004 Reading	Eastern	OF	4	15	2	3	0	0	2	4	0	.200
2004 Philadelphia a	N.L.	OF	127	448	66	115	17	0	24	84	2	.257
2005 Philadelphia	N.L.	OF	154	562	78	158	27	1	32	117	0	.281
2006 Philadelphia	N.L.	OF	144	462	80	119	24	1	29	95	0	.258
2007 Philadelphia	N.L.	OF	155	472	77	121	26	0	30	97	0	.256
2008 Philadelphia b	N.L.	OF	157	536	74	134	33	3	33	86	0	.250
2009 Charlotte	Fla.St.	DH	1	4	0	0	0	0	0	0	0	.000
2009 Montgomery	Southern	DH	2	9	1	1	0	0	0	0	0	.111
2009 Tampa Bay c	A.L.	DH-OF	122	412	45	91	16	1	14	64	2	.221
2010 Fresno	P.C.	OF	5	16	4	5	1	0	1	6	0	.313
2010 Tampa Bay	A.L.	DH	24	84	9	17	5	0	2	13	0	.202
2010 San Francisco d-e	N.L.	OF	96	289	41	77	16	0	18	51	0	.266
Major League Totals		11 Yrs.	1548	5320	750	1351	290	15	285	955	7	.254
Division Series												
2007 Philadelphia	N.L.	OF	3	11	1	2	0	0	1	1	0	.182
2008 Philadelphia	N.L.	OF	4	12	2	3	0	0	2	4	0	.250
2010 San Francisco	N.L.	OF	4	10	1	2	1	0	1	3	0	.200
Division Series Totals			11	33	4	7	1	0	4	8	0	.212
Championship Series												
2008 Philadelphia	N.L.	OF	5	18	1	6	0	0	1	3	0	.333

Year Club	Lea	Pos	G	AB	R	H	2B	3B	HR	RBI	SB	Avg
2010 San Francisco	N.L.	OF	6	19	3	4	2	0	0	1	0	.211
Championship Series Totals			11	37	4	10	2	0	1	4	0	.270
World Series Record												
2008 Philadelphia	N.L.	OF	5	14	0	1	1	0	0	1	0	.071
2010 San Francisco	N.L.	OF-DH	4	13	1	0	0	0	0	0	0	.000
World Series Totals			9	27	1	1	1	0	0	1	0	.037

a On disabled list from August 4 to September 3, 2004.
b Filed for free agency, November 6, 2008. Signed with Tampa Bay Rays, January 5, 2009.
c On disabled list from May 12 to June 12, 2009.
d Released by Tampa Bay Rays, May 16, 2010. Signed with San Francisco Giants, May 29, 2010.
e Filed for free agency, November 1, 2010, re-signed with San Francisco Giants, December 3, 2010.

BURRISS, EMMANUEL ALLEN

Born, Washington, District of Columbia, January 17, 1985.
Bats Both. Throws Right. Height, 6 feet. Weight, 190 pounds.

Year Club	Lea	Pos	G	AB	R	H	2B	3B	HR	RBI	SB	Avg
2006 Salem-Keizer .	Northwest	SS	65	254	50	78	8	2	1	27	35	.307
2007 San Jose	Calif.	SS	36	139	23	23	2	0	0	8	17	.165
2007 Augusta	So.Atl.	SS	89	365	64	117	14	4	0	38	51	.321
2008 Fresno	P.C.	2B-SS	14	62	6	16	1	1	0	6	2	.258
2008 San Francisco	N.L.	SS-2B-OF	95	240	37	68	6	1	1	18	13	.283
2009 Fresno	P.C.	2B	17	71	9	19	2	1	1	7	6	.268
2009 San Francisco a	N.L.	2B	61	202	18	48	6	0	0	13	11	.238
2010 San Jose	Calif.	SS	5	14	2	3	0	0	0	1	1	.214
2010 Fresno	P.C.	SS-2B	67	273	32	77	11	2	0	22	11	.282
2010 San Francisco b	N.L.	2B	7	5	3	2	0	0	0	0	0	.400
Major League Totals		3 Yrs.	163	447	58	118	12	1	1	31	24	.264

a On disabled list from September 1 to November 10, 2009.
b On disabled list from March 26 to June 25, 2010.

BUTLER, BILLY RAY

Born, Orange Park, Florida, April 18, 1986.
Bats Right. Throws Right. Height, 6 feet, 1 inch. Weight, 240 pounds.

Year Club	Lea	Pos	G	AB	R	H	2B	3B	HR	RBI	SB	Avg
2004 Idaho Falls	Pioneer	3B	72	260	74	97	22	3	10	68	5	.373
2005 High Desert	Calif.	3B-OF	92	379	70	132	30	2	25	91	0	.348
2005 Wichita.........	Texas	OF	29	112	14	35	9	0	5	19	0	.313
2006 Wichita.........	Texas	OF	119	477	82	158	33	1	15	96	1	.331
2007 Omaha	P.C.	OF-1B	57	203	40	59	10	1	13	46	1	.291
2007 Kansas City	A.L.	DH-1B-OF	92	329	38	96	23	2	8	52	0	.292
2008 Omaha	P.C.	1B	26	101	18	34	6	1	5	13	0	.337
2008 Kansas City	A.L.	DH-1B	124	443	44	122	22	0	11	55	0	.275
2009 Kansas City	A.L.	1B	159	608	78	183	51	1	21	93	1	.301
2010 Kansas City	A.L.	1B	158	595	77	189	45	0	15	78	0	.318
Major League Totals		4 Yrs.	533	1975	237	590	141	3	55	278	1	.299

BYRD, MARLON JERRARD

Born, Boynton Beach, Florida, August 30, 1977.
Bats Right. Throws Right. Height, 6 feet. Weight, 235 pounds.

Year Club	Lea	Pos	G	AB	R	H	2B	3B	HR	RBI	SB	Avg
1999 Batavia.........	N.Y.-Penn.	OF	65	239	39	70	7	6	13	49	8	.293
2000 Piedmont..........	So.Atl.	OF	133	515	104	159	29	13	17	93	41	.309
2001 Reading	Eastern	OF	137	510	108	161	22	8	28	89	32	.316
2002 Scranton-WB	Int.	OF	136	538	103	160	37	7	15	63	15	.297
2002 Philadelphia	N.L.	OF	10	35	2	8	2	0	1	1	0	.229
2003 Scranton-WB	Int.	OF	1	4	1	3	1	0	0	0	0	.750
2003 Reading	Eastern	OF	3	16	3	5	0	0	1	3	0	.313
2003 Philadelphia a.........	N.L.	OF	135	495	86	150	28	4	7	45	11	.303
2004 Scranton/WB	Int.	OF	37	152	13	40	11	1	2	17	2	.263
2004 Philadelphia	N.L.	OF	106	346	48	79	13	2	5	33	2	.228
2005 New Orleans...........	P.C.	OF	21	81	19	33	6	0	5	11	4	.407
2005 Scranton/WB	Int.	OF	5	19	4	7	1	0	3	5	0	.368
2005 Philadelphia-Washington b-c	N.L.	OF	79	229	20	61	15	2	2	26	5	.266
2006 New Orleans...........	P.C.	OF	46	155	20	42	9	0	7	29	3	.271
2006 Washington d.........	N.L.	OF	78	197	28	44	8	1	5	18	3	.223

Year	Club	Lea	Pos	G	AB	R	H	2B	3B	HR	RBI	SB	Avg
2007	Oklahoma	P.C.	OF	44	176	29	63	15	2	6	32	3	.358
2007	Texas	A.L.	OF	109	414	60	127	17	8	10	70	5	.307
2008	Oklahoma	P.C.	OF	4	16	3	5	2	0	0	3	0	.313
2008	Texas e	A.L.	OF	122	403	70	120	28	4	10	53	7	.298
2009	Texas f	A.L.	OF	146	547	66	155	43	2	20	89	8	.283
2010	Chicago	N.L.	OF	152	580	84	170	39	2	12	66	5	.293
Major League Totals			9 Yrs.	937	3246	464	914	193	25	72	401	46	.282

a On disabled list from April 14 to April 29, 2003.
b On disabled list from March 29 to May 3, 2005.
c Traded to Washington Nationals for outfielder Endy Chavez, May 14, 2005.
d Filed for free agency, October 2, 2006. Signed with Texas Rangers, December 8, 2006.
e On disabled list from April 17 to May 14, 2008.
f Filed for free agency, November 5, 2009. Signed with Chicago Cubs, December 31, 2009.

CABRERA, ASDRUBAL JOSE

Born, Puerto La Cruz, Venezuela, November 13, 1985.
Bats Both. Throws Right. Height, 6 feet. Weight, 170 pounds.

Year	Club	Lea	Pos	G	AB	R	H	2B	3B	HR	RBI	SB	Avg
2004	Everett	Northwest	SS-2B-3B	63	239	44	65	16	3	5	41	7	.272
2005	Inland Empire	Calif.	SS	55	225	31	64	15	6	1	26	3	.284
2005	Wisconsin	Midwest	2B-SS-3B	51	192	26	61	12	3	4	30	2	.318
2005	Tacoma	P.C.	SS	6	23	4	5	0	1	0	3	0	.217
2006	Buffalo	Int.	SS	52	190	26	50	11	0	1	14	5	.263
2006	Tacoma a	P.C.	SS	60	203	27	48	12	2	3	22	7	.236
2007	Akron	Eastern	SS-2B	96	368	78	114	23	3	8	54	23	.310
2007	Buffalo	Int.	SS-2B	9	38	6	12	3	0	0	3	2	.316
2007	Cleveland	A.L.	2B-SS-3B	45	159	30	45	9	2	3	22	0	.283
2008	Buffalo	Int.	SS-2B	34	141	25	46	7	1	4	13	2	.326
2008	Cleveland	A.L.	2B-SS	114	352	48	91	20	0	6	47	4	.259
2009	Akron	Eastern	SS	4	16	5	4	1	0	0	0	2	.250
2009	Cleveland b	A.L.	SS-2B	131	523	81	161	42	4	6	68	17	.308
2010	Mahoning Valley	N.Y.-Penn.	SS	2	6	0	2	1	0	0	2	0	.333
2010	Akron	Eastern	SS	4	14	4	5	2	0	1	1	2	.357
2010	Cleveland c	A.L.	SS	97	381	39	105	16	1	3	29	6	.276
Major League Totals			4 Yrs.	387	1415	198	402	87	7	18	166	27	.284
	Division Series												
2007	Cleveland	A.L.	2B	4	17	3	3	0	0	1	2	0	.176
	Championship Series												
2007	Cleveland	A.L.	2B	7	29	2	7	0	0	0	4	0	.241

a Traded to Cleveland Indians by Seattle Mariners for outfielder Eduardo Perez, June 30, 2006.
b On disabled list from June 3 to June 28, 2009.
c On disabled list from May 18 to July 20, 2010.

CABRERA, EVERTH

Born, Nandaime, Nicaragua, November 17, 1986.
Bats Both. Throws Right. Height, 5 feet, 10 inches. Weight, 175 pounds.

Year	Club	Lea	Pos	G	AB	R	H	2B	3B	HR	RBI	SB	Avg
2006	Casper	Pioneer	2B	54	185	30	47	4	2	0	14	18	.254
2007	Modesto	Calif.	2B	4	15	3	4	0	1	0	2	1	.267
2007	Tri-City	Northwest	2B-SS	42	150	29	45	8	3	1	23	12	.300
2008	Asheville a	So.Atl.	2B-SS	121	479	80	136	25	6	6	38	73	.284
2009	Lake Elsinore	Calif.	SS-2B	7	23	7	9	1	1	0	4	4	.391
2009	Portland	P.C.	SS	7	27	5	9	2	0	0	0	1	.333
2009	San Diego b	N.L.	SS	103	377	59	96	18	8	2	31	25	.255
2010	Lake Elsinore	Calif.	SS	3	10	1	3	0	0	0	1	1	.300
2010	Portland	P.C.	SS	8	31	7	8	1	0	0	3	3	.258
2010	San Diego c	N.L.	SS-2B	76	212	22	44	6	3	1	22	10	.208
Major League Totals			2 Yrs.	179	589	81	140	24	11	3	53	35	.238

a Selected by San Diego Padres from Colorado Rockies in Rule V draft, December 11, 2008.
b On disabled list from April 20 to June 19, 2009.
c On disabled list from April 27 to May 14 and May 24 to June 25, 2010.

CABRERA, JOSE MIGUEL (MIGUEL)

Born, Maracay, Venezuela, April 18, 1983.
Bats Right. Throws Right. Height, 6 feet, 2 inches. Weight, 240 pounds.

Year	Club	Lea	Pos	G	AB	R	H	2B	3B	HR	RBI	SB	Avg
2000	Marlins	Gulf Coast	SS	57	219	38	57	10	2	2	22	1	.260
2000	Utica	N.Y.-Penn	SS	8	32	3	8	2	0	0	6	0	.250
2001	Kane County	Midwest	SS	110	422	61	134	19	4	7	66	3	.318
2002	Jupiter	Fla.St.	3B	124	478	77	134	43	1	9	75	10	.274
2003	Carolina	Southern	3B-OF	69	266	46	97	29	3	10	59	9	.365
2003	Florida	N.L.	OF-3B	87	314	39	84	21	3	12	62	0	.268
2004	Florida	N.L.	OF	160	603	101	177	31	1	33	112	5	.294
2005	Florida	N.L.	OF-3B	158	613	106	198	43	2	33	116	1	.323
2006	Florida	N.L.	3B	158	576	112	195	50	2	26	114	9	.339
2007	Florida a	N.L.	3B	157	588	91	188	38	2	34	119	2	.320
2008	Detroit	A.L.	1B-3B	160	616	85	180	36	2	*37	127	1	.292
2009	Detroit	A.L.	1B	160	611	96	198	34	0	34	103	6	.324
2010	Detroit	A.L.	1B	150	548	111	180	45	1	38	*126	3	.328
Major League Totals			8 Yrs.	1190	4469	741	1400	298	13	247	879	27	.313
	Division Series												
2003	Florida	N.L.	3B	4	14	1	4	2	0	0	3	0	.286
	Championship Series												
2003	Florida	N.L.	OF-3B-SS	7	30	9	10	0	0	3	6	0	.333
	World Series Record												
2003	Florida	N.L.	OF	6	24	1	4	0	0	1	3	0	.167

a Traded to Detroit Tigers with pitcher Dontrelle Willis for pitcher Burke Badenhop, pitcher Eulogio De La Cruz, pitcher Andrew Miller, catcher Mike Rabelo and outfielder Cameron Maybin, December 5, 2007.

CABRERA, MELKY

Born, Santo Domingo, Dominican Republic, August 11, 1984.
Bats Both. Throws Left. Height, 5 feet, 11 inches. Weight, 200 pounds.

Year	Club	Lea	Pos	G	AB	R	H	2B	3B	HR	RBI	SB	Avg
2003	Staten Island	N.Y.-Penn.	OF	67	279	34	79	10	2	2	31	13	.283
2004	Tampa	Fla.St.	OF	85	333	48	96	20	3	8	51	3	.288
2004	Battle Creek	Midwest	OF	42	171	35	57	16	3	0	16	7	.333
2005	New York	A.L.	OF	6	19	1	4	0	0	0	0	0	.211
2005	Columbus	Int.	OF	26	101	15	25	3	0	3	17	2	.248
2005	Trenton	Eastern	OF	106	426	57	117	22	3	10	60	11	.275
2006	Columbus	Int.	OF	31	122	19	47	6	2	4	24	3	.385
2006	New York	A.L.	OF	130	460	75	129	26	2	7	50	12	.280
2007	New York	A.L.	OF	150	545	66	149	24	8	8	73	13	.273
2008	Scranton-WB	Int.	OF	15	57	8	19	2	0	0	5	1	.333
2008	New York	A.L.	OF	129	414	42	103	12	1	8	37	9	.249
2009	New York a	A.L.	OF	154	485	66	133	28	1	13	68	10	.274
2010	Atlanta b	N.L.	OF	147	458	50	117	27	3	4	42	7	.255
Major League Totals			6 Yrs.	716	2381	300	635	117	15	40	270	51	.267
	Division Series												
2006	New York	A.L.	OF	2	3	0	0	0	0	0	0	0	.000
2007	New York	A.L.	OF	4	16	2	3	0	0	1	2	0	.188
2009	New York	A.L.	OF	3	12	1	2	0	0	0	0	0	.167
2010	Atlanta	N.L.	OF	3	8	1	0	0	0	0	1	0	.000
Division Series Totals				12	39	4	5	0	0	1	3	0	.128
	Championship Series												
2009	New York	A.L.	OF	6	23	3	9	2	0	0	4	0	.391
	World Series Record												
2009	New York	A.L.	OF	4	13	1	2	0	0	0	0	0	.154

a Traded to Atlanta Braves with pitcher Arodys Vizcaino, pitcher Michael Dunn and cash for pitcher Javier Vazquez and pitcher Boone Logan, December 22, 2009.

b Released by Atlanta Braves, October 18, 2010. Signed with Kansas City Royals, December 10, 2010.

CABRERA, ORLANDO LUIS

Born, Cartagena, Colombia, November 2, 1974.
Bats Right. Throws Right. Height, 5 feet, 9 inches. Weight, 180 pounds.

Year	Club	Lea	Pos	G	AB	R	H	2B	3B	HR	RBI	SB	Avg
1994	Expos	Gulf Coast	2B-SS-OF	22	73	13	23	4	1	0	11	6	.315
1995	Wst Plm Bch	Fla. St.	SS	3	5	0	1	0	0	0	0	0	.200
1995	Vermont	N.Y.-Penn.	2B-SS	65	248	37	70	12	5	3	33	15	.282
1996	Delmarva	So. Atl.	SS-2B	134	512	86	129	28	4	14	65	51	.252
1997	Wst Plm Bch	Fla. St.	SS-2B	69	279	56	77	19	2	5	26	32	.276

Year	Club	Lea	Pos	G	AB	R	H	2B	3B	HR	RBI	SB	Avg
1997	Harrisburg	Eastern	SS-2B	35	133	34	41	13	2	5	20	7	.308
1997	Ottawa	Int.	SS-2B	31	122	17	32	5	2	2	14	8	.262
1997	Montreal	N.L.	SS-2B	16	18	4	4	0	0	0	2	1	.222
1998	Ottawa	Int.	SS-2B	66	272	31	63	9	4	0	26	19	.232
1998	Montreal	N.L.	SS-2B	79	261	44	73	16	5	3	22	6	.280
1999	Montreal a	N.L.	SS	104	382	48	97	23	5	8	39	2	.254
2000	Ottawa	Int.	SS	2	6	1	4	0	0	0	0	1	.667
2000	Montreal b	N.L.	SS-2B	125	422	47	100	25	1	13	55	4	.237
2001	Montreal	N.L.	SS	*162	626	64	173	41	6	14	96	19	.276
2002	Montreal	N.L.	SS	153	563	64	148	43	1	7	56	25	.263
2003	Montreal	N.L.	SS	*162	626	95	186	47	2	17	80	24	.297
2004	Montreal	N.L.	SS	103	390	41	96	19	2	4	31	12	.246
2004	Boston c-d-e	A.L.	SS	58	228	33	67	19	1	6	31	4	.294
2005	Los Angeles f	A.L.	SS	141	540	70	139	28	3	8	57	21	.257
2006	Los Angeles	A.L.	SS	153	607	95	171	45	1	9	72	27	.282
2007	Los Angeles g	A.L.	SS	155	638	101	192	35	1	8	86	20	.301
2008	Chicago h	A.L.	SS	161	661	93	186	33	1	8	57	19	.281
2009	Oakland-Minnesota i-j	A.L.	SS	160	656	83	186	36	3	9	77	13	.284
2010	Dayton	Midwest	SS	1	3	0	0	0	0	0	0	0	.000
2010	Cincinnati k-l	N.L.	SS	123	494	64	130	33	0	4	42	11	.263
Major League Totals			14 Yrs.	1855	7112	946	1948	443	32	118	803	208	.274
	Division Series												
2004	Boston	A.L.	SS	3	13	1	2	1	0	0	3	0	.154
2005	Los Angeles	A.L.	SS	5	21	3	5	2	0	0	3	0	.238
2007	Los Angeles	A.L.	SS	3	12	0	3	1	0	0	1	0	.250
2008	Chicago	A.L.	SS	4	16	1	2	0	0	0	0	0	.125
2009	Minnesota	A.L.	SS	3	13	1	2	0	0	0	0	1	.154
2010	Cincinnati	N.L.	SS	3	8	0	1	0	0	0	0	0	.125
Division Series Totals				21	83	6	15	4	0	0	7	1	.181
	Championship Series												
2004	Boston	A.L.	SS	7	29	5	11	2	0	0	5	1	.379
2005	Los Angeles	A.L.	SS	5	20	1	4	1	0	1	3	0	.200
Championship Series Totals				12	49	6	15	3	0	1	8	1	.306
	World Series Record												
2004	Boston	A.L.	SS	4	17	3	4	1	0	0	3	0	.235

a On disabled list from August 9 to October 13, 1999.
b On disabled list from July 15 to August 14, 2000.
c Traded to Chicago Cubs for infielder Alex Gonzalez, infielder Brendan Harris and pitcher Francis Beltran, July 31, 2004.
d Traded to Boston Red Sox with infielder Doug Mientkiewicz for infielder Nomar Garciaparra and outfielder Matt Murton, July 31, 2004.
e Filed for free agency, November 1, 2004. Signed with Anaheim Angels, December 20, 2004.
f On disabled list from June 27 to July 16, 2005.
g Traded to Chicago White Sox for pitcher Jon Garland, November 19, 2007.
h Filed for free agency, November 1, 2008. Signed with Oakland Athletics, March 6, 2009.
i Traded to Minnesota Twins with cash for infielder Tyler Ladendorf, July 31, 2009.
j Filed for free agency, November 9, 2009. Signed with Cincinnati Reds, February 1, 2010.
k On disabled list from August 3 to September 3, 2010.
l Filed for free agency, November 3, 2010.

CAIN, LORENZO LAMAR

Born, Valdosta, Georgia, April 13, 1986.
Bats Right. Throws Right. Height, 6 feet, 2 inches. Weight, 200 pounds.

Year	Club	Lea	Pos	G	AB	R	H	2B	3B	HR	RBI	SB	Avg
2005	Brewers	Arizona	OF	50	205	45	73	18	5	5	37	12	.356
2005	Helena	Pioneer	OF	6	24	4	5	0	0	0	1	0	.208
2006	West Tenn	So.Atl.	OF	132	527	91	162	36	4	6	60	34	.307
2007	Brevard County	Fla.St.	OF	126	482	67	133	21	3	2	44	24	.276
2008	Brevard County	Fla.St.	OF	80	317	50	91	22	4	7	41	19	.287
2008	Nashville	P.C.	OF	6	19	0	3	0	0	0	2	0	.158
2008	Huntsville	Southern	OF	40	148	21	41	9	5	4	17	6	.277
2009	Brewers	Arizona	OF	3	9	1	4	1	0	0	1	0	.444
2009	Wisconsin	Midwest	OF	15	52	3	10	4	0	0	3	0	.192
2009	Huntsville	Southern	OF	42	145	17	31	6	0	4	15	3	.214
2010	Huntsville	Southern	OF	62	244	45	79	6	6	3	18	21	.324
2010	Nashville	P.C.	OF	22	87	13	26	5	3	0	9	5	.299
2010	Milwaukee a	N.L.	OF	43	147	17	45	11	1	1	13	7	.306

a Traded to Kansas City Royals with infielder Alcides Escobar, pitcher Jeremy Jeffress and pitcher Jake Odorizzi for outfielder Yuniesky Betancourt and pitcher Zack Greinke, December 19, 2010.

CAIRO, MIGUEL JESUS

Born, Anaco, Venezuela, May 4, 1974.

Bats Right. Throws Right. Height, 6 feet, 1 inch. Weight, 225 pounds.

Year	Club	Lea	Pos	G	AB	R	H	2B	3B	HR	RBI	SB	Avg
1992	Dodgers	Gulf Coast	SS-3B	21	76	10	23	5	2	0	9	1	.303
1992	Vero Beach	Fla.St.	2B-SS	36	125	7	28	0	0	0	7	5	.224
1993	Vero Beach	Fla.St.	2B-SS-3B	90	346	50	109	10	1	1	23	23	.315
1994	Bakersfield	Calif.	2B-SS	133	533	76	155	23	4	2	48	44	.291
1995	San Antonio a	Texas	2B-SS	107	435	53	121	20	1	1	41	33	.278
1996	Syracuse	Int.	2B-3B-SS	120	465	71	129	14	4	3	48	27	.277
1996	Toronto b	A.L.	2B	9	27	5	6	2	0	0	1	0	.222
1997	Iowa	A.A.	2B-SS	135	569	82	159	35	4	5	46	40	.279
1997	Chicago c	N.L.	2B-SS	16	29	7	7	1	0	0	1	0	.241
1998	Tampa Bay	A.L.	2B	150	515	49	138	26	5	5	46	19	.268
1999	Tampa Bay	A.L.	2B	120	465	61	137	15	5	3	36	22	.295
1999	Orlando	Southern	2B	3	13	1	5	2	0	0	1	0	.385
1999	St. Petersburg d	Fla.St.	2B	3	13	2	5	0	0	0	0	1	.385
2000	Tampa Bay	A.L.	2B	119	375	49	98	18	2	1	34	28	.261
2001	Iowa	P.C.	2B-SS-3B	34	123	22	37	7	1	3	14	3	.301
2001	Chicago-St. Louis e-f-g	N.L.	3B-2B-OF-SS	93	156	25	46	8	1	3	16	2	.295
2002	St. Louis	N.L.	OF-2B-3B-SS	108	184	28	46	9	2	2	23	1	.250
2003	Memphis	P.C.	2B	3	13	2	3	1	0	0	0	0	.231
2003	St. Louis h-i	N.L.	2B-OF-3B-SS	92	261	41	64	15	2	5	32	4	.245
2004	New York	A.L.	2B-3B-SS-1B	122	360	48	105	17	5	6	42	11	.292
2005	St. Lucie	Fla.St.	DH	1	4	0	1	0	0	0	0	0	.250
2005	Mets	Gulf Coast	2B	3	13	3	4	1	0	0	0	0	.308
2005	New York j-k	N.L.	2B-1B-3B-OF	100	327	31	82	18	0	2	19	13	.251
2006	New York l-m	A.L.	2B-1B-SS-3B	81	222	28	53	12	3	0	30	13	.239
2007	New York	A.L.	1B-SS-3B-2B	54	107	12	27	7	0	0	10	8	.252
2007	Memphis	P.C.	3B-SS-OF-1B	9	31	8	9	2	0	0	3	2	.290
2007	St. Louis n-o	N.L.	3B-2B-1B-OF	28	67	8	17	2	2	0	5	2	.254
2008	Seattle p	A.L.	1B-3B-2B-OF	108	221	34	55	14	2	0	23	5	.249
2009	Lehigh Valley	Int.	SS-2B-3B-1B	78	296	44	85	12	2	5	33	8	.287
2009	Philadelphia q-r	N.L.	2B-SS-3B	27	45	6	12	2	1	1	2	0	.267
2010	Cincinnati s	N.L.	3B-1B-2B-SS	91	200	30	58	12	0	4	28	4	.290
Major League Totals			15 Yrs.	1318	3561	462	951	178	30	32	348	132	.267
	Division Series												
2001	St. Louis	N.L.	OF	3	5	0	1	0	0	0	0	1	.200
2002	St. Louis	N.L.	3B	2	4	2	4	1	0	0	3	0	1.000
2004	New York	A.L.	2B	4	14	3	3	1	0	0	1	0	.214
2009	Philadelphia	N.L.	OF-3B	2	3	0	0	0	0	0	0	0	.000
2010	Cincinnati	N.L.	PH	3	3	0	0	0	0	0	0	0	.000
Division Series Totals				14	29	5	8	2	0	0	4	1	.276
	Championship Series												
2002	St. Louis	N.L.	3B	3	13	2	5	0	0	1	2	0	.385
2004	New York	A.L.	2B	7	25	4	7	3	0	0	0	1	.280
2009	Philadelphia	N.L.	PH	2	2	0	0	0	0	0	0	0	.000
Championship Series Totals				12	40	6	12	3	0	1	2	1	.300

a Traded to Toronto Blue Jays with pitcher Bill Risley for pitcher Edwin Hurtado and pitcher Paul Menhart, December 18, 1995.

b Traded to Chicago Cubs for pitcher Jason Stevenson, November 20, 1996.

c Selected by Tampa Bay Devil Rays in expansion draft. November 18, 1997.

d On disabled list from April 24 to May 17 and July 26 to August 11, 1999.

e Released by Tampa Bay Devil Rays, November 27, 2000. Signed with Oakland Athletics organization, January 11, 2001.

f Traded to Chicago Cubs with pitcher Scott Chiasson for infielder Eric Hinske, March 28, 2001.

g Claimed on waivers by St. Louis Cardinals, August 10, 2001.

h On disabled list from June 19 to July 29, 2003.

i Filed for free agency, October 26, 2003. Signed with New York Yankees, December 19, 2003.

j Filed for free agency, October 28, 2004. Signed with New York Mets, January 10, 2005.

k On disabled list from June 15 to July 2, 2005.

l Filed for free agency, October 28, 2005. Signed with New York Yankees, January 5, 2006.

m On disabled list from August 6 to September 11, 2006.

n Filed for free agency, October 28, 2006, re-signed with New York Yankees, January 26, 2007.

o Released by New York Yankees, August 15, 2007. Signed with St. Louis Cardinals organization, August 19, 2007.

p Filed for free agency, October 29, 2007. Signed with Seattle Mariners organization, January 8, 2008.

q Filed for free agency, October 30, 2008. Signed with Philadelphia Phillies organization, February 15, 2009.

r Filed for free agency, November 6, 2009. Signed with Cincinnati Reds organization, January 27, 2010.

s Filed for free agency, November 1, 2010. Signed with Cincinnati Reds, December 8, 2010.

CALLASPO, ALBERTO JOSE

Born, Maracay, Venezuela, April 19, 1983.
Bats Both. Throws Right. Height, 5 feet, 10 inches. Weight, 180 pounds.

Year	Club	Lea	Pos	G	AB	R	H	2B	3B	HR	RBI	SB	Avg
2002	Provo	Pioneer	2B-SS	70	299	70	101	16	10	3	60	13	.338
2003	Cedar Rapids	Midwest	2B-SS	133	514	86	168	38	4	2	67	20	.327
2004	Arkansas	Texas	SS-2B	136	550	76	156	29	2	6	48	15	.284
2005	Salt Lake	P.C.	2B	50	212	28	67	21	2	1	31	2	.316
2005	Arkansas	Texas	2B	89	350	53	104	8	0	10	49	9	.297
2006	Tucson	P.C.	2B-SS-3B-OF	114	490	93	165	24	12	7	68	8	.337
2006	Arizona a	N.L.	SS-2B-3B	23	42	2	10	1	1	0	6	0	.238
2007	Tucson	P.C.	SS-2B-3B	59	226	48	77	15	2	5	30	1	.341
2007	Arizona b	N.L.	3B-2B-OF-SS	56	144	10	31	8	0	0	7	1	.215
2008	Omaha	P.C.	2B	4	16	5	3	0	0	0	0	0	.188
2008	Kansas City c	A.L.	2B-SS-OF-3B	74	213	21	65	8	3	0	16	2	.305
2009	Kansas City	A.L.	2B-3B-SS	155	576	79	173	41	8	11	73	2	.300
2010	Kansas City-LA d	A.L.	3B-2B-OF	146	562	61	149	27	2	10	56	5	.265
Major League Totals			5 Yrs.	454	1537	173	428	85	14	21	158	10	.278
Championship Series													
2007	Arizona	N.L.	PH	2	2	0	0	0	0	0	0	0	.000

a Traded by Los Angeles Angels to Arizona Diamondbacks for pitcher Jason Bulger, February 28, 2006.
b Traded to Kansas City Royals for pitcher Billy Buckner, December 14, 2007.
c On disabled list from June 28 to August 23, 2008.
d Traded to Anaheim Angels for pitcher Sean O'Sullivan and pitcher Will Smith, July 22, 2010.

CAMERON, MICHAEL TERRANCE (MIKE)

Born, La Grange, Georgia, January 8, 1973.
Bats Right. Throws Right. Height, 6 feet, 2 inches. Weight, 200 pounds.

Year	Club	Lea	Pos	G	AB	R	H	2B	3B	HR	RBI	SB	Avg
1991	White Sox	Gulf Coast	OF	44	136	20	30	3	0	0	11	13	.221
1992	Utica	N.Y.-Penn.	OF	28	87	15	24	1	4	2	12	3	.276
1992	South Bend	Midwest	OF	35	114	19	26	8	1	1	9	2	.228
1993	South Bend	Midwest	OF	122	411	52	98	14	5	0	30	19	.238
1994	Pr William	Carolina	OF	131	468	86	116	15	17	6	48	22	.248
1995	Birmingham	Southern	OF	107	350	64	87	20	5	11	60	21	.249
1995	Chicago	A.L.	OF	28	38	4	7	2	0	1	2	0	.184
1996	Birmingham	Southern	OF	123	473	120	142	34	12	28	77	39	.300
1996	Chicago	A.L.	OF	11	11	1	1	0	0	0	0	0	.091
1997	Nashville	A.A.	OF	30	120	21	33	7	3	6	17	4	.275
1997	Chicago	A.L.	OF	116	379	63	98	18	3	14	55	23	.259
1998	Chicago a	A.L.	OF	141	396	53	83	16	5	8	43	27	.210
1999	Cincinnati	N.L.	OF	146	542	93	139	34	9	21	66	38	.256
2000	Seattle b	A.L.	OF	155	543	96	145	28	4	19	78	24	.267
2001	Seattle	A.L.	OF	150	540	99	144	30	5	25	110	34	.267
2002	Seattle	A.L.	OF	158	545	84	130	26	5	25	80	31	.239
2003	Seattle c	A.L.	OF	147	534	74	135	31	5	18	76	17	.253
2004	New York	N.L.	OF	140	493	76	114	30	1	30	76	22	.231
2005	St. Lucie	Fla.St.	OF	4	10	3	3	2	0	0	0	0	.300
2005	Norfolk	Int.	OF	2	7	2	2	0	1	0	2	0	.286
2005	New York d-e	N.L.	OF	76	308	47	84	23	2	12	39	13	.273
2006	Lake Elsinore	Calif.	OF	2	6	1	2	1	0	0	1	0	.333
2006	San Diego f	N.L.	OF	141	552	88	148	34	9	22	83	25	.268
2007	San Diego g	N.L.	OF	151	571	88	138	33	6	21	78	18	.242
2008	Nashville	P.C.	OF	4	15	4	3	0	0	1	2	0	.200
2008	Milwaukee	N.L.	OF	120	444	69	108	25	2	25	70	17	.243
2009	Milwaukee h	N.L.	OF	149	544	78	136	32	3	24	70	7	.250
2010	Portland	Eastern	OF	3	13	4	5	2	0	2	3	0	.385
2010	Pawtucket	Int.	OF	5	14	3	4	1	0	1	3	0	.286
2010	Boston i	A.L.	OF	48	162	24	42	11	0	4	15	0	.259
Major League Totals			16 Yrs.	1877	6602	1037	1652	373	59	269	941	296	.250
Division Series													
2000	Seattle	A.L.	OF	3	12	2	3	0	0	0	2	1	.250
2001	Seattle	A.L.	OF	5	18	2	4	3	0	1	3	0	.222
2006	San Diego	N.L.	OF	4	14	1	2	1	0	0	1	1	.143
2008	Milwaukee	N.L.	OF	4	13	3	2	0	0	0	0	0	.154
Division Series Totals				16	57	8	11	4	0	1	6	2	.193
Championship Series													
2000	Seattle	A.L.	OF	6	18	3	2	0	0	0	1	1	.111

Year	Club	Lea	Pos	G	AB	R	H	2B	3B	HR	RBI	SB	Avg
2001	Seattle	A.L.	OF	5	17	3	3	2	0	0	0	0	.176
Championship Series Totals				11	35	6	5	2	0	0	1	1	.143

a Traded to Cincinnati Reds for infielder Paul Konerko, November 11, 1998.
b Traded to Seattle Mariners with pitcher Brett Tomko, infielder Antonio Perez and pitcher Jake Meyer for outfielder Ken Griffey, February 10, 2000.
c Filed for free agency, October 27, 2003. Signed with New York Mets, December 14, 2003.
d On disabled list from April 1 to May 5 and August 12 to October 31, 2005.
e Traded to San Diego Padres for infielder Xavier Nady, November 18, 2005.
f On disabled list from March 31 to April 23, 2006.
g Filed for free agency, October 31, 2007. Signed with Milwaukee Brewers, January 14, 2008.
h Filed for free agency, November 5, 2009. Signed with Boston Red Sox, December 16, 2009.
i On disabled list from April 19 to May 25 and July 31 to November 8, 2010.

CANO (MERCEDES), ROBINSON JOSE

Born, San Pedro de Macoris, Dominican Republic, October 22, 1982.
Bats Left. Throws Right. Height, 6 feet. Weight, 200 pounds.

Year	Club	Lea	Pos	G	AB	R	H	2B	3B	HR	RBI	SB	Avg
2001	Yankees	Gulf Coast	2B-SS-3B	57	200	37	46	14	2	3	34	11	.230
2001	Staten Island	N.Y.-Penn.	3B-SS	2	8	0	2	0	0	0	2	0	.250
2002	Staten Island	N.Y.-Penn.	2B-SS	22	87	11	24	5	1	1	15	6	.276
2002	Greensboro	So.Atl.	SS-2B	113	474	67	131	20	9	14	66	2	.276
2003	Trenton	Eastern	2B-SS-C	46	164	21	46	9	1	1	13	0	.280
2003	Tampa	Fla.St.	2B	90	366	50	101	16	3	5	50	1	.276
2004	Trenton	Eastern	2B-3B	74	292	43	88	20	8	7	44	2	.301
2004	Columbus	Int.	2B	61	216	22	56	9	2	6	30	0	.259
2005	Columbus	Int.	2B-3B	24	108	19	36	8	3	4	24	0	.333
2005	New York	A.L.	2B	132	522	78	155	34	4	14	62	1	.297
2006	Yankees	Gulf Coast	DH	1	5	0	2	0	0	0	1	0	.400
2006	Trenton	Eastern	2B	3	10	1	5	2	0	0	2	0	.500
2006	New York a	A.L.	2B	122	482	62	165	41	1	15	78	5	.342
2007	New York	A.L.	2B	160	617	93	189	41	7	19	97	4	.306
2008	New York	A.L.	2B	159	597	70	162	35	3	14	72	2	.271
2009	New York	A.L.	2B	*161	637	103	204	48	2	25	85	5	.320
2010	New York	A.L.	2B	160	626	103	200	41	3	29	109	3	.319
Major League Totals			6 Yrs.	894	3481	509	1075	240	20	116	503	20	.309
	Division Series												
2005	New York	A.L.	2B	5	19	3	5	3	0	0	5	0	.263
2006	New York	A.L.	2B	4	15	0	2	0	0	0	0	0	.133
2007	New York	A.L.	2B	4	15	3	5	1	0	2	3	0	.333
2009	New York	A.L.	2B	3	12	1	2	0	0	0	1	0	.167
2010	New York	A.L.	2B	3	12	3	4	0	1	0	1	0	.333
Division Series Totals				19	73	10	18	4	1	2	10	0	.247
	Championship Series												
2009	New York	A.L.	2B	6	23	4	6	1	2	0	4	0	.261
2010	New York	A.L.	2B	6	23	5	8	1	0	4	5	0	.348
Championship Series Totals				12	46	9	14	2	2	4	9	0	.304
	World Series Record												
2009	New York	A.L.	2B	6	22	0	3	0	0	0	1	0	.136

a On disabled list from June 26 to August 8, 2006.

CANTU (GUZMAN), JORGE LUIS

Born, McAllen, Texas, January 30, 1982.
Bats Right. Throws Right. Height, 6 feet, 3 inches. Weight, 200 pounds.

Year	Club	Lea	Pos	G	AB	R	H	2B	3B	HR	RBI	SB	Avg
1999	Hudson Valley	N.Y.-Penn.	SS	72	281	33	73	17	2	1	33	3	.260
2000	St. Petersburg	Fla.St.	SS	36	130	18	38	5	2	1	14	4	.292
2000	Charleston-Sc	So.Atl.	SS-2B	46	186	25	56	13	2	2	24	3	.301
2001	Orlando	Southern	SS	130	512	58	131	26	3	4	45	4	.256
2002	Orlando	Southern	SS-3B-2B	131	512	50	124	31	1	3	43	2	.242
2003	Durham	Int.	SS-3B	60	200	26	59	16	1	4	30	2	.295
2003	Orlando	Southern	3B-SS-2B	43	158	15	34	10	0	3	17	0	.215
2004	Durham	Int.	2B-SS-3B	95	368	57	111	33	1	22	80	3	.302
2004	Tampa Bay	A.L.	2B-3B-SS	50	173	25	52	20	1	2	17	0	.301
2005	Tampa Bay	A.L.	2B-3B	150	598	73	171	40	1	28	117	1	.286
2006	Montgomery	Southern	2B	8	31	4	6	0	0	2	8	0	.194
2006	Tampa Bay a	A.L.	2B	107	413	40	103	18	2	14	62	1	.249

Year	Club	Lea	Pos	G	AB	R	H	2B	3B	HR	RBI	SB	Avg
2007	Tampa Bay	A.L.	1B-2B	25	58	4	12	1	0	0	4	0	.207
2007	Durham	Int.	1B-2B-3B	24	91	12	22	5	1	1	10	0	.242
2007	Louisville	Int.	2B-1B	24	94	12	29	9	0	2	13	0	.309
2007	Cincinnati b	N.L.	1B-2B-3B	27	57	8	17	8	0	1	9	0	.298
2008	Florida c	N.L.	3B-1B	155	628	92	174	41	0	29	95	6	.277
2009	Florida	N.L.	1B-3B	149	585	67	169	42	0	16	100	3	.289
2010	Florida	N.L.	3B-1B	97	374	41	98	25	0	10	54	0	.262
2010	Texas d-e	A.L.	1B-3B-2B	30	98	9	23	4	1	1	2	0	.235
Major League Totals			7 Yrs.	790	2984	359	819	199	5	101	460	11	.274
	Division Series												
2010	Texas	A.L.	1B	1	4	0	0	0	0	0	0	0	.000
	Championship Series												
2010	Texas	A.L.	1B	1	3	0	0	0	0	0	0	0	.000
	World Series Record												
2010	Texas	A.L.	1B	1	1	0	0	0	0	0	0	0	.000

a On disabled list from April 24 to June 6, 2006.

b Traded to Cincinnati Reds with outfielder Shaun Cumberland and cash for pitchers Calvin Medlock and Brian Shackelford, July 28, 2007.

c Released by Cincinnati Reds, December 5, 2007. Signed with Florida Marlins organization, January 5, 2008.

d Traded to Texas Rangers with cash for pitcher Omar Poveda and pitcher Evan Reed, July 30, 2010.

e Filed for free agency, November 1, 2010.

CARROLL, JAMEY BLAKE

Born, Evansville, Indiana, February 18, 1974.

Bats Right. Throws Right. Height, 5 feet, 9 inches. Weight, 170 pounds.

Year	Club	Lea	Pos	G	AB	R	H	2B	3B	HR	RBI	SB	Avg
1996	Vermont	N.Y.-Penn.	SS-2B-3B	54	203	40	56	6	1	0	17	16	.276
1997	Wst Plm Bch	Fla.St.	SS-2B-3B	121	407	56	99	19	1	0	38	17	.243
1998	Jupiter	Fla.St.	2B-SS	55	222	40	58	5	0	0	14	11	.261
1998	Harrisburg	Eastern	2B-SS	75	261	43	66	11	3	0	20	11	.253
1999	Harrisburg	Eastern	2B	141	561	78	164	34	5	5	63	21	.292
2000	Harrisburg	Eastern	3B-SS-2B	45	169	23	49	5	3	0	18	8	.290
2000	Ottawa	Int.	2B-3B-SS	91	349	53	97	17	2	2	23	6	.278
2001	Ottawa	Int.	2B-SS-3B	83	267	26	64	8	2	0	16	5	.240
2002	Harrisburg	Eastern	2B	3	9	1	4	0	0	0	1	0	.444
2002	Ottawa	Int.	3B-2B-SS	117	421	57	118	19	2	8	49	6	.280
2002	Montreal	N.L.	3B-SS-2B	16	71	16	22	5	3	1	6	1	.310
2003	Montreal	N.L.	3B-SS-2B	105	227	31	59	10	1	1	10	5	.260
2004	Montreal	N.L.	2B-3B-SS-OF	102	218	36	63	14	2	0	16	5	.289
2005	Washington	N.L.	2B-SS-3B	113	303	44	76	8	1	0	22	3	.251
2006	Colorado a	N.L.	2B-SS-3B	136	463	84	139	23	5	5	36	10	.300
2007	Colorado b	N.L.	2B-3B-SS-OF	108	227	45	51	9	1	2	22	6	.225
2008	Cleveland	A.L.	2B-3B-OF	113	347	60	96	13	4	1	36	7	.277
2009	Columbus	Int.	2B-3B	3	11	2	3	1	0	0	0	0	.273
2009	Cleveland c-d	A.L.	2B-3B-OF	93	315	53	87	10	2	2	26	4	.276
2010	Los Angeles	N.L.	SS-2B-3B-OF	133	351	48	102	15	1	0	23	12	.291
Major League Totals			9 Yrs.	919	2522	417	695	107	20	12	197	53	.276
	Division Series												
2007	Colorado	N.L.	2B	1	0	0	0	0	0	0	0	0	.000
	Championship Series												
2007	Colorado	N.L.	3B	2	1	0	0	0	0	0	0	0	.000
	World Series Record												
2007	Colorado	N.L.	2B	1	1	0	0	0	0	0	0	0	.000

a Sold to Colorado Rockies, February 11, 2006.

b Traded to Cleveland Indians for player to be named later, December 8, 2007. Colorado Rockies received pitcher Sean Smith to complete trade, April 22, 2008

c On disabled list from April 5 to May 12, 2009.

d Filed for free agency, November 5, 2009. Signed with Los Angeles Dodgers, December 16, 2009.

CARTER, WILLIAM CHRIS (CHRIS)

Born, Fremont, California, September 16, 1982.

Bats Left. Throws Left. Height, 6 feet. Weight, 230 pounds.

Year	Club	Lea	Pos	G	AB	R	H	2B	3B	HR	RBI	SB	Avg
2004	Yakima	Northwest	OF-1B	70	257	47	86	15	1	15	63	2	.335
2005	Lancaster	Calif.	1B-OF	103	412	71	122	26	2	21	85	0	.296
2005	Tennessee	Southern	1B-OF	36	128	21	38	4	0	10	30	0	.297
2006	Tucson	P.C.	1B	136	509	87	153	30	3	19	97	10	.301
2007	Pawtucket	Int.	1B	12	47	6	11	1	0	1	4	0	.234

Year	Club	Lea	Pos	G	AB	R	H	2B	3B	HR	RBI	SB	Avg
2007	Tucson a-b	P.C.	1B-OF	126	503	74	163	39	3	18	84	2	.324
2008	Pawtucket	Int.	OF	121	470	65	141	25	2	24	81	0	.300
2008	Boston	A.L.	OF	9	18	5	6	0	0	0	3	0	.333
2009	Boston	A.L.	OF	4	5	0	0	0	0	0	1	0	.000
2009	Pawtucket c	Int.	OF-1B	116	428	50	126	25	0	16	61	0	.294
2010	Buffalo	Int.	OF-1B	29	113	17	38	9	2	6	22	0	.336
2010	New York d	N.L.	OF	100	167	15	44	9	0	4	24	1	.263
Major League Totals			3 Yrs.	113	190	20	50	9	0	4	28	1	.263

a Traded by Arizona Diamondbacks to Washington Nationals for pitcher Emiliano Fruto, August 21, 2007.
b Sent to Boston Red Sox to complete trade for Willy Mo Pena, August 21, 2007.
c Sent to New York Mets with infielder Eddie Lora to complete trade for Billy Wagner, October 7, 2009.
d Not offered contract, December 2, 2010. Signed with Tampa Bay Rays organization, January 5, 2011.

CASILLA (LORA), ALEXI

Born, San Cristobal, Dominican Republic, July 20, 1984.
Bats Both. Throws Right. Height, 5 feet, 9 inches. Weight, 180 pounds.

Year	Club	Lea	Pos	G	AB	R	H	2B	3B	HR	RBI	SB	Avg
2004	Angels	Arizona	2B-SS	45	163	29	42	1	4	0	10	24	.258
2004	Cedar Rapids	Midwest	2B	9	29	6	9	2	1	0	1	1	.310
2004	Provo	Pioneer	2B-3B	4	12	4	4	1	1	0	1	1	.333
2005	Cedar Rapids	Midwest	SS-2B	78	308	62	100	11	3	3	17	47	.325
2005	Salt Lake	P.C.	2B-SS	13	39	3	10	0	0	0	1	1	.256
2005	Arkansas a	Texas	SS-2B	7	19	4	4	0	0	0	4	1	.211
2006	Fort Myers	Fla.St.	2B-SS	78	323	56	107	12	6	0	33	31	.331
2006	New Britain	Eastern	SS	45	170	28	50	10	1	1	13	19	.294
2006	Minnesota	A.L.	2B-SS	9	4	1	1	0	0	0	0	0	.250
2007	Rochester	Int.	2B-SS	84	320	53	86	13	1	3	20	24	.269
2007	Minnesota	A.L.	2B-SS	56	189	15	42	5	1	0	9	11	.222
2008	Beloit	Midwest	2B	2	7	2	4	0	0	0	1	0	.571
2008	Rochester	Int.	SS-2B	32	96	11	21	3	0	0	2	4	.219
2008	Minnesota b	A.L.	2B-SS	98	385	58	108	15	0	7	50	7	.281
2009	Rochester	Int.	2B	40	156	21	53	3	4	2	17	9	.340
2009	Minnesota	A.L.	2B-SS	80	228	25	46	7	3	0	17	11	.202
2010	Twins	Gulf Coast	2B	5	14	1	2	1	0	0	0	0	.143
2010	Fort Myers	Fla.St.	2B-SS	3	12	0	2	0	0	0	1	1	.167
2010	New Britain	Eastern	2B-3B-SS	6	20	1	7	0	0	0	0	1	.350
2010	Minnesota c	A.L.	SS-2B-3B-OF	69	152	26	42	7	4	1	20	6	.276
Major League Totals			5 Yrs.	312	958	125	239	34	8	8	96	35	.249

a Traded to Minnesota Twins for pitcher J.C. Romero, December 9, 2005.
b On disabled list from July 29 to August 21, 2008.
c On disabled list from June 1 to July 22, 2010.

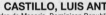

CASTILLO, LUIS ANTONIO

Born, San Pedro de Macoris, Dominican Republic, September 12, 1975.
Bats Both. Throws Right. Height, 5 feet, 11 inches. Weight, 190 pounds.

Year	Club	Lea	Pos	G	AB	R	H	2B	3B	HR	RBI	SB	Avg
1993	Florida	Dominican	2B	69	266	48	75	7	1	4	31	9	.282
1994	Marlins	Gulf Coast	2B-SS	57	216	49	57	8	0	0	16	31	.264
1995	Kane County	Midwest	2B	89	340	71	111	4	4	0	23	41	.326
1996	Portland	Eastern	2B	109	420	83	133	15	7	1	35	51	.317
1996	Florida	N.L.	2B	41	164	26	43	2	1	1	8	17	.262
1997	Florida	N.L.	2B	75	263	27	63	8	0	0	8	16	.240
1997	Charlotte	Int.	2B	37	130	25	46	5	0	0	5	8	.354
1998	Charlotte	Int.	2B	100	381	74	109	11	2	0	15	41	.286
1998	Florida	N.L.	2B	44	153	21	31	3	2	1	10	3	.203
1999	Florida	N.L.	2B	128	487	76	147	23	4	0	28	50	.302
2000	Calgary	P.C.	2B	4	13	4	4	1	1	0	0	1	.308
2000	Florida a	N.L.	2B	136	539	101	180	17	3	2	17	*62	.334
2001	Florida	N.L.	2B	134	537	76	141	16	10	2	45	33	.263
2002	Florida	N.L.	2B	146	606	86	185	18	5	2	39	48	.305
2003	Florida b	N.L.	2B	152	595	99	187	19	6	6	39	21	.314
2004	Florida	N.L.	2B	150	564	91	164	12	7	2	47	21	.291
2005	Florida c	N.L.	2B	122	439	72	132	12	4	4	30	10	.301
2006	Minnesota	A.L.	2B	142	584	84	173	22	6	3	49	25	.296
2007	Minnesota	A.L.	2B	85	349	54	106	11	3	0	18	9	.304
2007	New York d-e	N.L.	2B	50	199	37	59	8	2	1	20	10	.296
2008	Mets	Gulf Coast	2B	3	5	0	0	0	0	0	0	0	.000

Year Club	Lea	Pos	G	AB	R	H	2B	3B	HR	RBI	SB	Avg
2008 St. Lucie	Fla.St.	2B	5	15	1	1	0	0	0	0	0	.067
2008 Binghamton	Eastern	2B	5	16	1	4	0	0	0	2	0	.250
2008 New York f	N.L.	2B	87	298	46	73	7	1	3	28	17	.245
2009 New York	N.L.	2B	142	486	77	147	12	3	1	40	20	.302
2010 St. Lucie	Fla.St.	2B	4	13	3	2	1	0	0	0	0	.154
2010 New York g	N.L.	2B	86	247	28	58	4	2	0	17	8	.235
Major League Totals		15 Yrs.	1720	6510	1001	1889	194	59	28	443	370	.290
Division Series												
2003 Florida	N.L.	2B	4	17	2	5	3	0	0	1	0	.294
2006 Minnesota	A.L.	2B	3	11	0	3	0	0	0	0	0	.273
Division Series Totals			7	28	2	8	3	0	0	1	0	.286
Championship Series												
2003 Florida	N.L.	2B	7	28	3	6	1	0	0	2	2	.214
World Series Record												
2003 Florida	N.L.	2B	6	26	1	4	0	0	0	1	1	.154

a On disabled list from April 16 to May 5, 2000.
b Filed for free agency, November 6, 2003, re-signed with Florida Marlins, December 2, 2003.
c Traded to Minnesota Twins for pitcher Travis Bowyer and pitcher Scott Tyler, December 2, 2005.
d Traded to New York Mets for catcher Drew Butera and outfielder Dustin Martin, July 30, 2007.
e Filed for free agency, October 29, 2007, re-signed with New York Mets, November 19, 2007.
f On disabled list from July 3 to August 25, 2008.
g On disabled list from June 2 to July 19, 2010.

CASTRO, JASON MICHAEL

Born, Castro Valley, California, June 18, 1987.
Bats Left. Throws Right. Height, 6 feet, 3 inches. Weight, 210 pounds.

Year Club	Lea	Pos	G	AB	R	H	2B	3B	HR	RBI	SB	Avg
2008 Tri-City	N.Y.-Penn.	C	39	138	10	38	9	0	2	12	0	.275
2009 Lancaster	Calif.	C	56	207	27	64	20	1	7	44	1	.309
2009 Corpus Christi	Texas	C	63	239	38	70	11	1	3	29	2	.293
2010 Round Rock	P.C.	C	57	211	31	56	7	0	4	26	1	.265
2010 Houston	N.L.	C	67	195	26	40	8	1	2	8	0	.205

CASTRO, STARLIN DE JESUS

Born, Monte Cristi, Dominican Republic, March 24, 1990.
Bats Right. Throws Right. Height, 6 feet. Weight, 190 pounds.

Year Club	Lea	Pos	G	AB	R	H	2B	3B	HR	RBI	SB	Avg
2008 Cubs	Arizona	SS-2B-3B-OF	51	196	33	61	11	5	3	22	6	.311
2009 Daytona	Fla.St.	SS	96	358	45	108	17	3	3	35	22	.302
2009 Tennessee	Southern	SS	31	111	11	32	6	3	0	14	6	.288
2010 Tennessee	Southern	SS	26	109	20	41	8	5	1	20	4	.376
2010 Chicago	N.L.	SS	125	463	53	139	31	5	3	41	10	.300

CEDENO, RONNY ALEXANDER

Born, Puerto Cabello, Venezuela, February 2, 1983.
Bats Right. Throws Right. Height, 6 feet. Weight, 180 pounds.

Year Club	Lea	Pos	G	AB	R	H	2B	3B	HR	RBI	SB	Avg
2001 Cubs	Arizona	SS-2B-OF	52	206	36	72	13	4	1	17	17	.350
2001 Lansing	Midwest	2B-SS-3B	17	56	9	11	4	1	1	2	0	.196
2002 Lansing	Midwest	SS-2B	98	376	44	80	17	4	2	31	14	.213
2002 Boise	Northwest	SS-2B	29	110	17	24	5	2	0	6	8	.218
2003 Daytona	Fla.St.	SS-2B	107	380	43	80	18	1	4	36	19	.211
2004 West Tenn	Southern	SS	116	384	39	107	19	5	6	48	10	.279
2005 Iowa	P.C.	SS	65	245	42	87	14	1	8	36	11	.355
2005 Chicago	N.L.	SS-2B	41	80	13	24	3	0	1	6	1	.300
2006 Chicago	N.L.	SS-2B	151	534	51	131	18	7	6	41	8	.245
2007 Iowa	P.C.	SS	75	287	52	103	15	3	10	37	6	.359
2007 Chicago	N.L.	SS-2B-3B	38	74	6	15	2	0	4	13	2	.203
2008 Chicago	N.L.	2B-SS-3B-OF	99	216	36	58	12	0	2	28	4	.269
2009 Seattle	A.L.	SS-2B-OF-3B	59	186	15	31	4	2	5	17	3	.167
2009 Pittsburgh a-b	N.L.	SS	46	155	17	40	4	1	5	21	2	.258
2010 Pittsburgh	N.L.	SS	139	468	42	120	29	3	8	38	12	.256
Major League Totals		6 Yrs.	573	1713	180	419	72	13	31	164	32	.245
Division Series												
2007 Chicago	N.L.	PH	2	0	0	0	0	0	0	0	0	.000

Year	Club	Lea	Pos	G	AB	R	H	2B	3B	HR	RBI	SB	Avg
2008	Chicago	N.L.	PH	1	0	0	0	0	0	0	0	1	.000
Division Series Totals				3	0	0	0	0	0	0	0	1	.000

a Traded to Seattle Mariners with pitcher Garrett Olson for pitcher Aaron Heilman, January 28, 2009.
b Traded to Pittsburgh Pirates with outfielder Jeff Clement, pitcher Aaron Pribanic, pitcher Brett Lorin and pitcher Nathan Adcock for infielder Jack Wilson and pitcher Ian Snell, July 29, 2009.

CERVELLI, FRANCISCO

Born, Valencia, Venezuela, March 6, 1986.
Bats Right. Throws Right. Height, 6 feet, 1 inch. Weight, 210 pounds.

Year	Club	Lea	Pos	G	AB	R	H	2B	3B	HR	RBI	SB	Avg
2005	Yankees	Gulf Coast	C-OF	24	58	10	11	2	0	1	9	1	.190
2006	Staten Island	N.Y.-Penn.	C	42	136	21	42	10	0	2	16	0	.309
2007	Tampa	Fla.St.	C	89	290	34	81	24	2	2	32	4	.279
2008	Tampa	Fla.St.	C	3	10	2	3	0	0	0	1	0	.300
2008	Yankees	Gulf Coast	C	3	8	0	2	1	0	0	0	0	.250
2008	Trenton	Eastern	C	21	73	8	23	5	0	0	8	0	.315
2008	New York	A.L.	C	3	5	0	0	0	0	0	0	0	.000
2009	Trenton	Eastern	C	16	58	8	11	1	0	2	7	0	.190
2009	Yankees	Gulf Coast	C	2	6	1	1	0	0	0	0	0	.167
2009	Scranton/WB	Int.	C	21	69	7	19	5	0	1	7	0	.275
2009	New York	A.L.	C	42	94	13	28	4	0	1	11	0	.298
2010	New York	A.L.	C-3B	93	266	27	72	11	3	0	38	1	.271
Major League Totals			3 Yrs.	138	365	40	100	15	3	1	49	1	.274
	Division Series												
2009	New York	A.L.	C	1	0	0	0	0	0	0	0	0	.000
	Championship Series												
2009	New York	A.L.	PH	1	1	0	0	0	0	0	0	0	.000
2010	New York	A.L.	C	1	2	0	0	0	0	0	0	0	.000
Championship Series Totals				2	3	0	0	0	0	0	0	0	.000

CHOO, SHIN-SOO

Born, Pusan, South Korea, July 13, 1982.
Bats Left. Throws Left. Height, 5 feet, 11 inches. Weight, 200 pounds.

Year	Club	Lea	Pos	G	AB	R	H	2B	3B	HR	RBI	SB	Avg
2001	Mariners	Arizona	OF	51	199	51	60	10	10	4	35	12	.302
2001	Wisconsin	Midwest	OF	3	13	1	6	0	0	0	3	2	.462
2002	San Bernardino	Calif.	OF	11	39	14	12	5	1	1	9	3	.308
2002	Wisconsin	Midwest	OF	119	420	69	127	24	8	6	48	34	.302
2003	Inland Empire	Calif.	OF	110	412	62	118	18	13	9	55	18	.286
2004	San Antonio	Texas	OF	132	517	89	163	17	7	15	84	40	.315
2005	Tacoma	P.C.	OF	115	429	73	121	21	5	11	54	20	.282
2005	Seattle	A.L.	OF	10	18	1	1	0	0	0	1	0	.056
2006	Tacoma	P.C.	OF	94	375	71	121	21	3	13	48	26	.323
2006	Seattle-Cleveland a	A.L.	OF	49	157	23	44	12	3	3	22	5	.280
2007	Cleveland	A.L.	OF	6	17	5	5	0	0	0	5	0	.294
2007	Indians	Gulf Coast	OF	2	5	0	1	1	0	0	2	0	.200
2007	Buffalo	Int.	OF	59	208	34	54	11	2	3	26	10	.260
2008	Buffalo	Int.	OF	12	42	1	11	2	0	1	3	1	.262
2008	Cleveland b	A.L.	OF	94	317	68	98	28	3	14	66	4	.309
2009	Cleveland	A.L.	OF	156	583	87	175	38	6	20	86	21	.300
2010	Akron	Eastern	OF	3	11	1	1	0	0	0	0	1	.091
2010	Cleveland c	A.L.	OF	144	550	81	165	31	2	22	90	22	.300
Major League Totals			6 Yrs.	459	1642	265	488	109	14	59	270	52	.297

a Traded to Cleveland Indians with player to be named later for infielder Ben Broussard and cash, July 27, 2006. Cleveland Indians received pitcher Shawn Nottingham to complete trade, August 24, 2006.
b On disabled list from March 21 to May 30, 2008.
c On disabled list from July 3 to July 23, 2010.

CHURCH, RYAN MATTHEW

Born, Santa Barbara, California, October 14, 1978.
Bats Left. Throws Left. Height, 6 feet, 1 inch. Weight, 190 pounds.

Year	Club	Lea	Pos	G	AB	R	H	2B	3B	HR	RBI	SB	Avg
2000	Mahoning Valley	N.Y.-Penn.	OF	73	272	51	81	16	5	10	65	11	.298
2001	Kinston	Carolina	OF	24	83	16	20	7	0	5	15	1	.241
2001	Columbus	So.Atl.	OF	101	363	64	104	23	3	17	76	4	.287
2002	Kinston	Carolina	OF	53	181	30	59	12	1	10	30	4	.326

Year	Club	Lea	Pos	G	AB	R	H	2B	3B	HR	RBI	SB	Avg
2002	Akron	Eastern	OF	71	291	39	86	17	4	12	51	1	.296
2003	Akron	Eastern	OF	99	371	47	97	17	3	13	52	4	.261
2004	Edmonton	P.C.	OF	98	347	74	120	29	8	17	79	0	.346
2004	Montreal a	N.L.	OF	30	63	6	11	1	0	1	6	0	.175
2005	Harrisburg	Eastern	OF	4	18	2	5	1	0	0	0	0	.278
2005	Washington b	N.L.	OF	102	268	41	77	15	3	9	42	3	.287
2006	Harrisburg	Eastern	OF	5	19	3	4	0	0	2	3	1	.211
2006	New Orleans	P.C.	OF	53	175	29	43	6	0	7	29	5	.246
2006	Washington	N.L.	OF	71	196	22	54	17	1	10	35	6	.276
2007	Washington c	N.L.	OF	144	470	57	128	43	1	15	70	3	.272
2008	Mets	Gulf Coast	DH	2	6	0	1	0	0	0	1	0	.167
2008	Brooklyn	N.Y.-Penn.	OF	2	6	1	3	1	0	0	1	0	.500
2008	Binghamton	Eastern	OF	2	8	0	0	0	0	0	0	0	.000
2008	New Orleans	P.C.	OF	2	5	0	1	1	0	0	1	0	.200
2008	New York d	N.L.	OF	90	319	54	88	14	1	12	49	2	.276
2009	New York-Atlanta e-f-g	N.L.	OF	111	359	46	98	28	0	4	40	6	.273
2010	Pittsburgh-Arizona h-i	N.L.	OF	106	219	25	44	16	1	5	25	1	.201
Major League Totals			7 Yrs.	654	1894	251	500	134	7	56	267	21	.264

a Traded by Cleveland Indians to Montreal Expos with infielder Maicer Izturis for pitcher Scott Stewart, January 5, 2004.
b On disabled list from June 23 to July 13 and August 25 to September 9, 2005.
c Traded to New York Mets with catcher Brian Schneider for outfielder Lastings Milledge, November 30, 2007.
d On disabled list from June 6 to June 29 and July 6 to August 22, 2008.
e On disabled list from May 23 to June 7, 2009.
f Traded to Atlanta Braves for outfielder Jeff Francoeur and cash, July 10, 2009.
g Not offered contract, December 12, 2009. Signed with Pittsburgh Pirates, January 13, 2010.
h Traded to Arizona Diamondbacks with infielder Bobby Crosby and pitcher D.J. Carrasco for catcher Chris Snyder, infielder Pedro Ciriaco and cash, July 31, 2010.
i Not offered contract, December 2, 2010.

COGHLAN, CHRISTOPHER B. (CHRIS)

Born, Palm Harbor, Florida, June 18, 1985.
Bats Left. Throws Right. Height, 6 feet, 1 inch. Weight, 195 pounds.

Year	Club	Lea	Pos	G	AB	R	H	2B	3B	HR	RBI	SB	Avg
2006	Marlins	Gulf Coast	3B	2	7	2	2	0	0	0	3	0	.286
2006	Jamestown	N.Y.-Penn.	3B-2B	28	94	14	28	5	1	0	12	5	.298
2007	Jupiter	Fla.St.	2B	34	130	17	26	5	3	2	18	5	.200
2007	Greensboro	So.Atl.	2B	81	305	60	99	26	4	10	64	19	.325
2008	Carolina	Southern	2B-3B	132	483	83	144	32	5	7	74	34	.298
2009	New Orleans	P.C.	2B-3B-OF	25	96	21	33	9	1	3	22	9	.344
2009	Florida a	N.L.	OF-2B	128	504	84	162	31	6	9	47	8	.321
2010	Florida b	N.L.	OF	91	358	60	96	20	3	5	28	10	.268
Major League Totals			2 Yrs.	219	862	144	258	51	9	14	75	18	.299

a Selected Rookie of the Year in National League for 2009.
b On disabled list from July 26 to November 5, 2010.

COLVIN, TYLER EUGENE

Born, Augusta, Georgia, September 5, 1985.
Bats Left. Throws Left. Height, 6 feet, 3 inches. Weight, 210 pounds.

Year	Club	Lea	Pos	G	AB	R	H	2B	3B	HR	RBI	SB	Avg
2006	Boise	Northwest	OF	64	265	50	71	12	6	11	53	12	.268
2007	Daytona	Fla.St.	OF	63	245	38	75	24	3	7	50	10	.306
2007	Tennessee	Southern	OF	62	247	34	72	11	2	9	31	7	.291
2008	Tennessee	Southern	OF	137	540	68	138	27	11	14	80	7	.256
2009	Daytona	Fla.St.	OF	32	112	18	28	5	2	1	10	3	.250
2009	Tennessee	Southern	OF	84	307	51	92	13	7	14	50	5	.300
2009	Chicago	N.L.	OF	6	17	1	3	0	0	0	2	0	.176
2010	Chicago a	N.L.	OF	135	358	60	91	18	5	20	56	6	.254
Major League Totals			2 Yrs.	141	375	61	94	18	5	20	58	6	.251

a On disabled list from September 20 to October 6, 2010.

CONRAD, BROOKS LITCHFIELD

Born, San Diego, California, January 16, 1980.
Bats Both. Throws Right. Height, 5 feet, 11 inches. Weight, 190 pounds.

Year	Club	Lea	Pos	G	AB	R	H	2B	3B	HR	RBI	SB	Avg
2001	Pittsfield	N.Y.-Penn.	2B-3B	65	232	41	65	16	5	4	39	14	.280

Year	Club	Lea	Pos	G	AB	R	H	2B	3B	HR	RBI	SB	Avg
2002	Michigan	Midwest	2B	133	499	94	143	25	14	14	94	18	.287
2003	Salem	Carolina	2B	99	345	50	98	24	3	11	61	4	.284
2003	Lexington	So.Atl.	2B	38	140	20	26	5	2	3	11	7	.186
2004	Round Rock	Texas	2B	129	480	84	139	39	6	13	83	8	.290
2005	Round Rock	P.C.	2B	113	418	84	110	22	3	21	57	12	.263
2005	Corpus Christi	Texas	2B	22	77	13	18	6	1	2	11	8	.234
2006	Round Rock	P.C.	2B-3B	138	532	100	142	40	15	24	94	15	.267
2007	Round Rock a	P.C.	2B-3B-C	139	533	85	116	36	3	22	70	12	.218
2008	Oakland	A.L.	3B-2B	6	19	0	3	1	0	0	2	0	.158
2008	Sacramento	P.C.	2B-SS-OF-3B	117	465	86	113	29	5	28	91	4	.243
2009	Gwinnett	Int.	2B-SS-1B-3B	110	398	66	107	25	0	12	64	13	.269
2009	Atlanta b	N.L.	2B-3B	30	54	7	11	1	2	2	8	0	.204
2010	Atlanta	N.L.	3B-2B	103	156	31	39	11	1	8	33	5	.250
Major League Totals			3 Yrs.	139	229	38	53	13	3	10	43	5	.231
	Division Series												
2010	Atlanta	N.L.	2B	4	11	0	1	0	0	0	0	0	.091

a Filed for free agency from Houston Astros, October 29, 2007. Signed with Oakland Athletics organization, December 8, 2007.

b Filed for free agency, October 8, 2008. Signed with Atlanta Braves organization, January 22, 2009.

CORA, JOSE ALEXANDER (ALEX)

Born, Caguas, Puerto Rico, October 18, 1975.

Bats Left. Throws Right. Height, 6 feet. Weight, 200 pounds.

Year	Club	Lea	Pos	G	AB	R	H	2B	3B	HR	RBI	SB	Avg
1996	Vero Beach	Fla.St.	SS-OF	61	214	26	55	5	4	0	26	5	.257
1997	San Antonio	Texas	SS	127	448	52	105	20	4	3	48	12	.234
1998	Albuquerque	P.C.	SS-2B	81	299	42	79	16	6	5	45	10	.264
1998	Los Angeles	N.L.	SS-2B	29	33	1	4	0	1	0	0	0	.121
1999	Albuquerque	P.C.	SS	80	302	51	93	11	7	4	37	9	.308
1999	Los Angeles a	N.L.	SS-2B	11	30	2	5	1	0	0	3	0	.167
2000	Albuquerque	P.C.	SS	30	110	18	41	8	3	0	20	5	.373
2000	Los Angeles	N.L.	SS-2B	109	353	39	84	18	6	4	32	4	.238
2001	Los Angeles	N.L.	SS-2B	134	405	38	88	18	3	4	29	0	.217
2002	Los Angeles	N.L.	SS-2B	115	258	37	75	14	4	5	28	7	.291
2003	Los Angeles	N.L.	2B-SS	148	477	39	119	24	3	4	34	4	.249
2004	Los Angeles b	N.L.	2B	138	405	47	107	9	4	10	47	3	.264
2005	Cleveland-Boston c	A.L.	2B-SS-3B-OF	96	250	25	58	8	4	3	24	7	.232
2006	Boston d	A.L.	SS-2B-3B	96	235	31	56	7	2	1	18	6	.238
2007	Boston	A.L.	2B-SS-1B	83	207	30	51	10	5	3	18	1	.246
2008	Pawtucket	Int.	2B-SS	3	11	2	3	0	0	0	0	0	.273
2008	Boston e-f	A.L.	SS-2B	75	152	14	41	8	2	0	9	1	.270
2009	Buffalo	Int.	SS	3	14	0	3	1	0	0	0	0	.214
2009	New York g-h	N.L.	SS-2B-1B	82	271	31	68	11	1	1	18	8	.251
2010	Oklahoma	P.C.	2B-SS	6	22	5	4	1	0	1	2	1	.182
2010	New York	N.L.	2B-SS-1B	62	169	14	35	6	3	0	20	4	.207
2010	Texas i-j	A.L.	2B-3B	4	7	0	2	0	0	0	0	0	.286
Major League Totals			13 Yrs.	1182	3252	348	793	134	38	35	280	45	.244
	Division Series												
2004	Los Angeles	N.L.	2B	4	15	1	2	0	1	0	1	0	.133
2005	Boston	A.L.	SS	1	0	0	0	0	0	0	0	0	.000
2008	Boston	A.L.	SS	2	4	1	1	1	0	0	0	0	.250
Division Series Totals				7	19	2	3	1	1	0	1	0	.158
	Championship Series												
2007	Boston	A.L.	2B-SS	2	0	0	0	0	0	0	0	0	.000
2008	Boston	A.L.	SS	2	7	0	1	0	0	0	0	0	.143
Championship Series Totals				4	7	0	1	0	0	0	0	0	.143
	World Series Record												
2007	Boston	A.L.	2B-SS	2	0	0	0	0	0	0	0	0	.000

a On disabled list from March 25 to June 27, 1999.

b Not offered contract, December 21, 2004. Signed with Cleveland Indians, January 18, 2005.

c Traded to Boston Red Sox for infielder Ramon Vazquez, July 7, 2005.

d Filed for free agency, October 31, 2006, re-signed with Boston Red Sox, November 17, 2006.

e On disabled list from April 10 to May 11, 2008.

f Filed for free agency, October 30, 2008. Signed with New York Mets, January 22, 2009.

g On disabled list from May 18 to June 2 and August 18 to November 6, 2009.

h Filed for free agency, November 6, 2009, re-signed with New York Mets, November 30, 2009.

i Released by New York Mets, August 7, 2010. Signed with Texas Rangers organization, August 17, 2010.

j Released by Texas Rangers, September 7, 2010. Signed with Washington Nationals organization, January 17, 2011.

COUNSELL, CRAIG JOHN

Born, South Bend, Indiana, August 21, 1970.
Bats Left. Throws Right. Height, 6 feet. Weight, 185 pounds.

Year	Club	Lea	Pos	G	AB	R	H	2B	3B	HR	RBI	SB	Avg
1992	Bend	Northwest	2B-SS	18	61	11	15	6	1	0	8	1	.246
1993	Central Val	California	SS	131	471	79	132	26	3	5	59	14	.280
1994	New Haven	Eastern	SS-2B	83	300	47	84	20	1	5	37	4	.280
1995	Colo Sprngs	P.C.	SS	118	399	60	112	22	6	5	53	10	.281
1995	Colorado	N.L.	SS	3	1	0	0	0	0	0	0	0	.000
1996	Colo Sprngs	P.C.	2B-3B-SS	25	75	17	18	3	0	2	10	4	.240
1997	Colo Sprngs	P.C.	2B-SS	96	376	77	126	31	6	5	63	12	.335
1997	Colorado-Florida a	N.L.	2B	52	164	20	49	9	2	1	16	1	.299
1998	Florida b	N.L.	2B	107	335	43	84	19	5	4	40	3	.251
1999	Florida-Los Angeles c-d	N.L.	2B-SS	87	174	24	38	7	0	0	11	1	.218
2000	Tucson	P.C.	2B	50	198	45	69	14	3	3	27	4	.348
2000	Arizona	N.L.	2B-3B-SS	67	152	23	48	8	1	2	11	3	.316
2001	Arizona	N.L.	SS-2B-3B-1B	141	458	76	126	22	3	4	38	6	.275
2002	Arizona e	N.L.	3B-SS-2B	112	436	63	123	22	1	2	51	7	.282
2003	Tucson	P.C.	2B-SS-3B	5	23	8	10	2	0	0	2	0	.435
2003	Arizona f-g	N.L.	3B-SS-2B-1B	89	303	40	71	6	3	3	21	11	.234
2004	Milwaukee h	N.L.	SS-3B	140	473	59	114	19	5	2	23	17	.241
2005	Arizona	N.L.	2B-SS	150	578	85	148	34	4	9	42	26	.256
2006	Lancaster	Calif.	DH	1	3	1	3	1	0	0	0	0	1.000
2006	Tucson	P.C.	DH	2	11	2	2	0	0	0	0	0	.182
2006	Arizona i-j	N.L.	SS-3B-2B	105	372	56	95	14	4	4	30	15	.255
2007	Milwaukee	N.L.	3B-SS-2B	122	282	31	62	12	2	3	24	4	.220
2008	Milwaukee k	N.L.	3B-SS-2B	110	248	31	56	14	1	1	14	3	.226
2009	Milwaukee l	N.L.	2B-3B-SS	130	404	61	115	22	8	4	39	3	.285
2010	Milwaukee m	N.L.	SS-3B-2B	102	204	16	51	8	0	2	21	1	.250
Major League Totals			15 Yrs.	1517	4584	628	1180	216	39	41	381	101	.257
	Division Series												
1997	Florida	N.L.	2B	3	5	0	2	1	0	0	1	0	.400
2001	Arizona	N.L.	2B	5	16	2	3	0	0	1	3	0	.187
2008	Milwaukee	N.L.	2B-3B	4	12	0	2	0	0	0	1	0	.167
Division Series Totals				12	33	2	7	1	0	1	5	0	.212
	Championship Series												
1997	Florida	N.L.	2B	5	14	0	6	0	0	0	2	0	.429
2001	Arizona	N.L.	2B-SS	5	21	5	8	3	0	0	4	1	.381
Championship Series Totals				10	35	5	14	3	0	0	6	1	.400
	World Series Record												
1997	Florida	N.L.	2B	7	22	4	4	1	0	0	2	1	.182
2001	Arizona	N.L.	2B	6	24	1	2	0	0	1	1	0	.083
World Series Totals				13	46	5	6	1	0	1	3	1	.130

a Traded to Florida Marlins for pitcher Mark Hutton, July 27, 1997.
b On disabled list from August 4 to September 28, 1998.
c Traded to Los Angeles Dodgers for player to be named later, June 15, 1999. Florida Marlins received pitcher Ryan Moskau to complete trade, July 15, 1999.
d Released by Los Angeles Dodgers, March 17, 2000. Signed with Arizona Diamondbacks organization, March 20, 2000.
e On disabled list from August 9 to October 14, 2002.
f On disabled list from May 7 to July 7, 2003.
g Traded to Milwaukee Brewers with infielder Junior Spivey, infielder Lyle Overbay, catcher Chad Moeller, pitcher Chris Capuano and pitcher Jorge DeRosa for infielder Richie Sexson, pitcher Shane Nance and player to be named later. Arizona Diamondbacks received outfielder Gary Varner to complete trade, December 15, 2003.
h Filed for free agency, October 29, 2004. Signed with Arizona Diamondbacks December 15, 2004.
i On disabled list from July 15 to August 22, 2006.
j Filed for free agency, October 30, 2006. Signed with Milwaukee Brewers, November 29, 2006.
k Not offered contract, October 31, 2008. re-signed with Milwaukee Brewers, January 26, 2009.
l Filed for free agency, November 9, 2009, re-signed with Milwaukee Brewers, December 14, 2009.
m Filed for free agency, November 1, 2010, re-signed with Milwaukee Brewers, December 22, 2010.

CRAWFORD, CARL DEMONTE

Born, Houston, Texas, August 5, 1981.
Bats Left. Throws Left. Height, 6 feet, 2 inches. Weight, 220 pounds.

Year	Club	Lea	Pos	G	AB	R	H	2B	3B	HR	RBI	SB	Avg
1999	Princeton	Appal.	OF	60	260	62	83	14	4	0	25	17	.319
2000	Charleston-SC	So.Atl.	OF	135	564	99	170	21	11	6	57	55	.301
2001	Orlando	Southern	OF	132	537	64	147	24	3	4	51	36	.274
2002	Durham	Int.	OF	85	353	59	105	17	9	7	52	26	.297

Year Club	Lea	Pos	G	AB	R	H	2B	3B	HR	RBI	SB	Avg
2002 Tampa Bay	A.L.	OF	63	259	23	67	11	6	2	30	9	.259
2003 Tampa Bay	A.L.	OF	151	630	80	177	18	9	5	54	*55	.281
2004 Tampa Bay	A.L.	OF	152	626	104	185	26	*19	11	55	*59	.296
2005 Tampa Bay	A.L.	OF	156	644	101	194	33	*15	15	81	46	.301
2006 Tampa Bay	A.L.	OF	151	600	89	183	20	*16	18	77	*58	.305
2007 Tampa Bay	A.L.	OF	143	584	93	184	37	9	11	80	*50	.315
2008 Tampa Bay a..........	A.L.	OF	109	443	69	121	12	10	8	57	25	.273
2009 Tampa Bay	A.L.	OF	156	606	96	185	28	8	15	68	60	.305
2010 Tampa Bay b	A.L.	OF	154	600	110	184	30	*13	19	90	47	.307
Major League Totals		9 Yrs.	1235	4992	765	1480	215	105	104	592	409	.296
Division Series												
2008 Tampa Bay	N.L.	OF	4	14	2	3	0	0	0	2	3	.214
2010 Tampa Bay	N.L.	OF	5	21	1	3	0	0	1	1	1	.143
Division Series Totals			9	35	3	6	0	0	1	3	4	.171
Championship Series												
2008 Tampa Bay	N.L.	OF	7	29	3	10	2	1	0	4	3	.345
World Series Record												
2008 Tampa Bay	N.L.	OF	5	19	4	5	1	0	2	2	1	.263

a On disabled list from August 10 to September 26, 2008.

b Filed for free agency, November 1, 2010. Signed with Boston Red Sox, December 11, 2010.

CRISP, COVELLI LOYCE (COCO)

Born, Los Angeles, California, November 1, 1979.
Bats Both. Throws Right. Height, 6 feet. Weight, 180 pounds.

Year Club	Lea	Pos	G	AB	R	H	2B	3B	HR	RBI	SB	Avg
1999 Johnson City	Appal.	2B	65	229	55	59	5	4	3	22	27	.258
2000 New Jersey	N.Y.-Penn.	OF-2B	36	134	18	32	5	0	0	14	25	.239
2000 Peoria............	Midwest	OF	27	98	14	27	9	0	0	7	7	.276
2001 Potomac..........	Carolina	OF	139	530	80	162	23	3	11	47	39	.306
2002 New Haven.........	Eastern	OF	89	355	61	107	16	1	9	47	26	.301
2002 Akron.............	Eastern	OF	7	32	9	13	1	0	1	4	4	.406
2002 Buffalo	Int.	OF	4	21	3	5	1	0	0	2	1	.238
2002 Cleveland a...........	A.L.	OF	32	127	16	33	9	2	1	9	4	.260
2003 Buffalo	Int.	OF	56	225	42	81	19	6	1	24	20	.360
2003 Cleveland	A.L.	OF	99	414	55	110	15	6	3	27	15	.266
2004 Cleveland	A.L.	OF	139	491	78	146	24	2	15	71	20	.297
2005 Cleveland b	A.L.	OF	145	594	86	178	42	4	16	69	15	.300
2006 Pawtucket	Int.	OF	1	3	0	1	0	0	0	2	0	.333
2006 Boston c-d............	A.L.	OF	105	413	58	109	22	2	8	36	22	.264
2007 Boston	A.L.	OF	145	526	85	141	28	7	6	60	28	.268
2008 Boston e..............	A.L.	OF	118	361	55	102	18	3	7	41	20	.283
2009 Kansas City f-g........	A.L.	OF	49	180	30	41	8	5	3	14	13	.228
2010 Stockton.............	Calif.	OF	2	6	2	5	0	1	1	3	0	.833
2010 Sacramento	P.C.	OF	6	22	7	13	2	1	0	5	2	.591
2010 Oakland h............	A.L.	OF	75	290	51	81	14	4	8	38	32	.279
Major League Totals		9 Yrs.	907	3396	514	941	180	35	67	365	169	.277
Division Series												
2007 Boston	A.L.	OF	3	10	0	2	0	0	0	2	1	.200
2008 Boston	A.L.	OF	2	4	2	1	0	0	0	0	1	.250
Division Series Totals			5	14	2	3	0	0	0	2	2	.214
Championship Series												
2007 Boston	A.L.	OF	7	21	2	3	1	0	0	0	1	.143
2008 Boston	A.L.	OF	5	20	2	9	2	0	0	1	0	.450
Championship Series Totals			12	41	4	12	3	0	0	1	1	.293
World Series Record												
2007 Boston	A.L.	OF	3	2	1	1	0	0	0	0	0	.500

a Sent by St. Louis Cardinals to Cleveland Indians as player to be named later for pitcher Chuck Finley, August 6, 2002.

b On disabled list from May 18 to June 2, 2005.

c Traded to Boston Red Sox with pitcher David Riske and catcher Josh Bard for infielder Andy Marte, catcher Kelly Shoppach and pitcher Guillermo Mota, January 27, 2006.

d On disabled list from April 9 to May 28, 2006.

e Traded to Kansas City Royals for pitcher Ramon Ramirez, November 19, 2008.

f On disabled list from June 13 to November 9, 2009.

g Filed for free agency, November 9, 2009. Signed with Oakland Athletics, December 23, 2009.

h On disabled list from April 3 to May 21 and May 26 to June 22, 2010.

CROSBY, ROBERT EDWARD (BOBBY)

Born, Lakewood, California, January 12, 1980.
Bats Right. Throws Right. Height, 6 feet, 3 inches. Weight, 215 pounds.

Year Club	Lea	Pos	G	AB	R	H	2B	3B	HR	RBI	SB	Avg
2001 Modesto.....	California	SS	11	38	7	15	5	0	1	3	0	.395
2002 Modesto.....	California	SS	73	280	47	86	17	2	2	38	5	.307
2002 Midland	Texas	SS	59	228	31	64	16	0	7	31	9	.281
2003 Sacramento	P.C.	SS	127	465	86	143	32	6	22	90	24	.308
2003 Oakland	A.L.	SS	11	12	1	0	0	0	0	0	0	.000
2004 Oakland a.........	A.L.	SS	151	545	70	130	34	1	22	64	7	.239
2005 Stockton.....	California	SS	3	9	1	3	1	0	0	1	0	.333
2005 Sacramento	P.C.	SS	3	12	0	1	0	0	0	1	0	.083
2005 Oakland b.........	A.L.	SS	84	333	66	92	25	4	9	38	0	.276
2006 Oakland c.........	A.L.	SS	96	358	42	82	12	0	9	40	8	.229
2007 Oakland d.........	A.L.	SS	93	349	40	79	16	0	8	31	10	.226
2008 Oakland e.........	A.L.	SS	145	556	66	132	39	1	7	61	7	.237
2009 Oakland f-g	A.L.	1B-3B-SS-2B	97	238	35	53	10	2	6	29	2	.223
2010 Pittsburgh-Arizona h-i .	N.L.	SS-2B-3B-1B	70	168	9	37	10	0	1	13	0	.220
Major League Totals		8 Yrs.	747	2559	329	605	146	8	62	276	34	.236

a Selected Rookie of the Year in American League for 2004.
b On disabled list from April 5 to May 30 and August 28 to September 19, 2005.
c On disabled list from July 31 to August 18 and August 22 to October 25, 2006.
d On disabled list from July 15 to October 8, 2007.
e On disabled list from July 3 to July 18, 2008.
f On disabled list from August 18 to September 2, 2009.
g Filed for free agency, November 5, 2009. Signed with Pittsburgh Pirates, December 10, 2009.
h Traded to Arizona Diamondbacks with outfielder Ryan Church and pitcher D.J. Carrasco for catcher Chris Snyder, infielder Pedro Ciriaco and cash, July 31, 2010.
i Released by Arizona Diamondbacks, August 24, 2010.

CROWE, TREVOR THORNTON

Born, Portland, Oregon, November 17, 1983.
Bats Both. Throws Right. Height, 6 feet. Weight, 190 pounds.

Year Club	Lea	Pos	G	AB	R	H	2B	3B	HR	RBI	SB	Avg
2005 Akron.............	Eastern	OF	3	10	1	1	0	0	0	0	0	.100
2005 Mahoning Valley. .	N.Y.-Penn.	OF	12	51	9	13	2	1	1	6	4	.255
2005 Lake County	So.Atl.	OF	44	178	18	46	8	2	0	23	7	.258
2006 Kinston.	Carolina	OF	60	219	51	72	15	2	4	31	29	.329
2006 Akron	Eastern	OF-2B	39	154	20	36	7	2	1	13	16	.234
2006 Lake County	So.Atl.	OF	2	5	0	0	0	0	0	0	0	.000
2007 Akron.............	Eastern	OF	133	518	87	134	26	4	5	50	28	.259
2008 Akron.............	Eastern	OF	49	198	45	64	16	2	4	28	13	.323
2008 Buffalo	Int.	OF	35	146	25	40	12	2	5	13	5	.274
2009 Columbus............	Int.	OF	49	185	27	55	11	1	2	20	14	.297
2009 Cleveland a...........	A.L.	OF	68	183	22	43	9	3	1	17	6	.235
2010 Columbus............	Int.	OF	29	119	21	29	4	1	1	13	6	.244
2010 Cleveland	A.L.	OF	122	442	48	111	24	3	2	36	20	.251
Major League Totals		2 Yrs.	190	625	70	154	33	6	3	53	26	.246

a On disabled list from August 17 to September 4, 2009.

CRUZ, NELSON RAMON

Born, Monte Cristi, Dominican Republic, July 1, 1980.
Bats Right. Throws Right. Height, 6 feet, 3 inches. Weight, 230 pounds.

Year Club	Lea	Pos	G	AB	R	H	2B	3B	HR	RBI	SB	Avg
2001 Athletics a	Arizona	OF	23	88	11	22	3	1	3	16	6	.250
2002 Vancouver	Northwest	OF	63	214	23	59	14	0	4	25	12	.276
2003 Kane County.......	Midwest	OF	119	470	65	112	26	2	20	85	10	.238
2004 Modesto............	Calif.	OF	66	261	54	90	27	1	11	52	8	.345
2004 Sacramento	P.C.	OF	4	13	4	3	1	0	1	2	0	.231
2004 Midland b...........	Texas	OF	67	262	51	82	14	2	14	46	8	.313
2005 Huntsville........	Southern	OF	68	248	45	76	19	0	16	54	10	.306
2005 Nashville	P.C.	OF	60	208	33	56	13	0	11	27	9	.269
2005 Milwaukee	N.L.	OF	8	5	1	1	1	0	0	0	0	.200
2006 Nashville	P.C.	OF	104	371	68	112	22	1	20	73	17	.302
2006 Texas c.............	A.L.	OF	41	130	15	29	3	0	6	22	1	.223
2007 Oklahoma............	P.C.	OF	44	162	32	57	9	1	15	45	1	.352
2007 Texas	A.L.	OF	96	307	35	72	15	2	9	34	2	.235

Year	Club	Lea	Pos	G	AB	R	H	2B	3B	HR	RBI	SB	Avg
2008	Rangers	Arizona	OF	1	4	1	1	1	0	0	1	0	.250
2008	Oklahoma	P.C.	OF	103	383	93	131	18	3	37	99	24	.342
2008	Texas	A.L.	OF	31	115	19	38	9	1	7	26	3	.330
2009	Okla.	P.C.	OF	3	10	0	0	0	0	0	0	1	.000
2009	Texas d	A.L.	OF	128	462	75	120	21	1	33	76	20	.260
2010	Frisco	Texas	OF	3	11	1	4	1	0	0	1	1	.364
2010	Oklahoma	P.C.	OF	5	19	1	4	1	0	0	4	0	.211
2010	Texas e	A.L.	OF	108	399	60	127	31	3	22	78	17	.318
Major League Totals			6 Yrs.	412	1418	205	387	80	7	77	236	43	.273
	Division Series												
2010	Texas	A.L.	OF	5	20	5	8	2	0	3	3	1	.400
	Championship Series												
2010	Texas	A.L.	OF	6	20	6	7	3	0	2	5	0	.350
	World Series Record												
2010	Texas	A.L.	OF	5	20	2	4	2	0	1	3	0	.200

a Traded by New York Mets to Oakland Athletics for infielder Jorge Velandia, August 30, 2000.
b Traded to Milwaukee Brewers with pitcher Justin Lehr for infielder Keith Ginter, December 15, 2004.
c Traded to Texas Rangers with outfielder Carlos Lee for pitcher Francisco Cordero, outfielder Kevin Mench, outfielder Laynce Nix and pitcher Julian Cordero, July 28, 2006.
d On disabled list from August 4 to August 20, 2009.
e On disabled list from April 27 to May 14 and May 29 to June 22 and August 15 to August 30, 2010.

CUDDYER, MICHAEL BRENT

Born, Norfolk, Virginia, March 27, 1979.
Bats Right. Throws Right. Height, 6 feet, 2 inches. Weight, 220 pounds.

Year	Club	Lea	Pos	G	AB	R	H	2B	3B	HR	RBI	SB	Avg
1998	Fort Wayne	Midwest	SS-2B	129	497	82	137	37	7	12	81	16	.276
1999	Fort Myers	Fla.St.	3B	130	466	87	139	24	4	16	82	14	.298
2000	New Britain	Eastern	3B	138	490	72	129	30	8	6	61	5	.263
2001	New Britain	Eastern	3B-1B-OF	141	509	95	153	36	3	30	87	5	.301
2001	Minnesota	A.L.	1B-3B	8	18	1	4	2	0	0	1	1	.222
2002	Edmonton	P.C.	OF-1B-3B	86	330	70	102	16	9	20	53	12	.309
2002	Minnesota	A.L.	OF-3B-1B	41	112	12	29	7	0	4	13	2	.259
2003	Twins	Gulf Coast	OF	2	5	1	4	0	0	1	3	0	.800
2003	Rochester	Int.	OF-2B-3B-1B	53	186	25	57	17	0	3	34	5	.306
2003	Minnesota	A.L.	OF-3B-1B-2B	35	102	14	25	1	3	4	8	1	.245
2004	Minnesota	A.L.	2B-3B-OF-1B	115	339	49	89	22	1	12	45	5	.263
2005	Rochester	Int.	3B-1B	3	9	1	1	0	0	0	0	2	.111
2005	Minnesota a	A.L.	3B-OF-2B-1B	126	422	55	111	25	3	12	42	3	.263
2006	Minnesota	A.L.	OF-1B	150	557	102	158	41	5	24	109	6	.284
2007	Minnesota b	A.L.	OF-1B	144	547	87	151	28	5	16	81	5	.276
2008	Rochester	Int.	OF	4	10	3	3	2	0	0	1	0	.300
2008	Minnesota c	A.L.	OF-1B	71	249	30	62	13	4	3	36	5	.249
2009	Minnesota	A.L.	OF-1B-2B	153	588	93	162	34	7	32	94	6	.276
2010	Minnesota	A.L.	1B-OF-3B-2B	157	609	93	165	37	5	14	81	7	.271
Major League Totals			10 Yrs.	1000	3543	536	956	210	33	121	510	41	.270
	Division Series												
2002	Minnesota	A.L.	OF	5	13	1	5	1	0	0	1	0	.385
2003	Minnesota	A.L.	PH	1	4	0	1	0	0	0	1	0	.250
2004	Minnesota	A.L.	2B-1B	4	15	1	7	0	0	0	2	0	.467
2006	Minnesota	A.L.	OF	3	12	2	3	0	1	1	1	0	.250
2009	Minnesota	A.L.	1B	3	14	0	6	0	0	0	1	0	.429
2010	Minnesota	A.L.	1B	3	11	1	2	1	0	1	2	0	.182
Division Series Totals				19	69	5	24	2	1	2	8	0	.348
	Championship Series												
2002	Minnesota	A.L.	OF	3	5	0	1	0	0	0	0	0	.200

a On disabled list from June 30 to July 17, 2005.
b On disabled list from July 19 to August 3, 2007.
c On disabled list from April 5 to April 25 and June 28 to September 13, 2008.

CUST, JOHN JOSEPH (JACK)

Born, Flemington, New Jersey, January 16, 1979.
Bats Left. Throws Right. Height, 6 feet, 2 inches. Weight, 235 pounds.

Year	Club	Lea	Pos	G	AB	R	H	2B	3B	HR	RBI	SB	Avg
1997	Diamondbcks	Arizona	OF	35	121	26	37	11	1	3	33	2	.306
1998	South Bend	Midwest	1B	16	62	5	15	3	0	0	4	0	.242
1998	Lethbridge	Pioneer	OF-1B	73	223	75	77	20	2	11	56	15	.345

Year	Club	Lea	Pos	G	AB	R	H	2B	3B	HR	RBI	SB	Avg
1999	High Desert	Calif.	OF	125	455	107	152	42	3	32	112	1	.334
2000	El Paso	Texas	OF	129	447	100	131	32	6	20	75	12	.293
2001	Tucson	P.C.	OF	135	442	81	123	24	2	27	79	6	.278
2001	Arizona	N.L.	OF	3	2	0	1	0	0	0	0	0	.500
2002	Colorado Springs	P.C.	OF	105	359	74	95	24	0	23	55	6	.265
2002	Colorado a	N.L.	OF	35	65	8	11	2	0	1	8	0	.169
2003	Ottawa	Int.	OF	97	333	55	95	18	1	9	58	5	.285
2003	Baltimore b	A.L.	DH-OF	27	73	7	19	7	0	4	11	0	.260
2004	Baltimore	A.L.	DH	1	1	0	0	0	0	0	0	0	.000
2004	Ottawa c	Int.	OF	102	344	55	81	15	1	17	55	4	.235
2005	Sacramento d	P.C.	OF	134	479	95	123	28	1	19	75	2	.257
2006	Portland	P.C.	OF	138	441	97	129	23	0	30	77	0	.293
2006	San Diego	N.L.	OF	4	3	1	1	0	0	0	0	0	.333
2007	Portland	P.C.	OF	25	80	17	24	7	0	9	20	0	.300
2007	Oakland e	A.L.	OF	124	395	61	101	18	1	26	82	0	.256
2008	Oakland	A.L.	OF	148	481	77	111	19	0	33	77	0	.231
2009	Oakland f	A.L.	DH-OF	149	513	88	123	16	0	25	70	4	.240
2010	Sacramento	P.C.	OF	33	110	21	30	6	0	4	19	0	.273
2010	Oakland g	A.L.	DH-OF	112	349	50	95	19	0	13	52	2	.272
Major League Totals			9 Yrs.	603	1882	292	462	81	1	102	300	6	.245

a Traded to Colorado Rockies with catcher JD Closser for pitcher Mike Myers, January 7, 2002.
b Traded to Baltimore Orioles for outfielder Chris Richard and cash, March 11, 2003.
c Filed for free agency, October 27, 2004. Signed by Oakland Athletics organization, November 19, 2004.
d Filed for free agency, October 28, 2005. Signed by San Diego Padres organization, December 6, 2005.
e Sold to Oakland Athletics, May 3, 2007.
f Not offered contract, December 12, 2009, re-signed with Oakland Athletics, January 7, 2010.
g Not offered contract, December 2, 2010. Signed with Seattle Mariners, December 8, 2010.

DAMON, JOHNNY DAVID

Born, Fort Riley, Kansas, November 5, 1973.
Bats Left. Throws Left. Height, 6 feet, 2 Inches. Weight, 205 pounds.

Year	Club	Lea	Pos	G	AB	R	H	2B	3B	HR	RBI	SB	Avg
1992	Royals	Gulf Coast	OF	50	192	58	67	12	9	4	24	23	.349
1992	Baseball City	Fla. St.	OF	1	1	0	0	0	0	0	0	0	.000
1993	Rockford	Midwest	OF	127	511	82	148	25	13	5	50	59	.290
1994	Wilmington	Carolina	OF	119	472	96	149	25	13	6	75	44	.316
1995	Wichita	Texas	OF	111	423	83	145	15	9	16	54	26	.343
1995	Kansas City	A.L.	OF	47	188	32	53	11	5	3	23	7	.282
1996	Kansas City	A.L.	OF	145	517	61	140	22	5	6	50	25	.271
1997	Kansas City	A.L.	OF	146	472	70	130	12	8	8	48	16	.275
1998	Kansas City	A.L.	OF	161	642	104	178	30	10	18	66	26	.277
1999	Kansas City	A.L.	OF	145	583	101	179	39	9	14	77	36	.307
2000	Kansas City a	A.L.	OF	159	655	*136	214	42	10	16	88	*46	.327
2001	Oakland b	A.L.	OF	155	644	108	165	34	4	9	49	27	.256
2002	Boston	A.L.	OF	154	623	118	178	34	*11	14	63	31	.286
2003	Boston	A.L.	OF	145	608	103	166	32	6	12	67	30	.273
2004	Boston	A.L.	OF	150	621	123	189	35	6	20	94	19	.304
2005	Boston c	A.L.	OF	148	624	117	197	35	6	10	75	18	.316
2006	New York	A.L.	OF-1B	149	593	115	169	35	5	24	80	25	.285
2007	New York	A.L.	OF-1B	141	533	93	144	27	2	12	63	27	.270
2008	New York d	A.L.	OF-1B	143	555	95	168	27	5	17	71	29	.303
2009	New York e	A.L.	OF	143	550	107	155	36	3	24	82	12	.282
2010	Detroit f	A.L.	DH-OF	145	539	81	146	36	5	8	51	11	.271
Major League Totals			16 Yrs.	2276	8947	1564	2571	487	100	215	1047	385	.287
	Division Series												
2001	Oakland	A.L.	OF	5	22	3	9	2	1	0	0	2	.409
2003	Boston	A.L.	OF	5	19	2	6	2	0	1	3	2	.316
2004	Boston	A.L.	OF	3	15	4	7	1	0	0	0	3	.467
2005	Boston	A.L.	OF	3	13	2	3	1	0	0	0	0	.231
2006	New York	A.L.	OF	4	17	3	4	0	0	1	3	0	.235
2007	New York	A.L.	OF	4	18	2	5	0	0	2	5	0	.278
2009	New York	A.L.	OF	3	12	0	1	0	0	0	0	0	.083
Division Series Totals				27	116	16	35	6	1	4	11	7	.302
	Championship Series												
2003	Boston	A.L.	OF	5	20	1	4	1	0	0	1	1	.200
2004	Boston	A.L.	OF	7	35	5	6	0	0	2	7	2	.171
2009	New York	A.L.	OF	6	30	4	9	1	0	2	5	0	.300
Championship Series Totals				18	85	10	19	2	0	4	13	3	.224

Year	Club	Lea	Pos	G	AB	R	H	2B	3B	HR	RBI	SB	Avg
	World Series Record												
2004	Boston	A.L.	OF	4	21	4	6	2	1	1	2	0	.286
2009	New York	A.L.	OF	6	22	6	8	2	0	0	4	3	.364
World Series Totals				10	43	10	14	4	1	1	6	3	.326

a Traded to Oakland Athletics with infielder Mark Ellis for pitcher Roberto Hernandez, catcher A.J. Hinch, infielder Angel Berroa and cash, January 8, 2001.
b Filed for free agency, November 5, 2001. Signed with Boston Red Sox, December 21, 2001.
c Filed for free agency, October 28, 2005. Signed with New York Yankees, December 23, 2005.
d On disabled list from July 5 to July 21, 2008.
e Filed for free agency, November 9, 2009. Signed with Detroit Tigers, February 22, 2010.
f Filed for free agency, November 1, 2010.

DAVIS, ISAAC BENJAMIN (IKE)

Born, Edina, Minnesota, March 22, 1987.
Bats Left. Throws Left. Height, 6 feet, 4 inches. Weight, 215 pounds.

Year	Club	Lea	Pos	G	AB	R	H	2B	3B	HR	RBI	SB	Avg
2008	Brooklyn	N.Y.-Penn.	1B	58	215	17	55	15	0	0	17	0	.256
2009	Binghamton	Eastern	1B-OF	55	207	30	64	14	0	13	43	0	.309
2009	St. Lucie	Fla.St.	1B	59	222	28	64	17	3	7	28	0	.288
2010	Buffalo	Int.	1B	10	33	8	12	3	0	2	4	0	.364
2010	New York	N.L.	1B	147	523	73	138	33	1	19	71	3	.264

DAVIS, RAJAI LAVAE

Born, Norwich, Connecticut, October 19, 1980.
Bats Right. Throws Right. Height, 5 feet, 11 inches. Weight, 195 pounds.

Year	Club	Lea	Pos	G	AB	R	H	2B	3B	HR	RBI	SB	Avg
2001	Pirates	Gulf Coast	OF	26	84	19	22	1	0	0	4	11	.262
2001	Williamsport	N.Y.-Penn.	OF-2B	6	12	1	1	0	0	0	0	0	.083
2002	Pirates	Gulf Coast	OF	58	224	38	86	16	5	4	35	24	.384
2002	Williamsport	N.Y.-Penn.	OF	1	4	0	0	0	0	0	0	0	.000
2002	Hickory	So.Atl.	OF	6	14	4	6	0	0	0	3	2	.429
2003	Hickory	So.Atl.	OF	125	478	84	146	21	7	6	54	40	.305
2004	Lynchburg	Carolina	OF	127	509	91	160	27	7	5	38	57	.314
2005	Altoona	Eastern	OF	123	499	82	140	22	5	4	34	45	.281
2006	Indianapolis	Int.	OF	100	385	53	109	17	1	2	21	45	.283
2006	Pittsburgh	N.L.	OF	20	14	1	2	1	0	0	0	1	.143
2007	Indianapolis	Int.	OF	53	211	31	67	12	4	4	30	27	.318
2007	Pittsburgh-San Francisco a	N.L.	OF	75	190	32	53	11	2	1	9	22	.279
2008	San Francisco	N.L.	OF	12	18	2	1	0	0	0	0	4	.056
2008	Oakland b	A.L.	OF-2B	101	196	28	51	5	4	3	19	25	.260
2009	Oakland	A.L.	OF	125	390	65	119	27	5	3	48	41	.305
2010	Oakland c	A.L.	OF	143	525	66	149	28	3	5	52	50	.284
Major League Totals			5 Yrs.	476	1333	194	375	72	14	12	128	143	.281

a Traded to San Francisco Giants with player to be named later for pitcher Matt Morris, July 31, 2007. San Francisco Giants received pitcher Steve MacFarland to complete trade, August 27, 2007.
b Claimed on waivers by Oakland Athletics, April 23, 2008.
c Traded to Toronto Blue Jays for pitcher Daniel Farquhar and pitcher Trystan Magnuson, November 17, 2010.

DE JESUS, DAVID CHRISTOPHER

Born, Brooklyn, New York, December 20, 1979.
Bats Left. Throws Left. Height, 6 feet. Weight, 190 pounds.

Year	Club	Lea	Pos	G	AB	R	H	2B	3B	HR	RBI	SB	Avg
2001					INJURED—Did Not Play								
2002	Wilmington	Carolina	OF	87	334	69	99	22	6	4	41	15	.296
2002	Wichita a	Texas	OF	25	79	7	20	5	2	2	15	3	.253
2003	Wichita	Texas	OF	17	71	14	24	4	0	2	10	1	.338
2003	Omaha	P.C.	OF	59	215	49	64	16	3	5	23	8	.298
2003	Kansas City	A.L.	OF	12	7	0	2	0	1	0	0	0	.286
2004	Omaha	P.C.	OF	50	197	38	62	14	4	6	16	7	.315
2004	Kansas City	A.L.	OF	96	363	58	104	15	3	7	39	8	.287
2005	Kansas City	A.L.	OF	122	461	69	135	31	6	9	56	5	.293
2006	Omaha	P.C.	OF	3	13	0	5	0	0	0	2	0	.385
2006	Kansas City b	A.L.	OF	119	491	83	145	36	7	8	56	6	.295
2007	Kansas City	A.L.	OF	157	605	101	157	29	9	7	58	10	.260
2008	Kansas City	A.L.	OF	135	518	70	159	25	7	12	73	11	.307

Year	Club	Lea	Pos	G	AB	R	H	2B	3B	HR	RBI	SB	Avg
2009	Kansas City	A.L.	OF	144	558	74	157	28	9	13	71	4	.281
2010	Kansas City c-d	A.L.	OF	91	352	46	112	23	3	5	37	3	.318
Major League Totals	....		8 Yrs.	876	3355	501	971	187	45	61	390	47	.289

a On minor league disabled list from June 19 to September 17, 2001.
b On disabled list from April 19 to May 29, 2006.
c On disabled list from July 23 to November 10, 2010.
d Traded to Oakland Athletics for pitcher Vin Mazzaro and pitcher Justin Marks, November 10, 2010.

DENORFIA, CHRISTOPHER ANTHONY (CHRIS)

Born, Bristol, Connecticut, July 15, 1980.
Bats Right. Throws Right. Height, 6 feet, 1 inch. Weight, 205 pounds.

Year	Club	Lea	Pos	G	AB	R	H	2B	3B	HR	RBI	SB	Avg
2002	Reds...........	Gulf Coast	OF	57	200	38	68	9	2	0	19	18	.340
2002	Dayton	Midwest	OF	3	10	2	0	0	0	0	0	0	.000
2002	Chattanooga......	Southern	OF	3	7	0	3	2	1	0	0	0	.429
2003	Potomac..........	Carolina	OF	128	470	60	111	10	5	4	39	20	.236
2004	Potomac..........	Carolina	OF	75	269	52	84	18	4	11	51	10	.312
2004	Chattanooga......	Southern	OF	61	221	30	55	10	2	6	27	5	.249
2005	Chattanooga......	Southern	OF	46	188	40	62	17	3	7	26	4	.330
2005	Louisville	Int.	OF	91	323	50	100	12	6	13	61	8	.310
2005	Cincinnati............	N.L.	OF	18	38	8	10	3	0	1	2	1	.263
2006	Louisville	Int.	OF	83	312	46	109	19	1	7	45	15	.349
2006	Cincinnati............	N.L.	OF	49	106	14	30	6	0	1	7	1	.283
2007	Cincinnati............	N.L.	INJURED—Did Not Play										
2007	Oakland a-b	A.L.	INJURED—Did Not Play										
2008	Stockton.............	Calif.	OF	2	9	1	3	0	0	0	0	0	.333
2008	Sacramento	P.C.	OF	45	189	34	57	13	1	2	20	5	.302
2008	Oakland c.............	A.L.	OF	29	62	10	18	3	0	1	9	2	.290
2009	Oakland	A.L.	OF	4	2	1	0	0	0	0	1	0	.000
2009	Sacramento d..........	P.C.	OF	107	432	62	117	18	5	9	49	15	.271
2010	Portland..............	P.C.	OF	34	121	17	37	10	4	2	12	7	.306
2010	San Diego	N.L.	OF	99	284	41	77	15	2	9	36	8	.271
Major League Totals	....		5 Yrs.	199	492	74	135	27	2	12	55	12	.274

a On disabled list from March 24 to October 15, 2007.
b Traded to Oakland Athletics for pitcher Marcus McBeth and player to be named later, April 27, 2007. Cincinnati Reds received pitcher Ben Jukich to complete trade, June 12, 2007.
c On disabled list from May 7 to July 19, 2008.
d Filed for free agency, November 9, 2009. Signed with San Diego Padres organization, December 17, 2009.

DE ROSA, MARK THOMAS

Born, Passaic, New Jersey, February 26, 1975.
Bats Right. Throws Right. Height, 6 feet, 1 inch. Weight, 205 pounds.

Year	Club	Lea	Pos	G	AB	R	H	2B	3B	HR	RBI	SB	Avg
1996	Eugene......	Northwest	SS	70	255	43	66	13	1	2	28	3	.259
1997	Durham	Carolina	SS	92	346	51	93	11	3	8	37	6	.269
1998	Greenville.....	Southern	SS	125	461	67	123	26	2	8	49	7	.267
1998	Atlanta	N.L.	SS	5	3	2	1	0	0	0	0	0	.333
1999	Richmond	Int.	SS	105	364	41	99	16	2	1	40	7	.272
1999	Atlanta	N.L.	SS	7	8	0	0	0	0	0	0	0	.000
2000	Richmond	Int.	SS-2B-3B	101	370	62	108	22	3	3	35	13	.292
2000	Atlanta	N.L.	SS	22	13	9	4	1	0	0	3	0	.308
2001	Richmond	Int.	SS-3B-2B	49	186	31	55	18	0	2	17	7	.296
2001	Atlanta	N.L.	SS-2B-3B-OF	66	164	27	47	8	0	3	20	2	.287
2002	Myrtle Beach	Car.	2B	2	7	0	0	0	0	0	0	0	.000
2002	Richmond	Int.	2B-SS	16	55	9	14	3	0	0	6	2	.255
2002	Atlanta a..........	N.L.	2B-SS-OF-3B	72	212	24	63	9	2	5	23	2	.297
2003	Atlanta	N.L.	2B-3B-SS-OF	103	266	40	70	14	0	6	22	1	.263
2004	Atlanta b..........	N.L.	3B-SS-2B-OF	118	309	33	74	16	0	3	31	1	.239
2005	Texas	A.L.	OF-2B-SS-3B	66	148	26	36	5	0	8	20	1	.243
2006	Oklahoma.........	P.C.	2B-3B	3	12	2	6	1	0	0	0	0	.500
2006	Texas c-d	A.L.	OF-3B-2B-SS	136	520	78	154	40	2	13	74	4	.296
2007	Chicago	N.L.	2B-3B-OF-1B	149	502	64	147	28	3	10	72	1	.293
2008	Chicago e..........	N.L.	2B-OF-3B-1B	149	505	103	144	30	3	21	87	6	.285
2009	Cleveland	A.L.	3B-OF-1B	71	278	47	75	13	0	13	50	1	.270
2009	St. Louis f-g-h	N.L.	3B-1B-OF-2B	68	237	31	54	10	1	10	28	2	.228
2010	San Jose	Calif.	OF	1	4	0	0	0	0	0	0	0	.000
2010	Fresno	P.C.	2B-3B-OF	3	11	1	4	1	0	0	1	0	.364

Year	Club	Lea	Pos	G	AB	R	H	2B	3B	HR	RBI	SB	Avg
2010	San Francisco i	N.L.	OF-2B	26	93	9	18	3	0	1	10	0	.194
Major League Totals			13 Yrs.	1058	3258	493	887	177	11	93	440	21	.272
	Division Series												
2001	Atlanta	N.L.	SS	1	1	0	1	0	0	0	0	0	1.000
2002	Atlanta	N.L.	2B	4	7	2	3	1	1	0	3	0	.429
2003	Atlanta	N.L.	2B-3B	4	7	1	3	2	0	0	2	0	.429
2007	Chicago	N.L.	2B	3	9	2	3	0	0	0	0	0	.333
2008	Chicago	N.L.	2B-OF	3	12	2	4	2	0	1	4	0	.333
2009	St. Louis	N.L.	3B	3	13	1	5	1	0	0	1	0	.385
Division Series Totals				18	49	8	19	6	1	1	10	0	.388
	Championship Series												
2001	Atlanta	N.L.	SS	4	4	0	0	0	0	0	0	0	.000

a On disabled list from May 18 to July 17, 2002.
b Not offered contract, December 20, 2004. Signed with Texas Rangers organization, January 19, 2005.
c On disabled list from April 15 to April 30, 2006.
d Filed for free agency, October 28, 2006. Signed with Chicago Cubs, November 15, 2006.
e Traded to Cleveland Indians for pitcher Jeff Stevens, pitcher Chris Archer and pitcher John Gaub, December 31, 2008.
f Traded to St. Louis Cardinals for pitcher Chris Perez and player to be named later, June 27, 2009. Cleveland Indians received pitcher Jess Todd to complete trade, July 26, 2009.
g On disabled list from July 1 to July 18, 2009.
h Filed for free agency, November 5, 2009. Signed with San Francisco Giants, December 29, 2009.
i On disabled list from May 9 to November 9, 2010.

DESMOND, IAN M.

Born, Sarasota, Florida, September 20, 1985.
Bats Right. Throws Right. Height, 6 feet, 2 inches. Weight, 210 pounds.

Year	Club	Lea	Pos	G	AB	R	H	2B	3B	HR	RBI	SB	Avg
2004	Expos	Gulf Coast	SS	55	216	28	49	11	0	1	27	13	.227
2004	Vermont	N.Y.-Penn.	SS	4	12	2	3	0	0	1	1	0	.250
2005	Potomac	Carolina	SS	55	219	37	56	13	3	3	15	13	.256
2005	Savannah	So.Atl.	SS	73	296	37	73	10	2	4	23	20	.247
2006	Potomac	Carolina	SS	92	365	50	89	20	2	9	45	14	.244
2006	Harrisburg	Eastern	SS	37	121	8	22	4	1	0	3	4	.182
2007	Potomac	Carolina	SS	129	458	69	121	30	4	13	45	27	.264
2008	Harrisburg	Eastern	SS	93	323	42	81	14	0	12	44	12	.251
2008	Nationals	Gulf Coast	SS	3	13	1	5	1	0	0	2	3	.385
2009	Harrisburg	Eastern	SS	42	170	29	52	12	1	6	18	13	.306
2009	Syracuse	Int.	SS-OF	55	178	25	63	12	2	1	14	8	.354
2009	Washington	N.L.	SS-2B-OF	21	82	9	23	7	2	4	12	1	.280
2010	Washington	N.L.	SS-OF	154	525	59	141	27	4	10	65	17	.269
Major League Totals			2 Yrs.	175	607	68	164	34	6	14	77	18	.270

DEWITT, BLAKE ROBERT

Born, Sarasota, Florida, August 20, 1985.
Bats Left. Throws Right. Height, 5 feet, 11 inches. Weight, 190 pounds.

Year	Club	Lea	Pos	G	AB	R	H	2B	3B	HR	RBI	SB	Avg
2004	Ogden	Pioneer	3B	70	299	61	85	19	3	12	47	1	.284
2005	Vero Beach	Fla.St.	3B	8	31	4	13	3	0	1	7	0	.419
2005	Columbus	So.Atl.	3B	120	481	61	136	31	3	11	65	0	.283
2006	Vero Beach	Fla.St.	2B-3B	106	425	61	114	18	1	18	61	8	.268
2006	Jacksonville	Southern	3B-2B	26	104	6	19	1	0	1	6	0	.183
2007	Inland Empire	Calif.	3B	83	339	48	101	29	2	8	46	2	.298
2007	Jacksonville	Southern	3B	45	178	20	50	13	1	6	20	0	.281
2008	Las Vegas	P.C.	2B-3B-1B	27	111	16	34	4	2	4	18	1	.306
2008	Los Angeles	N.L.	3B-2B	117	368	45	97	13	2	9	52	3	.264
2009	Albuquerque	P.C.	2B-3B-SS	92	352	64	90	21	9	7	47	2	.256
2009	Los Angeles	N.L.	3B-2B-SS	31	49	4	10	3	0	2	4	0	.204
2010	Los Angeles-Chicago a	N.L.	2B-3B	135	440	47	115	24	5	5	52	3	.261
Major League Totals			3 Yrs.	283	857	96	222	40	7	16	108	6	.259
	Division Series												
2008	Los Angeles	N.L.	2B	3	11	2	3	2	0	0	1	0	.273
	Championship Series												
2008	Los Angeles	N.L.	2B	5	13	0	1	0	1	0	5	0	.077

a Traded to Chicago Cubs with pitcher Kyle Smit and pitcher Brett Wallach for pitcher Ted Lilly, infielder Ryan Theriot and cash, July 31, 2010.

DIAZ, MATTHEW EDWARD (MATT)

Born, Portland, Oregon, March 3, 1978.
Bats Right. Throws Right. Height, 6 feet, 1 inch. Weight, 205 pounds.

Year	Club	Lea	Pos	G	AB	R	H	2B	3B	HR	RBI	SB	Avg
1999	Hudson Valley	N.Y.-Penn.	OF	54	208	22	51	15	2	1	20	6	.245
2000	St. Petersburg	Fla.St.	OF	106	392	37	106	21	3	6	53	2	.270
2001	Bakersfield	Calif.	OF	131	524	79	172	40	2	17	81	11	.328
2002	Orlando	Southern	OF-1B	122	449	71	123	28	1	10	50	31	.274
2003	Orlando	Southern	OF	60	227	32	87	21	0	5	41	9	.383
2003	Durham	Int.	OF	67	253	35	83	18	3	8	45	6	.328
2003	Tampa Bay	A.L.	OF	4	9	2	1	0	0	0	0	0	.111
2004	Durham	Int.	OF	134	503	81	167	47	5	21	93	15	.332
2004	Tampa Bay	A.L.	OF	10	21	3	4	1	1	1	3	0	.190
2005	Royals	Arizona	OF	3	13	2	6	2	0	0	2	0	.462
2005	Wichita	Texas	OF	7	26	6	7	0	0	1	6	1	.269
2005	Omaha	P.C.	OF	65	259	48	96	22	4	14	56	10	.371
2005	Kansas City a-b-c	A.L.	OF	34	89	7	25	4	2	1	9	0	.281
2006	Atlanta	N.L.	OF	124	297	37	97	15	4	7	32	5	.327
2007	Atlanta	N.L.	OF-1B	135	358	44	121	21	0	12	45	4	.338
2008	Mississippi	Southern	OF	7	26	5	6	0	0	1	4	1	.231
2008	Richmond	Int.	OF	4	12	0	2	0	0	0	1	0	.167
2008	Atlanta d	N.L.	OF	43	135	9	33	2	0	2	14	4	.244
2009	Atlanta	N.L.	OF	125	371	56	116	18	4	13	58	12	.313
2010	Gwinnett	Int.	OF	3	12	2	3	1	0	0	3	0	.250
2010	Atlanta e-f	N.L.	OF	84	224	27	56	17	2	7	31	3	.250
Major League Totals			8 Yrs.	559	1504	185	453	78	13	43	192	28	.301
Division Series													
2010	Atlanta	N.L.	OF	4	10	0	1	0	0	0	0	0	.100

a Released by Tampa Bay Devil Rays, February 18, 2005. Signed with Kansas City Royals organization, February 24, 2005.
b On disabled list from June 11 to July 18, 2005.
c Traded to Atlanta Braves for pitcher Ricardo Rodriguez, December 20, 2005.
d On disabled list from May 28 to September 24, 2008.
e On disabled list from May 15 to June 29, 2010.
f Not offered contract, December 2, 2010. Signed with Pittsburgh Pirates, December 8, 2010.

DICKERSON, CHRISTOPHER CHARLES (CHRIS)

Born, Hollywood, California, April 10, 1982.
Bats Left. Throws Left. Height, 6 feet, 3 inches. Weight, 225 pounds.

Year	Club	Lea	Pos	G	AB	R	H	2B	3B	HR	RBI	SB	Avg
2003	Billings	Pioneer	OF	58	201	36	49	6	4	6	38	9	.244
2004	Potomac	Carolina	OF	15	45	5	9	2	0	0	5	3	.200
2004	Dayton	Midwest	OF	84	314	50	95	15	3	4	34	27	.303
2005	Sarasota	Fla.St.	OF	119	436	68	103	17	7	11	43	19	.236
2006	Chattanooga	Southern	OF	115	389	65	94	21	7	12	48	21	.242
2007	Louisville	Int.	OF	104	354	58	92	11	6	13	44	23	.260
2007	Chattanooga	Southern	OF	30	114	11	31	4	1	1	11	7	.272
2008	Louisville	Int.	OF	97	349	65	100	16	9	11	53	26	.287
2008	Cincinnati	N.L.	OF	31	102	20	31	9	2	6	15	5	.304
2009	Louisville	Int.	OF	4	12	2	3	0	0	0	1	2	.250
2009	Cincinnati a	N.L.	OF	97	255	31	70	13	3	2	15	11	.275
2010	Louisville	Int.	OF	13	43	12	19	5	0	3	7	6	.442
2010	Cincinnati-Milwaukee b-c	N.L.	OF	45	97	11	20	2	2	0	5	4	.206
Major League Totals			3 Yrs.	173	454	62	121	24	7	8	35	20	.267

a On disabled list from July 27 to August 11 and August 24 to September 30, 2009.
b On disabled list from April 30 to August 9, 2010.
c Traded to Milwaukee Brewers for outfielder Jim Edmonds, August 9, 2010.

DOBBS, GREGORY STUART (GREG)

Born, Los Angeles, California, July 2, 1978.
Bats Left. Throws Right. Height, 6 feet, 1 inch. Weight, 205 pounds.

Year	Club	Lea	Pos	G	AB	R	H	2B	3B	HR	RBI	SB	Avg
2001	San Bernardino	Calif.	OF	3	13	2	5	1	0	1	3	0	.385
2001	Everett	Northwest	1B-OF-3B	65	249	37	80	17	2	6	41	5	.321
2002	Wisconsin	Midwest	3B	86	320	43	88	16	2	10	48	13	.275
2002	San Antonio	Texas	OF-1B	27	96	13	35	2	0	5	15	1	.365
2003	San Antonio	Texas	3B	2	6	0	2	2	0	0	0	0	.333
2004	San Antonio	Texas	3B	51	203	25	66	14	4	5	34	5	.325

Year	Club	Lea	Pos	G	AB	R	H	2B	3B	HR	RBI	SB	Avg
2004	Tacoma	P.C.	3B	67	255	28	69	9	2	8	31	4	.271
2004	Seattle	A.L.	3B	18	53	4	12	1	0	1	9	0	.226
2005	Tacoma	P.C.	1B-3B-OF	50	190	27	61	9	0	3	22	5	.321
2005	Seattle	A.L.	DH-1B-OF-3B	59	142	8	35	7	1	1	20	1	.246
2006	Tacoma	P.C.	3B-1B-OF	99	379	60	119	19	3	9	55	14	.314
2006	Seattle	A.L.	1B-OF-3B	23	27	4	10	3	1	0	3	0	.370
2007	Philadelphia a	N.L.	3B-OF-1B-2B	142	324	45	88	20	4	10	55	3	.272
2008	Philadelphia	N.L.	3B-OF-1B	128	226	30	68	14	1	9	40	3	.301
2009	Philadelphia b	N.L.	3B-OF-1B	97	154	15	38	6	0	5	20	1	.247
2010	Lehigh Valley	Int.	OF-3B	16	62	10	13	3	1	2	9	2	.210
2010	Philadelphia c	N.L.	3B-1B-OF	88	163	13	32	7	0	5	15	1	.196
Major League Totals			7 Yrs.	555	1089	119	283	58	7	31	162	9	.260
	Division Series												
2007	Philadelphia	N.L.	3B	3	3	0	0	0	0	0	0	0	.000
2008	Philadelphia	N.L.	3B	3	5	0	3	0	0	0	0	0	.600
2009	Philadelphia	N.L.	PH	3	3	0	0	0	0	0	0	0	.000
Division Series Totals				9	11	0	3	0	0	0	0	0	.273
	Championship Series												
2008	Philadelphia	N.L.	3B	3	6	2	3	1	0	0	0	0	.500
2009	Philadelphia	N.L.	PH	2	1	0	0	0	0	0	0	0	.000
Championship Series Totals				5	7	2	3	1	0	0	0	0	.429
	World Series Record												
2008	Philadelphia	N.L.	DH	2	3	0	1	0	0	0	0	0	.333

a Claimed by Philadelphia Phillies on waivers, January 16, 2007.
b On disabled list from August 22 to September 16, 2009.
c Filed for free agency, October 28, 2010.

DONALD, JASON THOMAS

Born, Clovis, California, September 4, 1984.
Bats Right. Throws Right. Height, 6 feet, 1 inch. Weight, 195 pounds.

Year	Club	Lea	Pos	G	AB	R	H	2B	3B	HR	RBI	SB	Avg
2006	Batavia	N.Y.-Penn.	SS	63	213	33	56	14	2	1	24	12	.263
2007	Clearwater	Fla.St.	SS	83	293	48	88	22	5	8	41	3	.300
2007	Lakewood	So.Atl.	SS	51	197	41	61	9	3	4	30	2	.310
2008	Reading	Eastern	SS	92	362	57	111	19	4	14	54	11	.307
2009	Phillies	Gulf Coast	SS	9	26	4	6	1	1	0	1	1	.231
2009	Columbus	Int.	SS	10	35	10	9	2	0	1	1	1	.257
2009	Lehigh Valley a	Int.	SS-2B-3B	51	208	26	49	15	1	1	16	6	.236
2010	Columbus	Int.	2B-SS	37	137	27	38	10	2	2	17	10	.277
2010	Cleveland	A.L.	SS-2B	88	296	39	75	19	3	4	24	5	.253

a Traded by Philadelphia Phillies to Cleveland Indians with catcher Lou Marson, pitcher Jason Knapp and pitcher Carlos Carrasco for pitcher Cliff Lee and outfielder Ben Francisco, July 29, 2009.

DOUMIT, RYAN MATTHEW

Born, Moses Lake, Washington, April 3, 1981.
Bats Both. Throws Right. Height, 6 feet. Weight, 200 pounds.

Year	Club	Lea	Pos	G	AB	R	H	2B	3B	HR	RBI	SB	Avg
1999	Pirates	Gulf Coast	C	29	85	17	24	5	0	1	7	4	.282
2000	Williamsport	N.Y.-Penn.	C	66	246	25	77	15	5	2	40	2	.313
2001	Altoona	Eastern	C	2	4	0	1	0	0	0	2	0	.250
2001	Pirates	Gulf Coast	C	7	17	2	4	2	0	0	3	0	.235
2001	Hickory	So.Atl.	C	39	148	14	40	6	0	2	14	2	.270
2002	Hickory	So.Atl.	C	68	258	46	83	14	1	6	47	3	.322
2003	Lynchburg	Carolina	C	127	458	75	126	38	1	11	77	4	.275
2004	Altoona	Eastern	C	67	221	31	58	20	0	10	34	0	.262
2005	Indianapolis	Int.	C-OF	51	165	41	57	11	0	12	35	1	.345
2005	Pittsburgh	N.L.	C-OF	75	231	25	59	13	1	6	35	2	.255
2006	Pirates	Gulf Coast	C-1B	5	14	1	0	0	0	0	0	0	.000
2006	Altoona	Eastern	C-1B	4	15	4	5	3	0	0	4	0	.333
2006	Indianapolis	Int.	C	6	22	3	7	1	1	0	7	0	.318
2006	Pittsburgh a	N.L.	1B-C	61	149	15	31	9	0	6	17	0	.208
2007	Indianapolis	Int.	C	16	53	15	22	4	0	4	20	3	.415
2007	Pittsburgh b	N.L.	OF-C-1B	83	252	33	69	19	2	9	32	1	.274
2008	Altoona	Eastern	C	3	7	0	3	0	0	0	0	0	.429
2008	Pittsburgh c	N.L.	C-1B	116	431	71	137	34	0	15	69	2	.318
2009	Pirates	Gulf Coast	C	2	7	0	0	0	0	0	0	0	.000
2009	Indianapolis	Int.	C	5	17	1	2	0	0	0	0	0	.118

Year Club	Lea	Pos	G	AB	R	H	2B	3B	HR	RBI	SB	Avg
2009 Pittsburgh d..........	N.L.	C-OF	75	280	31	70	16	0	10	38	4	.250
2010 Indianapolis............	Int.	OF-C	4	12	2	2	1	0	1	2	0	.167
2010 Pittsburgh e..........	N.L.	C-OF-1B	124	406	42	102	22	1	13	45	1	.251
Major League Totals............		6 Yrs.	534	1749	217	468	113	4	59	236	10	.268

a On disabled list from April 12 to May 3 and June 5 to August 23, 2006.
b On disabled list from August 13 to September 8 and September 9 to November 13, 2007.
c On disabled list from May 14 to June 6, 2008.
d On disabled list from April 20 to July 10, 2009.
e On disabled list from July 22 to August 7, 2010.

DREW, DAVID JONATHAN (J.D.)

Born, Tallahassee, Florida, November 20, 1975.
Bats Left. Throws Right. Height, 6 feet, 1 inch. Weight, 200 pounds.

Year Club	Lea	Pos	G	AB	R	H	2B	3B	HR	RBI	SB	Avg
1997 St. Paul..........	Northern	OF	44	170	51	58	6	1	18	50	5	.341
1998 St. Paul..........	Northern	OF	30	114	27	44	11	2	9	33	8	.386
1998 Arkansas..........	Texas	OF	19	67	18	22	3	1	5	11	2	.328
1998 Memphis............	P.C.	OF	26	79	15	25	8	1	2	13	1	.316
1998 St. Louis............	N.L.	OF	14	36	9	15	3	1	5	13	0	.417
1999 St. Louis a..........	N.L.	OF	104	368	72	89	16	6	13	39	19	.242
2000 St. Louis b..........	N.L.	OF	135	407	73	120	17	2	18	57	17	.295
2001 Peoria............	Midwest	OF	3	11	3	6	2	0	0	0	0	.545
2001 St. Louis c..........	N.L.	OF	109	375	80	121	18	5	27	73	13	.323
2002 St. Louis d..........	N.L.	OF	135	424	61	107	19	1	18	56	8	.252
2003 Palm Beach..........	Fla.St.	OF	8	19	4	7	0	0	1	3	0	.368
2003 St. Louis e-f..........	N.L.	OF	100	287	60	83	13	3	15	42	2	.289
2004 Atlanta g............	N.L.	OF	145	518	118	158	28	8	31	93	12	.305
2005 Los Angeles h..........	N.L.	OF	72	252	48	72	12	1	15	36	1	.286
2006 Los Angeles i..........	N.L.	OF	146	494	84	140	34	6	20	100	2	.283
2007 Boston............	A.L.	OF	140	466	84	126	30	4	11	64	4	.270
2008 Boston j............	A.L.	OF	109	368	79	103	23	4	19	64	4	.280
2009 Boston............	A.L.	OF	137	452	84	126	30	4	24	68	2	.279
2010 Boston............	A.L.	OF	139	478	69	122	24	2	22	68	3	.255
Major League Totals............		13 Yrs.	1485	4925	921	1382	267	47	238	773	87	.281
Division Series												
2000 St. Louis............	N.L.	OF	2	6	1	1	0	0	0	0	2	.167
2001 St. Louis............	N.L.	OF	5	13	1	2	0	0	1	2	0	.154
2002 St. Louis............	N.L.	OF	2	9	1	2	0	0	1	1	0	.222
2004 Atlanta............	N.L.	OF	5	20	1	4	0	0	0	1	1	.200
2006 Los Angeles..........	N.L.	OF	3	13	1	2	0	0	0	0	0	.154
2007 Boston............	A.L.	OF	3	11	1	2	0	0	0	3	0	.182
2008 Boston............	A.L.	OF	4	14	2	4	1	0	1	3	0	.286
2009 Boston............	A.L.	OF	3	9	1	2	0	0	1	2	0	.222
Division Series Totals..........			27	95	9	19	1	0	4	12	3	.200
Championship Series												
2000 St. Louis............	N.L.	OF	5	12	2	4	1	0	0	1	0	.333
2002 St. Louis............	N.L.	OF	5	13	1	5	0	0	1	1	0	.385
2007 Boston............	A.L.	OF	7	25	5	9	1	0	1	6	0	.360
2008 Boston............	A.L.	OF	7	24	1	6	1	0	1	3	0	.250
Championship Series Totals......			24	74	9	24	3	0	3	11	0	.324
World Series Record												
2007 Boston............	A.L.	OF	4	15	1	5	2	0	0	2	0	.333

a On disabled list from May 16 to June 17, 1999.
b On disabled list from July 8 to July 26, 2000.
c On disabled list from June 18 to July 31, 2001.
d On disabled list from June 28 to July 13, 2002.
e On disabled list from March 21 to April 20 and August 9 to September 1, 2003.
f Traded to Atlanta Braves with catcher Eli Marrero for pitcher Jason Marquis, pitcher Ray King and pitcher Adam Wainwright, December 13, 2003.
g Filed for free agency, October 28, 2004. Signed with Los Angeles Dodgers, December 23, 2004.
h On disabled list from July 4 to October 7, 2005.
i Filed for free agency, November 10, 2006. Signed with Boston Red Sox, December 5, 2006.
j On disabled list from August 18 to September 8, 2008.

DREW, STEPHEN ORIS

Born, Hahira, Georgia, March 16, 1983.
Bats Left. Throws Right. Height, 6 feet, 1 inch. Weight, 185 pounds.

Year Club	Lea	Pos	G	AB	R	H	2B	3B	HR	RBI	SB	Avg
2005 Tennessee	Southern	SS	27	101	11	22	5	0	4	13	2	.218
2006 Tucson	P.C.	SS	83	342	55	97	16	3	13	51	3	.284
2006 Arizona..............	N.L.	SS	59	209	27	66	13	7	5	23	2	.316
2007 Arizona..............	N.L.	SS	150	543	60	129	28	4	12	60	9	.238
2008 Arizona..............	N.L.	SS	152	611	91	178	44	11	21	67	3	.291
2009 Reno	P.C.	SS	2	9	0	3	0	1	0	1	0	.333
2009 Arizona a	N.L.	SS	135	533	71	139	29	12	12	65	5	.261
2010 Arizona..............	N.L.	SS	151	565	83	157	33	12	15	61	10	.278
Major League Totals		5 Yrs.	647	2461	332	669	147	46	65	276	29	.272
Division Series												
2007 Arizona..............	N.L.	SS	3	14	4	7	1	1	2	4	1	.500
Championship Series												
2007 Arizona..............	N.L.	SS	4	17	2	5	0	0	0	0	0	.294

a On disabled list from April 25 to May 12, 2009.

DUNCAN, DAVID SHELLEY (SHELLEY)

Born, Tucson, Arizona, September 29, 1979.
Bats Right. Throws Right. Height, 6 feet, 5 inches. Weight, 225 pounds.

Year Club	Lea	Pos	G	AB	R	H	2B	3B	HR	RBI	SB	Avg
2001 Staten Island	N.Y.-Penn.	DH	70	273	43	67	17	2	8	39	5	.245
2002 Greensboro	So.Atl.	OF	101	356	58	95	23	2	14	56	15	.267
2003 Tampa	Fla.St.	OF	91	330	42	87	19	2	8	47	5	.264
2004 Tampa	Fla.St.	1B-OF	123	424	65	105	27	1	19	78	6	.248
2005 Trenton............	Eastern	1B	142	537	86	129	28	2	34	92	3	.240
2006 Trenton............	Eastern	1B-OF	92	351	47	90	24	0	19	61	3	.256
2006 Columbus.............	Int.	OF	12	43	1	8	1	0	1	4	0	.186
2007 Scranton/WB	Int.	OF-1B	91	336	58	99	18	1	25	79	2	.295
2007 New York	A.L.	DH-OF-1B	34	74	16	19	1	0	7	17	0	.257
2008 New York	A.L.	1B-OF	23	57	7	10	3	0	1	6	0	.175
2008 Yankees	Gulf Coast	DH	2	7	0	0	0	0	0	0	0	.000
2008 Scranton/WB	Int.	OF-1B	58	205	38	49	14	0	12	44	6	.239
2009 Scranton/WB	Int.	OF-1B	123	452	85	125	30	1	30	99	2	.277
2009 New York	A.L.	OF	11	15	1	3	0	0	0	1	0	.200
2010 Columbus.............	Int.	OF-1B	38	146	21	44	11	0	6	34	0	.301
2010 Cleveland a...........	A.L.	OF-1B	85	229	29	53	10	0	11	36	1	.231
Major League Totals		4 Yrs.	153	375	53	85	14	0	19	60	1	.227
Division Series												
2007 New York	A.L.	1B	3	4	1	2	0	0	0	0	0	.500

a Filed for free agency, November 25, 2009. Signed with Cleveland Indians organization, January 4, 2010.

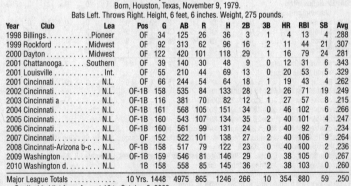

DUNN, ADAM TROY

Born, Houston, Texas, November 9, 1979.
Bats Left. Throws Right. Height, 6 feet, 6 inches. Weight, 275 pounds.

Year Club	Lea	Pos	G	AB	R	H	2B	3B	HR	RBI	SB	Avg
1998 Billings............	Pioneer	OF	34	125	26	36	3	1	4	13	4	.288
1999 Rockford	Midwest	OF	92	313	62	96	16	2	11	44	21	.307
2000 Dayton	Midwest	OF	122	420	101	118	29	1	16	79	24	.281
2001 Chattanooga......	Southern	OF	39	140	30	48	9	0	12	31	6	.343
2001 Louisville	Int.	OF	55	210	44	69	13	0	20	53	5	.329
2001 Cincinnati...........	N.L.	OF	66	244	54	64	18	1	19	43	4	.262
2002 Cincinnati...........	N.L.	OF-1B	158	535	84	133	28	2	26	71	19	.249
2003 Cincinnati a	N.L.	OF-1B	116	381	70	82	12	1	27	57	8	.215
2004 Cincinnati...........	N.L.	OF-1B	161	568	105	151	34	0	46	102	6	.266
2005 Cincinnati...........	N.L.	OF-1B	160	543	107	134	35	2	40	101	4	.247
2006 Cincinnati...........	N.L.	OF-1B	160	561	99	131	24	0	40	92	7	.234
2007 Cincinnati...........	N.L.	OF	152	522	101	138	27	2	40	106	9	.264
2008 Cincinnati-Arizona b-c ..	N.L.	OF-1B	158	517	79	122	23	0	40	100	2	.236
2009 Washington	N.L.	OF-1B	159	546	81	146	29	0	38	105	0	.267
2010 Washington d..........	N.L.	1B	158	558	85	145	36	2	38	103	0	.260
Major League Totals		10 Yrs.	1448	4975	865	1246	266	10	354	880	59	.250

a On disabled list from August 16 to October 2, 2003.

b Traded to Arizona Diamondbacks for pitcher Dallas Buck and two players to be named later, August 12, 2008. To complete trade, Cincinnati Reds received catcher Wilkin Castillo on August 14, 2008 and pitcher Micah Owings on September 10, 2008.

c Filed for free agency, November 1, 2008. Signed with Washington Nationals, February 11, 2009.
d Filed for free agency, November 1, 2010. Signed with Chicago White Sox, December 3, 2010.

ECKSTEIN, DAVID MARK

Born, Sanford, Florida, January 20, 1975.
Bats Right. Throws Right. Height, 5 feet, 7 inches. Weight, 165 pounds.

Year Club	Lea	Pos	G	AB	R	H	2B	3B	HR	RBI	SB	Avg
1997 Lowell	N.Y.-Penn.	2B	68	249	43	75	11	4	4	39	21	.301
1998 Sarasota............	Fla.St.	2B-SS	135	503	99	154	29	4	3	58	45	.306
1999 Trenton............	Eastern	2B	131	483	109	151	22	5	6	52	32	.313
2000 Pawtucket	Int.	2B-SS	119	422	77	104	20	0	1	31	11	.246
2000 Edmonton a...........	P.C.	2B	15	52	17	18	8	0	3	8	5	.346
2001 Anaheim.............	A.L.	SS-2B	153	582	82	166	26	2	4	41	29	.285
2002 Anaheim.............	A.L.	SS	152	608	107	178	22	6	8	63	21	.293
2003 Anaheim b...........	A.L.	SS	120	452	59	114	22	1	3	31	16	.252
2004 Anaheim c...........	A.L.	SS	142	566	92	156	24	1	2	35	16	.276
2005 St. Louis.............	N.L.	SS	158	630	90	185	26	7	8	61	11	.294
2006 St. Louis d...........	N.L.	SS	123	500	68	146	18	1	2	23	7	.292
2007 St. Louis e-f..........	N.L.	SS	117	434	58	134	23	0	3	31	10	.309
2008 Dunedin............	Fla.St.	SS	5	14	4	2	1	0	0	0	0	.143
2008 Toronto	A.L.	SS-2B	76	260	27	72	18	0	1	23	2	.277
2008 Arizona g-h-i	N.L.	2B	18	64	5	14	3	0	1	4	0	.219
2009 San Diego j...........	N.L.	2B	136	503	64	131	27	2	2	51	3	.260
2010 Fort Wayne........	Midwest	2B	3	9	1	3	1	0	0	3	0	.333
2010 San Diego k-l.........	N.L.	2B	116	442	49	118	23	0	1	29	8	.267
Major League Totals		10 Yrs.	1311	5041	701	1414	232	20	35	392	123	.280
Division Series												
2002 Anaheim.............	A.L.	SS	4	18	2	5	0	0	0	1	1	.278
2004 Anaheim.............	A.L.	SS	3	12	2	4	0	0	0	0	0	.333
2005 St. Louis.............	N.L.	SS	3	13	3	5	0	0	1	4	0	.385
2006 St. Louis.............	N.L.	SS	4	15	1	2	0	0	0	1	1	.133
Division Series Totals			14	58	8	16	0	0	1	6	2	.276
Championship Series												
2002 Anaheim.............	A.L.	SS	5	21	1	6	0	0	0	2	0	.286
2005 St. Louis.............	N.L.	SS	6	20	5	4	0	0	0	2	1	.200
2006 St. Louis.............	N.L.	SS	7	26	3	6	1	0	1	1	3	.231
Championship Series Totals ..			18	67	9	16	1	0	1	5	4	.239
World Series Record												
2002 Anaheim.............	A.L.	SS	7	29	6	9	0	0	0	3	1	.310
2006 St. Louis.............	N.L.	SS	5	22	3	8	3	0	0	4	0	.364
World Series Totals.........			12	51	9	17	3	0	0	7	1	.333

a Claimed on waivers by Anaheim Angels from Boston Red Sox, August 16, 2000.
b On disabled list from August 18 to September 9, 2003.
c Not offered contract, December 20, 2004. Signed with St. Louis Cardinals, December 23, 2004.
d On disabled list from August 19 to September 15, 2006.
e On disabled list from June 14 to July 13, 2007.
f Filed for free agency, October 29, 2007. Signed with Texas Rangers, December 14, 2007.
g On disabled list from May 7 to May 27, 2008.
h Traded to Arizona Diamondbacks for pitcher Chad Beck, August 31, 2008.
i Filed for free agency, October 30, 2008. Signed with San Diego Padres, January 15, 2009.
j On disabled list from July 6 to July 28, 2009.
k On disabled list from July 21 to August 21, 2010.
l Filed for free agency, November 1, 2010.

EDMONDS, JAMES PATRICK (JIM)

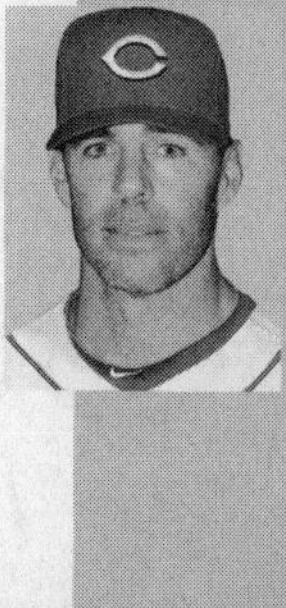

Born, Fullerton, California, June 27, 1970.
Bats Left. Throws Left. Height, 6 feet, 1 inch. Weight, 210 pounds.

Year Club	Lea	Pos	G	AB	R	H	2B	3B	HR	RBI	SB	Avg
1988 Bend..........	Northwest	OF	35	122	23	27	4	0	0	13	4	.221
1989 Quad City.........	Midwest	OF	31	92	11	24	4	0	1	4	1	.261
1990 Palm Sprngs	Calif.	OF	91	314	36	92	18	6	3	56	5	.293
1991 Palm Sprngs	Calif.	OF-1B-P	60	187	28	55	15	1	2	27	2	.294
1992 Midland	Texas	OF	70	246	42	77	15	2	8	32	3	.313
1992 Edmonton	P.C.	OF	50	194	37	58	15	2	6	36	3	.299
1993 Vancouver	P.C.	OF	95	356	59	112	28	4	9	74	6	.315
1993 California	A.L.	OF	18	61	5	15	4	1	0	4	0	.246
1994 California	A.L.	OF-1B	94	289	35	79	13	1	5	37	4	.273
1995 California	A.L.	OF	141	558	120	162	30	4	33	107	1	.290

Year Club	Lea	Pos	G	AB	R	H	2B	3B	HR	RBI	SB	Avg
1996 Lk Elsinore	Calif.	OF	5	15	4	6	2	0	1	4	0	.400
1996 California a	A.L.	OF	114	431	73	131	28	3	27	66	4	.304
1997 Anaheim b	A.L.	OF-1B	133	502	82	146	27	0	26	80	5	.291
1998 Anaheim	A.L.	OF	154	599	115	184	42	1	25	91	7	.307
1999 Lake Elsinore	Calif.	DH	5	19	4	8	2	0	0	3	2	.421
1999 Anaheim c	A.L.	OF-1B	55	204	34	51	17	2	5	23	5	.250
2000 St. Louis d	N.L.	OF-1B	152	525	129	155	25	0	42	108	10	.295
2001 St. Louis	N.L.	OF-1B	150	500	95	152	38	1	30	110	5	.304
2002 St. Louis e	N.L.	OF	144	476	96	148	31	2	28	83	4	.311
2003 St. Louis	N.L.	OF	137	447	89	123	32	2	39	89	1	.275
2004 St. Louis	N.L.	OF-1B	153	498	102	150	38	3	42	111	8	.301
2005 St. Louis	N.L.	OF	142	467	88	123	37	1	29	89	5	.263
2006 St. Louis f	N.L.	OF-1B	110	350	52	90	18	0	19	70	4	.257
2007 St. Louis g-h	N.L.	OF-1B	117	365	39	92	15	2	12	53	0	.252
2008 Lake Elsinore	Calif.	OF	2	6	0	2	0	0	0	0	0	.333
2008 San Diego-Chicago i-j	N.L.	OF	111	340	53	80	19	2	20	55	2	.235
2009					Did Not Play							
2010 Milwaukee-Cin. k-l-m-n-o	N.L.	OF-1B	86	246	44	68	23	0	11	23	2	.276
Major League Totals		17 Yrs.	2011	6858	1251	1949	437	25	393	1199	67	.284
Division Series												
2000 St. Louis	N.L.	OF	3	14	5	8	4	0	2	7	1	.571
2001 St. Louis	N.L.	OF	5	17	3	4	1	0	2	3	0	.235
2002 St. Louis	N.L.	OF	3	11	1	3	0	0	1	2	0	.273
2004 St. Louis	N.L.	OF	4	15	1	4	0	0	1	2	0	.267
2005 St. Louis	N.L.	OF	3	11	5	4	2	0	1	1	0	.364
2006 St. Louis	N.L.	OF	4	13	2	4	0	0	0	2	0	.308
2008 Chicago	N.L.	OF	3	10	1	2	1	0	0	1	0	.200
Division Series Totals			25	91	18	29	8	0	7	18	1	.319
Championship Series												
2000 St. Louis	N.L.	OF	5	22	1	5	1	0	1	5	0	.227
2002 St. Louis	N.L.	OF	5	20	2	8	2	0	1	4	0	.400
2004 St. Louis	N.L.	OF	7	24	2	7	2	0	2	7	0	.292
2005 St. Louis	N.L.	OF	6	19	2	4	1	0	0	0	1	.211
2006 St. Louis	N.L.	OF	7	22	5	5	0	0	2	4	0	.227
Championship Series Totals			30	107	12	29	6	0	6	20	1	.271
World Series Record												
2004 St. Louis	N.L.	OF	4	15	2	1	0	0	0	0	0	.067
2006 St. Louis	N.L.	OF	5	17	1	4	2	0	0	4	0	.235
World Series Totals			9	32	3	5	2	0	0	4	0	.156

a On disabled list from May 26 to June 10 and June 12 to July 18, 1996.
b On disabled list from July 31 to August 16, 1997.
c On disabled list from March 30 to August 2, 1999.
d Traded to St. Louis Cardinals for pitcher Kent Bottenfield and infielder Adam Kennedy, March 23, 2000.
e On disabled list from June 1 to June 16, 2002.
f Filed for free agency, November 2, 2006, re-signed with St. Louis Cardinals, November 10, 2006.
g On disabled list from June 16 to July 19, 2007.
h Traded to San Diego Padres for infielder David Freese, December 15, 2007.
i On disabled list from March 21 to April 5, 2008.
j Released by San Diego Padres, May 9, 2008.
k Signed with Milwaukee Brewers organization, January 28, 2010.
l On disabled list from May 16 to June 1, 2010.
m Traded to Cincinnati Reds for outfielder Chris Dickerson, August 9, 2010.
n On disabled list from August 24 to September 10, 2010.
o Filed for free agency, November 1, 2010.

ELLIS, MARK WILLIAM

Born, Rapid City, South Dakota, June 6, 1977.
Bats Right. Throws Right. Height, 5 feet, 11 inches. Weight, 195 pounds.

Year Club	Lea	Pos	G	AB	R	H	2B	3B	HR	RBI	SB	Avg
1999 Spokane	Northwest	SS	71	281	67	92	14	0	7	47	21	.327
2000 Wilmington	Carolina	SS-2B	132	484	83	146	27	4	6	62	25	.302
2000 Wichita	Texas	2B	7	22	4	7	1	0	0	4	1	.318
2001 Sacramento a	P.C.	SS	132	472	71	129	38	0	10	53	21	.273
2002 Sacramento	P.C.	SS	21	84	14	25	10	1	0	5	4	.298
2002 Oakland	A.L.	2B-SS-3B	98	345	58	94	16	4	6	35	4	.272
2003 Oakland	A.L.	2B	154	553	78	137	31	5	9	52	6	.248
2004 Oakland b	A.L.				INJURED—Did Not Play							
2005 Oakland	A.L.	2B-SS-1B	122	434	76	137	21	5	13	52	1	.316

Year	Club	Lea	Pos	G	AB	R	H	2B	3B	HR	RBI	SB	Avg
2006	Sacramento	P.C.	2B	4	12	1	2	0	0	0	2	0	.167
2006	Oakland c	A.L.	2B-1B	124	441	64	110	25	1	11	52	4	.249
2007	Oakland	A.L.	2B	150	583	84	161	33	3	19	76	9	.276
2008	Oakland d	A.L.	2B	117	442	55	103	20	3	12	41	14	.233
2009	Stockton	Calif.	2B	2	4	0	0	0	0	0	0	0	.000
2009	Sacramento	P.C.	2B	8	33	2	6	1	0	0	3	0	.182
2009	Oakland e	A.L.	2B	105	377	52	99	23	0	10	61	10	.263
2010	Stockton	Calif.	2B	2	5	0	1	0	0	0	1	0	.200
2010	Sacramento	P.C.	2B	1	4	0	1	0	0	0	0	0	.250
2010	Oakland f	A.L.	2B	124	436	45	127	24	0	5	49	7	.291
Major League Totals			8 Yrs.	994	3611	512	968	193	21	85	418	55	.268
	Division Series												
2002	Oakland	A.L.	2B	5	19	1	7	2	0	1	4	0	.368
2003	Oakland	A.L.	2B	5	17	2	2	0	0	0	0	0	.118
2006	Oakland	A.L.	2B	2	7	0	2	0	0	0	0	0	.286
Division Series Totals				12	43	3	11	2	0	1	4	0	.256

a Traded to Oakland Athletics by Kansas City Royals with outfielder Johnny Damon and player to be named later for pitcher Roberto Hernandez, catcher A.J. Hinch, infielder Angel Berroa and cash, January 8, 2001.
b On disabled list from March 26 to October 20, 2004.
c On disabled list from June 1 to June 30, 2006.
d On disabled list from September 21 to November 14, 2008.
e On disabled list from April 29 to June 28, 2009.
f On disabled list from April 21 to May 22, 2010.

ELLSBURY, JACOBY McCABE

Born, Madras, Oregon, September 11, 1983.
Bats Left. Throws Left. Height, 6 feet, 1 inch. Weight, 185 pounds.

Year	Club	Lea	Pos	G	AB	R	H	2B	3B	HR	RBI	SB	Avg
2005	Lowell	N.Y.-Penn.	OF	35	139	28	44	3	5	1	19	23	.317
2006	Wilmington	Carolina	OF	61	244	35	73	7	5	4	32	25	.299
2006	Portland	Eastern	OF	50	198	29	61	10	3	3	19	16	.308
2007	Portland	Eastern	OF	17	73	16	33	10	2	0	13	8	.452
2007	Pawtucket	Int.	OF	87	363	66	108	14	5	2	28	33	.298
2007	Boston	A.L.	OF	33	116	20	41	7	1	3	18	9	.353
2008	Boston	A.L.	OF	145	554	98	155	22	7	9	47	*50	.280
2009	Boston	A.L.	OF	153	624	94	188	27	*10	8	60	*70	.301
2010	Red Sox	Gulf Coast	OF	3	8	3	2	0	0	0	0	1	.250
2010	Portland	Eastern	OF	2	7	2	3	1	0	0	0	1	.429
2010	Pawtucket	Int.	OF	4	17	5	8	1	0	0	2	0	.471
2010	Boston a	A.L.	OF	18	78	10	15	4	0	0	5	7	.192
Major League Totals			4 Yrs.	349	1372	222	399	60	18	20	130	136	.291
	Division Series												
2007	Boston	A.L.	OF	2	1	1	0	0	0	0	0	0	.000
2008	Boston	A.L.	OF	4	18	2	6	3	0	0	6	3	.333
2009	Boston	A.L.	OF	3	12	2	3	0	1	0	0	0	.250
Division Series Totals				9	31	5	9	3	1	0	6	3	.290
	Championship Series												
2007	Boston	A.L.	OF	5	8	3	2	0	0	0	1	1	.250
2008	Boston	A.L.	OF	4	14	0	0	0	0	0	1	0	.000
Championship Series Totals				9	22	3	2	0	0	0	2	1	.091
	World Series Record												
2007	Boston	A.L.	OF	4	16	4	7	4	0	0	3	1	.438

a On disabled list from April 12 to May 22 and May 28 to August 4 and August 14 to November 8, 2010.

ENCARNACION, EDWIN ELPIDIO

Born, La Romana, Dominican Republic, January 7, 1983.
Bats Right. Throws Right. Height, 6 feet, 1 inch. Weight, 215 pounds.

Year	Club	Lea	Pos	G	AB	R	H	2B	3B	HR	RBI	SB	Avg
2000	Rangers	Gulf Coast	3B	51	177	31	55	6	3	0	36	3	.311
2001	Dayton	Midwest	3B	9	37	2	6	2	0	1	6	0	.162
2001	Billings	Pioneer	3B	52	211	27	55	8	2	5	26	8	.261
2001	Savannah a	So.Atl.	3B	45	170	23	52	9	2	4	25	3	.306
2002	Dayton	Midwest	3B-SS	136	517	80	146	32	4	17	73	25	.282
2003	Potomac	Carolina	3B	58	215	40	69	15	1	6	29	7	.321
2003	Chattanooga	Southern	3B-SS	67	254	40	69	13	1	5	36	8	.272
2004	Chattanooga	Southern	3B	120	469	73	132	35	1	13	76	17	.281
2005	Louisville	Int.	3B	78	290	44	91	23	0	15	54	7	.314

Year	Club	Lea	Pos	G	AB	R	H	2B	3B	HR	RBI	SB	Avg
2005	Cincinnati	N.L.	3B	69	211	25	49	16	0	9	31	3	.232
2006	Louisville	Int.	3B-1B	10	36	6	11	3	0	1	1	0	.306
2006	Cincinnati b	N.L.	3B-1B	117	406	60	112	33	1	15	72	6	.276
2007	Louisville	Int.	3B	11	46	12	19	3	0	3	7	1	.413
2007	Cincinnati	N.L.	3B	139	502	66	145	25	1	16	76	8	.289
2008	Cincinnati	N.L.	3B	146	506	75	127	29	1	26	68	1	.251
2009	Louisville	Int.	3B	11	37	5	10	1	0	2	8	0	.270
2009	Cincinnati	N.L.	3B	43	139	10	29	6	1	5	16	1	.209
2009	Toronto c-d-e	A.L.	3B	42	154	25	37	5	1	8	23	1	.240
2010	Dunedin	Fla.St.	3B	3	10	2	1	0	0	1	1	0	.100
2010	Las Vegas	P.C.	3B	7	32	9	14	2	0	3	13	0	.438
2010	Toronto f-g-h	A.L.	3B	96	332	47	81	16	0	21	51	1	.244
Major League Totals			6 Yrs.	652	2250	308	580	130	5	100	337	21	.258

a Traded by Texas Rangers to Cincinnati Reds with outfielder Ruben Mateo for pitcher Rob Bell, June 15, 2001.
b On disabled list from June 7 to July 6, 2006.
c On disabled list from April 28 to July 3, 2009.
d Traded to Toronto Blue Jays with pitcher Josh Roenicke and pitcher Zach Stewart for infielder Scott Rolen, July 31, 2009.
e On disabled list from August 21 to September 5, 2009.
f On disabled list from April 15 to May 18 and August 29 to September 13, 2010.
g Claimed on waivers by Oakland Athletics, November 12, 2010.
h Not offered contract, December 2, 2010. Signed with Toronto Blue Jays, December 16, 2010.

ESCOBAR, ALCIDES

Born, Lasabana, Venezuela, December 16, 1986.
Bats Right. Throws Right. Height, 6 feet, 1 inch. Weight, 180 pounds.

Year	Club	Lea	Pos	G	AB	R	H	2B	3B	HR	RBI	SB	Avg
2004	Helena	Pioneer	SS	67	231	38	65	8	0	2	24	20	.281
2005	West Virginia	So.Atl.	SS	127	520	80	141	25	8	2	36	30	.271
2006	Brevard County	Fla.St.	SS	87	350	47	90	9	1	2	33	28	.257
2007	Brevard County	Fla.St.	SS	63	268	37	87	8	3	0	25	18	.325
2007	Huntsville	Southern	SS	62	226	27	64	5	4	1	28	4	.283
2008	Huntsville	Southern	SS	131	546	95	179	24	5	8	76	34	.328
2008	Milwaukee	N.L.	SS	9	4	2	2	0	0	0	0	0	.500
2009	Nashville	P.C.	SS-2B	109	430	76	128	24	6	4	34	42	.298
2009	Milwaukee	N.L.	SS	38	125	20	38	3	1	1	11	4	.304
2010	Milwaukee a	N.L.	SS-OF	145	506	57	119	14	10	4	41	10	.235
Major League Totals			3 Yrs.	192	635	79	159	17	11	5	52	14	.250

a Traded to Kansas City Royals with outfielder Lorenzo Cain, pitcher Jeremy Jeffress and pitcher Jake Odorizzi for outfielder Yuniesky Betancourt and pitcher Zack Greinke, December 19, 2010.

ESCOBAR, YUNEL

Born, Havana, Cuba, November 2, 1982.
Bats Right. Throws Right. Height, 6 feet, 2 inches. Weight, 200 pounds.

Year	Club	Lea	Pos	G	AB	R	H	2B	3B	HR	RBI	SB	Avg
2005	Danville	Appal.	SS	8	30	9	12	2	1	2	8	0	.400
2005	Rome	So.Atl.	SS	48	198	30	62	13	3	4	19	0	.313
2006	Mississippi	Southern	SS-3B-2B	121	428	55	113	21	4	2	45	7	.264
2007	Richmond	Int.	SS	46	180	20	60	10	3	2	29	7	.333
2007	Atlanta	N.L.	SS-3B-2B	94	319	54	104	25	0	5	28	5	.326
2008	Atlanta	N.L.	SS	136	514	71	148	24	2	10	60	2	.288
2009	Atlanta	N.L.	SS	141	528	89	158	26	2	14	76	5	.299
2010	Gwinnett	Int.	SS	1	3	1	2	0	0	0	0	0	.667
2010	Atlanta	N.L.	SS	75	261	28	62	12	0	0	19	5	.238
2010	Toronto a-b	A.L.	SS	60	236	32	65	7	0	4	16	1	.275
Major League Totals			4 Yrs.	506	1858	274	537	94	4	33	199	18	.289

a On disabled list from April 30 to May 15, 2010.
b Traded to Toronto Blue Jays with pitcher Jo-Jo Reyes for infielder Alex Gonzalez, pitcher Tim Collins and infielder Tyler Pastornicky, July 14, 2010.

ETHIER, ANDRE EVERETT

Born, Phoenix, Arizona, April 10, 1982.
Bats Left. Throws Left. Height, 6 feet, 1 inch. Weight, 210 pounds.

Year	Club	Lea	Pos	G	AB	R	H	2B	3B	HR	RBI	SB	Avg
2003	Kane County	Midwest	OF	40	162	23	44	10	0	0	11	2	.272
2003	Vancouver	Northwest	OF	10	41	7	16	4	1	1	7	2	.390
2004	Modesto	Calif.	OF	99	419	72	131	23	5	7	53	2	.313

Year	Club	Lea	Pos	G	AB	R	H	2B	3B	HR	RBI	SB	Avg
2005	Sacramento	P.C.	OF	4	15	0	4	1	0	0	2	0	.267
2005	Midland a	Texas	OF	131	505	104	161	30	3	18	80	1	.319
2006	Las Vegas	P.C.	OF	25	86	15	30	4	3	1	12	2	.349
2006	Los Angeles	N.L.	OF	126	396	50	122	20	7	11	55	5	.308
2007	Los Angeles	N.L.	OF	153	447	50	127	32	2	13	64	0	.284
2008	Los Angeles	N.L.	OF	141	525	90	160	38	5	20	77	6	.305
2009	Los Angeles	N.L.	OF	160	596	92	162	42	3	31	106	6	.272
2010	Albuquerque	P.C.	OF	2	5	4	3	0	0	0	2	0	.600
2010	Los Angeles b	N.L.	OF-1B	139	517	71	151	33	1	23	82	2	.292
Major League Totals			5 Yrs.	719	2481	353	722	165	18	98	384	19	.291
Division Series													
2006	Los Angeles	N.L.	OF	2	1	0	0	0	0	0	0	0	.000
2008	Los Angeles	N.L.	OF	3	10	2	1	0	0	0	0	0	.100
2009	Los Angeles	N.L.	OF	3	12	5	6	2	1	2	3	0	.500
Division Series Totals				8	23	7	7	2	1	2	3	0	.304
Championship Series													
2008	Los Angeles	N.L.	OF	5	22	4	5	1	0	0	0	0	.227
2009	Los Angeles	N.L.	OF	5	19	2	5	1	0	1	3	0	.263
Championship Series Totals				10	41	6	10	2	0	1	3	0	.244

a Traded by Oakland Athletics to Los Angeles for outfielder Milton Bradley and infielder Antonio Perez, December 13, 2005.

b On disabled list from May 15 to May 31, 2010.

FELIZ, PEDRO JULIO

Born, Azua, Dominican Republic, April 27, 1975.

Bats Right. Throws Right. Height, 6 feet, 1 inch. Weight, 210 pounds.

Year	Club	Lea	Pos	G	AB	R	H	2B	3B	HR	RBI	SB	Avg
1994	Giants	Arizona	3B	38	119	7	23	0	0	0	3	2	.193
1995	Bellingham	Northwest	3B-1B	43	113	14	31	2	1	0	16	1	.274
1996	Burlington	Midwest	3B-1B	93	321	36	85	12	2	5	36	5	.265
1997	Bakersfield	California	3B	135	515	59	140	25	4	14	56	5	.272
1998	Shreveport	Texas	3B	100	364	39	96	23	2	12	50	0	.264
1998	Fresno	P.C.	3B	3	7	1	3	1	0	1	3	0	.429
1999	Shreveport	Texas	3B	131	491	52	124	24	6	13	77	4	.253
2000	Fresno	P.C.	3B	128	503	85	150	34	2	33	105	1	.298
2000	San Francisco	N.L.	3B	8	7	1	2	0	0	0	0	0	.286
2001	San Francisco	N.L.	3B	94	220	23	50	9	1	7	22	2	.227
2002	San Francisco	N.L.	3B-SS-OF	67	146	14	37	4	1	2	13	0	.253
2003	San Francisco	N.L.	3B-OF-1B	95	235	31	58	9	3	16	48	2	.247
2004	San Francisco	N.L.	1B-3B-SS-OF	144	503	72	139	33	3	22	84	5	.276
2005	San Francisco	N.L.	3B-OF-1B	156	569	69	142	30	4	20	81	0	.250
2006	San Francisco a	N.L.	3B-OF-SS	160	603	75	147	35	5	22	98	1	.244
2007	San Francisco b	N.L.	3B-1B-OF-C	150	557	61	141	28	2	20	72	2	.253
2008	Clearwater	Fla.St.	3B	1	3	0	0	0	0	0	0	0	.000
2008	Reading	Eastern	3B	2	8	2	4	0	0	2	2	0	.500
2008	Philadelphia c	N.L.	3B-SS	133	425	43	106	19	2	14	58	0	.249
2009	Philadelphia d	N.L.	3B-SS	158	580	62	154	30	2	12	82	0	.266
2010	Houston-St. Louis e-f	N.L.	3B-1B	137	409	36	89	12	2	5	40	1	.218
Major League Totals			11 Yrs.	1302	4254	487	1065	209	25	140	598	13	.250
Division Series													
2002	San Francisco	N.L.	PH	1	1	0	0	0	0	0	0	0	.000
2003	San Francisco	N.L.	PH	3	3	1	2	0	1	0	1	0	.667
2008	Philadelphia	N.L.	3B	4	13	1	3	1	0	0	1	0	.231
2009	Philadelphia	N.L.	3B	4	14	0	3	1	0	0	0	0	.214
Division Series Totals				12	31	2	8	2	1	0	2	0	.258
Championship Series													
2002	San Francisco	N.L.	PH	1	1	0	0	0	0	0	0	0	.000
2008	Philadelphia	N.L.	3B	5	13	0	2	0	0	0	1	0	.154
2009	Philadelphia	N.L.	3B	5	17	3	2	0	1	1	2	0	.118
Championship Series Totals				11	31	3	4	0	1	1	3	0	.129
World Series Record													
2002	San Francisco	N.L.	DH	3	5	0	0	0	0	0	0	0	.000
2008	Philadelphia	N.L.	3B	5	18	0	6	0	0	0	2	0	.333
2009	Philadelphia	N.L.	3B	6	23	2	4	1	0	1	2	0	.174
World Series Totals				14	46	2	10	1	0	1	4	0	.217

a Filed for free agency, November 1, 2006, re-signed with San Francisco Giants, December 4, 2006.

b Filed for free agency, October 29, 2007. Signed with Philadelphia Phillies, January 31, 2008.

c On disabled list from July 25 to August 20, 2008.
d Filed for free agency, November 9, 2009. Signed with Houston Astros, December 10, 2009.
e Traded to St. Louis Cardinals with cash for pitcher David Carpenter, August 19, 2010.
f Filed for free agency, November 1, 2010.

FIELDER, PRINCE SEMIEN

Born, Ontario, California, May 9, 1984.
Bats Left. Throws Right. Height, 6 feet. Weight, 260 pounds.

Year	Club	Lea	Pos	G	AB	R	H	2B	3B	HR	RBI	SB	Avg
2002	Beloit	Midwest	1B	32	112	15	27	7	0	3	11	0	.241
2002	Ogden	Pioneer	1B	41	146	35	57	12	0	10	40	3	.390
2003	Beloit	Midwest	1B	137	502	81	157	22	2	27	112	2	.313
2004	Huntsville	Southern	1B-OF	136	497	70	135	29	1	23	78	11	.272
2005	Nashville	P.C.	1B	103	378	68	110	21	0	28	86	8	.291
2005	Milwaukee	N.L.	1B	39	59	2	17	4	0	2	10	0	.288
2006	Milwaukee	N.L.	1B	157	569	82	154	35	1	28	81	7	.271
2007	Milwaukee	N.L.	1B	158	573	109	165	35	2	*50	119	2	.288
2008	Milwaukee	N.L.	1B	159	588	86	162	30	2	34	102	3	.276
2009	Milwaukee	N.L.	1B	*162	591	103	177	35	3	46	*141	2	.299
2010	Milwaukee	N.L.	1B	161	578	94	151	25	0	32	83	1	.261
Major League Totals			6 Yrs.	836	2958	476	826	164	8	192	536	15	.279
	Division Series												
2008	Milwaukee	N.L.	1B	4	14	1	1	0	0	1	2	0	.071

FIELDS, JOSHUA DEAN (JOSH)

Born, Ada, Oklahoma, December 14, 1982.
Bats Right. Throws Right. Height, 6 feet, 1 inch. Weight, 225 pounds.

Year	Club	Lea	Pos	G	AB	R	H	2B	3B	HR	RBI	SB	Avg
2004	Winston-Salem	Carolina	3B	66	256	36	73	12	4	7	39	0	.285
2005	Birmingham	Southern	3B-1B	134	477	76	120	27	0	16	79	7	.252
2006	Charlotte	Int.	3B	124	462	85	141	32	4	19	70	28	.305
2006	Chicago	A.L.	3B-OF	11	20	4	3	2	0	1	2	0	.150
2007	Charlotte	Int.	3B-SS	56	205	28	58	14	0	10	37	8	.283
2007	Chicago	A.L.	3B-OF	100	373	54	91	17	1	23	67	1	.244
2008	Winston-Salem	Carolina	3B	4	9	1	3	1	0	0	1	0	.333
2008	Charlotte	Int.	3B	75	276	41	68	15	3	10	35	8	.246
2008	Chicago	A.L.	3B	14	32	3	5	1	0	0	2	0	.156
2009	Charlotte	Int.	3B	27	98	15	26	5	0	5	13	1	.265
2009	Chicago a	A.L.	3B-1B	79	239	29	53	5	2	7	30	2	.222
2010	Royals	Arizona	DH	3	10	2	4	1	1	0	4	0	.400
2010	Northwest	Texas	3B	11	39	10	17	8	0	0	9	1	.436
2010	Kansas City b-c	A.L.	3B	13	49	5	15	0	0	3	6	0	.306
Major League Totals			5 Yrs.	217	713	95	167	25	3	34	107	3	.234

a Traded to Kansas City Royals with infielder Chris Getz for infielder Mark Teahen, November 6, 2009.
b On disabled list from March 28 to September 1, 2010.
c Not offered contract, December 2, 2010. Signed with Pittsburgh Pirates organization, December 20, 2010.

FIGGINS, DESMOND DECHONE (CHONE)

Born, Leary, Georgia, January 22, 1978.
Bats Both. Throws Right. Height, 5 feet, 7 inches. Weight, 180 pounds.

Year	Club	Lea	Pos	G	AB	R	H	2B	3B	HR	RBI	SB	Avg
1997	Rockies	Arizona	SS	54	214	41	60	5	6	1	23	30	.280
1998	Portland	Northwest	SS	69	269	41	76	9	3	1	26	25	.283
1999	Salem	Carolina	SS	123	444	65	106	12	3	0	22	27	.239
2000	Salem	Carolina	2B	134	522	92	145	26	14	3	48	37	.278
2001	Carolina	Southern	2B-SS	86	332	41	73	14	5	2	25	27	.220
2001	Arkansas a	Texas	2B-SS-3B	39	138	21	37	12	2	0	12	7	.268
2002	Salt Lake	P.C.	2B-SS	125	511	100	156	25	18	7	62	39	.305
2002	Anaheim	A.L.	2B	15	12	6	2	1	0	0	1	2	.167
2003	Salt Lake	P.C.	2B-SS-OF-3B	68	285	55	89	14	15	4	30	16	.312
2003	Anaheim	A.L.	OF-2B-SS	71	240	34	71	9	4	0	27	13	.296
2004	Anaheim	A.L.	3B-OF-2B-SS	148	577	83	171	22	17	5	60	34	.296
2005	Los Angeles	A.L.	OF-3B-2B-SS	158	642	113	186	25	10	8	57	*62	.290
2006	Los Angeles	A.L.	OF-3B-2B-SS	155	604	93	161	23	8	9	62	52	.267
2007	Salt Lake	P.C.	3B	4	14	3	5	1	0	0	1	0	.357
2007	Los Angeles b	A.L.	3B-OF-2B	115	442	81	146	24	6	3	58	41	.330
2008	Salt Lake	P.C.	3B	3	10	2	2	0	0	0	0	0	.200

Year Club	Lea	Pos	G	AB	R	H	2B	3B	HR	RBI	SB	Avg
2008 Los Angeles c.	A.L.	3B-2B	116	453	72	125	14	1	1	22	34	.276
2009 Los Angeles d	A.L.	3B-2B-OF	158	615	114	183	30	7	5	54	42	.298
2010 Seattle	A.L.	2B	161	602	62	156	21	2	1	35	42	.259
Major League Totals		9 Yrs.	1097	4187	658	1201	169	55	32	376	322	.287
Division Series												
2002 Anaheim.	A.L.	DH	1	0	1	0	0	0	0	0	1	.000
2004 Anaheim.	A.L.	2B-3B	3	14	0	2	0	0	0	0	1	.143
2005 Los Angeles	A.L.	3B-OF	5	21	2	3	1	1	0	2	0	.143
2007 Los Angeles	A.L.	OF	3	13	1	3	2	0	0	1	0	.231
2008 Los Angeles	A.L.	3B	4	21	2	7	1	1	0	1	1	.333
2009 Los Angeles	A.L.	3B	3	12	1	0	0	0	0	0	0	.000
Division Series Totals			19	81	7	15	4	2	0	4	3	.185
Championship Series												
2002 Anaheim.	A.L.	PH	3	1	2	1	0	0	0	0	0	1.000
2005 Los Angeles	A.L.	3B-OF	5	17	1	2	1	0	0	1	1	.118
2009 Los Angeles	A.L.	3B	6	23	2	3	0	0	0	1	0	.130
Championship Series Totals			14	41	5	6	1	0	0	2	1	.146
World Series Record												
2002 Anaheim.	A.L.	PH	2	0	1	0	0	0	0	0	0	.000

a Traded by Colorado Rockies to Anaheim Angels for outfielder Kimera Bartee, July 13, 2001.
b On disabled list from March 23 to April 30, 2007.
c On disabled list from May 4 to May 21 and May 22 to June 12, 2008.
d Filed for free agency, November 6, 2009. Signed with Seattle Mariners, December 8, 2009.

FONTENOT, MICHAEL EUGENE (MIKE)

Born, Slidell, Louisiana, June 9, 1980.
Bats Left. Throws Right. Height, 5 feet, 8 inches. Weight, 165 pounds.

Year Club	Lea	Pos	G	AB	R	H	2B	3B	HR	RBI	SB	Avg
2002 Frederick	Carolina	2B	122	481	61	127	16	4	8	53	13	.264
2003 Bowie.	Eastern	2B	126	449	63	146	24	5	12	66	16	.325
2004 Ottawa	Int.	2B	136	524	73	146	30	10	8	49	14	.279
2005 Iowa.	P.C.	2B-3B-SS-OF	111	379	60	103	22	10	6	39	3	.272
2005 Chicago a.	N.L.	PH	7	2	4	0	0	0	0	0	0	.000
2006 Iowa.	P.C.	2B-3B-SS	111	362	54	107	28	2	8	36	5	.296
2007 Iowa.	P.C.	SS-2B-3B-OF	55	211	46	71	17	4	6	34	3	.336
2007 Chicago	N.L.	2B-SS	86	234	32	65	12	4	3	29	5	.278
2008 Chicago	N.L.	2B-SS	119	243	42	74	22	1	9	40	2	.305
2009 Chicago	N.L.	2B-3B	135	377	38	89	22	2	9	43	4	.236
2010 Chicago-San Fran. b	N.L.	2B-3B-SS	103	240	24	68	13	3	1	25	1	.283
Major League Totals		5 Yrs.	450	1096	140	296	69	10	22	137	12	.270
Division Series												
2007 Chicago	N.L.	PH	2	2	0	0	0	0	0	0	0	.000
2008 Chicago	N.L.	2B	3	6	0	2	0	0	0	0	0	.333
2010 San Francisco	N.L.	3B	3	6	1	1	0	1	0	0	0	.167
Division Series Totals			8	14	1	3	0	1	0	0	0	.214
Championship Series												
2010 San Francisco	N.L.	3B	4	8	0	2	0	0	0	0	1	.250
World Series Record												
2010 San Francisco	N.L.	PH	1	0	0	0	0	0	0	0	0	.000

a Traded to Chicago Cubs by Baltimore Orioles with infielder Jerry Hairston and pitcher Dave Crouthers for outfielder Sammy Sosa, February 2, 2005.
b Traded to San Francisco Giants for outfielder Evan Crawford, August 11, 2010.

FOWLER, WILLIAM DEXTER (DEXTER)

Born, Atlanta, Georgia, March 22, 1986.
Bats Both. Throws Right. Height, 6 feet, 4 inches. Weight, 185 pounds.

Year Club	Lea	Pos	G	AB	R	H	2B	3B	HR	RBI	SB	Avg
2005 Casper	Pioneer	OF	62	220	43	60	10	4	4	23	18	.273
2006 Asheville.	So.Atl.	OF	99	405	92	120	31	6	8	46	43	.296
2007 Modesto.	Calif.	OF	65	245	43	67	7	5	2	23	20	.273
2008 Tulsa	Texas	OF	108	421	92	141	31	9	9	64	20	.335
2008 Colorado	N.L.	OF	13	26	3	4	0	0	0	0	0	.154
2009 Tulsa	Texas	OF	3	10	3	4	2	0	0	3	1	.400
2009 Colorado a	N.L.	OF	135	433	73	115	29	10	4	34	27	.266
2010 Colorado Springs	P.C.	OF	27	106	23	36	10	4	2	13	1	.340

Year Club	Lea	Pos	G	AB	R	H	2B	3B	HR	RBI	SB	Avg
2010 Colorado	N.L.	OF	132	439	73	114	20	*14	6	36	13	.260
Major League Totals		3 Yrs.	280	898	149	233	49	24	10	70	40	.259
Division Series												
2009 Colorado	N.L.	OF	4	14	1	3	0	0	0	2	0	.214

a On disabled list from August 25 to September 9, 2009.

FOX, JACOB QUIRIN (JAKE)

Born, Beech Grove, Indiana, July 20, 1982.
Bats Right. Throws Right. Height, 6 feet. Weight, 210 pounds.

Year Club	Lea	Pos	G	AB	R	H	2B	3B	HR	RBI	SB	Avg
2003 Cubs	Arizona	C-SS	15	50	4	12	5	0	1	6	0	.240
2003 Lansing	Midwest	C	29	100	13	26	8	0	5	12	0	.260
2004 Lansing	Midwest	C	97	366	49	105	19	3	14	55	2	.287
2005 Daytona	Fla.St.	C-OF	83	270	37	76	20	0	9	40	5	.281
2006 Daytona	Fla.St.	C	66	249	45	78	15	1	16	61	4	.313
2006 West Tenn	Southern	C-OF	55	193	20	52	17	0	5	25	0	.269
2007 Tennessee	Southern	1B-OF-C-3B	91	359	60	102	23	1	18	60	6	.284
2007 Chicago	N.L.	OF-1B	7	14	3	2	2	0	0	1	0	.143
2007 Iowa	P.C.	OF-1B	25	99	18	28	7	0	6	19	2	.283
2008 Iowa	P.C.	1B-OF-3B	29	117	17	26	10	1	6	26	3	.222
2008 Tennessee	Southern	1B-OF-3B	105	388	76	119	29	1	25	79	4	.307
2009 Iowa	P.C.	1B-OF-C-3B	45	164	44	67	14	3	17	53	2	.409
2009 Chicago a	N.L.	3B-OF-1B-C	82	216	23	56	12	0	11	44	0	.259
2010 Oakland-Baltimore b	A.L.	DH-C-OF-1B-3B	77	198	21	43	10	1	7	22	0	.217
Major League Totals		3 Yrs.	166	428	47	101	24	1	18	67	0	.236

a Traded to Oakland Athletics with infielder Aaron Miles and cash for pitcher Jeff Gray, pitcher Ronny Morla and outfielder Matt Spencer, December 3, 2009.
b Traded to Baltimore Orioles for pitcher Ross Wolf and cash, June 22, 2010.

FRANCISCO, LOUIS BEN (BEN)

Born, Santa Ana, California, October 23, 1981.
Bats Right. Throws Right. Height, 6 feet, 1 inch. Weight, 190 pounds.

Year Club	Lea	Pos	G	AB	R	H	2B	3B	HR	RBI	SB	Avg
2002 Mahoning Valley	N.Y.-Penn.	OF	58	235	55	82	23	2	3	23	22	.349
2003 Lake County	So.Atl.	OF	80	289	57	83	21	1	11	48	15	.287
2004 Akron	Eastern	OF	133	497	72	126	29	3	15	71	21	.254
2005 Akron	Eastern	OF	83	323	45	99	19	7	7	46	15	.307
2005 Buffalo	Int.	OF	4	16	4	8	1	0	0	3	1	.500
2006 Buffalo	Int.	OF	134	515	80	143	32	4	17	59	25	.278
2007 Buffalo	Int.	OF	95	377	60	120	27	2	12	51	22	.318
2007 Cleveland	A.L.	OF	25	62	10	17	5	0	3	12	0	.274
2008 Buffalo	Int.	OF	24	92	9	21	3	1	1	6	3	.228
2008 Cleveland	A.L.	OF	121	447	65	119	32	0	15	54	4	.266
2009 Cleveland	A.L.	OF	89	308	48	77	21	1	10	33	13	.250
2009 Philadelphia a	N.L.	OF	37	97	10	27	9	0	5	13	1	.278
2010 Philadelphia	N.L.	OF	88	179	24	48	13	0	6	28	8	.268
Major League Totals		4 Yrs.	360	1093	157	288	80	1	39	140	26	.263
Division Series												
2009 Philadelphia	N.L.	OF	3	1	0	0	0	0	0	0	0	.000
2010 Philadelphia	N.L.	PH	1	0	0	0	0	0	0	0	0	.000
Division Series Totals			4	1	0	0	0	0	0	0	0	.000
Championship Series												
2009 Philadelphia	N.L.	OF	4	3	0	0	0	0	0	0	0	.000
2010 Philadelphia	N.L.	OF	3	6	1	1	0	0	0	0	0	.167
Championship Series Totals			7	9	1	1	0	0	0	0	0	.111
World Series Record												
2009 Philadelphia	N.L.	OF	4	7	0	0	0	0	0	0	0	.000

a Traded to Philadelphia Phillies with pitcher Cliff Lee for catcher Lou Marson, pitcher Jason Knapp, infielder Jason Donald and pitcher Carlos Carrasco, July 29, 2009.

FRANCOEUR, JEFFREY BRADEN (JEFF)

Born, Atlanta, Georgia, January 8, 1984.
Bats Right. Throws Right. Height, 6 feet, 4 inches. Weight, 220 pounds.

Year Club	Lea	Pos	G	AB	R	H	2B	3B	HR	RBI	SB	Avg
2002 Danville	Appal.	OF	38	147	31	48	12	1	8	31	8	.327
2003 Rome	So.Atl.	OF	134	524	78	147	26	9	14	68	14	.281

Year	Club	Lea	Pos	G	AB	R	H	2B	3B	HR	RBI	SB	Avg
2004	Myrtle Beach	Carolina	OF	88	334	56	98	26	0	15	52	10	.293
2004	Greenville........	Southern	OF	18	76	8	15	2	0	3	9	1	.197
2005	Mississippi.......	Southern	OF	84	335	40	92	28	2	13	62	13	.275
2005	Atlanta..............	N.L.	OF	70	257	41	77	20	1	14	45	3	.300
2006	Atlanta..............	N.L.	OF	*162	651	83	169	24	6	29	103	1	.260
2007	Atlanta..............	N.L.	OF	*162	642	84	188	40	0	19	105	5	.293
2008	Mississippi.......	Southern	OF	3	13	3	7	0	1	0	2	0	.538
2008	Atlanta..............	N.L.	OF	155	599	70	143	33	3	11	71	0	.239
2009	Atlanta-New York a.....	N.L.	OF	157	593	72	166	32	4	15	76	6	.280
2010	New York............	N.L.	OF	124	401	43	95	16	2	11	54	8	.237
2010	Texas b-c............	A.L.	OF	15	53	9	18	2	0	2	11	0	.340
Major League Totals			6 Yrs.	845	3196	402	856	167	16	101	465	23	.268
	Division Series												
2005	Atlanta..............	N.L.	OF	4	17	2	4	1	1	0	1	0	.235
2010	Texas...............	A.L.	OF	2	8	1	1	1	0	0	1	0	.125
Division Series Totals				6	25	3	5	2	1	0	2	0	.200
	Championship Series												
2010	Texas...............	A.L.	OF	4	10	0	2	0	0	0	0	0	.200
	World Series Record												
2010	Texas...............	A.L.	OF	3	6	0	0	0	0	0	0	0	.000

a Traded to New York Mets with cash for outfielder Ryan Church, July 10, 2009.
b Traded to Texas Rangers for infielder Joaquin Arias, September 1, 2010.
c Filed for free agency, November 10, 2010. Signed with Kansas City Royals, December 8, 2010.

FREESE, DAVID RICHARD

Born, Corpus Christi, Texas, April 28, 1983.
Bats Right. Throws Right. Height, 6 feet, 2 inches. Weight, 220 pounds.

Year	Club	Lea	Pos	G	AB	R	H	2B	3B	HR	RBI	SB	Avg
2006	Fort Wayne........	Midwest	3B	53	204	27	61	13	3	8	44	1	.299
2006	Eugene.........	Northwest	3B	18	58	19	22	8	0	5	26	0	.379
2007	Lake Elsinore a........	Calif.	3B	128	503	104	152	31	6	17	96	6	.302
2008	Memphis.............	P.C.	3B	131	464	83	142	29	3	26	91	5	.306
2009	Cardinals.......	Gulf Coast	3B	4	11	2	5	2	0	1	6	0	.455
2009	Springfield..........	Texas	3B	4	16	3	6	1	0	1	5	0	.375
2009	Memphis.............	P.C.	3B-1B	56	200	34	60	15	0	10	37	1	.300
2009	St. Louis............	N.L.	3B-1B-C	17	31	3	10	2	0	1	7	0	.323
2010	Springfield..........	Texas	DH	1	2	0	1	1	0	0	0	0	.500
2010	St. Louis b...........	N.L.	3B-1B	70	240	28	71	12	1	4	36	1	.296
Major League Totals			2 Yrs.	87	271	31	81	14	1	5	43	1	.299

a Traded by San Diego Padres to St. Louis Cardinals for outfielder Jim Edmonds, December 15, 2007.
b On disabled list from June 28 to November 2, 2010.

FUKUDOME, KOSUKE

Born, Kagoshima, Japan, April 26, 1977.
Bats Left. Throws Right. Height, 6 feet. Weight, 185 pounds.

Year	Club	Lea	Pos	G	AB	R	H	2B	3B	HR	RBI	SB	Avg
1999	Chunichi.......	Japan Cent.	OF	132	461	76	131	25	2	16	52	4	.284
2000	Chunichi.......	Japan Cent.	OF	97	316	50	80	18	2	13	42	8	.253
2001	Chunichi.......	Japan Cent.	OF	120	375	51	94	22	2	15	56	8	.251
2002	Chunichi.......	Japan Cent.	OF	140	542	85	186	42	3	19	65	4	.343
2003	Chunichi.......	Japan Cent.	OF	140	528	107	165	30	11	34	96	10	.313
2004	Chunichi.......	Japan Cent.	OF	92	350	61	97	19	7	23	81	8	.277
2005	Chunichi.......	Japan Cent.	OF	142	515	102	169	39	6	28	103	1	.328
2006	Chunichi.......	Japan Cent.	OF	130	496	117	174	47	5	31	104	1	.351
2007	Chunichi a.....	Japan Cent.	OF	81	269	64	79	22	0	13	48	1	.294
2008	Chicago.............	N.L.	OF	150	501	79	129	25	3	10	58	12	.257
2009	Chicago.............	N.L.	OF	146	499	79	129	38	5	11	54	6	.259
2010	Chicago.............	N.L.	OF	130	358	45	94	20	2	13	44	7	.263
Major League Totals			3 Yrs.	426	1358	203	352	83	10	34	156	25	.259
	Division Series												
2008	Chicago.............	N.L.	OF	3	10	0	1	0	0	0	0	0	.100

a Signed with Chicago Cubs, December 12, 2007.

FURCAL, RAFAEL

Born, Loma de Cabrera, Dominican Republic, August 24, 1977.
Bats Both. Throws Right. Height, 5 feet, 8 inches. Weight, 195 pounds.

Year	Club	Lea	Pos	G	AB	R	H	2B	3B	HR	RBI	SB	Avg
1997	Braves	Gulf Coast	2B-OF	50	190	31	49	5	4	1	9	15	.258
1998	Danville	Appal.	2B	66	268	56	88	15	4	0	23	60	.328
1999	Myrtle Beach	Carolina	SS	43	184	32	54	9	3	0	12	23	.293
1999	Macon	So.Atl.	SS	83	335	73	113	15	1	1	29	73	.337
2000	Greenville	Southern	SS	3	10	1	2	0	0	1	3	0	.200
2000	Atlanta a-b	N.L.	SS-2B	131	455	87	134	20	4	4	37	40	.295
2001	Atlanta c	N.L.	SS	79	324	39	89	19	0	4	30	22	.275
2002	Atlanta	N.L.	SS-2B	154	636	95	175	31	8	8	47	27	.275
2003	Atlanta	N.L.	SS	156	664	130	194	35	*10	15	61	25	.292
2004	Atlanta	N.L.	SS-2B	143	563	103	157	24	5	14	59	29	.279
2005	Atlanta d	N.L.	SS	154	616	100	175	31	11	12	58	46	.284
2006	Los Angeles	N.L.	SS	159	654	113	196	32	9	15	63	37	.300
2007	Inland Empire	Calif.	SS	2	6	0	1	0	0	0	0	1	.167
2007	Los Angeles e	N.L.	SS	138	581	87	157	23	4	6	47	25	.270
2008	Las Vegas	P.C.	SS	1	3	0	1	1	0	0	1	0	.333
2008	Los Angeles f-g	N.L.	SS	36	143	34	51	12	2	5	16	8	.357
2009	Los Angeles	N.L.	SS	150	613	92	165	28	5	9	47	12	.269
2010	Inland Empire	Calif.	SS	2	4	0	0	0	0	0	0	0	.000
2010	Albuquerque	P.C.	SS	2	5	3	3	1	1	1	4	0	.600
2010	Los Angeles h	N.L.	SS	97	383	66	115	23	7	8	43	22	.300
Major League Totals			11 Yrs.	1397	5632	946	1608	278	65	100	508	293	.286
	Division Series												
2000	Atlanta	N.L.	SS	3	11	2	1	0	0	0	0	1	.091
2002	Atlanta	N.L.	SS	5	24	2	6	1	1	0	2	1	.250
2003	Atlanta	N.L.	SS	5	19	3	4	0	0	0	0	1	.211
2004	Atlanta	N.L.	SS	5	21	5	8	0	1	2	4	3	.381
2005	Atlanta	N.L.	SS	4	20	1	3	0	0	0	0	3	.150
2006	Los Angeles	N.L.	SS	3	11	1	2	0	0	0	1	2	.182
2008	Los Angeles	N.L.	SS	3	12	4	4	0	0	0	2	0	.333
2009	Los Angeles	N.L.	SS	3	12	2	6	0	1	0	2	0	.500
Division Series Totals				31	130	20	34	1	3	2	11	11	.262
	Championship Series												
2008	Los Angeles	N.L.	SS	5	19	5	4	0	0	1	1	0	.211
2009	Los Angeles	N.L.	SS	5	21	0	3	1	0	0	1	1	.143
Championship Series Totals				10	40	5	7	1	0	1	2	1	.175

a On disabled list from June 13 to June 28, 2000.
b Selected Rookie of the Year in National League for 2000.
c On disabled list from July 7 to November 6, 2001.
d Filed for free agency, October 31, 2005. Signed with Los Angeles Dodgers, December 7, 2005.
e On disabled list from March 23 to April 13, 2007.
f On disabled list from May 6 to September 24, 2008.
g Filed for free agency, November 3, 2008, re-signed with Los Angeles Dodgers, December 19, 2008.
h On disabled list from April 28 to May 25 and August 3 to September 3, 2010.

GAMEL, MATHEW LAWRENCE (MAT)

Born, Jacksonville, Florida, July 26, 1985.
Bats Left. Throws Right. Height, 6 feet. Weight, 200 pounds.

Year	Club	Lea	Pos	G	AB	R	H	2B	3B	HR	RBI	SB	Avg
2005	Helena	Pioneer	3B-1B	50	199	34	65	15	2	5	37	7	.327
2005	West Virginia	So.Atl.	3B	8	23	2	4	0	0	1	1	0	.174
2006	West Virginia	So.Atl.	3B	129	493	65	142	28	5	17	88	9	.288
2007	Brevard County	Fla.St.	3B	128	466	78	140	37	8	9	60	14	.300
2008	Huntsville	Southern	3B	127	508	96	167	35	7	19	96	6	.329
2008	Nashville	P.C.	3B	5	21	3	5	0	0	1	3	0	.238
2008	Milwaukee	N.L.	3B	2	2	0	1	1	0	0	0	0	.500
2009	Nashville	P.C.	3B	75	273	42	76	18	1	11	48	1	.278
2009	Milwaukee	N.L.	3B	61	128	11	31	6	1	5	20	1	.242
2010	Brevard County	Fla.St.	3B	6	20	3	2	1	0	0	2	0	.100
2010	Huntsville	Southern	3B	8	28	6	11	2	0	1	5	0	.393
2010	Nashville	P.C.	3B-OF-1B	82	311	54	96	24	0	13	67	3	.309
2010	Milwaukee a	N.L.	3B-OF	12	15	1	3	1	0	0	1	0	.200
Major League Totals			3 Yrs.	75	145	12	35	8	1	5	21	1	.241

a On disabled list from March 25 to June 4, 2010.

GARDNER, BRETT M.

Born, Holly Hill, South Carolina, August 24, 1983.
Bats Left. Throws Left. Height, 5 feet, 10 inches. Weight, 185 pounds.

Year	Club	Lea	Pos	G	AB	R	H	2B	3B	HR	RBI	SB	Avg
2005	Staten Island	N.Y.-Penn.	OF-3B	73	282	62	80	9	1	5	32	19	.284
2006	Trenton	Eastern	OF	55	217	41	59	4	3	0	13	28	.272
2006	Tampa	Fla.St.	OF	63	232	46	75	12	5	0	22	30	.323
2007	Trenton	Eastern	OF	54	203	43	61	14	5	0	17	18	.300
2007	Scranton/WB	Int.	OF	45	181	37	47	4	3	1	9	21	.260
2008	Scranton/WB	Int.	OF	94	341	68	101	12	11	3	32	37	.296
2008	New York	A.L.	OF	42	127	18	29	5	2	0	16	13	.228
2009	Scranton/WB	Int.	OF	4	11	3	1	0	0	0	0	3	.091
2009	New York a	A.L.	OF	108	248	48	67	6	6	3	23	26	.270
2010	New York	A.L.	OF	150	477	97	132	20	7	5	47	47	.277
Major League Totals			3 Yrs.	300	852	163	228	31	15	8	86	86	.268
	Division Series												
2009	New York	A.L.	OF	3	0	0	0	0	0	0	0	1	.000
2010	New York	A.L.	OF	3	10	1	2	0	0	0	1	1	.200
Division Series Totals				6	10	1	2	0	0	0	1	2	.200
	Championship Series												
2009	New York	A.L.	OF	6	3	2	2	0	0	0	0	0	.667
2010	New York	A.L.	OF	6	17	1	3	0	0	0	1	1	.176
Championship Series Totals				12	20	3	5	0	0	0	1	1	.250
	World Series Record												
2009	New York	A.L.	OF	5	10	1	0	0	0	0	0	0	.000

a On disabled list from July 26 to September 7, 2009.

GETZ, CHRISTOPHER RYAN (CHRIS)

Born, Southfield, Michigan, August 30, 1983.
Bats Left. Throws Right. Height, 6 feet. Weight, 185 pounds.

Year	Club	Lea	Pos	G	AB	R	H	2B	3B	HR	RBI	SB	Avg
2005	Great Falls	Pioneer	SS-2B	6	24	3	8	1	0	0	4	2	.333
2005	Kannapolis	So.Atl.	2B-SS	55	214	38	65	13	2	1	28	11	.304
2006	Birmingham	Southern	2B-SS	130	508	67	130	15	6	2	36	19	.256
2007	Birmingham	Southern	2B	72	278	40	83	10	2	3	29	13	.299
2008	Charlotte	Int.	2B-SS-OF-3B	111	404	60	122	24	1	11	52	11	.302
2008	Chicago	A.L.	2B	10	7	2	2	0	0	0	1	1	.286
2009	Charlotte	Int.	2B	5	15	4	4	0	0	0	0	2	.267
2009	Chicago a-b	A.L.	2B	107	375	49	98	18	4	2	31	25	.261
2010	Omaha	P.C.	2B	2	6	3	2	0	0	0	0	0	.333
2010	Kansas City c	A.L.	2B-3B	72	224	23	53	9	0	0	18	15	.237
Major League Totals			3 Yrs.	189	606	74	153	27	4	2	50	41	.252

a On disabled list from August 12 to September 1, 2009.
b Traded to Kansas City Royals with infielder Josh Fields for infielder Mark Teahen, November 6, 2009.
c On disabled list from April 15 to April 30, 2010.

GIAMBI, JASON GILBERT

Born, West Covina, California, January 8, 1971.
Bats Left. Throws Right. Height, 6 feet, 3 inches. Weight, 230 pounds.

Year	Club	Lea	Pos	G	AB	R	H	2B	3B	HR	RBI	SB	Avg
1992	South Oregon	Northwest	3B	13	41	9	13	3	0	3	13	1	.317
1993	Modesto	California	3B	89	313	72	91	16	2	12	60	2	.291
1994	Huntsville	Southern	3B-1B	56	193	31	43	9	0	6	30	0	.223
1994	Tacoma	P.C.	3B-1B-SS	52	176	28	56	20	0	4	38	1	.318
1995	Edmonton	P.C.	3B-1B	55	190	34	65	26	1	3	41	0	.342
1995	Oakland	A.L.	3B-1B	54	176	27	45	7	0	6	25	2	.256
1996	Oakland	A.L.	1B-OF-3B	140	536	84	156	40	1	20	79	0	.291
1997	Oakland	A.L.	OF-1B	142	519	66	152	41	2	20	81	0	.293
1998	Oakland	A.L.	1B	153	562	92	166	28	0	27	110	2	.295
1999	Oakland	A.L.	1B-3B	158	575	115	181	36	1	33	123	1	.315
2000	Oakland a	A.L.	1B	152	510	108	170	29	1	43	137	2	.333
2001	Oakland b	A.L.	1B	154	520	109	178	*47	2	38	120	2	.342
2002	New York	A.L.	1B	155	560	120	176	34	1	41	122	2	.314
2003	New York	A.L.	1B	156	535	97	134	25	0	41	107	2	.250
2004	Tampa	Fla.St.	1B	2	6	0	1	0	0	0	0	0	.167
2004	New York c	A.L.	1B	80	264	33	55	9	0	12	40	0	.208
2005	New York	A.L.	1B	139	417	74	113	14	0	32	87	0	.271

Year	Club	Lea	Pos	G	AB	R	H	2B	3B	HR	RBI	SB	Avg
2006	New York	A.L.	DH-1B	139	446	92	113	25	0	37	113	2	.253
2007	Tampa	Fla.St.	DH	5	13	0	4	1	0	0	1	0	.308
2007	Scranton-WB	Int.	1B	4	9	1	1	0	0	1	1	0	.111
2007	New York d	A.L.	DH-1B	83	254	31	60	8	0	14	39	1	.236
2008	New York e	A.L.	1B	145	458	68	113	19	1	32	96	2	.247
2009	Colorado Springs	P.C.	1B	6	18	4	8	1	0	2	4	0	.444
2009	Oakland	A.L.	1B	83	269	39	52	13	0	11	40	0	.193
2009	Colorado f-g-h	N.L.	1B	19	24	4	7	1	0	2	11	0	.292
2010	Colorado i	N.L.	1B	87	176	17	43	9	0	6	35	2	.244
Major League Totals			16 Yrs.	2039	6801	1176	1914	385	9	415	1365	20	.281
	Division Series												
2000	Oakland	A.L.	1B	5	14	2	4	0	0	0	1	1	.286
2001	Oakland	A.L.	1B	5	17	2	6	0	0	1	4	0	.353
2002	New York	A.L.	1B-DH	4	14	5	5	0	0	1	3	0	.357
2003	New York	A.L.	DH	4	16	1	4	2	0	0	2	0	.250
2005	New York	A.L.	1B-DH	5	19	1	8	3	0	0	2	0	.421
2006	New York	A.L.	DH-1B	3	8	1	1	0	0	1	2	1	.125
2007	New York	A.L.	1B	3	4	0	1	0	0	0	0	0	.250
2009	Colorado	N.L.	PH	3	3	1	1	0	0	0	1	0	.333
Division Series Totals				32	95	13	30	5	0	3	15	2	.316
	Championship Series												
2003	New York	A.L.	DH	7	26	4	6	0	0	3	3	0	.231
	World Series Record												
2003	New York	A.L.	1B	6	17	2	4	1	0	1	1	0	.235

a Selected Most Valuable Player in American League for 2000.
b Filed for free agency, November 5, 2001. Signed with New York Yankees, December 13, 2001.
c On disabled list from May 22 to June 6 and from July 26 to September 14, 2004.
d On disabled list from May 31 to August 7, 2007.
e Not offered contract, November 4, 2008. Signed with Oakland A's, January 7, 2009.
f On disabled list from July 20 to August 7, 2009.
g Released by Oakland Athletics, August 7, 2009. Signed with Colorado Rockies organization, August 24, 2009.
h Filed for free agency, November 5, 2009, re-signed with Colorado Rockies, January 28, 2010.
i Filed for free agency, November 1, 2010, re-signed with Colorado Rockies organization, January 17, 2011.

GLAUS, TROY EDWARD

Born, Tarzana, California, August 3, 1976.
Bats Right. Throws Right. Height, 6 feet, 5 inches. Weight, 240 pounds.

Year	Club	Lea	Pos	G	AB	R	H	2B	3B	HR	RBI	SB	Avg
1998	Midland	Texas	3B	50	188	51	58	11	2	19	51	4	.309
1998	Vancouver	P.C.	3B	59	219	33	67	16	0	16	42	3	.306
1998	Anaheim	A.L.	3B	48	165	19	36	9	0	1	23	1	.218
1999	Anaheim	A.L.	3B	154	551	85	132	29	0	29	79	5	.240
2000	Anaheim	A.L.	3B-SS	159	563	120	160	37	1	*47	102	14	.284
2001	Anaheim	A.L.	3B-SS	161	588	100	147	38	2	41	108	10	.250
2002	Anaheim	A.L.	3B-SS	156	569	99	142	24	1	30	111	10	.250
2003	Rancho Cucamonga	Calif.	DH	2	6	1	2	0	0	0	1	0	.333
2003	Anaheim a	A.L.	3B	91	319	53	79	17	2	16	50	7	.248
2004	Rancho Cucamonga	Calif.	DH	5	15	4	3	0	0	2	4	0	.200
2004	Anaheim b-c	A.L.	DH-3B	58	207	47	52	11	1	18	42	2	.251
2005	Arizona d	N.L.	3B	149	538	78	139	29	1	37	97	4	.258
2006	Toronto	A.L.	3B-SS	153	540	105	136	27	0	38	104	3	.252
2007	Toronto e-f	A.L.	3B	115	385	60	101	19	1	20	62	0	.262
2008	St. Louis	N.L.	3B-1B	151	544	69	147	33	1	27	99	0	.270
2009	Palm Beach	Fla.St.	1B-OF	6	25	2	5	1	0	0	4	0	.200
2009	Springfield	Texas	1B	3	9	1	2	0	0	0	2	0	.222
2009	Memphis	P.C.	3B-OF	15	51	10	11	0	0	3	8	1	.216
2009	St. Louis g-h	N.L.	3B-1B	14	29	2	5	2	0	0	2	0	.172
2010	Gwinnett	Int.	3B	8	30	10	10	2	0	2	8	0	.333
2010	Atlanta i-j	N.L.	1B-3B	128	412	52	99	18	0	16	71	0	.240
Major League Totals			13 Yrs.	1537	5410	889	1375	293	10	320	950	56	.254
	Division Series												
2002	Anaheim	A.L.	3B	4	16	4	5	0	0	3	3	0	.313
2004	Anaheim	A.L.	DH	3	11	3	4	2	0	2	3	0	.364
2009	St. Louis	N.L.	PH	2	2	0	0	0	0	0	0	0	.000
2010	Atlanta	N.L.	3B	3	4	0	0	0	0	0	0	0	.000
Division Series Totals				12	33	7	9	2	0	5	6	0	.273
	Championship Series												
2002	Anaheim	A.L.	3B	5	19	4	6	0	1	1	2	0	.316

Year	Club	Lea	Pos	G	AB	R	H	2B	3B	HR	RBI	SB	Avg
	World Series Record												
2002	Anaheim	A.L.	3B	7	26	7	10	3	0	3	8	0	.385

a On disabled list from July 22 to October 6, 2003.
b On disabled list from May 12 to August 29, 2004.
c Filed for free agency, October 28, 2004. Signed with Arizona Diamondbacks, December 9, 2004.
d Traded to Toronto Blue Jays with infielder Sergio Santos for infielder Orlando Hudson and pitcher Miguel Batista, December 27, 2005.
e On disabled list from April 13 to April 28 and September 14 to November 13, 2007.
f Traded to St. Louis Cardinals for infielder Scott Rolen, January 14, 2008.
g On disabled list from March 27 to September 1, 2009.
h Filed for free agency, November 5, 2009. Signed with Atlanta Braves, January 5, 2010.
i On disabled list from August 18 to September 2, 2010.
j Filed for free agency, November 1, 2010.

GLOAD, ROSS PETER

Born, Brooklyn, New York, April 5, 1976.
Bats Left. Throws Left. Height, 6 feet, 1 inches. Weight, 210 pounds.

Year	Club	Lea	Pos	G	AB	R	H	2B	3B	HR	RBI	SB	Avg
1997	Utica	N.Y.-Penn.	1B	68	245	28	64	15	2	3	43	1	.261
1998	Kane County	Midwest	1B	132	501	77	157	41	3	12	92	7	.313
1999	Brevard County	Fla.St.	1B	133	490	80	146	26	3	10	74	3	.298
2000	Portland	Eastern	OF-1B	100	401	60	114	28	4	16	65	4	.284
2000	Iowa	P.C.	OF	28	104	24	42	10	2	14	39	1	.404
2000	Chicago a	N.L.	OF-1B	18	31	4	6	0	1	1	3	0	.194
2001	Iowa b	P.C.	OF-1B	133	475	70	141	32	10	15	93	9	.297
2002	Colorado Springs	P.C.	1B-OF	104	442	69	139	28	6	16	71	9	.314
2002	Colorado c-d	N.L.	1B-OF	26	31	4	8	1	0	1	4	0	.258
2003	Charlotte e	Int.	1B-OF	133	508	72	160	40	6	18	70	6	.315
2004	Chicago	A.L.	1B-OF	110	234	28	75	16	0	7	44	0	.321
2005	Charlotte	Int.	1B-OF	60	236	45	86	22	1	15	45	0	.364
2005	Chicago f	A.L.	1B-OF	28	42	2	7	2	0	0	5	0	.167
2006	Chicago g	A.L.	1B-OF	77	156	22	51	8	2	3	18	6	.327
2007	Omaha	P.C.	DH	1	4	1	2	0	0	1	1	0	.500
2007	Kansas City h	A.L.	1B-OF	102	320	37	92	22	3	7	51	2	.287
2008	Kansas City	A.L.	1B-OF	122	388	46	106	18	1	3	37	3	.273
2009	Florida i-j	N.L.	1B-OF-P	125	230	33	60	10	2	6	30	0	.261
2010	Clearwater	Fla.St.	1B	2	8	1	1	0	0	1	1	0	.125
2010	Philadelphia k	N.L.	1B-OF	94	128	16	36	8	0	6	22	1	.281
	Major League Totals		9 Yrs.	702	1560	192	441	85	9	34	214	12	.283
	Championship Series												
2010	Philadelphia	N.L.	PH	6	5	0	0	0	0	0	0	0	.000

a Traded to Chicago Cubs with pitcher David Noyce for outfielder Henry Rodriguez and cash, July 31, 2000.
b Claimed on waivers by Colorado Rockies, September 12, 2001.
c Traded to New York Mets with pitcher Craig House and outfielder Alex Ochoa for outfielder Benny Agbayani and infielder Todd Zeile, January 21, 2002.
d Sold to Colorado Rockies, January 26, 2002.
e Traded to Chicago White Sox for pitcher Wade Parrish, March 31, 2003.
f On disabled list from April 25 to July 17, 2005.
g Traded to Kansas City Royals for pitcher Andy Sisco, December 16, 2006.
h On disabled list from May 14 to June 30, 2007.
i Traded to Florida Marlins for player to be named later, March 31, 2009. Kansas City Royals received pitcher Eric Basurto to complete trade, May 13, 2009.
j Filed for free agency, November 5, 2009. Signed with Philadelphia Phillies, December 15, 2009.
k On disabled list from August 19 to September 3, 2010.

GOMES, JONNY JOHNSON

Born, Petaluma, California, November 22, 1980.
Bats Right. Throws Right. Height, 6 feet, 1 inch. Weight, 225 pounds.

Year	Club	Lea	Pos	G	AB	R	H	2B	3B	HR	RBI	SB	Avg
2001	Princeton	Appal.	OF	62	206	58	60	11	2	16	44	15	.291
2002	Bakersfield	California	OF	133	446	102	123	24	9	30	72	15	.276
2003	Orlando	Southern	OF	120	442	68	110	28	3	17	56	23	.249
2003	Durham	Int.	OF	5	19	2	6	2	1	0	1	0	.316
2003	Tampa Bay	A.L.	DH	8	15	1	2	1	0	0	0	0	.133
2004	Durham	Int.	OF	114	389	73	100	27	1	26	78	8	.257
2004	Tampa Bay	A.L.	DH	5	14	0	1	0	0	0	1	0	.071
2005	Durham	Int.	OF	45	162	34	52	13	0	14	46	7	.321
2005	Tampa Bay	A.L.	OF	101	348	61	98	13	6	21	54	9	.282
2006	Tampa Bay a	A.L.	DH-OF	117	385	53	83	21	1	20	59	1	.216

Year Club	Lea	Pos	G	AB	R	H	2B	3B	HR	RBI	SB	Avg
2007 Durham	Int.	OF	13	43	6	13	2	0	1	7	4	.302
2007 Tampa Bay	A.L.	OF	107	348	48	85	20	2	17	49	12	.244
2008 Durham	Int.	OF	26	107	19	27	11	0	2	14	0	.252
2008 Tampa Bay b	A.L.	DH-OF	77	154	23	28	5	1	8	21	8	.182
2009 Louisville	Int.	OF	37	131	18	37	10	1	9	27	4	.282
2009 Cincinnati c	N.L.	OF	98	281	39	75	17	0	20	51	3	.267
2010 Cincinnati	N.L.	OF	148	511	77	136	24	3	18	86	5	.266
Major League Totals		8 Yrs.	661	2056	302	508	101	13	104	321	38	.247
Division Series												
2010 Cincinnati	N.L.	OF	2	6	0	0	0	0	0	0	0	.000

a On disabled list from August 22 to October 2, 2006.
b Not offered contract, December 12, 2008. Signed with Cincinnati Reds organization, January 19, 2009.
c Not offered contract, December 12, 2009, re-signed with Cincinnati Reds, February 22, 2010.

GOMEZ (PENA), CARLOS ARGELIS

Born, Santiago, Dominican Republic, December 4, 1985.
Bats Right. Throws Right. Height, 6 feet, 4 inches. Weight, 195 pounds.

Year Club	Lea	Pos	G	AB	R	H	2B	3B	HR	RBI	SB	Avg
2004 Kingsport	Appal.	OF	38	150	24	43	10	4	1	20	8	.287
2004 Mets	Gulf Coast	OF	19	71	10	19	7	0	0	11	9	.268
2005 Hagerstown	So.Atl.	OF	120	487	75	134	13	6	8	48	64	.275
2006 Binghamton	Eastern	OF	120	430	53	121	24	8	7	48	41	.281
2007 New Orleans	P.C.	OF	36	140	24	40	8	2	2	13	17	.286
2007 St. Lucie	Fla.St.	OF	5	13	1	2	0	0	0	0	2	.154
2007 New York a	N.L.	OF	58	125	14	29	3	0	2	12	12	.232
2008 Minnesota b	A.L.	OF	153	577	79	149	24	7	7	59	33	.258
2009 Minnesota c	A.L.	OF	137	315	51	72	15	5	3	28	14	.229
2010 Wisconsin	Midwest	OF	2	7	0	2	0	0	0	0	2	.286
2010 Nashville	P.C.	OF	8	28	7	8	0	0	0	2	2	.286
2010 Milwaukee d	N.L.	OF	97	291	38	72	11	3	5	24	18	.247
Major League Totals		4 Yrs.	445	1308	182	322	53	15	17	123	77	.246
Division Series												
2009 Minnesota	A.L.	OF	1	4	1	0	0	0	0	0	0	.000

a On disabled list from July 5 to September 7, 2007.
b Traded to Minnesota Twins with pitcher Philip Humber, pitcher Kevin Mulvey and pitcher Deolis Garcia for pitcher Johan Santana, February 2, 2008.
c Traded to Milwaukee Brewers for infielder J.J. Hardy, November 6, 2009.
d On disabled list from May 6 to May 21 and August 3 to August 24, 2010.

GONZALEZ, ADRIAN

Born, San Diego, California, May 8, 1982.
Bats Left. Throws Left. Height, 6 feet, 2 inches. Weight, 220 pounds.

Year Club	Lea	Pos	G	AB	R	H	2B	3B	HR	RBI	SB	Avg
2000 Marlins	Gulf Coast	1B	53	193	24	57	10	1	0	30	0	.295
2000 Utica	N.Y.-Penn.	1B	8	29	7	9	3	0	0	3	0	.310
2001 Kane County	Midwest	1B	127	516	86	161	37	1	17	103	5	.312
2002 Portland	Eastern	1B	138	508	70	135	34	1	17	96	6	.266
2003 Albuquerque	P.C.	1B	39	139	17	30	5	1	1	18	1	.216
2003 Carolina	Southern	1B	36	137	15	42	9	1	1	16	1	.307
2003 Frisco a	Texas	1B	45	173	16	49	6	2	3	17	0	.283
2004 Oklahoma	P.C.	1B	123	457	61	139	28	3	12	88	1	.304
2004 Texas	A.L.	1B	16	42	7	10	3	0	1	7	0	.238
2005 Oklahoma	P.C.	1B	84	328	61	111	17	1	18	65	0	.338
2005 Texas	A.L.	DH-1B-OF	43	150	17	34	7	1	6	17	0	.227
2006 San Diego b	N.L.	1B	156	570	83	173	38	1	24	82	0	.304
2007 San Diego	N.L.	1B	161	646	101	182	46	3	30	100	0	.282
2008 San Diego	N.L.	1B	*162	616	103	172	32	1	36	119	0	.279
2009 San Diego	N.L.	1B	160	552	90	153	27	2	40	99	1	.277
2010 San Diego c	N.L.	1B	160	591	87	176	33	0	31	101	0	.298
Major League Totals		7 Yrs.	858	3167	488	900	186	8	168	525	1	.284
Division Series												
2006 San Diego	N.L.	1B	4	14	2	5	0	0	0	0	0	.357

a Traded to Texas Rangers with pitcher Ryan Snare and outfielder Will Smith for pitcher Ugueth Urbina, July 11, 2003.
b Traded to San Diego Padres with pitcher Chris Young and outfielder Terrmel Sledge for pitcher Adam Eaton, pitcher Akinori Otsuka and catcher Billy Killian, January 4, 2006.
c Traded to Boston Red Sox for pitcher Casey Kelly, outfielder Reymond Fuentes, infielder Anthony Rizzo and player to be named later, December 5, 2010. San Diego Padres received outfielder Eric Patterson to complete trade, December 16, 2010.

GONZALEZ, ALBERTO RAMON

Born, Maracaibo, Venezuela, April 18, 1983.
Bats Right. Throws Right. Height, 5 feet, 11 inches. Weight, 195 pounds.

Year	Club	Lea	Pos	G	AB	R	H	2B	3B	HR	RBI	SB	Avg
2004	South Bend	Midwest	SS-2B-OF	100	319	39	76	15	6	2	25	9	.238
2005	South Bend	Midwest	SS-2B-3B	95	352	60	112	21	7	1	42	12	.318
2006	Tennessee	Southern	SS	129	434	67	126	20	3	6	50	5	.290
2006	Tucson	Pacific	SS	4	15	2	3	0	0	0	1	0	.200
2007	Trenton	Eastern	SS	28	109	18	36	10	1	0	16	1	.330
2007	Scranton-WB	Int.	SS-2B	106	384	44	95	21	10	1	35	11	.247
2007	New York a	A.L.	SS-3B	12	14	3	1	0	0	0	1	0	.071
2008	New York	A.L.	SS-3B-2B	28	52	4	9	2	0	0	1	0	.173
2008	Scranton-WB	Int.	SS	47	188	23	47	8	0	4	23	4	.250
2008	Columbus	Int.	SS	8	33	2	10	3	0	1	6	0	.303
2008	Washington b-c	N.L.	SS-3B	17	49	9	17	6	0	1	9	0	.347
2009	Syracuse	Int.	SS	23	90	5	28	3	1	0	8	1	.311
2009	Washington	N.L.	2B-SS-3B	105	291	31	77	16	3	1	33	1	.265
2010	Washington	N.L.	2B-3B-SS-1B	114	186	19	46	8	1	0	5	0	.247
Major League Totals			4 Yrs.	276	592	66	150	32	4	2	49	1	.253

a Traded by Arizona Diamondbacks to New York Yankees with pitcher Steven Jackson, pitcher Ross Ohlendorf and pitcher Luis Vizcaino for pitcher Randy Johnson, January 9, 2007.
b Traded to Washington Nationals for pitcher Jhonny Nunez, July 31, 2008.
c On disabled list from August 5 to September 1, 2008.

GONZALEZ, ALEXANDER (ALEX)

Born, Cagua, Venezuela, February 15, 1977.
Bats Right. Throws Right. Height, 6 feet. Weight, 200 pounds.

Year	Club	Lea	Pos	G	AB	R	H	2B	3B	HR	RBI	SB	Avg
1994	Florida	Dominican	SS	66	282	39	67	9	5	4	39	5	.238
1995	Brevard Cty	Fla.St.	SS	17	59	6	12	2	1	0	8	1	.203
1995	Marlins	Gulf Coast	SS	53	187	30	55	7	4	2	30	11	.294
1996	Marlins	Gulf Coast	SS	10	41	6	16	3	0	0	6	1	.390
1996	Kane County	Midwest	SS	4	10	2	2	0	0	0	0	0	.200
1996	Portland	Eastern	SS	11	34	4	8	0	1	0	1	0	.235
1997	Portland	Eastern	SS	133	449	69	114	16	4	19	65	4	.254
1998	Charlotte	Int.	SS	108	422	71	117	20	10	10	51	4	.277
1998	Florida	N.L.	SS	25	86	11	13	2	0	3	7	0	.151
1999	Florida	N.L.	SS	136	560	81	155	28	8	14	59	3	.277
2000	Brevard County	Fla.St.	SS	4	17	1	2	0	0	0	2	1	.118
2000	Florida a	N.L.	SS	109	385	35	77	17	4	7	42	7	.200
2001	Florida	N.L.	SS	145	515	57	129	36	1	9	48	2	.250
2002	Florida b	N.L.	SS	42	151	15	34	7	1	2	18	3	.225
2002	Marlins	Gulf Coast	SS	5	12	0	2	1	0	0	1	0	.167
2003	Florida	N.L.	SS	150	528	52	135	33	6	18	77	0	.256
2004	Florida	N.L.	SS	159	561	67	130	30	3	23	79	3	.232
2005	Florida c	N.L.	SS	130	435	45	115	30	0	5	45	5	.264
2006	Pawtucket	Int.	SS	1	3	0	1	0	0	0	0	0	.333
2006	Boston d-e	A.L.	SS	111	388	48	99	24	2	9	50	1	.255
2007	Cincinnati	N.L.	SS	110	393	55	107	27	1	16	55	0	.272
2008	Cincinnati f	N.L.			INJURED—Did Not Play								
2009	Louisville	Int.	SS	4	13	1	1	0	0	0	1	0	.077
2009	Cincinnati	N.L.	SS	68	243	16	51	12	0	3	26	0	.210
2009	Boston g-h-i	A.L.	SS	44	148	26	42	10	0	5	15	2	.284
2010	Toronto	A.L.	SS	85	328	47	85	25	1	17	50	1	.259
2010	Atlanta j	N.L.	SS	72	267	27	64	17	2	6	38	0	.240
Major League Totals			12 Yrs.	1386	4988	582	1236	298	29	137	609	27	.248
Division Series													
2003	Florida	N.L.	SS	4	16	2	1	0	0	0	0	0	.063
2009	Boston	A.L.	SS	3	6	1	1	0	0	0	0	0	.167
2010	Atlanta	N.L.	SS	4	15	1	3	1	0	0	2	0	.200
Division Series Totals				11	37	4	5	1	0	0	2	0	.135
Championship Series													
2003	Florida	N.L.	SS	7	24	1	3	2	0	0	4	0	.125
World Series Record													
2003	Florida	N.L.	SS	6	22	3	6	2	0	1	2	0	.273

a On disabled list from July 28 to August 31, 2000.
b On disabled list from May 19 to November 6, 2002.
c Filed for free agency, October 27, 2005. Signed with Boston Red Sox, February 6, 2006.
d On disabled list from August 19 to September 3, 2006.

e Filed for free agency, October 30, 2006. Signed with Cincinnati Reds, November 20, 2006.
f On disabled list from March 21 to November 6, 2008.
g On disabled list from June 19 to July 24, 2009.
h Traded to Boston Red Sox for infielder Kristopher Negron, August 14, 2009.
i Filed for free agency, November 9, 2009. Signed with Toronto Blue Jays, November 26, 2009.
j Traded to Atlanta Braves with pitcher Tim Collins and infielder Tyler Pastornicky for infielder Yunel Escobar and pitcher Jo-Jo Reyes, July 14, 2010.

GONZALEZ, CARLOS EDUARDO

Born, Maracaibo, Venezuela, October 17, 1985.
Bats Left. Throws Left. Height, 6 feet, 1 inch. Weight, 200 pounds.

Year	Club	Lea	Pos	G	AB	R	H	2B	3B	HR	RBI	SB	Avg
2003	Missoula	Pioneer	OF	72	275	45	71	14	4	6	25	12	.258
2004	South Bend	Midwest	OF	12	42	3	11	4	0	1	6	0	.262
2004	Yakima	Northwest	OF	73	300	44	83	15	2	9	44	2	.277
2005	South Bend	Midwest	OF	129	515	91	158	28	6	18	92	7	.307
2006	Lancaster	Calif.	OF	104	403	82	121	35	4	21	94	15	.300
2006	Tennessee	Southern	OF	18	61	11	13	6	0	2	5	1	.213
2007	Tucson	P.C.	OF	10	42	9	13	5	0	1	11	1	.310
2007	Mobile a	Southern	OF	120	458	63	131	33	3	16	75	9	.286
2008	Sacramento	P.C.	OF	46	173	23	49	9	1	4	28	1	.283
2008	Oakland b	A.L.	OF	85	302	31	73	22	1	4	26	4	.242
2009	Colorado Springs	P.C.	OF	48	192	43	65	12	7	10	59	6	.339
2009	Colorado	N.L.	OF	89	278	53	79	14	7	13	29	16	.284
2010	Colorado	N.L.	OF	145	587	111	*197	34	9	34	117	26	*.336
Major League Totals			3 Yrs.	319	1167	195	349	70	17	51	172	46	.299
	Division Series												
2009	Colorado	N.L.	OF	4	17	5	10	2	0	1	1	2	.588

a Traded by Arizona Diamondbacks to Oakland Athletics with pitcher Brett Anderson, pitcher Dana Eveland, pitcher Greg Smith, infielder Chris Carter and outfielder Aaron Cunningham for pitcher Danny Haren and pitcher Connor Robertson, December 14, 2007.
b Traded to Colorado Rockies with pitcher Greg Smith and pitcher Huston Street for outfielder Matt Holliday, November 12, 2008.

GORDON, ALEX JONATHAN

Born, Lincoln, Nebraska, February 10, 1984.
Bats Left. Throws Right. Height, 6 feet, 1 inch. Weight, 220 pounds.

Year	Club	Lea	Pos	G	AB	R	H	2B	3B	HR	RBI	SB	Avg
2006	Wichita	Texas	3B-1B	130	486	111	158	39	1	29	101	22	.325
2007	Kansas City	A.L.	3B-1B-SS	151	543	60	134	36	4	15	60	14	.247
2008	Kansas City a	A.L.	3B	134	493	72	128	35	1	16	59	9	.260
2009	Azl Royals	Arizona	3B	4	7	1	2	0	0	1	3	0	.286
2009	NW Arkansas	Texas	3B	8	30	4	11	3	0	2	10	0	.367
2009	Omaha	P.C.	3B	18	67	17	21	4	1	2	10	0	.313
2009	Kansas City b	A.L.	3B	49	164	28	38	6	0	6	22	5	.232
2010	Wilmington	Carolina	3B	7	17	7	4	3	0	0	2	1	.235
2010	Omaha	P.C.	OF	68	260	59	82	20	3	14	44	7	.315
2010	Kansas City c	A.L.	OF-3B-1B	74	242	34	52	10	0	8	20	1	.215
Major League Totals			4 Yrs.	408	1442	194	352	87	5	45	161	29	.244

a On disabled list from August 22 to September 12, 2008.
b On disabled list from April 16 to July 16, 2009.
c On disabled list from March 26 to April 17, 2010.

GRANDERSON, CURTIS

Born, Blue Island, Illinois, March 16, 1981.
Bats Left. Throws Right. Height, 6 feet, 1 inch. Weight, 185 pounds.

Year	Club	Lea	Pos	G	AB	R	H	2B	3B	HR	RBI	SB	Avg
2002	Oneonta	N.Y.-Penn.	OF	52	212	45	73	15	4	3	34	9	.344
2003	Lakeland	Fla.St.	OF	127	476	71	136	29	10	11	51	10	.286
2004	Erie	Eastern	OF	123	462	89	139	19	8	21	94	14	.301
2004	Detroit	A.L.	OF	9	25	2	6	1	1	0	0	0	.240
2005	Toledo	Int.	OF	111	445	79	129	29	13	15	65	22	.290
2005	Detroit	A.L.	OF	47	162	18	44	6	3	8	20	1	.272
2006	Detroit	A.L.	OF	159	596	90	155	31	9	19	68	8	.260
2007	Detroit	A.L.	OF	158	612	122	185	38	*23	23	74	26	.302
2008	West Michigan	Midwest	OF	3	11	1	4	0	2	0	1	0	.364
2008	Toledo	Int.	OF	2	9	1	3	1	0	0	0	0	.333

Year Club	Lea	Pos	G	AB	R	H	2B	3B	HR	RBI	SB	Avg
2008 Detroit a	A.L.	OF	141	553	112	155	26	*13	22	66	12	.280
2009 Detroit b	A.L.	OF	160	631	91	157	23	8	30	71	20	.249
2010 Scranton/WB	Int.	OF	5	16	0	4	0	0	0	2	0	.250
2010 New York c	A.L.	OF	136	466	76	115	17	7	24	67	12	.247
Major League Totals		7 Yrs.	810	3045	511	817	142	64	126	366	79	.268
Division Series												
2006 Detroit	A.L.	OF	4	17	3	5	0	1	2	5	1	.294
2010 New York	A.L.	OF	3	11	2	5	1	1	0	3	1	.455
Division Series Totals			7	28	5	10	1	2	2	8	2	.357
Championship Series												
2006 Detroit	A.L.	OF	4	15	4	5	2	0	1	2	1	.333
2010 New York	A.L.	OF	6	17	1	5	1	0	1	3	0	.294
Championship Series Totals			10	32	5	10	3	0	2	5	1	.313
World Series Record												
2006 Detroit	A.L.	OF	5	21	1	2	1	0	0	0	0	.095

a On disabled list from March 23 to April 23, 2008.
b Traded to New York Yankees for outfielder Austin Jackson, pitcher Phil Coke and pitcher Ian Kennedy, December 9, 2009.
c On disabled list from May 2 to May 28, 2010.

GRIFFEY, GEORGE KENNETH, JR. (KEN)

Born, Donora, Pennsylvania, November 21, 1969.
Bats Left. Throws Left. Height, 6 feet, 3 inches. Weight, 220 pounds.

Year Club	Lea	Pos	G	AB	R	H	2B	3B	HR	RBI	SB	Avg
1987 Bellingham	Northwest	OF	54	182	43	57	9	1	14	40	13	.313
1988 San Bernardino a	California	OF	58	219	50	74	13	3	11	42	32	.338
1988 Vermont	Eastern	OF	17	61	10	17	5	1	2	10	4	.279
1989 Seattle b	A.L.	OF	127	455	61	120	23	0	16	61	16	.264
1990 Seattle	A.L.	OF	155	597	91	179	28	7	22	80	16	.300
1991 Seattle	A.L.	OF	154	548	76	179	42	1	22	100	18	.327
1992 Seattle c	A.L.	OF	142	565	83	174	39	4	27	103	10	.308
1993 Seattle	A.L.	OF-1B	156	582	113	180	38	3	45	109	17	.309
1994 Seattle	A.L.	OF	111	433	94	140	24	4	*40	90	11	.323
1995 Tacoma	P.C.	DH	1	3	0	0	0	0	0	0	0	.000
1995 Seattle d	A.L.	OF	72	260	52	67	7	0	17	42	4	.258
1996 Seattle e	A.L.	OF	140	545	125	165	26	2	49	140	16	.303
1997 Seattle f	A.L.	OF	157	608	*125	185	34	3	*56	*147	15	.304
1998 Seattle	A.L.	OF-1B	161	633	120	180	33	3	*56	146	20	.284
1999 Seattle	A.L.	OF	160	606	123	173	26	3	*48	134	24	.285
2000 Cincinnati g	N.L.	OF	145	520	100	141	22	3	40	118	6	.271
2001 Cincinnati h	N.L.	OF	111	364	57	104	20	2	22	65	2	.286
2002 Cincinnati i	N.L.	OF	70	197	17	52	8	0	8	23	1	.264
2003 Cincinnati j	N.L.	OF	53	166	34	41	12	1	13	26	1	.247
2004 Cincinnati k	N.L.	OF	83	300	49	76	18	0	20	60	1	.253
2005 Cincinnati	N.L.	OF	128	491	85	148	30	0	35	92	0	.301
2006 Cincinnati l	N.L.	OF	109	428	62	108	19	0	27	72	0	.252
2007 Cincinnati	N.L.	OF	144	528	78	146	24	1	30	93	6	.277
2008 Cincinnati	N.L.	OF	102	359	51	88	20	1	15	53	0	.245
2008 Chicago m-n	A.L.	OF	41	131	16	34	10	0	3	18	0	.260
2009 Seattle	A.L.	DH-OF	117	387	44	83	19	0	19	57	0	.214
2010 Seattle o	A.L.	DH	33	98	6	18	2	0	0	7	0	.184
Major League Totals		22 Yrs.	2671	9801	1662	2781	524	38	630	1836	184	.284
Division Series												
1995 Seattle	A.L.	OF	5	23	9	9	0	0	5	7	1	.391
1997 Seattle	A.L.	OF	4	15	0	2	0	0	0	2	2	.133
2008 Chicago	A.L.	OF	3	10	1	2	0	0	0	0	0	.200
Division Series Totals			12	48	10	13	0	0	5	9	3	.271
Championship Series												
1995 Seattle	A.L.	OF	6	21	2	7	2	0	1	2	2	.333

a On disabled list from June 9 to August 15, 1988.
b On disabled list from July 24 to August 20, 1989.
c On disabled list from June 9 to June 25, 1992.
d On disabled list from May 27 to August 15, 1995.
e On disabled list from June 20 to July 13, 1996.
f Selected Most Valuable Player in American League for 1997.
g Traded to Cincinnati Reds for pitcher Brett Tomko, outfielder Mike Cameron, infielder Antonio Perez and pitcher Jake Meyer, February 10, 2000.
h On disabled list from April 29 to June 15, 2001.

i On disabled list from April 8 to May 24 and June 24 to July 22, 2002.
j On disabled list from April 6 to May 13 and July 18 to November 5, 2003.
k On disabled list from July 11 to August 3 and from August 12 to November 2, 2004.
l On disabled list from April 13 to May 11, 2006.
m Traded to Chicago White Sox for pitcher Nick Masset and infielder Danny Richar, July 31, 2008.
n Not offered contract, October 30, 2008. Signed with Seattle Mariners, February 18, 2009.
o Announced retirement, June 2, 2010.

GROSS, GABRIEL JORDAN (GABE)

Born, Baltimore, Maryland, October 21, 1979.
Bats Left. Throws Right. Height, 6 feet, 3 inches. Weight, 210 pounds.

Year	Club	Lea	Pos	G	AB	R	H	2B	3B	HR	RBI	SB	Avg
2001	Dunedin	Fla.St.	OF	35	126	23	38	9	2	4	15	4	.302
2001	Tennessee	Southern	OF	11	41	8	10	1	0	3	11	0	.244
2002	Tennessee	Southern	OF	112	403	57	96	17	5	10	54	8	.238
2003	New Haven	Eastern	OF	84	310	52	99	23	3	7	51	3	.319
2003	Syracuse	Int.	OF	53	182	22	48	16	2	5	23	1	.264
2004	Syracuse	Int.	OF	103	377	52	111	29	2	9	54	4	.294
2004	Toronto	A.L.	OF	44	129	18	27	4	0	3	16	2	.209
2005	Syracuse	Int.	OF	102	390	64	116	29	4	6	46	14	.297
2005	Toronto a	A.L.	OF	40	92	11	23	4	1	1	7	1	.250
2006	Milwaukee	N.L.	OF	117	208	42	57	15	0	9	38	1	.274
2007	Nashville	P.C.	OF	20	76	13	27	3	2	4	10	2	.355
2007	Milwaukee	N.L.	OF	93	183	28	43	12	2	7	24	3	.235
2008	Milwaukee	N.L.	OF	16	43	6	9	3	0	0	2	2	.209
2008	Tampa Bay b	A.L.	OF	127	302	40	73	13	3	13	38	2	.242
2009	Tampa Bay c	A.L.	OF	115	282	31	64	16	1	6	36	6	.227
2010	Oakland d	A.L.	OF	105	222	27	53	11	1	1	25	5	.239
Major League Totals			7 Yrs.	657	1461	203	349	78	8	40	186	22	.239
	Division Series												
2008	Tampa Bay	N.L.	OF	3	6	0	1	0	0	0	0	1	.167
	Championship Series												
2008	Tampa Bay	N.L.	OF	6	10	0	0	0	0	0	0	1	.000
	World Series Record												
2008	Tampa Bay	N.L.	OF	1	3	0	0	0	0	0	2	0	.000

a Traded to Milwaukee Brewers with pitcher Dave Bush and pitcher Zach Jackson for infielder Lyle Overbay and pitcher Ty Taubenheim, December 7, 2005.
b Traded to Tampa Bay Rays for pitcher Josh Butler, April 22, 2008.
c Not offered contract, December 12, 2009. Signed with Oakland Athletics, February 1, 2010.
d Filed for free agency, October 30, 2010.

GUERRERO, VLADIMIR NIZAO

Born, Nizao, Dominican Republic, February 9, 1976.
Bats Right. Throws Right. Height, 6 feet, 3 inches. Weight, 235 pounds.

Year	Club	Lea	Pos	G	AB	R	H	2B	3B	HR	RBI	SB	Avg
1994	Montreal	Dominican	OF	25	92	34	39	11	0	12	35	5	.424
1994	Expos	Gulf Coast	OF	37	137	24	43	13	3	5	25	0	.314
1995	Albany	So.Atl.	OF	110	421	77	140	21	10	16	63	12	.333
1996	Wst Plm Bch	Fla.St.	OF	20	80	16	29	8	0	5	18	2	.363
1996	Harrisburg	Eastern	OF	118	417	84	150	32	8	19	78	17	.360
1996	Montreal	N.L.	OF	9	27	2	5	0	0	1	1	0	.185
1997	Wst. Plm. Bch	Fla. St.	OF	3	10	0	4	2	0	0	2	1	.400
1997	Montreal a	N.L.	OF	90	325	44	98	22	2	11	40	3	.302
1998	Montreal	N.L.	OF	159	623	108	202	37	7	38	109	11	.324
1999	Montreal	N.L.	OF	160	610	102	193	37	5	42	131	14	.316
2000	Montreal	N.L.	OF	154	571	101	197	28	11	44	123	9	.345
2001	Montreal	N.L.	OF	159	599	107	184	45	4	34	108	37	.307
2002	Montreal	N.L.	OF	161	614	106	*206	37	2	39	111	40	.336
2003	Brevard County	Fla.St.	OF	3	6	2	3	0	0	1	1	0	.500
2003	Montreal b-c	N.L.	OF	112	394	71	130	20	3	25	79	9	.330
2004	Anaheim d	A.L.	OF	156	612	*124	206	39	2	39	126	15	.337
2005	Los Angeles e	A.L.	OF	141	520	95	165	29	2	32	108	13	.317
2006	Los Angeles	A.L.	OF	156	607	92	200	34	1	33	116	15	.329
2007	Los Angeles	A.L.	OF	150	574	89	186	45	1	27	125	2	.324
2008	Los Angeles	A.L.	OF	143	541	85	164	31	3	27	91	5	.303
2009	Rancho Cucamonga	Calif.	DH	2	6	2	3	2	0	0	2	0	.500
2009	Los Angeles f-g	A.L.	DH-OF	100	383	59	113	16	1	15	50	2	.295
2010	Texas h	A.L.	DH-OF	152	593	83	178	27	1	29	115	4	.300
Major League Totals			15 Yrs.	2002	7593	1268	2427	447	45	436	1433	179	.320

Year	Club	Lea	Pos	G	AB	R	H	2B	3B	HR	RBI	SB	Avg
	Division Series												
2004	Anaheim	A.L.	OF	3	12	1	2	0	0	1	6	0	.167
2005	Los Angeles	A.L.	OF	5	18	5	6	0	0	0	0	1	.333
2007	Los Angeles	A.L.	OF-DH	3	10	0	2	0	0	0	0	0	.200
2008	Los Angeles	A.L.	DH	4	15	2	7	1	0	0	0	1	.467
2009	Los Angeles	A.L.	DH	3	10	2	4	0	0	0	2	0	.400
2010	Texas	A.L.	DH	5	19	2	5	1	0	0	1	0	.263
Division Series Totals				23	84	12	26	2	0	1	9	2	.310
	Championship Series												
2005	Los Angeles	A.L.	OF-DH	5	20	0	1	0	0	0	1	0	.050
2009	Los Angeles	A.L.	DH	6	27	3	10	3	0	1	5	0	.370
2010	Texas	A.L.	DH	6	26	2	7	2	0	0	3	0	.269
Championship Series Totals				17	73	5	18	5	0	1	9	0	.247
	World Series Record												
2010	Texas	A.L.	DH-OF	4	14	0	1	0	0	0	2	0	.071

a On disabled list from April 1 to May 2 and June 6 to June 21 and July 12 to July 27, 1997.
b On disabled list from June 5 to July 21, 2003.
c Filed for free agency, October 27, 2003. Signed with Anaheim Angels, January 12, 2004.
d Selected Most Valuable Player in American League for 2004.
e On disabled list from May 21 to June 10, 2005.
f On disabled list from April 16 to May 25 and July 8 to August 4, 2009.
g Filed for free agency, November 6, 2009. Signed with the Texas Rangers, January 11, 2010.
h Filed for free agency, November 3, 2010.

GUILLEN, CARLOS ALFONSO

Born, Maracay, Venezuela, September 30, 1975.
Bats Both. Throws Right. Height, 6 feet, 1 inch. Weight, 215 pounds.

Year	Club	Lea	Pos	G	AB	R	H	2B	3B	HR	RBI	SB	Avg
1993	Houston	Domincan	SS	18	56	12	14	4	2	0	8	0	.250
1994	a		INJURED—Did Not Play										
1995	Astros	Gulf Coast	DH	30	105	17	31	4	2	2	15	17	.295
1996	Quad City b	Midwest	SS	29	112	23	37	7	1	3	17	13	.330
1997	Jackson	Texas	SS	115	390	47	99	16	1	10	39	6	.254
1997	New Orleans	A.A.	SS	3	13	3	4	1	0	0	0	0	.308
1998	New Orleans	P.C.	SS	100	374	67	109	18	4	12	51	3	.291
1998	Tacoma	P.C.	2B	24	92	8	21	1	1	1	4	1	.228
1998	Seattle c-d	A.L.	2B	10	39	9	13	1	1	0	5	2	.333
1999	Seattle e	A.L.	SS-2B	5	19	2	3	0	0	1	3	0	.158
2000	Tacoma	P.C.	3B	24	87	19	26	4	1	2	11	4	.299
2000	Seattle f	A.L.	3B-SS	90	288	45	74	15	2	7	42	1	.257
2001	Seattle	A.L.	SS	140	456	72	118	21	4	5	53	4	.259
2002	Seattle	A.L.	SS	134	475	73	124	24	6	9	56	4	.261
2003	Tacoma	P.C.	3B	4	14	2	5	1	0	2	4	0	.357
2003	Seattle g-h	A.L.	SS-3B	109	388	63	107	19	3	7	52	4	.276
2004	Detroit	A.L.	SS	136	522	97	166	37	10	20	97	12	.318
2005	Detroit i	A.L.	SS	87	334	48	107	15	4	5	23	2	.320
2006	Detroit	A.L.	SS-1B	153	543	100	174	41	5	19	85	20	.320
2007	Detroit	A.L.	SS-1B	151	564	86	167	35	9	21	102	13	.296
2008	Detroit	A.L.	3B-1B-OF	113	420	68	120	29	2	10	54	9	.286
2009	Lakeland	Fla.St.	OF	5	12	3	3	1	0	0	0	0	.250
2009	Toledo	Int.	DH	2	7	2	4	0	0	0	1	0	.571
2009	Detroit j	A.L.	OF-1B	81	277	36	67	10	3	11	41	1	.242
2010	West Michigan	Midwest	2B	2	6	0	2	0	0	0	0	0	.333
2010	Toledo	Int.	2B	5	18	5	6	3	0	1	2	0	.333
2010	Detroit k	A.L.	2B-OF	68	253	26	69	17	1	6	34	1	.273
Major League Totals			13 Yrs.	1277	4578	725	1309	264	50	121	647	73	.286
	Division Series												
2000	Seattle	A.L.	PH	1	1	0	1	0	0	0	1	0	1.000
2006	Detroit	A.L.	SS	4	14	3	8	3	0	1	2	0	.571
Division Series Totals				5	15	3	9	3	0	1	3	0	.600
	Championship Series												
2000	Seattle	A.L.	3B	2	5	1	1	0	0	1	2	0	.200
2001	Seattle	A.L.	SS	3	8	1	2	0	0	0	0	0	.250
2006	Detroit	A.L.	1B-SS	4	16	1	3	1	0	0	0	0	.188
Championship Series Totals				9	29	3	6	1	0	1	2	0	.207
	World Series Record												
2006	Detroit	A.L.	SS-1B	5	17	2	6	1	1	0	2	1	.353

a On disabled list from June 1 to September 12, 1994.

b On disabled list from May 21 to September 11, 1996.
c Traded by Houston Astros to Seattle Mariners with pitcher Freddy Garcia and player to be named later for pitcher Randy Johnson, July 31, 1998.
d Seattle Mariners received pitcher John Halama to complete trade, October 1, 1998.
e On disabled list from April 11 to November 12, 1999.
f On disabled list from April 13 to April 27, 2000.
g On disabled list from July 29 to August 23, 2003.
h Traded to Detroit Tigers for infielder Ramon Santiago and infielder Juan Gonzalez, January 8, 2004.
i On disabled list from June 8 to June 26 and August 11 to September 23, 2005.
j On disabled list from May 5 to July 24, 2009.
k On disabled list from April 23 to May 28 and July 25 to August 9 and August 17 to October 6, 2010.

GUILLEN, JOSE MANUEL

Born, San Cristobal, Dominican Republic, May 17, 1976.
Bats Right. Throws Right. Height, 5 feet, 11 inches. Weight, 195 pounds.

Year	Club	Lea	Pos	G	AB	R	H	2B	3B	HR	RBI	SB	Avg
1993	Pittsburgh	Dominican	OF	63	234	39	53	3	4	11	31	10	.226
1994	Pirates	Gulf Coast	OF	30	110	17	29	4	1	4	11	2	.264
1995	Erie	N.Y.-Penn.	OF	66	258	41	81	17	1	12	46	1	.314
1995	Augusta	So.Atl.	OF	10	34	6	8	1	1	2	6	0	.235
1996	Lynchburg	Carolina	OF	136	528	78	170	30	0	21	94	24	.322
1997	Pittsburgh	N.L.	OF	143	498	58	133	20	5	14	70	1	.267
1998	Pittsburgh	N.L.	OF	153	573	60	153	38	2	14	84	3	.267
1999	Pittsburgh	N.L.	OF	40	120	18	32	6	0	1	18	1	.267
1999	Nashville	P.C.	OF	35	132	28	44	10	0	5	22	0	.333
1999	Durham	Int.	OF	9	34	8	13	1	0	3	12	0	.382
1999	Tampa Bay a-b	A.L.	OF	47	168	24	41	10	0	2	13	0	.244
2000	Durham	Int.	OF	19	78	20	33	8	2	9	31	0	.423
2000	Tampa Bay c	A.L.	OF	105	316	40	80	16	5	10	41	3	.253
2001	Durham	Int.	OF	33	119	18	35	9	0	7	29	0	.294
2001	Tampa Bay d-e-f	A.L.	OF	41	135	14	37	5	0	3	11	2	.274
2002	Colorado Springs	P.C.	OF	5	17	2	7	3	0	0	5	0	.412
2002	Louisville	Int.	OF	8	29	4	9	4	0	2	8	0	.310
2002	Arizona-Cincinnati g	N.L.	OF	85	240	25	57	7	0	8	31	4	.237
2003	Louisville	Int.	OF	4	15	4	5	1	0	0	3	1	.333
2003	Cincinnati	N.L.	OF	91	315	52	106	21	1	23	63	1	.337
2003	Oakland h-i	A.L.	OF	45	170	25	45	7	1	8	23	0	.265
2004	Anaheim j	A.L.	OF	148	565	88	166	28	3	27	104	5	.294
2005	Washington	N.L.	OF	148	551	81	156	32	2	24	76	1	.283
2006	Potomac	Carolina	OF	3	6	2	3	0	0	2	3	0	.500
2006	Washington k-l	N.L.	OF	69	241	28	52	15	1	9	40	1	.216
2007	Seattle m	A.L.	OF	153	593	84	172	28	2	23	99	5	.290
2008	Kansas City	A.L.	OF	153	598	66	158	42	1	20	97	2	.264
2009	Kansas City n	A.L.	OF	81	281	30	68	8	0	9	40	1	.242
2010	Kansas City	A.L.	DH-OF	106	396	46	101	17	2	16	62	1	.255
2010	San Francisco o-p	N.L.	OF	42	128	9	34	5	0	3	15	0	.266
Major League Totals			14 Yrs.	1650	5888	748	1591	305	25	214	887	31	.270
	Division Series												
2003	Oakland	A.L.	OF	4	11	1	5	1	0	0	1	0	.455

a Traded to Tampa Bay Devil Rays with pitcher Jeff Sparks for catcher Joe Oliver and catcher Humberto Cota, July 23, 1999.
b On disabled list from July 23 to 30, 1999.
c On disabled list from March 28 to April 11, 2000.
d On disabled list from May 18 to June 24 and June 25 to July 30, 2001.
e On disabled list from August 7 to 24, 2001.
f Released by Tampa Bay Devil Rays, November 27, 2001. Signed with Arizona Diamondbacks, December 12, 2001.
g Released by Arizona Diamondbacks, July 22, 2002. Signed with Cincinnati Reds organization, July 26, 2002.
h Traded to Oakland Athletics for pitcher Aaron Harang, pitcher Joe Valentine and pitcher Jeff Bruksch, July 30, 2003.
i Filed for free agency, October 30, 2003. Signed with Anaheim Angels, December 19, 2003.
j Traded to Washington Nationals for outfielder Juan Rivera and infielder Maicer Izturis, November 19, 2004.
k On disabled list from May 26 to June 10 and July 19 to October 9, 2006.
l Filed for free agency, October 29, 2006. Signed with Seattle Mariners, December 4, 2006.
m Filed for free agency, November 12, 2007. Signed with Kansas City Royals, December 6, 2007.
n On disabled list from April 10 to April 25 and July 23 to September 1 and September 18 to November 16, 2009.
o Traded to San Francisco Giants for player to be named later, August 13, 2010. San Francisco Giants received pitcher Kevin Pucetas to complete trade, October 15, 2010.
p Filed for free agency, November 1, 2010.

GUTIERREZ, FRANKLIN RAFAEL

Born, Caracas, Venezuela, February 21, 1983.
Bats Right. Throws Right. Height, 6 feet, 2 inches. Weight, 180 pounds.

Year	Club	Lea	Pos	G	AB	R	H	2B	3B	HR	RBI	SB	Avg
2001	Dodgers	Gulf Coast	OF	56	234	38	63	16	0	4	30	9	.269
2002	Las Vegas	P.C.	OF	2	10	2	3	2	0	0	2	0	.300
2002	South Bend	So.Atl.	OF	92	361	61	102	18	4	12	45	13	.283
2003	Vero Beach	Fla.St.	OF	110	425	65	120	28	5	20	68	17	.282
2003	Jacksonville	Southern	OF	18	67	12	21	3	2	4	12	3	.313
2004	Akron	Eastern	OF	70	262	38	79	24	2	5	35	6	.302
2004	Buffalo a	Int.	DH	7	27	4	4	1	0	1	3	0	.148
2005	Akron	Eastern	OF	95	383	70	100	25	2	11	42	14	.261
2005	Buffalo	Int.	OF	19	67	10	17	6	2	0	7	2	.254
2005	Cleveland	A.L.	OF	7	1	2	0	0	0	0	0	0	.000
2006	Buffalo	Int.	OF	90	349	63	97	27	0	9	38	13	.278
2006	Cleveland	A.L.	OF	43	136	21	37	9	0	1	8	0	.272
2007	Buffalo	Int.	OF	30	129	29	44	7	0	4	16	7	.341
2007	Cleveland b	A.L.	OF	100	271	41	72	13	2	13	36	8	.266
2008	Cleveland c	A.L.	OF	134	399	54	99	26	2	8	41	9	.248
2009	Seattle	A.L.	OF	153	565	85	160	24	1	18	70	16	.283
2010	Seattle	A.L.	OF	152	568	61	139	25	3	12	64	25	.245
Major League Totals			6 Yrs.	589	1940	264	507	97	8	52	219	58	.261
	Division Series												
2007	Cleveland	A.L.	OF	4	10	2	2	0	0	0	0	0	.200
	Championship Series												
2007	Cleveland	A.L.	OF	6	19	3	4	0	0	1	4	0	.211

a Traded to Cleveland Indians with player to be named later for outfielder Milton Bradley, April 4, 2004. Cleveland Indians received pitcher Andrew Brown to complete trade, May 19, 2004.
b On disabled list from March 23 to April 13, 2007.
c Traded to Seattle Mariners for pitcher Luis Valbuena and pitcher Joe Smith, December 10, 2008.

GUZMAN, CRISTIAN

Born, Santo Domingo, Dominican Republic, March 21, 1978.
Bats Both. Throws Right. Height, 6 feet. Weight, 215 pounds.

Year	Club	Lea	Pos	G	AB	R	H	2B	3B	HR	RBI	SB	Avg
1995	Yankees	Domincan	SS	46	160	24	43	6	5	3	20	11	.269
1996	Yankees	Gulf Coast	SS	42	170	37	50	8	2	1	21	7	.294
1997	Tampa	Fla.St.	SS	4	14	4	4	0	0	0	1	0	.286
1997	Greensboro	So.Atl.	SS	124	495	68	135	21	4	4	52	23	.273
1998	New Britain a	Eastern	SS	140	566	68	157	29	5	1	40	23	.277
1999	Minnesota b	A.L.	SS	131	420	47	95	12	3	1	26	9	.226
2000	Minnesota	A.L.	SS	156	631	89	156	25	*20	8	54	28	.247
2001	Twins	Gulf Coast	SS	5	16	4	4	0	1	0	0	0	.250
2001	Minnesota c	A.L.	SS	118	493	80	149	28	*14	10	51	25	.302
2002	Minnesota	A.L.	SS	148	623	80	170	31	6	9	59	12	.273
2003	Minnesota	A.L.	SS	143	534	78	143	15	*14	3	53	18	.268
2004	Minnesota d	A.L.	SS	145	576	84	158	31	4	8	46	10	.274
2005	Washington	N.L.	SS	142	456	39	100	19	6	4	31	7	.219
2006	Washington e	N.L.	INJURED — Did Not Play										
2007	Washington f	N.L.	SS	46	174	31	57	6	6	2	14	2	.328
2008	Washington	N.L.	SS	138	579	77	183	35	5	9	55	6	.316
2009	Washington g	N.L.	SS	135	531	74	151	24	7	6	52	4	.284
2010	Frisco	Texas	SS-2B-3B	4	13	1	4	0	0	0	3	1	.308
2010	Washington	N.L.	2B-SS-OF	89	319	44	90	11	4	2	25	4	.282
2010	Texas h-i-j	A.L.	2B-SS	15	46	4	7	1	0	0	1	0	.152
Major League Totals			11 Yrs.	1406	5382	727	1459	238	89	62	467	125	.271
	Division Series												
2002	Minnesota	A.L.	SS	5	21	5	6	2	0	1	2	2	.286
2003	Minnesota	A.L.	SS	4	13	1	2	0	0	0	0	0	.154
2004	Minnesota	A.L.	SS	4	15	2	5	0	0	0	0	1	.333
Division Series Totals				13	49	8	13	2	0	1	2	3	.265
	Championship Series												
2002	Minnesota	A.L.	SS	5	18	1	3	1	0	0	0	0	.167

a Traded by New York Yankees to Minnesota Twins with pitcher Eric Milton, pitcher Danny Mota, outfielder Brian Buchanan and cash for infielder Chuck Knoblauch, February 6, 1998.
b On disabled list from May 27 to June 11, 1999.
c On disabled list from July 13 to August 17, 2001.
d Filed for free agency, October 29, 2004. Signed with Washington Nationals, November 16, 2004.
e On disabled list from March 24 to October 9, 2006.

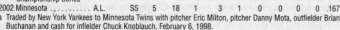

f On disabled list from April 3 to May 7 and June 25 to September 21, 2007.
g On disabled list from April 14 to April 29, 2009.
h Traded to Texas Rangers with cash for pitcher Ryan Tatusko and pitcher Tanner Roark, July 31, 2010.
i On disabled list from August 14 to September 1, 2010.
j Filed for free agency, November 1, 2010.

GWYNN, ANTHONY KEITH JR. (TONY)

Born, Long Beach, California, October 4, 1982.
Bats Left. Throws Right. Height, 6 feet. Weight, 195 pounds.

Year	Club	Lea	Pos	G	AB	R	H	2B	3B	HR	RBI	SB	Avg
2003	Beloit	Midwest	OF	61	236	35	66	8	0	1	33	14	.280
2004	Huntsville	Southern	OF	138	534	74	130	20	5	2	37	35	.243
2005	Huntsville	Southern	OF	133	509	83	138	21	5	1	41	34	.271
2006	Nashville	P.C.	OF	112	447	73	134	21	5	4	42	30	.300
2006	Milwaukee	N.L.	OF	32	77	5	20	2	1	0	4	3	.260
2007	Nashville	P.C.	OF	32	126	19	36	3	3	0	13	4	.286
2007	Milwaukee	N.L.	OF	69	123	13	32	3	2	0	10	8	.260
2008	Nashville	P.C.	OF	93	375	47	103	9	3	2	26	20	.275
2008	Milwaukee a	N.L.	OF	29	42	5	8	1	0	0	1	3	.190
2009	Nashville	P.C.	OF	38	152	34	47	8	1	1	9	15	.309
2009	San Diego b	N.L.	OF	119	393	59	106	11	6	2	21	11	.270
2010	San Diego c-d	N.L.	OF	117	289	30	59	9	3	3	20	17	.204
Major League Totals			5 Yrs.	366	924	112	225	26	12	5	56	42	.244
	Division Series												
2008	Milwaukee	N.L.	PH	3	3	0	1	0	0	0	0	0	.333

a On disabled list from April 4 to April 23, 2008.
b Traded to San Diego Padres for outfielder Jody Gerut, May 21, 2009.
c On disabled list from August 19 to September 13, 2010.
d Not offered contract, December 2, 2010. Signed with Los Angeles Dodgers, December 11, 2010.

HAFNER, TRAVIS LEE

Born, Jamestown, North Dakota, June 3, 1977.
Bats Left. Throws Right. Height, 6 feet, 3 inches. Weight, 240 pounds.

Year	Club	Lea	Pos	G	AB	R	H	2B	3B	HR	RBI	SB	Avg
1997	Rangers	Gulf Coast	1B-OF	55	189	38	54	14	0	5	24	7	.286
1998	Savannah	So.Atl.	1B-3B-OF	123	405	62	96	15	4	16	84	7	.237
1999	Savannah	So.Atl.	1B	134	480	94	140	30	4	28	111	5	.292
2000	Charlotte a	Fla.St.	1B-3B	122	436	90	151	34	1	22	109	0	.346
2001	Tulsa b	Texas	1B	88	323	59	91	25	0	20	74	3	.282
2002	Oklahoma	P.C.	1B	110	401	79	137	22	1	21	77	2	.342
2002	Texas c	A.L.	DH-1B	23	62	6	15	4	1	1	6	0	.242
2003	Buffalo	Int.	1B	29	100	15	27	4	0	2	10	2	.270
2003	Cleveland d	A.L.	DH-1B	91	291	35	74	19	3	14	40	2	.254
2004	Cleveland	A.L.	DH-1B	140	482	96	150	41	3	28	109	3	.311
2005	Akron	Eastern	DH	3	9	0	0	0	0	0	0	0	.000
2005	Cleveland e	A.L.	DH-1B	137	486	94	148	42	0	33	108	0	.305
2006	Cleveland	A.L.	DH-1B	129	454	100	140	31	1	42	117	0	.308
2007	Cleveland	A.L.	DH-1B	152	545	80	145	25	2	24	100	1	.266
2008	Buffalo	Int.	DH	7	22	4	7	3	0	0	4	0	.318
2008	Cleveland f	A.L.	DH	57	198	21	39	10	0	5	24	1	.197
2009	Columbus	Int.	DH	12	39	6	13	4	0	1	8	0	.333
2009	Cleveland g	A.L.	DH	94	338	46	92	19	0	16	49	0	.272
2010	Cleveland h	A.L.	DH	118	396	46	110	29	0	13	50	2	.278
Major League Totals			9 Yrs.	941	3252	524	913	220	10	176	603	9	.281
	Division Series												
2007	Cleveland	A.L.	DH	4	16	4	4	0	0	1	2	0	.250
	Championship Series												
2007	Cleveland	A.L.	DH	7	27	2	4	1	0	1	2	0	.148

a On disabled list from August 6 to 22, 2000.
b On disabled list from April 5 to May 11, 2001.
c Traded to Cleveland Indians with pitcher Aaron Myette for catcher Einar Diaz and pitcher Ryan Drese, December 6, 2002.
d On disabled list from May 10 to May 26, 2003.
e On disabled list from July 17 to August 4, 2005.
f On disabled list from May 26 to September 9, 2008.
g On disabled list from April 29 to June 5, 2009.
h On disabled list from July 29 to August 15, 2010.

HAIRSTON, JERRY WAYNE JR.

Born, Naperville, Illinois, May 29, 1976.
Bats Right. Throws Right. Height, 5 feet, 10 inches. Weight, 185 pounds.

Year	Club	Lea	Pos	G	AB	R	H	2B	3B	HR	RBI	SB	Avg
1997	Bluefield	Appal.	SS	59	221	44	73	13	4	2	36	13	.330
1998	Frederick	Carolina	SS-2B	80	293	56	83	22	3	5	33	13	.283
1998	Bowie	Eastern	2B-SS	55	221	42	72	12	3	5	37	6	.326
1998	Baltimore	A.L.	2B	6	7	2	0	0	0	0	0	0	.000
1999	Rochester	Int.	2B	107	413	65	120	24	5	7	48	19	.291
1999	Baltimore	A.L.	2B	50	175	26	47	12	1	4	17	9	.269
2000	Rochester	Int.	2B-SS	58	201	43	59	15	1	4	21	6	.294
2000	Orioles	Gulf Coast	2B	4	10	3	3	2	0	0	3	4	.300
2000	Frederick	Carolina	2B	2	8	1	3	2	0	0	1	0	.375
2000	Baltimore a	A.L.	2B	49	180	27	46	5	0	5	19	8	.256
2001	Baltimore	A.L.	2B	159	532	63	124	25	5	8	47	29	.233
2002	Baltimore	A.L.	2B	122	426	55	114	25	3	5	32	21	.268
2003	Aberdeen	N.Y.-Penn.	2B	2	3	2	1	0	0	0	0	1	.333
2003	Bowie	Eastern	2B	6	20	4	6	1	0	1	2	0	.300
2003	Baltimore b	A.L.	2B	58	218	25	59	12	2	2	21	14	.271
2004	Bowie	Eastern	2B	5	13	4	2	1	0	0	2	2	.154
2004	Baltimore c	A.L.	OF-2B-3B	86	287	43	87	19	1	2	24	13	.303
2005	Iowa	P.C.	2B-OF	5	22	3	7	0	1	0	2	3	.318
2005	Chicago d-e	N.L.	OF-2B-SS	114	380	51	99	25	2	4	30	8	.261
2006	Chicago	N.L.	2B-OF-1B	38	82	8	17	3	0	0	4	3	.207
2006	Texas f-g	A.L.	OF-SS-2B-3B	63	88	17	18	3	1	0	6	2	.205
2007	Frisco	Texas	DH	3	12	2	2	1	0	1	2	0	.167
2007	Oklahoma	P.C.	SS-OF	4	15	2	2	0	0	1	1	0	.133
2007	Texas h-i	A.L.	OF-2B-3B-SS	73	159	22	30	7	0	3	16	5	.189
2008	Louisville	Int.	OF-SS-3B-2B	20	79	11	30	8	2	4	19	1	.380
2008	Cincinnati j-k	N.L.	OF-SS-2B-3B	80	261	47	85	20	2	6	36	15	.326
2009	Cincinnati	N.L.	3B-SS-OF-2B	86	307	47	78	18	1	8	27	7	.254
2009	New York l-m	A.L.	OF-3B-SS-2B	45	76	15	18	5	0	2	12	0	.237
2010	San Diego n-o	N.L.	SS-2B-OF-3B	119	430	53	105	13	2	10	50	9	.244
Major League Totals			13 Yrs.	1148	3608	501	927	192	20	59	341	143	.257
	Division Series												
2009	New York	A.L.	PH	1	0	0	0	0	0	0	0	0	.000
	Championship Series												
2009	New York	A.L.	OF	2	2	1	1	0	0	0	0	0	.500
	World Series Record												
2009	New York	A.L.	OF	3	6	0	1	0	0	0	0	0	.167

a On disabled list from May 16 to July 4, 2000.
b On disabled list from May 21 to September 4, 2003.
c On disabled list from March 31 to May 11 and from August 18 to November 3, 2004.
d Traded to Chicago Cubs with infielder Mike Fontenot and pitcher Dave Crouthers for outfielder Sammy Sosa, February 2, 2005.
e On disabled list from August 4 to August 19, 2005.
f Traded to Texas Rangers for infielder Phil Nevin, May 31, 2006.
g Filed for free agency, October 13, 2006. re-signed with Texas Rangers organization, January 5, 2007.
h On disabled list from May 17 to June 5 and August 8 to August 29, 2007.
i Filed for free agency, October 30, 2007. Signed with Cincinnati Reds organization, March 3, 2008.
j On disabled list from June 10 to June 26 and July 14 to August 1 and August 18 to September 8, 2008.
k Filed for free agency, October 31, 2008, re-signed with Cincinnati Reds, January 7, 2009.
l Traded to New York Yankees for catcher Chase Weems, July 31, 2009.
m Filed for free agency, November 10, 2009. Signed with the San Diego Padres, January 18, 2010.
n On disabled list from August 28 to September 12, 2010.
o Filed for free agency, November 1, 2010. Signed with Washington Nationals, January 19, 2011.

HAIRSTON, SCOTT ALEXANDER

Born, Fort Worth, Texas, May 25, 1980.
Bats Right. Throws Right. Height, 6 feet. Weight, 190 pounds.

Year	Club	Lea	Pos	G	AB	R	H	2B	3B	HR	RBI	SB	Avg
2001	Missoula	Pioneer	2B	74	291	81	101	16	6	14	65	2	.347
2002	Lancaster	Calif.	2B-3B	18	79	20	32	11	1	6	26	1	.405
2002	South Bend	Midwest	2B-3B	109	394	79	131	35	4	16	72	9	.332
2003	Tucson	P.C.	DH	1	0	0	0	0	0	0	1	0	.000
2003	El Paso	Texas	2B	88	337	53	93	21	7	10	47	6	.276
2004	Tucson	P.C.	2B-OF	28	115	29	36	8	3	5	20	0	.313
2004	Arizona	N.L.	2B-OF	101	339	39	84	15	6	13	29	3	.248
2005	Arizona	N.L.	OF	15	20	0	2	1	0	0	0	0	.100
2005	Tucson a	P.C.	OF-2B	58	209	45	65	8	3	16	40	3	.311
2006	Tucson	P.C.	OF	98	381	83	123	22	1	26	81	3	.323

Year	Club	Lea	Pos	G	AB	R	H	2B	3B	HR	RBI	SB	Avg
2006	Arizona b	N.L.	OF	9	15	2	6	2	0	0	2	0	.400
2007	Arizona-San Diego c-d	N.L.	OF	107	263	37	64	18	2	11	36	2	.243
2008	San Diego e	N.L.	OF-2B	112	326	42	81	18	3	17	31	3	.248
2009	Lake Elsinore	Calif.	OF	3	10	1	1	0	0	0	0	0	.100
2009	San Diego	N.L.	OF	56	197	26	59	14	1	10	29	8	.299
2009	Oakland f-g-h	A.L.	OF	60	233	24	55	13	1	7	35	3	.236
2010	Lake Elsinore	Calif.	OF	3	7	1	4	1	0	0	1	0	.571
2010	San Diego i-j	N.L.	OF	104	295	34	62	10	0	10	36	6	.210
Major League Totals			7 Yrs.	564	1688	204	413	91	13	68	198	25	.245

a On disabled list from September 2 to November 14, 2005.
b On disabled list from June 20 to July 29, 2006.
c Traded to San Diego Padres for pitcher Leo Rosales, July 27, 2007.
d On disabled list from August 10 to September 8, 2007.
e On disabled list from August 28 to October 2, 2008.
f On disabled list from June 3 to June 23, 2009.
g Traded to Oakland Athletics for pitcher Ryan Webb, pitcher Craig Italiano and player to be named later, July 5, 2009. San Diego Padres received pitcher Sean Gallagher to complete trade, July 28, 2009.
h Traded to San Diego Padres with outfielder Aaron Cunningham for third baseman Kevin Kouzmanoff and infielder Eric Sogard, January 16, 2010.
i On disabled list from May 16 to June 2, 2010.
j Not offered contract, December 2, 2010.

HALL, WILLIAM (BILL)

Born, Tupelo, Mississippi, December 28, 1979.
Bats Right. Throws Right. Height, 6 feet. Weight, 210 pounds.

Year	Club	Lea	Pos	G	AB	R	H	2B	3B	HR	RBI	SB	Avg
1998	Helena	Pioneer	SS	29	85	11	15	3	0	0	5	5	.176
1999	Ogden	Pioneer	SS	69	280	41	81	15	2	6	31	19	.289
2000	Beloit	Midwest	SS	130	470	57	123	30	6	3	41	10	.262
2001	High Desert	California	SS	89	346	61	105	21	6	15	51	18	.303
2001	Huntsville	Southern	SS	41	160	14	41	8	1	3	14	5	.256
2002	Indianapolis	Int.	SS	134	465	35	106	20	1	4	31	17	.228
2002	Milwaukee	N.L.	SS-3B	19	36	3	7	1	1	1	5	0	.194
2003	Indianapolis	Int.	2B-SS-OF	89	354	57	100	25	2	5	32	10	.282
2003	Milwaukee	N.L.	2B-SS-3B	52	142	23	37	9	2	5	20	1	.261
2004	Milwaukee	N.L.	2B-SS-3B	126	390	43	93	20	3	9	53	12	.238
2005	Milwaukee	N.L.	SS-3B-2B	146	501	69	146	39	6	17	62	18	.291
2006	Milwaukee	N.L.	SS-3B-OF-2B	148	537	101	145	39	4	35	85	8	.270
2007	Azl Brewers	Arizona	OF	2	6	0	1	0	0	0	2	0	.167
2007	Milwaukee a	N.L.	OF	136	452	59	115	35	0	14	63	4	.254
2008	Milwaukee	N.L.	3B-2B	128	404	50	91	22	1	15	55	5	.225
2009	Nashville	P.C.	SS-OF	4	14	1	4	1	0	1	4	1	.286
2009	Milwaukee	N.L.	3B-OF	76	214	22	43	12	0	6	24	1	.201
2009	Seattle b-c	A.L.	OF-2B-3B	34	120	10	24	8	1	2	12	1	.200
2010	Boston d	A.L.	OF-2B-SS-3B	120	344	44	85	16	1	18	46	9	.247
Major League Totals			9 Yrs.	985	3140	424	786	201	19	122	425	59	.250
	Division Series												
2008	Milwaukee	N.L.	3B	3	8	1	2	0	0	0	0	0	.250

a On disabled list from July 6 to July 25, 2007.
b Traded to Seattle Mariners for pitcher Ruben Flores, August 19, 2009.
c Traded to Boston Red Sox with player to be named later for infielder Casey Kotchman, January 7, 2010. Boston Red Sox received pitcher Miguel Celestino to complete trade, March 18, 2010.
d Filed for free agency, November 4, 2010. Signed with Houston Astros, December 20, 2010.

HAMILTON, JOSHUA HOLT (JOSH)

Born, Raleigh, North Carolina, May 21, 1981.
Bats Left. Throws Left. Height, 6 feet, 4 inches. Weight, 235 pounds.

Year	Club	Lea	Pos	G	AB	R	H	2B	3B	HR	RBI	SB	Avg
1999	Princeton	Appal.	OF	56	236	49	82	20	4	10	48	17	.347
1999	Hudson Valley	N.Y.-Penn.	OF	16	72	7	14	3	0	0	7	1	.194
2000	Charleston-SC	So.Atl.	OF	96	391	62	118	23	3	13	61	14	.302
2001	Charleston-SC	So.Atl.	OF	4	11	3	4	1	0	1	2	0	.364
2001	Orlando	Southern	OF	23	89	5	16	5	0	0	4	2	.180
2002	Bakersfield	Calif.	OF	56	211	32	64	14	1	9	44	10	.303
2003-05							Did Not Play						
2006	Hudson Valley a	N.Y.-Penn.	OF	15	50	7	13	3	1	0	5	0	.260
2007	Louisville	Int.	OF	11	40	9	14	1	0	4	8	3	.350

Year Club	Lea	Pos	G	AB	R	H	2B	3B	HR	RBI	SB	Avg
2007 Cincinnati b-c..........	N.L.	OF	90	298	52	87	17	2	19	47	3	.292
2008 Texas	A.L.	OF	156	624	98	190	35	5	32	*130	9	.304
2009 Frisco..............	Texas	DH	1	4	1	1	0	0	0	1	1	.250
2009 Okla................	P.C.	OF	7	28	3	5	2	1	0	0	1	.179
2009 Texas d..............	A.L.	OF	89	336	43	90	19	2	10	54	8	.268
2010 Texas e..............	A.L.	OF	133	518	95	186	40	3	32	100	8	*.359
Major League Totals		4 Yrs.	468	1776	288	553	111	12	93	331	28	.311
Division Series												
2010 Texas	A.L.	OF	5	18	1	2	0	0	0	1	1	.111
Championship Series												
2010 Texas	A.L.	OF	6	20	6	7	1	0	4	7	3	.350
World Series Record												
2010 Texas	A.L.	OF	5	20	2	2	0	0	1	1	0	.100

a Selected by Chicago Cubs from Tampa Bay Devil Rays in Rule V draft, December 7, 2006. Sold to Cincinnati Reds, December 7, 2006.
b On disabled list from May 19 to June 4 and July 8 to August 12, 2007.
c Traded to Texas Rangers for pitcher Edinson Volquez and pitcher Danny Herrera, December 21, 2007.
d On disabled list from April 27 to May 12 and June 1 to July 6, 2009.
e Selected Most Valuable Player in American League for 2010.

HANIGAN, RYAN M.

Born, Washington, District of Columbia, August 16, 1980.
Bats Right. Throws Right. Height, 6 feet. Weight, 195 pounds.

Year Club	Lea	Pos	G	AB	R	H	2B	3B	HR	RBI	SB	Avg
2002 Dayton............	Midwest	C	6	11	1	3	1	0	0	0	0	.273
2003 Louisville..............	Int.	C	1	3	1	1	0	0	0	0	0	.333
2003 Dayton............	Midwest	C	92	311	43	86	12	0	1	31	3	.277
2004 Potomac...........	Carolina	C	119	429	58	127	21	0	5	56	6	.296
2005 Chattanooga.......	Southern	1B-C	100	333	45	107	14	1	4	29	4	.321
2006 Louisville..............	Int.	C-1B	8	13	2	2	0	0	0	1	0	.154
2006 Chattanooga.......	Southern	C-1B-OF	56	126	17	31	2	0	0	14	0	.246
2007 Chattanooga.......	Southern	C-1B	60	197	30	59	14	1	3	27	0	.299
2007 Louisville..............	Int.	C-1B	41	127	16	32	5	0	1	9	0	.252
2007 Cincinnati............	N.L.	C	5	10	3	3	1	0	0	2	0	.300
2008 Louisville..............	Int.	C-1B	75	272	37	88	14	0	4	35	1	.324
2008 Cincinnati............	N.L.	C	31	85	9	23	2	0	2	9	0	.271
2009 Louisville..............	Int.	C	5	18	4	7	2	0	0	2	0	.389
2009 Cincinnati a	N.L.	C	90	251	22	66	6	1	3	11	0	.263
2010 Louisville..............	Int.	C	13	46	6	11	3	0	0	2	0	.239
2010 Cincinnati b	N.L.	C	70	203	25	61	11	0	5	40	0	.300
Major League Totals		4 Yrs.	196	549	59	153	20	1	10	62	0	.279
Division Series												
2010 Cincinnati............	N.L.	C	2	4	0	0	0	0	0	0	0	.000

a On disabled list from August 24 to September 9, 2009.
b On disabled list from May 29 to July 9, 2010.

HARDY, JAMES JERRY (J.J.)

Born, Tucson, Arizona, August 19, 1982.
Bats Right. Throws Right. Height, 6 feet, 2 inches. Weight, 190 pounds.

Year Club	Lea	Pos	G	AB	R	H	2B	3B	HR	RBI	SB	Avg
2001 Brewers............	Arizona	SS	5	20	6	5	2	1	0	1	0	.250
2001 Ogden	Pioneer	SS	35	125	20	31	5	0	2	15	1	.248
2002 High Desert	California	SS	84	335	53	98	19	1	6	48	9	.293
2002 Huntsville.........	Southern	SS	38	145	14	33	7	0	1	13	1	.228
2003 Huntsville.........	Southern	SS	114	416	67	116	26	0	12	62	6	.279
2004 Indianapolis...........	Int.	SS	26	101	17	28	10	0	4	20	0	.277
2005 Milwaukee	N.L.	SS	124	372	46	92	22	1	9	50	0	.247
2006 Milwaukee a..........	N.L.	SS	35	128	13	31	5	0	5	14	1	.242
2007 Milwaukee	N.L.	SS	151	592	89	164	30	1	26	80	2	.277
2008 Milwaukee	N.L.	SS	146	569	78	161	31	4	24	74	2	.283
2009 Nashville	P.C.	SS	18	71	7	18	2	0	4	12	0	.254
2009 Milwaukee b..........	N.L.	SS	115	414	53	95	16	2	11	47	0	.229
2010 Beloit	Midwest	SS	3	10	0	2	0	0	0	0	0	.200
2010 Minnesota c-d	A.L.	SS	101	340	44	91	19	3	6	38	1	.268
Major League Totals		6 Yrs.	672	2415	323	634	123	11	81	303	6	.263
Division Series												
2008 Milwaukee	N.L.	SS	4	14	2	6	1	0	0	2	0	.429

Year	Club	Lea	Pos	G	AB	R	H	2B	3B	HR	RBI	SB	Avg
2010	Minnesota	A.L.	SS	3	10	0	1	1	0	0	0	0	.100
Division Series Totals				7	24	2	7	2	0	0	2	0	.292

a On disabled list from May 17 to October 31, 2006.
b Traded to Minnesota Twins for outfielder Carlos Gomez, November 6, 2009.
c On disabled list from May 5 to May 25 and June 7 to July 3, 2010.
d Traded to Baltimore Orioles with infielder Brendan Harris and cash for pitcher Jim Hoey and pitcher Brett Jacobson, December 9, 2010.

HARRIS, WILLIAM CHARLES (WILLIE)

Born, Cairo, Georgia, June 22, 1978.
Bats Left. Throws Right. Height, 5 feet, 9 inches. Weight, 175 pounds.

Year	Club	Lea	Pos	G	AB	R	H	2B	3B	HR	RBI	SB	Avg
1999	Bluefield	Appal.	2B	5	22	3	6	1	0	0	3	1	.273
1999	Delmarva	So.Atl.	2B-OF	66	272	42	72	13	3	2	32	17	.265
2000	Delmarva	So.Atl.	2B-OF-SS	133	474	106	130	27	10	6	60	38	.274
2001	Bowie	Eastern	2B-OF	133	525	83	160	27	4	9	49	54	.305
2001	Baltimore	A.L.	OF	9	24	3	3	1	0	0	0	0	.125
2002	Charlotte	Int.	2B-OF	89	360	54	102	16	5	5	33	32	.283
2002	Chicago a	A.L.	2B-OF	49	163	14	38	4	0	2	12	8	.233
2003	Charlotte	Int.	2B-OF	28	100	22	38	6	1	6	13	9	.380
2003	Chicago b	A.L.	OF-2B	79	137	19	28	3	1	0	5	12	.204
2004	Chicago	A.L.	2B-OF	129	409	68	107	15	2	2	27	19	.262
2005	Charlotte	Int.	2B	28	109	21	29	11	1	1	10	10	.266
2005	Chicago	A.L.	2B-SS	56	121	17	31	2	1	1	8	10	.256
2006	Boston c-d	A.L.	OF-2B	47	45	17	7	2	0	0	1	6	.156
2006	Pawtucket	Int.	OF-2B	60	218	32	48	6	1	8	17	11	.220
2007	Richmond	Int.	3B-2B-OF	17	58	17	21	7	2	1	7	7	.362
2007	Atlanta e	N.L.	OF-3B	117	344	56	93	20	8	2	32	17	.270
2008	Washington	N.L.	OF-2B-3B-SS	140	367	58	92	14	4	13	43	13	.251
2009	Syracuse	Int.	OF-2B	5	18	2	4	1	0	0	1	0	.222
2009	Washington f	N.L.	OF-2B-3B	137	323	47	76	18	6	7	27	11	.235
2010	Washington g	N.L.	OF-3B	132	224	25	41	6	2	10	32	5	.183
Major League Totals			10 Yrs.	895	2157	324	516	85	24	37	187	101	.239
	Division Series												
2005	Chicago	A.L.	2B	1	1	0	1	0	0	0	1	0	1.000
	World Series Record												
2005	Chicago	A.L.	2B	2	1	1	1	0	0	0	0	1	1.000

a Traded to Chicago White Sox for outfielder Chris Singleton, January 29, 2002.
b On disabled list from May 22 to June 16, 2003.
c Not offered contract, December 21, 2005. Signed with Boston Red Sox organization, January 19, 2006.
d Filed for free agency, October 2, 2006. Signed with Atlanta Braves organization, December 9, 2006.
e Released by Atlanta Braves, December 12, 2007. Signed with Washington Nationals, December 13, 2007.
f On disabled list from April 13 to April 28, 2009.
g Filed for free agency, November 1, 2010. Signed with New York Mets organization, January 17, 2011.

HART, JON COREY (COREY)

Born, Bowling Green, Kentucky, March 24, 1982.
Bats Right. Throws Right. Height, 6 feet, 6 inches. Weight, 215 pounds.

Year	Club	Lea	Pos	G	AB	R	H	2B	3B	HR	RBI	SB	Avg
2000	Ogden	Pioneer	1B	57	216	32	62	9	1	2	30	6	.287
2001	Ogden	Pioneer	1B-OF	69	262	53	89	18	1	11	62	14	.340
2002	High Desert	Calif.	3B-1B	100	393	76	113	26	10	22	84	24	.288
2002	Huntsville	Southern	3B-1B	28	94	16	25	3	0	2	15	3	.266
2003	Huntsville	Southern	3B-OF	130	493	70	149	40	1	13	94	25	.302
2004	Indianapolis	Int.	OF-1B	121	440	68	124	29	8	15	67	17	.282
2004	Milwaukee	N.L.	DH	1	1	0	0	0	0	0	0	0	.000
2005	Milwaukee	N.L.	OF	21	57	9	11	2	1	2	7	2	.193
2005	Nashville	P.C.	OF-1B	113	429	85	132	29	9	17	69	31	.308
2006	Milwaukee	N.L.	OF-1B	87	237	32	67	13	2	9	33	5	.283
2007	Milwaukee	N.L.	OF	140	505	86	149	33	9	24	81	23	.295
2008	Milwaukee	N.L.	OF	157	612	76	164	45	6	20	91	23	.268
2009	Nashville	P.C.	OF	4	10	5	5	1	0	1	3	0	.500
2009	Milwaukee a	N.L.	OF	115	419	64	109	24	3	12	48	11	.260
2010	Milwaukee	N.L.	OF	145	558	91	158	34	4	31	102	7	.283
Major League Totals			7 Yrs.	666	2389	358	658	151	25	98	362	71	.275
	Division Series												
2008	Milwaukee	N.L.	OF	4	13	0	3	0	0	0	0	0	.231

a On disabled list from August 2 to September 8, 2009.

HAWPE, BRADLEY BONTE (BRAD)

Born, Fort Worth, Texas, June 22, 1979.
Bats Left. Throws Left. Height, 6 feet, 3 inches. Weight, 205 pounds.

Year	Club	Lea	Pos	G	AB	R	H	2B	3B	HR	RBI	SB	Avg
2000	Portland	Northwest	OF-1B	62	205	38	59	19	2	7	29	2	.288
2001	Asheville	So.Atl.	OF-1B	111	393	78	105	22	3	22	72	7	.267
2002	Salem	Carolina	1B	122	450	87	156	38	2	22	97	1	.347
2003	Tulsa	Texas	OF-1B	93	346	52	96	27	0	17	68	1	.277
2004	Colorado Springs	P.C.	OF	92	345	62	111	19	1	31	86	3	.322
2004	Colorado	N.L.	OF	42	105	12	26	3	2	3	9	1	.248
2005	Colorado Springs	P.C.	OF	7	28	7	13	3	0	3	11	0	.464
2005	Colorado a	N.L.	OF	101	305	38	80	10	3	9	47	2	.262
2006	Colorado	N.L.	OF	150	499	67	146	33	6	22	84	5	.293
2007	Colorado	N.L.	OF	152	516	80	150	33	4	29	116	0	.291
2008	Colorado Springs	P.C.	OF	3	11	1	1	0	0	0	0	0	.091
2008	Colorado b	N.L.	OF	138	488	69	138	24	3	25	85	2	.283
2009	Colorado	N.L.	OF	145	501	82	143	42	3	23	86	1	.285
2010	Charlotte	Fla.St.	DH	3	6	0	1	0	0	0	0	0	.167
2010	Modesto	Calif.	OF	1	4	0	1	1	0	0	1	0	.250
2010	Colorado Springs	P.C.	OF	2	9	2	2	1	0	0	0	0	.222
2010	Colorado	N.L.	OF-1B	88	259	24	66	21	2	7	37	2	.255
2010	Tampa Bay c-d-e	A.L.	1B-OF	15	39	7	7	0	0	2	7	0	.179
Major League Totals			7 Yrs.	831	2712	379	756	166	23	120	471	13	.279
	Division Series												
2007	Colorado	N.L.	OF	3	11	1	3	0	0	0	0	0	.273
2009	Colorado	N.L.	OF	2	4	0	0	0	0	0	0	0	.000
Division Series Totals				5	15	1	3	0	0	0	0	0	.200
	Championship Series												
2007	Colorado	N.L.	OF	4	12	2	4	0	0	0	2	0	.333
	World Series Record												
2007	Colorado	N.L.	OF	4	16	1	4	0	1	1	2	0	.250

a On disabled list from July 12 to September 2, 2005.
b On disabled list from May 21 to June 6, 2008.
c On disabled list from April 25 to May 10, 2010.
d Released by Colorado Rockies, August 24, 2010. Signed with Tampa Bay Rays organization, August 29, 2010.
e Filed for free agency, November 1, 2010. Signed with San Diego Padres, January 3, 2011.

HEADLEY, CHASE JORDAN

Born, Fountain, Colorado, May 9, 1984.
Bats Both. Throws Right. Height, 6 feet, 2 inches. Weight, 195 pounds.

Year	Club	Lea	Pos	G	AB	R	H	2B	3B	HR	RBI	SB	Avg
2005	Fort Wayne	Midwest	3B	4	15	2	3	0	0	0	1	0	.200
2005	Eugene	Northwest	3B	57	220	29	59	14	3	6	33	1	.268
2006	Lake Elsinore	Calif.	3B	129	484	79	141	33	0	12	73	4	.291
2007	San Antonio	Texas	3B	121	433	82	143	38	5	20	78	1	.330
2007	San Diego	N.L.	3B	8	18	1	4	1	0	0	0	0	.222
2008	Portland	P.C.	OF-3B	65	259	49	79	24	1	13	40	0	.305
2008	San Diego	N.L.	OF-3B	91	331	34	89	19	2	9	38	4	.269
2009	San Diego	N.L.	OF-3B-1B	156	543	62	142	31	2	12	64	10	.262
2010	San Diego	N.L.	3B	161	610	77	161	29	3	11	58	17	.264
Major League Totals			4 Yrs.	416	1502	174	396	80	7	32	160	31	.264

HEISEY, CHRISTOPHER J. (CHRIS)

Born, Lancaster, Pennsylvania, December 14, 1984.
Bats Right. Throws Right. Height, 6 feet. Weight, 215 pounds.

Year	Club	Lea	Pos	G	AB	R	H	2B	3B	HR	RBI	SB	Avg
2006	Billings	Pioneer	OF	70	245	46	70	10	0	6	37	11	.286
2007	Sarasota	Fla.St.	OF	12	43	6	15	1	0	1	5	3	.349
2007	Dayton	Midwest	OF	104	374	60	108	24	2	9	46	19	.289
2008	Sarasota	Fla.St.	OF	117	436	77	125	31	7	7	51	27	.287
2008	Chattanooga	Southern	OF	19	79	11	25	6	1	2	10	5	.316
2009	Louisville	Int.	OF	63	245	37	68	17	1	9	37	8	.278
2009	Carolina	Southern	OF	71	271	54	94	18	2	13	40	13	.347
2010	Louisville	Int.	OF	20	79	6	19	3	0	4	13	2	.241
2010	Cincinnati	N.L.	OF	97	201	33	51	10	1	8	21	1	.254
	Division Series												
2010	Cincinnati	N.L.	OF	1	2	0	0	0	0	0	0	0	.000

HELMS, WESLEY RAY (WES)

Born, Gastonia, North Carolina, May 12, 1976.
Bats Right. Throws Right. Height, 6 feet, 4 inches. Weight, 230 pounds.

Year	Club	Lea	Pos	G	AB	R	H	2B	3B	HR	RBI	SB	Avg
1994	Braves	Gulf Coast	3B	56	184	22	49	15	1	4	29	6	.266
1995	Macon	So.Atl.	3B	136	539	89	149	32	1	11	85	2	.276
1996	Durham	Carolina	3B	67	258	40	83	19	2	13	54	1	.322
1996	Greenville	Southern	3B	64	231	24	59	13	2	4	22	2	.255
1997	Richmond	Int.	3B	32	110	11	21	4	0	3	15	1	.191
1997	Greenville	Southern	3B	86	314	50	93	14	1	11	44	3	.296
1998	Richmond	Int.	3B	125	451	56	124	27	1	13	75	6	.275
1998	Atlanta	N.L.	3B	7	13	2	4	1	0	1	2	0	.308
1999	Braves	Gulf Coast	DH	9	33	1	15	2	0	0	10	0	.455
1999	Greenville a-b	Southern	1B	30	113	15	34	6	0	8	26	1	.301
2000	Richmond	Int.	3B	136	539	74	155	27	7	20	88	0	.288
2000	Atlanta	N.L.	3B	6	5	0	1	0	0	0	0	0	.200
2001	Atlanta	N.L.	1B-3B-OF	100	216	28	48	10	3	10	36	1	.222
2002	Atlanta c-d	N.L.	1B-3B-OF	85	210	20	51	16	0	6	22	1	.243
2003	Indianapolis	Int.	3B	2	5	0	2	0	0	0	0	0	.400
2003	Milwaukee e	N.L.	3B	134	476	56	124	21	0	23	67	0	.261
2004	Indianapolis	Int.	3B	6	19	4	6	1	0	0	1	0	.316
2004	Milwaukee f	N.L.	3B-1B	92	274	24	72	13	1	4	28	0	.263
2005	Milwaukee g	N.L.	3B-1B	95	168	18	50	13	1	4	24	0	.298
2006	Florida h	N.L.	1B-3B-OF	140	240	30	79	19	5	10	47	0	.329
2007	Philadelphia	N.L.	3B-1B	112	280	21	69	19	0	5	39	0	.246
2008	Florida i	N.L.	3B-1B-OF	132	251	28	61	11	0	5	31	0	.243
2009	Florida	N.L.	3B-1B	113	214	18	58	11	0	3	33	1	.271
2010	Florida	N.L.	3B-1B	127	254	25	56	12	4	4	39	0	.220
Major League Totals			12 Yrs.	1143	2601	270	673	146	14	75	368	3	.259
	Division Series												
2002	Atlanta	N.L.	1B	1	0	0	0	0	0	0	0	0	.000
2007	Philadelphia	N.L.	3B	2	2	1	0	0	0	0	0	0	.000
Division Series Totals				3	2	1	0	0	0	0	0	0	.000

a On Atlanta disabled list from April 3 to July 15 and September 4 to November 1, 1999.
b On Greenville disabled list from August 15 to September 4, 1999.
c On disabled list from August 10 to September 10, 2002.
d Traded to Milwaukee Brewers with pitcher John Foster for pitcher Ray King, December 16, 2002.
e On disabled list from August 6 to August 22, 2003.
f On disabled list from May 19 to June 28, 2004.
g Filed for free agency, October 27, 2005. Signed with Florida Marlins, December 30, 2005.
h Filed for free agency, October 28, 2006. Signed with Philadelphia Phillies, November 17, 2006.
i Sold to Florida Marlins, April 5, 2008.

HELTON, TODD LYNN

Born, Knoxville, Tennessee, August 20, 1973.
Bats Left. Throws Left. Height, 6 feet, 2 inches. Weight, 210 pounds.

Year	Club	Lea	Pos	G	AB	R	H	2B	3B	HR	RBI	SB	Avg
1995	Asheville	So. Atl.	1B	54	201	24	51	11	1	1	15	1	.254
1996	New Haven	Eastern	1B	93	319	46	106	24	2	7	51	2	.332
1996	Colo Sprngs	P.C.	1B-OF	21	71	13	25	4	1	2	13	0	.352
1997	Colo Sprngs	P.C.	1B-OF	99	392	87	138	31	2	16	88	3	.352
1997	Colorado	N.L.	OF-1B	35	93	13	26	2	1	5	11	0	.280
1998	Colorado	N.L.	1B	152	530	78	167	37	1	25	97	3	.315
1999	Colorado	N.L.	1B	159	578	114	185	39	5	35	113	7	.320
2000	Colorado	N.L.	1B	160	580	138	*216	*59	2	42	*147	5	*.372
2001	Colorado	N.L.	1B	159	587	132	197	54	2	49	146	7	.336
2002	Colorado	N.L.	1B	156	553	107	182	39	4	30	109	5	.329
2003	Colorado	N.L.	1B	160	583	135	209	49	5	33	117	0	.358
2004	Colorado	N.L.	1B	154	547	115	190	49	2	32	96	3	.347
2005	Colo Sprngs	P.C.	2B	2	5	1	3	2	0	0	1	0	.600
2005	Colorado a	N.L.	1B	144	509	92	163	45	2	20	79	3	.320
2006	Colorado Springs	P.C.	1B	2	6	0	2	0	0	0	0	0	.333
2006	Colorado b	N.L.	1B	145	546	94	165	40	5	15	81	3	.302
2007	Colorado	N.L.	1B	154	557	86	178	42	2	17	91	0	.320
2008	Colorado c	N.L.	1B	83	299	39	79	16	0	7	29	0	.264
2009	Colorado	N.L.	1B	151	544	79	177	38	3	15	86	0	.325
2010	Casper	Pioneer	1B	3	10	1	5	1	0	0	5	0	.500
2010	Colorado d	N.L.	1B	118	398	48	102	18	1	8	37	0	.256
Major League Totals			14 Yrs.	1930	6904	1270	2236	527	35	333	1239	36	.324

Year	Club	Lea	Pos	G	AB	R	H	2B	3B	HR	RBI	SB	Avg
	Division Series												
2007	Colorado	N.L.	1B	3	12	1	1	0	1	0	0	0	.083
2009	Colorado	N.L.	1B	4	16	5	3	0	0	0	2	0	.188
Division Series Totals				7	28	6	4	0	1	0	2	0	.143
	Championship Series												
2007	Colorado	N.L.	1B	4	14	3	3	0	0	0	1	0	.214
	World Series Record												
2007	Colorado	N.L.	1B	4	15	2	5	2	0	0	1	0	.333

a On disabled list from July 26 to August 10, 2005.
b On disabled list from April 20 to May 5, 2006.
c On disabled list from July 3 to September 12, 2008.
d On disabled list from July 7 to August 3, 2010.

HERMIDA, JEREMY RYAN

Born, Atlanta, Georgia, January 30, 1984.
Bats Left. Throws Right. Height, 6 feet, 3 inches. Weight, 210 pounds.

Year	Club	Lea	Pos	G	AB	R	H	2B	3B	HR	RBI	SB	Avg
2002	Marlins	Gulf Coast	OF	38	134	15	30	7	3	0	14	5	.224
2002	Jamestown	N.Y.-Penn.	OF	13	47	8	15	2	1	0	7	1	.319
2003	Albuquerque	P.C.	OF	1	3	0	0	0	0	0	0	0	.000
2003	Greensboro	So.Atl.	OF	133	468	73	133	23	5	6	49	28	.284
2004	Jupiter	Fla.St.	OF	91	340	53	101	17	1	10	50	10	.297
2005	Carolina	Southern	OF	118	386	77	113	29	2	18	63	23	.293
2005	Florida	N.L.	OF	23	41	9	12	2	0	4	11	2	.293
2006	Jupiter	Fla.St.	OF	6	17	3	3	1	0	0	2	0	.176
2006	Florida a	N.L.	OF	99	307	37	77	19	1	5	28	4	.251
2007	Jupiter	Fla.St.	OF	3	12	4	4	0	1	2	5	0	.333
2007	Albuquerque	P.C.	OF	2	5	0	1	0	0	0	2	0	.200
2007	Florida b	N.L.	OF	123	429	54	127	32	1	18	63	3	.296
2008	Jupiter	Fla.St.	OF	5	15	6	5	1	0	1	1	0	.333
2008	Florida c	N.L.	OF	142	502	74	125	22	3	17	61	6	.249
2009	Florida d	N.L.	OF	129	429	48	111	14	2	13	47	5	.259
2010	Portland	Eastern	OF	3	11	1	3	2	0	0	3	0	.273
2010	Sacramento	P.C.	OF	3	13	3	4	2	0	0	3	0	.308
2010	Pawtucket	Int.	OF	19	66	7	19	1	0	2	12	0	.288
2010	Boston-Oakland e-f-g	A.L.	OF	73	222	19	48	12	0	6	29	1	.216
Major League Totals			6 Yrs.	589	1930	241	500	101	7	63	239	21	.259

a On disabled list from April 12 to May 22, 2006.
b On disabled list from March 23 to May 14, 2007.
c On disabled list from March 21 to April 9, 2008.
d Traded to Boston Red Sox for pitcher Jose Alvarez and pitcher Hunter Jones, November 5, 2009.
e On disabled list from June 10 to July 22, 2010.
f Released by Boston Red Sox, August 31, 2010. Signed with Oakland Athletics organization, September 3, 2010.
g Filed for free agency, October 12, 2010. Signed with Cincinnati Reds organization, January 4, 2011.

HERNANDEZ (MARIN), RAMON JOSE

Born, Caracas, Venezuela, May 20, 1976.
Bats Right. Throws Right. Height, 6 feet. Weight, 225 pounds.

Year	Club	Lea	Pos	G	AB	R	H	2B	3B	HR	RBI	SB	Avg
1994	Oakland	Domincan	C	42	134	24	33	2	0	2	18	1	.246
1995	Athletics	Arizona	C-1B-3B	48	143	37	52	9	6	4	37	6	.364
1996	W Michigan	Midwest	C-1B	123	447	62	114	26	2	12	68	2	.255
1997	Visalia	California	C-1B	86	332	57	120	21	2	15	85	2	.361
1997	Huntsville	Southern	C-1B-3B	44	161	27	31	3	0	4	24	0	.193
1998	Huntsville	Southern	DH-C-1B	127	479	83	142	24	1	15	98	4	.296
1999	Vancouver	P.C.	C	77	291	38	76	11	3	13	55	1	.261
1999	Oakland a	A.L.	C	40	136	13	38	7	0	3	21	1	.279
2000	Oakland	A.L.	C	143	419	52	101	19	0	14	62	1	.241
2001	Oakland	A.L.	C-1B	136	453	55	115	25	0	15	60	1	.254
2002	Oakland	A.L.	C	136	403	51	94	20	0	7	42	0	.233
2003	Oakland b	A.L.	C	140	483	70	132	24	1	21	78	0	.273
2004	Portland	P.C.	C	7	19	2	6	1	0	0	6	0	.316
2004	San Diego c	N.L.	C	111	384	45	106	23	0	18	63	1	.276
2005	San Diego d-e	N.L.	C	99	369	36	107	19	2	12	58	1	.290
2006	Baltimore	A.L.	C-1B	144	501	66	138	29	2	23	91	1	.275
2007	Aberdeen	N.Y.-Penn.	C	2	4	2	2	1	0	0	0	1	.500
2007	Frederick	Carolina	C	2	6	0	2	1	0	0	0	0	.333

Year	Club	Lea	Pos	G	AB	R	H	2B	3B	HR	RBI	SB	Avg
2007	Baltimore f	A.L.	C-1B	106	364	40	94	18	0	9	62	1	.258
2008	Baltimore g	A.L.	C-1B	133	463	49	119	22	1	15	65	0	.257
2009	Cincinnati h	N.L.	C-1B-3B	81	287	25	74	13	1	5	37	1	.258
2010	Cincinnati i-j	N.L.	C-1B	97	313	30	93	18	1	7	48	0	.297
Major League Totals			12 Yrs.	1366	4575	532	1211	237	8	149	687	8	.265
	Division Series												
2000	Oakland	A.L.	C	5	16	3	6	2	0	0	3	0	.375
2001	Oakland	A.L.	C	5	10	0	0	0	0	0	0	0	.000
2002	Oakland	A.L.	C	5	17	0	1	0	0	0	0	0	.059
2003	Oakland	A.L.	C	4	15	1	3	0	0	0	2	0	.200
2005	San Diego	N.L.	C	3	11	2	5	0	0	1	1	0	.455
2010	Cincinnati	N.L.	C	3	7	0	1	1	0	0	0	0	.143
Division Series Totals				25	76	6	16	3	0	1	6	0	.211

a On disabled list from July 26 to August 27, 1999.
b Traded to San Diego Padres with outfielder Terrence Long for outfielder Mark Kotsay, November 26, 2003.
c On disabled list from June 21 to July 26, 2004.
d On disabled list from June 18 to July and July 25 to September 2, 2005.
e Filed for free agency, October 27, 2005. Signed with Baltimore Orioles, December 13, 2005.
f On disabled list from March 31 to April 26 and June 7 to June 22, 2007.
g Traded to Cincinnati Reds with cash for outfielder Ryan Freel, infielder Brandon Waring and infielder Justin Turner, December 9, 2008.
h On disabled list from July 17 to September 19, 2009.
i On disabled list from July 5 to July 22, 2010.
j Filed for free agency, November 1, 2010, re-signed with Cincinnati Reds, November 15, 2010.

HERRERA, JONATHAN ALEJANDRO

Born, Maracaibo, Venezuela, November 3, 1984.
Bats Both. Throws Right. Height, 5 feet, 9 inches. Weight, 150 pounds.

Year	Club	Lea	Pos	G	AB	R	H	2B	3B	HR	RBI	SB	Avg
2003	Casper	Pioneer	2B	39	159	27	49	7	1	1	25	12	.308
2004	Asheville	So.Atl.	SS	95	380	71	106	20	2	6	35	21	.279
2005	Modesto	Calif.	SS-2B	73	310	48	80	9	4	2	30	9	.258
2005	Asheville	So.Atl.	SS-2B	19	87	17	27	2	0	0	5	6	.310
2006	Modesto	Calif.	SS-2B-3B	127	487	87	151	20	8	7	77	34	.310
2007	Tulsa	Texas	SS	131	509	65	131	24	4	3	40	18	.257
2008	Colorado	N.L.	2B-SS	28	61	5	14	1	1	0	3	1	.230
2008	Colorado Springs a	P.C.	SS-2B	66	226	40	70	7	0	3	31	15	.310
2009	Colorado Springs	P.C.	SS-2B	119	381	63	102	11	5	2	33	16	.268
2010	Colorado Springs	P.C.	SS-2B-3B	58	222	30	58	6	1	2	17	3	.261
2010	Colorado	N.L.	2B-3B-SS	76	222	34	63	6	2	1	21	2	.284
Major League Totals			2 Yrs.	104	283	39	77	7	3	1	24	3	.272

a Not offered contract, December 12, 2008, re-signed with Colorado Rockies, December 13, 2008.

HEYWARD, JASON ADENOLITH

Born, Ridgewood, New Jersey, August 9, 1989.
Bats Left. Throws Left. Height, 6 feet, 5 inches. Weight, 240 pounds.

Year	Club	Lea	Pos	G	AB	R	H	2B	3B	HR	RBI	SB	Avg
2007	Danville	Appal.	OF	4	16	3	5	1	0	0	1	0	.313
2007	Braves	Gulf Coast	OF	8	27	1	8	4	0	1	5	1	.296
2008	Myrtle Beach	Carolina	OF	7	22	3	4	2	0	0	4	0	.182
2008	Rome	So.Atl.	OF	120	449	88	145	27	6	11	52	15	.323
2009	Myrtle Beach	Carolina	OF	49	189	34	56	12	0	10	31	4	.296
2009	Gwinnett	Int.	OF	3	11	3	4	0	0	0	2	1	.364
2009	Mississippi	Southern	OF	47	162	32	57	13	4	7	30	5	.352
2010	Atlanta a	N.L.	OF	142	520	83	144	29	5	18	72	11	.277
	Division Series												
2010	Atlanta	N.L.	OF	4	16	0	2	0	0	0	0	0	.125

a On disabled list from June 27 to July 15, 2010.

HILL, AARON WALTER

Born, Visalia, California, March 21, 1982.
Bats Right. Throws Right. Height, 5 feet, 11 inches. Weight, 195 pounds.

Year	Club	Lea	Pos	G	AB	R	H	2B	3B	HR	RBI	SB	Avg
2003	Dunedin	Fla.St.	SS	32	119	26	34	7	0	0	11	1	.286
2003	Auburn	N.Y.-Penn.	SS	33	122	22	44	4	0	4	34	1	.361
2004	New Hampshire	Eastern	SS	135	479	78	134	26	2	11	80	3	.280

Year	Club	Lea	Pos	G	AB	R	H	2B	3B	HR	RBI	SB	Avg
2005	Syracuse	Int.	SS	38	156	22	47	11	0	5	18	2	.301
2005	Toronto	A.L.	3B-2B-SS	105	361	49	99	25	3	3	40	2	.274
2006	Toronto	A.L.	2B-SS	155	546	70	159	28	3	6	50	5	.291
2007	Toronto	A.L.	2B	160	608	87	177	47	2	17	78	4	.291
2008	Toronto a	A.L.	2B	55	205	19	54	14	0	2	20	4	.263
2009	Toronto	A.L.	2B	158	*682	103	195	37	0	36	108	6	.286
2010	Toronto b	A.L.	2B	138	528	70	108	22	0	26	68	2	.205
Major League Totals			6 Yrs.	771	2930	398	792	173	8	90	364	23	.270

a On disabled list from June 5 to November 14, 2008.

b On disabled list from April 8 to April 23, 2010.

HILL, KOYIE DOLAN

Born, Tulsa, Oklahoma, March 9, 1979.

Bats Both. Throws Right. Height, 6 feet. Weight, 190 pounds.

Year	Club	Lea	Pos	G	AB	R	H	2B	3B	HR	RBI	SB	Avg
2001	Wilmington	So.Atl.	C	134	498	65	150	20	2	8	79	21	.301
2002	Jacksonville	Southern	C	130	468	67	127	25	1	11	64	5	.271
2003	Jacksonville	Southern	C	25	101	9	23	7	0	0	7	2	.228
2003	Las Vegas	P.C.	C-1B	85	312	48	98	18	0	3	36	5	.314
2003	Los Angeles	N.L.	PH	3	3	0	1	1	0	0	0	0	.333
2004	Las Vegas	P.C.	C-1B-3B	91	350	57	100	26	0	13	54	0	.286
2004	Arizona a-b	N.L.	C	13	36	3	9	1	0	1	6	1	.250
2005	Tucson	P.C.	C	50	168	22	41	9	1	5	26	3	.244
2005	Arizona	N.L.	C	34	78	6	17	5	0	0	6	0	.218
2006	Columbus c-d	Int.	C	20	70	4	10	2	0	1	5	0	.143
2007	Chicago	N.L.	C-OF	36	93	7	15	4	0	2	12	0	.161
2007	Iowa	P.C.	C-1B	47	149	22	48	16	0	2	24	1	.322
2008	Iowa	P.C.	C-1B	113	364	56	100	24	2	17	64	3	.275
2008	Chicago	N.L.	C	10	21	0	2	1	0	0	1	0	.095
2009	Chicago	N.L.	C-3B	83	253	26	60	12	2	2	24	0	.237
2010	Chicago	N.L.	C-3B	77	215	18	46	13	1	1	17	1	.214
Major League Totals			7 Yrs.	256	699	60	150	37	3	6	66	2	.215

a Traded to Arizona Diamondbacks with pitcher Bill Murphy and outfielder Reggie Abercrombie for outfielder Steve Finley and catcher Brent Mayne, July 31, 2004.

b On disabled list from August 18 to October 4, 2004.

c Claimed on waivers by New York Yankees, April 6, 2006.

d Filed for free agency, October 2, 2006. Signed with Chicago Cubs organization, December 16, 2006.

HINSKE, ERIC SCOTT

Born, Menasha, Wisconsin, August 5, 1977.

Bats Left. Throws Right. Height, 6 feet, 2 inches. Weight, 235 pounds.

Year	Club	Lea	Pos	G	AB	R	H	2B	3B	HR	RBI	SB	Avg
1998	Williamsprt.	N.Y.-Penn.	1B	68	248	46	74	20	0	9	57	19	.298
1998	Rockford	Midwest	1B-OF	6	20	8	9	4	0	1	4	1	.450
1999	Daytona	Fla.St.	3B	130	445	76	132	28	6	19	79	16	.297
1999	Iowa	P.C.	1B	4	15	3	4	0	1	1	2	0	.267
2000	West Tenn	Southern	3B-1B-OF	131	436	76	113	21	9	20	73	14	.259
2001	Sacramento a-b-c	P.C.	3B-2B	121	436	71	123	27	1	25	79	20	.282
2002	Toronto d	A.L.	3B	151	566	99	158	38	2	24	84	13	.279
2003	Syracuse	Int.	3B	2	8	2	4	1	0	1	2	0	.500
2003	Toronto e	A.L.	3B	124	449	74	109	45	3	12	63	12	.243
2004	Toronto	A.L.	3B	155	570	66	140	23	3	15	69	12	.246
2005	Toronto	A.L.	1B	147	477	79	125	31	2	15	68	8	.262
2006	Toronto-Boston f	A.L.	OF-1B-3B	109	277	43	75	17	2	13	34	2	.271
2007	Boston g	A.L.	1B-OF	84	186	25	38	12	3	6	21	3	.204
2008	Tampa Bay h	A.L.	OF-1B-3B	133	381	59	94	21	1	20	60	10	.247
2009	Pittsburgh	N.L.	OF-1B-3B	54	106	18	27	9	0	1	11	0	.255
2009	New York i-j	A.L.	OF-3B	39	84	13	19	3	0	7	14	1	.226
2010	Atlanta k	N.L.	OF-1B-3B	131	281	38	72	21	1	11	51	0	.256
Major League Totals			9 Yrs.	1127	3377	514	857	220	17	124	475	61	.254
Division Series													
2007	Boston	A.L.	PH	1	1	0	0	0	0	0	0	0	.000
2010	Atlanta	N.L.	PH	4	3	1	1	0	0	1	2	0	.333
Division Series Totals				5	4	1	1	0	0	1	2	0	.250
Championship Series													
2007	Boston	A.L.	PH	1	0	1	0	0	0	0	0	0	.000

Year	Club	Lea	Pos	G	AB	R	H	2B	3B	HR	RBI	SB	Avg
	World Series Record												
2007	Boston	A.L.	PH	1	1	0	0	0	0	0	0	0	.000
2008	Tampa Bay	N.L.	PH	2	2	1	1	0	0	1	1	0	.500
2009	New York	A.L.	PH	1	0	1	0	0	0	0	0	0	.000
World Series Totals				4	3	2	1	0	0	1	1	0	.333

a Traded by Chicago Cubs with pitcher Scott Chiasson to Oakland A's for infielder Miguel Cairo, March 28, 2001.
b On disabled list from May 1 to 12, 2001.
c Traded by Oakland A's to Toronto Blue Jays with pitcher Justin Miller for pitcher Billy Koch, December 7, 2001.
d Selected Rookie of the Year in American League for 2002.
e On disabled list from May 2 to June 26, 2003.
f Sold to Boston Red Sox, August 17, 2006.
g Filed for free agency, October 30, 2007. Signed with Tampa Bay Rays organization, February 7, 2008.
h Filed for free agency, November 1, 2008. Signed with Pittsburgh Pirates, January 30, 2009.
i Traded to New York Yankees for outfielder Eric Fryer and pitcher Casey Erickson, June 30, 2009.
j Filed for free agency, November 9, 2009. Signed with Atlanta Braves, January 12, 2010.
k Filed for free agency, November 1, 2010, re-signed with Atlanta Braves, December 2, 2010.

HOLLIDAY, MATTHEW THOMAS (MATT)

Born, Stillwater, Oklahoma, January 15, 1980.
Bats Right. Throws Right. Height, 6 feet, 4 inches. Weight, 235 pounds.

Year	Club	Lea	Pos	G	AB	R	H	2B	3B	HR	RBI	SB	Avg
1998	Rockies	Arizona	3B	32	117	20	40	4	1	5	23	2	.342
1999	Asheville	So.Atl.	3B	121	444	76	117	28	0	16	64	10	.264
2000	Salem	Carolina	3B	123	460	64	126	28	2	7	72	11	.274
2001	Salem	Carolina	OF	72	255	36	70	16	1	11	52	11	.275
2002	Carolina	Southern	OF	130	463	79	128	19	2	10	64	16	.276
2003	Tulsa	Texas	OF	135	522	65	132	28	5	12	72	15	.253
2004	Colorado Springs	P.C.	OF	6	22	8	8	5	0	2	4	2	.364
2004	Colorado	N.L.	OF	121	400	65	116	31	3	14	57	3	.290
2005	Tulsa	Texas	OF	7	26	6	14	3	0	1	6	1	.538
2005	Colorado a	N.L.	OF	125	479	68	147	24	7	19	87	14	.307
2006	Colorado	N.L.	OF	155	602	119	196	45	5	34	114	10	.326
2007	Colorado	N.L.	OF	158	636	120	*216	*50	6	36	*137	11	*.340
2008	Colorado Springs	P.C.	OF	3	10	4	6	1	0	1	3	0	.600
2008	Colorado b-c	N.L.	OF	139	539	107	173	38	2	25	88	28	.321
2009	Oakland	A.L.	OF	93	346	52	99	23	1	11	54	12	.286
2009	St. Louis d-e	N.L.	OF	63	235	42	83	16	2	13	55	2	.353
2010	St. Louis	N.L.	OF	158	596	95	186	45	1	28	103	9	.312
Major League Totals			7 Yrs.	1012	3833	668	1216	272	27	180	695	89	.317
	Division Series												
2007	Colorado	N.L.	OF	3	13	2	3	0	0	2	3	0	.231
2009	St. Louis	N.L.	OF	3	12	1	2	0	0	1	1	0	.167
Division Series Totals				6	25	3	5	0	0	3	4	0	.200
	Championship Series												
2007	Colorado	N.L.	OF	4	15	3	5	0	0	2	4	0	.333
	World Series Record												
2007	Colorado	N.L.	OF	4	17	1	5	0	0	1	3	0	.294

a On disabled list from June 9 to July 19, 2005.
b On disabled list from May 25 to June 10, 2008.
c Traded to Oakland Athletics for outfielder Carlos Gonzalez, pitcher Greg Smith and pitcher Huston Street, November 12, 2008.
d Traded to St. Louis Cardinals for pitcher Clayton Mortensen, infielder Brett Wallace and outfielder Shane Peterson, July 24, 2009.
e Filed for free agency, November 5, 2009, re-signed with St. Louis Cardinals, January 5, 2010.

HOWARD, RYAN JAMES

Born, St. Louis, Missouri, November 19, 1979.
Bats Left. Throws Left. Height, 6 feet, 4 inches. Weight, 250 pounds.

Year	Club	Lea	Pos	G	AB	R	H	2B	3B	HR	RBI	SB	Avg
2001	Batavia	N.Y.-Penn.	1B	48	169	26	46	7	3	6	35	0	.272
2002	Lakewood	So.Atl.	1B	135	493	56	138	20	6	19	87	5	.280
2003	Clearwater	Fla.St.	1B	130	490	67	149	32	1	23	82	0	.304
2004	Reading	Eastern	1B	102	374	73	111	18	1	37	102	1	.297
2004	Scranton/W.B.	Int.	1B	29	111	21	30	10	0	9	29	0	.270
2004	Philadelphia	N.L.	1B	19	39	5	11	5	0	2	5	0	.282
2005	Scranton/WB.	Int.	1B	61	210	38	78	19	0	16	54	0	.371
2005	Philadelphia a	N.L.	1B	88	312	52	90	17	2	22	63	0	.288

Year	Club	Lea	Pos	G	AB	R	H	2B	3B	HR	RBI	SB	Avg
2006	Philadelphia b	N.L.	1B	159	581	104	182	25	1	*58	*149	0	.313
2007	Lakewood	So.Atl.	1B	2	6	1	2	1	0	1	4	0	.333
2007	Philadelphia c	N.L.	1B	144	529	94	142	26	0	47	136	1	.268
2008	Philadelphia	N.L.	1B	*162	610	105	153	26	4	*48	*146	1	.251
2009	Philadelphia	N.L.	1B	160	616	105	172	37	4	45	*141	8	.279
2010	Lakewood	So.Atl.	1B	1	2	0	1	1	0	0	1	0	.500
2010	Philadelphia d	N.L.	1B	143	550	87	152	23	5	31	108	1	.276
Major League Totals			7 Yrs.	875	3237	552	902	159	16	253	748	11	.279
	Division Series												
2007	Philadelphia	N.L.	1B	3	12	1	3	0	0	1	1	0	.250
2008	Philadelphia	N.L.	1B	4	11	1	2	1	0	0	1	0	.182
2009	Philadelphia	N.L.	1B	4	16	3	6	3	0	0	6	0	.375
2010	Philadelphia	N.L.	1B	3	11	0	3	0	0	0	0	0	.273
Division Series Totals				14	50	5	14	4	0	1	8	0	.280
	Championship Series												
2008	Philadelphia	N.L.	1B	5	20	4	6	1	0	0	2	0	.300
2009	Philadelphia	N.L.	1B	5	15	5	5	1	1	2	8	0	.333
2010	Philadelphia	N.L.	1B	6	22	1	7	4	0	0	0	0	.318
Championship Series Totals				16	57	10	18	6	1	2	10	0	.316
	World Series Record												
2008	Philadelphia	N.L.	1B	5	21	3	6	1	0	3	6	0	.286
2009	Philadelphia	N.L.	1B	6	23	3	4	2	0	1	3	1	.174
World Series Totals				11	44	6	10	3	0	4	9	1	.227

a Selected Rookie of the Year in National League for 2005.
b Selected Most Valuable Player in National League for 2006.
c On disabled list from May 10 to May 25, 2007.
d On disabled list from August 2 to August 21, 2010.

HUDSON, ORLANDO THILL

Born, Darlington, South Carolina, December 12, 1977.
Bats Both. Throws Right. Height, 6 feet. Weight, 185 pounds.

Year	Club	Lea	Pos	G	AB	R	H	2B	3B	HR	RBI	SB	Avg
1998	Medicine Hat	Pioneer	2B	65	242	50	71	18	1	8	42	6	.293
1999	Hagerstown	So.Atl.	3B	132	513	66	137	36	6	7	74	8	.267
2000	Dunedin	Fla.St.	3B-2B-SS	96	358	54	102	16	2	7	48	9	.285
2000	Tennessee	Southern	3B	39	134	17	32	4	3	2	15	3	.239
2001	Syracuse	Int.	2B-3B	55	194	31	59	14	3	4	27	11	.304
2001	Tennessee	Southern	2B-3B	84	306	51	94	22	8	4	52	8	.307
2002	Syracuse	Int.	2B	100	417	63	127	27	3	10	37	8	.305
2002	Toronto	A.L.	2B	54	192	20	53	10	5	4	23	0	.276
2003	Toronto	A.L.	2B	142	474	54	127	21	6	9	57	5	.268
2004	Toronto a	A.L.	2B	135	489	73	132	32	7	12	58	7	.270
2005	Toronto b	A.L.	2B	131	461	62	125	25	5	10	63	7	.271
2006	Arizona	N.L.	2B	157	579	87	166	34	9	15	67	9	.287
2007	Arizona	N.L.	2B	139	517	69	152	28	9	10	63	10	.294
2008	Arizona c-d	N.L.	2B	107	407	54	124	29	3	8	41	4	.305
2009	Los Angeles e	N.L.	2B	149	551	74	156	35	6	9	62	8	.283
2010	Minnesota f-g	A.L.	2B	126	497	80	133	24	5	6	37	10	.268
Major League Totals			9 Yrs.	1140	4167	573	1168	238	55	83	471	60	.280
	Division Series												
2009	Los Angeles	N.L.	2B	3	0	0	0	0	0	0	0	0	.000
2010	Minnesota	A.L.	2B	3	12	2	4	0	0	1	2	0	.333
Division Series Totals				6	12	2	4	0	0	1	2	0	.333
	Championship Series												
2009	Los Angeles	N.L.	2B	5	4	1	1	0	0	1	1	0	.250

a On disabled list from May 24 to June 16, 2004.
b Traded to Arizona Diamondbacks with pitcher Miguel Batista for infielder Troy Glaus and infielder Sergio Santos, December 27, 2005.
c On disabled list from August 10 to November 1, 2008.
d Filed for free agency, November 1, 2008. Signed with Los Angeles Dodgers, February 21, 2009.
e Filed for free agency, November 5, 2009. Signed with Minnesota Twins, February 4, 2010.
f On disabled list from May 31 to June 18 and July 24 to August 8, 2010.
g Filed for free agency, November 1, 2010. Signed with San Diego Padres, December 20, 2010.

HUFF, AUBREY LEWIS

Born, Marion, Ohio, December 20, 1976.
Bats Left. Throws Right. Height, 6 feet, 4 inches. Weight, 230 pounds.

Year	Club	Lea	Pos	G	AB	R	H	2B	3B	HR	RBI	SB	Avg
1998	Chston-SC	So.Atl.	3B	69	265	38	85	19	1	13	54	3	.321
1999	Orlando	Southern	3B	133	491	85	148	40	3	22	78	2	.301
2000	Durham	Int.	3B	108	408	73	129	36	3	20	76	2	.316
2000	Tampa Bay	A.L.	3B	39	122	12	35	7	0	4	14	0	.287
2001	Durham	Int.	3B	17	66	14	19	6	0	3	10	0	.288
2001	Tampa Bay	A.L.	3B-1B	111	411	42	102	25	1	8	45	1	.248
2002	Durham	Int.	1B	32	126	18	41	9	0	3	20	0	.325
2002	Tampa Bay	A.L.	DH-1B-3B	113	454	67	142	25	0	23	59	4	.313
2003	Tampa Bay	A.L.	OF-1B-3B	162	636	91	198	47	3	34	107	2	.311
2004	Tampa Bay	A.L.	3B-1B-OF	157	600	92	178	27	2	29	104	5	.297
2005	Tampa Bay	A.L.	OF-1B-3B	154	575	70	150	26	2	22	92	8	.261
2006	Visalia	Calif.	3B	2	8	2	2	1	0	0	1	0	.250
2006	Tampa Bay	A.L.	3B	63	230	26	65	15	1	8	28	0	.283
2006	Houston a-b-c	N.L.	OF-3B-1B	68	224	31	56	10	1	13	38	0	.250
2007	Baltimore	A.L.	DH-1B-3B	151	550	68	154	34	5	15	72	1	.280
2008	Baltimore	A.L.	DH-3B-1B	154	598	96	182	48	2	32	108	4	.304
2009	Baltimore-Detroit d-e	A.L.	1B	150	536	59	129	30	1	15	85	0	.241
2010	San Francisco f	N.L.	1B-OF	157	569	100	165	35	5	26	86	7	.290
Major League Totals			11 Yrs.	1479	5505	754	1556	329	23	229	838	32	.283
	Division Series												
2010	San Francisco	N.L.	1B	4	15	1	4	0	0	0	1	0	.267
	Championship Series												
2010	San Francisco	N.L.	1B	6	24	3	6	0	0	0	3	0	.250
	World Series Record												
2010	San Francisco	N.L.	1B-DH	5	17	3	5	2	0	1	4	0	.294

a On disabled list from April 12 to May 5, 2006.
b Traded to Houston Astros with cash for pitcher Mitch Talbot and infielder Ben Zobrist, July 12, 2006.
c Filed for free agency, October 28, 2006. Signed with Baltimore Orioles, December 30, 2006.
d Traded to Detroit Tigers for pitcher Brett Jacobson, August 17, 2009.
e Filed for free agency, November 5, 2009. Signed with San Francisco Giants, January 13, 2010.
f Filed for free agency, November 1, 2010, re-signed with San Francisco Giants, November 23, 2010.

HUNDLEY, NICHOLAS JOHN (NICK)

Born, Corvallis, Oregon, September 8, 1983.
Bats Right. Throws Right. Height, 6 feet, 1 inch. Weight, 210 pounds.

Year	Club	Lea	Pos	G	AB	R	H	2B	3B	HR	RBI	SB	Avg
2005	Fort Wayne	Midwest	C	10	36	2	8	2	0	0	5	0	.222
2005	Eugene	Northwest	C	43	148	30	37	7	1	7	22	1	.250
2006	Lake Elsinore	Calif.	C	47	176	18	49	13	0	3	23	1	.278
2006	Fort Wayne	Midwest	C	57	215	29	59	19	0	8	44	1	.274
2007	San Antonio	Texas	C	101	373	55	92	23	1	20	72	0	.247
2008	Portland	P.C.	C	58	224	33	52	13	0	12	39	0	.232
2008	San Diego	N.L.	C	60	198	21	47	7	1	5	24	0	.237
2009	Portland	P.C.	C	5	16	2	4	1	0	1	2	0	.250
2009	San Diego a	N.L.	C-OF	78	256	23	61	15	2	8	30	5	.238
2010	San Diego	N.L.	C	85	273	33	68	18	2	8	43	0	.249
Major League Totals			3 Yrs.	223	727	77	176	40	5	21	97	5	.242

a On disabled list from June 18 to August 12, 2009.

HUNTER, TORII KEDAR

Born, Pine Bluff, Arkansas, July 18, 1975.
Bats Right. Throws Right. Height, 6 feet, 2 inches. Weight, 215 pounds.

Year	Club	Lea	Pos	G	AB	R	H	2B	3B	HR	RBI	SB	Avg
1993	Twins	Gulf Coast	OF	28	100	6	19	3	0	0	8	4	.190
1994	Fort Wayne	Midwest	OF	91	335	57	98	17	1	10	50	8	.293
1995	Fort Myers	Fla.St.	OF	113	391	64	96	15	2	7	36	7	.246
1996	Ft. Myers	Fla.St.	OF	4	16	1	3	0	0	0	1	1	.188
1996	New Britain	Eastern	OF	99	342	49	90	20	3	7	33	7	.263
1997	New Britain	Eastern	OF	127	471	57	109	22	2	8	56	8	.231
1997	Minnesota	A.L.	OF	1	0	0	0	0	0	0	0	0	.000
1998	New Britain	Eastern	OF	82	308	42	87	24	3	6	32	11	.282
1998	Salt Lake	P.C.	OF	26	92	15	31	7	0	4	20	2	.337
1998	Minnesota	A.L.	OF	6	17	0	4	1	0	0	2	0	.235
1999	Minnesota	A.L.	OF	135	384	52	98	17	2	9	35	10	.255

Year Club	Lea	Pos	G	AB	R	H	2B	3B	HR	RBI	SB	Avg
2000 Salt Lake	P.C.	OF	55	209	58	77	17	2	18	61	11	.368
2000 Minnesota	A.L.	OF	99	336	44	94	14	7	5	44	4	.280
2001 Minnesota a	A.L.	OF	148	564	82	147	32	5	27	92	9	.261
2002 Minnesota	A.L.	OF	148	561	89	162	37	4	29	94	23	.289
2003 Minnesota	A.L.	OF	154	581	83	145	31	4	26	102	6	.250
2004 Minnesota b	A.L.	OF	138	520	79	141	37	0	23	81	21	.271
2005 Minnesota c	A.L.	OF	98	372	63	100	24	1	14	56	23	.269
2006 Minnesota d	A.L.	OF	147	557	86	155	21	2	31	98	12	.278
2007 Minnesota e	A.L.	OF	160	600	94	172	45	1	28	107	18	.287
2008 Los Angeles	A.L.	OF	146	551	85	153	37	2	21	78	19	.278
2009 Rancho Cucamonga	Calif.	OF	3	9	3	3	0	0	1	3	1	.333
2009 Los Angeles f	A.L.	OF	119	451	74	135	26	1	22	90	18	.299
2010 Los Angeles	A.L.	OF	152	573	76	161	36	0	23	90	9	.281
Major League Totals		14 Yrs.	1651	6067	907	1667	358	29	258	969	172	.275
Division Series												
2002 Minnesota	A.L.	OF	5	20	4	6	4	0	0	2	0	.300
2003 Minnesota	A.L.	OF	4	14	3	6	0	1	1	2	0	.429
2004 Minnesota	A.L.	OF	4	17	5	6	1	0	1	2	2	.353
2006 Minnesota	A.L.	OF	3	11	1	3	1	0	1	2	0	.273
2008 Los Angeles	A.L.	OF	4	18	0	7	0	0	0	5	0	.389
2009 Los Angeles	A.L.	OF	3	10	2	2	1	0	1	3	0	.200
Division Series Totals			23	90	15	30	7	1	4	16	2	.333
Championship Series												
2002 Minnesota	A.L.	OF	5	18	2	3	2	0	0	0	0	.167
2009 Los Angeles	A.L.	OF	6	23	2	7	1	0	0	2	1	.304
Championship Series Totals			11	41	4	10	3	0	0	2	1	.244

a On disabled list from April 6 to April 21, 2001.
b On disabled list from April 7 to April 25, 2004.
c On disabled list from July 30 to October 6, 2005.
d On disabled list from July 16 to July 31, 2006.
e Filed for free agency, October 29, 2007. Signed with Los Angeles Angels, November 21, 2007.
f On disabled list from July 8 to August 16, 2009.

IANNETTA, CHRISTOPHER DOMENIC (CHRIS)

Born, Providence, Rhode Island, April 8, 1983.
Bats Right. Throws Right. Height, 5 feet, 11 inches. Weight, 225 pounds.

Year Club	Lea	Pos	G	AB	R	H	2B	3B	HR	RBI	SB	Avg
2004 Asheville	So.Atl.	C	36	121	23	38	5	1	5	17	0	.314
2005 Tulsa	Texas	C	19	60	7	14	3	1	2	11	0	.233
2006 Tulsa	Texas	C	44	156	38	50	10	2	11	26	1	.321
2006 Colorado Springs	P.C.	C	47	151	23	53	11	2	3	22	0	.351
2006 Colorado	N.L.	C	21	77	12	20	4	0	2	10	0	.260
2007 Colorado Springs	P.C.	C	16	54	8	16	3	0	1	7	0	.296
2007 Colorado	N.L.	C	67	197	22	43	8	3	4	27	0	.218
2008 Colorado	N.L.	C-3B	104	333	50	88	22	2	18	65	0	.264
2009 Colorado Springs	P.C.	C	4	15	3	5	2	0	1	3	0	.333
2009 Colorado a	N.L.	C	93	289	41	66	15	2	16	52	0	.228
2010 Colorado Springs	P.C.	C-1B	17	63	17	22	7	0	5	21	0	.349
2010 Colorado	N.L.	C-1B-3B	61	188	20	37	6	1	9	27	1	.197
Major League Totals		5 Yrs.	346	1084	145	254	55	8	49	181	1	.234

a On disabled list from May 24 to June 9, 2009.

IBANEZ, RAUL JAVIER

Born, New York, New York, June 2, 1972.
Bats Left. Throws Right. Height, 6 feet, 2 inches. Weight, 220 pounds.

Year Club	Lea	Pos	G	AB	R	H	2B	3B	HR	RBI	SB	Avg
1992 Mariners	Arizona	DH-1B-C-OF	33	120	25	37	8	2	1	16	1	.308
1993 Appleton	Midwest	DH-1B-OF-C	52	157	26	43	9	0	5	21	0	.274
1993 Bellingham	Northwest	C	43	134	16	38	5	2	0	15	0	.284
1994 Appleton	Midwest	DH-C-1B-OF	91	327	55	102	30	3	7	59	10	.312
1995 Riverside	California	C-1B	95	361	59	120	23	9	20	108	4	.332
1996 Port City	Southern	OF-1B-C	19	76	12	28	8	1	1	13	3	.368
1996 Seattle	A.L.	DH	4	5	0	0	0	0	0	0	0	.000
1996 Tacoma	P.C.	OF-1B	111	405	59	115	20	3	11	47	7	.284
1997 Tacoma	P.C.	OF	111	438	84	133	30	5	15	84	7	.304
1997 Seattle	A.L.	OF	11	26	3	4	0	1	1	4	0	.154
1998 Tacoma	P.C.	OF	52	190	24	41	8	1	6	25	1	.216

Year Club	Lea	Pos	G	AB	R	H	2B	3B	HR	RBI	SB	Avg
1998 Seattle	A.L.	OF-1B	37	98	12	25	7	1	2	12	0	.255
1999 Tacoma	P.C.	OF	8	31	6	11	1	0	3	5	1	.355
1999 Seattle a	A.L.	OF-1B-C	87	209	23	54	7	0	9	27	5	.258
2000 Tacoma	P.C.	OF	10	40	3	10	4	0	0	6	0	.250
2000 Seattle b-c	A.L.	OF-1B	92	140	21	32	8	0	2	15	2	.229
2001 Omaha	P.C.	OF-SS	8	27	3	4	1	0	2	5	0	.148
2001 Kansas City	A.L.	OF-1B-3B	104	279	44	78	11	5	13	54	0	.280
2002 Kansas City	A.L.	OF-1B	137	497	70	146	37	6	24	103	5	.294
2003 Kansas City d	A.L.	OF-1B	157	608	95	179	33	5	18	90	8	.294
2004 Tacoma	P.C.	OF	4	17	2	4	1	0	0	1	0	.235
2004 Seattle e	A.L.	OF-1B	123	481	67	146	31	1	16	62	1	.304
2005 Seattle	A.L.	DH-OF-1B	*162	614	92	172	32	2	20	89	9	.280
2006 Seattle	A.L.	OF	159	626	103	181	33	5	33	123	2	.289
2007 Seattle	A.L.	OF	149	573	80	167	35	5	21	105	0	.291
2008 Seattle f	A.L.	OF	162	635	85	186	43	3	23	110	2	.293
2009 Reading	Eastern	OF	1	2	1	0	0	0	0	0	0	.000
2009 Lehigh Valley	Int.	OF	2	5	1	2	1	0	0	2	0	.400
2009 Philadelphia g	N.L.	OF	134	500	93	136	32	3	34	93	4	.272
2010 Philadelphia	N.L.	OF-1B	155	561	75	154	37	5	16	83	4	.275
Major League Totals		15 Yrs.	1673	5852	863	1660	346	42	232	970	42	.284
Division Series												
2000 Seattle	A.L.	OF	3	8	2	3	0	0	0	0	0	.375
2009 Philadelphia	N.L.	OF	4	13	2	4	1	0	0	5	0	.308
2010 Philadelphia	N.L.	OF	3	12	0	3	1	0	0	0	0	.250
Division Series Totals			10	33	4	10	2	0	0	5	0	.303
Championship Series												
2000 Seattle	A.L.	OF	6	9	0	0	0	0	0	0	0	.000
2009 Philadelphia	N.L.	OF	5	18	4	3	1	0	1	4	0	.167
2010 Philadelphia	N.L.	OF	5	19	1	4	1	0	0	0	0	.211
Championship Series Totals			16	46	5	7	2	0	1	4	0	.152
World Series Record												
2009 Philadelphia	N.L.	OF-DH	6	23	2	7	4	0	1	4	0	.304

a On disabled list from May 18 to June 3, 1999.
b On disabled list from August 7 to August 21, 2000.
c Not offered contract, December 21, 2000. Signed with Kansas City Royals organization, January 13, 2001.
d Filed for free agency, October 27, 2003. Signed with Seattle Mariners, November 19, 2003.
e On disabled list from June 3 to July 10, 2004.
f Filed for free agency, October 30, 2008. Signed with Philadelphia Phillies, December 16, 2008.
g On disabled list from June 18 to July 10, 2009.

INFANTE, OMAR RAFAEL

Born, Puerto La Cruz, Venezuela, December 26, 1981.
Bats Right. Throws Right. Height, 6 feet. Weight, 180 pounds.

Year Club	Lea	Pos	G	AB	R	H	2B	3B	HR	RBI	SB	Avg
1999 Tigers	Gulf Coast	SS	21	75	9	20	0	0	0	4	4	.267
2000 Lakeland	Fla.St.	SS	79	259	35	71	11	0	2	24	11	.274
2000 West Michigan	Midwest	SS-2B	12	48	7	11	0	0	0	5	1	.229
2001 Erie	Eastern	SS	132	540	86	163	21	4	2	62	27	.302
2002 Toledo	Int.	SS	120	436	49	117	16	8	4	51	19	.268
2002 Detroit	A.L.	SS-2B	18	72	4	24	3	0	1	6	0	.333
2003 Toledo	Int.	SS	64	224	28	50	10	0	2	18	22	.223
2003 Detroit	A.L.	SS-3B-2B	69	221	24	49	6	1	0	8	6	.222
2004 Detroit	A.L.	2B-SS-3B-OF	142	503	69	133	27	9	16	55	13	.264
2005 Detroit	A.L.	2B-SS	121	406	36	90	28	2	9	43	8	.222
2006 Detroit	A.L.	2B-SS-3B	78	224	35	62	11	4	4	25	3	.277
2007 Toledo	Int.	SS-2B	10	38	3	14	2	0	0	4	1	.368
2007 Detroit a-b	A.L.	2B-OF-SS-3B	66	166	24	45	6	1	2	17	4	.271
2008 Richmond	Int.	OF	3	11	3	4	1	0	0	3	0	.364
2008 Atlanta c	N.L.	OF-3B-SS-2B	96	317	45	93	24	3	3	40	0	.293
2009 Rome	So.Atl.	2B-3B-SS-OF	5	17	1	5	0	0	0	0	1	.294
2009 Gwinnett	Int.	SS	1	3	1	1	0	0	1	2	0	.333
2009 Atlanta d	N.L.	2B-OF-3B-SS	70	203	24	62	9	1	2	27	2	.305
2010 Atlanta e	N.L.	2B-3B-OF-SS	134	471	65	151	15	3	8	47	7	.321
Major League Totals		9 Yrs.	794	2583	326	709	129	24	45	268	43	.274
Division Series												
2010 Atlanta	N.L.	3B-2B	4	18	1	4	1	0	0	0	0	.222
Championship Series												
2006 Detroit	A.L.	DH	1	2	0	1	0	0	0	0	1	.500

Year	Club	Lea	Pos	G	AB	R	H	2B	3B	HR	RBI	SB	Avg
	World Series Record												
2006	Detroit	A.L.	PH	1	1	0	0	0	0	0	0	0	.000

a Traded to Chicago Cubs for outfielder Jacque Jones, November 12, 2007.
b Traded to Atlanta Braves with pitcher Will Ohman for pitcher Jose Ascanio, December 4, 2007.
c On disabled list from March 21 to May 8 and July 7 to July 22, 2008.
d On disabled list from May 21 to August 11, 2009.
e Traded to Florida Marlins with pitcher Michael Dunn for infielder Dan Uggla, November 16, 2010.

INGE, CHARLES BRANDON (BRANDON)

Born, Lynchburg, Virginia, May 19, 1977.
Bats Both. Throws Right. Height, 5 feet, 11 inches. Weight, 190 pounds.

Year	Club	Lea	Pos	G	AB	R	H	2B	3B	HR	RBI	SB	Avg
1998	Jamestown	N.Y.-Penn.	C	51	191	24	44	10	1	8	29	8	.230
1999	West Michigan	Midwest	C	100	352	54	86	25	2	9	46	15	.244
2000	Toledo	Int.	C	55	190	24	42	9	3	5	20	2	.221
2000	Jacksonville	Southern	C-OF	78	298	39	77	25	1	6	53	10	.258
2001	Tigers	Gulf Coast	C	3	10	1	1	0	0	1	2	0	.100
2001	West Michigan	Midwest	C	4	16	3	3	1	0	0	2	0	.188
2001	Toledo	Int.	C	27	90	11	26	11	1	2	15	1	.289
2001	Detroit a	A.L.	C	79	189	13	34	11	0	0	15	1	.180
2002	Toledo	Int.	C	21	65	10	17	2	4	3	13	1	.262
2002	Detroit b	A.L.	C	95	321	27	65	15	3	7	24	1	.202
2003	Toledo	Int.	C	39	142	15	39	9	0	5	15	3	.275
2003	Detroit	A.L.	C	104	330	32	67	15	3	8	30	4	.203
2004	Detroit c	A.L.	3B-C-OF	131	408	43	117	15	7	13	64	5	.287
2005	Detroit	A.L.	3B-OF	160	616	75	161	31	9	16	72	7	.261
2006	Detroit	A.L.	3B	159	542	83	137	29	2	27	83	7	.253
2007	Detroit	A.L.	3B	151	508	64	120	25	2	14	71	9	.236
2008	Toledo	Int.	C-3B	3	10	2	3	0	0	1	4	0	.300
2008	Detroit d	A.L.	C-3B-OF	113	347	41	71	16	4	11	51	4	.205
2009	Detroit	A.L.	3B	*161	562	71	129	16	1	27	84	2	.230
2010	West Michigan	Midwest	3B	1	5	0	2	2	0	0	1	0	.400
2010	Detroit e	A.L.	3B	144	514	47	127	28	5	13	70	4	.247
	Major League Totals		10 Yrs.	1297	4337	496	1028	201	36	136	564	44	.237
	Division Series												
2006	Detroit	A.L.	3B	4	15	1	2	0	0	0	0	0	.133
	Championship Series												
2006	Detroit	A.L.	3B	4	12	3	4	1	0	1	3	0	.333
	World Series Record												
2006	Detroit	A.L.	3B	5	17	0	6	2	0	0	1	0	.353

a On disabled list from June 25 to August 6, 2001.
b On disabled list from May 12 to May 27, 2002.
c On disabled list from June 26 to July 15, 2004.
d On disabled list from June 23 to July 10, 2008.
e On disabled list from July 20 to August 4, 2010.

INGLETT, JOSEPH STEVEN (JOE)

Born, Sacramento, California, June 29, 1978.
Bats Left. Throws Right. Height, 5 feet, 10 inches. Weight, 175 pounds.

Year	Club	Lea	Pos	G	AB	R	H	2B	3B	HR	RBI	SB	Avg
2000	Mahoning Valley	N.Y.-Penn.	2B-OF-1B	56	202	37	58	12	4	2	37	4	.287
2001	Columbus	So.Atl.	2B	62	237	34	71	9	2	2	33	5	.300
2002	Kinston	Carolina	2B	66	238	24	67	12	0	0	29	5	.282
2002	Columbus	So.Atl.	3B-2B	60	235	44	73	18	5	2	46	5	.311
2003	Kinston	Carolina	2B	28	85	21	28	10	1	0	15	1	.329
2003	Akron	Eastern	2B-OF	71	276	41	78	16	1	4	25	1	.283
2004	Akron	Eastern	2B	66	266	49	85	19	7	1	20	3	.320
2005	Buffalo	Int.	2B-OF-SS	95	327	57	108	20	9	2	40	13	.330
2006	Akron	Eastern	SS	18	64	20	33	9	0	3	9	7	.516
2006	Buffalo	Int.	2B-SS-OF	40	157	21	47	7	2	1	13	3	.299
2006	Cleveland	A.L.	2B-OF-SS	64	201	26	57	8	3	2	21	5	.284
2007	Buffalo	Int.	2B-OF-SS	107	392	45	99	15	9	4	57	7	.253
2007	Toronto a-b	A.L.	3B	2	5	0	3	0	1	0	2	1	.600
2008	Syracuse	Int.	2B-OF	15	54	12	22	2	2	1	6	1	.407
2008	Toronto	A.L.	2B-OF-3B-SS	109	344	45	102	15	7	3	39	9	.297
2009	Las Vegas	P.C.	2B-SS-OF	40	161	29	58	14	1	3	25	4	.360
2009	Toronto c	A.L.	OF-2B	36	89	11	25	4	1	0	6	3	.281

Year	Club	Lea	Pos	G	AB	R	H	2B	3B	HR	RBI	SB	Avg
2010	Milwaukee d-e	N.L.	OF-2B-P	102	142	15	36	8	5	1	8	1	.254
Major League Totals			5 Yrs.	313	781	97	223	35	17	6	76	19	.286

a On disabled list from March 23 to April 17, 2007.
b Claimed on waivers by Toronto Blue Jays, September 14, 2007.
c Claimed on waivers by Texas Rangers, December 4, 2009.
d Claimed on waivers by Milwaukee Brewers, January 27, 2010.
e Not offered contract, December 2, 2010.

ISHIKAWA, TRAVIS TAKASHI

Born, Seattle, Washington, September 24, 1983.
Bats Left. Throws Left. Height, 6 feet, 3 inches. Weight, 225 pounds.

Year	Club	Lea	Pos	G	AB	R	H	2B	3B	HR	RBI	SB	Avg
2002	Giants	Arizona	1B-OF	19	68	10	19	4	2	1	10	7	.279
2002	Salem-Keizer	Northwest	1B	23	88	14	27	2	1	1	17	1	.307
2003	Salem-Keizer	Northwest	1B	66	248	53	63	17	4	3	31	0	.254
2003	Hagerstown	So.Atl.	1B	57	194	20	40	5	0	3	22	3	.206
2004	San Jose	Calif.	1B	16	56	10	13	7	0	1	10	0	.232
2004	Hagerstown	So.Atl.	1B	98	358	59	92	19	2	15	54	10	.257
2005	San Jose	Calif.	1B	127	432	87	122	28	7	22	79	1	.282
2006	San Francisco	N.L.	1B	12	24	1	7	3	1	0	4	0	.292
2006	Connecticut	Eastern	1B	86	298	33	69	13	4	10	42	0	.232
2007	San Jose	Calif.	1B	56	198	35	53	15	1	13	34	0	.268
2007	Connecticut	Eastern	1B	48	173	17	37	3	1	3	17	0	.214
2008	Connecticut	Eastern	1B	64	234	34	68	16	0	8	48	10	.291
2008	Fresno	P.C.	1B	48	171	35	53	19	3	16	46	0	.310
2008	San Francisco	N.L.	1B	33	95	12	26	6	0	3	15	1	.274
2009	San Francisco	N.L.	1B	120	326	49	85	10	2	9	39	2	.261
2010	San Francisco	N.L.	1B	116	158	18	42	11	0	3	22	0	.266
Major League Totals			4 Yrs.	281	603	80	160	30	3	15	80	3	.265
	Division Series												
2010	San Francisco	N.L.	1B	3	2	1	0	0	0	0	0	0	.000
	Championship Series												
2010	San Francisco	N.L.	1B	5	4	0	1	0	0	0	0	0	.250
	World Series Record												
2010	San Francisco	N.L.	1B	2	4	1	1	1	0	0	1	0	.250

IWAMURA, AKINORI

Born, Ehime, Japan, February 9, 1979.
Bats Left. Throws Right. Height, 5 feet, 9 inches. Weight, 175 pounds.

Year	Club	Lea	Pos	G	AB	R	H	2B	3B	HR	RBI	SB	Avg
1998	Yakult	Japan Pac.	3B	1	3	0	0	0	0	0	0	0	.000
1999	Yakult	Japan Pac.	3B	83	252	28	74	11	4	11	35	7	.341
2000	Yakult	Japan Pac.	3B	130	436	67	121	13	9	18	66	13	.342
2001	Yakult	Japan Pac.	3B	136	520	79	149	24	4	18	81	15	.329
2002	Yakult	Japan Pac.	3B	140	510	79	163	35	2	23	71	5	.390
2003	Yakult	Japan Pac.	3B	60	232	43	61	6	2	12	35	5	.328
2004	Yakult	Japan Pac.	3B	138	533	99	160	19	0	44	103	8	.383
2005	Yakult	Japan Pac.	3B	144	548	83	175	31	4	30	102	6	.388
2006	Yakult a	Japan Pac.	3B	145	546	84	170	27	2	32	77	8	389
2007	Tampa Bay b	A.L.	3B-2B	123	491	82	140	21	10	7	34	12	.285
2008	Tampa Bay	A.L.	2B	152	627	91	172	30	9	6	48	8	.274
2009	Durham	Int.	2B	11	33	9	10	3	0	0	2	0	.303
2009	Tampa Bay c-d	A.L.	2B-3B	69	231	28	67	16	2	1	22	9	.290
2010	Indianapolis	Int.	3B-2B	50	163	26	43	10	1	3	16	0	.264
2010	Pittsburgh	N.L.	2B	54	165	18	30	6	1	2	9	3	.182
2010	Oakland e-f	A.L.	3B	10	31	3	4	1	0	0	4	0	.129
Major League Totals			4 Yrs.	408	1545	222	413	74	22	16	117	32	.267
	Division Series												
2008	Tampa Bay	N.L.	2B	4	18	3	7	1	1	1	4	0	.389
	Championship Series												
2008	Tampa Bay	N.L.	2B	7	29	4	6	2	0	0	0	2	.207
	World Series Record												
2008	Tampa Bay	N.L.	2B	5	19	1	5	1	0	0	1	0	.263

a Signed with Tampa Bay Devil Rays, December 15, 2006.
b On disabled list from April 24 to May 28, 2007.
c On disabled list from May 25 to August 29, 2009.
d Traded to Pittsburgh Pirates for pitcher Jesse Chavez, November 3, 2009.

e Released by Pittsburgh Pirates, September 10, 2010. Signed with Oakland Athletics, September 13, 2010.
f Released by Oakland Athletics, October 4, 2010. Signed with Rakuten Eagles (Japan), November 14, 2010.

IZTURIS, CESAR DAVID

Born, Barquisimeto, Venezuela, February 10, 1980.
Bats Both. Throws Right. Height, 5 feet, 9 inches. Weight, 190 pounds.

Year	Club	Lea	Pos	G	AB	R	H	2B	3B	HR	RBI	SB	Avg
1997	St.Cathrnes	N.Y.-Penn.	2B-SS	70	231	32	44	3	0	1	11	6	.190
1998	Hagerstown	So.Atl.	SS-2B-3B	130	413	56	108	13	1	1	38	20	.262
1999	Dunedin	Fla.St.	SS-2B-3B	131	536	77	165	28	12	3	77	32	.308
2000	Syracuse	Int.	SS	132	435	54	95	16	5	0	27	21	.218
2001	Syracuse	Int.	SS-2B	87	342	32	100	16	3	2	35	24	.292
2001	Toronto a	A.L.	2B-SS	46	134	19	36	6	2	2	9	8	.269
2002	Los Angeles	N.L.	SS-2B	135	439	43	102	24	2	1	31	7	.232
2003	Los Angeles	N.L.	SS	158	558	47	140	21	6	1	40	10	.251
2004	Los Angeles	N.L.	SS	159	670	90	193	32	9	4	62	25	.288
2005	Los Angeles b	N.L.	SS	106	444	48	114	19	2	2	31	8	.257
2006	Las Vegas	P.C.	SS-2B	15	59	9	16	3	0	0	3	0	.271
2006	Los Angeles-Chicago c-d-e	N.L.	3B-SS-2B	54	192	14	47	9	1	1	18	1	.245
2007	Chicago-Pittsburgh f-g	N.L.	SS-3B	110	314	31	81	14	2	0	16	3	.258
2008	St. Louis h-i	N.L.	SS-3B	135	414	50	109	10	3	1	24	24	.263
2009	Bowie	Eastern	SS	2	6	2	2	0	0	0	0	1	.333
2009	Baltimore j	A.L.	SS	114	387	34	99	14	4	2	30	12	.256
2010	Baltimore k	A.L.	SS	150	473	42	109	13	1	1	28	11	.230
Major League Totals			10 Yrs.	1167	4025	418	1030	162	32	15	289	109	.256
Division Series													
2004	Los Angeles	N.L.	SS	4	17	1	3	1	0	0	0	0	.176

a Traded to Los Angeles Dodgers with pitcher Paul Quantrill for pitcher Luke Prokopec and pitcher Chad Ricketts, December 13, 2001.
b On disabled list from June 30 to July 15 and August 23 to October 7, 2005.
c On disabled list from March 28 to June 20, 2006.
d Traded to Chicago Cubs for pitcher Greg Maddux, July 31, 2006.
e On disabled list from August 22 to September 6, 2006.
f Sold to Pittsburgh Pirates, July 19, 2007.
g Filed for free agency, November 12, 2007. Signed with St. Louis Cardinals, November 30, 2007.
h On disabled list from June 21 to July 6, 2008.
i Filed for free agency, October 30, 2008. Signed with Baltimore Orioles, December 15, 2008.
j On disabled list from June 4 to July 10, 2009.
k Filed for free agency, November 1, 2010, re-signed with Baltimore Orioles, January 5, 2011.

IZTURIS, MAICER

Born, Barquisimeto, Venezuela, September 12, 1980.
Bats Both. Throws Right. Height, 5 feet, 8 inches. Weight, 160 pounds.

Year	Club	Lea	Pos	G	AB	R	H	2B	3B	HR	RBI	SB	Avg
1998	Burlington	Appal.	SS	55	217	33	63	8	2	2	33	16	.290
1999	Columbus	So.Atl.	SS	57	220	46	66	5	3	4	23	14	.300
2000	Columbus	So.Atl.	SS	10	29	4	8	1	0	0	1	0	.276
2001	Kinston	Carolina	2B	114	433	47	104	16	6	1	39	32	.240
2002	Kinston	Carolina	2B	58	233	28	61	13	1	1	30	24	.262
2002	Akron	Eastern	2B	67	253	34	70	12	7	0	32	8	.277
2003	Akron	Eastern	2B-SS-OF	54	218	31	61	11	5	1	20	14	.280
2003	Buffalo	Int.	SS-2B	85	301	43	79	16	4	2	29	14	.262
2004	Edmonton	P.C.	SS-2B	99	376	65	127	19	2	3	36	14	.338
2004	Montreal a-b	N.L.	SS-2B	32	107	10	22	5	2	1	4	4	.206
2005	Salt Lake	P.C.	SS-3B-2B	10	31	10	14	4	0	0	2	4	.452
2005	Los Angeles c	A.L.	3B-SS-2B-OF	77	191	18	47	8	4	1	15	9	.246
2006	Salt Lake	P.C.	SS-3B-2B	9	36	5	11	5	1	0	5	1	.306
2006	Los Angeles d	A.L.	3B-SS-2B	104	352	64	103	21	3	5	44	14	.293
2007	Rancho Cucamonga	Calif.	3B	7	22	5	7	1	0	0	3	0	.318
2007	Salt Lake	P.C.	2B-SS	5	17	3	6	1	0	0	0	0	.353
2007	Los Angeles e	A.L.	3B-2B-SS	102	336	47	97	17	2	6	51	7	.289
2008	Rancho Cucamonga	Calif.	2B	1	2	0	1	0	0	0	0	0	.500
2008	Los Angeles f	A.L.	SS-2B-3B	79	290	44	78	14	2	3	37	11	.269
2009	Los Angeles	A.L.	2B-SS-3B-OF	114	387	74	116	22	3	8	65	13	.300
2010	Salt Lake	P.C.	3B-SS	2	7	1	2	0	0	0	1	0	.286
2010	Los Angeles g	A.L.	3B-2B-SS	61	212	27	53	13	1	3	27	7	.250
Major League Totals			7 Yrs.	569	1875	284	516	100	17	27	243	65	.275

Year	Club	Lea	Pos	G	AB	R	H	2B	3B	HR	RBI	SB	Avg
	Division Series												
2007	Los Angeles	A.L.	3B	3	12	1	4	2	0	0	0	2	.333
2009	Los Angeles	A.L.	2B	2	7	1	1	0	0	0	1	1	.143
Division Series Totals				5	19	2	5	2	0	0	1	3	.263
	Championship Series												
2005	Los Angeles	A.L.	SS	1	0	0	0	0	0	0	0	0	.000
2009	Los Angeles	A.L.	2B	4	10	1	1	1	0	0	1	0	.100
Championship Series Totals				5	10	1	1	1	0	0	1	0	.100

a Traded by Cleveland Indians to Montreal Expos with outfielder Ryan Church for pitcher Scott Stewart, January 5, 2004.
b Traded to Anaheim Angels with outfielder Juan Rivera for outfielder Jose Guillen, November 19, 2004.
c On disabled list from April 26 to June 18, 2005.
d On disabled list from April 24 to June 9, 2006.
e On disabled list from April 30 to May 15 and May 21 to July 3, 2007.
f On disabled list from April 28 to May 13 and August 14 to October 9, 2008.
g On disabled list from May 6 to May 25 and June 16 to July 18 and August 20 to September 27, 2010.

JACKSON, AUSTIN JARRIEL

Born, Denton, Texas, February 1, 1987.
Bats Right. Throws Right. Height, 6 feet, 1 inch. Weight, 185 pounds.

Year	Club	Lea	Pos	G	AB	R	H	2B	3B	HR	RBI	SB	Avg
2005	Yankees	Gulf Coast	OF	40	148	32	45	11	2	0	14	11	.304
2006	Charleston	So.Atl.	OF	134	535	90	139	24	5	4	47	37	.260
2007	Tampa	Fla.St.	OF	67	258	53	89	15	6	10	34	13	.345
2007	Scranton/WB	Int.	OF	1	3	2	1	1	0	0	0	1	.333
2007	Charleston	So.Atl.	OF	60	235	33	61	16	1	3	25	19	.260
2008	Trenton	Eastern	OF	131	520	75	148	33	5	9	69	19	.285
2009	Scranton/WB a	Int.	OF	132	504	67	151	23	9	4	65	24	.300
2010	Detroit	A.L.	OF	151	618	103	181	34	10	4	41	27	.293

a Traded by New York Yankees to Detroit Tigers with pitcher Phil Coke and pitcher Ian Kennedy for outfielder Curtis Granderson, December 9, 2009.

JACKSON, CONOR SIMS

Born, Austin, Texas, May 7, 1982.
Bats Right. Throws Right. Height, 6 feet, 2 inches. Weight, 225 pounds.

Year	Club	Lea	Pos	G	AB	R	H	2B	3B	HR	RBI	SB	Avg
2003	Yakima	Northwest	OF	68	257	44	82	35	1	6	60	3	.319
2004	Lancaster	Calif.	OF	67	258	64	89	19	2	11	54	4	.345
2004	El Paso	Texas	OF-3B	60	226	33	68	13	2	6	37	3	.301
2005	Tucson	P.C.	1B-OF	93	333	66	118	38	2	8	73	3	.354
2005	Arizona	N.L.	1B-OF	40	85	8	17	3	0	2	8	0	.200
2006	Arizona	N.L.	1B	140	485	75	141	26	1	15	79	1	.291
2007	Arizona	N.L.	1B-3B-OF	130	415	56	118	29	1	15	60	2	.284
2008	Arizona	N.L.	OF-1B	144	540	87	162	31	6	12	75	10	.300
2009	Visalia	Calif.	OF	3	10	1	0	0	0	0	1	0	.000
2009	Arizona a	N.L.	OF-1B	30	99	8	18	4	0	1	14	5	.182
2010	Athletics	Arizona	OF	3	7	0	0	0	0	0	1	0	.000
2010	Stockton	Calif.	OF	2	7	1	2	1	0	0	2	0	.286
2010	Reno	P.C.	OF	3	11	4	3	0	0	1	2	0	.273
2010	Sacramento	P.C.	OF	2	8	1	0	0	0	0	0	0	.000
2010	Arizona	N.L.	OF-1B	42	151	19	36	11	0	1	11	4	.238
2010	Oakland b-c-d	A.L.	OF	18	57	6	13	2	0	1	5	2	.228
Major League Totals			6 Yrs.	544	1832	259	505	106	8	47	252	24	.276
	Division Series												
2007	Arizona	N.L.	1B	3	8	0	1	1	0	0	1	0	.125
	Championship Series												
2007	Arizona	N.L.	1B	3	9	1	3	0	0	0	1	0	.333

a On disabled list from May 12 to November 20, 2009.
b On disabled list from April 19 to May 8, 2010.
c Traded to Oakland Athletics with cash for pitcher Sam Demel, June 15, 2010.
d On disabled list from July 1 to August 16 and August 20 to November 4, 2010.

JANISH, PAUL RYAN

Born, Houston, Texas, October 12, 1982.
Bats Right. Throws Right. Height, 6 feet, 2 inches. Weight, 195 pounds.

Year	Club	Lea	Pos	G	AB	R	H	2B	3B	HR	RBI	SB	Avg
2004	Billings	Pioneer	SS	66	205	39	54	11	0	2	22	7	.263
2005	Dayton	Midwest	SS	55	208	30	51	10	2	5	29	5	.245
2006	Sarasota	Fla.St.	SS	91	335	53	93	17	2	9	55	8	.278
2006	Dayton	Midwest	SS	26	98	19	39	6	0	5	18	0	.398
2006	Chattanooga	Southern	SS	4	15	1	4	1	0	0	2	0	.267
2007	Louisville	Int.	SS	55	199	20	44	8	1	3	19	2	.221
2007	Chattanooga	Southern	SS-2B-3B	88	324	46	79	21	2	1	20	10	.244
2008	Louisville	Int.	SS-2B	92	318	45	80	20	1	7	42	2	.252
2008	Cincinnati	N.L.	SS	38	80	5	15	2	0	1	6	0	.188
2009	Cincinnati	N.L.	SS-P-3B	90	256	36	54	21	0	1	16	2	.211
2010	Cincinnati	N.L.	SS-3B-2B	82	200	23	52	10	0	5	25	1	.260
Major League Totals			3 Yrs.	210	536	64	121	33	0	7	47	3	.226
	Division Series												
2010	Cincinnati	N.L.	SS	1	1	0	0	0	0	0	0	0	.000

JASO, JOHN EDWARD

Born, Chula Vista, California, September 19, 1983.
Bats Left. Throws Right. Height, 6 feet, 2 inches. Weight, 205 pounds.

Year	Club	Lea	Pos	G	AB	R	H	2B	3B	HR	RBI	SB	Avg
2003	Hudson Valley	N.Y.-Penn.	C	47	154	20	34	7	0	2	20	2	.221
2004	Hudson Valley	N.Y.-Penn.	C-1B-SS	57	199	34	60	17	2	2	35	1	.302
2005	Sw Michigan	Midwest	C-1B	92	332	61	102	25	1	14	50	3	.307
2006	Visalia	Calif.	C	95	366	58	113	22	0	10	55	1	.309
2007	Montgomery	Southern	C	109	380	62	120	24	2	12	71	2	.316
2008	Montgomery	Southern	C	85	284	51	77	13	2	7	43	1	.271
2008	Durham	Int.	C	31	108	14	30	7	0	5	24	1	.278
2008	Tampa Bay	A.L.	C	5	10	2	2	0	0	0	0	0	.200
2009	Durham	Int.	C	104	331	42	88	14	2	5	30	1	.266
2010	Durham	Int.	C	3	11	1	4	1	0	0	2	0	.364
2010	Tampa Bay	A.L.	C-1B	109	339	57	89	18	3	5	44	4	.263
Major League Totals			2 Yrs.	114	349	59	91	18	3	5	44	4	.261
	Division Series												
2010	Tampa Bay	N.L.	C	3	10	0	3	0	0	0	1	0	.300

JAY, JONATHAN HENRY (JON)

Born, Miami, Florida, March 15, 1985.
Bats Left. Throws Left. Height, 5 feet, 11 inches. Weight, 200 pounds.

Year	Club	Lea	Pos	G	AB	R	H	2B	3B	HR	RBI	SB	Avg
2006	Quad Cities	Midwest	OF	60	234	42	80	13	3	3	45	9	.342
2007	Palm Beach	Fla.St.	OF	32	126	19	36	8	0	2	10	5	.286
2007	Cardinals	Gulf Coast	DH	1	2	0	1	0	0	0	0	0	.500
2007	Springfield	Texas	OF	26	102	17	24	4	2	2	11	4	.235
2008	Memphis	P.C.	OF	16	58	8	20	4	1	1	10	0	.345
2008	Springfield	Texas	OF	96	372	57	114	17	3	11	47	10	.306
2009	Memphis	P.C.	OF-1B	136	505	72	142	23	2	10	54	20	.281
2010	Memphis	P.C.	OF-1B	42	165	31	53	16	0	4	32	13	.321
2010	St. Louis	N.L.	OF	105	287	47	86	19	2	4	27	2	.300

JETER, DEREK SANDERSON

Born, Pequannock, New Jersey, June 26, 1974.
Bats Right. Throws Right. Height, 6 feet, 3 inches. Weight, 195 pounds.

Year	Club	Lea	Pos	G	AB	R	H	2B	3B	HR	RBI	SB	Avg
1992	Tampa Yankees	Gulf C.	SS	47	173	19	35	10	0	3	25	2	.202
1992	Greensboro	So. Atl.	SS	11	37	4	9	0	0	1	4	0	.243
1993	Greensboro	So. Atl.	SS	128	515	85	152	14	11	5	71	18	.295
1994	Tampa	Fla. St.	SS	69	292	61	96	13	8	0	39	28	.329
1994	Albany	Eastern	SS	34	122	17	46	7	2	2	13	12	.377
1994	Columbus	Int.	SS	35	126	25	44	7	1	3	16	10	.349
1995	Columbus	Int.	SS	123	486	96	154	27	9	2	45	20	.317
1995	New York	A.L.	SS	15	48	5	12	4	1	0	7	0	.250
1996	New York a	A.L.	SS	157	582	104	183	25	6	10	78	14	.314
1997	New York	A.L.	SS	159	654	116	190	31	7	10	70	23	.291
1998	Columbus	Int.	SS	1	5	2	2	2	0	0	0	0	.400

Year	Club	Lea	Pos	G	AB	R	H	2B	3B	HR	RBI	SB	Avg
1998	New York b	A.L.	SS	149	626	*127	203	25	8	19	84	30	.324
1999	New York	A.L.	SS	158	627	134	219	37	9	24	102	19	.349
2000	Tampa	Fla.St.	SS	1	3	2	2	1	0	0	0	0	.667
2000	New York c	A.L.	SS	148	593	119	201	31	4	15	73	22	.339
2001	New York d	A.L.	SS	150	614	110	191	35	3	21	74	27	.311
2002	New York	A.L.	SS	157	644	124	191	26	0	18	75	32	.297
2003	Trenton	Eastern	SS	5	18	2	8	1	1	0	5	0	.444
2003	New York e	A.L.	SS	119	482	87	156	25	3	10	52	11	.324
2004	New York	A.L.	SS	154	643	111	188	44	1	23	78	23	.292
2005	New York	A.L.	SS	159	654	122	202	25	5	19	70	14	.309
2006	New York	A.L.	SS	154	623	118	214	39	3	14	97	34	.343
2007	New York	A.L.	SS	156	639	102	206	39	4	12	73	15	.322
2008	New York	A.L.	SS	150	596	88	179	25	3	11	69	11	.300
2009	New York	A.L.	SS	153	634	107	212	27	1	18	66	30	.334
2010	New York f	A.L.	SS	157	663	111	179	30	3	10	67	18	.270
Major League Totals			16 Yrs.	2295	9322	1685	2926	468	61	234	1135	323	.314
	Division Series												
1996	New York	A.L.	SS	4	17	2	7	1	0	0	1	0	.412
1997	New York	A.L.	SS	5	21	6	7	1	0	2	2	1	.333
1998	New York	A.L.	SS	3	9	0	1	0	0	0	0	0	.111
1999	New York	A.L.	SS	3	11	3	5	1	1	0	0	0	.455
2000	New York	A.L.	SS	5	19	1	4	0	0	0	2	0	.211
2001	New York	A.L.	SS	5	18	2	8	1	0	0	1	0	.444
2002	New York	A.L.	SS	4	16	6	8	0	0	2	3	0	.500
2003	New York	A.L.	SS	4	14	2	6	0	0	1	1	1	.429
2004	New York	A.L.	SS	4	19	3	6	1	0	1	4	1	.316
2005	New York	A.L.	SS	5	21	4	7	0	0	2	5	1	.333
2006	New York	A.L.	SS	4	16	4	8	4	0	1	1	0	.500
2007	New York	A.L.	SS	4	17	0	3	0	0	0	1	0	.176
2009	New York	A.L.	SS	3	10	4	4	2	0	1	2	0	.400
2010	New York	A.L.	SS	3	14	0	4	0	0	0	1	1	.286
Division Series Totals				56	222	37	78	11	1	10	24	5	.351
	Championship Series												
1996	New York	A.L.	SS	5	24	5	10	2	0	1	1	2	.417
1998	New York	A.L.	SS	6	25	3	5	1	1	0	2	3	.200
1999	New York	A.L.	SS	5	20	3	7	1	0	1	3	0	.350
2000	New York	A.L.	SS	6	22	6	7	0	0	2	5	1	.318
2001	New York	A.L.	SS	5	17	0	2	0	0	0	2	0	.118
2003	New York	A.L.	SS	7	30	3	7	2	0	1	2	1	.233
2004	New York	A.L.	SS	7	30	5	6	1	0	0	5	1	.200
2009	New York	A.L.	SS	6	27	5	7	0	0	2	3	0	.259
2010	New York	A.L.	SS	6	26	2	6	3	1	0	1	0	.231
Championship Series Totals				53	221	32	57	10	2	7	24	8	.258
	World Series												
1996	New York	A.L.	SS	6	20	5	5	0	0	0	1	1	.250
1998	New York	A.L.	SS	4	17	4	6	0	0	0	1	0	.353
1999	New York	A.L.	SS	4	17	4	6	1	0	0	1	3	.353
2000	New York	A.L.	SS	5	22	6	9	2	1	2	2	0	.409
2001	New York	A.L.	SS	7	27	3	4	0	0	1	1	0	.148
2003	New York	A.L.	SS	6	26	5	9	3	0	0	2	0	.346
2009	New York	A.L.	SS	6	27	5	11	3	0	0	1	0	.407
World Series Totals				38	156	32	50	9	1	3	9	4	.321

a Selected Rookie of the Year in American League for 1996.
b On disabled list from June 4 to June 19, 1998.
c On disabled list from May 12 to May 26, 2000.
d On disabled list from March 23 to April 7, 2001.
e On disabled list from April 1 to May 13, 2003.
f Filed for free agency, November 1, 2010, re-signed with New York Yankees, December 7, 2010.

JOHNSON, CHRISTOPHER DALTON (CHRIS)

Born, Naples, Florida, October 1, 1984.
Bats Right. Throws Right. Height, 6 feet, 3 inches. Weight, 220 pounds.

Year	Club	Lea	Pos	G	AB	R	H	2B	3B	HR	RBI	SB	Avg
2006	Tri-City	N.Y.-Penn.	3B-1B	60	222	18	47	7	1	1	29	7	.212
2007	Salem	Carolina	3B-1B	60	224	24	59	11	0	6	38	1	.263
2007	Lexington	So.Atl.	3B-SS-1B	64	255	37	66	14	0	8	44	3	.259
2008	Round Rock	P.C.	3B	30	101	10	22	2	1	1	9	0	.218
2008	Corpus Christi	Texas	3B	84	330	43	107	24	0	12	58	5	.324

Year	Club	Lea	Pos	G	AB	R	H	2B	3B	HR	RBI	SB	Avg
2009	Lancaster	Calif.	3B	4	16	5	7	5	0	0	6	0	.438
2009	Round Rock	P.C.	3B	104	384	48	108	20	5	13	42	2	.281
2009	Houston	N.L.	3B	11	22	1	2	0	0	0	1	0	.091
2010	Round Rock	P.C.	3B	38	149	26	49	10	1	8	33	0	.329
2010	Houston a	N.L.	3B	94	341	40	105	22	2	11	52	3	.308
Major League Totals			2 Yrs.	105	363	41	107	22	2	11	53	3	.295

a On disabled list from April 18 to May 8, 2010.

JOHNSON, KELLY ANDREW

Born, Austin, Texas, February 22, 1982.

Bats Left. Throws Right. Height, 6 feet, 1 inch. Weight, 205 pounds.

Year	Club	Lea	Pos	G	AB	R	H	2B	3B	HR	RBI	SB	Avg
2000	Braves	Gulf Coast	SS-3B	53	193	27	52	12	3	4	29	6	.269
2001	Macon	So.Atl.	SS	124	415	75	120	22	1	23	66	25	.289
2002	Myrtle Beach	Carolina	SS-3B	126	482	62	123	21	5	12	49	12	.255
2003	Braves	Gulf Coast	SS	6	26	10	10	1	1	1	3	1	.385
2003	Greenville	Southern	SS	98	334	46	92	22	5	6	45	10	.275
2004	Greenville	Southern	OF-3B-2B	135	479	70	135	35	3	16	50	9	.282
2005	Richmond	Int.	OF-3B-SS	44	155	35	48	12	3	8	22	7	.310
2005	Atlanta	N.L.	OF	87	290	46	70	12	3	9	40	2	.241
2006	Richmond	Int.	OF	10	39	3	13	4	0	1	7	1	.333
2006	Rome a	So.Atl.	OF	5	19	5	9	2	1	1	3	2	.474
2007	Atlanta	N.L.	2B	147	521	91	144	26	10	16	68	9	.276
2008	Atlanta	N.L.	2B	150	547	86	157	39	6	12	69	11	.287
2009	Gwinnett	Int.	2B	13	52	9	16	2	2	3	16	1	.308
2009	Atlanta b-c	N.L.	2B	106	303	47	68	20	3	8	29	7	.224
2010	Arizona	N.L.	2B	154	585	93	166	36	5	26	71	13	.284
Major League Totals			5 Yrs.	644	2246	363	605	133	27	71	277	42	.269
Division Series													
2005	Atlanta	N.L.	PH	4	2	0	0	0	0	0	0	0	.000

a On disabled list from March 24 to November 1, 2006.
b On disabled list from July 3 to July 23, 2009.
c Not offered contract, December 12, 2009. Signed with Arizona Diamondbacks, December 30, 2009.

JOHNSON, REED CAMERON

Born, Riverside, California, December 8, 1976.

Bats Right. Throws Right. Height, 5 feet, 10 inches. Weight, 180 pounds.

Year	Club	Lea	Pos	G	AB	R	H	2B	3B	HR	RBI	SB	Avg
1999	St. Catharines	N.Y.-Penn.	OF	60	189	24	44	8	2	2	23	5	.233
2000	Dunedin	Fla.St.	OF	36	133	26	42	9	2	4	28	3	.316
2000	Hagerstown	So.Atl.	OF	95	324	66	94	24	5	8	70	14	.290
2001	Tennessee	Southern	OF	136	554	104	174	29	4	13	74	42	.314
2002	Dunedin	Fla.St.	OF	8	33	7	9	3	0	0	6	0	.273
2002	Syracuse	Int.	OF	44	159	27	37	8	3	2	10	1	.233
2003	Syracuse	Int.	OF	26	101	14	33	4	1	2	16	3	.327
2003	Toronto	A.L.	OF	114	412	79	121	21	2	10	52	5	.294
2004	Toronto	A.L.	OF	141	537	68	145	25	2	10	61	6	.270
2005	Toronto	A.L.	OF	142	398	55	107	21	6	8	58	5	.269
2006	Toronto	A.L.	OF	134	461	86	147	34	2	12	49	8	.319
2007	Dunedin	Fla.St.	OF	4	12	1	4	1	0	1	1	0	.333
2007	Syracuse	Int.	OF	2	8	1	3	0	0	0	1	0	.375
2007	Toronto a	A.L.	OF	79	275	31	65	13	2	2	14	4	.236
2008	Chicago b-c	N.L.	OF	109	333	52	101	21	0	6	50	5	.303
2009	Peoria	Midwest	OF	3	6	2	2	0	0	0	0	0	.333
2009	Chicago d-e	N.L.	OF	65	165	23	42	10	2	4	22	2	.255
2010	Inland Empire	Calif.	OF	2	6	2	3	1	0	0	0	0	.500
2010	Los Angeles f-g	N.L.	OF	102	202	24	53	11	2	2	15	2	.262
Major League Totals			8 Yrs.	886	2783	418	781	156	18	54	321	37	.281

a On disabled list from April 12 to July 6, 2007.
b Released by Toronto Blue Jays, March 23, 2008. Signed with Chicago Cubs, March 25, 2008.
c On disabled list from June 18 to July 3, 2008.
d On disabled list from June 21 to July 6 and July 30 to September 21, 2009.
e Filed for free agency, November 5, 2009. Signed with Los Angeles Dodgers, February 1, 2010.
f On disabled list from July 9 to August 4, 2010.
g Filed for free agency, November 1, 2010. Signed with Chicago Cubs organization, January 12, 2011.

JOHNSON, ROBERT JAMES (ROB)

Born, Anaconda, Montana, July 22, 1983.
Bats Right. Throws Right. Height, 6 feet, 1 inch. Weight, 215 pounds.

Year	Club	Lea	Pos	G	AB	R	H	2B	3B	HR	RBI	SB	Avg
2004	Mariners	Arizona	DH	8	27	4	6	1	0	0	1	1	.222
2004	Everett	Northwest	C-OF	20	77	17	18	3	1	1	7	6	.234
2005	Inland Empire	Calif.	C	19	70	15	22	3	0	2	12	2	.314
2005	Wisconsin	Midwest	C-OF	77	305	41	83	19	1	9	51	10	.272
2006	Tacoma	P.C.	C-OF	97	337	28	78	9	4	4	33	14	.231
2007	Tacoma	P.C.	C	112	422	57	113	26	0	6	40	7	.268
2007	Seattle	A.L.	C	6	3	1	1	0	0	0	0	1	.333
2008	Tacoma	P.C.	C-OF	112	417	55	127	30	0	9	49	7	.305
2008	Seattle	A.L.	C	14	31	2	4	0	0	1	2	0	.129
2009	Seattle	A.L.	C	80	258	21	55	19	2	2	27	1	.213
2010	Tacoma	P.C.	C	19	64	9	19	7	0	1	8	0	.297
2010	Seattle a	A.L.	C	61	178	24	34	10	0	2	13	1	.191
Major League Totals			4 Yrs.	161	470	48	94	29	2	5	42	3	.200

a Traded to San Diego Padres for player to be named later, December 21, 2010.

JONES, ADAM LA MARQUE

Born, San Diego, California, August 1, 1985.
Bats Right. Throws Right. Height, 6 feet, 2 inches. Weight, 200 pounds.

Year	Club	Lea	Pos	G	AB	R	H	2B	3B	HR	RBI	SB	Avg
2003	Mariners	Arizona	SS	28	109	18	31	5	1	0	8	5	.284
2003	Everett	Northwest	SS	3	13	2	6	1	0	0	4	0	.462
2004	Wisconsin	Midwest	SS-3B	130	510	76	136	23	7	11	72	8	.267
2005	Inland Empire	Calif.	SS	68	271	43	80	20	5	8	46	4	.295
2005	San Antonio	Texas	SS-OF	63	228	33	68	10	3	7	20	9	.298
2006	Tacoma	P.C.	OF	96	380	69	109	19	4	16	62	13	.287
2006	Seattle	A.L.	OF	32	74	6	16	4	0	1	8	3	.216
2007	Tacoma	P.C.	OF	101	420	75	132	27	6	25	84	8	.314
2007	Seattle	A.L.	OF	41	65	16	16	2	1	2	4	2	.246
2008	Baltimore a-b	A.L.	OF	132	477	61	129	21	7	9	57	10	.270
2009	Baltimore c	A.L.	OF	119	473	83	131	22	3	19	70	10	.277
2010	Baltimore	A.L.	OF	149	581	76	165	25	5	19	69	7	.284
Major League Totals			5 Yrs.	473	1670	242	457	74	16	50	208	32	.274

a Traded to Baltimore Orioles with pitcher Tony Butler, pitcher Kam Mickolio, pitcher George Sherrill and pitcher Chris Tillman for pitcher Erik Bedard, February 8, 2008.
b On disabled list from August 3 to September 1, 2008.
c On disabled list from September 2 to November 6, 2009.

JONES, ANDRUW RUDOLF

Born, Willemstad, Curacao, Netherlands Antillies, April 23, 1977.
Bats Right. Throws Right. Height, 6 feet, 1 inch. Weight, 240 pounds.

Year	Club	Lea	Pos	G	AB	R	H	2B	3B	HR	RBI	SB	Avg
1994	Braves	Gulf Coast	OF	27	95	22	21	5	1	2	10	5	.221
1994	Danville	Appal.	OF	36	143	20	48	9	2	1	16	16	.336
1995	Macon	So.Atl.	OF	139	537	104	149	41	5	25	100	56	.277
1996	Durham	Carolina	OF	66	243	65	76	14	3	17	43	16	.313
1996	Greenville	Southern	OF	38	157	39	58	10	1	12	37	12	.369
1996	Richmond	Int.	OF	12	45	11	17	3	1	5	12	2	.378
1996	Atlanta	N.L.	OF	31	106	11	23	7	1	5	13	3	.217
1997	Atlanta	N.L.	OF	153	399	60	92	18	1	18	70	20	.231
1998	Atlanta	N.L.	OF	159	582	89	158	33	8	31	90	27	.271
1999	Atlanta	N.L.	OF	162	592	97	163	35	5	26	84	24	.275
2000	Atlanta	N.L.	OF	161	*656	122	199	36	6	36	104	21	.303
2001	Atlanta	N.L.	OF	161	625	104	157	25	2	34	104	11	.251
2002	Atlanta	N.L.	OF	154	560	91	148	34	0	35	94	8	.264
2003	Atlanta	N.L.	OF	156	595	101	165	28	2	36	116	4	.277
2004	Atlanta	N.L.	OF	154	570	85	149	34	4	29	91	6	.261
2005	Atlanta	N.L.	OF	160	586	95	154	24	3	*51	*128	5	.263
2006	Atlanta	N.L.	OF	156	565	107	148	29	0	41	129	4	.262
2007	Atlanta a	N.L.	OF	154	572	83	127	27	2	26	94	5	.222
2008	Las Vegas	P.C.	1B-OF	11	31	7	10	0	0	4	11	2	.323
2008	Los Angeles b-c	N.L.	OF	75	209	21	33	8	1	3	14	0	.158
2009	Frisco	Texas	1B	3	9	0	2	0	0	0	0	1	.222
2009	Texas d-e	A.L.	DH-OF-1B	82	281	43	60	18	0	17	43	5	.214
2010	Chicago f	A.L.	OF	107	278	41	64	12	1	19	48	9	.230
Major League Totals			15 Yrs.	2025	7176	1150	1840	368	36	407	1222	152	.256

Year	Club	Lea	Pos	G	AB	R	H	2B	3B	HR	RBI	SB	Avg
	Division Series												
1996	Atlanta	N.L.	OF	3	0	0	0	0	0	0	0	0	.000
1997	Atlanta	N.L.	OF	3	5	1	0	0	0	0	1	0	.000
1998	Atlanta	N.L.	OF	3	9	2	0	0	0	0	1	2	.000
1999	Atlanta	N.L.	OF	4	18	1	4	1	0	0	2	0	.222
2000	Atlanta	N.L.	OF	3	9	3	1	0	0	1	1	0	.111
2001	Atlanta	N.L.	OF	3	12	2	6	0	0	1	1	0	.500
2002	Atlanta	N.L.	OF	5	19	4	6	1	0	0	2	0	.316
2003	Atlanta	N.L.	OF	5	17	1	1	0	0	0	1	0	.059
2004	Atlanta	N.L.	OF	5	19	4	10	2	0	2	5	1	.526
2005	Atlanta	N.L.	OF	4	17	5	8	3	0	1	5	0	.471
Division Series Totals				38	125	23	36	7	0	5	19	3	.288
	Championship Series												
1996	Atlanta	N.L.	OF	5	9	3	2	0	0	1	3	0	.222
1997	Atlanta	N.L.	OF	5	9	0	4	0	0	0	1	0	.444
1998	Atlanta	N.L.	OF	6	22	3	6	0	0	1	2	1	.273
1999	Atlanta	N.L.	OF	6	23	5	5	0	0	0	1	0	.217
2001	Atlanta	N.L.	OF	5	17	4	3	0	0	1	1	0	.176
Championship Series Totals				27	80	15	20	0	0	3	8	1	.250
	World Series												
1996	Atlanta	N.L.	OF	6	20	4	8	1	0	2	6	1	.400
1999	Atlanta	N.L.	OF	4	13	1	1	0	0	0	0	0	.077
World Series Totals				10	33	5	9	1	0	2	6	1	.273

a Filed for free agency, October 31, 2007. Signed with Los Angeles Dodgers, December 12, 2007.
b On disabled list from May 24 to July 4 and August 10 to September 1 and September 13 to November 4, 2008.
c Released, January 15, 2009. Signed with Texas Rangers organization, February 8, 2009.
d On disabled list from August 24 to September 8, 2009.
e Filed for free agency, November 6, 2009. Signed with Chicago White Sox, November 25, 2009.
f Filed for free agency, November 1, 2010.

JONES, GARRETT THOMAS

Born, Harvey, Illinois, June 21, 1981.
Bats Left. Throws Left. Height, 6 feet, 4 inches. Weight, 245 pounds.

Year	Club	Lea	Pos	G	AB	R	H	2B	3B	HR	RBI	SB	Avg
1999	Braves	Gulf Coast	1B	46	170	17	41	3	0	3	18	1	.241
2000	Danville	Appal.	1B	40	138	12	24	7	2	0	16	0	.174
2001	Danville	Appal.	1B	40	149	13	43	11	0	3	23	0	.289
2002	Quad Cities a	Midwest	1B-OF	63	223	21	45	8	0	10	32	3	.202
2003	Fort Myers	Fla.St.	1B-OF	117	404	52	89	12	5	18	67	5	.220
2004	New Britain	Eastern	1B	122	450	68	140	33	2	30	92	11	.311
2004	Fort Myers	Fla.St.	1B	19	66	6	16	5	0	1	6	2	.242
2005	Rochester	Int.	1B-OF	134	488	71	119	22	2	24	72	5	.244
2006	Rochester	Int.	1B-OF	140	525	72	125	32	3	21	92	3	.238
2007	Rochester	Int.	OF-1B	107	400	57	112	32	3	13	70	2	.280
2007	Minnesota	A.L.	DH-1B-OF	31	77	7	16	2	1	2	5	1	.208
2008	Rochester b	Int.	1B-OF	138	527	82	147	33	3	23	92	9	.279
2009	Indianapolis	Int.	OF-1B	72	277	44	85	18	0	12	49	14	.307
2009	Pittsburgh	N.L.	OF-1B	82	314	45	92	21	1	21	44	10	.293
2010	Pittsburgh	N.L.	1B-OF	158	592	64	146	34	1	21	86	7	.247
Major League Totals			3 Yrs.	271	983	116	254	57	3	44	135	18	.258

a Released by Atlanta Braves, May 21,2002. Signed with Minnesota Twins organization, May 24, 2002.
b Filed for free agency, November 3, 2008. Signed with Pittsburgh Pirates organization, December 16, 2008.

JONES, LARRY WAYNE (CHIPPER)

Born, Deland, Florida, April 24, 1972.
Bats Both. Throws Right. Height, 6 feet, 4 inches. Weight, 210 pounds.

Year	Club	Lea	Pos	G	AB	R	H	2B	3B	HR	RBI	SB	Avg
1990	Bradenton Braves	Gulf C.	SS	44	140	20	32	1	1	1	18	5	.229
1991	Macon	So. Atl.	SS	136	473	*104	154	24	11	15	98	40	.326
1992	Durham	Carolina	SS	70	264	43	73	22	1	4	31	10	.277
1992	Greenville	Southern	SS	67	266	43	92	17	11	9	42	14	.346
1993	Richmond	Int.	SS	139	536	97	174	31	12	13	89	23	.325
1993	Atlanta	N.L.	SS	8	3	2	2	1	0	0	0	0	.667
1994	Atlanta a	N.L.				INJURED—Did Not Play							
1995	Atlanta	N.L.	3B-OF	140	524	87	139	22	3	23	86	8	.265
1996	Atlanta b	N.L.	3B-SS-OF	157	598	114	185	32	5	30	110	14	.309
1997	Atlanta	N.L.	3B-OF	157	597	100	176	41	3	21	111	20	.295

Year Club	Lea	Pos	G	AB	R	H	2B	3B	HR	RBI	SB	Avg
1998 Atlanta	N.L.	3B	160	601	123	188	29	5	34	107	16	.313
1999 Atlanta c	N.L.	3B-SS	157	567	116	181	41	1	45	110	25	.319
2000 Atlanta	N.L.	3B-SS	156	579	118	180	38	1	36	111	14	.311
2001 Atlanta	N.L.	3B-OF	159	572	113	189	33	5	38	102	9	.330
2002 Atlanta	N.L.	OF	158	548	90	179	35	1	26	100	8	.327
2003 Atlanta	N.L.	OF	153	555	103	169	33	2	27	106	2	.305
2004 Rome	So.Atl.	OF	1	4	0	0	0	0	0	0	0	.000
2004 Atlanta d	N.L.	3B-OF	137	472	69	117	20	1	30	96	2	.248
2005 Rome	So.Atl.	3B	3	6	1	3	0	0	0	2	0	.500
2005 Atlanta e	N.L.	3B	109	358	66	106	30	0	21	72	5	.296
2006 Mississippi	Southern	3B	2	6	1	1	0	0	0	0	0	.167
2006 Atlanta f	N.L.	3B	110	411	87	133	28	3	26	86	6	.324
2007 Atlanta g	N.L.	3B-SS	134	513	108	173	42	4	29	102	5	.337
2008 Atlanta h	N.L.	3B	128	439	82	160	24	1	22	75	4	*.364
2009 Atlanta	N.L.	3B	143	488	80	129	23	2	18	71	4	.264
2010 Atlanta i	N.L.	3B	95	317	47	84	21	0	10	46	5	.265
Major League Totals		17 Yrs.	2261	8142	1505	2490	493	37	436	1491	147	.306
Division Series												
1995 Atlanta	N.L.	3B	4	18	4	7	2	0	2	4	0	.389
1996 Atlanta	N.L.	3B	3	9	2	2	0	0	1	2	1	.222
1997 Atlanta	N.L.	3B	3	8	3	4	0	0	1	2	1	.500
1998 Atlanta	N.L.	3B	3	10	2	2	0	0	0	1	0	.200
1999 Atlanta	N.L.	3B	4	13	2	3	0	0	0	1	0	.231
2000 Atlanta	N.L.	3B	3	12	2	4	1	0	0	1	0	.333
2001 Atlanta	N.L.	3B	3	9	2	4	0	0	2	5	0	.444
2002 Atlanta	N.L.	OF	5	17	3	5	0	0	0	2	0	.294
2003 Atlanta	N.L.	OF	5	18	3	3	0	0	2	6	0	.167
2004 Atlanta	N.L.	3B	5	20	4	4	0	0	0	0	0	.200
2005 Atlanta	N.L.	3B	4	17	3	3	2	0	1	2	0	.176
Division Series Totals			42	151	30	41	5	0	9	26	2	.272
Championship Series												
1995 Atlanta	N.L.	3B	4	16	3	7	0	0	1	3	1	.438
1996 Atlanta	N.L.	3B	7	25	6	11	2	0	0	4	1	.440
1997 Atlanta	N.L.	3B	6	24	5	7	1	0	2	4	0	.292
1998 Atlanta	N.L.	3B	6	24	2	5	1	0	0	1	0	.208
1999 Atlanta	N.L.	3B	6	19	3	5	2	0	0	1	3	.263
2001 Atlanta	N.L.	3B	5	19	1	5	1	0	0	2	0	.263
Championship Series Totals			34	127	20	40	7	0	3	15	5	.315
World Series Record												
1995 Atlanta	N.L.	3B	6	21	3	6	3	0	0	1	0	.286
1996 Atlanta	N.L.	3B-SS	6	21	3	6	3	0	0	3	1	.286
1999 Atlanta	N.L.	3B	4	13	2	3	0	0	1	2	0	.231
World Series Totals			16	55	8	15	6	0	1	6	1	.273

a On disabled list from March 20 to end of 1994 season.
b On disabled list from April 1 to April 6, 1996.
c Selected Most Valuable Player in National League for 1999.
d On disabled list from April 19 to May 8, 2004.
e On disabled list from June 6 to July 18, 2005.
f On disabled list from April 10 to April 25 and July 30 to August 13 and September 4 to September 19, 2006.
g On disabled list from May 24 to June 13, 2007.
h On disabled list from July 24 to August 8, 2008.
i On disabled list from August 11 to October 19, 2010.

JOYCE, MATTHEW R. (MATT)

Born, Tampa, Florida, August 3, 1984.
Bats Left. Throws Right. Height, 6 feet, 2 inches. Weight, 205 pounds.

Year Club	Lea	Pos	G	AB	R	H	2B	3B	HR	RBI	SB	Avg
2005 Oneonta	N.Y.-Penn.	OF	65	245	51	81	10	4	4	45	9	.331
2006 West Michigan	Midwest	OF	122	465	75	120	30	5	11	86	5	.258
2007 Erie	Eastern	OF	130	456	61	117	33	3	17	70	4	.257
2008 Toledo	Int.	OF	56	200	36	54	13	2	13	41	2	.270
2008 Detroit a	A.L.	OF	92	242	40	61	16	3	12	33	0	.252
2009 Tampa Bay	A.L.	OF	11	32	3	6	1	0	3	7	1	.188
2009 Durham	Int.	OF	111	417	73	114	35	2	16	66	14	.273
2010 Charlotte	Fla.St.	OF	10	29	6	11	5	0	2	8	1	.379
2010 Durham	Int.	OF	25	92	18	27	8	0	3	12	1	.293
2010 Tampa Bay b	A.L.	OF	77	216	30	52	15	3	10	40	2	.241
Major League Totals		3 Yrs.	180	490	73	119	32	6	25	80	3	.243

Year	Club	Lea	Pos	G	AB	R	H	2B	3B	HR	RBI	SB	Avg
	Division Series												
2010	Tampa Bay	N.L.	OF	4	9	0	2	0	0	0	0	1	.222

a Traded to Tampa Bay Rays for pitcher Edwin Jackson, December 10, 2008.
b On disabled list from March 26 to May 31, 2010.

KALISH, RYAN MICHAEL

Born, Northridge, California, March 28, 1988.
Bats Left. Throws Left. Height, 6 feet, 1 inch. Weight, 205 pounds.

Year	Club	Lea	Pos	G	AB	R	H	2B	3B	HR	RBI	SB	Avg
2006	Red Sox	Gulf Coast	OF	6	20	6	6	2	0	1	2	0	.300
2006	Lowell	N.Y.-Penn.	OF	11	35	8	7	0	1	0	4	2	.200
2007	Lowell	N.Y.-Penn.	OF	23	87	27	32	4	1	3	13	18	.368
2008	Lancaster	Calif.	OF	18	73	6	17	6	0	2	14	1	.233
2008	Greenville	So.Atl.	OF	96	360	51	101	16	1	3	32	18	.281
2009	Salem	Carolina	OF	32	115	21	35	5	2	5	21	7	.304
2009	Portland	Eastern	OF	103	391	63	106	19	4	13	56	14	.271
2010	Portland	Eastern	OF	41	150	35	44	9	1	8	29	13	.293
2010	Pawtucket	Int.	OF	37	143	22	42	9	1	5	18	12	.294
2010	Boston	A.L.	OF	53	163	26	41	11	1	4	24	10	.252

KEARNS, AUSTIN RYAN

Born, Lexington, Kentucky, May 20, 1980.
Bats Right. Throws Right. Height, 6 feet, 3 inches. Weight, 235 pounds.

Year	Club	Lea	Pos	G	AB	R	H	2B	3B	HR	RBI	SB	Avg
1998	Billings	Pioneer	OF-3B	30	108	17	34	9	0	1	14	1	.315
1999	Rockford	Midwest	OF	124	426	72	110	36	5	13	48	21	.258
2000	Dayton	Midwest	OF	136	484	110	148	37	2	27	104	18	.306
2001	Reds	Gulf Coast	OF	6	17	2	3	2	0	0	4	0	.176
2001	Chattanooga a	Southern	OF	59	205	30	55	11	2	6	36	7	.268
2002	Chattanooga	Southern	OF	12	41	10	11	2	0	5	13	1	.268
2002	Louisville	Int.	OF	1	4	3	3	2	0	0	2	0	.750
2002	Cincinnati b	N.L.	OF	107	372	66	117	24	3	13	56	6	.315
2003	Chattanooga	Southern	OF	3	5	2	1	0	0	0	1	0	.200
2003	Cincinnati c	N.L.	OF	82	292	39	77	11	0	15	58	5	.264
2004	Louisville	Int.	OF	25	83	19	28	7	1	2	15	3	.337
2004	Cincinnati d	N.L.	OF	64	217	28	50	10	2	9	32	2	.230
2005	Louisville	Int.	OF	28	111	24	38	15	1	7	21	0	.342
2005	Cincinnati	N.L.	OF	112	387	62	93	26	1	18	67	0	.240
2006	Cincinnati-Washington e	N.L.	OF	150	537	86	142	33	2	24	86	9	.264
2007	Washington	N.L.	OF	161	587	84	156	35	1	16	74	2	.266
2008	Hagerstown	So.Atl.	DH	2	3	2	1	0	0	0	1	0	.333
2008	Columbus	Int.	OF	5	14	2	6	1	1	1	6	0	.429
2008	Washington f	N.L.	OF	86	313	40	68	10	0	7	32	2	.217
2009	Washington g-h	N.L.	OF	80	174	20	34	6	2	3	17	1	.195
2010	Cleveland-New York i-j-k	A.L.	OF	120	403	55	106	21	1	10	49	4	.263
Major League Totals			9 Yrs.	962	3282	480	843	176	12	115	471	31	.257

a On disabled list from May 27 to August 13, 2001.
b On disabled list from August 27 to September 30, 2002.
c On disabled list from July 9 to November 5, 2003.
d On disabled list from April 27 to May 19 and from June 2 to August 24, 2004.
e Traded to Washington Nationals with infielder Felipe Lopez and pitcher Ryan Wagner for pitcher Gary Majewski, pitcher Bill Bray, infielder Royce Clayton, infielder Brendan Harris and pitcher Daryl Thompson, July 13, 2006.
f On disabled list from May 22 to July 3 and August 25 to October 3, 2008.
g On disabled list from August 4 to October 13, 2009.
h Filed for free agency, November 6, 2009. Signed with Cleveland Indians organization, January 5, 2010.
i Traded to New York Yankees for player to be named later, July 31, 2010.
j Cleveland Indians received pitcher Zach McAllister to complete trade, August 20, 2010.
k Filed for free agency, November 1, 2010. Signed with Cleveland Indians, December 20, 2010.

KELLY, DONALD THOMAS (DON)

Born, Butler, Pennsylvania, February 15, 1980.
Bats Left. Throws Right. Height, 6 feet, 4 inches. Weight, 190 pounds.

Year	Club	Lea	Pos	G	AB	R	H	2B	3B	HR	RBI	SB	Avg
2001	Oneonta	N.Y.-Penn.	SS	67	262	41	75	8	3	0	25	8	.286
2002	West Michigan	Midwest	SS	128	455	72	130	21	5	1	59	9	.286
2003	Erie	Eastern	SS-1B	22	83	14	22	5	1	1	13	0	.265

Year Club	Lea	Pos	G	AB	R	H	2B	3B	HR	RBI	SB	Avg
2003 Lakeland	Fla.St.	3B-SS-1B-2B	87	303	48	96	17	4	1	38	15	.317
2004 Erie	Eastern	SS	28	101	17	23	6	2	0	9	3	.228
2004 Tigers	Gulf Coast	SS	3	10	2	4	0	0	0	0	1	.400
2005 Erie	Eastern	3B-SS	82	329	54	112	22	3	9	54	10	.340
2005 Toledo	Int.	SS-3B-OF	43	160	22	40	8	0	1	13	8	.250
2006 Erie	Eastern	2B-SS-3B-1B	58	207	30	57	11	1	0	24	5	.275
2006 Toledo	Int.	SS-1B-2B	66	237	23	54	14	3	0	19	18	.228
2007 Pittsburgh	N.L.	SS-2B-OF	25	27	2	4	0	0	0	0	0	.148
2007 Indianapolis a-b	Int.	OF-SS-2B-3B	52	150	20	37	5	2	0	11	6	.247
2008 Tucson	P.C.	2B-SS-3B-OF	124	436	61	120	24	5	8	55	2	.275
2009 Toledo	Int.	OF-1B-3B-2B	105	372	57	123	20	6	6	40	27	.331
2009 Detroit c	A.L.	OF-3B-1B-2B	31	56	8	14	3	1	0	3	1	.250
2010 Detroit	A.L.	OF-1B-3B	119	238	30	58	4	0	9	27	3	.244
Major League Totals		3 Yrs.	175	321	40	76	7	1	9	30	4	.237

a Filed for free agency from Detroit Tigers, October 3, 2006. Signed with Pittsburgh Pirates organization, November 16, 2006.
b Filed for free agency, October 4, 2007. Signed with Arizona Diamondbacks organization, November 24, 2007.
c Filed for free agency, November 3, 2008. Signed with Detroit Tigers organization, January 14, 2009.

KEMP, MATTHEW RYAN (MATT)

Born, Midwest City, Oklahoma, September 23, 1984.
Bats Right. Throws Right. Height, 6 feet, 2 inches. Weight, 230 pounds.

Year Club	Lea	Pos	G	AB	R	H	2B	3B	HR	RBI	SB	Avg
2003 Dodgers	Gulf Coast	OF	42	159	11	43	5	2	1	17	2	.270
2004 Vero Beach	Fla.St.	OF	11	37	5	13	5	0	1	9	2	.351
2004 Columbus	So.Atl.	OF	112	423	67	122	22	8	17	66	8	.288
2005 Vero Beach	Fla.St.	OF	109	418	76	128	21	4	27	90	23	.306
2006 Jacksonville	Southern	OF	48	199	38	65	15	2	7	34	11	.327
2006 Las Vegas	P.C.	OF	44	182	37	67	14	6	3	36	14	.368
2006 Los Angeles	N.L.	OF	52	154	30	39	7	1	7	23	6	.253
2007 Las Vegas	P.C.	OF	39	161	32	53	16	3	4	20	9	.329
2007 Los Angeles a	N.L.	OF	98	292	47	100	12	5	10	42	10	.342
2008 Los Angeles	N.L.	OF	155	606	93	176	38	5	18	76	35	.290
2009 Los Angeles	N.L.	OF	159	606	97	180	25	7	26	101	34	.297
2010 Los Angeles	N.L.	OF	*162	602	82	150	25	6	28	89	19	.249
Major League Totals		5 Yrs.	626	2260	349	645	107	24	89	331	104	.285
Division Series												
2008 Los Angeles	N.L.	OF	3	13	0	2	2	0	0	1	0	.154
2009 Los Angeles	N.L.	OF	3	14	2	2	0	0	1	2	0	.143
Division Series Totals			6	27	2	4	2	0	1	3	0	.148
Championship Series												
2008 Los Angeles	N.L.	OF	5	15	1	5	1	0	0	0	0	.333
2009 Los Angeles	N.L.	OF	5	20	2	5	0	0	1	2	0	.250
Championship Series Totals			10	35	3	10	1	0	1	2	0	.286

a On disabled list from April 10 to April 27, 2007.

KENDALL, JASON DANIEL

Born, San Diego, California, June 26, 1974.
Bats Right. Throws Right. Height, 6 feet. Weight, 205 pounds.

Year Club	Lea	Pos	G	AB	R	H	2B	3B	HR	RBI	SB	Avg
1992 Pirates	Gulf Coast	C	33	111	7	29	2	0	0	10	2	.261
1993 Augusta	So.Atl.	C	102	366	43	101	17	4	1	40	8	.276
1994 Salem	Carolina	C	101	371	68	118	19	2	7	66	14	.318
1994 Carolina	Southern	C	13	47	6	11	2	0	0	6	0	.234
1995 Carolina	Southern	C	117	429	87	140	26	1	8	71	10	.326
1996 Pittsburgh	N.L.	C	130	414	54	124	23	5	3	42	5	.300
1997 Pittsburgh	N.L.	C	144	486	71	143	36	4	8	49	18	.294
1998 Pittsburgh	N.L.	C	149	535	95	175	36	3	12	75	26	.327
1999 Pittsburgh a	N.L.	C	78	280	61	93	20	3	8	41	22	.332
2000 Pittsburgh	N.L.	C	152	579	112	185	33	6	14	58	22	.320
2001 Pittsburgh	N.L.	C-OF	157	606	84	161	22	2	10	53	13	.266
2002 Pittsburgh	N.L.	C	145	545	59	154	25	3	3	44	15	.283
2003 Pittsburgh	N.L.	C	150	587	84	191	29	3	6	58	8	.325
2004 Pittsburgh b	N.L.	C	147	574	86	183	32	0	3	51	11	.319
2005 Oakland	A.L.	C	150	601	70	163	28	1	0	53	8	.271
2006 Oakland	A.L.	C	143	552	76	163	23	0	1	50	11	.295
2007 Oakland	A.L.	C-OF	80	292	24	66	10	0	2	22	3	.226

Year	Club	Lea	Pos	G	AB	R	H	2B	3B	HR	RBI	SB	Avg
2007	Chicago c-d	N.L.	C	57	174	21	47	10	1	1	19	0	.270
2008	Milwaukee	N.L.	C	151	516	46	127	30	2	2	49	8	.246
2009	Milwaukee e	N.L.	C	134	452	48	109	19	2	2	43	7	.241
2010	Kansas City f	A.L.	C	118	434	39	111	18	0	0	37	12	.256
Major League Totals			15 Yrs.	2085	7627	1030	2195	394	35	75	744	189	.288
	Division Series												
2006	Oakland	A.L.	C	3	14	1	3	1	0	0	1	0	.214
2007	Chicago	N.L.	C	1	4	0	1	0	0	0	1	0	.250
2008	Milwaukee	N.L.	C	4	14	0	2	0	0	0	1	0	.143
Division Series Totals				8	32	1	6	1	0	0	3	0	.188
	Championship Series												
2006	Oakland	A.L.	C	4	17	0	5	0	0	0	0	0	.294

a On disabled list from July 5 to November 17, 1999.
b Traded to Oakland Athletics with cash for pitcher Mark Redman and pitcher Arthur Rhodes, November 25, 2004.
c Traded to Chicago Cubs with cash for pitcher Jerry Blevins and catcher Rob Bowen, July 17, 2007.
d Filed for free agency, October 30, 2007. Signed with Milwaukee Brewers, November 28, 2007.
e Filed for free agency, November 5, 2009. Signed with Kansas City Royals, December 11, 2009.
f On disabled list from September 3 to November 10, 2010.

KENDRICK, HOWARD JOSEPH (HOWIE)

Born, Jacksonville, Florida, July 12, 1983.
Bats Right. Throws Right. Height, 5 feet, 10 inches. Weight, 195 pounds.

Year	Club	Lea	Pos	G	AB	R	H	2B	3B	HR	RBI	SB	Avg
2002	Angels	Arizona	2B	42	157	24	50	6	4	0	13	12	.318
2003	Provo	Pioneer	2B	63	234	65	86	20	3	3	36	8	.368
2004	Angels	Arizona	2B	3	12	1	3	1	0	0	0	2	.250
2004	Cedar Rapids	Midwest	2B	75	313	66	115	24	6	10	49	15	.367
2005	Rancho Cucamonga	Calif.	2B	63	279	69	107	23	6	12	47	13	.384
2005	Arkansas	Texas	2B	46	190	35	65	20	2	7	42	12	.342
2006	Salt Lake	P.C.	2B-3B	69	290	57	107	25	6	13	62	11	.369
2006	Los Angeles	A.L.	1B-2B-3B	72	267	25	76	21	1	4	30	6	.285
2007	Rancho Cucamonga	Calif.	DH	1	4	0	1	0	0	0	0	0	.250
2007	Salt Lake	P.C.	2B	13	50	9	15	1	0	3	11	1	.300
2007	Los Angeles a	A.L.	2B	88	338	55	109	24	2	5	39	5	.322
2008	Rancho Cucamonga	Calif.	2B	2	6	3	5	0	0	2	2	1	.833
2008	Salt Lake	P.C.	2B	2	5	0	1	0	0	0	1	0	.200
2008	Los Angeles b	A.L.	2B	92	340	43	104	26	2	3	37	11	.306
2009	Salt Lake	P.C.	2B	20	78	11	27	6	1	2	11	4	.346
2009	Los Angeles	A.L.	2B	105	374	61	109	21	3	10	61	11	.291
2010	Los Angeles	A.L.	2B-1B-OF	158	616	67	172	41	4	10	75	14	.279
Major League Totals			5 Yrs.	515	1935	251	570	133	12	32	242	47	.295
	Division Series												
2007	Los Angeles	A.L.	2B	3	10	0	2	0	0	0	1	2	.200
2008	Los Angeles	A.L.	2B	4	17	0	2	0	0	0	0	0	.118
2009	Los Angeles	A.L.	2B	2	5	1	1	0	0	0	0	1	.200
Division Series Totals				9	32	1	5	0	0	0	1	3	.156
	Championship Series												
2009	Los Angeles	A.L.	2B	4	14	3	4	0	1	1	1	0	.286

a On disabled list from April 18 to May 23 and July 8 to August 20, 2007.
b On disabled list from April 14 to May 30 and August 28 to September 22, 2008.

KENNEDY, ADAM THOMAS

Born, Riverside, California, January 10, 1976.
Bats Left. Throws Right. Height, 6 feet. Weight, 185 pounds.

Year	Club	Lea	Pos	G	AB	R	H	2B	3B	HR	RBI	SB	Avg
1997	New Jersey	N.Y.-Penn.	SS	29	114	20	39	6	3	0	19	9	.342
1997	Pr William	Carolina	SS	35	154	24	48	9	3	1	27	4	.312
1998	Pr William	Carolina	2B-SS	17	69	9	18	6	0	0	7	5	.261
1998	Arkansas	Texas	SS-2B	52	205	35	57	11	2	6	24	6	.278
1998	Memphis	P.C.	SS-2B	74	305	36	93	22	7	4	41	15	.305
1999	Memphis	P.C.	2B	91	367	69	120	22	4	10	63	20	.327
1999	St. Louis	N.L.	2B	33	102	12	26	10	1	1	16	0	.255
2000	Anaheim a	A.L.	2B	156	598	82	159	33	11	9	72	22	.266
2001	Rancho Cucamonga	Calif.	2B	3	8	3	3	2	0	0	1	3	.375
2001	Anaheim b	A.L.	2B	137	478	48	129	25	3	6	40	12	.270
2002	Anaheim	A.L.	2B-OF	144	474	65	148	32	6	7	52	17	.312

Year Club	Lea	Pos	G	AB	R	H	2B	3B	HR	RBI	SB	Avg
2003 Rancho Cucamonga	Calif.	2B	3	11	3	3	1	0	1	1	0	.273
2003 Anaheim c	A.L.	2B	143	449	71	121	17	1	13	49	22	.269
2004 Anaheim	A.L.	2B	144	468	70	130	20	5	10	48	15	.278
2005 Rancho Cucamonga	Calif.	2B	2	5	1	2	0	0	0	1	1	.400
2005 Salt Lake	P.C.	2B	4	17	4	7	1	0	0	4	2	.412
2005 Los Angeles d	A.L.	2B	129	416	49	125	23	0	2	37	19	.300
2006 Los Angeles e	A.L.	2B	139	451	50	123	26	6	4	55	16	.273
2007 St. Louis f	N.L.	2B-SS-OF	87	279	27	61	9	1	3	18	6	.219
2008 St. Louis	N.L.	2B-OF-1B	115	339	42	95	17	4	2	36	7	.280
2009 Durham	Int.	2B-1B-3B	23	82	11	23	4	0	3	9	2	.280
2009 Oakland g-h-i	A.L.	3B-2B-1B-OF	129	529	65	153	29	1	11	63	20	.289
2010 Washington j	N.L.	2B-1B-3B	135	342	43	85	16	1	3	31	14	.249
Major League Totals		12 Yrs.	1491	4925	624	1355	257	40	71	517	170	.275
Division Series												
2002 Anaheim	A.L.	2B	4	8	4	4	1	0	1	3	1	.500
2005 Los Angeles	A.L.	2B	5	17	0	4	0	1	0	2	0	.235
Division Series Totals			9	25	4	8	1	1	1	5	1	.320
Championship Series												
2002 Anaheim	A.L.	2B	4	14	5	5	0	0	3	5	0	.357
2005 Los Angeles	A.L.	2B	5	14	3	4	0	0	0	1	0	.286
Championship Series Totals			9	28	8	9	0	0	3	6	0	.321
World Series Record												
2002 Anaheim	A.L.	2B	7	25	1	7	2	0	0	2	0	.280

a Traded to Anaheim Angels with pitcher Kent Bottenfield for outfielder Jim Edmonds, March 23, 2000.
b On disabled list from March 23 to April 13, 2001.
c On disabled list from April 7 to April 22, 2003.
d On disabled list from March 25 to May 2, 2005.
e Filed for free agency, October 29, 2006. Signed with St. Louis Cardinals, November 28, 2006.
f On disabled list from August 12 to November 2, 2007.
g Released by St. Louis Cardinals, February 9, 2009. Signed with Tampa Bay Rays organization, February 17, 2009.
h Traded to Oakland Athletics for player to be named later, May 8, 2009. Tampa Bay Rays received infielder Joe Dillon to complete trade, May 9, 2009.
i Filed for free agency, November 5, 2009. Signed with Washington Nationals, February 12, 2010.
j Filed for free agency, November 3, 2010. Signed with Seattle Mariners organization, January 10, 2011.

KEPPINGER, JEFFREY SCOTT (JEFF)

Born, Miami, Florida, April 21, 1980.
Bats Right. Throws Right. Height, 6 feet. Weight, 180 pounds.

Year Club	Lea	Pos	G	AB	R	H	2B	3B	HR	RBI	SB	Avg
2002 Hickory	So.Atl.	2B	126	478	75	132	23	4	10	73	6	.276
2003 Lynchburg	Carolina	2B-3B-1B	92	342	55	111	21	2	3	51	3	.325
2004 Altoona	Eastern	2B	82	323	45	108	17	2	1	33	10	.334
2004 Binghamton	Eastern	2B-3B	14	47	14	17	3	1	0	5	2	.362
2004 Norfolk	Int.	2B	6	19	1	6	1	0	0	2	0	.316
2004 New York a	N.L.	2B	33	116	9	33	2	0	3	9	2	.284
2005 Norfolk b	Int.	2B-3B-SS	64	255	40	86	15	3	3	29	5	.337
2006 Norfolk	Int.	2B-OF-3B	87	323	36	97	13	0	2	26	0	.300
2006 Omaha	P.C.	2B-3B-1B-SS	32	127	21	45	6	1	2	17	0	.354
2006 Kansas City c	A.L.	3B-1B-2B-OF	22	60	11	16	2	0	2	8	0	.267
2007 Sarasota	Fla.St.	3B-2B	3	12	1	4	2	0	0	1	0	.333
2007 Louisville	Int.	3B-2B-OF-1B	57	228	31	84	15	1	2	18	1	.368
2007 Cincinnati d-e	N.L.	SS-3B-2B-OF	67	241	39	80	16	2	5	32	2	.332
2008 Sarasota	Fla.St.	3B	2	7	1	2	0	0	0	1	0	.286
2008 Louisville	Int.	3B-SS	6	22	3	11	2	0	1	2	0	.500
2008 Cincinnati f	N.L.	SS-3B-1B-2B	121	459	45	122	24	2	3	43	3	.266
2009 Houston g	N.L.	3B-2B-SS-OF	107	305	35	78	13	3	7	29	0	.256
2010 Corpus Christi	Texas	2B	2	5	0	2	0	0	0	1	0	.400
2010 Houston h	N.L.	2B-SS	137	514	62	148	34	1	6	59	4	.288
Major League Totals		6 Yrs.	487	1695	201	477	91	8	26	180	11	.281

a Traded to New York Mets with pitcher Kris Benson for infielder Ty Wigginton, pitcher Matt Peterson and infielder Jose Bautista, July 30, 2004.
b On disabled list from September 9 to October 31, 2005.
c Traded to Kansas City Royals for infielder Ruben Gotay, July 19, 2006.
d Traded to Cincinnati Reds for pitcher Russ Haltiwanger, January 11, 2007.
e On disabled list from March 23 to April 22, 2007.
f On disabled list from May 14 to June 22, 2008.
g Traded to Houston Astros for player to be named later, March 31, 2009. Cincinnati Reds received infielder Drew Sutton to complete trade, April 16, 2009.
h On disabled list from August 17 to September 1, 2010.

KINSLER, IAN MICHAEL

Born, Tucson, Arizona, June 22, 1982.
Bats Right. Throws Right. Height, 6 feet. Weight, 200 pounds.

Year	Club	Lea	Pos	G	AB	R	H	2B	3B	HR	RBI	SB	Avg
2003	Spokane	Northwest	SS	51	188	32	52	10	6	1	15	11	.277
2004	Clinton	Midwest	SS	60	227	52	91	30	1	11	53	16	.401
2004	Frisco	Texas	SS	71	277	51	83	21	1	9	46	7	.300
2005	Oklahoma	P.C.	2B-SS-3B	131	530	102	145	28	2	23	94	19	.274
2006	Oklahoma	P.C.	2B	10	39	7	10	3	0	2	6	1	.256
2006	Texas a	A.L.	2B	120	423	65	121	27	1	14	55	11	.286
2007	Oklahoma	P.C.	2B	3	13	1	5	0	0	0	3	2	.385
2007	Texas b	A.L.	2B	130	483	96	127	22	2	20	61	23	.263
2008	Texas c	A.L.	2B	121	518	102	165	41	4	18	71	26	.319
2009	Frisco	Texas	2B	2	7	1	0	0	0	0	0	0	.000
2009	Texas d	A.L.	2B	144	566	101	143	32	4	31	86	31	.253
2010	Frisco	Texas	2B	6	19	3	5	0	1	0	6	2	.263
2010	Texas e	A.L.	2B	103	391	73	112	20	1	9	45	15	.286
Major League Totals			5 Yrs.	618	2381	437	668	142	12	92	318	106	.281
	Division Series												
2010	Texas	A.L.	2B	5	18	5	8	0	0	3	6	0	.444
	Championship Series												
2010	Texas	A.L.	2B	6	20	1	5	1	1	0	3	2	.250
	World Series Record												
2010	Texas	A.L.	2B	5	16	1	3	1	0	0	0	1	.188

a On disabled list from April 12 to May 25, 2006.
b On disabled list from July 2 to July 31, 2007.
c On disabled list from August 18 to November 14, 2008.
d On disabled list from July 29 to August 14, 2009.
e On disabled list from March 26 to April 30 and July 28 to September 1, 2010.

KONERKO, PAUL HENRY

Born, Providence, Rhode Island, March 5, 1976.
Bats Right. Throws Right. Height, 6 feet, 2 inches. Weight, 220 pounds.

Year	Club	Lea	Pos	G	AB	R	H	2B	3B	HR	RBI	SB	Avg
1994	Yakima	Northwest	C	67	257	25	74	15	2	6	58	1	.288
1995	San Berndno	California	C	118	448	77	124	21	1	19	77	3	.277
1996	San Antonio	Texas	1B	133	470	78	141	23	2	29	86	1	.300
1996	Albuquerque	P.C.	1B	4	14	2	6	0	0	1	2	0	.429
1997	Albuquerque	P.C.	3B-1B-2B	130	483	97	156	31	1	37	127	2	.323
1997	Los Angeles	N.L.	1B-3B	6	7	0	1	0	0	0	0	0	.143
1998	Albuquerque	P.C.	OF-1B-3B	24	87	16	33	10	0	6	26	0	.379
1998	Indianapols	Int.	3B	39	150	25	49	8	0	8	39	1	.327
1998	Los Angeles-Cinc. a-b	N.L.	1B-3B-OF	75	217	21	47	4	0	7	29	0	.217
1999	Chicago	A.L.	1B-3B	142	513	71	151	31	4	24	81	1	.294
2000	Chicago	A.L.	1B-3B	143	524	84	156	31	1	21	97	1	.298
2001	Chicago	A.L.	1B	156	582	92	164	35	0	32	99	1	.282
2002	Chicago	A.L.	1B	151	570	81	173	30	0	27	104	0	.304
2003	Chicago	A.L.	1B	137	444	49	104	19	0	18	65	0	.234
2004	Chicago	A.L.	1B	155	563	84	156	22	0	41	117	1	.277
2005	Chicago c	A.L.	1B	158	575	98	163	24	0	40	100	0	.283
2006	Chicago	A.L.	1B	152	566	97	177	30	0	35	113	1	.313
2007	Chicago	A.L.	1B	151	549	71	142	34	0	31	90	0	.259
2008	Charlotte	Int.	1B	4	11	3	5	2	0	0	3	0	.455
2008	Chicago d	A.L.	1B	122	438	59	105	19	1	22	62	2	.240
2009	Chicago	A.L.	1B	152	546	75	151	30	1	28	88	1	.277
2010	Chicago e	A.L.	1B	149	548	89	171	30	1	39	111	0	.312
Major League Totals			14 Yrs.	1849	6642	971	1861	339	8	365	1156	8	.280
	Division Series												
2000	Chicago	A.L.	1B	3	9	1	0	0	0	0	0	0	.000
2005	Chicago	A.L.	1B	3	12	3	3	0	0	2	4	0	.250
2008	Chicago	A.L.	1B	4	16	3	5	0	0	2	2	0	.313
Division Series Totals				10	37	7	8	0	0	4	6	0	.216
	Championship Series												
2005	Chicago	A.L.	1B	5	21	2	6	1	0	2	7	0	.286
	World Series Record												
2005	Chicago	A.L.	1B	4	16	1	4	1	0	1	4	0	.250

a Traded to Cincinnati Reds with pitcher Dennis Reyes for pitcher Jeff Shaw, July 4, 1998.
b Traded to Chicago White Sox for outfielder Mike Cameron, November 11, 1998.

c Filed for free agency, October 27, 2005, re-signed with Chicago White Sox, November 30, 2005.
d On disabled list from June 15 to July 8, 2008.
e Filed for free agency, November 1, 2010. Signed with Chicago White Sox, December 8, 2010.

KOTCHMAN, CASEY JOHN

Born, St. Petersburg, Florida, February 22, 1983.
Bats Left. Throws Left. Height, 6 feet, 3 inches. Weight, 215 pounds.

Year Club	Lea	Pos	G	AB	R	H	2B	3B	HR	RBI	SB	Avg
2001 Angels	Arizona	1B	4	15	5	9	1	0	1	5	0	.600
2001 Provo	Pioneer	1B	7	22	6	11	3	0	0	7	0	.500
2002 Cedar Rapids	Midwest	1B	81	288	42	81	30	1	5	50	2	.281
2003 Angels	Arizona	1B	7	27	5	9	1	0	2	6	0	.333
2003 Rancho Cucamonga	Calif.	1B	57	206	42	72	12	0	8	28	2	.350
2004 Arkansas	Texas	1B	28	114	19	42	11	0	3	18	0	.368
2004 Anaheim	A.L.	1B	38	116	7	26	6	0	0	15	3	.224
2004 Salt Lake	P.C.	1B	49	199	32	74	22	0	5	38	0	.372
2005 Salt Lake	P.C.	1B	94	363	62	105	23	1	10	58	0	.289
2005 Los Angeles	A.L.	1B	47	126	16	35	5	0	7	22	1	.278
2006 Salt Lake	P.C.	1B	3	7	0	0	0	0	0	1	0	.000
2006 Los Angeles a	A.L.	1B	29	79	6	12	2	0	1	6	0	.152
2007 Los Angeles	A.L.	1B	137	443	64	131	37	3	11	68	2	.296
2008 Los Angeles	A.L.	1B	100	373	47	107	24	0	12	54	2	.287
2008 Atlanta b	N.L.	1B	43	152	18	36	4	1	2	20	0	.237
2009 Gwinnett	Int.	1B	2	3	2	0	0	0	0	3	0	.000
2009 Atlanta	N.L.	1B	87	298	28	84	20	0	6	41	0	.282
2009 Boston c-d-e	A.L.	1B	39	87	9	19	3	0	1	7	1	.218
2010 Seattle f	A.L.	1B	125	414	37	90	20	1	9	51	0	.217
Major League Totals		7 Yrs.	645	2088	232	540	121	5	49	284	9	.259
Division Series												
2004 Anaheim	A.L.	PH	2	1	0	0	0	0	0	0	0	.000
2005 Los Angeles	A.L.	PH	2	2	0	0	0	0	0	0	0	.000
2007 Los Angeles	A.L.	1B	2	5	1	0	0	0	0	0	0	.000
2009 Boston	A.L.	1B	3	1	0	0	0	0	0	0	0	.000
Division Series Totals			9	9	1	0	0	0	0	0	0	.000
Championship Series												
2005 Los Angeles	A.L.	DH	2	7	0	2	1	0	0	1	0	.286

a On disabled list from May 9 to October 2, 2006.
b Traded to Atlanta Braves with pitcher Steve Marek for infielder Mark Teixeira, July 29, 2008.
c On disabled list from June 1 to June 16, 2009.
d Traded to Boston Red Sox for infielder Adam LaRoche, July 31, 2009. Boston Red Sox received pitcher Miguel Celestino to complete trade, March 18, 2010.
e Traded to Seattle Mariners for infielder Bill Hall and player to be named later, January 7, 2010.
f Filed for free agency, November 4, 2010.

KOTSAY, MARK STEVEN

Born, Whittier, California, December 2, 1975.
Bats Left. Throws Left. Height, 6 feet. Weight, 205 pounds.

Year Club	Lea	Pos	G	AB	R	H	2B	3B	HR	RBI	SB	Avg
1996 Kane County	Midwest	OF	17	60	16	17	5	0	2	8	3	.283
1997 Florida	N.L.	OF	14	52	5	10	1	1	0	4	3	.192
1997 Portland	Eastern	OF	114	438	103	134	27	2	20	77	17	.306
1998 Florida	N.L.	OF-1B	154	578	72	161	25	7	11	68	10	.279
1999 Florida	N.L.	OF-1B	148	495	57	134	23	9	8	50	7	.271
2000 Florida	N.L.	OF-1B	152	530	87	158	31	5	12	57	19	.298
2001 San Diego a-b	N.L.	OF	119	406	67	118	29	1	10	58	13	.291
2002 San Diego	N.L.	OF	153	578	82	169	27	7	17	61	11	.292
2003 San Diego c-d	N.L.	OF	128	482	64	128	28	4	7	38	6	.266
2004 Oakland	A.L.	OF	148	606	78	190	37	3	15	63	8	.314
2005 Oakland	A.L.	OF	139	582	75	163	35	1	15	82	5	.280
2006 Oakland	A.L.	OF-1B	129	502	57	138	29	3	7	59	6	.275
2007 Sacramento	P.C.	OF	10	37	2	10	1	0	0	2	2	.270
2007 Oakland e-f	A.L.	OF	56	206	20	44	14	0	1	20	1	.214
2008 Mississippi	Southern	OF	5	18	4	6	1	0	0	1	0	.333
2008 Atlanta	N.L.	OF	88	318	39	92	17	3	6	37	2	.289
2008 Boston g-h-i	A.L.	OF-1B	22	84	6	19	8	1	0	12	0	.226
2009 Pawtucket	Int.	OF-1B	10	33	2	10	1	0	0	5	1	.303
2009 Boston-Chicago j-k	A.L.	1B-OF	67	187	16	52	9	0	4	23	3	.278
2010 Chicago l	A.L.	DH-1B-OF	107	327	30	78	17	2	8	31	1	.239
Major League Totals		14 Yrs.	1624	5933	755	1654	330	47	121	663	95	.279

Year Club	Lea	Pos	G	AB	R	H	2B	3B	HR	RBI	SB	Avg
Division Series												
2006 Oakland	A.L.	OF	3	14	2	2	0	0	1	2	0	.143
2008 Boston	A.L.	1B	3	10	1	3	0	0	0	0	0	.300
Division Series Totals			6	24	3	5	0	0	1	2	0	.208
Championship Series												
2006 Oakland	A.L.	OF	4	16	3	4	2	0	0	0	0	.250
2008 Boston	A.L.	1B	7	30	1	7	3	0	0	0	0	.233
Championship Series Totals			11	46	4	11	5	0	0	0	0	.239

a Traded to San Diego Padres with outfielder Cesar Crespo for pitcher Matt Clement, pitcher Omar Ortiz and outfielder Eric Owens, March 28, 2001
b On disabled list from April 16 to May 1, 2001.
c On disabled list from May 19 to June 5, 2003.
d Traded to Oakland Athletics for catcher Ramon Hernandez and outfielder Terrence Long, November 26, 2003.
e On disabled list from March 23 to June 1 and August 15 to October 8, 2007.
f Traded to Atlanta Braves for pitcher Joey Devine, pitcher Jamie Richmond and cash, January 14, 2008.
g On disabled list from May 26 to July 1, 2008.
h Traded to Boston Red Sox for outfielder Luis Sumoza, August 29, 2008.
i Filed for free agency, November 1, 2008, re-signed with Boston Red Sox, January 15, 2009.
j On disabled list from March 27 to June 2, 2009.
k Traded to Chicago White Sox for outfielder Brian Anderson, July 28, 2009.
l Filed for free agency, November 1, 2010.

KOTTARAS, GEORGE

Born, Scarborough, Ontario, Canada, May 16, 1983.
Bats Left. Throws Right. Height, 6 feet. Weight, 185 pounds.

Year Club	Lea	Pos	G	AB	R	H	2B	3B	HR	RBI	SB	Avg
2003 Idaho Falls	Pioneer	C-1B	42	143	27	37	8	1	7	24	1	.259
2004 Fort Wayne	Midwest	C	78	271	40	84	18	1	7	46	0	.310
2005 Lake Elsinore	Calif.	C	91	337	54	102	29	0	9	50	2	.303
2005 Mobile	Southern	C	29	101	16	29	7	0	2	15	0	.287
2006 Portland	P.C.	C	33	119	14	25	10	1	2	17	0	.210
2006 Mobile a	Southern	C	78	257	40	71	19	1	8	33	0	.276
2007 Pawtucket	Int.	C	87	294	32	71	22	0	9	39	1	.241
2008 Pawtucket	Int.	C	107	395	63	96	18	0	22	65	0	.243
2008 Boston	A.L.	C	3	5	1	1	1	0	0	0	0	.200
2009 Pawtucket	Int.	C	10	24	1	7	3	0	0	0	0	.292
2009 Boston b-c	A.L.	C-3B	45	93	15	22	11	0	1	10	0	.237
2010 Milwaukee	N.L.	C-1B-OF	67	212	24	43	12	1	9	26	2	.203
Major League Totals		3 Yrs.	115	310	40	66	24	1	10	36	2	.213

a Sent by San Diego Padres to Boston Red Sox as player to be named later for pitcher David Wells, September 5, 2006.
b On disabled list from July 30 to September 1, 2009.
c Claimed on waivers by Milwaukee Brewers, November 18, 2009.

KOUZMANOFF, KEVIN

Born, Newport Beach, California, July 25, 1981.
Bats Right. Throws Right. Height, 6 feet, 1 inch. Weight, 210 pounds.

Year Club	Lea	Pos	G	AB	R	H	2B	3B	HR	RBI	SB	Avg
2003 Mahoning Valley	N.Y.-Penn.	3B	54	206	31	56	8	1	8	33	2	.272
2004 Akron	Eastern	3B	7	24	3	5	1	1	1	6	0	.208
2004 Lake County	So.Atl.	3B	123	473	74	156	35	5	16	87	5	.330
2005 Kinston	Carolina	3B	68	254	47	86	20	4	12	58	3	.339
2005 Mahoning Valley	N.Y.-Penn.	3B	3	7	0	1	0	0	0	0	0	.143
2006 Akron	Eastern	3B	67	244	46	95	19	1	15	55	2	.389
2006 Buffalo	Int.	3B-1B	27	102	22	36	9	0	7	20	2	.353
2006 Cleveland a	A.L.	DH-3B	16	56	4	12	2	0	3	11	0	.214
2007 San Diego	N.L.	3B	145	484	57	133	30	2	18	74	1	.275
2008 San Diego	N.L.	3B	154	624	71	162	31	4	23	84	0	.260
2009 San Diego b	N.L.	3B	141	529	50	135	31	1	18	88	1	.255
2010 Oakland	A.L.	3B	143	551	59	136	32	1	16	71	2	.247
Major League Totals		5 Yrs.	599	2244	241	578	126	8	78	328	4	.258

a Traded to San Diego Padres with pitcher Andrew Brown for infielder Josh Barfield, November 8, 2006.
b Traded to Oakland Athletics with infielder Eric Sogard for outfielders Scott Hairston and Aaron Cunningham, January 16, 2010.

KUBEL, JASON JAMES

Born, Belle Fourche, South Dakota, May 25, 1982.
Bats Left. Throws Right. Height, 5 feet, 11 inches. Weight, 200 pounds.

Year	Club	Lea	Pos	G	AB	R	H	2B	3B	HR	RBI	SB	Avg
2000	Twins	Gulf Coast	OF	23	78	17	22	3	2	0	13	0	.282
2001	Twins	Gulf Coast	OF	37	124	14	41	10	4	1	30	3	.331
2002	Quad Cities	Midwest	OF	115	424	60	136	26	4	17	69	3	.321
2003	Fort Myers	Fla.St.	OF	116	420	56	125	20	4	5	82	4	.298
2004	New Britain	Eastern	OF	37	138	25	52	14	4	6	29	0	.377
2004	Rochester	Int.	OF	90	350	71	120	28	0	16	71	16	.343
2004	Minnesota	A.L.	OF	23	60	10	18	2	0	2	7	1	.300
2005	Minnesota a	A.L.					INJURED—Did Not Play						
2006	Rochester	Int.	OF	30	120	18	34	7	2	4	22	2	.283
2006	Minnesota	A.L.	OF	73	220	23	53	8	0	8	26	2	.241
2007	Minnesota	A.L.	OF	128	418	49	114	31	2	13	65	5	.273
2008	Minnesota	A.L.	DH-OF	141	463	74	126	22	5	20	78	0	.272
2009	Minnesota	A.L.	DH-OF	146	514	73	154	35	2	28	103	1	.300
2010	Minnesota	A.L.	OF	143	518	68	129	23	3	21	92	0	.249
Major League Totals			6 Yrs.	654	2193	297	594	121	12	92	371	9	.271
	Division Series												
2004	Minnesota	A.L.	DH	2	7	0	1	1	0	0	0	0	.143
2009	Minnesota	A.L.	OF-DH	3	14	0	1	0	0	0	0	0	.071
2010	Minnesota	A.L.	OF	3	8	0	0	0	0	0	0	0	.000
Division Series Totals				8	29	0	2	1	0	0	0	0	.069

a On disabled list from March 15 to October 14, 2005.

LAIRD, GERALD LEE

Born, Westminster, California, November 13, 1979.
Bats Right. Throws Right. Height, 6 feet, 1 inch. Weight, 225 pounds.

Year	Club	Lea	Pos	G	AB	R	H	2B	3B	HR	RBI	SB	Avg
1999	Southern Oregon	Northwest	C	60	228	45	65	7	2	2	39	10	.285
2000	Athletics	Arizona	C	14	50	10	15	2	1	0	9	2	.300
2000	Visalia	Calif.	C	33	103	14	25	3	0	0	13	7	.243
2001	Modesto	Calif.	C-OF-1B-2B	119	443	71	113	13	5	5	46	10	.255
2002	Tulsa a	Texas	C-OF	123	442	70	122	21	4	11	67	8	.276
2003	Oklahoma	P.C.	C	99	338	50	88	20	5	9	42	9	.260
2003	Texas	A.L.	C	19	44	9	12	2	1	1	4	0	.273
2004	Texas	A.L.	C	49	147	20	33	6	0	1	16	0	.224
2004	Oklahoma b	P.C.	C	6	22	2	4	2	0	0	2	1	.182
2005	Rangers	Arizona	C	8	26	4	5	2	2	0	3	1	.192
2005	Oklahoma	P.C.	C	75	281	51	87	12	4	17	55	12	.310
2005	Texas	A.L.	C-OF	13	40	7	9	2	0	1	4	0	.225
2006	Texas	A.L.	C-OF	78	243	46	72	20	1	7	22	3	.296
2007	Texas	A.L.	C-OF	120	407	48	91	18	3	9	47	6	.224
2008	Oklahoma	P.C.	C	4	12	1	0	0	0	0	2	0	.000
2008	Texas c-d	A.L.	C-3B	95	344	54	95	24	0	6	41	2	.276
2009	Detroit	A.L.	C-1B	135	413	49	93	23	2	4	33	5	.225
2010	Detroit e	A.L.	C	89	270	22	56	11	0	5	25	3	.207
Major League Totals			8 Yrs.	598	1908	255	461	106	7	34	192	19	.242

a Traded to Texas Rangers with pitcher Mario Ramos, outfielder Ryan Ludwick and infielder Jason Hart for pitcher Mike Venafro and outfielder Carlos Pena, January 14, 2002.
b On disabled list from May 21 to July 23, 2004.
c On disabled list from June 21 to July 26, 2008.
d Traded to Detroit Tigers for pitcher Guillermo Moscoso and pitcher Carlos Melo, December 9, 2008.
e Filed for free agency, November 1, 2010. Signed with St. Louis Cardinals, December 14, 2010.

LANGERHANS, RYAN DAVID

Born, San Antonio, Texas, February 20, 1980.
Bats Left. Throws Left. Height, 6 feet, 3 inches. Weight, 220 pounds.

Year	Club	Lea	Pos	G	AB	R	H	2B	3B	HR	RBI	SB	Avg
1998	Braves	Gulf Coast	OF	43	148	15	41	10	4	2	19	2	.277
1999	Macon	So.Atl.	OF	121	448	66	120	30	1	9	49	19	.268
2000	Myrtle Beach	Carolina	OF	116	392	55	83	14	7	6	37	25	.212
2001	Myrtle Beach	Carolina	OF	125	450	66	129	30	3	7	48	22	.287
2002	Greenville	Southern	OF	109	391	57	98	23	2	9	62	10	.251
2002	Atlanta	N.L.	OF	1	1	0	0	0	0	0	0	0	.000
2003	Greenville	Southern	OF	94	336	42	85	23	2	6	38	10	.253
2003	Richmond	Int.	OF	38	132	13	37	10	2	4	11	2	.280

Year	Club	Lea	Pos	G	AB	R	H	2B	3B	HR	RBI	SB	Avg
2003	Atlanta	N.L.	OF	16	15	2	4	0	0	0	0	0	.267
2004	Richmond	Int.	OF	135	456	103	136	34	3	20	72	5	.298
2005	Atlanta	N.L.	OF	128	326	48	87	22	3	8	42	0	.267
2006	Atlanta	N.L.	OF	131	315	46	76	16	3	7	28	1	.241
2007	Oakland	A.L.	OF	2	4	0	0	0	0	0	0	0	.000
2007	Columbus	Int.	OF	14	51	11	14	3	0	1	2	1	.275
2007	Atlanta-Washington a-b	N.L.	OF	123	206	27	35	7	2	6	23	3	.170
2008	Columbus	Int.	OF-1B	62	213	40	66	16	2	3	31	12	.310
2008	Washington c	N.L.	OF-1B	73	111	17	26	5	2	3	12	2	.234
2009	Syracuse	Int.	OF-1B	64	205	34	57	16	0	9	40	7	.278
2009	Seattle d-e	A.L.	OF	38	101	12	22	6	1	3	10	0	.218
2010	Tacoma	P.C.	OF-1B	12	39	8	11	5	0	0	3	3	.282
2010	Seattle f	A.L.	OF-1B	60	107	16	21	2	1	3	4	4	.196
Major League Totals			8 Yrs.	572	1186	168	271	58	12	30	119	10	.228
	Division Series												
2005	Atlanta	N.L.	OF	4	12	1	4	1	0	0	0	1	.333

a Sold to Oakland Athletics, April 29, 2007.
b Traded to Washington Nationals for outfielder Chris Snelling, May 2, 2007.
c Filed for free agency, October 23, 2008, re-signed with Washington Nationals organization, December 13, 2008.
d Traded to Seattle Mariners for infielder Mike Morse, June 28, 2009.
e Not offered contract, December 12, 2009, re-signed with Seattle Mariners, December 18, 2009.
f Filed for free agency, November 4, 2010, re-signed with Seattle Mariners organization, December 15, 2010.

LA PORTA, MATTHEW VINCENT (MATT)

Born, Port Charlotte, Florida, January 8, 1985.
Bats Right. Throws Right. Height, 6 feet, 2 inches. Weight, 210 pounds.

Year	Club	Lea	Pos	G	AB	R	H	2B	3B	HR	RBI	SB	Avg
2007	Helena	Pioneer	OF	7	27	4	7	1	0	2	4	0	.259
2007	West Virginia	So.Atl.	OF	23	88	18	28	8	0	10	27	0	.318
2008	Akron	Eastern	OF	17	60	6	14	1	0	2	8	0	.233
2008	Huntsville a	Southern	OF-1B	84	302	56	87	23	2	20	66	2	.288
2009	Columbus	Int.	1B-OF	93	338	63	101	23	2	17	60	1	.299
2009	Cleveland	A.L.	OF-1B	52	181	29	46	13	0	7	21	2	.254
2010	Columbus	Int.	OF-1B	18	69	7	25	4	0	5	16	0	.362
2010	Cleveland	A.L.	1B-OF	110	376	41	83	15	1	12	41	0	.221
Major League Totals			2 Yrs.	162	557	70	129	28	1	19	62	2	.232

a Traded by Milwaukee Brewers to Cleveland Indians with pitcher Zach Jackson, pitcher Rob Bryson and player to be named later for pitcher C.C. Sabathia, July 7, 2008. Cleveland Indians received outfielder Michael Brantley to complete trade, October 3, 2008.

LA ROCHE, ANDREW CHRISTIAN (ANDY)

Born, Fort Scott, Kansas, September 13, 1983.
Bats Right. Throws Right. Height, 6 feet, 1 inch. Weight, 215 pounds.

Year	Club	Lea	Pos	G	AB	R	H	2B	3B	HR	RBI	SB	Avg
2003	Ogden	Pioneer	DH	6	19	1	4	1	0	0	5	0	.211
2004	Vero Beach	Fla.St.	3B	62	219	26	52	13	0	10	34	2	.237
2004	Columbus	So.Atl.	3B	65	244	52	69	20	0	13	42	12	.283
2005	Vero Beach	Fla.St.	3B	63	249	54	83	14	1	21	51	6	.333
2005	Jacksonville	Southern	3B-1B	64	227	41	62	12	0	9	43	2	.273
2006	Las Vegas	P.C.	3B	55	202	35	65	14	1	10	35	3	.322
2006	Jacksonville	Southern	3B	62	230	42	71	13	0	9	46	6	.309
2007	Las Vegas	P.C.	3B-OF	73	265	55	82	18	1	18	48	2	.309
2007	Los Angeles	N.L.	3B-OF	35	93	16	21	5	0	1	10	2	.226
2008	Jacksonville	Southern	3B	6	22	5	7	1	0	0	1	1	.318
2008	Las Vegas	P.C.	3B-2B-1B	39	123	35	36	3	0	5	28	2	.293
2008	Los Angeles-Pittsburgh a-b	N.L.	3B-2B-1B	76	223	17	37	5	0	5	18	2	.166
2009	Pittsburgh	N.L.	3B	150	524	64	135	29	5	12	64	3	.258
2010	Pittsburgh c	N.L.	3B-2B-1B	102	247	26	51	8	0	4	16	1	.206
Major League Totals			4 Yrs.	363	1087	123	244	47	5	22	108	8	.224

a On disabled list from March 21 to May 3, 2008.
b Traded to Pittsburgh Pirates with pitcher Bryan Morris for outfielder Manny Ramirez, July 31, 2008.
c Filed for free agency, November 29, 2010.

LA ROCHE, DAVID ADAM (ADAM)

Born, Orange Co., California, November 6, 1979.
Bats Left. Throws Left. Height, 6 feet, 3 inches. Weight, 200 pounds.

Year	Club	Lea	Pos	G	AB	R	H	2B	3B	HR	RBI	SB	Avg
2000	Danville	Appal.	1B	56	201	38	62	13	3	7	45	4	.308
2001	Myrtle Beach	Carolina	1B-OF	126	471	49	118	31	0	7	47	10	.251
2002	Myrtle Beach	Carolina	1B	69	250	30	84	17	0	9	53	0	.336
2002	Greenville	Southern	1B	45	173	17	50	9	0	4	19	1	.289
2003	Greenville	Southern	1B	61	219	42	62	12	1	12	37	1	.283
2003	Richmond	Int.	1B	72	264	33	78	21	0	8	35	1	.295
2004	Richmond	Int.	1B	4	11	1	2	0	0	1	2	0	.182
2004	Atlanta a	N.L.	1B	110	324	45	90	27	1	13	45	0	.278
2005	Atlanta	N.L.	1B	141	451	53	117	28	0	20	78	0	.259
2006	Atlanta b	N.L.	1B	149	492	89	140	38	1	32	90	0	.285
2007	Pittsburgh	N.L.	1B	152	563	71	153	42	0	21	88	1	.272
2008	Hickory	So.Atl.	1B	3	10	2	6	1	0	1	4	0	.600
2008	Pittsburgh c	N.L.	1B	136	492	66	133	32	3	25	85	1	.270
2009	Boston	A.L.	1B	6	19	2	5	2	0	1	3	0	.263
2009	Pittsburgh-Atlanta d-e-f	N.L.	1B	144	536	76	149	36	2	24	80	2	.278
2010	Arizona g	N.L.	1B	151	560	75	146	37	2	25	100	0	.261
Major League Totals			7 Yrs.	989	3437	477	933	242	9	161	569	4	.271
	Division Series												
2004	Atlanta	N.L.	1B	5	17	1	4	1	0	1	4	0	.235
2005	Atlanta	N.L.	1B	3	8	2	4	1	0	1	6	0	.500
Division Series Totals				8	25	3	8	2	0	2	10	0	.320

a On disabled list from May 29 to July 2, 2004.
b Traded to Pittsburgh Pirates with outfielder Jamie Romak for pitcher Mike Gonzalez and infielder Brent Lillibridge, January 17, 2007.
c On disabled list from July 28 to August 14, 2008.
d Traded to Boston Red Sox for infielder Argenis Diaz and pitcher Hunter Strickland, July 22, 2009.
e Traded to Atlanta Braves for infielder Casey Kotchman, July 31, 2009.
f Filed for free agency, November 5, 2009. Signed with Arizona Diamondbacks, January 15, 2010.
g Filed for free agency, November 2, 2010. Signed with Washington Nationals, January 7, 2011.

LEE, CARLOS

Born, Aguadulce, Panama, June 20, 1976.
Bats Right. Throws Right. Height, 6 feet, 2 inches. Weight, 240 pounds.

Year	Club	Lea	Pos	G	AB	R	H	2B	3B	HR	RBI	SB	Avg
1994	White Sox	Gulf Coast	3B	29	56	6	7	1	0	0	1	0	.125
1995	Hickory	So.Atl.	3B-SS	63	218	18	54	9	1	4	30	1	.248
1995	Bristol	Appal.	3B-1B	67	269	43	93	17	1	7	45	17	.346
1996	Hickory	So.Atl.	3B-1B	119	480	65	150	23	6	8	70	18	.313
1997	Winston-Sal	Carolina	3B	139	546	81	173	50	4	17	82	11	.317
1998	Birmingham	Southern	3B	138	549	77	166	33	2	21	106	11	.302
1999	Charlotte	Int.	3B	25	94	16	33	5	0	4	20	2	.351
1999	Chicago	A.L.	OF-1B	127	492	66	144	32	2	16	84	4	.293
2000	Chicago	A.L.	OF	152	572	107	172	29	2	24	92	13	.301
2001	Chicago	A.L.	OF	150	558	75	150	33	3	24	84	17	.269
2002	Chicago	A.L.	OF	140	492	82	130	26	2	26	80	1	.264
2003	Chicago	A.L.	OF	158	623	100	181	35	1	31	113	18	.291
2004	Chicago a	A.L.	OF	153	591	103	180	37	0	31	99	11	.305
2005	Milwaukee	N.L.	OF	*162	618	85	164	41	0	32	114	13	.265
2006	Milwaukee	N.L.	OF	102	388	60	111	18	0	28	81	12	.286
2006	Texas b-c	A.L.	OF	59	236	42	76	19	1	9	35	7	.322
2007	Houston	N.L.	OF	*162	627	93	190	43	1	32	119	10	.303
2008	Houston d	N.L.	OF	115	436	61	137	27	0	28	100	4	.314
2009	Houston	N.L.	OF-1B	160	610	65	183	35	1	26	102	5	.300
2010	Houston	N.L.	OF-1B	157	605	67	149	29	1	24	89	3	.246
Major League Totals			12 Yrs.	1797	6848	1006	1967	404	14	331	1192	118	.287
	Division Series												
2000	Chicago	A.L.	OF	3	11	0	1	1	0	0	1	0	.091

a Traded to Milwaukee Brewers for outfielder Scott Podsednik, pitcher Luis Vizcaino and player to be named later, December 13, 2004. Chicago White Sox received infielder Travis Hinton to complete trade, January 10, 2005.
b Traded to Texas Rangers with outfielder Nelson Cruz for pitcher Francisco Cordero, outfielder Kevin Mench, outfielder Laynce Nix and pitcher Julian Cordero, July 28, 2006.
c Filed for free agency, October 30, 2006. Signed with Houston Astros, November 24, 2006.
d On disabled list from August 10 to September 30, 2008.

LEE, DERREK LEON

Born, Sacramento, California, September 6, 1975.
Bats Right. Throws Right. Height, 6 feet, 5 inches. Weight, 245 pounds.

Year	Club	Lea	Pos	G	AB	R	H	2B	3B	HR	RBI	SB	Avg
1993	Padres	Arizona	1B	15	52	11	17	1	1	2	5	4	.327
1993	Rancho Cucamonga	Calif.	1B	20	73	13	20	5	1	1	10	0	.274
1994	Rancho Cucamonga	Calif.	3B-1B	126	442	66	118	19	2	8	53	18	.267
1995	Rancho Cucamonga	Calif.	1B	128	502	82	151	25	2	23	95	14	.301
1995	Memphis	Southern	1B	2	9	0	1	0	0	0	1	0	.111
1996	Memphis	Southern	1B-3B	134	500	98	140	39	2	34	104	13	.280
1997	Las Vegas	P.C.	1B	124	468	85	152	29	2	13	64	17	.325
1997	San Diego a	N.L.	1B	22	54	9	14	3	0	1	4	0	.259
1998	Florida	N.L.	1B	141	454	62	106	29	1	17	74	5	.233
1999	Calgary	P.C.	1B	89	339	60	96	20	1	19	73	3	.283
1999	Florida	N.L.	1B	70	218	21	45	9	1	5	20	2	.206
2000	Florida	N.L.	1B	158	477	70	134	18	3	28	70	0	.281
2001	Florida	N.L.	1B	158	561	83	158	37	4	21	75	4	.282
2002	Florida	N.L.	1B	*162	581	95	157	35	7	27	86	19	.270
2003	Florida b	N.L.	1B	155	539	91	146	31	2	31	92	21	.271
2004	Chicago	N.L.	1B	161	605	90	168	39	1	32	98	12	.278
2005	Chicago	N.L.	1B	158	594	120	*199	*50	3	46	107	15	*.335
2006	Iowa	P.C.	1B	1	4	0	1	0	0	0	1	0	.250
2006	Chicago c	N.L.	1B	50	175	30	50	9	0	8	30	8	.286
2007	Chicago	N.L.	1B	150	567	91	180	43	1	22	82	6	.317
2008	Chicago	N.L.	1B	155	623	93	181	41	3	20	90	8	.291
2009	Chicago	N.L.	1B	141	532	91	163	36	2	35	111	1	.306
2010	Chicago-Atlanta d-e	N.L.	1B	148	547	80	142	35	0	19	80	1	.260
Major League Totals			14 Yrs.	1829	6527	1026	1843	415	28	312	1019	102	.282
	Division Series												
2003	Florida	N.L.	1B	4	16	2	4	1	0	0	2	1	.250
2007	Chicago	N.L.	1B	3	12	1	4	0	0	0	0	0	.333
2008	Chicago	N.L.	1B	3	11	2	6	3	0	0	0	0	.545
2010	Atlanta	N.L.	1B	4	16	2	2	0	0	0	0	0	.125
Division Series Totals				14	55	7	16	4	0	0	2	1	.291
	Championship Series												
2003	Florida	N.L.	1B	7	32	2	6	2	0	1	4	1	.188
	World Series Record												
2003	Florida	N.L.	1B	6	24	2	5	0	0	0	2	0	.208

a Traded to Florida Marlins with pitcher Rafael Medina and pitcher Steve Hoff for pitcher Kevin Brown, December 15, 1997.
b Traded to Chicago Cubs for infielder Hee Seop Choi and player to be named later, November 25, 2003. Florida Marlins received pitcher Mike Nannini to complete trade, December 15, 2003.
c On disabled list from April 20 to June 25 and July 24 to August 28, 2006.
d Traded to Atlanta Braves with cash for pitcher Tyrelle Harris, pitcher Robinson Lopez and pitcher Jeffrey Lorick, August 18, 2010.
e Filed for free agency, November 1, 2010. Signed with Baltimore Orioles, January 6, 2011.

LEWIS, FREDERICK DESHAUN (FRED)

Born, Hattiesburg, Mississippi, December 9, 1980.
Bats Left. Throws Right. Height, 6 feet, 2 inches. Weight, 190 pounds.

Year	Club	Lea	Pos	G	AB	R	H	2B	3B	HR	RBI	SB	Avg
2002	Salem-Keizer	Northwest	OF	58	239	43	77	9	3	1	23	9	.322
2003	Hagerstown	So.Atl.	OF	114	420	61	105	17	8	1	27	30	.250
2004	San Jose	Calif.	OF	115	439	88	132	20	11	8	57	33	.301
2004	Fresno	P.C.	OF	6	23	3	7	1	0	1	2	1	.304
2005	Norwich	Eastern	OF	137	512	79	140	28	7	7	47	30	.273
2006	Fresno	P.C.	OF	120	439	85	121	20	11	12	56	18	.276
2006	San Francisco	N.L.	OF	13	11	5	5	1	0	0	2	0	.455
2007	Fresno	P.C.	OF	42	171	31	50	8	6	8	32	9	.292
2007	San Francisco a	N.L.	OF	58	157	34	45	6	2	3	19	5	.287
2008	San Francisco	N.L.	OF	133	468	81	132	25	11	9	40	21	.282
2009	San Francisco	N.L.	OF	122	295	49	76	21	3	4	20	8	.258
2010	Fresno	P.C.	OF	7	22	6	9	3	1	1	6	2	.409
2010	Toronto b-c-d	A.L.	OF	110	428	70	112	31	5	8	36	17	.262
Major League Totals			5 Yrs.	436	1359	239	370	84	21	24	117	51	.272

a On disabled list from June 9 to June 30, 2007.
b On disabled list from March 27 to April 15, 2010.
c Sold to Toronto Blue Jays, April 16, 2010.
d Not offered contract, December 2, 2010. Signed with Cincinnati Reds, January 10, 2011.

LILLIBRIDGE, BRENT STUART

Born, Everett, Washington, September 18, 1983.
Bats Right. Throws Right. Height, 5 feet, 11 inches. Weight, 190 pounds.

Year	Club	Lea	Pos	G	AB	R	H	2B	3B	HR	RBI	SB	Avg
2005	Williamsport. .	N.Y.-Penn.	SS	42	169	19	41	12	4	4	18	10	.243
2006	Lynchburg	Carolina	SS	54	201	47	63	10	3	2	28	24	.313
2006	Hickory.	So.Atl.	SS-2B	74	274	59	82	18	5	11	43	29	.299
2007	Richmond	Int.	SS	87	321	47	92	14	2	10	41	28	.287
2007	Mississippi a . .	Southern	SS	52	204	31	56	8	3	3	17	14	.275
2008	Richmond	Int.	SS	90	355	46	78	18	7	4	39	23	.220
2008	Atlanta b.	N.L.	SS-3B	29	80	9	16	6	1	1	8	2	.200
2009	Charlotte	Int.	SS-OF-2B	67	246	34	62	9	4	3	24	17	.252
2009	Chicago	A.L.	2B-OF-SS-3B	46	95	9	15	2	0	0	3	6	.158
2010	Charlotte	Int.	SS-2B-OF	48	185	26	50	8	0	4	16	19	.270
2010	Chicago	A.L.	2B-OF-SS	64	98	19	22	5	2	2	16	5	.224
Major League Totals			3 Yrs.	139	273	37	53	13	3	3	27	13	.194

a Traded by Pittsburgh Pirates to Atlanta Braces with pitcher Mike Gonzalez for infielder Adam LaRoche and of Jamie Romak, January 18, 2007.

b Traded to Chicago White Sox with catcher Tyler Flowers, infielder Jonathan Gilmore and pitcher Santos Rodriguez for pitcher Javier Vazquez and pitcher Boone Logan, December 4, 2008.

LIND, ADAM ALAN

Born, Anderson, Indiana, July 17, 1983.
Bats Left. Throws Left. Height, 6 feet, 2 inches. Weight, 195 pounds.

Year	Club	Lea	Pos	G	AB	R	H	2B	3B	HR	RBI	SB	Avg
2004	Auburn.	N.Y.-Penn.	OF	70	266	43	82	23	0	7	50	1	.308
2005	Dunedin	Fla.St.	OF	126	495	80	155	42	4	12	84	2	.313
2006	New Hampshire	Eastern	OF	91	348	43	108	24	0	19	71	2	.310
2006	Syracuse	Int.	OF	34	109	20	43	7	0	5	18	1	.394
2006	Toronto	A.L.	DH-OF	18	60	8	22	8	0	2	8	0	.367
2007	Syracuse	Int.	OF	46	174	20	52	8	2	6	28	0	.299
2007	Toronto	A.L.	OF	89	290	34	69	14	0	11	46	1	.238
2008	Syracuse	Int.	OF-1B	51	189	24	62	17	2	6	50	1	.328
2008	Toronto	A.L.	OF	88	326	48	92	16	4	9	40	2	.282
2009	Toronto	A.L.	DH-OF	151	587	93	179	46	0	35	114	1	.305
2010	Toronto	A.L.	DH-OF-1B	150	569	57	135	32	3	23	72	0	.237
Major League Totals			5 Yrs.	496	1832	240	497	116	7	80	280	4	.271

LONEY, JAMES ANTHONY

Born, Houston, Texas, May 7, 1984.
Bats Left. Throws Left. Height, 6 feet, 3 inches. Weight, 220 pounds.

Year	Club	Lea	Pos	G	AB	R	H	2B	3B	HR	RBI	SB	Avg
2002	Vero Beach.	Fla.St.	1B	17	67	6	20	6	0	0	5	0	.299
2002	Great Falls	Pioneer	1B	47	170	33	63	22	3	5	30	5	.371
2003	Vero Beach.	Fla.St.	1B-OF	125	468	64	129	31	3	7	46	9	.276
2004	Jacksonville	Southern	1B	104	395	39	94	19	2	4	35	6	.238
2005	Jacksonville	Southern	1B-OF	138	504	74	143	31	2	11	65	1	.284
2006	Las Vegas.	P.C.	1B-OF	98	366	64	139	33	2	8	67	9	.380
2006	Los Angeles	N.L.	1B-OF	48	102	20	29	6	5	4	18	1	.284
2007	Las Vegas.	P.C.	1B-OF	58	233	28	65	19	1	1	32	2	.279
2007	Los Angeles	N.L.	1B-OF	96	344	41	114	18	4	15	67	0	.331
2008	Los Angeles	N.L.	1B	161	595	66	172	35	6	13	90	7	.289
2009	Los Angeles	N.L.	1B	158	576	73	162	25	2	13	90	7	.281
2010	Los Angeles	N.L.	1B	161	588	67	157	41	2	10	88	10	.267
Major League Totals			5 Yrs.	624	2205	267	634	125	19	55	353	25	.288
	Division Series												
2006	Los Angeles	N.L.	1B	1	4	0	3	0	0	0	3	0	.750
2008	Los Angeles	N.L.	1B	3	14	2	3	1	0	1	6	0	.214
2009	Los Angeles	N.L.	1B	3	12	0	3	0	0	0	0	0	.250
Division Series Totals				7	30	2	9	1	0	1	9	0	.300
	Championship Series												
2008	Los Angeles	N.L.	1B	5	16	0	7	2	0	0	2	0	.438
2009	Los Angeles	N.L.	1B	5	17	3	6	0	0	2	3	0	.353
Championship Series Totals				10	33	3	13	2	0	2	5	0	.394

LONGORIA, EVAN MICHAEL

Born, Downey, California, October 7, 1985.
Bats Right. Throws Right. Height, 6 feet, 2 inches. Weight, 210 pounds.

Year	Club	Lea	Pos	G	AB	R	H	2B	3B	HR	RBI	SB	Avg
2006	Visalia	Calif.	3B	28	110	22	36	8	0	8	28	1	.327
2006	Hudson Valley	N.Y.-Penn.	3B	8	33	5	14	1	1	4	11	1	.424
2006	Montgomery	Southern	3B	26	105	14	28	5	0	6	19	2	.267
2007	Durham	Int.	3B	31	104	19	28	8	0	5	19	0	.269
2007	Montgomery	Southern	3B	105	381	78	117	21	0	21	76	4	.307
2008	Durham	Int.	3B	7	25	2	5	0	0	0	1	0	.200
2008	Tampa Bay a-b	A.L.	3B-SS	122	448	67	122	31	2	27	85	7	.272
2009	Tampa Bay	A.L.	3B	157	584	100	164	44	0	33	113	9	.281
2010	Tampa Bay	A.L.	3B	151	574	96	169	46	5	22	104	15	.294
Major League Totals			3 Yrs.	430	1606	263	455	121	7	82	302	31	.283
	Division Series												
2008	Tampa Bay	N.L.	3B	4	15	2	4	0	0	2	3	1	.267
2010	Tampa Bay	N.L.	3B	5	20	2	4	2	0	1	2	0	.200
Division Series Totals				9	35	4	8	2	0	3	5	1	.229
	Championship Series												
2008	Tampa Bay	N.L.	3B	7	27	8	7	3	0	4	8	0	.259
	World Series Record												
2008	Tampa Bay	N.L.	3B	5	20	0	1	0	0	0	2	0	.050

a On disabled list from August 8 to September 6, 2008.
b Selected Rookie of the Year in American League for 2008.

LOPEZ, FELIPE

Born, Bayamon, Puerto Rico, May 12, 1980.
Bats Both. Throws Right. Height, 6 feet, 1 Inch. Weight, 205 pounds.

Year	Club	Lea	Pos	G	AB	R	H	2B	3B	HR	RBI	SB	Avg
1998	St.Cathrnes	N.Y.-Penn.	SS	19	83	14	31	5	2	1	11	4	.373
1998	Dunedin	Fla.St.	SS	4	13	3	5	0	1	1	1	0	.385
1999	Hagerstown	So.Atl.	SS	134	537	87	149	27	4	14	80	21	.277
2000	Tennessee	Southern	SS	127	463	52	119	18	4	9	41	12	.257
2001	Tennessee	Southern	SS-2B	19	72	12	16	2	1	2	4	4	.222
2001	Syracuse	Int.	SS-2B-3B	89	358	65	100	19	7	16	44	13	.279
2001	Toronto	A.L.	3B-SS	49	177	21	46	5	4	5	23	4	.260
2002	Toronto	A.L.	SS-3B	85	282	35	64	15	3	8	34	5	.227
2002	Syracuse a	Int.	SS	43	173	35	55	11	2	3	16	13	.318
2003	Cincinnati	N.L.	SS-3B-2B	59	197	28	42	7	2	2	13	8	.213
2003	Louisville	Int.	SS-2B	35	143	22	40	11	0	2	18	2	.280
2004	Louisville	Int.	SS-2B-3B	75	293	50	80	11	3	9	44	2	.273
2004	Cincinnati	N.L.	SS-3B-2B	79	264	35	64	18	2	7	31	1	.242
2005	Cincinnati	N.L.	SS-2B-3B	148	580	97	169	34	5	23	85	15	.291
2006	Cincinnati-Wash. b	N.L.	SS	156	617	98	169	27	3	11	52	44	.274
2007	Washington	N.L.	SS-2B	154	603	70	148	25	6	9	50	24	.245
2008	Wash.-St. Louis c-d	N.L.	2B-OF-3B-SS	143	481	64	136	28	2	6	46	8	.283
2009	Arizona-Milwaukee e-f	N.L.	2B	151	604	88	187	38	3	9	57	6	.310
2010	St. Louis	N.L.	3B-2B-SS-1B	109	376	50	87	18	1	7	36	8	.231
2010	Boston g-h-i	A.L.	2B-3B-SS	4	15	2	4	0	0	1	1	0	.267
Major League Totals			10 Yrs.	1137	4196	588	1116	215	31	88	428	123	.266

a Traded by Toronto Blue Jays to Cincinnati Reds in four team deal. Cincinnati sent pitcher Elmer Dessens to Arizona Diamondbacks, who sent infield Eurbiel Durazo to Oakland A's, who sent pitcher Jamie Arnold to Toronto Blue Jays, December 15, 2002.
b Traded to Washington Nationals with outfielder Austin Kearns and pitcher Ryan Wagner for pitcher Gary Majewski, pitcher Bill Bray, infielder Royce Clayton, infielder Brendan Harris and pitcher Daryl Thompson, July 13, 2006.
c Released by Washington Nationals, July 31, 2008. Signed with St. Louis Cardinals, August 5, 2008.
d Filed for free agency, October 30, 2008. Signed with Arizona Diamondbacks, December 12, 2008.
e Traded to Milwaukee Brewers for outfielder Cole Gillespie and pitcher Roque Mercedes, July 20, 2009.
f Filed for free agency, November 5, 2009. Signed with St. Louis Cardinals, February 27, 2010.
g On disabled list from April 26 to May 16, 2010.
h Released by St. Louis Cardinals, September 21, 2010. Signed with Boston Red Sox, September 25, 2010.
i Filed for free agency, November 4, 2010.

LOPEZ, JOSE CELESTINO

Born, Barcelona, Venezuela, November 24, 1983.
Bats Right. Throws Right. Height, 6 feet. Weight, 200 pounds.

Year	Club	Lea	Pos	G	AB	R	H	2B	3B	HR	RBI	SB	Avg
2001	Everett	Northwest	SS-2B	70	289	42	74	15	0	2	20	13	.256
2002	San Bernardino	Calif.	SS-2B	123	522	82	169	39	5	8	60	31	.324

Year	Club	Lea	Pos	G	AB	R	H	2B	3B	HR	RBI	SB	Avg
2003	San Antonio	Texas	SS-2B-3B	132	538	82	139	35	2	13	69	18	.258
2004	Tacoma	P.C.	SS-3B-2B	74	275	40	81	19	0	13	39	5	.295
2004	Mariners	Arizona	3B-SS-2B	4	12	3	2	1	0	0	1	1	.167
2004	Seattle	A.L.	SS-3B	57	207	28	48	13	0	5	22	0	.232
2005	Tacoma	P.C.	2B	44	182	29	58	19	0	5	31	2	.319
2005	Seattle	A.L.	2B-3B	54	190	18	47	19	0	2	25	4	.247
2006	Seattle	A.L.	2B	151	603	78	170	28	8	10	79	5	.282
2007	Seattle	A.L.	2B-3B	149	524	58	132	17	2	11	62	2	.252
2008	Seattle	A.L.	2B-1B	159	644	80	191	41	1	17	89	6	.297
2009	Seattle	A.L.	2B-1B	153	613	69	167	42	0	25	96	3	.272
2010	Seattle a	A.L.	3B	150	593	49	142	29	0	10	58	3	.239
Major League Totals			7 Yrs.	873	3374	380	897	189	11	80	431	23	.266

a Traded to Colorado Rockies for pitcher Chaz Roe, December 2, 2010.

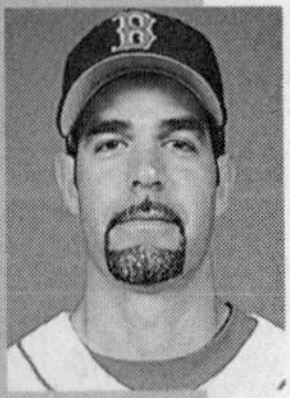

LOWELL, MICHAEL AVERETT (MIKE)

Born, San Juan, Puerto Rico, February 24, 1974.
Bats Right. Throws Right. Height, 6 feet, 3 inches. Weight, 210 pounds.

Year	Club	Lea	Pos	G	AB	R	H	2B	3B	HR	RBI	SB	Avg
1995	Oneonta	N.Y.-Penn.	3B	72	281	36	73	18	0	1	27	3	.260
1996	Greensboro	So.Atl.	3B-SS-P	113	433	58	122	33	0	8	64	10	.282
1996	Tampa	Fla.St.	3B	24	78	8	22	5	0	0	11	1	.282
1997	Norwich	Eastern	3B-SS	78	285	60	98	17	0	15	47	2	.344
1997	Columbus	Int.	3B-SS	57	210	36	58	13	1	15	45	2	.276
1998	Columbus	Int.	3B-1B-SS	126	510	79	155	34	3	26	99	4	.304
1998	New York	A.L.	3B	8	15	1	4	0	0	0	0	0	.267
1999	Calgary	P.C.	3B	24	83	11	26	3	0	2	9	0	.313
1999	Florida a-b	N.L.	3B	97	308	32	78	15	0	12	47	0	.253
2000	Florida c	N.L.	3B	140	508	73	137	38	0	22	91	4	.270
2001	Florida	N.L.	3B	146	551	65	156	37	0	18	100	1	.283
2002	Florida	N.L.	3B	160	597	88	165	44	0	24	92	4	.276
2003	Florida d	N.L.	3B	130	492	76	136	27	1	32	105	3	.276
2004	Florida	N.L.	3B	158	598	87	175	44	1	27	85	5	.293
2005	Florida e	N.L.	3B-2B	150	500	56	118	36	1	8	58	4	.236
2006	Boston	A.L.	3B	153	573	79	163	47	1	20	80	2	.284
2007	Boston f	A.L.	3B	154	589	79	191	37	2	21	120	3	.324
2008	Pawtucket	Int.	3B	3	13	0	3	0	0	0	3	0	.231
2008	Boston g	A.L.	3B	113	419	58	115	27	0	17	73	2	.274
2009	Boston h	A.L.	3B	119	445	54	129	29	1	17	75	2	.290
2010	Pawtucket	Int.	1B-3B	5	22	5	11	4	0	4	10	0	.500
2010	Boston i	A.L.	1B-3B	73	218	23	52	13	0	5	26	0	.239
Major League Totals			13 Yrs.	1601	5813	771	1619	394	7	223	952	30	.279
	Division Series												
2003	Florida	N.L.	3B	2	3	0	0	0	0	0	0	0	.000
2007	Boston	A.L.	3B	3	9	1	3	2	0	0	3	0	.333
2008	Boston	A.L.	3B	2	8	0	0	0	0	0	0	0	.000
2009	Boston	A.L.	3B	3	10	1	2	0	0	0	1	0	.200
Division Series Totals				10	30	2	5	2	0	0	4	0	.167
	Championship Series												
2003	Florida	N.L.	3B	7	20	5	4	0	0	2	3	0	.200
2007	Boston	A.L.	3B	7	27	3	9	2	0	1	8	0	.333
Championship Series Totals				14	47	8	13	2	0	3	11	0	.277
	World Series Record												
2003	Florida	N.L.	3B	6	23	1	5	1	0	0	2	0	.217
2007	Boston	A.L.	3B	4	15	6	6	3	0	1	4	1	.400
World Series Totals				10	38	7	11	4	0	1	6	1	.289

a Traded to Florida Marlins for pitcher Ed Yarnall, pitcher Mark Johnson and pitcher Todd Noel, February 1, 1999.
b On disabled list from March 26 to May 29, 1999.
c On disabled list from May 13 to May 28, 2000.
d On disabled list from August 31 to September 28, 2003.
e Traded to Boston Red Sox with pitcher Josh Beckett and pitcher Guillermo Mota for infielder Hanley Ramirez, pitcher Anibal Sanchez and pitcher Jesus Delgado, November 24, 2005.
f Filed for free agency, November 6, 2007, re-signed with Boston Red Sox, November 20, 2007.
g On disabled list from April 10 to April 29 and August 13 to September 5, 2008.
h On disabled list from June 28 to July 17, 2009.
i On disabled list from June 23 to August 3, 2010.

LOWRIE, JED CARLSON

Born, Salem, Oregon, April 17, 1984.
Bats Both. Throws Right. Height, 6 feet. Weight, 180 pounds.

Year	Club	Lea	Pos	G	AB	R	H	2B	3B	HR	RBI	SB	Avg
2005	Lowell	N.Y.-Penn.	SS-2B	53	201	36	66	12	0	4	32	7	.328
2006	Wilmington	Carolina	SS	97	374	43	98	21	6	3	50	2	.262
2007	Portland	Eastern	SS-2B	93	337	61	100	31	7	8	49	5	.297
2007	Pawtucket	Int.	SS-2B-3B	40	160	21	48	16	1	5	21	0	.300
2008	Pawtucket	Int.	SS-2B-3B	53	198	35	53	14	2	5	32	1	.268
2008	Boston	A.L.	SS-3B-2B	81	260	34	67	25	3	2	46	1	.258
2009	Portland	Eastern	SS	1	5	1	3	1	0	0	2	0	.600
2009	Lowell	N.Y.-Penn.	SS	3	11	2	2	2	0	0	1	0	.182
2009	Pawtucket	Int.	SS	22	68	9	12	3	0	3	8	0	.176
2009	Boston	A.L.	SS-3B-2B	32	68	5	10	2	0	2	11	0	.147
2010	Lowell	N.Y.-Penn.	SS	6	15	2	6	1	0	0	5	0	.400
2010	Pawtucket	Int.	2B-3B-SS	4	15	3	5	3	0	1	4	1	.333
2010	Boston a	A.L.	2B-SS-1B-3B	55	171	31	49	14	0	9	24	1	.287
Major League Totals			3 Yrs.	168	499	70	126	41	3	13	81	2	.253
	Division Series												
2008	Boston	A.L.	SS-3B	3	11	2	4	0	0	0	1	0	.364
2009	Boston	A.L.	SS	3	2	0	0	0	0	0	0	0	.000
Division Series Totals				6	13	2	4	0	0	0	1	0	.308
	Championship Series												
2008	Boston	A.L.	SS	6	18	2	2	1	0	0	1	0	.111

a On disabled list from March 26 to July 21, 2010.

LUCROY, JONATHAN CHARLES

Born, Eustis, Pennsylvania, June 13, 1986.
Bats Right. Throws Right. Height, 6 feet. Weight, 195 pounds.

Year	Club	Lea	Pos	G	AB	R	H	2B	3B	HR	RBI	SB	Avg
2007	Helena	Pioneer	C	61	234	35	80	18	2	4	39	0	.342
2008	Brevard County	Fla.St.	C	64	236	31	69	12	1	10	44	1	.292
2008	West Tenn	So.Atl.	C	65	239	45	74	16	1	10	33	8	.310
2009	Huntsville	Southern	C	125	419	61	112	32	2	9	66	1	.267
2010	Huntsville	Southern	C	10	42	8	19	3	0	0	5	0	.452
2010	Nashville	P.C.	C	21	80	8	19	4	0	2	11	0	.237
2010	Milwaukee	N.L.	C	75	277	24	70	9	0	4	26	4	.253

LUDWICK, RYAN ANDREW

Born, Satellite Beach, Florida, July 13, 1978.
Bats Right. Throws Left. Height, 6 feet, 3 inches. Weight, 220 pounds.

Year	Club	Lea	Pos	G	AB	R	H	2B	3B	HR	RBI	SB	Avg
1999	Modesto	Calif.	OF	43	171	28	47	11	3	4	34	2	.275
2000	Modesto	Calif.	OF	129	493	86	130	26	3	29	102	10	.264
2001	Sacramento	P.C.	OF	17	57	10	13	3	0	1	7	2	.228
2001	Midland	Texas	OF	119	443	82	119	23	3	25	96	9	.269
2002	Oklahoma	P.C.	OF	78	305	62	87	27	4	15	52	2	.285
2002	Texas a	A.L.	OF	23	81	10	19	6	0	1	9	2	.235
2003	Oklahoma	P.C.	OF	81	317	51	96	24	3	17	63	1	.303
2003	Texas-Cleveland b-c	A.L.	OF	47	162	17	40	8	1	7	26	2	.247
2004	Akron	Eastern	OF	8	26	4	7	2	0	1	5	0	.269
2004	Buffalo	Int.	OF	44	166	25	45	15	0	8	30	0	.271
2004	Cleveland d	A.L.	OF	15	50	3	11	2	0	2	4	0	.220
2005	Cleveland	A.L.	OF	19	41	8	9	0	0	4	5	0	.220
2005	Buffalo	Int.	OF	54	188	27	36	10	2	4	16	0	.191
2006	Toledo e-f	Int.	OF	134	508	81	135	34	2	28	80	2	.266
2007	Memphis	P.C.	OF	29	106	27	36	8	0	8	36	1	.340
2007	St. Louis	N.L.	OF	120	303	42	81	22	0	14	52	4	.267
2008	St. Louis	N.L.	OF	152	538	104	161	40	3	37	113	4	.299
2009	St. Louis g	N.L.	OF	139	486	63	129	20	1	22	97	4	.265
2010	Memphis	P.C.	OF	3	9	2	3	1	0	2	5	0	.333
2010	St. Louis-San Diego h-i	N.L.	OF	136	490	63	123	27	2	17	69	0	.251
Major League Totals			8 Yrs.	651	2151	310	573	125	7	104	375	16	.266
	Division Series												
2009	St. Louis	N.L.	OF	3	12	1	4	0	0	0	1	0	.333

a Traded to Texas Rangers by Oakland Athletics with pitcher Mario Ramos, infielder Jason Hart and catcher Gerald Laird for pitcher Mike Venafro and infielder Carlos Pena, January 14, 2002.

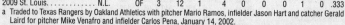

b Traded to Cleveland Indians for outfielder Shane Spencer and pitcher Ricardo Rodriguez, July 18, 2003.
c On disabled list from September 9 to October 28, 2003.
d On disabled list from April 2 to July 5, 2004.
e Filed for free agency, October 28, 2005. Signed with Detroit Tigers organization, January 4, 2006.
f Filed for free agency, October 15, 2006. Signed with St. Louis Cardinals organization, December 1, 2006.
g On disabled list from May 13 to May 29, 2009.
h On disabled list from June 26 to July 24, 2010.
i Traded to San Diego Padres for pitcher Nick Greenwood and pitcher Corey Kluber, July 31, 2010.

LUGO, JULIO CESAR

Born, Barahona, Dominican Republic, November 16, 1975.
Bats Right. Throws Right. Height, 6 feet, 1 Inch. Weight, 175 pounds.

Year Club Lea	Pos	G	AB	R	H	2B	3B	HR	RBI	SB	Avg
1995 Auburn......N.Y.-Penn.	2B-SS-OF	59	230	36	67	6	3	1	16	17	.291
1996 Quad City..... Midwest	SS-2B-3B	101	393	60	116	18	2	10	50	24	.295
1997 Kissimmee...... Fla.St.	SS-2B-3B	125	505	89	135	22	14	7	61	35	.267
1998 Kissimmee...... Fla.St.	SS	128	509	81	154	20	14	7	62	51	.303
1999 Jackson a....... Texas	SS	116	445	77	142	24	5	10	42	25	.319
2000 New Orleans.......P.C.	2B	24	101	22	33	4	1	3	12	12	.327
2000 Houston..........N.L.	SS-2B-OF	116	420	78	119	22	5	10	40	22	.283
2001 Houston..........N.L.	SS-OF-2B	140	513	93	135	20	3	10	37	12	.263
2002 Houston b ........N.L.	SS	88	322	45	84	15	1	8	35	9	.261
2003 Houston..........N.L.	SS	22	65	6	16	3	0	0	2	2	.246
2003 Tampa Bay c.......A.L.	SS	117	433	58	119	13	4	15	53	10	.275
2004 Tampa Bay........A.L.	SS-2B	157	581	83	160	41	4	7	75	21	.275
2005 Tampa Bay........A.L.	SS	158	616	89	182	36	6	6	57	39	.295
2006 Tampa Bay d ......A.L.	SS	73	289	53	89	17	1	12	27	18	.308
2006 Los Angeles e-f ....N.L.	2B-3B-SS-OF	49	146	16	32	5	1	0	10	6	.219
2007 Boston...........A.L.	SS	147	570	71	135	36	2	8	73	33	.237
2008 Boston g .........A.L.	SS-OF	82	261	27	70	13	0	1	22	12	.268
2009 Pawtucket .... Int.	SS	4	17	1	4	1	0	0	0	0	.235
2009 Boston...........A.L.	SS	37	109	16	31	4	1	1	8	3	.284
2009 St. Louis h-i.......N.L.	2B-SS	51	148	24	41	9	4	2	13	6	.277
2010 Baltimore j-k ......A.L.	2B-SS-3B-OF	93	241	26	60	4	2	0	20	5	.249
Major League Totals	11 Yrs.	1330	4714	685	1273	238	34	80	472	198	.270
Division Series											
2001 Houston..........N.L.	SS	3	8	1	0	0	0	0	0	0	.000
2006 Los Angeles.......N.L.	2B-3B	2	4	0	1	1	0	0	0	0	.250
2007 Boston...........A.L.	SS	3	10	2	3	0	0	0	0	1	.300
2009 St. Louis..........N.L.	2B	3	5	1	2	1	0	0	0	2	.400
Division Series Totals		11	27	4	6	2	0	0	0	3	.222
Championship Series											
2007 Boston...........A.L.	SS	7	25	3	5	2	0	0	2	0	.200
World Series Record											
2007 Boston...........A.L.	SS	4	13	2	5	1	0	0	1	0	.385

a On disabled list from July 21 to 29, 1999.
b On disabled list from August 13 to September 30, 2002.
c Released by Houston Astros, May 13, 2003. Signed with Tampa Bay Devil Rays, May 15, 2003.
d On disabled list from April 4 to May 5, 2006.
e Traded to Los Angeles Dodgers for infielder Joel Guzman and outfielder Sergio Pedroza, July 31, 2006.
f Filed for free agency, October 28, 2006. Signed with Boston Red Sox, December 13, 2006.
g On disabled list from July 12 to November 5, 2008.
h On disabled list from March 27 to April 27, 2009.
i Traded to St. Louis Cardinals with cash for outfielder Chris Duncan, July 22, 2009.
j Sold to Baltimore Orioles, April 1, 2010.
k Filed for free agency, November 1, 2010.

MAIER, MITCHELL WILLIAM (MITCH)

Born, Petoskey, Michigan, June 30, 1982.
Bats Left. Throws Right. Height, 6 feet, 2 inches. Weight, 210 pounds.

Year Club Lea	Pos	G	AB	R	H	2B	3B	HR	RBI	SB	Avg
2003 Royals 1...........Arizona	C	51	203	41	71	14	6	2	45	7	.350
2004 Wilmington .... Carolina	3B-OF	51	174	25	46	9	2	3	17	9	.264
2004 Burlington .... Midwest	3B	82	317	41	95	24	3	4	36	34	.300
2005 High Desert ....Calif.	OF	50	211	42	71	26	1	8	32	6	.336
2005 Wichita............. Texas	OF-3B	80	322	55	82	21	5	7	49	10	.255
2006 Wichita............. Texas	OF	138	543	95	166	35	7	14	92	13	.306
2006 Kansas City .... A.L.	OF	5	13	3	2	0	0	0	0	0	.154
2007 Omaha...............P.C.	OF	140	544	75	152	29	5	14	62	7	.279

Year	Club	Lea	Pos	G	AB	R	H	2B	3B	HR	RBI	SB	Avg
2008	Omaha	P.C.	OF	85	345	57	109	24	1	9	41	12	.316
2008	Kansas City a	A.L.	OF	34	91	9	26	1	1	0	9	0	.286
2009	Omaha	P.C.	OF	12	51	8	16	3	0	2	10	1	.314
2009	Kansas City	A.L.	OF	127	341	42	83	15	3	3	31	9	.243
2010	Kansas City	A.L.	OF-1B	117	373	41	98	15	6	5	39	3	.263
Major League Totals			4 Yrs.	283	818	95	209	31	10	8	79	12	.256

a On disabled list from August 21 to September 12, 2008.

MANZELLA, THOMAS SAMUEL (TOMMY)

Born, Chalmette, Louisiana, April 16, 1983.
Bats Right. Throws Right. Height, 6 feet, 2 inches. Weight, 200 pounds.

Year	Club	Lea	Pos	G	AB	R	H	2B	3B	HR	RBI	SB	Avg
2005	Tri-City	N.Y.-Penn.	SS	53	220	24	51	6	4	0	18	5	.232
2006	Lexington	So.Atl.	SS	99	338	50	93	22	1	7	43	16	.275
2007	Salem	Carolina	SS	57	223	28	53	13	0	0	24	5	.238
2007	Corpus Christi	Texas	SS	64	228	35	66	12	3	1	15	10	.289
2008	Round Rock	P.C.	SS	61	228	19	50	15	1	0	15	0	.219
2008	Corpus Christi	Texas	SS	54	224	27	67	11	5	4	34	4	.299
2009	Round Rock	P.C.	SS	133	530	68	153	31	5	9	56	12	.289
2009	Houston	N.L.	SS	7	5	0	1	0	0	0	0	0	.200
2010	Corpus Christi	Texas	SS	5	14	4	6	1	0	0	1	0	.429
2010	Round Rock	P.C.	SS	6	27	4	9	2	0	1	4	0	.333
2010	Houston a	N.L.	SS	83	258	17	58	7	0	1	21	0	.225
Major League Totals			2 Yrs.	90	263	17	59	7	0	1	21	0	.224

a On disabled list from June 23 to August 19, 2010.

MARKAKIS, NICHOLAS WILLIAM (NICK)

Born, Woodstock, Georgia, November 17, 1983.
Bats Left. Throws Left. Height, 6 feet, 2 inches. Weight, 195 pounds.

Year	Club	Lea	Pos	G	AB	R	H	2B	3B	HR	RBI	SB	Avg
2003	Aberdeen	N.Y.-Penn.	OF	59	205	22	58	14	3	1	28	13	.283
2004	Delmarva	So.Atl.	OF	96	355	57	106	22	3	11	64	12	.299
2005	Frederick	Carolina	OF	91	350	59	105	25	1	12	62	2	.300
2005	Bowie	Eastern	OF	33	124	19	42	16	2	3	30	0	.339
2006	Baltimore	A.L.	OF	147	491	72	143	25	2	16	62	2	.291
2007	Baltimore	A.L.	OF	161	637	97	191	43	3	23	112	18	.300
2008	Baltimore	A.L.	OF	157	595	106	182	48	1	20	87	10	.306
2009	Baltimore	A.L.	OF	*161	642	94	188	45	2	18	101	6	.293
2010	Baltimore	A.L.	OF	160	629	79	187	45	3	12	60	7	.297
Major League Totals			5 Yrs.	786	2994	448	891	206	11	89	422	43	.298

MARSON, LOUIS GLENN (LOU)

Born, Scottsdale, Arizona, June 26, 1986.
Bats Right. Throws Right. Height, 6 feet, 1 inch. Weight, 200 pounds.

Year	Club	Lea	Pos	G	AB	R	H	2B	3B	HR	RBI	SB	Avg
2004	Phillies	Gulf Coast	C	38	113	18	29	3	0	4	8	4	.257
2005	Batavia	N.Y.-Penn.	C	60	220	25	54	11	3	5	25	0	.245
2006	Lakewood	So.Atl.	C	104	350	44	85	16	5	4	39	4	.243
2007	Clearwater	Fla.St.	C	111	393	68	113	24	1	7	63	3	.288
2008	Reading	Eastern	C	94	322	55	101	18	0	5	46	3	.314
2008	Philadelphia	N.L.	C	1	4	2	2	0	0	1	2	0	.500
2009	Philadelphia	N.L.	C	7	17	3	4	1	0	0	0	0	.235
2009	Lehigh Valley	Int.	C	63	211	32	62	13	0	1	24	3	.294
2009	Columbus	Int.	C	28	103	10	25	5	1	1	9	1	.243
2009	Cleveland a	A.L.	C	14	44	6	11	6	0	0	4	0	.250
2010	Columbus	Int.	C	37	124	19	25	7	1	4	14	5	.202
2010	Cleveland	A.L.	C	87	262	29	51	15	0	3	22	8	.195
Major League Totals			3 Yrs.	109	327	40	68	22	0	4	28	8	.208

a Traded to Cleveland Indians with pitcher Jason Knapp, infielder Jason Donald and pitcher Carlos Carrasco for pitcher Cliff Lee and outfielder Ben Francisco, July 29, 2009.

MARTE, ANDY MANUEL

Born, Villa Tapia, Dominican Republic, October 21, 1983.
Bats Right. Throws Right. Height, 6 feet, 1 inch. Weight, 205 pounds.

Year	Club	Lea	Pos	G	AB	R	H	2B	3B	HR	RBI	SB	Avg
2001	Danville	Appal.	3B-2B	37	125	12	25	6	0	1	12	3	.200
2002	Macon	So.Atl.	3B	126	488	69	137	32	4	21	105	2	.281
2003	Myrtle Beach	Carolina	3B	130	463	69	132	35	1	16	63	5	.285
2004	Braves	Gulf Coast	2B-3B	3	15	4	7	4	0	1	6	0	.467
2004	Greenville	Southern	3B	107	387	52	104	28	1	23	68	1	.269
2005	Richmond	Int.	3B	109	389	51	107	26	2	20	74	0	.275
2005	Atlanta a	N.L.	3B	24	57	3	8	2	1	0	4	0	.140
2006	Buffalo	Int.	3B	96	357	49	93	23	0	15	46	1	.261
2006	Cleveland b	A.L.	3B	50	164	20	37	15	1	5	23	0	.226
2007	Buffalo	Int.	3B	96	352	47	94	17	1	16	60	0	.267
2007	Cleveland c	A.L.	3B	20	57	3	11	4	0	1	8	0	.193
2008	Cleveland	A.L.	3B-1B	80	235	21	52	11	1	3	17	1	.221
2009	Columbus	Int.	3B-1B	82	300	48	98	24	1	18	66	3	.327
2009	Cleveland	A.L.	1B	47	155	20	36	6	1	6	25	0	.232
2010	Lake County	So.Atl.	3B	1	4	2	2	0	0	0	0	0	.500
2010	Cleveland d-e	A.L.	3B-1B-P	81	170	18	39	7	2	5	19	0	.229
Major League Totals			6 Yrs.	302	838	85	183	45	6	20	96	1	.218

a Traded to Boston Red Sox for infielder Edgar Renteria and cash, December 7, 2005.
b Traded to Cleveland Indians with catcher Kelly Shoppach and pitcher Guillermo Mota for outfielder Coco Crisp, pitcher David Riske and catcher Josh Bard, January 27, 2006.
c On disabled list from April 23 to May 19, 2007.
d On disabled list from May 12 to June 7, 2010.
e Filed for free agency, November 6, 2010. Signed with Seattle Mariners organization, December 1, 2010.

MARTIN, RUSSELL NATHAN

Born, East York, Ontario, Canada, February 15, 1983.
Bats Right. Throws Right. Height, 5 feet, 10 inches. Weight, 210 pounds.

Year	Club	Lea	Pos	G	AB	R	H	2B	3B	HR	RBI	SB	Avg
2002	Dodgers	Gulf Coast	3B-SS	41	126	22	36	3	3	0	10	7	.286
2003	Ogden	Pioneer	C	52	188	25	51	13	0	6	36	3	.271
2003	South Bend	So.Atl.	C-OF-3B	25	98	15	28	4	1	3	14	5	.286
2004	Vero Beach	Fla.St.	C	122	416	74	104	24	1	15	64	9	.250
2005	Jacksonville	Southern	C-OF	129	409	83	127	17	1	9	61	15	.311
2006	Las Vegas	P.C.	C	23	74	14	22	9	0	0	9	0	.297
2006	Los Angeles	N.L.	C	121	415	65	117	26	4	10	65	10	.282
2007	Los Angeles	N.L.	C	151	540	87	158	32	3	19	87	21	.293
2008	Los Angeles	N.L.	C-3B	155	553	87	155	25	0	13	69	18	.280
2009	Los Angeles	N.L.	C-3B	143	505	63	126	19	0	7	53	11	.250
2010	Los Angeles a-b	N.L.	C	97	331	45	82	13	0	5	26	6	.248
Major League Totals			5 Yrs.	667	2344	347	638	115	7	54	300	66	.272
	Division Series												
2006	Los Angeles	N.L.	C	3	12	2	4	0	0	0	0	0	.333
2008	Los Angeles	N.L.	C	3	13	2	4	3	0	1	5	0	.308
2009	Los Angeles	N.L.	C	3	9	0	1	0	0	0	1	0	.111
Division Series Totals				9	34	4	9	3	0	1	6	0	.265
	Championship Series												
2008	Los Angeles	N.L.	C	5	17	3	2	0	0	0	1	1	.118
2009	Los Angeles	N.L.	C	5	16	2	4	1	0	0	2	0	.250
Championship Series Totals				10	33	5	6	1	0	0	3	1	.182

a On disabled list from August 4 to November 2, 2010.
b Not offered contract, December 2, 2010. Signed with New York Yankees, December 16, 2010.

MARTINEZ, VICTOR JESUS

Born, Ciudad Bolivar, Venezuela, December 23, 1978.
Bats Both. Throws Right. Height, 6 feet, 2 inches. Weight, 210 pounds.

Year	Club	Lea	Pos	G	AB	R	H	2B	3B	HR	RBI	SB	Avg
1997	Maracay-1	Venzuelan	C	53	122	21	42	12	0	0	26	6	.344
1998	Guacara-2	Venzuelan	C	55	160	28	43	13	0	1	27	8	.269
1999	Mahoning Valley	N.Y.-Penn.	C	64	235	37	65	9	0	4	36	0	.277
2000	Kinston	Carolina	C	26	83	9	18	7	0	0	8	1	.217
2000	Columbus a	So.Atl.	C	21	70	11	26	9	1	2	12	0	.371
2001	Kinston	Carolina	C	114	420	59	138	33	2	10	57	3	.329
2002	Akron	Eastern	C	121	443	84	149	40	0	22	85	3	.336

Year	Club	Lea	Pos	G	AB	R	H	2B	3B	HR	RBI	SB	Avg
2002	Cleveland	A.L.	C	12	32	2	9	1	0	1	5	0	.281
2003	Buffalo	Int.	C-1B	73	274	42	90	19	0	7	45	3	.328
2003	Akron	Eastern	C	3	12	1	4	2	0	0	2	0	.333
2003	Cleveland b	A.L.	C	49	159	15	46	4	0	1	16	1	.289
2004	Cleveland	A.L.	C	141	520	77	147	38	1	23	108	0	.283
2005	Cleveland	A.L.	C	147	547	73	167	33	0	20	80	0	.305
2006	Cleveland	A.L.	C-1B	153	572	82	181	37	0	16	93	0	.316
2007	Cleveland	A.L.	C-1B	147	562	78	169	40	0	25	114	0	.301
2008	Akron	Eastern	DH	2	6	1	2	0	0	1	1	0	.333
2008	Buffalo	Int.	C	6	20	2	6	2	0	0	2	0	.300
2008	Cleveland c	A.L.	C-1B	73	266	30	74	17	0	2	35	0	.278
2009	Cleveland-Boston d	A.L.	C-1B	155	588	88	178	33	1	23	108	1	.303
2010	Boston e-f	A.L.	C-1B	127	493	64	149	32	1	20	79	1	.302
Major League Totals			9 Yrs.	1004	3739	509	1120	235	3	131	638	3	.300
	Division Series												
2007	Cleveland	A.L.	C-1B	4	17	2	6	1	0	1	4	0	.353
2009	Boston	A.L.	C	3	11	0	2	0	0	0	2	0	.182
Division Series Totals				7	28	2	8	1	0	1	6	0	.286
	Championship Series												
2007	Cleveland	A.L.	C-1B	7	27	4	8	1	0	1	3	0	.296

a On minor league disabled list from May 25 to July 19, 2000.
b On disabled list from August 9 to September 2, 2003.
c On disabled list from June 12 to August 29, 2008.
d Traded to Boston Red Sox for pitcher Justin Masterson, pitcher Nick Hagadone and pitcher Bryan Price, July 31, 2009.
e On disabled list from June 28 to July 26, 2010.
f Filed for free agency, November 1, 2010. Signed with Detroit Tigers, November 26, 2010.

MATHIS, JEFFERY STEPHEN (JEFF)

Born, Marianna, Florida, March 31, 1983.
Bats Right. Throws Right. Height, 6 feet. Weight, 180 pounds.

Year	Club	Lea	Pos	G	AB	R	H	2B	3B	HR	RBI	SB	Avg
2001	Angels	Arizona	C-OF	7	23	1	7	1	0	0	3	0	.304
2001	Provo	Pioneer	C	22	77	14	23	6	3	0	18	1	.299
2002	Cedar Rapids	Midwest	C	128	491	75	141	41	3	10	73	7	.287
2003	Rancho Cucamonga	Calif.	C	98	378	74	122	28	3	11	54	5	.323
2003	Arkansas	Texas	C	24	95	19	27	11	0	2	14	1	.284
2004	Arkansas	Texas	C	117	432	57	98	24	3	14	55	2	.227
2005	Salt Lake	P.C.	C	112	427	78	118	26	3	21	73	4	.276
2005	Los Angeles	A.L.	C	5	3	1	1	0	0	0	0	0	.333
2006	Salt Lake	P.C.	C	99	384	62	111	33	3	5	45	3	.289
2006	Los Angeles	A.L.	C	23	55	9	8	2	0	2	6	0	.145
2007	Salt Lake	P.C.	C	66	250	39	61	14	2	5	26	3	.244
2007	Los Angeles	A.L.	C	59	171	24	36	12	0	4	23	0	.211
2008	Los Angeles	A.L.	C	94	283	35	55	8	0	9	42	2	.194
2009	Los Angeles	A.L.	C	84	237	26	50	8	0	5	28	2	.211
2010	Salt Lake	P.C.	C	9	33	6	8	1	1	1	5	0	.242
2010	Los Angeles a	A.L.	C	68	205	19	40	6	1	3	18	3	.195
Major League Totals			6 Yrs.	333	954	114	190	36	1	23	117	7	.199
	Division Series												
2007	Los Angeles	A.L.	C	2	3	0	0	0	0	0	1	0	.000
2008	Los Angeles	A.L.	C	1	2	0	1	0	0	0	0	0	.500
2009	Los Angeles	A.L.	C	2	3	0	1	0	0	0	0	0	.333
Division Series Totals				5	8	0	2	0	0	0	1	0	.250
	Championship Series												
2009	Los Angeles	A.L.	C	5	12	2	7	5	0	0	1	0	.583

a On disabled list from April 20 to June 17, 2010.

MATSUI, HIDEKI

Born: Ishikawa, Japan June 12, 1974
Bats Left, Throws Right, Height 6 feet two inches, Weight 230 pounds

Year	Club	Lea	Pos	G	AB	R	H	2B	3B	HR	RBI	SB	Avg
1993	Yomiuri Giants	Japan Cent.	OF	57	184	27	41	9	0	11	27	1	223
1994	Yomiuri Giants	Japan Cent.	OF	130	503	70	148	23	4	20	66	6	.294
1995	Yomiuri Giants	Japan Cent.	OF	131	501	76	142	31	1	22	80	9	283
1996	Yomiuri Giants	Japan Cent.	OF	130	487	97	153	34	1	38	99	7	.314
1997	Yomiuri Giants	Japan Cent.	OF	135	484	93	144	18	0	37	103	9	.298

Year	Club	Lea	Pos	G	AB	R	H	2B	3B	HR	RBI	SB	Avg
1998	Yomiuri Giants	Japan Cent.	OF	135	487	103	142	24	3	34	100	3	.292
1999	Yomiuri Giants	Japan Cent.	OF	135	471	100	143	24	2	42	95	0	.304
2000	Yomiuri Giants	Japan Cent.	OF	135	474	116	150	32	1	42	108	5	.316
2001	Yomiuri Giants	Japan Cent.	OF	140	481	107	160	23	3	36	104	3	.333
2002	Yomiuri Giants a	Japan Cent.	OF	140	500	112	167	27	1	50	107	3	.334
Japan Central Totals			10 years	1268	4572	901	1390	245	16	332	889	46	.304
2003	New York	A.L.	OF	*163	623	82	179	42	1	16	106	2	.287
2004	New York	A.L.	OF	*162	584	109	174	34	2	31	108	3	.298
2005	New York	A.L.	OF	*162	629	108	192	45	3	23	116	2	.305
2006	New York b.	A.L.	OF	51	172	32	52	9	0	8	29	1	.302
2007	Tampa	Fla.St.	OF	2	6	1	2	0	0	0	0	0	.333
2007	New York c.	A.L.	OF	143	547	100	156	28	4	25	103	4	.285
2008	Tampa	Fla.St.	DH	3	8	1	2	0	0	1	1	0	.250
2008	New York d.	A.L.	DH-OF	93	337	43	99	17	0	9	45	0	.294
2009	New York e.	A.L.	DH	142	456	62	125	21	1	28	90	0	.274
2010	Los Angeles f.	A.L.	DH-OF	145	482	55	132	24	1	21	84	0	.274
Major League Totals			8 Yrs.	1061	3830	591	1109	220	12	161	681	12	.290
	Division Series												
2003	New York	A.L.	OF	4	15	2	4	1	0	1	3	0	.267
2004	New York	A.L.	OF	4	17	3	7	1	0	1	3	0	.412
2005	New York	A.L.	OF	5	20	4	4	1	0	1	1	0	.200
2006	New York	A.L.	OF-DH	4	16	1	4	1	0	0	1	0	.250
2007	New York	A.L.	DH	4	11	4	2	0	0	0	0	0	.182
2009	New York	A.L.	DH	3	9	1	2	0	0	1	2	0	.222
Division Series Totals				24	88	15	23	4	0	4	10	0	.261
	Championship Series												
2003	New York	A.L.	OF	7	26	3	8	3	0	0	4	0	.308
2004	New York	A.L.	OF	7	34	9	14	6	1	2	10	0	.412
2009	New York	A.L.	DH	6	21	1	5	1	0	0	3	0	.238
Championship Series Totals				20	81	13	27	10	1	2	17	0	.333
	World Series Record												
2003	New York	A.L.	OF	6	23	1	6	0	0	1	4	0	.261
2009	New York	A.L.	DH	6	13	3	8	1	0	3	8	0	.615
World Series Totals				12	36	4	14	1	0	4	12	0	.389

a Reached agreement with New York Yankees on three year contract, December 19, 2002.
b On disabled list from May 12 to September 12, 2006.
c On disabled list from April 8 to April 23, 2007.
d On disabled list from June 23 to August 19 and September 22 to November 14, 2008.
e Filed for free agency, November 9, 2009. Signed with Los Angeles Angels, December 16, 2009.
f Filed for free agency, November 1, 2010. Signed with Oakland Athletics, December 14, 2010.

MAUER, JOSEPH PATRICK (JOE)

Born, St. Paul, Minnesota, April 19, 1983.
Bats Left. Throws Right. Height, 6 feet, 4 inches. Weight, 220 pounds.

Year	Club	Lea	Pos	G	AB	R	H	2B	3B	HR	RBI	SB	Avg
2001	Elizabethton	Appal.	C	32	110	14	44	6	2	0	14	4	.400
2002	Quad Cities	Midwest	C-1B	110	411	58	124	23	1	4	62	0	.302
2003	Fort Myers	Fla.St.	C-1B	62	233	25	78	13	1	1	44	3	.335
2003	New Britain	Eastern	C	73	276	48	94	17	1	4	41	0	.341
2004	Fort Myers	Fla.St.	C	2	6	0	4	0	0	0	2	0	.667
2004	Rochester	Int.	C	5	19	1	6	3	0	0	2	0	.316
2004	Minnesota a	A.L.	C	35	107	18	33	8	1	6	17	1	.308
2005	Minnesota	A.L.	C	131	489	61	144	26	2	9	55	13	.294
2006	Minnesota	A.L.	C	140	521	86	181	36	4	13	84	8	*.347
2007	Fort Myers	Fla.St.	C	1	3	0	0	0	0	0	0	0	.000
2007	Minnesota b	A.L.	C	109	406	62	119	27	3	7	60	7	.293
2008	Minnesota	A.L.	C	146	536	98	176	31	4	9	85	1	*.328
2009	Fort Myers	Fla.St.	C	5	15	2	6	2	0	0	4	0	.400
2009	Minnesota c-d	A.L.	C	138	523	94	191	30	1	28	96	4	*.365
2010	Minnesota	A.L.	C	137	510	88	167	43	1	9	75	1	.327
Major League Totals			7 Yrs.	836	3092	507	1011	201	16	81	472	35	.327
	Division Series												
2006	Minnesota	A.L.	C	3	11	0	2	0	0	0	0	0	.182
2009	Minnesota	A.L.	C	3	12	1	5	1	0	0	1	0	.417
2010	Minnesota	A.L.	C	3	12	0	3	0	0	0	0	0	.250
Division Series Totals				9	35	1	10	1	0	0	1	0	.286

a On disabled list from April 7 to June 2 and from July 16 to October 11, 2004.

b On disabled list from May 5 to June 8, 2007.
c On disabled list from March 27 to May 1, 2009.
d Selected Most Valuable Player in American League for 2009.

MAXWELL, JUSTIN ADAM

Born, Olney, Maryland, November 6, 1983.
Bats Right. Throws Right. Height, 6 feet, 5 inches. Weight, 235 pounds.

Year	Club	Lea	Pos	G	AB	R	H	2B	3B	HR	RBI	SB	Avg
2006	Vermont	N.Y.-Penn.	OF	74	271	36	73	11	3	4	33	20	.269
2006	Savannah	So.Atl.	OF	17	58	8	10	2	2	1	7	1	.172
2007	Hagerstown	So.Atl.	OF	56	209	51	63	12	2	14	40	14	.301
2007	Potomac	Carolina	OF	58	228	35	60	13	0	13	43	21	.263
2007	Washington	N.L.	OF	15	26	5	7	0	0	2	5	0	.269
2008	Harrisburg a	Eastern	OF	43	146	35	34	6	3	7	28	13	.233
2009	Syracuse	Int.	OF	111	384	68	93	10	5	13	42	35	.242
2009	Washington	N.L.	OF	40	89	13	22	4	1	4	9	6	.247
2010	Syracuse	Int.	OF	66	230	34	66	17	0	6	21	16	.287
2010	Washington	N.L.	OF	67	104	16	15	6	0	3	12	5	.144
Major League Totals		3 Yrs.		122	219	34	44	10	1	9	26	11	.201

a On disabled list from September 2 to September 29, 2008.

MAYBIN, CAMERON KEITH

Born, Asheville, North Carolina, April 4, 1987.
Bats Right. Throws Right. Height, 6 feet, 4 inches. Weight, 205 pounds.

Year	Club	Lea	Pos	G	AB	R	H	2B	3B	HR	RBI	SB	Avg
2006	West Michigan	Midwest	OF	101	385	59	117	20	6	9	69	27	.304
2007	Tigers	Gulf Coast	OF	2	7	1	4	0	0	0	1	0	.571
2007	Lakeland	Fla.St.	OF	83	296	58	90	14	5	10	44	25	.304
2007	Erie	Eastern	OF	6	20	9	8	1	0	4	8	0	.400
2007	Detroit a	A.L.	OF	24	49	8	7	3	0	1	2	5	.143
2008	Carolina	Southern	OF	108	390	73	108	15	8	13	49	21	.277
2008	Florida	N.L.	OF	8	32	9	16	2	0	0	2	4	.500
2009	New Orleans	P.C.	OF	82	298	44	95	18	8	3	39	8	.319
2009	Florida	N.L.	OF	54	176	30	44	12	2	4	13	1	.250
2010	Marlins	Gulf Coast	OF	3	11	4	4	1	0	1	5	0	.364
2010	New Orleans	P.C.	OF	33	130	21	44	6	2	4	23	5	.338
2010	Florida b	N.L.	OF	82	291	46	68	7	3	8	28	9	.234
Major League Totals		4 Yrs.		168	548	93	135	24	5	13	45	19	.246

a Traded to Florida Marlins with pitcher Burke Badenhop, pitcher Eulogio De La Cruz, pitcher Andrew Miller and catcher Mike Rabelo for pitcher Dontrelle Willis and infielder Miguel Cabrera, December 5, 2007.
b Traded to San Diego Padres for pitcher Edward Mujica and pitcher Ryan Webb, November 13, 2010.

MC CANN, BRIAN MICHAEL

Born, Athens, Georgia, February 20, 1984.
Bats Left. Throws Right. Height, 6 feet, 3 inches. Weight, 230 pounds.

Year	Club	Lea	Pos	G	AB	R	H	2B	3B	HR	RBI	SB	Avg
2002	Braves	Gulf Coast	C	29	100	9	22	5	0	2	11	0	.220
2003	Rome	So.Atl.	C	115	424	40	123	31	3	12	71	7	.290
2004	Myrtle Beach	Carolina	C	111	385	45	107	35	0	16	66	2	.278
2005	Mississippi	Southern	C	48	166	27	44	13	2	6	26	2	.265
2005	Atlanta	N.L.	C	59	180	20	50	7	0	5	23	1	.278
2006	Rome	So.Atl.	DH	2	7	0	2	0	0	0	0	0	.286
2006	Atlanta a	N.L.	C	130	442	61	147	34	0	24	93	2	.333
2007	Atlanta	N.L.	C	139	504	51	136	38	0	18	92	0	.270
2008	Atlanta	N.L.	C	145	509	68	153	42	1	23	87	5	.301
2009	Myrtle Beach	Carolina	DH	2	6	1	2	2	0	0	1	0	.333
2009	Gwinnett	Int.	C	1	3	0	1	1	0	0	1	0	.333
2009	Atlanta b	N.L.	C	138	488	63	137	35	1	21	94	4	.281
2010	Atlanta	N.L.	C	143	479	63	129	25	0	21	77	5	.269
Major League Totals		6 Yrs.		754	2602	326	752	181	2	112	466	17	.289
	Division Series												
2005	Atlanta	N.L.	C	3	16	2	3	0	0	2	5	0	.188
2010	Atlanta	N.L.	C	4	14	2	6	1	0	1	3	0	.429
Division Series Totals				7	30	4	9	1	0	3	8	0	.300

a On disabled list from May 24 to June 9, 2006.
b On disabled list from April 23 to May 8, 2009.

MC CUTCHEN, ANDREW STEFAN

Born, Fort Meade, Florida, October 10, 1986.
Bats Right. Throws Right. Height, 5 feet, 11 inches. Weight, 175 pounds.

Year	Club	Lea	Pos	G	AB	R	H	2B	3B	HR	RBI	SB	Avg
2005	Pirates	Gulf Coast	OF	45	158	36	47	9	3	2	30	13	.297
2005	Williamsport	N.Y.-Penn.	OF	13	52	12	18	3	1	0	5	4	.346
2006	Altoona	Eastern	OF	20	78	12	24	4	0	3	12	1	.308
2006	Hickory	So.Atl.	OF	114	453	77	132	20	4	14	62	22	.291
2007	Altoona	Eastern	OF	118	446	70	115	20	3	10	48	17	.258
2007	Indianapolis	Int.	OF	17	67	7	21	4	0	1	5	4	.313
2008	Indianapolis	Int.	OF	135	512	75	145	26	3	9	50	34	.283
2009	Indianapolis	Int.	OF	49	201	41	61	10	8	4	20	10	.303
2009	Pittsburgh	N.L.	OF	108	433	74	124	26	9	12	54	22	.286
2010	Pittsburgh	N.L.	OF	154	570	94	163	35	5	16	56	33	.286
Major League Totals			2 Yrs.	262	1003	168	287	61	14	28	110	55	.286

MC DONALD, DARNELL TYRONE

Born, Fort Collins, Colorado, November 17, 1978.
Bats Right. Throws Right. Height, 5 feet, 11 inches. Weight, 205 pounds.

Year	Club	Lea	Pos	G	AB	R	H	2B	3B	HR	RBI	SB	Avg
1998	Delmarva	So.Atl.	OF	134	528	87	138	24	5	6	44	35	.261
1998	Frederick	Carolina	OF	4	18	3	4	2	0	1	2	2	.222
1999	Frederick	Carolina	OF	130	507	81	135	23	5	6	73	26	.266
2000	Bowie	Eastern	OF	116	459	59	111	13	5	6	43	11	.242
2001	Bowie	Eastern	OF	30	117	16	33	7	1	3	21	3	.282
2001	Rochester	Int.	OF	104	391	37	93	19	2	2	35	13	.238
2002	Bowie	Eastern	OF	37	144	21	42	9	1	4	15	9	.292
2002	Rochester	Int.	OF	91	332	43	96	21	6	6	35	11	.289
2003	Ottawa	Int.	OF	40	152	19	45	7	1	0	20	5	.296
2004	Ottawa	Int.	OF	107	410	44	96	32	1	7	44	12	.234
2004	Baltimore	A.L.	OF	17	32	3	5	1	0	0	1	1	.156
2005	Buffalo	Int.	OF	26	74	11	20	7	0	1	4	0	.270
2005	Durham a-b	Int.	OF	73	285	45	81	13	2	12	34	7	.284
2006	Durham c-d	Int.	OF	136	538	80	157	33	1	14	57	30	.292
2007	Columbus	Int.	OF	73	267	39	84	17	4	2	41	14	.315
2007	Minnesota	A.L.	OF	4	10	0	1	0	0	0	0	0	.100
2007	Rochester e	Int.	OF	61	224	32	62	12	2	5	32	19	.277
2008	Rochester f	Int.	OF	93	369	53	99	25	4	11	57	19	.268
2009	Louisville	Int.	OF	73	280	42	88	22	7	9	40	8	.314
2009	Cincinnati g	N.L.	OF	47	105	12	28	6	1	2	10	1	.267
2010	Pawtucket	Int.	OF	10	41	6	14	6	1	2	8	1	.341
2010	Boston	A.L.	OF	117	319	40	86	18	3	9	34	9	.270
Major League Totals			4 Yrs.	185	466	55	120	25	4	11	45	11	.258

a Filed for free agency, October 15, 2004. Signed with Cleveland Indians organization, January 25, 2005.
b Released by Cleveland Indians, June 4, 2005. Signed with Tampa Bay Devil Rays, June 10, 2005,
c Filed for free agency, October 15, 2005, re-signed with Tampa Bay Devil Rays organization, January 4, 2006.
d Filed for free agency, October 15, 2006. Signed with Washington Nationals organization, November 6, 2006.
e Traded to Minnesota Twins for pitcher Levale Speigner, June 24, 2007.
f Filed for free agency, November 3, 2008. Signed with Cincinnati Reds organization, December 2, 2008.
g Filed for free agency, November 9, 2009. Signed with Boston Red Sox organization, November 24, 2009.

MC DONALD, JOHN JOSEPH

Born, New London, Connecticut, September 24, 1974.
Bats Right. Throws Right. Height, 5 feet, 11 inches. Weight, 175 pounds.

Year	Club	Lea	Pos	G	AB	R	H	2B	3B	HR	RBI	SB	Avg
1996	Watertown	N.Y.-Penn.	SS	75	278	48	75	11	0	2	26	11	.270
1997	Kinston	Carolina	SS	130	541	77	140	27	3	5	53	6	.259
1998	Akron	Eastern	SS	132	514	68	118	18	2	2	43	17	.230
1999	Akron	Eastern	SS	55	226	31	67	12	0	1	26	7	.296
1999	Buffalo	Int.	SS	66	237	30	75	12	1	0	25	6	.316
1999	Cleveland	A.L.	2B-SS	18	21	2	7	0	0	0	0	0	.333
2000	Buffalo	Int.	SS-2B	75	286	37	77	17	2	1	36	4	.269
2000	Mahoning Valley	N.Y.-Penn.	SS	5	17	0	2	1	0	0	1	0	.118
2000	Cleveland	A.L.	SS-2B	9	9	0	4	0	0	0	0	0	.444
2000	Kinston a	Carolina	SS	1	3	0	1	0	0	0	0	0	.333
2001	Buffalo	Int.	SS-2B-3B	116	410	52	100	17	1	2	33	17	.244
2001	Cleveland b	A.L.	SS-2B-3B	17	22	1	2	1	0	0	0	0	.091
2002	Cleveland	A.L.	2B-SS-3B	93	264	35	66	11	3	1	12	3	.250

Year	Club	Lea	Pos	G	AB	R	H	2B	3B	HR	RBI	SB	Avg
2003	Lake County	So.Atl.	SS	1	3	0	0	0	0	0	0	0	.000
2003	Mahoning Valley	N.Y.-Penn.	SS	1	2	1	0	0	0	0	0	0	.000
2003	Cleveland c	A.L.	2B-SS-3B	82	214	21	46	9	1	1	14	3	.215
2004	Cleveland d	A.L.	SS-2B-3B	66	93	17	19	5	1	2	7	0	.204
2005	Toronto-Detroit e-f	A.L.	SS-2B-3B	68	166	18	46	6	1	0	16	6	.277
2006	Toronto g	A.L.	SS-2B-3B	104	260	35	58	7	3	3	23	7	.223
2007	Toronto	A.L.	SS-3B	123	327	32	82	20	2	1	31	7	.251
2008	Dunedin	Fla.St.	SS	3	11	2	4	0	0	0	1	0	.364
2008	Toronto h	A.L.	SS-3B-2B	84	186	21	39	8	0	1	18	3	.210
2009	Toronto i	A.L.	SS-3B-2B-OF	73	151	18	39	7	0	4	13	0	.258
2010	Toronto	A.L.	2B-3B-SS-OF	63	152	27	38	9	2	6	23	2	.250
Major League Totals			12 Yrs.	800	1865	227	446	83	13	19	157	31	.239

a On disabled list from April 27 to May 9 and May 10 to June 22, 2000.
b On disabled list from May 10 to 17, 2001.
c On disabled list from June 30 to July 17 and August 27 to October 3, 2003.
d Traded to Toronto Blue Jays for player to be named later, December 2, 2004. Cleveland received pitcher Tom Mastny to complete deal, December 13, 2004.
e Sold to Detroit Tigers, July 22, 2005.
f Sold to Toronto Blue Jays, November 10, 2005.
g On disabled list from May 28 to June 12, 2006.
h On disabled list from May 7 to June 7, 2008.
i Filed for free agency, November 6, 2009, re-signed with Toronto Blue Jays, November 25, 2009.

MC GEHEE, CASEY MICHAEL

Born, Santa Cruz, California, October 12, 1982.
Bats Right. Throws Right. Height, 6 feet, 1 inch. Weight, 195 pounds.

Year	Club	Lea	Pos	G	AB	R	H	2B	3B	HR	RBI	SB	Avg
2003	Lansing	Midwest	3B	64	243	24	66	18	1	3	23	2	.272
2004	Daytona	Fla.St.	3B-C	119	449	56	117	30	0	10	66	2	.261
2005	West Tenn	Southern	3B-1B-2B	124	455	67	135	31	1	8	72	2	.297
2006	Iowa	P.C.	3B-1B-2B-SS	135	497	56	139	28	1	11	68	0	.280
2007	Iowa	P.C.	3B-1B	18	52	3	9	2	0	1	5	0	.173
2007	Tennessee	Southern	3B-C-1B	105	384	53	105	26	2	9	54	1	.273
2008	Iowa	P.C.	3B-C-1B-2B	133	497	68	147	30	0	12	92	0	.296
2008	Chicago a	N.L.	3B	9	24	1	4	1	0	0	5	0	.167
2009	Milwaukee	N.L.	3B-2B-1B-OF	116	355	58	107	20	1	16	66	0	.301
2010	Milwaukee	N.L.	3B-1B	157	610	70	174	38	1	23	104	1	.285
Major League Totals			3 Yrs.	282	989	129	285	59	2	39	175	1	.288

a Claimed on waivers by Milwaukee Brewers, October 29, 2008.

MC LOUTH, NATHAN RICHARD (NATE)

Born, Muskegon, Michigan, October 28, 1981.
Bats Left. Throws Right. Height, 5 feet, 11 inches. Weight, 185 pounds.

Year	Club	Lea	Pos	G	AB	R	H	2B	3B	HR	RBI	SB	Avg
2001	Hickory	So.Atl.	OF-2B	96	351	59	100	17	5	12	54	21	.285
2002	Lynchburg	Carolina	OF	114	393	58	96	23	4	9	46	20	.244
2003	Lynchburg	Carolina	OF	117	440	85	132	27	2	6	33	40	.300
2004	Altoona	Eastern	OF	133	515	93	166	40	4	8	73	31	.322
2005	Indianapolis	Int.	OF	110	397	64	118	20	3	5	39	34	.297
2005	Pittsburgh	N.L.	OF	41	109	20	28	6	0	5	12	2	.257
2006	Pittsburgh a	N.L.	OF	106	270	50	63	16	2	7	16	10	.233
2007	Pittsburgh	N.L.	OF	137	329	62	85	21	3	13	38	22	.258
2008	Pittsburgh	N.L.	OF	152	597	113	165	*46	4	26	94	23	.276
2009	Rome	So.Atl.	OF	1	2	0	0	0	0	0	0	0	.000
2009	Mississippi	Southern	OF	2	3	1	0	0	0	0	0	0	.000
2009	Pittsburgh-Atlanta b-c	N.L.	OF	129	507	86	130	27	2	20	70	19	.256
2010	Gwinnett	Int.	OF	34	128	18	30	1	0	6	18	7	.234
2010	Atlanta d	N.L.	OF	85	242	30	46	12	1	6	24	7	.190
Major League Totals			6 Yrs.	650	2054	361	517	128	12	77	254	83	.2520
Division Series													
2010	Atlanta	N.L.	OF	3	2	0	1	0	0	0	0	0	.500

a On disabled list from August 12 to October 3, 2006.
b Traded to Atlanta Braves for outfielder Gorkys Hernandez, pitcher Jeff Locke and pitcher Charlie Morton, June 3, 2009.
c On disabled list from August 16 to September 4, 2009.
d On disabled list from June 10 to July 21, 2010.

MICHAELS, JASON DREW

Born, Tampa, Florida, May 4, 1976.
Bats Right. Throws Right. Height, 6 feet. Weight, 205 pounds.

Year	Club	Lea	Pos	G	AB	R	H	2B	3B	HR	RBI	SB	Avg
1998	Batavia	N.Y.-Penn.	OF	67	235	45	63	14	3	11	49	4	.268
1999	Clearwater	Fla.St.	OF	122	452	91	138	31	6	14	65	10	.305
2000	Reading	Eastern	OF	113	437	71	129	30	4	10	74	7	.295
2001	Scranton-WB	Int.	OF	109	418	58	109	19	3	17	69	11	.261
2001	Philadelphia a	N.L.	OF	6	6	0	1	0	0	0	1	0	.167
2002	Scranton-WB	Int.	OF	9	32	3	9	2	0	0	7	1	.281
2002	Philadelphia	N.L.	OF-3B	81	105	16	28	10	3	2	11	1	.267
2003	Clearwater	Fla.St.	OF	4	14	1	0	0	0	0	0	0	.000
2003	Philadelphia b	N.L.	OF	76	109	20	36	11	0	5	17	0	.330
2004	Philadelphia	N.L.	OF	115	299	44	82	12	0	10	40	2	.274
2005	Philadelphia	N.L.	OF	105	289	54	88	16	2	4	31	3	.304
2006	Buffalo	Int.	OF	2	7	1	3	0	0	1	1	0	.429
2006	Cleveland c-d	A.L.	OF	123	494	77	132	32	1	9	55	9	.267
2007	Cleveland	A.L.	OF	105	267	43	72	11	1	7	39	3	.270
2008	Cleveland	A.L.	OF	21	58	3	12	4	0	0	9	1	.207
2008	Pittsburgh e-f	N.L.	OF	102	228	25	52	9	1	8	44	1	.228
2009	Houston g	N.L.	OF	102	135	17	32	12	1	4	16	1	.237
2010	Houston	N.L.	OF	106	186	23	47	14	1	8	26	0	.253
Major League Totals			10 Yrs.	942	2176	322	582	131	10	57	289	21	.267
	Division Series												
2007	Cleveland	A.L.	OF	1	1	0	1	1	0	0	0	0	1.000
	Championship Series												
2007	Cleveland	A.L.	PH	1	0	1	0	0	0	0	0	0	.000

a On disabled list from May 1 to 10, 2001.
b On disabled list from March 21 to April 14, 2003.
c Traded to Cleveland Indians for pitcher Arthur Rhodes, January 27, 2006.
d On disabled list from June 16 to July 4, 2006.
e Sold to Pittsburgh Pirates, May 8, 2008.
f Not offered contract, October 31, 2008. Signed with Houston Astros, December 15, 2008.
g Filed for free agency, November 5, 2009, re-signed with Houston Astros, December 14, 2009.

MILES, AARON WADE

Born, Pittsburg, California, December 15, 1976.
Bats Both. Throws Right. Height, 5 feet, 8 inches. Weight, 175 pounds.

Year	Club	Lea	Pos	G	AB	R	H	2B	3B	HR	RBI	SB	Avg
1995	Astros	Gulf Coast	SS-2B	47	171	32	44	9	3	0	18	9	.257
1996	Astros	Gulf Coast	2B	55	214	48	63	3	2	0	15	14	.294
1997	Quad City	Midwest	2B	97	370	55	97	13	2	1	35	18	.262
1998	Quad City	Midwest	2B-3B-OF	108	369	42	90	22	6	2	37	28	.244
1999	Michigan	Midwest	2B	112	470	72	149	28	8	10	71	17	.317
2000	Kissimmee a	Fla.St.	2B	75	295	40	86	20	1	2	36	11	.292
2001	Birmingham b	Southern	3B-2B	84	343	53	89	16	3	8	42	3	.259
2002	Birmingham c	Southern	2B-3B	138	531	67	171	39	1	9	68	25	.322
2003	Charlotte	Int.	2B-3B	133	546	80	166	34	5	11	50	8	.304
2003	Chicago d	A.L.	2B	8	12	3	4	3	0	0	2	0	.333
2004	Colorado Springs	P.C.	2B	12	54	8	18	3	0	0	8	2	.333
2004	Colorado	N.L.	2B	134	522	75	153	15	3	6	47	12	.293
2005	Colorado Springs	P.C.	2B	8	32	6	7	0	1	0	1	1	.219
2005	Colorado e-f	N.L.	2B-SS	99	324	37	91	12	3	2	28	4	.281
2006	St. Louis	N.L.	2B-SS-3B	135	426	48	112	20	5	2	30	2	.263
2007	St. Louis g	N.L.	2B-SS-3B-P	133	414	55	120	16	1	2	32	2	.290
2008	St. Louis h	N.L.	2B-SS-3B-OF	134	379	49	120	15	2	4	31	3	.317
2009	Iowa	P.C.	2B-3B-SS	21	87	8	22	4	0	0	8	1	.253
2009	Chicago i-j	N.L.	2B-SS-3B	74	157	17	29	7	1	0	5	3	.185
2010	Springfield	Texas	2B-SS-3B	16	61	11	17	4	0	0	13	0	.279
2010	St. Louis k-l-m	N.L.	2B-SS-3B-P	79	139	14	39	5	0	0	9	0	.281
Major League Totals			8 Yrs.	796	2373	298	668	93	15	16	184	26	.282
	Division Series												
2006	St. Louis	N.L.	2B	2	2	0	1	0	0	0	0	0	.500
	Championship Series												
2006	St. Louis	N.L.	2B	3	3	0	2	0	1	0	0	0	.667
	World Series Record												
2006	St. Louis	N.L.	2B	2	6	2	1	0	0	0	0	1	.167

a Selected by Chicago White Sox organization from Houston Astros organization in Rule V draft, December 11, 2000.
b Filed for free agency, October 15, 2001, re-signed with Chicago White Sox, November 16, 2001.

c Filed for free agency, October 15, 2002, re-signed with Chicago White Sox, October 25, 2002.
d Traded to Colorado Rockies for infielder Juan Uribe, December 2, 2003.
e On disabled list from May 26 to June 28, 2005.
f Traded to St. Louis Cardinals with outfielder Larry Bigbie for pitcher Ray King, December 7, 2005.
g Not offered contract, December 12, 2007, re-signed with St. Louis Cardinals organization, January 4, 2008.
h Not offered contract, December 12, 2008. Signed with Chicago Cubs, December 31, 2008.
i On disabled list from May 26 to June 10 and June 21 to August 5, 2009.
j Traded to Oakland Athletics with infielder Jake Fox and cash for pitcher Jeff Gray, pitcher Ronny Morla and outfielder Matt Spencer, December 3, 2009.
k Traded to Cincinnati Reds for infielder Adam Rosales and outfielder Willy Taveras, February 1, 2010.
l Released by Cincinnati Reds, April 12, 2010. Signed with St. Louis Cardinals organization, April 30, 2010.
m Filed for free agency, November 1, 2010.

MILLEDGE, LASTINGS DARNELL

Born, Bradenton, Florida, April 5, 1985.
Bats Right. Throws Right. Height, 6 feet, 1 inch. Weight, 205 pounds.

Year Club	Lea	Pos	G	AB	R	H	2B	3B	HR	RBI	SB	Avg
2003 Kingsport	Appal.	DH	7	26	4	6	2	0	0	2	5	.231
2004 St. Lucie	Fla.St.	OF	22	81	6	19	6	2	2	8	3	.235
2004 Capital City	So.Atl.	OF	65	262	66	89	22	1	13	58	23	.340
2005 Binghamton	Eastern	OF	48	193	33	65	17	0	4	24	11	.337
2005 St. Lucie	Fla.St.	OF	62	232	48	70	15	0	4	22	18	.302
2006 Norfolk	Int.	OF	84	307	52	85	21	4	7	36	13	.277
2006 New York	N.L.	OF	56	166	14	40	7	2	4	22	1	.241
2007 Mets	Gulf Coast	OF	2	7	1	1	1	0	0	0	0	.143
2007 St. Lucie	Fla.St.	OF	1	4	2	1	0	0	0	0	0	.250
2007 Binghamton	Eastern	OF	5	23	7	10	1	1	3	8	1	.435
2007 New Orleans	P.C.	OF	11	39	9	13	1	0	1	5	5	.333
2007 New York a	N.L.	OF	59	184	27	50	9	1	7	29	3	.272
2008 Nationals	Gulf Coast	OF	2	4	1	1	0	0	1	1	0	.250
2008 Columbus	Int.	OF	3	13	0	1	0	0	0	2	0	.077
2008 Washington b	N.L.	OF	138	523	65	140	24	2	14	61	24	.268
2009 Nationals	Gulf Coast	OF	3	5	1	1	0	0	1	3	1	.200
2009 Pirates	Gulf Coast	OF	4	12	1	4	2	0	0	0	1	.333
2009 Lynchburg	Carolina	OF	3	12	3	3	1	0	2	4	0	.250
2009 Indianapolis	Int.	OF	17	60	7	20	6	0	0	7	3	.333
2009 Syracuse	Int.	OF	22	79	11	20	5	0	0	4	6	.253
2009 Washington-Pittsburgh c	N.L.	OF	65	244	21	68	11	0	4	21	7	.279
2010 Pittsburgh d	N.L.	OF	113	379	38	105	21	3	4	34	5	.277
Major League Totals		5 Yrs.	431	1496	165	403	72	8	33	167	40	.269

a Traded to Washington Nationals for outfielder Ryan Church and catcher Brian Schneider, November 30, 2007.
b On disabled list from June 28 to July 24, 2008.
c Traded to Pittsburgh Pirates with pitcher Joel Hanrahan for outfielder Nyjer Morgan and pitcher Sean Burnett, June 30, 2009.
d Not offered contract, December 2, 2010.

MOLINA, BENJAMIN JOSE (BENGIE)

Born, Rio Piedras, Puerto Rico, July 20, 1974.
Bats Right. Throws Right. Height, 5 feet, 11 inches. Weight, 225 pounds.

Year Club	Lea	Pos	G	AB	R	H	2B	3B	HR	RBI	SB	Avg
1993 Angels	Arizona	DH-C	27	80	9	21	6	2	0	10	0	.262
1994 Cedar Rapds	Midwest	C	48	171	14	48	8	0	3	16	1	.281
1995 Vancouver	P.C.	C	1	2	0	0	0	0	0	0	0	.000
1995 Cedar Rapds	Midwest	C	39	133	15	39	9	0	4	17	1	.293
1995 Lk Elsinore	California	C	27	96	21	37	7	2	2	12	0	.385
1996 Midland	Texas	C	108	365	45	100	21	2	8	54	0	.274
1997 Lk Elsinore	California	C	36	149	18	42	10	2	4	33	0	.282
1997 Midland	Texas	DH-C	29	106	18	35	8	0	6	30	0	.330
1998 Midland	Texas	C	41	154	28	55	8	0	9	39	0	.357
1998 Vancouver	P.C.	C	49	184	13	54	9	1	1	22	1	.293
1998 Anaheim a	A.L.	C	2	1	0	0	0	0	0	0	0	.000
1999 Edmonton	P.C.	C	65	241	28	69	16	0	7	41	1	.286
1999 Anaheim b	A.L.	C	31	101	8	26	5	0	1	10	0	.257
2000 Anaheim	A.L.	C	130	473	59	133	20	2	14	71	1	.281
2001 Salt Lake	P.C.	C	5	18	2	5	1	0	0	3	0	.278
2001 Rancho Cucamonga	Calif.	C	3	11	1	6	1	0	0	2	0	.545
2001 Anaheim c	A.L.	C	96	325	31	85	11	0	6	40	0	.262
2002 Rancho Cucamonga	Calif.	C	1	2	0	1	0	0	0	0	0	.500
2002 Anaheim d	A.L.	C	122	428	34	105	18	0	5	47	0	.245

Year Club	Lea	Pos	G	AB	R	H	2B	3B	HR	RBI	SB	Avg
2003 Anaheim e	A.L.	C	119	409	37	115	24	0	14	71	1	.281
2004 Anaheim f	A.L.	C	97	337	36	93	13	0	10	54	0	.276
2005 Los Angeles g-h	A.L.	C	119	410	45	121	17	0	15	69	0	.295
2006 Toronto i	A.L.	C	117	433	44	123	20	1	19	57	1	.284
2007 San Francisco	N.L.	C	134	497	38	137	19	1	19	81	0	.276
2008 San Francisco	N.L.	C	145	530	46	155	33	0	16	95	0	.292
2009 San Francisco j	N.L.	C	132	491	52	130	25	1	20	80	0	.265
2010 San Francisco	N.L.	C	61	202	17	52	6	0	3	17	0	.257
2010 Texas k-l	A.L.	C	57	175	10	42	6	1	2	19	0	.240
Major League Totals		13 Yrs.	1362	4812	457	1317	217	6	144	711	3	.274
Division Series												
2002 Anaheim	A.L.	C	4	15	0	4	2	0	0	2	0	.267
2004 Anaheim	A.L.	C	3	6	0	1	0	0	0	0	0	.167
2005 Los Angeles	A.L.	C	5	18	5	8	0	0	3	5	0	.444
2010 Texas	A.L.	C	4	14	1	5	0	0	1	2	1	.357
Division Series Totals			16	53	6	18	2	0	4	9	1	.340
Championship Series												
2002 Anaheim	A.L.	C	5	14	0	3	0	1	0	2	0	.214
2005 Los Angeles	A.L.	C-DH	5	17	0	2	0	0	0	1	0	.118
2010 Texas	A.L.	C	5	16	3	5	1	0	1	5	0	.313
Championship Series Totals			15	47	3	10	1	1	1	8	0	.213
World Series Record												
2002 Anaheim	A.L.	C	7	21	2	6	2	0	0	2	0	.286
2010 Texas	A.L.	C	4	11	3	2	1	0	0	1	0	.182
World Series Totals			11	32	5	8	3	0	0	3	0	.250

a On disabled list from May 13 to 22, 1998.
b On disabled list from June 4 to 14, 1999.
c On disabled list from May 5 to June 27, 2001.
d On disabled list from July 17 to August 1, 2002.
e On disabled list from September 4 to October 6, 2003.
f On disabled list from June 4 to June 19 and from August 1 to August 17, 2004.
g On disabled list from April 18 to May 13, 2005.
h Filed for free agency, October 27, 2005. Signed with Toronto Blue Jays, February 28, 2006.
i Filed for free agency, November 31, 2006, re-signed with San Francisco Giants, December 6, 2006.
j Filed for free agency, November 6, 2009, re-signed with San Francisco Giants, January 19, 2010.
k Traded to Texas Rangers with cash for pitcher Chris Ray and pitcher Michael Main, July 1, 2010.
l Filed for free agency, November 1, 2010.

MOLINA (MATTA), JOSE BENJAMIN

Born, Bayamon, Puerto Rico, June 3, 1975.
Bats Right. Throws Right. Height, 6 feet, 2 inch. Weight, 245 pounds.

Year Club	Lea	Pos	G	AB	R	H	2B	3B	HR	RBI	SB	Avg
1993 Cubs	Gulf Coast	C-1B	33	78	5	17	2	0	0	4	3	.218
1993 Daytona	Fla.St.	C	3	7	0	1	0	0	0	1	0	.143
1994 Peoria	Midwest	C	78	253	31	58	13	1	1	33	4	.229
1995 Daytona	Fla.St.	C	82	233	27	55	9	1	1	19	1	.236
1996 Rockford	Midwest	C	96	305	35	69	10	1	2	27	2	.226
1997 Iowa	A.A.	C	1	3	0	1	0	0	0	0	0	.333
1997 Daytona	Fla.St.	C	55	179	17	45	9	1	0	23	4	.251
1997 Orlando	Southern	C	37	99	10	17	3	0	1	15	0	.172
1998 West Tenn	Southern	C-1B	109	320	33	71	10	1	2	28	1	.222
1999 West Tenn	Southern	C	14	35	2	6	3	0	0	5	0	.171
1999 Iowa	P.C.	C	74	240	24	63	11	1	4	26	0	.262
1999 Chicago	N.L.	C	10	19	3	5	1	0	0	1	0	.263
2000 Iowa	P.C.	C-1B	76	248	22	58	9	0	1	17	1	.234
2001 Salt Lake	P.C.	C	61	213	29	64	11	1	5	31	1	.300
2001 Anaheim a-b	A.L.	C	15	37	8	10	3	0	2	4	0	.270
2002 Salt Lake	P.C.	C	79	290	30	89	14	2	4	43	0	.307
2002 Anaheim	A.L.	C	29	70	5	19	3	0	0	5	0	.271
2003 Anaheim	A.L.	C	53	114	12	21	4	0	0	6	0	.184
2004 Anaheim	A.L.	C-1B	73	203	26	53	10	2	3	25	4	.261
2005 Los Angeles	A.L.	C-1B	75	184	14	42	4	0	6	25	2	.228
2006 Los Angeles	A.L.	C-1B	78	225	18	54	17	0	4	22	1	.240
2007 Los Angeles-New York c-d	A.L.	C	69	191	18	49	13	0	1	19	2	.257
2008 New York	A.L.	C-1B	100	268	32	58	17	0	3	18	0	.216
2009 Trenton	Eastern	C	3	7	0	0	0	0	0	0	0	.000
2009 Scranton/WB	Int.	C	2	4	0	1	1	0	0	1	0	.250
2009 New York e-f	A.L.	C-1B-3B	52	138	15	30	4	0	1	11	0	.217

Year Club	Lea	Pos	G	AB	R	H	2B	3B	HR	RBI	SB	Avg
2010 Toronto	A.L.	C	57	167	13	41	4	0	6	12	1	.246
Major League Totals		11 Yrs.	611	1616	164	382	80	2	26	148	10	.236
Division Series												
2004 Anaheim	A.L.	C	2	3	2	1	0	0	0	0	0	.333
2005 Los Angeles	A.L.	C	1	1	1	1	0	0	0	1	0	1.000
2009 New York	A.L.	C	1	1	0	0	0	0	0	0	0	.000
Division Series Totals			4	5	3	2	0	0	0	1	0	.400
Championship Series												
2002 Anaheim	A.L.	C	3	1	0	0	0	0	0	0	0	.000
2005 Los Angeles	A.L.	C	1	3	0	1	0	0	0	0	0	.333
2009 New York	A.L.	C	2	3	0	1	0	0	0	0	0	.333
Championship Series Totals			6	7	0	2	0	0	0	0	0	.286
World Series Record												
2002 Anaheim	A.L.	C	3	0	0	0	0	0	0	0	0	.000
2009 New York	A.L.	C	2	2	0	0	0	0	0	0	0	.000
World Series Totals			5	2	0	0	0	0	0	0	0	.000

a Released by Chicago Cubs November 27, 2000. Signed with Anaheim Angels organization, January 15, 2001.
b On disabled list from May 21 to July 2, 2001.
c Traded to New York Yankees for pitcher Jeff Kennard, July 21, 2007.
d Filed for free agency, October 30, 2007, re-signed with New York Yankees, December 3, 2007.
e On disabled list from May 8 to July 8, 2009.
f Filed for free agency, November 9, 2009. Signed with Toronto Blue Jays, February 19, 2010.

MOLINA, YADIER BENJAMIN

Born, Bayamon, Puerto Rico, July 13, 1982.
Bats Right. Throws Right. Height, 5 feet, 11 inches. Weight, 225 pounds.

Year Club	Lea	Pos	G	AB	R	H	2B	3B	HR	RBI	SB	Avg
2001 Johnson City	Appal.	C	44	158	18	41	11	0	4	18	1	.259
2002 Peoria	Midwest	C	112	393	39	110	20	0	7	50	2	.280
2003 Tennessee	Southern	C	104	364	32	100	13	1	2	51	0	.275
2004 Memphis	P.C.	C	37	129	19	39	6	0	1	14	0	.302
2004 St. Louis	N.L.	C	51	135	12	36	6	0	2	15	0	.267
2005 St. Louis a	N.L.	C-1B	114	385	36	97	15	1	8	49	2	.252
2006 St. Louis	N.L.	C-1B	129	417	29	90	26	0	6	49	1	.216
2007 St. Louis b	N.L.	C-1B	111	353	30	97	15	0	6	40	1	.275
2008 St. Louis	N.L.	C-1B	124	444	37	135	18	0	7	56	0	.304
2009 St. Louis	N.L.	C-1B	140	481	45	141	23	1	6	54	9	.293
2010 St. Louis	N.L.	C-1B	136	465	34	122	19	0	6	62	8	.262
Major League Totals		7 Yrs.	805	2680	223	718	122	2	41	325	21	.268
Division Series												
2005 St. Louis	N.L.	C	3	13	1	3	0	0	0	3	0	.231
2006 St. Louis	N.L.	C	4	13	0	4	1	0	0	1	0	.308
2009 St. Louis	N.L.	C	3	13	0	4	1	0	0	0	0	.308
Division Series Totals			10	39	1	11	2	0	0	4	0	.282
Championship Series												
2004 St. Louis	N.L.	C	1	4	0	1	0	0	0	0	0	.250
2005 St. Louis	N.L.	C	6	22	1	7	3	0	0	0	0	.318
2006 St. Louis	N.L.	C	7	23	2	8	1	0	2	6	0	.348
Championship Series Totals			14	49	3	16	4	0	2	6	0	.327
World Series Record												
2004 St. Louis	N.L.	C	3	3	0	0	0	0	0	0	0	.000
2006 St. Louis	N.L.	C	5	17	3	7	2	0	0	1	0	.412
World Series Totals			8	20	3	7	2	0	0	1	0	.350

a On disabled list from July 9 to August 18, 2005.
b On disabled list from May 30 to June 28, 2007.

MONTERO, MIGUEL ANGEL

Born, Caracas, Venezuela, July 9, 1983.
Bats Left. Throws Right. Height, 5 feet, 11 inches. Weight, 195 pounds.

Year Club	Lea	Pos	G	AB	R	H	2B	3B	HR	RBI	SB	Avg
2002 Missoula	Pioneer	C-3B-1B	50	152	21	40	10	1	3	14	2	.263
2003 Missoula	Pioneer	C	59	196	24	59	10	2	4	32	2	.301
2004 South Bend	Midwest	C-1B-SS	115	403	47	106	22	2	11	59	8	.263
2005 Lancaster	Calif.	C-1B	85	355	73	124	24	1	24	82	1	.349
2005 Tennessee	Southern	C-1B	30	108	13	27	1	2	2	13	1	.250

Year	Club	Lea	Pos	G	AB	R	H	2B	3B	HR	RBI	SB	Avg
2006	Tennessee	Southern	C	81	289	24	78	18	0	10	46	0	.270
2006	Tucson	P.C.	C	36	134	21	43	5	0	7	29	1	.321
2006	Arizona	N.L.	C	6	16	0	4	1	0	0	3	0	.250
2007	Arizona	N.L.	C	84	214	30	48	7	0	10	37	0	.224
2008	Tucson	P.C.	C	11	32	3	9	2	0	1	5	0	.281
2008	Arizona a	N.L.	C	70	184	24	47	16	1	5	18	0	.255
2009	Arizona	N.L.	C	128	425	61	125	30	0	16	59	1	.294
2010	Reno	P.C.	C	4	15	1	5	0	0	0	2	0	.333
2010	Arizona b	N.L.	C	85	297	36	79	20	2	9	43	0	.266
Major League Totals			5 Yrs.	373	1136	151	303	74	3	40	160	1	.267
	Division Series												
2007	Arizona	N.L.	C	1	2	1	0	0	0	0	0	0	.000
	Championship Series												
2007	Arizona	N.L.	C	3	5	0	2	0	0	0	0	0	.400

a On disabled list from March 23 to April 23, 2008.
b On disabled list from April 11 to June 12, 2010.

MOORE, ADAM ROSS

Born, Longview, Texas, May 8, 1984.
Bats Right. Throws Right. Height, 6 feet, 3 inches. Weight, 220 pounds.

Year	Club	Lea	Pos	G	AB	R	H	2B	3B	HR	RBI	SB	Avg
2006	Wisconsin	Midwest	C	44	165	21	44	6	0	7	24	0	.267
2006	Everett	Northwest	C	16	63	8	20	9	0	0	9	0	.317
2007	High Desert	Calif.	C-1B	115	433	74	133	30	3	22	102	1	.307
2008	West Tenn	Southern	C	119	429	60	137	34	2	14	71	0	.319
2009	West Tenn	Southern	C	27	95	14	25	5	0	3	13	0	.263
2009	Tacoma	P.C.	C	91	340	41	100	19	0	9	43	1	.294
2009	Seattle	A.L.	C	6	23	4	5	1	0	1	2	1	.217
2010	Tacoma	P.C.	C	36	134	18	43	8	1	3	15	1	.321
2010	Seattle a	A.L.	C	60	205	12	40	6	0	4	15	0	.195
Major League Totals			2 Yrs.	66	228	16	45	7	0	5	17	1	.197

a On disabled list from May 16 to June 25, 2010.

MORA, MELVIN

Born, Agua Negra, Venezuela, February 2, 1972.
Bats Right. Throws Right. Height, 5 feet, 11 inches. Weight, 200 pounds.

Year	Club	Lea	Pos	G	AB	R	H	2B	3B	HR	RBI	SB	Avg
1992	Astros	Gulf Coast	OF-2B-3B	49	144	28	32	3	0	0	8	16	.222
1993	Asheville	So.Atl.	2B-OF-3B	108	365	66	104	22	2	2	31	20	.285
1994	Osceola	Fla.St.	OF-3B-2B	118	425	57	120	29	4	8	46	24	.282
1995	Jackson	Texas	OF-2B-3B	123	467	63	139	32	0	3	45	22	.298
1995	Tucson	P.C.	OF	2	5	3	3	0	1	0	1	1	.600
1996	Tucson	P.C.	3B-OF-2B	62	228	35	64	11	2	3	26	3	.281
1996	Jackson	Texas	OF-2B-SS-3B	70	255	36	73	6	1	5	23	4	.286
1997	New Orleans	A.A.	OF-3B-2B-SS	119	370	55	95	15	3	2	38	7	.257
1998	St. Lucie	Fla.St.	2B-SS-OF	17	55	5	15	0	0	0	8	1	.273
1998	Norfolk a	Int.	3B-OF-2B	11	28	5	5	1	0	0	2	0	.179
1999	Norfolk	Int.	SS	82	304	55	92	17	2	8	36	18	.303
1999	New York b	N.L.	OF-2B-3B-SS	66	31	6	5	0	0	0	1	2	.161
2000	Norfolk	Int.	OF	8	27	7	9	2	0	0	7	2	.333
2000	New York	N.L.	SS-OF-2B-3B	79	215	35	56	13	2	6	30	7	.260
2000	Baltimore c	A.L.	SS-2B	53	199	25	58	9	3	2	17	5	.291
2001	Baltimore	A.L.	OF-SS-2B	128	436	49	109	28	0	7	48	11	.250
2002	Baltimore	A.L.	OF-SS-2B	149	557	86	130	30	4	19	64	16	.233
2003	Bowie	Eastern	OF	6	21	3	6	0	0	2	5	0	.286
2003	Baltimore d	A.L.	OF-SS-2B-1B	96	344	68	109	17	1	15	48	6	.317
2004	Baltimore e	A.L.	3B-SS	140	550	111	187	41	0	27	104	11	.340
2005	Baltimore	A.L.	3B	149	593	86	168	30	1	27	88	7	.283
2006	Baltimore	A.L.	3B-2B	155	624	96	171	25	0	16	83	11	.274
2007	Orioles	Gulf Coast	DH	2	7	1	2	1	0	0	1	0	.286
2007	Baltimore f	A.L.	3B	126	467	67	128	23	1	14	58	9	.274
2008	Baltimore	A.L.	3B-SS	135	513	77	146	29	2	23	104	3	.285
2009	Baltimore g-h	A.L.	3B	125	450	44	117	20	0	8	48	3	.260
2010	Colorado i	N.L.	3B-1B-2B-OF	113	316	39	90	12	5	7	45	2	.285
Major League Totals			12 Yrs.	1514	5295	789	1474	277	19	171	738	93	.278
	Division Series												
1999	New York	N.L.	OF	3	1	1	0	0	0	0	0	0	.000

Year	Club	Lea	Pos	G	AB	R	H	2B	3B	HR	RBI	SB	Avg
	Championship Series												
1999	New York	N.L.	OF	6	14	3	6	0	0	1	2	2	.429

a Filed for free agency from Houston Astros, October 17, 1997. Signed with New York Mets, July 24, 1998.
b Filed for free agency, October 16, 1998, re-signed with New York Mets, February 2, 1999.
c Traded to Baltimore Orioles with infielder Mike Kinkade, pitcher Pat Gorman and pitcher Leslie Brea for infielder Mike Bordick, July 28, 2000.
d On disabled list from August 1 to September 2, 2003.
e On disabled list from July 3 to July 18, 2004.
f On disabled list from July 13 to August 5, 2007.
g On disabled list from April 13 to April 28, 2009.
h Filed for free agency, November 5, 2009. Signed with Colorado Rockies, February 5, 2010.
i Filed for free agency, November 1, 2010. Signed with Arizona Diamondbacks, December 6, 2010.

MORALES, KENDRYS (KENDRY)

Born, Fomento, Cuba, June 20, 1983.
Bats Both. Throws Right. Height, 6 feet, 1 inch. Weight, 225 pounds.

Year	Club	Lea	Pos	G	AB	R	H	2B	3B	HR	RBI	SB	Avg
2005	Rancho Cucamonga	Calif.	1B-3B-OF	22	90	18	31	3	0	5	17	0	.344
2005	Arkansas	Texas	1B-OF	74	281	47	86	12	0	17	54	2	.306
2006	Salt Lake	P.C.	1B	66	256	41	82	13	1	12	52	0	.320
2006	Los Angeles	A.L.	1B	57	197	21	46	10	1	5	22	1	.234
2007	Salt Lake	P.C.	1B	64	255	42	87	20	1	5	37	0	.341
2007	Los Angeles	A.L.	1B-OF	43	119	12	35	10	0	4	15	0	.294
2008	Angels	Arizona	OF	5	21	4	11	3	0	1	10	0	.524
2008	Salt Lake	P.C.	1B-OF	78	317	46	108	19	0	15	64	1	.341
2008	Los Angeles	A.L.	OF-1B	27	61	7	13	2	0	3	8	0	.213
2009	Los Angeles	A.L.	1B	152	566	86	173	43	2	34	108	3	.306
2010	Los Angeles a	A.L.	1B	51	193	29	56	5	0	11	39	0	.290
Major League Totals			5 Yrs.	330	1136	155	323	70	3	57	192	4	.284
	Division Series												
2007	Los Angeles	A.L.	1B-DH	3	9	1	1	0	0	0	0	0	.111
2008	Los Angeles	A.L.	PH	4	4	0	2	1	0	0	0	0	.500
2009	Los Angeles	A.L.	1B	3	10	1	2	0	0	1	3	0	.200
Division Series Totals				10	23	2	5	1	0	1	3	0	.217
	Championship Series												
2009	Los Angeles	A.L.	1B	6	24	1	4	0	0	1	4	0	.167

a On disabled list from May 30 to November 2, 2010.

MORELAND, MITCHELL AUSTIN (MITCH)

Born, Amory, Mississippi, September 6, 1985.
Bats Left. Throws Left. Height, 6 feet, 2 inches. Weight, 230 pounds.

Year	Club	Lea	Pos	G	AB	R	H	2B	3B	HR	RBI	SB	Avg
2007	Spokane	Northwest	1B-OF	27	108	10	28	7	1	2	15	1	.259
2008	Clinton	Midwest	1B-OF	123	466	64	151	37	4	18	99	2	.324
2009	Bakersfield	Calif.	1B-OF	43	170	34	58	19	0	8	26	1	.341
2009	Frisco	Texas	OF-1B	73	301	51	98	19	3	8	59	1	.326
2010	Oklahoma	P.C.	OF-1B	95	353	52	102	29	2	12	65	2	.289
2010	Texas	A.L.	1B-OF	47	145	20	37	4	0	9	25	3	.255
	Division Series												
2010	Texas	A.L.	1B	4	15	1	3	3	0	0	1	0	.200
	Championship Series												
2010	Texas	A.L.	1B	6	18	3	7	0	0	0	3	0	.389
	World Series Record												
2010	Texas	A.L.	1B	5	13	1	6	1	0	1	3	0	.462

MORGAN, NYJER JAMID

Born, San Francisco, California, July 2, 1980.
Bats Left. Throws Left. Height, 6 feet. Weight, 170 pounds.

Year	Club	Lea	Pos	G	AB	R	H	2B	3B	HR	RBI	SB	Avg
2003	Williamsport	N.Y.-Penn.	OF	72	268	49	92	7	4	0	23	26	.343
2004	Hickory	So.Atl.	OF	134	514	83	131	16	7	4	41	55	.255
2005	Lynchburg	Carolina	OF	60	252	36	72	12	3	0	24	24	.286
2006	Lynchburg	Carolina	OF	61	228	43	69	7	3	0	22	38	.303
2006	Altoona	Eastern	OF	56	219	39	67	6	5	1	10	21	.306
2007	Pirates	Gulf Coast	OF	4	13	3	4	0	0	1	1	0	.308
2007	Indianapolis	Int.	OF	44	164	30	50	4	2	0	10	26	.305

Year	Club	Lea	Pos	G	AB	R	H	2B	3B	HR	RBI	SB	Avg
2007	Pittsburgh a	N.L.	OF	28	107	15	32	3	4	1	7	7	.299
2008	Indianapolis	Int.	OF	82	322	54	96	13	4	1	33	44	.298
2008	Pittsburgh	N.L.	OF	58	160	26	47	13	0	0	7	9	.294
2009	Pittsburgh-Washington b-c	N.L.	OF	120	469	74	144	15	7	3	39	42	.307
2010	Hagerstown	So.Atl.	OF	1	3	0	0	0	0	0	0	0	.000
2010	Potomac	Carolina	DH	1	3	0	0	0	0	0	0	0	.000
2010	Washington d	N.L.	OF	136	509	60	129	17	7	0	24	34	.253
Major League Totals			4 Yrs.	342	1245	175	352	48	18	4	77	92	.283

a On minor league disabled list from May 14 through August 23, 2007.
b Traded to Washington Nationals with pitcher Sean Burnett for outfielder Lastings Milledge and pitcher Joel Hanrahan, June 30, 2009.
c On disabled list from August 28 to October 13, 2009.
d On disabled list from August 4 to August 19, 2010.

MORNEAU, JUSTIN ERNEST GEORGE

Born, New Westminster, British Columbia, Canada, May 15, 1981.
Bats Left. Throws Right. Height, 6 feet, 4 inches. Weight, 225 pounds.

Year	Club	Lea	Pos	G	AB	R	H	2B	3B	HR	RBI	SB	Avg
1999	Twins	Gulf Coast	DH	17	53	3	16	5	0	0	9	0	.302
2000	Twins	Gulf Coast	1B-C-OF	52	194	47	78	21	0	10	58	3	.402
2000	Elizabethton	Appal.	C	6	23	4	5	0	0	1	3	0	.217
2001	Quad Cities	Midwest	1B	64	236	50	84	17	2	12	53	0	.356
2001	Fort Myers	Fla.St.	1B	53	197	25	58	10	3	4	40	0	.294
2001	New Britain	Eastern	1B	10	38	3	6	1	0	0	4	0	.158
2002	New Britain	Eastern	1B	126	494	72	147	31	4	16	80	7	.298
2003	New Britain	Eastern	1B	20	79	14	26	3	1	6	13	0	.329
2003	Rochester	Int.	1B	71	265	39	71	11	1	16	42	0	.268
2003	Minnesota	A.L.	DH-1B	40	106	14	24	4	0	4	16	0	.226
2004	Rochester	Int.	1B	72	288	51	88	23	0	22	63	1	.306
2004	Minnesota	A.L.	1B	74	280	39	76	17	0	19	58	0	.271
2005	Minnesota a	A.L.	1B	141	490	62	117	23	4	22	79	0	.239
2006	Minnesota b	A.L.	1B	157	592	97	190	37	1	34	130	3	.321
2007	Minnesota	A.L.	1B	157	590	84	160	31	3	31	111	1	.271
2008	Minnesota	A.L.	1B	*163	623	97	187	47	4	23	129	0	.300
2009	Minnesota	A.L.	1B	135	508	85	139	31	1	30	100	0	.274
2010	Minnesota c	A.L.	1B	81	296	53	102	25	1	18	56	0	.345
Major League Totals			8 Yrs.	948	3485	531	995	215	14	181	679	4	.286
	Division Series												
2004	Minnesota	A.L.	1B	4	17	1	4	2	0	0	2	0	.235
2006	Minnesota	A.L.	1B	3	12	3	5	1	0	2	2	0	.417
Division Series Totals				7	29	4	9	3	0	2	4	0	.310

a On disabled list from April 7 to April 22, 2005.
b Selected Most Valuable Player in American League for 2006.
c On disabled list from July 8 to November 2, 2010.

MORRISON, JUSTIS LOGAN (LOGAN)

Born, Kansas City, Missouri, August 25, 1987.
Bats Left. Throws Left. Height, 6 feet, 3 inches. Weight, 235 pounds.

Year	Club	Lea	Pos	G	AB	R	H	2B	3B	HR	RBI	SB	Avg
2006	Marlins	Gulf Coast	1B	26	89	10	24	4	0	1	7	1	.270
2006	Jamestown	N.Y.-Penn.	1B	23	74	6	15	3	0	1	11	0	.203
2007	Greensboro	So.Atl.	1B	128	453	71	121	22	2	24	86	2	.267
2008	Jupiter	Fla.St.	1B	130	488	71	162	38	1	13	74	9	.332
2009	Jupiter	Fla.St.	1B	3	11	0	3	1	0	0	2	0	.273
2009	Jacksonville	Southern	1B-OF	79	278	48	77	18	2	8	47	9	.277
2010	Jupiter	Fla.St.	1B	5	21	3	8	2	2	0	2	0	.381
2010	New Orleans	P.C.	1B-OF	68	238	36	73	17	4	6	45	1	.307
2010	Florida	N.L.	OF	62	244	43	69	20	7	2	18	0	.283

MORSE, MICHAEL JOHN (MIKE)

Born, Fort Lauderdale, Florida, March 22, 1982.
Bats Right. Throws Right. Height, 6 feet, 4 inches. Weight, 230 pounds.

Year	Club	Lea	Pos	G	AB	R	H	2B	3B	HR	RBI	SB	Avg
2000	White Sox	Arizona	SS	45	180	32	46	6	1	2	24	5	.256
2001	Bristol	Appal.	SS	57	181	23	41	7	3	4	27	6	.227

Year	Club	Lea	Pos	G	AB	R	H	2B	3B	HR	RBI	SB	Avg
2002	Kannapolis	So.Atl.	SS-3B	113	417	43	107	30	4	2	56	7	.257
2003	Winston-Salem	Carolina	SS	122	432	45	106	30	2	10	55	4	.245
2004	Birmingham	Southern	SS	54	209	30	60	9	5	11	38	0	.287
2004	San Antonio a	Texas	SS	41	157	18	43	10	1	6	33	0	.274
2005	Tacoma	P.C.	SS	49	182	20	46	12	2	4	23	1	.253
2005	Seattle	A.L.	SS-OF	72	230	27	64	10	1	3	23	3	.278
2006	Tacoma	P.C.	1B-3B-SS-OF	57	206	23	51	15	1	5	34	0	.248
2006	Seattle	A.L.	OF-3B-1B-SS	21	43	5	16	5	0	0	11	1	.372
2007	Mariners	Arizona	3B-SS	5	15	2	3	1	0	0	2	0	.200
2007	Tacoma	P.C.	3B-SS-OF	76	291	48	90	26	0	6	39	5	.309
2007	Seattle	A.L.	1B-3B-SS-OF	9	18	1	8	2	0	0	3	0	.444
2008	Seattle b	A.L.	OF	5	9	0	2	1	0	0	0	0	.222
2009	Tacoma	P.C.	SS-2B-3B-OF	66	260	38	81	14	0	10	52	0	.312
2009	Syracuse	Int.	1B-3B-OF-SS	44	165	21	56	12	3	6	34	2	.339
2009	Washington c	N.L.	1B-OF-3B	32	52	4	13	3	0	3	10	0	.250
2010	Syracuse	Int.	1B-OF-3B	15	51	12	13	2	0	3	8	0	.255
2010	Washington d	N.L.	OF-1B	98	266	36	77	12	2	15	41	0	.289
Major League Totals			6 Yrs.	237	618	73	180	33	3	21	88	4	.291

a Traded by Chicago White Sox to Seattle Mariners with catcher Miguel Olivo and outfielder Jeremy Reed for pitcher Freddy Garcia, catcher Ben Davis and cash, June 27, 2004.
b On disabled list from April 14 to September 29, 2008.
c Traded to Washington Nationals for outfielder Ryan Langerhans, June 28, 2009.
d On disabled list from April 11 to May 16, 2010.

MURPHY, DAVID MATTHEW

Born, Houston, Texas, October 18, 1981.
Bats Left. Throws Left. Height, 6 feet, 4 inches. Weight, 205 pounds.

Year	Club	Lea	Pos	G	AB	R	H	2B	3B	HR	RBI	SB	Avg
2003	Sarasota	Fla.St.	OF	45	153	18	37	5	1	1	18	6	.242
2003	Lowell	N.Y.-Penn.	OF	21	78	13	27	4	0	0	13	4	.346
2004	Sarasota	Fla.St.	OF	73	272	35	71	11	0	4	38	3	.261
2004	Red Sox	Gulf Coast	OF	5	18	3	5	1	0	0	1	1	.278
2005	Portland	Eastern	OF	135	484	71	133	25	4	14	75	13	.275
2006	Portland	Eastern	OF	42	172	22	47	17	1	3	25	4	.273
2006	Pawtucket	Int.	OF	84	318	45	85	23	5	8	44	3	.267
2006	Boston	A.L.	OF	20	22	4	5	1	0	1	2	0	.227
2007	Oklahoma	P.C.	OF	2	7	0	2	0	0	0	0	0	.286
2007	Pawtucket	Int.	OF	100	400	50	112	20	5	9	47	8	.280
2007	Boston-Texas a	A.L.	OF	46	105	17	36	12	2	2	14	0	.343
2008	Texas b	A.L.	OF	108	415	64	114	28	3	15	74	7	.275
2009	Texas	A.L.	OF	128	432	61	116	24	1	17	57	9	.269
2010	Texas	A.L.	OF	138	419	54	122	26	2	12	65	14	.291
Major League Totals			5 Yrs.	440	1393	200	393	91	8	47	212	30	.282
	Division Series												
2010	Texas	A.L.	OF	2	7	0	1	0	0	0	0	0	.143
	Championship Series												
2010	Texas	A.L.	OF	6	13	6	3	1	0	1	2	0	.231
	World Series Record												
2010	Texas	A.L.	OF	3	7	0	1	0	0	0	1	0	.143

a Traded to Texas Rangers with pitcher Kason Gabbard and outfielder Engle Beltre for pitcher Eric Gagne, July 31, 2007.
b On disabled list from August 7 to October 2, 2008.

NADY, XAVIER CLIFFORD

Born, Salinas, California, November 14, 1978.
Bats Right. Throws Right. Height, 6 feet, 2 inches. Weight, 220 pounds.

Year	Club	Lea	Pos	G	AB	R	H	2B	3B	HR	RBI	SB	Avg
2000	San Diego	N.L.	PH	1	1	1	1	0	0	0	0	0	1.000
2001	Lake Elsinore	California	1B	137	524	96	158	38	1	26	100	6	.302
2002	Lake Elsinore	California	OF	45	169	41	47	6	3	13	37	2	.278
2002	Portland	P.C.	OF	85	315	46	89	12	1	10	43	0	.283
2003	Portland	P.C.	OF	37	136	19	36	7	0	7	23	0	.265
2003	San Diego	N.L.	OF	110	371	50	99	17	1	9	39	6	.267
2004	Portland	P.C.	OF-1B	74	291	52	96	19	1	22	70	3	.330
2004	San Diego	N.L.	OF	34	77	7	19	4	0	3	9	0	.247
2005	San Diego a	N.L.	OF-1B-3B	124	326	40	85	15	2	13	43	2	.261
2006	Norfolk	Int.	OF	3	11	2	4	1	0	0	3	0	.364

Year	Club	Lea	Pos	G	AB	R	H	2B	3B	HR	RBI	SB	Avg
2006	New York-Pittsburgh b-c	N.L.	OF-1B	130	468	57	131	28	1	17	63	3	.280
2007	Pittsburgh	N.L.	OF	125	431	55	120	23	1	20	72	3	.278
2008	Pittsburgh	N.L.	OF	89	327	50	108	26	1	13	57	1	.330
2008	New York d	A.L.	OF-1B	59	228	26	61	11	0	12	40	1	.268
2009	Scranton/WB	Int.	OF	2	5	0	1	1	0	0	0	0	.200
2009	New York e-f	A.L.	OF	7	28	4	8	4	0	0	2	0	.286
2010	Chicago g	N.L.	1B-OF	119	317	33	81	13	0	6	33	0	.256
Major League Totals			9 Yrs.	798	2574	323	713	141	6	93	358	16	.277
	Division Series												
2005	San Diego	N.L.	1B	2	3	0	1	0	0	0	2	0	.333

a Traded to New York Mets for outfielder Mike Cameron, November 18, 2005.
b On disabled list from May 30 to June 18, 2006.
c Traded to Pittsburgh Pirates for pitcher Oliver Perez and pitcher Roberto Hernandez, July 31, 2006.
d Traded to New York Yankees with pitcher Damaso Marte for outfielder Jose Tabata, pitcher Ross Ohlendorf, pitcher Jeff Karstens and pitcher Dan McCutchen, July 26, 2008.
e On disabled list from April 15 to November 9, 2009.
f Filed for free agency, November 9, 2009. Signed with Chicago Cubs, January 29, 2010.
g Filed for free agency, November 1, 2010. Signed with Arizona Diamondbacks, December 17, 2010.

NAPOLI, MICHAEL ANTHONY (MIKE)

Born, Hollywood, Florida, October 31, 1981.
Bats Right. Throws Right. Height, 6 feet. Weight, 205 pounds.

Year	Club	Lea	Pos	G	AB	R	H	2B	3B	HR	RBI	SB	Avg
2000	Butte	Pioneer	1B-C	10	26	3	6	2	0	0	3	1	.231
2001	Rancho Cucamonga	Calif.	C	7	20	3	4	0	0	1	4	0	.200
2001	Cedar Rapids	Midwest	C-1B	43	155	23	36	10	1	5	18	3	.232
2002	Cedar Rapids	Midwest	C-1B-3B	106	362	57	91	19	1	10	50	6	.251
2003	Rancho Cucamonga	Calif.	C-1B	47	165	28	44	10	1	4	26	5	.267
2004	Rancho Cucamonga	Calif.	C-1B-3B	132	482	94	136	29	4	29	118	9	.282
2005	Arkansas	Texas	C-1B	131	439	96	104	22	2	31	99	12	.237
2006	Salt Lake	P.C.	C-1B	21	78	12	19	6	0	3	10	1	.244
2006	Los Angeles	A.L.	C	99	268	47	61	13	0	16	42	2	.228
2007	Los Angeles a	A.L.	C	75	219	40	54	11	1	10	34	5	.247
2008	Rancho Cucamonga	Calif.	C	5	14	3	8	3	0	1	4	0	.571
2008	Los Angeles b	A.L.	C	78	227	39	62	9	1	20	49	7	.273
2009	Los Angeles	A.L.	C	114	382	60	104	22	1	20	56	3	.272
2010	Los Angeles	A.L.	1B-C	140	453	60	108	24	1	26	68	4	.238
Major League Totals			5 Yrs.	506	1549	246	389	79	4	92	249	21	.251
	Division Series												
2007	Los Angeles	A.L.	C	3	6	0	1	0	0	0	0	0	.167
2008	Los Angeles	A.L.	C	4	12	3	3	0	0	2	4	0	.250
2009	Los Angeles	A.L.	C	2	4	1	1	1	0	0	0	0	.250
Division Series Totals				9	22	4	5	1	0	2	4	0	.227
	Championship Series												
2009	Los Angeles	A.L.	C	5	9	0	1	0	0	0	0	0	.111

a On disabled list from July 2 to July 18 and July 28 to September 1, 2007.
b On disabled list from July 6 to August 8, 2008.

NAVA, DANIEL JAMES

Born, Redwood City, California, February 22, 1983.
Bats Both. Throws Left. Height, 5 feet, 10 inches. Weight, 200 pounds.

Year	Club	Lea	Pos	G	AB	R	H	2B	3B	HR	RBI	SB	Avg
2007	Chico a	Golden	OF	72	256	70	95	23	3	12	59	18	.371
2008	Lancaster b	Calif.	OF	85	323	54	110	27	1	10	59	4	.341
2009	Salem	Carolina	OF	29	109	18	37	12	1	1	13	0	.339
2009	Portland	Eastern	OF	32	118	25	43	10	1	4	23	0	.364
2010	Pawtucket	Int.	OF	77	284	41	82	16	1	10	48	4	.289
2010	Boston	A.L.	OF	60	161	23	39	14	1	1	26	1	.242

a Signed by independent Chico, 2007.
b Signed by Boston Red Sox organization, January 17, 2008.

NIX, JAYSON TRUITT EDWARD

Born, Dallas, Texas, August 26, 1982.
Bats Right. Throws Right. Height, 5 feet, 11 inches. Weight, 185 pounds.

Year	Club	Lea	Pos	G	AB	R	H	2B	3B	HR	RBI	SB	Avg
2001	Casper	Pioneer	SS	42	153	28	45	10	1	5	24	1	.294
2002	Asheville	So.Atl.	2B	132	487	73	120	29	2	14	79	14	.246
2003	Visalia	Calif.	2B	137	562	107	158	46	0	21	86	24	.281
2004	Tulsa	Texas	2B	123	456	58	97	17	1	14	58	14	.213
2005	Tulsa	Texas	2B	131	501	68	118	27	0	11	47	10	.236
2006	Colorado Springs	P.C.	2B-3B	103	358	39	90	14	1	2	26	15	.251
2007	Colorado Springs	P.C.	2B-3B	124	439	80	128	33	2	11	58	24	.292
2008	Colorado	N.L.	2B	22	56	2	7	2	0	0	2	1	.125
2008	Colorado Springs a	P.C.	2B-3B	67	264	63	80	21	2	17	51	11	.303
2009	Birmingham	Southern	SS	3	10	1	3	0	0	0	3	0	.300
2009	Charlotte	Int.	SS-2B	5	20	4	9	1	0	0	5	1	.450
2009	Chicago b	A.L.	2B-SS-3B-OF	94	255	36	57	11	0	12	32	10	.224
2010	Chicago-Cleveland c	A.L.	3B-2B-OF-SS	102	331	32	74	15	0	14	34	1	.224
Major League Totals			3 Yrs.	218	642	70	138	28	0	26	68	12	.215

a Filed for free agency, October 15, 2008. Signed with Chicago White Sox, October 24, 2008.
b On disabled list from March 27 to May 1, 2009.
c Claimed on waivers by Cleveland Indians, June 25, 2010.

NIX, LAYNCE MICHAEL

Born, Houston, Texas, October 30, 1980.
Bats Left. Throws Left. Height, 6 feet. Weight, 220 pounds.

Year	Club	Lea	Pos	G	AB	R	H	2B	3B	HR	RBI	SB	Avg
2000	Rangers	Gulf Coast	OF	51	199	34	45	7	1	2	25	4	.226
2001	Charlotte	Fla.St.	OF	9	37	4	11	3	1	0	2	0	.297
2001	Savannah	So.Atl.	OF	104	407	50	113	26	8	8	59	9	.278
2002	Charlotte	Fla.St.	OF	137	512	86	146	27	3	21	110	17	.285
2003	Frisco	Texas	OF	87	335	52	95	23	0	15	63	9	.284
2003	Texas	A.L.	OF	53	184	25	47	10	0	8	30	3	.255
2004	Frisco	Texas	OF	7	26	2	7	1	0	0	2	0	.269
2004	Texas a	A.L.	OF	115	371	58	92	20	4	14	46	1	.248
2005	Oklahoma	P.C.	OF	10	36	8	12	1	1	3	6	0	.333
2005	Texas b	A.L.	OF	63	229	28	55	12	3	6	32	2	.240
2006	Texas	A.L.	OF	9	32	1	3	1	0	0	4	0	.094
2006	Oklahoma	P.C.	OF	77	286	39	77	14	1	10	55	4	.269
2006	Nashville	P.C.	OF	18	68	16	28	5	1	7	13	0	.412
2006	Milwaukee c-d	N.L.	OF	10	35	2	8	1	0	1	6	0	.229
2007	Huntsville	Southern	OF	4	11	2	4	1	0	1	6	0	.364
2007	Nashville	P.C.	OF	95	347	60	93	20	1	24	74	5	.268
2007	Milwaukee e	N.L.	OF	10	12	0	0	0	0	0	0	0	.000
2008	Nashville	P.C.	OF	103	380	63	108	22	3	23	60	5	.284
2008	Milwaukee f	N.L.	OF	10	12	1	1	0	0	0	0	0	.083
2009	Cincinnati g-h	N.L.	OF	116	309	42	74	26	1	15	46	0	.239
2010	Cincinnati i-j	N.L.	OF	97	165	16	48	11	2	4	18	0	.291
Major League Totals			8 Yrs.	483	1349	173	328	81	10	48	182	6	.243
Division Series													
2010	Cincinnati	N.L.	OF	1	3	1	0	0	0	0	0	0	.000

a On disabled list from June 14 to July 10, 2004.
b On disabled list from July 15 to October 12, 2005.
c Traded to Milwaukee Brewers with pitcher Francisco Cordero, outfielder Kevin Mench and pitcher Julian Cordero for outfielder Carlos Lee and outfielder Nelson Cruz, July 28, 2006.
d On disabled list from September 9 to October 2, 2006.
e On disabled list from March 23 to May 14, 2007.
f Filed for free agency, October 9, 2008. Signed with Cincinnati Reds organization, December 15, 2008.
g On disabled list from August 31 to September 15, 2009.
h Filed for free agency, November 20, 2009, re-signed with Cincinnati Reds organization, December 18, 2009.
i On disabled list from August 26 to September 18, 2010.
j Filed for free agency, November 9, 2010.

OLIVO (PENA), MIGUEL EDUARDO

Born, Villa Vasquez, Dominican Republic, July 15, 1978.
Bats Right. Throws Right. Height, 6 feet. Weight, 220 pounds.

Year	Club	Lea	Pos	G	AB	R	H	2B	3B	HR	RBI	SB	Avg
1997	Oakland-East	Dominican	C	63	221	37	60	11	4	6	57	6	.271
1998	Athletics	Arizona	C-OF	46	164	30	51	11	3	2	23	2	.311

Year Club	Lea	Pos	G	AB	R	H	2B	3B	HR	RBI	SB	Avg
1999 Modesto.........	California	C	73	243	46	74	13	6	9	42	4	.305
2000 Modesto.........	California	C	58	227	40	64	11	5	5	35	5	.282
2000 Midland a-b-c........	Texas	C	19	59	8	14	2	0	1	9	0	.237
2001 Birmingham d	Southern	C	93	316	45	82	23	1	14	55	6	.259
2002 Birmingham......	Southern	C	106	359	51	110	24	10	6	49	29	.306
2002 Chicago e............	A.L.	C	6	19	2	4	1	0	1	5	0	.211
2003 Chicago	A.L.	C	114	317	37	75	19	1	6	27	6	.237
2004 Everett	Northwest	C	2	6	0	0	0	0	0	0	0	.000
2004 Chicago-Seattle f-g	A.L.	C	96	301	46	70	15	4	13	40	7	.233
2005 Tacoma	P.C.	C	24	90	13	21	4	1	3	21	8	.233
2005 Seattle	A.L.	C	54	152	14	23	4	0	5	18	1	.151
2005 San Diego h..........	N.L.	C	37	115	16	35	7	1	4	16	6	.304
2006 Florida i	N.L.	C-1B	127	430	52	113	22	3	16	58	2	.263
2007 Florida j	N.L.	C	122	452	43	107	20	4	16	60	3	.237
2008 Kansas City	A.L.	C	84	306	29	78	22	0	12	41	7	.255
2009 Kansas City k.........	A.L.	C	114	390	51	97	15	5	23	65	5	.249
2010 Colorado l-m	N.L.	C	112	394	55	106	17	6	14	58	7	.269
Major League Totals		9 Yrs.	866	2876	345	708	142	24	110	388	44	.246
Division Series												
2005 San Diego	N.L.	PH	1	1	0	0	0	0	0	0	0	.000

a On disabled list from August 8 to September 29, 2000.
b Chicago White Sox traded pitcher Chad Bradford to Oakland Athletics for player to be named later, December 7, 2000.
c Sent by Oakland Athletics to Chicago White Sox to complete trade, December 12, 2000.
d On disabled list from April 22 to May 2, 2001.
e On disabled list from June 4 to 11, 2002.
f Traded to Seattle Mariners with outfielder Jeremy Reed and infielder Michael Morse for pitcher Freddy Garcia, catcher Ben Davis and cash, June 27, 2004.
g On disabled list from June 30 to July 15, 2004.
h Traded to San Diego Padres for catcher Miguel Ojeda and pitcher Nathaniel Mateo, July 31, 2005.
i Filed for free agency, December 21, 2005. Signed with Florida Marlins, January 3, 2006.
j Not offered contract, December 12, 2007. Signed with Kansas City Royals, December 27, 2007.
k Filed for free agency, November 6, 2009. Signed with Colorado Rockies, January 4, 2010.
l Traded to Toronto Blue Jays for player to be named later, November 4, 2010.
m Filed for free agency, November 4, 2010. Signed with Seattle Mariners, December 10, 2010.

ORDONEZ, MAGGLIO JOSE

Born, Caracas, Venezuela, January 28, 1974.
Bats Right. Throws Right. Height, 6 feet. Weight, 215 pounds.

Year Club	Lea	Pos	G	AB	R	H	2B	3B	HR	RBI	SB	Avg
1993 Hickory............	So. Atl.	OF	84	273	32	59	14	4	3	20	5	.216
1994 Hickory............	So. Atl.	OF	132	490	86	144	24	5	11	69	16	.294
1995 Pr William	Carolina	OF	131	487	61	116	24	2	12	65	11	.238
1996 Birmingham......	Southern	OF	130	479	66	126	41	0	18	67	9	.263
1997 Nashville	A.A.	OF	135	523	65	172	29	3	14	90	14	.329
1997 Chicago	A.L.	OF	21	69	12	22	6	0	4	11	1	.319
1998 Chicago	A.L.	OF	145	535	70	151	25	2	14	65	9	.282
1999 Chicago	A.L.	OF	157	624	100	188	34	3	30	117	13	.301
2000 Chicago	A.L.	OF	153	588	102	185	34	3	32	126	18	.315
2001 Chicago	A.L.	OF	160	593	97	181	40	1	31	113	25	.305
2002 Chicago	A.L.	OF	153	590	116	189	47	1	38	135	7	.320
2003 Chicago	A.L.	OF	160	606	95	192	46	3	29	99	9	.317
2004 Chicago a-b	A.L.	OF	52	202	32	59	8	2	9	37	0	.292
2005 Toledo	Int.	OF	4	14	3	3	1	0	1	2	0	.214
2005 Detroit c..............	A.L.	OF	82	305	38	92	17	0	8	46	0	.302
2006 Detroit	A.L.	OF	155	593	82	177	32	1	24	104	1	.298
2007 Detroit	A.L.	OF	157	595	117	216	*54	0	28	139	4	*.363
2008 West Michigan.....	Midwest	DH	1	4	1	1	0	0	0	0	0	.250
2008 Detroit d..............	A.L.	OF	146	561	72	178	32	2	21	103	1	.317
2009 Detroit	A.L.	OF	131	465	54	144	24	2	9	50	3	.310
2010 Detroit e-f............	A.L.	OF	84	323	56	98	17	1	12	59	1	.303
Major League Totals		14 Yrs.	1756	6649	1043	2072	416	21	289	1204	92	.312
Division Series												
2000 Chicago	A.L.	OF	3	11	0	2	0	1	0	1	1	.182
2006 Detroit	A.L.	OF	4	15	3	4	1	0	1	2	0	.267
Division Series Totals			7	26	3	6	1	1	1	3	1	.231
Championship Series												
2006 Detroit	A.L.	OF	4	17	3	4	0	0	2	6	0	.235

Year	Club	Lea	Pos	G	AB	R	H	2B	3B	HR	RBI	SB	Avg
	World Series Record												
2006	Detroit	A.L.	OF	5	19	2	2	0	0	0	0	0	.105

a On disabled list from May 26 to July 8 and from July 22 to October 12, 2004.
b Filed for free agency, October 28, 2004. Signed with Detroit Tigers organization, February 7, 2005.
c On disabled list from April 13 to July 1, 2005.
d On disabled list from June 29 to July 17, 2008.
e On disabled list from July 25 to October 6, 2010.
f Filed for free agency, November 1, 2010, re-signed with Detroit Tigers, December 17, 2010.

ORTIZ (ARIAS), DAVID AMERICO

Born, Santo Domingo, Dominican Republic, November 18, 1975.
Bats Left. Throws Left. Height, 6 feet, 4 inches. Weight, 230 pounds.

Year	Club	Lea	Pos	G	AB	R	H	2B	3B	HR	RBI	SB	Avg
1993	Seattle	Dominican	1B	61	201	37	53	17	1	7	31	1	.264
1994	Mariners...........	Arizona	1B	53	167	14	41	10	1	2	20	1	.246
1995	Mariners...........	Arizona	1B	48	184	30	61	18	4	4	37	2	.332
1996	Wisconsin a	Midwest	1B	129	485	89	156	34	2	18	93	3	.322
1997	Salt Lake	P.C.	1B	10	42	5	9	1	0	4	10	0	.214
1997	New Britain	Eastern	DH-1B	69	258	40	83	22	2	14	56	2	.322
1997	Ft. Myers	Fla.St.	1B	61	239	45	79	15	0	13	58	2	.331
1997	Minnesota	A.L.	1B	15	49	10	16	3	0	1	6	0	.327
1998	Salt Lake	P.C.	1B	11	37	5	9	3	0	2	6	0	.243
1998	Minnesota b..........	A.L.	1B	86	278	47	77	20	0	9	46	1	.277
1999	Salt Lake	P.C.	1B	130	476	85	150	35	3	30	110	2	.315
1999	Minnesota	A.L.	1B	10	20	1	0	0	0	0	0	0	.000
2000	Minnesota	A.L.	DH-1B	130	415	59	117	36	1	10	63	1	.282
2001	Twins	Gulf Coast	DH	4	10	3	4	0	0	0	1	1	.400
2001	Fort Myers	Fla.St.	1B	1	3	0	0	0	0	0	0	0	.000
2001	New Britain	Eastern	1B	9	37	3	9	4	0	0	1	0	.243
2001	Minnesota c..........	A.L.	DH-1B	89	303	46	71	17	1	18	48	1	.234
2002	Minnesota d-e	A.L.	DH-1B	125	412	52	112	32	1	20	75	1	.272
2003	Boston	A.L.	DH-1B	128	448	79	129	39	2	31	101	0	.288
2004	Boston	A.L.	DH-1B	150	582	94	175	47	3	41	139	0	.301
2005	Boston	A.L.	DH-1B	159	601	119	180	40	1	47	*148	1	.300
2006	Boston	A.L.	DH-1B	151	558	115	160	29	2	*54	*137	1	.287
2007	Boston	A.L.	DH-1B	149	549	116	182	52	1	35	117	3	.332
2008	Portland	Eastern	DH	3	8	2	2	0	0	0	1	0	.250
2008	Pawtucket	Int.	DH	3	9	4	3	0	0	3	5	0	.333
2008	Boston f.............	A.L.	DH	109	416	74	110	30	1	23	89	1	.264
2009	Boston	A.L.	DH-1B	150	541	77	129	35	1	28	99	0	.238
2010	Boston	A.L.	DH-1B	145	518	86	140	36	1	32	102	0	.270
Major League Totals			14 Yrs.	1596	5690	975	1598	416	15	349	1170	10	.281
	Division Series												
2002	Minnesota	A.L.	DH	4	13	0	3	2	0	0	2	0	.231
2003	Boston	A.L.	DH	5	21	0	2	1	0	0	2	0	.095
2004	Boston	A.L.	DH	3	11	4	6	2	0	1	4	0	.545
2005	Boston	A.L.	DH	3	12	2	4	2	0	1	1	0	.333
2007	Boston	A.L.	DH	3	7	5	5	0	0	2	3	0	.714
2008	Boston	A.L.	DH	4	17	1	4	1	0	0	1	0	.235
2009	Boston	A.L.	DH	3	12	0	1	0	0	0	0	0	.083
Division Series Totals				25	93	12	25	8	0	4	13	0	.269
	Championship Series												
2002	Minnesota	A.L.	DH	5	16	0	5	1	0	0	2	0	.313
2003	Boston	A.L.	DH	7	26	4	7	1	0	2	6	0	.269
2004	Boston	A.L.	DH	7	31	6	12	0	1	3	11	0	.387
2007	Boston	A.L.	DH	7	24	7	7	3	0	1	3	0	.292
2008	Boston	A.L.	DH	7	26	3	4	1	1	1	4	0	.154
Championship Series Totals				33	123	20	35	6	2	7	26	0	.285
	World Series Record												
2004	Boston	A.L.	1B-DH	4	13	3	4	1	0	1	4	0	.308
2007	Boston	A.L.	1B-DH	4	15	4	5	3	0	0	4	0	.333
World Series Totals..............				8	28	7	9	4	0	1	8	0	.321

a Sent to Minnesota Twins by Seattle Mariners to complete trade for infielder Dave Hollins, September 13, 1996.
b On disabled list from May 10 to July 9, 1998.
c On disabled list from May 5 to July 21, 2001.
d On disabled list from April 20 to May 13, 2002.
e Released by Minnesota Twins, December 16, 2002. Signed with Boston Red Sox, January 22, 2003.
f On disabled list from June 1 to July 25, 2008.

OVERBAY, LYLE STEFAN

Born, Centralia, Washington, January 28, 1977.
Bats Left. Throws Left. Height, 6 feet, 2 inches. Weight, 235 pounds.

Year	Club	Lea	Pos	G	AB	R	H	2B	3B	HR	RBI	SB	Avg
1999	Missoula	Pioneer	1B	75	306	66	105	25	7	12	101	10	.343
2000	South Bend	Midwest	1B	71	259	47	86	19	3	6	47	9	.332
2000	El Paso	Texas	1B	62	244	43	86	16	2	8	49	3	.352
2001	El Paso	Texas	1B-OF	138	532	82	187	49	3	13	100	5	.352
2001	Arizona	N.L.	PH	2	2	0	1	0	0	0	0	0	.500
2002	Tucson	P.C.	1B	134	525	83	180	40	0	19	109	0	.343
2002	Arizona	N.L.	PH	10	10	0	1	0	0	0	1	0	.100
2003	Tucson	P.C.	1B	35	119	24	34	11	0	4	16	0	.286
2003	Arizona a	N.L.	1B	86	254	23	70	20	0	4	28	1	.276
2004	Milwaukee	N.L.	1B	159	579	83	174	*53	1	16	87	2	.301
2005	Milwaukee b	N.L.	1B	158	537	80	148	34	1	19	72	1	.276
2006	Toronto	A.L.	1B	157	581	82	181	46	1	22	92	5	.312
2007	New Hampshire	Eastern	1B	4	15	2	4	1	0	1	5	0	.267
2007	Toronto c	A.L.	1B	122	425	49	102	30	2	10	44	2	.240
2008	Toronto	A.L.	1B	158	544	74	147	32	2	15	69	1	.270
2009	Toronto	A.L.	1B	132	423	57	112	35	1	16	64	0	.265
2010	Toronto d	A.L.	1B	154	534	75	130	37	2	20	67	1	.243
Major League Totals			10 Yrs.	1138	3889	523	1066	287	10	122	524	13	.274

a Traded to Milwaukee Brewers with infielder Junior Spivey, infielder Craig Counsell, catcher Chad Moeller, pitcher Chris Capuano and pitcher Jorge De La Rosa for infielder Richie Sexson, pitcher Shane Nance and player to be named later, December 1, 2003. Arizona Diamondbacks received outfielder Gary Varner to complete trade, December 15, 2003.
b Traded to Toronto Blue Jays with pitcher Ty Taubenheim for pitcher Dave Bush, outfielder Gabe Gross and pitcher Zach Jackson, December 7, 2005.
c On disabled list from June 4 to July 12, 2007.
d Filed for free agency, November 1, 2010. Signed with Pittsburgh Pirates, December 14, 2010.

PAGAN, ANGEL ANTHONY

Born, Rio Piedras, Puerto Rico, July 2, 1981.
Bats Both. Throws Right. Height, 6 feet, 1 inch. Weight, 195 pounds.

Year	Club	Lea	Pos	G	AB	R	H	2B	3B	HR	RBI	SB	Avg
2000	Kingsport	Appal.	OF	19	72	13	26	5	1	0	8	6	.361
2001	Brooklyn	N.Y.-Penn.	OF	62	238	46	75	10	2	0	15	30	.315
2001	Columbia	So.Atl.	OF	15	57	4	17	1	1	0	5	3	.298
2002	St. Lucie	Fla.St.	OF	16	67	12	23	2	1	1	7	10	.343
2002	Columbia	So.Atl.	OF	108	458	79	128	14	5	1	36	52	.279
2003	St. Lucie	Fla.St.	OF	113	441	64	110	15	5	1	33	35	.249
2004	Binghamton	Eastern	OF	112	448	71	129	25	8	4	63	29	.288
2004	Norfolk	Int.	OF	12	45	13	13	3	3	0	1	4	.289
2005	Norfolk	Int.	OF	129	516	69	140	20	10	8	40	27	.271
2006	Cubs	Arizona	OF	3	9	1	1	0	0	0	0	1	.111
2006	Iowa	P.C.	OF	4	15	2	4	1	0	0	0	1	.267
2006	Chicago a-b	N.L.	OF	77	170	28	42	6	2	5	18	4	.247
2007	Iowa	P.C.	OF	33	116	18	29	4	3	3	9	6	.250
2007	Chicago c-d	N.L.	OF	71	148	21	39	10	2	4	21	4	.264
2008	Mets	Gulf Coast	OF	2	5	1	3	1	0	0	0	2	.600
2008	Brooklyn	N.Y.-Penn.	OF	4	13	0	4	0	0	0	1	3	.308
2008	St. Lucie	Fla.St.	OF	1	4	1	0	0	0	0	0	0	.000
2008	New York e	N.L.	OF	31	91	12	25	7	1	0	13	4	.275
2009	St. Lucie	Fla.St.	OF	4	12	4	5	2	0	0	3	2	.417
2009	Buffalo	Int.	OF	3	14	2	4	0	2	0	2	0	.286
2009	New York f	N.L.	OF	88	343	54	105	22	11	6	32	14	.306
2010	New York	N.L.	OF	151	579	80	168	31	7	11	69	37	.290
Major League Totals			5 Yrs.	418	1331	195	379	76	23	26	153	63	.285

a Sold to Chicago by New York Mets, January 25, 2006.
b On disabled list from April 16 to June 30, 2006.
c On disabled list from August 8 to November 1, 2007.
d Traded to New York Mets for pitcher Ryan Meyers and outfielder Corey Coles, January 5, 2008.
e On disabled list from May 13 to November 3, 2008.
f On disabled list from March 27 to May 16 and June 1 to July 10, 2009.

PARRA, GERARDO ENRIQUE

Born, Santa Barbara Del Zulia, Venezuela, May 6, 1987.
Bats Left. Throws Left. Height, 5 feet, 11 inches. Weight, 195 pounds.

Year Club	Lea	Pos	G	AB	R	H	2B	3B	HR	RBI	SB	Avg
2006 Missoula	Pioneer	OF	69	271	46	89	18	4	4	43	23	.328
2007 Visalia	Calif.	OF	24	102	11	29	2	1	2	14	2	.284
2007 South Bend	Midwest	OF	110	444	64	142	25	4	6	57	24	.320
2008 Visalia	Calif.	OF	50	196	26	59	8	4	2	19	12	.301
2008 Mobile	Southern	OF	73	265	35	73	14	6	4	33	16	.275
2009 Mobile	Southern	OF	29	108	23	39	3	1	3	12	7	.361
2009 Arizona	N.L.	OF	120	455	59	132	21	8	5	60	5	.290
2010 Reno	P.C.	OF	9	36	8	15	4	0	1	7	3	.417
2010 Arizona	N.L.	OF	133	364	31	95	19	6	3	30	1	.261
Major League Totals		2 Yrs.	253	819	90	227	40	14	8	90	6	.277

PATTERSON, DONALD COREY (COREY)

Born, Atlanta, Georgia, August 13, 1979.
Bats Left. Throws Right. Height, 5 feet, 10 inches. Weight, 180 pounds.

Year Club	Lea	Pos	G	AB	R	H	2B	3B	HR	RBI	SB	Avg
1999 Lansing	Midwest	OF	112	475	94	152	35	17	20	79	33	.320
2000 West Tenn	Southern	OF	118	444	73	116	26	5	22	82	27	.261
2000 Chicago	N.L.	OF	11	42	9	7	1	0	2	2	1	.167
2001 Iowa	P.C.	OF	89	367	63	93	22	3	7	32	19	.253
2001 Chicago	N.L.	OF	59	131	26	29	3	0	4	14	4	.221
2002 Chicago	N.L.	OF	153	592	71	150	30	5	14	54	18	.253
2003 Chicago a	N.L.	OF	83	329	49	98	17	7	13	55	16	.298
2004 Chicago	N.L.	OF	157	631	91	168	33	6	24	72	32	.266
2005 Iowa	P.C.	OF	24	91	16	27	4	0	5	12	6	.297
2005 Chicago	N.L.	OF	126	451	47	97	15	3	13	34	15	.215
2006 Baltimore b	A.L.	OF	135	463	75	128	19	5	16	53	45	.276
2007 Baltimore	A.L.	OF	132	461	65	124	26	2	8	45	37	.269
2008 Louisville	Int.	OF	5	22	3	9	2	0	0	0	1	.409
2008 Cincinnati c-d	N.L.	OF	135	366	46	75	17	2	10	34	14	.205
2009 Syracuse	Int.	OF	84	263	30	72	16	1	7	40	14	.274
2009 Nashville	P.C.	OF	29	124	24	41	12	3	5	22	7	.331
2009 Washington-Milwaukee e-f	N.L.	OF	16	29	0	3	0	0	0	0	2	.103
2010 Norfolk	Int.	OF	14	57	6	21	5	1	0	2	3	.368
2010 Baltimore g-h	A.L.	OF	90	308	43	83	16	1	8	32	21	.269
Major League Totals		11 Yrs.	1097	3803	522	962	177	31	112	395	205	.253

a On disabled list from July 7 to October 31, 2003.
b Traded to Baltimore Orioles for infielder Nate Spears and pitcher Carlos Perez, January 9, 2006.
c Filed for free agency, October 31, 2007. Signed with Cincinnati Reds organization, March 3, 2008.
d Filed for free agency, November 3, 2008. Signed with Washington Nationals organization, December 18, 2008.
e Released by Washington Nationals, July 29, 2009. Signed with Milwaukee Brewers organization, August 1, 2009.
f Filed for free agency, November 5, 2009. Signed with Seattle Mariners organization, December 10, 2009.
g Released by Seattle Mariners, April 1, 2010. Signed with Baltimore Orioles organization, April 21, 2010.
h Filed for free agency, November 1, 2010. Signed with Toronto Blue Jays organization, December 21, 2010.

PATTERSON, ERIC SCOTT

Born, Tallahassee, Florida, April 8, 1983.
Bats Left. Throws Right. Height, 5 feet, 11 inches. Weight, 170 pounds.

Year Club	Lea	Pos	G	AB	R	H	2B	3B	HR	RBI	SB	Avg
2005 Peoria	Midwest	2B	110	432	90	144	26	11	13	71	40	.333
2005 West Tenn	Southern	2B	9	30	5	6	2	0	0	2	3	.200
2006 Iowa	P.C.	2B	17	67	14	24	1	1	2	12	8	.358
2006 West Tenn	Southern	2B-OF	121	441	66	116	22	9	8	48	38	.263
2007 Iowa	P.C.	2B-OF	128	516	94	153	28	6	14	65	24	.297
2007 Chicago	N.L.	OF	7	8	0	2	1	0	0	0	0	.250
2008 Chicago	N.L.	OF-2B	13	38	5	9	1	0	1	7	2	.237
2008 Iowa	P.C.	2B-OF	52	203	33	65	16	3	6	28	11	.320
2008 Sacramento	P.C.	2B-OF	25	109	18	36	8	2	4	19	8	.330
2008 Oakland a	A.L.	2B-OF	30	92	11	16	3	0	0	8	8	.174
2009 Sacramento	P.C.	2B-OF-3B-1B	110	466	91	143	29	11	12	56	43	.307
2009 Oakland	A.L.	OF-2B	39	94	15	27	5	1	1	11	6	.287
2010 Pawtucket	Int.	2B-OF	4	17	4	4	2	1	0	0	3	.235
2010 Oakland-Boston b-c-d	A.L.	OF-2B	90	187	26	40	8	5	6	16	11	.214
Major League Totals		4 Yrs.	179	419	57	94	18	6	8	42	27	.224

a Traded to Oakland Athletics with pitcher Sean Gallagher, outfielder Matt Murton and catcher Josh Donaldson for pitcher Rich Harden and pitcher Chad Gaudin, July 8, 2008.
b Traded to Boston Red Sox for pitcher Fabian Williamson, June 26, 2010.
c On disabled list from August 16 to September 1, 2010.
d Sent to San Diego Padres to complete trade for Adrian Gonzalez, December 16, 2010.

PAULINO, RONNY LEONEL

Born, Santo Domingo, Dominican Republic, April 21, 1981.
Bats Right. Throws Right. Height, 6 feet, 3 inches. Weight, 245 pounds.

Year	Club	Lea	Pos	G	AB	R	H	2B	3B	HR	RBI	SB	Avg
1998	Pittsburgh	Dominican	C	53	170	18	40	5	0	4	26	6	.235
1999	Pirates	Gulf Coast	C	29	83	6	21	2	4	1	13	1	.253
2000	Hickory	So.Atl.	C-1B-3B	88	301	38	87	16	2	6	39	3	.289
2001	Lynchburg	Carolina	C	103	352	30	102	16	1	6	51	4	.290
2002	Lynchburg	Carolina	C-1B	119	442	63	116	26	2	12	55	2	.262
2003	Lynchburg	Carolina	C	23	81	8	19	3	0	1	12	1	.235
2003	Altoona a	Eastern	C	46	159	19	36	6	1	6	19	0	.226
2004	Altoona	Eastern	C-1B	99	369	54	105	23	2	15	60	3	.285
2005	Altoona	Eastern	C	43	168	24	49	6	0	6	20	3	.292
2005	Indianapolis	Int.	C	77	273	49	86	18	2	13	42	3	.315
2005	Pittsburgh	N.L.	C	2	4	1	2	0	0	0	0	0	.500
2006	Indianapolis	Int.	C	8	29	2	7	3	0	0	4	1	.241
2006	Pittsburgh	N.L.	C	129	442	37	137	19	0	6	55	0	.310
2007	Pittsburgh	N.L.	C	133	457	56	120	25	0	11	55	2	.263
2008	Pirates	Gulf Coast	C	8	28	3	8	1	0	1	6	0	.286
2008	Indianapolis	Int.	C	30	111	16	34	13	1	4	18	0	.306
2008	Pittsburgh b	N.L.	C	40	118	8	25	5	0	2	18	0	.212
2009	Florida c-d	N.L.	C	80	239	24	65	10	1	8	27	1	.272
2010	Florida e	N.L.	C	91	316	31	82	18	0	4	37	1	.259
Major League Totals			6 Yrs.	475	1576	157	431	77	1	31	192	4	.273

a Selected by Kansas City Royals from Pittsburgh Pirates in Rule V draft, December 16, 2002. Returned to Pittsburgh Pirates, March 13, 2003.
b Traded to Philadelphia Phillies for catcher Jason Jaramillo, December 10, 2008.
c Traded to San Francisco Giants for pitcher Jack Taschner, March 27, 2009.
d Traded to Florida Marlins for pitcher Hector Correa, March 28, 2009.
e Not offered contract, December 2, 2010. Signed with New York Mets, December 9, 2010.

PEARCE, STEVEN WAYNE (STEVE)

Born, Lakeland, Florida, April 13, 1983.
Bats Right. Throws Right. Height, 5 feet, 11 inches. Weight, 215 pounds.

Year	Club	Lea	Pos	G	AB	R	H	2B	3B	HR	RBI	SB	Avg
2005	Williamsport	N.Y.-Penn.	1B	72	272	48	82	26	0	7	52	2	.301
2006	Lynchburg	Carolina	1B	90	328	48	87	27	1	14	60	7	.265
2006	Hickory	So.Atl.	1B	41	160	35	46	13	1	12	38	1	.287
2007	Lynchburg	Carolina	1B	19	75	19	26	4	1	11	24	2	.347
2007	Altoona	Eastern	1B	81	290	57	97	27	2	14	72	7	.334
2007	Indianapolis	Int.	1B-OF	34	122	18	39	9	1	6	17	5	.320
2007	Pittsburgh	N.L.	OF-1B	23	68	13	20	5	1	0	6	2	.294
2008	Indianapolis	Int.	OF-1B	103	386	47	97	26	1	12	60	10	.251
2008	Pittsburgh	N.L.	OF	37	109	6	27	7	0	4	15	2	.248
2009	Indianapolis	Int.	1B-OF	77	273	37	78	18	1	13	54	3	.286
2009	Pittsburgh	N.L.	1B-OF	60	165	19	34	13	1	4	16	1	.206
2010	Bradenton	Fla.St.	1B	2	7	2	3	2	0	0	2	0	.429
2010	Indianapolis	Int.	1B-3B-OF	35	129	25	42	14	2	3	15	7	.326
2010	Pittsburgh a	N.L.	1B	15	29	4	8	2	1	0	5	0	.276
Major League Totals			4 Yrs.	135	371	42	89	27	3	8	42	5	.240

a On disabled list from May 25 to November 3, 2010.

PEDROIA, DUSTIN LUIS

Born, Woodland, California, August 17, 1983.
Bats Right. Throws Right. Height, 5 feet, 9 inches. Weight, 180 pounds.

Year	Club	Lea	Pos	G	AB	R	H	2B	3B	HR	RBI	SB	Avg
2004	Sarasota	Fla.St.	SS	30	107	23	36	8	3	2	14	0	.336
2004	Augusta	So.Atl.	SS	12	50	11	20	5	0	1	5	2	.400
2005	Portland	Eastern	2B-SS	66	256	39	83	19	2	8	40	7	.324
2005	Pawtucket	Int.	2B-SS	51	204	39	52	9	1	5	24	1	.255
2006	Pawtucket	Int.	SS-2B-3B	111	423	55	129	30	3	5	50	1	.305
2006	Boston	A.L.	2B-SS	31	89	5	17	4	0	2	7	0	.191

Year	Club	Lea	Pos	G	AB	R	H	2B	3B	HR	RBI	SB	Avg
2007	Boston a	A.L.	2B	139	520	86	165	39	1	8	50	7	.317
2008	Boston b	A.L.	2B	157	653	*118	*213	*54	2	17	83	20	.326
2009	Boston	A.L.	2B	154	626	*115	185	48	1	15	72	20	.296
2010	Pawtucket	Int.	2B	2	6	1	1	0	0	0	0	0	.167
2010	Boston c	A.L.	2B	75	302	53	87	24	1	12	41	9	.288
Major League Totals			5 Yrs.	556	2190	377	667	169	5	54	253	56	.305
	Division Series												
2007	Boston	A.L.	2B	3	13	2	2	2	0	0	1	0	.154
2008	Boston	A.L.	2B	4	17	0	1	1	0	0	1	0	.059
2009	Boston	A.L.	2B	3	12	1	2	1	0	0	2	0	.167
Division Series Totals				10	42	3	5	4	0	0	4	0	.119
	Championship Series												
2007	Boston	A.L.	2B	7	29	8	10	3	0	1	5	0	.345
2008	Boston	A.L.	2B	7	26	9	9	1	0	3	5	2	.346
Championship Series Totals				14	55	17	19	4	0	4	10	2	.345
	World Series Record												
2007	Boston	A.L.	2B	4	18	2	5	1	0	1	4	0	.278

a Selected Rookie of the Year in American League for 2007.
b Selected Most Valuable Player in American League for 2008.
c On disabled list from June 26 to August 17 and August 19 to October 13, 2010.

PENA, BRAYAN EDUARDO

Born, Havana, Cuba, January 7, 1982.
Bats Both. Throws Right. Height, 5 feet, 11 inches. Weight, 245 pounds.

Year	Club	Lea	Pos	G	AB	R	H	2B	3B	HR	RBI	SB	Avg
2001	Danville	Appal.	C	64	235	39	87	16	2	1	33	3	.370
2002	Myrtle Beach	Carolina	C	6	19	3	4	1	0	0	1	0	.211
2002	Macon	So.Atl.	C	81	271	26	62	10	0	3	25	0	.229
2003	Myrtle Beach	Carolina	C	82	286	24	84	14	1	2	27	2	.294
2004	Greenville	Southern	C	77	277	30	87	10	4	2	30	3	.314
2005	Richmond	Int.	C-1B	81	282	27	92	21	2	0	25	3	.326
2005	Atlanta	N.L.	C	18	39	2	7	2	0	0	4	0	.179
2006	Richmond	Int.	C	87	325	32	98	18	1	1	33	6	.302
2006	Atlanta	N.L.	C-3B	23	41	9	11	2	0	1	5	0	.268
2007	Richmond	Int.	C-1B-OF-3B	94	345	42	104	20	2	6	48	5	.301
2007	Atlanta a	N.L.	C	16	33	2	7	0	0	1	3	0	.212
2008	Atlanta	N.L.	PH	14	14	3	4	1	0	0	0	0	.286
2008	Omaha b-c	P.C.	C-OF-3B	60	234	33	71	17	1	6	31	7	.303
2009	Omaha	P.C.	OF-C	22	88	11	27	6	1	4	18	2	.307
2009	Kansas City	A.L.	C	64	165	17	45	10	0	6	18	0	.273
2010	Kansas City	A.L.	C	60	158	11	40	10	0	1	19	2	.253
Major League Totals			6 Yrs.	195	450	44	114	25	0	9	49	2	.253

a On disabled list from May 2 to May 17, 2007.
b On disabled list from May 5 to May 23, 2008.
c Claimed on waivers by Kansas City Royals, May 30, 2008.

PENA, CARLOS FELIPE

Born, Santo Domingo, Dominican Republic, May 17, 1978.
Bats Left. Throws Left. Height, 6 feet, 2 inches. Weight, 210 pounds.

Year	Club	Lea	Pos	G	AB	R	H	2B	3B	HR	RBI	SB	Avg
1998	Rangers	Gulf Coast	1B	2	5	1	2	0	0	0	0	1	.400
1998	Savannah	So.Atl.	1B-OF	30	117	22	38	14	0	6	20	3	.325
1998	Charlotte	Fla.St.	1B	7	22	1	6	1	0	0	3	0	.273
1999	Charlotte	Fla.St.	1B	136	501	85	128	31	8	18	103	2	.255
2000	Tulsa	Texas	1B	138	529	117	158	36	2	28	105	12	.299
2001	Oklahoma	P.C.	1B	119	431	71	124	38	3	23	74	11	.288
2001	Texas	A.L.	1B	22	62	6	16	4	1	3	12	0	.258
2002	Sacramento	P.C.	1B	44	175	30	42	10	1	10	33	3	.240
2002	Oakland-Detroit a-b	A.L.	1B	115	397	43	96	17	4	19	52	2	.242
2003	Toledo	Int.	1B	8	30	4	10	4	1	0	5	0	.333
2003	Detroit c	A.L.	1B	131	452	51	112	21	6	18	50	4	.248
2004	Detroit	A.L.	1B	142	481	89	116	22	4	27	82	7	.241
2005	Toledo	Int.	1B	71	257	43	80	17	1	12	45	3	.311
2005	Detroit	A.L.	1B	79	260	37	61	9	0	18	44	0	.235
2006	Columbus	Int.	1B	105	381	65	99	17	0	19	66	4	.260
2006	Pawtucket	Int.	1B	11	37	7	17	3	0	4	8	0	.459

Year	Club	Lea	Pos	G	AB	R	H	2B	3B	HR	RBI	SB	Avg
2006	Boston d-e-f	A.L.	1B-OF	18	33	3	9	2	0	1	3	0	.273
2007	Tampa Bay	A.L.	1B	148	490	99	138	29	1	46	121	1	.282
2008	Vero Beach	Fla.St.	DH	1	4	0	0	0	0	0	1	0	.000
2008	Tampa Bay g	A.L.	1B	139	490	76	121	24	2	31	102	1	.247
2009	Tampa Bay h	A.L.	1B	135	471	91	107	25	2	*39	100	3	.227
2010	Charlotte	Fla.St.	DH	1	3	1	2	0	0	0	1	0	.667
2010	Tampa Bay i-j	A.L.	1B	144	484	64	95	18	0	28	84	5	.196
Major League Totals			10 Yrs.	1073	3620	559	871	171	20	230	650	23	.241
	Division Series												
2008	Tampa Bay	N.L.	1B	3	10	0	5	0	0	0	2	2	.500
2010	Tampa Bay	N.L.	1B	4	14	4	4	1	1	1	4	0	.286
Division Series Totals				7	24	4	9	1	1	1	6	2	.375
	Championship Series												
2008	Tampa Bay	N.L.	1B	7	26	8	7	1	0	3	6	1	.269
	World Series Record												
2008	Tampa Bay	N.L.	1B	5	17	1	2	1	0	0	2	0	.118

a Traded to Oakland Athletics with pitcher Mike Venafro for pitcher Mario Ramos, outfielder Ryan Ludwick, infielder Jason Hart and catcher Gerald Laird, January 14, 2002.
b Traded to Detroit Tigers with pitcher Franklyn German and player to be named later for pitcher Jeff Weaver, July 5, 2002. Detroit Tigers received pitcher Jeremy Bonderman to complete trade, August 22, 2002.
c On disabled list from June 2 to June 27, 2003.
d Released by Detroit Tigers, March 26, 2006. Signed with New York Yankees organization, April 15, 2006.
e Filed for free agency, August 16, 2006. Signed with Boston Red Sox organization, August 17, 2006.
f Filed for free agency, October 13, 2006. Signed with Tampa Bay Devil Rays organization, February 1, 2007.
g On disabled list from June 4 to June 27, 2008.
h On disabled list from September 7 to November 19, 2009.
i On disabled list from August 1 to August 16, 2010.
j Filed for free agency, November 1, 2010. Signed with Chicago Cubs, December 8, 2010.

PENA (GUANA), RAMIRO GUANA

Born, Monterrey, Mexico, July 18, 1985.
Bats Both. Throws Right. Height, 5 feet, 11 inches. Weight, 165 pounds.

Year	Club	Lea	Pos	G	AB	R	H	2B	3B	HR	RBI	SB	Avg
2005	Trenton	Eastern	SS	68	236	28	59	5	2	0	12	4	.250
2005	Tampa	Fla.St.	SS	23	73	11	18	4	1	1	6	1	.247
2006	Trenton	Eastern	SS	26	86	6	17	2	0	0	6	0	.198
2006	Tampa	Fla.St.	SS	54	218	31	61	4	2	0	23	8	.280
2007	Trenton	Eastern	SS	52	202	23	51	7	1	0	10	7	.252
2008	Trenton	Eastern	SS	111	443	57	118	20	7	2	45	8	.266
2009	Scranton/WB	Int.	SS-2B-OF-3B	43	156	18	36	9	0	2	9	5	.231
2009	New York	A.L.	SS-3B-2B	69	115	17	33	6	1	1	10	4	.287
2010	New York	A.L.	3B-SS-2B-OF	85	154	18	35	1	1	0	18	7	.227
Major League Totals			2 Yrs.	154	269	35	68	7	2	1	28	11	.253

PENCE, HUNTER ANDREW

Born, Arlington, Texas, April 13, 1983.
Bats Right. Throws Right. Height, 6 feet, 4 inches. Weight, 210 pounds.

Year	Club	Lea	Pos	G	AB	R	H	2B	3B	HR	RBI	SB	Avg
2004	Tri-City	N.Y.-Penn.	OF	51	199	36	59	18	1	8	37	3	.296
2005	Lexington	So.Atl.	OF	80	302	59	102	14	3	25	60	8	.338
2005	Salem	Carolina	OF	41	151	24	46	8	1	6	30	1	.305
2006	Corpus Christi	Texas	OF	136	523	97	148	31	8	28	95	17	.283
2007	Round Rock	P.C.	OF	25	95	17	31	11	1	3	21	2	.326
2007	Houston a	N.L.	OF	108	456	57	147	30	9	17	69	11	.322
2008	Houston	N.L.	OF	157	595	78	160	34	4	25	83	11	.269
2009	Houston	N.L.	OF	159	585	76	165	26	5	25	72	14	.282
2010	Houston	N.L.	OF	156	614	93	173	29	3	25	91	18	.282
Major League Totals			4 Yrs.	580	2250	304	645	119	21	92	315	54	.287

a On disabled list from July 23 to August 21, 2007.

PENNINGTON, CLIFTON RANDOLPH (CLIFF)

Born, Corpus Christi, Texas, June 15, 1984.
Bats Both. Throws Right. Height, 5 feet, 11 inches. Weight, 190 pounds.

Year	Club	Lea	Pos	G	AB	R	H	2B	3B	HR	RBI	SB	Avg
2005	Kane County	Midwest	SS	69	290	49	80	15	0	3	29	25	.276
2006	Athletics	Arizona	SS	9	28	3	13	3	1	0	6	0	.464

Year	Club	Lea	Pos	G	AB	R	H	2B	3B	HR	RBI	SB	Avg
2006	Stockton	Calif.	SS	46	177	36	36	7	0	2	21	7	.203
2007	Stockton	Calif.	SS-2B	68	286	50	73	17	3	6	36	9	.255
2007	Midland	Texas	SS-2B	70	271	41	68	13	2	2	21	8	.251
2008	Midland	Texas	SS-2B	50	204	42	53	7	2	0	18	20	.260
2008	Sacramento	P.C.	SS-2B-3B	65	236	47	70	9	3	2	16	11	.297
2008	Oakland	A.L.	2B-SS-3B	36	99	14	24	5	0	0	9	4	.242
2009	Sacramento	P.C.	SS-2B-3B-OF	99	360	48	95	22	3	3	40	27	.264
2009	Oakland	A.L.	SS	60	208	27	58	11	3	4	21	7	.279
2010	Oakland	A.L.	SS	156	508	64	127	26	8	6	46	29	.250
Major League Totals			3 Yrs.	252	815	105	209	42	11	10	76	40	.256

PERALTA, JHONNY ANTONIO

Born, Santiago, Dominican Republic, May 28, 1982.
Bats Right. Throws Right. Height, 6 feet, 1 inch. Weight, 210 pounds.

Year	Club	Lea	Pos	G	AB	R	H	2B	3B	HR	RBI	SB	Avg
2001	Kinston	Carolina	SS	125	441	57	106	24	2	7	47	4	.240
2002	Akron	Eastern	SS	130	470	62	132	28	5	15	62	4	.281
2003	Buffalo	Int.	SS-3B	63	237	25	61	12	1	1	21	1	.257
2003	Cleveland	A.L.	SS-3B	77	242	24	55	10	1	4	21	1	.227
2004	Buffalo	Int.	SS-3B	138	556	109	181	44	2	15	86	8	.326
2004	Cleveland	A.L.	SS-3B	8	25	2	6	1	0	0	2	0	.240
2005	Cleveland	A.L.	SS	141	504	82	147	35	4	24	78	0	.292
2006	Cleveland	A.L.	SS	149	569	84	146	28	3	13	68	0	.257
2007	Cleveland	A.L.	SS	152	574	87	155	27	1	21	72	4	.270
2008	Cleveland	A.L.	SS-3B	154	605	104	167	42	4	23	89	3	.276
2009	Cleveland	A.L.	3B-SS	151	582	57	148	35	1	11	83	0	.254
2010	Cleveland-Detroit a-b	A.L.	3B-SS-1B	148	551	60	137	30	2	15	81	1	.249
Major League Totals			8 Yrs.	980	3652	500	961	208	16	111	494	9	.263
	Division Series												
2007	Cleveland	A.L.	SS	4	15	2	7	3	0	0	2	1	.467
	Championship Series												
2007	Cleveland	A.L.	SS	7	27	4	7	2	0	2	8	0	.259

a Traded to Detroit Tigers for pitcher Giovanni Soto, July 28, 2010.
b Filed for free agency, November 2, 2010, re-signed with Detroit Tigers, November 8, 2010.

PHILLIPS, BRANDON EMIL

Born, Raleigh, North Carolina, June 28, 1981.
Bats Right. Throws Right. Height, 6 feet. Weight, 195 pounds.

Year	Club	Lea	Pos	G	AB	R	H	2B	3B	HR	RBI	SB	Avg
1999	Expos	Gulf Coast	SS	47	169	23	49	11	3	1	21	12	.290
2000	Cape Fear	So.Atl.	SS-2B	126	484	74	117	17	8	11	72	23	.242
2001	Harrisburg	Eastern	SS-2B-3B	67	265	35	79	19	0	7	36	13	.298
2001	Jupiter	Fla.St.	SS	55	194	36	55	12	2	4	23	17	.284
2002	Harrisburg	Eastern	SS	60	245	40	80	13	2	9	35	6	.327
2002	Ottawa	Int.	SS	10	35	1	9	4	0	1	5	0	.257
2002	Buffalo	Int.	SS-2B	55	223	30	63	14	0	8	27	8	.283
2002	Cleveland a-b	A.L.	2B	11	31	5	8	3	1	0	4	0	.258
2003	Cleveland	A.L.	2B	112	370	36	77	18	1	6	33	4	.208
2003	Buffalo	Int.	2B	43	154	14	27	7	0	3	13	7	.175
2004	Buffalo	Int.	2B-SS	135	521	83	158	34	4	8	50	14	.303
2004	Cleveland	A.L.	2B	6	22	1	4	2	0	0	1	0	.182
2005	Cleveland	A.L.	2B-SS	6	9	1	0	0	0	0	0	0	.000
2005	Buffalo	Int.	SS	112	465	79	119	24	1	15	46	7	.256
2006	Cincinnati c-d	N.L.	2B-SS	149	536	65	148	28	1	17	75	25	.276
2007	Cincinnati	N.L.	2B-SS	158	650	107	187	26	6	30	94	32	.288
2008	Cincinnati e	N.L.	2B	141	559	80	146	24	7	21	78	23	.261
2009	Cincinnati	N.L.	2B	153	584	78	161	30	5	20	98	25	.276
2010	Cincinnati	N.L.	2B	155	626	100	172	33	5	18	59	16	.275
Major League Totals			9 Yrs.	891	3387	473	903	164	26	112	442	125	.267
	Division Series												
2010	Cincinnati	N.L.	2B	3	12	2	4	1	0	1	1	0	.333

a Traded to Cleveland Indians with infielder Lee Stevens, outfielder Grady Sizemore and pitcher Cliff Lee for pitcher Bartolo Colon and player to be named later, June 27, 2002.
b Montreal Expos received pitcher Tim Drew to complete trade, June 28, 2002.
c Traded to Cincinnati Reds for player to be named later, April 7, 2006.
d Cleveland Indians received pitcher Jeff Stevens to complete trade, June 13, 2006.
e On disabled list from September 12 to November 6, 2008.

PIE, FELIX

Born, LaRomana, Dominican Republic, February 8, 1985.
Bats Left. Throws Left. Height, 6 feet, 2 inches. Weight, 170 pounds.

Year Club	Lea	Pos	G	AB	R	H	2B	3B	HR	RBI	SB	Avg
2002 Cubs	Arizona	OF	55	218	42	70	16	13	4	37	17	.321
2002 Boise	Northwest	OF	2	8	1	1	1	0	0	1	0	.125
2003 Lansing	Midwest	OF	124	505	72	144	22	9	4	47	19	.285
2004 Daytona	Fla.St.	OF	105	412	79	123	17	9	8	47	31	.299
2005 West Tenn	Southern	OF	59	240	41	73	17	5	11	25	13	.304
2006 Iowa	P.C.	OF	141	559	78	158	33	8	15	57	17	.283
2007 Iowa	P.C.	OF	55	229	51	83	9	5	9	43	9	.362
2007 Chicago	N.L.	OF	87	177	26	38	9	3	2	20	8	.215
2008 Cubs	Arizona	OF	1	3	3	2	0	0	1	5	0	.667
2008 Iowa	P.C.	OF	85	335	57	96	20	5	10	55	11	.287
2008 Chicago	N.L.	OF	43	83	9	20	2	1	1	10	3	.241
2009 Baltimore a	A.L.	OF	101	252	38	67	10	3	9	29	1	.266
2010 Orioles	Gulf Coast	DH	2	8	1	1	0	0	0	0	0	.125
2010 Frederick	Carolina	OF	3	12	3	5	0	0	0	2	0	.417
2010 Bowie	Eastern	OF	6	23	2	8	2	1	0	1	1	.348
2010 Baltimore b	A.L.	OF	82	288	39	79	15	5	5	31	5	.274
Major League Totals		4 Yrs.	313	800	112	204	36	12	17	90	17	.255
Division Series												
2007 Chicago	N.L.	PH	1	1	0	0	0	0	0	0	0	.000
2008 Chicago	N.L.	PH	1	0	0	0	0	0	0	0	0	.000
Division Series Totals			2	1	0	0	0	0	0	0	0	.000

a Traded to Baltimore Orioles for pitcher Garrett Olson and pitcher Hank Williamson, January 18, 2009.
b On disabled list from April 16 to July 6, 2010.

PIERRE, JUAN D'VAUGHN

Born, Mobile, Alabama, August 14, 1977.
Bats Left. Throws Left. Height, 6 feet. Weight, 180 pounds.

Year Club	Lea	Pos	G	AB	R	H	2B	3B	HR	RBI	SB	Avg
1998 Portland	Northwest	OF	64	264	55	93	9	2	0	30	38	.352
1999 Asheville	So.Atl.	OF	140	585	93	187	28	5	1	55	66	.320
2000 Carolina	Southern	OF	107	439	63	143	16	4	0	32	46	.326
2000 Colorado Spgs	P.C.	OF	4	17	3	8	0	1	0	1	1	.471
2000 Colorado	N.L.	OF	51	200	26	62	2	0	0	20	7	.310
2001 Colorado	N.L.	OF	156	617	108	202	26	11	2	55	*46	.327
2002 Colorado a	N.L.	OF	152	592	90	170	20	5	1	35	47	.287
2003 Florida	N.L.	OF	*162	*668	100	204	28	7	1	41	*65	.305
2004 Florida	N.L.	OF	*162	*678	100	*221	22	*12	3	49	45	.326
2005 Florida b	N.L.	OF	*162	656	96	181	19	13	2	47	57	.276
2006 Chicago c	N.L.	OF	*162	*699	87	*204	32	13	3	40	58	.292
2007 Los Angeles	N.L.	OF	*162	668	96	196	24	8	0	41	64	.293
2008 Las Vegas	P.C.	OF	2	6	2	3	1	0	0	0	0	.500
2008 Los Angeles d	N.L.	OF	119	375	44	106	10	2	1	28	40	.283
2009 Los Angeles e	N.L.	OF	145	380	57	117	16	8	0	31	30	.308
2010 Chicago	A.L.	OF	160	651	96	179	18	3	1	47	*68	.275
Major League Totals		11 Yrs.	1593	6184	900	1842	217	82	14	434	527	.298
Division Series												
2003 Florida	N.L.	OF	4	19	5	5	1	0	0	3	1	.263
2008 Los Angeles	N.L.	OF	1	1	1	0	0	0	0	0	0	.000
2009 Los Angeles	N.L.	OF	3	0	1	0	0	0	0	0	0	.000
Division Series Totals			8	20	7	5	1	0	0	3	1	.250
Championship Series												
2003 Florida	N.L.	OF	7	33	5	10	1	2	0	1	1	.303
2008 Los Angeles	N.L.	OF	1	3	1	2	1	0	0	0	0	.667
2009 Los Angeles	N.L.	OF	4	2	1	0	0	0	0	0	0	.000
Championship Series Totals			12	38	7	12	2	2	0	1	1	.316
World Series Record												
2003 Florida	N.L.	OF	6	21	2	7	2	0	0	3	1	.333

a Traded to Florida Marlins with pitcher Mike Hampton for outfielder Preston Wilson, catcher Charles Johnson, pitcher Vic Darensbourg and infielder Pablo Ozuna, November 16, 2002.
b Traded to Chicago Cubs for pitcher Sergio Mitre, pitcher Ricky Nolasco and pitcher Renyel Pinto, December 7, 2005.
c Filed for free agency, October 29, 2006. Signed with Los Angeles Dodgers, November 22, 2006.
d On disabled list from June 30 to July 25, 2008.
e Traded with cash to Chicago White Sox for pitcher John Ely and pitcher Jon Link, December 15, 2009.

PIERZYNSKI, ANTHONY JOHN (A.J.)

Born, Bridgehampton, New York, December 30, 1976.
Bats Left. Throws Right. Height, 6 feet, 3 inches. Weight, 235 pounds.

Year	Club	Lea	Pos	G	AB	R	H	2B	3B	HR	RBI	SB	Avg
1994	Twins	Gulf Coast	C	43	152	21	44	8	1	1	19	0	.289
1995	Ft. Wayne	Midwest	C	22	84	10	26	5	1	2	14	0	.310
1995	Elizabethtn	Appal.	C-1B	56	205	29	68	13	1	7	45	0	.332
1996	Ft. Wayne	Midwest	C-OF	114	431	48	118	30	3	7	70	0	.274
1997	Ft. Myers	Fla.St.	C-1B	118	412	49	115	23	1	9	64	2	.279
1998	New Britain	Eastern	C	59	212	30	63	11	0	3	17	0	.297
1998	Salt Lake	P.C.	C	59	208	29	53	7	2	7	30	3	.255
1998	Minnesota	A.L.	C	7	10	1	3	0	0	0	1	0	.300
1999	Salt Lake	P.C.	C	67	228	29	59	10	0	1	25	0	.259
1999	Minnesota a	A.L.	C	9	22	3	6	2	0	0	3	0	.273
2000	New Britain	Eastern	C	62	228	36	68	17	2	4	34	0	.298
2000	Salt Lake	P.C.	C	41	155	22	52	14	1	4	25	1	.335
2000	Minnesota	A.L.	C	33	88	12	27	5	1	2	11	1	.307
2001	Minnesota	A.L.	C	114	381	51	110	33	2	7	55	1	.289
2002	Minnesota	A.L.	C	130	440	54	132	31	6	6	49	1	.300
2003	Minnesota b	A.L.	C	137	487	63	152	35	3	11	74	3	.312
2004	San Francisco c	N.L.	C	131	471	45	128	28	2	11	77	0	.272
2005	Chicago	A.L.	C	128	460	61	118	21	0	18	56	0	.257
2006	Chicago	A.L.	C	140	509	65	150	24	0	16	64	1	.295
2007	Chicago	A.L.	C	136	472	54	124	24	0	14	50	1	.263
2008	Chicago	A.L.	C	134	534	66	150	31	1	13	60	1	.281
2009	Chicago	A.L.	C	138	504	57	151	22	1	13	49	1	.300
2010	Chicago d	A.L.	C	128	474	43	128	29	0	9	56	3	.270
Major League Totals			13 Yrs.	1365	4852	575	1379	285	16	120	605	13	.284
	Division Series												
2002	Minnesota	A.L.	C	5	16	4	7	0	1	1	4	0	.438
2003	Minnesota	A.L.	C	4	13	1	3	0	0	1	1	0	.231
2005	Chicago	A.L.	C	3	9	5	4	2	0	2	4	1	.444
2008	Chicago	A.L.	C	4	13	1	5	1	0	0	1	0	.385
Division Series Totals				16	51	11	19	3	1	4	10	1	.373
	Championship Series												
2002	Minnesota	A.L.	C	5	16	1	4	0	0	0	2	0	.250
2005	Chicago	A.L.	C	5	18	1	3	0	0	1	2	0	.167
Championship Series Totals				10	34	2	7	0	0	1	4	0	.206
	World Series Record												
2005	Chicago	A.L.	C	4	15	3	4	2	0	0	3	1	.267

a On disabled list from August 24 to September 30, 1999.
b Traded to San Francisco Giants with cash for pitcher Joe Nathan, pitcher Boof Bonser and pitcher Francisco Liriano, November 14, 2003.
c Released by San Francisco Giants, December 16, 2004. Signed with Chicago White Sox, January 5, 2005.
d Filed for free agency, November 1, 2010, re-signed with Chicago White Sox, December 3, 2010.

PODSEDNIK, SCOTT ERIC

Born, West, Texas, March 18, 1976.
Bats Left. Throws Left. Height, 6 feet, 1 Inch. Weight, 190 pounds.

Year	Club	Lea	Pos	G	AB	R	H	2B	3B	HR	RBI	SB	Avg
1994	Rangers	Gulf Coast	OF	60	211	34	48	7	1	1	17	18	.227
1995	Hudson Val a	N.Y.-Penn.	OF	65	252	42	67	3	0	0	20	20	.266
1996	Brevard Cty	Fla.St.	OF	108	383	39	100	9	2	0	30	20	.261
1997	Kane County b	Midwest	OF	135	531	80	147	23	4	3	49	28	.277
1998	Tulsa	Texas	OF	17	75	9	18	4	1	0	4	5	.240
1998	Charlotte	Fla.St.	OF	81	302	55	86	12	4	4	39	26	.285
1999	Rangers	Gulf Coast	OF	5	17	6	7	2	0	0	5	1	.412
1999	Tulsa	Texas	OF	37	116	10	18	4	0	0	1	6	.155
2000	Tulsa c-d	Texas	OF	49	169	20	42	7	2	2	13	19	.249
2001	Tacoma	P.C.	OF	66	269	46	78	15	4	3	30	12	.290
2001	Seattle e	A.L.	OF	5	6	1	1	0	1	0	3	0	.167
2002	Tacoma	P.C.	OF	125	438	63	122	25	6	9	61	35	.279
2002	Seattle f	A.L.	OF	14	20	2	4	0	0	1	5	0	.200
2003	Milwaukee	N.L.	OF	154	558	100	175	29	8	9	58	43	.314
2004	Milwaukee g	N.L.	OF	154	640	85	156	27	7	12	39	*70	.244
2005	Charlotte	Int.	OF	2	9	2	2	2	0	0	1	0	.222
2005	Chicago h	A.L.	OF	129	507	80	147	28	1	0	25	59	.290
2006	Chicago	A.L.	OF	139	524	86	137	27	6	3	45	40	.261
2007	Charlotte	Int.	OF	20	73	12	21	5	0	1	6	2	.288

Year	Club	Lea	Pos	G	AB	R	H	2B	3B	HR	RBI	SB	Avg
2007	Chicago i-j	A.L.	OF	62	214	30	52	13	4	2	11	12	.243
2008	Colorado Springs	P.C.	OF	4	16	2	7	0	0	0	3	3	.438
2008	Colorado k-l	N.L.	OF	93	162	22	41	8	1	1	15	12	.253
2009	Charlotte	Int.	OF	10	42	6	11	4	0	0	2	1	.262
2009	Chicago m-n	A.L.	OF	132	537	75	163	25	6	7	48	30	.304
2010	Kansas City	A.L.	OF	95	390	46	121	8	6	5	44	30	.310
2010	Los Angeles o-p	N.L.	OF	39	149	17	39	6	1	1	7	5	.262
Major League Totals			10 Yrs.	1016	3707	544	1036	171	41	41	300	301	.279
	Division Series												
2005	Chicago	A.L.	OF	3	11	3	3	1	0	1	4	1	.273
	Championship Series												
2005	Chicago	A.L.	OF	5	17	4	5	0	1	0	0	3	.294
	World Series Record												
2005	Chicago	A.L.	OF	4	21	2	6	0	2	1	2	2	.286

a Sent to Florida Marlins by Texas Rangers to complete trade for pitcher Bobby Witt, August 8, 1995.
b Selected by Texas Rangers organization in Rule V draft, December 15, 1997.
c On disabled list from April 6 to May 22, 2000.
d Filed for free agency, October 15, 2000. Signed with Seattle Mariners organization, November 7, 2000.
e On disabled list from May 4 to June 12 and August 14 to 26, 2001.
f Claimed on waivers by Milwaukee Brewers, October 11, 2002.
g Traded to Chicago White Sox with pitcher Luis Vizcaino and player to be named later for outfielder Carlos Lee, December 13, 2004. Chicago White Sox received infielder Travis Hinton to complete trade, January 10, 2005.
h On disabled list from August 13 to August 29, 2005.
i On disabled list from April 16 to June 23 and July 2 to July 24, 2007.
j Released by Chicago White Sox, November 28, 2007. Signed with Colorado Rockies organization, February 5, 2008.
k On disabled list from July 28 to August 22, 2008.
l Filed for free agency, November 1, 2008, re-signed with Colorado Rockies organization, January 14, 2009.
m Released by Colorado Rockies, April 1, 2009. Signed with Chicago White Sox organization, April 14, 2009.
n Filed for free agency, November 5, 2009. Signed with Kansas City Royals, January 8, 2010.
o Traded to Los Angeles Dodgers for catcher Lucas May and pitcher Elisaul Pimentel, July 29, 2010.
p Filed for free agency, November 4, 2010.

POLANCO, PLACIDO ENRIQUE

Born, Santo Domingo, Dominican Republic, October 10, 1975.
Bats Right. Throws Right. Height, 5 feet, 10 inches. Weight, 195 pounds.

Year	Club	Lea	Pos	G	AB	R	H	2B	3B	HR	RBI	SB	Avg
1994	Cardinals	Arizona	SS-2B	32	127	17	27	4	0	1	10	4	.213
1995	Peoria	Midwest	SS-2B	103	361	43	96	7	4	2	41	7	.266
1996	St. Pete	Fla.St.	2B	137	540	65	157	29	5	0	51	4	.291
1997	Arkansas	Texas	2B	129	508	71	148	16	3	2	51	19	.291
1998	Memphis	P.C.	2B-SS	70	246	36	69	19	1	1	21	6	.280
1998	St. Louis	N.L.	SS-2B	45	114	10	29	3	2	1	11	2	.254
1999	Memphis	P.C.	2B	29	120	18	33	4	1	0	10	2	.275
1999	St. Louis	N.L.	2B-3B-SS	88	220	24	61	9	3	1	19	1	.277
2000	St. Louis a	N.L.	2B-3B-SS-1B	118	323	50	102	12	3	5	39	4	.316
2001	St. Louis	N.L.	3B-SS-2B	144	564	87	173	26	4	3	38	12	.307
2002	St. Louis-Phil. b	N.L.	3B-SS-2B	147	548	75	158	32	2	9	49	5	.288
2003	Philadelphia c	N.L.	2B-3B	122	492	87	142	30	3	14	63	14	.289
2004	Reading	Eastern	2B	1	3	0	2	0	0	0	0	0	.667
2004	Scranton/W.B.	Int.	2B	1	3	1	0	0	0	0	0	0	.000
2004	Philadelphia d-e	N.L.	2B-3B	126	503	74	150	21	0	17	55	7	.298
2005	Philadelphia	N.L.	2B-3B-OF-SS	43	158	26	50	7	0	3	20	0	.316
2005	Detroit f-g	A.L.	2B-3B	86	343	58	116	20	2	6	36	4	.338
2006	Detroit h	A.L.	2B	110	461	58	136	18	1	4	52	1	.295
2007	Detroit	A.L.	2B	142	587	105	200	36	3	9	67	7	.341
2008	Detroit	A.L.	2B	141	580	90	178	34	3	8	58	7	.307
2009	Detroit i	A.L.	2B	153	618	82	176	31	4	10	72	7	.285
2010	Phillies	Gulf Coast	2B	1	3	1	3	1	0	0	2	0	1.000
2010	Clearwater	Fla.St.	3B	1	4	1	1	0	0	0	0	0	.250
2010	Philadelphia j	N.L.	3B-2B	132	554	76	165	27	2	6	52	5	.298
Major League Totals			13 Yrs.	1597	6065	902	1836	306	32	96	631	76	.303
	Division Series												
2000	St. Louis	N.L.	3B	3	10	1	3	0	0	0	3	1	.300
2001	St. Louis	N.L.	3B	5	15	1	4	0	0	0	1	1	.267
2006	Detroit	A.L.	2B	4	17	3	7	1	0	0	2	0	.412
2010	Philadelphia	N.L.	3B	2	9	1	1	0	0	0	0	0	.111
Division Series Totals				14	51	6	15	1	0	0	6	2	.294
	Championship Series												
2000	St. Louis	N.L.	3B	4	5	0	1	0	0	0	0	0	.200

Year	Club	Lea	Pos	G	AB	R	H	2B	3B	HR	RBI	SB	Avg
2006	Detroit	A.L.	2B	4	17	2	9	1	0	0	2	0	.529
2010	Philadelphia	N.L.	3B	6	20	3	5	2	0	0	5	1	.250
Championship Series Totals				14	42	5	15	3	0	0	7	1	.357
	World Series Record												
2006	Detroit	A.L.	2B	5	17	0	0	0	0	0	0	0	.000

a On disabled list from July 1 to July 15, 2000.
b Traded to Philadelphia Phillies with pitcher Bud Smith and pitcher Mike Timlin for infielder Scott Rolen and pitcher Doug Nickle, July 29, 2002.
c On disabled list from April 16 to May 1, 2003.
d On disabled list from May 8 to June 7, 2004.
e Filed for free agency, October 29, 2004, re-signed with Philadelphia Phillies, December 19, 2004.
f Traded to Detroit Tigers for pitcher Ugueth Urbina and infielder Ramon Martinez, June 8, 2005.
g On disabled list from July 12 to July 27, 2005.
h On disabled list from August 16 to September 22, 2006.
i Filed for free agency, November 5, 2009. Signed with Philadelphia Phillies, December 3, 2009.
j On disabled list from June 26 to July 17, 2010.

POSADA, JORGE RAFAEL

Born, Santurce, Puerto Rico, August 17, 1971.
Bats Both. Throws Right. Height, 6 feet, 2 inches. Weight, 205 pounds

Year	Club	Lea	Pos	G	AB	R	H	2B	3B	HR	RBI	SB	Avg
1991	Oneonta	N.Y.-Penn	2B-C	71	217	34	51	5	5	4	33	6	.235
1992	Greensboro	So. Atl.	DH-C-3B	101	339	60	94	22	4	12	58	11	.277
1993	Pr William	Carolina	C-3B	118	410	71	106	27	2	17	61	17	.259
1993	Albany	Eastern	C	7	25	3	7	0	0	0	0	0	.280
1994	Columbus	Int.	C-OF	92	313	46	75	13	3	11	48	5	.240
1995	Columbus	Int.	C	108	368	60	94	32	5	8	51	4	.255
1995	New York	A.L.	C	1	0	0	0	0	0	0	0	0	.000
1996	Columbus	Int.	C-OF	106	354	76	96	22	6	11	62	3	.271
1996	New York	A.L.	C	8	14	1	1	0	0	0	0	0	.071
1997	New York	A.L.	C	60	188	29	47	12	0	6	25	1	.250
1998	New York	A.L.	C-1B	111	358	56	96	23	0	17	63	0	.268
1999	New York	A.L.	C-1B	112	379	50	93	19	2	12	57	1	.245
2000	New York	A.L.	C-1B	151	505	92	145	35	1	28	86	2	.287
2001	New York	A.L.	C-1B	138	484	59	134	28	1	22	95	2	.277
2002	New York	A.L.	C	143	511	79	137	40	1	20	99	1	.268
2003	New York	A.L.	C	142	481	83	135	24	0	30	101	2	.281
2004	New York	A.L.	C	137	449	72	122	31	0	21	81	1	.272
2005	New York	A.L.	C	142	474	67	124	23	0	19	71	1	.262
2006	New York	A.L.	C-1B	143	465	65	129	27	2	23	93	3	.277
2007	New York a	A.L.	C-1B	144	506	91	171	42	1	20	90	2	.338
2008	New York b	A.L.	C-1B	51	168	18	45	13	1	3	22	0	.268
2009	New York c	A.L.	C-1B	111	383	55	109	25	0	22	81	1	.285
2010	New York d	A.L.	C-1B	120	383	49	95	23	1	18	57	3	.248
Major League Totals			16 Yrs.	1714	5748	866	1583	365	10	261	1021	20	.275
	Division Series												
1995	New York	A.L.	C	1	0	1	0	0	0	0	0	0	.000
1997	New York	A.L.	C	2	2	0	0	0	0	0	0	0	.000
1998	New York	A.L.	C	1	2	1	0	0	0	0	0	0	.000
1999	New York	A.L.	C	1	4	0	1	1	0	0	0	0	.250
2000	New York	A.L.	C	5	17	2	4	2	0	0	1	0	.235
2001	New York	A.L.	C	5	18	3	8	1	0	1	2	1	.444
2002	New York	A.L.	C	4	17	2	4	0	0	1	3	0	.235
2003	New York	A.L.	C	4	17	1	3	1	0	0	0	0	.176
2004	New York	A.L.	C	4	18	2	4	0	0	0	0	0	.222
2005	New York	A.L.	C	5	13	3	3	1	0	1	2	0	.231
2006	New York	A.L.	C	4	14	2	7	1	0	1	2	0	.500
2007	New York	A.L.	C	4	15	1	2	1	0	0	0	0	.133
2009	New York	A.L.	C	3	11	1	4	0	0	1	2	0	.364
2010	New York	A.L.	C	3	11	2	3	0	0	0	2	0	.273
Division Series Totals				46	159	21	43	8	0	5	14	1	.270
	Championship Series												
1998	New York	A.L.	C	5	11	1	2	0	0	1	2	0	.182
1999	New York	A.L.	C	3	10	1	1	0	0	1	2	0	.100
2000	New York	A.L.	C	6	19	2	3	1	0	0	3	0	.158
2001	New York	A.L.	C	5	14	4	3	1	0	0	0	0	.214
2003	New York	A.L.	C	7	27	5	8	4	0	1	6	0	.296
2004	New York	A.L.	C	7	27	4	7	1	0	0	2	0	.259
2009	New York	A.L.	C	6	20	3	4	1	0	1	1	1	.200

Year Club	Lea	Pos	G	AB	R	H	2B	3B	HR	RBI	SB	Avg
2010 New York	A.L.	C	6	19	1	5	2	0	0	1	0	.263
Championship Series Totals			45	147	21	33	10	0	4	17	1	.224
World Series Record												
1998 New York	A.L.	C	3	9	2	3	0	0	1	2	0	.333
1999 New York	A.L.	C	2	8	0	2	1	0	0	1	0	.250
2000 New York	A.L.	C	5	18	2	4	1	0	0	1	0	.222
2001 New York	A.L.	C	7	23	2	4	1	0	1	1	0	.174
2003 New York	A.L.	C	6	19	0	3	1	0	0	1	1	.158
2009 New York	A.L.	C	6	19	1	5	1	0	0	5	0	.263
World Series Totals			29	96	7	21	5	0	2	11	1	.219

a Filed for free agency, October 29, 2007, re-signed with New York Yankees, November 29, 2007.
b On disabled list from April 27 to June 4 and July 21 to November 14, 2008.
c On disabled list from May 5 to May 29, 2009.
d On disabled list from May 17 to June 2, 2010.

POSEY, GERALD DEMP (BUSTER)

Born, Leesburg, Georgia, March 27, 1987.
Bats Right. Throws Right. Height, 6 feet, 1 inch. Weight, 205 pounds.

Year Club	Lea	Pos	G	AB	R	H	2B	3B	HR	RBI	SB	Avg
2008 Giants.	Arizona	C	7	26	8	10	3	1	1	4	0	.385
2008 Salem-Keizer	Northwest	C	3	11	2	3	2	0	0	2	0	.273
2009 San Jose	Calif.	C	80	291	63	95	23	0	13	58	6	.326
2009 Fresno	P.C.	C	35	131	21	42	8	1	5	22	0	.321
2009 San Francisco	N.L.	C	7	17	1	2	0	0	0	0	0	.118
2010 Fresno	P.C.	C-1B	47	172	31	60	13	2	6	32	1	.349
2010 San Francisco a	N.L.	C-1B	108	406	58	124	23	2	18	67	0	.305
Major League Totals		2 Yrs.	115	423	59	126	23	2	18	67	0	.298
Division Series												
2010 San Francisco	N.L.	C	4	16	3	6	1	0	0	0	1	.375
Championship Series												
2010 San Francisco	N.L.	C	6	23	1	5	2	0	0	3	0	.217
World Series Record												
2010 San Francisco	N.L.	C	5	20	2	6	0	0	1	2	0	.300

a Selected Rookie of the Year in National League for 2010.

PRADO, MARTIN MANUEL

Born, Maracay, Venezuela, October 27, 1983.
Bats Right. Throws Right. Height, 6 feet, 1 inch. Weight, 170 pounds.

Year Club	Lea	Pos	G	AB	R	H	2B	3B	HR	RBI	SB	Avg
2003 Braves	Gulf Coast	2B-3B	59	220	28	63	2	6	0	23	9	.286
2004 Rome	So.Atl.	2B	107	429	68	135	25	6	3	38	14	.315
2005 Myrtle Beach . .	Carolina	2B	75	297	44	91	13	3	4	34	9	.306
2005 Mississippi. . . .	Southern	2B	39	143	17	40	7	1	1	11	3	.280
2006 Richmond	Int.	2B-3B	60	241	30	68	12	1	2	23	2	.282
2006 Mississippi. . . .	Southern	2B-3B	43	176	17	49	6	2	1	15	2	.278
2006 Atlanta	N.L.	2B-3B	24	42	3	11	1	1	1	9	0	.262
2007 Richmond	Int.	2B-3B-SS	103	395	61	125	23	3	4	41	5	.316
2007 Atlanta	N.L.	2B-3B	28	59	5	17	3	0	0	2	0	.288
2008 Mississippi. . . .	Southern	2B-3B-SS-OF	5	19	2	5	2	0	0	3	0	.263
2008 Atlanta a.	N.L.	3B-1B-2B-OF	78	228	36	73	18	4	2	33	3	.320
2009 Atlanta	N.L.	2B-3B-1B-OF	128	450	64	138	38	0	11	49	1	.307
2010 Gwinnett.	Int.	2B-3B	1	4	0	1	0	0	0	0	0	.250
2010 Atlanta b.	N.L.	2B-3B-1B	140	599	100	184	40	3	15	66	5	.307
Major League Totals		5 Yrs.	398	1378	208	423	100	8	29	159	9	.307

a On disabled list from May 5 to July 3, 2008.
b On disabled list from July 31 to August 17, 2010.

PUJOLS, JOSE ALBERTO (ALBERT)

Born, Santo Domingo, Dominican Republic, January 16, 1980.
Bats Right. Throws Right. Height, 6 feet, 3 inches. Weight, 225 pounds.

Year Club	Lea	Pos	G	AB	R	H	2B	3B	HR	RBI	SB	Avg
2000 Potomac.	Carolina	3B	21	81	11	23	8	1	2	10	1	.284
2000 Peoria.	Midwest	3B	109	395	62	128	32	6	17	84	2	.324
2000 Memphis	P.C.	3B-OF	3	14	1	3	1	0	0	2	1	.214
2001 St. Louis a	N.L.	OF-3B-1B	161	590	112	194	47	4	37	130	1	.329

Year Club	Lea	Pos	G	AB	R	H	2B	3B	HR	RBI	SB	Avg
2002 St. Louis..........	N.L.	OF-3B-1B-SS	157	590	118	185	40	2	34	127	2	.314
2003 St. Louis..........	N.L.	OF-1B	157	591	*137	*212	*51	1	43	124	5	*.359
2004 St. Louis..........	N.L.	1B	154	592	*133	196	51	2	46	123	5	.331
2005 St. Louis b........	N.L.	1B	161	591	*129	195	38	2	41	117	16	.330
2006 St. Louis c........	N.L.	1B	143	535	119	177	33	1	49	137	7	.331
2007 St. Louis..........	N.L.	1B	158	565	99	185	38	1	32	103	2	.327
2008 St. Louis d-e......	N.L.	1B-2B	148	524	100	187	44	0	37	116	7	.357
2009 St. Louis f........	N.L.	1B	160	568	*124	186	45	1	*47	135	16	.327
2010 St. Louis..........	N.L.	1B	159	587	*115	183	39	1	*42	*118	14	.312
Major League Totals............		10 Yrs.	1558	5733	1186	1900	426	15	408	1230	75	.331
Division Series												
2001 St. Louis..........	N.L.	1B-OF	5	18	1	2	0	0	1	2	0	.111
2002 St. Louis..........	N.L.	OF-1B-3B	3	10	3	3	0	1	0	3	0	.300
2004 St. Louis..........	N.L.	1B	4	15	4	5	0	0	2	5	0	.333
2005 St. Louis..........	N.L.	1B	3	9	4	5	2	0	0	2	0	.556
2006 St. Louis..........	N.L.	1B	4	15	3	5	1	0	1	3	0	.333
2009 St. Louis..........	N.L.	1B	3	10	0	3	0	0	0	1	0	.300
Division Series Totals...........			22	77	15	23	3	1	4	16	0	.299
Championship Series												
2002 St. Louis..........	N.L.	OF-3B-1B	5	19	2	5	1	0	1	2	0	.263
2004 St. Louis..........	N.L.	1B	7	28	10	14	2	0	4	9	0	.500
2005 St. Louis..........	N.L.	1B	6	23	3	7	0	0	2	6	0	.304
2006 St. Louis..........	N.L.	1B	7	22	5	7	1	0	1	1	0	.318
Championship Series Totals......			25	92	20	33	4	0	8	18	0	.359
World Series Record												
2004 St. Louis..........	N.L.	1B	4	15	1	5	2	0	0	0	0	.333
2006 St. Louis..........	N.L.	1B	5	15	3	3	1	0	1	2	0	.200
World Series Totals..........			9	30	4	8	3	0	1	2	0	.267

a Selected Rookie of the Year in National League for 2001.
b Selected Most Valuable Player in National League for 2005.
c On disabled list from June 4 to June 22, 2006.
d On disabled list from June 11 to June 26, 2008.
e Selected Most Valuable Player in National League for 2008.
f Selected Most Valuable Player in National League for 2009.

PUNTO, NICHOLAS PAUL (NICK)

Born, San Diego, California, November 8, 1977.
Bats Both. Throws Right. Height, 5 feet, 9 inches. Weight, 185 pounds.

Year Club	Lea	Pos	G	AB	R	H	2B	3B	HR	RBI	SB	Avg
1998 Batavia.......	N.Y.-Penn.	SS-2B	72	279	51	69	9	4	1	20	19	.247
1999 Clearwater......	Fla.St.	SS	106	400	65	122	18	6	1	48	16	.305
2000 Reading.......	Eastern	SS	121	456	77	116	15	4	5	47	33	.254
2001 Scranton-WB......	Int.	SS	123	463	57	106	19	5	1	39	33	.229
2001 Philadelphia.......	N.L.	SS	4	5	0	2	0	0	0	0	0	.400
2002 Philadelphia.......	N.L.	2B-SS	9	6	0	1	0	0	0	0	0	.167
2002 Scranton-WB......	Int.	SS	115	443	74	120	12	5	1	29	42	.271
2003 Philadelphia.......	N.L.	2B-3B-SS	64	92	14	20	2	0	1	4	2	.217
2003 Scranton/WB a.....	Int.	SS	25	111	19	35	7	1	0	9	7	.315
2004 Minnesota........	A.L.	2B-SS-3B-OF	38	91	17	23	0	0	2	12	6	.253
2004 Quad Cities b..	Midwest	SS-2B-3B	4	16	4	7	1	0	1	6	1	.438
2005 Rochester.........	Int.	2B	4	15	2	3	1	0	0	1	0	.200
2005 Minnesota c.......	A.L.	2B-SS-3B-OF	112	394	45	94	18	4	4	26	13	.239
2006 Minnesota........	A.L.	3B-SS-2B-OF	135	459	73	133	21	7	1	45	17	.290
2007 Minnesota........	A.L.	3B-SS-2B	150	472	53	99	18	4	1	25	16	.210
2008 Fort Myers......	Fla.St.	SS	3	12	0	3	0	0	0	1	1	.250
2008 Minnesota d-e.....	A.L.	SS-2B-3B-OF	99	338	43	96	19	4	2	28	15	.284
2009 Minnesota f.......	A.L.	2B-SS-3B	125	359	56	82	15	1	1	38	16	.228
2010 Minnesota g-h.....	A.L.	3B-SS-2B	88	252	24	60	11	1	1	20	6	.238
Major League Totals............		10 Yrs.	824	2468	325	610	104	21	13	198	91	.247
Division Series												
2006 Minnesota........	A.L.	3B	3	12	0	2	0	0	0	0	0	.167
2009 Minnesota........	A.L.	2B	3	9	0	4	1	0	0	1	0	.444
Division Series Totals...........			6	21	0	6	1	0	0	1	0	.286

a Traded to Minnesota Twins with pitcher Carlos Silva and cash for pitcher Eric Milton, December 3, 2003.
b On disabled list from May 9 to June 30 and July 27 to October 28, 2004.
c On disabled list from June 3 to July 3, 2005.
d On disabled list from May 8 to May 31 and June 6 to June 24, 2008.

e Filed for free agency, October 30, 2008, re-signed with Minnesota Twins, December 11, 2008.
f On disabled list from May 28 to June 12, 2009.
g On disabled list from April 16 to May 1 and July 29 to August 17 and August 20 to September 10, 2010.
h Filed for free agency, November 1, 2010.

QUENTIN, CARLOS JOSE

Born, Bellflower, California, August 28, 1982.
Bats Right. Throws Right. Height, 6 feet, 1 inch. Weight, 225 pounds.

Year	Club	Lea	Pos	G	AB	R	H	2B	3B	HR	RBI	SB	Avg
2004	Lancaster	Calif.	OF	65	242	64	75	14	1	15	51	5	.310
2004	El Paso	Texas	OF	60	210	39	75	19	0	6	38	0	.357
2005	Tucson	P.C.	OF	136	452	98	136	28	4	21	89	9	.301
2006	Tucson	P.C.	OF	85	318	66	92	30	3	9	52	5	.289
2006	Arizona	N.L.	OF	57	166	23	42	13	3	9	32	1	.253
2007	Tucson	P.C.	OF	33	115	30	40	12	1	4	27	0	.348
2007	Arizona a-b	N.L.	OF	81	229	29	49	16	0	5	31	2	.214
2008	Chicago	A.L.	OF	130	480	96	138	26	1	36	100	7	.287
2009	Kannapolis	So.Atl.	OF	2	3	0	1	1	0	0	1	0	.333
2009	Charlotte	Int.	OF	12	37	10	14	3	0	1	9	0	.378
2009	Chicago c	A.L.	OF	99	351	47	83	14	0	21	56	3	.236
2010	Chicago	A.L.	OF	131	453	73	110	25	2	26	87	2	.243
Major League Totals			5 Yrs.	498	1679	268	422	94	6	97	306	15	.251

a On disabled list from March 23 to April 16 and August 2 to September 1, 2007.
b Traded to Chicago White Sox for infielder Chris Carter, December 3, 2007.
c On disabled list from May 26 to July 20, 2009.

QUINTERO, HUMBERTO

Born, Maracaibo, Venezuela, August 2, 1979.
Bats Right. Throws Right. Height, 5 feet, 9 inches. Weight, 205 pounds.

Year	Club	Lea	Pos	G	AB	R	H	2B	3B	HR	RBI	SB	Avg
1997	Guacara-1	Venzuelan	C	24	42	4	11	2	0	0	0	1	.262
1998	Miranda	Venzuelan	C	30	73	6	15	1	0	0	1	0	.205
1999	Bristol	Appal.	C	48	155	30	43	5	2	0	15	11	.277
2000	White Sox	Arizona	C-OF	15	56	13	22	2	2	0	8	1	.393
2000	Burlington	Midwest	C	75	248	23	59	12	2	0	24	10	.238
2001	Winston-Salem	Carolina	C	43	154	15	37	6	0	0	12	9	.240
2001	Kannapolis	So.Atl.	C	60	197	32	53	7	1	1	20	7	.269
2001	Birmingham	Southern	C	5	19	0	4	0	0	0	2	0	.211
2002	Winston-Salem	Carolina	C	52	160	15	31	1	1	0	12	2	.194
2002	Charlotte	Int.	C	15	41	2	9	1	0	0	5	0	.220
2002	Birmingham	Southern	C	4	12	1	6	0	0	0	3	1	.500
2002	Mobile a	Southern	C	37	125	11	30	8	0	1	14	0	.240
2003	Mobile	Southern	C	110	386	37	115	26	0	3	52	0	.298
2003	San Diego	N.L.	C	12	23	1	5	0	0	0	2	0	.217
2004	Portland	P.C.	C	68	259	36	82	25	0	5	30	0	.317
2004	San Diego	N.L.	C	23	72	7	18	3	0	2	10	0	.250
2005	Corpus Christi	Texas	C	4	11	0	2	1	0	0	1	0	.182
2005	Round Rock	P.C.	C	52	191	23	55	13	0	8	31	2	.288
2005	Houston b-c	N.L.	C-1B	18	54	6	10	1	0	1	8	0	.185
2006	Round Rock	P.C.	C	82	292	39	87	21	2	4	37	4	.298
2006	Houston	N.L.	C	11	21	2	7	2	0	0	2	0	.333
2007	Round Rock	P.C.	C-1B	53	177	22	59	12	1	5	22	0	.333
2007	Houston	N.L.	C	29	53	2	12	2	0	0	1	0	.226
2008	Round Rock	P.C.	C-1B	32	118	13	28	2	2	3	18	0	.237
2008	Corpus Christi	Texas	C	3	12	0	3	2	0	0	1	0	.250
2008	Houston d	N.L.	C	59	168	16	38	6	0	2	12	0	.226
2009	Round Rock	P.C.	C	4	10	0	1	1	0	0	1	0	.100
2009	Houston e	N.L.	C	60	157	11	37	8	1	4	14	0	.236
2010	Houston	N.L.	C	88	265	13	62	10	0	4	20	0	.234
Major League Totals			8 Yrs.	300	813	58	189	32	1	13	69	0	.232

a Traded by Chicago White Sox to San Diego Padres with outfielder Alex Fernandez for infielder D'Angelo Jimenez, July 12, 2002.
b Traded to Houston Astros for pitcher Tim Redding and cash, March 28, 2005.
c On disabled list from June 19 to July 16, 2005.
d On disabled list from July 2 to July 22, 2008.
e On disabled list from April 25 to May 12, 2009.

RABURN, RYAN NEIL

Born, Tampa, Florida, April 17, 1981.
Bats Right. Throws Right. Height, 6 feet. Weight, 185 pounds.

Year	Club	Lea	Pos	G	AB	R	H	2B	3B	HR	RBI	SB	Avg
2001	Tigers	Gulf Coast	3B	19	58	4	9	2	0	1	5	2	.155
2001	Oneonta	N.Y.-Penn.	3B-2B	44	171	25	62	17	8	8	42	1	.363
2002	Tigers	Gulf Coast	3B	8	30	4	9	3	1	1	5	0	.300
2002	West Michigan	Midwest	3B	40	150	27	33	10	1	6	28	0	.220
2003	Lakeland	Fla.St.	3B	95	325	52	72	14	3	12	56	2	.222
2003	West Michigan	Midwest	3B	16	57	14	20	7	0	3	12	1	.351
2004	Lakeland	Fla.St.	2B	3	11	1	3	1	0	1	3	0	.273
2004	Erie	Eastern	2B	98	366	66	110	29	4	16	63	3	.301
2004	Detroit	A.L.	2B	12	29	4	4	1	0	0	1	1	.138
2005	Toledo	Int.	2B-OF	130	471	62	119	22	4	19	64	8	.253
2006	Toledo	Int.	OF-2B	118	451	68	124	29	4	20	79	16	.275
2007	Toledo	Int.	OF-2B	85	315	60	92	21	3	17	64	12	.292
2007	Detroit	A.L.	OF-2B-3B	49	138	28	42	12	2	4	27	3	.304
2008	Toledo	Int.	OF	5	19	6	6	2	0	2	6	0	.316
2008	Detroit	A.L.	OF-3B-2B	92	182	26	43	10	1	4	20	3	.236
2009	Toledo	Int.	OF	12	47	11	12	3	0	5	9	2	.255
2009	Detroit	A.L.	OF-1B-3B	113	261	44	76	11	2	16	45	5	.291
2010	Toledo	Int.	OF	7	27	5	12	6	0	0	2	1	.444
2010	Detroit	A.L.	OF-2B-3B-1B	113	371	54	104	25	1	15	62	2	.280
Major League Totals			5 Yrs.	379	981	156	269	59	6	39	155	14	.274

RAMIREZ, ALEXEI FERNANDO

Born, Pinar Del Rio, Cuba, September 22, 1981.
Bats Right. Throws Right. Height, 6 feet, 3 inches. Weight, 185 pounds.

Year	Club	Lea	Pos	G	AB	R	H	2B	3B	HR	RBI	SB	Avg
2008	Chicago a-b	A.L.	2B-SS-OF-3B	136	480	65	139	22	2	21	77	13	.290
2009	Chicago	A.L.	SS	148	542	71	150	14	1	15	68	14	.277
2010	Chicago	A.L.	SS	156	585	83	165	29	2	18	70	13	.282
Major League Totals			3 Yrs.	440	1607	219	454	65	5	54	215	40	.283
	Division Series												
2008	Chicago	A.L.	2B	4	12	1	3	0	0	0	2	0	.250

a Played in Cuba 2001-2007.
b Signed with Chicago White Sox, January 1, 2008.

RAMIREZ (NIN), ARAMIS

Born, Santo Domingo, Dominican Republic, June 25, 1978.
Bats Right. Throws Right. Height, 6 feet, 1 inch. Weight, 215 pounds.

Year	Club	Lea	Pos	G	AB	R	H	2B	3B	HR	RBI	SB	Avg
1995	Pittsburgh	Dominican	3B	64	214	41	63	13	0	11	54	2	.294
1996	Erie	N.Y.-Penn.	3B	61	223	37	68	14	4	9	42	0	.305
1996	Augusta	So.Atl.	3B	6	20	3	4	1	0	1	2	0	.200
1997	Lynchburg	Carolina	3B	137	482	85	134	24	2	29	114	5	.278
1998	Nashville	P.C.	3B-SS	47	168	19	46	10	0	5	18	0	.274
1998	Pittsburgh a	N.L.	3B	72	251	23	59	9	1	6	24	0	.235
1999	Nashville	P.C.	3B	131	460	92	151	35	1	21	74	5	.328
1999	Pittsburgh	N.L.	3B	18	56	2	10	2	1	0	7	0	.179
2000	Nashville	P.C.	3B	44	167	28	59	12	2	4	26	2	.353
2000	Pittsburgh b	N.L.	3B	73	254	19	65	15	2	6	35	0	.256
2001	Pittsburgh	N.L.	3B	158	603	83	181	40	0	34	112	5	.300
2002	Pittsburgh	N.L.	3B	142	522	51	122	26	0	18	71	2	.234
2003	Pittsburgh-Chicago c-d	N.L.	3B	159	607	75	165	32	2	27	106	2	.272
2004	Chicago	N.L.	3B	145	547	99	174	32	1	36	103	0	.318
2005	Chicago e	N.L.	3B	123	463	72	140	30	0	31	92	0	.302
2006	Chicago f	N.L.	3B	157	594	93	173	38	4	38	119	2	.291
2007	Chicago g	N.L.	3B	132	506	72	157	35	4	26	101	0	.310
2008	Chicago	N.L.	3B	149	554	97	160	44	1	27	111	2	.289
2009	Peoria	Midwest	3B	3	6	2	3	1	0	0	1	0	.500
2009	Chicago h	N.L.	3B	82	306	46	97	14	1	15	65	2	.317
2010	Peoria	Midwest	3B	2	6	1	1	0	0	0	1	0	.167
2010	Chicago i	N.L.	3B	124	465	61	112	21	1	25	83	0	.241
Major League Totals			13 Yrs.	1534	5728	793	1615	338	18	289	1029	15	.282
	Division Series												
2003	Chicago	N.L.	3B	5	18	2	5	1	0	1	3	0	.278
2007	Chicago	N.L.	3B	3	12	0	0	0	0	0	0	0	.000

Year	Club	Lea	Pos	G	AB	R	H	2B	3B	HR	RBI	SB	Avg
2008	Chicago	N.L.	3B	3	11	1	2	1	0	0	0	0	.182
Division Series Totals.				11	41	3	7	2	0	1	3	0	.171
	Championship Series												
2003	Chicago	N.L.	3B	7	26	4	6	0	1	3	7	0	.231

a On disabled list from August 10 to September 4, 1998.
b On disabled list from August 29 to October 1, 2000.
c Traded to Chicago Cubs with outfielder Kenny Lofton for infielder Jose Hernandez, pitcher Matt Bruback and player to be named later, July 22, 2003.
d Pittsburgh Pirates received infielder Bobby Hill to complete trade, August 15, 2003.
e On disabled list from August 25 to October 3, 2005.
f Filed for free agency, October 30, 2006, re-signed with Chicago Cubs, November 12, 2006.
g On disabled list from June 7 to June 22, 2007.
h On disabled list from May 9 to July 6, 2009.
i On disabled list from June 8 to June 25, 2010.

RAMIREZ, HANLEY

Born, Samana, Dominican Republic, December 23, 1983.
Bats Right. Throws Right. Height, 6 feet, 3 inches. Weight, 195 pounds.

Year	Club	Lea	Pos	G	AB	R	H	2B	3B	HR	RBI	SB	Avg
2002	Red Sox	Gulf Coast	SS-2B-3B	45	164	29	56	11	3	6	26	8	.341
2002	Lowell	N.Y.-Penn.	SS	22	97	17	36	9	2	1	19	4	.371
2003	Augusta	So.Atl.	SS	111	422	69	116	24	3	8	50	36	.275
2004	Portland	Eastern	SS	32	129	26	40	7	2	5	15	12	.310
2004	Sarasota.	Fla.St.	SS	62	239	33	74	8	4	1	24	12	.310
2004	Red Sox	Gulf Coast	SS-2B	6	20	5	8	0	1	0	7	1	.400
2005	Portland	Eastern	SS-2B-3B	122	465	66	126	21	7	6	52	26	.271
2005	Boston a.	A.L.	SS	2	2	0	0	0	0	0	0	0	.000
2006	Florida b.	N.L.	SS	158	633	119	185	46	11	17	59	51	.292
2007	Florida	N.L.	SS	154	639	125	212	48	6	29	81	51	.332
2008	Florida	N.L.	SS	153	589	*125	177	34	4	33	67	35	.301
2009	Florida	N.L.	SS	151	576	101	197	42	1	24	106	27	*.342
2010	Florida	N.L.	SS	142	543	92	163	28	2	21	76	32	.300
Major League Totals			6 Yrs.	760	2982	562	934	198	24	124	389	196	.313

a Traded to Florida Marlins with pitcher Anibal Sanchez and pitcher Jesus Delgado for pitcher Josh Beckett, infielder Mike Lowell and pitcher Guillermo Mota, November 24, 2005.
b Selected Rookie of the Year in National League for 2006.

RAMIREZ, MANUEL ARISTIDES (MANNY)

Born, Santo Domingo, Domininican Republic, May 30, 1972.
Bats Right. Throws Right. Height, 6 feet. Weight, 200 pounds.

Year	Club	Lea	Pos	G	AB	R	H	2B	3B	HR	RBI	SB	Avg
1991	Burlington	Appal.	OF	59	215	44	70	11	4	19	63	7	.326
1992	Kinston a	Carolina	OF	81	291	52	81	18	4	13	63	1	.278
1993	Canton	Eastern	OF	89	344	67	117	32	0	17	79	2	.340
1993	Charlotte	Int.	OF	40	145	38	46	12	0	14	36	1	.317
1993	Cleveland	A.L.	DH-OF	22	53	5	9	1	0	2	5	0	.170
1994	Cleveland	A.L.	OF	91	290	51	78	22	0	17	60	4	.269
1995	Cleveland	A.L.	OF	137	484	85	149	26	1	31	107	6	.308
1996	Cleveland	A.L.	OF	152	550	94	170	45	3	33	112	8	.309
1997	Cleveland	A.L.	OF	150	561	99	184	40	0	26	88	2	.328
1998	Cleveland	A.L.	OF	150	571	108	168	35	2	45	145	5	.294
1999	Cleveland	A.L.	OF	147	522	131	174	34	3	44	*165	2	.333
2000	Akron	Eastern	PH	1	2	1	1	0	0	1	2	0	.500
2000	Buffalo	Int.	PH	5	11	5	5	1	0	3	7	0	.455
2000	Cleveland b-c	A.L.	OF	118	439	92	154	34	2	38	122	1	.351
2001	Boston	A.L.	DH-OF	142	529	93	162	33	2	41	125	0	.306
2002	Pawtucket	Int.	OF	11	30	2	3	1	0	1	2	0	.100
2002	Boston d	A.L.	OF	120	436	84	152	31	0	33	107	0	*.349
2003	Boston	A.L.	OF	154	569	117	185	36	1	37	104	3	.325
2004	Boston	A.L.	OF	152	568	108	175	44	0	*43	130	2	.308
2005	Boston	A.L.	OF	152	554	112	162	30	1	45	144	1	.292
2006	Boston	A.L.	OF	130	449	79	144	27	1	35	102	0	.321
2007	Boston	A.L.	OF	133	483	84	143	33	1	20	88	0	.296
2008	Boston	A.L.	OF	100	365	66	109	22	1	20	68	1	.299
2008	Los Angeles e-f-g.	N.L.	OF	53	187	36	74	14	0	17	53	2	.396
2009	Inland Empire.	Calif.	OF	3	7	2	3	0	0	1	1	0	.429
2009	Albuquerque.	P.C.	OF	2	3	0	0	0	0	0	0	0	.000
2009	Los Angeles	N.L.	OF	104	352	62	102	24	2	19	63	0	.290

Year Club	Lea	Pos	G	AB	R	H	2B	3B	HR	RBI	SB	Avg
2010 Inland Empire	Calif.	OF	8	19	1	2	0	0	0	1	0	.105
2010 Los Angeles	N.L.	OF	66	196	32	61	15	0	8	40	1	.311
2010 Chicago h-i-j	A.L.	DH	24	69	6	18	1	0	1	2	0	.261
Major League Totals		18 Yrs.	2297	8227	1544	2573	547	20	555	1830	38	.313
Division Series												
1995 Cleveland	A.L.	OF	3	12	1	0	0	0	0	0	0	.000
1996 Cleveland	A.L.	OF	4	16	4	6	2	0	2	2	0	.375
1997 Cleveland	A.L.	OF	5	21	2	3	1	0	0	3	0	.143
1998 Cleveland	A.L.	OF	4	14	2	5	2	0	2	3	0	.357
1999 Cleveland	A.L.	OF	5	18	5	1	1	0	0	1	0	.056
2003 Boston	A.L.	OF	5	20	2	4	0	0	1	3	0	.200
2004 Boston	A.L.	OF	3	13	3	5	2	0	1	7	0	.385
2005 Boston	A.L.	OF	3	10	2	3	0	0	2	4	0	.300
2007 Boston	A.L.	OF	3	8	3	3	0	0	2	4	0	.375
2008 Los Angeles	N.L.	OF	3	10	5	5	0	0	2	3	0	.500
2009 Los Angeles	N.L.	OF	3	13	0	4	3	0	0	2	0	.308
Division Series Totals			41	155	29	39	11	0	12	32	0	.252
Championship Series												
1995 Cleveland	A.L.	OF	6	21	2	6	0	0	2	2	0	.286
1997 Cleveland	A.L.	OF	6	21	3	6	1	0	2	3	0	.286
1998 Cleveland	A.L.	OF	6	21	2	7	1	0	2	4	0	.333
2003 Boston	A.L.	OF	7	29	6	9	1	0	2	4	0	.310
2004 Boston	A.L.	OF	7	30	3	9	1	0	0	0	0	.300
2007 Boston	A.L.	OF	7	22	5	9	1	0	2	10	0	.409
2008 Los Angeles	N.L.	OF	5	15	4	8	2	0	2	7	0	.533
2009 Los Angeles	N.L.	OF	5	19	3	5	0	0	1	2	0	.263
Championship Series Totals			49	178	28	59	7	0	13	32	0	.331
World Series Record												
1995 Cleveland	A.L.	OF	6	18	2	4	0	0	1	2	1	.222
1997 Cleveland	A.L.	OF	7	26	3	4	0	0	2	6	0	.154
2004 Boston	A.L.	OF	4	17	2	7	0	0	1	4	0	.412
2007 Boston	A.L.	OF	4	16	3	4	1	0	0	2	0	.250
World Series Totals			21	77	10	19	1	0	4	14	1	.247

a On disabled list from July 10 to end of 1992 season.
b On disabled list from May 30 to July 12, 2000.
c Filed for free agency, October 27, 2000. Signed with Boston Red Sox, December 13, 2000.
d On disabled list from May 14 to June 25, 2002.
e Traded to Pittsburgh Pirates with outfielder Brandon Moss and pitcher Craig Hansen for outfielder Jason Bay, July 31, 2008.
f Traded to Los Angeles Dodgers for infielder Andy LaRoche and pitcher Bryan Morris, July 31, 2008.
g Filed for free agency, October 30, 2008, re-signed with Los Angeles Dodgers, March 4, 2009.
h On disabled list from April 23 to May 8 and June 30 to July 14 and July 16 to August 21, 2010.
i Claimed on waivers by Chicago White Sox, August 30, 2010.
j Filed for free agency, November 1, 2010.

RASMUS, COLBY RYAN

Born, Columbus, Georgia, August 11, 1986.
Bats Left. Throws Left. Height, 6 feet, 2 inches. Weight, 200 pounds.

Year Club	Lea	Pos	G	AB	R	H	2B	3B	HR	RBI	SB	Avg
2005 Johnson City	Appal.	OF	62	216	47	64	16	5	7	27	13	.296
2006 Palm Beach	Fla.St.	OF	53	193	22	49	4	5	5	35	11	.254
2006 Quad Cities	Midwest	OF	78	303	49	94	22	3	11	50	17	.310
2007 Springfield	Texas	OF	128	472	93	130	37	3	29	72	18	.275
2008 Palm Beach	Fla.St.	OF	3	9	1	0	0	0	0	0	0	.000
2008 Cardinals	Gulf Coast	OF	3	9	1	5	1	0	1	2	0	.556
2008 Memphis	P.C.	OF	90	331	56	83	15	0	11	36	15	.251
2009 St. Louis	N.L.	OF	147	474	72	119	22	2	16	52	3	.251
2010 St. Louis	N.L.	OF	144	464	85	128	28	3	23	66	12	.276
Major League Totals		2 Yrs.	291	938	157	247	50	5	39	118	15	.263
Division Series												
2009 St. Louis	N.L.	OF	3	9	1	4	3	0	0	1	0	.444

RENTERIA, EDGAR ENRIQUE

Born, Barranquilla, Colombia, August 7, 1976.
Bats Right. Throws Right. Height, 6 feet, 1 inch. Weight, 200 pounds.

Year Club	Lea	Pos	G	AB	R	H	2B	3B	HR	RBI	SB	Avg
1992 Marlins	Gulf Coast	SS	43	163	25	47	8	1	0	9	10	.288

Year Club	Lea	Pos	G	AB	R	H	2B	3B	HR	RBI	SB	Avg
1993 Kane County.......	Midwest	SS	116	384	40	78	8	0	1	35	7	.203
1994 Brevard Cty	Fla. St.	SS	128	439	46	111	15	1	0	36	6	.253
1995 Portland	Eastern	SS	135	508	70	147	15	7	7	68	30	.289
1996 Charlotte	Int.	SS	35	132	17	37	8	0	2	16	10	.280
1996 Florida a.............	N.L.	SS	106	431	68	133	18	3	5	31	16	.309
1997 Florida	N.L.	SS	154	617	90	171	21	3	4	52	32	.277
1998 Florida b-c	N.L.	SS	133	517	79	146	18	2	3	31	41	.282
1999 St. Louis.............	N.L.	SS	154	585	92	161	36	2	11	63	37	.275
2000 St. Louis.............	N.L.	SS	150	562	94	156	32	1	16	76	21	.278
2001 St. Louis.............	N.L.	SS-1B	141	493	54	128	19	3	10	57	17	.260
2002 St. Louis.............	N.L.	SS	152	544	77	166	36	2	11	83	22	.305
2003 St. Louis.............	N.L.	SS	157	587	96	194	47	1	13	100	34	.330
2004 St. Louis d	N.L.	SS	149	586	84	168	37	0	10	72	17	.287
2005 Boston e.............	A.L.	SS	153	623	100	172	36	4	8	70	9	.276
2006 Atlanta	N.L.	SS	149	598	100	175	40	2	14	70	17	.293
2007 Atlanta f-g	N.L.	SS	124	494	87	164	30	1	12	57	11	.332
2008 Detroit h.............	A.L.	SS	138	503	69	136	22	2	10	55	6	.270
2009 San Francisco	N.L.	SS	124	460	50	115	19	1	5	48	7	.250
2010 Fresno	P.C.	SS	2	4	2	3	0	0	0	3	0	.750
2010 San Francisco i-j	N.L.	SS	72	243	26	67	11	2	3	22	3	.276
Major League Totals		15 Yrs.	2056	7843	1166	2252	422	29	135	887	290	.287
Division Series												
1997 Florida	N.L.	SS	3	13	1	2	0	0	0	1	0	.154
2000 St. Louis.............	N.L.	SS	3	10	5	2	0	0	0	0	2	.200
2001 St. Louis.............	N.L.	SS	5	17	2	4	1	0	1	1	0	.235
2002 St. Louis.............	N.L.	SS	3	12	3	3	0	0	0	0	2	.250
2004 St. Louis.............	N.L.	SS	4	11	4	5	2	0	0	4	1	.455
2005 Boston	A.L.	SS	3	13	1	3	2	0	0	0	0	.231
2010 San Francisco	N.L.	SS	2	2	0	2	0	0	0	0	0	1.000
Division Series Totals			23	78	16	21	5	0	1	6	5	.269
Championship Series												
1997 Florida	N.L.	SS	6	22	4	5	1	0	0	0	1	.227
2000 St. Louis.............	N.L.	SS	5	20	4	6	1	0	0	4	3	.300
2002 St. Louis.............	N.L.	SS	5	19	0	3	0	0	0	1	0	.158
2004 St. Louis.............	N.L.	SS	7	24	1	4	0	0	0	2	0	.167
2010 San Francisco	N.L.	SS	4	16	1	1	0	0	0	0	0	.063
Championship Series Totals			27	101	10	19	2	0	0	7	4	.188
World Series Record												
1997 Florida	N.L.	SS	7	31	3	9	2	0	0	3	0	.290
2004 St. Louis.............	N.L.	SS	4	15	2	5	3	0	0	1	0	.333
2010 San Francisco	N.L.	SS	5	17	6	7	0	0	2	6	0	.412
World Series Totals.............			16	63	11	21	5	0	2	10	0	.333

a On disabled list from June 24 to July 11, 1996
b On disabled list from August 25 to September 9, 1998.
c Traded to St. Louis Cardinals for infielder Pablo Ozuna, pitcher Armando Almanza and pitcher Braden Looper, December 14, 1998.
d Filed for free agency, October 29, 2004. Signed with Boston Red Sox, December 17, 2004.
e Traded to Atlanta Braves with cash for infielder Andy Marte, December 7, 2005.
f On disabled list from August 3 to August 22 and from August 23 to September 7, 2007.
g Traded to Detroit Tigers for pitcher Jair Jurrjens and outfielder Gorkys Hernandez, October 29, 2007.
h Not offered contract, October 30, 2008. Signed with San Francisco Giants, December 4, 2008.
i On disabled list from May 7 to May 22 and May 26 to June 16 and August 11 to September 1, 2010.
j Filed for free agency, November 4, 2010. Signed with Cincinnati Reds, January 10, 2011.

REYES, JOSE BERNABE

Born, Villa Gonzalez, Dominican Republic, June 11, 1983.
Bats Both. Throws Right. Height, 6 feet. Weight, 200 pounds.

Year Club	Lea	Pos	G	AB	R	H	2B	3B	HR	RBI	SB	Avg
2000 Kingsport	Appal.	SS-3B-2B-OF	49	132	22	33	3	3	0	8	10	.250
2001 Columbia	So.Atl.	SS	108	407	71	125	22	15	5	48	30	.307
2002 Binghamton	Eastern	SS	65	275	46	79	16	8	2	24	27	.287
2002 St. Lucie.........	Fla.St.	SS	69	288	58	83	10	11	6	38	31	.288
2003 Norfolk...........	Int.	SS	42	160	28	43	6	4	0	13	26	.269
2003 New York a........	N.L.	SS	69	274	47	84	12	4	5	32	13	.307
2004 St. Lucie.........	Fla.St.	2B	6	23	3	6	2	0	0	1	2	.261
2004 Binghamton	Eastern	2B	4	18	2	2	0	0	0	3	3	.111
2004 New York b........	N.L.	2B-SS	53	220	33	56	16	2	2	14	19	.255
2005 New York..........	N.L.	SS	161	*696	99	190	24	*17	7	58	*60	.273

Year	Club	Lea	Pos	G	AB	R	H	2B	3B	HR	RBI	SB	Avg
2006	New York	N.L.	SS	153	647	*122	194	30	17	19	81	*64	.300
2007	New York	N.L.	SS	160	681	119	191	36	12	12	57	*78	.280
2008	New York	N.L.	SS	159	*688	113	*204	37	*19	16	68	56	.297
2009	New York c	N.L.	SS	36	147	18	41	7	2	2	15	11	.279
2010	St. Lucie	Fla.St.	SS	1	4	0	0	0	0	0	1	0	.000
2010	New York d	N.L.	SS	133	563	83	159	29	10	11	54	30	.282
Major League Totals			8 Yrs.	924	3916	634	1119	191	83	74	379	331	.286
	Division Series												
2006	New York	N.L.	SS	3	12	2	2	0	0	0	3	1	.167
	Championship Series												
2006	New York	N.L.	SS	7	32	5	9	1	1	1	2	2	.281

a On disabled list from September 1 to November 6, 2003.
b On disabled list from March 26 to June 19 and August 12 to September 24, 2004.
c On disabled list from May 21 to October 14, 2009.
d On disabled list from March 26 to April 8, 2010.

REYNOLDS, MARK ANDREW

Born, Pikeville, Kentucky, August 3, 1983.
Bats Right. Throws Right. Height, 6 feet, 1 inch. Weight, 220 pounds.

Year	Club	Lea	Pos	G	AB	R	H	2B	3B	HR	RBI	SB	Avg
2004	Lancaster	Calif.	3B-SS	4	12	1	1	0	0	0	1	0	.083
2004	South Bend	Midwest	3B	4	15	0	1	1	0	0	0	0	.067
2004	Yakima	Northwest	SS-3B-2B	64	234	58	64	19	1	12	41	5	.274
2005	South Bend	Midwest	SS-3B	118	434	65	110	26	2	19	76	4	.253
2006	Lancaster	Calif.	SS-3B-2B-1B	76	273	64	92	18	2	23	77	1	.337
2006	Tennessee	Southern	OF-3B-2B	30	114	23	31	7	0	8	21	0	.272
2007	Mobile	Southern	3B-2B	37	134	28	41	9	2	6	22	2	.306
2007	Arizona	N.L.	3B-2B-OF	111	366	62	102	20	4	17	62	0	.279
2008	Arizona	N.L.	3B-1B	152	539	87	129	28	3	28	97	11	.239
2009	Arizona	N.L.	3B-1B	155	578	98	150	30	1	44	102	24	.260
2010	Arizona a	N.L.	3B-1B	145	499	79	99	17	2	32	85	7	.198
Major League Totals			4 Yrs.	563	1982	326	480	95	10	121	346	42	.242
	Division Series												
2007	Arizona	N.L.	3B	3	10	2	2	0	0	1	1	0	.200
	Championship Series												
2007	Arizona	N.L.	3B	4	16	1	2	0	0	1	1	0	.125

a Traded to Baltimore Orioles with player to be named later for pitcher Kam Mickolio and pitcher David Hernandez, December 6, 2010.

RHYMES, WILLIAM DANIEL (WILL)

Born, Houston, Texas, April 1, 1983.
Bats Left. Throws Right. Height, 5 feet, 9 inches. Weight, 155 pounds.

Year	Club	Lea	Pos	G	AB	R	H	2B	3B	HR	RBI	SB	Avg
2005	Oneonta	N.Y.-Penn.	2B	61	250	48	82	11	3	2	27	14	.328
2006	West Michigan	Midwest	2B	126	506	80	132	19	2	3	39	23	.261
2007	Erie	Eastern	2B	39	155	21	41	6	0	1	21	5	.265
2007	Lakeland	Fla.St.	2B-SS	88	326	43	99	12	2	4	35	24	.304
2008	Erie	Eastern	2B-SS-3B	131	516	76	158	21	7	3	60	17	.306
2008	Toledo	Int.	2B	6	25	5	8	0	1	0	2	0	.320
2009	Toledo	Int.	2B-3B-SS-OF	109	404	48	105	17	6	3	41	20	.260
2010	Toledo	Int.	2B-3B-SS-OF	95	364	59	111	20	7	2	35	22	.305
2010	Detroit	A.L.	2B	54	191	30	58	12	3	1	19	0	.304

RIOS, ALEXIS ISRAEL

Born, Coffee County, Alabama, February 18, 1981.
Bats Right. Throws Right. Height, 6 feet, 5 inches. Weight, 195 pounds.

Year	Club	Lea	Pos	G	AB	R	H	2B	3B	HR	RBI	SB	Avg
1999	Medicine Hat	Pioneer	OF	67	234	35	63	7	3	0	13	8	.269
2000	Hagerstown	So.Atl.	DH	22	74	5	17	3	1	0	5	2	.230
2000	Queens	N.Y.-Penn.	OF	50	206	22	55	9	2	1	25	5	.267
2001	Charleston-W.V.	So.Atl.	OF	130	480	40	126	20	9	2	58	22	.262
2002	Dunedin	Fla.St.	OF	111	456	60	139	22	8	3	61	14	.305
2003	New Haven	Eastern	OF	127	514	86	181	32	11	11	82	11	.352
2004	Syracuse	Int.	OF	46	185	14	48	10	1	3	23	2	.259
2004	Toronto	A.L.	OF	111	426	55	122	24	7	1	28	15	.286
2005	Toronto	A.L.	OF	146	481	71	126	23	6	10	59	14	.262

Year	Club	Lea	Pos	G	AB	R	H	2B	3B	HR	RBI	SB	Avg
2006	Syracuse	Int.	OF	3	10	0	3	1	0	0	1	0	.300
2006	Toronto a	A.L.	OF	128	450	68	136	33	6	17	82	15	.302
2007	Toronto	A.L.	OF	161	643	114	191	43	7	24	85	17	.297
2008	Toronto	A.L.	OF	155	635	91	185	47	8	15	79	32	.291
2009	Toronto-Chicago b	A.L.	OF	149	582	63	144	31	2	17	71	24	.247
2010	Chicago	A.L.	OF	147	567	89	161	29	3	21	88	34	.284
Major League Totals			7 Yrs.	997	3784	551	1065	230	39	105	492	151	.281

a On disabled list from June 28 to July 28, 2006.
b Claimed on waivers by Chicago White Sox, August 10, 2009.

RIVERA, JUAN LUIS

Born, Guarenas, Venezuela, July 3, 1978.
Bats Right. Throws Right. Height, 6 feet, 2 inches. Weight, 225 pounds.

Year	Club	Lea	Pos	G	AB	R	H	2B	3B	HR	RBI	SB	Avg
1996	NY Yankees	Dominican	OF	10	18	0	3	0	0	0	2	0	.167
1997	Maracay-2	Venzuelan	OF	52	142	25	40	9	0	0	14	12	.282
1998	Yankees	Gulf Coast	OF	57	210	43	70	9	1	12	45	8	.333
1998	Oneonta	N.Y.-Penn.	OF	6	18	2	5	0	0	1	3	1	.278
1999	Tampa	Fla.St.	OF	109	427	50	112	20	2	14	77	5	.262
1999	Yankees	Gulf Coast	OF	5	18	7	6	0	0	1	4	0	.333
2000	Norwich	Eastern	OF	17	62	9	14	5	0	2	12	0	.226
2000	Tampa	Fla.St.	OF-1B	115	409	62	113	26	1	14	69	11	.276
2001	Norwich	Eastern	OF	77	316	50	101	18	3	14	58	5	.320
2001	Columbus	Int.	OF	55	199	39	65	11	1	14	40	4	.327
2001	New York	A.L.	OF	3	4	0	0	0	0	0	0	0	.000
2002	Columbus	Int.	OF	65	265	40	86	21	1	8	47	5	.325
2002	New York a	A.L.	OF	28	83	9	22	5	0	1	6	1	.265
2003	Columbus	Int.	OF	79	308	47	100	21	0	7	37	1	.325
2003	New York b	A.L.	OF	57	173	22	46	14	0	7	26	0	.266
2004	Montreal c	N.L.	OF	134	391	48	120	24	1	12	49	6	.307
2005	Los Angeles	A.L.	OF	106	350	46	95	17	1	15	59	1	.271
2006	Salt Lake	P.C.	OF	2	9	3	5	3	0	1	6	0	.556
2006	Los Angeles d	A.L.	OF	124	448	65	139	27	0	23	85	0	.310
2007	Rancho Cucamonga	Calif.	OF	3	10	3	4	1	0	0	2	0	.400
2007	Salt Lake	P.C.	OF	15	61	4	16	8	0	0	17	0	.262
2007	Los Angeles e	A.L.	OF	14	43	3	12	1	0	2	8	0	.279
2008	Los Angeles f	A.L.	OF-1B-2B	89	256	31	63	13	0	12	45	1	.246
2009	Los Angeles	A.L.	OF	138	529	72	152	24	1	25	88	0	.287
2010	Los Angeles	A.L.	OF-1B	124	416	53	105	20	0	15	52	2	.252
Major League Totals			10 Yrs.	817	2693	349	754	145	3	112	418	11	.280
	Division Series												
2002	New York	A.L.	OF	4	12	2	3	0	0	0	3	0	.250
2003	New York	A.L.	OF	4	12	2	4	0	0	0	0	0	.333
2005	Los Angeles	A.L.	DH	5	17	3	6	1	0	1	1	0	.353
2007	Los Angeles	A.L.	DH	2	3	0	1	0	0	0	0	0	.333
2008	Los Angeles	A.L.	OF	3	8	1	1	0	0	0	1	0	.125
2009	Los Angeles	A.L.	OF	3	11	1	3	1	0	0	2	1	.273
Division Series Totals				21	63	9	18	2	0	1	7	1	.286
	Championship Series												
2003	New York	A.L.	OF	2	2	0	0	0	0	0	0	0	.000
2005	Los Angeles	A.L.	OF-DH	3	9	1	1	1	0	0	0	0	.111
2009	Los Angeles	A.L.	OF	6	25	0	5	1	0	0	0	0	.200
Championship Series Totals				11	36	1	6	2	0	0	0	0	.167
	World Series Record												
2003	New York	A.L.	OF	4	6	0	1	1	0	0	1	0	.167

a On disabled list from June 8 to August 19, 2002.
b Traded to Montreal Expos with infielder Nick Johnson and pitcher Randy Choate for pitcher Javier Vazquez, December 4, 2003.
c Traded to Anaheim Angels with infielder Maicer Izturis for outfielder Jose Guillen, November 19, 2004.
d On disabled list from April 17 to May 8, 2006.
e On disabled list from March 23 to September 2, 2007.
f Filed for free agency, October 31, 2008, re-signed with Los Angeles Angels, December 19, 2008.

ROBERTS, BRIAN MICHAEL

Born, Durham, North Carolina, October 9, 1977.
Bats Both. Throws Right. Height, 5 feet, 9 inches. Weight, 175 pounds.

Year	Club	Lea	Pos	G	AB	R	H	2B	3B	HR	RBI	SB	Avg
1999	Delmarva a	So.Atl.	SS	47	167	22	40	12	1	0	21	17	.240
2000	Frederick	Carolina	SS	48	163	27	49	6	3	0	16	13	.301
2000	Orioles b	Gulf Coast	SS	9	29	8	9	1	2	1	3	7	.310
2001	Bowie	Eastern	2B-SS	22	81	12	24	7	0	1	7	10	.296
2001	Rochester	Int.	SS	44	161	16	43	4	1	1	12	23	.267
2001	Baltimore	A.L.	SS-2B	75	273	42	69	12	3	2	17	12	.253
2002	Rochester	Int.	2B	78	313	49	86	9	7	3	30	22	.275
2002	Baltimore	A.L.	2B	38	128	18	29	6	0	1	11	9	.227
2003	Ottawa	Int.	2B-SS	44	178	36	56	13	1	0	15	19	.315
2003	Baltimore	A.L.	2B-SS	112	460	65	124	22	4	5	41	23	.270
2004	Baltimore	A.L.	2B	159	641	107	175	*50	2	4	53	29	.273
2005	Baltimore	A.L.	2B	143	561	92	176	45	7	18	73	27	.314
2006	Bowie	Eastern	2B	2	5	0	1	0	0	0	0	0	.200
2006	Baltimore c	A.L.	2B	138	563	85	161	34	3	10	55	36	.286
2007	Baltimore	A.L.	2B	156	621	103	180	42	5	12	57	*50	.290
2008	Baltimore	A.L.	2B	155	611	107	181	51	8	9	57	40	.296
2009	Baltimore	A.L.	2B	159	632	110	179	*56	1	16	79	30	.283
2010	Orioles	Gulf Coast	2B	5	15	1	8	1	0	0	0	0	.533
2010	Bowie	Eastern	2B	3	14	3	6	2	0	0	3	0	.429
2010	Baltimore d	A.L.	2B	59	230	28	64	14	0	4	15	12	.278
Major League Totals			10 Yrs.	1194	4720	757	1338	332	33	81	458	268	.283

a Drafted by Baltimore Orioles with choice received for Texas Rangers signing infielder Rafael Palmeiro, June 2, 1999.
b On disabled list from April 19 to July 13, 2000.
c On disabled list from April 30 to May 24, 2006.
d On disabled list from April 10 to July 23, 2010.

RODRIGUEZ, ALEXANDER EMMANUEL (ALEX)

Born, New York, New York, July 27, 1975.
Bats Right. Throws Right. Height, 6 feet, 3 inches. Weight, 225 pounds.

Year	Club	Lea	Pos	G	AB	R	H	2B	3B	HR	RBI	SB	Avg
1994	Appleton	Midwest	SS	65	248	49	79	17	6	14	55	16	.319
1994	Jacksonville	Southern	SS	17	59	7	17	4	1	1	8	2	.288
1994	Seattle	A.L.	SS	17	54	4	11	0	0	0	2	3	.204
1994	Calgary	P.C.	SS	32	119	22	37	7	4	6	21	2	.311
1995	Tacoma	P.C.	SS	54	214	37	77	12	3	15	45	2	.360
1995	Seattle	A.L.	SS	48	142	15	33	6	2	5	19	4	.232
1996	Tacoma a	P.C.	SS	2	5	0	1	0	0	0	0	0	.200
1996	Seattle	A.L.	SS	146	601	*141	215	*54	1	36	123	15	*.358
1997	Seattle b	A.L.	SS	141	587	100	176	40	3	23	84	29	.300
1998	Seattle	A.L.	SS	161	*686	123	*213	35	5	42	124	46	.310
1999	Seattle c	A.L.	SS	129	502	110	143	25	0	42	111	21	.285
2000	Seattle d-e	A.L.	SS	148	554	134	175	34	2	41	132	15	.316
2001	Texas	A.L.	SS	*162	632	*133	201	34	1	*52	135	18	.318
2002	Texas	A.L.	SS	*162	624	125	187	27	2	*57	*142	9	.300
2003	Texas	A.L.	SS	161	607	*124	181	30	6	*47	118	17	.298
2004	New York f-g	A.L.	3B-SS	155	601	112	172	24	2	36	106	28	.286
2005	New York h	A.L.	3B-SS	*162	605	*124	194	29	1	*48	130	21	.321
2006	New York	A.L.	3B	154	572	113	166	26	1	35	121	15	.290
2007	New York i-j	A.L.	3B	158	583	*143	183	31	0	*54	*156	24	.314
2008	New York k	A.L.	3B	138	510	104	154	33	0	35	103	18	.302
2009	New York l	A.L.	3B	124	444	78	127	17	1	30	100	14	.286
2010	New York m	A.L.	3B	137	522	74	141	29	2	30	125	4	.270
Major League Totals			17 Yrs.	2303	8826	1757	2672	474	29	613	1831	301	.303
	Division Series												
1995	Seattle	A.L.	SS	1	1	1	0	0	0	0	0	0	.000
1997	Seattle	A.L.	SS	4	16	1	5	1	0	1	1	0	.313
2000	Seattle	A.L.	SS	3	13	0	4	0	0	0	2	0	.308
2004	New York	A.L.	3B	4	19	3	8	3	0	1	3	2	.421
2005	New York	A.L.	3B	5	15	2	2	1	0	0	0	1	.133
2006	New York	A.L.	3B	4	14	0	1	0	0	0	0	0	.071
2007	New York	A.L.	3B	4	15	2	4	0	0	1	1	0	.267
2009	New York	A.L.	3B	3	11	4	5	0	0	2	6	0	.455
2010	New York	A.L.	3B	3	11	1	3	0	0	0	1	1	.273
Division Series Totals				31	115	14	32	5	0	5	14	4	.278
	Championship Series												
1995	Seattle	A.L.	PH	1	1	0	0	0	0	0	0	0	.000

Year Club	Lea	Pos	G	AB	R	H	2B	3B	HR	RBI	SB	Avg
2000 Seattle	A.L.	SS	6	22	4	9	2	0	2	5	1	.409
2004 New York	A.L.	3B	7	31	8	8	2	0	2	5	0	.258
2009 New York	A.L.	3B	6	21	6	9	2	0	3	6	1	.429
2010 New York	A.L.	3B	6	21	4	4	2	0	0	2	1	.190
Championship Series Totals			26	96	22	30	8	0	7	18	3	.313
World Series Record												
2009 New York	A.L.	3B	6	20	5	5	3	0	1	6	1	.250

a On disabled list from April 22 to May 7, 1996.
b On disabled list from June 12 to June 27, 1997.
c On disabled list from April 7 to May 14, 1999.
d On disabled list from July 8 to July 23, 2000.
e Filed for free agency, October 30, 2000. Signed with Texas Rangers, December 11, 2000.
f Traded to New York Yankees for infielder Alfonso Soriano and player to be named later, February 16, 2004.
g Texas Rangers received infielder Joaquin Arias to complete trade, March 23, 2004.
h Selected Most Valuable Player in American League for 2005.
i Filed for free agency, October 29, 2007, re-signed with New York Yankees, December 13, 2007.
j Selected Most Valuable Player in American League for 2007.
k On disabled list from April 30 to May 20, 2008.
l On disabled list from March 27 to May 8, 2009.
m On disabled list from August 21 to September 5, 2010.

RODRIGUEZ (TORRES), IVAN

Born, Manati, Puerto Rico, November 27, 1971.
Bats Right. Throws Right. Height, 5 feet, 9 inches. Weight, 195 pounds.

Year Club	Lea	Pos	G	AB	R	H	2B	3B	HR	RBI	SB	Avg
1989 Gastonia	So. Atl.	C	112	386	38	92	22	1	7	42	2	.238
1990 Charlotte	Fla. St.	C	109	408	48	117	17	7	2	55	1	.287
1991 Tulsa	Texas	C	50	175	16	48	7	2	3	28	1	.274
1991 Texas	A.L.	C	88	280	24	74	16	0	3	27	0	.264
1992 Texas a	A.L.	C	123	420	39	109	16	1	8	37	0	.260
1993 Texas	A.L.	C	137	473	56	129	28	4	10	66	8	.273
1994 Texas	A.L.	C	99	363	56	108	19	1	16	57	6	.298
1995 Texas	A.L.	C	130	492	56	149	32	2	12	67	0	.303
1996 Texas	A.L.	C	153	639	116	192	47	3	19	86	5	.300
1997 Texas	A.L.	C	150	597	98	187	34	4	20	77	7	.313
1998 Texas	A.L.	C	145	579	88	186	40	4	21	91	9	.321
1999 Texas b	A.L.	C	144	600	116	199	29	1	35	113	25	.332
2000 Texas c	A.L.	C	91	363	66	126	27	4	27	83	5	.347
2001 Texas d	A.L.	C	111	442	70	136	24	2	25	65	10	.308
2002 Charlotte	Fla.St.	C	3	9	1	3	0	0	0	0	0	.333
2002 Texas e-f	A.L.	C	108	408	67	128	32	2	19	60	5	.314
2003 Florida g	N.L.	C	144	511	90	152	36	3	16	85	10	.297
2004 Detroit	A.L.	C	135	527	72	176	32	2	19	86	7	.334
2005 Detroit	A.L.	C	129	504	71	139	33	5	14	50	7	.276
2006 Detroit	A.L.	C-1B-2B	136	547	74	164	28	4	13	69	8	.300
2007 Detroit	A.L.	C	129	502	50	141	31	3	11	63	2	.281
2008 Detroit-New York h-i	A.L.	C	115	398	44	110	20	3	7	35	10	.276
2009 Houston	N.L.	C	93	327	41	82	15	2	8	34	0	.251
2009 Texas j-k	A.L.	C	28	98	14	24	8	0	2	13	1	.245
2010 Potomac	Carolina	C	1	3	0	0	0	0	0	0	0	.000
2010 Washington l	N.L.	C	111	398	32	106	18	1	4	49	2	.266
Major League Totals		20 Yrs.	2499	9468	1340	2817	565	51	309	1313	127	.298
Division Series												
1996 Texas	A.L.	C	4	16	1	6	1	0	0	2	0	.375
1998 Texas	A.L.	C	3	10	0	1	0	0	0	1	0	.100
1999 Texas	A.L.	C	3	12	0	3	1	0	0	0	1	.250
2003 Florida	N.L.	C	4	17	3	6	1	0	1	6	0	.353
2006 Detroit	A.L.	C	4	13	3	3	1	0	0	3	0	.231
Division Series Totals			18	68	7	19	4	0	1	12	1	.279
Championship Series												
2003 Florida	N.L.	C	7	28	5	9	2	0	2	10	0	.321
2006 Detroit	A.L.	C	4	16	2	2	0	0	1	1	0	.125
Championship Series Totals			11	44	7	11	2	0	3	11	0	.250
World Series Record												
2003 Florida	N.L.	C	6	22	2	6	2	0	0	1	0	.273
2006 Detroit	A.L.	C	5	19	1	3	1	0	0	1	0	.158
World Series Totals			11	41	3	9	3	0	0	2	0	.220

a On disabled list from June 6 to June 27, 1992.

b Selected Most Valuable Player in American League for 1999.
c On disabled list from July 25 to October 1, 2000.
d On disabled list from May 2 to May 17 and August 31 to November 19, 2001.
e On disabled list from April 17 to June 7, 2002.
f Filed for free agency, October 28, 2002. Signed with Florida Marlins, January 24, 2003
g Filed for free agency, November 2, 2003. Signed with Detroit Tigers, February 2, 2004.
h Traded to New York Yankees for pitcher Kyle Farnsworth, July 30, 2008.
i Filed for free agency, October 30, 2008. Signed with Houston Astros, March 20, 2009.
j Traded to Texas Rangers for pitcher Matt Nevarez, and player to be named later, August 18, 2009. Houston Astros received infielder Jose Vallejo to complete trade, August 20, 2009.
k Filed for free agency, November 5, 2009. Signed with Washington Nationals, December 11, 2009.
l On disabled list from May 23 to June 8, 2010.

RODRIGUEZ, SEAN JOHN

Born, Miami, Florida, April 26, 1985.
Bats Right. Throws Right. Height, 6 feet, 1 inch. Weight, 215 pounds.

Year Club	Lea	Pos	G	AB	R	H	2B	3B	HR	RBI	SB	Avg
2003 Angels	Arizona	SS-3B-2B-OF	54	216	30	58	8	5	2	25	11	.269
2004 Cedar Rapids ..	Midwest	2B-OF-3B-SS	57	196	35	49	8	4	4	17	14	.250
2004 Provo	Pioneer	SS-OF	64	225	64	76	14	4	10	55	9	.338
2005 Cedar Rapids ..	Midwest	SS-3B-OF-2B	124	448	86	112	29	3	14	45	27	.250
2006 Rancho Cucamonga ..	Calif.	SS-OF	116	455	78	137	29	5	24	77	15	.301
2006 Salt Lake	P.C.	SS	1	2	0	0	0	0	0	0	0	.000
2006 Arkansas	Texas	SS	18	65	16	23	5	0	5	9	0	.354
2007 Arkansas	Texas	SS-OF	136	508	84	129	31	2	17	73	15	.254
2008 Salt Lake	P.C.	2B-SS-OF	66	248	68	76	19	1	21	52	4	.306
2008 Los Angeles	A.L.	2B-SS-3B	59	167	18	34	8	1	3	10	3	.204
2009 Los Angeles	A.L.	OF-2B	12	25	4	5	0	0	2	4	0	.200
2009 Salt Lake	P.C.	2B-SS-OF	103	365	81	109	17	6	29	93	9	.299
2009 Durham a.........	Int.	2B-3B	5	20	6	4	2	0	1	5	0	.200
2010 Tampa Bay........	A.L.	2B-OF-3B-SS	118	343	53	86	19	2	9	40	13	.251
Major League Totals		3 Yrs.	189	535	75	125	27	3	14	54	16	.234
Division Series												
2010 Tampa Bay........	N.L.	2B	4	10	2	2	0	0	0	0	0	.200

a Sent to Tampa Bay Rays as player to be named later for pitcher Scott Kazmir, September 1, 2009.

ROLEN, SCOTT BRUCE

Born, Evansville, Indiana, April 4, 1975.
Bats Right. Throws Right. Height, 6 feet, 4 inches. Weight, 240 pounds.

Year Club	Lea	Pos	G	AB	R	H	2B	3B	HR	RBI	SB	Avg
1993 Martinsville	Appal.	3B	25	80	8	25	5	0	0	12	3	.313
1994 Spartanburg.........	So.Atl.	3B	138	513	83	151	34	5	14	72	6	.294
1995 Clearwater	Fla.St.	3B	66	238	45	69	13	2	10	39	4	.290
1995 Reading	Eastern	3B	20	76	16	22	3	0	3	15	1	.289
1996 Reading	Eastern	3B	61	230	44	83	22	2	9	42	8	.361
1996 Scranton-WB	Int.	3B	45	168	23	46	17	0	2	19	4	.274
1996 Philadelphia	N.L.	3B	37	130	10	33	7	0	4	18	0	.254
1997 Philadelphia a..........	N.L.	3B	156	561	93	159	35	3	21	92	16	.283
1998 Philadelphia	N.L.	3B	160	601	120	174	45	4	31	110	14	.290
1999 Philadelphia	N.L.	3B	112	421	74	113	28	1	26	77	12	.268
2000 Philadelphia b	N.L.	3B	128	483	88	144	32	6	26	89	8	.298
2001 Philadelphia	N.L.	3B	151	554	96	160	39	1	25	107	16	.289
2002 Philadelphia-St. Louis c .	N.L.	3B	155	580	89	154	29	8	31	110	8	.266
2003 St. Louis.............	N.L.	3B	154	559	98	160	49	1	28	104	13	.286
2004 St. Louis.............	N.L.	3B	142	500	109	157	32	4	34	124	4	.314
2005 St. Louis d	N.L.	3B	56	196	28	46	12	1	5	28	1	.235
2006 St. Louis.............	N.L.	3B	142	521	94	154	48	1	22	95	7	.296
2007 St. Louis e-f..........	N.L.	3B	112	392	55	104	24	2	8	58	5	.265
2008 Dunedin	Fla.St.	3B	3	9	0	0	0	0	0	0	0	.000
2008 Toronto g	A.L.	3B	115	408	58	107	30	3	11	50	5	.262
2009 Louisville	Int.	3B	2	6	1	2	0	0	0	1	0	.333
2009 Toronto	A.L.	3B	88	338	52	108	29	0	8	43	4	.320
2009 Cincinnati h-i	N.L.	3B	40	137	24	37	7	1	3	24	1	.270
2010 Cincinnati...........	N.L.	3B	133	471	66	134	34	3	20	83	1	.285
Major League Totals		15 Yrs.	1881	6852	1154	1944	480	39	303	1212	115	.284
Division Series												
2002 St. Louis.............	N.L.	3B	2	7	1	3	0	0	1	2	0	.429
2004 St. Louis.............	N.L.	3B	4	12	1	0	0	0	0	0	0	.000

Year	Club	Lea	Pos	G	AB	R	H	2B	3B	HR	RBI	SB	Avg
2006	St. Louis	N.L.	3B	3	11	0	1	1	0	0	0	0	.091
2010	Cincinnati	N.L.	3B	3	11	0	1	0	0	0	0	0	.091
Division Series Totals				12	41	2	5	1	0	1	2	0	.122
	Championship Series												
2004	St. Louis	N.L.	3B	7	29	6	9	2	0	3	6	0	.310
2006	St. Louis	N.L.	3B	7	21	4	5	1	0	0	0	0	.238
Championship Series Totals				14	50	10	14	3	0	3	6	0	.280
	World Series Record												
2004	St. Louis	N.L.	3B	4	15	0	0	0	0	0	1	0	.000
2006	St. Louis	N.L.	3B	5	19	5	8	3	0	1	2	0	.421
World Series Totals				9	34	5	8	3	0	1	3	0	.235

a Selected Rookie of the Year in National League for 1997.
b On disabled list from May 24 to June 8, 2000.
c Traded to St. Louis Cardinals with pitcher Doug Nickle for infielder Placido Polanco, pitcher Bud Smith and pitcher Mike Timlin, July 29, 2002.
d On disabled list from May 11 to June 18 and July 22 to October 31, 2005.
e On disabled list from August 29 to November 2, 2007.
f Traded to Toronto Blue Jays for infielder Troy Glaus, January 14, 2008.
g On disabled list from March 21 to April 25 and from August 11 to August 26, 2008.
h Traded to Cincinnati Reds for infielder Edwin Encarnacion, pitcher Josh Roenicke and pitcher Zach Stewart, July 31, 2009.
i On disabled list from August 8 to August 23, 2009.

ROLLINS, JAMES CALVIN (JIMMY)

Born, Oakland, California, November 27, 1978.
Bats Both. Throws Right. Height, 5 feet, 8 inches. Weight, 170 pounds.

Year	Club	Lea	Pos	G	AB	R	H	2B	3B	HR	RBI	SB	Avg
1996	Martinsvlle	Appal.	SS	49	172	22	41	3	1	1	16	11	.238
1997	Piedmont	So.Atl.	SS	139	560	94	151	22	8	6	59	46	.270
1998	Clearwater	Fla.St.	SS	119	495	72	121	18	9	6	35	23	.244
1999	Reading	Eastern	SS	133	532	81	145	21	8	11	56	24	.273
1999	Scranton-WB	Int.	SS	4	13	0	1	1	0	0	0	1	.077
2000	Scranton-WB	Int.	SS	133	470	67	129	28	11	12	69	24	.274
2000	Philadelphia	N.L.	SS	14	53	5	17	1	1	0	5	3	.321
2001	Philadelphia	N.L.	SS	158	*656	97	180	29	*12	14	54	*46	.274
2002	Philadelphia	N.L.	SS-2B	154	*637	82	156	33	*10	11	60	31	.245
2003	Philadelphia	N.L.	SS	156	628	85	165	42	6	8	62	20	.263
2004	Philadelphia	N.L.	SS	154	657	119	190	43	*12	14	73	30	.289
2005	Philadelphia	N.L.	SS	158	677	115	196	38	11	12	54	41	.290
2006	Philadelphia	N.L.	SS	158	689	127	191	45	9	25	83	36	.277
2007	Philadelphia a	N.L.	SS	*162	*716	*139	212	38	*20	30	94	41	.296
2008	Clearwater	Fla.St.	SS	1	3	2	0	0	0	0	0	0	.000
2008	Philadelphia b	N.L.	SS	137	556	76	154	38	9	11	59	47	.277
2009	Philadelphia	N.L.	SS	155	*672	100	168	43	5	21	77	31	.250
2010	Clearwater	Fla.St.	SS	5	14	2	2	0	0	0	2	0	.143
2010	Philadelphia c	N.L.	SS	88	350	48	85	16	3	8	41	17	.243
Major League Totals			11 Yrs.	1494	6291	993	1714	366	98	154	662	343	.272
	Division Series												
2007	Philadelphia	N.L.	SS	3	11	1	2	0	1	1	4	1	.182
2008	Philadelphia	N.L.	SS	4	16	2	6	2	0	1	1	1	.375
2009	Philadelphia	N.L.	SS	4	19	1	5	1	0	0	0	0	.263
2010	Philadelphia	N.L.	SS	3	11	1	1	0	0	0	0	0	.091
Division Series Totals				14	57	5	14	3	1	2	5	2	.246
	Championship Series												
2008	Philadelphia	N.L.	SS	5	21	4	3	0	0	1	1	2	.143
2009	Philadelphia	N.L.	SS	5	22	5	5	2	0	0	3	0	.227
2010	Philadelphia	N.L.	SS	6	23	0	6	1	0	0	4	2	.261
Championship Series Totals				16	66	9	14	3	0	1	8	4	.212
	World Series Record												
2008	Philadelphia	N.L.	SS	5	22	4	5	2	0	0	0	0	.227
2009	Philadelphia	N.L.	SS	6	23	3	5	0	0	0	2	3	.217
World Series Totals				11	45	7	10	2	0	0	2	3	.222

a Selected Most Valuable Player in National League for 2007.
b On disabled list from April 20 to May 9, 2008.
c On disabled list from April 13 to May 17 and May 22 to June 22, 2010.

ROSALES, ADAM M.

Born, Chicago, Illinois, May 20, 1983.
Bats Right. Throws Right. Height, 6 feet, 1 inch. Weight, 195 pounds.

Year	Club	Lea	Pos	G	AB	R	H	2B	3B	HR	RBI	SB	Avg
2005	Dayton	Midwest	SS	32	134	24	44	8	0	9	21	3	.328
2005	Billings	Pioneer	SS	34	140	29	45	14	0	5	25	2	.321
2006	Sarasota	Fla.St.	SS	34	122	15	26	8	2	2	14	3	.213
2006	Dayton	Midwest	SS	55	222	36	60	9	3	6	29	5	.270
2007	Sarasota	Fla.St.	1B-SS	69	248	47	73	23	5	5	48	9	.294
2007	Chattanooga	Southern	1B-3B-SS-OF	67	255	51	71	18	6	13	31	4	.278
2008	Louisville	Int.	3B-SS-1B-2B	117	432	70	124	29	7	11	58	7	.287
2008	Cincinnati	N.L.	3B-2B	18	29	0	6	1	0	0	2	1	.207
2009	Louisville	Int.	3B-SS-2B-1B	30	109	27	38	8	2	5	20	4	.349
2009	Cincinnati	N.L.	3B-1B-SS-2B	87	230	23	49	10	1	4	19	1	.213
2010	Oakland a-b	A.L.	2B-SS-1B-3B	80	255	31	69	8	2	7	31	2	.271
Major League Totals			3 Yrs.	185	514	54	124	19	3	11	52	4	.241

a Traded to Oakland Athletics with outfielder Willy Taveras for infielder Aaron Miles, February 1, 2010.
b On disabled list from August 13 to November 4, 2010.

ROSS, CODY JOSEPH

Born, Portales, New Mexico, December 23, 1980.
Bats Right. Throws Left. Height, 5 feet, 9 inches. Weight, 205 pounds.

Year	Club	Lea	Pos	G	AB	R	H	2B	3B	HR	RBI	SB	Avg
1999	Tigers	Gulf Coast	OF	42	142	19	31	8	3	4	18	3	.218
2000	West Michigan	Midwest	OF	122	434	71	116	17	9	7	68	11	.267
2001	Lakeland	Fla.St.	OF	127	482	84	133	34	5	15	80	28	.276
2002	Erie	Eastern	OF	105	400	73	112	28	3	19	72	16	.280
2003	Toledo	Int.	OF	124	470	74	135	35	6	20	61	15	.287
2003	Detroit	A.L.	OF	6	19	1	4	1	0	1	5	0	.211
2004	Las Vegas a	P.C.	OF	60	238	44	65	17	2	14	49	2	.273
2005	Los Angeles	N.L.	OF	14	25	1	4	1	0	0	1	0	.160
2005	Las Vegas	P.C.	OF	115	393	79	105	21	4	22	63	4	.267
2006	L.A.-Cin.-Florida b-c-d-e	N.L.	OF	101	269	34	61	12	2	13	46	1	.227
2007	Jupiter	Fla.St.	OF	7	23	2	6	1	0	2	3	0	.261
2007	Florida f	N.L.	OF	66	173	35	58	19	0	12	39	2	.335
2008	Florida	N.L.	OF	145	461	59	120	29	5	22	73	6	.260
2009	Florida	N.L.	OF-P	151	559	73	151	37	1	24	90	5	.270
2010	Florida-San Francisco g	N.L.	OF	153	525	71	141	28	3	14	65	9	.269
Major League Totals			7 Yrs.	636	2031	274	539	127	11	86	319	23	.265
	Division Series												
2010	San Francisco	N.L.	OF	4	14	2	4	1	0	1	3	0	.286
	Championship Series												
2010	San Francisco	N.L.	OF	6	20	4	7	3	0	3	5	0	.350
	World Series Record												
2010	San Francisco	N.L.	OF	5	17	5	4	1	0	1	2	0	.235

a Traded to Los Angeles Dodgers for pitcher Steve Cuyler and player to be named later, April 1, 2004.
b Traded to Cincinnati Reds for player to be named later, April 24, 2006.
c Los Angeles Dodgers received pitcher Ben Kozlowski to complete trade, June 1, 2006.
d On disabled list from April 29 to May 23, 2006.
e Sold to Florida Marlins, May 27, 2006.
f On disabled list from May 6 to July 19, 2007.
g Claimed on waivers by San Francisco Giants, August 22, 2010.

ROSS, DAVID WADE

Born, Bainbridge, Georgia, March 19, 1977.
Bats Right. Throws Right. Height, 6 feet, 2 inches. Weight, 240 pounds.

Year	Club	Lea	Pos	G	AB	R	H	2B	3B	HR	RBI	SB	Avg
1998	Yakima	Northwest	C	59	191	31	59	14	1	6	25	2	.309
1999	Vero Beach	Fla.St.	C-1B-OF	114	375	47	85	19	1	7	39	5	.227
2000	San Bernardino	Calif.	C	51	191	27	49	11	1	7	21	3	.257
2000	San Antonio	Texas	C	24	67	11	14	2	1	3	12	1	.209
2001	Jacksonville	Southern	C	74	246	35	65	13	1	11	45	1	.264
2002	Las Vegas	P.C.	C	92	293	48	87	16	2	15	68	1	.297
2002	Los Angeles	N.L.	C	8	10	2	2	1	0	1	2	0	.200
2003	Las Vegas	P.C.	C	24	86	12	19	4	0	5	16	0	.221
2003	Los Angeles	N.L.	C	40	124	19	32	7	0	10	18	0	.258
2004	Los Angeles	N.L.	C	70	165	13	28	3	1	5	15	0	.170
2005	Indianapolis	Int.	C	6	19	1	4	1	0	0	1	0	.211

Year Club	Lea	Pos	G	AB	R	H	2B	3B	HR	RBI	SB	Avg
2005 Portland	P.C.	C	6	21	3	3	1	0	0	1	0	.143
2005 Pittsburgh-San Diego a-b	N.L.	C	51	125	11	30	8	1	3	15	0	.240
2006 Chattanooga	Southern	C	2	6	0	2	0	0	0	2	0	.333
2006 Cincinnati c-d	N.L.	C	90	247	37	63	15	1	21	52	0	.255
2007 Louisville	Int.	C	3	9	0	2	1	0	0	0	0	.222
2007 Cincinnati e	N.L.	C	112	311	32	63	10	0	17	39	0	.203
2008 Sarasota	Fla.St.	C	4	11	2	2	0	0	0	1	0	.182
2008 Louisville	Int.	C	9	30	4	5	1	1	1	2	0	.167
2008 Cincinnati	N.L.	C	52	134	17	31	9	0	3	13	0	.231
2008 Pawtucket	Int.	C	6	28	4	7	1	0	1	3	0	.250
2008 Boston f-g-h	A.L.	C	8	8	1	1	0	0	0	0	0	.125
2009 Rome	So.Atl.	C	2	6	1	3	0	0	1	4	0	.500
2009 Atlanta i	N.L.	C	54	128	18	35	9	0	7	20	0	.273
2010 Atlanta	N.L.	C	59	121	15	35	13	2	2	28	0	.289
Major League Totals		9 Yrs.	544	1373	165	320	75	5	69	202	0	.233
Division Series												
2004 Los Angeles	N.L.	C	2	3	0	0	0	0	0	0	0	.000
2008 Boston	A.L.	C	1	0	0	0	0	0	0	0	0	.000
2010 Atlanta	N.L.	C	2	0	0	0	0	0	0	0	0	.000
Division Series Totals			5	3	0	0	0	0	0	0	0	.000

a Sold to Pittsburgh Pirates, March 30, 2005.
b Traded to San Diego Padres for infielder J.J. Furmaniak, July 28, 2005.
c Traded to Cincinnati Reds for pitcher Bobby Basham, March 21, 2006.
d On disabled list from July 8 to July 26, 2006.
e On disabled list from August 13 to August 28, 2007.
f On disabled list from March 30 to April 23, 2008.
g Released by Cincinnati Reds, August 19, 2008. Signed with Boston Red Sox organization, August 22, 2008.
h Filed for free agency, October 30, 2008. Signed with Atlanta Braves, December 5, 2008.
i On disabled list from April 1 to April 16, 2009.

ROWAND, AARON RYAN

Born, Portland, Oregon, August 29, 1977.
Bats Right. Throws Right. Height, 6 feet. Weight, 220 pounds.

Year Club	Lea	Pos	G	AB	R	H	2B	3B	HR	RBI	SB	Avg
1998 Hickory a	So.Atl.	OF	60	218	42	75	13	3	5	32	7	.344
1999 Winston-Salem	Carolina	OF	133	512	96	143	37	3	24	88	15	.279
2000 Birmingham	Southern	OF	139	532	80	137	26	5	20	98	22	.258
2001 Charlotte	Int.	OF	82	329	54	97	28	0	16	48	8	.295
2001 Chicago	A.L.	OF	63	123	21	36	5	0	4	20	5	.293
2002 Chicago	A.L.	OF	126	302	41	78	16	2	7	29	0	.258
2003 Charlotte	Int.	OF	32	120	15	29	9	0	3	13	0	.242
2003 Chicago	A.L.	OF	93	157	22	45	8	0	6	24	0	.287
2004 Chicago	A.L.	OF	140	487	94	151	38	2	24	69	17	.310
2005 Chicago b	A.L.	OF	157	578	77	156	30	5	13	69	16	.270
2006 Philadelphia c	N.L.	OF	109	405	59	106	24	3	12	47	10	.262
2007 Philadelphia d	N.L.	OF	161	612	105	189	45	0	27	89	6	.309
2008 San Francisco	N.L.	OF	152	549	57	149	37	0	13	70	2	.271
2009 San Francisco	N.L.	OF	144	499	61	130	30	2	15	64	4	.261
2010 San Francisco e	N.L.	OF	105	331	42	76	12	2	11	34	5	.230
Major League Totals		10 Yrs.	1250	4043	579	1116	245	16	132	515	65	.276
Division Series												
2005 Chicago	A.L.	OF	3	10	3	4	2	0	0	2	1	.400
2007 Philadelphia	N.L.	OF	3	12	1	1	0	0	1	1	0	.083
2010 San Francisco	N.L.	PH	2	2	0	1	0	0	0	0	0	.500
Division Series Totals			8	24	4	6	2	0	1	3	1	.250
Championship Series												
2005 Chicago	A.L.	OF	5	18	3	3	3	0	0	1	0	.167
2010 San Francisco	N.L.	OF	3	5	1	1	1	0	0	0	0	.200
Championship Series Totals			8	23	4	4	4	0	0	1	0	.174
World Series Record												
2005 Chicago	A.L.	OF	4	17	2	5	1	0	0	0	0	.294
2010 San Francisco	N.L.	OF	2	4	1	1	0	1	0	2	0	.250
World Series Totals			6	21	3	6	1	1	0	2	0	.286

a Drafted by Chicago White Sox with choice received for Tampa Bay Devil Rays signing of outfielder Dave Martinez, June 2, 1998.
b Traded to Philadelphia Phillies with pitcher Dan Haigwood and player to be named later for infielder Jim Thome, November 25, 2005. Philadelphia Phillies received pitcher Giovany Gonzalez to complete trade, December 8, 2005.

c On disabled list from May 12 to May 27 and August 22 to October 4, 2006.
d Filed for free agency, October 29, 2007. Signed with San Francisco Giants, December 12, 2007.
e On disabled list from April 17 to May 2, 2010.

RUIZ, CARLOS JOAQUIN

Born, David, Panama, January 22, 1979.
Bats Right. Throws Right. Height, 5 feet, 10 inches. Weight, 200 pounds.

Year	Club	Lea	Pos	G	AB	R	H	2B	3B	HR	RBI	SB	Avg
2000	Phillies	Gulf Coast	C	38	130	11	36	7	1	1	22	3	.277
2001	Lakewood	So.Atl.	C-OF	73	249	21	65	14	3	4	32	5	.261
2002	Clearwater	Fla.St.	C	92	342	35	73	18	3	5	32	3	.213
2003	Reading	Eastern	C-OF	52	169	22	45	6	0	2	16	1	.266
2003	Clearwater	Fla.St.	C	15	54	5	17	0	0	2	9	2	.315
2004	Reading	Eastern	C	101	349	45	99	15	2	17	50	8	.284
2005	Scranton-WB	Int.	C-1B	100	347	50	104	25	9	4	40	4	.300
2006	Scranton-WB	Int.	C	100	368	56	113	25	0	16	69	4	.307
2006	Philadelphia	N.L.	C	27	69	5	18	1	1	3	10	0	.261
2007	Philadelphia	N.L.	C	115	374	42	97	29	2	6	54	6	.259
2008	Philadelphia	N.L.	C-3B	117	320	47	70	14	0	4	31	1	.219
2009	Lehigh Valley	Int.	C	4	13	1	3	1	0	0	2	0	.231
2009	Philadelphia a	N.L.	C	107	322	32	82	26	1	9	43	3	.255
2010	Lakewood	So.Atl.	C	2	8	1	4	2	0	0	1	0	.500
2010	Lehigh Valley	Int.	C	1	2	0	0	0	0	0	0	0	.000
2010	Philadelphia b	N.L.	C	121	371	43	112	28	1	8	53	0	.302
Major League Totals			5 Yrs.	487	1456	169	379	98	5	30	191	10	.260
	Division Series												
2007	Philadelphia	N.L.	C	3	9	1	3	1	0	0	0	1	.333
2008	Philadelphia	N.L.	C	4	14	1	1	0	0	0	0	0	.071
2009	Philadelphia	N.L.	C	4	13	0	4	0	0	0	3	0	.308
2010	Philadelphia	N.L.	C	3	8	1	2	1	0	0	1	0	.250
Division Series Totals				14	44	3	10	2	0	0	4	1	.227
	Championship Series												
2008	Philadelphia	N.L.	C	5	16	3	5	1	0	0	1	0	.313
2009	Philadelphia	N.L.	C	5	13	4	5	1	0	1	4	1	.385
2010	Philadelphia	N.L.	C	6	18	2	3	0	0	1	1	0	.167
Championship Series Totals				16	47	9	13	2	0	2	6	1	.277
	World Series Record												
2008	Philadelphia	N.L.	C	5	16	2	6	2	0	1	3	1	.375
2009	Philadelphia	N.L.	C	6	18	4	6	2	1	1	2	0	.333
World Series Totals				11	34	6	12	4	1	2	5	1	.353

a On disabled list from April 11 to May 2, 2009.
b On disabled list from June 19 to July 10, 2010.

RYAL, RUSTY ALLEN

Born, Ponca City, Oklahoma, March 16, 1983.
Bats Right. Throws Right. Height, 6 feet, 2 inches. Weight, 200 pounds.

Year	Club	Lea	Pos	G	AB	R	H	2B	3B	HR	RBI	SB	Avg
2005	Missoula	Pioneer	3B-2B	72	294	59	98	22	4	6	46	11	.333
2006	Lancaster	Calif.	3B-SS	97	350	53	97	17	6	11	42	8	.277
2007	Visalia	Calif.	3B-2B-SS	70	276	46	83	15	3	11	46	2	.301
2007	Mobile	Southern	2B-3B	47	168	18	40	6	2	6	21	4	.238
2008	Mobile	Southern	2B-3B	128	460	65	126	22	4	16	66	4	.274
2009	Reno	P.C.	2B-3B-SS-OF	103	404	65	117	33	6	17	70	5	.290
2009	Arizona	N.L.	2B-1B	30	59	11	16	6	2	3	9	0	.271
2010	Arizona a	N.L.	OF-1B-3B	104	207	19	54	7	1	3	11	0	.261
Major League Totals			2 Yrs.	134	266	30	70	13	3	6	20	0	.263

a Sold to Yomiuri Giants (Japan), December 23, 2010.

RYAN, BRENDAN WOOD

Born, Los Angeles, California, March 26, 1982.
Bats Right. Throws Right. Height, 6 feet, 2 inches. Weight, 195 pounds.

Year	Club	Lea	Pos	G	AB	R	H	2B	3B	HR	RBI	SB	Avg
2003	New Jersey	N.Y.-Penn.	SS-3B	53	193	20	60	14	4	0	13	11	.311
2004	Peoria	Midwest	SS	105	426	72	137	21	4	2	59	30	.322
2005	Palm Beach	Fla.St.	SS	49	188	29	57	17	0	1	16	8	.303
2005	Springfield	Texas	SS	43	154	28	42	8	1	2	9	6	.273
2006	Palm Beach	Fla.St.	SS	3	14	2	6	1	0	0	1	1	.429

Year	Club	Lea	Pos	G	AB	R	H	2B	3B	HR	RBI	SB	Avg
2006	State College	N.Y.-Penn.	SS	8	34	5	8	0	0	0	3	1	.235
2006	Memphis	P.C.	SS	7	26	4	4	0	0	1	6	1	.154
2006	Springfield	Texas	SS	10	43	6	13	1	0	0	3	1	.302
2007	Memphis	P.C.	SS	81	323	55	88	9	5	1	15	17	.272
2007	St. Louis	N.L.	SS-3B-2B	67	180	30	52	9	0	4	12	7	.289
2008	Palm Beach	Fla.St.	SS	3	12	1	3	1	0	0	0	1	.250
2008	Springfield	Texas	3B-2B-SS	4	19	5	7	3	0	1	3	1	.368
2008	Memphis	P.C.	OF-2B-SS	21	80	13	19	5	0	3	10	1	.237
2008	St. Louis a	N.L.	SS-2B-3B-OF	80	197	30	48	9	0	0	10	7	.244
2009	Memphis	P.C.	SS	3	11	0	0	0	0	0	0	0	.000
2009	St. Louis b	N.L.	SS-2B	129	390	55	114	19	7	3	37	14	.292
2010	St. Louis c	N.L.	SS	139	439	50	98	19	3	2	36	11	.223
Major League Totals			4 Yrs.	415	1206	165	312	56	10	9	95	39	.259
Division Series													
2009	St. Louis	N.L.	SS	3	12	0	1	1	0	0	0	0	.083

a On disabled list from March 21 to April 23, 2008.
b On disabled list from April 30 to May 15, 2009.
c Traded to Seattle Mariners for pitcher Maikel Cleto, December 12, 2010.

SALAZAR, OSCAR ENRIQUE

Born, Maracay, Venezuela, June 27, 1978.
Bats Right. Throws Right. Height, 5 feet, 11 inches. Weight, 195 pounds.

Year	Club	Lea	Pos	G	AB	R	H	2B	3B	HR	RBI	SB	Avg
1998	Athletics	Arizona	3B-SS-2B	26	102	29	33	7	5	2	18	4	.324
1998	Sou Oregon	Northwest	3B-2B-SS	28	101	19	32	4	1	5	28	5	.317
1999	Modesto	Calif.	2B-3B-SS-1B	130	525	100	155	26	18	18	105	14	.295
2000	Sacramento	P.C.	SS	4	13	0	2	1	0	0	1	1	.154
2000	Midland	Texas	SS-OF-3B	111	427	70	128	27	1	13	57	4	.300
2001	Sacramento	P.C.	2B-3B	5	16	0	1	0	0	0	1	0	.063
2001	Midland	Texas	SS-3B-2B-OF	130	521	75	139	31	4	18	95	10	.267
2002	Toledo	Int.	SS-2B	8	19	0	6	0	0	0	1	0	.316
2002	Detroit	A.L.	2B-3B-SS	8	21	2	4	1	0	1	3	0	.190
2002	Erie	Eastern	2B-SS-OF-1B	53	191	16	41	18	1	6	26	2	.215
2002	Binghamton a-b	Eastern	2B-3B	28	75	6	13	2	0	1	5	0	.173
2003	Salt Lake	P.C.	2B	7	26	5	8	2	1	1	4	0	.308
2003	Arkansas	Texas	2B-SS-3B-OF	39	143	22	47	6	2	4	21	2	.329
2003	Wichita c-d	Texas	2B-SS-3B-OF	78	287	34	80	15	2	7	43	4	.279
2004	Akron e	Eastern	SS-2B-1B-3B	44	163	18	36	6	0	6	21	2	.221
2005	Cancun f	Mexican	1B	71	264	39	72	12	2	6	32	2	.273
2007	Bowie g-h	Eastern	3B-2B-1B-OF	136	532	73	154	39	2	22	96	3	.289
2008	Norfolk	Int.	1B-3B-2B-OF	112	443	73	140	42	3	13	85	8	.316
2008	Baltimore	A.L.	1B-3B-SS	34	81	13	23	3	0	5	15	0	.284
2009	Norfolk	Int.	1B-OF	50	199	31	74	17	1	10	43	0	.372
2009	Baltimore	A.L.	3B-1B-SS-OF	17	31	4	13	0	0	2	6	0	.419
2009	San Diego i	N.L.	OF-1B-2B	55	108	12	29	8	2	3	19	0	.269
2010	Lake Elsinore	Calif.	1B-2B-3B-OF	7	25	3	7	1	0	1	4	0	.280
2010	San Diego j	N.L.	OF-1B-2B-3B	85	131	19	31	4	0	3	19	1	.237
Major League Totals			4 Yrs.	199	372	50	100	16	2	14	62	1	.269

a Claimed on waivers by Detroit Tigers from Oakland Athletics, January 24, 2002.
b Claimed on waivers by New York Mets, July 31, 2002.
c Filed for free agency, October 15, 2002. Signed with Anaheim Angels organization, February 17, 2003.
d Released by Anaheim Angels, May 24, 2003. Signed with Kansas City Royals organization, May 31, 2003.
e Filed for free agency, October 15, 2003. Signed with Cleveland Indians organization, January 26, 2004.
f Released by Cleveland Indians, June 18, 2004. Signed with Cancun (Mexico) for 2005.
g Played in Italy in 2006. Signed with Baltimore Orioles organization, November 24. 2006
h Filed for free agency, October 29, 2007, re-signed with Baltimore Orioles organization, 2007.
i Traded to San Diego Padres for pitcher Cla Meredith, July 20, 2009.
j On disabled list from July 30 to September 1, 2010.

SANCHEZ, ANGEL LUIS

Born, Humacao, Puerto Rico, September 20, 1983.
Bats Right. Throws Right. Height, 6 feet, 2 inches. Weight, 205 pounds.

Year	Club	Lea	Pos	G	AB	R	H	2B	3B	HR	RBI	SB	Avg
2001	Royals	Gulf Coast	SS-3B-2B	30	95	10	23	4	0	0	6	3	.242
2002	Royals	Gulf Coast	2B-SS-3B	49	175	21	44	4	0	0	12	9	.251
2003	Burlington	Midwest	SS-2B	106	408	54	110	8	1	2	35	14	.270
2004	Burlington	Midwest	SS	96	357	37	90	13	1	2	25	16	.252

Year Club	Lea	Pos	G	AB	R	H	2B	3B	HR	RBI	SB	Avg
2005 High Desert	Calif.	SS	133	585	102	183	33	4	5	70	10	.313
2006 Wichita	Texas	SS	133	542	105	153	24	1	4	57	8	.282
2006 Kansas City	A.L.	2B-SS	8	27	2	6	0	0	0	1	0	.222
2007 Kansas City a	A.L.	INJURED—Did Not Play										
2008 Omaha	P.C.	SS	38	131	13	29	7	1	1	13	1	.221
2008 NW Arkansas b-c	Texas	SS	63	241	28	63	7	2	1	23	4	.261
2009 Las Vegas	P.C.	SS-2B	126	449	67	137	29	4	6	60	1	.305
2010 Pawtucket	Int.	SS-2B-3B	62	223	26	61	10	1	0	17	6	.274
2010 Boston d-e	A.L.	SS	1	3	0	0	0	0	0	0	0	.000
2010 Houston	N.L.	SS-2B	65	250	30	70	9	4	0	25	0	.280
Major League Totals		2 Yrs.	74	280	32	76	9	4	0	26	0	.271

a On disabled list from March 28 to November 13, 2007.
b On disabled list from September 2 to September 29, 2008.
c Claimed on waivers by Toronto Blue Jays, November 3, 2008.
d Filed for free agency, November 9, 2009. Signed with Boston Red Sox organization, January 15, 2010.
e Traded to Houston Astros for catcher Kevin Cash, July 1, 2010.

SANCHEZ, FREDERICK PHILLIP (FREDDY)

Born, Hollywood, California, December 21, 1977.
Bats Right. Throws Right. Height, 5 feet, 10 inches. Weight, 185 pounds.

Year Club	Lea	Pos	G	AB	R	H	2B	3B	HR	RBI	SB	Avg
2000 Lowell	N.Y.-Penn.	SS	34	132	24	38	13	2	1	14	2	.288
2000 Augusta	So.Atl.	SS	30	109	17	33	7	0	0	15	4	.303
2001 Trenton	Eastern	SS	44	178	25	58	20	0	2	19	3	.326
2001 Sarasota	Fla.St.	SS	69	280	40	95	19	4	1	24	5	.339
2002 Trenton	Eastern	SS-2B	80	311	60	102	23	1	3	38	19	.328
2002 Pawtucket	Int.	SS-2B	45	183	25	55	10	1	4	28	5	.301
2002 Boston	A.L.	2B-SS	12	16	3	3	0	0	0	2	0	.188
2003 Pawtucket	Int.	SS-2B-3B	58	211	46	72	17	0	5	25	8	.341
2003 Boston	A.L.	3B-SS-2B	20	34	6	8	2	0	0	2	0	.235
2003 Nashville a	P.C.	2B	1	5	1	2	1	0	0	0	0	.400
2004 Nashville	P.C.	2B-SS	44	125	10	33	7	1	1	11	4	.264
2004 Pittsburgh b	N.L.	SS-2B-3B	9	19	2	3	0	0	0	2	0	.158
2005 Pittsburgh	N.L.	3B-2B-SS	132	453	54	132	26	4	5	35	2	.291
2006 Pittsburgh	N.L.	3B-SS-2B	157	582	85	200	*53	2	6	85	3	*.344
2007 Indianapolis	Int.	2B	1	2	1	1	1	0	0	0	0	.500
2007 Pittsburgh c	N.L.	2B-SS	147	602	77	183	42	4	11	81	0	.304
2008 Pittsburgh	N.L.	2B	145	569	75	154	26	2	9	52	0	.271
2009 Fresno	P.C.	2B	3	9	1	3	1	0	0	0	0	.333
2009 Pittsburgh-San Fran. d-e	N.L.	2B	111	457	56	134	29	3	7	41	5	.293
2010 San Jose	Calif.	2B	3	9	6	6	5	0	0	4	0	.667
2010 Fresno	P.C.	2B	4	11	1	3	0	0	0	0	0	.273
2010 San Francisco f	N.L.	2B	111	431	55	126	22	1	7	47	3	.292
Major League Totals		9 Yrs.	844	3163	413	943	200	16	45	347	13	.298
Division Series												
2010 San Francisco	N.L.	2B	4	16	2	2	0	0	0	0	0	.125
Championship Series												
2010 San Francisco	N.L.	2B	6	25	1	9	1	0	0	1	0	.360
World Series Record												
2010 San Francisco	N.L.	2B	5	22	2	6	3	0	0	3	0	.273

a Traded to Pittsburgh Pirates with pitcher Mike Gonzalez and cash for pitcher Jeff Suppan, pitcher Brandon Lyon and pitcher Anastacio Martinez, July 31, 2003.
b On disabled list from March 26 to July 9, 2004.
c On disabled list from March 23 to April 8, 2007.
d Traded to San Francisco Giants for pitcher Tim Alderson, July 30, 2009.
e On disabled list from August 18 to September 7, 2009.
f On disabled list from March 26 to May 19, 2010.

SANCHEZ, GABRIEL (GABY)

Born, Miami, Florida, September 2, 1983.
Bats Right. Throws Right. Height, 6 feet, 2 inches. Weight, 225 pounds.

Year Club	Lea	Pos	G	AB	R	H	2B	3B	HR	RBI	SB	Avg
2005 Jamestown	N.Y.-Penn.	3B-1B-C	62	234	34	83	16	0	5	42	11	.355
2006 Jupiter	Fla.St.	1B-3B-C	16	55	13	10	3	1	1	7	1	.182
2006 Marlins	Gulf Coast	1B	3	6	1	2	1	0	0	3	0	.333
2006 Greensboro	So.Atl.	1B-C	55	189	43	60	12	0	14	40	6	.317
2007 Jupiter	Fla.St.	1B-3B-C	133	473	89	132	40	3	9	70	6	.279

Year	Club	Lea	Pos	G	AB	R	H	2B	3B	HR	RBI	SB	Avg
2008	Carolina	Southern	1B-3B	133	478	70	150	42	1	17	92	17	.314
2008	Florida	N.L.	1B	5	8	0	3	2	0	0	1	0	.375
2009	New Orleans	P.C.	1B-3B	85	318	55	92	11	0	16	56	5	.289
2009	Florida	N.L.	1B	21	21	2	5	0	0	2	3	0	.238
2010	Florida	N.L.	1B	151	572	72	156	37	3	19	85	5	.273
Major League Totals			3 Yrs.	177	601	74	164	39	3	21	89	5	.273

SANDOVAL, PABLO E.

Born, Puerto Cabello, Venezuela, August 11, 1986.
Bats Both. Throws Right. Height, 5 feet, 11 inches. Weight, 245 pounds.

Year	Club	Lea	Pos	G	AB	R	H	2B	3B	HR	RBI	SB	Avg
2004	Giants	Arizona	C	46	177	21	47	9	5	0	26	4	.266
2005	Salem-Keizer	Northwest	3B-1B-C	75	294	46	97	15	2	3	50	2	.330
2006	Augusta	So.Atl.	1B-3B	117	438	43	116	20	1	1	49	3	.265
2007	San Jose	Calif.	C-1B	102	401	56	115	33	5	11	52	3	.287
2008	San Jose	Calif.	C-1B	68	273	61	98	25	2	12	59	2	.359
2008	Connecticut	Eastern	C-1B	44	175	29	59	13	0	8	37	0	.337
2008	San Francisco	N.L.	1B-3B-C	41	145	24	50	10	1	3	24	0	.345
2009	San Francisco	N.L.	3B-1B-C	153	572	79	189	44	5	25	90	5	.330
2010	San Francisco	N.L.	3B-1B	152	563	61	151	34	3	13	63	3	.268
Major League Totals			3 Yrs.	346	1280	164	390	88	9	41	177	8	.305
	Division Series												
2010	San Francisco	N.L.	3B	2	6	0	1	0	0	0	0	0	.167
	Championship Series												
2010	San Francisco	N.L.	3B	3	8	0	2	1	0	0	2	0	.250
	World Series Record												
2010	San Francisco	N.L.	DH	1	3	0	0	0	0	0	0	0	.000

SANTIAGO, RAMON D.

Born, Las Matas de Farfan, Dominican Republic, August 31, 1979.
Bats Both. Throws Right. Height, 5 feet, 11 inches. Weight, 150 pounds.

Year	Club	Lea	Pos	G	AB	R	H	2B	3B	HR	RBI	SB	Avg
1999	Tigers	Gulf Coast	SS	35	134	25	43	9	2	0	11	20	.321
1999	Oneonta	N.Y.-Penn.	SS	12	50	9	17	1	2	1	8	5	.340
2000	West Michigan	Midwest	SS	98	379	69	103	15	1	1	42	39	.272
2001	Lakeland	Fla.St.	DH	120	429	64	115	15	3	2	46	34	.268
2002	Erie	Eastern	SS	22	75	9	21	0	2	1	7	6	.280
2002	Toledo	Int.	SS	9	28	8	12	1	0	2	6	0	.429
2002	Detroit	A.L.	SS	65	222	33	54	5	5	4	20	8	.243
2003	Detroit	A.L.	SS-2B	141	444	41	100	18	1	2	29	10	.225
2004	Tacoma	P.C.	SS-2B	71	243	35	47	7	2	1	24	9	.193
2004	Seattle a	A.L.	SS	19	39	8	7	1	0	0	2	0	.179
2005	Tacoma	P.C.	2B-SS-3B-C	129	441	68	111	22	3	10	50	18	.252
2005	Seattle	A.L.	2B-SS	8	8	2	1	0	0	0	0	0	.125
2006	Toledo	Int.	2B-SS	25	83	13	21	6	0	2	12	2	.253
2006	Detroit b	A.L.	SS-2B-3B	43	80	9	18	1	1	0	3	2	.225
2007	Toledo	Int.	SS-2B	91	365	40	96	19	4	3	30	8	.263
2007	Detroit	A.L.	SS	32	67	10	19	5	1	0	7	3	.284
2008	Toledo	Int.	SS	8	28	3	6	2	0	0	3	0	.214
2008	Detroit c	A.L.	SS-2B-3B	58	124	30	35	6	2	4	18	1	.282
2009	Detroit	A.L.	SS-2B-3B	93	262	29	70	6	2	7	35	1	.267
2010	Detroit	A.L.	SS-2B	112	320	38	84	9	1	3	22	2	.262
Major League Totals			9 Yrs.	571	1566	200	388	51	13	20	136	27	.248
	Championship Series												
2006	Detroit	A.L.	SS	3	7	0	0	0	0	0	0	0	.000
	World Series Record												
2006	Detroit	A.L.	SS	3	5	0	1	0	0	0	0	0	.200

a Traded to Seattle Mariners with infielder Juan Gonzalez for infielder Carlos Guillen, January 8, 2004.
b Released by Seattle Mariners, November 18, 2005. Signed with Detroit Tigers organization, January 4, 2006.
c On disabled list from June 5 to July 8, 2008.

SAUNDERS, MICHAEL EDWARD BRETT

Born, Victoria, British Columbia, Canada, November 19, 1986.
Bats Left. Throws Right. Height, 6 feet, 4 inches. Weight, 210 pounds.

Year	Club	Lea	Pos	G	AB	R	H	2B	3B	HR	RBI	SB	Avg
2005	Everett	Northwest	OF	56	196	24	53	13	3	7	39	2	.270
2006	Wisconsin	Midwest	OF	104	359	48	86	10	8	4	39	22	.240
2007	High Desert	Calif.	OF	108	431	91	129	25	4	14	77	27	.299
2007	West Tenn	Southern	OF	15	52	8	15	1	2	1	7	2	.288
2008	Tacoma	P.C.	OF	24	95	12	23	4	1	3	16	1	.242
2008	West Tenn	Southern	OF	67	248	46	72	18	3	8	30	11	.290
2009	Tacoma	P.C.	OF	64	248	58	77	15	2	13	32	6	.310
2009	Seattle	A.L.	OF	46	122	13	27	1	3	0	4	4	.221
2010	Tacoma	P.C.	OF	21	80	6	16	1	0	0	5	4	.200
2010	Seattle	A.L.	OF	100	289	29	61	11	2	10	33	6	.211
Major League Totals			2 Yrs.	146	411	42	88	12	5	10	37	10	.214

SCHIERHOLTZ, NATHAN JOHN (NATE)

Born, Reno, Nevada, February 15, 1984.
Bats Left. Throws Right. Height, 6 feet, 2 inches. Weight, 215 pounds.

Year	Club	Lea	Pos	G	AB	R	H	2B	3B	HR	RBI	SB	Avg
2003	Giants	Arizona	3B-1B	11	45	5	18	0	2	0	5	4	.400
2003	Salem-Keizer	Northwest	3B	35	124	23	38	6	2	3	29	0	.306
2004	San Jose	Calif.	3B-OF	62	258	39	76	18	9	3	31	3	.295
2004	Hagerstown	So.Atl.	3B	59	235	41	70	22	0	15	54	1	.298
2005	San Jose	Calif.	OF	128	502	83	160	37	8	15	86	5	.319
2006	Connecticut	Eastern	OF	125	470	55	127	25	7	14	54	8	.270
2007	Fresno	P.C.	OF	109	411	67	137	31	7	16	68	10	.333
2007	San Francisco	N.L.	OF	39	112	9	34	5	3	0	10	3	.304
2008	Fresno	P.C.	OF	93	350	62	112	22	10	18	73	9	.320
2008	San Francisco	N.L.	OF	19	75	12	24	8	1	1	5	0	.320
2009	Fresno	P.C.	OF	5	18	2	4	1	0	0	1	1	.222
2009	San Francisco a	N.L.	OF	116	285	33	76	19	2	5	29	3	.267
2010	San Francisco	N.L.	OF	137	227	34	55	13	3	3	17	4	.242
Major League Totals			4 Yrs.	311	699	88	189	45	9	9	61	10	.270
	Division Series												
2010	San Francisco	N.L.	OF	4	4	0	1	0	0	0	0	0	.250
	Championship Series												
2010	San Francisco	N.L.	OF	4	3	1	0	0	0	0	0	0	.000
	World Series Record												
2010	San Francisco	N.L.	OF	3	5	1	1	0	0	0	1	0	.200

a On disabled list from July 27 to August 12, 2009.

SCHUMAKER, JARED MICHAEL (SKIP)

Born, Torrance, California, February 3, 1980.
Bats Left. Throws Right. Height, 5 feet, 10 inches. Weight, 195 pounds.

Year	Club	Lea	Pos	G	AB	R	H	2B	3B	HR	RBI	SB	Avg
2001	New Jersey	N.Y.-Penn.	OF	49	162	22	41	10	1	0	14	11	.253
2002	Potomac	Carolina	OF	136	551	71	158	22	4	2	44	26	.287
2003	Tennessee	Southern	OF	91	342	43	86	20	3	2	22	6	.251
2004	Tennessee	Southern	OF-3B	138	516	78	163	29	6	4	43	19	.316
2005	Memphis	P.C.	OF	115	443	66	127	24	3	7	34	14	.287
2005	St. Louis	N.L.	OF	27	24	9	6	1	0	0	1	1	.250
2006	Memphis	P.C.	OF	95	369	47	113	13	3	3	27	11	.306
2006	St. Louis	N.L.	OF	28	54	3	10	1	0	1	2	2	.185
2007	Memphis	P.C.	OF	59	232	34	71	16	0	7	31	2	.306
2007	St. Louis	N.L.	OF	88	177	19	59	12	2	2	19	1	.333
2008	St. Louis	N.L.	OF	153	540	87	163	22	5	8	46	8	.302
2009	St. Louis	N.L.	2B-OF	153	532	85	161	34	1	4	35	2	.303
2010	St. Louis	N.L.	2B-OF	137	476	66	126	18	1	5	42	5	.265
Major League Totals			6 Yrs.	586	1803	269	525	88	9	20	145	19	.291
	Division Series												
2009	St. Louis	N.L.	2B-OF	2	6	1	2	1	0	0	1	0	.333

SCOTT, LUKE BRANDON

Born, DeLeon Springs, Florida, June 25, 1978.
Bats Left. Throws Right. Height, 6 feet. Weight, 210 pounds.

Year	Club	Lea	Pos	G	AB	R	H	2B	3B	HR	RBI	SB	Avg
2001	Kinston a	Carolina	INJURED — Did Not Play										
2002	Kinston	Carolina	OF-1B	48	163	22	39	7	1	8	30	2	.239
2002	Columbus	So.Atl.	OF	49	171	28	44	15	4	7	32	9	.257
2003	Kinston	Carolina	OF	67	241	37	67	12	1	13	44	6	.278
2003	Akron	Eastern	OF	50	183	21	50	13	1	7	37	0	.273
2004	Salem	Carolina	OF	66	241	45	67	20	1	8	35	6	.278
2004	Round Rock b	Texas	OF	63	208	45	62	17	0	19	62	0	.298
2005	Round Rock	P.C.	OF	103	398	69	114	25	4	31	87	2	.286
2005	Houston	N.L.	OF	34	80	6	15	4	2	0	4	1	.188
2006	Round Rock	P.C.	OF	87	318	63	95	15	1	20	63	6	.299
2006	Houston	N.L.	OF	65	214	31	72	19	6	10	37	2	.336
2007	Houston c	N.L.	OF	132	369	49	94	28	5	18	64	3	.255
2008	Baltimore	A.L.	OF	148	475	67	122	29	2	23	65	2	.257
2009	Delmarva	So.Atl.	OF	2	4	1	3	0	0	1	1	0	.750
2009	Baltimore d	A.L.	DH-OF-1B	128	449	61	116	26	1	25	77	0	.258
2010	Orioles	Gulf Coast	OF	3	9	1	2	0	0	0	2	0	.222
2010	Baltimore e	A.L.	DH-1B-OF	131	447	70	127	29	1	27	72	2	.284
Major League Totals			6 Yrs.	638	2034	284	546	135	17	103	319	10	.268
	Division Series												
2005	Houston	N.L.	OF	2	2	1	0	0	0	0	0	0	.000
	World Series Record												
2005	Houston	N.L.	PH	0	0	0	0	0	0	0	0	0	.000

a On disabled list from June 21 to September 14, 2001.
b Traded by Cleveland Indians to Houston Astros with outfielder Willy Taveras for pitcher Jeriome Robertston, March 31, 2004.
c Traded to Baltimore Orioles with pitcher Troy Patton, pitcher Matt Albers, pitcher Dennis Sarfate and infielder Michael Costanzo for infielder Miguel Tejada, December 12, 2007.
d On disabled list from May 11 to May 27, 2009.
e On disabled list from July 1 to July 19, 2010.

SCUTARO, MARCOS (MARCO)

Born, San Felipe, Venezuela, October 30, 1975.
Bats Right. Throws Right. Height, 5 feet, 10 inches. Weight, 190 pounds.

Year	Club	Lea	Pos	G	AB	R	H	2B	3B	HR	RBI	SB	Avg
1995	Cleveland	Dominican	3B	66	262	71	103	18	6	0	38	32	.393
1996	Columbus	So.Atl.	2B-SS-3B	85	315	66	79	12	3	10	45	6	.251
1997	Buffalo	A.A.	2B-3B-SS	21	57	8	15	3	0	1	6	0	.263
1997	Kinston	Carolina	2B-3B	97	378	58	103	17	6	10	59	23	.272
1998	Buffalo	Int.	2B-3B	8	26	3	6	3	0	0	4	0	.231
1998	Akron	Eastern	2B-SS	124	462	68	146	27	6	11	62	33	.316
1999	Buffalo	Int.	2B-SS	129	462	76	126	24	2	8	51	21	.273
2000	Buffalo	Int.	2B-SS	124	425	67	117	20	5	5	54	9	.275
2000	Indianapolis a	Int.	2B-SS	4	13	5	7	1	1	1	3	1	.538
2001	Indianapolis	Int.	2B-3B-SS	132	495	87	146	29	3	11	50	11	.295
2002	Norfolk	Int.	2B-SS-OF-3B	97	354	48	113	22	6	7	28	7	.319
2002	New York b	N.L.	2B-SS-3B-OF	27	36	2	8	0	1	1	6	0	.222
2003	Norfolk	Int.	3B-2B-SS-OF	70	244	42	76	18	3	9	32	11	.311
2003	New York c	N.L.	2B-SS	48	75	10	16	4	0	2	6	2	.213
2004	Oakland	A.L.	2B-SS-3B	137	455	50	124	32	1	7	43	0	.273
2005	Oakland	A.L.	SS-2B-3B-OF	118	381	48	94	22	3	9	37	5	.247
2006	Oakland	A.L.	SS-2B-3B-OF	117	365	52	97	21	6	5	41	5	.266
2007	Oakland d	A.L.	SS-3B-2B-OF	104	338	49	88	13	0	7	41	2	.260
2008	Toronto	A.L.	SS-2B-3B-1B	145	517	76	138	23	1	7	60	7	.267
2009	Toronto e	A.L.	SS-2B	144	574	100	162	35	1	12	60	14	.282
2010	Boston	A.L.	SS-2B	150	632	92	174	38	0	11	56	5	.275
Major League Totals			9 Yrs.	990	3373	479	901	188	13	61	350	40	.267
	Division Series												
2006	Oakland	A.L.	SS	3	12	1	4	4	0	0	6	0	.333
	Championship Series												
2006	Oakland	A.L.	SS	4	15	0	1	0	0	0	0	0	.067

a Sent by Cleveland Indians to Milwaukee Brewers as player to be named later in Richie Sexson trade, August 30, 2000.
b Claimed on waivers by New York Mets, April 3, 2002.
c Claimed on waivers by Oakland Athletics, October 9, 2003.
d Traded to Toronto Blue Jays for pitcher Kristian Bell and pitcher Graham Godfrey, November 18, 2007.
e Filed for free agency, November 6, 2009. Signed with Boston Red Sox, December 4, 2009.

SHOPPACH, KELLY BRIAN

Born, Fort Worth, Texas, April 29, 1980.
Bats Right. Throws Right. Height, 6 feet, 1 inch. Weight, 210 pounds.

Year Club	Lea	Pos	G	AB	R	H	2B	3B	HR	RBI	SB	Avg
2002 Sarasota	Fla.St.	C	116	414	54	112	35	1	10	66	2	.271
2003 Portland	Eastern	C	92	340	45	96	30	2	12	60	0	.282
2004 Pawtucket	Int.	C	113	399	62	93	25	0	22	64	0	.233
2005 Pawtucket	Int.	C	102	371	60	94	16	0	26	75	0	.253
2005 Boston	A.L.	C	9	15	1	0	0	0	0	0	0	.000
2006 Buffalo	Int.	C	21	78	11	22	8	0	4	9	0	.282
2006 Cleveland a	A.L.	C	41	110	7	27	6	0	3	16	0	.245
2007 Cleveland	A.L.	C	59	161	26	42	13	0	7	30	0	.261
2008 Cleveland	A.L.	C	112	352	67	92	27	0	21	55	0	.261
2009 Cleveland b	A.L.	C	89	271	33	58	14	0	12	40	0	.214
2010 Durham	Int.	C	4	13	0	4	0	0	0	2	0	.308
2010 Tampa Bay c	A.L.	C	63	158	17	31	8	0	5	17	0	.196
Major League Totals		6 Yrs.	373	1067	151	250	68	0	48	158	0	.234
Division Series												
2007 Cleveland	A.L.	C	1	3	1	2	2	0	0	0	0	.667
2010 Tampa Bay	N.L.	C	3	9	0	0	0	0	0	0	0	.000
Division Series Totals			4	12	1	2	2	0	0	0	0	.167
Championship Series												
2007 Cleveland	A.L.	C	1	3	0	1	0	0	0	0	0	.333

a Traded to Cleveland Indians with infielder Andy Marte and pitcher Guillermo Mota for outfielder Coco Crisp, pitcher David Riske and catcher Josh Bard, January 27, 2006.
b Traded to Tampa Bay Rays for player to be named later, December 1, 2009. Cleveland Indians received pitcher Mitch Talbot to complete the trade, December 21, 2009.
c On disabled list from April 11 to June 4, 2010.

SIZEMORE, GRADY

Born, Seattle, Washington, August 2, 1982.
Bats Left. Throws Left. Height, 6 feet, 2 inches. Weight, 200 pounds.

Year Club	Lea	Pos	G	AB	R	H	2B	3B	HR	RBI	SB	Avg
2000 Expos	Gulf Coast	OF	55	205	31	60	8	3	1	14	16	.293
2001 Clinton	Midwest	OF	123	451	64	121	16	4	2	61	32	.268
2002 Kinston	Carolina	OF	47	172	31	59	9	3	3	20	14	.343
2002 Brevard County a	Fla.St.	OF	75	256	37	66	15	4	0	26	9	.258
2003 Akron	Eastern	OF-2B	128	496	96	151	26	11	13	78	10	.304
2004 Buffalo	Int.	OF	101	418	73	120	23	8	8	51	15	.287
2004 Cleveland	A.L.	OF	43	138	15	34	6	2	4	24	2	.246
2005 Cleveland	A.L.	OF	158	640	111	185	37	11	22	81	22	.289
2006 Cleveland	A.L.	OF	*162	655	*134	190	*53	11	28	76	22	.290
2007 Cleveland	A.L.	OF	*162	628	118	174	34	5	24	78	33	.277
2008 Cleveland	A.L.	OF	157	634	101	170	39	5	33	90	38	.268
2009 Cleveland b	A.L.	OF	106	436	73	108	20	6	18	64	13	.248
2010 Cleveland c	A.L.	OF	33	128	15	27	6	2	0	13	4	.211
Major League Totals		7 Yrs.	821	3259	567	888	195	42	129	426	134	.272
Division Series												
2007 Cleveland	A.L.	OF	4	16	3	6	0	1	1	1	1	.375
Championship Series												
2007 Cleveland	A.L.	OF	7	27	6	6	2	0	1	2	1	.222

a Traded by Montreal Expos to Cleveland Indians with infielder Lee Stevens, infielder Brandon Phillips and pitcher Cliff Lee for pitcher Bartolo Colon and player to be named later, June 27, 2002. Montreal Expos received pitcher Tim Drew to complete trade, June 28, 2002.
b On disabled list from May 31 to June 23 and September 4 to October 14, 2009.
c On disabled list from May 17 to November 9, 2010.

SMITH, GARRY SETH (SETH)

Born, Jackson, Mississippi, September 30, 1982.
Bats Left. Throws Left. Height, 6 feet, 3 inches. Weight, 215 pounds.

Year Club	Lea	Pos	G	AB	R	H	2B	3B	HR	RBI	SB	Avg
2004 Tri-Cities	Northwest	OF	9	27	6	7	1	1	2	5	0	.259
2004 Casper	Pioneer	OF	56	233	46	86	21	3	9	61	9	.369
2005 Modesto	Calif.	OF	129	533	87	160	45	6	9	72	5	.300
2006 Tulsa	Texas	OF	130	524	79	154	46	4	15	71	4	.294
2007 Colorado Springs	P.C.	OF	129	451	68	143	32	6	17	82	7	.317
2007 Colorado	N.L.	OF	7	8	4	5	0	1	0	0	0	.625
2008 Colorado Springs	P.C.	OF	68	248	55	80	16	2	10	53	11	.323

Year	Club	Lea	Pos	G	AB	R	H	2B	3B	HR	RBI	SB	Avg
2008	Colorado	N.L.	OF	67	108	13	28	7	0	4	15	1	.259
2009	Colorado a	N.L.	OF	133	335	61	98	20	4	15	55	4	.293
2010	Colorado	N.L.	OF	133	358	55	88	19	5	17	52	2	.246
Major League Totals			4 Yrs.	340	809	133	219	46	10	36	122	7	.271
	Division Series												
2007	Colorado	N.L.	PH	2	2	1	1	0	0	0	0	0	.500
2009	Colorado	N.L.	OF	3	5	0	1	0	0	0	0	0	.200
Division Series Totals				5	7	1	2	0	0	0	0	0	.286
	Championship Series												
2007	Colorado	N.L.	PH	2	2	1	1	1	0	0	2	0	.500
	World Series Record												
2007	Colorado	N.L.	PH	2	2	0	1	0	0	0	0	0	.500

a On disabled list from September 1 to November 13, 2009.

SMOAK, JUSTIN KYLE

Born, Goose Creek, South Carolina, December 5, 1986.
Bats Both. Throws Left. Height, 6 feet, 4 inches. Weight, 220 pounds.

Year	Club	Lea	Pos	G	AB	R	H	2B	3B	HR	RBI	SB	Avg
2008	Clinton	Midwest	1B	14	56	9	17	3	0	3	6	0	.304
2009	Rangers	Arizona	1B	2	6	3	4	0	1	2	5	0	.667
2009	Okla.	P.C.	1B	54	197	25	48	11	0	4	23	0	.244
2009	Frisco	Texas	1B	50	183	30	60	10	0	6	29	0	.328
2010	Oklahoma	P.C.	1B	15	50	10	15	6	0	2	5	0	.300
2010	Tacoma	P.C.	1B	35	133	23	36	7	0	7	25	0	.271
2010	Texas-Seattle a	A.L.	1B	100	348	40	76	14	0	13	48	1	.218
Major League Totals			1 Yrs.	100	348	40	76	14	0	13	48	1	.218

a Traded to Seattle Mariners with pitcher Blake Beavan, pitcher Josh Lueke and infielder Matt Lawson for pitcher Cliff Lee, pitcher Mark Lowe and cash, July 9, 2010.

SNIDER, TRAVIS JAMES

Born, Kirkland, Washington, February 2, 1988.
Bats Left. Throws Left. Height, 5 feet, 11 inches. Weight, 245 pounds.

Year	Club	Lea	Pos	G	AB	R	H	2B	3B	HR	RBI	SB	Avg
2006	Pulaski	Appal.	OF	54	194	36	63	12	1	11	41	6	.325
2007	Lansing	Midwest	OF	118	457	72	143	35	7	16	93	3	.313
2008	Dunedin	Fla.St.	DH	17	61	15	17	5	0	4	7	1	.279
2008	New Hampshire	Eastern	OF	98	362	65	95	21	0	17	67	1	.262
2008	Syracuse	Int.	OF	18	64	9	22	5	0	2	17	1	.344
2008	Toronto	A.L.	OF	24	73	9	22	6	0	2	13	0	.301
2009	Las Vegas	P.C.	OF	48	175	32	59	13	1	14	40	2	.337
2009	Toronto	A.L.	OF	77	241	34	58	14	1	9	29	1	.241
2010	Blue Jays	Gulf Coast	OF	4	14	2	4	0	0	0	1	1	.286
2010	Dunedin	Fla.St.	DH	1	4	0	0	0	0	0	0	0	.000
2010	New Hampshire	Eastern	OF	20	81	14	24	5	0	5	17	3	.296
2010	Toronto a	A.L.	OF	82	298	36	76	20	0	14	32	6	.255
Major League Totals			3 Yrs.	183	612	79	156	40	1	25	74	7	.255

a On disabled list from May 15 to July 17, 2010.

SNYDER, CHRISTOPHER RYAN (CHRIS)

Born, Houston, Texas, February 12, 1981.
Bats Right. Throws Right. Height, 6 feet, 3 inches. Weight, 245 pounds.

Year	Club	Lea	Pos	G	AB	R	H	2B	3B	HR	RBI	SB	Avg
2002	Lancaster	Calif.	C	60	217	32	56	16	0	9	44	0	.258
2003	Lancaster	Calif.	C	69	245	53	77	16	2	10	53	0	.314
2003	El Paso	Texas	C	53	188	21	38	14	0	4	26	0	.202
2004	El Paso	Texas	C-1B	99	346	66	104	31	0	15	57	3	.301
2004	Arizona	N.L.	C	29	96	10	23	6	0	5	15	0	.240
2005	Arizona	N.L.	C	115	326	24	66	14	0	6	28	0	.202
2006	Arizona	N.L.	C	61	184	19	51	9	0	6	32	0	.277
2007	Arizona	N.L.	C-1B-OF	110	326	37	82	20	0	13	47	0	.252
2008	Visalia	Calif.	C	1	5	1	2	0	0	1	4	0	.400
2008	Arizona a	N.L.	C	115	334	47	79	22	1	16	64	0	.237
2009	Visalia	Calif.	C	3	7	1	1	0	0	0	0	0	.143
2009	Reno	P.C.	C	3	13	2	4	1	0	1	4	0	.308
2009	Arizona b	N.L.	C-1B	61	165	20	33	7	0	6	22	0	.200

Year Club	Lea	Pos	G	AB	R	H	2B	3B	HR	RBI	SB	Avg
2010 Arizona-Pittsburgh c ...	N.L.	C	105	319	34	66	9	0	15	48	0	.207
Major League Totals		7 Yrs.	596	1750	191	400	87	1	67	256	0	.229
Division Series												
2007 Arizona..............	N.L.	C	3	7	2	1	0	0	0	0	0	.143
Championship Series												
2007 Arizona..............	N.L.	C	3	12	1	4	2	0	1	3	0	.333

a On disabled list from July 1 to July 20, 2008.
b On disabled list from June 21 to July 28 and August 27 to October 15, 2009.
c Traded to Pittsburgh Pirates with infielder Pedro Ciriaco and cash for infielder Bobby Crosby, outfielder Ryan Church and pitcher D.J. Carrasco, July 31, 2010.

SORIANO, ALFONSO GUILLEARD

Born, San Pedro de Macoris, Dominican Republic, January 7, 1976.
Bats Right. Throws Right. Height, 6 feet, 1 inch. Weight, 180 pounds.

Year Club	Lea	Pos	G	AB	R	H	2B	3B	HR	RBI	SB	Avg
1995 Hiroshima	Dominican	SS	63	227	52	83	12	3	4	55	8	.366
1996 Hiroshima	Japan East	SS	57	131	11	28	0	0	0	13	0	.214
1997 Hiroshima	Japan Cent.	SS	9	17	2	2	0	0	0	2	0	.118
1998 a						Did Not Play						
1999 Norwich...........	Eastern	SS	89	361	57	110	20	3	15	68	24	.305
1999 Yankees	Gulf Coast	SS	5	19	7	5	2	0	1	5	0	.263
1999 Columbus.............	Int.	SS	20	82	8	15	5	1	2	11	1	.183
1999 New York b...........	A.L.	SS	9	8	2	1	0	0	1	1	0	.125
2000 Columbus.............	Int.	SS-2B	111	459	90	133	32	6	12	66	14	.290
2000 New York	A.L.	3B-SS-2B	22	50	5	9	3	0	2	3	2	.180
2001 New York	A.L.	2B	158	574	77	154	34	3	18	73	43	.268
2002 New York	A.L.	2B	156	*696	*128	*209	51	2	39	102	41	.300
2003 New York	A.L.	2B	156	*682	114	198	36	5	38	91	35	.290
2004 Texas c-d	A.L.	2B	145	608	77	170	32	4	28	91	18	.280
2005 Texas e..............	A.L.	2B	156	637	102	171	43	2	36	104	30	.268
2006 Washington f	N.L.	OF	159	647	119	179	41	2	46	95	41	.277
2007 Chicago g............	N.L.	OF-2B	135	579	97	173	42	5	33	70	19	.299
2008 Azl Cubs...........	Arizona	DH	1	2	1	0	0	0	0	0	0	.000
2008 Iowa.................	P.C.	OF	1	3	0	1	0	0	0	0	0	.333
2008 Chicago h............	N.L.	OF-2B	109	453	76	127	27	0	29	75	19	.280
2009 Chicago i	N.L.	OF-2B-3B	117	477	64	115	25	1	20	55	9	.241
2010 Chicago	N.L.	OF	147	496	67	128	40	3	24	79	5	.258
Major League Totals		12 Yrs.	1469	5907	928	1634	374	27	314	839	262	.277
Division Series												
2001 New York	A.L.	2B	5	18	2	4	0	0	0	3	2	.222
2002 New York	A.L.	2B	4	17	2	2	1	0	1	2	1	.118
2003 New York	A.L.	2B	4	19	2	7	1	0	0	4	2	.368
2007 Chicago	N.L.	OF	3	14	0	2	0	0	0	0	0	.143
2008 Chicago	N.L.	OF	3	14	0	1	0	0	0	0	0	.071
Division Series Totals			19	82	6	16	2	0	1	9	5	.195
Championship Series												
2001 New York	A.L.	2B	5	15	5	6	0	0	1	2	2	.500
2003 New York	A.L.	2B	7	30	0	4	1	0	0	3	2	.133
Championship Series Totals			12	45	5	10	1	0	1	5	4	.222
World Series Record												
2001 New York	A.L.	2B	7	25	1	6	0	0	1	2	0	.240
2003 New York	A.L.	2B-OF	6	22	2	5	0	0	1	2	1	.227
World Series Totals..........			13	47	3	11	0	0	2	4	1	.234

a Signed by New York Yankees as free agent, September 29, 1998.
b On disabled list from July 15 to August 15, 1999.
c Traded to Texas Rangers with player to be named later for infielder Alex Rodriguez, February 16, 2004.
d Texas Rangers received infielder Joaquin Arias to complete trade, March 23, 2004.
e Traded to Washington Nationals for outfielder Brad Wilkerson, outfielder Terrmel Sledge and pitcher Armando Galarraga, December 13, 2005.
f Filed for free agency, October 29, 2006. Signed with Chicago Cubs, November 20, 2006.
g On disabled list from August 6 to August 28, 2007.
h On disabled list from April 16 to May 1 and June 12 to July 23, 2008.
i On disabled list from September 4 to October 14, 2009.

SOTO, GEOVANY

Born, San Juan, Puerto Rico, January 20, 1983.
Bats Right. Throws Right. Height, 6 feet, 1 inch. Weight, 230 pounds.

Year Club	Lea	Pos	G	AB	R	H	2B	3B	HR	RBI	SB	Avg
2001 Cubs	Arizona	C-1B-3B-OF	41	150	18	39	16	0	1	20	1	.260
2002 Cubs	Arizona	C-1B	44	156	24	42	10	2	3	24	0	.269
2002 Boise	Northwest	C	1	5	1	2	0	0	0	0	0	.400
2003 Daytona	Fla.St.	C-3B	89	297	26	72	12	2	2	38	0	.242
2004 West Tenn	Southern	C-1B	104	332	47	90	16	0	9	48	1	.271
2005 Iowa	P.C.	C	91	292	30	74	14	0	4	39	0	.253
2005 Chicago	N.L.	PH	1	1	0	0	0	0	0	0	0	.000
2006 Iowa	P.C.	C	108	342	34	93	21	0	6	38	0	.272
2006 Chicago	N.L.	C	11	25	1	5	1	0	0	2	0	.200
2007 Iowa	P.C.	C-1B	110	385	75	136	31	3	26	109	0	.353
2007 Chicago	N.L.	C	18	54	12	21	6	0	3	8	0	.389
2008 Chicago a	N.L.	C	141	494	66	141	35	2	23	86	0	.285
2009 Azl Cubs	Arizona	DH	1	3	0	1	1	0	0	2	0	.333
2009 Tennessee	Southern	C	3	9	2	3	0	0	2	4	0	.333
2009 Chicago b	N.L.	C	102	331	27	72	19	1	11	47	1	.218
2010 Chicago c	N.L.	C	105	322	47	90	19	0	17	53	0	.280
Major League Totals		6 Yrs.	378	1227	153	329	80	3	54	196	1	.268
Division Series												
2007 Chicago	N.L.	C	2	6	1	1	0	0	1	2	0	.167
2008 Chicago	N.L.	C	3	11	0	2	1	0	0	0	0	.182
Division Series Totals			5	17	1	3	1	0	1	2	0	.176

a Selected Rookie of the Year in National League for 2008.
b On disabled list from July 7 to August 7, 2009.
c On disabled list from August 7 to August 23 and September 19 to October 6, 2010.

SPAN, KEIUNTA DENARD (DENARD)

Born, Tampa, Florida, February 17, 1984.
Bats Left. Throws Left. Height, 6 feet. Weight, 205 pounds.

Year Club	Lea	Pos	G	AB	R	H	2B	3B	HR	RBI	SB	Avg
2003 Elizabethton	Appal.	OF	50	207	34	56	5	1	1	18	14	.271
2004 Twins	Gulf Coast	OF	5	16	1	6	2	0	0	1	0	.375
2004 Quad Cities	Midwest	OF	64	240	29	64	4	3	0	14	15	.267
2005 New Britain	Eastern	OF	68	267	47	76	6	5	0	26	10	.285
2005 Fort Myers	Fla.St.	OF	49	186	38	63	3	3	1	19	13	.339
2006 New Britain	Eastern	OF	134	536	80	153	16	6	2	45	24	.285
2007 Rochester	Int.	OF	139	487	59	130	20	7	3	55	25	.267
2008 Rochester	Int.	OF	40	156	32	53	11	1	3	14	15	.340
2008 Minnesota	A.L.	OF	93	347	70	102	16	7	6	47	18	.294
2009 Rochester	Int.	OF	2	6	1	2	1	0	0	0	1	.333
2009 Minnesota a	A.L.	OF	145	578	97	180	16	*10	8	68	23	.311
2010 Minnesota	A.L.	OF	153	629	85	166	24	10	3	58	26	.264
Major League Totals		3 Yrs.	391	1554	252	448	56	27	17	173	67	.288
Division Series												
2009 Minnesota	A.L.	OF	3	15	1	6	1	0	0	1	1	.400
2010 Minnesota	A.L.	OF	3	13	0	4	0	0	0	0	0	.308
Division Series Totals			6	28	1	10	1	0	0	1	1	.357

a On disabled list from June 10 to June 25, 2009.

SPILBORGHS, RYAN ADAM

Born, Santa Barbara, California, September 5, 1979.
Bats Right. Throws Right. Height, 6 feet, 1 inch. Weight, 190 pounds.

Year Club	Lea	Pos	G	AB	R	H	2B	3B	HR	RBI	SB	Avg
2002 Tri-City	Northwest	OF	71	261	34	60	11	1	4	34	11	.230
2003 Asheville	So.Atl.	OF	119	434	78	122	22	2	15	61	10	.281
2004 Visalia	Calif.	OF-SS	125	444	59	115	26	3	8	57	8	.259
2005 Tulsa	Texas	OF	71	255	52	87	23	3	6	54	10	.341
2005 Colorado	N.L.	OF	1	4	0	2	0	0	0	1	0	.500
2005 Colorado Springs a	P.C.	OF	60	227	49	77	23	5	5	30	7	.339
2006 Colorado Springs	P.C.	OF	68	269	50	91	20	1	5	34	8	.338
2006 Colorado	N.L.	OF	67	167	26	48	6	3	4	21	5	.287
2007 Colorado Springs	P.C.	OF-1B	34	124	25	40	7	1	5	17	4	.323
2007 Colorado	N.L.	OF	97	264	40	79	14	1	11	51	4	.299
2008 Colorado Springs	P.C.	OF	11	30	9	9	1	0	1	4	0	.300

Year	Club	Lea	Pos	G	AB	R	H	2B	3B	HR	RBI	SB	Avg
2008	Colorado b	N.L.	OF	89	233	38	73	14	2	6	36	7	.313
2009	Colorado	N.L.	OF	133	352	55	85	24	3	8	48	9	.241
2010	Colorado	N.L.	OF	134	341	41	95	20	2	10	39	4	.279
Major League Totals			6 Yrs.	521	1361	200	382	78	11	39	196	29	.281
	Division Series												
2007	Colorado	N.L.	OF	3	8	2	2	0	0	0	0	0	.250
2009	Colorado	N.L.	OF	4	9	1	2	1	0	0	0	0	.222
Division Series Totals				7	17	3	4	1	0	0	0	0	.235
	Championship Series												
2007	Colorado	N.L.	OF	2	2	1	1	0	0	0	0	0	.500
	World Series Record												
2007	Colorado	N.L.	OF-DH	4	10	0	0	0	0	0	0	0	.000

a Not offered contract, December 21, 2005, re-signed with Colorado Rockies organization, December 22, 2005.
b On disabled list from July 9 to September 1, 2008.

STAIRS, MATTHEW WADE (MATT)

Born, St. John, New Brunswick, Canada, February 27, 1969.
Bats Left. Throws Right. Height, 5 feet, 9 inches. Weight, 215 pounds.

Year	Club	Lea	Pos	G	AB	R	H	2B	3B	HR	RBI	SB	Avg
1989	Jamestown	N.Y.Penn.	2B-3B	14	43	8	11	1	0	1	5	1	.256
1989	West Palm Bch.	Fla. St.	3B-SS-2B	36	111	12	21	3	1	1	9	0	.189
1989	Rockford	Midwest	3B	44	141	20	40	9	2	2	14	5	.284
1990	West Palm Bch.	Fla. St.	3B-SS	55	183	30	62	9	3	3	30	15	.339
1990	Jacksonville	Southern	3B-OF-2B	79	280	26	71	17	0	3	34	5	.254
1991	Harrisburg	Eastern	2B-3B-OF	129	505	87	168	30	10	13	78	23	.333
1992	Montreal	N.L.	OF	13	30	2	5	2	0	0	5	0	.167
1992	Indianapolis	A.A.	OF	110	401	57	107	23	4	11	56	11	.267
1993	Ottawa a - b	Int.	OF	34	125	18	35	4	2	3	20	4	.280
1993	Montreal	N.L.	OF	6	8	1	3	1	0	0	2	0	.375
1993	Chunichi	Japan Cent.	OF	60	132	10	33	6	0	6	23	1	.250
1994	New Britain	Eastern	OF-1B	93	317	44	98	25	2	9	61	10	.309
1995	Pawtucket	Int.	OF	75	271	40	77	17	0	13	56	3	.284
1995	Boston c	A.L.	OF	39	88	8	23	7	1	1	17	0	.261
1996	Edmonton	P.C.	DH-OF-1B	51	180	35	62	16	1	8	41	0	.344
1996	Oakland	A.L.	OF-1B	61	137	21	38	5	1	10	23	1	.277
1997	Oakland	A.L.	OF-1B	133	352	62	105	19	0	27	73	3	.298
1998	Oakland	A.L.	DH-OF-1B	149	523	88	154	33	1	26	106	8	.294
1999	Oakland	A.L.	OF-1B	146	531	94	137	26	3	38	102	2	.258
2000	Oakland d	A.L.	OF-1B	143	476	74	108	26	0	21	81	5	.227
2001	Chicago e	N.L.	1B-OF-2B	128	340	48	85	21	0	17	61	2	.250
2002	Milwaukee f-g	N.L.	OF	107	270	41	66	15	0	16	41	2	.244
2003	Nashville	P.C.	OF-1B	7	18	4	3	0	0	2	3	0	.167
2003	Pittsburgh h-i	N.L.	OF-1B	121	305	49	89	20	1	20	57	0	.292
2004	Kansas City j	A.L.	OF-1B	126	439	48	117	21	3	18	66	1	.267
2005	Kansas City	A.L.	1B-OF	127	396	55	109	26	1	13	66	1	.275
2006	K.C.-Texas-Detroit k-l-m	A.L.	DH-1B-OF	117	348	42	86	21	0	13	51	0	.247
2007	Toronto n	A.L.	OF-1B	125	357	58	103	28	1	21	64	2	.289
2008	Toronto	A.L.	DH-OF	105	320	42	80	11	1	11	44	1	.250
2008	Philadelphia o	N.L.	OF	16	17	4	5	1	0	2	5	0	.294
2009	Philadelphia p	N.L.	OF	99	103	15	20	4	0	5	17	0	.194
2010	San Diego q-r	N.L.	OF-1B	78	99	14	23	6	0	6	16	2	.232
Major League Totals			18 Yrs.	1839	5139	766	1356	293	13	265	897	30	.264
	Division Series												
1995	Boston	A.L.	PH	1	1	0	0	0	0	0	0	0	.000
2000	Oakland	A.L.	OF	3	9	0	1	1	0	0	0	0	.111
2008	Philadelphia	N.L.	PH	2	2	0	0	0	0	0	0	0	.000
2009	Philadelphia	N.L.	PH	2	1	0	0	0	0	0	0	0	.000
Division Series Totals				8	13	0	1	1	0	0	0	0	.077
	Championship Series												
2008	Philadelphia	N.L.	PH	1	1	1	1	0	0	1	2	0	1.000
2009	Philadelphia	N.L.	PH	2	1	0	0	0	0	0	0	0	.000
Championship Series Totals				3	2	1	1	0	0	1	2	0	.500
	World Series Record												
2008	Philadelphia	N.L.	PH	1	1	0	0	0	0	0	0	0	.000
2009	Philadelphia	N.L.	DH	5	8	0	1	0	0	0	1	0	.125
World Series Totals				6	9	0	1	0	0	0	1	0	.111

a Released, June 8, 1993, played in Japan, re-signed by Montreal Expos organization, December 15, 1993.

b Traded to Boston Red Sox with pitcher Pete Young for player to be named later and cash, February 18, 1994.
c Filed for free agency, October 14, 1995. Signed by Oakland Athletics organization, December 1, 1995.
d Traded to Chicago Cubs for pitcher Eric Ireland, November 20, 2000.
e Filed for free agency, November 5, 2001. Signed with Milwaukee Brewers, January 25, 2002.
f On disabled list from May 16 to June 3, 2002.
g Filed for free agency, October 28, 2002. Signed with Pittsburgh Pirates, December 15, 2002.
h On disabled list from May 19 to June 10, 2003.
i Filed for free agency, October 31, 2003. Signed with Kansas City Royals, December 9, 2003.
j On disabled list from August 7 to August 22, 2004.
k Traded to Texas Rangers for pitcher Joselo Diaz, July 31, 2006.
l Claimed on waivers by Detroit Tigers, September 15, 2006.
m Filed for free agency, October 30, 2006. Signed with Toronto Blue Jays organization, December 12, 2006.
n Filed for free agency, October 29, 2007, re-signed with Toronto Blue Jays, November 2, 2007.
o Traded to Philadelphia Phillies August 30, 2008. Toronto Blue Jays received pitcher Fabio Castro to complete trade, September 29, 2008.
p Filed for free agency, November 9, 2009. Signed with San Diego Padres organization, January 26, 2010.
q On disabled list from June 7 to July 1, 2010.
r Filed for free agency, November 1, 2010. Signed with Washington Nationals organization, December 14, 2010.

STANTON, GIANCARLO CRUZ-MICHAEL (MIKE)

Born, Panorama, California, November 8, 1989.
Bats Right. Throws Right. Height, 6 feet, 5 inches. Weight, 235 pounds.

Year	Club	Lea	Pos	G	AB	R	H	2B	3B	HR	RBI	SB	Avg
2007	Marlins	Gulf Coast	OF	8	26	6	7	2	0	0	1	0	.269
2007	Jamestown	N.Y.-Penn.	OF	9	30	2	2	1	0	1	2	0	.067
2008	Greensboro	So.Atl.	OF	125	468	89	137	26	3	39	97	4	.293
2009	Jupiter	Fla.St.	OF	50	180	27	53	9	3	12	39	2	.294
2009	Jacksonville	Southern	OF	79	299	49	69	15	2	16	53	1	.231
2010	Jacksonville	Southern	OF	53	192	42	60	13	2	21	52	1	.313
2010	Florida	N.L.	OF	100	359	45	93	21	1	22	59	5	.259

STAVINOHA, NICHOLAS LEE (NICK)

Born, Houston, Texas, May 3, 1982.
Bats Right. Throws Right. Height, 6 feet, 2 inches. Weight, 240 pounds.

Year	Club	Lea	Pos	G	AB	R	H	2B	3B	HR	RBI	SB	Avg
2005	Quad Cities	Midwest	OF-1B	65	250	54	86	9	2	14	53	4	.344
2006	Springfield	Texas	OF	111	417	55	124	26	3	12	73	2	.297
2007	Memphis	P.C.	OF	139	501	50	131	17	0	13	49	7	.261
2008	Memphis	P.C.	OF	112	427	67	144	23	3	16	74	2	.337
2008	St. Louis	N.L.	OF	29	57	4	11	1	0	0	4	0	.193
2009	St. Louis	N.L.	OF	39	87	6	20	7	0	2	17	1	.230
2009	Memphis	P.C.	1B-OF-C	72	259	39	73	17	2	11	56	2	.282
2010	Memphis	P.C.	OF-1B	23	100	19	39	9	1	6	28	0	.390
2010	St. Louis a	N.L.	OF-1B-C	79	121	11	31	4	0	2	9	0	.256
Major League Totals		3 Yrs.		147	265	21	62	12	0	4	30	1	.234

a On disabled list from July 12 to July 31, 2010.

STEWART, IAN KENNETH

Born, Long Beach, California, April 5, 1985.
Bats Left. Throws Right. Height, 6 feet, 3 inches. Weight, 205 pounds.

Year	Club	Lea	Pos	G	AB	R	H	2B	3B	HR	RBI	SB	Avg
2003	Casper	Pioneer	3B	57	224	40	71	14	5	10	43	4	.317
2004	Asheville	So.Atl.	3B	131	505	92	161	31	9	30	101	19	.319
2005	Modesto	Calif.	3B	112	435	83	119	32	7	17	86	2	.274
2006	Tulsa	Texas	3B	120	462	75	124	41	7	10	71	3	.268
2007	Colorado Springs	P.C.	3B	112	414	72	126	23	2	15	65	11	.304
2007	Colorado	N.L.	3B	35	43	3	9	4	0	1	9	0	.209
2008	Colorado Springs	P.C.	3B-2B	69	257	65	72	15	6	19	57	7	.280
2008	Colorado	N.L.	3B-2B	81	266	33	69	18	2	10	41	1	.259
2009	Colorado	N.L.	3B-2B-OF	147	425	74	97	19	3	25	70	7	.228
2010	Colorado a	N.L.	3B	121	386	54	99	14	2	18	61	5	.256
Major League Totals		4 Yrs.		384	1120	164	274	55	7	54	181	13	.245
	Division Series												
2009	Colorado	N.L.	3B	2	1	0	0	0	0	0	0	0	.000

a On disabled list from August 26 to September 17, 2010.

STUBBS, ANDREW ROBERT (DREW)

Born, Texarkana, Texas, October 4, 1984.
Bats Right. Throws Right. Height, 6 feet, 4 inches. Weight, 205 pounds.

Year	Club	Lea	Pos	G	AB	R	H	2B	3B	HR	RBI	SB	Avg
2006	Billings	Pioneer	OF	56	210	39	53	7	3	6	24	19	.252
2007	Dayton	Midwest	OF	129	497	93	134	29	5	12	43	23	.270
2008	Sarasota	Fla.St.	OF	86	303	49	79	21	4	5	38	27	.261
2008	Louisville	Int.	OF	19	75	14	22	4	2	2	10	3	.293
2008	Chattanooga	Southern	OF	26	92	12	29	8	0	0	9	3	.315
2009	Louisville	Int.	OF	107	411	57	110	25	2	3	39	46	.268
2009	Cincinnati	N.L.	OF	42	180	27	48	5	1	8	17	10	.267
2010	Cincinnati	N.L.	OF	150	514	91	131	19	6	22	77	30	.255
Major League Totals			2 Yrs.	192	694	118	179	24	7	30	94	40	.258
Division Series													
2010	Cincinnati	N.L.	OF	3	9	0	1	0	0	0	0	0	.111

SUZUKI, ICHIRO

Born, Kasugai, Japan, October 22, 1973.
Bats Left. Throws Right. Height, 5 feet, 9 inches. Weight, 170 pounds.

Year	Club	Lea	Pos	G	AB	R	H	2B	3B	HR	RBI	SB	Avg
1992	Orix	Japan Pac.	OF	40	95	9	24	5	0	0	5	3	.253
1993	Orix	Japan Pac.	OF	43	64	4	12	2	0	1	2	0	.188
1994	Orix	Japan Pac.	OF	130	546	111	210	41	5	13	54	29	.385
1995	Orix	Japan Pac.	OF	130	524	104	179	23	4	25	80	49	.342
1996	Orix	Japan Pac.	OF	130	542	104	193	24	4	16	84	35	.356
1997	Orix	Japan Pac.	OF	135	536	94	185	31	4	17	91	39	.345
1998	Orix	Japan Pac.	OF	135	506	79	181	36	3	13	71	11	.358
1999	Orix	Japan Pac.	OF	103	411	80	141	27	2	21	68	12	.343
2000	Orix a	Japan Pac.	OF	105	395	73	153	22	1	12	73	21	.387
2001	Seattle b-c	A.L.	OF	157	*692	127	*242	34	8	8	69	*56	*.350
2002	Seattle	A.L.	OF	157	647	111	208	27	8	8	51	31	.321
2003	Seattle	A.L.	OF	159	679	111	212	29	8	13	62	34	.312
2004	Seattle	A.L.	OF	161	*704	101	*262	24	5	8	60	36	*.372
2005	Seattle	A.L.	OF	*162	679	111	206	21	12	15	68	33	.303
2006	Seattle	A.L.	OF	161	*695	110	*224	20	9	9	49	45	.322
2007	Seattle	A.L.	OF	161	*678	111	*238	22	7	6	68	37	.351
2008	Seattle	A.L.	OF	162	*686	103	*213	20	7	6	42	43	.310
2009	Seattle d	A.L.	OF	146	639	88	*225	31	4	11	46	26	.352
2010	Seattle	A.L.	OF	*162	*680	74	*214	30	3	6	43	42	.315
Major League Totals			10 Yrs.	1588	6779	1047	2244	258	71	90	558	383	.331
Division Series													
2001	Seattle	A.L.	OF	5	20	4	12	1	0	0	2	1	.600
Championship Series													
2001	Seattle	A.L.	OF	5	18	3	4	1	0	0	1	2	.222

a Signed by Seattle Mariners as free agent, November 18, 2000.
b Selected Rookie of the Year in American League for 2001.
c Selected Most Valuable Player in American League for 2001.
d On disabled list from March 31 to April 15, 2009.

SUZUKI, KURT KIYOSHI

Born, Wailuku, Hawaii, October 4, 1983.
Bats Right. Throws Right. Height, 6 feet. Weight, 205 pounds.

Year	Club	Lea	Pos	G	AB	R	H	2B	3B	HR	RBI	SB	Avg
2004	Vancouver	Northwest	C	46	175	27	52	10	3	3	31	0	.297
2005	Stockton	Calif.	C	114	441	85	122	26	5	12	65	5	.277
2006	Midland	Texas	C-1B	99	376	64	107	26	1	7	55	5	.285
2007	Sacramento	P.C.	C	55	211	32	59	9	0	3	27	0	.280
2007	Oakland	A.L.	C	68	213	27	53	13	0	7	39	0	.249
2008	Oakland	A.L.	C	148	530	54	148	25	1	7	42	2	.279
2009	Oakland	A.L.	C	147	570	74	156	37	1	15	88	8	.274
2010	Sacramento	P.C.	C	3	8	4	3	2	0	1	5	0	.375
2010	Oakland a	A.L.	C	131	495	55	120	18	2	13	71	3	.242
Major League Totals			4 Yrs.	494	1808	210	477	93	4	42	240	13	.264

a On disabled list from April 24 to May 16, 2010.

SWEENEY, RYAN JOSEPH

Born, Cedar Rapids, Iowa, February 20, 1985.
Bats Left. Throws Left. Height, 6 feet, 4 inches. Weight, 200 pounds.

Year	Club	Lea	Pos	G	AB	R	H	2B	3B	HR	RBI	SB	Avg
2003	Bristol	Appal.	OF	19	67	11	21	3	0	2	5	3	.313
2003	Great Falls	Pioneer	OF	10	34	0	12	2	0	0	4	0	.353
2004	Winston-Salem	Carolina	OF	134	515	71	146	22	3	7	66	8	.283
2005	Birmingham	Southern	OF	113	429	64	128	22	3	1	47	6	.298
2006	Charlotte	Int.	OF	118	449	64	133	25	3	13	70	7	.296
2006	Chicago	A.L.	OF	18	35	1	8	0	0	0	5	0	.229
2007	Chicago	A.L.	OF	15	45	5	9	3	0	1	5	0	.200
2007	Charlotte	Int.	OF	105	397	50	107	17	2	10	47	8	.270
2008	Azl Athletics	Arizona	DH	1	3	0	0	0	0	0	0	0	.000
2008	Sacramento	P.C.	OF	8	34	5	14	4	0	1	5	0	.412
2008	Oakland a-b	A.L.	OF	115	384	53	110	18	2	5	45	9	.286
2009	Oakland c	A.L.	OF	134	484	68	142	31	3	6	53	6	.293
2010	Oakland d	A.L.	OF	82	303	41	89	20	2	1	36	1	.294
Major League Totals			5 Yrs.	364	1251	168	358	72	7	13	144	16	.286

a Traded to Oakland Athletics with pitcher Gio Gonzalez and pitcher Fautino de los Santos for outfielder Nick Swisher, January 3, 2008.
b On disabled list from May 29 to June 13 and August 13 to August 28, 2008.
c On disabled list from June 3 to June 18, 2009.
d On disabled list from July 12 to November 4, 2010.

SWISHER, NICHOLAS THOMPSON (NICK)

Born, Columbus, Ohio, January 25, 1980.
Bats Both. Throws Left. Height, 6 feet. Weight, 215 pounds.

Year	Club	Lea	Pos	G	AB	R	H	2B	3B	HR	RBI	SB	Avg
2002	Visalia	California	OF	49	183	22	44	13	2	4	23	3	.240
2002	Vancouver	Northwest	OF	13	44	10	11	3	0	2	12	3	.250
2003	Modesto	California	OF-1B	51	189	38	56	14	2	10	43	0	.296
2003	Midland	Texas	OF-1B	76	287	36	66	24	2	5	43	0	.230
2004	Sacramento	P.C.	OF-1B	125	443	109	119	28	2	29	92	3	.269
2004	Oakland	A.L.	OF-1B	20	60	11	15	4	0	2	8	0	.250
2005	Sacramento	P.C.	OF-1B	6	23	4	9	3	0	0	1	0	.391
2005	Oakland a	A.L.	OF-1B	131	462	66	109	32	1	21	74	0	.236
2006	Oakland	A.L.	1B-OF	157	556	106	141	24	2	35	95	1	.254
2007	Oakland b	A.L.	OF-1B	150	539	84	141	36	1	22	78	3	.262
2008	Chicago c	A.L.	OF-1B	153	497	86	109	21	1	24	69	3	.219
2009	New York	A.L.	OF-1B-P	150	498	84	124	35	1	29	82	0	.249
2010	New York	A.L.	OF-1B	150	566	91	163	33	3	29	89	1	.288
Major League Totals			7 Yrs.	911	3178	528	802	185	9	162	495	8	.252
	Division Series												
2006	Oakland	A.L.	1B	3	10	3	3	2	0	0	1	0	.300
2008	Chicago	A.L.	OF-1B	3	4	1	1	0	0	0	0	0	.250
2009	New York	A.L.	OF	3	12	0	1	1	0	0	1	0	.083
2010	New York	A.L.	OF	3	12	3	4	2	0	1	1	0	.333
Division Series Totals				12	38	7	9	5	0	1	3	0	.237
	Championship Series												
2006	Oakland	A.L.	1B	4	10	0	1	0	0	0	0	0	.100
2009	New York	A.L.	OF	6	20	2	3	0	0	0	0	0	.150
2010	New York	A.L.	OF-1B	6	22	3	2	1	0	1	1	0	.091
Championship Series Totals				16	52	5	6	1	0	1	1	0	.115
	World Series Record												
2009	New York	A.L.	OF	5	15	3	2	1	0	1	1	0	.133

a On disabled list from May 2 to May 25, 2005.
b Traded to Chicago White Sox for pitcher Gio Gonzalez, pitcher Fautino de los Santos and outfielder Ryan Sweeney, January 3, 2008.
c Traded to New York Yankees with pitcher Kaneoka Texeira for infielder Wilson Betemit, pitcher Jeff Marquez and pitcher Jhonny Nunez, November 13, 2008.

TABATA, JOSE NICOLAS

Born, El Tigre, Venezuela, August 12, 1988.
Bats Right. Throws Right. Height, 5 feet, 11 inches. Weight, 210 pounds.

Year	Club	Lea	Pos	G	AB	R	H	2B	3B	HR	RBI	SB	Avg
2005	Yankees	Gulf Coast	OF	44	156	30	49	5	1	3	25	22	.314
2006	Charleston	So.Atl.	OF	86	319	50	95	22	1	5	51	15	.298
2007	Tampa	Fla.St.	OF	103	411	56	126	16	2	5	54	15	.307

Year	Club	Lea	Pos	G	AB	R	H	2B	3B	HR	RBI	SB	Avg
2008	Altoona	Eastern	OF	22	89	16	31	6	2	3	13	8	.348
2008	Trenton	Eastern	OF	79	294	40	73	9	0	3	36	10	.248
2008	Pirates a	Gulf Coast	OF	4	11	4	5	1	0	2	7	0	.455
2009	Altoona	Eastern	OF	61	228	31	69	15	1	2	25	7	.303
2009	Indianapolis	Int.	OF	32	134	21	37	7	1	3	10	4	.276
2010	Indianapolis	Int.	OF	53	224	42	69	13	2	3	19	25	.308
2010	Pittsburgh	N.L.	OF	102	405	61	121	21	4	4	35	19	.299

a Traded by New York Yankees to Pittsburgh Pirates with pitcher Ross Ohlendorf, pitcher Jeff Karstens and pitcher Dan McCutchen for outfielder Xavier Nady and pitcher Damaso Marte, July 26, 2008.

TEAHEN, MARK THOMAS

Born, Redlands, California, September 6, 1981.
Bats Left. Throws Right. Height, 6 feet, 3 inches. Weight, 220 pounds.

Year	Club	Lea	Pos	G	AB	R	H	2B	3B	HR	RBI	SB	Avg
2002	Modesto	California	3B	59	234	25	56	9	1	1	26	1	.239
2002	Vancouver	Northwest	3B	13	57	10	23	5	1	0	6	4	.404
2003	Modesto	California	3B	121	453	68	128	27	4	3	71	4	.283
2004	Omaha	P.C.	3B	66	246	33	69	15	1	8	31	0	.280
2004	Sacramento	P.C.	3B	20	69	9	19	8	0	0	10	0	.275
2004	Midland a	Texas	3B	53	197	31	66	15	4	6	36	0	.335
2005	Omaha	P.C.	3B	8	27	4	7	2	0	0	4	0	.259
2005	Kansas City b	A.L.	3B	130	447	60	110	29	4	7	55	7	.246
2006	Omaha	P.C.	3B	24	79	14	30	8	4	2	14	0	.380
2006	Kansas City	A.L.	3B	109	393	70	114	21	7	18	69	10	.290
2007	Kansas City c	A.L.	OF-1B	144	544	78	155	31	8	7	60	13	.285
2008	Kansas City	A.L.	OF-3B-1B	149	572	66	146	31	4	15	59	4	.255
2009	Kansas City d	A.L.	3B-OF-1B-2B	144	524	69	142	34	1	12	50	8	.271
2010	Charlotte	Int.	3B-OF-1B	11	33	7	12	2	0	0	4	0	.364
2010	Chicago e	A.L.	3B-OF-1B	77	233	31	60	13	2	4	25	3	.258
Major League Totals			6 Yrs.	753	2713	374	727	159	26	63	318	45	.268

a Traded to Kansas City Royals with pitcher Mike Wood for outfielder Octavio Dotel and cash, June 24, 2004.
b On disabled list from April 12 to May 3, 2005.
c On disabled list from August 19 to September 3, 2007.
d Traded to Chicago White Sox for infielder Josh Fields and infielder Chris Getz, November 6, 2009.
e On disabled list from May 31 to August 13, 2010.

TEIXEIRA, MARK CHARLES

Born, Annapolis, Maryland, April 11, 1980.
Bats Both. Throws Right. Height, 6 feet, 3 inches. Weight, 220 pounds.

Year	Club	Lea	Pos	G	AB	R	H	2B	3B	HR	RBI	SB	Avg
2002	Charlotte	Fla.St.	3B	38	150	32	48	10	2	9	41	2	.320
2002	Tulsa	Texas	3B	48	171	31	54	11	3	10	28	3	.316
2003	Texas	A.L.	1B-OF-3B	146	529	66	137	29	5	26	84	1	.259
2004	Frisco	Texas	1B	1	3	0	0	0	0	0	0	0	.000
2004	Texas a	A.L.	1B-OF	145	545	101	153	34	2	38	112	4	.281
2005	Texas	A.L.	1B	*162	644	112	194	41	3	43	144	4	.301
2006	Texas	A.L.	1B	*162	628	99	177	45	1	33	110	2	.282
2007	Frisco	Texas	1B	1	2	0	0	0	0	0	0	0	.000
2007	Texas	A.L.	1B	78	286	48	85	24	1	13	49	0	.297
2007	Atlanta b-c	N.L.	1B	54	208	38	66	9	1	17	56	0	.317
2008	Atlanta	N.L.	1B	103	381	63	108	27	0	20	78	0	.283
2008	Los Angeles d-e	A.L.	1B	54	193	39	69	14	0	13	43	2	.358
2009	New York	A.L.	1B	156	609	103	178	43	3	*39	*122	2	.292
2010	New York	A.L.	1B	158	601	*113	154	36	0	33	108	0	.256
Major League Totals			8 Yrs.	1218	4624	782	1321	302	16	275	906	15	.286
	Division Series												
2008	Los Angeles	A.L.	1B	4	15	4	7	0	0	0	1	0	.467
2009	New York	A.L.	1B	3	12	3	2	0	0	1	1	0	.167
2010	New York	A.L.	1B	3	13	2	4	1	0	1	3	0	.308
Division Series Totals				10	40	9	13	1	0	2	5	0	.325
	Championship Series												
2009	New York	A.L.	1B	6	27	2	6	1	0	0	4	0	.222
2010	New York	A.L.	1B	4	14	1	0	0	0	0	0	0	.000
Championship Series Totals				10	41	3	6	1	0	0	4	0	.146
	World Series Record												
2009	New York	A.L.	1B	6	22	5	3	1	0	1	3	0	.136

a On disabled list from April 13 to April 29, 2004.
b On disabled list from June 9 to July 13, 2007.
c Traded to Atlanta Braves with pitcher Ron Mahay for catcher Jarrod Saltalamacchia, infielder Elvis Andrus, pitcher Neftali Feliz, pitcher Matt Harrison and pitcher Beau James, July 31, 2007.
d Traded to Los Angeles Angels for infielder Casey Kotchman and pitcher Steve Marek, July 29, 2008.
e Filed for free agency, October 30, 2008. Signed with New York Yankees, January 6, 2009.

TEJADA, MIGUEL ODALIS

Born, Bani, Dominican Republic, May 25, 1976.
Bats Right. Throws Right. Height, 5 feet, 9 inches. Weight, 215 pounds.

Year	Club	Lea	Pos	G	AB	R	H	2B	3B	HR	RBI	SB	Avg
1994	Oakland	Dominican	2B	74	218	51	64	9	1	18	62	13	.294
1995	Sou. Oregon	Northwest	SS	74	269	45	66	15	5	8	44	19	.245
1996	Modesto	California	SS-3B	114	458	97	128	12	5	20	72	27	.279
1997	Huntsville	Southern	SS	128	502	85	138	20	3	22	97	15	.275
1997	Oakland	A.L.	SS	26	99	10	20	3	2	2	10	2	.202
1998	Edmonton	P.C.	SS	1	3	0	0	0	0	0	0	0	.000
1998	Huntsville	Southern	SS	15	52	9	17	6	0	2	7	1	.327
1998	Oakland a	A.L.	SS	105	365	53	85	20	1	11	45	5	.233
1999	Oakland	A.L.	SS	159	593	93	149	33	4	21	84	8	.251
2000	Oakland	A.L.	SS	160	607	105	167	32	1	30	115	6	.275
2001	Oakland	A.L.	SS	*162	622	107	166	31	3	31	113	11	.267
2002	Oakland b	A.L.	SS	*162	662	108	204	30	0	34	131	7	.308
2003	Oakland c	A.L.	SS	162	636	98	177	42	0	27	106	10	.278
2004	Baltimore	A.L.	SS	*162	653	107	203	40	2	34	*150	4	.311
2005	Baltimore	A.L.	SS	*162	654	89	199	*50	5	26	98	5	.304
2006	Baltimore	A.L.	SS	*162	648	99	214	37	0	24	100	6	.330
2007	Frederick	Carolina	3B	1	2	1	2	0	0	1	1	0	1.000
2007	Bowie	Eastern	SS	1	3	0	0	0	0	0	1	0	.000
2007	Baltimore d-e	A.L.	SS	133	514	72	152	19	1	18	81	2	.296
2008	Houston	N.L.	SS	158	632	92	179	38	3	13	66	7	.283
2009	Houston f	N.L.	SS	158	635	83	199	*46	1	14	86	5	.313
2010	Baltimore	A.L.	3B	97	401	40	108	16	0	7	39	0	.269
2010	San Diego g-h	N.L.	SS-3B	59	235	31	63	10	0	8	32	2	.268
Major League Totals			14 Yrs.	2027	7956	1187	2285	447	23	300	1256	80	.287
	Division Series												
2000	Oakland	A.L.	SS	5	20	5	7	2	0	0	1	1	.350
2001	Oakland	A.L.	SS	5	21	1	6	3	0	0	1	0	.286
2002	Oakland	A.L.	SS	5	21	3	3	1	0	1	4	0	.143
2003	Oakland	A.L.	SS	5	23	0	2	1	0	0	2	0	.087
Division Series Totals				20	85	9	18	7	0	1	8	1	.212

a On disabled list from March 31 to May 20, 1998.
b Selected Most Valuable Player in American League for 2002.
c Filed for free agency, October 27, 2003. Signed with Baltimore Orioles, December 14, 2003.
d On disabled list from June 22 to July 27, 2007.
e Traded to Houston Astros for pitcher Troy Patton, outfielder Luke Scott, pitcher Matt Albers, pitcher Dennis Sarfate and infielder Michael Costanzo, December 12, 2007.
f Filed for free agency, November 6, 2009. Signed with Baltimore Orioles, January 26, 2010.
g Traded to San Diego Padres with cash for pitcher Wynn Pelzer, July 29, 2010.
h Filed for free agency, November 1, 2010. Signed with San Francisco Giants, November 30, 2010.

TEJADA, RUBEN DARIO

Born, Veraguas, Panama, September 1, 1989.
Bats Right. Throws Right. Height, 5 feet, 11 inches. Weight, 160 pounds.

Year	Club	Lea	Pos	G	AB	R	H	2B	3B	HR	RBI	SB	Avg
2007	Mets	Gulf Coast	SS-2B	35	120	13	34	4	3	0	16	2	.283
2008	St. Lucie	Fla.St.	SS	131	497	55	114	19	4	2	37	8	.229
2009	Binghamton	Eastern	SS-2B	134	488	59	141	24	3	5	46	19	.289
2010	Buffalo	Int.	SS-2B	65	218	25	61	11	0	1	16	1	.280
2010	New York	N.L.	2B-SS	78	216	28	46	12	0	1	15	2	.213

THAMES, MARCUS MARKLEY

Born, Louisville, Mississippi, March 6, 1977.
Bats Right. Throws Right. Height, 6 feet, 2 inches. Weight, 220 pounds.

Year	Club	Lea	Pos	G	AB	R	H	2B	3B	HR	RBI	SB	Avg
1997	Yankees	Gulf Coast	OF	57	195	51	67	17	4	7	36	6	.344
1997	Greensboro	So.Atl.	OF	4	16	2	5	1	0	0	2	1	.313
1998	Tampa	Fla.St.	OF	122	457	62	130	18	3	11	59	13	.284

Year	Club	Lea	Pos	G	AB	R	H	2B	3B	HR	RBI	SB	Avg
1999	Norwich	Eastern	OF	51	182	25	41	6	2	4	26	0	.225
1999	Tampa	Fla.St.	OF	69	266	47	65	12	4	11	38	3	.244
2000	Norwich	Eastern	OF	131	474	72	114	30	2	15	79	1	.241
2001	Norwich	Eastern	OF	139	520	114	167	43	4	31	97	10	.321
2002	Columbus	Int.	OF	107	386	51	80	21	3	13	45	5	.207
2002	New York	A.L.	OF	7	13	2	3	1	0	1	2	0	.231
2003	Columbus	Int.	OF	52	194	26	54	15	2	2	28	3	.278
2003	Oklahoma	P.C.	OF	18	66	9	17	4	0	2	7	1	.258
2003	Texas a-b	A.L.	OF	30	73	12	15	2	0	1	4	0	.205
2004	Toledo	Int.	OF	64	234	57	77	21	1	24	59	4	.329
2004	Detroit	A.L.	OF	61	165	24	42	12	0	10	33	0	.255
2005	Toledo	Int.	OF	73	265	53	90	18	3	22	56	4	.340
2005	Detroit	A.L.	OF	38	107	11	21	2	0	7	16	0	.196
2006	Detroit	A.L.	OF	110	348	61	89	20	2	26	60	1	.256
2007	Toledo	Int.	1B	2	8	2	3	0	0	1	2	0	.375
2007	Detroit c	A.L.	OF-1B	86	269	37	65	15	0	18	54	2	.242
2008	Detroit	A.L.	OF-1B	103	316	50	76	12	0	25	56	0	.241
2009	Toledo	Int.	OF	12	49	6	12	0	0	2	6	0	.245
2009	Detroit d-e	A.L.	DH-OF-1B	87	258	33	65	11	1	13	36	0	.252
2010	Scranton/WB	Int.	OF	4	15	0	3	0	0	0	1	0	.200
2010	New York f-g	A.L.	DH-OF-3B	82	212	22	61	7	0	12	33	0	.288
Major League Totals			9 Yrs.	604	1761	252	437	82	3	113	294	3	.248
	Division Series												
2006	Detroit	A.L.	DH	4	15	2	5	2	0	0	1	0	.333
2010	New York	A.L.	DH	2	7	1	2	0	0	1	2	0	.286
Division Series Totals				6	22	3	7	2	0	1	3	0	.318
	Championship Series												
2006	Detroit	A.L.	DH	2	5	1	0	0	0	0	0	0	.000
2010	New York	A.L.	DH-OF	6	16	0	2	0	0	0	1	0	.125
Championship Series Totals				8	21	1	2	0	0	0	1	0	.095
	World Series Record												
2006	Detroit	A.L.	OF	2	1	0	0	0	0	0	0	0	.000

a Traded to Texas Rangers for outfielder Ruben Sierra, June 6, 2003.
b Filed for free agency, October 14, 2003. Signed with Detroit Tigers organization, December 7, 2003.
c On disabled list from July 19 to August 9, 2007.
d On disabled list from April 19 to June 7, 2009.
e Filed for free agency, November 6, 2009. Signed with New York Yankees organization, February 8, 2010.
f On disabled list from June 13 to July 4, 2010.
g Filed for free agency, November 1, 2010. Signed with Los Angeles Dodgers, January 18, 2011.

THERIOT, RYAN STEWART

Born, Baton Rouge, Louisiana, December 7, 1979.
Bats Right. Throws Right. Height, 5 feet, 11 inches. Weight, 175 pounds.

Year	Club	Lea	Pos	G	AB	R	H	2B	3B	HR	RBI	SB	Avg
2001	Daytona	Fla.St.	SS	30	103	20	21	5	0	0	9	2	.204
2002	Lansing	Midwest	2B-SS	130	489	75	123	19	4	1	37	32	.252
2003	Lansing	Midwest	2B-SS	58	220	29	57	8	1	1	17	21	.259
2003	West Tenn	Southern	SS	53	178	20	42	3	0	1	9	9	.236
2004	Daytona	Fla.St.	2B-SS-3B	103	330	47	90	14	3	1	34	13	.273
2005	West Tenn	Southern	2B-SS-3B	120	448	52	136	28	4	1	53	24	.304
2005	Chicago	N.L.	2B	9	13	3	2	1	0	0	0	0	.154
2006	Iowa	P.C.	SS-2B-OF-3B	73	280	41	85	11	5	0	22	14	.304
2006	Chicago	N.L.	2B-SS-3B	53	134	34	44	11	3	3	16	13	.328
2007	Chicago	N.L.	SS-2B-3B-OF	148	537	80	143	30	2	3	45	28	.266
2008	Chicago	N.L.	SS	149	580	85	178	19	4	1	38	22	.307
2009	Chicago	N.L.	SS	154	602	81	171	20	5	7	54	21	.284
2010	Chicago-Los Angeles a-b	N.L.	2B-SS	150	586	72	158	15	2	2	29	20	.270
Major League Totals			6 Yrs.	663	2452	355	696	96	16	16	182	104	.284
	Division Series												
2007	Chicago	N.L.	SS	3	12	0	3	0	0	0	1	1	.250
2008	Chicago	N.L.	SS	3	11	0	3	0	0	0	0	0	.273
Division Series Totals				6	23	0	6	0	0	0	1	1	.261

a Traded to Los Angeles Dodgers with pitcher Ted Lilly and cash for infielder Blake Dewitt, pitcher Kyle Smit and pitcher Brett Wallach, July 31, 2010.
b Traded to St. Louis Cardinals for pitcher Blake Hawksworth, November 30, 2010.

THOLE, JOSHUA MICHAEL (JOSH)

Born, Breese, Illinois, October 28, 1986.
Bats Left. Throws Right. Height, 6 feet, 1 inch. Weight, 205 pounds.

Year	Club	Lea	Pos	G	AB	R	H	2B	3B	HR	RBI	SB	Avg
2005	Mets	Gulf Coast	1B-C	35	104	14	28	2	1	1	12	1	.269
2006	Kingsport	Appal.	1B-C	36	98	13	23	4	0	1	12	1	.235
2007	Savannah	So.Atl.	1B-C	117	389	46	104	17	0	0	36	4	.267
2008	St. Lucie	Fla.St.	C-1B	111	347	49	104	25	2	5	56	2	.300
2009	Binghamton	Eastern	C-1B	103	384	48	126	29	2	1	46	8	.328
2009	New York	N.L.	C	17	53	2	17	2	1	0	9	1	.321
2010	Buffalo	Int.	C	48	165	20	44	19	1	2	17	0	.267
2010	New York	N.L.	C	73	202	17	56	7	1	3	17	1	.277
Major League Totals			2 Yrs.	90	255	19	73	9	2	3	26	2	.286

THOME, JAMES HOWARD (JIM)

Born, Peoria, Illinois, August 27, 1970.
Bats Left. Throws Right. Height, 6 feet, 4 inches. Weight, 245 pounds.

Year	Club	Lea	Pos	G	AB	R	H	2B	3B	HR	RBI	SB	Avg
1989	Indians	Gulf Coast	SS-3B	55	186	22	44	5	3	0	22	6	.237
1990	Burlington	Appal.	3B	34	118	31	44	7	1	12	34	6	.373
1990	Kinston	Carolina	3B	33	117	19	36	4	1	4	16	4	.308
1991	Canton	Eastern	3B	84	294	47	99	20	2	5	45	8	.337
1991	Colorado Springs	P.C.	3B	41	151	20	43	7	3	2	28	0	.285
1991	Cleveland	A.L.	3B	27	98	7	25	4	2	1	9	1	.255
1992	Colorado Springs	P.C.	3B	12	48	11	15	4	1	2	14	0	.313
1992	Cleveland a	A.L.	3B	40	117	8	24	3	1	2	12	2	.205
1993	Charlotte	Int.	3B	115	410	85	136	21	4	25	*102	1	*.332
1993	Cleveland	A.L.	3B	47	154	28	41	11	0	7	22	2	.266
1994	Cleveland	A.L.	3B	98	321	58	86	20	1	20	52	3	.268
1995	Cleveland	A.L.	3B	137	452	92	142	29	3	25	73	4	.314
1996	Cleveland	A.L.	3B	151	505	122	157	28	5	38	116	2	.311
1997	Cleveland	A.L.	1B	147	496	104	142	25	0	40	102	1	.286
1998	Cleveland b	A.L.	1B	123	440	89	129	34	2	30	85	1	.293
1999	Cleveland	A.L.	1B	146	494	101	137	27	2	33	108	0	.277
2000	Cleveland	A.L.	1B	158	557	106	150	33	1	37	106	1	.269
2001	Cleveland	A.L.	1B	156	526	101	153	26	1	49	124	0	.291
2002	Cleveland c	A.L.	1B	147	480	101	146	19	2	52	118	1	.304
2003	Philadelphia	N.L.	1B	159	578	111	154	30	3	*47	131	0	.266
2004	Philadelphia	N.L.	1B	143	508	97	139	28	1	42	105	0	.274
2005	Clearwater	Fla.St.	DH	5	12	2	4	0	0	1	3	0	.333
2005	Philadelphia d-e	N.L.	1B	59	193	26	40	7	0	7	30	0	.207
2006	Chicago	A.L.	DH-1B	143	490	108	141	26	0	42	109	0	.288
2007	Charlotte	Int.	DH	5	14	2	3	1	0	0	5	0	.214
2007	Chicago f	A.L.	DH-1B	130	432	79	119	19	0	35	96	0	.275
2008	Chicago	A.L.	DH	149	503	93	123	28	0	34	90	1	.245
2009	Chicago	A.L.	DH	107	345	55	86	15	0	23	74	0	.249
2009	Los Angeles g-h	N.L.	PH	17	17	0	4	0	0	0	3	0	.235
2010	Minnesota i	A.L.	DH	108	276	48	78	16	2	25	59	0	.283
Major League Totals			20 Yrs.	2392	7982	1534	2216	428	26	589	1624	19	.278
	Division Series												
1995	Cleveland	A.L.	3B	3	13	1	2	0	0	1	3	0	.154
1996	Cleveland	A.L.	3B	4	10	1	3	0	0	0	0	0	.300
1997	Cleveland	A.L.	1B	5	15	1	3	0	0	0	1	0	.200
1998	Cleveland	A.L.	1B-DH	4	15	2	2	0	0	2	2	0	.133
1999	Cleveland	A.L.	1B	5	17	7	6	0	0	4	10	0	.353
2001	Cleveland	A.L.	1B	5	19	2	3	0	0	1	1	0	.158
2008	Chicago	A.L.	DH	4	16	1	2	1	0	0	1	0	.125
2009	Los Angeles	N.L.	PH	3	2	0	0	0	0	0	0	0	.000
2010	Minnesota	A.L.	DH	3	10	2	1	0	0	0	0	0	.100
Division Series Totals				35	117	17	22	1	0	8	18	0	.188
	Championship Series												
1995	Cleveland	A.L.	3B	5	15	2	4	0	0	2	5	0	.267
1997	Cleveland	A.L.	1B	6	14	3	1	0	0	0	0	0	.071
1998	Cleveland	A.L.	1B-DH	6	23	4	7	0	0	4	8	0	.304
2009	Los Angeles	N.L.	PH	2	1	0	1	0	0	0	0	0	1.000
Championship Series Totals				19	53	9	13	0	0	6	13	0	.245
	World Series Record												
1995	Cleveland	A.L.	3B	6	19	1	4	1	0	1	2	0	.211

Year	Club	Lea	Pos	G	AB	R	H	2B	3B	HR	RBI	SB	Avg
1997	Cleveland	A.L.	1B	7	28	8	8	0	1	2	4	0	.286
World Series Totals				13	47	9	12	1	1	3	6	0	.255

a On disabled list from March 28 to May 18 and May 29 to June 15, 1992.
b On disabled list from August 8 to September 16, 1998.
c Filed for free agency, October 28, 2002. Signed with Philadelphia Phillies, December 3, 2002.
d On disabled list from May 1 to May 21 and July 1 to November 1, 2005.
e Traded to Chicago White Sox for outfielder Aaron Rowand, pitcher Dan Haigwood and player to be named later, November 25, 2005. Philadelphia Phillies received pitcher Giovany Gonzalez to complete trade, December 8, 2005.
f On disabled list from April 28 to May 20, 2007.
g Traded to Los Angeles Dodgers with cash for infielder Justin Fuller, August 31, 2009.
h Filed for free agency, November 6, 2009. Signed with Minnesota Twins, February 5, 2010.
i Filed for free agency, November 1, 2010, re-signed with Minnesota Twins, January 14, 2011.

TORREALBA, YORVIT ADOLFO

Born, Caracas, Venezuela, July 19, 1978.
Bats Right. Throws Right. Height, 5 feet, 11 inches. Weight, 200 pounds.

Year	Club	Lea	Pos	G	AB	R	H	2B	3B	HR	RBI	SB	Avg
1995	Bellingham	Northwest	C	26	71	2	11	3	0	0	8	0	.155
1996	San Jose	California	C	2	5	0	0	0	0	0	0	0	.000
1996	Burlington	Midwest	C	1	4	0	0	0	0	0	0	0	.000
1996	Bellingham	Northwest	C	48	150	23	40	4	0	1	10	4	.267
1997	Bakersfield	California	C	119	446	52	122	15	3	4	40	4	.274
1998	San Jose	California	C	21	70	10	20	2	0	0	10	2	.286
1998	Shreveport	Texas	C	59	196	18	46	7	0	0	13	0	.235
1998	Fresno	P.C.	C	4	11	1	2	1	0	0	1	0	.182
1999	San Jose	California	C	19	73	10	23	3	0	2	14	0	.315
1999	Fresno	P.C.	C	17	63	9	16	2	0	2	10	0	.254
1999	Shreveport	Texas	C	65	217	25	53	10	1	4	19	0	.244
2000	Shreveport	Texas	C	108	398	50	114	21	1	4	32	2	.286
2001	Fresno	P.C.	C	115	394	56	108	23	3	8	36	2	.274
2001	San Francisco	N.L.	C	3	4	0	2	0	1	0	2	0	.500
2002	San Francisco	N.L.	C	53	136	17	38	10	0	2	14	0	.279
2003	San Francisco	N.L.	C-OF	66	200	22	52	10	2	4	29	1	.260
2004	San Francisco	N.L.	C	64	172	19	39	7	3	6	23	2	.227
2005	San Francisco	N.L.	C	34	93	18	21	8	0	1	7	1	.226
2005	Seattle a-b	A.L.	C	42	108	14	26	4	0	2	8	0	.241
2006	Colorado Springs	P.C.	C	10	36	0	6	2	0	0	2	0	.167
2006	Colorado c	N.L.	C	65	223	23	55	16	3	7	43	4	.247
2007	Colorado d	N.L.	C	113	396	47	101	22	1	8	47	2	.255
2008	Colorado e	N.L.	C	70	236	19	58	17	0	6	31	0	.246
2009	Colorado Springs	P.C.	C-1B	4	15	1	4	0	0	0	1	0	.267
2009	Colorado f	N.L.	C	64	213	27	62	11	1	2	31	1	.291
2010	San Diego g	N.L.	C	95	325	31	88	14	0	7	37	7	.271
Major League Totals			10 Yrs.	669	2106	237	542	119	11	45	272	18	.257
	Division Series												
2003	San Francisco	N.L.	C	2	3	0	0	0	0	0	1	0	.000
2007	Colorado	N.L.	C	3	10	3	5	1	0	0	3	0	.500
2009	Colorado	N.L.	C	4	14	1	5	2	0	1	4	0	.357
Division Series Totals				9	27	4	10	3	0	1	8	0	.370
	Championship Series												
2007	Colorado	N.L.	C	4	15	2	3	1	0	1	4	0	.200
	World Series Record												
2007	Colorado	N.L.	C	4	14	0	2	0	0	0	1	0	.143

a Traded to Seattle Mariners with pitcher Jesse Foppert for outfielder Randy Winn, July 31, 2005.
b Traded to Colorado Rockies for player to be named later, December 7, 2005. Seattle Mariners received pitcher Marcos Carvajal to complete trade, December 8, 2005.
c On disabled list from March 24 to June 2 and September 10 to November 1, 2006.
d Filed for free agency, October 31, 2007, re-signed with Colorado Rockies, November 29, 2007.
e On disabled list from August 26 to October 1, 2008.
f Filed for free agency, November 6, 2009. Signed with San Diego Padres, February 9, 2010.
g Filed for free agency, November 1, 2010. Signed with Texas Rangers, December 19, 2010.

TORRES, ANDRES VUNGO

Born, Aguadilla, Puerto Rico, January 26, 1978.
Bats Both. Throws Right. Height, 5 feet, 10 inches. Weight, 190 pounds.

Year	Club	Lea	Pos	G	AB	R	H	2B	3B	HR	RBI	SB	Avg
1998	Jamestown	N.Y.-Penn.	OF	48	192	28	45	2	6	1	21	13	.234

Year	Club	Lea	Pos	G	AB	R	H	2B	3B	HR	RBI	SB	Avg
1999	West Michigan	Midwest	OF	117	407	72	96	20	5	2	34	39	.236
2000	Lakeland	Fla.St.	OF	108	398	82	118	11	11	3	33	65	.296
2000	Jacksonville	Southern	OF	14	54	3	8	0	0	0	0	2	.148
2001	Erie	Eastern	OF	64	252	54	74	16	3	1	23	19	.294
2002	Toledo	Int.	OF	115	462	80	123	17	8	4	42	42	.266
2002	Detroit	A.L.	OF	19	70	7	14	1	1	0	3	2	.200
2003	Toledo	Int.	OF	70	271	36	69	13	3	2	16	27	.255
2003	Detroit	A.L.	OF	59	168	23	37	4	3	1	9	5	.220
2004	Detroit	A.L.	OF	3	0	1	0	0	0	0	0	1	.000
2004	Charlotte	Int.	OF	87	322	49	95	11	4	8	26	23	.295
2004	Bristol a-b	Appal.	OF	6	22	8	8	0	0	1	2	5	.364
2005	Oklahoma	P.C.	OF	15	63	12	19	3	1	0	1	6	.302
2005	Texas c	A.L.	OF	8	19	2	3	1	0	0	1	1	.158
2006	Rochester	Int.	OF	116	348	46	82	17	9	2	30	19	.236
2007	Erie	Eastern	OF	85	305	53	89	15	11	6	35	17	.292
2007	Toledo d-e	Int.	OF	42	168	23	49	6	9	4	17	5	.292
2008	Iowa f	P.C.	OF	118	409	91	125	27	10	11	51	29	.306
2009	Azl Giants	Arizona	OF	3	6	1	2	1	0	0	1	1	.333
2009	San Jose	Calif.	OF	3	10	0	1	1	0	0	0	0	.100
2009	Fresno	P.C.	OF	11	43	7	13	1	1	1	2	1	.302
2009	San Francisco g	N.L.	OF	75	152	30	41	6	8	6	23	6	.270
2010	San Francisco	N.L.	OF	139	507	84	136	43	8	16	63	26	.268
Major League Totals			6 Yrs.	303	916	147	231	55	20	23	99	41	.252
	Division Series												
2010	San Francisco	N.L.	OF	4	16	0	2	0	0	0	0	1	.125
	Championship Series												
2010	San Francisco	N.L.	OF	6	20	2	7	0	0	0	0	0	.350
	World Series Record												
2010	San Francisco	N.L.	OF	5	22	4	7	4	0	1	3	1	.318

a Filed for free agency, April 22, 2004. Signed with Chicago White Sox organization, April 26, 2004.
b Field for free agency, October 15, 2004. Signed with Texas Rangers organization, November 19, 2004.
c Filed for free agency, October 6, 2005. Signed with Minnesota Twins organization, December 20, 2005.
d Filed for free agency, October 15, 2006. Signed with Detroit Tigers organization, March 2, 2007.
e Filed for free agency, October 29, 2007. Signed with Chicago Cubs organization, November 20, 2007.
f Filed for free agency, November 3, 2008. Signed with San Francisco Giants organization, January 9, 2009.
g On disabled list from April 28 to May 26 July 31 to September 1, 2009.

TRACY, CHAD AUSTIN

Born, Charlotte, North Carolina, May 22, 1980.
Bats Left. Throws Right. Height, 6 feet, 2 inches. Weight, 215 pounds.

Year	Club	Lea	Pos	G	AB	R	H	2B	3B	HR	RBI	SB	Avg
2001	South Bend	Midwest	3B-1B	54	215	43	73	11	0	4	36	3	.340
2001	Yakima	Northwest	3B	10	36	2	10	1	0	0	5	1	.278
2002	El Paso	Texas	3B-1B	129	514	80	177	39	5	8	74	2	.344
2003	Tucson	P.C.	3B	133	522	91	169	31	4	10	80	0	.324
2004	Tucson	P.C.	3B-OF	11	40	7	16	4	0	2	11	2	.400
2004	Arizona	N.L.	3B-1B-OF	143	481	45	137	29	3	8	53	2	.285
2005	Arizona	N.L.	1B-OF	145	503	73	155	34	4	27	72	3	.308
2006	Arizona	N.L.	3B-1B	154	597	91	168	41	0	20	80	5	.281
2007	Tucson	P.C.	3B	3	15	3	7	2	0	1	4	0	.467
2007	Arizona a	N.L.	3B-1B	76	227	30	60	18	2	7	35	0	.264
2008	Tucson	P.C.	3B-1B	12	49	5	15	2	0	0	6	0	.306
2008	Arizona b	N.L.	1B-3B	88	273	25	73	16	0	8	39	0	.267
2009	Reno	P.C.	1B-3B	10	35	4	10	1	1	0	4	0	.286
2009	Arizona c-d	N.L.	1B-3B	98	257	29	61	15	0	8	39	1	.237
2010	Iowa	P.C.	3B	26	91	21	36	8	0	5	18	0	.396
2010	Scranton/WB	Int.	3B-1B	18	68	14	22	5	0	6	18	0	.324
2010	Chicago-Florida e-f	N.L.	3B-1B	69	146	11	36	8	0	1	15	0	.247
Major League Totals			7 Yrs.	773	2484	304	690	161	9	79	333	11	.278

a On disabled list from May 16 to June 10 and August 13 to September 16, 2007.
b On disabled list from March 23 to May 26, 2008.
c On disabled list from May 30 to June 30, 2009.
d Filed for free agency, November 5, 2009. Signed with Chicago Cubs organization, January 27, 2010.
e Released by Chicago Cubs, July 1, 2010. Signed with Florida Marlins, August 5, 2010.
f Filed for free agency, November 1, 2010.

TREANOR, MATTHEW AARON (MATT)

Born, Garden Grove, California, March 3, 1976.
Bats Right. Throws Right. Height, 6 feet, 2 inches. Weight, 205 pounds.

Year	Club	Lea	Pos	G	AB	R	H	2B	3B	HR	RBI	SB	Avg
1994	Royals	Gulf Coast	C-2B-OF	46	99	17	18	5	0	1	12	1	.182
1995	Springfield	Midwest	C	75	211	17	39	6	2	3	19	1	.185
1996	Lansing	Midwest	C-OF	119	384	56	100	18	2	6	33	5	.260
1997	Wilmington	Carolina	C	80	257	22	51	6	1	5	25	1	.198
1997	Brevard Cty a	Fla.St.	C	23	70	11	15	4	1	0	3	0	.214
1998	Brevard Cty	Fla.St.	C-1B-3B	80	243	24	57	8	0	3	28	3	.235
1999	Kane County	Midwest	C	86	308	56	88	21	1	10	53	4	.286
2000	Brevard County b	Fla.St.	C-1B	109	350	51	86	17	0	3	37	3	.246
2001	Portland	Eastern	C-1B	35	89	7	14	2	0	2	8	1	.157
2001	Marlins	Gulf Coast	C	11	34	10	14	4	0	1	4	3	.412
2001	Kane County	Midwest	C	1	1	2	1	0	0	0	0	0	1.000
2002	Portland	Eastern	C	50	156	24	39	5	1	9	28	3	.250
2002	Calgary c	P.C.	C-1B	36	95	10	27	8	0	1	18	1	.284
2003	Albuquerque d	P.C.	C	98	315	45	86	18	1	11	40	9	.273
2004	Albuquerque	P.C.	C	62	198	32	51	8	0	8	38	2	.258
2004	Florida	N.L.	C	29	55	7	13	2	0	0	1	0	.236
2005	Florida	N.L.	C	58	134	10	27	8	0	0	13	0	.201
2006	Florida e	N.L.	C	67	157	12	36	6	1	2	14	0	.229
2007	Florida	N.L.	C	55	171	16	46	7	1	4	19	0	.269
2008	Jupiter	Fla.St.	C	5	16	7	5	1	0	1	5	0	.313
2008	Florida f-g	N.L.	C	65	206	18	49	7	0	2	23	1	.238
2009	Detroit h-i	A.L.	C	4	13	0	0	0	0	0	0	0	.000
2010	Oklahoma	P.C.	C	5	15	2	3	0	0	0	2	0	.200
2010	Texas j-k-l	A.L.	C	82	237	22	50	6	1	5	27	1	.211
Major League Totals			7 Yrs.	360	973	85	221	36	3	13	97	2	.227
	Division Series												
2010	Texas	A.L.	C	1	1	1	0	0	0	0	0	0	.000
	Championship Series												
2010	Texas	A.L.	C	2	6	2	2	0	0	1	2	0	.333
	World Series Record												
2010	Texas	A.L.	C	1	3	0	0	0	0	0	0	0	.000

a Traded by Kansas City Royals to Florida Marlins for pitcher Matt Whisenant, July 29, 1997.
b Filed for free agency, October 15, 2000, re-signed with Florida Marlins, November 13, 2000.
c Filed for free agency, October 15, 2002, re-signed with Florida Marlins organization, November 25, 2002.
d Filed for free agency, October 15, 2003, re-signed with Florida Marlins, December 4, 2003.
e On disabled list from August 2 to August 16, 2006.
f On disabled list from July 8 to August 6, 2008.
g Released by Florida Marlins, December 10, 2008. Signed with Detroit Tigers, December 18, 2008.
h On disabled list from April 24 to November 6, 2009.
i Filed for free agency, November 9, 2009. Signed with Milwaukee Brewers organization, December 18, 2009.
j Traded to Texas Rangers for infielder Ray Olmedo, March 22, 2010.
k On disabled list from July 24 to August 23, 2010.
l Filed for free agency, November 1, 2010. Re-signed with Texas Rangers, December 13, 2010.

TULOWITZKI, TROY TREVER

Born, Santa Clara, California, October 10, 1984.
Bats Right. Throws Right. Height, 6 feet, 3 inches. Weight, 205 pounds.

Year	Club	Lea	Pos	G	AB	R	H	2B	3B	HR	RBI	SB	Avg
2005	Modesto	Calif.	SS	22	94	17	25	6	0	4	14	1	.266
2006	Tulsa	Texas	SS	104	423	75	123	34	2	13	61	6	.291
2006	Colorado	N.L.	SS	25	96	15	23	2	0	1	6	3	.240
2007	Colorado	N.L.	SS	155	609	104	177	33	5	24	99	7	.291
2008	Modesto	Calif.	SS	5	12	3	4	3	0	0	1	0	.333
2008	Tulsa	Texas	SS	5	21	5	7	0	0	2	3	0	.333
2008	Colorado Springs	P.C.	SS	2	7	2	3	1	0	0	1	1	.429
2008	Colorado a	N.L.	SS	101	377	48	99	24	2	8	46	1	.263
2009	Colorado	N.L.	SS	151	543	101	161	25	9	32	92	20	.297
2010	Tulsa	Texas	SS	2	7	1	1	1	0	0	1	0	.143
2010	Colorado Springs	P.C.	SS	2	4	1	1	0	0	0	0	0	.250
2010	Colorado b	N.L.	SS	122	470	89	148	32	3	27	95	11	.315
Major League Totals			5 Yrs.	554	2095	357	608	116	19	92	338	42	.290
	Division Series												
2007	Colorado	N.L.	SS	3	12	1	2	1	0	1	2	0	.167
2009	Colorado	N.L.	SS	4	16	0	4	2	0	0	3	0	.250
Division Series Totals				7	28	1	6	3	0	1	5	0	.214

Year	Club	Lea	Pos	G	AB	R	H	2B	3B	HR	RBI	SB	Avg
	Championship Series												
2007	Colorado	N.L.	SS	4	16	1	3	0	0	0	0	0	.188
	World Series Record												
2007	Colorado	N.L.	SS	4	13	1	3	2	0	0	1	0	.231

a On disabled list from April 30 to June 20 and July 5 to July 21, 2008.
b On disabled list from June 18 to July 27, 2010.

UGGLA, DANIEL COOLEY (DAN)

Born, Louisville, Kentucky, March 11, 1980.
Bats Right. Throws Right. Height, 5 feet, 11 inches. Weight, 200 pounds.

Year	Club	Lea	Pos	G	AB	R	H	2B	3B	HR	RBI	SB	Avg
2001	Yakima	Northwest	2B	72	278	39	77	21	0	5	40	8	.277
2002	Lancaster	Calif.	2B-3B	54	184	21	42	7	2	3	16	3	.228
2002	South Bend	Midwest	3B-2B	53	171	16	34	5	1	2	10	0	.199
2003	Lancaster	Calif.	3B-2B	134	534	104	155	31	7	23	90	24	.290
2004	Lancaster	Calif.	2B-3B-SS-1B	37	140	29	47	13	3	6	38	2	.336
2004	El Paso	Texas	3B-OF-2B	83	295	29	76	12	2	4	30	10	.258
2005	Tennessee a	Southern	2B-3B-1B-SS	135	498	88	148	33	3	21	87	15	.297
2006	Florida	N.L.	2B	154	611	105	172	26	7	27	90	6	.282
2007	Florida	N.L.	2B	159	632	113	155	49	3	31	88	2	.245
2008	Florida	N.L.	2B	146	531	97	138	37	1	32	92	5	.260
2009	Florida	N.L.	2B	158	564	84	137	27	1	31	90	2	.243
2010	Florida b	N.L.	2B	159	589	100	169	31	0	33	105	4	.287
Major League Totals			5 Yrs.	776	2927	499	771	170	12	154	465	19	.263

a Selected by Florida Marlins from Arizona Diamondbacks in Rule V draft, December 8, 2005.
b Traded to Atlanta Braves for infielder Omar Infante and pitcher Michael Dunn, November 16, 2010.

UPTON, JUSTIN IRVIN

Born, Norfolk, Virginia, August 25, 1987.
Bats Right. Throws Right. Height, 6 feet, 3 inches. Weight, 205 pounds.

Year	Club	Lea	Pos	G	AB	R	H	2B	3B	HR	RBI	SB	Avg
2006	South Bend	Midwest	OF	113	438	71	115	28	1	12	66	15	.263
2007	Visalia	Calif.	OF	32	126	27	43	6	2	5	17	9	.341
2007	Mobile	Southern	OF	71	259	48	80	17	4	13	53	10	.309
2007	Arizona	N.L.	OF	43	140	17	31	8	3	2	11	2	.221
2008	Tucson	P.C.	OF	15	61	13	17	3	1	3	10	2	.279
2008	Arizona a	N.L.	OF	108	356	52	89	19	6	15	42	1	.250
2009	Visalia	Calif.	OF	2	8	1	2	0	0	1	6	1	.250
2009	Arizona b	N.L.	OF	138	526	84	158	30	7	26	86	20	.300
2010	Arizona	N.L.	OF	133	495	73	135	27	3	17	69	18	.273
Major League Totals			4 Yrs.	422	1517	226	413	84	19	60	208	41	.272
	Division Series												
2007	Arizona	N.L.	OF	2	5	2	3	0	0	0	1	1	.600
	Championship Series												
2007	Arizona	N.L.	OF	4	9	0	2	1	1	0	0	0	.222

a On disabled list from July 9 to August 29, 2008.
b On disabled list from August 6 to August 26, 2009.

UPTON, MELVIN EMANUEL (B.J.)

Born, Norfolk, Virginia, August 21, 1984.
Bats Right. Throws Right. Height, 6 feet, 3 inches. Weight, 180 pounds.

Year	Club	Lea	Pos	G	AB	R	H	2B	3B	HR	RBI	SB	Avg
2003	Charleston	So.Atl.	SS	101	384	70	116	22	6	7	46	38	.302
2003	Orlando	Southern	SS	29	105	14	29	8	0	1	16	2	.276
2004	Montgomery	Southern	SS	29	104	21	34	7	1	2	15	3	.327
2004	Durham	Int.	SS	69	264	65	82	17	1	12	36	17	.311
2004	Tampa Bay	A.L.	SS-3B-OF	45	159	19	41	8	2	4	12	4	.258
2005	Durham	Int.	SS	139	545	98	165	36	6	18	74	44	.303
2006	Durham	Int.	SS-3B	106	398	72	107	18	4	8	41	46	.269
2006	Tampa Bay	A.L.	3B	50	175	20	43	5	0	1	10	11	.246
2007	Vero Beach	Fla.St.	2B-OF	7	17	4	4	0	0	1	3	0	.235
2007	Durham	Int.	2B	2	7	1	3	0	0	1	1	0	.429
2007	Tampa Bay a	A.L.	OF-2B	129	474	86	142	25	1	24	82	22	.300
2008	Tampa Bay	A.L.	OF	145	531	85	145	37	2	9	67	44	.273
2009	Charlotte	Fla.St.	OF	3	9	1	4	0	0	0	2	4	.444
2009	Tampa Bay b	A.L.	OF	144	560	79	135	33	4	11	55	42	.241

Year	Club	Lea	Pos	G	AB	R	H	2B	3B	HR	RBI	SB	Avg
2010	Tampa Bay	A.L.	OF	154	536	89	127	38	4	18	62	42	.237
Major League Totals			6 Yrs.	667	2435	378	633	146	13	67	288	165	.260
	Division Series												
2008	Tampa Bay	N.L.	OF	4	18	5	5	0	1	3	4	0	.278
2010	Tampa Bay	N.L.	OF	5	21	0	4	2	0	0	2	2	.190
Division Series Totals				9	39	5	9	2	1	3	6	2	.231
	Championship Series												
2008	Tampa Bay	N.L.	OF	7	28	8	9	1	0	4	11	2	.321
	World Series Record												
2008	Tampa Bay	N.L.	OF	5	20	3	5	0	0	0	1	4	.250

a On disabled list from June 9 to July 13, 2007.
b On disabled list from March 27 to April 13, 2009.

URIBE (TENA), JUAN C.

Born, Bani, Dominican Republic, July 22, 1979.
Bats Right. Throws Right. Height, 6 feet. Weight, 220 pounds.

Year	Club	Lea	Pos	G	AB	R	H	2B	3B	HR	RBI	SB	Avg
1997	Colorado	Domincan	SS	65	234	32	63	12	0	0	29	7	.269
1998	Rockies	Arizona	SS	40	148	25	41	5	3	0	17	8	.277
1999	Asheville	So.Atl.	SS	125	430	57	115	28	3	9	46	11	.267
2000	Salem	Carolina	SS	134	485	64	124	22	7	13	65	22	.256
2001	Carolina	Southern	SS	3	13	1	3	1	0	0	1	1	.231
2001	Colo Sprngs	P.C.	SS	74	281	40	87	27	7	7	48	11	.310
2001	Colorado	N.L.	SS	72	273	32	82	15	11	8	53	3	.300
2002	Colorado	N.L.	SS	155	566	69	136	25	7	6	49	9	.240
2003	Visalia	California	2B-SS	2	9	4	5	1	0	0	1	0	.556
2003	Tulsa	Texas	2B-3B-SS-OF	5	20	3	5	2	0	1	4	0	.250
2003	Colorado a-b	N.L.	SS-2B-OF	87	316	45	80	19	3	10	33	7	.253
2004	Chicago	A.L.	2B-SS-3B	134	502	82	142	31	6	23	74	9	.283
2005	Chicago	A.L.	SS	146	481	58	121	23	3	16	71	4	.252
2006	Chicago	A.L.	SS	132	463	53	109	28	2	21	71	1	.235
2007	Chicago	A.L.	SS	150	513	55	120	18	2	20	68	1	.234
2008	Charlotte	Int.	2B-SS	3	11	0	2	0	0	0	2	0	.182
2008	Chicago c-d	A.L.	3B-2B-SS	110	324	38	80	22	1	7	40	1	.247
2009	San Francisco e	N.L.	3B-SS-2B	122	398	50	115	26	4	16	55	3	.289
2010	San Francisco f	N.L.	SS-3B-2B	148	521	64	129	24	2	24	85	1	.248
Major League Totals			10 Yrs.	1256	4357	546	1114	231	41	151	599	39	.256
	Division Series												
2005	Chicago	A.L.	SS	3	10	4	4	1	0	1	4	0	.400
2008	Chicago	A.L.	3B	4	12	0	2	0	0	0	1	1	.167
2010	San Francisco	N.L.	SS-3B	4	14	0	1	0	0	0	1	0	.071
Division Series Totals				11	36	4	7	1	0	1	6	1	.194
	Championship Series												
2005	Chicago	A.L.	SS	5	16	1	4	1	0	0	0	0	.250
2010	San Francisco	N.L.	SS-3B	5	14	1	3	0	0	1	3	0	.214
Championship Series Totals				10	30	2	7	1	0	1	3	0	.233
	World Series Record												
2005	Chicago	A.L.	SS	4	16	2	4	3	0	0	2	1	.250
2010	San Francisco	N.L.	3B	5	19	3	3	0	0	1	5	0	.158
World Series Totals				9	35	5	7	3	0	1	7	1	.200

a On disabled list from March 18 to June 3, 2003.
b Traded to Chicago White Sox for infielder Aaron Miles, December 2, 2003.
c On disabled list from May 16 to May 31, 2008.
d Filed for free agency, October 30, 2008. Signed with San Francisco Giants organization, January 29, 2009.
e Filed for free agency, November 5, 2009, re-signed with San Francisco Giants, January 5, 2010.
f Filed for free agency, November 1, 2010. Signed with Los Angeles Dodgers, November 30, 2010.

UTLEY, CHASE CAMERON

Born, Pasadena, California, December 17, 1978.
Bats Left. Throws Right. Height, 6 feet, 1 inch. Weight, 200 pounds.

Year	Club	Lea	Pos	G	AB	R	H	2B	3B	HR	RBI	SB	Avg
2000	Batavia	N.Y.-Penn.	2B	40	153	21	47	13	1	2	22	5	.307
2001	Clearwater	Fla.St.	2B	122	467	65	120	25	2	16	59	19	.257
2002	Scranton/W.B.	Int.	3B	125	464	73	122	39	1	17	70	8	.263
2003	Scranton/W.B.	Int.	2B	113	431	80	139	26	2	18	77	10	.323
2003	Philadelphia	N.L.	2B	43	134	13	32	10	1	2	21	2	.239

Year	Club	Lea	Pos	G	AB	R	H	2B	3B	HR	RBI	SB	Avg
2004	Scranton/W.B.	Int.	2B	33	123	23	35	8	1	6	25	4	.285
2004	Philadelphia	N.L.	2B-1B	94	267	36	71	11	2	13	57	4	.266
2005	Philadelphia	N.L.	2B-1B	147	543	93	158	39	6	28	105	16	.291
2006	Philadelphia	N.L.	2B-1B	160	658	*131	203	40	4	32	102	15	.309
2007	Reading	Eastern	2B	3	10	0	1	0	0	0	0	0	.100
2007	Philadelphia a	N.L.	2B-1B	132	530	104	176	48	5	22	103	9	.332
2008	Philadelphia	N.L.	2B-1B	159	607	113	177	41	4	33	104	14	.292
2009	Philadelphia	N.L.	2B	156	571	112	161	28	4	31	93	23	.282
2010	Clearwater	Fla.St.	2B	4	12	1	3	0	2	0	1	0	.250
2010	Philadelphia b	N.L.	2B	115	425	75	117	20	2	16	65	13	.275
Major League Totals			8 Yrs.	1006	3735	677	1095	237	28	177	650	96	.293
	Division Series												
2007	Philadelphia	N.L.	2B	3	11	0	2	0	0	0	0	0	.182
2008	Philadelphia	N.L.	2B	4	15	1	2	1	0	0	2	0	.133
2009	Philadelphia	N.L.	2B	4	14	5	6	0	0	1	1	2	.429
2010	Philadelphia	N.L.	2B	3	11	3	3	0	0	1	4	1	.273
Division Series Totals				14	51	9	13	1	0	2	7	3	.255
	Championship Series												
2008	Philadelphia	N.L.	2B	5	17	4	6	2	0	1	3	0	.353
2009	Philadelphia	N.L.	2B	5	19	3	4	0	0	0	1	0	.211
2010	Philadelphia	N.L.	2B	6	22	5	4	1	0	0	1	3	.182
Championship Series Totals				16	58	12	14	3	0	1	5	3	.241
	World Series Record												
2008	Philadelphia	N.L.	2B	5	18	5	3	0	0	2	4	3	.167
2009	Philadelphia	N.L.	2B	6	21	7	6	1	0	5	8	1	.286
World Series Totals				11	39	12	9	1	0	7	12	4	.231

a On disabled list from July 27 to August 27, 2007.
b On disabled list from June 29 to August 17, 2010.

VALBUENA, LUIS ADAN

Born, Caja Seca, Venezuela, November 30, 1985.
Bats Left. Throws Right. Height, 5 feet, 10 inches. Weight, 195 pounds.

Year	Club	Lea	Pos	G	AB	R	H	2B	3B	HR	RBI	SB	Avg
2005	Everett	Northwest	2B	74	287	47	75	10	3	12	51	14	.261
2005	Tacoma	P.C.	2B	3	4	0	0	0	0	0	0	0	.000
2006	Inland Empire	Calif.	2B-SS-3B	43	163	18	41	10	1	2	10	1	.252
2006	Wisconsin	Midwest	2B	89	325	45	93	16	6	3	38	21	.286
2007	West Tenn	Southern	2B	122	444	55	106	23	3	11	44	10	.239
2008	West Tenn	Southern	2B-3B	70	240	43	73	12	2	9	40	8	.304
2008	Tacoma	P.C.	2B-3B	58	212	41	64	9	0	2	20	10	.302
2008	Seattle a	A.L.	2B-SS	18	49	6	12	5	0	0	1	0	.245
2009	Columbus	Int.	2B-SS-3B	22	78	15	25	4	2	3	13	3	.321
2009	Cleveland	A.L.	2B-SS-3B	103	368	52	92	25	3	10	31	2	.250
2010	Columbus	Int.	SS-3B-2B	25	96	23	30	8	1	6	20	2	.313
2010	Cleveland	A.L.	2B-3B-SS-OF	91	275	22	53	12	0	2	24	1	.193
Major League Totals			3 Yrs.	212	692	80	157	42	3	12	56	3	.227

a Traded to Cleveland Indians with pitcher Joe Smith for outfielder Franklin Gutierrez, December 10, 2008.

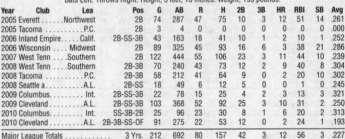

VALDEZ, WILSON ANTONIO

Born, Nizao, Dominican Republic, May 20, 1978.
Bats Right. Throws Right. Height, 5 feet, 11 inches. Weight, 170 pounds.

Year	Club	Lea	Pos	G	AB	R	H	2B	3B	HR	RBI	SB	Avg
1997	Montreal	Dominican	SS	62	244	39	74	13	1	2	29	19	.303
1998	Montreal	Dominican	SS	64	247	42	74	9	0	3	30	15	.300
1999	Expos	Gulf Coast	SS-2B	22	82	12	24	2	0	0	7	10	.293
1999	Vermont	N.Y.-Penn.	SS-2B	36	130	19	32	7	0	1	10	4	.246
2000	Vermont	N.Y.-Penn.	SS	65	248	32	66	8	1	1	30	16	.266
2000	Cape Fear	So.Atl.	2B-SS-C	15	49	6	12	2	0	0	3	3	.245
2001	Jupiter	Fla.St.	SS	64	233	34	58	13	2	2	19	7	.249
2001	Clinton	Midwest	SS	59	214	31	54	8	1	0	11	6	.252
2002	Portland a	Eastern	SS	114	375	51	98	19	5	1	30	18	.261
2003	Albuquerque	P.C.	SS-2B	90	338	45	97	12	4	0	18	33	.287
2003	Carolina	Southern	2B-SS	37	144	28	45	6	2	0	14	16	.313
2004	Albuquerque	P.C.	SS	66	285	36	91	11	3	2	25	19	.319
2004	Charlotte	Int.	SS	70	281	37	85	7	2	2	15	13	.302
2004	Chicago b	A.L.	SS-2B	19	43	8	10	1	0	1	4	1	.233
2005	Seattle	A.L.	SS	42	126	9	25	5	1	0	8	2	.198

Year Club	Lea	Pos	G	AB	R	H	2B	3B	HR	RBI	SB	Avg
2005 Tacoma	P.C.	SS	1	4	0	0	0	0	0	1	0	.000
2005 San Diego	N.L.	SS	9	13	0	3	2	0	0	1	0	.231
2005 Portland c-d-e-f	P.C.	SS	50	155	14	38	5	3	1	15	8	.245
2006 Las Vegas g	P.C.	SS-OF-2B	137	528	94	157	24	1	6	53	26	.297
2007 Las Vegas.........	P.C.	SS-OF-2B-3B	90	361	81	124	19	1	4	29	14	.343
2007 Los Angeles	N.L.	2B-SS-3B-OF	41	74	12	16	2	1	0	7	1	.216
2008 Kia	Korea	SS	47	156	17	34	9	1	1	16	13	.218
2008 Yakult h-i ...	Japan Pac.	SS-OF	29	78	8	20	1	0	1	8	4	.256
2009 Columbus.........	Int.	SS-OF-2B	41	121	17	24	1	0	0	6	5	.198
2009 Buffalo	Int.	SS-2B-OF	36	114	13	34	4	0	0	6	1	.298
2009 New York j-k.......	N.L.	SS-OF-2B-3B	41	86	11	22	3	2	0	7	0	.256
2010 Lehigh Valley	Int.	2B-SS	5	22	2	10	0	0	0	5	2	.455
2010 Philadelphia	N.L.	SS-2B-3B	111	333	37	86	16	3	4	35	7	.258
Major League Totals		5 Yrs.	263	675	77	162	29	7	5	62	11	.240
Division Series												
2010 Philadelphia	N.L.	3B	1	3	1	1	0	0	0	0	0	.333
Championship Series												
2010 Philadelphia	N.L.	PH	2	0	0	0	0	0	0	0	0	.000

a Claimed on waivers from Montreal Expos by Florida Marlins, March 29, 2002.
b Traded to Chicago White Sox for pitcher Billy Koch and cash, June 17, 2004.
c Claimed on waivers by New York Mets, March 29, 2005.
d Claimed on waivers by Seattle Mariners, April 1, 2005.
e Traded to San Diego Padres for pitcher Mike Bumstead and pitcher R.D. Spiehs, June 9, 2005.
f Filed for free agency, October 3, 2005. Signed with Kansas City Royals organization, November 18, 2005.
g Traded to Los Angeles Dodgers for pitcher Jarod Plummer, March 31, 2006.
h Sold to Kia (Korea) January 8, 2008. Signed with Yakult (Japan), 2008.
i Signed with Cleveland Indians organization, December 15,2008.
j Sold to New York Mets, May 26, 2009.
k Filed for free agency, October 27, 2009. Signed with Philadelphia Phillies organization, November 25, 2009.

VALENCIA, DANIEL PAUL (DANNY)

Born, Miami, Florida, September 19, 1984.
Bats Right. Throws Right. Height, 6 feet, 2 inches. Weight, 210 pounds.

Year Club	Lea	Pos	G	AB	R	H	2B	3B	HR	RBI	SB	Avg
2006 Elizabethton	Appal.	1B-3B	48	190	30	59	13	0	8	29	0	.311
2007 Fort Myers	Fla.St.	3B	61	230	28	67	8	2	6	31	1	.291
2007 Beloit	Midwest	3B-1B	66	242	44	73	15	0	11	35	3	.302
2008 New Britain	Eastern	3B-1B	69	266	40	77	18	2	10	32	2	.289
2008 Fort Myers	Fla.St.	3B-SS	60	220	35	74	19	3	5	44	2	.336
2009 New Britain	Eastern	3B	57	218	44	62	14	4	7	29	0	.284
2009 Rochester.............	Int.	3B	71	269	35	77	24	0	7	41	0	.286
2010 Rochester.............	Int.	3B	49	185	22	54	15	0	0	24	2	.292
2010 Minnesota	A.L.	3B	85	299	30	93	18	1	7	40	2	.311
Division Series												
2010 Minnesota	A.L.	3B	3	9	1	2	1	0	0	2	0	.222

VARITEK, JASON ANDREW

Born, Rochester, Minnesota, April 11, 1972.
Bats Both. Throws Right. Height, 6 feet, 2 inches. Weight, 230 pounds.

Year Club	Lea	Pos	G	AB	R	H	2B	3B	HR	RBI	SB	Avg
1995 Port City.........	Southern	C	104	352	42	79	14	2	10	44	0	.224
1996 Port City.........	Southern	C-3B-OF	134	503	63	132	34	1	12	67	7	.262
1997 Tacoma	P.C.	C	87	307	54	78	13	0	15	48	0	.254
1997 Pawtucket	Int.	C	20	66	6	13	5	0	1	5	0	.197
1997 Boston a.............	A.L.	C	1	1	0	1	0	0	0	0	0	1.000
1998 Boston	A.L.	C	86	221	31	56	13	0	7	33	2	.253
1999 Boston	A.L.	C	144	483	70	130	39	2	20	76	1	.269
2000 Boston	A.L.	C	139	448	55	111	31	1	10	65	1	.248
2001 Boston b	A.L.	C	51	174	19	51	11	1	7	25	0	.293
2002 Boston	A.L.	C	132	467	58	124	27	1	10	61	4	.266
2003 Boston	A.L.	C	142	451	63	123	31	1	25	85	3	.273
2004 Boston c.............	A.L.	C	137	463	67	137	30	1	18	73	10	.296
2005 Boston	A.L.	C	133	470	70	132	30	1	22	70	2	.281
2006 Pawtucket	Int.	C	2	7	2	3	0	0	1	1	0	.429
2006 Boston d	A.L.	C	103	365	46	87	19	2	12	55	1	.238
2007 Boston	A.L.	C	131	435	57	111	15	3	17	68	1	.255
2008 Boston e.............	A.L.	C	131	423	37	93	20	0	13	43	0	.220
2009 Boston	A.L.	C	109	364	41	76	24	0	14	51	0	.209

Year	Club	Lea	Pos	G	AB	R	H	2B	3B	HR	RBI	SB	Avg
2010	Pawtucket	Int.	C	2	5	0	2	0	0	0	1	0	.400
2010	Boston f-g	A.L.	C	39	112	18	26	6	0	7	16	0	.232
Major League Totals			14 Yrs.	1478	4877	632	1258	296	13	182	721	25	.258
	Division Series												
1998	Boston	A.L.	C	1	4	0	1	0	0	0	1	0	.250
1999	Boston	A.L.	C	5	21	7	5	3	0	1	3	0	.238
2003	Boston	A.L.	C	5	14	4	4	0	0	2	2	0	.286
2004	Boston	A.L.	C	3	12	3	2	0	0	1	2	0	.167
2005	Boston	A.L.	C	3	10	1	3	0	0	0	1	0	.300
2007	Boston	A.L.	C	3	11	1	2	1	0	0	1	0	.182
2008	Boston	A.L.	C	4	14	2	3	0	0	0	0	0	.214
Division Series Totals				24	86	18	20	4	0	4	10	0	.233
	Championship Series												
1999	Boston	A.L.	C	5	20	1	4	1	1	1	1	0	.200
2003	Boston	A.L.	C	6	20	4	6	2	0	2	3	0	.300
2004	Boston	A.L.	C	7	28	5	9	1	0	2	7	0	.321
2007	Boston	A.L.	C	7	26	3	7	3	0	1	4	0	.269
2008	Boston	A.L.	C	6	20	2	1	0	0	1	1	0	.050
Championship Series Totals				31	114	15	27	7	1	7	16	0	.237
	World Series Record												
2004	Boston	A.L.	C	4	13	2	2	0	1	0	2	0	.154
2007	Boston	A.L.	C	4	15	2	5	1	0	0	5	0	.333
World Series Totals				8	28	4	7	1	1	0	7	0	.250

a Traded to Boston Red Sox by Seattle Mariners with pitcher Derek Lowe for pitcher Heathcliff Slocumb, July 31, 1997.
b On disabled list from June 8 to November 7, 2001.
c Filed for free agency, November 1, 2004, re-signed with Boston Red Sox, December 24, 2004.
d On disabled list from August 1 to September 3, 2006.
e Filed for free agency, October 30, 2008, re-signed with Boston Red Sox, February 6, 2009.
f On disabled list from July 1 to September 6, 2010.
g Filed for free agency, November 1, 2010, re-signed with Boston Red Sox, December 10, 2010.

VENABLE, WILLIAM DION (WILL)

Born, Greenbrae, California, October 29, 1982.
Bats Left. Throws Left. Height, 6 feet, 2 inches. Weight, 205 pounds.

Year	Club	Lea	Pos	G	AB	R	H	2B	3B	HR	RBI	SB	Avg
2005	Padres	Arizona	OF	15	59	13	19	4	2	1	12	4	.322
2005	Eugene	Northwest	OF	42	139	17	30	5	2	2	14	2	.216
2006	Fort Wayne	Midwest	OF	124	472	86	148	34	5	11	91	18	.314
2007	San Antonio	Texas	OF	134	515	66	143	19	3	8	68	21	.278
2008	Portland	P.C.	OF	120	442	70	129	26	4	14	58	7	.292
2008	San Diego	N.L.	OF	28	110	16	29	4	2	2	10	1	.264
2009	Portland	P.C.	OF	53	200	33	52	10	3	12	30	1	.260
2009	San Diego	N.L.	OF	95	293	38	75	14	2	12	38	6	.256
2010	Lake Elsinore	Calif.	OF	5	14	0	1	1	0	0	0	1	.071
2010	San Antonio	Texas	OF	2	6	2	2	0	0	0	1	2	.333
2010	San Diego a	N.L.	OF-1B	131	392	60	96	11	7	13	51	29	.245
Major League Totals			3 Yrs.	254	795	114	200	29	11	27	99	36	.252

a On disabled list from July 2 to July 21, 2010.

VICIEDO (PEREZ), DAYAN

Born, Remedios, Cuba, March 10, 1989.
Bats Right. Throws Right. Height, 5 feet, 11 inches. Weight, 240 pounds.

Year	Club	Lea	Pos	G	AB	R	H	2B	3B	HR	RBI	SB	Avg
2009	Birmingham	Southern	3B-1B	130	504	72	141	20	0	12	78	5	.280
2010	Charlotte	Int.	1B-3B	86	343	42	94	15	0	20	47	1	.274
2010	Chicago a	A.L.	3B-1B	38	104	17	32	7	0	5	13	1	.308

a Played in Cuba 2006 and 2007.

VICTORINO, SHANE PATRICK

Born, Wailuku, Hawaii, November 30, 1980.
Bats Both. Throws Right. Height, 5 feet, 9 inches. Weight, 180 pounds.

Year	Club	Lea	Pos	G	AB	R	H	2B	3B	HR	RBI	SB	Avg
1999	Great Falls	Pioneer	OF	55	225	53	63	7	6	2	25	20	.280
2000	Yakima	Northwest	2B-SS	61	236	32	58	7	2	2	20	21	.246

Year	Club	Lea	Pos	G	AB	R	H	2B	3B	HR	RBI	SB	Avg
2001	Vero Beach	Fla.St.	OF	2	6	2	1	0	0	0	0	0	.167
2001	Wilmington	So.Atl.	OF	112	435	71	123	21	9	4	32	47	.283
2002	Jacksonville	Southern	OF	122	481	61	124	15	1	4	34	45	.258
2003	Jacksonville	Southern	OF	66	266	37	75	9	4	2	15	16	.282
2003	Las Vegas	P.C.	OF	11	41	6	16	1	2	1	9	0	.390
2003	San Diego a	N.L.	OF	36	73	8	11	2	0	0	4	7	.151
2004	Las Vegas	P.C.	OF-2B	55	200	28	47	9	1	3	20	7	.235
2004	Jacksonville b	Southern	OF	75	293	70	96	13	7	16	43	9	.328
2005	Scranton/WB	Int.	OF	126	494	93	153	25	16	18	70	17	.310
2005	Philadelphia	N.L.	OF	21	17	5	5	0	0	2	8	0	.294
2006	Philadelphia	N.L.	OF	153	415	70	119	19	8	6	46	4	.287
2007	Lakewood	So.Atl.	DH	1	5	1	1	0	0	0	0	0	.200
2007	Reading	Eastern	OF	2	6	0	2	0	0	0	1	1	.333
2007	Philadelphia c	N.L.	OF	131	456	78	128	23	3	12	46	37	.281
2008	Clearwater	Fla.St.	OF	2	5	1	2	0	0	0	1	0	.400
2008	Reading	Eastern	OF	1	3	0	1	0	0	0	0	0	.333
2008	Lehigh Valley	Int.	OF	2	8	0	3	0	0	0	0	0	.375
2008	Philadelphia d	N.L.	OF	146	570	102	167	30	8	14	58	36	.293
2009	Philadelphia	N.L.	OF	156	620	102	181	39	*13	10	62	25	.292
2010	Lehigh Valley	Int.	OF	2	6	1	4	0	1	1	3	0	.667
2010	Philadelphia e	N.L.	OF	147	587	84	152	26	10	18	69	34	.259
Major League Totals			7 Yrs.	790	2738	449	763	139	42	62	293	143	.279
	Division Series												
2007	Philadelphia	N.L.	OF	3	9	2	2	0	0	1	1	1	.222
2008	Philadelphia	N.L.	OF	4	14	2	5	3	0	1	5	3	.357
2009	Philadelphia	N.L.	OF	4	17	4	6	1	0	1	1	1	.353
2010	Philadelphia	N.L.	OF	3	13	2	3	1	0	0	3	1	.231
Division Series Totals				14	53	10	16	5	0	3	10	6	.302
	Championship Series												
2008	Philadelphia	N.L.	OF	5	18	2	4	0	1	1	6	0	.222
2009	Philadelphia	N.L.	OF	5	19	4	7	1	1	2	6	1	.368
2010	Philadelphia	N.L.	OF	6	24	3	5	1	0	0	2	1	.208
Championship Series Totals				16	61	9	16	2	2	3	14	2	.262
	World Series Record												
2008	Philadelphia	N.L.	OF	5	20	1	5	0	0	0	2	0	.250
2009	Philadelphia	N.L.	OF	6	22	3	4	1	0	0	2	0	.182
World Series Totals				11	42	4	9	1	0	0	4	0	.214

a Selected by San Diego Padres from Los Angeles Dodgers in Rule V draft, December 16, 2002. Returned to Los Angeles Dodgers, May 28, 2003.
b Selected by Philadelphia Phillies in Rule V draft, December 13, 2004.
c On disabled list from July 31 to August 22, 2007.
d On disabled list from April 13 to April 29, 2008.
e On disabled list from July 28 to August 12, 2010.

VIZQUEL, OMAR ENRIQUE

Born, Caracas, Venezuela, April 24, 1967.
Bats Both. Throws Right. Height, 5 feet, 9 inches. Weight, 175 pounds.

Year	Club	Lea	Pos	G	AB	R	H	2B	3B	HR	RBI	SB	Avg
1984	Butte a	Pioneer	SS-2B	15	45	7	14	2	0	0	4	2	.311
1985	Bellingham	Northwest	SS-2B	50	187	24	42	9	0	5	17	4	.225
1986	Wausau	Midwest	SS-2B	105	352	60	75	13	2	4	28	19	.213
1987	Salinas	California	SS-2B	114	407	61	107	12	8	0	38	25	.263
1988	Vermont	Eastern	SS	103	375	54	95	18	2	2	35	30	.253
1988	Calgary	P.C.	SS	33	107	10	24	2	3	1	12	2	.224
1989	Seattle	A.L.	SS	143	387	45	85	7	3	1	20	1	.220
1989	Calgary	P.C.	SS	7	28	3	6	2	0	0	3	0	.214
1990	San Bernardino	California	SS	6	28	5	7	0	0	0	3	1	.250
1990	Calgary	P.C.	SS	48	150	18	35	6	2	0	8	4	.233
1990	Seattle b	A.L.	SS	81	255	19	63	3	2	2	18	4	.247
1991	Seattle	A.L.	SS-2B	142	426	42	98	16	4	1	41	7	.230
1992	Seattle c	A.L.	SS	136	483	49	142	20	4	0	21	15	.294
1992	Calgary	P.C.	SS	6	22	0	6	1	0	0	2	0	.273
1993	Seattle d	A.L.	SS	158	560	68	143	14	2	2	31	12	.255
1994	Charlotte	Int.	SS	7	26	3	7	1	0	0	1	1	.269
1994	Cleveland e	A.L.	SS	69	286	39	78	10	1	1	33	13	.273
1995	Cleveland	A.L.	SS	136	542	87	144	28	0	6	56	29	.266
1996	Cleveland	A.L.	SS	151	542	98	161	36	1	9	64	35	.297
1997	Cleveland	A.L.	SS	153	565	89	158	23	6	5	49	43	.280

Year Club	Lea	Pos	G	AB	R	H	2B	3B	HR	RBI	SB	Avg
1998 Cleveland	A.L.	SS	151	576	86	166	30	6	2	50	37	.288
1999 Cleveland	A.L.	SS-OF	144	574	112	191	36	4	5	66	42	.333
2000 Cleveland	A.L.	SS	156	613	101	176	27	3	7	66	22	.287
2001 Cleveland	A.L.	SS	155	611	84	156	26	8	2	50	13	.255
2002 Cleveland	A.L.	SS	151	582	85	160	31	5	14	72	18	.275
2003 Lake County	So.Atl.	SS	4	14	0	1	0	0	0	0	1	.071
2003 Cleveland f	A.L.	SS	64	250	43	61	13	2	2	19	8	.244
2004 Cleveland g	A.L.	SS	148	567	82	165	28	3	7	59	19	.291
2005 San Francisco	N.L.	SS	152	568	66	154	28	4	3	45	24	.271
2006 San Francisco	N.L.	SS	153	579	88	171	22	10	4	58	24	.295
2007 San Francisco	N.L.	SS	145	513	54	126	18	3	4	51	14	.246
2008 San Jose	Calif.	SS	3	8	3	3	0	0	0	1	0	.375
2008 Fresno	P.C.	SS	2	5	0	1	0	0	0	0	0	.200
2008 San Francisco h-i	N.L.	SS	92	266	24	59	10	1	0	23	5	.222
2009 Texas j	A.L.	SS-3B-2B	62	177	17	47	7	2	1	14	4	.266
2010 Chicago	A.L.	3B-2B-SS	108	344	36	95	11	1	2	30	11	.276
Major League Totals		22 Yrs.	2850	10266	1414	2799	444	75	80	936	400	.273
Division Series												
1995 Cleveland	A.L.	SS	3	12	2	2	1	0	0	4	1	.167
1996 Cleveland	A.L.	SS	4	14	4	6	1	0	0	2	4	.429
1997 Cleveland	A.L.	SS	5	18	3	9	0	0	0	1	4	.500
1998 Cleveland	A.L.	SS	4	15	1	1	0	0	0	0	0	.067
1999 Cleveland	A.L.	SS	5	21	3	5	1	1	0	3	0	.238
2001 Cleveland	A.L.	SS	5	22	2	9	1	1	0	6	1	.409
Division Series Totals			26	102	15	32	4	2	0	16	10	.314
Championship Series												
1995 Cleveland	A.L.	SS	6	23	2	2	1	0	0	2	3	.087
1997 Cleveland	A.L.	SS	6	25	1	1	0	0	0	0	0	.040
1998 Cleveland	A.L.	SS	6	25	2	11	0	1	0	0	4	.440
Championship Series Totals			18	73	5	14	1	1	0	2	7	.192
World Series Record												
1995 Cleveland	A.L.	SS	6	23	3	4	0	1	0	1	1	.174
1997 Cleveland	A.L.	SS	7	30	5	7	2	0	0	1	5	.233
World Series Totals			13	53	8	11	2	1	0	2	6	.208

a Batted righthanded only from 1984 through 1988 season.
b On disabled list from April 7 to May 14, 1990.
c On disabled list from April 13 to May 11, 1992.
d Traded to Cleveland Indians for shortstop Felix Fermin and first baseman Reggie Jefferson, December 20, 1993.
e On disabled list from April 23 to June 13, 1994.
f On disabled list from June 12 to August 26 and September 6 to October 28, 2003.
g Filed for free agency, October 29, 2004. Signed with San Francisco Giants, November 14, 2004.
h On disabled list from March 21 to May 10, 2008.
i Not offered contract, November 3, 2008. Signed with Texas Rangers organization, January 21, 2009.
j Filed for free agency, November 6, 2009. Signed with Chicago White Sox, November 23, 2009.

VOTTO, JOSEPH DANIEL (JOEY)

Born, Toronto, Ontario, Canada, September 10, 1983.
Bats Left. Throws Right. Height, 6 feet, 3 inches. Weight, 220 pounds.

Year Club	Lea	Pos	G	AB	R	H	2B	3B	HR	RBI	SB	Avg
2002 Reds	Gulf Coast	3B-C-OF	50	175	29	47	13	3	9	33	7	.269
2003 Dayton	Midwest	1B	60	195	19	45	8	0	1	20	2	.231
2003 Billings	Pioneer	1B	70	240	47	76	17	3	6	37	4	.317
2004 Potomac	Carolina	1B	24	84	11	25	7	0	5	20	1	.298
2004 Dayton	Midwest	1B	111	391	60	118	26	2	14	73	9	.302
2005 Sarasota	Fla.St.	1B	124	464	64	119	23	2	17	83	4	.256
2006 Chattanooga	Southern	1B	136	508	85	162	46	2	22	77	24	.319
2007 Louisville	Int.	1B-OF	133	496	74	146	21	2	22	92	17	.294
2007 Cincinnati	N.L.	1B-OF	24	84	11	27	7	0	4	17	1	.321
2008 Cincinnati	N.L.	1B	151	526	69	156	32	3	24	84	7	.297
2009 Dayton	Midwest	1B	2	7	3	3	0	0	1	3	1	.429
2009 Sarasota	Fla.St.	1B	1	2	0	0	0	0	0	0	0	.000
2009 Cincinnati a	N.L.	1B	131	469	82	151	38	1	25	84	4	.322
2010 Cincinnati b	N.L.	1B	150	547	106	177	36	2	37	113	16	.324
Major League Totals		4 Yrs.	456	1626	268	511	113	6	90	298	28	.314
Division Series												
2010 Cincinnati	N.L.	1B	3	10	0	1	0	0	0	1	0	.100

a On disabled list from May 30 to June 23, 2009.
b Selected Most Valuable Player in National League for 2010.

WALKER, NEIL MARTIN

Born, Pittsburgh, Pennsylvania, September 10, 1985.
Bats Both. Throws Right. Height, 6 feet, 3 inches. Weight, 210 pounds.

Year	Club	Lea	Pos	G	AB	R	H	2B	3B	HR	RBI	SB	Avg
2004	Pirates	Gulf Coast	C	52	192	28	52	12	3	4	20	3	.271
2004	Williamsport	N.Y.-Penn.	C	8	33	2	10	3	0	0	7	1	.303
2005	Lynchburg	Carolina	C	9	42	4	11	2	1	0	12	0	.262
2005	Hickory	So.Atl.	C	120	485	78	146	33	2	12	68	7	.301
2006	Lynchburg	Carolina	C	72	264	32	75	22	1	3	35	3	.284
2006	Altoona	Eastern	C	10	31	5	5	0	0	2	3	0	.161
2007	Altoona	Eastern	3B	117	431	77	124	30	3	13	66	9	.288
2007	Indianapolis	Int.	3B	19	64	7	13	3	0	0	0	1	.203
2008	Indianapolis	Int.	3B	133	505	69	122	25	7	16	80	10	.242
2009	Pirates	Gulf Coast	3B	8	30	2	5	2	0	1	1	0	.167
2009	Indianapolis	Int.	3B	95	356	38	94	31	2	14	69	5	.264
2009	Pittsburgh	N.L.	3B	17	36	5	7	1	0	0	0	1	.194
2010	Indianapolis	Int.	2B-OF-1B-3B	43	168	25	54	18	2	6	26	10	.321
2010	Pittsburgh	N.L.	2B-3B	110	426	57	126	29	3	12	66	2	.296
Major League Totals			2 Yrs.	127	462	62	133	30	3	12	66	3	.288

WALLACE, BRETT ALEXANDER

Born, Marin, California, August 26, 1986.
Bats Left. Throws Right. Height, 6 feet, 2 inches. Weight, 205 pounds.

Year	Club	Lea	Pos	G	AB	R	H	2B	3B	HR	RBI	SB	Avg
2008	Quad Cities	Midwest	3B	41	153	28	50	8	1	5	25	0	.327
2008	Springfield	Texas	3B	13	49	13	18	5	0	3	11	0	.367
2009	Memphis	P.C.	3B-1B	62	222	22	65	11	0	6	19	0	.293
2009	Sacramento	P.C.	3B-1B	44	182	32	55	10	0	9	28	1	.302
2009	Springfield a-b	Texas	3B	32	128	22	36	5	0	5	16	0	.281
2010	Las Vegas	P.C.	1B	95	385	64	116	24	1	18	61	1	.301
2010	Houston c	N.L.	1B	51	144	14	32	6	1	2	13	0	.222

a Traded by St. Louis Cardinals to Oakland Athletics with pitcher Clayton Mortensen and outfielder Shane Peterson for outfielder Matt Holliday, July 24, 2009.
b Traded to Philadelphia Phillies for pitcher Michael Taylor, December 16, 2009.
c Traded to Houston Astros for outfielder Anthony Gose, July 29, 2010.

WEEKS, RICKIE DARNELL

Born, Altamonte Springs, Florida, September 13, 1982.
Bats Right. Throws Right. Height, 6 feet. Weight, 205 pounds.

Year	Club	Lea	Pos	G	AB	R	H	2B	3B	HR	RBI	SB	Avg
2003	Brewers	Arizona	DH	1	4	0	2	0	0	0	4	1	.500
2003	Beloit	Midwest	2B	20	63	13	22	8	1	1	16	2	.349
2003	Milwaukee	N.L.	2B	7	12	1	2	1	0	0	0	0	.167
2004	Huntsville	Southern	2B	133	479	67	124	35	6	8	42	11	.259
2005	Nashville	P.C.	2B	55	203	43	65	14	9	12	48	10	.320
2005	Milwaukee	N.L.	2B	96	360	56	86	13	2	13	42	15	.239
2006	Milwaukee a	N.L.	2B	95	359	73	100	15	3	8	34	19	.279
2007	Nashville	P.C.	2B	6	22	5	10	3	1	0	3	1	.455
2007	Milwaukee b	N.L.	2B	118	409	87	96	21	6	16	36	25	.235
2008	Milwaukee c	N.L.	2B	129	475	89	111	22	7	14	46	19	.234
2009	Milwaukee d	N.L.	2B	37	147	28	40	5	2	9	24	2	.272
2010	Milwaukee	N.L.	2B	160	*651	112	175	32	4	29	83	11	.269
Major League Totals			7 Yrs.	642	2413	446	610	109	24	89	265	91	.253
Division Series													
2008	Milwaukee	N.L.	2B	3	4	0	0	0	0	0	0	0	.000

a On disabled list from July 29 to October 31, 2006.
b On disabled list from May 30 to June 18, 2007.
c On disabled list from June 7 to June 22, 2008.
d On disabled list from May 17 to November 6, 2009.

WELLS, VERNON M.

Born, Shreveport, Louisiana, December 8, 1978.
Bats Right. Throws Right. Height, 6 feet, 1 inch. Weight, 225 pounds.

Year	Club	Lea	Pos	G	AB	R	H	2B	3B	HR	RBI	SB	Avg
1997	St.Catherines	N.Y.-Penn.	OF	66	264	52	81	20	1	10	31	8	.307
1998	Hagerstown	So.Atl.	OF	134	509	86	145	35	2	11	65	13	.285
1999	Dunedin	Fla.St.	OF	70	265	43	91	16	2	11	43	13	.343

Year Club	Lea	Pos	G	AB	R	H	2B	3B	HR	RBI	SB	Avg
1999 Knoxville	Southern	OF	26	106	18	36	6	2	3	17	6	.340
1999 Syracuse	Int.	OF	33	129	20	40	8	1	4	21	5	.310
1999 Toronto	A.L.	OF	24	88	8	23	5	0	1	8	1	.261
2000 Syracuse	Int.	OF	127	493	76	120	31	7	16	66	23	.243
2000 Toronto	A.L.	OF	3	2	0	0	0	0	0	0	0	.000
2001 Syracuse	Int.	OF	107	413	57	116	27	4	12	52	15	.281
2001 Toronto a	A.L.	OF	30	96	14	30	8	0	1	6	5	.313
2002 Toronto	A.L.	OF	159	608	87	167	34	4	23	100	9	.275
2003 Toronto	A.L.	OF	161	678	118	*215	*49	5	33	117	4	.317
2004 Toronto b	A.L.	OF	134	536	82	146	34	2	23	67	9	.272
2005 Toronto	A.L.	OF	156	620	78	167	30	3	28	97	8	.269
2006 Toronto	A.L.	OF	154	611	91	185	40	5	32	106	17	.303
2007 Toronto c	A.L.	OF	149	584	85	143	36	4	16	80	10	.245
2008 Dunedin	Fla.St.	OF	2	8	3	4	0	0	0	4	0	.500
2008 Syracuse	Int.	OF	2	6	0	0	0	0	0	0	0	.000
2008 Toronto d	A.L.	OF	108	427	63	128	22	1	20	78	4	.300
2009 Toronto	A.L.	OF	158	630	84	164	37	3	15	66	17	.260
2010 Toronto	A.L.	OF	157	590	79	161	44	3	31	88	6	.273
Major League Totals		12 Yrs.	1393	5470	789	1529	339	30	223	813	90	.280

a On disabled list from April 14 to 24, 2001.
b On disabled list from June 16 to July 16, 2004.
c On disabled list from September 22 to November 13, 2007.
d On disabled list from May 10 to June 7 and July 10 to August 10, 2008.

WERTH, JAYSON RICHARD GOWAN

Born, Springfield, Illinois, May 20, 1979.
Bats Right. Throws Right. Height, 6 feet, 5 inches. Weight, 220 pounds.

Year Club	Lea	Pos	G	AB	R	H	2B	3B	HR	RBI	SB	Avg
1997 Orioles	Gulf Coast	C-1B-OF	32	88	16	26	6	0	1	8	7	.295
1998 Delmarva	So.Atl.	C	120	408	71	108	20	3	8	53	21	.265
1998 Bowie.............	Eastern	C	5	19	2	3	2	0	0	1	1	.158
1999 Frederick	Carolina	C	66	236	41	72	10	1	3	30	16	.305
1999 Bowie.............	Eastern	C-OF	35	121	18	33	5	1	1	11	7	.273
2000 Frederick	Carolina	C	24	83	16	23	3	0	2	18	5	.277
2000 Bowie a	Eastern	C-OF	85	276	47	63	16	2	5	26	9	.228
2001 Dunedin	Fla.St.	C	21	70	9	14	3	0	2	14	1	.200
2001 Tennessee	Southern	C-1B	104	369	51	105	23	1	18	69	12	.285
2002 Syracuse	Int.	OF-C	127	443	65	114	25	2	18	82	24	.257
2002 Toronto	A.L.	OF	15	46	4	12	2	1	0	6	1	.261
2003 Dunedin	Fla.St.	OF	18	62	10	23	5	0	4	18	1	.371
2003 Toronto	A.L.	OF	26	48	7	10	4	0	2	10	1	.208
2003 Syracuse b	Int.	OF	64	236	37	56	19	1	9	34	11	.237
2004 Los Angeles	N.L.	OF	89	290	56	76	11	3	16	47	4	.262
2004 Las Vegas c-d	P.C.	OF	14	51	13	21	2	1	5	20	2	.412
2005 Las Vegas.............	P.C.	OF	15	49	9	18	0	0	3	10	6	.367
2005 Los Angeles e.........	N.L.	OF	102	337	46	79	22	2	7	43	11	.234
2006 Los Angeles f-g	N.L.			INJURED—Did Not Play								
2007 Clearwater	Fla.St.	OF	4	13	3	1	0	0	0	0	0	.077
2007 Philadelphia h	N.L.	OF-1B	94	255	43	76	11	3	8	49	7	.298
2008 Clearwater	Fla.St.	OF	2	6	0	1	0	0	0	0	0	.167
2008 Philadelphia i	N.L.	OF	134	418	73	114	16	3	24	67	20	.273
2009 Philadelphia	N.L.	OF	159	571	98	153	26	1	36	99	20	.268
2010 Philadelphia j	N.L.	OF	156	554	106	164	*46	2	27	85	13	.296
Major League Totals		8 Yrs.	775	2519	433	684	138	15	120	406	77	.272
Division Series												
2004 Los Angeles	N.L.	OF	4	14	3	4	1	0	2	3	0	.286
2007 Philadelphia	N.L.	OF	2	3	0	0	0	0	0	0	0	.000
2008 Philadelphia	N.L.	OF	4	16	3	5	3	1	1	1	1	.313
2009 Philadelphia	N.L.	OF	4	14	5	5	0	1	2	4	0	.357
2010 Philadelphia	N.L.	OF	3	12	2	2	0	0	0	1	1	.167
Division Series Totals			17	59	13	16	4	2	5	9	2	.271
Championship Series												
2008 Philadelphia	N.L.	OF	5	21	2	4	1	0	0	0	0	.190
2009 Philadelphia	N.L.	OF	5	18	5	4	0	0	3	6	0	.222
2010 Philadelphia	N.L.	OF	6	18	3	4	1	0	2	5	0	.222
Championship Series Totals			16	57	10	12	2	0	5	11	0	.211
World Series Record												
2008 Philadelphia	N.L.	OF	5	18	4	8	3	0	1	3	3	.444

Year	Club	Lea	Pos	G	AB	R	H	2B	3B	HR	RBI	SB	Avg
2009	Philadelphia	N.L.	OF	6	19	3	5	0	0	2	3	0	.263
World Series Totals				11	37	7	13	3	0	3	6	3	.351

a Traded to Toronto Blue Jays by Baltimore Orioles for pitcher John Bale, December 11, 2000.
b On disabled list from March 21 to April 11, 2003.
c On disabled list from April 6 to June 4, 2004.
d Traded to Los Angeles Dodgers for pitcher Jason Frasor, March 30, 2004.
e On disabled list from March 25 to May 25 and from July 27 to August 11, 2005.
f On disabled list from April 1 to November 2, 2006.
g Not offered contract, December 12, 2006. Signed with Philadelphia Phillies, December 19, 2006.
h On disabled list from June 29 to August 1, 2007.
i On disabled list from May 23 to June 7, 2008.
j Filed for free agency, November 1, 2010. Signed with Washington Nationals, December 5, 2010.

WIETERS, MATTHEW RICHARD (MATT)

Born, Goose Creek, South Carolina, May 21, 1986.
Bats Both. Throws Right. Height, 6 feet, 5 inches. Weight, 230 pounds.

Year	Club	Lea	Pos	G	AB	R	H	2B	3B	HR	RBI	SB	Avg
2008	Frederick	Carolina	C	69	229	48	79	8	0	15	40	1	.345
2008	Bowie	Eastern	C	61	208	41	76	14	2	12	51	1	.365
2009	Norfolk	Int.	C	39	141	25	43	9	2	5	30	0	.305
2009	Baltimore	A.L.	C	96	354	35	102	15	1	9	43	0	.288
2010	Baltimore a	A.L.	C	130	446	37	111	22	1	11	55	0	.249
Major League Totals			2 Yrs.	226	800	72	213	37	2	20	98	0	.266

a On disabled list from July 10 to July 25, 2010.

WIGGINTON, TY ALLEN (TY)

Born, San Diego, California, October 11, 1977.
Bats Right. Throws Right. Height, 6 feet. Weight, 225 pounds.

Year	Club	Lea	Pos	G	AB	R	H	2B	3B	HR	RBI	SB	Avg
1998	Pittsfield	N.Y.-Penn.	2B-3B-OF	70	272	39	65	14	4	8	29	11	.239
1999	St. Lucie	Fla.St.	2B	123	456	69	133	23	5	21	73	9	.292
2000	Binghamton	Eastern	2B-3B	122	453	64	129	27	3	20	77	5	.285
2001	Binghamton	Eastern	2B-3B	8	28	5	8	3	0	0	0	1	.286
2001	St. Lucie	Fla.St.	2B	3	9	1	3	1	0	0	1	0	.333
2001	Norfolk	Int.	3B-2B-1B-OF	78	260	29	65	12	0	7	24	3	.250
2002	Norfolk	Int.	3B-2B-OF-1B	104	383	49	115	26	3	6	48	5	.300
2002	New York	N.L.	3B-1B-2B-OF	46	116	18	35	8	0	6	18	2	.302
2003	New York	N.L.	3B	156	573	73	146	36	6	11	71	12	.255
2004	St. Lucie	Fla.St.	3B	2	8	1	3	0	0	0	0	0	.375
2004	N.Y.-Pittsburgh a-b	N.L.	3B-2B-1B	144	494	63	129	30	2	17	66	7	.261
2005	Indianapolis	Int.	3B-1B-2B	72	280	53	82	18	0	14	52	8	.293
2005	Pittsburgh c	N.L.	3B-1B-2B	57	155	20	40	9	1	7	25	0	.258
2006	Durham	Int.	1B	2	8	2	3	2	0	1	2	0	.375
2006	Tampa Bay d	A.L.	1B-2B-3B-OF	122	444	55	122	25	1	24	79	4	.275
2007	Tampa Bay	A.L.	2B-3B-1B	98	378	47	104	21	0	16	49	1	.275
2007	Houston e	N.L.	3B-OF-1B	50	169	24	48	12	0	6	18	2	.284
2008	Round Rock	P.C.	3B	3	9	1	1	0	1	0	1	0	.111
2008	Houston f-g	N.L.	3B-OF	111	386	50	110	22	1	23	58	4	.285
2009	Baltimore	A.L.	1B-3B-SS	122	410	44	112	19	0	11	41	1	.273
2010	Baltimore h	A.L.	1B-2B-3B	154	581	63	144	29	1	22	76	0	.248
Major League Totals			9 Yrs.	1060	3706	457	990	211	12	143	501	33	.267

a On disabled list from April 21 to May 7, 2004.
b Traded to Pittsburgh Pirates with pitcher Matt Peterson and infielder Jose Bautista for pitcher Kris Benson and infielder Jeff Keppinger, July 30, 2004.
c Released by Pittsburgh Pirates, December 8, 2005. Signed with Tampa Bay Devil Rays, January 10, 2006.
d On disabled list from July 31 to September 1, 2006.
e Traded to Houston Astros for pitcher Dan Wheeler, July 28, 2007.
f On disabled list from April 6 to May 2, 2008.
g Not offered contract, December 12, 2008. Signed with Baltimore Orioles, February 10, 2009.
h Filed for free agency, November 1, 2010. Signed with Colorado Rockies, December 7, 2010.

WILLINGHAM, JOSHUA DAVID (JOSH)

Born, Florence, Alabama, February 17, 1979.
Bats Right. Throws Right. Height, 6 feet, 1 inch. Weight, 215 pounds.

Year	Club	Lea	Pos	G	AB	R	H	2B	3B	HR	RBI	SB	Avg
2000	Utica	N.Y.-Penn.	OF-2B-3B-SS	65	205	37	54	16	0	6	29	9	.263
2001	Kane County	Midwest	3B-OF-2B	97	320	57	83	20	2	7	36	24	.259

Year	Club	Lea	Pos	G	AB	R	H	2B	3B	HR	RBI	SB	Avg
2002	Jupiter	Fla.St.	1B-3B-OF	107	376	72	103	21	4	17	69	18	.274
2003	Jupiter	Fla.St.	C-1B-OF-3B	59	193	46	51	17	1	12	34	9	.264
2003	Marlins	Gulf Coast	DH	2	7	3	3	1	0	1	3	0	.429
2003	Carolina	Southern	1B-C-3B-OF	22	67	15	20	2	1	5	14	0	.299
2004	Carolina	Southern	C-1B-OF-3B	112	338	81	95	24	0	24	76	6	.281
2004	Florida	N.L.	C-OF	12	25	2	5	0	0	1	1	0	.200
2005	Jupiter	Fla.St.	C	2	9	1	2	1	0	0	1	0	.222
2005	Albuquerque	P.C.	C-3B	66	219	56	71	14	3	19	54	5	.324
2005	Florida a	N.L.	C-OF	16	23	3	7	1	0	0	4	0	.304
2006	Carolina	Southern	OF	2	8	0	2	0	0	0	0	0	.250
2006	Florida b	N.L.	OF-C-1B	142	502	62	139	28	2	26	74	2	.277
2007	Florida	N.L.	OF	144	521	75	138	32	4	21	89	8	.265
2008	Carolina	Southern	OF	8	26	6	6	2	0	0	5	0	.231
2008	Florida c-d	N.L.	OF	102	351	54	89	21	5	15	51	3	.254
2009	Washington	N.L.	OF-1B	133	427	70	111	29	0	24	61	4	.260
2010	Washington e-f	N.L.	OF	114	370	54	99	19	2	16	56	8	.268
Major League Totals			7 Yrs.	663	2219	320	588	130	13	103	336	25	.265

a On disabled list from June 30 to September 2, 2005.
b On disabled list from June 7 to June 22, 2006.
c On disabled list from April 28 to June 23, 2008.
d Traded to Washington Nationals with pitcher Scott Olsen for infielder Emilio Bonifacio, pitcher P.J. Dean and infielder Jake Smolinkski, November 11, 2008.
e On disabled list from August 18 to November 10, 2010.
f Traded to Oakland Athletics for pitcher Henry Rodriguez and outfielder Corey Brown, December 16, 2010.

WILLITS, REGGIE GENE

Born, Chickasha, Oklahoma, May 30, 1981.
Bats Both. Throws Right. Height, 5 feet, 11 inches. Weight, 185 pounds.

Year	Club	Lea	Pos	G	AB	R	H	2B	3B	HR	RBI	SB	Avg
2003	Provo	Pioneer	OF	59	230	53	69	14	4	4	27	14	.300
2004	Rancho Cucamonga	Calif.	OF	135	526	99	150	17	5	5	52	45	.285
2005	Arkansas	Texas	OF	123	487	75	148	23	6	2	46	40	.304
2006	Salt Lake	P.C.	OF	97	352	85	115	18	4	3	39	31	.327
2006	Los Angeles	A.L.	OF	28	45	12	12	1	0	0	2	4	.267
2007	Los Angeles	A.L.	OF	136	430	74	126	20	1	0	34	27	.293
2008	Salt Lake	P.C.	OF	10	37	7	14	2	1	0	4	1	.378
2008	Rancho Cucamonga	Calif.	OF	4	14	4	5	0	0	0	0	2	.357
2008	Los Angeles a	A.L.	OF	82	108	21	21	4	0	0	7	2	.194
2009	Salt Lake	P.C.	OF	62	234	40	61	10	1	1	27	11	.261
2009	Los Angeles	A.L.	OF	49	80	16	17	2	0	0	6	5	.213
2010	Rancho Cucamonga	Calif.	OF	5	15	3	4	1	0	0	1	2	.267
2010	Los Angeles b	A.L.	OF	97	159	23	41	7	0	0	8	2	.258
Major League Totals			5 Yrs.	392	822	146	217	34	1	0	57	40	.264
	Division Series												
2007	Los Angeles	A.L.	OF	3	4	0	0	0	0	0	0	1	.000
2008	Los Angeles	A.L.	OF	3	0	0	0	0	0	0	0	0	.000
2009	Los Angeles	A.L.	OF	1	0	0	0	0	0	0	0	0	.000
Division Series Totals				7	4	0	0	0	0	0	0	1	.000
	Championship Series												
2009	Los Angeles	A.L.	OF	3	0	0	0	0	0	0	0	0	.000

a On disabled list from August 9 to August 27, 2008.
b On disabled list from March 30 to April 14, 2010.

WILSON, JACK EUGENE

Born, Westlake Village, California, December 29, 1977.
Bats Right. Throws Right. Height, 6 feet. Weight, 185 pounds.

Year	Club	Lea	Pos	G	AB	R	H	2B	3B	HR	RBI	SB	Avg
1998	Johnson Cty	Appal.	SS	61	241	50	90	18	4	4	29	22	.373
1999	Potomac	Carolina	SS	64	257	44	76	10	1	2	18	7	.296
1999	Peoria	Midwest	SS	64	251	47	86	22	4	3	28	11	.343
2000	Potomac	Carolina	SS	13	47	7	13	0	1	2	7	2	.277
2000	Altoona	Eastern	SS	33	139	17	35	7	2	1	16	1	.252
2000	Arkansas a	Texas	SS	88	343	65	101	20	8	6	34	2	.294
2001	Nashville	P.C.	SS	27	103	20	38	6	1	1	6	2	.369
2001	Pittsburgh	N.L.	SS	108	390	44	87	17	1	3	25	1	.223
2002	Pittsburgh	N.L.	SS	147	527	77	133	22	4	4	47	5	.252
2003	Pittsburgh	N.L.	SS	150	558	58	143	21	3	9	62	5	.256
2004	Pittsburgh	N.L.	SS	157	652	82	201	41	*12	11	59	8	.308

Year Club	Lea	Pos	G	AB	R	H	2B	3B	HR	RBI	SB	Avg
2005 Pittsburgh	N.L.	SS	158	587	60	151	24	7	8	52	7	.257
2006 Pittsburgh	N.L.	SS	142	543	70	148	27	1	8	35	4	.273
2007 Pittsburgh	N.L.	SS	135	477	67	141	29	2	12	56	2	.296
2008 Altoona	Eastern	SS	7	19	1	6	0	0	0	0	1	.316
2008 Indianapolis	Int.	SS	4	12	2	4	1	0	0	2	0	.333
2008 Pittsburgh b	N.L.	SS	87	305	24	83	18	1	1	22	2	.272
2009 Indianapolis	Int.	SS	2	6	0	2	2	0	0	3	0	.333
2009 Pittsburgh	N.L.	SS	75	266	26	71	18	1	4	31	2	.267
2009 Seattle c-d	A.L.	SS	31	107	11	24	5	0	1	8	1	.224
2010 West Tenn	Southern	DH	1	2	1	1	0	0	0	0	0	.500
2010 Tacoma	P.C.	SS	9	33	3	10	2	0	1	4	2	.303
2010 Seattle e	A.L.	SS	61	193	17	48	11	1	0	14	1	.249
Major League Totals		10 Yrs.	1251	4605	536	1230	233	33	61	411	38	.267

a Traded by St. Louis Cardinals to Pittsburgh Pirates for pitcher Jason Christiansen, July 30, 2000.
b On disabled list from April 4 to May 27, 2008.
c On disabled list from April 25 to May 12, 2009.
d Traded to Seattle Mariners with pitcher Ian Snell for outfielder Jeff Clement, infielder Ronny Cedeno, pitcher Aaron Pribanic, pitcher Brett Lorin and pitcher Nathan Adcock, July 29, 2009.
e On disabled list from May 6 to June 20 and August 8 to October 8, 2010.

WILSON, JOSHUA AARON (JOSH)

Born, Pittsburgh, Pennsylvania, March 26, 1981.
Bats Right. Throws Right. Height, 6 feet, 1 inch. Weight, 175 pounds.

Year Club	Lea	Pos	G	AB	R	H	2B	3B	HR	RBI	SB	Avg
1999 Marlins	Gulf Coast	SS	53	203	29	54	9	4	0	27	14	.266
2000 Kane County	Midwest	SS-2B-3B	13	52	2	14	3	1	1	6	0	.269
2000 Utica	N.Y.-Penn.	SS	66	259	43	89	13	6	3	43	9	.344
2001 Kane County	Midwest	2B-SS-3B	123	506	65	144	28	5	4	61	17	.285
2002 Portland	Eastern	SS	12	41	5	14	3	0	2	5	0	.341
2002 Jupiter	Fla.St.	SS-2B-3B	111	398	51	102	17	1	11	50	7	.256
2003 Carolina	Southern	SS-2B	118	434	53	110	30	6	3	58	6	.253
2004 Albuquerque	P.C.	SS	56	240	32	67	12	2	5	23	6	.279
2004 Carolina	Southern	SS	81	311	63	98	21	1	10	41	8	.315
2005 Albuquerque	P.C.	SS-2B	143	526	88	135	31	6	17	82	17	.257
2005 Florida	N.L.	SS-2B	11	10	2	1	1	0	0	0	0	.100
2006 Colorado Springs a-b-c	P.C.	SS-3B-2B	89	335	61	103	18	4	10	45	15	.307
2007 Washington	N.L.	SS	15	19	3	1	0	0	0	0	0	.053
2007 Tampa Bay d-e	A.L.	SS-2B-3B-P	90	263	25	66	15	3	2	24	6	.251
2008 Indianapolis	Int.	SS-2B-3B-OF	97	293	28	81	18	1	5	32	11	.276
2008 Pawtucket f-g	Int.	SS-2B-3B	27	112	16	25	6	0	2	10	2	.223
2009 Reno	P.C.	SS	15	50	5	13	3	1	1	10	1	.260
2009 Arizona-San Diego	N.L.	SS-P-3B	27	64	3	10	3	0	0	3	0	.156
2009 Tacoma	P.C.	SS-2B	16	53	10	13	2	0	1	3	1	.245
2009 Seattle h-i-j	A.L.	SS-3B-2B	45	128	16	32	8	1	3	10	1	.250
2010 Tacoma	P.C.	SS-2B	20	81	7	27	11	1	0	11	0	.333
2010 Seattle	A.L.	SS-3B-1B-2B	108	361	22	82	14	2	2	25	5	.227
Major League Totals		4 Yrs.	296	845	71	192	41	6	7	62	12	.227

a Sold to Colorado Rockies, January 6, 2006.
b On disabled list from March 28 to June 7, 2006.
c Filed for free agency, November 1, 2006. Signed with Washington Nationals, November 6, 2006.
d Claimed on waivers by Tampa Bay Devil Rays, May 10, 2007.
e Claimed on waivers by Pittsburgh Pirates, December 3, 2007.
f Sold to Boston Red Sox, August 2, 2008.
g Filed for free agency, October 14, 2008, signed with Arizona Diamondbacks organization, December 5, 2008.
h Claimed on waivers by San Diego Padres, May 15, 2009.
i Claimed on waivers by Seattle Mariners, June 19, 2009.
j Filed for free agency, November 23, 2009, re-signed with Seattle Mariners organization, December 10, 2009.

WINN, DWIGHT RANDOLPH (RANDY)

Born, Los Angeles, California, June 9, 1974.
Bats Both. Throws Right. Height, 6 feet, 2 inches. Weight, 195 pounds.

Year Club	Lea	Pos	G	AB	R	H	2B	3B	HR	RBI	SB	Avg
1995 Elmira a	N.Y.-Penn.	OF	51	213	38	67	7	4	0	22	19	.315
1996 Kane County	Midwest	OF	130	514	90	139	16	3	0	35	30	.270
1997 Brevard Cty	Fla.St.	OF	36	143	26	45	8	2	0	15	16	.315
1997 Portland b	Eastern	OF	96	384	66	112	15	6	8	36	35	.292
1998 Durham	Int.	OF	29	123	25	35	5	2	1	16	10	.285
1998 Tampa Bay	A.L.	OF	109	338	51	94	9	9	1	17	26	.278
1999 Tampa Bay	A.L.	OF	79	303	44	81	16	4	2	24	9	.267

Year	Club	Lea	Pos	G	AB	R	H	2B	3B	HR	RBI	SB	Avg
1999	Durham	Int.	OF	46	207	38	73	20	3	3	30	9	.353
2000	Durham	Int.	OF	79	303	67	100	24	5	7	40	18	.330
2000	Tampa Bay	A.L.	OF	51	159	28	40	5	0	1	16	6	.252
2001	Tampa Bay	A.L.	OF	128	429	54	117	25	6	6	50	12	.273
2002	Tampa Bay c	A.L.	OF	152	607	87	181	39	9	14	75	27	.298
2003	Seattle	A.L.	OF	157	600	103	177	37	4	11	75	23	.295
2004	Seattle	A.L.	OF	157	626	84	179	34	6	14	81	21	.286
2005	Seattle	A.L.	OF	102	386	46	106	25	1	6	37	12	.275
2005	San Francisco d	N.L.	OF	58	231	39	83	22	5	14	26	7	.359
2006	San Francisco	N.L.	OF	149	573	82	150	34	5	11	56	10	.262
2007	San Francisco	N.L.	OF-3B	155	593	73	178	42	1	14	65	15	.300
2008	San Francisco	N.L.	OF	155	598	84	183	38	2	10	64	25	.306
2009	San Francisco e	N.L.	OF	149	538	65	141	33	5	2	51	16	.262
2010	New York	A.L.	OF	29	61	7	13	0	1	1	8	1	.213
2010	St. Louis f-g	N.L.	OF	87	144	16	36	8	1	3	17	5	.250
Major League Totals			13 Yrs.	1717	6186	863	1759	367	59	110	662	215	.284

a On disabled list from August 22 to September 11, 1995.
b Selected in expansion draft by Tampa Bay Devil Rays, November 18, 1997.
c Traded to Seattle Mariners for infielder Antonio Perez and manager Lou Piniella, October 28, 2002.
d Traded to San Francisco Giants for pitcher Jesse Foppert and catcher Yorvit Torrealba, July 31, 2005.
e Filed for free agency, November 5, 2009. Signed with New York Yankees, February 2, 2010.
f Released by New York Yankees, June 2, 2010. Signed with St. Louis Cardinals, June 5, 2010.
g Filed for free agency, November 1, 2010.

WOOD, RICHARD BRANDON (BRANDON)

Born, Austin, Texas, March 2, 1985.
Bats Right. Throws Right. Height, 6 feet, 3 inches. Weight, 210 pounds.

Year	Club	Lea	Pos	G	AB	R	H	2B	3B	HR	RBI	SB	Avg
2003	Angels	Arizona	SS-3B	19	78	14	24	8	2	0	13	3	.308
2003	Provo	Pioneer	SS-3B	42	162	25	45	13	2	5	31	1	.278
2004	Cedar Rapids	Midwest	SS	125	478	65	120	30	5	11	64	21	.251
2005	Rancho Cucamonga	Calif.	SS	130	536	109	172	51	4	43	115	7	.321
2005	Salt Lake	P.C.	SS	4	19	1	6	2	1	0	1	0	.316
2006	Arkansas	Texas	SS	118	453	74	125	42	4	25	83	19	.276
2007	Salt Lake	P.C.	3B-SS	111	437	73	119	27	1	23	77	10	.272
2007	Los Angeles	A.L.	3B-SS	13	33	2	5	1	0	1	3	0	.152
2008	Salt Lake	P.C.	SS-3B	103	395	82	117	21	2	31	84	6	.296
2008	Los Angeles	A.L.	3B-SS	55	150	12	30	4	0	5	13	4	.200
2009	Salt Lake	P.C.	3B-SS-1B	99	386	65	113	28	4	22	72	1	.293
2009	Los Angeles	A.L.	3B-SS-1B	18	41	5	8	1	0	1	3	0	.195
2010	Salt Lake	P.C.	3B-1B-SS	13	51	4	10	0	0	1	2	0	.196
2010	Los Angeles a	A.L.	3B-SS-1B	81	226	20	33	2	0	4	14	1	.146
Major League Totals			4 Yrs.	167	450	39	76	8	0	11	33	5	.169

a On disabled list from May 24 to June 15, 2010.

WRIGHT, DAVID ALLEN

Born, Norfolk, Virginia, December 20, 1982.
Bats Right. Throws Right. Height, 6 feet. Weight, 215 pounds.

Year	Club	Lea	Pos	G	AB	R	H	2B	3B	HR	RBI	SB	Avg
2001	Kingsport	Appal.	3B	35	116	27	35	7	0	4	16	9	.302
2002	Columbia	So.Atl.	3B	135	496	85	132	30	2	11	93	21	.266
2003	St. Lucie	Fla.St.	3B	133	466	69	126	39	2	15	75	19	.270
2004	Binghamton	Eastern	3B	60	223	44	81	27	0	10	40	20	.363
2004	Norfolk	Int.	3B	31	114	18	34	8	0	8	17	2	.298
2004	New York	N.L.	3B	69	263	41	77	17	1	14	40	6	.293
2005	New York	N.L.	3B	160	575	99	176	42	1	27	102	17	.306
2006	New York	N.L.	3B	154	582	96	181	40	5	26	116	20	.311
2007	New York	N.L.	3B	160	604	113	196	42	1	30	107	34	.325
2008	New York	N.L.	3B	160	626	115	189	42	2	33	124	15	.302
2009	New York a	N.L.	3B	144	535	88	164	39	3	10	72	27	.307
2010	New York	N.L.	3B	157	587	87	166	36	3	29	103	19	.283
Major League Totals			7 Yrs.	1004	3772	639	1149	258	16	169	664	138	.305
	Division Series												
2006	New York	N.L.	3B	3	12	1	4	2	0	0	4	0	.333
	Championship Series												
2006	New York	N.L.	3B	7	25	2	4	1	0	1	2	0	.160

a On disabled list from August 16 to September 1, 2009.

YOUKILIS, KEVIN EDMUND

Born, Cincinnati, Ohio, March 15, 1979.
Bats Right. Throws Right. Height, 6 feet, 1 inch. Weight, 220 pounds.

Year Club	Lea	Pos	G	AB	R	H	2B	3B	HR	RBI	SB	Avg
2001 Lowell	N.Y.-Penn.	3B	59	183	52	58	14	2	3	28	4	.317
2001 Augusta	So.Atl.	3B	5	12	0	2	0	0	0	0	0	.167
2002 Augusta	So.Atl.	3B	15	53	5	15	5	0	0	6	0	.283
2002 Sarasota	Fla.St.	1B-3B	76	268	45	79	16	0	3	48	0	.295
2002 Trenton	Eastern	3B	44	160	34	55	10	0	5	26	5	.344
2003 Portland	Eastern	3B	94	312	74	102	23	1	6	37	7	.327
2003 Pawtucket	Int.	3B	32	109	9	18	3	0	2	15	0	.165
2004 Lowell	N.Y.-Penn.	3B	2	4	1	3	1	1	0	0	0	.750
2004 Pawtucket	Int.	3B-1B	38	154	25	41	12	0	3	18	2	.266
2004 Boston a	A.L.	3B	72	208	38	54	11	0	7	35	0	.260
2005 Pawtucket	Int.	3B-1B-2B	43	152	30	49	15	1	8	27	1	.322
2005 Boston	A.L.	3B-1B-2B	44	79	11	22	7	0	1	9	0	.278
2006 Boston	A.L.	1B-OF-3B	147	569	100	159	42	2	13	72	5	.279
2007 Boston	A.L.	1B-3B	145	528	85	152	35	2	16	83	4	.288
2008 Boston	A.L.	1B-3B-OF	145	538	91	168	43	4	29	115	3	.312
2009 Pawtucket	Int.	1B	2	6	0	0	0	0	0	0	0	.000
2009 Boston b	A.L.	1B-3B-OF	136	491	99	150	36	1	27	94	7	.305
2010 Boston c	A.L.	1B-3B	102	362	77	111	26	5	19	62	4	.307
Major League Totals		7 Yrs.	791	2775	501	816	200	14	112	470	23	.294
Division Series												
2004 Boston	A.L.	3B	1	2	0	0	0	0	0	0	0	.000
2007 Boston	A.L.	1B	3	12	3	3	1	0	1	2	0	.250
2008 Boston	A.L.	1B-3B	4	18	2	4	1	0	0	1	0	.222
2009 Boston	A.L.	1B-3B	3	12	0	1	1	0	0	0	0	.083
Division Series Totals			11	44	5	8	3	0	1	3	0	.182
Championship Series												
2007 Boston	A.L.	1B	7	28	10	14	1	1	3	7	0	.500
2008 Boston	A.L.	3B	7	30	4	10	3	0	2	6	0	.333
Championship Series Totals			14	58	14	24	4	1	5	13	0	.414
World Series Record												
2007 Boston	A.L.	1B	4	9	3	2	2	0	0	1	0	.222

a On disabled list from August 16 to September 1, 2004.
b On disabled list from May 5 to May 21, 2009.
c On disabled list from August 3 to November 8, 2010.

YOUNG, CHRISTOPHER BRANDON (CHRIS)

Born, Houston, Texas, September 5, 1983.
Bats Right. Throws Right. Height, 6 feet, 2 inches. Weight, 200 pounds.

Year Club	Lea	Pos	G	AB	R	H	2B	3B	HR	RBI	SB	Avg
2002 White Sox	Arizona	OF	55	184	26	40	13	1	5	17	7	.217
2003 Bristol	Appal.	OF	64	238	47	69	18	3	7	28	21	.290
2003 Great Falls	Pioneer	OF	10	34	5	6	3	0	0	0	0	.176
2004 Kannapolis	So.Atl.	OF	136	467	83	122	31	5	24	56	31	.261
2005 Birmingham a	Southern	OF	126	466	100	129	41	3	26	77	32	.277
2006 Tucson	P.C.	OF	100	402	78	111	32	4	21	77	17	.276
2006 Arizona	N.L.	OF	30	70	10	17	4	0	2	10	2	.243
2007 Arizona	N.L.	OF	148	569	85	135	29	3	32	68	27	.237
2008 Arizona	N.L.	OF	160	625	85	155	42	7	22	85	14	.248
2009 Reno	P.C.	OF	13	54	17	20	5	1	3	9	2	.370
2009 Arizona	N.L.	OF	134	433	54	92	28	4	15	42	11	.212
2010 Arizona	N.L.	OF	156	584	94	150	33	0	27	91	28	.257
Major League Totals		5 Yrs.	628	2281	328	549	136	14	98	296	82	.241
Division Series												
2007 Arizona	N.L.	OF	3	11	3	3	0	0	2	4	1	.273
Championship Series												
2007 Arizona	N.L.	OF	4	14	1	4	1	0	0	1	0	.286

a Traded to Arizona Diamondbacks by Chicago White Sox with pitcher Orlando Hernandez and pitcher Luis Vizcaino for pitcher Javier Vazquez, December 20, 2005.

YOUNG, DELMON DAMARCUS

Born, Birmingham, Alabama, September 14, 1985.
Bats Right. Throws Right. Height, 6 feet, 3 inches. Weight, 205 pounds.

Year Club	Lea	Pos	G	AB	R	H	2B	3B	HR	RBI	SB	Avg
2004 Charleston	So.Atl.	OF	131	513	95	165	26	5	25	116	21	.322
2005 Durham	Int.	OF	52	228	33	65	13	3	6	28	7	.285

Year	Club	Lea	Pos	G	AB	R	H	2B	3B	HR	RBI	SB	Avg
2005	Montgomery	Southern	OF	84	330	59	111	13	4	20	71	25	.336
2006	Durham	Int.	OF	86	342	50	108	22	4	8	59	22	.316
2006	Tampa Bay	A.L.	OF	30	126	16	40	9	1	3	10	2	.317
2007	Tampa Bay a	A.L.	OF	*162	645	65	186	38	0	13	93	10	.288
2008	Minnesota	A.L.	OF	152	575	80	167	28	4	10	69	14	.290
2009	Minnesota	A.L.	OF	108	395	50	112	16	2	12	60	2	.284
2010	Minnesota	A.L.	OF	153	570	77	170	46	1	21	112	5	.298
Major League Totals			5 Yrs.	605	2311	288	675	137	8	59	344	33	.292
	Division Series												
2009	Minnesota	A.L.	OF	3	12	1	1	1	0	0	0	1	.083
2010	Minnesota	A.L.	OF	3	12	1	4	0	1	0	0	0	.333
Division Series Totals				6	24	2	5	1	1	0	0	1	.208

a Traded to Minnesota Twins with infielder Brendan Harris and outfielder Jason Pridie for infielder Jason Bartlett, pitcher Matt Garza and pitcher Eduardo Morlan, November 28, 2007.

YOUNG, DELWYN RUDY

Born, Los Angeles, California, June 30, 1982.

Bats Both. Throws Right. Height, 5 feet, 8 inches. Weight, 210 pounds.

Year	Club	Lea	Pos	G	AB	R	H	2B	3B	HR	RBI	SB	Avg
2002	Great Falls	Pioneer	2B-1B	59	240	42	72	18	1	10	41	4	.300
2003	South Bend	So.Atl.	2B	119	443	67	143	38	7	15	73	5	.323
2004	Vero Beach	Fla.St.	2B	129	470	76	132	36	3	22	85	11	.281
2005	Las Vegas	P.C.	2B	36	160	23	52	12	0	4	14	0	.325
2005	Jacksonville	Southern	2B-3B-OF	95	371	52	110	25	1	16	62	1	.296
2006	Las Vegas	P.C.	OF-2B	140	532	76	145	42	1	18	98	3	.273
2006	Los Angeles	N.L.	OF	8	5	0	0	0	0	0	0	0	.000
2007	Las Vegas	P.C.	OF	121	490	107	165	54	5	17	97	4	.337
2007	Los Angeles	N.L.	OF-2B	19	34	4	13	1	1	2	3	1	.382
2008	Las Vegas	P.C.	OF	13	49	14	17	5	1	3	10	0	.347
2008	Los Angeles a	N.L.	OF-2B	83	126	10	31	9	0	1	7	0	.246
2009	Albuquerque	P.C.	OF	3	9	0	1	0	0	0	0	0	.111
2009	Pittsburgh b-c	N.L.	2B-OF	124	354	40	94	16	2	7	43	2	.266
2010	Pittsburgh d	N.L.	OF-2B-3B	110	191	22	45	11	1	7	28	1	.236
Major League Totals			5 Yrs.	344	710	76	183	37	4	17	81	4	.258

a On disabled list from July 24 to September 1, 2008.

b On disabled list from March 27 to April 13, 2009.

c Traded to Pittsburgh Pirates for two players to be named later, April 15, 2009. Dodgers received pitcher Eric Krebs and cash to complete trade, May 22, 2009.

d Filed for free agency, November 29, 2010. Signed with Philadelphia Phillies organization, January 6, 2011.

YOUNG, ERIC ORLANDO JR.

Born, New Brunswick, New Jersey, May 25, 1985.

Bats Both. Throws Right. Height, 5 feet, 10 inches. Weight, 180 pounds.

Year	Club	Lea	Pos	G	AB	R	H	2B	3B	HR	RBI	SB	Avg
2004	Casper	Pioneer	2B	23	87	20	23	5	1	0	7	14	.264
2005	Casper	Pioneer	2B	63	219	48	66	7	7	3	25	25	.301
2006	Asheville	So.Atl.	2B	128	482	92	142	28	6	5	49	87	.295
2007	Modesto	Calif.	2B	130	540	113	157	29	11	8	63	73	.291
2008	Tulsa	Texas	2B-OF	105	403	74	117	24	4	3	33	46	.290
2009	Colorado Springs	P.C.	2B-OF	119	472	118	141	21	10	7	43	58	.299
2009	Colorado	N.L.	2B-OF	30	57	7	14	1	0	1	1	4	.246
2010	Tulsa	Texas	2B	4	13	2	3	0	0	0	0	0	.231
2010	Colorado Springs	P.C.	2B-OF	33	123	20	31	5	1	1	9	10	.252
2010	Colorado a	N.L.	2B-OF	51	172	26	42	5	1	0	8	17	.244
Major League Totals			2 Yrs.	81	229	33	56	6	1	1	9	21	.245
	Division Series												
2009	Colorado	N.L.	PH	2	1	0	0	0	0	0	0	0	.000

a On disabled list from May 13 to July 31, 2010.

YOUNG, MICHAEL BRIAN

Born, Covina, California, October 19, 1976.

Bats Right. Throws Right. Height, 6 feet, 1 Inch. Weight, 200 pounds.

Year	Club	Lea	Pos	G	AB	R	H	2B	3B	HR	RBI	SB	Avg
1997	St.Catherines	N.Y.-Penn.	SS-2B	74	276	49	85	18	3	9	48	9	.308
1998	Hagerstown	So.Atl.	2B-SS-OF	140	522	86	147	33	5	16	87	16	.282
1999	Dunedin	Fla.St.	2B	129	495	86	155	36	3	5	83	30	.313

Year	Club	Lea	Pos	G	AB	R	H	2B	3B	HR	RBI	SB	Avg
2000	Tennessee	Southern	2B-SS	91	345	51	95	24	5	6	47	16	.275
2000	Tulsa	Texas	SS	43	188	30	60	13	5	1	32	9	.319
2000	Texas a..............	A.L.	2B	2	2	0	0	0	0	0	0	0	.000
2001	Oklahoma.............	P.C.	2B-SS	47	189	28	55	8	0	8	28	3	.291
2001	Texas	A.L.	2B	106	386	57	96	18	4	11	49	3	.249
2002	Texas	A.L.	2B-SS-3B	156	573	77	150	26	8	9	62	6	.262
2003	Texas	A.L.	2B-SS	160	666	106	204	33	9	14	72	13	.306
2004	Texas	A.L.	SS	160	690	114	216	33	9	22	99	12	.313
2005	Texas	A.L.	SS	159	668	*114	*221	40	5	24	91	5	*.331
2006	Texas	A.L.	SS	*162	691	93	217	52	3	14	103	7	.314
2007	Texas	A.L.	SS	156	639	80	201	37	1	9	94	13	.315
2008	Texas	A.L.	SS	155	645	102	183	36	2	12	82	10	.284
2009	Texas	A.L.	3B	135	541	76	174	36	2	22	68	8	.322
2010	Texas	A.L.	3B	157	656	99	186	36	3	21	91	4	.284
Major League Totals	....		11 Yrs.	1508	6157	918	1848	347	46	158	811	81	.300
	Division Series												
2010	Texas	A.L.	3B	5	20	1	3	0	0	1	3	0	.150
	Championship Series												
2010	Texas	A.L.	3B	6	27	3	9	3	0	0	4	0	.333
	World Series Record												
2010	Texas	A.L.	3B	5	20	0	5	0	0	0	0	0	.250

a Traded by Toronto Blue Jays to Texas Rangers with pitcher Darwin Cubillan for pitcher Esteban Loaiza, July 19, 2000.

ZIMMERMAN, RYAN WALLACE

Born, Washington, North Carolina, September 28, 1984.
Bats Right. Throws Right. Height, 6 feet, 3 inches. Weight, 230 pounds.

Year	Club	Lea	Pos	G	AB	R	H	2B	3B	HR	RBI	SB	Avg
2005	Savannah..........	So.Atl.	1B-SS	4	17	5	8	2	1	2	6	0	.471
2005	Harrisburg	Eastern	3B-SS	63	233	40	76	20	0	9	32	1	.326
2005	Washington	N.L.	3B-SS	20	58	6	23	10	0	0	6	0	.397
2006	Washington	N.L.	3B	157	614	84	176	47	3	20	110	11	.287
2007	Washington	N.L.	3B	*162	653	99	174	43	5	24	91	4	.266
2008	Potomac..........	Carolina	DH	2	10	1	3	2	0	0	0	0	.300
2008	Columbus.............	Int.	3B	4	15	4	4	1	0	1	3	0	.267
2008	Washington a.........	N.L.	3B	106	428	51	121	24	1	14	51	1	.283
2009	Washington	N.L.	3B	157	610	110	178	37	3	33	106	2	.292
2010	Washington	N.L.	3B	142	525	85	161	32	0	25	85	4	.307
Major League Totals	....		6 Yrs.	744	2888	435	833	193	12	116	449	22	.288

a On disabled list from May 26 to July 22, 2008.

ZOBRIST, BENJAMIN THOMAS (BEN)

Born, Eureka, Illinois, May 26, 1981.
Bats Both. Throws Right. Height, 6 feet, 3 inches. Weight, 200 pounds.

Year	Club	Lea	Pos	G	AB	R	H	2B	3B	HR	RBI	SB	Avg
2004	Tri-City......	N.Y.-Penn.	SS	68	257	50	87	14	3	4	45	15	.339
2005	Salem.........	Carolina	SS	42	141	25	47	12	1	3	13	2	.333
2005	Lexington.......	So.Atl.	SS	68	247	45	75	17	2	2	32	16	.304
2006	Corpus Christi ...	Texas	SS-3B	83	315	57	103	25	6	3	30	9	.327
2006	Durham	Int.	SS	18	69	12	21	3	1	0	6	4	.304
2006	Tampa Bay a.......	A.L.	SS	52	183	10	41	6	2	2	18	2	.224
2007	Durham	Int.	SS	61	222	42	62	14	2	7	22	8	.279
2007	Tampa Bay b	A.L.	SS	31	97	8	15	2	0	1	9	2	.155
2008	Vero Beach......	Fla.St.	2B-3B-SS	4	14	1	4	1	0	0	2	0	.286
2008	Durham	Int.	SS-3B-2B	20	71	15	26	3	0	4	13	4	.366
2008	Tampa Bay c.......	A.L.	SS-OF-2B-3B	62	198	32	50	10	2	12	30	3	.253
2009	Tampa Bay	A.L.	2B-OF-SS-1B	152	501	91	149	28	7	27	91	17	.297
2010	Tampa Bay	A.L.	OF-2B-1B-3B	151	541	77	129	28	2	10	75	24	.238
Major League Totals	....		5 Yrs.	448	1520	218	384	74	13	52	223	48	.253
	Division Series												
2010	Tampa Bay	N.L.	OF-2B-1B	5	20	2	6	2	0	1	2	0	.300
	Championship Series												
2008	Tampa Bay	N.L.	OF-SS	3	4	0	0	0	0	0	0	0	.000
	World Series Record												
2008	Tampa Bay	N.L.	OF	4	7	0	1	0	0	0	0	0	.143

a Traded by Houston Astros to Tampa Bay Devil Rays with pitcher Mitch Talbot for infielder Aubrey Huff and cash, July 12, 2006.
b On disabled list from August 19 to November 12, 2007.
c On disabled list from March 25 to May 13, 2008.

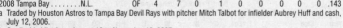

PITCHERS

AARDSMA, DAVID ALLAN

Born, Denver, Colorado, December 27, 1981.
Bats Right. Throws Right. Height, 6 feet, 5 inches. Weight, 205 pounds.

Year	Club	Lea	G	IP	W	L	Pct	SO	BB	H	ERA	SAVES
2003	San Jose	Calif.	18	18 1/3	1	1	.500	28	7	14	1.96	8
2004	San Francisco	N.L.	11	10 2/3	1	0	1.000	5	10	20	6.75	0
2004	Fresno	P.C.	44	55 1/3	6	4	.600	53	29	46	3.09	11
2005	Norwich	Eastern	9	46	6	2	.750	30	13	44	2.93	0
2005	West Tenn a	Southern	33	50 2/3	4	1	.800	43	32	48	3.91	2
2006	Iowa	P.C.	29	36 1/3	2	3	.400	36	15	31	3.22	8
2006	Chicago b	N.L.	45	53	3	0	1.000	49	28	41	4.08	0
2007	Chicago	A.L.	25	32 1/3	2	1	.667	36	17	39	6.40	0
2007	Charlotte	Int.	28	35 1/3	3	2	.600	45	11	26	4.33	15
2008	Pawtucket	Int.	2	2	0	0	.000	2	2	0	0.00	0
2008	Boston c-d	A.L.	47	48 2/3	4	2	.667	49	35	49	5.55	0
2009	Seattle e	A.L.	73	71 1/3	3	6	.333	80	34	49	2.52	38
2010	Seattle	A.L.	53	49 2/3	0	6	.000	49	25	33	3.44	31
Major League Totals		6 Yrs.	254	265 2/3	13	15	.464	268	149	231	4.20	69

a Traded to Chicago Cubs with pitcher Jerome Williams for pitcher La Troy Hawkins, May 28, 2005.
b Traded to Chicago White Sox with pitcher Carlos Vazquez for pitcher Neal Cotts, November 16, 2006.
c Traded to Boston Red Sox for pitcher Willy Mota and pitcher Miguel Socolovich, January 29, 2008.
d On disabled list from July 19 to August 8 and August 21 to September 10, 2008.
e Traded to Seattle Mariners for pitcher Fabian Williamson, January 20, 2009.

ADAMS, JON MICHAEL (MIKE)

Born, Corpus Christi, Texas, July 29, 1978.
Bats Right. Throws Right. Height, 6 feet, 5 inches. Weight, 190 pounds.

Year	Club	Lea	G	IP	W	L	Pct	SO	BB	H	ERA	SAVES
2001	Ogden	Pioneer	23	32	2	2	.500	44	6	26	2.81	12
2002	High Desert	Calif.	10	14	2	1	.667	23	7	9	2.57	5
2002	Beloit	Midwest	11	15 1/3	0	0	.000	21	2	13	2.93	5
2002	Huntsville	Southern	13	18 2/3	1	0	1.000	17	12	14	3.38	1
2003	Huntsville	Southern	45	74 1/3	3	7	.300	83	33	58	3.15	14
2004	Indianapolis	Int.	10	31	2	0	1.000	37	4	23	2.61	0
2004	Milwaukee	N.L.	46	53	2	3	.400	39	14	50	3.40	0
2005	Milwaukee	N.L.	13	13 1/3	0	1	.000	14	10	12	2.70	1
2005	Nashville	P.C.	26	36	3	4	.429	45	12	35	5.75	2
2006	Milwaukee	N.L.	2	2 1/3	0	0	.000	1	2	4	11.57	0
2006	Nashville	P.C.	15	16 1/3	1	1	.500	18	8	17	3.31	2
2006	Norfolk	Int.	13	14 2/3	0	0	.000	12	7	13	4.91	0
2006	Buffalo	Int.	3	4 2/3	0	0	.000	3	0	4	1.93	0
2006	Portland a-b-c	P.C.	17	23 2/3	0	2	.000	15	7	29	4.18	0
2007					INJURED—Did Not Play							
2008	Portland	P.C.	12	14 2/3	3	1	.750	16	9	21	5.52	0
2008	San Diego d	N.L.	54	65 1/3	2	3	.400	74	19	49	2.48	0
2009	San Antonio	Texas	4	4	1	0	1.000	6	2	3	2.25	0
2009	Portland	P.C.	4	5	0	0	.000	0	1	4	5.40	0
2009	San Diego e	N.L.	37	37	0	0	.000	45	8	14	0.73	0
2010	San Antonio	Texas	1	1	0	0	.000	1	0	0	0.00	0
2010	San Diego f	N.L.	70	66 2/3	4	1	.800	73	23	48	1.75	0
Major League Totals		6 Yrs.	222	237 2/3	8	8	.500	246	76	177	2.31	1

a Traded to New York Mets for pitcher Jeremi Gonzalez, May 26, 2006.
b Claimed on waivers by Cleveland Indians, July 6, 2006.
c Traded to San Diego Padres for pitcher Brian Sikorski, July 18, 2006.
d Released by San Diego Padres, March 14, 2007, re-signed with San Diego Padres organization, April 12, 2007.
e On disabled list from April 1 to June 8 and August 22 to September 17, 2009.
f On disabled list from July 12 to August 7, 2010.

AFFELDT, JEREMY DAVID

Born, Phoenix, Arizona, June 6, 1979.
Bats Left. Throws Left. Height, 6 feet, 4 inches. Weight, 225 pounds.

Year	Club	Lea	G	IP	W	L	Pct	SO	BB	H	ERA	SAVES
1997	Royals	Gulf Coast	10	40	2	0	1.000	36	21	34	4.50	0
1998	Royals	Gulf Coast	12	56	4	3	.571	67	24	50	2.89	0

Year	Club	Lea	G	IP	W	L	Pct	SO	BB	H	ERA	SAVES
1998	Lansing	Midwest	6	17	0	3	.000	8	12	27	9.53	0
1999	Charleston-WV	So.Atl.	27	143 1/3	7	7	.500	111	80	140	3.83	0
2000	Wilmington	Carolina	27	147 1/3	5	15	.250	92	59	158	4.09	0
2001	Wichita	Texas	25	145 1/3	10	6	.625	128	46	153	3.90	0
2002	Wichita	Texas	3	6	0	0	.000	3	3	1	1.50	0
2002	Kansas City a	A.L.	34	77 2/3	3	4	.429	67	37	85	4.64	0
2003	Kansas City b	A.L.	36	126	7	6	.538	98	38	126	3.93	4
2004	Omaha	P.C.	4	4	0	0	.000	5	0	2	0.00	3
2004	Kansas City c	A.L.	38	76 1/3	3	4	.429	49	32	91	4.95	13
2005	Omaha	P.C.	9	8 1/3	0	1	.000	9	6	9	6.48	0
2005	Kansas City d	A.L.	49	49 2/3	0	2	.000	39	29	56	5.26	0
2006	Kansas City	A.L.	27	70	4	6	.400	28	42	71	5.91	0
2006	Colorado e	N.L.	27	27 1/3	4	2	.667	20	13	30	6.91	1
2007	Colorado f	N.L.	75	59	4	3	.571	46	33	47	3.51	0
2008	Cincinnati g	N.L.	74	78 1/3	1	1	.500	80	25	78	3.33	0
2009	San Francisco	N.L.	74	62 1/3	2	2	.500	55	31	42	1.73	0
2010	San Jose	Calif.	2	3	0	0	.000	4	1	2	0.00	0
2010	San Francisco h	N.L.	53	50	4	3	.571	44	24	56	4.14	4
Major League Totals		9 Yrs.	487	676 2/3	32	33	.492	526	304	683	4.26	22
	Division Series											
2007	Colorado	N.L.	1	1	0	0	.000	2	0	1	9.00	0
	Championship Series											
2007	Colorado	N.L.	2	1 1/3	0	0	.000	0	0	0	0.00	0
2010	San Francisco	N.L.	3	2 2/3	0	0	.000	4	1	0	3.38	0
Championship Series Totals			5	4	0	0	.000	4	1	0	2.25	0
	World Series Record											
2007	Colorado	N.L.	4	3	0	0	.000	2	1	2	0.00	0
2010	San Francisco	N.L.	2	1 1/3	0	0	.000	0	1	1	6.75	0
World Series Totals			6	4 1/3	0	0	.000	2	2	3	2.08	0

a On disabled list from June 9 to August 1, 2002.
b On disabled list from April 20 to May 6, 2003.
c On disabled list from June 27 to August 21, 2004.
d On disabled list from April 16 to June 4 and June 19 to July 7, 2005.
e Traded to Colorado Rockies with pitcher Denny Bautista for infielder Ryan Shealy and pitcher Scott Dohmann, July 31, 2006.
f Filed for free agency, October 29, 2007. Signed with Cincinnati Reds, January 23, 2008.
g Filed for free agency, October 30, 2008. Signed with San Francisco Giants, November 17, 2008.
h On disabled list from July 21 to August 18, 2010.

ALBERS, MATTHEW JAMES (MATT)

Born, Houston, Texas, January 20, 1983.
Bats Left. Throws Right. Height, 6 feet. Weight, 205 pounds.

Year	Club	Lea	G	IP	W	L	Pct	SO	BB	H	ERA	SAVES
2002	Martinsville	Appal.	13	59 2/3	2	3	.400	72	38	61	5.13	0
2003	Tri-City	N.Y.-Penn.	15	86 1/3	5	4	.556	94	25	69	2.92	0
2004	Lexington	So.Atl.	22	111 1/3	8	3	.727	140	57	95	3.31	0
2005	Salem	Carolina	28	148 2/3	8	12	.400	146	62	161	4.66	0
2006	Corpus Christi	Texas	19	116	10	2	.833	95	47	96	2.17	0
2006	Round Rock	P.C.	4	25	2	1	.667	26	10	24	3.96	0
2006	Houston	N.L.	4	15	0	2	.000	11	7	17	6.00	0
2007	Round Rock	P.C.	9	53	2	3	.400	43	22	50	3.74	0
2007	Houston a	N.L.	31	110 2/3	4	11	.267	71	50	127	5.86	0
2008	Aberdeen	N.Y.-Penn.	2	2	0	0	.000	4	1	1	0.00	0
2008	Baltimore b	A.L.	28	49	3	3	.500	26	22	43	3.49	0
2009	Norfolk	Int.	10	12 2/3	1	0	1.000	12	5	19	5.68	0
2009	Baltimore	A.L.	56	67	3	6	.333	49	36	80	5.51	0
2010	Baltimore d	A.L.	62	75 2/3	5	3	.625	49	34	78	4.52	0
Major League Totals		5 Yrs.	181	317 1/3	15	25	.375	206	149	345	5.11	0

a Traded to Baltimore Orioles with pitcher Troy Patton, outfielder Luke Scott, pitcher Dennis Sarfate and infielder Michael Costanzo for infielder Miguel Tejada, December 12, 2007.
b On disabled list from June 26 to October 21, 2008.
d Not offered contract, December 2, 2010. Signed with Boston Red Sox, December 16, 2010.

ANDERSON, BRETT FRANKLIN

Born, Midland, Texas, February 1, 1988.
Bats Left. Throws Left. Height, 6 feet, 4 inches. Weight, 215 pounds.

Year	Club	Lea	G	IP	W	L	Pct	SO	BB	H	ERA	SAVES
2007	Visalia	Calif.	9	39	3	3	.500	40	11	50	4.85	0
2007	South Bend a	Midwest	14	81 1/3	8	4	.667	85	10	76	2.21	0
2008	Stockton	Calif.	14	74	9	4	.692	80	18	68	4.14	0
2008	Midland	Texas	6	31	2	1	.667	38	9	27	2.61	0
2009	Oakland	A.L.	30	175 1/3	11	11	.500	150	45	180	4.06	0
2010	Athletics	Arizona	2	6	0	0	.000	6	0	11	3.00	0
2010	Sacramento	P.C.	3	13 1/3	1	0	1.000	12	3	19	4.05	0
2010	Oakland b	A.L.	19	112 1/3	7	6	.538	75	22	112	2.80	0
Major League Totals		2 Yrs.	49	287 2/3	18	17	.514	225	67	292	3.57	0

a Traded by Arizona Diamonbacks to Oakland Athletics with pitcher Dana Eveland, pitcher Greg Smith, infielder Chris Carter, outfielder Aaron Cunningham and outfielder Carlos Gonzalez for pitcher Danny Haren and pitcher Connor Robertson, December 14, 2007.
b On disabled list from April 25 to May 29 and June 4 to July 30, 2010.

ARRIETA, JACOB JOSEPH (JAKE)

Born, Farmington, Missouri, March 6, 1986.
Bats Right. Throws Right. Height, 6 feet, 4 inches. Weight, 225 pounds.

Year	Club	Lea	G	IP	W	L	Pct	SO	BB	H	ERA	SAVES
2008	Frederick	Carolina	20	113	6	5	.545	120	51	80	2.87	0
2009	Bowie	Eastern	11	59	6	3	.667	70	23	45	2.59	0
2009	Norfolk	Int.	17	91 2/3	5	8	.385	78	33	97	3.93	0
2010	Norfolk	Int.	12	73	6	2	.750	64	34	48	1.85	0
2010	Baltimore	A.L.	18	100 1/3	6	6	.500	52	48	106	4.66	0

ARROYO, BRONSON ANTHONY

Born, Key West, Florida, February 24, 1977.
Bats Right. Throws Right. Height, 6 feet, 5 inches. Weight, 190 pounds.

Year	Club	Lea	G	IP	W	L	Pct	SO	BB	H	ERA	SAVES
1995	Pirates	Gulf Coast	13	61 1/3	5	4	.556	48	9	72	4.26	1
1996	Augusta	So.Atl.	26	135 2/3	8	6	.571	107	36	123	3.52	0
1997	Lynchburg	Carolina	24	160 1/3	12	4	.750	121	33	154	3.31	0
1998	Carolina a	Southern	23	127	9	8	.529	90	51	158	5.46	0
1999	Altoona	Eastern	25	153	15	4	.789	100	58	167	3.65	0
1999	Nashville	P.C.	3	13	0	2	.000	11	10	22	10.38	0
2000	Nashville	P.C.	13	88 2/3	8	2	.800	52	25	82	3.65	0
2000	Pittsburgh	N.L.	20	71 2/3	2	6	.250	50	36	88	6.40	0
2000	Lynchburg	Carolina	1	7	0	0	.000	3	2	8	3.86	0
2001	Pittsburgh	N.L.	24	88 1/3	5	7	.417	39	34	99	5.09	0
2001	Nashville	P.C.	9	66 1/3	6	2	.750	49	15	63	3.93	0
2002	Nashville	P.C.	22	143	8	6	.571	116	28	126	2.96	0
2002	Pittsburgh	N.L.	9	27	2	1	.667	22	15	30	4.00	0
2003	Pawtucket	Int.	24	149 2/3	12	6	.667	155	23	148	3.43	0
2003	Boston b	A.L.	6	17 1/3	0	0	.000	14	4	10	2.08	1
2004	Boston	A.L.	32	178 2/3	10	9	.526	142	47	171	4.03	0
2005	Boston	A.L.	35	205 1/3	14	10	.583	100	54	213	4.51	0
2006	Cincinnati c	N.L.	35	*240 2/3	14	11	.560	184	64	222	3.29	0
2007	Cincinnati	N.L.	34	210 2/3	9	15	.375	156	63	232	4.23	0
2008	Cincinnati	N.L.	34	200	15	11	.577	163	68	219	4.77	0
2009	Cincinnati	N.L.	33	220 1/3	15	13	.536	127	65	214	3.84	0
2010	Cincinnati	N.L.	33	215 2/3	17	10	.630	121	59	188	3.88	0
Major League Totals		11 Yrs.	295	1675 2/3	103	93	.526	1118	509	1686	4.19	1
	Division Series											
2004	Boston	A.L.	1	6	0	0	.000	7	2	3	3.00	0
2005	Boston	A.L.	1	1	0	0	.000	1	2	2	18.00	0
2010	Cincinnati	N.L.	1	5 1/3	0	0	.000	2	3	4	1.69	0
Division Series Totals			3	12 1/3	0	0	.000	10	7	9	3.65	0
	Championship Series											
2003	Boston	A.L.	3	3 1/3	0	0	.000	5	2	2	2.70	0
2004	Boston	A.L.	3	4	0	0	.000	3	2	8	15.75	0
Championship Series Totals			6	7 1/3	0	0	.000	8	4	10	9.82	0
	World Series Record											
2004	Boston	A.L.	2	2 2/3	0	0	.000	4	1	4	6.75	0

a On minor league disabled list from May 18 to June 7 and June 18 to July 4, 1998.
b Claimed on waivers by Boston Red Sox, February 4, 2003.
c Traded to Cincinnati Reds for outfielder Wily Mo Pena, March 20, 2006.

ATCHISON, SCOTT BARHAM

Born, Denton, Texas, March 29, 1976.
Bats Right. Throws Right. Height, 6 feet, 2 inches. Weight, 200 pounds.

Year	Club	Lea	G	IP	W	L	Pct	SO	BB	H	ERA	SAVES
1999	Wisconsin	Midwest	15	$81\frac{2}{3}$	4	5	.444	85	25	67	3.42	0
2000	Lancaster	Calif.	19	$97\frac{2}{3}$	5	5	.500	77	21	117	3.69	0
2000	Tacoma	P.C.	5	26	1	1	.500	18	6	22	3.81	0
2001	San Antonio	Texas	24	136	9	10	.474	83	28	171	4.24	0
2002	Tacoma	P.C.	27	$124\frac{1}{3}$	5	10	.333	112	31	123	4.63	2
2003	Tacoma	P.C.	39	$108\frac{2}{3}$	6	9	.400	83	37	114	4.31	1
2004	Tacoma	P.C.	40	$69\frac{1}{3}$	5	3	.625	76	26	71	4.15	7
2004	Seattle	A.L.	25	$30\frac{2}{3}$	2	3	.400	36	14	29	3.52	0
2005	Mariners	Arizona	4	5	0	0	.000	9	1	7	5.40	0
2005	San Antonio	Texas	5	6	0	0	.000	8	2	3	0.00	0
2005	Tacoma	P.C.	10	13	0	0	.000	17	5	13	4.15	0
2005	Seattle a	A.L.	6	$6\frac{2}{3}$	0	0	.000	9	1	7	6.75	0
2006	Tacoma b	P.C.	30	50	4	0	1.000	39	15	49	2.34	1
2007	Fresno	P.C.	38	$53\frac{2}{3}$	3	2	.600	51	8	44	2.01	4
2007	San Francisco c	N.L.	22	$30\frac{2}{3}$	0	0	.000	25	10	32	4.11	0
2008	Hanshin	Japan Pac.	42	$104\frac{2}{3}$	7	6	.538	85	26	104	3.70	0
2009	Hanshin d	Japan Pac.	75	90	5	3	.625	81	20	60	1.70	0
2010	Pawtucket	Int.	11	$13\frac{1}{3}$	1	0	1.000	17	5	13	4.05	0
2010	Boston	A.L.	43	60	2	3	.400	41	19	58	4.50	0
Major League Totals		4 Yrs.	96	128	4	6	.400	111	44	126	4.29	0

a On disabled list from April 2 to September 3, 2005.
b Filed for free agency October 15, 2006. Signed with San Francisco Giants organization, November 13, 2006.
c Filed for free agency, November 28, 2007. Signed with Boston Red Sox organization, December 12, 2007.
d Sold to Hanshin (Japan), December 19, 2007. Signed with Boston Red Sox, December 5, 2009.

ATILANO, LUIS A.

Born, Santurce, Puerto Rico, May 10, 1985.
Bats Right. Throws Right. Height, 6 feet, 2 inches. Weight, 220 pounds.

Year	Club	Lea	G	IP	W	L	Pct	SO	BB	H	ERA	SAVES
2003	Braves	Gulf Coast	12	54	3	2	.600	24	7	61	3.83	0
2004	Danville	Appal.	13	$64\frac{1}{3}$	5	1	.833	54	10	64	4.20	0
2005	Rome	So.Atl.	24	136	8	9	.471	66	32	138	4.17	0
2006	Myrtle Beach a	Carolina	19	116	6	7	.462	45	27	134	4.50	0
2007	Nationals	Gulf Coast	1	$1\frac{1}{3}$	0	0	.000	2	1	1	6.75	0
2008	Potomac	Carolina	15	62	5	2	.714	39	14	50	2.32	0
2008	Harrisburg	Eastern	2	6	0	1	.000	3	2	6	1.50	0
2008	Hagerstown	So.Atl.	7	$25\frac{2}{3}$	0	0	.000	13	7	29	3.16	0
2009	Harrisburg	Eastern	21	$114\frac{2}{3}$	7	8	.467	61	27	143	4.16	0
2009	Syracuse	Int.	2	11	2	0	1.000	5	1	11	2.45	0
2010	Syracuse	Int.	3	$13\frac{1}{3}$	2	1	.667	9	5	17	4.72	0
2010	Washington b	N.L.	16	$85\frac{2}{3}$	6	7	.462	40	32	96	5.15	0

a Traded by Atlanta Braves to Washington Nationals for outfielder Daryle Ward, August 31, 2006.
b On disabled list from July 21 to November 10, 2010.

AXFORD, JOHN BERTON

Born, Simcoe, Ontario, Canada, April 1, 1983.
Bats Right. Throws Right. Height, 6 feet, 5 inches. Weight, 195 pounds.

Year	Club	Lea	G	IP	W	L	Pct	SO	BB	H	ERA	SAVES
2007	Tampa	Fla.St.	5	$11\frac{1}{3}$	0	0	.000	15	7	6	2.38	2
2007	Scranton/WB	Int.	1	$0\frac{2}{3}$	0	0	.000	1	1	2	13.50	0
2007	Staten Island	N.Y.-Penn.	8	$24\frac{1}{3}$	1	1	.500	30	15	13	2.22	2
2007	Charleston	So.Atl.	13	$26\frac{2}{3}$	0	3	.000	21	22	29	4.39	0
2008	Brevard County a	Fla.St.	26	95	5	10	.333	89	73	86	4.55	0
2009	Brevard County	Fla.St.	19	$27\frac{2}{3}$	4	1	.800	43	16	14	1.63	0
2009	Huntsville	Southern	4	$7\frac{2}{3}$	0	0	.000	9	3	7	3.52	1
2009	Nashville	P.C.	22	33	5	0	1.000	37	19	23	3.55	0
2009	Milwaukee	N.L.	7	$7\frac{2}{3}$	0	0	.000	9	6	5	3.52	1
2010	Nashville	P.C.	12	$13\frac{1}{3}$	3	2	.600	19	5	14	2.03	2
2010	Milwaukee	N.L.	50	58	8	2	.800	76	27	42	2.48	24
Major League Totals		2 Yrs.	57	$65\frac{2}{3}$	8	2	.800	85	33	47	2.60	25

a Released by New York Yankees, December 14, 2007. Signed with Milwaukee Brewers organization, March 4, 2008.

BADENHOP, BURKE HEINRICH

Born, Atlanta, Georgia, February 8, 1983.
Bats Right. Throws Right. Height, 6 feet, 5 inches. Weight, 220 pounds.

Year	Club	Lea	G	IP	W	L	Pct	SO	BB	H	ERA	SAVES
2005	Oneonta	N.Y.-Penn.	14	77	6	4	.600	55	26	69	2.92	0
2006	West Michigan	Midwest	27	171	14	3	.824	124	31	170	2.84	0
2007	Erie	Eastern	3	$18^2/_3$	2	0	1.000	12	3	8	1.45	0
2007	Lakeland a	Fla.St.	23	$135^1/_3$	10	6	.625	78	34	130	3.13	0
2008	Carolina	Southern	1	$6^1/_3$	1	0	1.000	3	0	6	0.00	0
2008	Florida	N.L.	13	$47^1/_3$	2	3	.400	35	21	55	6.08	0
2008	Marlins	Gulf Coast	1	3	0	0	.000	2	0	1	0.00	0
2009	Marlins	Gulf Coast	2	3	0	1	.000	4	0	2	0.00	0
2009	Jupiter	Fla.St.	2	8	0	0	.000	8	1	2	0.00	0
2009	New Orleans	P.C.	2	$9^1/_3$	0	1	.000	6	4	14	6.75	0
2009	Florida b	N.L.	35	72	7	4	.636	57	24	71	3.75	0
2010	New Orleans	P.C.	12	16	0	1	.000	9	7	16	2.81	0
2010	Florida	N.L.	53	$67^2/_3$	2	5	.286	47	21	62	3.99	1
Major League Totals		3 Yrs.	101	187	11	12	.478	139	66	188	4.43	1

a Traded by Detroit Tigers to Florida Marlins with pitcher Eulogio De La Cruz, pitcher Andrew Miller, catcher Mike Rabelo and outfielder Cameron Maybin for pitcher Dontrelle Willis and infielder Miguel Cabrera, December 5, 2007.
b On disabled list from August 2 to September 1, 2009.

BAEZ, DANYS

Born, Pinar Del Rio, Cuba, September 10, 1977.
Bats Right. Throws Right. Height, 6 feet, 3 inches. Weight, 235 pounds.

Year	Club	Lea	G	IP	W	L	Pct	SO	BB	H	ERA	SAVES
2000	Kinston	Carolina	9	$49^2/_3$	2	2	.500	56	20	45	4.71	0
2000	Akron a-b	Eastern	18	$102^2/_3$	4	9	.308	77	32	98	3.68	0
2001	Buffalo	Int.	16	$25^1/_3$	2	0	1.000	30	9	18	3.20	3
2001	Akron	Eastern	1	2	0	0	.000	2	0	1	0.00	0
2001	Cleveland	A.L.	43	$50^1/_3$	5	3	.625	52	20	34	2.50	0
2002	Cleveland	A.L.	39	$165^1/_3$	10	11	.476	130	82	160	4.41	6
2003	Cleveland c	A.L.	73	$75^2/_3$	2	9	.182	66	23	65	3.81	25
2004	Tampa Bay d	A.L.	62	68	4	4	.500	52	29	60	3.57	30
2005	Tampa Bay	A.L.	67	$72^1/_3$	5	4	.556	51	30	66	2.86	41
2006	Los Angeles-Atlanta e-f-g	N.L.	57	$59^2/_3$	5	6	.455	39	17	60	4.53	9
2007	Bowie	Eastern	3	4	0	0	.000	4	2	3	2.25	0
2007	Baltimore h	A.L.	53	$50^1/_3$	0	6	.000	29	29	50	6.44	3
2008	Baltimore i	A.L.			INJURED—Did Not Play							
2009	Baltimore j	A.L.	59	$71^2/_3$	4	6	.400	40	22	59	4.02	0
2010	Lehigh Valley	Int.	1	1	0	0	.000	0	0	2	9.00	0
2010	Philadelphia k	N.L.	51	$47^2/_3$	3	4	.429	28	23	55	5.48	0
Major League Totals		9 Yrs.	504	661	38	53	.418	487	275	609	4.14	114
	Division Series											
2001	Cleveland	A.L.	3	$3^2/_3$	0	0	.000	6	0	4	2.45	0

a Played in Cuba in 1999. Signed with Cleveland Indians organization, November 6, 1999.
b On disabled list from June 19 to July 4, 2000.
c Not offered contract, November 14, 2003, re-signed with Cleveland Indians, November 18, 2003.
d Not offered contract, December 21, 2003. Signed with Tampa Bay Devil Rays, January 6, 2004.
e Traded to Atlanta Braves with infielder Willy Aybar and cash for outfielder Wilson Betemit, July 28, 2006.
f On disabled list from August 23 to October 3, 2006.
g Filed for free agency, October 28, 2006. Signed with Baltimore Orioles, November 27, 2006.
h On disabled list from June 16 to July 12, 2007.
i On disabled list from March 21 to October 21, 2008.
j Filed for free agency, November 5, 2009. Signed with Philadelphia Phillies, December 31, 2009.
k On disabled list from August 25 to September 9, 2010.

BAILEY, ANDREW SCOTT

Born, Voorhees, New Jersey, May 31, 1984.
Bats Right. Throws Right. Height, 6 feet, 3 inches. Weight, 235 pounds.

Year	Club	Lea	G	IP	W	L	Pct	SO	BB	H	ERA	SAVES
2006	Vancouver	Northwest	13	58	2	5	.286	53	20	39	2.02	0
2007	Stockton	Calif.	11	66	3	4	.429	72	31	56	3.82	0
2007	Kane County	Midwest	11	51	1	4	.200	74	22	42	3.35	0
2007	Sacramento	P.C.	1	8	1	0	1.000	4	1	3	1.13	0
2008	Midland	Texas	37	$110^1/_3$	5	9	.357	110	56	99	4.32	0
2009	Oakland a	A.L.	68	$83^1/_3$	6	3	.667	91	24	49	1.84	26
2010	Sacramento	P.C.	1	$0^2/_3$	0	0	.000	1	0	3	27.00	0

Year	Club	Lea	G	IP	W	L	Pct	SO	BB	H	ERA	SAVES
2010	Oakland b	A.L.	47	49	1	3	.250	42	13	34	1.47	25
Major League Totals		2 Yrs.	115	132 1/3	7	6	.538	133	37	83	1.70	51

a Selected Rookie of the Year in American League for 2009.
b On disabled list from July 21 to August 22, 2010.

BAILEY, DAVID DEWITT (HOMER)

Born, LaGrange, Texas, May 3, 1986.
Bats Right. Throws Right. Height, 6 feet, 4 inches. Weight, 210 pounds.

Year	Club	Lea	G	IP	W	L	Pct	SO	BB	H	ERA	SAVES
2004	Reds	Gulf Coast	6	12 1/3	0	1	.000	9	3	14	4.38	0
2005	Dayton	Midwest	28	103 2/3	8	4	.667	125	62	89	4.43	0
2006	Sarasota	Fla.St.	13	70 2/3	3	5	.375	79	22	49	3.31	0
2006	Chattanooga	Southern	13	68	7	1	.875	77	28	50	1.59	0
2007	Louisville	Int.	12	67 1/3	6	3	.667	59	32	49	3.07	0
2007	Sarasota	Fla.St.	2	8	0	1	.000	7	5	15	10.13	0
2007	Cincinnati	N.L.	9	45 1/3	4	2	.667	28	28	43	5.76	0
2008	Cincinnati	N.L.	8	36 1/3	0	6	.000	18	17	59	7.93	0
2008	Louisville	Int.	19	111 1/3	4	7	.364	96	46	118	4.77	0
2009	Louisville	Int.	14	89 2/3	8	5	.615	82	27	87	2.71	0
2009	Cincinnati	N.L.	20	113 1/3	8	5	.615	86	52	115	4.53	0
2010	Dayton	Midwest	1	4	0	1	.000	5	1	4	6.75	0
2010	Louisville	Int.	4	19	2	0	1.000	15	5	15	2.37	0
2010	Cincinnati a	N.L.	19	109	4	3	.571	100	40	109	4.46	0
Major League Totals		4 Yrs.	56	304	16	16	.500	232	137	326	5.09	0
Division Series												
2010	Cincinnati	N.L.	1	2	0	0	.000	2	0	2	0.00	0

a On disabled list from May 24 to August 15, 2010.

BAKER, TIMOTHY SCOTT (SCOTT)

Born, Shreveport, Louisiana, September 19, 1981.
Bats Right. Throws Right. Height, 6 feet, 4 inches. Weight, 210 pounds.

Year	Club	Lea	G	IP	W	L	Pct	SO	BB	H	ERA	SAVES
2003	Quad Cities	Midwest	11	50 2/3	3	1	.750	47	8	45	2.49	0
2004	New Britain	Eastern	10	70 1/3	5	3	.625	72	13	44	2.43	0
2004	Fort Myers	Fla.St.	7	45	4	2	.667	37	6	40	2.40	0
2004	Rochester	Int.	9	54 1/3	1	3	.250	36	15	65	4.97	0
2005	Rochester	Int.	22	134 2/3	5	8	.385	107	26	123	3.01	0
2005	Minnesota	A.L.	10	53 2/3	3	3	.500	32	14	48	3.35	0
2006	Rochester	Int.	12	84 1/3	5	4	.556	68	25	77	2.67	0
2006	Minnesota	A.L.	16	83 1/3	5	8	.385	62	16	114	6.37	0
2007	Rochester	Int.	7	42 2/3	3	2	.600	41	4	34	3.16	1
2007	Minnesota	A.L.	24	143 2/3	9	9	.500	102	29	162	4.26	0
2008	Fort Myers	Fla.St.	1	5	1	0	1.000	4	0	7	5.40	0
2008	Minnesota a	A.L.	28	172 1/3	11	4	.733	141	42	161	3.45	0
2009	Fort Myers	Fla.St.	1	7	1	0	1.000	3	1	5	1.29	0
2009	Minnesota b	A.L.	33	200	15	9	.625	162	48	190	4.36	0
2010	Minnesota	A.L.	29	170 1/3	12	9	.571	148	43	186	4.49	0
Major League Totals		6 Yrs.	140	823 1/3	55	42	.567	647	192	861	4.32	0
Division Series												
2010	Minnesota	A.L.	1	2 1/3	0	0	.000	2	0	3	3.86	0

a On disabled list from May 4 to June 5, 2008.
b On disabled list from March 28 to April 15, 2009.

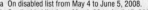

BALFOUR, GRANT ROBERT

Born, Sydney, New South Wales,Australia, December 30, 1977.
Bats Right. Throws Right. Height, 6 feet, 2 inches. Weight, 190 pounds.

Year	Club	Lea	G	IP	W	L	Pct	SO	BB	H	ERA	SAVES
1997	Twins	Gulf Coast	13	67	2	4	.333	43	20	73	3.76	0
1998	Elizabethtn	Appal.	13	77 2/3	7	2	.778	75	27	70	3.36	0
1999	Quad Cities	Midwest	19	91 2/3	8	5	.615	95	37	66	3.53	1
2000	Fort Myers	Fla.St.	35	89	8	5	.615	90	34	91	4.25	6
2001	New Britain	Eastern	35	50	2	1	.667	72	22	26	1.08	13
2001	Minnesota	A.L.	2	2 2/3	0	0	.000	2	3	3	13.50	0
2001	Edmonton	P.C.	11	16 1/3	2	2	.500	17	10	18	5.51	0
2002	Edmonton	P.C.	58	71 1/3	2	4	.333	88	30	60	4.16	8

Year	Club	Lea	G	IP	W	L	Pct	SO	BB	H	ERA	SAVES
2003	Rochester	Int.	21	71	5	2	.714	87	16	48	2.41	5
2003	Minnesota	A.L.	17	26	1	0	1.000	30	14	23	4.15	0
2004	Minnesota a	A.L.	36	$39\frac{1}{3}$	4	1	.800	42	21	35	4.35	0
2005	Minnesota b	A.L.			INJURED—Did Not Play							
2006	Sarasota	Fla.St.	5	$5\frac{2}{3}$	0	0	.000	7	3	8	7.94	0
2006	Reds	Gulf Coast	2	$1\frac{1}{3}$	0	0	.000	2	3	1	13.50	0
2006	Dayton c-d	Midwest	2	2	0	0	.000	3	0	0	0.00	0
2007	Huntsville	Southern	8	$11\frac{1}{3}$	0	0	.000	21	4	8	2.38	2
2007	Nashville	P.C.	24	32	1	1	.500	47	11	17	1.69	5
2007	Milwaukee e-f	N.L.	3	$2\frac{2}{3}$	0	2	.000	3	4	4	20.25	0
2007	Tampa Bay	A.L.	22	22	1	0	1.000	27	16	26	6.14	0
2008	Durham	Int.	15	$23\frac{2}{3}$	1	0	1.000	39	10	5	0.38	8
2008	Tampa Bay	A.L.	51	$58\frac{1}{3}$	6	2	.750	82	24	28	1.54	4
2009	Tampa Bay	A.L.	73	$67\frac{1}{3}$	5	4	.556	69	33	59	4.81	4
2010	Charlotte	Fla.St.	2	$1\frac{2}{3}$	0	1	.000	2	3	2	10.80	0
2010	Tampa Bay g-h	A.L.	57	$55\frac{1}{3}$	2	1	.667	56	17	43	2.28	0
Major League Totals		7 Yrs.	261	$273\frac{2}{3}$	19	10	.655	311	132	221	3.81	8
	Division Series											
2004	Minnesota	A.L.	2	$2\frac{2}{3}$	0	0	.000	2	0	0	0.00	0
2008	Tampa Bay	N.L.	3	$3\frac{1}{3}$	0	0	.000	4	1	2	0.00	0
2010	Tampa Bay	N.L.	3	$3\frac{2}{3}$	0	0	.000	1	0	2	0.00	0
Division Series Totals			8	$9\frac{2}{3}$	0	0	.000	7	1	4	0.00	0
	Championship Series											
2008	Tampa Bay	N.L.	4	$2\frac{1}{3}$	0	0	.000	1	4	5	19.29	0
	World Series Record											
2008	Tampa Bay	N.L.	3	3	0	0	.000	2	3	4	3.00	0

a On disabled list from April 4 to May 14 and August 2 to August 17, 2004.
b On disabled list from March 25 to October 14, 2005.
c Filed for free agency, October 15, 2005. Signed with Cincinnati Reds organization, January 12, 2006.
d On disabled list from March 31 to October 3, 2006.
e Claimed on waivers by Milwaukee Brewers, October 5, 2006.
f Traded to Tampa Bay Devil Rays for pitcher Seth McClung, July 27, 2007.
g On disabled list from July 30 to September 1, 2010.
h Filed for free agency, November 1, 2010. Signed with Oakland Athletics, January 18, 2011.

BANNISTER, BRIAN PATRICK

Born, Scottsdale, Arizona, February 28, 1981.
Bats Right. Throws Right. Height, 6 feet, 2 inches. Weight, 210 pounds.

Year	Club	Lea	G	IP	W	L	Pct	SO	BB	H	ERA	SAVES
2003	Brooklyn	N.Y.-Penn.	12	46	4	1	.800	42	18	27	2.15	1
2004	Binghamton	Eastern	8	$44\frac{1}{3}$	3	3	.500	28	17	45	4.06	0
2004	St. Lucie	Fla.St.	20	$110\frac{1}{3}$	5	7	.417	106	27	111	4.32	0
2005	Binghamton	Eastern	18	109	9	4	.692	94	27	91	2.56	0
2005	Norfolk	Int.	8	$45\frac{1}{3}$	4	1	.800	48	13	48	3.18	0
2006	St. Lucie	Fla.St.	2	12	1	0	1.000	9	4	10	1.50	0
2006	Norfolk	Int.	6	$30\frac{1}{3}$	3	3	.500	24	5	34	3.86	0
2006	New York a-b	N.L.	8	38	2	1	.667	19	22	34	4.26	0
2007	Omaha	P.C.	4	$20\frac{2}{3}$	1	1	.500	14	4	16	2.61	0
2007	Kansas City	A.L.	27	165	12	9	.571	77	44	156	3.87	0
2008	Kansas City	A.L.	32	$182\frac{2}{3}$	9	16	.360	113	58	215	5.76	0
2009	Omaha	P.C.	3	13	0	1	.000	8	1	12	3.46	0
2009	Kansas City	A.L.	26	154	7	12	.368	98	50	161	4.73	0
2010	Omaha	P.C.	3	$7\frac{1}{3}$	0	1	.000	3	0	10	3.68	0
2010	Kansas City c-d	A.L.	24	$127\frac{2}{3}$	7	12	.368	77	50	158	6.34	0
Major League Totals		5 Yrs.	117	$667\frac{1}{3}$	37	50	.425	384	224	724	5.08	0

a On disabled list from April 27 to August 25, 2006.
b Traded to Kansas City Royals for pitcher Ambiorix Burgos, December 6, 2006.
c On disabled list from August 8 to September 3, 2010.
d Filed for free agency, November 10, 2010. Signed with Yomiuri Giants (Japan), January 6, 2011.

BARD, DANIEL PAUL

Born, Houston, Texas, June 25, 1985.
Bats Right. Throws Right. Height, 6 feet, 4 inches. Weight, 200 pounds.

Year	Club	Lea	G	IP	W	L	Pct	SO	BB	H	ERA	SAVES
2007	Lancaster	Calif.	5	$13\frac{1}{3}$	0	2	.000	9	22	21	10.13	0
2007	Greenville	So.Atl.	17	$61\frac{2}{3}$	3	5	.375	38	56	55	6.42	0
2008	Portland	Eastern	31	$49\frac{2}{3}$	4	1	.800	64	26	30	1.99	7

Year	Club	Lea	G	IP	W	L	Pct	SO	BB	H	ERA	SAVES
2008	Greenville	So.Atl.	15	28	1	0	1.000	43	4	12	0.64	0
2009	Pawtucket	Int.	11	16	1	0	1.000	29	5	6	1.13	6
2009	Boston	A.L.	49	49 1/3	2	2	.500	63	22	41	3.65	1
2010	Boston	A.L.	73	74 2/3	1	2	.333	76	30	45	1.93	3
Major League Totals		2 Yrs.	122	124	3	4	.429	139	52	86	2.61	4
	Division Series											
2009	Boston	A.L.	2	3	0	0	.000	4	0	0	0.00	0

BATISTA, MIGUEL JEREZ

Born, Santo Domingo, Dominican Republic, February 19, 1971.
Bats Right. Throws Right. Height, 6 feet, 1 Inch. Weight, 195 pounds.

Year	Club	Lea	G	IP	W	L	Pct	SO	BB	H	ERA	SAVES
1990	Expos	Gulf Coast	9	39 1/3	4	3	.571	21	17	33	2.06	0
1990	Rockford	Midwest	3	12 1/3	0	1	.000	7	5	16	8.76	0
1991	Rockford a	Midwest	23	133 2/3	11	5	.688	90	57	126	4.04	0
1992	Pittsburgh b	N.L.	1	2	0	0	.000	1	3	4	9.00	0
1992	Wst Plm Bch	Fla. St.	24	135 1/3	7	7	.500	92	54	130	3.79	0
1993	Harrisburg	Eastern	26	141	13	5	.722	91	86	139	4.34	0
1994	Harrisburg c-d-e	Eastern	3	11 1/3	0	1	.000	5	9	8	2.38	0
1995	Charlotte	Int.	34	116 1/3	6	12	.333	58	60	118	4.80	0
1996	Charlotte	Int.	47	77	4	3	.571	56	39	93	5.38	4
1996	Florida f	N.L.	9	11 1/3	0	0	.000	6	7	9	5.56	0
1997	Iowa	A.A.	31	122	9	4	.692	95	38	117	4.20	0
1997	Chicago g	N.L.	11	36 1/3	0	5	.000	27	24	36	5.70	0
1998	Montreal	N.L.	56	135	3	5	.375	92	65	141	3.80	0
1999	Ottawa h	Int.	3	8	0	1	.000	7	4	3	2.25	0
2000	Montreal i	N.L.	4	8 1/3	0	1	.000	7	3	19	14.04	0
2000	Omaha	P.C.	18	28 1/3	2	2	.500	27	7	35	6.04	3
2000	Kansas City j	A.L.	14	57	2	6	.250	30	34	66	7.74	0
2001	Arizona	N.L.	48	139 1/3	11	8	.579	90	60	113	3.36	0
2002	Arizona	N.L.	36	184 2/3	8	9	.471	112	70	172	4.29	0
2003	Arizona k	N.L.	36	193 1/3	10	9	.526	142	60	197	3.54	0
2004	Toronto	A.L.	38	198 2/3	10	13	.435	104	*96	206	4.80	5
2005	Toronto l	A.L.	71	74 2/3	5	8	.385	54	27	80	4.10	31
2006	Arizona m	N.L.	34	206 1/3	11	8	.579	110	84	231	4.58	0
2007	Seattle	A.L.	33	193	16	11	.593	133	85	209	4.29	0
2008	Seattle	A.L.	44	115	4	14	.222	73	79	135	6.26	1
2009	Seattle n	A.L.	56	71 1/3	7	4	.636	52	39	79	4.04	1
2010	Washington o	N.L.	58	82 2/3	1	2	.333	55	39	71	3.70	2
Major League Totals		16 Yrs.	588	1843 2/3	96	110	.466	1183	833	1914	4.51	41
	Division Series											
2001	Arizona	N.L.	2	6 2/3	1	0	1.000	4	1	3	2.70	0
2002	Arizona	N.L.	1	3 2/3	0	1	.000	1	3	5	9.82	0
Division Series Totals			3	10 1/3	1	1	.500	5	4	8	5.23	0
	Championship Series											
2001	Arizona	N.L.	2	7	0	1	.000	3	2	5	5.14	0
	World Series Record											
2001	Arizona	N.L.	2	8	0	0	.000	6	5	5	0.00	0

a Selected by Pittsburgh Pirates from Montreal Expos in Rule V draft, December 9, 1991.
b Returned to Montreal Expos by Pittsburgh Pirates, April 23, 1992.
c On disabled list April 14 to 30 and May 7 to September 26, 1994.
d Released by Montreal Expos, November 18, 1994.
e Signed as free agent by Florida Marlins organization, December 9, 1994.
f Claimed on waivers by Chicago Cubs, December 10, 1996.
g Traded to Montreal Expos for outfielder Henry Rodriguez, December 12, 1997.
h On disabled list from July 16 to August 10, 1999.
i Traded to Kansas City Royals for pitcher Brad Rigby, April 25, 2000.
j Filed for free agency, October 2, 2000. Signed with Arizona Diamondbacks, November 15, 2000.
k Filed for free agency, November 7, 2003. Signed with Toronto Blue Jays, December 12, 2003.
l Traded to Arizona Diamondbacks with infielder Orlando Hudson for infielder Troy Glaus and infielder Sergio Santos, December 27, 2005.
m Filed for free agency, October 30, 2006. Signed with Seattle Mariners, December 14, 2006.
n Filed for free agency, November 6, 2009. Signed with Washington Nationals organization, January 29, 2010.
o Filed for free agency, November 1, 2010. Signed with St. Louis Cardinals organization, January 14, 2011.

BECKETT, JOSHUA PATRICK (JOSH)

Born, Spring, Texas, May 15, 1980.
Bats Right. Throws Right. Height, 6 feet, 5 inches. Weight, 220 pounds.

Year	Club	Lea	G	IP	W	L	Pct	SO	BB	H	ERA	SAVES
2000	Kane County	Midwest	13	59 1/3	2	3	.400	61	15	45	2.12	0
2001	Brevard County	Fla.St.	13	65 2/3	6	0	1.000	101	15	32	1.23	0
2001	Portland	Eastern	13	74 1/3	8	1	.889	102	19	50	1.82	0
2001	Florida	N.L.	4	24	2	2	.500	24	11	14	1.50	0
2002	Marlins	Gulf Coast	1	4	0	0	.000	7	1	5	4.50	0
2002	Jupiter	Fla.St.	1	6	1	0	1.000	12	1	4	0.00	0
2002	Florida a	N.L.	23	107 2/3	6	7	.462	113	44	93	4.10	0
2003	Carolina	Southern	1	4	0	0	.000	7	0	4	4.50	0
2003	Jupiter	Fla.St.	1	3	0	0	.000	5	0	2	0.00	0
2003	Florida b	N.L.	24	142	9	8	.529	152	56	132	3.04	0
2004	Florida c	N.L.	26	156 2/3	9	9	.500	152	54	137	3.79	0
2005	Florida d-e	N.L.	29	178 2/3	15	8	.652	166	58	153	3.38	0
2006	Boston	A.L.	33	204 2/3	16	11	.593	158	74	191	5.01	0
2007	Boston f	A.L.	30	200 2/3	*20	7	.741	194	40	189	3.27	0
2008	Boston g	A.L.	27	174 1/3	12	10	.545	172	34	173	4.03	0
2009	Boston	A.L.	32	212 1/3	17	6	.739	199	55	198	3.86	0
2010	Pawtucket	Int.	2	8	0	0	.000	7	1	7	4.50	0
2010	Boston h	A.L.	21	127 2/3	6	6	.500	116	45	151	5.78	0
Major League Totals		10 Yrs.	249	1528 2/3	112	74	.602	1446	471	1431	3.96	0
	Division Series											
2003	Florida	N.L.	1	7	0	1	.000	9	5	2	1.29	0
2007	Boston	A.L.	1	9	1	0	1.000	8	0	4	0.00	0
2008	Boston	A.L.	1	5	0	0	.000	6	4	9	7.20	0
2009	Boston	A.L.	1	6 2/3	0	1	.000	3	1	5	5.40	0
Division Series Totals			4	27 2/3	1	2	.333	26	10	20	2.93	0
	Championship Series											
2003	Florida	N.L.	3	19 1/3	1	0	1.000	19	2	11	3.26	0
2007	Boston	A.L.	2	14	2	0	1.000	18	1	9	1.93	0
2008	Boston	A.L.	2	9 1/3	1	0	1.000	8	2	13	9.64	0
Championship Series Totals			7	42 2/3	4	0	1.000	45	5	33	4.22	0
	World Series Record											
2003	Florida	N.L.	2	16 1/3	1	1	.500	19	5	8	1.10	0
2007	Boston	A.L.	1	7	1	0	1.000	9	1	6	1.29	0
World Series Totals			3	23 1/3	2	1	.667	28	6	14	1.16	0

a On disabled list from April 29 to May 14 and June 5 to July 16 and August 23 to September 11, 2002.
b On disabled list from May 8 to July 1, 2003.
c On disabled list from May 31 to June 17 and from June 18 to July 5 and July 6 to July 30, 2004.
d On disabled list from June 15 to June 30 and July 6 to July 23, 2005.
e Traded to Boston Red Sox with infielder Mike Lowell and pitcher Guillermo Mota for infielder Hanley Ramirez, pitcher Anibal Sanchez and pitcher Jesus Delgado, November 24, 2005.
f On disabled list from May 14 to May 29, 2007.
g On disabled list from March 19 to April 6 and August 18 to September 5, 2008.
h On disabled list from May 19 to July 23, 2010.

BEIMEL, JOSEPH RONALD (JOE)

Born, St. Marys, Pennsylvania, April 19, 1977.
Bats Left. Throws Left. Height, 6 feet, 2 inches. Weight, 215 pounds.

Year	Club	Lea	G	IP	W	L	Pct	SO	BB	H	ERA	SAVES
1998	Erie	N.Y.-Penn.	17	47	1	4	.200	37	22	56	6.32	0
1999	Hickory	So.Atl.	29	130	5	11	.313	102	43	146	4.43	0
2000	Lynchburg	Carolina	18	120 2/3	10	6	.625	82	44	111	3.36	0
2000	Altoona	Eastern	10	62 2/3	1	6	.143	28	21	72	4.16	0
2001	Pittsburgh	N.L.	42	115 1/3	7	11	.389	58	49	131	5.23	0
2002	Pittsburgh	N.L.	53	85 1/3	2	5	.286	53	45	88	4.64	0
2003	Pittsburgh	N.L.	69	62 1/3	1	3	.250	42	33	69	5.05	0
2004	Rochester	Int.	49	62	2	4	.333	44	24	83	6.97	2
2004	Minnesota a	A.L.	3	1 2/3	0	0	.000	2	2	8	43.20	0
2005	Durham	Int.	48	52 2/3	1	2	.333	36	21	58	3.93	0
2005	Tampa Bay b-c	A.L.	7	11	0	0	.000	3	4	15	3.27	0
2006	Las Vegas	P.C.	10	13	3	0	1.000	9	4	9	1.38	0
2006	Los Angeles	N.L.	62	70	2	1	.667	30	21	70	2.96	2
2007	Los Angeles	N.L.	83	67 1/3	4	2	.667	39	24	63	3.88	1
2008	Los Angeles d	N.L.	71	49	5	1	.833	32	21	50	2.02	0
2009	Potomac	Carolina	1	1	0	0	.000	0	0	7	45.00	0
2009	Washington-Colorado e-f-g	N.L.	71	55 1/3	1	6	.143	35	19	57	3.58	1

Year	Club	Lea	G	IP	W	L	Pct	SO	BB	H	ERA	SAVES
2010	Colorado Springs	P.C.	2	2⅔	0	0	.000	2	0	2	0.00	0
2010	Colorado h	N.L.	71	45	1	2	.333	21	15	46	3.40	0
Major League Totals		10 Yrs.	532	562⅓	23	31	.426	315	233	597	4.16	4
	Division Series											
2009	Colorado	N.L.	3	0⅔	0	0	.000	0	0	1	0.00	0
	Championship Series											
2008	Los Angeles	N.L.	3	0⅔	0	0	.000	0	2	0	0.00	0

a Released by Pittsburgh Pirates, March 31, 2004. Signed with Minnesota Twins organization, April 11, 2004.
b Filed for free agency, October 9, 2004. Signed with Tampa Bay Devil Rays organization, November 21, 2005.
c Released by Tampa Bay Devil Rays, November 22, 2005. Signed with Los Angeles Dodgers organization, January 23, 2006.
d Filed for free agency, October 30, 2008. Signed with Washington Nationals, March 18, 2009.
e On disabled list from April 21 to May 6, 2009.
f Traded to Colorado Rockies for pitcher Ryan Mattheus and pitcher Robinson Fabian, July 31, 2009.
g Filed for free agency, November 9, 2009, re-signed with Colorado Rockies organization, March 23, 2010.
h Filed for free agency, November 1, 2010.

BELISARIO, RONALD J.

Born, Maracay, Venezuela, December 31, 1982.
Bats Right. Throws Right. Height, 6 feet, 3 inches. Weight, 235 pounds.

Year	Club	Lea	G	IP	W	L	Pct	SO	BB	H	ERA	SAVES
2001	Marlins	Gulf Coast	13	73	4	6	.400	54	20	62	2.34	0
2002	Kane County	Midwest	23	140⅓	6	5	.545	98	56	131	3.46	0
2003	Jupiter	Fla.St.	6	18⅓	1	2	.333	13	8	20	4.91	0
2003	Greensboro	So.Atl.	10	48	5	1	.833	45	18	41	3.00	0
2004	Jupiter	Fla.St.	6	8⅔	1	1	.500	7	5	2	0.00	1
2004	Marlins	Gulf Coast	2	2	0	0	.000	2	0	1	0.00	0
2004	Carolina	Southern	15	73	3	5	.375	58	43	75	5.55	0
2005	a					INJURED—Did Not Play						
2006	b					Did Not Play						
2007	Lynchburg	Carolina	19	34⅓	0	3	.000	19	13	38	4.46	4
2007	Altoona	Eastern	18	24⅔	1	0	1.000	21	14	23	3.28	0
2008	Altoona c	Eastern	38	57	4	4	.500	36	25	63	4.74	9
2009	Inland Empire	Calif.	2	2	0	0	.000	3	1	2	0.00	0
2009	Los Angeles d-e	N.L.	69	70⅔	4	3	.571	64	29	52	2.04	0
2010	Inland Empire	Calif.	2	2	0	0	.000	1	2	1	4.50	0
2010	Los Angeles	N.L.	59	55⅓	3	1	.750	38	19	52	5.04	2
Major League Totals		2 Yrs.	128	126	7	4	.636	102	48	104	3.36	2
	Division Series											
2009	Los Angeles	N.L.	2	1⅓	0	0	.000	0	0	0	0.00	0
	Championship Series											
2009	Los Angeles	N.L.	4	3⅓	0	0	.000	0	1	5	10.80	0

a On minor league disabled list April 7 to September 15, 2005.
b Filed for free agency, October 15, 2006. Signed with Pittsburgh Pirates organization, November 9, 2006.
c Filed for free agency, October 30, 2008.
d Signed with Los Angeles Dodgers organization, January 16, 2009.
e On disabled list from July 6 to August 8, 2009.

BELISLE, MATTHEW THOMAS (MATT)

Born, Austin, Texas, June 6, 1980.
Bats Right. Throws Right. Height, 6 feet, 3 inches. Weight, 225 pounds.

Year	Club	Lea	G	IP	W	L	Pct	SO	BB	H	ERA	SAVES
1999	Danville	Appal.	14	71⅓	2	5	.286	60	23	86	4.67	0
2000	Myrtle Beach	Carolina	12	78⅔	3	4	.429	71	11	72	3.43	0
2000	Macon	So.Atl.	15	102⅓	9	5	.643	97	18	79	2.37	0
2001	a					INJURED—Did Not Play						
2002	Greenville	Southern	26	159⅓	5	9	.357	123	39	162	4.35	0
2003	Greenville	Southern	21	125⅓	6	8	.429	94	42	128	3.52	0
2003	Richmond	Int.	3	20	1	1	.500	10	0	17	2.25	0
2003	Louisville	Int.	4	26	1	3	.250	15	5	31	3.81	0
2003	Cincinnati b	N.L.	6	8⅔	1	1	.500	6	2	10	5.19	0
2004	Louisville	Int.	28	162⅔	9	11	.450	106	51	192	5.26	0
2005	Cincinnati	N.L.	60	85⅔	4	8	.333	59	26	101	4.41	1
2006	Dayton	Midwest	2	4	1	0	1.000	3	0	3	0.00	1
2006	Chattanooga	Southern	2	3⅓	0	0	.000	4	0	3	0.00	0
2006	Louisville	Int.	8	9	1	0	1.000	9	1	4	0.00	0
2006	Cincinnati c	N.L.	30	40	2	0	1.000	26	19	43	3.60	0

Year	Club	Lea	G	IP	W	L	Pct	SO	BB	H	ERA	SAVES
2007	Louisville	Int.	1	6	0	1	.000	7	2	7	3.00	0
2007	Cincinnati	N.L.	30	177 2/3	8	9	.471	125	43	212	5.32	0
2008	Sarasota	Fla.St.	1	8 2/3	1	0	1.000	3	0	2	0.00	0
2008	Chattanooga	Southern	1	9	1	0	1.000	3	0	7	2.00	0
2008	Cincinnati	N.L.	6	29 2/3	1	4	.200	14	6	47	7.28	0
2008	Louisville d-e	Int.	26	38	5	1	.833	27	11	43	4.26	4
2009	Colorado Springs	P.C.	33	58 1/3	1	1	.500	47	15	58	3.09	9
2009	Colorado f	N.L.	24	31	3	1	.750	22	5	35	5.52	0
2010	Colorado	N.L.	76	92	7	5	.583	91	16	84	2.93	1
Major League Totals		7 Yrs.	232	464 2/3	26	28	.481	343	117	532	4.67	2
Division Series												
2009	Colorado	N.L.	2	2	0	0	.000	2	1	0	0.00	0

a On minor league disabled list from April 6 to September 18, 2001.

b Sent by Atlanta Braves to Cincinnati Reds as player to be named later for pitcher Kent Mercker, August 14, 2003.

c On disabled list from May 28 to June 27 and July 10 to August 20, 2006.

d On disabled list from March 21 to April 21, 2008.

e On disabled list from September 9 to November 6, 2008.

f Not offered contract, December 12, 2008. Signed with Colorado Rockies organization, January 14, 2009.

BELL, HEATH JUSTIN

Born, Oceanside, California, September 29, 1977.

Bats Right. Throws Right. Height, 6 feet, 3 inches. Weight, 240 pounds.

Year	Club	Lea	G	IP	W	L	Pct	SO	BB	H	ERA	SAVES
1998	Kingsport	Appal.	22	46	1	0	1.000	61	11	40	2.54	8
1999	Columbia	So.Atl.	55	62 1/3	1	7	.125	68	17	47	2.60	25
2000	St. Lucie	Fla.St.	48	60	5	1	.833	75	21	43	2.55	23
2001	Binghamton	Eastern	43	61 1/3	3	1	.750	55	19	82	6.02	4
2002	Binghamton	Eastern	24	38	1	0	1.000	49	6	22	1.18	6
2002	Norfolk	Int.	22	31 2/3	3	4	.429	28	9	38	4.26	5
2003	Norfolk	Int.	40	49 2/3	2	3	.400	54	8	54	4.71	3
2004	Binghamton	Eastern	1	2	0	0	.000	0	0	2	0.00	0
2004	Norfolk	Int.	45	55 2/3	3	1	.750	68	24	42	3.23	16
2004	New York	N.L.	17	24 1/3	0	2	.000	27	6	22	3.33	0
2005	Norfolk	Int.	13	26 2/3	1	0	1.000	29	5	15	1.69	6
2005	New York	N.L.	42	46 2/3	1	3	.250	43	13	56	5.59	0
2006	Norfolk	Int.	30	35	3	3	.500	56	8	27	1.29	12
2006	New York a	N.L.	22	37	0	0	.000	35	11	51	5.11	0
2007	San Diego	N.L.	81	93 2/3	6	4	.600	102	30	60	2.02	2
2008	San Diego	N.L.	74	78	6	6	.500	71	28	66	3.58	0
2009	San Diego	N.L.	68	69 2/3	6	4	.600	79	24	54	2.71	*42
2010	San Diego	N.L.	67	70	6	1	.857	86	28	56	1.93	47
Major League Totals		7 Yrs.	371	419 1/3	25	20	.556	443	140	365	3.16	91

a Traded to San Diego Padres with pitcher Royce Ring for pitcher Jon Adkins and outfielder Ben Johnson, November 15, 2006.

BELL, TREVOR D.

Born, N.Hollywood, California, October 12, 1986.

Bats Left. Throws Right. Height, 6 feet, 2 inches. Weight, 185 pounds.

Year	Club	Lea	G	IP	W	L	Pct	SO	BB	H	ERA	SAVES
2005	Angels	Arizona	4	8	0	0	.000	7	3	10	4.50	0
2006	Orem	Pioneer	16	82 1/3	4	2	.667	53	15	82	3.50	0
2007	Cedar Rapids	Midwest	21	115 1/3	8	4	.667	90	23	136	4.14	0
2008	Rancho Cucamonga	Calif.	36	100 1/3	6	8	.429	80	39	106	4.22	0
2008	Cedar Rapids	Midwest	3	17	1	0	1.000	13	4	13	2.12	0
2009	Arkansas	Texas	11	68 2/3	4	3	.571	51	20	54	2.23	0
2009	Salt Lake	P.C.	11	71 1/3	3	4	.429	38	15	67	3.15	0
2009	Los Angeles	A.L.	8	20 1/3	1	2	.333	14	11	40	9.74	0
2010	Salt Lake	P.C.	6	30	2	0	1.000	19	6	30	3.00	0
2010	Los Angeles	A.L.	25	61	2	5	.286	45	21	77	4.72	0
Major League Totals		2 Yrs.	33	81 1/3	3	7	.300	59	32	117	5.98	0

BENOIT (PENA), JOAQUIN ANTONIO

Born, Santiago, Dominican Republic, July 26, 1977.
Bats Right. Throws Right. Height, 6 feet, 3 inches. Weight, 220 pounds.

Year Club	Lea	G	IP	W	L	Pct	SO	BB	H	ERA	SAVES
1996 Texas	Dominican	14	75	6	5	.545	63	23	63	2.28	0
1997 Rangers	Gulf Coast	10	44	3	3	.500	38	11	40	2.05	0
1998 Savannah	So.Atl.	15	80	4	3	.571	68	18	79	3.83	0
1999 Charlotte	Fla.St.	22	105	7	4	.636	83	50	117	5.31	0
2000 Tulsa	Texas	16	$82\tfrac{1}{3}$	4	4	.500	72	30	73	3.83	0
2001 Tulsa	Texas	4	$21\tfrac{2}{3}$	1	0	1.000	23	6	23	3.32	0
2001 Oklahoma	P.C.	24	131	9	5	.643	142	73	113	4.19	0
2001 Texas	A.L.	1	5	0	0	.000	4	3	8	10.80	0
2002 Oklahoma	P.C.	16	$98\tfrac{2}{3}$	8	4	.667	103	37	74	3.56	0
2002 Texas	A.L.	17	$84\tfrac{2}{3}$	4	5	.444	59	58	91	5.31	1
2002 Charlotte	Fla.St.	1	5	0	0	.000	8	3	1	0.00	0
2003 Oklahoma	P.C.	6	33	2	1	.667	31	11	28	3.82	0
2003 Texas a	A.L.	25	105	8	5	.615	87	51	99	5.49	0
2004 Texas	A.L.	28	103	3	5	.375	95	31	113	5.68	0
2004 Frisco b	Texas	1	2	0	0	.000	6	0	0	0.00	0
2005 Oklahoma	P.C.	3	5	0	1	.000	2	4	4	5.40	0
2005 Rangers	Arizona	1	2	0	0	.000	4	1	0	0.00	0
2005 Texas c	A.L.	32	87	4	4	.500	78	38	69	3.72	0
2006 Texas	A.L.	56	$79\tfrac{2}{3}$	1	1	.500	85	38	68	4.86	0
2007 Texas	A.L.	70	82	7	4	.636	87	28	68	2.85	6
2008 Frisco	Texas	3	$1\tfrac{2}{3}$	0	0	.000	2	4	4	16.20	0
2008 Oklahoma	P.C.	2	3	1	0	1.000	3	0	1	0.00	0
2008 Texas d	A.L.	44	45	3	2	.600	43	35	40	5.00	1
2009 Texas e-f	A.L.	INJURED—Did Not Play									
2010 Durham	Int.	8	$9\tfrac{2}{3}$	0	1	.000	17	3	8	2.79	2
2010 Tampa Bay g	A.L.	63	$60\tfrac{1}{3}$	1	2	.333	75	11	30	1.34	1
Major League Totals	9 Yrs.	336	$651\tfrac{2}{3}$	31	28	.525	613	293	586	4.47	9
Division Series											
2010 Tampa Bay	N.L.	3	$3\tfrac{2}{3}$	1	0	1.000	3	0	0	0.00	0

a On disabled list from June 1 to June 22, 2003.
b On disabled list from August 23 to September 7, 2004.
c On disabled list from March 25 to May 2 and June 9 to June 28, 2005.
d On disabled list from July 3 to August 6, 2008.
e On disabled list from April 5 to November 5, 2009.
f Filed for free agency, November 5, 2009. Signed with Tampa Bay Rays organization, February 15, 2010.
g Filed for free agency, November 1, 2010. Signed with Detroit Tigers, November 19, 2010.

BERGESEN, BRADLEY STEVEN (BRAD)

Born, Fairfield, California, September 25, 1985.
Bats Left. Throws Right. Height, 6 feet, 2 inches. Weight, 215 pounds.

Year Club	Lea	G	IP	W	L	Pct	SO	BB	H	ERA	SAVES
2004 Bluefield	Appal.	5	$7\tfrac{1}{3}$	0	0	.000	6	3	7	6.14	0
2005 Aberdeen	N.Y.-Penn.	15	71	1	3	.250	54	14	89	4.82	0
2006 Delmarva	So.Atl.	18	$86\tfrac{1}{3}$	5	4	.556	49	10	97	4.27	0
2007 Frederick	Carolina	10	$56\tfrac{1}{3}$	3	6	.333	35	9	78	5.75	0
2007 Delmarva	So.Atl.	15	$94\tfrac{1}{3}$	7	3	.700	73	17	75	2.19	0
2008 Frederick	Carolina	4	$17\tfrac{1}{3}$	1	1	.500	15	6	15	2.08	0
2008 Bowie	Eastern	24	148	15	6	.714	72	27	143	3.22	0
2009 Norfolk	Int.	2	11	1	1	.500	9	3	6	2.45	0
2009 Baltimore a	A.L.	19	$123\tfrac{1}{3}$	7	5	.583	65	32	126	3.43	0
2010 Norfolk	Int.	3	$14\tfrac{2}{3}$	1	0	1.000	10	3	17	4.30	0
2010 Baltimore	A.L.	30	170	8	12	.400	81	51	193	4.98	0
Major League Totals	2 Yrs.	49	$293\tfrac{1}{3}$	15	17	.469	146	83	319	4.33	0

a On disabled list from July 31 to November 6, 2009.

BERKEN, JASON THOMAS

Born, Green Bay, Wisconsin, November 27, 1983.
Bats Right. Throws Right. Height, 6 feet. Weight, 175 pounds.

Year Club	Lea	G	IP	W	L	Pct	SO	BB	H	ERA	SAVES
2006 Aberdeen	N.Y.-Penn.	9	45	1	4	.200	46	5	39	2.80	0
2007 Frederick	Carolina	27	151	9	9	.500	124	49	160	4.53	0
2008 Bowie	Eastern	26	$145\tfrac{2}{3}$	12	4	.750	125	38	141	3.58	0
2009 Bowie	Eastern	2	8	1	1	.500	8	6	4	5.63	0
2009 Norfolk	Int.	5	$25\tfrac{2}{3}$	2	0	1.000	16	6	19	1.05	0

Year	Club	Lea	G	IP	W	L	Pct	SO	BB	H	ERA	SAVES
2009	Baltimore	A.L.	24	119⅔	6	12	.333	66	44	164	6.54	0
2010	Baltimore a	A.L.	41	62⅓	3	3	.500	45	19	64	3.03	0
Major League Totals		2 Yrs.	65	182	9	15	.375	111	63	228	5.34	0

a On disabled list from August 13 to November 4, 2010.

BETANCOURT, RAFAEL JOSE

Born, Cumana, Venezuela, April 29, 1975.
Bats Right. Throws Right. Height, 6 feet, 2 inches. Weight, 200 pounds.

Year	Club	Lea	G	IP	W	L	Pct	SO	BB	H	ERA	SAVES
1997	Michigan	Midwest	27	32⅓	0	3	.000	52	2	26	1.95	11
1998	Red Sox	Gulf Coast	4	5	0	2	.000	4	1	6	7.20	0
1998	Sarasota	Fla.St.	20	28	3	1	.750	33	6	22	3.54	2
1998	Trenton	Eastern	7	9⅓	0	0	.000	9	3	9	6.75	0
1999	Sarasota	Fla.St.	6	7	0	0	.000	6	1	5	0.00	4
1999	Trenton a	Eastern	39	54⅔	6	2	.750	57	10	50	3.62	13
2000	Yokohama	Japan Cen.	11	29	1	2	.333	16	11	30	4.08	0
2000	Searex b	Japan East	20	23	1	0	1.000	29	6	17	1.17	6
2001	Trenton	Eastern	16	24	0	1	.000	27	3	28	5.63	4
2002	Trenton	Eastern	INJURED—Did Not Play									
2003	Akron	Eastern	31	45⅓	0	0	.000	75	13	33	1.39	16
2003	Buffalo	Int.	4	6⅔	0	0	.000	6	2	6	4.05	1
2003	Cleveland c	A.L.	33	38	2	2	.500	36	13	27	2.13	1
2004	Akron	Eastern	1	1	0	0	.000	2	1	0	0.00	0
2004	Cleveland d	A.L.	68	66⅔	5	6	.455	76	18	71	3.92	4
2005	Cleveland e	A.L.	54	67⅔	4	3	.571	73	17	57	2.79	1
2006	Akron f	Eastern	1	1	0	0	.000	2	1	0	0.00	0
2007	Cleveland	A.L.	68	79⅓	5	1	.833	80	9	51	1.47	3
2008	Cleveland	A.L.	69	71	3	4	.429	64	25	76	5.07	4
2009	Columbus	Int.	3	3⅓	1	0	1.000	4	1	0	0.00	0
2009	Cleveland g-h-i	A.L.	29	30⅔	1	2	.333	32	15	25	3.52	1
2009	Colorado	N.L.	32	25⅓	3	1	.750	29	5	17	1.78	1
2010	Colorado	N.L.	72	62⅓	5	1	.833	89	8	52	3.61	1
Major League Totals		8 Yrs.	475	497⅔	31	24	.564	527	121	428	3.22	19
	Division Series											
2007	Cleveland	A.L.	2	2	0	0	.000	3	0	1	0.00	0
2009	Colorado	N.L.	3	2⅓	0	0	.000	3	1	2	3.86	0
Division Series Totals			5	4⅓	0	0	.000	6	1	3	2.08	0
	Championship Series											
2007	Cleveland	A.L.	5	8	0	0	.000	6	1	6	6.75	0

a Sold by Boston Red Sox to Yokohama, November 18,1999.
b Sold to Boston Red Sox, December 13, 2000.
c Filed for free agency, October 15, 2001. Signed with Cleveland Indians organization, January 20, 2003.
d On disabled list from June 26 to July 11, 2004.
e On disabled list from June 30 to July 18, 2005.
f On disabled list from April 20 to May 16, 2006.
g On disabled list from June 1 to July 9, 2009.
h Traded to Colorado Rockies for pitcher Connor Graham, July 23, 2009.
i Filed for free agency, November 14, 2009. Accepted arbitration, December 7, 2009.

BILLINGSLEY, CHAD RYAN

Born, Defiance, Ohio, July 29, 1984.
Bats Right. Throws Right. Height, 6 feet. Weight, 245 pounds.

Year	Club	Lea	G	IP	W	L	Pct	SO	BB	H	ERA	SAVES
2003	Ogden	Pioneer	11	54	5	4	.556	62	15	49	2.83	0
2004	Vero Beach	Fla.St.	18	92	7	4	.636	111	49	68	2.35	0
2004	Jacksonville	Southern	8	42⅓	4	0	1.000	47	22	32	2.98	0
2005	Jacksonville	Southern	28	146	13	6	.684	162	50	116	3.51	0
2006	Las Vegas	P.C.	13	70⅔	6	3	.667	78	32	57	3.95	0
2006	Los Angeles	N.L.	18	90	7	4	.636	59	58	92	3.80	0
2007	Los Angeles	N.L.	43	147	12	5	.706	141	64	131	3.31	0
2008	Los Angeles	N.L.	35	200⅔	16	10	.615	201	80	188	3.14	0
2009	Los Angeles	N.L.	33	196⅓	12	11	.522	179	86	173	4.03	0
2010	Los Angeles a	N.L.	31	191⅔	12	11	.522	171	69	176	3.57	0
Major League Totals		5 Yrs.	160	825⅔	59	41	.590	751	357	760	3.55	0
	Division Series											
2006	Los Angeles	N.L.	2	2	0	0	.000	3	0	1	0.00	0

Year	Club	Lea	G	IP	W	L	Pct	SO	BB	H	ERA	SAVES
2008	Los Angeles	N.L.	1	6 2/3	1	0	1.000	7	1	5	1.35	0
Division Series Totals			3	8 2/3	1	0	1.000	10	1	6	1.04	0
	Championship Series											
2008	Los Angeles	N.L.	2	5	0	2	.000	9	7	12	18.00	0
2009	Los Angeles	N.L.	1	3 1/3	0	0	.000	3	2	2	5.40	0
Championship Series Totals			3	8 1/3	0	2	.000	12	9	14	12.96	0

a On disabled list from June 12 to June 28, 2010.

BLACKBURN, ROBERT NICHOLAS (NICK)

Born, Ada, Oklahoma, February 24, 1982.

Bats Right. Throws Right. Height, 6 feet, 4 inches. Weight, 225 pounds.

Year	Club	Lea	G	IP	W	L	Pct	SO	BB	H	ERA	SAVES
2002	Elizabethton	Appal.	13	66 2/3	3	3	.500	62	21	70	4.99	0
2003	Quad Cities	Midwest	16	76	2	9	.182	40	18	78	4.86	1
2004	Fort Myers	Fla.St.	9	37 1/3	3	3	.500	21	7	51	6.27	0
2004	Quad Cities	Midwest	20	84 1/3	6	4	.600	66	23	69	2.77	1
2005	New Britain	Eastern	7	49	2	4	.333	27	10	35	1.84	0
2005	Fort Myers	Fla.St.	15	93 2/3	7	5	.583	55	16	95	3.36	0
2005	Rochester	Int.	3	14	0	0	.000	7	3	20	5.14	0
2006	New Britain	Eastern	30	132 1/3	7	8	.467	81	37	141	4.42	0
2007	New Britain	Eastern	8	38	3	1	.750	18	7	36	3.08	0
2007	Rochester	Int.	17	110 2/3	7	3	.700	57	12	96	2.11	0
2007	Minnesota	A.L.	6	11 2/3	0	2	.000	8	2	19	7.71	0
2008	Minnesota	A.L.	33	193 1/3	11	11	.500	96	39	224	4.05	0
2009	Minnesota	A.L.	33	205 2/3	11	11	.500	98	41	*240	4.03	0
2010	Rochester	Int.	4	21 2/3	1	0	1.000	13	6	19	2.49	0
2010	Minnesota	A.L.	28	161	10	12	.455	68	40	194	5.42	0
Major League Totals		4 Yrs.	100	571 2/3	32	36	.471	270	122	677	4.50	0
	Division Series											
2009	Minnesota	A.L.	1	5 2/3	0	0	.000	3	2	3	1.59	0

BLANTON, JOSEPH MATTHEW (JOE)

Born, Bowling Green, Kentucky, December 11, 1980.

Bats Right. Throws Right. Height, 6 feet, 3 inches. Weight, 255 pounds.

Year	Club	Lea	G	IP	W	L	Pct	SO	BB	H	ERA	SAVES
2002	Modesto	California	2	6	0	1	.000	6	6	8	7.50	0
2002	Vancouver	Northwest	4	14 1/3	1	1	.500	15	2	11	3.14	0
2003	Kane County	Midwest	21	133	8	7	.533	144	19	110	2.57	0
2003	Midland	Texas	7	35 2/3	3	1	.750	30	7	21	1.26	1
2004	Sacramento	P.C.	28	176 1/3	11	8	.579	143	34	199	4.19	0
2004	Oakland	A.L.	3	8	0	0	.000	6	2	6	5.63	0
2005	Oakland	A.L.	33	201 1/3	12	12	.500	116	67	178	3.53	0
2006	Oakland	A.L.	32	194 1/3	16	12	.571	107	58	241	4.82	0
2007	Oakland	A.L.	34	230	14	10	.583	140	40	*240	3.95	0
2008	Oakland	A.L.	20	127	5	12	.294	62	35	145	4.96	0
2008	Philadelphia a	N.L.	13	70 2/3	4	0	1.000	49	31	66	4.20	0
2009	Philadelphia	N.L.	31	195 1/3	12	8	.600	163	59	198	4.05	0
2010	Lakewood	So.Atl.	1	2	0	0	.000	2	0	0	0.00	0
2010	Reading	Eastern	2	8	0	1	.000	5	2	9	5.63	0
2010	Philadelphia b	N.L.	29	175 2/3	9	6	.600	134	43	206	4.82	0
Major League Totals		7 Yrs.	195	1202 1/3	72	60	.545	777	335	1280	4.30	0
	Division Series											
2008	Philadelphia	N.L.	1	6	1	0	1.000	7	0	5	1.50	0
2009	Philadelphia	N.L.	2	3 2/3	0	0	.000	1	0	4	4.91	0
Division Series Totals			3	9 2/3	1	0	1.000	8	0	9	2.79	0
	Championship Series											
2006	Oakland	A.L.	1	2	0	0	.000	2	2	0	0.00	0
2008	Philadelphia	N.L.	1	5	0	0	.000	4	4	7	5.40	0
2009	Philadelphia	N.L.	1	6	0	0	.000	2	2	6	4.50	0
2010	Philadelphia	N.L.	1	4 2/3	0	0	.000	3	1	5	5.79	0
Championship Series Totals			4	17 2/3	0	0	.000	11	9	18	4.58	0
	World Series Record											
2008	Philadelphia	N.L.	1	6	1	0	1.000	7	2	4	3.00	0
2009	Philadelphia	N.L.	1	6	0	0	.000	7	2	5	6.00	0
World Series Totals			2	12	1	0	1.000	14	4	9	4.50	0

a Traded to Philadelphia Phillies for pitcher Josh Outman, infielder Adrian Cardenas and outfielder Matt Spencer, July 17, 2008.

b On disabled list from March 26 to May 3, 2010.

BLEVINS, JERRY RICHARD

Born, Johnson City, Tennessee, September 6, 1983.
Bats Left. Throws Left. Height, 6 feet, 6 inches. Weight, 180 pounds.

Year Club	Lea	G	IP	W	L	Pct	SO	BB	H	ERA	SAVES
2004 Boise	Northwest	23	33 1/3	6	1	.857	42	21	17	1.62	5
2005 Peoria	Midwest	48	76 1/3	3	7	.300	96	38	75	5.54	14
2006 Daytona	Fla.St.	8	11	0	1	.000	9	4	18	9.00	1
2006 Boise	Northwest	16	22 1/3	1	2	.333	19	8	27	6.04	0
2006 West Tenn	Southern	5	6 1/3	0	0	.000	8	1	5	1.42	1
2007 Daytona	Fla.St.	15	23 2/3	1	0	1.000	32	5	13	0.38	6
2007 Tennessee	Southern	23	29 1/3	2	2	.500	37	8	23	1.53	3
2007 Midland	Texas	17	21 2/3	1	3	.250	29	5	18	3.32	1
2007 Sacramento	P.C.	1	2 2/3	1	0	1.000	4	0	1	0.00	0
2007 Oakland a	A.L.	6	4 2/3	0	1	.000	3	2	8	9.64	0
2008 Sacramento	P.C.	28	32 1/3	2	2	.500	36	6	31	2.78	10
2008 Oakland	A.L.	36	37 2/3	1	3	.250	35	13	32	3.11	0
2009 Sacramento	P.C.	45	63 1/3	5	3	.625	62	18	65	3.84	2
2009 Oakland	A.L.	20	22 1/3	0	0	.000	23	6	19	4.84	0
2010 Oakland	A.L.	63	48 2/3	2	1	.667	46	18	54	3.70	1
Major League Totals	4 Yrs.	125	113 1/3	3	5	.375	107	39	113	3.97	1

a Traded by Chicago Cubs to Oakland Athletics with catcher Rob Bowen for catcher Jason Kendall and cash, July 17, 2007.

BOGGS, MITCHELL THOMAS

Born, Dalton, Georgia, February 15, 1984.
Bats Right. Throws Right. Height, 6 feet, 4 inches. Weight, 215 pounds.

Year Club	Lea	G	IP	W	L	Pct	SO	BB	H	ERA	SAVES
2005 New Jersey	N.Y.-Penn.	15	71 2/3	4	4	.500	61	24	77	3.89	0
2006 Palm Beach	Fla.St.	27	145	10	6	.625	126	51	153	3.41	0
2007 Springfield	Texas	26	152 1/3	11	7	.611	117	62	167	3.84	0
2008 St. Louis	N.L.	8	34	3	2	.600	13	22	42	7.41	0
2008 Memphis	P.C.	21	125 1/3	9	3	.750	81	46	107	3.45	0
2009 Memphis	P.C.	14	76 1/3	6	4	.600	58	32	90	4.83	0
2009 St. Louis	N.L.	16	58	2	3	.400	46	33	71	4.19	0
2010 St. Louis	N.L.	61	67 1/3	2	3	.400	52	27	60	3.61	0
Major League Totals	3 Yrs.	85	159 1/3	7	8	.467	111	82	173	4.63	0
Division Series											
2009 St. Louis	N.L.	1	1	0	0	.000	1	2	0	0.00	0

BONDERMAN, JEREMY ALLEN

Born, Kennewick, Washington, October 28, 1982.
Bats Right. Throws Right. Height, 6 feet, 2 inches. Weight, 220 pounds.

Year Club	Lea	G	IP	W	L	Pct	SO	BB	H	ERA	SAVES
2002 Modesto	California	25	144 2/3	9	8	.529	160	55	129	3.61	0
2002 Lakeland a	Fla.St.	2	12	0	1	.000	10	4	11	6.00	0
2003 Detroit	A.L.	33	162	6	19	.240	108	58	193	5.56	0
2004 Detroit	A.L.	33	184	11	13	.458	168	73	168	4.89	0
2005 Detroit	A.L.	29	189	14	13	.519	145	57	199	4.57	0
2006 Detroit	A.L.	34	214	14	8	.636	202	64	214	4.08	0
2007 Detroit b	A.L.	28	174 1/3	11	9	.550	145	48	193	5.01	0
2008 Detroit c	A.L.	12	71 1/3	3	4	.429	44	36	75	4.29	0
2009 West Michigan	Midwest	1	7	1	0	1.000	4	1	6	2.57	0
2009 Toledo	Int.	14	34	1	4	.200	26	7	40	4.24	1
2009 Detroit d	A.L.	8	10 1/3	0	1	.000	5	8	16	8.71	0
2010 Detroit e	A.L.	30	171	8	10	.444	112	60	187	5.53	0
Major League Totals	8 Yrs.	207	1176	67	77	.465	929	404	1245	4.89	0
Division Series											
2006 Detroit	A.L.	1	8 1/3	1	0	1.000	4	1	5	2.16	0
Championship Series											
2006 Detroit	A.L.	1	6 2/3	0	0	.000	3	2	6	4.05	0
World Series Record											
2006 Detroit	A.L.	1	5 1/3	0	0	.000	4	4	6	3.38	0

a Sent by Oakland Athletics to Detroit Tigers to complete trade involving Jeff Weaver, Carlos Pena and Ted Lilly, August 22, 2002.
b On disabled list from May 9 to May 24, 2007.
c On disabled list from June 7 to September 30, 2008.
d On disabled list from March 30 to June 8 and June 9 to September 1, 2009.
e Filed for free agency, November 1, 2010.

BONINE, EDDIE KEITH

Born, Columbus, Georgia, June 6, 1981.
Bats Right. Throws Right. Height, 6 feet, 5 inches. Weight, 220 pounds.

Year	Club	Lea	G	IP	W	L	Pct	SO	BB	H	ERA	SAVES
2003	Eugene	Northwest	31	33 1/3	1	2	.333	33	10	32	3.78	14
2004	Lake Elsinore	Calif.	21	112 1/3	5	10	.333	96	39	121	5.45	0
2004	Fort Wayne	Midwest	5	27 1/3	2	1	.667	31	3	25	1.98	0
2005	Lake Elsinore	Calif.	36	104 1/3	5	6	.455	77	42	142	6.47	0
2005	Portland a	P.C.	1	2	1	0	1.000	5	0	0	0.00	0
2006	Erie	Eastern	1	6	0	1	.000	2	0	8	9.00	0
2006	Lakeland	Fla.St.	41	106 1/3	4	4	.500	83	27	108	3.98	1
2007	Erie	Eastern	25	154 2/3	14	5	.737	73	24	159	3.90	0
2007	Toledo	Int.	1	8	1	0	1.000	4	1	7	2.25	0
2008	Detroit	A.L.	5	26 2/3	2	1	.667	9	5	36	5.40	0
2008	Erie	Eastern	1	3 2/3	0	1	.000	1	2	4	2.45	0
2008	Toledo	Int.	17	106 1/3	12	4	.750	69	18	107	4.15	0
2009	Toledo	Int.	17	102	4	5	.444	51	16	112	4.41	0
2009	Detroit	A.L.	10	34 1/3	1	1	.500	19	12	40	4.46	0
2010	Detroit b	A.L.	47	68	4	1	.800	26	22	84	4.63	0
Major League Totals		3 Yrs.	62	129	7	3	.700	54	39	160	4.74	0

a Selected by Detroit Tigers from San Diego Padres in Rule V draft, December 8, 2005.
b Filed for free agency, November 6, 2010. Signed with Philadelphia Phillies organization, November 12, 2010.

BOYER, BLAINE THOMAS

Born, Atlanta, Georgia, July 11, 1981.
Bats Right. Throws Right. Height, 6 feet, 3 inches. Weight, 215 pounds.

Year	Club	Lea	G	IP	W	L	Pct	SO	BB	H	ERA	SAVES
2000	Braves	Gulf Coast	11	32 1/3	1	3	.250	27	19	24	2.51	1
2001	Danville	Appal.	13	50	4	5	.444	57	19	48	4.32	0
2002	Macon	So.Atl.	43	70 1/3	5	9	.357	73	39	52	3.07	1
2003	Rome	So.Atl.	30	136 2/3	12	8	.600	115	58	146	3.69	0
2004	Myrtle Beach	Carolina	28	154	10	10	.500	95	49	138	2.98	0
2005	Mississippi	Southern	14	48 1/3	2	4	.333	40	18	62	5.03	0
2005	Atlanta	N.L.	43	37 2/3	4	2	.667	33	17	32	3.11	0
2006	Atlanta a	N.L.	2	0 2/3	0	0	.000	0	1	4	40.50	0
2007	Atlanta	N.L.	5	5 1/3	0	0	.000	3	1	10	3.38	0
2007	Richmond	Int.	21	73 1/3	4	3	.571	62	50	76	4.30	2
2008	Atlanta	N.L.	76	72	2	6	.250	67	25	73	5.88	1
2009	Atlanta-St. Louis-Arizona b-c	N.L.	48	54 2/3	0	2	.000	29	20	56	4.12	0
2010	Reno	P.C.	5	6	1	0	1.000	9	1	5	1.50	2
2010	Arizona d	N.L.	54	57	3	2	.600	29	29	59	4.26	0
Major League Totals		6 Yrs.	228	227 1/3	9	12	.429	161	93	234	4.63	1

a On disabled list from June 24 to November 1, 2006.
b Traded to St. Louis Cardinals for outfielder Brian Barton, April 20, 2009.
c Claimed on waivers by Arizona Diamondbacks, June 8, 2009.
d Not offered contract, December 2, 2010.

BRADEN, DALLAS LEE

Born, Phoenix, Arizona, August 13, 1983.
Bats Left. Throws Left. Height, 6 feet, 1 inch. Weight, 195 pounds.

Year	Club	Lea	G	IP	W	L	Pct	SO	BB	H	ERA	SAVES
2004	Kane County	Midwest	5	23	2	1	.667	33	6	22	4.70	0
2004	Vancouver	Northwest	8	19 1/3	2	0	1.000	26	3	15	2.33	2
2005	Stockton	Calif.	7	43 2/3	6	0	1.000	64	11	31	2.68	0
2005	Midland	Texas	16	97	9	5	.643	71	32	104	3.90	0
2006	Athletics	Arizona	6	21	2	0	1.000	36	3	12	0.86	0
2006	Stockton	Calif.	3	13	2	0	1.000	17	5	12	6.23	0
2006	Midland	Texas	1	3 1/3	0	0	.000	2	0	9	16.20	0
2007	Midland	Texas	2	12	1	0	1.000	13	3	5	2.25	0

Year	Club	Lea	G	IP	W	L	Pct	SO	BB	H	ERA	SAVES
2007	Sacramento	P.C.	11	64	2	3	.400	74	18	51	2.95	0
2007	Oakland	A.L.	20	72 1/3	1	8	.111	55	26	91	6.72	0
2008	Sacramento	P.C.	11	53 1/3	3	1	.750	54	11	49	2.36	0
2008	Oakland	A.L.	19	71 2/3	5	4	.556	41	25	77	4.14	0
2009	Oakland a	A.L.	22	136 2/3	8	9	.471	81	42	144	3.89	0
2010	Stockton	Calif.	1	4	0	0	.000	4	1	7	6.75	0
2010	Oakland b-c	A.L.	30	192 2/3	11	14	.440	113	43	180	3.50	0
Major League Totals		4 Yrs.	91	473 1/3	25	35	.417	290	136	492	4.20	0

a On disabled list from August 1 to November 4, 2009.
b Pitched no-hit, no-run perfect game against Tampa Bay Rays, May 9, 2010.
c On disabled list from June 23 to July 20, 2010.

BRESLOW, CRAIG ANDREW

Born, New Haven, Connecticut, August 8, 1980.
Bats Left. Throws Left. Height, 6 feet, 1 inch. Weight, 185 pounds.

Year	Club	Lea	G	IP	W	L	Pct	SO	BB	H	ERA	SAVES
2002	Ogden	Pioneer	23	54 1/3	6	2	.750	56	24	42	1.82	2
2003	Beloit	Midwest	33	65	3	4	.429	80	27	64	5.12	2
2004	High Desert	Calif.	23	41 1/3	1	3	.250	41	24	54	7.19	0
2004	New Jersey a	Northeast	19	26 1/3	3	1	.750	37	13	19	4.10	0
2005	Mobile	Southern	40	52 1/3	2	1	.667	47	17	38	2.75	0
2005	Portland	P.C.	7	9	0	1	.000	9	1	11	4.00	0
2005	San Diego b	N.L.	14	16 1/3	0	0	.000	14	13	15	2.20	0
2006	Pawtucket	Int.	39	67	7	1	.875	77	24	49	2.69	7
2006	Boston c	A.L.	13	12	0	2	.000	12	6	12	3.75	0
2007	Pawtucket	Int.	49	68 2/3	2	3	.400	73	25	70	4.06	1
2008	Cleveland-Minnesota d-e	A.L.	49	47	0	2	.000	39	19	34	1.91	1
2009	Minnesota-Oakland f	A.L.	77	69 2/3	8	7	.533	55	29	48	3.36	0
2010	Oakland	A.L.	75	74 2/3	4	4	.500	71	29	53	3.01	5
Major League Totals		5 Yrs.	228	219 2/3	12	15	.444	191	96	162	2.87	6

a Released by Milwaukee Brewers, July 6, 2004. Signed with independent New Jersey (Northeast), July 2004.
b Signed with San Diego Padres organization, March 6, 2005.
c Not offered contract, December 21, 2005. Signed with Boston Red Sox organization, February 1, 2006.
d Claimed on waivers by Cleveland Indians, March 23, 2008.
e Claimed on waivers by Minnesota Twins, May 29, 2008.
f Claimed on waivers by Oakland Athletics, May 20, 2009.

BROXTON, JONATHAN ROY

Born, Augusta, Georgia, June 16, 1984.
Bats Right. Throws Right. Height, 6 feet, 4 inches. Weight, 290 pounds.

Year	Club	Lea	G	IP	W	L	Pct	SO	BB	H	ERA	SAVES
2002	Great Falls	Pioneer	11	29 1/3	2	0	1.000	33	16	22	2.76	2
2003	South Bend	So.Atl.	9	37 1/3	4	2	.667	30	22	27	3.13	0
2004	Vero Beach	Fla.St.	23	128 1/3	11	6	.647	144	43	110	3.23	0
2005	Jacksonville	Southern	33	96 2/3	5	3	.625	107	31	79	3.17	5
2005	Los Angeles	N.L.	14	13 2/3	1	0	1.000	22	12	13	5.93	0
2006	Las Vegas	P.C.	11	11 1/3	1	0	1.000	18	3	6	0.00	5
2006	Los Angeles	N.L.	68	76 1/3	4	1	.800	97	33	61	2.59	3
2007	Los Angeles	N.L.	83	82	4	4	.500	99	25	69	2.85	2
2008	Los Angeles	N.L.	70	69	3	5	.375	88	27	54	3.13	14
2009	Los Angeles	N.L.	73	76	7	2	.778	114	29	44	2.61	36
2010	Los Angeles	N.L.	64	62 1/3	5	6	.455	73	28	64	4.04	22
Major League Totals		6 Yrs.	372	379 1/3	24	18	.571	493	154	305	3.11	77
	Division Series											
2006	Los Angeles	N.L.	2	2	0	1	.000	3	2	5	13.50	0
2008	Los Angeles	N.L.	3	3 1/3	0	0	.000	5	2	0	0.00	1
2009	Los Angeles	N.L.	3	3 2/3	0	0	.000	4	0	4	2.45	1
Division Series Totals			8	9	0	1	.000	12	4	9	4.00	2
	Championship Series											
2008	Los Angeles	N.L.	2	2 1/3	0	0	.000	2	1	3	3.86	0
2009	Los Angeles	N.L.	3	3	0	1	.000	1	1	2	6.00	1
Championship Series Totals			5	5 1/3	0	1	.000	3	2	5	5.06	1

BUCHHOLZ, CLAY DANIEL

Born, Nederland, Texas, August 14, 1984.
Bats Left. Throws Right. Height, 6 feet, 3 inches. Weight, 190 pounds.

Year	Club	Lea	G	IP	W	L	Pct	SO	BB	H	ERA	SAVES
2005	Lowell	N.Y.-Penn.	15	41⅓	0	1	.000	45	9	34	2.61	0
2006	Wilmington	Carolina	3	16	2	0	1.000	23	4	10	1.13	0
2006	Greenville	So.Atl.	21	103	9	4	.692	117	29	78	2.62	0
2007	Portland	Eastern	16	86⅔	7	2	.778	116	22	55	1.77	0
2007	Pawtucket	Int.	8	38⅔	1	3	.250	55	13	32	3.96	0
2007	Boston a	A.L.	4	22⅔	3	1	.750	22	10	14	1.59	0
2008	Portland	Eastern	2	15	1	0	1.000	18	1	7	1.80	0
2008	Pawtucket	Int.	9	43⅔	4	2	.667	43	17	36	2.47	0
2008	Boston b	A.L.	16	76	2	9	.182	72	41	93	6.75	0
2009	Pawtucket	Int.	17	99	7	2	.778	89	30	67	2.36	0
2009	Boston	A.L.	16	92	7	4	.636	68	36	91	4.21	0
2010	Pawtucket	Int.	1	3⅔	0	0	.000	2	1	4	4.91	0
2010	Boston c	A.L.	28	173⅔	17	7	.708	120	67	142	2.33	0
Major League Totals		4 Yrs.	64	364⅓	29	21	.580	282	154	340	3.68	0
Division Series												
2009	Boston	A.L.	1	5	0	0	.000	3	1	6	3.60	0

a Pitched no-hit, no-run game against Baltimore Orioles, September 1, 2007.
b On disabled list from May 13 to May 31, 2008.
c On disabled list from June 27 to July 21, 2010.

BUEHRLE, MARK ANTHONY

Born, St. Charles, Missouri, March 23, 1979.
Bats Left. Throws Left. Height, 6 feet, 2 inches. Weight, 225 pounds.

Year	Club	Lea	G	IP	W	L	PCT	SO	BB	H	ERA	SAVES
1999	Burlington	Midwest	20	98⅔	7	4	.636	91	16	105	4.10	3
2000	Birmingham	Southern	16	118⅔	8	4	.667	68	17	95	2.28	0
2000	Chicago	A.L.	28	51⅓	4	1	.800	37	19	55	4.21	0
2001	Chicago	A.L.	32	221⅓	16	8	.667	126	48	188	3.29	0
2002	Chicago	A.L.	34	239	19	12	.613	134	61	236	3.58	0
2003	Chicago	A.L.	35	230⅓	14	14	.500	119	61	250	4.14	0
2004	Chicago	A.L.	35	*245⅓	16	10	.615	165	51	257	3.89	0
2005	Chicago	A.L.	33	*236⅔	16	8	.667	149	40	*240	3.12	0
2006	Chicago	A.L.	32	204	12	13	.480	98	48	*247	4.99	0
2007	Chicago a	A.L.	30	201	10	9	.526	115	45	208	3.63	0
2008	Chicago	A.L.	34	218⅔	15	12	.556	140	52	*240	3.79	0
2009	Chicago b	A.L.	33	213⅓	13	10	.565	105	45	222	3.84	0
2010	Chicago	A.L.	33	210⅓	13	13	.500	99	49	*246	4.28	0
Major League Totals		11 Yrs.	359	2271⅓	148	110	.574	1287	519	2389	3.85	0
Division Series												
2000	Chicago	A.L.	1	0⅓	0	0	.000	1	0	2	0.00	0
2005	Chicago	A.L.	1	7	1	0	1.000	2	1	8	5.14	0
2008	Chicago	A.L.	1	7	0	1	.000	3	0	10	6.43	0
Division Series Totals			3	14⅓	1	1	.500	6	1	20	5.65	0
Championship Series												
2005	Chicago	A.L.	1	9	1	0	1.000	4	0	5	1.00	0
World Series Record												
2005	Chicago	A.L.	2	7⅓	0	0	.000	6	0	7	4.91	1

a Pitched no-hit, no-run game against Texas Rangers, April 18, 2007.
b Pitched no-hit, no-run perfect game against Tampa Bay Rays, July 23, 2009.

BUMGARNER, MADISON K.

Born, Hickory, North Carolina, August 1, 1989.
Bats Right. Throws Left. Height, 6 feet, 4 inches. Weight, 215 pounds.

Year	Club	Lea	G	IP	W	L	Pct	SO	BB	H	ERA	SAVES
2008	Augusta	So.Atl.	24	141⅔	15	3	.833	164	21	111	1.46	0
2009	San Jose	Calif.	5	24⅓	3	1	.750	23	4	20	1.48	0
2009	Connecticut	Eastern	20	107	9	1	.900	69	30	80	1.93	0
2009	San Francisco	N.L.	4	10	0	0	.000	10	3	8	1.80	0
2010	Fresno	P.C.	14	82⅔	7	1	.875	59	22	88	3.16	0
2010	San Francisco	N.L.	18	111	7	6	.538	86	26	119	3.00	0
Major League Totals		2 Yrs.	22	121	7	6	.538	96	29	127	2.90	0
Division Series												
2010	San Francisco	N.L.	1	6	1	0	1.000	5	1	6	3.00	0

Year	Club	Lea	G	IP	W	L	Pct	SO	BB	H	ERA	SAVES
	Championship Series											
2010	San Francisco	N.L.	2	6⅔	0	0	.000	7	2	9	4.05	0
	World Series Record											
2010	San Francisco	N.L.	1	8	1	0	1.000	6	2	3	0.00	0

BURNETT, ALEX JAMES

Born, Anaheim, California, July 26, 1987.
Bats Right. Throws Right. Height, 6 feet. Weight, 210 pounds.

Year	Club	Lea	G	IP	W	L	Pct	SO	BB	H	ERA	SAVES
2005	Twins	Gulf Coast	13	48⅓	4	2	.667	33	14	50	4.10	0
2006	Elizabethton	Appal.	13	71⅓	4	3	.571	71	13	66	4.04	0
2007	Beloit	Midwest	27	155	9	8	.529	117	38	140	3.02	0
2008	Fort Myers	Fla.St.	28	143⅔	8	6	.571	84	36	151	3.76	0
2009	New Britain	Eastern	40	55⅓	1	2	.333	52	19	36	1.79	9
2009	Fort Myers	Fla.St.	18	22⅔	2	1	.667	26	7	14	1.99	4
2010	Rochester	Int.	14	19⅔	0	2	.000	18	8	26	5.49	2
2010	Minnesota	A.L.	41	47⅔	2	2	.500	37	23	52	5.29	0

BURNETT, ALLAN JAMES (A.J.)

Born, North Little Rock, Arkansas, January 3, 1977.
Bats Right. Throws Right. Height, 6 feet, 4 inches. Weight, 230 pounds.

Year	Club	Lea	G	IP	W	L	Pct	SO	BB	H	ERA	SAVES
1995	Mets	Gulf Coast	9	33⅔	2	3	.400	26	23	27	4.28	0
1996	Kingsport	Appal.	12	58	4	0	1.000	68	54	31	3.88	0
1997	Mets	Gulf Coast	3	11⅓	0	1	.000	15	8	8	3.18	0
1997	Pittsfield	N.Y.-Penn.	9	44	3	1	.750	48	35	28	4.70	0
1998	Kane County a	Midwest	20	119	10	4	.714	186	45	74	1.97	0
1999	Portland	Eastern	26	120⅔	6	12	.333	121	71	132	5.52	0
1999	Florida	N.L.	7	41⅓	4	2	.667	33	25	37	3.48	0
2000	Brevard County	Fla.St.	2	7⅓	0	0	.000	6	6	4	3.68	0
2000	Calgary	P.C.	1	5	0	0	.000	6	3	0	0.00	0
2000	Florida b	N.L.	13	82⅔	3	7	.300	57	44	80	4.79	0
2001	Brevard County	Fla.St.	2	9⅓	0	0	.000	10	4	4	1.93	0
2001	Florida c-d	N.L.	27	173⅓	11	12	.478	128	83	145	4.05	0
2002	Florida e	N.L.	31	204⅓	12	9	.571	203	90	153	3.30	0
2003	Florida f	N.L.	4	23	0	2	.000	21	18	18	4.70	0
2004	Jupiter	Fla.St.	1	4	0	0	.000	4	2	2	0.00	0
2004	Albuquerque	P.C.	1	3⅓	0	0	.000	6	2	7	10.80	0
2004	Florida g	N.L.	20	120	7	6	.538	113	38	102	3.68	0
2005	Florida h	N.L.	32	209	12	12	.500	198	79	184	3.44	0
2006	Dunedin	Fla.St.	2	8	0	0	.000	6	2	9	3.38	0
2006	New Hampshire	Eastern	1	6	1	0	1.000	9	3	2	1.50	0
2006	Syracuse	Int.	1	5	1	0	1.000	7	1	0	0.00	0
2006	Toronto i	A.L.	21	135⅔	10	8	.556	118	39	138	3.98	0
2007	Syracuse	Int.	1	5	0	0	.000	7	1	3	1.80	0
2007	Toronto j	A.L.	25	165⅔	10	8	.556	176	66	131	3.75	0
2008	Toronto k	A.L.	35	221⅓	18	10	.643	*231	86	211	4.07	0
2009	New York	A.L.	33	207	13	9	.591	195	*97	193	4.04	0
2010	New York	A.L.	33	186⅔	10	15	.400	145	78	204	5.26	0
Major League Totals		12 Yrs.	281	1770	110	100	.524	1618	743	1596	3.99	0
	Division Series											
2009	New York	A.L.	1	6	0	0	.000	6	5	3	1.50	0
	Championship Series											
2009	New York	A.L.	2	12⅓	0	0	.000	7	5	11	5.84	0
2010	New York	A.L.	1	6	0	1	.000	4	3	6	7.50	0
Championship Series Totals			3	18⅓	0	1	.000	11	8	17	6.38	0
	World Series Record											
2009	New York	A.L.	2	9	1	1	.500	11	6	8	7.00	0

a Traded to Florida Marlins by New York Mets with pitcher Jesus Sanchez and outfielder Robert Stratton for pitcher Al Leiter and infielder Ralph Milliard, February 6, 1998.
b On disabled list from March 17 to July 19, 2000.
c On disabled list from March 23 to May 7, 2001.
d Pitched no-hit, no-run game against San Diego Padres, May 12, 2001.
e On disabled list from August 19 to September 14, 2002.
f On disabled list from March 21 to April 9 and April 26 to September 29, 2003.
g On disabled list from March 26 to June 3, 2004.
h Filed for free agency, October 27, 2005. Signed with Toronto Blue Jays, December 6, 2005.

i On disabled list from March 24 to April 15 and April 22 to June 22, 2006.
j On disabled list from June 13 to June 28 and June 29 to August 12, 2007.
k Filed for free agency, November 13, 2008. Signed with New York Yankees, December 18, 2008.

BURNETT, SEAN RICHARD

Born, Dunedin, Florida, September 17, 1982.
Bats Left. Throws Left. Height, 5 feet, 11 inches. Weight, 190 pounds.

Year Club	Lea	G	IP	W	L	Pct	SO	BB	H	ERA	SAVES
2000 Pirates	Gulf Coast	8	31	2	1	.667	24	3	31	4.06	0
2001 Hickory	So.Atl.	26	$161^1/_3$	11	8	.579	134	33	164	2.62	0
2002 Lynchburg	Carolina	26	$155^1/_3$	13	4	.765	96	33	118	1.80	0
2003 Altoona	Eastern	27	$159^2/_3$	14	6	.700	86	29	158	3.21	0
2004 Nashville	P.C.	10	47	1	5	.167	25	17	58	5.36	0
2004 Pittsburgh a	N.L.	13	$71^2/_3$	5	5	.500	30	28	86	5.02	0
2005 Pittsburgh b	N.L.	INJURED—Did Not Play									
2006 Indianapolis	Int.	25	$120^1/_3$	8	11	.421	46	46	136	5.16	0
2007 Indianapolis	Int.	15	$70^1/_3$	4	5	.444	31	39	83	4.48	0
2008 Indianapolis	Int.	12	$17^1/_3$	1	1	.500	15	8	9	1.04	3
2008 Pittsburgh	N.L.	58	$56^2/_3$	1	1	.500	42	34	57	4.76	0
2009 Pittsburgh-Washington c	N.L.	71	$57^2/_3$	2	3	.400	43	28	36	3.12	1
2010 Washington	N.L.	73	63	1	7	.125	62	20	52	2.14	3
Major League Totals	4 Yrs.	215	249	9	16	.360	177	110	231	3.80	4

a On disabled list from August 22 to October 4, 2004.
b On disabled list from April 2 to October 3, 2005.
c Traded to Washington Nationals with outfielder Nyjer Morgan for outfielder Lastings Milledge and pitcher Joel Hanrahan, June 30, 2009.

BURRES, BRIAN JAMES

Born, Oregon City, Oregon, April 8, 1981.
Bats Left. Throws Left. Height, 6 feet, 1 inch. Weight, 190 pounds.

Year Club	Lea	G	IP	W	L	Pct	SO	BB	H	ERA	SAVES
2001 Salem-Keizer	Northwest	14	$40^2/_3$	3	1	.750	38	11	43	3.10	1
2002 Hagerstown	So.Atl.	32	$119^1/_3$	5	10	.333	119	53	114	4.75	1
2003 San Jose	Calif.	39	$60^2/_3$	3	3	.500	64	36	55	3.86	1
2004 San Jose	Calif.	36	$123^2/_3$	12	1	.923	114	30	115	2.84	0
2005 Norwich	Eastern	26	$128^2/_3$	9	6	.600	105	57	130	4.20	0
2006 Ottawa	Int.	26	139	10	6	.625	110	57	133	3.76	0
2006 Baltimore a	A.L.	11	8	0	0	.000	6	1	6	2.25	0
2007 Norfolk	Int.	2	4	1	0	1.000	5	1	2	2.25	0
2007 Baltimore	A.L.	37	121	6	8	.429	96	66	140	5.95	0
2008 Norfolk	Int.	4	11	1	0	1.000	11	1	9	0.82	0
2008 Baltimore	A.L.	31	$129^2/_3$	7	10	.412	63	50	165	6.04	0
2009 Toronto	A.L.	2	$6^1/_3$	0	2	.000	4	5	12	14.21	0
2009 Las Vegas b	P.C.	19	$107^2/_3$	6	7	.462	84	30	121	4.76	0
2010 Indianapolis	Int.	15	82	5	4	.556	61	34	75	4.50	0
2010 Pittsburgh c-d	N.L.	20	$79^1/_3$	4	5	.444	45	34	87	4.99	0
Major League Totals	5 Yrs.	101	$344^1/_3$	17	25	.405	214	156	410	5.83	0

a Claimed on waivers from San Francisco Giants by Baltimore Orioles, January 6, 2006.
b Claimed on waivers by Toronto Blue Jays, February 4, 2009.
c Filed for free agency, October 6, 2009. Signed with Pittsburgh Pirates organization, January 4, 2010.
d Not offered contract, December 2, 2010, re-signed with Pittsburgh Pirates organization, January 3, 2011.

BUSH, DAVID THOMAS (DAVE)

Born, Pittsburgh, Pennsylvania, November 9, 1979.
Bats Right. Throws Right. Height, 6 feet, 2 inches. Weight, 210 pounds.

Year Club	Lea	G	IP	W	L	Pct	SO	BB	H	ERA	SAVES
2002 Auburn	N.Y.-Penn.	18	$22^1/_3$	1	1	.500	39	7	13	2.82	10
2002 Dunedin	Fla.St.	7	$13^1/_3$	0	1	.000	9	2	10	2.03	0
2003 Dunedin	Fla.St.	14	77	7	3	.700	75	9	64	2.81	0
2003 New Haven	Eastern	14	81	7	3	.700	73	19	73	2.78	0
2004 Syracuse	Int.	16	$99^2/_3$	6	6	.500	88	20	108	4.06	0
2004 Toronto	A.L.	16	$97^2/_3$	5	4	.556	64	25	95	3.69	0
2005 Syracuse	Int.	9	55	2	2	.500	40	9	65	4.42	0
2005 Toronto a	A.L.	25	$136^1/_3$	5	11	.313	75	29	142	4.49	0
2006 Milwaukee	N.L.	34	210	12	11	.522	166	38	201	4.41	0
2007 Milwaukee	N.L.	33	$186^1/_3$	12	10	.545	134	44	217	5.12	0
2008 Nashville	P.C.	1	6	0	0	.000	7	2	3	1.50	0

Year	Club	Lea	G	IP	W	L	Pct	SO	BB	H	ERA	SAVES
2008	Milwaukee	N.L.	31	185	9	10	.474	109	48	163	4.18	0
2009	Wisconsin	Midwest	2	$7\frac{2}{3}$	0	0	.000	9	1	4	0.00	0
2009	Huntsville	Southern	2	$6\frac{1}{3}$	0	2	.000	4	5	7	9.95	0
2009	Milwaukee b	N.L.	22	$114\frac{1}{3}$	5	9	.357	89	37	131	6.38	0
2010	Milwaukee c	N.L.	32	$174\frac{1}{3}$	8	13	.381	107	65	198	4.54	0
Major League Totals		7 Yrs.	193	1104	56	68	.452	744	286	1147	4.66	0
	Division Series											
2008	Milwaukee	N.L.	1	$5\frac{1}{3}$	1	0	1.000	3	0	5	1.69	0

a Traded to Milwaukee Brewers with outfielder Gabe Gross and pitcher Zach Jackson for infielder Lyle Overbay and pitcher Ty Taubenheim, December 7, 2005.
b On disabled list from June 21 to August 27, 2009.
c Filed for free agency, November 1, 2010.

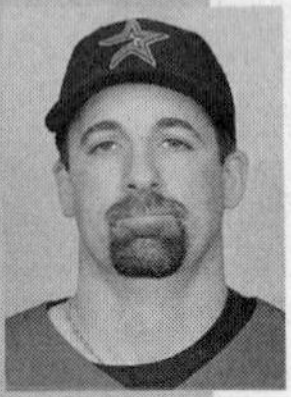

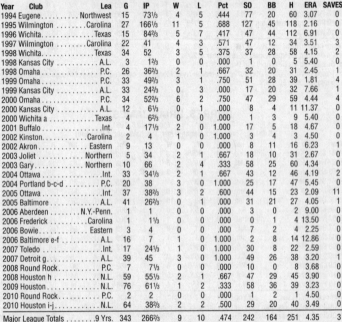

BYRDAK, TIMOTHY CHRISTOPHER (TIM)

Born, Oak Lawn, Illinois, October 31, 1973.
Bats Left. Throws Left. Height, 5 feet, 11 inches. Weight, 195 pounds.

Year	Club	Lea	G	IP	W	L	Pct	SO	BB	H	ERA	SAVES
1994	Eugene	Northwest	15	$73\frac{1}{3}$	4	5	.444	77	20	60	3.07	0
1995	Wilmington	Carolina	27	$166\frac{1}{3}$	11	5	.688	127	45	118	2.16	0
1996	Wichita	Texas	15	$84\frac{2}{3}$	5	7	.417	47	44	112	6.91	0
1997	Wilmington	Carolina	22	41	4	3	.571	47	12	34	3.51	3
1998	Wichita	Texas	34	52	3	5	.375	37	28	58	4.15	2
1998	Kansas City	A.L.	3	$1\frac{2}{3}$	0	0	.000	1	0	5	5.40	0
1998	Omaha	P.C.	26	$36\frac{2}{3}$	2	1	.667	32	20	31	2.45	1
1999	Omaha	P.C.	33	$49\frac{2}{3}$	3	1	.750	51	28	39	1.81	4
1999	Kansas City	A.L.	33	$24\frac{2}{3}$	0	3	.000	17	20	32	7.66	1
2000	Omaha	P.C.	34	$52\frac{2}{3}$	6	2	.750	47	29	59	4.44	4
2000	Kansas City	A.L.	12	$6\frac{1}{3}$	0	1	.000	8	4	11	11.37	0
2000	Wichita a	Texas	4	$6\frac{2}{3}$	0	0	.000	1	3	9	5.40	0
2001	Buffalo	Int.	4	$17\frac{1}{3}$	2	0	1.000	17	5	18	4.67	0
2002	Kinston	Carolina	2	4	1	0	1.000	3	4	3	4.50	0
2002	Akron	Eastern	9	13	0	0	.000	8	11	16	6.23	1
2003	Joliet	Northern	5	34	2	1	.667	18	10	31	2.67	0
2003	Gary	Northern	10	66	2	4	.333	58	25	60	4.34	0
2004	Ottawa	Int.	33	$34\frac{1}{3}$	2	1	.667	43	12	46	4.19	2
2004	Portland b-c-d	P.C.	20	38	3	0	1.000	25	17	47	5.45	0
2005	Ottawa	Int.	37	$38\frac{2}{3}$	3	2	.600	44	15	23	2.09	11
2005	Baltimore	A.L.	41	$26\frac{2}{3}$	0	1	.000	31	21	27	4.05	1
2006	Aberdeen	N.Y.-Penn.	1	1	0	0	.000	3	0	2	9.00	0
2006	Frederick	Carolina	1	$1\frac{1}{3}$	0	0	.000	0	1	4	13.50	0
2006	Bowie	Eastern	3	4	0	0	.000	7	2	4	2.25	0
2006	Baltimore e-f	A.L.	16	7	1	0	1.000	2	8	14	12.86	0
2007	Toledo	Int.	17	$24\frac{1}{3}$	1	0	1.000	30	8	22	2.59	0
2007	Detroit g	A.L.	39	45	3	0	1.000	49	26	38	3.20	1
2008	Round Rock	P.C.	7	$7\frac{1}{3}$	0	0	.000	10	0	8	3.68	0
2008	Houston h	N.L.	59	$55\frac{1}{3}$	2	1	.667	47	29	45	3.90	0
2009	Houston	N.L.	76	$61\frac{1}{3}$	1	2	.333	58	36	39	3.23	0
2010	Round Rock	P.C.	2	2	0	0	.000	1	2	1	4.50	0
2010	Houston i-j	N.L.	64	$38\frac{2}{3}$	2	2	.500	29	20	40	3.49	0
Major League Totals		9 Yrs.	343	$266\frac{2}{3}$	9	10	.474	242	164	251	4.35	3

a Not offered contract, December 1, 2000. Signed with Cleveland Indians organization, December 24, 2000.
b Released by Cleveland Indians, June 28, 2002. Signed with San Diego Padres organization, January 30, 2004.
c Sold to Baltimore Orioles, June 22, 2004.
d Filed for free agency, October 15, 2004, re-signed with Baltimore Orioles organization, November 16, 2004.
e On disabled list from April 19 to July 30, 2006.
f Filed for free agency, October 15, 2006. Signed with Detroit Tigers organization, November 18, 2006.
g On disabled list from June 27 to July 25, 2007.
h Released by Detroit Tigers, March 26, 2008. Signed with Houston Astros organization, April 3, 2008.
i On disabled list from May 4 to May 24, 2010.
j Filed for free agency, November 29, 2010.

CAHILL, TREVOR JOHN

Born, Oceanside, California, March 1, 1988.
Bats Right. Throws Right. Height, 6 feet, 3 inches. Weight, 210 pounds.

Year	Club	Lea	G	IP	W	L	Pct	SO	BB	H	ERA	SAVES
2006	Athletics	Arizona	4	9	0	0	.000	11	7	2	3.00	0
2007	Kane County	Midwest	20	$105\frac{1}{3}$	11	4	.733	117	40	85	2.73	0
2008	Stockton	Calif.	14	$87\frac{1}{3}$	5	4	.556	103	31	52	2.78	0

Year	Club	Lea	G	IP	W	L	Pct	SO	BB	H	ERA	SAVES
2008	Midland	Texas	7	37	6	1	.857	33	19	24	2.19	0
2009	Oakland	A.L.	32	178⅔	10	13	.435	90	72	185	4.63	0
2010	Sacramento	P.C.	2	8⅔	1	0	1.000	8	5	7	1.04	0
2010	Oakland a	A.L.	30	196⅔	18	8	.692	118	63	155	2.97	0
Major League Totals		2 Yrs.	62	375⅓	28	21	.571	208	135	340	3.76	0

a On disabled list from April 4 to April 20, 2010.

CAIN, MATTHEW THOMAS (MATT)

Born, Dothan, Alabama, October 1, 1984.
Bats Right. Throws Right. Height, 6 feet, 3 inches. Weight, 235 pounds.

Year	Club	Lea	G	IP	W	L	Pct	SO	BB	H	ERA	SAVES
2002	Giants	Arizona	8	19⅓	0	1	.000	20	11	13	3.72	0
2003	Hagerstown	So.Atl.	14	74	4	4	.500	90	24	57	2.55	0
2004	San Jose	Calif.	13	72⅔	7	1	.875	89	17	58	1.86	0
2004	Norwich	Eastern	15	86	6	4	.600	72	40	73	3.35	0
2005	Fresno	P.C.	26	145⅔	10	5	.667	176	73	118	4.39	0
2005	San Francisco	N.L.	7	46⅓	2	1	.667	30	19	24	2.33	0
2006	San Francisco	N.L.	32	190⅔	13	12	.520	179	87	157	4.15	0
2007	San Francisco	N.L.	32	200	7	16	.304	163	79	173	3.65	0
2008	San Francisco	N.L.	34	217⅔	8	14	.364	186	91	206	3.76	0
2009	San Francisco	N.L.	33	217⅔	14	8	.636	171	73	184	2.89	0
2010	San Francisco	N.L.	33	223⅓	13	11	.542	177	61	181	3.14	0
Major League Totals		6 Yrs.	171	1095⅔	57	62	.479	906	410	925	3.45	0
	Division Series											
2010	San Francisco	N.L.	1	6⅔	0	0	.000	6	2	7	0.00	0
	Championship Series											
2010	San Francisco	N.L.	1	7	1	0	1.000	5	3	2	0.00	0
	World Series Record											
2010	San Francisco	N.L.	1	7⅔	1	0	1.000	2	2	4	0.00	0

CAMP, SHAWN ANTHONY

Born, Fairfax, Virginia, November 18, 1975.
Bats Right. Throws Right. Height, 6 feet, 1 inch. Weight, 205 pounds.

Year	Club	Lea	G	IP	W	L	Pct	SO	BB	H	ERA	SAVES
1997	Idaho Falls	Pioneer	30	32⅔	2	1	.667	41	14	41	5.51	12
1998	Clinton	Midwest	47	55	3	5	.375	62	20	48	2.62	13
1999	Rancho Cucamonga	Calif.	53	66	1	5	.167	78	25	68	3.95	6
2000	Rancho Cucamonga	Calif.	14	18⅔	1	0	1.000	18	5	10	1.45	6
2000	Mobile	Southern	45	59⅓	3	3	.500	53	30	47	2.43	1
2001	Altoona	Eastern	8	23⅓	4	0	1.000	19	8	25	4.24	0
2001	Nashville	P.C.	11	17	0	0	.000	15	8	11	2.12	0
2001	Portland	P.C.	4	7	1	0	1.000	6	1	2	0.00	0
2001	Mobile a	Southern	35	48⅔	6	2	.750	55	15	46	4.44	0
2002	Nashville	P.C.	39	58⅓	4	1	.800	59	15	50	3.24	2
2003	Altoona	Eastern	18	29	0	2	.000	35	11	26	4.34	0
2003	Nashville b	P.C.	33	43⅓	0	1	.000	36	15	50	4.98	0
2004	Kansas City	A.L.	42	66⅔	2	2	.500	51	16	74	3.92	2
2004	Omaha	P.C.	15	22	1	1	.500	21	6	26	5.32	1
2005	Omaha	P.C.	21	67⅔	3	6	.333	42	22	71	3.86	1
2005	Kansas City	A.L.	29	49	1	4	.200	28	13	69	6.43	0
2006	Tampa Bay c	A.L.	75	75	7	4	.636	53	19	93	4.68	4
2007	Tampa Bay	A.L.	50	40	0	3	.000	36	18	63	7.20	0
2007	Durham	Int.	12	15⅓	0	1	.000	16	2	13	1.17	4
2008	Syracuse	Int.	7	10	1	0	1.000	13	0	4	0.00	4
2008	Toronto d	A.L.	40	39⅓	3	1	.750	31	11	40	4.12	0
2009	Toronto	A.L.	59	79⅔	2	6	.250	58	29	73	3.50	1
2010	Toronto	A.L.	70	72⅓	4	3	.571	46	18	71	2.99	2
Major League Totals		7 Yrs.	365	422	19	23	.452	303	124	483	4.44	9

a Traded by San Diego Padres to Pittsburgh Pirates for outfielder Emil Brown, July 10, 2001.
b Filed for free agency, October 15, 2003. Signed with Kansas City Royals organization, October 29, 2003.
c Not offered contract, December 21, 2005. Signed with Tampa Bay Devil Rays, January 17, 2006.
d Filed for free agency, October 31, 2007. Signed with Toronto Blue Jays organization, January 7, 2008.

CAPPS, MATTHEW DICUS (MATT)

Born, Douglasville, Georgia, September 3, 1983.
Bats Right. Throws Right. Height, 6 feet, 2 inches. Weight, 240 pounds.

Year	Club	Lea	G	IP	W	L	Pct	SO	BB	H	ERA	SAVES
2002	Pirates	Gulf Coast	7	13	1	0	1.000	8	6	13	0.69	1
2003	Lynchburg	Carolina	1	5	0	0	.000	5	4	3	5.40	0
2003	Pirates	Gulf Coast	10	62 2/3	5	1	.833	54	9	40	1.87	0
2004	Williamsport	N.Y.-Penn.	11	65	3	5	.375	33	4	84	4.85	0
2004	Hickory	So.Atl.	12	42	2	3	.400	27	16	82	10.07	0
2005	Hickory	So.Atl.	35	53 2/3	3	4	.429	39	5	47	2.52	14
2005	Altoona	Eastern	17	20	0	2	.000	26	1	21	2.70	7
2005	Pittsburgh	N.L.	4	4	0	0	.000	3	0	5	4.50	0
2006	Pittsburgh	N.L.	85	80 2/3	9	1	.900	56	12	81	3.79	1
2007	Pittsburgh	N.L.	76	79	4	7	.364	64	16	64	2.28	18
2008	Pirates	Gulf Coast	2	2	0	0	.000	2	0	2	0.00	0
2008	Altoona	Eastern	3	3	0	0	.000	5	1	0	0.00	0
2008	Indianapolis	Int.	1	1 2/3	0	0	.000	1	3	0	0.00	0
2008	Pittsburgh a	N.L.	49	53 2/3	2	3	.400	39	5	47	3.02	21
2009	Pittsburgh b	N.L.	57	54 1/3	4	8	.333	46	17	73	5.80	27
2010	Washington	N.L.	47	46	3	3	.500	38	9	51	2.74	26
2010	Minnesota c	A.L.	27	27	2	0	1.000	21	8	24	2.00	16
Major League Totals		6 Yrs.	345	344 2/3	24	22	.522	267	67	345	3.37	109
	Division Series											
2010	Minnesota	A.L.	1	1	0	0	.000	0	0	2	9.00	0

a On disabled list from July 2 to August 23, 2008.
b Not offered contract, December 12, 2009. Signed with Washington Nationals, December 24, 2009.
c Traded to Minnesota Twins for catcher Wilson Ramos, pitcher Joe Testa and cash, July 30, 2010.

CAPUANO, CHRISTOPHER FRANK (CHRIS)

Born, Springfield, Massachusetts, August 19, 1978.
Bats Left. Throws Left. Height, 6 feet, 3 inches. Weight, 225 pounds.

Year	Club	Lea	G	IP	W	L	Pct	SO	BB	H	ERA	SAVES
2000	South Bend	Midwest	18	101 2/3	10	4	.714	105	45	68	2.21	0
2001	El Paso	Texas	28	159 1/3	10	11	.476	167	75	184	5.31	0
2002	Tucson	P.C.	6	36 1/3	4	1	.800	29	11	30	2.72	0
2003	Tucson	P.C.	23	142 2/3	9	5	.643	108	43	133	3.34	0
2003	Arizona a	N.L.	9	33	2	4	.333	23	11	27	4.64	0
2004	Milwaukee	N.L.	17	88 1/3	6	8	.429	80	37	91	4.99	0
2004	Beloit	Midwest	1	2 2/3	0	0	.000	4	1	3	3.38	0
2004	Indianapolis	Int.	2	8 2/3	0	1	.000	9	5	10	8.31	0
2004	High Desert b	Calif.	1	2	0	1	.000	2	3	6	27.00	0
2005	Milwaukee	N.L.	35	219	18	12	.600	176	91	212	3.99	0
2006	Milwaukee	N.L.	34	221 1/3	11	12	.478	174	47	229	4.03	0
2007	Milwaukee c	N.L.	29	150	5	12	.294	132	54	170	5.10	0
2008	Milwaukee d-e	N.L.	INJURED—Did Not Play									
2009	Brewers	Arizona	3	3	0	0	.000	4	2	5	6.00	0
2009	Helena	Pioneer	2	4	0	0	.000	3	0	2	0.00	0
2010	Brevard County	Fla.St.	3	14 2/3	2	0	1.000	17	0	12	1.23	0
2010	Nashville	P.C.	4	25	1	1	.500	16	4	21	1.80	0
2010	Milwaukee f	N.L.	24	66	4	4	.500	54	21	65	3.95	0
Major League Totals		6 Yrs.	148	777 2/3	46	52	.469	639	261	794	4.35	0

a Traded to Milwaukee Brewers with infielder Junior Spivey, infielder Craig Counsell, infielder Lyle Overbay, catcher Chad Moeller and pitcher Jorge DeRosa for infielder Richie Sexson, pitcher Shane Nance and player to be named later, December 1, 2003. Arizona Diamondbacks received outfielder Noochie Varner to complete trade, December 15, 2003.
b On disabled list from April 19 to May 26 and May 27 to June 12 and August 25 to October 6, 2004.
c On disabled list from June 9 to July 1, 2007.
d Not offered contract, December 12, 2008, re-signed with Milwaukee Brewers organization, December 16, 2008.
e On disabled list from March 21 to September 29, 2008.
f Filed for free agency, November 1, 2010. Signed with New York Mets, January 3, 2011.

CARMONA, FAUSTO C.

Born, Santo Domingo, Dominican Republic, December 7, 1983.
Bats Right. Throws Right. Height, 6 feet, 4 inches. Weight, 220 pounds.

Year	Club	Lea	G	IP	W	L	Pct	SO	BB	H	ERA	SAVES
2002	Burlington	Appal.	13	76 1/3	2	4	.333	42	10	89	3.30	1
2002	Mahoning Valley	N.Y.-Penn.	3	4	0	0	.000	0	1	2	0.00	0
2003	Akron	Eastern	1	6	0	0	.000	3	0	8	4.50	0

Year Club	Lea	G	IP	W	L	Pct	SO	BB	H	ERA	SAVES
2003 Lake County	So.Atl.	24	148 1/3	17	4	.810	83	14	117	2.06	0
2004 Kinston	Carolina	13	70	5	2	.714	57	20	68	2.83	0
2004 Akron	Eastern	15	87	4	8	.333	63	21	114	4.97	0
2004 Buffalo	Int.	1	6	1	0	1.000	2	3	6	6.00	0
2005 Akron	Eastern	14	90 2/3	6	5	.545	57	20	100	4.07	0
2005 Buffalo	Int.	13	83	7	4	.636	49	15	76	3.25	0
2006 Buffalo	Int.	6	27 2/3	1	3	.250	28	8	28	5.53	0
2006 Cleveland	A.L.	38	74 2/3	1	10	.091	58	31	88	5.42	0
2007 Cleveland	A.L.	32	215	19	8	.704	137	61	199	3.06	0
2008 Lake County	So.Atl.	1	4	0	0	.000	3	0	1	0.00	0
2008 Akron	Eastern	1	5	1	0	1.000	2	0	9	1.80	0
2008 Cleveland a	A.L.	22	120 2/3	8	7	.533	58	70	126	5.44	0
2009 Lake County	So.Atl.	1	6 1/3	1	0	1.000	7	1	1	0.00	0
2009 Akron	Eastern	1	7	1	0	1.000	5	0	4	1.29	0
2009 Columbus	Int.	5	33	1	3	.250	27	6	32	3.55	0
2009 Cleveland	A.L.	24	125 1/3	5	12	.294	79	70	151	6.32	0
2010 Cleveland	A.L.	33	210 1/3	13	14	.481	124	72	203	3.77	0
Major League Totals	5 Yrs.	149	746	46	51	.474	456	304	767	4.43	0
Division Series											
2007 Cleveland	A.L.	1	9	0	0	.000	5	2	3	1.00	0
Championship Series											
2007 Cleveland	A.L.	2	6	0	1	.000	7	9	10	16.50	0

a On disabled list from May 24 to July 26, 2008.

CARPENTER, CHRISTOPHER JOHN (CHRIS)

Born, Exeter, New Hampshire, April 27, 1975.
Bats Right. Throws Right. Height, 6 feet, 6 inches. Weight, 230 pounds.

Year Club	Lea	G	IP	W	L	Pct	SO	BB	H	ERA	SAVES
1994 Medicne Hat	Pioneer	15	84 2/3	6	3	.667	80	39	76	2.76	0
1995 Dunedin	Fla.St.	15	99 1/3	3	5	.375	56	50	83	2.17	0
1995 Knoxville	Southern	12	64 1/3	3	7	.300	53	31	71	5.18	0
1996 Knoxville	Southern	28	171 1/3	7	9	.438	150	91	161	3.94	0
1997 Syracuse	Int.	19	120	4	9	.308	97	53	113	4.50	0
1997 Toronto	A.L.	14	81 1/3	3	7	.300	55	37	108	5.09	0
1998 Toronto	A.L.	33	175	12	7	.632	136	61	177	4.37	0
1999 Toronto	A.L.	24	150	9	8	.529	106	48	177	4.38	0
1999 St. Catharines a	N.Y.-Penn.	1	4	0	0	.000	6	1	5	4.50	0
2000 Toronto	A.L.	34	175 1/3	10	12	.455	113	83	204	6.26	0
2001 Toronto	A.L.	34	215 2/3	11	11	.500	157	75	229	4.09	0
2002 Toronto	A.L.	13	73 1/3	4	5	.444	45	27	89	5.28	0
2002 Tennessee	Southern	5	18 2/3	0	1	.000	9	8	26	8.20	0
2002 Syracuse b-c	Int.	1	6	0	1	.000	6	2	8	4.50	0
2003 Palm Beach	Fla.St.	4	7	0	1	.000	6	1	6	1.29	0
2003 Memphis	P.C.	3	8 1/3	0	0	.000	4	2	11	5.40	0
2003 Tennessee d-e	Southern	1	3 1/3	0	1	.000	2	2	7	13.50	0
2004 St. Louis	N.L.	28	182	15	5	.750	152	38	169	3.46	0
2005 St. Louis f	N.L.	33	241 2/3	21	5	*.808	213	51	204	2.83	0
2006 St. Louis g	N.L.	32	221 2/3	15	8	.652	184	43	194	3.09	0
2007 Palm Beach	Fla.St.	2	4 1/3	0	1	.000	4	1	7	6.23	0
2007 St. Louis h	N.L.	1	6	0	1	.000	3	1	9	7.50	0
2008 Springfield	Texas	1	4	0	0	.000	4	4	1	0.00	0
2008 Memphis	P.C.	1	5 2/3	0	1	.000	5	1	4	3.18	0
2008 St. Louis i	N.L.	4	15 1/3	0	1	.000	7	4	16	1.76	0
2009 St. Louis j	N.L.	28	192 2/3	17	4	*.810	144	38	156	*2.24	0
2010 St. Louis	N.L.	35	235	16	9	.640	179	63	214	3.22	0
Major League Totals	13 Yrs.	313	1965	133	83	.616	1494	569	1946	3.80	0
Division Series											
2005 St. Louis	N.L.	1	6	1	0	1.000	3	3	3	0.00	0
2006 St. Louis	N.L.	2	13 1/3	2	0	1.000	12	4	12	2.03	0
2009 St. Louis	N.L.	1	5	0	1	.000	3	4	9	7.20	0
Division Series Totals		4	24 1/3	3	1	.750	18	11	24	2.59	0
Championship Series											
2005 St. Louis	N.L.	2	15	1	0	1.000	9	4	14	3.00	0
2006 St. Louis	N.L.	2	11	0	1	.000	5	4	13	5.73	0
Championship Series Totals		4	26	1	1	.500	14	8	27	4.15	0
World Series Record											
2006 St. Louis	N.L.	1	8	1	0	1.000	6	0	3	0.00	0

a On disabled list from June 3 to June 28, 1999.

b On disabled list from April 2 to April 20 and April 22 to June 21 and August 14 to October 7, 2002.
c Filed for free agency, October 9, 2002. Signed with St. Louis Cardinals, December 15, 2002.
d On disabled list from March 27 to September 30, 2003.
e Filed for free agency, November 3, 2003, re-signed with St. Louis Cardinals, December 1, 2003.
f Selected Cy Young Award Winner in National League for 2005.
g On disabled list from May 22 to June 6, 2006.
h On disabled list from April 2 to November 2, 2007.
i On disabled list from March 21 to July 30 and August 11 to September 1, 2008.
j On disabled list from April 15 to May 20, 2009.

CARRASCO, CARLOS LUIS

Born, Barquisimeto, Venezuela, March 21, 1987.
Bats Right. Throws Right. Height, 6 feet, 3 inches. Weight, 220 pounds.

Year	Club	Lea	G	IP	W	L	Pct	SO	BB	H	ERA	SAVES
2004	Phillies	Gulf Coast	11	48	5	4	.556	34	15	53	3.56	0
2005	Phillies	Gulf Coast	2	5	0	0	.000	2	1	3	1.80	0
2005	Batavia	N.Y.-Penn.	4	15 1/3	0	3	.000	12	5	29	13.50	0
2005	Lakewood	So.Atl.	13	62 2/3	1	7	.125	46	28	78	7.04	0
2006	Lakewood	So.Atl.	26	159 1/3	12	6	.667	159	65	103	2.26	0
2007	Reading	Eastern	14	70 1/3	6	4	.600	49	46	65	4.86	0
2007	Clearwater	Fla.St.	12	69 2/3	6	2	.750	53	22	49	2.84	0
2008	Reading	Eastern	20	114 2/3	7	7	.500	109	45	109	4.32	0
2008	Lehigh Valley	Int.	6	36 2/3	2	2	.500	46	13	37	1.72	0
2009	Lehigh Valley	Int.	20	114 2/3	6	9	.400	112	38	118	5.18	0
2009	Columbus	Int.	6	42 1/3	5	1	.833	36	7	31	3.19	0
2009	Cleveland a	A.L.	5	22 1/3	0	4	.000	11	11	40	8.87	0
2010	Columbus	Int.	25	150 1/3	10	6	.625	133	46	139	3.65	0
2010	Cleveland	A.L.	7	44 2/3	2	2	.500	38	14	47	3.83	0
Major League Totals		2 Yrs.	12	67	2	6	.250	49	25	87	5.51	0

a Traded by Philadelphia Phillies to Cleveland Indians with catcher Lou Marson, pitcher Jason Knapp and infielder Jason Donald for pitcher Cliff Lee and outfielder Ben Francisco, July 29, 2009.

CARRASCO, DANIEL (D.J.)

Born, Safford, Arizona, April 12, 1977.
Bats Right. Throws Right. Height, 6 feet, 1 inch. Weight, 220 pounds.

Year	Club	Lea	G	IP	W	L	Pct	SO	BB	H	ERA	SAVES
1998	Watertown a	N.Y.-Penn.	13	31 2/3	1	1	.500	38	14	36	5.40	2
1999	Lynchburg	Carolina	2	5 2/3	0	1	.000	4	3	9	6.35	0
1999	Williamsport b	N.Y.-Penn.	18	51 2/3	4	2	.667	49	23	43	2.96	0
2000	Lynchburg	Carolina	8	10 1/3	1	0	1.000	10	8	8	3.48	2
2000	Altoona	Eastern	9	14	1	1	.500	10	13	16	8.36	0
2000	Hickory	So.Atl.	27	40 1/3	5	4	.556	40	20	35	1.34	6
2001	Lynchburg	Carolina	22	36	4	0	1.000	40	14	18	1.50	7
2001	Altoona	Eastern	27	37	2	2	.500	35	25	34	4.14	1
2002	Lynchburg c	Carolina	55	72 2/3	4	4	.500	83	18	52	1.61	29
2003	Kansas City	A.L.	50	80 1/3	6	5	.545	57	40	82	4.82	2
2004	Omaha	P.C.	32	56 1/3	2	1	.667	50	18	60	3.20	3
2004	Kansas City	A.L.	30	35 1/3	2	2	.500	22	15	41	4.84	0
2005	Omaha	P.C.	11	27 2/3	3	2	.600	21	11	24	2.28	0
2005	Kansas City	A.L.	21	114 2/3	6	8	.429	49	51	129	4.79	0
2006	Fukuoka d-e	Japan Pac.	3	10 1/3	0	3	.000	9	10	22	14.81	0
2007	Tucson	P.C.	34	137 1/3	5	14	.263	103	60	185	6.68	0
2008	Charlotte	Int.	8	25	2	1	.667	24	7	24	2.88	1
2008	Chicago f	A.L.	31	38 2/3	1	0	1.000	30	14	30	3.96	0
2009	Chicago g	A.L.	49	93 1/3	5	1	.833	62	29	103	3.76	0
2010	Pittsburgh-Arizona h-i	N.L.	63	78 1/3	3	2	.600	65	34	68	3.68	0
Major League Totals		6 Yrs.	244	440 2/3	23	18	.561	285	183	453	4.31	2

a Released by Baltimore Orioles organization, June 14, 1998. Signed with Cleveland Indians organization, June 18, 1998.
b Released by Cleveland Indians organization, August 21, 1998. Signed with Pittsburgh Pirates organization, March 29, 1999.
c Selected by Kansas City Royals in Rule V draft, December 16, 2002.
d Released by Kansas City Royals, December 7, 2005. Signed with Fukoka (Japan) for 2006.
e Signed with Arizona Diamondbacks organization, December 22, 2006.
f Filed for free agency, October 29, 2007. Signed with Chicago White Sox organization, January 11, 2008.
g Not offered contract, December 12, 2009. Signed with Pittsburgh Pirates organization, January 16, 2010.
h Traded to Arizona Diamondbacks with infielder Bobby Crosby and outfielder Ryan Church for catcher Chris Snyder, infielder Pedro Ciriaco and cash, July 31, 2010.
i Not offered contract, December 2, 2010. Signed with New York Mets organization, December 9, 2010.

CASHNER, ANDREW BURTON

Born, Conroe, Texas, September 11, 1986.
Bats Right. Throws Right. Height, 6 feet, 6 inches. Weight, 210 pounds.

Year	Club	Lea	G	IP	W	L	Pct	SO	BB	H	ERA	SAVES
2008	Cubs	Arizona	1	1	0	0	.000	2	0	1	0.00	0
2008	Daytona	Fla.St.	1	2 2/3	0	1	.000	1	4	4	13.50	0
2008	Boise	Northwest	6	16 1/3	1	1	.500	16	19	19	4.96	0
2009	Daytona	Fla.St.	12	42	0	0	.000	34	15	31	1.50	0
2009	Tennessee	Southern	12	58 1/3	3	4	.429	41	27	45	3.39	0
2010	Tennessee	Southern	6	36	3	1	.750	42	13	22	2.75	0
2010	Iowa	P.C.	5	21	3	0	1.000	17	2	17	0.86	0
2010	Chicago	N.L.	53	54 1/3	2	6	.250	50	30	55	4.80	0

CASILLA, SANTIAGO

Born, Don Gregorio, Dominican Republic, June 25, 1980.
Bats Right. Throws Right. Height, 6 feet. Weight, 200 pounds.

Year	Club	Lea	G	IP	W	L	Pct	SO	BB	H	ERA	SAVES
2001	Athletics	Arizona	12	47 1/3	4	2	.667	50	6	37	2.85	0
2002	Athletics	Arizona	13	59	2	1	.667	66	17	56	2.44	1
2002	Vancouver	Northwest	3	12 1/3	0	3	.000	16	7	15	7.30	0
2003	Kane County	Midwest	14	42 1/3	0	1	.000	28	19	40	2.55	0
2004	Kane County	Midwest	25	30	1	0	1.000	49	6	16	0.30	16
2004	Midland	Texas	13	18	2	0	1.000	32	15	10	1.50	2
2004	Sacramento	P.C.	11	13 2/3	1	2	.333	21	9	10	3.95	1
2004	Oakland	A.L.	4	5 2/3	0	0	.000	5	9	5	12.71	0
2005	Midland	Texas	10	16 2/3	0	0	.000	30	9	9	1.08	6
2005	Sacramento	P.C.	44	48 1/3	3	6	.333	73	20	45	4.47	20
2005	Oakland a	A.L.	3	3	0	0	.000	1	1	2	3.00	0
2006	Oakland	A.L.	2	2 1/3	0	0	.000	2	2	2	11.57	0
2006	Sacramento	P.C.	25	33	2	0	1.000	32	10	25	3.27	4
2007	Sacramento	P.C.	22	24	2	1	.667	29	14	18	4.13	3
2007	Oakland	A.L.	46	50 2/3	3	1	.750	52	23	43	4.44	2
2008	Stockton	Calif.	1	1	0	0	.000	2	0	0	0.00	0
2008	Sacramento	P.C.	2	2 2/3	0	0	.000	5	1	3	3.38	0
2008	Oakland b	A.L.	51	50 1/3	2	1	.667	43	20	60	3.93	2
2009	Stockton	Calif.	1	1	0	0	.000	0	0	0	0.00	0
2009	Sacramento	P.C.	1	1	0	0	.000	0	0	0	0.00	0
2009	Oakland c	A.L.	46	48 1/3	1	2	.333	35	25	61	5.96	0
2010	Fresno	P.C.	4	4	0	0	.000	7	2	2	0.00	2
2010	San Francisco	N.L.	52	55 1/3	7	2	.778	56	26	40	1.95	2
Major League Totals		7 Yrs.	204	215 2/3	13	6	.684	194	106	213	4.30	6
	Division Series											
2010	San Francisco	N.L.	1	1 2/3	0	0	.000	2	0	1	0.00	0
	Championship Series											
2010	San Francisco	N.L.	2	1 2/3	0	0	.000	2	1	2	5.40	0
	World Series Record											
2010	San Francisco	N.L.	1	1 1/3	0	0	.000	1	0	0	0.00	0

a Played under name of Jairo Garcia 2001-2005

b On disabled list from May 16 to June 19, 2008.

c Released by Oakland Athletics, December 10, 2009. Signed with San Francisco Giants organization, January 21, 2010.

CECIL, BRETT AARION

Born, Dunkirk, Maryland, July 2, 1986.
Bats Right. Throws Left. Height, 6 feet, 2 inches. Weight, 225 pounds.

Year	Club	Lea	G	IP	W	L	Pct	SO	BB	H	ERA	SAVES
2007	Auburn	N.Y.-Penn.	14	49 2/3	1	0	1.000	56	11	36	1.27	0
2008	New Hampshire	Eastern	18	77 2/3	6	2	.750	87	23	66	2.55	0
2008	Dunedin	Fla.St.	4	10 1/3	0	0	.000	11	2	6	1.74	0
2008	Syracuse	Int.	6	30 2/3	2	3	.400	31	16	28	4.11	0
2009	Las Vegas	P.C.	9	49	1	5	.167	32	19	53	5.69	0
2009	Toronto	A.L.	18	93 1/3	7	4	.636	69	38	116	5.30	0
2010	Las Vegas	P.C.	2	11	2	0	1.000	11	2	13	2.45	0
2010	Toronto	A.L.	28	172 2/3	15	7	.682	117	54	175	4.22	0
Major League Totals		2 Yrs.	46	266	22	11	.667	186	92	291	4.60	0

CHACIN (MOLINA), JHOULYS JOSE

Born, Maracaibo, Venezuela, January 7, 1988.
Bats Right. Throws Right. Height, 6 feet, 3 inches. Weight, 215 pounds.

Year	Club	Lea	G	IP	W	L	Pct	SO	BB	H	ERA	SAVES
2007	Casper	Pioneer	16	73	6	5	.545	77	26	85	3.13	0
2008	Asheville	So.Atl.	16	111 1/3	10	1	.909	98	30	82	1.86	0
2008	Modesto	Calif.	12	66 1/3	8	2	.800	62	12	61	2.31	0
2009	Tulsa	Texas	18	103 1/3	8	6	.571	86	35	87	3.14	0
2009	Colorado Springs	P.C.	4	14 1/3	1	2	.333	11	13	11	3.77	0
2009	Colorado	N.L.	9	11	0	1	.000	13	11	6	4.91	0
2010	Colorado Springs	P.C.	7	35 2/3	3	2	.600	34	17	27	1.51	0
2010	Colorado	N.L.	28	137 1/3	9	11	.450	138	61	114	3.28	0
Major League Totals		2 Yrs.	37	148 1/3	9	12	.429	151	72	120	3.40	0

CHAMBERLAIN, JUSTIN LOUIS (JOBA)

Born, Lincoln, Nebraska, September 23, 1985.
Bats Right. Throws Right. Height, 6 feet, 2 inches. Weight, 230 pounds.

Year	Club	Lea	G	IP	W	L	Pct	SO	BB	H	ERA	SAVES
2007	Tampa	Fla.St.	7	40	4	0	1.000	51	11	25	2.03	0
2007	Trenton	Eastern	8	40 1/3	4	2	.667	66	15	32	3.35	0
2007	Scranton-WB	Int.	3	8	1	0	1.000	18	1	5	0.00	0
2007	New York	A.L.	19	24	2	0	1.000	34	6	12	0.38	1
2008	New York a	A.L.	42	100 1/3	4	3	.571	118	39	87	2.60	0
2009	New York	A.L.	32	157 1/3	9	6	.600	133	76	167	4.75	0
2010	New York	A.L.	73	71 2/3	3	4	.429	77	22	71	4.40	3
Major League Totals		4 Yrs.	166	353 1/3	18	13	.581	362	143	337	3.77	4
	Division Series											
2007	New York	A.L.	2	3 2/3	0	0	.000	4	3	3	4.91	0
2009	New York	A.L.	3	1 2/3	0	0	.000	1	0	2	0.00	0
Division Series Totals			5	5 1/3	0	0	.000	5	3	5	3.38	0
	Championship Series											
2009	New York	A.L.	4	1 2/3	0	0	.000	2	0	5	5.40	0
2010	New York	A.L.	3	3 1/3	0	0	.000	3	2	4	2.70	0
Championship Series Totals			7	5	0	0	.000	5	2	9	3.60	0
	World Series Record											
2009	New York	A.L.	3	3	1	0	1.000	4	1	2	3.00	0

a On disabled list from August 5 to September 2, 2008.

CHAPMAN, ALBERTIN AROLDIS (AROLDIS)

Born, Holguin, Cuba, February 28, 1988.
Bats Left. Throws Left. Height, 6 feet, 4 inches. Weight, 185 pounds.

Year	Club	Lea	G	IP	W	L	Pct	SO	BB	H	ERA	SAVES
2010	Louisville	Int.	39	95 2/3	9	6	.600	125	52	77	3.57	8
2010	Cincinnati a	N.L.	15	13 1/3	2	2	.500	19	5	9	2.03	0
	Division Series											
2010	Cincinnati	N.L.	2	1 2/3	0	1	.000	1	0	3	0.00	0

a Played in Cuba 2005 through 2009. Signed with Cincinnati Reds, January 12, 2010.

CHAVEZ, JESSE DAVID

Born, Victorville, California, August 21, 1983.
Bats Right. Throws Right. Height, 6 feet, 2 inches. Weight, 170 pounds.

Year	Club	Lea	G	IP	W	L	Pct	SO	BB	H	ERA	SAVES
2003	Spokane	Northwest	17	55 1/3	2	2	.500	48	31	63	4.55	1
2004	Clinton	Midwest	27	123	6	10	.375	96	35	149	4.68	0
2005	Bakersfield	Calif.	11	24 1/3	0	0	.000	31	9	16	2.22	2
2005	Frisco	Texas	31	57	4	3	.571	27	25	71	5.68	1
2006	Indianapolis	Int.	12	17	2	1	.667	15	9	18	4.24	0
2006	Oklahoma	P.C.	1	2	0	0	.000	3	0	3	4.50	0
2006	Frisco a	Texas	38	59	2	5	.286	70	28	54	4.42	4
2007	Indianapolis	Int.	46	80 1/3	3	3	.500	65	17	94	3.92	2
2008	Indianapolis	Int.	51	68 2/3	2	6	.250	70	22	58	3.80	14
2008	Pittsburgh	N.L.	15	15	0	1	.000	16	9	20	6.60	0
2009	Pittsburgh b-c	N.L.	73	67 1/3	1	4	.200	47	22	69	4.01	0
2010	Atlanta	N.L.	28	36 2/3	3	2	.600	29	12	40	5.89	0

Year	Club	Lea	G	IP	W	L	Pct	SO	BB	H	ERA	SAVES
2010	Kansas City d	A.L.	23	26	2	3	.400	16	11	29	5.88	0
Major League Totals		3 Yrs.	139	145	6	10	.375	108	54	158	5.09	0

a Traded by Texas Rangers to Pittsburgh Pirates for pitcher Kip Wells, July 31, 2006.
b Traded to Tampa Bay Rays for infielder Akinori Iwamura, November 3, 2009.
c Traded to Atlanta Braves for pitcher Rafael Soriano, December 11, 2009.
d Traded to Kansas City Royals with outfielder Gregor Blanco and pitcher Tim Collins for outfielder Rick Ankiel, pitcher Kyle Farnsworth and cash, July 31, 2010.

CHEN, BRUCE KASTULO

Born, Panama City, Panama, June 19, 1977.
Bats Left. Throws Left. Height, 6 feet, 2 inches. Weight, 215 pounds.

Year	Club	Lea	G	IP	W	L	Pct	SO	BB	H	ERA	SAVES
1994	Braves	Gulf Coast	9	$42\frac{2}{3}$	1	4	.200	26	3	42	3.80	1
1995	Danville	Appal.	14	$70\frac{1}{3}$	4	4	.500	56	19	78	3.97	0
1996	Eugene	Northwest	11	$35\frac{2}{3}$	4	1	.800	55	14	23	2.27	0
1997	Macon	So.Atl.	28	$146\frac{1}{3}$	12	7	.632	182	44	120	3.51	0
1998	Greenville	Southern	24	$139\frac{1}{3}$	13	7	.650	164	48	106	3.29	0
1998	Richmond	Int.	4	24	2	1	.667	29	19	17	1.88	0
1998	Atlanta	N.L.	4	$20\frac{1}{3}$	2	0	1.000	17	9	23	3.98	0
1999	Richmond	Int.	14	78	6	3	.667	90	26	73	3.81	0
1999	Atlanta	N.L.	16	51	2	2	.500	45	27	38	5.47	0
2000	Richmond	Int.	1	6	1	0	1.000	6	1	5	0.00	0
2000	Atlanta-Philadelphia a	N.L.	37	134	7	4	.636	112	46	116	3.29	0
2001	Reading	Eastern	1	6	1	0	1.000	7	0	3	0.00	0
2001	Scranton-WB	Int.	3	$18\frac{2}{3}$	1	0	1.000	14	5	14	3.86	0
2001	Philadelphia-New York b	N.L.	27	146	7	7	.500	126	59	146	4.87	0
2002	NY-Montreal-Cincinnati c-d	N.L.	55	$77\frac{2}{3}$	2	5	.286	80	43	85	5.56	0
2003	Houston	N.L.	11	12	0	0	.000	8	8	14	6.00	0
2003	Boston	A.L.	5	$12\frac{1}{3}$	0	1	.000	12	2	12	5.11	0
2003	Pawtucket e-f-g	Int.	16	85	5	5	.500	73	15	80	4.24	1
2004	Syracuse	Int.	3	$10\frac{1}{3}$	0	1	.000	8	5	17	8.71	0
2004	Ottawa	Int.	22	95	4	3	.571	108	30	85	3.22	0
2004	Baltimore h	A.L.	8	$47\frac{2}{3}$	2	1	.667	32	16	39	3.02	0
2005	Baltimore	A.L.	34	$197\frac{1}{3}$	13	10	.565	133	63	187	3.83	0
2006	Baltimore	A.L.	40	$98\frac{2}{3}$	0	7	.000	70	35	137	6.93	0
2007	Texas	A.L.	5	10	0	0	.000	7	6	11	7.20	0
2007	Oklahoma i	P.C.	4	16	1	1	.500	12	3	17	5.63	0
2008							Did Not Play					
2009	Omaha	P.C.	14	82	4	2	.667	69	23	57	3.40	0
2009	Kansas City j-k-l	A.L.	17	$62\frac{1}{3}$	1	6	.143	45	25	74	5.78	0
2010	Omaha	P.C.	3	$20\frac{2}{3}$	0	1	.000	20	5	13	1.31	0
2010	Kansas City m	A.L.	33	$140\frac{1}{3}$	12	7	.632	98	57	136	4.17	1
Major League Totals		12 Yrs.	292	$1009\frac{2}{3}$	48	50	.490	785	396	1018	4.64	1

a Traded to Philadelphia Phillies with pitcher Jim Osting for pitcher Andy Ashby, July 12, 2000.
b Traded to New York Mets with pitcher Adam Walker for pitcher Turk Wendell and pitcher Dennis Cook, July 27, 2001.
c Traded to Montreal Expos with pitcher Dicky Gonzalez, infielder Luis Figueroa and player to be named later for pitcher Scott Strickland, pitcher Paul Seubel and outfielder Matt Watson, April 5, 2002.
d Traded to Cincinnati Reds for pitcher Jim Brower, June 14, 2002.
e Released by Cincinnati Reds, March 12, 2003. Signed with Houston Astros organization, March 14, 2003.
f Claimed on waivers by Boston Red Sox, May 7, 2003.
g Filed for free agency, October 3, 2003. Signed with Toronto Blue Jays organization, November 26, 2003.
h Sold to Baltimore Orioles, May 1, 2004.
i Filed for free agency, October 29, 2006. Signed with Texas Rangers organization, February 6, 2007.
j Filed for free agency, October 15, 2007. Signed with Kansas City Royals organization, March 1, 2009.
k On disabled list from September 23 to November 6, 2009.
l Filed for free agency, November 6, 2009, re-signed with Kansas City Royals organization, December 11, 2009.
m Filed for free agency, November 1, 2010, re-signed with Kansas City Royals, January 15, 2011.

CHOATE, RANDOL DOYLE (RANDY)

Born, San Antonio, Texas, September 5, 1975.
Bats Left. Throws Left. Height, 6 feet, 3 inches. Weight, 200 pounds.

Year	Club	Lea	G	IP	W	L	Pct	SO	BB	H	ERA	SAVES
1997	Oneonta	N.Y.-Penn.	10	$62\frac{1}{3}$	5	1	.833	61	12	49	1.73	0
1998	Tampa	Fla.St.	13	70	1	8	.111	55	22	83	5.27	0
1998	Greensboro	So.Atl.	8	39	1	5	.167	32	7	46	3.00	0

Year	Club	Lea	G	IP	W	L	Pct	SO	BB	H	ERA	SAVES
1999	Tampa	Fla.St.	47	50	2	2	.500	62	24	51	4.50	1
2000	Columbus	Int.	33	35 1/3	2	0	1.000	37	14	34	2.04	1
2000	New York	A.L.	22	17	0	1	.000	12	8	14	4.76	0
2001	New York	A.L.	37	48 1/3	3	1	.750	35	27	34	3.35	0
2001	Columbus	Int.	4	4 1/3	1	1	.500	4	3	7	2.08	0
2002	New York	A.L.	18	22 1/3	0	0	.000	17	15	18	6.04	0
2002	Columbus	Int.	31	36 2/3	3	2	.600	32	15	25	1.72	1
2003	Columbus	Int.	54	71 1/3	3	5	.375	56	24	75	3.91	1
2003	New York a	A.L.	5	3 2/3	0	0	.000	0	1	7	7.36	0
2004	Arizona	N.L.	74	50 2/3	2	4	.333	49	28	52	4.62	0
2004	Tucson b	P.C.	15	12 2/3	0	0	.000	7	8	10	5.68	1
2005	Arizona	N.L.	8	7	0	0	.000	4	5	8	9.00	0
2005	Tucson	P.C.	47	40	1	1	.500	20	22	44	3.38	3
2006	Tucson	P.C.	43	45 2/3	6	0	1.000	44	10	39	2.17	8
2006	Arizona	N.L.	30	16	0	1	.000	12	3	21	3.94	0
2007	Arizona	N.L.	2	0	0	0	.000	0	0	3	0.00	0
2007	Tucson c-d-e	P.C.	55	63 1/3	3	1	.750	61	16	68	2.98	3
2008	Brevard County	Fla.St.	1	1	0	0	.000	1	0	0	0.00	0
2008	Nashville f-g	P.C.	26	39	0	4	.000	31	20	42	5.08	2
2009	Durham	Int.	21	19 1/3	3	0	1.000	15	9	16	3.72	0
2009	Tampa Bay	A.L.	61	36 1/3	1	0	1.000	28	11	28	3.47	5
2010	Tampa Bay h	A.L.	*85	44 2/3	4	3	.571	40	17	41	4.23	0
Major League Totals		10 Yrs.	342	246	10	10	.500	197	115	226	4.39	5
	Division Series											
2000	New York	A.L.	1	1 1/3	0	0	.000	1	1	0	6.75	0
2010	Tampa Bay	N.L.	3	1	0	0	.000	0	0	0	0.00	0
Division Series Totals			4	2 1/3	0	0	.000	1	1	0	3.86	0
	Championship Series											
2000	New York	A.L.	1	0 1/3	0	0	.000	1	0	0	0.00	0
	World Series Record											
2001	New York	A.L.	2	3 2/3	0	0	.000	2	1	7	2.45	0

a Traded to Montreal Expos with infielder Nick Johnson and outfielder Juan Rivera for pitcher Javier Vazquez, December 4, 2003.

b Traded to Arizona Diamondbacks for pitcher John Patterson, March 25, 2004.

c Filed for free agency, October 31, 2006. Signed with Minnesota Twins organization, January 29, 2007.

d Released by Minnesota Twins, March 23, 2007. Signed with Arizona Diamondbacks organization, April 17, 2007.

e Filed for free agency, October 4, 2007. Signed with Milwaukee Brewers, November 13, 2007.

f On disabled list from March 21 to July 10, 2008.

g Filed for free agency, October 1, 2008. Signed with Tampa Bay Rays organization, December 23, 2008.

h Filed for free agency, November 1, 2010. Signed with Florida Marlins organization, December 15, 2010.

CLIPPARD, TYLER LEE

Born, Lexington, Kentucky, February 14, 1985.

Bats Right. Throws Right. Height, 6 feet, 4 inches. Weight, 200 pounds.

Year	Club	Lea	G	IP	W	L	Pct	SO	BB	H	ERA	SAVES
2003	Yankees	Gulf Coast	11	43 2/3	3	3	.500	56	5	33	2.89	0
2004	Battle Creek	Midwest	26	149	10	10	.500	145	32	153	3.44	0
2005	Tampa	Fla.St.	26	147 1/3	10	9	.526	169	34	118	3.18	0
2005	Columbus	Int.	1	1	0	0	.000	2	0	0	0.00	0
2005	Charleston	So.Atl.	1	6	0	1	.000	10	0	9	7.50	0
2006	Trenton	Eastern	28	166 1/3	12	10	.545	175	55	118	3.35	0
2007	New York	A.L.	6	27	3	1	.750	18	17	29	6.33	0
2007	Scranton/WB	Int.	14	69 1/3	4	4	.500	55	35	82	4.15	0
2007	Trenton a	Eastern	6	26 2/3	2	1	.667	28	12	22	5.40	0
2008	Washington	N.L.	2	10 1/3	1	1	.500	8	7	12	4.35	0
2008	Columbus	Int.	27	143	6	13	.316	125	66	129	4.66	0
2009	Syracuse	Int.	24	39	4	1	.800	42	15	20	0.92	1
2009	Washington	N.L.	41	60 1/3	4	2	.667	67	32	36	2.69	0
2010	Washington	N.L.	78	91	11	8	.579	112	41	69	3.07	1
Major League Totals		4 Yrs.	127	188 2/3	19	12	.613	205	97	146	3.48	1

a Traded to Washington Nationals for pitcher Jonathan Albaladejo, December 5, 2007.

COFFEY, JUSTIN TODD (TODD)

Born, Shelby, North Carolina, September 9, 1980.
Bats Right. Throws Right. Height, 6 feet, 5 inches. Weight, 240 pounds.

Year	Club	Lea	G	IP	W	L	Pct	SO	BB	H	ERA	SAVES
1998	Billings	Pioneer	3	12	0	0	.000	8	1	13	3.00	0
1999	Reds	Gulf Coast	5	16	1	1	.500	14	14	9	3.38	0
2000	a			INJURED—Did Not Play								
2001	Reds	Gulf Coast	3	12 2/3	0	1	.000	15	5	11	4.26	0
2001	Billings	Pioneer	14	33 1/3	2	2	.500	33	15	34	3.51	1
2002	Dayton	Midwest	38	80 1/3	6	4	.600	62	25	78	3.59	2
2003	Potomac	Carolina	11	23	0	2	.000	21	3	16	1.96	2
2003	Dayton	Midwest	39	56	3	3	.500	53	14	61	2.25	9
2004	Louisville	Int.	15	13 2/3	1	0	1.000	11	2	15	5.27	4
2004	Chattanooga	Southern	40	45 1/3	4	1	.800	53	4	36	2.38	20
2005	Louisville	Int.	8	8 2/3	0	0	.000	5	2	8	5.19	3
2005	Cincinnati	N.L.	57	58	4	1	.800	26	11	84	4.50	1
2006	Cincinnati	N.L.	81	78	6	7	.462	60	27	85	3.58	8
2007	Louisville	Int.	19	27	2	0	1.000	25	5	17	1.33	1
2007	Cincinnati	N.L.	58	51	2	1	.667	43	19	70	5.82	0
2008	Louisville	Int.	34	39 1/3	3	3	.500	43	15	49	4.35	2
2008	Cincinnati-Milwaukee b	N.L.	26	26 2/3	1	0	1.000	15	8	31	4.39	0
2009	Milwaukee	N.L.	78	83 2/3	4	4	.500	65	21	76	2.90	2
2010	Nashville	P.C.	1	1	0	0	.000	1	0	0	0.00	0
2010	Milwaukee c-d	N.L.	69	62 1/3	2	4	.333	56	23	65	4.76	0
Major League Totals		6 Yrs.	369	359 2/3	19	17	.528	265	109	411	4.15	11

a On minor league disabled list, June 19 to September 27, 2000.
b Claimed on waivers by Milwaukee Brewers, September 10, 2008.
c On disabled list from May 30 to June 20, 2010.
d Not offered contract, December 2, 2010.

COKE, PHILLIP DOUGLAS (PHIL)

Born, Sonora, California, July 19, 1982.
Bats Left. Throws Left. Height, 6 feet, 1 inch. Weight, 210 pounds.

Year	Club	Lea	G	IP	W	L	Pct	SO	BB	H	ERA	SAVES
2003	Yankees	Gulf Coast	10	12	0	0	.000	5	3	13	3.75	0
2004	Yankees	Gulf Coast	7	11 1/3	0	1	.000	13	3	18	3.97	0
2004	Staten Island	N.Y.-Penn.	3	8	0	0	.000	7	3	9	6.75	0
2005	Charleston	So.Atl.	24	103	8	11	.421	68	34	122	5.42	0
2006	Tampa	Fla.St.	22	110	5	7	.417	88	35	101	3.60	0
2006	Charleston	So.Atl.	5	17	0	1	.000	19	4	10	0.53	1
2007	Tampa	Fla.St.	17	99	7	3	.700	76	37	93	3.09	0
2008	Trenton	Eastern	23	118 1/3	9	4	.692	115	39	105	2.51	0
2008	Scranton-WB	Int.	14	17 1/3	2	2	.500	22	5	19	4.67	0
2008	New York	A.L.	12	14 2/3	1	0	1.000	14	2	8	0.61	0
2009	New York a	A.L.	72	60	4	3	.571	49	20	44	4.50	2
2010	Detroit	A.L.	74	64 2/3	7	5	.583	53	26	67	3.76	2
Major League Totals		3 Yrs.	158	139 1/3	12	8	.600	116	48	119	3.75	4
	Division Series											
2009	New York	A.L.	2	0 2/3	0	0	.000	1	0	0	0.00	0
	Championship Series											
2009	New York	A.L.	2	0 2/3	0	0	.000	1	1	1	0.00	0
	World Series Record											
2009	New York	A.L.	2	1 1/3	0	0	.000	1	0	3	13.50	0

a Traded to Detroit Tigers with outfielder Austin Jackson and pitcher Ian Kennedy for outfielder Curtis Granderson, December 9, 2009.

COLEMAN, JOSEPH CASEY (CASEY)

Born, Fort Myers, Florida, July 3, 1987.
Bats Left. Throws Right. Height, 6 feet. Weight, 180 pounds.

Year	Club	Lea	G	IP	W	L	Pct	SO	BB	H	ERA	SAVES
2008	Daytona	Fla.St.	1	5	1	0	1.000	2	2	4	0.00	0
2008	Peoria	Midwest	5	23 1/3	2	2	.500	18	4	25	2.70	0
2008	Boise	Northwest	7	26 2/3	1	1	.500	24	7	27	4.05	0
2009	Tennessee	Southern	27	149	14	6	.700	84	58	142	3.68	0
2010	Iowa	P.C.	20	117 1/3	10	7	.588	59	35	106	4.07	0
2010	Chicago	N.L.	12	57	4	2	.667	27	25	56	4.11	0

CONTRERAS, JOSE ARIEL

Born, Las Martinas, Cuba, December 6, 1971.
Bats Right. Throws Right. Height, 6 feet, 4 inches. Weight, 245 pounds.

Year	Club	Lea	G	IP	W	L	Pct	SO	BB	H	ERA	SAVES
2003	Staten Island	N.Y.-Penn.	1	7	0	0	.000	15	0	2	0.00	0
2003	Tampa	Fla.St.	1	4	0	0	.000	5	3	4	4.50	0
2003	Trenton	Eastern	1	1 2/3	0	0	.000	3	2	1	0.00	0
2003	Columbus	Int.	3	15	2	0	1.000	18	2	10	1.20	0
2003	New York a-b-c	A.L.	18	71	7	2	.778	72	30	52	3.30	0
2004	New York-Chicago d	A.L.	31	170 1/3	13	9	.591	150	84	166	5.50	0
2005	Chicago	A.L.	32	204 2/3	15	7	.682	154	75	177	3.61	0
2006	Chicago e	A.L.	30	196	13	9	.591	134	55	194	4.27	0
2007	Chicago	A.L.	32	189	10	17	.370	113	62	232	5.57	0
2008	Charlotte	Int.	1	5	0	0	.000	4	3	4	5.40	0
2008	Chicago f	A.L.	20	121	7	6	.538	70	35	130	4.54	0
2009	Charlotte	Int.	5	33 1/3	3	1	.750	27	16	19	2.70	0
2009	Chicago	A.L.	21	114 2/3	5	13	.278	89	45	121	5.42	0
2009	Colorado g-h	N.L.	7	17	1	0	1.000	17	8	20	1.59	0
2010	Philadelphia i	N.L.	67	56 2/3	6	4	.600	57	16	53	3.34	4
Major League Totals		8 Yrs.	258	1140 1/3	77	67	.535	856	410	1145	4.55	4
	Division Series											
2005	Chicago	A.L.	1	7 2/3	1	0	1.000	6	0	8	2.35	0
2009	Colorado	N.L.	2	2	0	0	.000	3	2	3	4.50	0
2010	Philadelphia	N.L.	1	1	1	0	1.000	1	0	0	0.00	0
Division Series Totals			4	10 2/3	2	0	1.000	10	2	11	2.53	0
	Championship Series											
2003	New York	A.L.	4	4 2/3	0	1	.000	7	2	6	5.79	0
2005	Chicago	A.L.	2	17 1/3	1	1	.500	6	2	12	3.12	0
2010	Philadelphia	N.L.	3	3	0	0	.000	3	0	1	0.00	0
Championship Series Totals			9	25	1	2	.333	16	4	19	3.24	0
	World Series Record											
2003	New York	A.L.	4	6 1/3	0	1	.000	10	5	5	5.68	0
2005	Chicago	A.L.	1	7	1	0	1.000	2	0	6	3.86	0
World Series Totals			5	13 1/3	1	1	.500	12	5	11	4.72	0

a Played in Cuba 1996 through 2002.
b Signed as free agent by New York Yankees, February 6, 2003.
c On disabled list from June 7 to August 24, 2003.
d Traded to Chicago White Sox for pitcher Esteban Loaiza, July 31, 2004.
e On disabled list from May 5 to May 21, 2006.
f On disabled list from July 18 to August 9 and August 10 to October 17, 2008.
g Traded to Colorado Rockies with cash for pitcher Brandon Hynick, August 31, 2009.
h Filed for free agency, November 9, 2009. Signed with Philadelphia Phillies, January 28, 2010.
i Filed for free agency, November 1, 2010, re-signed with Philadelphia Phillies, November 16, 2010.

COOK, AARON LANE

Born, Fort Campbell, Kentucky, February 8, 1979.
Bats Right. Throws Right. Height, 6 feet, 3 inches. Weight, 215 pounds.

Year	Club	Lea	G	IP	W	L	Pct	SO	BB	H	ERA	SAVES
1997	Rockies	Arizona	9	46	1	3	.250	35	17	48	3.13	0
1998	Portland	Northwest	15	79 1/3	5	8	.385	38	39	87	4.88	0
1999	Asheville	So.Atl.	25	121 2/3	4	12	.250	73	42	157	6.44	0
2000	Salem	Carolina	7	43	1	6	.143	37	12	52	5.44	0
2000	Asheville	So.Atl.	21	142 2/3	10	7	.588	118	23	130	2.96	0
2001	Salem	Carolina	27	155	11	11	.500	122	38	157	3.08	0
2002	Carolina	Southern	14	95	7	2	.778	58	19	73	1.42	0
2002	Colorado Springs	P.C.	10	64 1/3	4	4	.500	32	18	67	3.78	0
2002	Colorado	N.L.	9	35 2/3	2	1	.667	14	13	41	4.54	0
2003	Colorado Springs	P.C.	2	16	1	1	.500	12	4	10	2.25	0
2003	Colorado	N.L.	43	124	4	6	.400	43	57	160	6.02	0
2004	Colorado Springs	P.C.	7	46	3	1	.750	25	8	34	2.74	0
2004	Colorado a	N.L.	16	96 2/3	6	4	.600	40	39	112	4.28	0
2005	Tri-City	Northwest	2	7	0	0	.000	0	0	1	0.00	0
2005	Modesto	California	1	5	1	0	1.000	5	0	5	1.80	0
2005	Tulsa	Texas	1	3 2/3	0	1	.000	1	1	10	17.18	0
2005	Colorado Springs	P.C.	3	16 1/3	1	0	1.000	11	7	18	5.51	0
2005	Colorado b	N.L.	13	83 1/3	7	2	.778	24	16	101	3.67	0
2006	Colorado	N.L.	32	212 2/3	9	15	.375	92	55	242	4.23	0
2007	Colorado Springs	P.C.	1	1	0	1	.000	0	1	4	27.00	0
2007	Colorado c	N.L.	25	166	8	7	.533	61	44	178	4.12	0

Year	Club	Lea	G	IP	W	L	Pct	SO	BB	H	ERA	SAVES
2008	Colorado	N.L.	32	211 1/3	16	9	.640	96	48	*236	3.96	0
2009	Colorado d	N.L.	27	158	11	6	.647	78	47	175	4.16	0
2010	Tulsa	Texas	2	10 2/3	1	1	.500	10	3	8	2.53	0
2010	Colorado e	N.L.	23	127 2/3	6	8	.429	62	52	147	5.08	0
Major League Totals		9 Yrs.	220	1215 1/3	69	58	.543	510	371	1392	4.41	0
	Division Series											
2009	Colorado	N.L.	1	5	1	0	1.000	4	2	7	5.40	0
	World Series Record											
2007	Colorado	N.L.	1	6	0	1	.000	2	0	6	4.50	0

a On disabled list from August 8 to November 3, 2004.
b On disabled list from March 25 to July 30, 2005.
c On disabled list from August 16 to October 10, 2007.
d On disabled list from August 22 to September 25, 2009.
e On disabled list from August 4 to September 3 and September 9 to October 4, 2010.

CORDERO, FRANCISCO JAVIER

Born, Santo Domingo, Dominican Republic, May 11, 1975.
Bats Right. Throws Right. Height, 6 feet, 2 inches. Weight, 235 pounds.

Year	Club	Lea	G	IP	W	L	Pct	SO	BB	H	ERA	SAVES
1994	Detroit	Dominican	12	60	4	3	.571	36	27	65	3.90	0
1995	Fayettevlle	So.Atl.	4	20	0	3	.000	19	12	26	6.30	0
1995	Jamestown	N.Y.-Penn.	15	88	4	7	.364	54	37	96	5.22	0
1996	Fayettevlle	So.Atl.	2	7	0	0	.000	7	6	2	2.57	0
1996	Jamestown a	N.Y.-Penn.	2	11	0	0	.000	10	2	5	0.82	0
1997	W Michigan	Midwest	50	54 1/3	6	1	.857	67	15	36	0.99	35
1998	Jacksnville	Southern	17	16 2/3	1	1	.500	18	9	19	4.86	8
1998	Lakeland b	Fla.St.	1	0	0	0	.000	0	0	1	0.00	0
1999	Jacksonville	Southern	47	52 1/3	4	1	.800	58	22	35	1.38	27
1999	Detroit c	A.L.	20	19	2	2	.500	19	18	19	3.32	0
2000	Texas	A.L.	56	77 1/3	1	2	.333	49	48	87	5.35	0
2000	Oklahoma	P.C.	3	4 1/3	0	0	.000	5	3	7	4.15	1
2001	Oklahoma	P.C.	12	15 1/3	0	1	.000	20	3	8	0.59	6
2001	Texas d	A.L.	3	2 1/3	0	1	.000	1	2	3	3.86	0
2002	Oklahoma	P.C.	11	12 1/3	0	2	.000	21	7	15	5.84	2
2002	Texas e	A.L.	39	45 1/3	2	0	1.000	41	13	33	1.79	10
2003	Texas	A.L.	73	82 2/3	5	8	.385	90	38	70	2.94	15
2004	Texas	A.L.	67	71 2/3	3	4	.429	79	32	60	2.13	49
2005	Texas	A.L.	69	69	3	1	.750	79	30	61	3.39	37
2006	Texas	A.L.	49	48 2/3	7	4	.636	54	16	49	4.81	6
2006	Milwaukee f	N.L.	28	26 2/3	3	1	.750	30	16	20	1.69	16
2007	Milwaukee g	N.L.	66	63 1/3	0	4	.000	86	18	52	2.98	44
2008	Cincinnati	N.L.	72	70 1/3	5	4	.556	78	38	61	3.33	34
2009	Cincinnati	N.L.	68	66 2/3	2	6	.250	58	30	58	2.16	39
2010	Cincinnati	N.L.	75	72 2/3	6	5	.545	59	36	68	3.84	40
Major League Totals		12 Yrs.	685	715 2/3	39	42	.481	723	335	641	3.24	290

a On disabled list from June 28 to September 30, 1996.
b On disabled list from May 22 to June 18 and June 26 to September 30, 1998.
c Traded to Texas Rangers with pitcher Justin Thompson, pitcher Alan Webb, outfielder Gabe Kapler, catcher Bill Haselman and infielder Frank Catalanotto for outfielder Juan Gonzalez, pitcher Danny Patterson and catcher Gregg Zaun, November 2, 1999.
d On disabled list from March 23 to June 22 and June 26 to October 11, 2001.
e On disabled list from June 25 to July 27, 2002.
f Traded to Milwaukee Brewers with outfielder Kevin Mench, outfielder Laynce Nix and pitcher Julian Cordero for outfielder Carlos Lee and outfielder Nelson Cruz, July 28, 2006.
g Filed for free agency, October 29, 2007. Signed with Cincinnati Reds, November 28, 2007.

CORMIER, LANCE ROBERT

Born, Lafayette, Louisiana, August 19, 1980.
Bats Right. Throws Right. Height, 6 feet, 1 inch. Weight, 200 pounds.

Year	Club	Lea	G	IP	W	L	Pct	SO	BB	H	ERA	SAVES
2002	South Bend	Midwest	11	27 2/3	3	0	1.000	17	2	29	2.93	1
2002	Yakima	Northwest	1	1	0	0	.000	3	0	4	27.00	0
2003	Lancaster	Calif.	15	94 1/3	6	5	.545	59	16	102	3.82	0
2003	Tucson	P.C.	5	27 2/3	1	1	.500	11	5	26	2.60	0
2003	El Paso	Texas	9	41 1/3	2	3	.400	26	22	59	6.10	0
2004	El Paso	Texas	10	63	2	3	.400	58	17	66	2.29	0
2004	Tucson	P.C.	8	50 1/3	3	3	.500	37	17	50	2.68	0
2004	Arizona	N.L.	17	45 1/3	1	4	.200	24	25	62	8.14	0

Year	Club	Lea	G	IP	W	L	Pct	SO	BB	H	ERA	SAVES
2005	Tucson	P.C.	1	$3\frac{2}{3}$	0	1	.000	5	5	6	14.73	0
2005	Arizona a	N.L.	67	$79\frac{1}{3}$	7	3	.700	63	43	86	5.11	0
2006	Rome	So.Atl.	1	1	0	0	.000	2	0	0	0.00	0
2006	Richmond	Int.	9	$54\frac{2}{3}$	4	3	.571	27	14	65	3.95	0
2006	Atlanta b	N.L.	29	$73\frac{2}{3}$	4	5	.444	43	39	90	4.89	0
2007	Rome	So.Atl.	1	2	0	0	.000	4	0	5	4.50	0
2007	Mississippi	Southern	2	8	1	1	.500	6	0	8	4.50	0
2007	Richmond	Int.	10	52	4	2	.667	31	15	56	3.46	0
2007	Atlanta c	N.L.	10	$45\frac{2}{3}$	2	6	.250	27	22	56	7.09	0
2008	Norfolk	Int.	9	$18\frac{2}{3}$	1	1	.500	12	5	12	0.96	0
2008	Baltimore d-e	A.L.	45	$71\frac{2}{3}$	3	3	.500	46	34	78	4.02	1
2009	Tampa Bay	A.L.	53	$77\frac{1}{3}$	3	3	.500	36	25	75	3.26	2
2010	Tampa Bay f	A.L.	60	62	4	3	.571	30	34	68	3.92	0
Major League Totals		7 Yrs.	281	455	24	27	.471	269	222	515	4.93	3

a Traded to Atlanta Braves with pitcher Oscar Villarreal for catcher Johnny Estrada, December 7, 2005.
b On disabled list from May 3 to May 18, 2006.
c On disabled list from March 31 to June 3 and June 9 to June 30, 2007.
d Released by Atlanta Braves, December 7, 2007. Signed with Baltimore Orioles organization, January 22, 2008.
e Not offered contract, December 13, 2008. Signed with Tampa Bay Rays, January 16, 2009.
f Not offered contract, December 2, 2010.

CORPAS, MANUEL

Born, Panama City, Panama, December 3, 1982.
Bats Right. Throws Right. Height, 6 feet, 3 inches. Weight, 170 pounds.

Year	Club	Lea	G	IP	W	L	Pct	SO	BB	H	ERA	SAVES
2002	Casper	Pioneer	29	33	2	4	.333	42	18	37	5.73	2
2003	Tri-Cities	Northwest	15	84	5	6	.455	47	22	98	5.79	0
2004	Asheville	So.Atl.	43	$44\frac{1}{3}$	2	2	.500	52	13	48	3.05	3
2005	Modesto	Calif.	47	69	3	2	.600	52	14	83	3.78	2
2006	Tulsa	Texas	34	$36\frac{2}{3}$	2	1	.667	35	4	22	0.98	19
2006	Colorado Springs	P.C.	8	$8\frac{2}{3}$	0	0	.000	7	2	5	1.04	0
2006	Colorado	N.L.	35	$32\frac{1}{3}$	1	2	.333	27	8	36	3.62	0
2007	Colorado	N.L.	78	78	4	2	.667	58	20	63	2.08	19
2008	Colorado	N.L.	76	$79\frac{2}{3}$	3	4	.429	50	23	93	4.52	4
2009	Colorado Springs	P.C.	3	$2\frac{2}{3}$	0	0	.000	3	1	2	0.00	0
2009	Colorado a	N.L.	35	$33\frac{2}{3}$	1	3	.250	24	7	44	5.88	1
2010	Colorado b-c	N.L.	56	$62\frac{1}{3}$	3	5	.375	47	22	66	4.62	10
Major League Totals		5 Yrs.	280	286	12	16	.429	206	80	302	3.93	34
	Division Series											
2007	Colorado	N.L.	3	$3\frac{1}{3}$	0	0	.000	3	0	2	0.00	3
	Championship Series											
2007	Colorado	N.L.	4	$5\frac{1}{3}$	1	0	1.000	3	0	3	1.69	2
	World Series Record											
2007	Colorado	N.L.	2	$1\frac{2}{3}$	0	0	.000	1	0	1	0.00	0

a On disabled list from June 19 to July 16 and July 21 to November 6, 2009.
b On disabled list from August 26 to November 2, 2010.
c Released by Colorado Rockies, November 16, 2010.

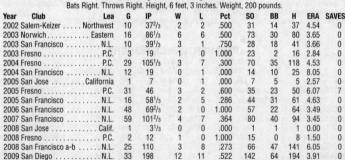

CORREIA, KEVIN JOHN

Born, San Diego, California, August 24, 1980.
Bats Right. Throws Right. Height, 6 feet, 3 inches. Weight, 200 pounds.

Year	Club	Lea	G	IP	W	L	Pct	SO	BB	H	ERA	SAVES
2002	Salem-Keizer	Northwest	10	$37\frac{2}{3}$	2	2	.500	31	14	37	4.54	0
2003	Norwich	Eastern	16	$86\frac{1}{3}$	6	6	.500	73	30	80	3.65	0
2003	San Francisco	N.L.	10	$39\frac{1}{3}$	3	1	.750	28	18	41	3.66	0
2003	Fresno	P.C.	3	19	1	0	1.000	23	2	16	2.84	0
2004	Fresno	P.C.	29	$105\frac{1}{3}$	3	7	.300	70	35	118	4.53	0
2004	San Francisco	N.L.	12	19	0	1	.000	14	10	25	8.05	0
2005	San Jose	California	1	7	0	1	.000	7	5	5	2.57	0
2005	Fresno	P.C.	31	46	3	2	.600	35	23	50	6.07	7
2005	San Francisco	N.L.	16	$58\frac{1}{3}$	2	5	.286	44	31	61	4.63	0
2006	San Francisco	N.L.	48	$69\frac{2}{3}$	2	0	1.000	57	22	64	3.49	0
2007	San Francisco	N.L.	59	$101\frac{2}{3}$	4	7	.364	80	40	94	3.45	0
2008	San Jose	Calif.	1	$3\frac{1}{3}$	0	0	.000	1	1	1	0.00	0
2008	Fresno	P.C.	2	12	1	0	1.000	15	0	8	1.50	0
2008	San Francisco a-b	N.L.	25	110	3	8	.273	66	47	141	6.05	0
2009	San Diego	N.L.	33	198	12	11	.522	142	64	194	3.91	0

Year	Club	Lea	G	IP	W	L	Pct	SO	BB	H	ERA	SAVES
2010	San Diego c	N.L.	28	145	10	10	.500	115	64	152	5.40	0
Major League Totals		8 Yrs.	231	741	36	43	.456	546	296	772	4.57	0

a On disabled list from April 27 to June 15, 2008.
b Filed for free agency, October 14, 2008. Signed with San Diego Padres organization, December 24, 2008.
c Filed for free agency, November 1, 2010. Signed with Pittsburgh Pirates, December 7, 2010.

CRAIN, JESSE ALAN

Born, Toronto, Ontario, Canada, July 5, 1981.
Bats Right. Throws Right. Height, 6 feet, 1 inch. Weight, 205 pounds.

Year	Club	Lea	G	IP	W	L	Pct	SO	BB	H	ERA	SAVES
2002	Elizabethton	Appal.	9	15 2/3	2	1	.667	18	7	4	0.57	2
2002	Quad Cities	Midwest	9	12	1	1	.500	11	4	6	1.50	1
2003	New Britain	Eastern	22	39	1	1	.500	56	10	13	0.69	9
2003	Fort Myers	Fla.St.	10	19	2	1	.667	25	5	10	2.84	0
2003	Rochester	Int.	23	26	3	1	.750	33	10	24	3.12	10
2004	Rochester	Int.	41	50 2/3	3	2	.600	64	17	38	2.49	19
2004	Minnesota	A.L.	22	27	3	0	1.000	14	12	17	2.00	0
2005	Minnesota	A.L.	75	79 2/3	12	5	.706	25	29	61	2.71	1
2006	Minnesota	A.L.	68	76 2/3	4	5	.444	60	18	79	3.52	1
2007	Minnesota a	A.L.	18	16 1/3	1	2	.333	10	4	19	5.51	0
2008	Minnesota	A.L.	66	62 2/3	5	4	.556	50	24	62	3.59	0
2009	Rochester	Int.	12	17 2/3	1	0	1.000	22	8	13	2.55	1
2009	Minnesota b	A.L.	56	51 2/3	7	4	.636	43	27	48	4.70	0
2010	Minnesota c	A.L.	71	68	1	1	.500	62	27	53	3.04	1
Major League Totals		7 Yrs.	376	382	33	21	.611	264	141	339	3.42	3
	Division Series											
2004	Minnesota	A.L.	1	0 1/3	0	0	.000	0	0	1	0.00	0
2006	Minnesota	A.L.	2	1	0	0	.000	1	1	3	9.00	0
2010	Minnesota	A.L.	1	0 1/3	0	1	.000	0	0	3	54.00	0
Division Series Totals			4	1 2/3	0	1	.000	1	1	7	16.20	0

a On disabled list from May 16 to October 10, 2007.
b On disabled list from April 18 to May 4, 2009.
c Filed for free agency, November 1, 2010. Signed with Chicago White Sox, December 20, 2010.

CUETO (ORTIZ), JOHNNY

Born, San Pedro de Macoris, Dominican Republic, February 15, 1985.
Bats Right. Throws Right. Height, 5 feet, 10 inches. Weight, 185 pounds.

Year	Club	Lea	G	IP	W	L	Pct	SO	BB	H	ERA	SAVES
2005	Sarasota	Fla.St.	2	6	0	1	.000	6	2	5	3.00	0
2005	Reds	Gulf Coast	13	43	2	2	.500	38	8	49	5.02	1
2006	Sarasota	Fla.St.	12	61 2/3	7	2	.778	61	23	48	3.50	0
2006	Dayton	Midwest	14	76 1/3	8	1	.889	82	15	52	2.59	0
2007	Sarasota	Fla.St.	14	78 1/3	4	5	.444	72	21	72	3.33	0
2007	Louisville	Int.	4	22	2	1	.667	21	2	22	2.05	0
2007	Chattanooga	Southern	10	61	6	3	.667	77	11	52	3.10	0
2008	Cincinnati	N.L.	31	174	9	14	.391	158	68	178	4.81	0
2009	Cincinnati a	N.L.	30	171 1/3	11	11	.500	132	61	172	4.41	0
2010	Cincinnati	N.L.	31	185 2/3	12	7	.632	138	56	181	3.64	0
Major League Totals		3 Yrs.	92	531	32	32	.500	428	185	531	4.27	0
	Division Series											
2010	Cincinnati	N.L.	1	5	0	1	.000	2	1	5	1.80	0

a On disabled list from August 16 to August 31, 2009.

DANKS, JOHN WILLIAM

Born, Austin, Texas, April 15, 1985.
Bats Left. Throws Left. Height, 6 feet, 1 inch. Weight, 200 pounds.

Year	Club	Lea	G	IP	W	L	Pct	SO	BB	H	ERA	SAVES
2003	Rangers	Arizona	5	13	1	0	1.000	22	4	6	0.69	0
2003	Spokane	Northwest	5	12 2/3	0	2	.000	13	7	12	8.53	0
2004	Stockton	Calif.	13	55	1	4	.200	48	26	62	5.24	0
2004	Clinton	Midwest	14	49 2/3	3	2	.600	64	14	38	2.17	0
2005	Bakersfield	Calif.	10	57 2/3	3	3	.500	53	16	50	2.50	0
2005	Frisco	Texas	18	98 1/3	4	10	.286	85	34	117	5.49	0
2006	Oklahoma	P.C.	14	70 2/3	4	5	.444	72	34	67	4.33	0
2006	Frisco a	Texas	13	69 1/3	5	4	.556	82	22	74	4.15	0

Year	Club	Lea	G	IP	W	L	Pct	SO	BB	H	ERA	SAVES
2007	Chicago	A.L.	26	139	6	13	.316	109	54	160	5.50	0
2008	Chicago	A.L.	33	195	12	9	.571	159	57	182	3.32	0
2009	Chicago	A.L.	32	200 1/3	13	11	.542	149	73	184	3.77	0
2010	Chicago	A.L.	32	213	15	11	.577	162	70	189	3.72	0
Major League Totals		4 Yrs.	123	747 1/3	46	44	.511	579	254	715	3.96	0
	Division Series											
2008	Chicago	A.L.	1	6 2/3	1	0	1.000	7	3	7	4.05	0

a Traded to Chicago White Sox by Texas Rangers with pitcher Nick Masset and pitcher Jacob Rasner for pitcher Brandon McCarthy and outfielder David Paisano, December 23, 2006.

DAVIES, HIRAM KYLE (KYLE)

Born, Decatur, Georgia, September 9, 1983.
Bats Right. Throws Right. Height, 6 feet, 2 inches. Weight, 205 pounds.

Year	Club	Lea	G	IP	W	L	Pct	SO	BB	H	ERA	SAVES
2001	Braves	Gulf Coast	12	56	4	2	.667	53	8	47	2.25	0
2001	Macon	So.Atl.	1	5 2/3	1	0	1.000	7	1	2	0.00	0
2002	Danville	Appal.	14	69 1/3	5	3	.625	62	23	73	3.50	0
2002	Macon	So.Atl.	2	6	0	1	.000	4	4	6	6.00	0
2003	Rome	So.Atl.	27	146 1/3	8	8	.500	148	53	128	2.89	0
2004	Myrtle Beach	Carolina	14	75 1/3	9	2	.818	95	32	55	2.63	0
2004	Richmond	Int.	1	5	0	1	.000	5	3	5	9.00	0
2004	Greenville	Southern	11	62	4	0	1.000	73	22	40	2.32	0
2005	Richmond	Int.	13	73 1/3	5	2	.714	62	34	66	3.44	0
2005	Atlanta	N.L.	21	87 2/3	7	6	.538	62	49	98	4.93	0
2006	Mississippi	Southern	4	14	1	1	.500	9	5	11	4.50	0
2006	Richmond	Int.	2	15	2	0	1.000	8	3	7	0.60	0
2006	Atlanta a	N.L.	14	63 1/3	3	7	.300	51	33	90	8.38	0
2007	Richmond	Int.	2	10	0	1	.000	12	6	11	4.50	0
2007	Atlanta	N.L.	17	86	4	8	.333	59	44	92	5.76	0
2007	Kansas City b	A.L.	11	50	3	7	.300	40	26	63	6.66	0
2008	Omaha	P.C.	11	57 2/3	6	2	.750	38	21	47	2.03	0
2008	Kansas City	A.L.	21	113	9	7	.563	71	43	121	4.06	0
2009	Omaha	P.C.	8	46 1/3	4	2	.667	44	14	47	2.14	0
2009	Kansas City	A.L.	22	123	8	9	.471	86	66	122	5.27	0
2010	Kansas City	A.L.	32	183 2/3	8	12	.400	126	80	206	5.34	0
Major League Totals		6 Yrs.	138	706 2/3	42	56	.429	495	341	792	5.49	0

a On disabled list from May 16 to September 1, 2006.
b Traded to Kansas City Royals for pitcher Octavio Dotel, July 31, 2007.

DAVIS, WADE ALLEN

Born, Lake Wales, Florida, September 7, 1985.
Bats Right. Throws Right. Height, 6 feet, 5 inches. Weight, 220 pounds.

Year	Club	Lea	G	IP	W	L	Pct	SO	BB	H	ERA	SAVES
2004	Princeton	Appal.	13	57 2/3	3	5	.375	38	19	71	5.93	0
2005	Hudson Valley	N.Y.-Penn.	15	86	7	4	.636	97	23	75	2.72	0
2006	SW Michigan	Midwest	27	146	7	12	.368	165	64	124	3.02	0
2007	Vero Beach	Fla.St.	13	78 1/3	3	0	1.000	88	21	54	1.84	0
2007	Montgomery	Southern	14	80	7	3	.700	81	30	74	3.15	0
2008	Durham	Int.	9	53	4	2	.667	55	24	39	2.72	0
2008	Montgomery	Southern	19	107 2/3	9	6	.600	81	42	104	3.85	0
2009	Durham	Int.	28	158 2/3	10	8	.556	140	60	139	3.40	0
2009	Tampa Bay	A.L.	6	36 1/3	2	2	.500	36	13	33	3.72	0
2010	Tampa Bay a	A.L.	29	168	12	10	.545	113	62	165	4.07	0
Major League Totals		2 Yrs.	35	204 1/3	14	12	.538	149	75	198	4.01	0
	Division Series											
2010	Tampa Bay	N.L.	1	5	1	0	1.000	7	3	7	3.60	0

a On disabled list from August 6 to August 24, 2010.

DE LA ROSA, JORGE ALBERTO

Born, Monterrey, Nuevo Leon, Mexico, April 5, 1981.
Bats Left. Throws Left. Height, 6 feet, 1 inch. Weight, 210 pounds.

Year	Club	Lea	G	IP	W	L	Pct	SO	BB	H	ERA	SAVES
1998	Arizona	Dominican	13	14	1	0	1.000	21	8	8	4.50	1
1999	Diamondbacks	Arizona	8	14	0	0	.000	17	3	12	3.21	2
1999	High Desert	California	2	3	0	0	.000	3	2	1	0.00	0
1999	Missoula	Pioneer	13	14 2/3	0	1	.000	14	9	22	7.98	2

Year	Club	Lea	G	IP	W	L	Pct	SO	BB	H	ERA	SAVES
2000	Monterrey a	Mexican	37	39	3	2	.600	50	32	38	6.28	1
2001	Trenton	Eastern	29	37	1	3	.250	27	20	56	5.84	0
2001	Sarasota b	Fla.St.	12	29 2/3	0	1	.000	27	12	13	1.21	2
2002	Trenton	Eastern	4	18	1	2	.333	15	9	17	5.50	0
2002	Sarasota	Fla.St.	23	120 2/3	7	7	.500	95	52	105	3.65	0
2003	Portland	Eastern	22	99 2/3	6	3	.667	102	36	87	2.80	1
2003	Pawtucket c-d	Int.	5	24	1	2	.333	17	12	27	3.75	0
2004	Indianapolis	Int.	20	85 2/3	5	6	.455	86	36	80	4.52	0
2004	Milwaukee	N.L.	5	22 2/3	0	3	.000	5	14	29	6.35	0
2005	Milwaukee	N.L.	38	42 1/3	2	2	.500	42	38	48	4.46	0
2006	Huntsville	Southern	6	30	3	1	.750	23	3	31	2.40	0
2006	Milwaukee	N.L.	18	30 1/3	2	2	.500	31	22	32	8.60	0
2006	Kansas City e-f	A.L.	10	48 2/3	3	4	.429	36	32	49	5.18	0
2007	Wichita	Texas	3	5 2/3	0	1	.000	7	4	10	11.12	0
2007	Kansas City g	A.L.	26	130	8	12	.400	82	53	160	5.82	0
2008	Omaha	P.C.	4	22	3	0	1.000	23	7	18	1.64	0
2008	Colorado h	N.L.	28	130	10	8	.556	128	62	128	4.92	0
2009	Colorado	N.L.	33	185	16	9	.640	193	83	172	4.38	0
2010	Colorado Springs	P.C.	3	14 2/3	1	2	.333	15	4	17	5.52	0
2010	Colorado i-j	N.L.	20	121 2/3	8	7	.533	113	55	105	4.22	0
Major League Totals		7 Yrs.	178	710 2/3	49	47	.510	630	359	723	5.02	0

a Sold by Arizona Diamondbacks to Monterrey, April 2, 2000.
b Sold to Boston Red Sox, February 22, 2001.
c Traded by Boston Red Sox to Arizona Diamondbacks with pitcher Casey Fossum, pitcher Brandon Lyon and outfielder Michael Goss for pitcher Curt Schilling, November 28, 2003.
d Traded to Milwaukee Brewers with infielder Junior Spivey, infielder Craig Counsell, infielder Lyle Overbay, catcher Chad Moeller and pitcher Chris Capuano for infielder Richie Sexson, pitcher Shane Nance and player to be named later, December 1, 2003. Arizona Diamondbacks received outfielder Noochie Varner to complete trade, December 15, 2003.
e On disabled list from June 10 to July 25, 2006.
f Traded to Kansas City Royals for infielder Tony Graffanino, July 25, 2006.
g On disabled list from August 1 to September 11, 2007.
h Sent to Colorado Rockies as player to be named later for pitcher Ramon Ramirez, April 30, 2008.
i On disabled list from April 26 to July 9, 2010.
j Filed for free agency, November 1, 2010, re-signed with Colorado Rockies, December 3, 2010.

DELCARMEN, MANUEL (MANNY)

Born, Boston, Massachusetts, February 16, 1982.
Bats Right. Throws Right. Height, 6 feet, 2 inches. Weight, 205 pounds.

Year	Club	Lea	G	IP	W	L	Pct	SO	BB	H	ERA	SAVES
2001	Red Sox	Gulf Coast	11	46	4	2	.667	62	19	35	2.54	1
2002	Augusta	So.Atl.	26	136	7	8	.467	136	56	124	4.10	0
2003	Sarasota	Fla.St.	4	23	1	1	.500	16	7	16	3.13	0
2004	Sarasota	Fla.St.	19	73	3	6	.333	76	20	84	4.68	0
2005	Portland	Eastern	31	39	4	4	.500	49	20	31	3.23	3
2005	Pawtucket	Int.	15	21	3	1	.750	23	13	17	1.29	2
2005	Boston	A.L.	10	9	0	0	.000	9	7	8	3.00	0
2006	Pawtucket	Int.	10	17	0	1	.000	19	6	9	2.12	0
2006	Boston	A.L.	50	53 1/3	2	0	1.000	45	17	68	5.06	0
2007	Boston	A.L.	44	44	0	0	.000	41	17	28	2.05	1
2008	Boston	A.L.	73	74 1/3	1	2	.333	72	28	55	3.27	2
2009	Boston	A.L.	64	59 2/3	5	2	.714	44	34	64	4.53	0
2010	Portland	Eastern	1	1	0	0	.000	0	0	0	0.00	0
2010	Boston	A.L.	48	44	3	2	.600	32	28	33	4.70	0
2010	Colorado a-b-c	N.L.	9	8 1/3	0	2	.000	6	4	12	6.48	0
Major League Totals		6 Yrs.	298	292 2/3	11	8	.579	249	135	268	3.97	3
	Division Series											
2007	Boston	A.L.	1	1 1/3	0	0	.000	1	0	0	0.00	0
2008	Boston	A.L.	2	2 1/3	1	0	1.000	1	0	1	0.00	0
Division Series Totals			3	3 2/3	1	0	1.000	2	0	1	0.00	0
	Championship Series											
2007	Boston	A.L.	3	1 2/3	0	0	.000	3	2	4	16.20	0
2008	Boston	A.L.	3	2	0	0	.000	2	5	3	31.50	0
Championship Series Totals			6	3 2/3	0	0	.000	5	7	7	24.55	0
	World Series Record											
2007	Boston	A.L.	2	1 1/3	0	0	.000	1	1	3	6.75	0

a On disabled list from July 1 to July 17, 2010.
b Traded to Colorado Rockies for pitcher Chris Balcom-Miller, August 31, 2010.
c Not offered contract, December 2, 2010.

DEMPSTER, RYAN SCOTT

Born, Sechelt, British Columbia, Canada, May 3, 1977.
Bats Right. Throws Right. Height, 6 feet, 2 inches. Weight, 215 pounds.

Year	Club	Lea	G	IP	W	L	Pct	SO	BB	H	ERA	SAVES
1995	Rangers	Gulf Coast	8	34 1/3	3	1	.750	37	17	34	2.36	0
1995	Hudson Val.	N.Y.-Penn.	1	5 2/3	1	0	1.000	6	1	7	3.18	0
1996	Chston-SC	So.Atl.	23	144 1/3	7	11	.389	141	58	120	3.30	0
1996	Kane County a	Midwest	4	26 1/3	2	1	.667	16	18	18	2.73	0
1997	Brevard Cty	Fla.St.	28	165 1/3	10	9	.526	131	46	190	4.90	0
1998	Portland	Eastern	7	44 2/3	4	3	.571	33	15	34	3.22	0
1998	Florida	N.L.	14	54 2/3	1	5	.167	35	38	72	7.08	0
1998	Charlotte	Int.	5	33	3	1	.750	24	12	33	3.27	0
1999	Calgary	P.C.	5	30 2/3	1	1	.500	29	10	30	4.99	0
1999	Florida	N.L.	25	147	7	8	.467	126	93	146	4.71	0
2000	Florida	N.L.	33	226 1/3	14	10	.583	209	97	210	3.66	0
2001	Florida	N.L.	34	211 1/3	15	12	.556	171	112	218	4.94	0
2002	Florida-Cincinnati b	N.L.	33	209	10	13	.435	153	93	228	5.38	0
2003	Cincinnati	N.L.	22	115 2/3	3	7	.300	84	70	134	6.54	0
2003	Louisville c	Int.	2	13 2/3	1	1	.500	9	3	13	3.29	0
2004	Lansing	Midwest	5	18 1/3	0	0	.000	21	2	20	1.96	0
2004	Iowa	P.C.	6	21	1	1	.500	20	10	19	3.86	0
2004	Chicago d-e	N.L.	23	20 2/3	1	1	.500	18	13	16	3.92	2
2005	Chicago	N.L.	63	92	5	3	.625	89	49	83	3.13	33
2006	Chicago	N.L.	74	75	1	9	.100	67	36	77	4.80	24
2007	Iowa	P.C.	2	2	0	0	.000	4	1	1	0.00	0
2007	Chicago f	N.L.	66	66 2/3	2	7	.222	55	30	59	4.72	28
2008	Chicago g	N.L.	33	206 2/3	17	6	.739	187	76	174	2.96	0
2009	Chicago h	N.L.	31	200	11	9	.550	172	65	196	3.65	0
2010	Chicago	N.L.	34	215 1/3	15	12	.556	208	86	198	3.85	0
Major League Totals		13 Yrs.	485	1840 1/3	102	102	.500	1574	858	1811	4.37	87
	Division Series											
2007	Chicago	N.L.	1	1	0	0	.000	2	0	0	0.00	0
2008	Chicago	N.L.	1	4 2/3	0	1	.000	2	7	4	7.71	0
Division Series Totals			2	5 2/3	0	1	.000	4	7	4	6.35	0

a Traded by Texas Rangers to Florida Marlins with player to be named later for pitcher John Burkett, August 8, 1996. Florida Marlins received pitcher Rick Helling to complete trade, September 3, 1996.
b Traded to Cincinnati Reds for outfielder Juan Encarnacion, infielder Wilton Guerrero and pitcher Ryan Snare, July 11, 2002.
c On disabled list from May 23 to June 7 and July 29 to November 3, 2003.
d Waived by Cincinnati Reds, November 4, 2003. Signed with Chicago Cubs, January 21, 2004.
e On disabled list from March 26 to August 1, 2004.
f On disabled list from June 23 to July 20, 2007.
g Filed for free agency, October 30, 2008, re-signed with Chicago Cubs, November 18, 2008.
h On disabled list from July 7 to July 28, 2009.

DESSENS (JUSAINO), ELMER

Born, Hermosillo, Mexico, January 13, 1971.
Bats Right. Throws Right. Height, 6 feet. Weight, 200 pounds.

Year	Club	Lea	G	IP	W	L	Pct	SO	BB	H	ERA	SAVES
1993	Mexico City Reds	Mexican	14	31	3	1	.750	16	5	31	2.32	2
1994	Mexico City Reds	Mexican	37	127 2/3	11	4	.733	51	32	121	2.04	3
1995	Carolina	Southern	27	152	15	8	.652	68	21	170	2.49	0
1996	Calgary	P.C.	6	34 1/3	2	2	.500	15	15	40	3.15	0
1996	Mexico City Reds	Mexican	7	50	7	0	1.000	17	10	44	1.26	0
1996	Carolina	Southern	5	11 2/3	0	1	.000	7	4	15	5.40	0
1996	Pittsburgh a-b	N.L.	15	25	0	2	.000	13	4	40	8.28	0
1997	Mexico City Reds	Mexican	26	159 1/3	16	5	.762	61	51	156	3.56	0
1997	Pittsburgh	N.L.	3	3 1/3	0	0	.000	2	0	2	0.00	0
1998	Nashville	P.C.	6	30	3	1	.750	13	6	32	3.30	0
1998	Pittsburgh c	N.L.	43	74 2/3	2	6	.250	43	25	90	5.67	0
1999	Yomiuri d-e	Japan Cent.	6	16 1/3	0	1	.000	6	4	24	3.86	0
2000	Louisville	Int.	4	22 2/3	2	0	1.000	14	7	24	3.18	0
2000	Cincinnati	N.L.	40	147 1/3	11	5	.688	85	43	170	4.28	1
2001	Cincinnati	N.L.	34	205	10	14	.417	128	56	221	4.48	0
2002	Cincinnati f-g	N.L.	30	178	7	8	.467	93	49	173	3.03	0
2003	Arizona	N.L.	34	175 2/3	8	8	.500	113	57	212	5.07	0
2004	Arizona-Los Angeles h-i	N.L.	50	105	2	6	.250	73	31	123	4.46	2
2005	Las Vegas	P.C.	3	8	0	0	.000	6	2	6	3.38	0
2005	Los Angeles j-k	N.L.	28	65 2/3	1	2	.333	37	19	63	3.56	0
2006	Kansas City	A.L.	43	54	5	7	.417	36	13	63	4.50	2

Year	Club	Lea	G	IP	W	L	Pct	SO	BB	H	ERA	SAVES
2006	Las Vegas	P.C.	1	$0\frac{2}{3}$	0	1	.000	0	1	2	13.50	0
2006	Los Angeles l-m	N.L.	19	23	0	1	.000	16	9	23	4.70	0
2007	Nashville	P.C.	3	$11\frac{2}{3}$	1	0	1.000	10	0	7	1.54	0
2007	Colorado Springs	P.C.	1	3	1	0	1.000	1	1	1	0.00	0
2007	Milwaukee-Colorado n-o-p	N.L.	17	34	2	2	.500	22	12	45	7.15	0
2008	Mexico City Reds	Mexican	20	105	10	2	.833	51	17	129	4.03	0
2008	Atlanta q-r-s	N.L.	4	4	0	1	.000	2	4	10	22.50	0
2009	Buffalo	Int.	27	35	3	2	.600	28	9	26	2.31	11
2009	New York t-u	N.L.	28	$32\frac{2}{3}$	0	0	.000	14	10	24	3.31	0
2010	Buffalo	Int.	13	17	5	0	1.000	18	3	20	2.12	6
2010	New York v	N.L.	53	47	4	2	.667	16	16	41	2.30	0
Major League Totals		14 Yrs.	441	$1174\frac{1}{3}$	52	64	.448	693	348	1300	4.44	5
	Division Series											
2004	Los Angeles	N.L.	1	$1\frac{1}{3}$	0	0	.000	1	0	1	6.75	0

a Loaned by Pirates to Mexico City Reds for 1993, 1994 and 1996.
b On disabled list from July 31 to September 10, 1996.
c On disabled list from April 8 to April 24, 1998.
d Sold to Yomiuri (Japan), March 31, 1999.
e Signed by Cincinnati Reds, December 15, 1999.
f On disabled list from August 2 to August 27, 2002.
g Traded to Arizona Diamondbacks in four team deal. Arizona sent infielder Erubiel Durazo to Oakland A's, who sent pitcher Jamie Arnold to Toronto Blue Jays, who sent infielder Felipe Lopez to Cincinnati, December 15, 2002.
h Traded to Los Angeles Dodgers for outfielder Jeremy Milons, August 19, 2004.
i Filed for free agency, October 29, 2004, re-signed with Los Angeles Dodgers, December 7, 2004.
j On disabled list from April 20 to June 15, 2005.
k Filed for free agency, November 3, 2005. Signed with Kansas City Royals, December 8, 2005.
l On disabled list from August 7 to August 18, 2006.
m Traded to Los Angeles Dodgers for pitcher Odalis Perez, pitcher Blake Johnson, pitcher Julio Pimental and cash, July 25, 2006.
n Traded to Milwaukee Brewers for outfielder Brady Clark, March 26, 2007.
o On disabled list from May 19 to August 1, 2007.
p Released by Milwaukee Brewers, August 8, 2007. Signed with Colorado Rockies organization, August 10, 2007.
q Filed for free agency, October 30, 2007. Signed with Pittsburgh Pirates organization, February 8, 2008.
r Released by Pittsburgh Pirates, March 27, 2008. Signed with Mexico City Reds for 2008.
s Signed with Atlanta Braves, August 27, 2008.
t Filed for free agency, November 4, 2008. Signed with New York Mets organization, February 5, 2009.
u Filed for free agency, November 10, 2009, re-signed with New York Mets organization, December 11, 2009.
v Filed for free agency, November 1, 2010.

DETWILER, ROSS EMERY

Born, St.Louis, Missouri, March 6, 1986.
Bats Right. Throws Right. Height, 6 feet, 5 inches. Weight, 185 pounds.

Year	Club	Lea	G	IP	W	L	Pct	SO	BB	H	ERA	SAVES
2007	Nationals	Gulf Coast	4	12	0	0	.000	15	3	11	2.25	0
2007	Potomac	Carolina	5	$21\frac{1}{3}$	2	2	.500	13	9	27	4.22	0
2007	Washington	N.L.	1	1	0	0	.000	1	0	0	0.00	0
2008	Potomac	Carolina	26	124	8	8	.500	114	57	140	4.86	0
2009	Harrisburg	Eastern	6	$27\frac{1}{3}$	0	3	.000	28	10	28	2.96	0
2009	Syracuse	Int.	10	$49\frac{1}{3}$	4	2	.667	42	20	56	3.10	0
2009	Washington	N.L.	15	$75\frac{2}{3}$	1	6	.143	43	33	87	5.00	0
2010	Potomac	Carolina	2	6	0	0	.000	6	1	6	1.50	0
2010	Harrisburg	Eastern	7	$32\frac{2}{3}$	2	2	.500	31	7	38	2.48	0
2010	Syracuse	Int.	1	5	1	0	1.000	2	1	5	1.80	0
2010	Washington a	N.L.	8	$29\frac{2}{3}$	1	3	.250	17	14	34	4.25	0
Major League Totals		3 Yrs.	24	$106\frac{1}{3}$	2	9	.182	61	47	121	4.74	0

a On disabled list from April 4 to June 21 and August 6 to September 7, 2010.

DICKEY, ROBERT ALAN (R.A.)

Born, Nashville, Tennessee, October 29, 1974.
Bats Right. Throws Right. Height, 6 feet, 3 inches. Weight, 220 pounds.

Year	Club	Lea	G	IP	W	L	Pct	SO	BB	H	ERA	SAVES
1997	Charlotte	Fla.St.	8	35	1	4	.200	32	12	51	6.94	0
1998	Charlotte	Fla.St.	57	60	1	5	.167	53	22	58	3.30	38
1999	Oklahoma	P.C.	6	$22\frac{2}{3}$	2	2	.500	17	7	23	4.37	0
1999	Tulsa	Texas	35	95	6	7	.462	59	40	105	4.55	10
2000	Oklahoma	P.C.	30	$158\frac{1}{3}$	8	9	.471	85	65	167	4.49	1
2001	Oklahoma	P.C.	24	163	11	7	.611	120	45	164	3.75	0

Year	Club	Lea	G	IP	W	L	Pct	SO	BB	H	ERA	SAVES
2001	Texas	A.L.	4	12	0	1	.000	4	7	13	6.75	0
2002	Oklahoma	P.C.	37	154	8	7	.533	109	47	176	4.09	0
2003	Oklahoma	P.C.	3	15	1	1	.500	4	3	14	1.20	0
2003	Texas	A.L.	38	116⅔	9	8	.529	94	38	135	5.09	1
2004	Frisco	Texas	4	13⅔	1	1	.500	9	1	16	1.98	0
2004	Texas a	A.L.	25	104⅓	6	7	.462	57	33	136	5.61	1
2005	Oklahoma	P.C.	19	121⅔	10	6	.625	81	39	152	5.99	0
2005	Texas b	A.L.	9	29⅔	1	2	.333	15	17	29	6.67	0
2006	Texas	A.L.	1	3⅓	0	1	.000	1	1	8	18.90	0
2006	Oklahoma	P.C.	22	131⅔	9	8	.529	61	46	134	4.92	1
2007	Nashville c-d-e	P.C.	31	169⅓	13	6	.684	119	60	159	3.72	0
2008	Tacoma	P.C.	7	49⅔	2	5	.286	30	8	58	3.44	0
2008	Seattle f-g	A.L.	32	112⅓	5	8	.385	58	51	124	5.21	0
2009	Rochester	Int.	5	33⅓	2	1	.667	18	9	39	5.13	0
2009	Minnesota h	A.L.	35	64⅓	1	1	.500	42	30	74	4.62	0
2010	Buffalo	Int.	8	60⅔	4	2	.667	37	8	55	2.23	0
2010	New York	N.L.	27	174⅓	11	9	.550	104	42	165	2.84	0
Major League Totals		8 Yrs.	171	617	33	37	.471	375	219	684	4.70	2

a On disabled list from June 25 to July 19 and July 30 to August 23, 2004.
b On disabled list from April 13 to May 25, 2005.
c Filed for free agency, October 11, 2006. Signed with Milwaukee Brewers organization, January 10, 2007.
d Filed for free agency, October 29, 2007. Signed with Minnesota Twins organization, November 29, 2007.
e Selected by Seattle Mariners in Rule V draft, December 6, 2007.
f Seattle retained rights to Dickey for catcher Jair Fernandez, March 29, 2008.
g Filed for free agency, December 9, 2008. Signed with Minnesota Twins organization, December 26, 2008.
h Filed for free agency, October 6, 2009. Signed with New York Mets organization, December 23, 2009.

DOTEL (DIAZ), OCTAVIO EDUARDO

Born, Santo Domingo, Dominican Republic, November 25, 1973.
Bats Right. Throws Right. Height, 6 feet. Weight, 215 pounds.

Year	Club	Lea	G	IP	W	L	Pct	SO	BB	H	ERA	SAVES
1993	Mets	Dominican	15	59⅓	6	2	.750	48	38	46	4.10	0
1994	Mets	Dominican	15	81⅓	5	0	1.000	95	31	84	4.32	0
1995	Mets	Gulf Coast	13	74⅓	7	4	.636	86	17	48	2.18	0
1995	St. Lucie	Fla.St.	3	8	1	0	1.000	9	4	10	5.63	0
1996	Columbia	So.Atl.	22	115⅓	11	3	.786	142	49	89	3.59	0
1997	Mets	Gulf Coast	3	9⅓	0	0	.000	7	2	9	0.96	1
1997	St. Lucie	Fla.St.	9	50	5	2	.714	39	23	44	2.52	0
1997	Binghamton	Eastern	12	55⅔	3	4	.429	40	38	66	5.98	0
1998	Binghamton	Eastern	10	68⅔	4	2	.667	82	24	41	1.97	0
1998	Norfolk	Int.	17	99	8	6	.571	118	43	82	3.45	0
1999	Norfolk	Int.	13	70⅓	5	2	.714	90	34	52	3.84	0
1999	New York a	N.L.	19	85⅓	8	3	.727	85	49	69	5.38	0
2000	Houston	N.L.	50	125	3	7	.300	142	61	127	5.40	16
2001	Houston	N.L.	61	105	7	5	.583	145	47	79	2.66	2
2002	Houston	N.L.	83	97⅓	6	4	.600	118	27	58	1.85	6
2003	Houston	N.L.	76	87	6	4	.600	97	31	53	2.48	4
2004	Houston	N.L.	32	34⅔	0	4	.000	50	15	27	3.12	14
2004	Oakland b-c	A.L.	45	50⅔	6	2	.750	72	18	41	4.09	22
2005	Oakland d-e	A.L.	15	15⅓	1	2	.333	16	11	10	3.52	7
2006	Staten Island	N.Y.-Penn.	1	1	0	0	.000	1	0	2	0.00	0
2006	Yankees	Gulf Coast	3	3	0	0	.000	6	1	0	0.00	0
2006	Tampa	Fla.St.	2	2	0	0	.000	2	0	1	0.00	0
2006	Trenton	Eastern	2	2	0	0	.000	3	0	1	0.00	0
2006	Columbus	Int.	5	5⅓	0	0	.000	8	0	6	3.38	0
2006	New York f-g	A.L.	14	10	0	0	.000	7	11	18	10.80	0
2007	Wichita	Texas	3	3	0	1	.000	4	0	2	3.00	1
2007	Kansas City	A.L.	24	23	2	1	.667	29	11	24	3.91	11
2007	Atlanta h-i-j	N.L.	9	7⅔	0	0	.000	12	1	5	4.70	0
2008	Chicago	A.L.	72	67	4	4	.500	92	29	52	3.76	1
2009	Chicago k	A.L.	62	62⅓	3	3	.500	75	36	54	3.32	0
2010	Pitt-LA-Col l-m-n	N.L.	68	64	3	4	.429	75	32	52	4.08	22
Major League Totals		12 Yrs.	630	834⅓	49	43	.533	1015	379	669	3.75	105
	Division Series											
1999	New York	N.L.	1	0⅓	0	0	.000	0	2	1	54.00	0
2001	Houston	N.L.	2	3⅓	0	0	.000	5	0	5	5.40	0
2008	Chicago	A.L.	4	1⅓	0	0	.000	3	0	2	13.50	0
Division Series Totals			7	5	0	0	.000	8	2	8	10.80	0

Year	Club	Lea	G	IP	W	L	Pct	SO	BB	H	ERA	SAVES
	Championship Series											
1999	New York	N.L.	1	3	1	0	1.000	5	2	4	3.00	0

a Traded with Roger Cedeno and Kyle Kessel to Houston for Mike Hampton and Derek Bell December 23, 1999.
b Traded to Kansas City Royals with catcher John Buck for outfielder Carlos Beltran, June 24, 2004.
c Traded to Oakland Athletics with cash for pitcher Mike Wood and infielder Mark Teahen, June 24, 2004.
d On disabled list from May 19 to October 28, 2005.
e Filed for free agency, October 28, 2005. Signed with New York Yankees, December 29, 2005.
f On disabled list from March 24 to August 16, 2006.
g Filed for free agency, October 28, 2006. Signed with Kansas City Royals, December 8, 2006.
h On disabled list from March 30 to May 22, 2007 and August 8 to September 20, 2007.
i Traded to Atlanta Braves for pitcher Kyle Davies, July 31, 2007.
j Filed for free agency, November 6, 2007. Signed with Chicago White Sox, January 22, 2008.
k Filed for free agency, November 9, 2009. Signed with Pittsburgh Pirates, January 21, 2010.
l Traded to Los Angeles Dodgers for pitcher James McDonald and outfielder Andrew Lambo, July 31, 2010.
m Traded to Colorado Rockies for player to be named later, September 18, 2010. Los Angeles Dodgers received outfielder Anthony Jackson to complete trade, November 15, 2010.
n Filed for free agency, November 3, 2010. Signed with Toronto Blue Jays, January 4, 2011.

DOWNS, SCOTT JEREMY

Born, Louisville, Kentucky, March 17, 1976.
Bats Left. Throws Left. Height, 6 feet, 2 inches. Weight, 210 pounds.

Year	Club	Lea	G	IP	W	L	Pct	SO	BB	H	ERA	SAVES
1997	Williamsprt.	N.Y.-Penn.	5	23	0	2	.000	28	7	15	2.74	0
1997	Rockford	Midwest	5	36	3	0	1.000	43	8	17	1.25	0
1998	Daytona a	Fla.St.	27	161 2/3	8	9	.471	117	55	179	3.90	0
1999	New Britain	Eastern	6	19 2/3	0	0	.000	22	10	33	8.69	0
1999	Daytona	Fla.St.	7	48	5	0	1.000	41	11	41	1.88	0
1999	Fort Myers	Fla.St.	2	9 2/3	0	1	.000	9	6	7	0.00	0
1999	West Tenn b	Southern	13	80	8	1	.889	101	28	56	1.35	0
2000	Chicago-Montreal c-d	N.L.	19	97	4	3	.571	63	40	122	5.29	0
2001	Montreal e	N.L.				INJURED—Did Not Play						
2002	Brevard County	Fla.St.	7	9	0	0	.000	7	2	7	3.00	1
2002	Ottawa f	Int.	17	23 1/3	2	1	.667	15	3	31	5.79	0
2003	Edmonton	P.C.	21	121 2/3	8	9	.471	54	39	119	4.29	0
2003	Montreal	N.L.	1	3	0	1	.000	4	3	5	15.00	0
2004	Edmonton	P.C.	22	135 1/3	10	6	.625	67	26	143	3.52	0
2004	Montreal g	N.L.	12	63	3	6	.333	38	23	79	5.14	0
2005	Syracuse	Int.	7	39 1/3	2	3	.400	35	3	45	4.81	0
2005	Toronto	A.L.	26	94	4	3	.571	75	34	93	4.31	0
2006	Toronto	A.L.	59	77	6	2	.750	61	30	73	4.09	1
2007	Toronto	A.L.	*81	58	4	2	.667	57	24	47	2.17	1
2008	Toronto h	A.L.	66	70 2/3	0	3	.000	57	27	54	1.78	5
2009	Dunedin	Fla.St.	3	2 1/3	0	0	.000	2	1	3	3.86	0
2009	Toronto i	A.L.	48	46 2/3	1	3	.250	43	13	46	3.09	9
2010	Toronto j	A.L.	67	61 1/3	5	5	.500	48	14	47	2.64	0
Major League Totals		9 Yrs.	379	570 2/3	27	28	.491	446	208	566	3.79	16

a Sent by Chicago Cubs to Minnesota Twins as player to be named later for pitcher Mike Morgan, November 3, 1998.
b Traded to Chicago Cubs with pitcher Rick Aguilera for pitcher Jason Ryan and pitcher Kyle Lohse, May 21, 1999.
c On disabled list from August 9 to October 1, 2000.
d Traded to Montreal Expos for outfielder Rondell White, July 31, 2000.
e On disabled list from March 23 to November 14, 2001.
f On disabled list from March 27 to June 10, 2002.
g Released by Montreal Expos, November 29, 2004. Signed with Toronto Blue Jays organization, December 16, 2004.
h On disabled list from September 20 to October 2, 2008.
i On disabled list from June 17 to July 8 and August 1 to August 24, 2009.
j Filed for free agency, November 1, 2010. Signed with Los Angeles Angels, December 10, 2010.

DRABEK, KYLE JORDAN

Born, The Woodlands, Texas, December 8, 1987.
Bats Right. Throws Right. Height, 6 feet, 1 inch. Weight, 190 pounds.

Year	Club	Lea	G	IP	W	L	Pct	SO	BB	H	ERA	SAVES
2006	Phillies	Gulf Coast	6	23 1/3	1	3	.250	14	11	33	7.71	0
2007	Lakewood	So.Atl.	11	54	5	1	.833	46	23	50	4.33	0
2008	Phillies	Gulf Coast	4	12	0	1	.000	6	6	6	2.25	0
2008	Williamsport	N.Y.-Penn.	4	20 1/3	1	2	.333	10	6	11	2.21	0
2009	Reading	Eastern	15	96 1/3	8	2	.800	76	31	92	3.64	0
2009	Clearwater a	Fla.St.	10	61 2/3	4	1	.800	74	19	49	2.48	0
2010	New Hampshire	Eastern	27	162	14	9	.609	132	68	126	2.94	0
2010	Toronto	A.L.	3	17	0	3	.000	12	5	18	4.76	0

a Traded by Philadelphia Phillies to Toronto Blue Jays with pitcher Michael Taylor and catcher Travis D'Arnaud for pitcher Roy Halladay, December 16, 2009.

DUENSING, BRIAN MATTHEW

Born, Marysville, Kansas, February 22, 1983.
Bats Left. Throws Left. Height, 5 feet, 11 inches. Weight, 195 pounds.

Year Club	Lea	G	IP	W	L	Pct	SO	BB	H	ERA	SAVES
2005 Elizabethton	Appal.	12	$50^{1}/_{3}$	4	3	.571	55	16	49	2.32	0
2006 New Britain	Eastern	10	$49^{1}/_{3}$	1	2	.333	30	18	51	3.65	0
2006 Fort Myers	Fla.St.	7	$40^{1}/_{3}$	2	5	.286	33	8	47	4.24	0
2006 Beloit	Midwest	11	$70^{1}/_{3}$	2	3	.400	55	14	68	2.94	0
2007 New Britain	Eastern	9	$50^{2}/_{3}$	4	1	.800	38	7	47	2.66	0
2007 Rochester	Int.	19	$116^{2}/_{3}$	11	5	.688	86	30	115	3.24	0
2008 Rochester	Int.	25	$138^{2}/_{3}$	5	11	.313	77	34	150	4.28	0
2009 Rochester	Int.	13	$75^{1}/_{3}$	4	6	.400	44	19	87	4.66	0
2009 Minnesota	A.L.	24	84	5	2	.714	53	31	84	3.64	0
2010 Minnesota	A.L.	53	$130^{2}/_{3}$	10	3	.769	78	35	122	2.62	0
Major League Totals	2 Yrs.	77	$214^{2}/_{3}$	15	5	.750	131	66	206	3.02	0
Division Series											
2009 Minnesota	A.L.	1	$4^{2}/_{3}$	0	1	.000	3	1	7	9.64	0
2010 Minnesota	A.L.	1	$3^{1}/_{3}$	0	1	.000	1	1	7	13.50	0
Division Series Totals		2	8	0	2	.000	4	2	14	11.25	0

DUKE, ZACHARY THOMAS (ZACH)

Born, Clifton, Texas, April 19, 1983.
Bats Left. Throws Left. Height, 6 feet, 2 inches. Weight, 220 pounds.

Year Club	Lea	G	IP	W	L	Pct	SO	BB	H	ERA	SAVES
2002 Pirates	Gulf Coast	11	60	8	1	.889	48	18	38	1.95	0
2003 Hickory	So.Atl.	26	$141^{2}/_{3}$	8	7	.533	113	46	124	3.11	0
2004 Lynchburg	Carolina	17	97	10	5	.667	106	20	73	1.39	0
2004 Altoona	Eastern	9	$51^{1}/_{3}$	5	1	.833	36	10	41	1.58	0
2005 Indianapolis	Int.	16	108	12	3	.800	66	23	108	2.92	0
2005 Pittsburgh a	N.L.	14	$84^{2}/_{3}$	8	2	.800	58	23	79	1.81	0
2006 Pittsburgh	N.L.	34	$215^{1}/_{3}$	10	15	.400	117	68	*255	4.47	0
2007 Pirates	Gulf Coast	2	$6^{2}/_{3}$	0	0	.000	3	2	5	1.35	0
2007 State College	NY-Penn	1	$5^{2}/_{3}$	1	0	1.000	3	2	3	1.59	0
2007 Indianapolis	Int.	1	$3^{2}/_{3}$	0	1	.000	1	2	7	4.91	0
2007 Pittsburgh b	N.L.	20	$107^{1}/_{3}$	3	8	.273	41	25	161	5.53	0
2008 Pittsburgh	N.L.	31	185	5	14	.263	87	47	230	4.82	0
2009 Pittsburgh	N.L.	32	213	11	*16	.407	106	49	231	4.06	0
2010 Altoona	Eastern	2	7	0	0	.000	1	1	5	2.57	0
2010 Pittsburgh c-d	N.L.	29	159	8	15	.348	96	51	212	5.72	0
Major League Totals	6 Yrs.	160	$964^{1}/_{3}$	45	70	.391	505	263	1168	4.54	0

a On disabled list from August 24 to September 16, 2005.
b On disabled list from June 29 to September 11, 2007.
c On disabled list from June 17 to July 12, 2010.
d Traded to Arizona Diamondbacks for player to be named later, November 24, 2010. Pittsburgh Pirates received pitcher Cesar Valdez to complete trade, December 9, 2010.

DUNN, MICHAEL G.

Born, Farmington, New Mexico, May 23, 1985.
Bats Left. Throws Left. Height, 6 feet, 1 inch. Weight, 195 pounds.

Year Club	Lea	G	IP	W	L	Pct	SO	BB	H	ERA	SAVES
2006 Yankees	Gulf Coast	11	$24^{2}/_{3}$	3	0	1.000	26	9	13	0.73	4
2006 Staten Island	N.Y.-Penn.	3	$6^{1}/_{3}$	0	0	.000	7	7	3	5.68	0
2007 Charleston	So.Atl.	27	$144^{2}/_{3}$	12	5	.706	138	45	136	3.42	0
2008 Trenton	Eastern	1	$1^{2}/_{3}$	1	0	1.000	2	1	1	0.00	0
2008 Tampa	Fla.St.	30	$124^{2}/_{3}$	4	7	.364	118	58	124	4.55	1
2009 Trenton	Eastern	26	$53^{1}/_{3}$	3	3	.500	76	32	41	3.71	2
2009 Scranton/WB	Int.	12	20	1	0	1.000	23	14	17	2.25	0
2009 New York a	A.L.	4	4	0	0	.000	5	5	3	6.75	0
2010 Gwinnett	Int.	38	$47^{1}/_{3}$	2	0	1.000	64	25	31	1.52	7
2010 Atlanta b	N.L.	25	19	2	0	1.000	27	17	15	1.89	0
Major League Totals	2 Yrs.	29	23	2	0	1.000	32	22	18	2.74	0
Division Series											
2010 Atlanta	N.L.	3	$1^{1}/_{3}$	0	0	.000	2	0	2	0.00	0

a Traded to Atlanta Braves with outfielder Melky Cabrera, pitcher Arodys Vizcaino and cash for pitcher Javier Vazquez and pitcher Boone Logan, December 22, 2009.

b Traded to Florida Marlins with infielder Omar Infante for infielder Dan Uggla, November 16, 2010.

DURBIN, CHAD GRIFFIN

Born, Spring Valley, Illinois, December 3, 1977.

Bats Both. Throws Right. Height, 6 feet, 2 inches. Weight, 200 pounds.

Year Club	Lea	G	IP	W	L	Pct	SO	BB	H	ERA	SAVES
1996 Royals	Gulf Coast	11	44 1/3	3	2	.600	43	25	34	4.26	0
1997 Lansing	Midwest	26	144 2/3	5	8	.385	116	53	157	4.79	0
1998 Wilmington	Carolina	26	147 2/3	10	7	.588	162	59	126	2.93	0
1999 Wichita	Texas	28	157	8	10	.444	122	49	154	4.64	0
1999 Kansas City	A.L.	1	2 1/3	0	0	.000	3	1	1	0.00	0
2000 Kansas City	A.L.	16	72 1/3	2	5	.286	37	43	91	8.21	0
2000 Omaha	P.C.	12	72 2/3	4	4	.500	53	22	75	4.46	0
2001 Omaha	P.C.	5	27	2	2	.500	35	6	22	3.33	0
2001 Kansas City	A.L.	29	179	9	16	.360	95	58	201	4.93	0
2002 Omaha	P.C.	1	1 2/3	0	1	.000	2	0	4	10.80	0
2002 Royals	Gulf Coast	3	6	0	0	.000	5	1	4	0.00	0
2002 Wichita	Texas	3	5 1/3	0	0	.000	6	4	5	5.06	0
2002 Kansas City	A.L.	2	8 1/3	0	1	.000	5	4	13	11.88	0
2003 Mahoning Valley	N.Y.-Penn.	2	12	1	1	.500	8	3	9	2.25	0
2003 Akron	Eastern	3	12	2	0	1.000	11	1	7	1.50	0
2003 Buffalo	Int.	10	58 2/3	3	6	.333	64	16	51	4.60	0
2003 Cleveland a	A.L.	3	8 2/3	0	1	.000	8	3	18	7.27	0
2004 Cleveland	A.L.	17	51 1/3	5	6	.455	38	24	63	6.66	0
2004 Buffalo	Int.	9	52	3	3	.500	40	16	55	3.46	0
2004 Arizona b-c	N.L.	7	9 1/3	1	1	.500	10	11	9	8.68	0
2005 New Orleans	P.C.	26	115 1/3	4	5	.444	99	48	121	5.77	0
2006 Toledo	Int.	28	185	11	8	.579	149	46	169	3.11	0
2006 Detroit d	A.L.	3	6	0	0	.000	3	0	6	1.50	0
2007 Detroit e	A.L.	36	127 2/3	8	7	.533	66	49	133	4.72	1
2008 Philadelphia	N.L.	71	87 2/3	5	4	.556	63	35	81	2.87	1
2009 Clearwater	Fla.St.	2	3	0	0	.000	4	1	3	0.00	0
2009 Lehigh Valley	Int.	1	1	0	0	.000	1	0	1	0.00	0
2009 Philadelphia f	N.L.	59	69 2/3	2	2	.500	62	47	56	4.39	2
2010 Clearwater	Fla.St.	2	3	1	0	1.000	3	0	0	0.00	0
2010 Philadelphia g-h	N.L.	64	68 2/3	4	1	.800	63	27	63	3.80	0
Major League Totals	11 Yrs.	308	691	36	44	.450	453	302	735	5.05	4
Division Series											
2008 Philadelphia	N.L.	1	0 2/3	0	0	.000	1	0	3	0.00	0
2009 Philadelphia	N.L.	1	1	1	0	1.000	0	0	0	0.00	0
2010 Philadelphia	N.L.	1	0 1/3	0	0	.000	0	1	0	0.00	0
Division Series Totals		3	2	1	0	1.000	1	1	3	0.00	0
Championship Series											
2008 Philadelphia	N.L.	3	2	0	0	.000	2	2	3	4.50	0
2009 Philadelphia	N.L.	4	3	1	0	1.000	1	0	0	0.00	0
2010 Philadelphia	N.L.	1	1	0	0	.000	1	2	2	18.00	0
Championship Series Totals		8	6	1	0	1.000	4	4	5	4.50	0
World Series Record											
2008 Philadelphia	N.L.	2	0 2/3	0	0	.000	0	1	1	0.00	0
2009 Philadelphia	N.L.	2	1 1/3	0	0	.000	2	2	3	27.00	0
World Series Totals		4	2	0	0	.000	2	3	4	18.00	0

a Not offered contract, December 20, 2002. Signed with Cleveland Indians organization, February 17, 2003.

b Claimed on waivers by Arizona Diamondbacks, August 13, 2004.

c Filed for free agency, October 11, 2004. Signed with Washington Nationals organization, December 23, 2004.

d Filed for free agency, October 28, 2005. Signed with Detroit Tigers organization, January 10, 2006.

e Not offered contract, December 12, 2007. Signed with Philadelphia Phillies, December 20, 2007.

f On disabled list from July 23 to August 10, 2009.

g On disabled list from June 24 to July 13, 2010.

h Filed for free agency, November 1, 2010.

ELY, JOHN DANIEL

Born, Harvey, Illinois, May 13, 1986.

Bats Right. Throws Right. Height, 6 feet, 2 inches. Weight, 200 pounds.

Year Club	Lea	G	IP	W	L	Pct	SO	BB	H	ERA	SAVES
2007 Great Falls	Pioneer	13	56	6	1	.857	56	14	55	3.86	0
2008 Winston-Salem	Carolina	27	145 1/3	10	12	.455	134	46	142	4.71	0

Year Club	Lea	G	IP	W	L	Pct	SO	BB	H	ERA	SAVES
2009 Birmingham a	Southern	27	$156^{1}/_{3}$	14	2	.875	125	50	140	2.82	0
2010 Albuquerque	P.C.	13	68	5	4	.556	56	29	70	6.22	0
2010 Los Angeles	N.L.	18	100	4	10	.286	76	40	105	5.49	0

a Traded by Chicago White Sox to Los Angeles Dodgers with pitcher Jon Link for outfielder Juan Pierre, December 15, 2009.

ENRIGHT, BARRY R.

Born, Stockton, California, March 30, 1986.
Bats Right. Throws Right. Height, 6 feet, 3 inches. Weight, 220 pounds.

Year Club	Lea	G	IP	W	L	Pct	SO	BB	H	ERA	SAVES
2007 Visalia	Calif.	4	5	0	0	.000	4	2	3	0.00	1
2007 South Bend	Midwest	1	2	0	0	.000	1	0	1	0.00	1
2007 Yakima	Northwest	5	8	0	0	.000	12	3	4	0.00	0
2008 Visalia	Calif.	29	$164^{1}/_{3}$	12	8	.600	143	35	185	4.44	0
2009 Mobile	Southern	27	156	10	9	.526	103	37	171	3.98	0
2010 Mobile	Southern	14	$93^{2}/_{3}$	4	1	.800	83	15	81	2.88	0
2010 Arizona	N.L.	17	99	6	7	.462	49	29	97	3.91	0

FARNSWORTH, KYLE LYNN

Born, Wichita, Kansas, April 14, 1976.
Bats Right. Throws Right. Height, 6 feet, 4 inches. Weight, 230 pounds.

Year Club	Lea	G	IP	W	L	Pct	SO	BB	H	ERA	SAVES
1995 Cubs	Gulf Coast	16	31	3	2	.600	18	11	22	0.87	1
1996 Rockford	Midwest	20	112	9	6	.600	82	35	122	3.70	0
1997 Daytona	Fla.St.	27	$156^{1}/_{3}$	10	10	.500	105	47	178	4.09	0
1998 West Tenn	Southern	13	$81^{1}/_{3}$	8	2	.800	73	21	70	2.77	0
1998 Iowa	P.C.	18	$102^{2}/_{3}$	5	9	.357	79	36	129	6.93	0
1999 Iowa	P.C.	6	$39^{1}/_{3}$	2	2	.500	29	9	38	3.20	0
1999 Chicago	N.L.	27	130	5	9	.357	70	52	140	5.05	0
2000 Chicago	N.L.	46	77	2	9	.182	74	50	90	6.43	1
2000 Iowa	P.C.	22	$25^{1}/_{3}$	0	2	.000	22	18	24	3.20	9
2001 Chicago	N.L.	76	82	4	6	.400	107	29	65	2.74	2
2002 Iowa	P.C.	2	3	0	1	.000	2	0	3	6.00	0
2002 Chicago a	N.L.	45	$46^{2}/_{3}$	4	6	.400	46	24	53	7.33	1
2003 Chicago	N.L.	77	$76^{1}/_{3}$	3	2	.600	92	36	53	3.30	0
2004 Chicago b	N.L.	72	$66^{2}/_{3}$	4	5	.444	78	33	67	4.72	0
2005 Detroit	A.L.	46	$42^{2}/_{3}$	1	1	.500	55	20	29	2.32	6
2005 Atlanta c-d-e	N.L.	26	$27^{1}/_{3}$	0	0	.000	32	7	15	1.98	10
2006 New York	A.L.	72	66	3	6	.333	75	28	62	4.36	6
2007 New York	A.L.	64	60	2	1	.667	48	27	60	4.80	0
2008 New York-Detroit f-g	A.L.	61	$60^{1}/_{3}$	2	3	.400	61	22	70	4.48	1
2009 Omaha	P.C.	2	2	0	0	.000	2	0	0	0.00	0
2009 NW Arkansas	Texas	3	$3^{2}/_{3}$	0	0	.000	3	1	1	0.00	0
2009 Kansas City h	A.L.	41	$37^{1}/_{3}$	1	5	.167	42	14	43	4.58	0
2010 Kansas City	A.L.	37	$44^{2}/_{3}$	3	0	1.000	36	12	40	2.42	0
2010 Atlanta i-j	N.L.	23	20	0	2	.000	25	7	15	5.40	0
Major League Totals	12 Yrs.	713	837	34	55	.382	841	361	802	4.39	27
Division Series											
2003 Chicago	N.L.	3	$2^{2}/_{3}$	0	0	.000	2	1	1	0.00	0
2005 Atlanta	N.L.	2	3	0	0	.000	4	1	2	9.00	0
2006 New York	A.L.	2	2	0	0	.000	1	1	1	0.00	0
2007 New York	A.L.	1	1	0	0	.000	2	0	1	0.00	0
2010 Atlanta	N.L.	2	2	1	0	1.000	1	1	1	0.00	0
Division Series Totals		10	$10^{2}/_{3}$	1	0	1.000	10	4	6	2.53	0
Championship Series											
2003 Chicago	N.L.	5	$5^{1}/_{3}$	0	0	.000	7	2	6	10.13	0

a On disabled list from April 10 to June 4, 2002.
b On disabled list from August 28 to September 12, 2004.
c Traded to Detroit Tigers for pitcher Roberto Novoa, infielder Scott Moore and outfielder Clarence Flowers, February 9, 2005.
d Traded to Atlanta Braves for pitcher Roman Colon and pitcher Zach Miner, July 26, 2005.
e Filed for free agency, October 31, 2005. Signed with New York Yankees, December 5, 2005.
f Traded to Detroit Tigers for catcher Ivan Rodriguez, July 30, 2008.
g Filed for free agency, November 3, 2008. Signed with Kansas City Royals, December 13, 2008.
h On disabled list from June 25 to August 18, 2009.
i Traded to Atlanta Braves with outfielder Rick Ankiel and cash for outfielder Gregor Blanco, pitcher Jesse Chavez and pitcher Tim Collins, July 31, 2010.
j Filed for free agency, November 1, 2010. Signed with Tampa Bay Rays, January 15, 2011.

FELDMAN, SCOTT WAYNE

Born, Kailua, Hawaii, February 7, 1983.
Bats Left. Throws Right. Height, 6 feet, 5 inches. Weight, 210 pounds.

Year	Club	Lea	G	IP	W	L	Pct	SO	BB	H	ERA	SAVES
2003	Rangers	Arizona	3	6⅓	1	1	.500	7	1	4	4.26	0
2004	Rangers	Arizona	4	7	0	0	.000	5	1	2	0.00	0
2005	Bakersfield	Calif.	6	9	0	0	.000	11	2	5	0.00	3
2005	Frisco	Texas	46	61	1	2	.333	41	23	43	2.36	14
2005	Texas	A.L.	8	9⅓	0	1	.000	4	2	9	0.96	0
2006	Oklahoma	P.C.	23	27⅓	2	2	.500	24	9	20	1.98	4
2006	Texas	A.L.	36	41⅓	0	2	.000	30	10	42	3.92	0
2007	Oklahoma	P.C.	21	30	1	1	.500	24	12	28	4.50	2
2007	Texas	A.L.	29	39	1	2	.333	19	32	44	5.77	0
2008	Frisco	Texas	2	12⅔	2	0	1.000	4	2	11	4.26	0
2008	Texas	A.L.	28	151⅓	6	8	.429	74	56	161	5.29	0
2009	Texas	A.L.	34	189⅔	17	8	.680	113	65	178	4.08	0
2010	Oklahoma	P.C.	1	4	0	0	.000	3	0	5	4.50	0
2010	Texas a	A.L.	29	141⅓	7	11	.389	75	45	181	5.48	0
Major League Totals		6 Yrs.	164	572	31	32	.492	315	210	615	4.80	0

a On disabled list from August 22 to September 7, 2010.

FELICIANO (MOLINA), PEDRO JUAN

Born, Rio Piedras, Puerto Rico, August 25, 1976.
Bats Left. Throws Left. Height, 5 feet, 10 inches. Weight, 185 pounds.

Year	Club	Lea	G	IP	W	L	Pct	SO	BB	H	ERA	SAVES
1995	Great Falls	Pioneer	6	6⅔	0	0	.000	9	7	12	13.50	0
1996	Great Falls	Pioneer	22	41	2	3	.400	39	26	50	5.71	3
1997	Savannah	So.Atl.	36	105⅔	3	7	.300	94	39	90	2.64	4
1997	Vero Beach	Fla.St.	1	2	0	0	.000	1	0	3	4.50	0
1998	Vero Beach	Fla.St.	22	68⅓	2	5	.286	51	30	68	4.61	2
1999	a					INJURED—Did Not Play						
2000	Vero Beach	Fla.St.	25	61⅓	4	5	.444	48	24	76	3.82	0
2000	Albuquerque	P.C.	1	1	0	0	.000	2	1	3	18.00	0
2000	San Antonio	Texas	9	9⅓	0	0	.000	11	4	7	1.93	2
2001	Las Vegas	P.C.	6	8⅔	0	1	.000	5	5	16	7.27	0
2001	Jacksonville b	Southern	54	60⅓	5	4	.556	55	11	41	1.94	17
2002	Chattanooga	Southern	28	38⅔	2	1	.667	26	11	33	2.56	4
2002	Louisville	Int.	20	26⅔	1	1	.500	19	4	35	3.04	0
2002	Norfolk	Int.	5	9	0	0	.000	11	1	14	7.00	2
2002	New York c-d-e	N.L.	6	6	0	0	.000	4	1	9	7.50	0
2003	Norfolk	Int.	15	22⅔	3	2	.600	18	6	20	3.97	1
2003	New York f-g	N.L.	23	48⅓	0	0	.000	43	21	52	3.35	0
2004	Norfolk	Int.	32	35⅔	4	3	.571	25	15	35	5.30	2
2004	New York	N.L.	22	18⅓	1	1	.500	14	12	14	5.40	0
2005	Fukuoka h-i	Japan Pac.	37	37	3	2	.600	36	13	30	3.89	0
2006	Norfolk	Int.	3	4⅓	0	0	.000	5	1	4	6.23	0
2006	New York	N.L.	64	60⅓	7	2	.778	54	20	56	2.09	0
2007	New York	N.L.	78	64	2	2	.500	61	31	47	3.09	2
2008	New York	N.L.	*86	53⅓	3	4	.429	50	26	57	4.05	2
2009	New York	N.L.	*88	59⅓	6	4	.600	59	18	51	3.03	0
2010	New York j	N.L.	*92	62⅔	3	6	.333	56	30	66	3.30	0
Major League Totals		8 Yrs.	459	372⅓	22	19	.537	341	159	352	3.31	4
	Division Series											
2006	New York	N.L.	3	1⅔	1	0	1.000	2	2	0	0.00	0
	Championship Series											
2006	New York	N.L.	3	3	0	0	.000	1	0	2	3.00	0

a On minor league disabled list from April 8 to September 22, 1999.
b Filed for free agency from Los Angeles Dodgers, October 15, 2001. Signed with Cincinnati Reds organization, December 21, 2001.
c Traded to New York Mets with outfielder Elvin Andujar, player to be named later and two players to be named later for pitcher Shawn Estes and cash, August 16, 2002.
d New York Mets received outfielder Raul Gonzalez (August 20, 2002) and Brady Clark to complete trade, September 9, 2002.
e Claimed on waivers by Detroit Tigers, October 11, 2002.
f Released by Detroit Tigers, December 17, 2002. Signed with New York Mets organization, April 3, 2003.
g Not offered contract, December 21, 2003, re-signed with New York Mets organization, December 22, 2003.
h Sold to Fukuoka Daiei Hawks (Japan), January 21, 2005.
i Signed with New York Mets organization, December 19, 2005.
j Filed for free agency, November 1, 2010. Signed with New York Yankees, January 3, 2011.

FELIZ (ANTONIO), NEFTALI

Born, Azua, Dominican Republic, May 2, 1988.
Bats Right. Throws Right. Height, 6 feet, 3 inches. Weight, 190 pounds.

Year	Club	Lea	G	IP	W	L	Pct	SO	BB	H	ERA	SAVES
2006	Braves	Gulf Coast	11	29	0	2	.000	42	14	20	4.03	2
2007	Danville	Appal.	8	$27^1/_3$	2	0	1.000	28	12	18	1.98	0
2007	Spokane a	Northwest	8	15	0	2	.000	27	12	13	3.60	0
2008	Clinton	Midwest	17	82	6	3	.667	106	28	55	2.52	0
2008	Frisco	Texas	10	$45^1/_3$	4	3	.571	47	23	34	2.98	0
2009	Okla.	P.C.	25	$77^1/_3$	4	6	.400	75	30	69	3.49	0
2009	Texas	A.L.	20	31	1	0	1.000	39	8	13	1.74	2
2010	Texas b	A.L.	70	$69^1/_3$	4	3	.571	71	18	43	2.73	40
Major League Totals		2 Yrs.	90	$100^1/_3$	5	3	.625	110	26	56	2.42	42
	Division Series											
2010	Texas	A.L.	2	$1^1/_3$	0	0	.000	2	3	2	6.75	0
	Championship Series											
2010	Texas	A.L.	3	3	0	0	.000	5	2	0	0.00	0
	World Series Record											
2010	Texas	A.L.	2	3	0	0	.000	4	0	1	0.00	1

a Traded by Atlanta Braves to Texas Rangers with catcher Jarrod Saltalamacchia, infielder Elvis Andrus, pitcher Matt Harrison and pitcher Beau James for infielder Mark Teixeira and pitcher Ron Mahay, July 31, 2007.

b Selected Rookie of the Year in American League for 2010.

FIGUEROA, NELSON

Born, Brooklyn, New York, May 18, 1974.
Bats Both. Throws Right. Height, 6 feet, 1 inch. Weight, 205 pounds.

Year	Club	Lea	G	IP	W	L	Pct	SO	BB	H	ERA	SAVES
1995	Kingsport	Appal.	12	$76^1/_3$	7	3	.700	79	22	57	3.07	0
1996	Columbia	So.Atl.	26	$185^1/_3$	14	7	.667	200	58	119	2.04	0
1997	Binghamton	Eastern	33	143	5	11	.313	116	68	137	4.34	0
1998	Binghamton	Eastern	21	$123^2/_3$	12	3	.800	116	44	133	4.66	0
1998	Tucson a	P.C.	7	$41^1/_3$	2	2	.500	29	16	46	3.70	0
1999	Diamondbacks	Arizona	1	3	0	1	.000	2	0	3	0.00	0
1999	Tucson b	P.C.	24	128	11	6	.647	106	41	128	3.94	0
2000	Tucson	P.C.	17	112	9	4	.692	78	28	101	2.81	0
2000	Arizona	N.L.	3	$15^2/_3$	0	1	.000	7	5	17	7.47	0
2000	Scranton-WB c	Int.	8	50	4	3	.571	35	11	50	3.78	0
2001	Scranton-WB	Int.	13	$87^1/_3$	4	2	.667	74	18	74	2.47	0
2001	Philadelphia	N.L.	19	89	4	5	.444	61	37	95	3.94	0
2002	Milwaukee	N.L.	30	93	1	7	.125	51	37	96	5.03	0
2002	Indianapolis d-e-f	Int.	6	$39^2/_3$	5	0	1.000	25	13	39	3.63	0
2003	Nashville	P.C.	23	$151^1/_3$	12	5	.706	121	37	144	2.97	0
2003	Pittsburgh	N.L.	12	$35^1/_3$	2	1	.667	23	13	28	3.31	0
2004	Nashville	P.C.	25	$152^1/_3$	12	8	.600	129	36	168	4.19	0
2004	Pittsburgh	N.L.	10	$28^1/_3$	0	3	.000	10	11	32	5.72	0
2005					Did Not Play							
2006	Long Island	Atlantic	2	10	0	1	.000	9	3	9	2.70	
2006	New Orleans g-h	P.C.	16	76	3	5	.375	44	21	76	4.38	0
2007	Chihuahua i-j	Mexican	19	$153^2/_3$	8	6	.571	94	36	163	3.87	0
2008	New Orleans	P.C.	20	$113^2/_3$	4	7	.364	97	33	120	4.43	0
2008	New York k-l	N.L.	16	$45^1/_3$	3	3	.500	36	26	48	4.57	0
2009	Buffalo	Int.	17	112	7	5	.583	94	24	91	2.25	0
2009	New York m	N.L.	16	$70^1/_3$	3	8	.273	59	24	80	4.09	0
2010	Lehigh Valley	Int.	3	19	3	0	1.000	18	3	10	0.95	0
2010	Philadelphia-Houston n-o	N.L.	31	93	7	4	.636	73	34	84	3.29	1
Major League Totals		8 Yrs.	137	470	20	32	.385	320	187	480	4.29	1

a Traded by New York Mets to Arizona Diamondbacks with outfielder Bernard Gilkey and cash for pitcher Willie Blair, catcher Jorge Fabregas and player to be named later, July 31, 1998. New York Mets received cash to complete trade, September 3, 1998.

b On disabled list from June 12 to 23 and July 6 to 30, 1999.

c Traded to Philadelphia Phillies with infielder Travis Lee, pitcher Omar Daal and pitcher Vicente Padilla for pitcher Curt Schilling, July 26, 2000.

d Claimed on waivers by Milwaukee Brewers, April 3, 2002.

e On disabled list from May 6 to May 21, 2002.

f Filed for free agency, October 11, 2002. Signed with Pittsburgh Pirates organization, December 27, 2002.

g Released by Pittsburgh Pirates, October 12, 2004. Signed with Long Island for 2006.

h Signed with Washington Nationals organization, May 9, 2006.

i Filed for free agency, October 15, 2006. Signed with Seattle Mariners organization, March 30, 2007.

j Signed with Chihuahua, then Uni-President (Taiwan) for 2007.

k Signed with New York Mets organization, February 4, 2008.

l Filed for free agency, November 3, 2008, re-signed with New York Mets, December 3, 2008.
m Released by New York Mets, April 22, 2009, re-signed with New York Mets organization, April 25, 2009.
n Claimed on waivers by Philadelphia Phillies, April 7, 2010.
o Claimed on waivers by Houston Astros, July 21, 2010.

FISTER, DOUGLAS WILDES (DOUG)

Born, Merced, California, February 4, 1984.
Bats Left. Throws Right. Height, 6 feet, 8 inches. Weight, 200 pounds.

Year	Club	Lea	G	IP	W	L	Pct	SO	BB	H	ERA	SAVES
2006	Everett	Northwest	20	40	3	5	.375	35	11	35	2.25	4
2007	West Tenn	Southern	24	131	7	8	.467	85	32	156	4.60	0
2008	West Tenn	Southern	31	134⅓	6	14	.300	104	45	155	5.43	0
2009	West Tenn	Southern	2	5⅔	1	0	1.000	5	1	2	0.00	0
2009	Tacoma	P.C.	22	106⅓	6	4	.600	79	11	132	3.81	0
2009	Seattle	A.L.	11	61	3	4	.429	36	15	63	4.13	0
2010	Tacoma	P.C.	1	4	0	0	.000	3	0	4	4.50	0
2010	Seattle a	A.L.	28	171	6	14	.300	93	32	187	4.11	0
Major League Totals		2 Yrs.	39	232	9	18	.333	129	47	250	4.11	0

a On disabled list from June 1 to June 25, 2010.

FLORES, RANDY ALAN

Born, Bellflower, California, July 31, 1975.
Bats Left. Throws Left. Height, 6 feet. Weight, 190 pounds.

Year	Club	Lea	G	IP	W	L	Pct	SO	BB	H	ERA	SAVES
1997	Oneonta	N.Y.-Penn.	13	74⅔	4	4	.500	70	23	64	3.25	0
1998	Tampa	Fla.St.	5	23⅔	1	2	.333	15	16	28	6.46	0
1998	Greensboro	So.Atl.	21	130⅔	12	7	.632	139	33	119	2.62	0
1999	Norwich	Eastern	4	25	0	1	.000	19	11	32	6.48	0
1999	Tampa	Fla.St.	21	135	11	4	.733	99	38	118	2.87	0
2000	Norwich	Eastern	31	141	10	9	.526	97	58	138	2.94	1
2000	Columbus	Int.	4	23⅓	1	2	.333	16	7	43	7.33	0
2001	Norwich	Eastern	25	158⅔	14	6	.700	115	63	156	2.78	0
2001	Columbus a	Int.	3	5⅔	0	1	.000	4	2	5	4.76	0
2002	Oklahoma	P.C.	15	20⅓	1	1	.500	16	5	22	5.75	1
2002	Texas	A.L.	20	12	0	0	.000	7	8	11	4.50	1
2002	Colorado Springs	P.C.	7	35⅔	2	2	.500	27	18	36	3.28	0
2002	Colorado b	N.L.	8	17	0	2	.000	7	8	29	9.53	0
2003	Colorado Springs c	P.C.	28	142⅔	10	8	.556	116	67	156	4.98	0
2004	Memphis	P.C.	36	122⅔	5	7	.417	99	46	115	3.82	2
2004	St. Louis	N.L.	9	14	1	0	1.000	7	3	13	1.93	0
2005	Memphis	P.C.	6	7	1	0	1.000	6	0	8	6.43	0
2005	St. Louis d	N.L.	50	41⅔	3	1	.750	43	13	37	3.46	1
2006	St. Louis	N.L.	65	41⅔	1	1	.500	40	22	49	5.62	0
2007	St. Louis	N.L.	70	55	3	0	1.000	47	15	71	4.25	1
2008	Memphis	P.C.	15	18⅓	0	1	.000	14	6	20	2.45	1
2008	St. Louis e	N.L.	43	25⅔	1	0	1.000	17	20	34	5.26	1
2009	Colorado Springs	P.C.	38	31⅔	0	2	.000	33	11	37	4.26	0
2009	Colorado f	N.L.	27	12	0	1	.000	14	2	14	5.25	0
2010	Colorado	N.L.	47	27⅓	2	0	1.000	18	13	22	2.96	0
2010	Minnesota g-h	A.L.	11	3⅔	0	0	.000	2	2	10	4.91	0
Major League Totals		8 Yrs.	350	250	11	5	.688	202	106	290	4.61	4
	Division Series											
2005	St. Louis	N.L.	3	2	0	0	.000	3	0	2	4.50	0
2006	St. Louis	N.L.	2	1	0	0	.000	1	1	2	0.00	0
Division Series Totals			5	3	0	0	.000	4	1	4	3.00	0
	Championship Series											
2005	St. Louis	N.L.	2	1⅓	0	0	.000	0	1	0	0.00	0
2006	St. Louis	N.L.	4	3⅔	1	0	1.000	3	0	2	0.00	0
Championship Series Totals			6	5	1	0	1.000	3	1	2	0.00	0
	World Series Record											
2006	St. Louis	N.L.	1	1	0	0	.000	0	0	1	0.00	0

a Sent by New York Yankees to Texas Rangers with pitcher Rosman Garcia to complete trade for Randy Velarde, October 12, 2001.
b Claimed on waivers by Colorado Rockies, July 17, 2002.
c Filed for free agency, October 15, 2003. Signed with St. Louis Cardinals organization, November 20, 2003.
d On disabled list from June 24 to July 9, 2005.
e On disabled list from June 26 to July 18, 2008.

f Not offered contract, December 12, 2008. Signed with Colorado Rockies organization, February 11, 2009.
g Claimed on waivers by Minnesota Twins, August 25, 2010.
h Filed for free agency, November 1, 2010.

FLOYD, GAVIN CHRISTOPHER

Born, Annapolis, Maryland, January 27, 1983.
Bats Right. Throws Right. Height, 6 feet, 4 inches. Weight, 230 pounds.

Year	Club	Lea	G	IP	W	L	Pct	SO	BB	H	ERA	SAVES
2002	Lakewood	So.Atl.	27	166	11	10	.524	140	64	119	2.77	0
2003	Clearwater	Fla.St.	24	138	7	8	.467	115	45	128	3.00	0
2004	Reading	Eastern	20	119	6	6	.500	94	46	93	2.57	0
2004	Scranton-WB	Int.	5	$30\frac{2}{3}$	1	3	.250	18	9	39	4.99	0
2004	Philadelphia	N.L.	6	$28\frac{1}{3}$	2	0	1.000	24	16	25	3.49	0
2005	Scranton-WB	Int.	24	$137\frac{1}{3}$	6	9	.400	97	66	155	6.16	0
2005	Philadelphia	N.L.	7	26	1	2	.333	17	16	30	10.04	0
2006	Philadelphia	N.L.	11	$54\frac{1}{3}$	4	3	.571	34	32	70	7.29	0
2006	Scranton-WB a	Int.	17	115	7	4	.636	85	38	117	4.23	0
2007	Charlotte	Int.	17	$106\frac{2}{3}$	7	3	.700	96	35	93	3.12	0
2007	Chicago	A.L.	16	70	1	5	.167	49	19	85	5.27	0
2008	Chicago	A.L.	33	$206\frac{1}{3}$	17	8	.680	145	70	190	3.84	0
2009	Chicago	A.L.	30	193	11	11	.500	163	59	178	4.06	0
2010	Chicago	A.L.	31	$187\frac{1}{3}$	10	13	.435	151	58	199	4.08	0
Major League Totals		7 Yrs.	134	$765\frac{1}{3}$	46	42	.523	583	270	777	4.53	0
	Division Series											
2008	Chicago	A.L.	1	3	0	1	.000	4	2	5	12.00	0

a Traded to Chicago White Sox with player to be named later for pitcher Freddy Garcia, December 6, 2006. Chicago White Sox received pitcher Gio Gonzalez to complete trade, December 7, 2006.

FRANCIS, JEFFREY WILLIAM (JEFF)

Born, Vancouver, British Columbia, Canada, January 8, 1981.
Bats Left. Throws Left. Height, 6 feet, 5 inches. Weight, 220 pounds.

Year	Club	Lea	G	IP	W	L	Pct	SO	BB	H	ERA	SAVES
2002	Tri-City	Northwest	4	$10\frac{2}{3}$	0	0	.000	16	4	5	0.00	0
2002	Asheville	So.Atl.	4	20	0	0	.000	23	4	16	1.80	0
2003	Visalia	Calif.	27	$160\frac{2}{3}$	12	9	.571	153	45	135	3.47	0
2004	Tulsa	Texas	17	$113\frac{2}{3}$	13	1	.929	147	22	73	1.98	0
2004	Colorado Springs	P.C.	7	41	3	2	.600	49	7	35	2.85	0
2004	Colorado	N.L.	7	$36\frac{2}{3}$	3	2	.600	32	13	42	5.15	0
2005	Colorado	N.L.	33	$183\frac{2}{3}$	14	12	.538	128	70	228	5.68	0
2006	Colorado	N.L.	32	199	13	11	.542	117	69	187	4.16	0
2007	Colorado	N.L.	34	$215\frac{1}{3}$	17	9	.654	165	63	234	4.22	0
2008	Tulsa	Texas	3	$14\frac{1}{3}$	1	0	1.000	19	2	12	0.63	0
2008	Colorado a	N.L.	24	$143\frac{2}{3}$	4	10	.286	94	49	164	5.01	0
2009	Colorado b	N.L.			INJURED—Did Not Play							
2010	Tulsa	Texas	2	$11\frac{2}{3}$	0	0	.000	5	2	11	1.54	0
2010	Colorado Springs	P.C.	1	3	0	0	.000	3	1	1	0.00	0
2010	Colorado c-d	N.L.	20	$104\frac{1}{3}$	4	6	.400	67	23	119	5.00	0
Major League Totals		6 Yrs.	150	$882\frac{2}{3}$	55	50	.524	603	287	974	4.77	0
	Division Series											
2007	Colorado	N.L.	1	6	1	0	1.000	8	2	4	3.00	0
	Championship Series											
2007	Colorado	N.L.	1	$6\frac{2}{3}$	1	0	1.000	4	1	7	1.35	0
	World Series Record											
2007	Colorado	N.L.	1	4	0	1	.000	3	3	10	13.50	0

a On disabled list from June 29 to August 6, 2008.
b On disabled list from March 27 to November 13, 2009.
c On disabled list from April 2 to May 16 and August 12 to September 7, 2010.
d Filed for free agency, November 3, 2010. Signed with Kansas City Royals, January 14, 2011.

FRANCISCO, FRANKLIN (FRANK)

Born, Santo Domingo, Dominican Republic, September 11, 1979.
Bats Right. Throws Right. Height, 6 feet, 2 inches. Weight, 235 pounds.

Year	Club	Lea	G	IP	W	L	Pct	SO	BB	H	ERA	SAVES
1997					INJURED—Did Not Play							
1998	Co-op	Dominican	16	48	0	5	.000	53	76	44	10.31	0
1999	Red Sox	Gulf Coast	12	$53\frac{1}{3}$	2	4	.333	48	35	58	4.56	0
2000	Red Sox	Gulf Coast	1	1	0	0	.000	1	2	2	18.00	0

Year	Club	Lea	G	IP	W	L	Pct	SO	BB	H	ERA	SAVES
2001	Augusta	So.Atl.	37	68	4	3	.571	90	30	40	2.91	2
2002	Winston-Salem	Carolina	6	$25\frac{2}{3}$	0	4	.000	25	18	31	8.06	0
2002	Trenton	Eastern	9	16	2	2	.500	18	16	10	5.63	0
2002	Sarasota a	Fla.St.	16	53	1	5	.167	58	27	33	2.55	0
2003	Winston-Salem	Carolina	16	$78\frac{1}{3}$	7	3	.700	67	36	59	3.56	0
2003	Frisco b	Texas	7	$35\frac{1}{3}$	2	3	.400	22	18	43	8.41	0
2004	Frisco	Texas	15	$17\frac{2}{3}$	1	3	.250	30	10	7	2.55	6
2004	Texas	A.L.	45	$51\frac{1}{3}$	5	1	.833	60	28	36	3.33	0
2005	Oklahoma	P.C.	2	3	0	0	.000	4	2	2	3.00	1
2005	Frisco c	Texas	4	$3\frac{1}{3}$	0	1	.000	3	2	4	8.10	0
2006	Frisco	Texas	13	$14\frac{2}{3}$	0	0	.000	22	4	10	1.84	0
2006	Spokane	Northwest	4	4	0	0	.000	6	0	3	0.00	0
2006	Texas d	A.L.	8	$7\frac{1}{3}$	0	1	.000	6	2	8	4.91	0
2007	Oklahoma	P.C.	5	6	1	0	1.000	14	3	0	0.00	2
2007	Texas	A.L.	59	$59\frac{1}{3}$	1	1	.500	49	38	57	4.55	0
2008	Oklahoma	P.C.	8	9	0	0	.000	16	3	3	0.00	5
2008	Texas	A.L.	58	$63\frac{1}{3}$	3	5	.375	83	26	47	3.13	5
2009	Frisco	Texas	2	2	0	0	.000	1	0	1	0.00	0
2009	Texas e	A.L.	51	$49\frac{1}{3}$	2	3	.400	57	15	40	3.83	25
2010	Texas f-g	A.L.	56	$52\frac{2}{3}$	6	4	.600	60	18	49	3.76	2
Major League Totals		6 Yrs.	277	$283\frac{1}{3}$	17	15	.531	315	127	237	3.75	32

a Traded to Chicago White Sox by Boston Red Sox with pitcher Byeong An for pitcher Bob Howry, July 31, 2002.
b Sent to Texas Rangers as one of the players to be named later for outfielder Carl Everett, July 23, 2003.
c On disabled list from March 25 to October 12, 2005.
d On disabled list from March 24 to June 19, 2006.
e On disabled list from May 7 to May 22 and June 4 to June 20 and July 11 to August 2, 2009.
f On disabled list from August 28 to November 1, 2010.
g Filed for free agency, November 1, 2010, accepted arbitration to remain with Texas Rangers, November 30, 2010.

FRANKLIN, RYAN RAY

Born, Fort Smith, Arkansas, March 5, 1973.
Bats Right. Throws Right. Height, 6 feet, 3 inches. Weight, 190 pounds.

Year	Club	Lea	G	IP	W	L	Pct	SO	BB	H	ERA	SAVES
1993	Bellingham	Northwest	15	74	5	3	.625	55	27	72	2.92	0
1994	Appleton	Midwest	18	118	9	6	.600	102	23	105	3.13	0
1994	Calgary	P.C.	1	$5\frac{2}{3}$	0	0	.000	2	1	9	7.94	0
1994	Riverside	California	8	$61\frac{2}{3}$	4	2	.667	35	8	61	3.06	0
1995	Port City	Southern	31	146	6	10	.375	102	43	153	4.32	0
1996	Port City	Southern	28	182	6	12	.333	127	37	186	4.01	0
1997	Memphis	Southern	11	$59\frac{1}{3}$	4	2	.667	49	14	45	3.03	0
1997	Tacoma	P.C.	14	$90\frac{1}{3}$	5	5	.500	59	24	97	4.18	0
1998	Tacoma	P.C.	34	$127\frac{2}{3}$	5	6	.455	90	32	148	4.51	1
1999	Tacoma	P.C.	29	$135\frac{2}{3}$	6	9	.400	94	33	142	4.71	2
1999	Seattle	A.L.	6	$11\frac{1}{3}$	0	0	.000	6	8	10	4.76	0
2000	Tacoma	P.C.	31	164	11	5	.688	142	35	147	3.90	0
2001	Tacoma	P.C.	1	$3\frac{2}{3}$	0	0	.000	3	0	2	0.00	0
2001	Seattle	A.L.	38	$78\frac{1}{3}$	5	1	.833	60	24	76	3.56	0
2002	Everett	Northwest	1	$2\frac{2}{3}$	0	0	.000	1	0	2	0.00	0
2002	Seattle a	A.L.	41	$118\frac{2}{3}$	7	5	.583	65	22	117	4.02	0
2003	Seattle	A.L.	32	212	11	13	.458	99	61	199	3.57	0
2004	Seattle	A.L.	32	$200\frac{1}{3}$	4	16	.200	104	61	224	4.90	0
2005	Seattle b	A.L.	32	$190\frac{2}{3}$	8	15	.348	93	62	212	5.10	0
2006	Philadelphia-Cincinnati c-d	N.L.	66	$77\frac{1}{3}$	6	7	.462	43	33	86	4.54	0
2007	St. Louis	N.L.	69	80	4	4	.500	44	11	70	3.04	1
2008	St. Louis	N.L.	74	$78\frac{2}{3}$	6	6	.500	51	30	86	3.55	17
2009	St. Louis	N.L.	62	61	4	3	.571	44	24	49	1.92	38
2010	St. Louis	N.L.	59	65	6	2	.750	42	10	57	3.46	27
Major League Totals		11 Yrs.	511	$1173\frac{1}{3}$	61	72	.459	651	346	1186	4.03	83
	Division Series											
2009	St. Louis	N.L.	2	$1\frac{1}{3}$	0	1	.000	1	2	3	0.00	0

a On disabled list from June 28 to July 15, 2002.
b Not offered contract, December 21, 2005. Signed with Philadelphia Phillies, January 5, 2006.
c Traded to Cincinnati Reds for pitcher Zac Scott, August 7, 2006.
d Filed for free agency, October 30, 2006. Signed with St. Louis Cardinals, January 11, 2007.

FRASOR, JASON ANDREW

Born, Chicago, Illinois, August 9, 1977.
Bats Right. Throws Right. Height, 5 feet, 10 inches. Weight, 170 pounds.

Year	Club	Lea	G	IP	W	L	Pct	SO	BB	H	ERA	SAVES
1999	Oneonta	N.Y.-Penn.	12	$58\frac{2}{3}$	3	3	.500	69	22	36	1.69	0
1999	West Michigan	Midwest	4	24	2	1	.667	33	9	17	2.63	0
2000	West Michigan	Midwest	14	$71\frac{1}{3}$	5	3	.625	65	29	55	3.28	0
2001	West Michigan a	Midwest			INJURED—Did Not Play							
2002	Lakeland b	Fla.St.	24	117	5	6	.455	87	46	112	3.54	0
2003	Vero Beach	Fla.St.	15	$24\frac{1}{3}$	1	0	1.000	36	4	16	1.85	6
2003	Jacksonville	Southern	35	$36\frac{2}{3}$	1	0	1.000	50	14	33	2.95	17
2004	Syracuse	Int.	3	4	0	0	.000	6	5	1	2.25	0
2004	Toronto c	A.L.	63	$68\frac{1}{3}$	4	6	.400	54	36	64	4.08	17
2005	Toronto	A.L.	67	$74\frac{2}{3}$	3	5	.375	62	28	67	3.25	1
2006	Syracuse	Int.	18	$20\frac{1}{3}$	3	1	.750	33	13	21	3.98	1
2006	Toronto	A.L.	51	50	3	2	.600	51	17	47	4.32	0
2007	Toronto	A.L.	51	57	1	5	.167	59	23	47	4.58	3
2008	Toronto	A.L.	49	$47\frac{1}{3}$	1	2	.333	42	32	36	4.18	0
2009	Toronto	A.L.	61	$57\frac{2}{3}$	7	3	.700	56	16	43	2.50	11
2010	Toronto d	A.L.	69	$63\frac{2}{3}$	3	4	.429	65	27	61	3.68	4
Major League Totals		7 Yrs.	411	$418\frac{2}{3}$	22	27	.449	389	179	365	3.76	36

a On minor league disabled list, April 5 to September 14, 2001.
b Sent by Detroit Tigers to Los Angeles Dodgers as player to be named later for infielder Hiram Bocachica, September 18, 2002.
c Traded to Toronto Blue Jays for outfielder Jayson Werth, March 30, 2004.
d Filed for free agency, November 1, 2010, accepted arbitration to remain with Toronto Blue Jays, November 30, 2010.

FRENCH, LUCAS STEPHEN (LUKE)

Born, Salina, Kansas, September 13, 1985.
Bats Left. Throws Left. Height, 6 feet, 4 inches. Weight, 220 pounds.

Year	Club	Lea	G	IP	W	L	Pct	SO	BB	H	ERA	SAVES
2004	Tigers	Gulf Coast	11	$49\frac{1}{3}$	1	3	.250	49	19	43	2.74	0
2005	Lakeland	Fla.St.	4	$22\frac{1}{3}$	3	1	.750	17	9	29	4.43	0
2005	Tigers	Gulf Coast	2	$10\frac{2}{3}$	1	0	1.000	9	0	16	7.59	0
2005	West Michigan	Midwest	6	$34\frac{2}{3}$	1	2	.333	24	14	42	5.45	0
2006	West Michigan	Midwest	26	$157\frac{1}{3}$	11	8	.579	94	44	156	3.72	0
2007	Lakeland	Fla.St.	27	149	5	14	.263	93	47	172	4.05	0
2008	Erie	Eastern	27	170	9	11	.450	88	60	195	4.02	0
2009	Toledo	Int.	13	$81\frac{2}{3}$	4	4	.500	72	20	71	2.98	0
2009	Detroit-Seattle a	A.L.	15	$67\frac{1}{3}$	4	5	.444	42	28	87	5.21	0
2010	Tacoma	P.C.	17	$113\frac{1}{3}$	11	3	.786	63	23	109	2.94	0
2010	Seattle	A.L.	16	$87\frac{2}{3}$	5	7	.417	37	29	88	4.83	0
Major League Totals		2 Yrs.	31	155	9	12	.429	79	57	175	4.99	0

a Traded to Seattle Mariners with pitcher Mauricio Robles for pitcher Jarrod Washburn, July 31, 2009.

FUENTES, BRIAN CHRISTOPHER

Born, Merced, California, August 9, 1975.
Bats Left. Throws Left. Height, 6 feet, 4 inches. Weight, 230 pounds.

Year	Club	Lea	G	IP	W	L	Pct	SO	BB	H	ERA	SAVES
1996	Everett	Northwest	13	$26\frac{2}{3}$	0	1	.000	26	13	23	4.39	0
1997	Wisconsin	Midwest	22	$118\frac{2}{3}$	6	7	.462	153	59	84	3.56	0
1998	Lancaster a	California	24	$118\frac{2}{3}$	7	7	.500	137	81	121	4.17	0
1999	New Haven b	Eastern	15	60	3	3	.500	66	46	53	4.95	0
2000	New Haven	Eastern	26	$139\frac{2}{3}$	7	12	.368	152	70	127	4.51	0
2001	Tacoma	P.C.	35	52	3	2	.600	70	25	35	2.94	6
2001	Seattle c-d	A.L.	10	$11\frac{2}{3}$	1	1	.500	10	8	6	4.63	0
2002	Colorado Springs	P.C.	41	$49\frac{1}{3}$	3	3	.500	62	32	44	3.65	1
2002	Colorado	N.L.	31	$26\frac{2}{3}$	2	0	1.000	38	13	25	4.72	0
2003	Colorado	N.L.	75	$75\frac{1}{3}$	3	3	.500	82	34	64	2.75	4
2004	Colorado Springs	P.C.	5	5	0	0	.000	6	3	1	0.00	0
2004	Colorado e	N.L.	47	$44\frac{2}{3}$	2	4	.333	48	19	46	5.64	0
2005	Colorado	N.L.	78	$74\frac{1}{3}$	2	5	.286	91	34	59	2.91	31
2006	Colorado	N.L.	66	$65\frac{1}{3}$	3	4	.429	73	26	50	3.44	30
2007	Asheville	So.Atl.	1	1	0	0	.000	2	0	0	0.00	0
2007	Colorado Springs	P.C.	2	2	0	0	.000	2	0	2	0.00	0
2007	Colorado f	N.L.	64	$61\frac{1}{3}$	3	5	.375	56	23	46	3.08	20
2008	Colorado g	N.L.	67	$62\frac{2}{3}$	1	5	.167	82	22	47	2.73	30

Year	Club	Lea	G	IP	W	L	Pct	SO	BB	H	ERA	SAVES
2009	Los Angeles	A.L.	65	55	1	5	.167	46	24	53	3.93	*48
2010	Rancho Cucamonga	Calif.	1	1	0	0	.000	1	0	0	0.00	0
2010	LA-Minnesota h-i-j	A.L.	48	48	4	1	.800	47	20	31	2.81	24
Major League Totals		10 Yrs.	551	525	22	33	.400	573	223	427	3.41	187
	Division Series											
2007	Colorado	N.L.	3	2 1/3	1	0	1.000	4	3	1	0.00	0
2009	Los Angeles	A.L.	2	1 2/3	0	0	.000	0	1	0	0.00	2
2010	Minnesota	A.L.	2	2 2/3	0	0	.000	2	0	1	0.00	0
Division Series Totals			7	6 2/3	1	0	1.000	6	4	2	0.00	2
	Championship Series											
2007	Colorado	N.L.	4	3 2/3	0	0	.000	6	0	7	7.36	0
2009	Los Angeles	A.L.	3	3	0	0	.000	3	3	1	3.00	1
Championship Series Totals			7	6 2/3	0	0	.000	9	3	8	5.40	1
	World Series Record											
2007	Colorado	N.L.	3	3 2/3	0	0	.000	1	2	6	9.82	0

a On disabled list from April 2 to 20, 1998.
b On disabled list from June 9 to August 22, 1999.
c On disabled list from August 26 to September 29, 2001.
d Traded to Colorado Rockies with pitcher Dennis Stark and pitcher Jose Paniagua for infielder Jeff Cirillo, December 15, 2001.
e On disabled list from June 7 to August 15, 2004.
f On disabled list from July 4 to August 14, 2007.
g Filed for free agency, November 1, 2008. Signed with Los Angeles Angels, December 31, 2008.
h On disabled list from April 6 to April 21, 2010.
i Traded to Minnesota Twins for player to be named later, August 27, 2010. Los Angeles Angels received pitcher Loek Van Mil to complete trade, September 1, 2010.
j Filed for free agency, November 1, 2010. Signed with Oakland Athletics, January 19, 2011.

FULCHINO, JEFFREY JOSEPH (JEFF)

Born, Titusville, Florida, November 26, 1979.
Bats Right. Throws Right. Height, 6 feet, 5 inches. Weight, 275 pounds.

Year	Club	Lea	G	IP	W	L	Pct	SO	BB	H	ERA	SAVES
2001	Utica	N.Y.-Penn.	14	60 2/3	3	8	.273	33	31	48	3.56	0
2002	Kane County	Midwest	24	132 2/3	5	5	.500	94	51	114	3.87	0
2003	Jupiter	Fla.St.	17	78	2	4	.333	47	32	76	4.04	0
2003	Greensboro	So.Atl.	5	24 2/3	1	2	.333	16	7	28	4.01	0
2004	Jupiter	Fla.St.	8	43	2	2	.500	28	16	39	2.72	0
2004	Carolina	Southern	17	90 2/3	6	5	.545	84	37	93	4.47	0
2005	Albuquerque	P.C.	29	153	11	7	.611	101	67	179	5.06	0
2006	Florida	N.L.	1	0 1/3	0	0	.000	0	1	0	0.00	0
2006	Albuquerque	P.C.	25	140	6	10	.375	109	56	144	4.50	0
2007	Albuquerque	P.C.	16	88	6	2	.750	55	39	108	5.83	0
2008	NW Arkansas	Texas	2	3 1/3	0	0	.000	6	1	3	5.40	1
2008	Omaha	P.C.	25	61 1/3	3	4	.429	53	27	71	4.84	5
2008	Kansas City a-b	A.L.	12	14	0	1	.000	12	8	21	9.00	0
2009	Round Rock	P.C.	2	4	0	0	.000	3	2	3	6.75	0
2009	Houston	N.L.	61	82	6	4	.600	71	27	70	3.40	0
2010	Round Rock	P.C.	4	4	0	0	.000	2	1	3	0.00	0
2010	Houston c	N.L.	50	47 1/3	2	1	.667	46	22	53	5.51	0
Major League Totals		4 Yrs.	124	143 2/3	8	6	.571	129	58	144	4.64	0

a Filed for free agency, October 29, 2007. Signed with Kansas City Royals, February 8, 2008.
b Claimed on waivers by Houston Astros, December 9, 2008.
c On disabled list from June 29 to August 2, 2010.

GALARRAGA, ARMANDO ANTONIO

Born, Cumana, Venezuela, January 15, 1982.
Bats Right. Throws Right. Height, 6 feet, 4 inches. Weight, 180 pounds.

Year	Club	Lea	G	IP	W	L	Pct	SO	BB	H	ERA	SAVES
2001	Expos	Gulf Coast	14	34 2/3	1	3	.250	24	15	37	3.12	2
2002	Expos	Gulf Coast	2	3 2/3	0	0	.000	1	0	1	2.45	0
2003	Expos	Gulf Coast	5	15	1	1	.500	7	5	13	1.80	0
2004	Savannah	So.Atl.	23	110 1/3	5	5	.500	94	31	104	4.65	0
2005	Potomac	Carolina	14	80	3	4	.429	79	23	69	2.48	0
2005	Harrisburg a	Eastern	13	76 1/3	3	4	.429	58	21	80	5.19	0
2006	Rangers	Arizona	6	16 1/3	0	2	.000	16	6	18	3.31	0
2006	Bakersfield	Calif.	2	8 2/3	0	1	.000	7	7	6	6.23	0

Year Club	Lea	G	IP	W	L	Pct	SO	BB	H	ERA	SAVES
2006 Spokane	Northwest	1	4	0	1	.000	3	0	4	4.50	0
2006 Frisco	Texas	9	41	1	6	.143	38	13	56	5.49	0
2007 Frisco	Texas	23	$127\frac{2}{3}$	9	6	.600	114	47	122	4.02	0
2007 Oklahoma	P.C.	4	$24\frac{2}{3}$	2	2	.500	21	11	23	4.74	0
2007 Texas	A.L.	3	$8\frac{2}{3}$	0	0	.000	6	7	8	6.23	0
2008 Toledo	Int.	2	12	2	0	1.000	11	1	7	2.25	0
2008 Detroit b	A.L.	30	$178\frac{2}{3}$	13	7	.650	126	61	152	3.73	0
2009 Detroit	A.L.	29	$143\frac{2}{3}$	6	10	.375	95	67	158	5.64	0
2010 Toledo	Int.	8	$44\frac{1}{3}$	4	2	.667	40	14	40	3.65	0
2010 Detroit	A.L.	25	$144\frac{1}{3}$	4	9	.308	74	51	143	4.49	0
Major League Totals	4 Yrs.	87	$475\frac{1}{3}$	23	26	.469	301	186	461	4.58	0

a Traded by Washington Nationals to Texas Rangers with outfielder Brad Wilkerson and outfielder Terrmel Sledge for infielder Alfonso Soriano, December 13, 2005.

b Traded to Detroit Tigers for outfielder Michael Hernandez, February 5, 2008.

GALLAGHER, SEAN PATRICK

Born, Boston, Massachusetts, December 30, 1985.
Bats Right. Throws Right. Height, 6 feet, 2 inches. Weight, 235 pounds.

Year Club	Lea	G	IP	W	L	Pct	SO	BB	H	ERA	SAVES
2004 Cubs	Arizona	10	$34\frac{2}{3}$	1	2	.333	44	11	38	3.12	0
2005 Daytona	Fla.St.	1	5	0	0	.000	7	0	6	1.80	0
2005 Peoria	Midwest	26	146	14	5	.737	139	55	107	2.71	0
2006 Daytona	Fla.St.	13	$78\frac{1}{3}$	4	0	1.000	80	21	75	2.30	0
2006 West Tenn	Southern	15	$86\frac{1}{3}$	7	5	.583	91	55	74	2.71	0
2007 Tennessee	Southern	11	61	7	2	.778	54	24	54	3.39	0
2007 Iowa	P.C.	8	$40\frac{2}{3}$	3	1	.750	37	13	33	2.66	0
2007 Chicago	N.L.	8	$14\frac{2}{3}$	0	0	.000	5	12	19	8.59	1
2008 Iowa	P.C.	5	29	2	2	.500	30	9	21	3.10	0
2008 Chicago	N.L.	12	$58\frac{2}{3}$	3	4	.429	49	22	58	4.45	0
2008 Oakland a-b	A.L.	11	$56\frac{2}{3}$	2	3	.400	54	36	60	5.88	0
2009 Sacramento	P.C.	5	$20\frac{2}{3}$	1	0	1.000	15	6	12	1.74	0
2009 Oakland	A.L.	6	$14\frac{1}{3}$	1	2	.333	10	7	21	8.16	0
2009 Portland	P.C.	1	1	0	1	.000	1	0	3	27.00	0
2009 San Diego c	N.L.	8	$5\frac{1}{3}$	2	0	1.000	4	5	5	0.00	0
2010 Portland	P.C.	3	11	0	2	.000	12	4	14	4.91	0
2010 San Diego-Pittsburgh d-e	N.L.	46	$57\frac{2}{3}$	2	1	.667	43	41	62	5.77	0
Major League Totals	4 Yrs.	91	$207\frac{1}{3}$	10	10	.500	165	123	225	5.64	1

a Traded to Oakland Athletics with outfielder Matt Murton, outfielder Eric Patterson and catcher Josh Donaldson for pitcher Rich Harden and pitcher Chad Gaudin, July 8, 2008.

b On disabled list from August 20 to September 10, 2008.

c Sent to San Diego Padres to complete trade for Scott Hairston, July 28, 2009.

d On disabled list from May 4 to May 28, 2010.

e Sold to Pittsburgh Pirates, July 7, 2010.

GALLARDO, YOVANI

Born, La Piedad, Mexico, February 27, 1986.
Bats Right. Throws Right. Height, 6 feet, 1 inch. Weight, 210 pounds.

Year Club	Lea	G	IP	W	L	Pct	SO	BB	H	ERA	SAVES
2004 Brewers	Arizona	6	$19\frac{1}{3}$	0	0	.000	23	4	14	0.47	0
2004 Beloit	Midwest	2	$7\frac{1}{3}$	0	1	.000	8	4	12	12.27	0
2005 West Virginia	So.Atl.	26	$121\frac{1}{3}$	8	3	.727	110	51	100	2.74	1
2006 Brevard County	Fla.St.	13	$77\frac{2}{3}$	6	3	.667	103	23	54	2.09	0
2006 Huntsville	Southern	13	$77\frac{1}{3}$	5	2	.714	85	28	50	1.63	0
2007 Nashville	P.C.	13	$77\frac{2}{3}$	8	3	.727	110	28	53	2.90	0
2007 Milwaukee	N.L.	20	$110\frac{1}{3}$	9	5	.643	101	37	103	3.67	0
2008 Nashville	P.C.	3	$15\frac{2}{3}$	0	1	.000	18	5	20	5.17	0
2008 Milwaukee a	N.L.	4	24	0	0	.000	20	8	22	1.88	0
2009 Milwaukee	N.L.	30	$185\frac{2}{3}$	13	12	.520	204	94	150	3.73	0
2010 Milwaukee b	N.L.	31	185	14	7	.667	200	75	178	3.84	0
Major League Totals	4 Yrs.	85	505	36	24	.600	525	214	453	3.67	0
Division Series											
2008 Milwaukee	N.L.	2	7	0	1	.000	4	5	4	0.00	0

a On disabled list from March 21 to April 20 and May 2 to September 23, 2008.

b On disabled list from July 5 to July 22, 2010.

GARCIA, FREDDY ANTONIO

Born, Caracas, Venezuela, October 6, 1976.
Bats Right. Throws Right. Height, 6 feet, 4 inches. Weight, 250 pounds.

Year Club	Lea	G	IP	W	L	Pct	SO	BB	H	ERA	SAVES
1994 Hou/Mil	Dominican	16	85	4	6	.400	68	38	80	5.29	0
1995 Astros	Gulf Coast	11	58 1/3	6	3	.667	58	14	60	4.47	0
1996 Quad City	Midwest	13	60 2/3	5	4	.556	50	27	57	3.12	0
1997 Kissimmee	Fla.St.	27	179	10	8	.556	131	49	165	2.56	0
1998 Jackson	Texas	19	119 1/3	6	7	.462	115	58	94	3.24	0
1998 New Orleans	P.C.	2	14 1/3	1	0	1.000	13	1	14	3.14	0
1998 Tacoma a	P.C.	5	32 2/3	3	1	.750	30	13	30	3.86	0
1999 Seattle	A.L.	33	201 1/3	17	8	.680	170	90	205	4.07	0
2000 Seattle	A.L.	21	124 1/3	9	5	.643	79	64	112	3.91	0
2000 Everett	Northwest	2	10	0	0	.000	15	2	11	4.50	0
2000 Tacoma b	P.C.	1	7	1	0	1.000	11	2	5	2.57	0
2001 Seattle	A.L.	34	*238 2/3	18	6	.750	163	69	199	*3.05	0
2002 Seattle	A.L.	34	223 2/3	16	10	.615	181	63	227	4.39	0
2003 Seattle	A.L.	33	201 1/3	12	14	.462	144	71	196	4.51	0
2004 Seattle-Chicago c	A.L.	31	210	13	11	.542	184	64	192	3.81	0
2005 Chicago	A.L.	33	228	14	8	.636	146	60	225	3.87	0
2006 Chicago d	A.L.	33	216 1/3	17	9	.654	135	48	228	4.53	0
2007 Philadelphia	N.L.	11	58	1	5	.167	50	19	74	5.90	0
2007 Phillies	Gulf Coast	1	2	0	0	.000	2	0	2	4.50	0
2007 Clearwater e	Fla.St.	2	6 1/3	0	0	.000	8	1	5	0.00	0
2008 Lakeland	Fla.St.	1	2	0	0	.000	1	1	3	0.00	0
2008 Toledo	Int.	1	3	0	0	.000	4	0	2	0.00	0
2008 Detroit f	A.L.	3	15	1	1	.500	12	6	11	4.20	0
2009 Buffalo	Int.	2	11	0	2	.000	6	5	12	8.18	0
2009 Kannapolis	So.Atl.	1	3	0	0	.000	3	1	2	0.00	0
2009 Bristol	Appal.	2	11	0	0	.000	7	0	6	1.64	0
2009 Charlotte	Int.	1	6	0	1	.000	9	0	8	3.00	0
2009 Chicago g-h	A.L.	9	56	3	4	.429	37	12	56	4.34	0
2010 Chicago i	A.L.	28	157	12	6	.667	89	45	171	4.64	0
Major League Totals	12 Yrs.	303	1929 2/3	133	87	.605	1390	611	1896	4.13	0
Division Series											
2000 Seattle	A.L.	1	3 1/3	0	0	.000	2	3	6	10.80	0
2001 Seattle	A.L.	2	11 2/3	1	1	.500	13	3	13	3.86	0
2005 Chicago	A.L.	1	5	1	0	1.000	1	4	5	5.40	0
Division Series Totals		4	20	2	1	.667	16	10	24	5.40	0
Championship Series											
2000 Seattle	A.L.	2	11 2/3	2	0	1.000	11	4	10	1.54	0
2001 Seattle	A.L.	1	7 1/3	0	1	.000	6	4	7	3.68	0
2005 Chicago	A.L.	1	9	1	0	1.000	5	1	6	2.00	0
Championship Series Totals		4	28	3	1	.750	22	9	23	2.25	0
World Series Record											
2005 Chicago	A.L.	1	7	1	0	1.000	7	3	4	0.00	0

a Traded by Houston Astros to Seattle Mariners with infielder Carlos Guillen and player to be named later for pitcher Randy Johnson, July 31, 1998. Seattle Mariners received pitcher John Halama to complete trade, October 1, 1998.
b On disabled list from April 22 to July 6, 2000.
c Traded to Chicago White Sox with catcher Ben Davis and cash for catcher Miguel Olivo, outfielder Jeremy Reed and infielder Michael Morse, June 27, 2004.
d Traded to Philadelphia Phillies for pitcher Gavin Floyd and player to be named later, December 6, 2006. Chicago White Sox received pitcher Gio Gonzalez to complete trade, December 7, 2006.
e On disabled list from March 23 to April 16 and June 9 to October 31, 2007.
f Filed for free agency, October 31, 2007. Signed with Detroit Tigers organization, August 12, 2008.
g Filed for free agency, October 30, 2008. Signed with New York Mets organization, January 22, 2009.
h Released by New York Mets, April 28, 2009. Signed with Chicago White Sox organization, June 9, 2009.
i Filed for free agency, November 1, 2010.

GARCIA, JAIME OMAR

Born, Reynosa, Mexico, July 8, 1986.
Bats Left. Throws Left. Height, 6 feet, 2 inches. Weight, 215 pounds.

Year Club	Lea	G	IP	W	L	Pct	SO	BB	H	ERA	SAVES
2006 Palm Beach	Fla.St.	12	77 1/3	5	4	.556	51	16	84	3.84	0
2006 Quad Cities	Midwest	13	77 2/3	5	4	.556	80	18	67	2.90	0
2007 Springfield	Texas	18	103 1/3	5	9	.357	97	45	93	3.75	0
2008 Springfield	Texas	6	35	3	2	.600	41	16	26	2.06	0
2008 Memphis	P.C.	13	71	4	4	.500	59	26	74	4.44	0
2008 St. Louis a	N.L.	10	16	1	1	.500	8	8	14	5.63	0

Year Club	Lea	G	IP	W	L	Pct	SO	BB	H	ERA	SAVES
2009 Palm Beach	Fla.St.	3	12 2/3	0	1	.000	16	4	4	0.71	0
2009 Cardinals	Gulf Coast	2	4	0	1	.000	3	1	4	4.50	0
2009 Memphis b............	P.C.	4	21	2	0	1.000	22	9	17	3.86	0
2010 St. Louis..............	N.L.	28	163 1/3	13	8	.619	132	64	151	2.70	0
Major League Totals	2 Yrs.	38	179 1/3	14	9	.609	140	72	165	2.96	0

a On disabled list from August 27 to October 8, 2008.
b On disabled list from March 27 to August 20, 2009.

GARLAND, JON STEVEN

Born, Valencia, California, September 27, 1979.
Bats Right. Throws Right. Height, 6 feet, 6 inches. Weight, 215 pounds.

Year Club	Lea	G	IP	W	L	Pct	SO	BB	H	ERA	SAVES
1997 Cubs..............	Arizona	10	40	3	2	.600	39	10	37	2.70	0
1998 Rockford	Midwest	19	107 1/3	4	7	.364	70	45	124	5.03	0
1998 Hickory a	So.Atl.	5	26 2/3	1	4	.200	19	13	36	5.40	0
1999 Winston-Salem	Carolina	19	119	5	7	.417	84	39	109	3.33	0
1999 Birmingham.......	Southern	7	39	3	1	.750	27	18	39	4.38	0
2000 Charlotte	Int.	16	103 2/3	9	2	.818	63	32	99	2.26	0
2000 Birmingham.......	Southern	1	6	0	0	.000	10	1	4	0.00	0
2000 Chicago b............	A.L.	15	69 2/3	4	8	.333	42	40	82	6.46	0
2001 Charlotte	Int.	5	33	0	3	.000	26	11	31	2.73	0
2001 Chicago	A.L.	35	117	6	7	.462	61	55	123	3.69	1
2002 Chicago	A.L.	33	192 2/3	12	12	.500	112	83	188	4.58	0
2003 Chicago	A.L.	32	191 2/3	12	13	.480	108	74	188	4.51	0
2004 Chicago	A.L.	34	217	12	11	.522	113	76	223	4.89	0
2005 Chicago	A.L.	32	221	18	10	.643	115	47	212	3.50	0
2006 Chicago	A.L.	33	211 1/3	18	7	.720	112	41	*247	4.51	0
2007 Chicago c............	A.L.	32	208 1/3	10	13	.435	98	57	219	4.23	0
2008 Los Angeles d	A.L.	32	196 2/3	14	8	.636	90	59	237	4.90	0
2009 Arizona-Los Angeles e-f..	N.L.	33	204	11	13	.458	109	61	225	4.01	0
2010 San Diego g	N.L.	33	200	14	12	.538	136	87	176	3.46	0
Major League Totals	11 Yrs.	344	2029 1/3	131	114	.535	1096	680	2120	4.32	1
Championship Series											
2005 Chicago	A.L.	1	9	1	0	1.000	7	1	4	2.00	0
World Series Record											
2005 Chicago	A.L.	1	7	0	0	.000	4	2	7	2.57	0

a Traded by Chicago Cubs to Chicago White Sox for pitcher Matt Karchner, July 29, 1998.
b On disabled list from August 19 to September 2, 2000.
c Traded to Los Angeles Angels for infielder Orlando Cabrera, November 19, 2007.
d Filed for free agency, October 30, 2008. Signed with Arizona Diamondbacks, January 29, 2009.
e Traded to Los Angeles Dodgers for player to be named later, August 31, 2009. Arizona Diamondbacks received infielder Tony Abreu to complete trade, October 9, 2009.
f Filed for free agency, November 5, 2009. Signed with San Diego Padres, January 26, 2010.
g Filed for free agency, November 1, 2010. Signed with Los Angeles Dodgers, November 26, 2010.

GARZA, MATTHEW SCOTT (MATT)

Born, Selma, California, November 11, 1983.
Bats Right. Throws Right. Height, 6 feet, 4 inches. Weight, 205 pounds.

Year Club	Lea	G	IP	W	L	Pct	SO	BB	H	ERA	SAVES
2005 Elizabethton	Appal.	4	19 2/3	1	1	.500	25	6	14	3.66	0
2006 Fort Myers	Fla.St.	8	44 1/3	5	1	.833	53	11	27	1.42	0
2006 New Britain	Eastern	10	57 1/3	6	2	.750	68	14	40	2.51	0
2006 Rochester..............	Int.	5	34	3	1	.750	33	7	20	1.85	0
2006 Minnesota	A.L.	10	50	3	6	.333	38	23	62	5.76	0
2007 Rochester..............	Int.	16	92	4	6	.400	95	31	93	3.62	0
2007 Minnesota a	A.L.	16	83	5	7	.417	67	32	96	3.69	0
2008 Vero Beach..........	Fla.St.	1	3 2/3	0	0	.000	4	3	8	9.82	0
2008 Tampa Bay b	A.L.	30	184 2/3	11	9	.550	128	59	170	3.70	0
2009 Tampa Bay	A.L.	32	203	8	12	.400	189	79	177	3.95	0
2010 Tampa Bay c-d.........	A.L.	33	204 2/3	15	10	.600	150	63	193	3.91	1
Major League Totals	5 Yrs.	121	725 1/3	42	44	.488	572	256	698	3.97	1
Division Series											
2008 Tampa Bay	N.L.	1	6	0	1	.000	4	4	7	7.50	0
2010 Tampa Bay	N.L.	1	6	0	0	.000	4	2	5	1.50	0
Division Series Totals		2	12	0	1	.000	8	6	12	4.50	0
Championship Series											
2008 Tampa Bay	N.L.	2	13	2	0	1.000	14	6	8	1.38	0

Year Club	Lea	G	IP	W	L	Pct	SO	BB	H	ERA	SAVES
World Series Record											
2008 Tampa Bay	N.L.	1	6	0	0	.000	7	2	6	6.00	0

a Traded to Tampa Bay Devil Rays with infielder Jason Bartlett and pitcher Eduardo Morlan for infielder Brendan Harris, outfielder Jason Pridie and outfielder Delmon Young, November 28, 2007.
b On disabled list from April 9 to April 25, 2008.
c Pitched no-hit, no-run game against Detroit Tigers, July 26, 2010.
d Traded to Chicago Cubs with outfielder Fernando Perez and pitcher Zachary Russcup for infielder Hak-Ju Lee, outfielder Brandon Guyer, pitcher Chris Archer, catcher Robinson Chirinos and outfielder Sam Fuld, January 8, 2011.

GAUDIN, CHAD EDWARD

Born, Metairie, Louisiana, March 24, 1983.
Bats Right. Throws Right. Height, 5 feet, 11 inches. Weight, 190 pounds.

Year Club	Lea	G	IP	W	L	Pct	SO	BB	H	ERA	SAVES
2002 Charleston-SC	So.Atl.	26	$119\frac{1}{3}$	4	6	.400	106	37	106	2.26	1
2003 Bakersfield	Calif.	14	$80\frac{1}{3}$	5	3	.625	70	23	63	2.13	0
2003 Orlando	Southern	3	19	2	0	1.000	23	3	8	0.47	0
2003 Tampa Bay	A.L.	15	40	2	0	1.000	23	16	37	3.60	0
2004 Tampa Bay	A.L.	26	$42\frac{2}{3}$	1	2	.333	30	16	59	4.85	0
2004 Durham a	Int.	17	$47\frac{2}{3}$	1	3	.250	52	17	48	4.72	2
2005 Toronto	A.L.	5	13	1	3	.250	12	6	31	13.15	0
2005 Syracuse b-c	Int.	23	$150\frac{1}{3}$	9	8	.529	113	35	140	3.35	0
2006 Sacramento	P.C.	4	$24\frac{1}{3}$	3	0	1.000	26	8	14	0.37	0
2006 Oakland	A.L.	55	64	4	2	.667	36	42	51	3.09	2
2007 Oakland	A.L.	34	$199\frac{1}{3}$	11	13	.458	154	100	205	4.42	0
2008 Oakland	A.L.	26	$62\frac{2}{3}$	5	3	.625	44	17	63	3.59	0
2008 Chicago d-e	N.L.	24	$27\frac{1}{3}$	4	2	.667	27	10	29	6.26	0
2009 Portland	P.C.	2	$8\frac{2}{3}$	0	0	.000	10	2	4	0.00	0
2009 San Diego	N.L.	20	$105\frac{1}{3}$	4	10	.286	105	56	105	5.13	0
2009 New York f-g	A.L.	11	42	2	0	1.000	34	20	41	3.43	0
2010 Oakland-New York h-i-j	A.L.	42	$65\frac{1}{3}$	1	4	.200	53	25	73	5.65	0
Major League Totals	8 Yrs.	258	$661\frac{2}{3}$	35	39	.473	518	308	694	4.61	2
Championship Series											
2006 Oakland	A.L.	3	$3\frac{1}{3}$	0	0	.000	1	3	2	0.00	0
2009 New York	A.L.	1	1	0	0	.000	0	0	0	0.00	0
Championship Series Totals		4	$4\frac{1}{3}$	0	0	.000	1	3	2	0.00	0

a Traded to Toronto Blue Jays for catcher Kevin Cash, December 13, 2004.
b Traded to Oakland Athletics for player to be named later, December 5, 2005.
c Toronto Blue Jays received outfielder Dustin Majewski to complete trade, December 8, 2005.
d On disabled list from March 19 to April 8, 2008.
e Traded to Chicago Cubs with pitcher Rich Harden for pitcher Sean Gallagher, outfielder Matt Murton, outfielder Eric Patterson and catcher Josh Donaldson, July 8, 2008.
f Released by Chicago Cubs, April 5, 2009. Signed with San Diego Padres organization, April 12, 2009.
g Sold to New York Yankees, August 6, 2009.
h Filed for free agency, November 1, 2010. Signed with Oakland Athletics, March 28, 2009.
i Released by Oakland Athletics, May 21, 2010. Signed with New York Yankees, May 26, 2010.
j Filed for free agency, November 2, 2010. Signed with Washington Nationals, December 17, 2010.

GONZALEZ, GIOVANY A. (GIO)

Born, Hialeah, Florida, September 19, 1985.
Bats Right. Throws Left. Height, 5 feet, 11 inches. Weight, 195 pounds.

Year Club	Lea	G	IP	W	L	Pct	SO	BB	H	ERA	SAVES
2004 Bristol	Appal.	7	24	1	2	.333	36	8	17	2.25	0
2004 Kannapolis	So.Atl.	8	$40\frac{2}{3}$	1	2	.333	34	20	39	3.76	0
2005 Winston-Salem	Carolina	13	$73\frac{1}{3}$	8	3	.727	79	25	61	3.56	0
2005 Kannapolis a	So.Atl.	11	$57\frac{2}{3}$	5	3	.625	84	22	36	1.87	0
2006 Reading b	Eastern	27	$154\frac{2}{3}$	7	12	.368	166	81	140	4.66	0
2007 Birmingham	Southern	27	150	9	7	.563	185	57	116	3.18	0
2008 Sacramento	P.C.	23	123	8	7	.533	128	61	106	4.24	0
2008 Oakland c	A.L.	10	34	1	4	.200	34	25	32	7.68	0
2009 Sacramento	P.C.	12	61	4	1	.800	71	34	42	2.51	0
2009 Oakland	A.L.	20	$98\frac{2}{3}$	6	7	.462	109	56	113	5.75	0
2010 Oakland	A.L.	33	$200\frac{2}{3}$	15	9	.625	171	92	171	3.23	0
Major League Totals	3 Yrs.	63	$333\frac{1}{3}$	22	20	.524	314	173	316	4.43	0

a Sent by Chicago White Sox to Philadelphia as player to be named later for infielder Jim Thome, December 8, 2005.
b Sent to Chicago White Sox as player to be named later for pitcher Freddy Garcia, December 7, 2006.
c Traded to Oakland Athletics with pitcher Fautino de los Santos and outfielder Ryan Sweeney for outfielder Nick Swisher, January 3, 2008.

GORZELANNY, THOMAS STEPHEN (TOM)

Born, Evergreen Park, Illinois, July 12, 1982.

Bats Left. Throws Left. Height, 6 feet, 2 inches. Weight, 205 pounds.

Year	Club	Lea	G	IP	W	L	Pct	SO	BB	H	ERA	SAVES
2003	Williamsport	N.Y.-Penn.	8	$30\frac{1}{3}$	1	2	.333	22	10	23	1.78	0
2004	Lynchburg	Carolina	10	$55\frac{2}{3}$	3	5	.375	61	19	54	4.85	0
2004	Hickory	So.Atl.	16	93	7	2	.778	106	34	63	2.23	0
2005	Altoona	Eastern	23	$129\frac{2}{3}$	8	5	.615	124	46	114	3.26	0
2005	Pittsburgh	N.L.	3	6	0	1	.000	3	3	10	12.00	0
2006	Indianapolis	Int.	16	$99\frac{2}{3}$	6	5	.545	94	27	67	2.35	0
2006	Pittsburgh a	N.L.	11	$61\frac{2}{3}$	2	5	.286	40	31	50	3.79	0
2007	Pittsburgh	N.L.	32	$201\frac{2}{3}$	14	10	.583	135	68	214	3.88	0
2008	Indianapolis	Int.	7	35	3	1	.750	33	4	28	2.06	0
2008	Pittsburgh b	N.L.	21	$105\frac{1}{3}$	6	9	.400	67	70	120	6.66	0
2009	Indianapolis	Int.	15	87	4	3	.571	85	30	73	2.48	0
2009	Pittsburgh-Chicago c	N.L.	22	47	7	3	.700	47	17	45	5.55	0
2010	Chicago d	N.L.	29	$136\frac{1}{3}$	7	9	.438	119	68	136	4.09	1
Major League Totals		6 Yrs.	118	558	36	37	.493	411	257	575	4.68	1

a On disabled list from August 18 to September 16, 2006.

b On disabled list from September 24 to November 13, 2008.

c Traded to Chicago Cubs with pitcher John Grabow for pitcher Kevin Hart, pitcher Jose Ascanio and infielder Josh Harrison, July 30, 2009.

d Traded to Washington Nationals for outfielder Michael Burgess, pitcher Graham Hicks and pitcher A.J. Morris, January 19, 2011.

GREGERSON, LUKE J.

Born, Park Ridge, Illinois, May 14, 1984.

Bats Left. Throws Right. Height, 6 feet, 3 inches. Weight, 200 pounds.

Year	Club	Lea	G	IP	W	L	Pct	SO	BB	H	ERA	SAVES
2006	Johnson City	Appal.	15	$16\frac{1}{3}$	0	1	.000	24	6	14	3.86	5
2006	State College	N.Y.-Penn.	12	$15\frac{2}{3}$	6	1	.857	22	9	9	1.72	4
2007	Palm Beach	Fla.St.	53	64	3	4	.429	69	20	42	1.97	29
2007	Springfield	Texas	1	1	0	0	.000	3	0	1	0.00	0
2008	Springfield	Texas	57	$75\frac{1}{3}$	7	6	.538	78	26	62	3.35	10
2009	San Diego a-b	N.L.	72	75	2	4	.333	93	31	62	3.24	1
2010	San Diego	N.L.	80	$78\frac{1}{3}$	4	7	.364	89	18	47	3.22	2
Major League Totals		2 Yrs.	152	$153\frac{1}{3}$	6	11	.353	182	49	109	3.23	3

a Sent by St. Louis Cardinals to San Diego Padres as player to be named later for Khalil Greene, March 23, 2009.

b On disabled list from June 8 to July 6, 2009.

GREGG, KEVIN MARSCHALL

Born, Corvallis, Oregon, June 20, 1978.

Bats Right. Throws Right. Height, 6 feet, 6 inches. Weight, 235 pounds.

Year	Club	Lea	G	IP	W	L	Pct	SO	BB	H	ERA	SAVES
1996	Athletics	Arizona	11	$40\frac{2}{3}$	3	3	.500	48	21	30	3.10	0
1997	Visalia	California	25	$115\frac{1}{3}$	6	8	.429	136	74	116	5.70	0
1998	Modesto	California	30	144	8	7	.533	141	76	139	3.81	1
1999	Visalia	California	13	64	4	4	.500	48	23	60	3.80	1
1999	Midland	Texas	16	$91\frac{1}{3}$	4	7	.364	66	31	75	3.74	0
1999	Vancouver	P.C.	1	5	1	0	1.000	4	2	6	3.60	0
2000	Midland	Texas	28	$140\frac{2}{3}$	5	14	.263	97	73	171	6.40	0
2001	Midland	Texas	44	$81\frac{1}{3}$	5	5	.500	72	40	88	4.54	1
2002	Midland	Texas	11	$37\frac{2}{3}$	3	3	.500	45	18	31	4.30	0
2002	Sacramento	P.C.	16	$58\frac{2}{3}$	2	5	.286	45	23	82	7.52	0
2002	Visalia a	California	3	$17\frac{1}{3}$	2	1	.667	11	9	8	2.08	0
2003	Arkansas	Texas	15	$66\frac{1}{3}$	4	3	.571	60	19	60	3.53	0
2003	Salt Lake	P.C.	15	$91\frac{2}{3}$	7	4	.636	75	18	90	4.03	0
2003	Anaheim	A.L.	5	$24\frac{2}{3}$	2	0	1.000	14	8	18	3.28	0
2004	Anaheim	A.L.	55	$87\frac{2}{3}$	5	2	.714	84	28	86	4.21	1
2005	Salt Lake	P.C.	7	$34\frac{2}{3}$	3	1	.750	36	10	36	3.89	0
2005	Los Angeles	A.L.	33	$64\frac{1}{3}$	1	2	.333	52	29	70	5.04	0
2006	Salt Lake	P.C.	3	10	1	0	1.000	8	4	5	0.00	0
2006	Los Angeles b	A.L.	32	$78\frac{1}{3}$	3	4	.429	71	21	88	4.14	0
2007	Florida	N.L.	74	84	0	5	.000	87	40	63	3.54	32
2008	Florida c	N.L.	72	$68\frac{2}{3}$	7	8	.467	58	37	51	3.41	29
2009	Chicago d	N.L.	72	$68\frac{2}{3}$	5	6	.455	71	30	60	4.72	23
2010	Toronto e	A.L.	63	59	2	6	.250	58	30	52	3.51	37
Major League Totals		8 Yrs.	406	$535\frac{1}{3}$	25	33	.431	495	223	488	4.03	122

Year	Club	Lea	G	IP	W	L	Pct	SO	BB	H	ERA	SAVES
	Division Series											
2004	Anaheim	A.L.	1	2	0	0	.000	0	1	3	0.00	0
	Championship Series											
2005	Los Angeles	A.L.	1	2	0	0	.000	3	1	1	0.00	0

a Filed for free agency from Oakland Athletics, October 15, 2002. Signed with Anaheim Angels organization, November 20, 2002.
b Traded to Florida Marlins for pitcher Chris Resop, November 20, 2006.
c Traded to Chicago Cubs for pitcher Jose Ceda, November 13, 2008.
d Filed for free agency, November 9, 2009. Signed with Toronto Blue Jays, February 5, 2010.
e Filed for free agency, November 4, 2010. Signed with Baltimore Orioles, January 5, 2011.

GREINKE, DONALD ZACKARY (ZACK)

Born, Orlando, Florida, October 21, 1983.
Bats Right. Throws Right. Height, 6 feet, 2 inches. Weight, 185 pounds.

Year	Club	Lea	G	IP	W	L	Pct	SO	BB	H	ERA	SAVES
2002	Wilmington	Carolina	1	2	0	0	.000	0	0	1	0.00	0
2002	Royals	Gulf Coast	3	$4\frac{2}{3}$	0	0	.000	4	3	3	1.93	0
2002	Spokane	Northwest	2	$4\frac{2}{3}$	0	0	.000	5	0	9	7.71	0
2003	Wilmington	Carolina	14	87	11	1	.917	78	13	56	1.14	0
2003	Wichita	Texas	9	53	4	3	.571	34	5	58	3.23	0
2004	Omaha	P.C.	6	$28\frac{2}{3}$	1	1	.500	23	6	25	2.51	0
2004	Kansas City	A.L.	24	145	8	11	.421	100	26	143	3.97	0
2005	Kansas City	A.L.	33	183	5	17	.227	114	53	233	5.80	0
2006	Wichita	Texas	18	$105\frac{2}{3}$	8	3	.727	94	27	96	4.34	0
2006	Kansas City a	A.L.	3	$6\frac{1}{3}$	1	0	1.000	5	3	7	4.26	0
2007	Kansas City	A.L.	52	122	7	7	.500	106	36	122	3.69	1
2008	Kansas City	A.L.	32	$202\frac{1}{3}$	13	10	.565	183	56	202	3.47	0
2009	Kansas City b	A.L.	33	$229\frac{1}{3}$	16	8	.667	242	51	195	*2.16	0
2010	Kansas City c	A.L.	33	220	10	14	.417	181	55	219	4.17	0
Major League Totals		7 Yrs.	210	1108	60	67	.472	931	280	1121	3.82	1

a On disabled list from April 1 to June 21, 2006.
b Selected Cy Young Award Winner in American League for 2009.
c Traded to Milwaukee Brewers with outfielder Yuniesky Betancourt for outfielder Lorenzo Cain, infielder Alcides Escobar, pitcher Jeremy Jeffress and pitcher Jake Odorizzi, December 19, 2010.

GUERRIER, MATTHEW OLSON (MATT)

Born, Cleveland, Ohio, August 2, 1978.
Bats Right. Throws Right. Height, 6 feet, 3 inches. Weight, 195 pounds.

Year	Club	Lea	G	IP	W	L	Pct	SO	BB	H	ERA	SAVES
1999	Bristol	Appal.	21	$25\frac{2}{3}$	5	0	1.000	37	14	18	1.05	10
1999	Winston-Salem	Carolina	4	$3\frac{1}{3}$	0	0	.000	5	0	3	5.40	2
2000	Winston-Salem	Carolina	30	$34\frac{2}{3}$	0	3	.000	35	12	25	1.30	19
2000	Birmingham	Southern	23	$23\frac{1}{3}$	3	1	.750	19	12	17	2.70	7
2001	Charlotte	Int.	12	$81\frac{1}{3}$	7	1	.875	43	18	75	3.54	0
2001	Birmingham	Southern	15	$98\frac{2}{3}$	11	3	.786	75	32	85	3.10	0
2002	Nashville a	P.C.	27	157	7	12	.368	130	47	154	4.59	0
2003	Nashville b	P.C.	20	$105\frac{1}{3}$	4	6	.400	78	18	108	4.53	0
2004	Rochester	Int.	24	144	5	10	.333	97	25	135	3.19	0
2004	Minnesota	A.L.	9	19	0	1	.000	11	6	22	5.68	0
2005	Minnesota	A.L.	43	$71\frac{2}{3}$	0	3	.000	46	24	71	3.39	0
2006	New Britain	Eastern	4	$8\frac{2}{3}$	2	0	1.000	10	3	3	1.04	0
2006	Minnesota c	A.L.	39	$69\frac{2}{3}$	1	0	1.000	37	21	78	3.36	1
2007	Minnesota	A.L.	73	88	2	4	.333	68	21	71	2.35	1
2008	Minnesota	A.L.	*76	$76\frac{1}{3}$	6	9	.400	59	37	84	5.19	1
2009	Minnesota	A.L.	*79	$76\frac{1}{3}$	5	1	.833	47	16	58	2.36	1
2010	Minnesota d	A.L.	74	71	5	7	.417	42	22	56	3.17	1
Major League Totals		7 Yrs.	393	472	19	25	.432	310	147	440	3.38	5
	Division Series											
2006	Minnesota	A.L.	1	1	0	0	.000	0	0	0	0.00	0
2009	Minnesota	A.L.	2	2	0	0	.000	2	0	0	0.00	0
2010	Minnesota	A.L.	2	$1\frac{2}{3}$	0	0	.000	2	1	1	0.00	0
Division Series Totals			5	$4\frac{2}{3}$	0	0	.000	4	1	1	0.00	0

a Traded by Chicago White Sox to Pittsburgh Pirates for pitcher Damaso Marte and infielder Edwin Yan, March 27, 2002.
b Claimed on waivers by Minnesota Twins, November 20, 2003.
c On disabled list from June 9 to August 1, 2006.
d Filed for free agency, November 1, 2010. Signed with Los Angeles Dodgers, December 16, 2010.

GUTHRIE, JEREMY SHANE

Born, Roseburg, Oregon, April 8, 1979.
Bats Right. Throws Right. Height, 6 feet, 1 inch. Weight, 200 pounds.

Year	Club	Lea	G	IP	W	L	Pct	SO	BB	H	ERA	SAVES
2003	Akron	Eastern	10	$62^{2}/_{3}$	6	2	.750	35	14	44	1.44	0
2003	Buffalo	Int.	18	$96^{2}/_{3}$	4	9	.308	62	30	129	6.52	0
2004	Buffalo	Int.	4	$19^{1}/_{3}$	1	2	.333	10	18	23	7.91	0
2004	Akron	Eastern	23	$130^{1}/_{3}$	8	8	.500	94	42	145	4.21	0
2004	Cleveland	A.L.	6	$11^{2}/_{3}$	0	0	.000	7	6	9	4.63	0
2005	Cleveland	A.L.	1	6	0	0	.000	3	2	9	6.00	0
2005	Buffalo	Int.	25	$136^{1}/_{3}$	12	10	.545	100	49	152	5.08	0
2006	Buffalo	Int.	21	$123^{1}/_{3}$	9	5	.643	88	48	104	3.14	0
2006	Cleveland	A.L.	9	$19^{1}/_{3}$	0	0	.000	14	15	24	6.98	0
2007	Baltimore a	A.L.	32	$175^{1}/_{3}$	7	5	.583	123	47	165	3.70	0
2008	Baltimore b	A.L.	30	$190^{2}/_{3}$	10	12	.455	120	58	176	3.63	0
2009	Baltimore	A.L.	33	200	10	*17	.370	110	60	224	5.04	0
2010	Baltimore	A.L.	32	$209^{1}/_{3}$	11	14	.440	119	50	193	3.83	0
Major League Totals		7 Yrs.	143	$812^{1}/_{3}$	38	48	.442	496	238	800	4.15	0

a Claimed on waivers by Baltimore Orioles, January 29, 2007.
b On disabled list from September 6 to September 27, 2008.

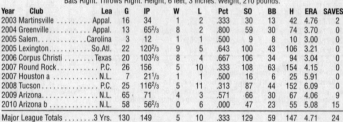

GUTIERREZ, JUAN CARLOS

Born, Puerto La Cruz, Venezuela, July 14, 1983.
Bats Right. Throws Right. Height, 6 feet, 3 inches. Weight, 210 pounds.

Year	Club	Lea	G	IP	W	L	Pct	SO	BB	H	ERA	SAVES
2003	Martinsville	Appal.	16	34	1	2	.333	30	13	42	4.76	2
2004	Greenville	Appal.	13	$65^{2}/_{3}$	8	2	.800	59	30	74	3.70	0
2005	Salem	Carolina	3	12	1	1	.500	9	8	10	3.00	0
2005	Lexington	So.Atl.	22	$120^{2}/_{3}$	9	5	.643	100	43	106	3.21	0
2006	Corpus Christi	Texas	20	$103^{2}/_{3}$	8	4	.667	106	34	94	3.04	0
2007	Round Rock	P.C.	26	156	5	10	.333	108	63	154	4.15	0
2007	Houston a	N.L.	7	$21^{1}/_{3}$	1	1	.500	16	6	25	5.91	0
2008	Tucson	P.C.	25	$116^{2}/_{3}$	5	11	.313	87	44	152	6.09	0
2009	Arizona	N.L.	65	71	4	3	.571	66	30	67	4.06	9
2010	Arizona b	N.L.	58	$56^{2}/_{3}$	0	6	.000	47	23	55	5.08	15
Major League Totals		3 Yrs.	130	149	5	10	.333	129	59	147	4.71	24

a Traded to Arizona Diamondbacks with pitcher Chad Qualls and outfielder Chris Burke for pitcher Jose Valverde, December 14, 2007.
b On disabled list from August 3 to August 18, 2010.

HALLADAY, HARRY LEROY (ROY)

Born, Denver, Colorado, May 14, 1977.
Bats Right. Throws Right. Height, 6 feet, 6 inches. Weight, 225 pounds.

Year	Club	Lea	G	IP	W	L	Pct	SO	BB	H	ERA	SAVES
1995	Blue Jays	Gulf Coast	10	$50^{1}/_{3}$	3	5	.375	48	16	35	3.40	0
1996	Dunedin	Fla.St.	27	$164^{2}/_{3}$	15	7	.682	109	46	158	2.73	0
1997	Knoxville	Southern	7	$36^{2}/_{3}$	2	3	.400	30	11	46	5.40	0
1997	Syracuse	Int.	22	$125^{2}/_{3}$	7	10	.412	64	53	132	4.58	0
1998	Syracuse	Int.	21	$116^{1}/_{3}$	9	5	.643	71	53	107	3.79	0
1998	Toronto	A.L.	2	14	1	0	1.000	13	2	9	1.93	0
1999	Toronto	A.L.	36	$149^{1}/_{3}$	8	7	.533	82	79	156	3.92	1
2000	Syracuse	Int.	11	$73^{2}/_{3}$	2	3	.400	38	21	85	5.50	0
2000	Toronto	A.L.	19	$67^{2}/_{3}$	4	7	.364	44	42	107	10.64	0
2001	Dunedin	Fla.St.	13	$22^{2}/_{3}$	0	1	.000	15	3	28	3.97	2
2001	Tennessee	Southern	5	34	2	1	.667	29	6	25	2.12	0
2001	Syracuse	Int.	2	14	1	0	1.000	13	0	12	3.21	0
2001	Toronto	A.L.	17	$105^{1}/_{3}$	5	3	.625	96	25	97	3.16	0
2002	Toronto	A.L.	34	*$239^{1}/_{3}$	19	7	.731	168	62	223	2.93	0
2003	Toronto a	A.L.	36	*266	*22	7	*.759	204	32	*253	3.25	0
2004	Toronto b	A.L.	21	133	8	8	.500	95	39	140	4.20	0
2005	Toronto c	A.L.	19	$141^{2}/_{3}$	12	4	.750	108	18	118	2.41	0
2006	Toronto	A.L.	32	220	16	5	*.762	132	34	208	3.19	0
2007	Toronto d	A.L.	31	$225^{1}/_{3}$	16	7	.696	139	48	232	3.71	0
2008	Toronto	A.L.	34	*246	20	11	.645	206	39	220	2.78	0
2009	Toronto e-f	A.L.	32	239	17	10	.630	208	35	234	2.79	0
2010	Philadelphia g-h-i	N.L.	33	*$250^{2}/_{3}$	*21	10	.677	219	30	*231	2.44	0
Major League Totals		13 Yrs.	346	$2297^{1}/_{3}$	169	86	.663	1714	485	2228	3.32	1

Year	Club	Lea	G	IP	W	L	Pct	SO	BB	H	ERA	SAVES
	Division Series											
2010	Philadelphia	N.L.	1	9	1	0	1.000	8	1	0	0.00	0
	Championship Series											
2010	Philadelphia	N.L.	2	13	1	1	.500	12	2	14	4.15	0

a Selected Cy Young Award Winner in American League for 2003.
b On disabled list from May 28 to June 12 and from July 17 to September 21, 2004.
c On disabled list from July 9 to October 3, 2005.
d On disabled list from May 11 to May 31, 2007.
e On disabled list from June 13 to June 28, 2009.
f Traded to Philadelphia Phillies for pitcher Kyle Drabek, pitcher Michael Taylor and catcher Travis D'Arnaud, December 16, 2009.
g Pitched no-hit, no-run perfect game against Florida Marlins, May 29, 2010.
h Pitched no-hit, no-run game against Cincinnati Reds in divisional playoff, October 6, 2010.
i Selected Cy Young Award Winner in National League for 2010.

HAMELS, COLBERT RICHARD (COLE)

Born, San Diego, California, December 27, 1983.
Bats Left. Throws Left. Height, 6 feet, 4 inches. Weight, 195 pounds.

Year	Club	Lea	G	IP	W	L	Pct	SO	BB	H	ERA	SAVES
2003	Clearwater	Fla.St.	5	26 1/3	0	2	.000	32	14	29	2.73	0
2003	Lakewood	So.Atl.	13	74 2/3	6	1	.857	115	25	32	0.84	0
2004	Clearwater	Fla.St.	4	16	1	0	1.000	24	4	10	1.13	0
2005	Reading	Eastern	3	19	2	0	1.000	19	12	10	2.37	0
2005	Clearwater	Fla.St.	3	16	2	0	1.000	18	7	7	2.25	0
2006	Lakewood	So.Atl.	1	5 2/3	0	0	.000	3	2	3	1.59	0
2006	Clearwater	Fla.St.	4	20 1/3	1	1	.500	29	9	16	1.77	0
2006	Scranton/WB	Int.	3	23	2	0	1.000	36	1	10	0.39	0
2006	Philadelphia a	N.L.	23	132 1/3	9	8	.529	145	48	117	4.08	0
2007	Philadelphia b	N.L.	28	183 1/3	15	5	.750	177	43	163	3.39	0
2008	Philadelphia	N.L.	33	227 1/3	14	10	.583	196	53	193	3.09	0
2009	Philadelphia	N.L.	32	193 2/3	10	11	.476	168	43	206	4.32	0
2010	Philadelphia	N.L.	33	208 2/3	12	11	.522	211	61	185	3.06	0
Major League Totals		5 Yrs.	149	945 1/3	60	45	.571	897	248	864	3.53	0
	Division Series											
2007	Philadelphia	N.L.	1	6 2/3	0	1	.000	7	4	3	4.05	0
2008	Philadelphia	N.L.	1	8	1	0	1.000	9	1	2	0.00	0
2009	Philadelphia	N.L.	1	5	0	1	.000	5	0	7	7.20	0
2010	Philadelphia	N.L.	1	9	1	0	1.000	9	0	5	0.00	0
Division Series Totals			4	28 2/3	2	2	.500	30	5	17	2.20	0
	Championship Series											
2008	Philadelphia	N.L.	2	14	2	0	1.000	13	5	11	1.93	0
2009	Philadelphia	N.L.	2	9 2/3	1	0	1.000	7	2	13	6.52	0
2010	Philadelphia	N.L.	1	6	0	1	.000	8	1	5	4.50	0
Championship Series Totals			5	29 2/3	3	1	.750	28	8	29	3.94	0
	World Series Record											
2008	Philadelphia	N.L.	2	13	1	0	1.000	8	3	10	2.77	0
2009	Philadelphia	N.L.	1	4 1/3	0	1	.000	3	2	5	10.38	0
World Series Totals			3	17 1/3	1	1	.500	11	5	15	4.67	0

a On disabled list from May 19 to June 6, 2006.
b On disabled list from August 17 to September 18, 2007.

HAMMEL, JASON AARON

Born, Greenville, South Carolina, September 2, 1982.
Bats Right. Throws Right. Height, 6 feet, 6 inches. Weight, 220 pounds.

Year	Club	Lea	G	IP	W	L	Pct	SO	BB	H	ERA	SAVES
2002	Princeton	Appal.	2	5 1/3	0	0	.000	5	0	7	0.00	1
2002	Hudson Valley	N.Y.-Penn.	13	51 2/3	1	5	.167	38	14	71	5.23	1
2003	Charleston	So.Atl.	14	76 2/3	6	2	.750	50	27	70	3.40	0
2004	Bakersfield	Calif.	11	71 1/3	6	2	.750	65	20	52	1.89	0
2004	Charleston	So.Atl.	18	94 2/3	4	7	.364	88	27	94	3.23	0
2005	Durham	Int.	10	54 2/3	3	2	.600	48	27	57	4.12	0
2005	Montgomery	Southern	12	81 1/3	8	2	.800	76	19	70	2.66	0
2006	Durham	Int.	24	127 2/3	5	9	.357	117	36	133	4.23	0
2006	Tampa Bay	A.L.	9	44	0	6	.000	32	21	61	7.77	0
2007	Durham	Int.	13	76 1/3	4	5	.444	75	28	61	3.42	0
2007	Tampa Bay	A.L.	24	85	3	5	.375	64	40	100	6.14	0
2008	Tampa Bay	A.L.	40	78 1/3	4	4	.500	44	35	83	4.60	2

Year Club	Lea	G	IP	W	L	Pct	SO	BB	H	ERA	SAVES
2009 Colorado a	N.L.	34	$176^{2}/_{3}$	10	8	.556	133	42	203	4.33	0
2010 Colorado Springs	P.C.	1	7	1	0	1.000	6	1	9	5.14	0
2010 Colorado b	N.L.	30	$177^{2}/_{3}$	10	9	.526	141	47	201	4.81	0
Major League Totals	5 Yrs.	137	$561^{2}/_{3}$	27	32	.458	414	185	648	5.06	2
Division Series											
2009 Colorado	N.L.	1	$3^{2}/_{3}$	0	0	.000	5	3	4	9.82	0

a Traded to Colorado Rockies for pitcher Aneury Rodriguez, April 4, 2009.
b On disabled list from April 27 to May 15, 2010.

HANRAHAN, JOEL RYAN

Born, Des Moines, Iowa, October 6, 1981.
Bats Right. Throws Right. Height, 6 feet, 3 inches. Weight, 250 pounds.

Year Club	Lea	G	IP	W	L	Pct	SO	BB	H	ERA	SAVES
2000 Great Falls	Pioneer	12	55	3	1	.750	40	23	49	4.75	0
2001 Wilmington	So.Atl.	27	144	9	11	.450	116	55	136	3.38	0
2002 Vero Beach	Fla.St.	25	$143^{2}/_{3}$	10	6	.625	139	51	129	4.20	0
2002 Jacksonville	Southern	3	11	1	1	.500	10	7	15	10.64	0
2003 Las Vegas	P.C.	5	25	1	2	.333	13	20	36	10.08	0
2003 Jacksonville	Southern	23	$133^{1}/_{3}$	10	4	.714	130	53	117	2.43	0
2004 Las Vegas	P.C.	25	$119^{1}/_{3}$	7	7	.500	97	75	128	5.05	0
2005 Vero Beach	Fla.St.	5	$21^{1}/_{3}$	1	0	1.000	25	11	25	5.91	0
2005 Jacksonville	Southern	23	$111^{2}/_{3}$	9	8	.529	102	55	118	4.92	0
2006 Las Vegas	P.C.	14	$74^{1}/_{3}$	4	3	.571	46	39	70	4.48	0
2006 Jacksonville a	Southern	12	$66^{1}/_{3}$	7	2	.778	67	38	49	2.58	0
2007 Columbus	Int.	15	$75^{1}/_{3}$	5	4	.556	71	36	65	3.70	0
2007 Washington	N.L.	12	51	5	3	.625	43	38	59	6.00	0
2008 Washington	N.L.	69	$84^{1}/_{3}$	6	3	.667	93	42	73	3.95	9
2009 Washington-Pittsburgh b	N.L.	67	64	1	4	.200	72	34	73	4.78	5
2010 Bradenton	Fla.St.	2	2	0	0	.000	3	0	0	0.00	0
2010 Pittsburgh c	N.L.	72	$69^{2}/_{3}$	4	1	.800	100	26	58	3.62	6
Major League Totals	4 Yrs.	220	269	16	11	.593	308	140	263	4.45	20

a Filed for free agency from Los Angeles Dodgers, October 15, 2006. Signed with Washington Nationals organization, November 6, 2006.
b Traded to Pittsburgh Pirates with outfielder Lastings Milledge for outfielder Nyjer Morgan and pitcher Sean Burnett, June 30, 2009.
c On disabled list from March 26 to April 12, 2010.

HANSON, THOMAS J. (TOMMY)

Born, Tulsa, Oklahoma, August 28, 1986.
Bats Right. Throws Right. Height, 6 feet, 6 inches. Weight, 220 pounds.

Year Club	Lea	G	IP	W	L	Pct	SO	BB	H	ERA	SAVES
2006 Danville	Appal.	13	$51^{2}/_{3}$	4	1	.800	56	9	42	2.09	0
2007 Myrtle Beach	Carolina	11	60	3	3	.500	64	32	53	4.20	0
2007 Rome	So.Atl.	15	73	2	6	.250	90	26	51	2.59	0
2008 Myrtle Beach	Carolina	7	40	3	1	.750	49	11	15	0.90	0
2008 Mississippi	Southern	18	98	8	4	.667	114	41	70	3.03	0
2009 Gwinnett	Int.	11	$66^{1}/_{3}$	3	3	.500	90	17	40	1.49	0
2009 Atlanta	N.L.	21	$127^{2}/_{3}$	11	4	.733	116	46	105	2.89	0
2010 Atlanta	N.L.	34	$202^{2}/_{3}$	10	11	.476	173	56	182	3.33	0
Major League Totals	2 Yrs.	55	$330^{1}/_{3}$	21	15	.583	289	102	287	3.16	0
Division Series											
2010 Atlanta	N.L.	1	4	0	0	.000	5	1	5	9.00	0

HAPP, JAMES ANTHONY (J.A.)

Born, Spring Valley, Illinois, October 19, 1982.
Bats Left. Throws Left. Height, 6 feet, 6 inches. Weight, 200 pounds.

Year Club	Lea	G	IP	W	L	Pct	SO	BB	H	ERA	SAVES
2004 Batavia	N.Y.-Penn.	11	$35^{2}/_{3}$	1	2	.333	37	18	22	2.02	0
2005 Reading	Eastern	1	6	1	0	1.000	8	2	3	1.50	0
2005 Lakewood	So.Atl.	14	$72^{1}/_{3}$	4	4	.500	70	26	57	2.36	0
2006 Reading	Eastern	12	$74^{2}/_{3}$	6	2	.750	81	29	58	2.65	0
2006 Clearwater	Fla.St.	13	80	3	7	.300	77	19	63	2.81	0
2006 Scranton/WB	Int.	1	6	1	0	1.000	4	1	3	1.50	0
2007 Philadelphia	N.L.	1	4	0	1	.000	5	2	7	11.25	0
2007 Ottawa	Int.	24	$118^{1}/_{3}$	4	6	.400	117	62	118	5.02	0
2008 Lehigh Valley	Int.	24	135	8	7	.533	151	48	116	3.60	0

Year	Club	Lea	G	IP	W	L	Pct	SO	BB	H	ERA	SAVES
2008	Philadelphia	N.L.	8	$31\frac{2}{3}$	1	0	1.000	26	14	28	3.69	0
2009	Philadelphia	N.L.	35	166	12	4	.750	119	56	149	2.93	0
2010	Clearwater	Fla.St.	1	3	0	1	.000	2	0	3	6.00	0
2010	Reading	Eastern	3	$12\frac{1}{3}$	1	0	1.000	10	4	18	8.03	0
2010	Lehigh Valley	Int.	5	$22\frac{1}{3}$	0	1	.000	22	15	26	4.84	0
2010	Philadelphia-Houston a-b	N.L.	16	$87\frac{1}{3}$	6	4	.600	70	47	73	3.40	0
Major League Totals		4 Yrs.	60	289	19	9	.679	220	119	257	3.27	0
	Division Series											
2009	Philadelphia	N.L.	2	3	0	0	.000	4	2	6	9.00	0
	Championship Series											
2008	Philadelphia	N.L.	1	3	0	0	.000	2	2	4	3.00	0
2009	Philadelphia	N.L.	3	$0\frac{2}{3}$	0	0	.000	0	3	0	0.00	0
Championship Series Totals			4	$3\frac{2}{3}$	0	0	.000	2	5	4	2.45	0
	World Series Record											
2009	Philadelphia	N.L.	2	$2\frac{2}{3}$	0	0	.000	4	1	2	3.38	0

a On disabled list from April 16 to July 6, 2010.

b Traded to Houston Astros with outfielder Anthony Gose and infielder Jonathan Villar for pitcher Roy Oswalt and cash, July 29, 2010.

HARANG, AARON MICHAEL

Born, San Diego, California, May 9, 1978.

Bats Right. Throws Right. Height, 6 feet, 7 inches. Weight, 270 pounds.

Year	Club	Lea	G	IP	W	L	Pct	SO	BB	H	ERA	SAVES
1999	Pulaski	Appal.	16	$78\frac{1}{3}$	9	2	.818	87	17	64	2.30	1
2000	Charlotte a	Fla.St.	28	157	13	5	.722	136	50	128	3.32	0
2001	Midland	Texas	27	150	10	8	.556	112	37	173	4.14	0
2002	Midland	Texas	3	$16\frac{2}{3}$	2	0	1.000	21	7	12	1.08	0
2002	Sacramento	P.C.	8	$38\frac{2}{3}$	3	3	.500	39	9	41	3.26	0
2002	Oakland	A.L.	16	$78\frac{1}{3}$	5	4	.556	64	45	78	4.83	0
2003	Louisville	Int.	1	3	0	1	.000	4	2	5	15.00	0
2003	Sacramento	P.C.	12	$69\frac{2}{3}$	8	2	.800	60	17	62	2.71	0
2003	Oakland	A.L.	7	$30\frac{1}{3}$	1	3	.250	16	9	41	5.34	0
2003	Cincinnati b	N.L.	9	46	4	3	.571	26	10	48	5.28	0
2004	Louisville	Int.	1	3	0	1	.000	3	3	9	12.00	0
2004	Cincinnati c	N.L.	28	161	10	9	.526	125	53	177	4.86	0
2005	Cincinnati	N.L.	32	$211\frac{2}{3}$	11	13	.458	163	51	217	3.83	0
2006	Cincinnati	N.L.	36	$234\frac{1}{3}$	*16	11	.593	*216	56	242	3.76	0
2007	Cincinnati	N.L.	34	$231\frac{2}{3}$	16	6	.727	218	52	213	3.73	0
2008	Louisville	Int.	1	6	1	0	1.000	6	0	5	0.00	0
2008	Cincinnati d	N.L.	30	$184\frac{1}{3}$	6	*17	.261	153	50	205	4.78	0
2009	Cincinnati e	N.L.	26	$162\frac{1}{3}$	6	14	.300	142	43	186	4.21	0
2010	Louisville	Int.	2	11	0	2	.000	10	2	14	9.00	0
2010	Cincinnati f-g	N.L.	22	$111\frac{2}{3}$	6	7	.462	82	38	139	5.32	0
Major League Totals		9 Yrs.	240	$1451\frac{2}{3}$	81	87	.482	1205	407	1546	4.33	0

a Traded by Texas Rangers to Oakland Athletics with pitcher Ryan Cullen for infielder Randy Velarde, November 17, 2000.

b Traded to Cincinnati Reds with pitcher Joe Valentine and pitcher Jeff Bruksch for outfielder Jose Guillen, July 30, 2003.

c On disabled list from June 2 to June 26, 2004.

d On disabled list from July 9 to August 10, 2008.

e On disabled list from August 21 to October 14, 2009.

f On disabled list from July 1 to August 31, 2010.

g Filed for free agency, November 3, 2010. Signed with San Diego Padres, December 6, 2010.

HARDEN, JAMES RICHARD (RICH)

Born, Victoria, British Columbia, Canada, November 30, 1981.

Bats Left. Throws Right. Height, 6 feet, 1 inch. Weight, 195 pounds.

Year	Club	Lea	G	IP	W	L	Pct	SO	BB	H	ERA	SAVES
2001	Vancouver	Northwest	18	$74\frac{1}{3}$	2	4	.333	100	38	47	3.39	0
2002	Visalia	California	12	68	4	3	.571	85	24	49	2.91	0
2002	Midland	Texas	16	$85\frac{1}{3}$	8	3	.727	102	52	67	2.95	0
2003	Midland	Texas	2	13	2	0	1.000	17	0	0	0.00	0
2003	Sacramento	P.C.	16	$88\frac{2}{3}$	9	4	.692	91	35	72	3.15	0
2003	Oakland	A.L.	15	$74\frac{2}{3}$	5	4	.556	67	40	72	4.46	0
2004	Sacramento	P.C.	1	5	0	0	.000	6	3	6	5.40	0
2004	Oakland	A.L.	31	$189\frac{2}{3}$	11	7	.611	167	81	171	3.99	0
2005	Sacramento	P.C.	1	3	0	0	.000	7	0	1	0.00	0

Year	Club	Lea	G	IP	W	L	Pct	SO	BB	H	ERA	SAVES
2005	Oakland a	A.L.	22	128	10	5	.667	121	43	93	2.53	0
2006	Sacramento	P.C.	1	2	0	0	.000	3	0	1	0.00	0
2006	Oakland b	A.L.	9	$46\frac{2}{3}$	4	0	1.000	49	26	31	4.24	0
2007	Sacramento	P.C.	1	1	0	0	.000	1	0	1	0.00	0
2007	Oakland c	A.L.	7	$25\frac{2}{3}$	1	2	.333	27	11	18	2.45	0
2008	Stockton	Calif.	1	6	1	0	1.000	9	0	3	0.00	0
2008	Sacramento	P.C.	1	$3\frac{2}{3}$	0	0	.000	4	0	3	2.45	0
2008	Oakland	A.L.	13	77	5	1	.833	92	31	57	2.34	0
2008	Chicago d-e	N.L.	12	71	5	1	.833	89	30	39	1.77	0
2009	Iowa	P.C.	1	$4\frac{2}{3}$	0	0	.000	6	2	3	1.93	0
2009	Chicago f-g	N.L.	26	141	9	9	.500	171	67	122	4.09	0
2010	Oklahoma	P.C.	5	$23\frac{1}{3}$	0	2	.000	34	8	21	3.86	0
2010	Texas h-i	A.L.	20	92	5	5	.500	75	62	91	5.58	0
Major League Totals		8 Yrs.	155	$845\frac{2}{3}$	55	34	.618	858	391	694	3.63	0
	Division Series											
2003	Oakland	A.L.	2	$1\frac{1}{3}$	1	1	.500	1	2	2	13.50	0
2008	Chicago	N.L.	1	$4\frac{1}{3}$	0	1	.000	4	3	5	6.23	0
Division Series Totals			3	$5\frac{2}{3}$	1	2	.333	5	5	7	7.94	0
	Championship Series											
2006	Oakland	A.L.	1	$5\frac{2}{3}$	0	1	.000	4	5	5	4.76	0

a On disabled list from May 14 to June 21, 2005.
b On disabled list from April 27 to June 4 and June 5 to September 21, 2006.
c On disabled list from April 16 to June 22 and July 8 to October 8, 2007.
d On disabled list from April 3 to May 11, 2008.
e Traded to Chicago Cubs with pitcher Chad Gaudin for pitcher Sean Gallagher, outfielder Matt Murton, outfielder Eric Patterson and catcher Josh Donaldson, July 8, 2008.
f On disabled list from May 18 to June 13, 2009.
g Filed for free agency, November 5, 2009. Signed with Texas Rangers, December 10, 2009.
h On disabled list from June 12 to July 31 and August 15 to August 23, 2010.
i Released by Texas Rangers, October 8, 2010. Signed with Oakland Athletics, December 21, 2010.

HAREN, DANIEL JOHN (DANNY)

Born, Monterey Park, California, September 17, 1980.
Bats Right. Throws Right. Height, 6 feet, 5 inches. Weight, 220 pounds.

Year	Club	Lea	G	IP	W	L	Pct	SO	BB	H	ERA	SAVES
2001	New Jersey	N.Y.-Penn.	12	$52\frac{1}{3}$	3	3	.500	57	8	47	3.10	1
2002	Potomac	Carolina	14	92	3	6	.333	82	19	90	3.62	0
2002	Peoria	Midwest	14	$101\frac{2}{3}$	7	3	.700	89	12	89	1.95	0
2003	Memphis	P.C.	8	$45\frac{2}{3}$	2	1	.667	35	8	50	4.93	0
2003	Tennessee	Southern	8	55	6	0	1.000	49	6	36	0.82	0
2003	St. Louis	N.L.	14	$72\frac{2}{3}$	3	7	.300	43	22	84	5.08	0
2004	Memphis	P.C.	21	128	11	4	.733	150	33	136	4.15	0
2004	St. Louis a	N.L.	14	46	3	3	.500	32	17	45	4.50	0
2005	Oakland	A.L.	34	217	14	12	.538	163	53	212	3.73	0
2006	Oakland	A.L.	34	223	14	13	.519	176	45	224	4.12	0
2007	Oakland b	A.L.	34	$222\frac{2}{3}$	15	9	.625	192	55	214	3.07	0
2008	Arizona	N.L.	33	216	16	8	.667	206	40	204	3.33	0
2009	Arizona	N.L.	33	$229\frac{1}{3}$	14	10	.583	223	38	192	3.14	0
2010	Arizona	N.L.	21	141	7	8	.467	141	29	161	4.60	0
2010	Los Angeles c	A.L.	14	94	5	4	.556	75	25	84	2.87	0
Major League Totals		8 Yrs.	231	$1461\frac{2}{3}$	91	74	.552	1251	324	1420	3.66	0
	Division Series											
2004	St. Louis	N.L.	1	2	1	0	1.000	3	1	1	0.00	0
2006	Oakland	A.L.	1	6	1	0	1.000	2	1	9	3.00	0
Division Series Totals			2	8	2	0	1.000	5	2	10	2.25	0
	Championship Series											
2004	St. Louis	N.L.	2	$1\frac{2}{3}$	0	0	.000	2	0	3	10.80	0
2006	Oakland	A.L.	1	5	0	0	.000	7	2	7	5.40	0
Championship Series Totals			3	$6\frac{2}{3}$	0	0	.000	9	2	10	6.75	0
	World Series Record											
2004	St. Louis	N.L.	2	$4\frac{2}{3}$	0	0	.000	2	3	4	0.00	0

a Traded to Oakland Athletics with pitcher Kiko Calero and catcher Daric Barton for pitcher Mark Mulder, December 18, 2004.
b Traded to Arizona Diamondbacks with pitcher Connor Robertson for pitcher Brett Anderson, pitcher Dana Eveland, pitcher Greg Smith, infielder Chris Carter, outfielder Aaron Cunningham and outfielder Carlos Gonzalez, December 14, 2007.
c Traded to Los Angeles Angels for pitcher Joe Saunders, pitcher Rafael Rodriguez, pitcher Patrick Corbin and player to be named later, July 25, 2010. Arizona Diamondbacks received pitcher Tyler Skaggs to complete trade, August 7, 2010.

HARRISON, MATTHEW REID (MATT)

Born, Durham, North Carolina, August 16, 1985.
Bats Left. Throws Left. Height, 6 feet, 4 inches. Weight, 225 pounds.

Year	Club	Lea	G	IP	W	L	Pct	SO	BB	H	ERA	SAVES
2003	Braves	Gulf Coast	11	39	3	1	.750	33	9	40	3.69	1
2004	Danville	Appal.	13	66	4	4	.500	49	10	72	4.09	0
2005	Rome	So.Atl.	27	167	12	7	.632	118	30	151	3.23	0
2006	Myrtle Beach	Carolina	13	81 1/3	8	4	.667	60	16	77	3.10	0
2006	Mississippi	Southern	13	77 1/3	3	4	.429	54	17	83	3.61	0
2007	Mississippi a	Southern	20	116 2/3	5	7	.417	78	34	118	3.39	0
2008	Frisco	Texas	9	46	3	2	.600	35	14	49	3.33	0
2008	Oklahoma	P.C.	6	38	3	1	.750	20	14	40	3.55	0
2008	Texas	A.L.	15	83 2/3	9	3	.750	42	31	100	5.49	0
2009	Frisco	Texas	3	9	0	1	.000	7	4	9	3.00	0
2009	Texas b	A.L.	11	63 1/3	4	5	.444	34	23	81	6.11	0
2010	Frisco	Texas	2	3	0	0	.000	4	0	3	3.00	1
2010	Oklahoma	P.C.	1	4 1/3	0	1	.000	4	1	9	6.23	0
2010	Texas c	A.L.	37	78 1/3	3	2	.600	46	39	80	4.71	2
Major League Totals		3 Yrs.	63	225 1/3	16	10	.615	122	93	261	5.39	2

a Traded to Texas Rangers with catcher Jarrod Saltalamacchia, infielder Elvis Andrus, pitcher Neftali Feliz and pitcher Beau James for infielder Mark Teixeira and pitcher Ron Mahay, July 31, 2007.
b On disabled list from May 26 to June 17 and June 24 to November 13, 2009.
c On disabled list from May 7 to May 29, 2010.

HAWKSWORTH, BLAKE EDWARD

Born, N.Vancouver, British Columbia, Canada, March 1, 1983.
Bats Right. Throws Right. Height, 6 feet, 3 inches. Weight, 195 pounds.

Year	Club	Lea	G	IP	W	L	Pct	SO	BB	H	ERA	SAVES
2002	Johnson City	Appal.	13	66	2	4	.333	61	18	58	3.14	0
2002	New Jersey	N.Y.-Penn.	2	9 2/3	1	0	1.000	8	2	6	0.00	0
2003	Palm Beach	Fla.St.	6	32	1	3	.250	32	11	28	3.94	0
2003	Peoria	Midwest	10	54 2/3	5	1	.833	57	12	37	2.30	0
2004	Palm Beach	Fla.St.	2	10 2/3	1	0	1.000	11	3	10	5.91	0
2005	New Jersey	N.Y.-Penn.	7	14 2/3	0	3	.000	12	10	18	7.98	0
2006	Palm Beach	Fla.St.	14	83 2/3	7	2	.778	55	19	75	2.47	0
2006	Springfield	Texas	13	79 2/3	4	2	.667	66	31	72	3.39	0
2007	Memphis	P.C.	25	129 2/3	4	13	.235	88	41	150	5.28	0
2008	Cardinals	Gulf Coast	2	7	0	0	.000	6	2	2	0.00	0
2008	Memphis	P.C.	18	88 2/3	5	7	.417	83	38	111	6.09	0
2009	Memphis	P.C.	12	73	5	4	.556	57	20	61	3.58	0
2009	St. Louis	N.L.	30	40	4	0	1.000	20	15	29	2.03	0
2010	St. Louis a	N.L.	45	90 1/3	4	8	.333	61	35	113	4.98	0
Major League Totals		2 Yrs.	75	130 1/3	8	8	.500	81	50	142	4.07	0
	Division Series											
2009	St. Louis	N.L.	1	1	0	0	.000	1	1	1	0.00	0

a Traded to Los Angeles Dodgers for infielder Ryan Theriot, November 30, 2010.

HEILMAN, AARON MICHAEL

Born, Logansport, Indiana, November 12, 1978.
Bats Right. Throws Right. Height, 6 feet, 5 inches. Weight, 220 pounds.

Year	Club	Lea	G	IP	W	L	Pct	SO	BB	H	ERA	SAVES
2001	St. Lucie	Fla.St.	7	38 1/3	0	1	.000	39	13	26	2.35	0
2002	Binghamton	Eastern	17	96 2/3	4	4	.500	97	28	85	3.82	0
2002	Norfolk	Int.	10	49 1/3	2	3	.400	35	16	42	3.28	0
2003	Norfolk	Int.	16	94 1/3	6	4	.600	71	32	99	3.24	0
2003	New York	N.L.	14	65 1/3	2	7	.222	51	41	79	6.75	0
2004	Norfolk	Int.	26	151 2/3	7	10	.412	123	66	156	4.33	0
2004	New York	N.L.	5	28	1	3	.250	22	13	27	5.46	0
2005	New York	N.L.	53	108	5	3	.625	106	37	87	3.17	5
2006	New York	N.L.	74	87	4	5	.444	73	28	73	3.62	0
2007	New York	N.L.	81	86	7	7	.500	63	20	72	3.03	1
2008	New York a	N.L.	78	76	3	8	.273	80	46	75	5.21	3
2009	Chicago b-c	N.L.	70	72 1/3	4	4	.500	65	34	68	4.11	1
2010	Arizona d	N.L.	70	72	5	8	.385	55	26	73	4.50	6
Major League Totals		8 Yrs.	445	594 2/3	31	45	.408	515	245	554	4.25	16
	Division Series											
2006	New York	N.L.	3	3	0	0	.000	1	0	3	3.00	0

Year	Club	Lea	G	IP	W	L	Pct	SO	BB	H	ERA	SAVES
	Championship Series											
2006	New York	N.L.	3	4 1/3	0	1	.000	5	1	4	4.15	0

a Traded to Seattle Mariners with outfielder Endy Chavez, pitcher Jason Vargas, infielder Mike Carp, outfielder Ezequiel Carrera and pitcher Maikel Cleto for pitcher J.J. Putz, pitcher Sean Green and infielder Jeremy Reed, December 10, 2008.
b Traded to Chicago Cubs for pitcher Garrett Olson and infielder Ronny Cedeno, January 28, 2009.
c Traded to Arizona Diamondbacks for pitcher Scott Maine and infielder Ryne White, November 19, 2009.
d Filed for free agency, November 1, 2010, re-signed with Arizona Diamondbacks, January 18, 2011.

HELLICKSON, JEREMY ROBERT

Born, Des Moines, Iowa, April 8, 1987.
Bats Right. Throws Right. Height, 6 feet, 1 inch. Weight, 185 pounds.

Year	Club	Lea	G	IP	W	L	Pct	SO	BB	H	ERA	SAVES
2005	Princeton	Appal.	4	6	0	0	.000	11	1	6	6.00	0
2006	Hudson Valley	N.Y.-Penn.	15	77 2/3	3	3	.500	96	16	55	2.43	0
2007	Columbus	So.Atl.	21	111 1/3	13	3	.813	106	34	87	2.67	0
2008	Vero Beach	Fla.St.	14	76 2/3	7	1	.875	83	5	64	2.00	0
2008	Montgomery	Southern	13	75 1/3	4	4	.500	79	15	84	3.94	0
2009	Durham	Int.	9	57 1/3	6	1	.857	70	15	31	2.51	0
2009	Montgomery	Southern	11	56 2/3	3	1	.750	62	14	41	2.38	0
2010	Charlotte	Fla.St.	1	1 2/3	0	0	.000	4	2	4	21.60	0
2010	Durham	Int.	21	117 2/3	12	3	.800	123	35	103	2.45	0
2010	Tampa Bay	A.L.	10	36 1/3	4	0	1.000	33	8	32	3.47	0

HENDRICKSON, MARK ALLAN

Born, Mount Vernon, Washington, June 23, 1974.
Bats Left. Throws Left. Height, 6 feet, 9 inches. Weight, 230 pounds.

Year	Club	Lea	G	IP	W	L	Pct	SO	BB	H	ERA	SAVES
1998	Dunedin	Fla.St.	16	49 1/3	4	3	.571	38	26	44	2.37	1
1999	Knoxville	Southern	12	55 2/3	2	7	.222	39	21	73	6.63	0
2000	Dunedin	Fla.St.	12	51 1/3	2	2	.500	38	29	63	5.61	0
2000	Tennessee	Southern	6	39 2/3	3	1	.750	29	12	32	3.63	0
2001	Syracuse	Int.	38	73 1/3	2	9	.182	33	18	80	4.66	0
2002	Syracuse	Int.	19	92	7	5	.583	68	22	90	3.52	0
2002	Toronto a	A.L.	16	36 2/3	3	0	1.000	21	12	25	2.45	0
2003	Syracuse	Int.	1	6	0	0	.000	5	1	8	4.50	0
2003	Dunedin	Fla.St.	1	5 2/3	1	0	1.000	3	4	5	1.59	0
2003	Toronto b-c	A.L.	30	158 1/3	9	9	.500	76	40	207	5.51	0
2004	Tampa Bay	A.L.	32	183 1/3	10	15	.400	87	46	211	4.81	0
2005	Tampa Bay d	A.L.	31	178 1/3	11	8	.579	89	49	227	5.90	0
2006	Tampa Bay	A.L.	13	89 2/3	4	8	.333	51	34	81	3.81	0
2006	Los Angeles e-f	N.L.	18	75	2	7	.222	48	28	92	4.68	0
2007	Los Angeles g	N.L.	39	122 2/3	4	8	.333	92	29	142	5.21	0
2008	Florida h	N.L.	36	133 2/3	7	8	.467	81	48	148	5.45	0
2009	Baltimore i	A.L.	53	105	6	5	.545	61	33	116	4.37	1
2010	Baltimore j	A.L.	52	75 1/3	1	6	.143	55	20	97	5.26	0
Major League Totals		9 Yrs.	320	1158	57	74	.435	661	339	1346	5.02	1
	Division Series											
2006	Los Angeles	N.L.	3	2 2/3	0	0	.000	1	1	1	0.00	0

a On disabled list from June 18 to July 12, 2002.
b Traded to Colorado Rockies for pitcher Justin Speier, December 14, 2003.
c Traded to Tampa Bay Devil Rays for pitcher Joe Kennedy, December 14, 2003.
d On disabled list from April 14 to April 30, 2005.
e On disabled list from April 7 to April 25, 2006.
f Traded to Los Angeles Dodgers with catcher Toby Hall and cash for catcher Dioner Navarro and pitcher Jae Seo, June 27, 2006.
g Not offered contract, December 12, 2007. Signed with Florida Marlins, January 16, 2008.
h Filed for free agency, October 31, 2008. Signed with Baltimore Orioles, December 31, 2008.
i Filed for free agency, November 5, 2009, re-signed with Baltimore Orioles, February 9, 2010.
j Filed for free agency, November 2, 2010.

HENSLEY, CLAYTON ALLEN (CLAY)

Born, Tomball, Texas, August 31, 1979.
Bats Right. Throws Right. Height, 5 feet, 11 inches. Weight, 190 pounds.

Year	Club	Lea	G	IP	W	L	Pct	SO	BB	H	ERA	SAVES
2002	Salem-Keizer	Northwest	15	81 2/3	7	0	1.000	84	25	72	2.53	0
2003	Lake Elsinore	Calif.	8	44 1/3	3	4	.429	40	14	51	3.45	0
2003	San Jose	Calif.	5	29 1/3	2	3	.400	25	9	38	5.83	0

Year	Club	Lea	G	IP	W	L	Pct	SO	BB	H	ERA	SAVES
2003	Hagerstown	So.Atl.	12	68	4	3	.571	74	20	56	3.18	0
2004	Mobile	Southern	27	159	11	10	.524	125	48	167	4.30	0
2005	Portland	P.C.	15	90⅓	2	2	.500	71	22	63	2.99	0
2005	San Diego	N.L.	24	47⅔	1	1	.500	28	17	33	1.70	0
2006	San Diego	N.L.	37	187	11	12	.478	122	76	174	3.71	0
2007	Portland	P.C.	13	71	2	7	.222	50	34	102	6.72	0
2007	San Diego a	N.L.	13	50	2	3	.400	30	32	62	6.84	0
2008	Lake Elsinore	Calif.	1	1	1	0	1.000	1	0	1	0.00	0
2008	Portland	P.C.	16	48	1	1	.500	34	16	46	3.94	0
2008	San Diego b	N.L.	32	39	1	2	.333	26	25	36	5.31	0
2009	New Orleans	P.C.	19	114	8	4	.667	82	38	105	3.24	0
2009	Round Rock c-d-e	P.C.	6	10	1	0	1.000	5	7	12	7.20	0
2010	Jupiter	Fla.St.	2	2⅔	0	0	.000	2	1	1	0.00	0
2010	Florida f	N.L.	68	75	3	4	.429	77	29	54	2.16	7
Major League Totals		5 Yrs.	174	398⅔	18	22	.450	283	179	359	3.72	7
	Division Series											
2005	San Diego	N.L.	3	4⅔	0	0	.000	1	3	4	3.86	0
2006	San Diego	N.L.	2	2⅔	0	0	.000	0	1	2	0.00	0
Division Series Totals			5	7⅓	0	0	.000	1	4	6	2.45	0

a On disabled list from May 3 to June 1 and September 25 to November 1, 2007.
b On disabled list from March 21 to June 6, 2008.
c Not offered contract, December 12, 2008. Signed with Houston Astros organization, January 5, 2009.
d Released by Houston Astros, April 28, 2009. Signed with Florida Marlins organization, May 25, 2009.
e Filed for free agency, November 9, 2009, re-signed with Florida Marlins, December 14, 2009.
f On disabled list from June 12 to July 2, 2010.

HERNANDEZ, DAVID JESUS

Born, Sacramento, California, May 13, 1985.
Bats Right. Throws Right. Height, 6 feet, 3 inches. Weight, 215 pounds.

Year	Club	Lea	G	IP	W	L	Pct	SO	BB	H	ERA	SAVES
2005	Aberdeen	N.Y.-Penn.	12	41⅔	1	2	.333	47	17	41	3.89	0
2006	Delmarva	So.Atl.	28	145⅓	7	8	.467	154	71	134	4.15	0
2007	Frederick	Carolina	28	145⅓	7	11	.389	168	47	139	4.95	0
2008	Bowie	Eastern	27	141	10	4	.714	166	71	112	2.68	0
2009	Bowie	Eastern	1	4	0	0	.000	4	1	2	2.25	0
2009	Norfolk	Int.	11	57⅓	3	2	.600	79	18	42	3.30	0
2009	Baltimore	A.L.	20	101⅓	4	10	.286	68	46	118	5.42	0
2010	Bowie	Eastern	2	2	0	0	.000	3	0	1	0.00	0
2010	Baltimore a-b	A.L.	41	79⅓	8	8	.500	72	42	72	4.31	2
Major League Totals		2 Yrs.	61	180⅔	12	18	.400	140	88	190	4.93	2

a On disabled list from August 5 to September 7, 2010.
b Traded to Baltimore Orioles with pitcher Kam Mickolio for infielder Mark Reynolds and player to be named later, December 6, 2010.

HERNANDEZ, EISLER LIVAN

Born, Villa Clara, Cuba, February 20, 1975.
Bats Right. Throws Right. Height, 6 feet, 2 inches. Weight, 245 pounds.

Year	Club	Lea	G	IP	W	L	Pct	SO	BB	H	ERA	SAVES
1996	Charlotte	Int.	10	49	2	4	.333	45	34	61	5.14	0
1996	Portland	Eastern	15	93⅓	9	2	.818	95	34	81	4.34	0
1996	Florida	N.L.	1	3	0	0	.000	2	2	3	0.00	0
1997	Portland	Eastern	1	4	0	0	.000	2	7	2	2.25	0
1997	Charlotte	Int.	14	81⅓	5	3	.625	58	38	76	3.98	0
1997	Florida	N.L.	17	96⅓	9	3	.750	72	38	81	3.18	0
1998	Florida	N.L.	33	234⅓	10	12	.455	162	104	*265	4.72	0
1999	Florida-San Francisco a	N.L.	30	199⅔	8	12	.400	144	76	227	4.64	0
2000	San Francisco	N.L.	33	240	17	11	.607	165	73	*254	3.75	0
2001	San Francisco	N.L.	34	226⅔	13	15	.464	138	85	*266	5.24	0
2002	San Francisco	N.L.	33	216	12	*16	.429	134	71	233	4.38	0
2003	Montreal b-c	N.L.	33	*233⅓	15	10	.600	178	57	225	3.20	0
2004	Montreal	N.L.	35	*255	11	15	.423	186	83	234	3.60	0
2005	Washington	N.L.	35	*246⅓	15	10	.600	147	84	*268	3.98	0
2006	Washington-Arizona d	N.L.	34	216	13	13	.500	128	78	246	4.83	0
2007	Arizona e	N.L.	33	204⅓	11	11	.500	90	79	*247	4.93	0
2008	Minnesota	A.L.	23	139⅔	10	8	.556	54	29	199	5.48	0
2008	Colorado f-g	N.L.	8	40⅓	3	3	.500	13	14	58	8.03	0
2009	New York-Washington h-i	N.L.	31	183⅔	9	12	.429	102	67	220	5.44	0

Year	Club	Lea	G	IP	W	L	Pct	SO	BB	H	ERA	SAVES
2010	Washington	N.L.	33	211 2/3	10	12	.455	114	64	216	3.66	0
Major League Totals		15 Yrs.	446	2946 1/3	166	163	.505	1829	1004	3242	4.39	0
	Division Series											
1997	Florida	N.L.	1	4	0	0	.000	3	0	3	2.25	0
2000	San Francisco	N.L.	1	7 2/3	1	0	1.000	5	5	5	1.17	0
2002	San Francisco	N.L.	1	8 1/3	1	0	1.000	6	2	8	3.24	0
2007	Arizona	N.L.	1	6	1	0	1.000	2	5	5	1.50	0
Division Series Totals			4	26	3	0	1.000	16	12	21	2.08	0
	Championship Series											
1997	Florida	N.L.	2	10 2/3	2	0	1.000	16	2	5	0.84	0
2002	San Francisco	N.L.	1	6 1/3	0	0	.000	0	1	9	2.84	0
2007	Arizona	N.L.	1	5 2/3	0	1	.000	4	2	8	6.35	0
Championship Series Totals			4	22 2/3	2	1	.667	20	5	22	2.78	0
	World Series Record											
1997	Florida	N.L.	2	13 2/3	2	0	1.000	7	10	15	5.27	0
2002	San Francisco	N.L.	2	5 2/3	0	2	.000	4	9	9	14.29	0
World Series Totals			4	19 1/3	2	2	.500	11	19	24	7.91	0

a Traded to San Francisco Giants for pitcher Jason Grilli and pitcher Nathan Bump, July 24, 1999.
b Traded to Montreal Expos with catcher Edwards Guzman for pitcher Jim Brower and player to be named later, March 24, 2003.
c San Francisco Giants received pitcher Matt Blank to complete trade, April 30, 2003.
d Traded to Arizona Diamondbacks with cash for pitcher Garrett Mock and pitcher Matt Chico, August 7, 2006.
e Filed for free agency, October 29, 2007. Signed with Minnesota Twins, February 12, 2008.
f Claimed on waivers by Colorado Rockies, August 6, 2008.
g Filed for free agency, November 1, 2008. Signed with New York Mets organization, February 14, 2009.
h Released by New York Mets, August 20, 2009. Signed with Washington Nationals, August 26, 2009.
i Filed for free agency, November 5, 2009.

HERNANDEZ, FELIX ABRAHAM

Born, Valencia, Venezuela, April 8, 1986.
Bats Right. Throws Right. Height, 6 feet, 3 inches. Weight, 230 pounds.

Year	Club	Lea	G	IP	W	L	Pct	SO	BB	H	ERA	SAVES
2003	Wisconsin	Midwest	2	14	0	0	.000	18	3	9	1.93	0
2003	Everett	Northwest	11	55	7	2	.778	73	24	43	2.29	0
2004	Inland Empire	California	16	92	9	3	.750	114	26	85	2.74	0
2004	San Antonio	Texas	10	57 1/3	5	1	.833	58	21	47	3.30	0
2005	Tacoma	P.C.	19	88	9	4	.692	100	48	62	2.25	0
2005	Seattle	A.L.	12	84 1/3	4	4	.500	77	23	61	2.67	0
2006	Seattle	A.L.	31	191	12	14	.462	176	60	195	4.52	0
2007	Seattle a	A.L.	30	190 1/3	14	7	.667	165	53	209	3.92	0
2008	Seattle b	A.L.	31	200 2/3	9	11	.450	175	80	198	3.45	0
2009	Seattle	A.L.	34	238 2/3	*19	5	*.792	217	71	200	2.49	0
2010	Seattle c	A.L.	34	*249 2/3	13	12	.520	232	70	194	*2.27	0
Major League Totals		6 Yrs.	172	1154 2/3	71	53	.573	1042	357	1057	3.20	0

a On disabled list from April 19 to May 15, 2007.
b On disabled list from June 24 to July 11, 2008.
c Selected Cy Young Award Winner in American League for 2010.

HERNDON, KENNETH DAVID (DAVID)

Born, Panama City, Florida, September 4, 1985.
Bats Right. Throws Right. Height, 6 feet, 5 inches. Weight, 230 pounds.

Year	Club	Lea	G	IP	W	L	Pct	SO	BB	H	ERA	SAVES
2006	Orem	Pioneer	14	69 1/3	5	2	.714	36	10	65	2.21	0
2007	Cedar Rapids	Midwest	25	152 1/3	13	8	.619	83	20	175	4.02	0
2008	Rancho Cucamonga	Calif.	43	100 2/3	3	7	.300	70	16	120	5.01	17
2009	Arkansas a	Texas	50	65 1/3	5	6	.455	35	14	70	3.03	11
2010	Philadelphia	N.L.	47	52 1/3	1	3	.250	29	17	67	4.30	0

a Selected by Philadelphia Phillies from Los Angeles Angels in Rule V draft, December 20, 2009.

HERRERA, DANIEL RAY (DANNY)

Born, Odessa, Texas, October 21, 1984.
Bats Left. Throws Left. Height, 5 feet, 6 inches. Weight, 165 pounds.

Year	Club	Lea	G	IP	W	L	Pct	SO	BB	H	ERA	SAVES
2006	Rangers	Arizona	3	8 2/3	0	1	.000	11	0	5	2.08	2
2006	Bakersfield	Calif.	14	53 1/3	4	2	.667	61	12	39	1.35	1

Year	Club	Lea	G	IP	W	L	Pct	SO	BB	H	ERA	SAVES
2007	Bakersfield	Calif.	7	11	2	0	1.000	11	5	14	3.27	1
2007	Frisco a	Texas	34	52 1/3	5	2	.714	64	20	43	3.78	0
2008	Chattanooga	Southern	10	17 2/3	3	0	1.000	10	7	12	2.55	0
2008	Louisville	Int.	47	55	4	4	.500	50	10	47	2.78	6
2008	Cincinnati	N.L.	7	7 1/3	0	0	.000	8	3	10	7.36	0
2009	Cincinnati	N.L.	70	61 2/3	4	4	.500	44	24	63	3.06	0
2010	Louisville	Int.	26	37 2/3	2	2	.500	34	5	31	4.30	5
2010	Cincinnati	N.L.	36	23	1	3	.250	14	6	31	3.91	0
Major League Totals		3 Yrs.	113	92	5	7	.417	66	33	104	3.62	0

a Traded by Texas Rangers to Cincinnati Reds with pitcher Edinson Volquez for outfielder Josh Hamilton, December 21, 2007.

HOCHEVAR, LUKE ANTHONY

Born, Denver, Colorado, September 15, 1983.
Bats Right. Throws Right. Height, 6 feet, 5 inches. Weight, 205 pounds.

Year	Club	Lea	G	IP	W	L	Pct	SO	BB	H	ERA	SAVES
2006	Burlington	Midwest	4	15 1/3	0	1	.000	16	2	8	1.17	0
2007	Wichita	Texas	17	94	3	6	.333	94	26	110	4.69	0
2007	Omaha	P.C.	10	58	1	3	.250	44	21	53	5.12	0
2007	Kansas City	A.L.	4	12 2/3	0	1	.000	5	4	11	2.13	0
2008	Omaha	P.C.	3	17 1/3	1	1	.500	12	6	11	2.60	0
2008	Kansas City a	A.L.	22	129	6	12	.333	72	47	143	5.51	0
2009	Omaha	P.C.	8	48	5	1	.833	36	12	41	1.50	0
2009	Kansas City	A.L.	25	143	7	13	.350	106	46	167	6.55	0
2010	Omaha	P.C.	2	5	0	0	.000	4	1	3	1.80	0
2010	Kansas City b	A.L.	18	103	6	6	.500	76	37	110	4.81	0
Major League Totals		4 Yrs.	69	387 2/3	19	32	.373	259	134	431	5.60	0

a On disabled list from August 20 to November 14, 2008.
b On disabled list from June 12 to September 3, 2010.

HOFFMAN, TREVOR WILLIAM

Born, Bellflower, California, October 13, 1967.
Bats Right. Throws Right. Height, 6 feet, 1 inch. Weight, 215 pounds.

Year	Club	Lea	G	IP	W	L	Pct	SO	BB	H	ERA	SAVES
1991	Cedar Rapids	Midwest	27	33 2/3	1	1	.500	52	13	22	1.87	12
1991	Chattanooga	Southern	14	14	1	0	1.000	23	7	10	1.93	8
1992	Chattanooga	Southern	6	29 2/3	3	0	1.000	31	11	22	1.52	0
1992	Nashville a	A.A.	42	65 1/3	4	6	.400	63	32	57	4.27	6
1993	Florida-San Diego b	N.L.	67	90	4	6	.400	79	39	80	3.90	5
1994	San Diego	N.L.	47	56	4	4	.500	68	20	39	2.57	20
1995	San Diego	N.L.	55	53 1/3	7	4	.636	52	14	48	3.88	31
1996	San Diego	N.L.	70	88	9	5	.643	111	31	50	2.25	42
1997	San Diego	N.L.	70	81 1/3	6	4	.600	111	24	59	2.66	37
1998	San Diego	N.L.	66	73	4	2	.667	86	21	41	1.48	*53
1999	San Diego	N.L.	64	67 1/3	2	3	.400	73	15	48	2.14	40
2000	San Diego	N.L.	70	72 1/3	4	7	.364	85	11	61	2.99	43
2001	San Diego	N.L.	62	60 1/3	3	4	.429	63	21	48	3.43	43
2002	San Diego	N.L.	61	59 1/3	2	5	.286	69	18	52	2.73	38
2003	Lake Elsinore	California	3	3	0	0	.000	4	0	2	0.00	0
2003	San Diego c	N.L.	9	9	0	0	.000	11	3	7	2.00	0
2004	San Diego	N.L.	55	54 2/3	3	3	.500	53	8	42	2.30	41
2005	San Diego d	N.L.	60	57 2/3	1	6	.143	54	12	52	2.97	43
2006	San Diego	N.L.	65	63	0	2	.000	50	13	48	2.14	*46
2007	San Diego	N.L.	61	57 1/3	4	5	.444	44	15	49	2.98	42
2008	San Diego e	N.L.	48	45 1/3	3	6	.333	46	9	38	3.77	30
2009	Nashville	P.C.	2	2	0	0	.000	2	0	4	9.00	0
2009	Milwaukee f	N.L.	55	54	3	2	.600	48	14	35	1.83	37
2010	Milwaukee g	N.L.	50	47 1/3	2	7	.222	30	19	49	5.89	10
Major League Totals		18 Yrs.	1035	1089 1/3	61	75	.449	1133	307	846	2.87	601
	Division Series											
1996	San Diego	N.L.	2	1 2/3	0	1	.000	2	1	3	10.80	0
1998	San Diego	N.L.	4	3	0	0	.000	4	1	3	0.00	2
2005	San Diego	N.L.	1	1	0	0	.000	0	0	1	0.00	0
2006	San Diego	N.L.	1	1	0	0	.000	1	0	0	0.00	1
Division Series Totals			8	6 2/3	0	1	.000	7	2	7	2.70	3
	Championship Series											
1998	San Diego	N.L.	3	4 1/3	1	0	1.000	7	2	2	2.08	1

Year	Club	Lea	G	IP	W	L	Pct	SO	BB	H	ERA	SAVES
	World Series Record											
1998	San Diego	N.L.	1	2	0	1	.000	0	1	2	9.00	0

Record as Position Player

Year	Club	Lea	Pos	G	AB	R	H	2B	3B	HR	RBI	SB	Avg
1989	Bellingham	Pioneer	SS	61	201	22	50	5	0	1	20	1	.249
1990	Charleston	So. Atl.	SS-3B	103	278	41	59	10	1	2	23	3	.212

a Selected by Florida Marlins from Cincinnati Reds organization in expansion draft, November 17, 1992.
b Traded to San Diego Padres with pitchers Andres Berumen and Jose Martinez for infielder Greg Sheffield and pitcher Rich Rodriguez, June 25, 1993.
c On disabled list from March 25 to September 2, 2003.
d Filed for free agency, October 28, 2005, re-signed with San Diego Padres, December 7, 2005.
e Filed for free agency, November 1, 2008. Signed with Milwaukee Brewers, January 13, 2009.
f On disabled list from March 27 to April 26, 2009.
g Filed for free agency, November 2, 2010. Announced retirement, January 11, 2011.

HOLLAND, DEREK LANE

Born, Newark, Ohio, October 9, 1986.
Bats Both. Throws Left. Height, 6 feet, 2 inches. Weight, 185 pounds.

Year	Club	Lea	G	IP	W	L	Pct	SO	BB	H	ERA	SAVES
2007	Spokane	Northwest	16	67	4	5	.444	83	21	57	3.22	0
2008	Bakersfield	Calif.	5	31	3	1	.750	37	5	20	3.19	0
2008	Clinton	Midwest	17	93⅔	7	0	1.000	91	29	77	2.40	0
2008	Frisco	Texas	4	26	3	0	1.000	29	6	14	0.69	0
2009	Okla.	P.C.	1	4	0	1	.000	5	3	5	9.00	0
2009	Texas	A.L.	33	138⅓	8	13	.381	107	47	160	6.12	0
2010	Rangers	Arizona	1	3	0	0	.000	6	0	0	0.00	0
2010	Oklahoma	P.C.	11	62⅔	6	2	.750	51	18	50	1.87	0
2010	Texas a	A.L.	14	57⅓	3	4	.429	54	24	55	4.08	0
Major League Totals		2 Yrs.	47	195⅔	11	17	.393	161	71	215	5.52	0
	Division Series											
2010	Texas	A.L.	2	4⅔	0	0	.000	4	1	6	5.79	0
	Championship Series											
2010	Texas	A.L.	2	5⅔	1	0	1.000	4	2	3	0.00	0
	World Series Record											
2010	Texas	A.L.	2	1	0	0	.000	1	4	0	27.00	0

a On disabled list from May 31 to August 1, 2010.

HUDSON, DANIEL CLAIRBORNE

Born, Lynchburg, Virginia, March 9, 1987.
Bats Right. Throws Right. Height, 6 feet, 4 inches. Weight, 220 pounds.

Year	Club	Lea	G	IP	W	L	Pct	SO	BB	H	ERA	SAVES
2008	Great Falls	Pioneer	14	69⅔	5	4	.556	90	22	52	3.36	0
2009	Kannapolis	So.Atl.	4	22	1	2	.333	30	2	15	1.23	0
2009	Winston-Salem	Carolina	8	45	4	3	.571	49	13	31	3.40	0
2009	Birmingham	Southern	9	56⅓	7	0	1.000	63	10	37	1.60	0
2009	Charlotte	Int.	5	24	2	0	1.000	24	9	22	3.00	0
2009	Chicago	A.L.	6	18⅔	1	1	.500	14	9	16	3.38	0
2010	Charlotte	Int.	17	93⅓	11	4	.733	108	31	81	3.47	0
2010	Chicago	A.L.	3	15⅔	1	1	.500	14	11	17	6.32	0
2010	Arizona a	N.L.	11	79⅔	7	1	.875	70	16	51	1.69	0
Major League Totals		2 Yrs.	20	114	9	3	.750	98	36	84	2.61	0

a Traded to Arizona Diamondbacks with pitcher David Holmberg for pitcher Edwin Jackson, July 30, 2010.

HUDSON, TIMOTHY ADAM (TIM)

Born, Columbus, Georgia, July 14, 1975.
Bats Right. Throws Right. Height, 6 feet, I Inch. Weight, 170 pounds.

Year	Club	Lea	G	IP	W	L	Pct	SO	BB	H	ERA	SAVES
1997	Sou Oregon	Northwest	8	28⅔	3	1	.750	37	15	12	2.51	0
1998	Modesto	California	8	37⅔	4	0	1.000	48	18	19	1.67	0
1998	Huntsville	Southern	22	134⅔	10	9	.526	104	71	136	4.54	0
1999	Midland	Texas	3	18	3	0	1.000	18	3	9	0.50	0
1999	Vancouver	P.C.	8	49	4	0	1.000	61	21	38	2.20	0
1999	Oakland	A.L.	21	136⅓	11	2	.846	132	62	121	3.23	0
2000	Oakland	A.L.	32	202⅓	*20	6	*.769	169	82	169	4.14	0
2001	Oakland	A.L.	35	235	18	9	.667	181	71	216	3.37	0
2002	Oakland	A.L.	34	238⅓	15	9	.625	152	62	237	2.98	0
2003	Oakland	A.L.	34	240	16	7	.696	162	61	197	2.70	0

Year	Club	Lea	G	IP	W	L	Pct	SO	BB	H	ERA	SAVES
2004	Sacramento	P.C.	1	3	0	0	.000	3	2	2	6.00	0
2004	Oakland a-b	A.L.	27	$188\frac{2}{3}$	12	6	.667	103	44	194	3.53	0
2005	Atlanta c	N.L.	29	192	14	9	.609	115	65	194	3.52	0
2006	Atlanta	N.L.	35	$218\frac{1}{3}$	13	12	.520	141	79	235	4.86	0
2007	Atlanta	N.L.	34	$224\frac{1}{3}$	16	10	.615	132	53	221	3.33	0
2008	Atlanta d	N.L.	23	142	11	7	.611	85	40	125	3.17	0
2009	Myrtle Beach	Carolina	2	$4\frac{2}{3}$	0	1	.000	3	2	5	5.79	0
2009	Gwinnett	Int.	4	$18\frac{2}{3}$	1	0	1.000	11	2	24	3.38	0
2009	Atlanta e	N.L.	7	$42\frac{1}{3}$	2	1	.667	30	13	49	3.61	0
2010	Atlanta	N.L.	34	$228\frac{2}{3}$	17	9	.654	139	74	189	2.83	0
Major League Totals		12 Yrs.	345	$2288\frac{1}{3}$	165	87	.655	1541	706	2147	3.42	0
	Division Series											
2000	Oakland	A.L.	1	8	0	1	.000	5	4	6	3.38	0
2001	Oakland	A.L.	2	$9\frac{2}{3}$	1	0	1.000	5	1	8	0.93	0
2002	Oakland	A.L.	2	$8\frac{2}{3}$	0	1	.000	8	4	13	6.23	0
2003	Oakland	A.L.	2	$7\frac{2}{3}$	0	0	.000	6	1	10	3.52	0
2005	Atlanta	N.L.	2	$13\frac{2}{3}$	0	1	.000	8	6	13	5.27	0
2010	Atlanta	N.L.	1	7	0	0	.000	5	4	4	0.00	0
Division Series Totals			10	$54\frac{2}{3}$	1	3	.250	37	20	54	3.46	0

a On disabled list from June 23 to August 7, 2004.
b Traded to Atlanta Braves for pitcher Juan Cruz, pitcher Dan Meyer and outfielder Charles Thomas, December 16, 2004.
c On disabled list from June 14 to July 16, 2005.
d On disabled list from July 27 to November 3, 2008.
e On disabled list from February 24 to September 1, 2009.

HUFF, DAVID GREGORY

Born, San Diego, California, August 22, 1984.
Bats Left. Throws Left. Height, 6 feet, 2 inches. Weight, 190 pounds.

Year	Club	Lea	G	IP	W	L	Pct	SO	BB	H	ERA	SAVES
2006	Mahoning Valley	N.Y.-Penn.	4	$7\frac{2}{3}$	0	1	.000	8	7	9	5.87	0
2007	Kinston	Carolina	11	$59\frac{2}{3}$	4	2	.667	46	15	57	2.72	0
2008	Akron	Eastern	11	$65\frac{2}{3}$	5	1	.833	62	14	44	1.92	0
2008	Buffalo	Int.	16	$80\frac{2}{3}$	6	4	.600	81	15	68	3.01	0
2009	Columbus	Int.	7	$39\frac{1}{3}$	5	1	.833	32	16	35	4.35	0
2009	Cleveland	A.L.	23	$128\frac{1}{3}$	11	8	.579	65	41	159	5.61	0
2010	Columbus	Int.	12	$74\frac{1}{3}$	8	2	.800	52	21	84	4.36	0
2010	Cleveland	A.L.	15	$79\frac{2}{3}$	2	11	.154	37	34	101	6.21	0
Major League Totals		2 Yrs.	38	208	13	19	.406	102	75	260	5.84	0

HUGHES, DUSTIN ROBERT (DUSTY)

Born, Tupelo, Mississippi, June 29, 1982.
Bats Left. Throws Left. Height, 5 feet, 10 inches. Weight, 185 pounds.

Year	Club	Lea	G	IP	W	L	Pct	SO	BB	H	ERA	SAVES
2003	Roy 1	Arizona	11	$50\frac{2}{3}$	5	2	.714	54	18	38	2.84	0
2004	Wilmington	Carolina	18	$108\frac{1}{3}$	5	5	.500	68	31	95	2.41	0
2004	Burlington	Midwest	8	52	4	2	.667	36	15	39	1.56	0
2005	High Desert	Calif.	19	92	5	7	.417	87	45	119	5.67	0
2006	a				INJURED—Did Not Play							
2007	Wichita	Texas	25	108	6	2	.750	77	45	98	3.08	1
2008	Omaha	P.C.	12	$55\frac{1}{3}$	3	2	.600	36	25	65	5.04	0
2008	NW Arkansas	Texas	20	$52\frac{2}{3}$	5	2	.714	43	16	47	2.91	3
2009	Omaha	P.C.	34	$87\frac{1}{3}$	3	3	.500	76	41	79	3.50	1
2009	Kansas City	A.L.	8	14	0	2	.000	15	8	13	5.14	0
2010	Kansas City	A.L.	57	$56\frac{1}{3}$	1	3	.250	34	24	59	3.83	0
Major League Totals		2 Yrs.	65	$70\frac{1}{3}$	1	5	.167	49	32	72	4.09	0

a On minor league disabled list, April 6 to September 8, 2006.

HUGHES, PHILIP JOSEPH

Born, Mission Viejo, California, June 24, 1986.
Bats Right. Throws Right. Height, 6 feet, 5 inches. Weight, 220 pounds.

Year	Club	Lea	G	IP	W	L	Pct	SO	BB	H	ERA	SAVES
2004	Yankees	Gulf Coast	3	5	0	0	.000	8	0	4	0.00	0
2005	Tampa	Fla.St.	5	$17\frac{2}{3}$	2	0	1.000	21	4	8	3.06	0
2005	Charleston	So.Atl.	12	$68\frac{2}{3}$	7	1	.875	72	16	46	1.97	0
2006	Trenton	Eastern	21	116	10	3	.769	138	32	73	2.25	0

Year	Club	Lea	G	IP	W	L	Pct	SO	BB	H	ERA	SAVES
2006	Tampa	Fla.St.	5	30	2	3	.400	30	2	19	1.80	0
2007	Tampa	Fla.St.	1	2	0	0	.000	3	2	0	0.00	0
2007	Trenton	Eastern	2	7	0	0	.000	11	2	5	1.29	0
2007	Scranton-WB	Int.	5	28⅔	4	1	.800	28	8	16	2.20	0
2007	New York a	A.L.	13	72⅔	5	3	.625	58	29	64	4.46	0
2008	Charleston	So.Atl.	2	6⅔	2	0	1.000	6	2	3	0.00	0
2008	Scranton-WB	Int.	6	29	1	0	1.000	31	9	34	5.90	0
2008	New York b	A.L.	8	34	0	4	.000	23	15	43	6.62	0
2009	Scranton/WB	Int.	3	19⅓	3	0	1.000	19	3	17	1.86	0
2009	New York	A.L.	51	86	8	3	.727	96	28	68	3.03	3
2010	New York	A.L.	31	176⅓	18	8	.692	146	58	162	4.19	0
Major League Totals		4 Yrs.	103	369	31	18	.633	323	130	337	4.20	3
	Division Series											
2007	New York	A.L.	2	5⅔	1	0	1.000	6	0	3	1.59	0
2009	New York	A.L.	3	2	0	0	.000	3	1	5	9.00	0
2010	New York	A.L.	1	7	1	0	1.000	6	1	4	0.00	0
Division Series Totals			6	14⅔	2	0	1.000	15	2	12	1.84	0
	Championship Series											
2009	New York	A.L.	3	2⅔	0	1	.000	3	1	4	3.38	0
2010	New York	A.L.	2	8⅔	0	2	.000	6	7	14	11.42	0
Championship Series Totals			5	11⅓	0	3	.000	9	8	18	9.53	0
	World Series Record											
2009	New York	A.L.	3	1⅔	0	0	.000	1	2	2	16.20	0

a On disabled list from May 2 to August 4, 2007.
b On disabled list from April 30 to July 30, 2008.

HUNTER, RAYMOND THOMAS (TOMMY)

Born, Tuscaloosa, Alabama, July 3, 1986.
Bats Right. Throws Right. Height, 6 feet, 3 inches. Weight, 255 pounds.

Year	Club	Lea	G	IP	W	L	Pct	SO	BB	H	ERA	SAVES
2007	Spokane	Northwest	10	17⅔	2	3	.400	13	1	15	2.55	1
2008	Bakersfield	Calif.	9	58⅓	5	4	.556	50	8	63	3.55	0
2008	Frisco	Texas	8	52⅓	4	2	.667	28	17	52	3.78	0
2008	Texas	A.L.	3	11	0	2	.000	9	3	23	16.36	0
2008	Oklahoma	P.C.	8	53	4	2	.667	28	9	55	2.89	0
2009	Frisco	Texas	5	21⅔	1	0	1.000	16	4	30	4.98	0
2009	Okla.	P.C.	8	49⅓	3	2	.600	35	16	53	3.83	0
2009	Texas	A.L.	19	112	9	6	.600	64	33	113	4.10	0
2010	Oklahoma	P.C.	6	26⅔	1	2	.333	14	11	28	4.05	0
2010	Texas a	A.L.	23	128	13	4	.765	68	33	126	3.73	0
Major League Totals		3 Yrs.	45	251	22	12	.647	141	69	262	4.45	0
	Division Series											
2010	Texas	A.L.	1	4	0	1	.000	7	0	6	4.50	0
	Championship Series											
2010	Texas	A.L.	1	3⅓	0	0	.000	5	0	5	8.10	0
	World Series Record											
2010	Texas	A.L.	1	4	0	1	.000	1	1	5	4.50	0

a On disabled list from March 26 to April 28, 2010.

JACKSON, EDWIN

Born, Neu-Ulm, West Germany, September 9, 1983.
Bats Right. Throws Right. Height, 6 feet, 3 inches. Weight, 210 pounds.

Year	Club	Lea	G	IP	W	L	Pct	SO	BB	H	ERA	SAVES
2001	Dodgers	Gulf Coast	12	22	2	1	.667	23	19	14	2.45	0
2002	South Bend	So.Atl.	19	104⅔	5	2	.714	85	33	79	1.98	0
2003	Jacksonville	Southern	27	148⅓	7	7	.500	157	53	121	3.70	0
2003	Los Angeles	N.L.	4	22	2	1	.667	19	11	17	2.45	0
2004	Las Vegas	P.C.	19	90⅔	6	4	.600	70	55	90	5.86	0
2004	Los Angeles a	N.L.	8	24⅔	2	1	.667	16	11	31	7.30	0
2005	Jacksonville	Southern	11	62	6	4	.600	44	18	52	3.48	0
2005	Las Vegas	P.C.	12	55⅓	3	7	.300	33	37	76	8.62	0
2005	Los Angeles	N.L.	7	28⅔	2	2	.500	13	17	31	6.28	0
2006	Durham	Int.	22	73	3	7	.300	66	35	84	5.55	5
2006	Tampa Bay b	A.L.	23	36⅓	0	0	.000	27	25	42	5.45	0
2007	Tampa Bay	A.L.	32	161	5	15	.250	128	88	195	5.76	0
2008	Tampa Bay c	A.L.	32	183⅓	14	11	.560	108	77	199	4.42	0
2009	Detroit d	A.L.	33	214	13	9	.591	161	70	200	3.62	0

Year	Club	Lea	G	IP	W	L	Pct	SO	BB	H	ERA	SAVES
2010	Chicago	A.L.	11	75	4	2	.667	77	18	73	3.24	0
2010	Arizona e-f	N.L.	21	134 1/3	6	10	.375	104	60	141	5.16	0
Major League Totals		8 Yrs.	171	879 1/3	48	51	.485	653	377	929	4.62	0
	Championship Series											
2008	Tampa Bay	N.L.	2	2 1/3	0	0	.000	4	2	0	0.00	0
	World Series Record											
2008	Tampa Bay c	N.L.	1	2	0	0	.000	1	1	2	4.50	0

a On disabled list from July 9 to September 7, 2004.
b Traded to Tampa Bay Devil Rays with pitcher Chuck Tiffany for pitcher Danys Baez and pitcher Lance Carter, January 14, 2006.
c Traded to Detroit Tigers for outfielder Matt Joyce, December 10, 2008.
d Traded to Arizona Diamondbacks with pitcher Ian Kennedy for pitcher Daniel Schlereth and pitcher Max Scherzer, December 9, 2009.
e Pitched no-hit, no-run game against Tampa Bay Rays, June 25, 2010.
f Traded to Chicago White Sox for pitcher Dan Hudson and pitcher David Holmberg, July 30, 2010.

JANSEN, KENLEY JERONIMO

Born, Curacao, Netherlands Antilles, September 30, 1987.
Bats Both. Throws Right. Height, 6 feet, 6 inches. Weight, 220 pounds.

Year	Club	Lea	G	IP	W	L	Pct	SO	BB	H	ERA	SAVES
2009	Inland Empire a	Calif.	12	11 2/3	0	0	.000	19	11	14	4.63	0
2010	Inland Empire	Calif.	11	18	1	1	.500	28	6	15	1.50	0
2010	Chattanooga	Southern	22	27	4	0	1.000	50	17	14	1.67	8
2010	Los Angeles	N.L.	25	27	1	0	1.000	41	15	12	0.67	4

a Played catcher in the Dodger organzation, 2005-2008.

JANSSEN, ROBERT CASEY (CASEY)

Born, Orange, California, September 17, 1981.
Bats Right. Throws Right. Height, 6 feet, 4 inches. Weight, 205 pounds.

Year	Club	Lea	G	IP	W	L	Pct	SO	BB	H	ERA	SAVES
2004	Auburn	N.Y.-Penn.	10	50	3	1	.750	45	10	47	3.60	0
2005	New Hampshire	Eastern	9	43	3	3	.500	47	4	49	2.93	0
2005	Dunedin	Fla.St.	10	59 2/3	6	1	.857	51	12	46	2.26	0
2005	Lansing	Midwest	7	46	4	0	1.000	38	4	27	1.37	0
2006	Syracuse	Int.	9	42 2/3	1	5	.167	32	8	47	4.85	0
2006	Toronto	A.L.	19	94	6	10	.375	44	21	103	5.07	0
2007	Toronto	A.L.	70	72 2/3	2	3	.400	39	20	67	2.35	6
2008	Toronto a	A.L.				INJURED—Did Not Play						
2009	Blue Jays	Gulf Coast	1	1	0	0	.000	0	0	2	9.00	0
2009	Dunedin	Fla.St.	4	13	0	0	.000	10	2	6	0.69	0
2009	New Hampshire	Eastern	6	15	1	0	1.000	12	5	12	2.40	0
2009	Las Vegas	P.C.	7	6 2/3	0	0	.000	7	1	4	5.40	0
2009	Toronto b	A.L.	21	40	2	4	.333	24	14	59	5.85	1
2010	Toronto	A.L.	56	68 2/3	5	2	.714	63	21	74	3.67	0
Major League Totals		4 Yrs.	166	275 1/3	15	19	.441	170	76	303	4.12	7

a On disabled list from March 17 to November 14, 2008.
b On disabled list from March 27 to April 30 and June 14 to July 23, 2009.

JENKS, ROBERT SCOTT (BOBBY)

Born, Mission Hills, California, March 14, 1981.
Bats Right. Throws Right. Height, 6 feet, 3 inches. Weight, 280 pounds.

Year	Club	Lea	G	IP	W	L	Pct	SO	BB	H	ERA	SAVES
2000	Butte	Pioneer	14	52 2/3	1	7	.125	42	44	61	7.86	0
2001	Cedar Rapids	Midwest	21	99	3	7	.300	98	64	90	5.27	0
2001	Arkansas	Texas	2	10	1	0	1.000	10	5	8	3.60	0
2002	Rancho Cucamonga	California	11	65 1/3	3	5	.375	64	46	50	4.82	0
2002	Arkansas	Texas	10	58	3	6	.333	58	44	49	4.66	0
2003	Angels	Arizona	1	4	0	0	.000	5	0	2	0.00	0
2003	Arkansas	Texas	16	83	7	2	.778	103	51	56	2.17	0
2004	Angels	Arizona	1	3 1/3	0	0	.000	5	3	2	8.10	0
2004	Rancho Cucamonga	California	1	3 2/3	0	1	.000	3	7	5	19.64	0
2004	Salt Lake a	P.C.	3	12 1/3	0	1	.000	13	6	19	8.76	0
2005	Birmingham	Southern	35	41	1	2	.333	48	20	34	2.85	19
2005	Chicago	A.L.	32	39 1/3	1	1	.500	50	15	34	2.75	6
2006	Chicago	A.L.	67	69 2/3	3	4	.429	80	31	66	4.00	41
2007	Chicago	A.L.	66	65	3	5	.375	56	13	45	2.77	40
2008	Winston-Salem	Carolina	1	1	0	0	.000	0	0	3	9.00	0

Year Club	Lea	G	IP	W	L	Pct	SO	BB	H	ERA	SAVES
2008 Birmingham	Southern	1	1	0	0	.000	3	0	0	0.00	0
2008 Chicago b	A.L.	57	$61\frac{2}{3}$	3	1	.750	38	17	51	2.63	30
2009 Chicago	A.L.	52	$53\frac{1}{3}$	3	4	.429	49	16	52	3.71	29
2010 Chicago c	A.L.	55	$52\frac{2}{3}$	1	3	.250	61	18	54	4.44	27
Major League Totals	6 Yrs.	329	$341\frac{2}{3}$	14	18	.438	334	110	302	3.40	173
Division Series											
2005 Chicago	A.L.	2	3	0	0	.000	1	1	1	0.00	2
2008 Chicago	A.L.	1	1	0	0	.000	1	0	1	0.00	1
Division Series Totals		3	4	0	0	.000	2	1	2	0.00	3
World Series Record											
2005 Chicago	A.L.	4	5	0	0	.000	7	2	3	3.60	2

a Claimed on waivers by Chicago White Sox from Anaheim Angels, December 17, 2004.
b On disabled list from June 30 to July 18, 2008.
c Not offered contract, December 2, 2010. Signed with Boston Red Sox, December 21, 2010.

JEPSEN, KEVIN MARTIN

Born, Anaheim, California, July 26, 1984.
Bats Right. Throws Right. Height, 6 feet, 3 inches. Weight, 215 pounds.

Year Club	Lea	G	IP	W	L	Pct	SO	BB	H	ERA	SAVES
2002 Angels	Arizona	8	$26\frac{1}{3}$	1	3	.250	19	12	29	6.84	0
2003 Cedar Rapids	Midwest	10	51	6	3	.667	42	28	32	2.65	0
2004 Cedar Rapids	Midwest	27	$144\frac{1}{3}$	8	10	.444	136	77	122	3.43	0
2005 Angels	Arizona	7	$14\frac{2}{3}$	0	1	.000	17	11	8	5.52	0
2005 Rancho Cucamonga....	Calif.	4	$12\frac{2}{3}$	0	1	.000	11	10	19	10.66	0
2006 Rancho Cucamonga....	Calif.	47	$50\frac{1}{3}$	4	4	.500	46	34	51	3.58	16
2007 Rancho Cucamonga....	Calif.	44	$53\frac{2}{3}$	1	5	.167	50	38	61	4.19	3
2008 Arkansas	Texas	25	$31\frac{2}{3}$	2	1	.667	35	18	22	1.42	11
2008 Salt Lake	P.C.	15	23	1	3	.250	21	12	17	2.35	2
2008 Los Angeles	A.L.	9	$8\frac{1}{3}$	0	1	.000	7	4	8	4.32	0
2009 Salt Lake	P.C.	14	18	1	0	1.000	20	16	30	9.00	2
2009 Los Angeles a..........	A.L.	54	$54\frac{2}{3}$	6	4	.600	48	19	63	4.94	1
2010 Los Angeles	A.L.	68	59	2	4	.333	61	29	54	3.97	0
Major League Totals	3 Yrs.	131	122	8	9	.471	116	52	125	4.43	1
Division Series											
2009 Los Angeles	A.L.	2	$1\frac{1}{3}$	0	0	.000	1	0	3	6.75	0
Championship Series											
2009 Los Angeles	A.L.	3	$3\frac{2}{3}$	1	0	1.000	2	2	5	2.45	0

a On disabled list from April 19 to May 4, 2009.

JIMENEZ, UBALDO

Born, Nagua, Dominican Republic, January 22, 1984.
Bats Right. Throws Right. Height, 6 feet, 4 inches. Weight, 200 pounds.

Year Club	Lea	G	IP	W	L	Pct	SO	BB	H	ERA	SAVES
2002 Casper	Pioneer	14	62	3	5	.375	65	29	72	6.53	0
2003 Visalia	Calif.	1	5	1	0	1.000	7	1	3	0.00	0
2003 Asheville............	So.Atl.	27	$153\frac{2}{3}$	10	6	.625	138	67	129	3.46	0
2004 Visalia	Calif.	9	$44\frac{1}{3}$	4	1	.800	61	12	29	2.23	0
2005 Modesto.............	Calif.	14	$72\frac{1}{3}$	5	3	.625	78	40	61	3.98	0
2005 Tulsa	Texas	12	63	2	5	.286	53	31	58	5.43	0
2006 Tulsa	Texas	13	$73\frac{1}{3}$	9	2	.818	86	40	49	2.45	0
2006 Colorado Springs.......	P.C.	13	$78\frac{1}{3}$	5	2	.714	64	43	74	5.06	0
2006 Colorado	N.L.	2	$7\frac{2}{3}$	0	0	.000	3	3	5	3.52	0
2007 Colorado Springs.......	P.C.	19	103	8	5	.615	89	62	110	5.85	0
2007 Colorado	N.L.	15	82	4	4	.500	68	37	70	4.28	0
2008 Colorado	N.L.	34	$198\frac{2}{3}$	12	12	.500	172	103	182	3.99	0
2009 Colorado	N.L.	33	218	15	12	.556	198	85	183	3.47	0
2010 Colorado	N.L.	33	$221\frac{2}{3}$	19	8	*.704	214	92	164	2.88	0
Major League Totals	5 Yrs.	117	728	50	36	.581	655	320	604	3.52	0
Division Series											
2007 Colorado	N.L.	1	$6\frac{1}{3}$	0	0	.000	5	4	3	1.42	0
2009 Colorado	N.L.	2	12	0	1	.000	11	3	15	5.25	0
Division Series Totals		3	$18\frac{1}{3}$	0	1	.000	16	7	18	3.93	0
Championship Series											
2007 Colorado	N.L.	1	5	0	0	.000	6	4	5	1.80	0
World Series Record											
2007 Colorado	N.L.	1	$4\frac{2}{3}$	0	1	.000	2	5	3	3.86	0

JOHNSON, JAMES ROBERT (JIM)

Born, Johnson City, New York, June 27, 1983.
Bats Right. Throws Right. Height, 6 feet, 5 inches. Weight, 230 pounds.

Year	Club	Lea	G	IP	W	L	Pct	SO	BB	H	ERA	SAVES
2001	Orioles	Gulf Coast	7	18 2/3	0	1	.000	19	7	17	3.86	0
2002	Bluefield	Appal.	11	55 2/3	4	2	.667	36	16	52	4.37	0
2003	Bluefield	Appal.	11	51 1/3	3	2	.600	46	18	62	3.68	0
2004	Frederick	Carolina	1	3	0	0	.000	6	1	6	9.00	0
2004	Delmarva	So.Atl.	20	106 2/3	8	7	.533	93	30	97	3.29	0
2005	Frederick	Carolina	28	159 2/3	12	9	.571	168	64	139	3.49	1
2005	Bowie	Eastern	1	7	0	0	.000	6	2	3	0.00	0
2006	Baltimore	A.L.	1	3	0	1	.000	0	3	9	24.00	0
2006	Bowie	Eastern	27	156	13	6	.684	124	57	165	4.44	0
2007	Baltimore	A.L.	1	2	0	0	.000	1	2	3	9.00	0
2007	Norfolk	Int.	26	148	6	12	.333	109	48	164	4.07	0
2008	Norfolk	Int.	1	4	0	1	.000	2	1	2	2.25	0
2008	Baltimore a	A.L.	54	68 2/3	2	4	.333	38	28	54	2.23	1
2009	Baltimore	A.L.	64	70	4	6	.400	49	23	73	4.11	10
2010	Orioles	Gulf Coast	4	4	0	0	.000	5	1	5	6.75	0
2010	Frederick	Carolina	2	3	0	0	.000	1	0	6	3.00	0
2010	Bowie	Eastern	4	5	0	0	.000	6	0	2	1.80	0
2010	Norfolk	Int.	1	1	0	0	.000	0	0	1	0.00	0
2010	Baltimore b	A.L.	26	26 1/3	1	1	.500	22	5	32	3.42	1
Major League Totals		5 Yrs.	146	170	7	12	.368	110	61	171	3.65	12

a On disabled list from September 1 to October 2, 2008.
b On disabled list from May 28 to August 27, 2010.

JOHNSON, JOSHUA MICHAEL (JOSH)

Born, Minneapolis, Minnesota, January 31, 1984.
Bats Left. Throws Right. Height, 6 feet, 7 inches. Weight, 230 pounds.

Year	Club	Lea	G	IP	W	L	Pct	SO	BB	H	ERA	SAVES
2002	Marlins	Gulf Coast	4	15	2	0	1.000	11	3	8	0.60	0
2003	Greensboro	So.Atl.	17	81 1/3	4	7	.364	59	29	69	3.61	0
2004	Jupiter	Fla.St.	23	114 1/3	5	12	.294	103	47	124	3.38	0
2005	Carolina	Southern	26	139 2/3	12	4	.750	113	50	139	3.87	0
2005	Florida	N.L.	4	12 1/3	0	0	.000	10	10	11	3.65	0
2006	Florida	N.L.	31	157	12	7	.632	133	68	136	3.10	0
2007	Carolina	Southern	2	10 1/3	0	0	.000	9	5	8	1.74	0
2007	Florida	N.L.	4	15 2/3	0	3	.000	14	12	26	7.47	0
2007	Jupiter a	Fla.St.	3	11 1/3	0	0	.000	13	0	9	0.79	0
2008	Greensboro	So.Atl.	1	5	0	1	.000	7	0	8	3.60	0
2008	Jupiter	Fla.St.	1	5 1/3	0	0	.000	2	2	6	5.06	0
2008	Carolina	Southern	3	19	1	1	.500	14	3	22	3.32	0
2008	Florida b	N.L.	14	87 1/3	7	1	.875	77	27	91	3.61	0
2009	Florida	N.L.	33	209	15	5	.750	191	58	184	3.23	0
2010	Florida	N.L.	28	183 2/3	11	6	.647	186	48	155	*2.30	0
Major League Totals		6 Yrs.	114	665	45	22	.672	611	223	603	3.10	0

a On disabled list from March 23 to June 18 and July 5 to November 12, 2007.
b On disabled list from March 21 to July 10, 2008.

JURRJENS, JAIR FRANCOISE

Born, Santa Maria, Curacao,Netherlands Antilles, January 29, 1986.
Bats Right. Throws Right. Height, 6 feet, 1 inch. Weight, 200 pounds.

Year	Club	Lea	G	IP	W	L	Pct	SO	BB	H	ERA	SAVES
2003	Tigers	Gulf Coast	7	28	2	1	.667	20	3	33	3.21	0
2004	Tigers	Gulf Coast	6	39 2/3	4	2	.667	39	10	25	2.27	0
2004	Oneonta	N.Y.-Penn.	7	39	1	5	.167	31	10	50	5.31	0
2005	West Michigan	Midwest	26	142 2/3	12	6	.667	108	36	132	3.41	0
2006	Erie	Eastern	12	67	4	3	.571	53	21	71	3.36	0
2006	Lakeland	Fla.St.	12	73 2/3	5	0	1.000	59	10	53	2.08	0
2007	Erie	Eastern	19	112 2/3	7	5	.583	94	31	112	3.20	0
2007	Detroit a-b	A.L.	7	30 2/3	3	1	.750	13	11	24	4.70	0
2008	Atlanta	N.L.	31	188 1/3	13	10	.565	139	70	188	3.68	0
2009	Atlanta	N.L.	34	215	14	10	.583	152	75	186	2.60	0
2010	Gwinnett	Int.	3	13	1	1	.500	9	6	20	5.54	0
2010	Atlanta c	N.L.	20	116 1/3	7	6	.538	86	42	120	4.64	0
Major League Totals		4 Yrs.	92	550 1/3	37	27	.578	390	198	518	3.52	0

a On disabled list from August 27 to September 11, 2007.
b Traded to Atlanta Braves with outfielder Gorkys Hernandez for infielder Edgar Renteria, October 29, 2007.
c On disabled list from April 30 to June 30, 2010.

KARSTENS, JEFFREY WAYNE (JEFF)

Born, San Diego, California, September 24, 1982.
Bats Right. Throws Right. Height, 6 feet, 3 inches. Weight, 185 pounds.

Year	Club	Lea	G	IP	W	L	Pct	SO	BB	H	ERA	SAVES
2003	Staten Island	N.Y.-Penn.	14	67⅓	4	2	.667	53	16	63	2.54	0
2004	Tampa	Fla.St.	24	138⅔	6	9	.400	116	31	151	4.02	0
2005	Trenton	Eastern	28	169	12	11	.522	147	42	192	4.15	0
2006	Trenton	Eastern	11	74	6	0	1.000	67	14	54	2.31	0
2006	Columbus	Int.	14	73⅔	5	5	.500	48	30	80	4.28	0
2006	New York	A.L.	8	42⅔	2	1	.667	16	11	40	3.80	0
2007	Tampa	Fla.St.	1	4	0	0	.000	5	1	3	0.00	0
2007	Yankees	Gulf Coast	1	3⅓	0	0	.000	2	1	3	0.00	0
2007	Staten Island	N.Y.-Penn.	1	5	1	0	1.000	8	0	4	1.80	0
2007	Trenton	Eastern	1	5	1	0	1.000	5	2	4	1.80	0
2007	Scranton/WB	Int.	6	31	3	0	1.000	27	9	25	1.74	0
2007	New York a	A.L.	7	14⅔	1	4	.200	5	9	27	11.05	0
2008	Scranton/WB	Int.	12	68⅔	6	4	.600	55	15	66	3.80	0
2008	Pittsburgh b-c	N.L.	9	51⅓	2	6	.250	23	13	56	4.03	0
2009	Indianapolis	Int.	3	6	0	0	.000	7	0	4	0.00	0
2009	Pittsburgh d	N.L.	39	108	4	6	.400	52	45	115	5.42	0
2010	Indianapolis	Int.	5	16	1	2	.333	12	2	21	7.31	0
2010	Pittsburgh	N.L.	26	122⅔	3	10	.231	72	27	146	4.92	0
Major League Totals		5 Yrs.	89	339⅓	12	27	.308	168	105	384	5.07	0

a On disabled list from March 26 to April 21 and April 29 to August 1, 2007.
b On disabled list from March 28 to May 20, 2008.
c Traded to Pittsburgh Pirates with outfielder Jose Tabata, pitcher Ross Ohlendorf and pitcher Dan McCutchen for outfielder Xavier Nady and pitcher Damaso Marte, July 26, 2008.
d On disabled list from August 25 to September 9, 2009.

KAWAKAMI, KENSHIN

Born, Tokushima, Japan, June 22, 1975.
Bats Right. Throws Right. Height, 5 feet, 11 inches. Weight, 200 pounds.

Year	Club	Lea	G	IP	W	L	Pct	SO	BB	H	ERA	SAVES
1998	Chunichi	Japan Cent.	26	161⅓	14	6	.700	124	51	123	2.57	0
1999	Chunichi	Japan Cent.	29	162	8	9	.471	102	43	173	4.44	1
2000	Chunichi	Japan Cent.	14	60⅓	2	3	.400	24	20	65	4.77	0
2001	Chunichi	Japan Cent.				INJURED—Did Not Play						
2002	Chunichi	Japan Cent.	27	187⅔	12	6	.667	149	34	170	2.35	0
2003	Chunichi	Japan Cent.	8	53⅔	4	3	.571	37	14	60	3.02	0
2004	Chunichi	Japan Cent.	27	192⅓	17	7	.708	176	38	173	3.32	0
2005	Chunichi	Japan Cent.	25	180⅓	11	8	.579	138	28	186	3.74	0
2006	Chunichi	Japan Cent.	29	215	17	7	.708	194	39	166	2.51	0
2007	Chunichi	Japan Cent.	26	167⅓	12	8	.600	145	23	175	3.55	0
2008	Chunichi	Japan Cent.	20	117⅓	9	5	.643	112	25	99	2.30	0
2009	Atlanta a	N.L.	32	156⅓	7	12	.368	105	57	153	3.86	1
2010	Atlanta	N.L.	18	87⅓	1	10	.091	59	32	98	5.15	0
Major League Totals		2 Yrs.	50	243⅔	8	22	.267	164	89	251	4.32	1

a Signed with Atlanta Braves, January 13, 2009.

KAZMIR, SCOTT EDWARD

Born, Houston, Texas, January 24, 1984.
Bats Left. Throws Left. Height, 6 feet. Weight, 190 pounds.

Year	Club	Lea	G	IP	W	L	Pct	SO	BB	H	ERA	SAVES
2002	Brooklyn	N.Y.-Penn.	5	18	0	1	.000	34	7	5	0.50	0
2003	St. Lucie	Fla.St.	7	33	1	2	.333	40	16	29	3.27	0
2003	Capital City	So.Atl.	18	76⅓	4	4	.500	105	28	50	2.36	0
2004	St. Lucie	Fla.St.	11	50	1	2	.333	51	22	49	3.42	0
2004	Binghamton	Eastern	4	26	2	1	.667	29	9	16	1.73	0
2004	Montgomery	Southern	4	25	1	2	.333	24	11	14	1.44	0
2004	Tampa Bay a	A.L.	8	33⅓	2	3	.400	41	21	33	5.67	0
2005	Tampa Bay	A.L.	32	186	10	9	.526	174	*100	172	3.77	0
2006	Tampa Bay b	A.L.	24	144⅔	10	8	.556	163	52	132	3.24	0
2007	Tampa Bay	A.L.	34	206⅔	13	9	.591	*239	89	196	3.48	0
2008	Vero Beach	Fla.St.	2	7⅔	0	1	.000	7	0	8	4.70	0

Year	Club	Lea	G	IP	W	L	Pct	SO	BB	H	ERA	SAVES
2008	Durham	Int.	1	5	0	0	.000	3	1	3	1.80	0
2008	Tampa Bay c	A.L.	27	152 1/3	12	8	.600	166	70	123	3.49	0
2009	Charlotte	Fla.St.	1	4 2/3	0	0	.000	5	1	3	0.00	0
2009	Durham	Int.	1	6	1	0	1.000	5	0	5	1.50	0
2009	Tampa Bay-Los Angeles d-e	A.L.	26	147 1/3	10	9	.526	117	60	149	4.89	0
2010	Rancho Cucamonga	Calif.	1	6 1/3	0	0	.000	6	0	8	4.26	0
2010	Los Angeles f	A.L.	28	150	9	15	.375	93	79	158	5.94	0
Major League Totals		7 Yrs.	179	1020 1/3	66	61	.520	993	471	963	4.14	0
	Division Series											
2008	Tampa Bay	N.L.	1	5 1/3	1	0	1.000	4	2	8	3.38	0
2009	Los Angeles	A.L.	1	6	0	0	.000	1	3	5	7.50	0
Division Series Totals			2	11 1/3	1	0	1.000	5	5	13	5.56	0
	Championship Series											
2008	Tampa Bay	N.L.	2	10 1/3	0	0	.000	9	6	8	4.35	0
2009	Los Angeles	A.L.	2	4 2/3	0	1	.000	3	5	6	7.71	0
Championship Series Totals			4	15	0	1	.000	12	11	14	5.40	0
	World Series Record											
2008	Tampa Bay	N.L.	2	10	0	1	.000	9	10	10	4.50	0

a Traded by New York Mets to Tampa Bay Devil Rays with pitcher Jose Diaz for pitcher Victor Zambrano and pitcher Bartolome Fortunato, July 30, 2004.

b On disabled list from July 31 to August 8 and August 23 to October 2, 2006.

c On disabled list from March 25 to May 4, 2008.

d On disabled list from May 21 to June 26, 2009.

e Traded to Los Angeles Angels for pitcher Alexander Torres, infielder Matthew Sweeney and player to be named later, August 28, 2009. Tampa Bay Rays received infielder Sean Rodriguez to complete trade, September 1, 2009.

f On disabled list from March 31 to April 15 and July 11 to August 7, 2010.

KELLEY, SHAWN ANDREW

Born, Louisville, Kentucky, April 26, 1984.

Bats Right. Throws Right. Height, 6 feet, 2 inches. Weight, 215 pounds.

Year	Club	Lea	G	IP	W	L	Pct	SO	BB	H	ERA	SAVES
2007	Wisconsin	Midwest	9	12	1	1	.500	14	4	16	2.25	0
2007	Everett	Northwest	3	3	1	0	1.000	4	0	2	3.00	0
2008	High Desert	Calif.	12	12	0	0	.000	12	3	8	0.00	3
2008	Wisconsin	Midwest	8	7 2/3	0	0	.000	12	2	10	3.52	3
2008	West Tenn	Southern	29	42 2/3	3	1	.750	44	17	31	2.11	9
2009	Azl Mariners	Arizona	2	2	0	0	.000	3	0	0	0.00	0
2009	Tacoma	P.C.	1	1	0	0	.000	0	0	0	0.00	0
2009	Seattle a	A.L.	41	46	5	4	.556	41	9	45	4.50	0
2010	Tacoma	P.C.	3	3 2/3	0	0	.000	6	3	1	4.91	1
2010	Seattle b	A.L.	22	25	3	1	.750	26	12	26	3.96	0
Major League Totals		2 Yrs.	63	71	8	5	.615	67	21	71	4.31	0

a On disabled list from May 6 to July 3, 2009.

b On disabled list from June 16 to October 8, 2010.

KENDRICK, KYLE RODNEY

Born, Houston, Texas, August 26, 1984.

Bats Right. Throws Right. Height, 6 feet, 3 inches. Weight, 190 pounds.

Year	Club	Lea	G	IP	W	L	Pct	SO	BB	H	ERA	SAVES
2003	Phillies	Gulf Coast	9	31 1/3	0	4	.000	26	12	40	5.46	0
2004	Batavia	N.Y.-Penn.	13	70 2/3	2	8	.200	53	18	94	5.48	0
2004	Lakewood	So.Atl.	15	66 2/3	3	8	.273	36	33	85	6.07	0
2005	Clearwater	Fla.St.	1	4	0	1	.000	1	2	5	0.00	0
2005	Batavia	N.Y.-Penn.	14	91 1/3	5	4	.556	70	22	94	3.74	0
2005	Lakewood	So.Atl.	5	22 2/3	0	3	.000	11	10	38	9.13	0
2006	Clearwater	Fla.St.	21	130	9	7	.563	79	37	117	3.53	0
2006	Lakewood	So.Atl.	7	46	3	2	.600	54	15	34	2.15	0
2007	Reading	Eastern	12	81 1/3	4	7	.364	50	18	82	3.21	0
2007	Philadelphia	N.L.	20	121	10	4	.714	49	25	129	3.87	0
2008	Philadelphia	N.L.	31	155 2/3	11	9	.550	68	57	194	5.49	0
2009	Lehigh Valley	Int.	24	143	9	7	.563	62	35	133	3.34	0
2009	Philadelphia	N.L.	9	26 1/3	3	1	.750	15	9	27	3.42	0
2010	Philadelphia	N.L.	33	180 2/3	11	10	.524	84	49	199	4.73	0
Major League Totals		4 Yrs.	93	483 2/3	35	24	.593	216	140	549	4.69	0
	Division Series											
2007	Philadelphia	N.L.	1	3 2/3	0	1	.000	2	2	5	12.27	0

KENNEDY, IAN PATRICK

Born, Huntington Beach, California, December 19, 1984.
Bats Right. Throws Right. Height, 6 feet. Weight, 195 pounds.

Year Club	Lea	G	IP	W	L	Pct	SO	BB	H	ERA	SAVES
2006 Staten Island	N.Y.-Penn.	1	2 2/3	0	0	.000	2	2	2	0.00	0
2007 Tampa	Fla.St.	11	63	6	1	.857	72	22	39	1.29	0
2007 Trenton	Eastern	9	48 2/3	5	1	.833	57	17	27	2.59	0
2007 Scranton/WB	Int.	6	34 2/3	1	1	.500	34	11	25	2.08	0
2007 New York	A.L.	3	19	1	0	1.000	15	9	13	1.89	0
2008 Yankees	Gulf Coast	1	3	1	0	1.000	7	0	3	3.00	0
2008 Tampa	Fla.St.	1	5	0	0	.000	4	1	2	0.00	0
2008 New York	A.L.	10	39 2/3	0	4	.000	27	26	50	8.17	0
2008 Scranton/WB a	Int.	13	69	5	3	.625	72	17	52	2.35	0
2009 Scranton/WB	Int.	4	22 2/3	1	0	1.000	25	7	18	1.59	0
2009 New York b-c	A.L.	1	1	0	0	.000	1	2	0	0.00	0
2010 Arizona	N.L.	32	194	9	10	.474	168	70	163	3.80	0
Major League Totals	4 Yrs.	46	253 2/3	10	14	.417	211	107	226	4.33	0

a On disabled list from May 28 to June 24, 2008.
b Traded to Detroit Tigers with outfielder Austin Jackson and pitcher Phil Coke for outfielder Curtis Granderson, December 9, 2009.
c Traded to Arizona Diamondbacks with pitcher Edwin Jackson for pitcher Daniel Schlereth and pitcher Max Scherzer, December 9, 2009.

KERSHAW, CLAYTON EDWARD

Born, Dallas, Texas, March 19, 1988.
Bats Left. Throws Left. Height, 6 feet, 3 inches. Weight, 220 pounds.

Year Club	Lea	G	IP	W	L	Pct	SO	BB	H	ERA	SAVES
2006 Dodgers	Gulf Coast	10	37	2	0	1.000	54	5	28	1.95	1
2007 Great Lakes	Midwest	20	97 1/3	7	5	.583	134	50	72	2.77	0
2007 Jacksonville	Southern	5	24 2/3	1	2	.333	29	17	17	3.65	0
2008 Jacksonville	Southern	13	61 1/3	2	3	.400	59	19	39	1.91	0
2008 Los Angeles	N.L.	22	107 2/3	5	5	.500	100	52	109	4.26	0
2009 Los Angeles	N.L.	31	171	8	8	.500	185	91	119	2.79	0
2010 Los Angeles	N.L.	32	204 1/3	13	10	.565	212	81	160	2.91	0
Major League Totals	3 Yrs.	85	483	26	23	.531	497	224	388	3.17	0
Division Series											
2009 Los Angeles	N.L.	1	6 2/3	0	0	.000	4	1	9	2.70	0
Championship Series											
2008 Los Angeles	N.L.	2	2	0	0	.000	1	2	1	4.50	0
2009 Los Angeles	N.L.	2	6 2/3	0	1	.000	6	6	5	9.45	0
Championship Series Totals		4	8 2/3	0	1	.000	7	8	6	8.31	0

KIMBREL, CRAIG M.

Born, Huntsville, Alabama, May 28, 1988.
Bats Right. Throws Right. Height, 5 feet, 11 inches. Weight, 205 pounds.

Year Club	Lea	G	IP	W	L	Pct	SO	BB	H	ERA	SAVES
2008 Danville	Appal.	12	19	1	2	.333	27	10	5	0.47	6
2008 Myrtle Beach	Carolina	2	3 2/3	0	0	.000	3	1	5	0.00	0
2008 Rome	So.Atl.	10	12 2/3	2	0	1.000	26	4	6	0.71	4
2009 Myrtle Beach	Carolina	19	26 1/3	0	2	.000	45	28	18	5.47	2
2009 Gwinnett	Int.	2	2	0	0	.000	3	4	0	0.00	0
2009 Rome	So.Atl.	16	20	0	0	.000	38	6	9	0.90	10
2009 Mississippi	Southern	12	11 2/3	2	1	.667	17	7	3	0.77	6
2010 Gwinnett	Int.	48	55 2/3	3	2	.600	83	35	28	1.62	23
2010 Atlanta	N.L.	21	20 2/3	4	0	1.000	40	16	9	0.44	1
Division Series											
2010 Atlanta	N.L.	4	4 1/3	0	1	.000	7	1	1	2.08	0

KUO, HONG-CHIH

Born, Tainan City, Taiwan, July 23, 1981.
Bats Left. Throws Left. Height, 6 feet. Weight, 235 pounds.

Year Club	Lea	G	IP	W	L	Pct	SO	BB	H	ERA	SAVES
2000 San Bernardino	Calif.	1	3	0	0	.000	7	0	0	0.00	0
2001 Dodgers	Gulf Coast	7	19 1/3	0	0	.000	21	4	13	2.33	0
2002 Vero Beach	Fla.St.	4	8	0	1	.000	8	2	11	6.75	0
2002 Dodgers	Gulf Coast	3	6	0	0	.000	9	1	4	4.50	0
2003 Columbus a	So.Atl	INJURED—Did Not Play									

Year Club	Lea	G	IP	W	L	Pct	SO	BB	H	ERA	SAVES
2004 Columbus	So.Atl.	3	6	1	0	1.000	10	4	8	4.50	0
2005 Vero Beach	Fla.St.	11	26	1	1	.500	42	10	19	2.08	0
2005 Jacksonville	Southern	17	28 1/3	1	1	.500	44	11	22	1.91	3
2005 Los Angeles	N.L.	9	5 1/3	0	1	.000	10	5	5	6.75	0
2006 Las Vegas	P.C.	23	53	4	3	.571	63	22	52	3.06	1
2006 Los Angeles	N.L.	28	59 2/3	1	5	.167	71	33	54	4.22	0
2007 Las Vegas	P.C.	7	20	0	1	.000	28	8	18	3.60	0
2007 Los Angeles b	N.L.	8	30 1/3	1	4	.200	27	14	35	7.42	0
2008 Los Angeles	N.L.	42	80	5	3	.625	96	21	60	2.14	1
2009 Azl Dodgers	Arizona	3	3	0	0	.000	5	1	2	0.00	0
2009 Inland Empire	Calif.	4	4	0	0	.000	6	0	3	0.00	0
2009 Albuquerque	P.C.	2	2	0	0	.000	1	1	2	4.50	0
2009 Los Angeles c	N.L.	35	30	2	0	1.000	32	13	21	3.00	0
2010 Inland Empire	Calif.	2	2	0	0	.000	3	0	0	0.00	0
2010 Los Angeles d	N.L.	56	60	3	2	.600	73	18	29	1.20	12
Major League Totals	6 Yrs.	178	265 1/3	12	15	.444	309	104	204	3.19	13
Division Series											
2006 Los Angeles	N.L.	1	4 1/3	0	1	.000	4	2	4	4.15	0
2009 Los Angeles	N.L.	1	1	0	0	.000	2	0	2	0.00	0
Division Series Totals		2	5 1/3	0	1	.000	6	2	6	3.38	0
Championship Series											
2008 Los Angeles	N.L.	3	3	0	0	.000	3	0	2	3.00	0
2009 Los Angeles	N.L.	4	4	1	0	1.000	6	0	2	2.25	0
Championship Series Totals		7	7	1	0	1.000	9	0	4	2.57	0

a On minor league disabled list from April 3 to September 8, 2003.
b On disabled list from March 23 to May 3 and June 30 to October 31, 2007.
c On disabled list from April 30 to July 27, 2009.
d On disabled list from March 26 to April 22, 2010.

KURODA, HIROKI

Born, Osaka, Japan, February 10, 1975.
Bats Right. Throws Right. Height, 6 feet, 1 inch. Weight, 210 pounds.

Year Club	Lea	G	IP	W	L	Pct	SO	BB	H	ERA	SAVES
1997 Hiroshima	Japan Cent.	23	135	6	9	.400	64	63	147	4.40	0
1998 Hiroshima	Japan Cent.	18	45	1	4	.200	25	24	53	6.60	0
1999 Hiroshima	Japan Cent.	21	87 2/3	5	8	.385	55	39	106	6.78	0
2000 Hiroshima	Japan Cent.	29	144	9	6	.600	116	61	147	4.31	0
2001 Hiroshima	Japan Cent.	27	190	12	8	.600	146	45	175	3.03	0
2002 Hiroshima	Japan Cent.	23	164 1/3	10	10	.500	144	34	166	3.67	0
2003 Hiroshima	Japan Cent.	28	205 2/3	13	9	.591	137	45	197	3.11	0
2004 Hiroshima	Japan Cent.	21	147	7	9	.438	138	29	187	4.65	0
2005 Hiroshima	Japan Cent.	29	212 2/3	15	12	.556	165	42	183	3.17	0
2006 Hiroshima	Japan Cent.	26	189 1/3	13	6	.684	144	21	169	1.85	1
2007 Hiroshima a	Japan Cent.	26	179 2/3	12	8	.600	123	42	176	3.56	0
2008 Los Angeles b	N.L.	31	183 1/3	9	10	.474	116	42	181	3.73	0
2009 Los Angeles c	N.L.	21	117 1/3	8	7	.533	87	24	110	3.76	0
2010 Los Angeles d	N.L.	31	196 1/3	11	13	.458	159	48	180	3.39	0
Major League Totals	3 Yrs.	83	497	28	30	.483	362	114	471	3.60	0
Division Series											
2008 Los Angeles	N.L.	1	6 1/3	1	0	1.000	4	2	6	0.00	0
Championship Series											
2008 Los Angeles	N.L.	1	6	1	0	1.000	3	1	5	3.00	0
2009 Los Angeles	N.L.	1	1 1/3	0	1	.000	1	0	6	40.50	0
Championship Series Totals		2	7 1/3	1	1	.500	4	1	11	9.82	0

a Signed with Los Angeles Dodgers, December 16, 2007.
b On disabled list from June 13 to July 2, 2008.
c On disabled list from April 7 to June 1 and August 16 to September 6, 2009.
d Filed for free agency, November 1, 2010, re-signed with Los Angeles Dodgers, November 15, 2010.

LACKEY, JOHN DERRAN

Born, Abilene, Texas, October 23, 1978.
Bats Right. Throws Right. Height, 6 feet, 6 inches. Weight, 235 pounds.

Year Club	Lea	G	IP	W	L	Pct	SO	BB	H	ERA	SAVES
1999 Boise	Northwest	15	81 1/3	6	2	.750	77	50	81	4.98	0
2000 Lake Elsinore	California	15	100 2/3	6	6	.500	74	42	94	3.40	0
2000 Erie	Eastern	8	57 1/3	6	1	.857	43	9	58	3.30	0
2000 Cedar Rapids	Midwest	5	30 1/3	3	2	.600	21	5	20	2.08	0

Year	Club	Lea	G	IP	W	L	Pct	SO	BB	H	ERA	SAVES
2001	Salt Lake	P.C.	10	57⅔	3	4	.429	42	16	75	6.71	0
2001	Arkansas	Texas	18	127⅓	9	7	.563	94	29	106	3.46	0
2002	Salt Lake	P.C.	16	101⅔	8	2	.800	82	28	89	2.57	0
2002	Anaheim	A.L.	18	108⅓	9	4	.692	69	33	113	3.66	0
2003	Anaheim	A.L.	33	204	10	16	.385	151	66	223	4.63	0
2004	Anaheim	A.L.	33	198⅓	14	13	.519	144	60	215	4.67	0
2005	Los Angeles	A.L.	33	209	14	5	.737	199	71	208	3.44	0
2006	Los Angeles	A.L.	33	217⅔	13	11	.542	190	72	203	3.56	0
2007	Los Angeles	A.L.	33	224	19	9	.679	179	52	219	*3.01	0
2008	Rancho Cucamonga	Calif.	3	9	0	0	.000	11	2	8	4.00	0
2008	Los Angeles a	A.L.	24	163⅓	12	5	.706	130	40	161	3.75	0
2009	Salt Lake	P.C.	2	9⅔	0	1	.000	8	1	6	2.79	0
2009	Los Angeles b-c	A.L.	27	176⅓	11	8	.579	139	47	177	3.83	0
2010	Boston	A.L.	33	215	14	11	.560	156	72	233	4.40	0
Major League Totals		9 Yrs.	267	1716	116	82	.586	1357	513	1752	3.89	0
	Division Series											
2002	Anaheim	A.L.	1	3	0	0	.000	3	1	3	0.00	0
2005	Los Angeles	A.L.	2	11⅓	0	0	.000	9	9	7	2.38	0
2007	Los Angeles	A.L.	1	6	0	1	.000	4	2	9	6.00	0
2008	Los Angeles	A.L.	2	13⅔	0	1	.000	6	4	11	2.63	0
2009	Los Angeles	A.L.	1	7⅓	1	0	1.000	4	1	4	0.00	0
Division Series Totals			7	41⅓	1	2	.333	26	17	34	2.40	0
	Championship Series											
2002	Anaheim	A.L.	1	7	1	0	1.000	7	0	3	0.00	0
2005	Los Angeles	A.L.	1	5	0	1	.000	3	1	8	9.00	0
2009	Los Angeles	A.L.	2	12⅓	0	1	.000	10	6	15	3.65	0
Championship Series Totals			4	24⅓	1	2	.333	20	7	26	3.70	0
	World Series Record											
2002	Anaheim	A.L.	3	12⅓	1	0	1.000	7	5	15	4.38	0

a On disabled list from March 21 to May 14, 2008.
b On disabled list from March 27 to May 16, 2009.
c Filed for free agency, November 5, 2009. Signed with Boston Red Sox, December 16, 2009.

LAFFEY, AARON STEVEN

Born, Cumberland, Maryland, April 15, 1985.
Bats Left. Throws Left. Height, 6 feet. Weight, 185 pounds.

Year	Club	Lea	G	IP	W	L	Pct	SO	BB	H	ERA	SAVES
2003	Burlington	Appal.	9	34	3	1	.750	46	15	22	2.91	0
2004	Mahoning Valley	N.Y.-Penn.	8	43⅔	3	1	.750	30	10	38	1.24	0
2004	Lake County	So.Atl.	19	74	3	7	.300	69	44	79	6.45	1
2005	Akron	Eastern	1	5	1	0	1.000	6	2	8	3.60	0
2005	Lake County	So.Atl.	25	142⅓	7	7	.500	69	52	123	3.22	1
2006	Kinston	Carolina	10	41⅓	4	1	.800	24	6	38	2.18	1
2006	Akron	Eastern	19	112⅓	8	3	.727	61	33	121	3.53	0
2007	Akron	Eastern	6	35	4	1	.800	24	7	29	2.31	0
2007	Buffalo	Int.	16	96⅓	9	3	.750	75	23	89	3.08	0
2007	Cleveland	A.L.	9	49⅓	4	2	.667	25	12	54	4.56	0
2008	Buffalo	Int.	11	61⅔	6	2	.750	47	18	72	4.38	0
2008	Cleveland	A.L.	16	93⅔	5	7	.417	43	31	103	4.23	0
2009	Akron	Eastern	2	7⅓	0	0	.000	6	7	6	3.68	0
2009	Columbus	Int.	3	10⅓	0	2	.000	4	5	21	11.32	0
2009	Cleveland a	A.L.	25	121⅔	7	9	.438	59	57	140	4.44	1
2010	Lake County	So.Atl.	2	2	0	0	.000	3	0	2	4.50	0
2010	Akron	Eastern	1	1	0	0	.000	0	0	1	0.00	0
2010	Columbus	Int.	10	27	0	1	.000	12	16	29	3.67	0
2010	Cleveland b	A.L.	29	55⅔	2	3	.400	28	28	62	4.53	0
Major League Totals		4 Yrs.	79	320⅓	18	21	.462	155	128	359	4.41	1
	Championship Series											
2007	Cleveland	A.L.	1	4⅔	0	0	.000	3	1	1	0.00	0

a On disabled list from May 23 to July 8, 2009.
b On disabled list from July 20 to August 31, 2010.

LANNAN, JOHN EDWARD

Born, Long Beach, New York, September 27, 1984.
Bats Left. Throws Left. Height, 6 feet, 5 inches. Weight, 225 pounds.

Year	Club	Lea	G	IP	W	L	Pct	SO	BB	H	ERA	SAVES
2005	Vermont	N.Y.-Penn.	14	63⅓	3	5	.375	41	31	74	5.26	0

Year	Club	Lea	G	IP	W	L	Pct	SO	BB	H	ERA	SAVES
2006	Savannah	So.Atl.	27	138	6	8	.429	114	54	149	4.76	0
2007	Potomac	Carolina	8	$50^2/_3$	6	0	1.000	35	15	31	2.13	0
2007	Harrisburg	Eastern	6	36	3	2	.600	20	15	31	3.25	0
2007	Columbus	Int.	7	38	3	1	.750	19	12	30	1.66	0
2007	Washington	N.L.	6	$34^2/_3$	2	2	.500	10	17	36	4.15	0
2008	Washington	N.L.	31	182	9	15	.375	117	72	172	3.91	0
2009	Washington	N.L.	33	$206^1/_3$	9	13	.409	89	68	210	3.88	0
2010	Harrisburg	Eastern	7	$40^2/_3$	1	4	.200	28	10	49	4.20	0
2010	Washington	N.L.	25	$143^1/_3$	8	8	.500	71	49	175	4.65	0
Major League Totals		4 Yrs.	95	$566^1/_3$	28	38	.424	287	206	593	4.10	0

LATOS, MATHEW A. (MAT)

Born, Alexandria, Virginia, December 9, 1987.
Bats Right. Throws Right. Height, 6 feet, 6 inches. Weight, 225 pounds.

Year	Club	Lea	G	IP	W	L	Pct	SO	BB	H	ERA	SAVES
2007	Eugene	Northwest	16	$56^1/_3$	1	4	.200	74	22	58	3.83	0
2008	Padres	Arizona	5	14	1	0	1.000	23	2	12	3.21	0
2008	Fort Wayne	Midwest	7	$24^2/_3$	0	3	.000	23	8	24	3.28	0
2008	Eugene	Northwest	3	$17^1/_3$	2	0	1.000	23	3	13	1.04	0
2009	Fort Wayne	Midwest	4	$25^1/_3$	3	0	1.000	27	3	10	0.36	0
2009	San Antonio	Texas	9	47	5	1	.833	46	9	32	1.91	0
2009	San Diego	N.L.	10	$50^2/_3$	4	5	.444	39	23	43	4.62	0
2010	San Diego a	N.L.	31	$184^2/_3$	14	10	.583	189	50	150	2.92	0
Major League Totals		2 Yrs.	41	$235^1/_3$	18	15	.545	228	73	193	3.29	0

a On disabled list from July 9 to July 24, 2010.

LEAGUE, BRANDON PAUL

Born, Sacramento, California, March 16, 1983.
Bats Right. Throws Right. Height, 6 feet, 3 inches. Weight, 200 pounds.

Year	Club	Lea	G	IP	W	L	Pct	SO	BB	H	ERA	SAVES
2001	Medicine Hat	Pioneer	9	$38^2/_3$	2	2	.500	38	11	36	4.66	0
2002	Auburn	N.Y.-Penn.	16	$85^2/_3$	7	2	.778	72	23	80	3.15	0
2003	Dunedin	Fla.St.	13	$66^1/_3$	4	3	.571	34	20	76	4.75	0
2003	Charleston	So.Atl.	12	$70^2/_3$	2	3	.400	61	18	58	1.91	0
2004	New Hampshire	Eastern	41	104	6	4	.600	90	41	92	3.38	2
2004	Toronto	A.L.	3	$4^2/_3$	1	0	1.000	2	1	3	0.00	0
2005	Syracuse	Int.	19	63	4	4	.500	35	18	78	5.71	0
2005	Toronto	A.L.	20	$35^2/_3$	1	0	1.000	17	20	42	6.56	0
2006	Syracuse	Int.	31	$54^2/_3$	3	2	.600	43	15	57	2.14	8
2006	Toronto	A.L.	33	$42^2/_3$	1	2	.333	29	9	34	2.53	1
2007	Syracuse	Int.	11	12	0	0	.000	10	6	12	3.00	0
2007	Blue Jays	Gulf Coast	1	1	0	0	.000	1	0	1	0.00	0
2007	Dunedin	Fla.St.	4	6	0	0	.000	6	2	5	4.50	0
2007	New Hampshire	Eastern	6	$7^2/_3$	1	1	.500	7	7	5	3.52	0
2007	Toronto a	A.L.	14	$11^2/_3$	0	0	.000	7	7	19	6.17	0
2008	Syracuse	Int.	20	$34^1/_3$	2	3	.400	32	10	36	3.93	2
2008	Toronto	A.L.	31	33	1	2	.333	23	15	28	2.18	1
2009	Toronto b	A.L.	67	$74^2/_3$	3	6	.333	76	21	72	4.58	0
2010	Seattle	A.L.	70	79	9	7	.563	56	27	67	3.42	6
Major League Totals		7 Yrs.	238	$281^1/_3$	16	17	.485	210	100	265	3.90	8

a On disabled list from March 31 to July 15 and August 5 to September 4, 2007.
b Traded to Seattle Mariners with outfielder Johermyn Chavez for pitcher Brandon Morrow, December 23, 2009.

LEAKE, MICHAEL RAYMOND (MIKE)

Born, San Diego, California, November 12, 1987.
Bats Right. Throws Right. Height, 6 feet, 1 inch. Weight, 190 pounds.

Year	Club	Lea	G	IP	W	L	Pct	SO	BB	H	ERA	SAVES
2010	Cincinnati a	N.L.	24	$138^1/_3$	8	4	.667	91	49	158	4.23	0

a On disabled list from August 25 to September 10, 2010.

LE BLANC, WADE MATTHEW

Born, Lake Charles, Louisiana, August 7, 1984.
Bats Left. Throws Left. Height, 6 feet, 3 inches. Weight, 200 pounds.

Year Club	Lea	G	IP	W	L	Pct	SO	BB	H	ERA	SAVES
2006 Fort Wayne	Midwest	7	32 2/3	4	1	.800	27	10	31	2.20	0
2006 Eugene	Northwest	7	21	1	0	1.000	20	6	19	4.29	0
2007 Lake Elsinore	Calif.	16	92	6	5	.545	90	17	72	2.64	0
2007 San Antonio	Texas	12	57 1/3	7	3	.700	55	19	48	3.45	0
2008 Portland	P.C.	26	138 2/3	11	9	.550	139	42	136	5.32	0
2008 San Diego	N.L.	5	21 1/3	1	3	.250	14	15	29	8.02	0
2009 Portland	P.C.	24	121	4	9	.308	95	31	109	3.87	0
2009 San Diego	N.L.	9	46 1/3	3	1	.750	30	19	35	3.69	0
2010 Portland	P.C.	2	10	0	1	.000	15	1	13	7.20	0
2010 San Diego	N.L.	26	146	8	12	.400	110	51	157	4.25	0
Major League Totals	3 Yrs.	40	213 2/3	12	16	.429	154	85	221	4.51	0

LEE, CLIFTON PHIFER (CLIFF)

Born, Benton, Arkansas, August 30, 1978.
Bats Left. Throws Left. Height, 6 feet, 3 inches. Weight, 190 pounds.

Year Club	Lea	G	IP	W	L	Pct	SO	BB	H	ERA	SAVES
2000 Cape Fear	So.Atl.	11	44 2/3	1	4	.200	63	36	50	5.24	0
2001 Jupiter	Fla.St.	21	109 2/3	6	7	.462	179	46	78	2.79	0
2002 Harrisburg	Eastern	15	86 1/3	7	2	.778	105	23	61	3.23	0
2002 Akron	Eastern	3	16 2/3	2	1	.667	18	10	11	5.40	0
2002 Buffalo	Int.	8	43	3	2	.600	30	22	36	3.77	0
2002 Cleveland a-b	A.L.	2	10 1/3	0	1	.000	6	8	6	1.74	0
2003 Buffalo	Int.	11	63 1/3	6	1	.857	61	31	62	3.27	0
2003 Kinston	Carolina	1	4 1/3	0	0	.000	4	3	0	0.00	0
2003 Akron	Eastern	2	12	1	0	1.000	13	4	7	1.50	0
2003 Cleveland c	A.L.	9	52 1/3	3	3	.500	44	20	41	3.61	0
2004 Cleveland	A.L.	33	179	14	8	.636	161	81	188	5.43	0
2005 Cleveland	A.L.	32	202	18	5	*.783	143	52	194	3.79	0
2006 Cleveland	A.L.	33	200 2/3	14	11	.560	129	58	224	4.40	0
2007 Kinston	Carolina	1	2	0	0	.000	4	0	1	0.00	0
2007 Akron	Eastern	1	5	1	0	1.000	7	1	2	0.00	0
2007 Buffalo	Int.	8	41	1	3	.250	50	25	32	3.51	0
2007 Cleveland d	A.L.	20	97 1/3	5	8	.385	66	36	112	6.29	0
2008 Cleveland e	A.L.	31	223 1/3	*22	3	*.880	170	34	214	*2.54	0
2009 Philadelphia	N.L.	12	79 2/3	7	4	.636	74	10	80	3.39	0
2009 Cleveland f-g	A.L.	22	152	7	9	.438	107	33	165	3.14	0
2010 Tacoma	P.C.	1	6	0	0	.000	4	0	3	0.00	0
2010 Seattle-Texas h-i-j	A.L.	28	212 1/3	12	9	.571	185	18	195	3.18	0
Major League Totals	9 Yrs.	222	1409	102	61	.626	1085	350	1419	3.85	0
Division Series											
2009 Philadelphia	N.L.	2	16 1/3	1	0	1.000	10	3	11	1.10	0
2010 Texas	A.L.	2	16	2	0	1.000	21	0	11	1.13	0
Division Series Totals		4	32 1/3	3	0	1.000	31	3	22	1.11	0
Championship Series											
2009 Philadelphia	N.L.	1	8	1	0	1.000	10	0	3	0.00	0
2010 Texas	A.L.	1	8	1	0	1.000	13	1	2	0.00	0
Championship Series Totals		2	16	2	0	1.000	23	1	5	0.00	0
World Series Record											
2009 Philadelphia	N.L.	2	16	2	0	1.000	13	3	13	2.81	0
2010 Texas	A.L.	2	11 2/3	0	2	.000	13	1	14	6.94	0
World Series Totals		4	27 2/3	2	2	.500	26	4	27	4.55	0

a Traded to Cleveland Indians with infielder Lee Stevens, infielder Brandon Phillips and outfielder Grady Sizemore for pitcher Bartolo Colon and player to be named later, June 27, 2002.
b Montreal Expos received pitcher Tim Drew to complete trade, June 28, 2002.
c On disabled list from March 29 to May 30, 2003.
d On disabled list from March 23 to May 3, 2007.
e Selected Cy Young Award Winner in American League for 2008.
f Traded to Philadelphia Phillies with outfielder Ben Francisco for catcher Lou Marson, pitcher Jason Knapp, infielder Jason Donald and pitcher Carlos Carrasco, July 29, 2009.
g Traded to Seattle Mariners for outfielder J.C. Ramirez, pitcher Phillippe Aumont and outfielder Tyson Gillies, December 16, 2009.
h On disabled list from March 26 to April 30, 2010.
i Traded to Texas Rangers with pitcher Mark Lowe and cash for infielder Justin Smoak, pitcher Blake Beavan, pitcher Josh Lueke and infielder Matt Lawson, July 9, 2010.
j Filed for free agency, November 1, 2010. Signed with Philadelphia Phillies, December 15, 2010.

LESTER, JONATHAN TYLER (JON)

Born, Tacoma, Washington, January 7, 1984.
Bats Left. Throws Left. Height, 6 feet, 2 inches. Weight, 190 pounds.

Year	Club	Lea	G	IP	W	L	Pct	SO	BB	H	ERA	SAVES
2002	Red Sox	Gulf Coast	1	$0\frac{2}{3}$	0	1	.000	1	1	5	13.50	0
2003	Augusta	So.Atl.	24	106	6	9	.400	71	44	102	3.65	0
2004	Sarasota	Fla.St.	21	$90\frac{1}{3}$	7	6	.538	97	37	82	4.28	0
2004	Red Sox	Gulf Coast	1	1	0	0	.000	1	2	0	0.00	0
2005	Portland	Eastern	26	$148\frac{1}{3}$	11	6	.647	163	57	114	2.61	0
2006	Pawtucket	Int.	11	$46\frac{2}{3}$	3	4	.429	43	25	43	2.70	0
2006	Boston a	A.L.	15	$81\frac{1}{3}$	7	2	.778	60	43	91	4.76	0
2007	Greenville	So.Atl.	3	13	0	0	.000	15	2	11	2.08	0
2007	Portland	Eastern	1	6	1	0	1.000	4	4	5	1.50	0
2007	Pawtucket	Int.	14	$71\frac{2}{3}$	4	5	.444	51	31	67	3.89	0
2007	Boston b	A.L.	12	63	4	0	1.000	50	31	61	4.57	0
2008	Boston c	A.L.	33	$210\frac{1}{3}$	16	6	.727	152	66	202	3.21	0
2009	Boston	A.L.	32	$203\frac{1}{3}$	15	8	.652	225	64	186	3.41	0
2010	Boston	A.L.	32	208	19	9	.679	225	83	167	3.25	0
Major League Totals		5 Yrs.	124	766	61	25	.709	712	287	707	3.55	0
	Division Series											
2008	Boston	A.L.	2	14	1	0	1.000	11	3	10	0.00	0
2009	Boston	A.L.	1	6	0	1	.000	5	4	4	4.50	0
Division Series Totals			3	20	1	1	.500	16	7	14	1.35	0
	Championship Series											
2007	Boston	A.L.	2	$3\frac{2}{3}$	0	0	.000	5	1	3	4.91	0
2008	Boston	A.L.	2	$12\frac{2}{3}$	0	2	.000	15	2	14	4.97	0
Championship Series Totals			4	$16\frac{1}{3}$	0	2	.000	20	3	17	4.96	0
	World Series Record											
2007	Boston	A.L.	1	$5\frac{2}{3}$	1	0	1.000	3	3	3	0.00	0

a On disabled list from August 24 to November 6, 2006.
b On disabled list from March 23 to June 11, 2007.
c Pitched no-hit, no-run game against Kansas City Royals, May 19, 2008.

LEWIS, COLBY PRESTON

Born, Bakersfield, California, August 2, 1979.
Bats Right. Throws Right. Height, 6 feet, 4 inches. Weight, 230 pounds.

Year	Club	Lea	G	IP	W	L	Pct	SO	BB	H	ERA	SAVES
1999	Pulaski	Appal.	14	$64\frac{2}{3}$	7	3	.700	84	27	46	1.95	0
2000	Charlotte	Fla.St.	28	$163\frac{2}{3}$	11	10	.524	153	45	169	4.07	0
2001	Charlotte	Fla.St.	1	$4\frac{1}{3}$	1	0	1.000	8	0	0	0.00	0
2001	Tulsa	Texas	25	156	10	10	.500	162	62	150	4.50	0
2002	Texas	A.L.	15	$34\frac{1}{3}$	1	3	.250	28	26	42	6.29	0
2002	Oklahoma	P.C.	20	$106\frac{2}{3}$	5	6	.455	99	28	100	3.63	0
2003	Texas	A.L.	26	127	10	9	.526	88	70	163	7.30	0
2003	Oklahoma	P.C.	7	$47\frac{2}{3}$	5	1	.833	43	19	36	3.02	0
2004	Texas a-b	A.L.	3	$15\frac{1}{3}$	1	1	.500	11	13	13	4.11	0
2005	Detroit c	A.L.	INJURED—Did Not Play									
2006	Toledo	Int.	24	$147\frac{2}{3}$	6	7	.462	104	36	154	3.96	0
2006	Detroit d	A.L.	2	3	0	0	.000	5	1	8	3.00	0
2007	Sacramento	P.C.	15	$95\frac{2}{3}$	8	3	.727	97	23	70	1.88	0
2007	Oakland e-f	A.L.	26	$37\frac{2}{3}$	0	2	.000	23	14	44	6.45	0
2008	Hiroshima g	Japan Cent.	26	178	15	8	.652	183	27	151	2.68	0
2009	Hiroshima	Japan Cent.	29	$176\frac{1}{3}$	11	9	.550	186	19	156	2.96	0
2010	Texas h	A.L.	32	201	12	13	.480	196	65	174	3.72	0
Major League Totals		6 Yrs.	104	$418\frac{1}{3}$	24	28	.462	351	189	444	5.27	0
	Division Series											
2010	Texas	A.L.	1	5	0	0	.000	5	5	2	0.00	0
	Championship Series											
2010	Texas	A.L.	2	$13\frac{2}{3}$	2	0	1.000	13	6	9	1.98	0
	World Series Record											
2010	Texas	A.L.	1	$7\frac{2}{3}$	1	0	1.000	6	2	5	2.35	0

a On disabled list from April 18 to October 6, 2004.
b Claimed on waivers by Detroit Tigers, October 8, 2004.
c On disabled list from April 2 to October 31, 2005.
d Filed for free agency, October 2, 2006. Signed with Washington Nationals organization, November 6, 2006.
e Released by Washington Nationals, March 19, 2007. Signed with Oakland Athletics organization, March 29, 2007.
f Claimed on waivers by Kansas City Royals, November 2, 2007.
g Released by Kansas City Royals, December 4, 2007. Signed with Hiroshima (Japan) for 2008.
h Signed with Texas Rangers, January 14, 2010.

LEWIS, JENSEN DANIEL

Born, Cincinnati, Ohio, May 16, 1984.
Bats Right. Throws Right. Height, 6 feet, 3 inches. Weight, 210 pounds.

Year	Club	Lea	G	IP	W	L	Pct	SO	BB	H	ERA	SAVES
2005	Mahoning Valley	N.Y.-Penn.	13	59	4	2	.667	59	11	58	3.20	0
2006	Kinston	Carolina	21	108 1/3	7	6	.538	94	29	110	3.99	0
2006	Akron	Eastern	7	39 1/3	1	2	.333	44	12	41	3.89	0
2007	Akron	Eastern	24	39	2	0	1.000	49	13	27	1.85	1
2007	Buffalo	Int.	10	13	1	0	1.000	12	4	5	1.38	1
2007	Cleveland	A.L.	26	29 1/3	1	1	.500	34	10	26	2.15	0
2008	Buffalo	Int.	11	20	1	2	.333	18	8	16	3.60	1
2008	Cleveland	A.L.	51	66	0	4	.000	52	27	68	3.82	13
2009	Columbus	Int.	12	18 2/3	1	0	1.000	28	7	13	0.00	0
2009	Cleveland	A.L.	47	66 1/3	2	4	.333	62	29	62	4.61	1
2010	Columbus	Int.	24	30 1/3	2	1	.667	30	8	29	2.67	2
2010	Cleveland	A.L.	37	36 1/3	4	2	.667	29	19	28	2.97	0
Major League Totals		4 Yrs.	161	198	7	11	.389	177	85	184	3.68	14
	Division Series											
2007	Cleveland	A.L.	2	2	0	0	.000	4	0	0	0.00	0
	Championship Series											
2007	Cleveland	A.L.	5	5 2/3	0	0	.000	3	0	6	6.35	0

LIDGE, BRADLEY THOMAS (BRAD)

Born, Sacramento, California, December 23, 1976.
Bats Right. Throws Right. Height, 6 feet, 5 inches. Weight, 210 pounds.

Year	Club	Lea	G	IP	W	L	Pct	SO	BB	H	ERA	SAVES
1998	Quad City a-b	Midwest	4	11	0	1	.000	6	5	10	3.27	0
1999	Kissimmee c	Fla.St.	6	21 1/3	0	2	.000	19	11	13	3.38	0
2000	Kissimmee d	Fla.St.	8	41 2/3	2	1	.667	46	15	28	2.81	0
2001	Round Rock e	Texas	5	26	2	0	1.000	42	7	21	1.73	0
2002	Round Rock	Texas	5	11	1	1	.500	18	3	9	2.45	0
2002	Houston	N.L.	6	8 2/3	1	0	1.000	12	9	12	6.23	0
2002	New Orleans	P.C.	24	111 2/3	5	5	.500	110	47	83	3.39	0
2003	Houston	N.L.	78	85	6	3	.667	97	42	60	3.60	1
2004	Houston	N.L.	80	94 2/3	6	5	.545	157	30	57	1.90	29
2005	Houston	N.L.	70	70 2/3	4	4	.500	103	23	58	2.29	42
2006	Houston	N.L.	78	75	1	5	.167	104	36	69	5.28	32
2007	Corpus Christi	Texas	1	1	0	0	.000	0	0	0	0.00	0
2007	Houston f-g	N.L.	66	67	5	3	.625	88	30	54	3.36	19
2008	Clearwater	Fla.St.	1	1	0	0	.000	2	1	2	9.00	0
2008	Philadelphia h	N.L.	72	69 1/3	2	0	1.000	92	35	50	1.95	41
2009	Clearwater	Fla.St.	1	1	0	0	.000	0	1	0	0.00	0
2009	Reading	Eastern	1	1	0	0	.000	2	0	1	0.00	0
2009	Philadelphia i	N.L.	67	58 2/3	0	8	.000	61	34	72	7.21	31
2010	Clearwater	Fla.St.	6	5 2/3	0	1	.000	5	2	5	7.94	0
2010	Reading	Eastern	2	3	0	0	.000	4	1	1	0.00	0
2010	Lehigh Valley	Int.	1	1	0	0	.000	0	1	0	0.00	0
2010	Philadelphia j	N.L.	50	45 2/3	1	1	.500	52	24	32	2.96	27
Major League Totals		9 Yrs.	567	574 2/3	26	29	.473	766	263	464	3.51	222
	Division Series											
2004	Houston	N.L.	3	4 1/3	0	0	.000	6	1	4	2.08	1
2005	Houston	N.L.	3	4	0	0	.000	5	4	2	0.00	0
2008	Philadelphia	N.L.	3	3	0	0	.000	4	1	3	3.00	2
2009	Philadelphia	N.L.	2	1 1/3	0	0	.000	1	2	0	0.00	2
2010	Philadelphia	N.L.	1	1	0	0	.000	0	1	0	0.00	1
Division Series Totals			12	13 2/3	0	0	.000	16	9	9	1.32	6
	Championship Series											
2004	Houston	N.L.	4	8	1	0	1.000	14	2	1	0.00	2
2005	Houston	N.L.	4	5	0	1	.000	7	2	6	7.20	3
2008	Philadelphia	N.L.	4	4 1/3	0	0	.000	6	2	2	0.00	3
2009	Philadelphia	N.L.	3	2 2/3	1	0	1.000	3	1	1	0.00	1
2010	Philadelphia	N.L.	3	3	0	0	.000	5	2	3	0.00	1
Championship Series Totals			18	23	2	1	.667	35	9	13	1.57	10
	World Series Record											
2005	Houston	N.L.	3	3 2/3	0	2	.000	6	0	4	4.91	0
2008	Philadelphia	N.L.	2	2	0	0	.000	3	0	1	0.00	2
2009	Philadelphia	N.L.	1	1	0	1	.000	1	0	3	27.00	0
World Series Totals			6	6 2/3	0	3	.000	10	0	8	6.75	2

a Drafted by Texas Rangers with choice received for Colorado Rockies signing pitcher Darryl Kile, June 2, 1998.

b On disabled list from August 18 to September 29, 1998.
c On disabled list from April 1 to June 1 and July 10 to September 29, 1999.
d On disabled list from April 24 to June 13 and July 1 to September 29, 2000.
e On disabled list from May 5 to September 29, 2001.
f On disabled list from June 16 to July 13, 2007.
g Traded to Philadelphia Phillies with infielder Eric Bruntlett for pitcher Geoff Geary, outfielder Michael Bourn and infielder Mike Costanzo, November 12, 2007.
h On disabled list from March 21 to April 5, 2008.
i On disabled list from June 7 to June 25, 2009.
j On disabled list from March 26 to April 30 and May 10 to May 31, 2010.

LILLY, THEODORE ROOSEVELT (TED)

Born, Lamita, California, January 4, 1976.
Bats Left. Throws Left. Height, 6 feet, 1 inch. Weight, 190 pounds.

Year	Club	Lea	G	IP	W	L	Pct	SO	BB	H	ERA	SAVES
1996	Yakima	Northwest	13	$53\frac{2}{3}$	4	0	1.000	75	14	25	0.84	0
1997	San Bernardino	California	23	$134\frac{2}{3}$	7	8	.467	158	32	116	2.81	0
1998	San Antonio	Texas	17	$111\frac{2}{3}$	8	4	.667	96	37	114	3.30	0
1998	Albuquerque	P.C.	5	31	1	3	.250	25	9	39	4.94	0
1998	Ottawa a	Int.	7	39	2	2	.500	49	19	45	4.85	0
1999	Ottawa	Int.	16	89	8	5	.615	78	23	81	3.84	0
1999	Montreal b-c	N.L.	9	$23\frac{2}{3}$	0	1	.000	28	9	30	7.61	0
2000	Tampa	Fla.St.	1	$6\frac{2}{3}$	0	0	.000	6	1	5	1.35	0
2000	Columbus	Int.	22	$137\frac{1}{3}$	8	11	.421	127	48	157	4.19	0
2000	New York d-e	A.L.	7	8	0	0	.000	11	5	8	5.63	0
2001	Columbus	Int.	5	$25\frac{1}{3}$	0	0	.000	30	8	16	2.84	0
2001	New York	A.L.	26	$120\frac{2}{3}$	5	6	.455	112	51	126	5.37	0
2002	New York-Oakland f-g	A.L.	22	100	5	7	.417	77	31	80	3.69	0
2003	Oakland h	A.L.	32	$178\frac{1}{3}$	12	10	.545	147	58	179	4.34	0
2004	Toronto	A.L.	32	$197\frac{1}{3}$	12	10	.545	168	89	171	4.06	0
2005	Syracuse	Int.	2	$8\frac{2}{3}$	0	1	.000	9	5	5	3.12	0
2005	Toronto i	A.L.	25	$126\frac{1}{3}$	10	11	.476	96	58	135	5.56	0
2006	Toronto j	A.L.	32	$181\frac{2}{3}$	15	13	.536	160	81	179	4.31	0
2007	Chicago	N.L.	34	207	15	8	.652	174	55	181	3.83	0
2008	Chicago	N.L.	34	$204\frac{2}{3}$	17	9	.654	184	64	187	4.09	0
2009	Peoria	Midwest	1	5	1	0	1.000	2	1	2	0.00	0
2009	Chicago k	N.L.	27	177	12	9	.571	151	36	151	3.10	0
2010	Peoria	Midwest	1	7	1	0	1.000	9	1	3	1.29	0
2010	Iowa	P.C.	1	4	0	0	.000	4	1	1	2.25	0
2010	Chicago-Los Angeles l-m	N.L.	30	$193\frac{2}{3}$	10	12	.455	166	44	165	3.62	0
Major League Totals		12 Yrs.	310	$1718\frac{1}{3}$	113	96	.541	1474	581	1592	4.18	0
	Division Series											
2002	Oakland	A.L.	2	4	0	1	.000	3	1	10	13.50	0
2003	Oakland	A.L.	2	9	0	0	.000	7	2	2	0.00	0
2007	Chicago	N.L.	1	$3\frac{1}{3}$	0	1	.000	4	4	7	16.20	0
Division Series Totals			5	$16\frac{1}{3}$	0	2	.000	14	7	19	6.61	0

a Traded by Los Angeles Dodgers to Montreal Expos with infielder Wilton Guerrero, outfielder Peter Bergeron and infielder Jonathan Tucker for infielder Mark Grudzielanek, outfielder Hiram Bocachica and pitcher Carlos Perez, July 31, 1998.
b On disabled list from June 21 to September 30, 1999.
c Montreal Expos traded pitcher Jake Westbrook and two players to be named later to New York Yankees for pitcher Hideki Irabu, December 22, 1999.
d Sent to New York Yankees with pitcher Christian Parker as players to be named later for Jake Westbrook, March 17 and March 22, 2000.
e On disabled list from March 25 to May 22, 2000.
f Traded to Oakland Athletics with pitcher Jason Arnold and outfielder John-Ford Griffin for pitcher Jeff Weaver, July 5, 2002.
g On disabled list from July 23 to September 10, 2002.
h Traded to Toronto Blue Jays for outfielder Bobby Kielty and cash, November 18, 2003.
i On disabled list from March 25 to April 10 and July 25 to September 6, 2005.
j Filed for free agency, October 28, 2006. Signed with Chicago Cubs, December 15, 2006.
k On disabled list from July 21 to August 17, 2009.
l On disabled list from March 26 to April 24, 2010.
m Traded to Los Angeles Dodgers with infielder Ryan Theriot and cash for infielder Blake Dewitt, pitcher Kyle Smit and pitcher Brett Wallach, July 31, 2010.

LINCECUM, TIMOTHY LEROY (TIM)

Born, Bellevue, Washington, June 15, 1984.
Bats Left. Throws Right. Height, 5 feet, 11 inches. Weight, 160 pounds.

Year	Club	Lea	G	IP	W	L	Pct	SO	BB	H	ERA	SAVES
2006	San Jose	Calif.	6	$27\frac{2}{3}$	2	0	1.000	48	12	13	1.95	0
2006	Salem-Keizer	Northwest	2	4	0	0	.000	10	0	1	0.00	0
2007	Fresno	P.C.	5	31	4	0	1.000	46	11	12	0.29	0
2007	San Francisco	N.L.	24	$146\frac{1}{3}$	7	5	.583	150	65	122	4.00	0
2008	San Francisco a	N.L.	34	227	18	5	*.783	*265	84	182	2.62	0
2009	San Francisco b	N.L.	32	$225\frac{1}{3}$	15	7	.682	*261	68	168	2.48	0
2010	San Francisco	N.L.	33	$212\frac{1}{3}$	16	10	.615	*231	76	194	3.43	0
	Major League Totals	4 Yrs.	123	811	56	27	.675	907	293	666	3.04	0
	Division Series											
2010	San Francisco	N.L.	1	9	1	0	1.000	14	1	2	0.00	0
	Championship Series											
2010	San Francisco	N.L.	3	$14\frac{1}{3}$	1	1	.500	16	4	12	3.14	0
	World Series Record											
2010	San Francisco	N.L.	2	$13\frac{2}{3}$	2	0	1.000	13	4	11	3.29	0

a Selected Cy Young Award Winner in National League for 2008.
b Selected Cy Young Award Winner in National League for 2009.

LINDSTROM, MATTHEW JAMES (MATT)

Born, Rexburg, Idaho, February 11, 1980.
Bats Right. Throws Right. Height, 6 feet, 4 inches. Weight, 210 pounds.

Year	Club	Lea	G	IP	W	L	Pct	SO	BB	H	ERA	SAVES
2002	Kingsport	Appal.	12	$48\frac{1}{3}$	0	6	.000	39	21	56	4.84	0
2003	Brooklyn	N.Y.-Penn.	14	$65\frac{1}{3}$	7	3	.700	52	27	61	3.44	0
2003	Capital City	So.Atl.	12	$56\frac{2}{3}$	2	3	.400	50	33	46	2.86	0
2004	St. Lucie	Fla.St.	14	$79\frac{2}{3}$	5	5	.500	50	20	83	3.73	0
2004	Capital City	So.Atl.	12	56	3	2	.600	64	10	47	3.21	0
2005	Binghamton	Eastern	35	$73\frac{1}{3}$	2	5	.286	58	55	90	5.40	0
2006	Binghamton	Eastern	35	$40\frac{2}{3}$	2	4	.333	54	14	42	3.76	11
2006	St. Lucie a	Fla.St.	11	18	1	0	1.000	16	7	14	2.50	2
2007	Florida	N.L.	71	67	3	4	.429	62	21	66	3.09	0
2008	Albuquerque	P.C.	3	4	0	0	.000	4	1	5	9.00	0
2008	Florida	N.L.	66	$57\frac{1}{3}$	3	3	.500	43	26	57	3.14	5
2009	Jupiter	Fla.St.	2	2	0	0	.000	1	0	1	0.00	0
2009	Jacksonville	Southern	2	2	0	1	.000	3	0	2	9.00	0
2009	Florida b-c	N.L.	54	$47\frac{1}{3}$	2	1	.667	39	24	54	5.89	15
2010	Corpus Christi	Texas	1	1	0	0	.000	1	0	0	0.00	0
2010	Houston d-e	N.L.	58	$53\frac{1}{3}$	2	5	.286	43	20	68	4.39	23
	Major League Totals	4 Yrs.	249	225	10	13	.435	187	91	245	4.00	43

a Traded to Florida Marlins by New York Mets with pitcher Henry Owens for pitcher Adam Bostick and pitcher Jason Vargas, November 20, 2006.
b On disabled list from June 24 to August 1, 2009.
c Traded to Houston Astros for infielder Luis Bryan and pitcher Robert Bono, December 9, 2009.
d On disabled list from August 17 to September 1, 2010.
e Traded to Colorado Rockies for pitcher Wes Musick and pitcher Jonnathan Aristil, December 23, 2010.

LINEBRINK, SCOTT CAMERON

Born, Austin, Texas, August 4, 1976.
Bats Right. Throws Right. Height, 6 feet, 2 inches. Weight, 215 pounds.

Year	Club	Lea	G	IP	W	L	Pct	SO	BB	H	ERA	SAVES
1997	Salem-Keizr	Northwest	3	10	0	0	.000	6	6	7	4.50	0
1997	San Jose	California	6	$28\frac{1}{3}$	2	1	.667	40	10	29	3.18	0
1998	Shreveport	Texas	21	113	10	8	.556	128	58	101	5.02	0
1999	Shreveport	Texas	10	$43\frac{1}{3}$	1	8	.111	33	14	48	6.44	0
2000	Fresno	P.C.	28	62	1	4	.200	49	12	54	5.23	4
2000	San Francisco-Houston	N.L.	11	12	0	0	.000	6	8	18	6.00	0
2000	New Orleans a	P.C.	11	15	2	0	1.000	22	7	15	1.80	1
2001	New Orleans	P.C.	50	72	7	6	.538	72	24	52	3.50	8
2001	Houston	N.L.	9	$10\frac{1}{3}$	0	0	.000	9	6	6	2.61	0
2002	Houston	N.L.	22	$24\frac{1}{3}$	0	0	.000	24	13	31	7.03	0
2002	New Orleans	P.C.	13	15	1	1	.500	16	11	17	6.00	0
2002	Round Rock b	Texas	2	2	0	0	.000	1	2	2	0.00	0
2003	New Orleans	P.C.	2	10	0	2	.000	6	5	8	2.70	0
2003	Houston-San Diego c-d	N.L.	52	$92\frac{1}{3}$	3	2	.600	68	36	93	3.31	0
2004	San Diego	N.L.	73	84	7	3	.700	83	26	61	2.14	0
2005	San Diego	N.L.	73	$73\frac{2}{3}$	8	1	.889	70	23	55	1.83	1

Year Club	Lea	G	IP	W	L	Pct	SO	BB	H	ERA	SAVES
2006 San Diego	N.L.	73	75 2/3	7	4	.636	68	22	70	3.57	2
2007 San Diego-Milwaukee e-f	N.L.	71	70 1/3	5	6	.455	50	25	68	3.71	1
2008 Chicago g	A.L.	50	46 1/3	2	2	.500	40	9	41	3.69	1
2009 Chicago	A.L.	57	56	3	7	.300	55	23	70	4.66	2
2010 Chicago h	A.L.	52	57 1/3	3	2	.600	52	17	59	4.40	0
Major League Totals	11 Yrs.	543	602 1/3	38	27	.585	525	208	572	3.50	7
Division Series											
2005 San Diego	N.L.	1	1	0	0	.000	1	0	2	0.00	0
2006 San Diego	N.L.	2	1 1/3	0	0	.000	0	1	1	6.75	0
2008 Chicago	A.L.	1	1	0	0	.000	1	1	1	0.00	0
Division Series Totals		4	3 1/3	0	0	.000	2	2	4	2.70	0

a Traded to Houston Astros for pitcher Doug Henry, July 30, 2000.
b On disabled list from May 20 to June 17, 2002.
c Filed for free agency, October 29, 2003, re-signed with Houston Astros, January 31, 2002.
d Claimed on waivers by San Diego Padres, May 29, 2003.
e Traded to Milwaukee Brewers for pitcher Will Inman, pitcher Joe Thatcher and pitcher Steve Garrison, July 25, 2007.
f Filed for free agency, October 29, 2007. Signed with Chicago White Sox, November 28, 2007.
g On disabled list from July 23 to September 1, 2008.
h Traded to Atlanta Braves for pitcher Kyle Cofield, December 3, 2010.

LIRIANO, FRANCISCO CASILLAS

Born, San Cristobal, Dominican Republic, October 26, 1983.
Bats Left. Throws Left. Height, 6 feet, 2 inches. Weight, 225 pounds.

Year Club	Lea	G	IP	W	L	Pct	SO	BB	H	ERA	SAVES
2001 Giants	Arizona	13	62	5	4	.556	67	24	51	3.63	0
2001 Salem-Keizer	Northwest	2	9	0	0	.000	12	1	7	5.00	0
2002 Hagerstown	So.Atl.	16	80	3	6	.333	85	31	61	3.49	0
2003 Giants	Arizona	4	8 1/3	0	1	.000	9	6	5	4.32	0
2003 San Jose a	Calif.	1	0 2/3	0	1	.000	0	2	5	54.00	0
2004 New Britain	Eastern	7	39 2/3	3	2	.600	49	17	45	3.18	0
2004 Fort Myers	Fla.St.	21	117	6	7	.462	125	43	118	4.00	0
2005 New Britain	Eastern	13	76 2/3	3	5	.375	92	26	70	3.64	0
2005 Rochester	Int.	14	91	9	2	.818	112	24	56	1.78	0
2005 Minnesota	A.L.	6	23 2/3	1	2	.333	33	7	19	5.70	0
2006 Minnesota b	A.L.	28	121	12	3	.800	144	32	89	2.16	1
2007 Minnesota c	A.L.			INJURED—Did Not Play							
2008 Fort Myers	Fla.St.	1	5 1/3	0	1	.000	8	2	6	6.75	0
2008 Rochester	Int.	19	118	10	2	.833	113	31	102	3.28	0
2008 Minnesota	A.L.	14	76	6	4	.600	67	32	74	3.91	0
2009 Minnesota d	A.L.	29	136 2/3	5	13	.278	122	65	147	5.80	0
2010 Minnesota	A.L.	31	191 2/3	14	10	.583	201	58	184	3.62	0
Major League Totals	5 Yrs.	108	549	38	32	.543	567	194	513	3.97	1
Division Series											
2009 Minnesota	A.L.	1	2	0	0	.000	1	1	1	4.50	0
2010 Minnesota	A.L.	1	5 2/3	0	0	.000	7	3	6	6.35	0
Division Series Totals		2	7 2/3	0	0	.000	8	4	7	5.87	0

a Traded by San Francisco Giants to Minnesota Twins with pitcher Joe Nathan and pitcher Boof Bonser for catcher A.J. Pierzynski, November 14, 2003.
b On disabled list from August 8 to September 11, 2006.
c On disabled list from March 24 to October 10, 2007.
d On disabled list from August 18 to September 9, 2009.

LOE, KAMERON DAVID

Born, Simi Valley, California, September 10, 1981.
Bats Right. Throws Right. Height, 6 feet, 8 inches. Weight, 240 pounds.

Year Club	Lea	G	IP	W	L	Pct	SO	BB	H	ERA	SAVES
2002 Pulaski	Appal.	14	58 1/3	4	4	.500	55	17	64	4.47	1
2003 Stockton	Calif.	9	37 2/3	3	0	1.000	31	6	26	0.96	1
2003 Clinton	Midwest	23	97	4	3	.571	94	19	78	1.95	2
2004 Frisco	Texas	19	113 1/3	7	7	.500	97	29	122	3.10	0
2004 Oklahoma	P.C.	8	52 1/3	5	2	.714	42	13	52	3.27	0
2004 Texas	A.L.	2	6 2/3	0	0	.000	3	6	6	5.40	0
2005 Oklahoma	P.C.	5	28 1/3	2	1	.667	23	10	32	5.08	0
2005 Texas	A.L.	48	92	9	6	.600	45	31	89	3.42	1
2006 Texas	A.L.	15	78 1/3	3	6	.333	34	22	105	5.86	0
2006 Frisco	Texas	2	7	0	1	.000	4	4	8	5.14	0

Year	Club	Lea	G	IP	W	L	Pct	SO	BB	H	ERA	SAVES
2006	Oklahoma a	P.C.	13	22 2/3	1	2	.333	21	13	32	9.13	1
2007	Frisco	Texas	1	3	0	0	.000	1	5	1	6.00	0
2007	Texas b	A.L.	28	136	6	11	.353	78	56	162	5.36	0
2008	Oklahoma	P.C.	26	58	3	5	.375	31	20	70	5.59	1
2008	Texas	A.L.	14	30 2/3	1	0	1.000	20	8	36	3.23	0
2009	Fukuoka c-d	Japan Pac.	5	27	0	4	.000	18	12	36	6.33	0
2010	Nashville	P.C.	10	62 2/3	4	3	.571	39	19	57	3.16	0
2010	Milwaukee	N.L.	53	58 1/3	3	5	.375	46	15	54	2.78	0
	Major League Totals	6 Yrs.	160	402	22	28	.440	226	138	452	4.48	1

a On disabled list from June 19 to August 3, 2006.
b On disabled list from July 30 to August 18, 2007.
c Released by Texas Rangers, November 28, 2008. Signed with Fukuoka (Japan) for 2009.
d Signed with Milwaukee Brewers organization, December 18, 2009.

LOGAN, BOONE

Born, San Antonio, Texas, August 13, 1984.
Bats Right. Throws Left. Height, 6 feet, 5 inches. Weight, 215 pounds.

Year	Club	Lea	G	IP	W	L	Pct	SO	BB	H	ERA	SAVES
2003	Great Falls	Pioneer	16	67	3	3	.500	48	31	76	6.58	0
2004	Great Falls	Pioneer	18	64 1/3	3	7	.300	48	31	74	5.60	1
2005	Winston-Salem	Carolina	4	5 1/3	0	0	.000	5	4	7	5.06	0
2005	Great Falls	Pioneer	21	35 1/3	1	1	.500	29	4	34	3.31	2
2006	Charlotte	Int.	38	42 2/3	3	1	.750	57	12	35	3.38	11
2006	Chicago	A.L.	21	17 1/3	0	0	.000	15	15	21	8.31	1
2007	Charlotte	Int.	4	8 1/3	0	1	.000	11	4	8	2.16	1
2007	Chicago	A.L.	68	50 2/3	2	1	.667	35	20	59	4.97	0
2008	Charlotte	Int.	5	9	0	1	.000	7	6	10	6.00	0
2008	Chicago a	A.L.	55	42 1/3	2	3	.400	42	14	57	5.95	0
2009	Gwinnett	Int.	29	35 2/3	4	2	.667	39	17	26	3.28	2
2009	Atlanta b	N.L.	20	17 1/3	1	1	.500	10	9	21	5.19	0
2010	Scranton/WB	Int.	14	21 1/3	0	1	.000	23	4	18	2.11	0
2010	New York	A.L.	51	40	2	0	1.000	38	20	34	2.93	0
	Major League Totals	5 Yrs.	215	167 2/3	7	5	.583	140	78	192	5.10	1
	Division Series											
2010	New York	A.L.	2	1	0	0	.000	0	0	1	0.00	0
	Championship Series											
2010	New York	A.L.	3	0 2/3	0	0	.000	1	1	2	27.00	0

a Traded to Atlanta Braves with pitcher Javier Vazquez for catcher Tyler Flowers, infielder Jonathan Gilmore, infielder Brent Lillibridge and pitcher Santos Rodriguez, December 4, 2008.
b Traded to New York Yankees with pitcher Javier Vazquez for outfielder Melky Cabrera, pitcher Arodys Vizcaino, pitcher Michael Dunn and cash, December 22, 2009.

LOHSE, KYLE MATTHEW

Born, Chico, California, October 4, 1978.
Bats Right. Throws Right. Height, 6 feet, 2 inches. Weight, 210 pounds.

Year	Club	Lea	G	IP	W	L	Pxt	SO	BB	H	ERA	SAVES
1997	Cubs	Arizona	12	47 2/3	2	2	.500	49	22	46	3.02	0
1998	Rockford	Midwest	28	170 2/3	13	8	.619	121	45	158	3.22	0
1999	New Britain	Eastern	11	70 1/3	3	4	.429	41	23	87	5.89	0
1999	Daytona	Fla.St.	9	53	5	3	.625	41	16	48	2.89	0
1999	Fort Myers a	Fla.St.	7	41 2/3	2	3	.400	33	9	47	5.18	0
2000	New Britain	Eastern	28	167	3	18	.143	124	55	196	6.04	0
2001	New Britain	Eastern	6	38	3	1	.750	32	4	32	2.37	0
2001	Edmonton	P.C.	8	49	4	2	.667	48	13	50	3.12	0
2001	Minnesota	A.L.	19	90 1/3	4	7	.364	64	29	102	5.68	0
2002	Minnesota	A.L.	32	180 2/3	13	8	.619	124	70	181	4.23	0
2003	Minnesota	A.L.	33	201	14	11	.560	130	45	211	4.61	0
2004	Minnesota	A.L.	35	194	9	13	.409	111	76	240	5.34	0
2005	Minnesota	A.L.	31	178 2/3	9	13	.409	86	44	211	4.18	0
2006	Rochester	Int.	4	24	2	1	.667	12	6	15	1.50	0
2006	Minnesota	A.L.	22	63 2/3	2	5	.286	46	25	80	7.07	0
2006	Cincinnati b	N.L.	12	63	3	5	.375	51	19	70	4.57	0
2007	Cincinnati-Philadelphia c-d	N.L.	34	192 2/3	9	12	.429	122	57	207	4.62	0
2008	St. Louis	N.L.	33	200	15	6	.714	119	49	211	3.78	0
2009	Springfield	Texas	1	4 2/3	0	0	.000	3	4	3	3.86	0
2009	Memphis	P.C.	1	6	1	0	1.000	6	2	2	0.00	0
2009	St. Louis e	N.L.	23	117 2/3	6	10	.375	77	36	125	4.74	0
2010	Springfield	Texas	1	5	0	1	.000	4	0	12	9.00	0

Year	Club	Lea	G	IP	W	L	Pct	SO	BB	H	ERA	SAVES
2010	Memphis	P.C.	3	14	1	0	1.000	14	2	9	3.21	0
2010	St. Louis f	N.L.	18	92	4	8	.333	54	35	129	6.55	0
Major League Totals		10 Yrs.	292	1573 2/3	88	98	.473	984	485	1767	4.79	0
	Division Series											
2002	Minnesota	A.L.	2	4	0	0	.000	5	0	2	0.00	0
2003	Minnesota	A.L.	1	5	0	1	.000	5	2	6	5.40	0
2004	Minnesota	A.L.	1	2	0	1	.000	3	0	1	4.50	0
2007	Philadelphia	N.L.	1	1 2/3	0	0	.000	1	0	1	6.75	0
Division Series Totals			5	12 2/3	0	2	.000	14	2	10	3.65	0
	Championship Series											
2002	Minnesota	A.L.	1	1	0	0	.000	1	0	0	0.00	0

a Traded by Chicago Cubs to Minnesota Twins with pitcher Jason Ryan for pitcher Rick Aguilera and pitcher Scott Downs, May 21, 1999.
b Traded to Cincinnati Reds for pitcher Zach Ward, July 31, 2006.
c Traded to Philadelphia Phillies for pitcher Matt Maloney, July 30, 2007.
d Filed for free agency, October 31, 2007. Signed with St. Louis Cardinals, March 14, 2008.
e On disabled list from June 4 to July 12 and August 22 to September 6, 2009.
f On disabled list from May 23 to August 15, 2010.

LOPEZ, JAVIER ALFONSO

Born, San Juan, Puerto Rico, July 11, 1977.
Bats Left. Throws Left. Height, 6 feet, 4 inches. Weight, 225 pounds.

Year	Club	Lea	G	IP	W	L	Pct	SO	BB	H	ERA	SAVES
1998	South Bend	Midwest	16	44	2	4	.333	31	30	60	6.55	0
1999	South Bend	Midwest	20	99	4	6	.400	70	43	122	6.00	0
2000	High Desert	Calif.	30	136 1/3	4	8	.333	98	57	152	5.22	2
2001	Lancaster	Calif.	17	24	1	3	.250	18	5	30	2.63	1
2001	El Paso	Texas	22	40	1	0	1.000	21	14	64	7.43	0
2002	El Paso a	Texas	61	46 1/3	2	2	.500	47	16	34	2.72	6
2003	Colorado b	N.L.	75	58 1/3	4	1	.800	40	12	58	3.70	1
2004	Colorado Springs	P.C.	8	9	0	1	.000	9	2	10	4.00	0
2004	Colorado	N.L.	64	40 2/3	1	2	.333	20	26	45	7.52	0
2005	Tucson	P.C.	27	24 1/3	0	1	.000	16	12	17	2.22	2
2005	Colorado-Arizona c	N.L.	32	16 1/3	1	1	.500	12	11	26	11.02	2
2006	Charlotte	Int.	26	33	2	1	.667	26	6	28	0.55	12
2006	Pawtucket	Int.	13	16 2/3	0	0	.000	12	8	20	4.86	4
2006	Boston d-e	A.L.	27	16 2/3	1	0	1.000	11	10	13	2.70	1
2007	Pawtucket	Int.	17	16 2/3	2	1	.667	15	8	19	3.78	0
2007	Boston	A.L.	61	40 2/3	2	1	.667	26	18	36	3.10	0
2008	Boston	A.L.	70	59 1/3	2	0	1.000	38	27	53	2.43	0
2009	Boston	A.L.	14	11 2/3	0	2	.000	5	9	20	9.26	0
2009	Pawtucket f	Int.	38	39 2/3	1	1	.500	23	13	35	3.18	0
2010	Pittsburgh-San Francisco g	N.L.	77	57 2/3	4	2	.667	38	20	50	2.34	0
Major League Totals		8 Yrs.	420	301 1/3	15	9	.625	190	133	301	4.18	4
	Division Series											
2007	Boston	A.L.	1	0 1/3	0	0	.000	0	0	0	0.00	0
2008	Boston	A.L.	1	1	0	1	.000	1	0	3	9.00	0
2010	San Francisco	N.L.	2	0 2/3	0	0	.000	2	0	0	0.00	0
Division Series Totals			4	2	0	1	.000	3	0	3	4.50	0
	Championship Series											
2007	Boston	A.L.	3	2	0	0	.000	0	2	3	18.00	0
2008	Boston	A.L.	2	1 2/3	0	0	.000	0	0	3	0.00	0
2010	San Francisco	N.L.	5	4 1/3	1	0	1.000	4	1	1	2.08	0
Championship Series Totals			10	8	1	0	1.000	4	3	7	5.63	0
	World Series Record											
2007	Boston	A.L.	1	0	0	0	.000	0	0	2	INF	0
2010	San Francisco	N.L.	2	0 2/3	0	0	.000	0	0	0	0.00	0
World Series Totals			3	0 2/3	0	0	.000	0	0	2	0.00	0

a Selected by Boston Red Sox from Arizona Diamondbacks in Rule V draft, December 16, 2002.
b Traded to Colorado Rockies for player to be named later, March 28, 2003. Boston Red Sox received pitcher Ryan Cameron to complete trade, March 29, 2003.
c Claimed on waivers by Arizona Diamondbacks, April 14, 2005.
d Filed for free agency, October 15, 2005. Signed with Chicago White Sox organization, January 19, 2006.
e Traded to Boston Red Sox for pitcher David Riske, June 15, 2006.
f Filed for free agency, October 5, 2009. Signed with Pittsburgh Pirates, December 18, 2009.
g Traded to San Francisco Giants for pitcher Joe Martinez and outfielder John Bowker, July 31, 2010.

LOPEZ (MUNOZ), RODRIGO

Born, Tlalnepantla, Mexico, December 14, 1975.
Bats Right. Throws Right. Height, 6 feet, 1 inch. Weight, 185 pounds.

Year	Club	Lea	G	IP	W	L	Pct	SO	BB	H	ERA	SAVES
1993	Veracruz	Mexican	2	1	0	0	.000	0	3	3	0.00	0
1994	Aguila	Mexican	10	12 2/3	0	0	.000	5	3	15	4.97	0
1995	Padres a	Arizona	11	34 2/3	1	1	.500	33	14	41	5.45	1
1996	Poza Rica	Mexican	7	20 1/3	1	1	.500	22	16	15	3.54	1
1996	Idaho Falls	Pioneer	15	71	4	4	.500	72	34	76	5.70	1
1997	Clinton	Midwest	37	121 2/3	6	8	.429	123	42	103	3.18	9
1998	Mexico	Mexican	26	163 2/3	10	6	.625	95	79	165	3.35	0
1998	Mobile	Southern	4	25 2/3	3	0	1.000	20	4	21	1.40	0
1999	Mobile	Southern	28	169 1/3	10	8	.556	138	58	187	4.41	0
2000	Las Vegas	P.C.	20	109 1/3	8	7	.533	100	45	123	4.69	0
2000	San Diego	N.L.	6	24 2/3	0	3	.000	17	13	40	8.76	0
2001	Lake Elsinore	Calif.	9	13	0	1	.000	9	4	15	0.69	0
2001	Portland b	P.C.	11	52 1/3	2	2	.500	37	15	45	3.44	0
2002	Baltimore	A.L.	33	196 2/3	15	9	.625	136	62	172	3.57	0
2003	Bowie	Eastern	1	6 1/3	1	0	1.000	13	0	3	0.00	0
2003	Baltimore c	A.L.	26	147	7	10	.412	103	43	188	5.82	0
2004	Baltimore	A.L.	37	170 2/3	14	9	.609	121	54	164	3.59	0
2005	Baltimore	A.L.	35	209 1/3	15	12	.556	118	63	232	4.90	0
2006	Baltimore	A.L.	36	189	9	18	.333	136	59	234	5.90	0
2007	Colorado Springs	P.C.	2	11 1/3	1	0	1.000	4	3	4	2.38	0
2007	Colorado d-e	N.L.	14	79 1/3	5	4	.556	43	21	83	4.42	0
2008	Braves	Gulf Coast	2	3	0	0	.000	4	0	2	0.00	0
2008	Rome f	So.Atl.	1	2	0	1	.000	1	2	8	40.50	0
2009	Philadelphia	N.L.	7	30	3	1	.750	19	11	42	5.70	0
2009	Lehigh Valley g-h	Int.	18	100 1/3	7	5	.583	71	14	122	4.31	0
2010	Arizona i	N.L.	33	200	7	*16	.304	116	56	227	4.99	0
Major League Totals		9 Yrs.	227	1246 2/3	75	82	.478	809	382	1382	4.85	0

a Signed by Veracruz (Mexico) for 1993. Sold to San Diego Padres, March 21, 1995.
b Filed for free agency, October 15, 2001. Signed with Baltimore Orioles organization, November 23, 2001.
c On disabled list from May 2 to June 15, 2003.
d Traded to Colorado Rockies for pitcher Jason Burch and pitcher Jim Miller, January 12, 2007.
e On disabled list from April 19 to May 29 and July 27 to October 31, 2007.
f Filed for free agency, October 31, 2007. Signed with Atlanta Braves organization, August 22, 2008.
g Released by Atlanta Braves, November 12, 2008. Signed with Philadelphia Phillies organization, March 6, 2009.
h Released by Philadelphia Phillies, September 8, 2009. Signed with Arizona Diamondbacks, December 16, 2009.
i Filed for free agency, November 1, 2010.

LOPEZ, WILTON

Born, Leon, Nicaragua, July 19, 1983.
Bats Right. Throws Right. Height, 6 feet. Weight, 190 pounds.

Year	Club	Lea	G	IP	W	L	Pct	SO	BB	H	ERA	SAVES
2002-03							Did Not Play					
2004	Tampa	Fla.St.	1	2	0	0	.000	2	1	2	4.50	0
2004	Yankees	Gulf Coast	4	5 2/3	1	0	1.000	6	0	2	0.00	1
2004	Battle Creek	Midwest	2	1 2/3	0	1	.000	2	1	4	0.00	0
2004	Staten Island	N.Y.-Penn.	2	3	0	0	.000	2	1	5	12.00	0
2005-06							Did Not Play					
2007	Lake Elsinore	Calif.	22	20 2/3	2	1	.667	19	1	35	6.10	3
2007	Fort Wayne a	Midwest	22	30	1	0	1.000	17	2	34	3.30	0
2008	Lake Elsinore	Calif.	30	30 2/3	2	1	.667	26	4	34	2.64	12
2008	Portland	P.C.	1	1	0	0	.000	1	2	1	9.00	0
2008	San Antonio	Texas	27	38 1/3	0	2	.000	24	9	41	4.93	0
2009	Corpus Christi	Texas	29	110 1/3	4	5	.444	69	13	133	4.73	0
2009	Houston b	N.L.	8	19 1/3	0	2	.000	9	8	32	8.38	0
2010	Round Rock	P.C.	3	5	2	1	.667	2	0	8	5.40	0
2010	Houston	N.L.	68	67	5	2	.714	50	5	66	2.96	1
Major League Totals		2 Yrs.	76	86 1/3	5	4	.556	59	13	98	4.17	1

a Released by New York Yankees, March 1, 2007. Signed with San Diego Padres organization, March 3, 2007.
b Claimed on waivers by Houston Astros, April 10, 2009.

LOWE, DEREK CHRISTOPHER

Born, Dearborn, Michigan, June 1, 1973.
Bats Right. Throws Right. Height, 6 feet, 6 inches. Weight, 230 pounds.

Year	Club	Lea	G	IP	W	L	Pct	SO	BB	H	ERA	SAVES
1991	Mariners	Arizona	12	71	5	3	.625	60	21	58	2.41	0
1992	Bellingham	Northwest	14	85⅔	7	3	.700	66	22	69	2.42	0
1993	Riverside	California	27	154	12	9	.571	80	60	189	5.26	0
1994	Jacksnville	Southern	26	151⅓	7	10	.412	75	50	177	4.94	0
1995	Mariners	Arizona	2	9⅔	1	0	1.000	11	2	5	0.93	0
1995	Port City	Southern	10	53⅓	1	6	.143	30	22	70	6.07	0
1996	Port City	Southern	10	65	5	3	.625	33	17	56	3.05	0
1996	Tacoma	P.C.	17	105	6	9	.400	54	37	118	4.54	0
1997	Tacoma	P.C.	10	57⅓	3	4	.429	49	20	53	3.45	0
1997	Pawtucket	Int.	6	30⅓	4	0	1.000	21	11	23	2.37	0
1997	Seattle-Boston a	A.L.	20	69	2	6	.250	52	23	74	6.13	0
1998	Boston	A.L.	63	123	3	9	.250	77	42	126	4.02	4
1999	Boston	A.L.	74	109⅓	6	3	.667	80	25	84	2.63	15
2000	Boston	A.L.	74	91⅓	4	4	.500	79	22	90	2.56	*42
2001	Boston	A.L.	67	91⅔	5	10	.333	82	29	103	3.53	24
2002	Boston b	A.L.	32	219⅔	21	8	.724	127	48	166	2.58	0
2003	Boston	A.L.	33	203⅓	17	7	.708	110	72	216	4.47	0
2004	Boston c	A.L.	33	182⅔	14	12	.538	105	71	224	5.42	0
2005	Los Angeles	N.L.	35	222	12	15	.444	146	55	223	3.61	0
2006	Los Angeles	N.L.	35	218	*16	8	.667	123	55	221	3.63	0
2007	Los Angeles	N.L.	33	199⅓	12	14	.462	147	59	194	3.88	0
2008	Los Angeles d	N.L.	34	211	14	11	.560	147	45	194	3.24	0
2009	Atlanta	N.L.	34	194⅔	15	10	.600	111	63	*232	4.67	0
2010	Atlanta	N.L.	33	193⅔	16	12	.571	136	61	204	4.00	0
Major League Totals		14 Yrs.	600	2328⅔	157	129	.549	1522	670	2351	3.85	85
	Division Series											
1998	Boston	A.L.	2	4⅓	0	0	.000	2	1	3	2.08	0
1999	Boston	A.L.	3	8⅓	1	1	.500	7	1	6	4.32	0
2003	Boston	A.L.	3	9⅔	0	1	.000	6	7	7	0.93	1
2004	Boston	A.L.	1	1	1	0	1.000	0	1	1	0.00	0
2006	Los Angeles	N.L.	1	5⅓	0	0	.000	6	2	6	6.75	0
2008	Los Angeles	N.L.	1	6	1	0	1.000	6	1	7	3.00	0
2010	Atlanta	N.L.	2	11⅔	0	2	.000	14	6	6	2.31	0
Division Series Totals			13	46⅓	3	4	.429	41	19	36	2.91	1
	Championship Series											
1999	Boston	A.L.	3	6⅓	0	0	.000	7	2	6	1.42	0
2003	Boston	A.L.	2	14	0	2	.000	5	7	14	6.43	0
2004	Boston	A.L.	2	11⅓	1	0	1.000	6	1	7	3.18	0
2008	Los Angeles	N.L.	2	10⅓	0	1	.000	6	2	12	3.48	0
Championship Series Totals			9	42	1	3	.250	24	12	39	4.07	0
	World Series Record											
2004	Boston	A.L.	1	7	1	0	1.000	4	1	3	0.00	0

a Traded to Boston Red Sox with catcher Jason Varitek for pitcher Heathcliff Slocumb, July 31, 1997.
b Pitched no-hit, no-run game against Tampa Bay Devil Rays, April 27, 2002.
c Filed for free agency, November 1, 2004. Signed with Los Angeles Dodgers, January 11, 2005.
d Filed for free agency, October 30, 2008. Signed with Atlanta Braves, January 13, 2009.

LYON, BRANDON JAMES

Born, Salt Lake City, Utah, August 10, 1979.
Bats Right. Throws Right. Height, 6 feet, 1 inch. Weight, 195 pounds.

Year	Club	Lea	G	IP	W	L	Pct	SO	BB	H	ERA	SAVES
2000	Queens	N.Y.-Penn.	15	60⅓	5	3	.625	55	6	43	2.39	0
2001	Tennessee	Southern	9	58⅔	5	0	1.000	45	9	57	3.68	0
2001	Syracuse	Int.	11	68⅓	5	3	.625	53	10	68	3.69	0
2001	Toronto	A.L.	11	63	5	4	.556	35	15	63	4.29	0
2002	Toronto	A.L.	15	62	1	4	.200	30	19	78	6.53	0
2002	Syracuse a	Int.	14	75⅔	4	9	.308	35	19	99	5.11	0
2003	Boston	A.L.	49	59	4	6	.400	50	19	73	4.12	9
2003	Pawtucket b-c-d-e	Int.	5	8⅓	0	0	.000	7	2	7	3.24	0
2004	Tucson f	P.C.	6	8⅓	2	3	.400	4	4	15	15.12	0
2005	Tucson	P.C.	5	5	0	1	.000	4	0	5	5.40	0
2005	Arizona g	N.L.	32	29⅓	0	2	.000	17	10	44	6.44	14
2006	Arizona	N.L.	68	69⅓	2	4	.333	46	22	68	3.89	0
2007	Arizona	N.L.	73	74	6	4	.600	40	22	70	2.68	2
2008	Arizona h	N.L.	61	59⅓	3	5	.375	44	13	75	4.70	26
2009	Detroit i	A.L.	65	78⅔	6	5	.545	57	31	56	2.86	3

Year	Club	Lea	G	IP	W	L	Pct	SO	BB	H	ERA	SAVES
2010	Houston	N.L.	79	78	6	6	.500	54	31	68	3.12	20
Major League Totals		9 Yrs.	453	$572\frac{2}{3}$	33	40	.452	373	182	595	4.05	74
	Division Series											
2007	Arizona	N.L.	3	3	0	0	.000	1	1	1	0.00	0
	Championship Series											
2007	Arizona	N.L.	2	3	0	0	.000	4	0	0	0.00	0

a Claimed on waivers by Boston Red Sox, October 9, 2002.
b Traded to Pittsburgh Pirates with pitcher Anastacio Martinez for pitcher Scott Sauerbeck and pitcher Mike Gonzalez, July 22, 2003.
c On disabled list from July 24 to September 1, 2003.
d Traded to Boston Red Sox with pitcher Jeff Suppan and pitcher Anastacio Martinez for infielder Freddy Sanchez, pitcher Mike Gonzalez and cash, July 31, 2003.
e Traded to Arizona Diamondbacks with pitcher Casey Fossum, pitcher Jorge DeRosa and outfielder Michael Goss for pitcher Curt Schilling, November 28, 2003.
f On disabled list from April 3 to October 4, 2004.
g On disabled list from May 13 to August 13, 2005.
h Filed for free agency, November 3, 2008. Signed with Detroit Tigers, January 24, 2009.
i Filed for free agency, November 9, 2009. Signed with Houston Astros, December 12, 2009.

MADSON, RYAN MICHAEL

Born, Long Beach, California, August 28, 1980.
Bats Left. Throws Right. Height, 6 feet, 6 inches. Weight, 195 pounds.

Year	Club	Lea	G	IP	W	L	Pct	SO	BB	H	ERA	SAVES
1998	Martinsvlle	Appal.	12	54	3	3	.500	52	20	57	4.83	0
1999	Batavia	N.Y.-Penn.	15	$87\frac{2}{3}$	5	5	.500	75	43	80	4.72	0
2000	Piedmont	So.Atl.	21	$135\frac{2}{3}$	14	5	.737	123	45	113	2.59	0
2001	Clearwater	Fla.St.	22	$117\frac{2}{3}$	9	9	.500	101	49	137	3.90	0
2002	Reading	Eastern	26	$171\frac{1}{3}$	16	4	.800	132	53	150	3.20	0
2003	Clearwater	Fla.St.	2	8	0	0	.000	9	2	11	5.63	0
2003	Scranton/WB	Int.	26	157	12	8	.600	138	42	157	3.50	0
2003	Philadelphia	N.L.	1	2	0	0	.000	0	0	0	0.00	0
2004	Reading	Eastern	2	2	0	0	.000	1	2	3	4.50	0
2004	Philadelphia	N.L.	52	77	9	3	.750	55	19	68	2.34	1
2005	Philadelphia	N.L.	78	87	6	5	.545	79	25	84	4.14	0
2006	Philadelphia	N.L.	50	$134\frac{1}{3}$	11	9	.550	99	50	176	5.69	2
2007	Reading	Eastern	2	3	0	0	.000	4	0	3	0.00	0
2007	Philadelphia a	N.L.	38	56	2	2	.500	43	23	48	3.05	1
2008	Philadelphia	N.L.	76	$82\frac{2}{3}$	4	2	.667	67	23	79	3.05	1
2009	Philadelphia	N.L.	79	$77\frac{1}{3}$	5	5	.500	78	22	73	3.26	10
2010	Clearwater	Fla.St.	2	2	0	1	.000	3	0	1	4.50	0
2010	Reading	Eastern	1	2	0	0	.000	1	0	2	0.00	0
2010	Lehigh Valley	Int.	2	$1\frac{2}{3}$	0	0	.000	2	2	1	5.40	0
2010	Philadelphia b	N.L.	55	53	6	2	.750	64	13	42	2.55	5
Major League Totals		8 Yrs.	429	$569\frac{1}{3}$	43	28	.606	485	175	570	3.71	20
	Division Series											
2008	Philadelphia	N.L.	3	4	0	0	.000	2	0	3	2.25	0
2009	Philadelphia	N.L.	3	$2\frac{2}{3}$	1	0	1.000	4	1	2	3.38	0
2010	Philadelphia	N.L.	1	1	0	0	.000	1	0	1	0.00	0
Division Series Totals			7	$7\frac{2}{3}$	1	0	1.000	7	1	6	2.35	0
	Championship Series											
2008	Philadelphia	N.L.	4	5	1	0	1.000	4	1	4	0.00	0
2009	Philadelphia	N.L.	4	$3\frac{1}{3}$	0	0	.000	4	3	6	5.40	0
2010	Philadelphia	N.L.	5	$6\frac{2}{3}$	0	1	.000	10	3	4	1.35	0
Championship Series Totals			13	15	1	1	.500	18	7	14	1.80	0
	World Series Record											
2008	Philadelphia	N.L.	4	$3\frac{2}{3}$	0	0	.000	6	0	3	4.91	0
2009	Philadelphia	N.L.	5	$4\frac{1}{3}$	0	0	.000	6	2	6	2.08	1
World Series Totals			9	8	0	0	.000	12	2	9	3.38	1

a On disabled list from May 4 to May 22 and July 30 to November 2, 2007.
b On disabled list from April 29 to July 8, 2010.

MAHAY, RONALD MATTHEW (RON)

Born, Crestwood, Illinois, June 28, 1971.
Bats Left. Throws Left. Height, 6 feet, 2 inches. Weight, 190 pounds.

Year	Club	Lea	G	IP	W	L	Pct	SO	BB	H	ERA	SAVES
1996	Sarasota	Fla.St.	31	$70\frac{2}{3}$	2	2	.500	68	35	61	3.82	2
1996	Trenton	Eastern	1	$3\frac{2}{3}$	0	1	.000	0	6	12	29.45	0

Year	Club	Lea	G	IP	W	L	Pct	SO	BB	H	ERA	SAVES
1997	Trenton	Eastern	17	$40\frac{2}{3}$	3	3	.500	47	13	29	3.10	5
1997	Pawtucket	Int.	2	$4\frac{2}{3}$	1	0	1.000	6	1	3	0.00	0
1997	Boston	A.L.	28	25	3	0	1.000	22	11	19	2.52	0
1998	Pawtucket	Int.	23	41	3	1	.750	41	19	37	4.17	3
1998	Boston	A.L.	29	26	1	1	.500	14	15	26	3.46	1
1999	Vancouver	P.C.	32	107	7	2	.778	73	45	116	4.29	0
1999	Oakland a	A.L.	6	$19\frac{1}{3}$	2	0	1.000	15	3	8	1.86	1
2000	Oakland	A.L.	5	16	0	1	.000	5	9	26	9.00	0
2000	Florida	N.L.	18	$25\frac{1}{3}$	1	0	1.000	27	16	31	6.04	0
2000	Calgary b-c	P.C.	8	13	0	1	.000	15	7	7	4.85	0
2001	Portland	P.C.	14	$16\frac{2}{3}$	1	2	.333	18	5	13	3.78	0
2001	Iowa	P.C.	36	$46\frac{2}{3}$	3	1	.750	52	10	29	2.31	14
2001	Chicago d	N.L.	17	$20\frac{2}{3}$	0	0	.000	24	15	14	2.61	0
2002	Iowa	P.C.	39	$46\frac{2}{3}$	0	1	.000	50	15	32	1.93	2
2002	Chicago e-f	N.L.	11	$14\frac{2}{3}$	2	0	1.000	14	8	13	8.59	0
2003	Oklahoma	P.C.	26	$42\frac{2}{3}$	4	2	.667	51	10	36	4.22	3
2003	Texas	A.L.	35	$45\frac{1}{3}$	3	3	.500	38	20	33	3.18	0
2004	Texas	A.L.	60	67	3	0	1.000	54	29	60	2.55	0
2005	Oklahoma	P.C.	3	$3\frac{2}{3}$	0	0	.000	5	1	2	0.00	0
2005	Texas	A.L.	30	$35\frac{2}{3}$	0	2	.000	30	16	47	6.81	1
2005	Frisco g	Texas	5	$19\frac{2}{3}$	1	3	.250	20	9	24	7.78	0
2006	Oklahoma	P.C.	5	$6\frac{1}{3}$	0	1	.000	11	0	5	1.42	2
2006	Texas	A.L.	62	57	1	3	.250	56	28	54	3.95	0
2007	Frisco	Texas	3	$4\frac{2}{3}$	0	0	.000	4	1	5	0.00	0
2007	Oklahoma	P.C.	4	$5\frac{2}{3}$	0	1	.000	5	4	10	11.12	0
2007	Texas h	A.L.	28	39	2	0	1.000	32	21	33	2.77	1
2007	Atlanta i-j	N.L.	30	28	1	0	1.000	23	16	19	2.25	0
2008	Kansas City k	A.L.	57	$64\frac{2}{3}$	5	0	1.000	49	29	61	3.48	0
2009	Kansas City-Minnesota l-m	A.L.	57	$50\frac{1}{3}$	2	1	.667	42	22	62	4.29	0
2010	Fort Myers	Fla.St.	4	$4\frac{2}{3}$	0	1	.000	4	1	5	1.93	0
2010	Minnesota n-o	A.L.	41	34	1	1	.500	25	8	33	3.44	0
Major League Totals		14 Yrs.	514	568	27	12	.692	470	266	539	3.83	4
	Division Series											
2009	Minnesota	A.L.	3	$1\frac{2}{3}$	0	0	.000	2	1	0	5.40	0

a Claimed on waivers by Oakland Athletics, March 30, 1999.
b Sold to Florida Marlins, May 11, 2000.
c Filed for free agency, October 2, 2000. Signed with San Diego Padres organization, November 20, 2000.
d Released by San Diego Padres, May 15, 2001. Signed with Chicago Cubs organization, May 19, 2001.
e On disabled list from May 24 to June 13, 2002.
f Filed for free agency, September 30, 2002. Signed with Texas Rangers organization, November 13, 2002.
g On disabled list from June 8 to June 24, 2005.
h On disabled list from May 12 to June 15, 2007.
i Traded to Atlanta Braves with infielder Mark Teixeira for catcher Jarrod Saltalamacchia, infielder Elvis Andrus, pitcher Neftali Feliz, pitcher Matt Harrison and pitcher Beau James, July 31, 2007.
j Filed for free agency, October 29, 2007. Signed with Kansas City Royals, December 20, 2007.
k On disabled list from August 16 to September 2, 2008.
l Released by Kansas City Royals, August 26, 2009. Signed with Minnesota Twins, August 29, 2009.
m Filed for free agency, November 5, 2009. re-signed with Minnesota Twins organization, March 24, 2010.
n On disabled list from August 22 to November 1, 2010.
o Filed for free agency, November 1, 2010.

MAHOLM, PAUL GURNER

Born, Greenwood, Mississippi, June 25, 1982.
Bats Left. Throws Left. Height, 6 feet, 2 inches. Weight, 230 pounds.

Year	Club	Lea	G	IP	W	L	Pct	SO	BB	H	ERA	SAVES
2003	Williamsport	N.Y.-Penn.	8	$34\frac{1}{3}$	2	1	.667	32	10	25	1.83	0
2004	Lynchburg	Carolina	8	44	1	3	.250	28	15	39	1.84	0
2004	Pirates	Gulf Coast	1	4	0	0	.000	2	1	5	2.25	0
2004	Hickory	So.Atl.	3	$12\frac{1}{3}$	0	2	.000	12	10	17	9.49	0
2005	Altoona	Eastern	16	$81\frac{2}{3}$	6	2	.750	75	26	73	3.20	0
2005	Indianapolis	Int.	6	$35\frac{2}{3}$	1	1	.500	21	12	40	3.53	0
2005	Pittsburgh	N.L.	6	$41\frac{1}{3}$	3	1	.750	26	17	31	2.18	0
2006	Pittsburgh	N.L.	30	176	8	10	.444	117	81	202	4.76	0
2007	Pittsburgh	N.L.	29	$177\frac{2}{3}$	10	15	.400	105	49	204	5.02	0
2008	Pittsburgh	N.L.	31	$206\frac{1}{3}$	9	9	.500	139	63	201	3.71	0
2009	Pittsburgh	N.L.	31	$194\frac{2}{3}$	8	9	.471	119	60	221	4.44	0
2010	Pittsburgh	N.L.	32	$185\frac{1}{3}$	9	15	.375	102	62	228	5.10	0
Major League Totals		6 Yrs.	159	$981\frac{1}{3}$	47	59	.443	608	332	1087	4.48	0

MARCUM, SHAUN MICHAL

Born, Kansas City, Missouri, December 14, 1981.
Bats Right. Throws Right. Height, 6 feet. Weight, 195 pounds.

Year	Club	Lea	G	IP	W	L	Pct	SO	BB	H	ERA	SAVES
2003	Auburn	N.Y.-Penn.	21	34	1	0	1.000	47	7	15	1.32	8
2004	Dunedin	Fla.St.	12	69 1/3	3	2	.600	72	4	74	3.12	0
2004	Charleston	So.Atl.	13	79	7	4	.636	83	16	64	3.19	0
2005	New Hampshire	Eastern	9	53 1/3	7	1	.875	40	10	44	2.53	0
2005	Syracuse	Int.	18	103 2/3	6	4	.600	90	18	112	4.95	0
2005	Toronto	A.L.	5	8	0	0	.000	4	4	6	0.00	0
2006	Syracuse	Int.	18	52 2/3	4	0	1.000	60	9	48	3.42	0
2006	Toronto	A.L.	21	78 1/3	3	4	.429	65	38	87	5.06	0
2007	Toronto	A.L.	38	159	12	6	.667	122	49	149	4.13	1
2008	Dunedin	Fla.St.	1	4	0	0	.000	6	0	0	0.00	0
2008	Syracuse	Int.	2	13	0	1	.000	15	3	10	2.77	0
2008	Toronto a	A.L.	25	151 1/3	9	7	.563	123	50	126	3.39	0
2009	New Hampshire	Eastern	2	7 2/3	0	1	.000	8	2	8	1.17	0
2009	Dunedin	Fla.St.	2	6	0	1	.000	5	0	7	3.00	0
2009	Las Vegas b	P.C.	1	2	0	0	.000	0	1	2	4.50	0
2010	Toronto c-d	A.L.	31	195 1/3	13	8	.619	165	43	181	3.64	0
Major League Totals		5 Yrs.	120	592	37	25	.597	479	184	549	3.85	1

a On disabled list from June 19 to July 22, 2008.
b On disabled list from March 27 to November 13, 2009.
c On disabled list from July 2 to July 18, 2010.
d Traded to Milwaukee Brewers for infielder Brett Lawrie, December 6, 2010.

MARMOL, CARLOS AGUSTIN

Born, Bonao, Dominican Republic, October 14, 1982.
Bats Right. Throws Right. Height, 6 feet, 2 inches. Weight, 180 pounds.

Year	Club	Lea	G	IP	W	L	Pct	SO	BB	H	ERA	SAVES
2002	Cubs	Arizona	1	1	0	0	.000	1	1	1	0.00	0
2003	Cubs	Arizona	15	64 1/3	3	5	.375	74	37	59	4.76	0
2004	Lansing	Midwest	26	154 2/3	14	8	.636	154	53	131	3.20	0
2005	Daytona	Fla.St.	13	72 1/3	6	2	.750	71	37	60	2.99	0
2005	West Tenn	Southern	14	81 1/3	3	4	.429	70	40	70	3.65	0
2006	West Tenn	Southern	11	58	3	2	.600	67	25	42	2.33	0
2006	Iowa	P.C.	2	3	0	0	.000	1	1	4	9.00	0
2006	Chicago a	N.L.	19	77	5	7	.417	59	59	71	6.08	0
2007	Iowa	P.C.	8	41	4	1	.800	48	12	30	3.95	0
2007	Chicago	N.L.	59	69 1/3	5	1	.833	96	35	41	1.43	1
2008	Chicago	N.L.	82	87 1/3	2	4	.333	114	41	40	2.68	7
2009	Chicago	N.L.	79	74	2	4	.333	93	65	43	3.41	15
2010	Chicago	N.L.	77	77 2/3	2	3	.400	138	52	40	2.55	38
Major League Totals		5 Yrs.	316	385 1/3	16	19	.457	500	252	235	3.25	61
	Division Series											
2007	Chicago	N.L.	2	3	0	1	.000	6	3	3	9.00	0
2008	Chicago	N.L.	2	2 2/3	0	0	.000	3	0	3	6.75	0
Division Series Totals			4	5 2/3	0	1	.000	9	3	6	7.94	0

a On disabled list from August 19 to September 4, 2006.

MARQUIS, JASON SCOTT

Born, Manhasset, New York, August 21, 1978.
Bats Left. Throws Right. Height, 6 feet, 1 inch. Weight, 210 pounds.

Year	Club	Lea	G	IP	W	L	Pct	SO	BB	H	ERA	SAVES
1996	Danville	Appal.	7	23 1/3	1	1	.500	24	7	30	4.63	0
1997	Macon	So.Atl.	28	141 2/3	14	10	.583	121	55	156	4.38	0
1998	Danville	Carolina	22	114 2/3	2	12	.143	135	41	120	4.87	0
1999	Myrtle Beach	Carolina	6	32	3	0	1.000	41	17	22	0.28	0
1999	Greenville a	Southern	12	55	3	4	.429	35	29	52	4.58	0
2000	Greenville	Southern	11	68	4	2	.667	49	23	68	3.57	0
2000	Atlanta	N.L.	15	23 1/3	1	0	1.000	17	12	23	5.01	0
2000	Richmond	Int.	6	20	0	3	.000	18	13	26	9.00	0
2001	Atlanta	N.L.	38	129 1/3	5	6	.455	98	59	113	3.48	0
2002	Richmond	Int.	1	5	0	1	.000	6	1	5	3.60	0
2002	Atlanta b	N.L.	22	114 1/3	8	9	.471	84	49	127	5.04	0
2003	Richmond	Int.	15	94	8	4	.667	75	34	93	3.35	0
2003	Atlanta c	N.L.	21	40 2/3	0	0	.000	19	18	43	5.53	1
2004	St. Louis	N.L.	32	201 1/3	15	7	.682	138	70	215	3.71	0

Year	Club	Lea	G	IP	W	L	Pct	SO	BB	H	ERA	SAVES
2005	St. Louis	N.L.	33	207	13	14	.481	100	69	206	4.13	0
2006	St. Louis d	N.L.	33	194 1/3	14	*16	.467	96	75	221	6.02	0
2007	Chicago	N.L.	34	191 2/3	12	9	.571	109	76	190	4.60	0
2008	Chicago e	N.L.	29	167	11	9	.550	91	70	172	4.53	0
2009	Colorado f	N.L.	33	216	15	13	.536	115	80	218	4.04	0
2010	Nationals	Gulf Coast	1	3	0	0	.000	4	0	2	0.00	0
2010	Potomac	Carolina	1	3 2/3	0	0	.000	3	1	6	7.36	0
2010	Harrisburg	Eastern	1	3 1/3	0	0	.000	3	1	5	8.10	0
2010	Syracuse	Int.	2	11	0	0	.000	11	3	7	4.09	0
2010	Washington g	N.L.	13	58 2/3	2	9	.182	31	24	76	6.60	0
Major League Totals		11 Yrs.	303	1543 2/3	96	92	.511	898	602	1604	4.56	1
	Division Series											
2004	St. Louis	N.L.	1	3 1/3	0	0	.000	0	4	4	8.10	0
2008	Chicago	N.L.	1	1	0	0	.000	1	0	1	9.00	0
2009	Colorado	N.L.	1	1	0	0	.000	0	0	1	0.00	0
Division Series Totals			3	5 1/3	0	0	.000	1	4	6	6.75	0
	Championship Series											
2001	Atlanta	N.L.	2	2	0	0	.000	3	2	2	0.00	0
2004	St. Louis	N.L.	1	4	0	0	.000	2	2	5	6.75	0
2005	St. Louis	N.L.	3	5 1/3	0	1	.000	4	3	6	3.38	0
Championship Series Totals			6	11 1/3	0	1	.000	9	7	13	3.97	0
	World Series Record											
2004	St. Louis	N.L.	2	7	0	1	.000	4	7	6	3.86	0

a On disabled list from July 5 to 31, 1999.
b On disabled list from April 15 to May 11, 2002.
c Traded to St. Louis Cardinals with pitcher Ray King and pitcher Adam Wainwright for catcher Eli Marrero and outfielder J.D. Drew, December 13, 2003.
d Filed for free agency, October 30, 2006. Signed with Chicago Cubs, December 19, 2006.
e Traded to Colorado Rockies for pitcher Luis Vizcaino, January 6, 2009.
f Filed for free agency, November 5, 2009. Signed with Washington Nationals, December 22, 2009.
g On disabled list from April 19 to August 8, 2010.

MARSHALL, SEAN CHRISTOPHER

Born, Richmond, Virginia, August 30, 1982.
Bats Left. Throws Left. Height, 6 feet, 7 inches. Weight, 220 pounds.

Year	Club	Lea	G	IP	W	L	Pct	SO	BB	H	ERA	SAVES
2003	Lansing	Midwest	1	7	1	0	1.000	11	0	5	0.00	0
2003	Boise	Northwest	14	73 2/3	5	6	.455	88	23	66	2.57	0
2004	Lansing	Midwest	7	48 2/3	2	0	1.000	51	4	29	1.11	0
2004	West Tenn	Southern	6	29	2	2	.500	23	12	36	5.90	0
2005	Daytona	Fla.St.	12	69	4	4	.500	61	26	63	2.74	0
2005	West Tenn	Southern	4	25	0	1	.000	24	5	16	2.52	0
2006	Iowa	P.C.	4	21 2/3	0	2	.000	21	14	17	3.32	0
2006	Chicago a	N.L.	24	125 2/3	6	9	.400	77	59	132	5.59	0
2007	Daytona	Fla.St.	1	6	1	0	1.000	4	1	7	3.00	0
2007	Iowa	P.C.	4	24 2/3	2	0	1.000	15	8	17	1.82	0
2007	Chicago	N.L.	21	103 1/3	7	8	.467	67	35	107	3.92	0
2008	Iowa	P.C.	7	31 2/3	1	1	.500	25	6	26	3.41	0
2008	Chicago	N.L.	34	65 1/3	3	5	.375	58	23	60	3.86	1
2009	Chicago	N.L.	55	85 1/3	3	7	.300	68	32	91	4.32	0
2010	Chicago	N.L.	80	74 2/3	7	5	.583	90	25	58	2.65	1
Major League Totals		5 Yrs.	214	454 1/3	26	34	.433	360	174	448	4.24	2
	Division Series											
2008	Chicago	N.L.	2	3 1/3	0	0	.000	5	1	2	2.70	0

a On disabled list from July 23 to September 1, 2006.

MARTIN, JOHN DALE (J.D.)

Born, Ridgecrest, California, January 2, 1983.
Bats Right. Throws Right. Height, 6 feet, 4 inches. Weight, 200 pounds.

Year	Club	Lea	G	IP	W	L	Pct	SO	BB	H	ERA	SAVES
2001	Burlington	Appal.	10	45 2/3	5	1	.833	72	11	26	1.38	0
2002	Columbus	So.Atl.	27	138 1/3	14	5	.737	131	46	141	3.90	0
2003	Kinston	Carolina	16	86 1/3	5	3	.625	57	30	95	4.27	0
2004	Kinston	Carolina	25	147 2/3	11	10	.524	98	41	139	4.39	0
2004	Buffalo	Int.	1	5	0	0	.000	2	2	9	10.80	0
2005	Akron	Eastern	10	56 2/3	3	1	.750	63	8	42	2.38	0
2006	Kinston	Carolina	3	11 1/3	1	0	1.000	11	1	6	0.00	0

Year	Club	Lea	G	IP	W	L	Pct	SO	BB	H	ERA	SAVES
2006	Mahoning Valley	N.Y.-Penn.	6	18	0	1	.000	13	1	11	1.50	0
2006	Lake County	So.Atl.	5	15	0	1	.000	16	3	13	4.20	0
2007	Akron	Eastern	9	42⅓	2	3	.400	23	16	42	4.25	0
2008	Akron	Eastern	31	79⅔	11	3	.786	71	19	73	2.49	0
2008	Buffalo a	Int.	4	10	1	0	1.000	8	2	6	1.80	0
2009	Syracuse	Int.	16	88	8	3	.727	63	10	75	2.66	0
2009	Washington	N.L.	15	77	5	4	.556	37	24	85	4.44	0
2010	Syracuse	Int.	7	41	2	2	.500	25	8	40	3.51	0
2010	Washington b	N.L.	9	48	1	5	.167	31	11	56	4.13	0
Major League Totals		2 Yrs.	24	125	6	9	.400	68	35	141	4.32	0

a Filed for free agency from Cleveland Indians, November 3, 2008. Signed with Washington Nationals, November 24, 2008.

b On disabled list from July 25 to November 10, 2010.

MASSET, NICHOLAS ALLEN (NICK)

Born, St. Petersburg, Florida, May 17, 1982.
Bats Right. Throws Right. Height, 6 feet, 4 inches. Weight, 235 pounds.

Year	Club	Lea	G	IP	W	L	Pct	SO	BB	H	ERA	SAVES
2001	Rangers	Gulf Coast	15	31	0	6	.000	32	7	34	4.35	0
2002	Savannah	So.Atl.	33	120⅓	5	8	.385	93	47	129	4.56	0
2003	Clinton	Midwest	30	123⅔	7	7	.500	63	43	144	4.08	2
2004	Stockton	Calif.	16	77	6	5	.545	43	19	71	3.51	0
2004	Frisco	Texas	2	10	1	0	1.000	8	4	8	1.80	0
2005	Frisco	Texas	29	157⅓	7	12	.368	105	61	197	6.18	0
2006	Frisco	Texas	8	48	2	2	.500	40	20	38	2.06	0
2006	Oklahoma	P.C.	24	67⅓	4	5	.444	65	28	79	4.81	3
2006	Texas a	A.L.	8	8⅔	0	0	.000	4	2	9	4.15	0
2007	Chicago	A.L.	27	39⅓	2	3	.400	21	26	52	7.09	0
2007	Charlotte	Int.	11	45⅓	0	4	.000	33	9	51	4.57	0
2008	Chicago	A.L.	32	44⅔	1	0	1.000	32	21	55	4.63	1
2008	Cincinnati b	N.L.	10	17⅓	1	0	1.000	11	5	16	2.08	0
2009	Cincinnati c	N.L.	74	76	5	1	.833	70	24	54	2.37	0
2010	Cincinnati	N.L.	82	76⅔	4	4	.500	85	33	64	3.40	2
Major League Totals		5 Yrs.	233	262⅔	13	8	.619	223	111	250	3.80	3
	Division Series											
2010	Cincinnati	N.L.	2	2	0	0	.000	1	2	2	4.50	0

a Traded to Chicago White Sox by Texas Rangers with pitcher John Danks and pitcher Jacob Rasner for pitcher Brandon McCarthy and outfielder David Paisano, December 23, 2006.

b Traded to Cincinnati Reds with infielder Danny Richar for outfielder Ken Griffey, July 31, 2008.

c On disabled list from May 11 to May 26, 2009.

MASTERSON, JUSTIN DANIEL

Born, Kingston, Jamaica, March 22, 1985.
Bats Right. Throws Right. Height, 6 feet, 6 inches. Weight, 250 pounds.

Year	Club	Lea	G	IP	W	L	Pct	SO	BB	H	ERA	SAVES
2006	Lowell	N.Y.-Penn.	14	31⅔	3	1	.750	33	2	20	0.85	0
2007	Lancaster	Calif.	17	95⅔	8	5	.615	56	22	103	4.33	0
2007	Portland	Eastern	10	58	4	3	.571	59	18	49	4.34	0
2008	Portland	Eastern	8	38⅓	1	3	.250	37	16	37	4.23	0
2008	Pawtucket	Int.	4	9⅓	1	0	1.000	8	1	6	2.89	0
2008	Boston	A.L.	36	88⅓	6	5	.545	68	40	68	3.16	0
2009	Boston-Cleveland a	A.L.	42	129⅓	4	10	.286	119	60	128	4.52	0
2010	Cleveland	A.L.	34	180	6	13	.316	140	73	197	4.70	0
Major League Totals		3 Yrs.	112	397⅔	16	28	.364	327	173	393	4.30	0
	Division Series											
2008	Boston	A.L.	4	4	0	0	.000	3	3	6	2.25	0
	Championship Series											
2008	Boston	A.L.	5	5⅔	1	0	1.000	6	2	4	1.59	0

a Traded to Cleveland Indians with pitcher Nick Hagadone and pitcher Bryan Price for catcher Victor Martinez, July 31, 2009.

MATSUZAKA, DAISUKE

Born, Tokyo, Japan, September 13, 1980.
Bats Right. Throws Right. Height, 6 feet. Weight, 185 pounds.

Year	Club	Lea	G	IP	W	L	Pct	SO	BB	H	ERA	SAVES
1999	Seibu	Japan Pac.	25	180	16	5	.762	151	87	124	2.60	0
2000	Seibu	Japan Pac.	27	167⅔	14	7	.667	144	95	132	3.97	1

Year	Club	Lea	G	IP	W	L	Pct	SO	BB	H	ERA	SAVES
2001	Seibu	Japan Pac.	33	240⅓	15	15	.500	214	117	184	3.60	0
2002	Seibu	Japan Pac.	14	73⅔	6	2	.750	78	15	60	3.68	0
2003	Seibu	Japan Pac.	29	194	16	7	.696	215	63	165	2.83	0
2004	Seibu	Japan Pac.	23	146	10	6	.625	127	42	127	2.90	0
2005	Seibu	Japan Pac.	28	215	14	13	.519	226	49	172	2.30	0
2006	Seibu a-b	Japan Pac.	25	186⅓	17	5	.773	200	34	138	2.13	0
2007	Boston	A.L.	32	204⅔	15	12	.556	201	80	191	4.40	0
2008	Pawtucket	Int.	1	5	1	0	1.000	5	1	4	3.60	0
2008	Boston c.	A.L.	29	167⅔	18	3	.857	154	*94	128	2.90	0
2009	Red Sox	Gulf Coast	1	3	0	0	.000	4	0	1	0.00	0
2009	Portland	Eastern	1	2	0	1	.000	2	3	4	22.50	0
2009	Pawtucket	Int.	4	16	0	1	.000	17	6	13	2.25	0
2009	Boston d	A.L.	12	59⅓	4	6	.400	54	30	81	5.76	0
2010	Pawtucket	Int.	3	16⅔	2	0	1.000	13	1	11	1.62	0
2010	Boston e.	A.L.	25	153⅔	9	6	.600	133	74	137	4.69	0
Major League Totals		4 Yrs.	98	585⅓	46	27	.630	542	278	537	4.18	0
	Division Series											
2007	Boston	A.L.	1	4⅔	0	0	.000	3	3	7	5.79	0
2008	Boston	A.L.	1	5	0	0	.000	5	3	8	5.40	0
Division Series Totals			2	9⅔	0	0	.000	8	6	15	5.59	0
	Championship Series											
2007	Boston	A.L.	2	9⅔	1	1	.500	9	2	12	5.59	0
2008	Boston	A.L.	2	11	1	0	1.000	11	6	9	4.09	0
Championship Series Totals			4	20⅔	2	1	.667	20	8	21	4.79	0
	World Series Record											
2007	Boston	A.L.	1	5⅓	1	0	1.000	5	3	3	3.38	0

a Signed with Boston Red Sox, December 14, 2006.
b World Baseball Classic most valuable player.
c On disabled list from May 28 to June 21, 2008.
d On disabled list from April 15 to May 22 and June 20 to September 15, 2009.
e On disabled list from April 4 to May 1 and June 8 to June 24, 2010.

MATUSZ, BRIAN ROBERT

Born, Grand Junction, Colorado, February 11, 1987.
Bats Left. Throws Left. Height, 6 feet, 5 inches. Weight, 200 pounds.

Year	Club	Lea	G	IP	W	L	Pct	SO	BB	H	ERA	SAVES
2009	Frederick	Carolina	11	66⅔	4	2	.667	75	21	56	2.16	0
2009	Bowie	Eastern	8	46⅓	7	0	1.000	46	11	31	1.55	0
2009	Baltimore	A.L.	8	44⅔	5	2	.714	38	14	52	4.63	0
2010	Baltimore	A.L.	32	175⅔	10	12	.455	143	63	173	4.30	0
Major League Totals		2 Yrs.	40	220⅓	15	14	.517	181	77	225	4.37	0

MAZZARO, VINCENT MICHAEL (VIN)

Born, Hackensack, New Jersey, September 27, 1986.
Bats Right. Throws Right. Height, 6 feet, 1 inch. Weight, 215 pounds.

Year	Club	Lea	G	IP	W	L	Pct	SO	BB	H	ERA	SAVES
2006	Kane County	Midwest	24	119⅓	9	9	.500	81	42	146	5.05	0
2007	Stockton	Calif.	28	153⅔	9	12	.429	115	71	159	5.33	0
2008	Sacramento	P.C.	6	33⅔	3	3	.500	27	9	49	6.15	0
2008	Midland	Texas	22	137⅓	12	3	.800	104	36	115	1.90	0
2009	Sacramento	P.C.	10	56⅔	2	2	.500	44	17	42	2.38	0
2009	Oakland a	A.L.	17	91⅓	4	9	.308	59	39	120	5.32	0
2010	Sacramento	P.C.	7	37⅓	3	1	.750	38	17	35	3.13	0
2010	Oakland b	A.L.	24	122⅓	6	8	.429	79	50	127	4.27	0
Major League Totals		2 Yrs.	41	213⅔	10	17	.370	138	89	247	4.72	0

a On disabled list from September 8 to November 4, 2009.
b Traded to Kansas City Royals with pitcher Justin Marks for outfielder David DeJesus, November 10, 2010.

MC CLELLAN, KYLE WILLIAM

Born, Florissant, Missouri, June 12, 1984.
Bats Right. Throws Right. Height, 6 feet, 4 inches. Weight, 205 pounds.

Year	Club	Lea	G	IP	W	L	Pct	SO	BB	H	ERA	SAVES
2002	Johnson City	Appal.	7	12	0	2	.000	8	7	17	11.25	0
2003	Johnson City	Appal.	12	67⅔	3	6	.333	44	16	74	3.99	0
2004	Peoria	Midwest	24	128	4	12	.250	84	34	143	5.34	0

Year	Club	Lea	G	IP	W	L	Pct	SO	BB	H	ERA	SAVES
2005	Quad Cities	Midwest	17	54	1	4	.200	36	26	59	4.83	1
2006	Johnson City	Appal.	3	$6\frac{2}{3}$	0	1	.000	4	3	7	9.45	0
2007	Palm Beach	Fla.St.	16	29	4	1	.800	24	4	22	1.24	0
2007	Springfield	Texas	24	$30\frac{2}{3}$	2	0	1.000	30	6	24	2.35	0
2008	St. Louis	N.L.	68	$75\frac{2}{3}$	2	7	.222	59	26	79	4.04	1
2009	St. Louis	N.L.	66	$66\frac{2}{3}$	4	4	.500	51	34	56	3.38	3
2010	St. Louis	N.L.	68	$75\frac{1}{3}$	1	4	.200	60	23	58	2.27	2
Major League Totals		3 Yrs.	202	$217\frac{2}{3}$	7	15	.318	170	83	193	3.23	6
	Division Series											
2009	St. Louis	N.L.	1	$0\frac{2}{3}$	0	0	.000	0	1	1	0.00	0

MC CUTCHEN, DANIEL THOMAS

Born, McKinney, Texas, September 26, 1982.

Bats Right. Throws Right. Height, 6 feet, 2 inches. Weight, 215 pounds.

Year	Club	Lea	G	IP	W	L	Pct	SO	BB	H	ERA	SAVES
2006	Staten Island	N.Y.-Penn.	2	8	1	0	1.000	11	1	4	1.13	0
2006	Charleston	So.Atl.	7	21	1	0	1.000	18	5	13	2.14	1
2007	Trenton	Eastern	7	41	3	2	.600	36	12	30	2.41	0
2007	Tampa	Fla.St.	17	101	11	2	.846	67	21	86	2.50	0
2008	Trenton	Eastern	9	53	4	3	.571	52	18	43	2.55	0
2008	Indianapolis	Int.	8	48	3	3	.500	41	7	49	4.69	0
2008	Scranton/WB a	Int.	11	$70\frac{1}{3}$	4	6	.400	58	11	73	3.58	0
2009	Indianapolis	Int.	24	$142\frac{2}{3}$	13	6	.684	110	29	145	3.47	0
2009	Pittsburgh	N.L.	6	$36\frac{1}{3}$	1	2	.333	19	11	38	4.21	0
2010	Indianapolis	Int.	13	79	4	8	.333	39	19	71	3.99	0
2010	Pittsburgh	N.L.	28	$67\frac{2}{3}$	2	5	.286	38	28	83	6.12	0
Major League Totals		2 Yrs.	34	104	3	7	.300	57	39	121	5.45	0

a Traded by New York Yankees to Pittsburgh Pirates with outfielder Jose Tabata, pitcher Ross Ohlendorf and pitcher Jeff Karstens for outfielder Xavier Nady and pitcher Damaso Marte, July 26, 2008.

MC DONALD, JAMES ZELL

Born, Long Beach, California, October 19, 1984.

Bats Left. Throws Right. Height, 6 feet, 5 inches. Weight, 195 pounds.

Year	Club	Lea	G	IP	W	L	Pct	SO	BB	H	ERA	SAVES
2003	Dodgers	Gulf Coast	12	$48\frac{2}{3}$	2	4	.333	47	15	39	3.33	0
2004	a					Did Not Pitch						
2005	Ogden	Pioneer	4	6	0	0	.000	9	2	4	1.50	0
2006	Columbus	So.Atl.	30	$142\frac{1}{3}$	5	10	.333	146	65	119	3.98	0
2007	Inland Empire	Calif.	16	82	6	7	.462	104	21	79	3.95	0
2007	Jacksonville	Southern	10	$52\frac{2}{3}$	7	2	.778	64	16	42	1.71	0
2008	Jacksonville	Southern	22	$118\frac{2}{3}$	5	3	.625	113	46	98	3.19	0
2008	Las Vegas	P.C.	5	$22\frac{1}{3}$	2	1	.667	28	7	17	3.63	0
2008	Los Angeles	N.L.	4	6	0	0	.000	2	1	5	0.00	0
2009	Albuquerque	P.C.	6	$30\frac{1}{3}$	1	0	1.000	40	14	21	3.26	0
2009	Los Angeles	N.L.	45	63	5	5	.500	54	34	60	4.00	0
2010	Dodgers	Arizona	2	$5\frac{2}{3}$	0	0	.000	8	3	3	1.59	0
2010	Albuquerque	P.C.	12	$63\frac{1}{3}$	6	1	.857	57	24	64	4.41	0
2010	Los Angeles-Pittsburgh b	N.L.	15	$71\frac{2}{3}$	4	6	.400	68	29	70	4.02	0
Major League Totals		3 Yrs.	64	$140\frac{2}{3}$	9	11	.450	124	64	135	3.84	0
	Championship Series											
2008	Los Angeles	N.L.	2	$5\frac{1}{3}$	0	0	.000	7	2	3	0.00	0

a Played outfield for Dodgers in the Gulf Coast League.

b Traded to Pittsburgh Pirates with outfielder Andrew Lambo for pitcher Octavio Dotel, July 31, 2010.

MECHE, GILBERT ALLEN (GIL)

Born, Lafayette, Louisiana, September 8, 1978.

Bats Right. Throws Right. Height, 6 feet, 3 inches. Weight, 220 pounds.

Year	Club	Lea	G	IP	W	L	Pct	SO	BB	H	ERA	SAVES
1996	Mariners	Arizona	2	3	0	1	.000	4	1	4	6.00	0
1997	Everett	Northwest	12	$74\frac{2}{3}$	3	4	.429	62	24	75	3.98	0
1997	Wisconsin	Midwest	2	12	0	2	.000	14	4	12	3.00	0
1998	Wisconsin	Midwest	26	149	8	7	.533	168	63	136	3.44	0
1999	New Haven	Eastern	10	59	3	4	.429	56	26	51	3.05	0
1999	Tacoma	P.C.	6	31	2	2	.500	24	13	31	3.19	0
1999	Seattle	A.L.	16	$85\frac{2}{3}$	8	4	.667	47	57	73	4.73	0

Year Club	Lea	G	IP	W	L	Pct	SO	BB	H	ERA	SAVES
2000 Seattle	A.L.	15	85 2/3	4	4	.500	60	40	75	3.78	0
2000 Tacoma	P.C.	3	14	1	1	.500	15	10	10	3.86	0
2000 Wisconsin	Midwest	1	5	0	0	.000	6	2	1	0.00	0
2000 Everett a	Northwest	1	1	0	1	.000	0	0	3	9.00	0
2001 Seattle b	A.L.	INJURED—Did Not Play									
2002 San Antonio	Texas	25	65	4	6	.400	56	32	68	6.51	0
2003 Seattle	A.L.	32	186 1/3	15	13	.536	130	63	187	4.59	0
2004 Tacoma	P.C.	10	57	1	3	.250	45	27	55	5.05	0
2004 Seattle	A.L.	23	127 2/3	7	7	.500	99	47	139	5.01	0
2005 Seattle c	A.L.	29	143 1/3	10	8	.556	83	72	153	5.09	0
2006 Seattle d	A.L.	32	186 2/3	11	8	.579	156	84	183	4.48	0
2007 Kansas City	A.L.	34	216	9	13	.409	156	62	218	3.67	0
2008 Kansas City	A.L.	34	210 1/3	14	11	.560	183	73	204	3.98	0
2009 Omaha	P.C.	2	8 2/3	1	1	.500	4	7	3	3.12	0
2009 Kansas City e	A.L.	23	129	6	10	.375	95	58	144	5.09	0
2010 Northwest	Texas	1	4	0	0	.000	3	3	2	0.00	0
2010 Omaha	P.C.	4	8 2/3	0	1	.000	6	4	10	8.31	0
2010 Kansas City f-g	A.L.	20	61 2/3	0	5	.000	41	38	65	5.69	0
Major League Totals	10 Yrs.	258	1432 1/3	84	83	.503	1050	594	1441	4.49	0

a On disabled list from May 29 to June 12 and July 31 to October 1, 2000.
b On disabled list from March 31 to November 6, 2001.
c On disabled list from August 20 to September 16, 2005.
d Filed for free agency, October 28, 2006. Signed with Kansas City Royals, December 7, 2006.
e On disabled list from July 12 to August 13, 2009.
f On disabled list from March 26 to April 11 and May 29 to September 1, 2010.
g Announced retirement, January 18, 2011.

MEDLEN, KRISTOPHER ALLEN (KRIS)

Born, Artesia, California, October 7, 1985.
Bats Both. Throws Right. Height, 5 feet, 10 inches. Weight, 190 pounds.

Year Club	Lea	G	IP	W	L	Pct	SO	BB	H	ERA	SAVES
2006 Danville	Appal.	20	22	1	0	1.000	36	2	14	0.41	10
2007 Myrtle Beach	Carolina	18	24	2	0	1.000	28	7	22	1.13	2
2007 Rome	So.Atl.	17	20 2/3	0	1	.000	33	3	13	0.87	8
2007 Mississippi	Southern	3	2 1/3	0	0	.000	2	2	4	11.57	1
2008 Mississippi	Southern	36	120 1/3	7	8	.467	120	27	121	3.52	1
2009 Gwinnett	Int.	8	37 2/3	5	0	1.000	44	10	20	1.19	0
2009 Atlanta	N.L.	37	67 2/3	3	5	.375	72	30	65	4.26	0
2010 Atlanta a	N.L.	31	107 2/3	6	2	.750	83	21	108	3.68	0
Major League Totals	2 Yrs.	68	175 1/3	9	7	.563	155	51	173	3.90	0

a On disabled list from August 5 to November 4, 2010.

MEEK, EVAN DAVID

Born, Bellevue, Washington, May 12, 1983.
Bats Right. Throws Right. Height, 6 feet. Weight, 220 pounds.

Year Club	Lea	G	IP	W	L	Pct	SO	BB	H	ERA	SAVES
2003 Elizabethton	Appal.	14	51	7	1	.875	47	24	33	2.47	1
2004 Elizabethton	Appal.	11	21 1/3	1	2	.333	23	25	18	8.44	0
2004 Quad Cities	Midwest	3	5 2/3	0	0	.000	3	15	7	11.12	0
2005 Beloit a	Midwest	13	18	0	1	.000	11	36	15	10.00	0
2006 Lake Elsinore	Calif.	26	119 1/3	6	6	.500	113	62	136	4.98	0
2006 Visalia b	Calif.	2	5	0	1	.000	7	4	6	9.00	0
2007 Montgomery c	Southern	44	67	2	1	.667	69	34	74	4.30	1
2008 Pittsburgh	N.L.	9	13	0	1	.000	7	12	11	6.92	0
2008 Altoona	Eastern	9	16	1	1	.500	17	3	14	2.81	2
2008 Indianapolis	Int.	23	41 1/3	0	0	.000	34	14	30	2.40	2
2009 Indianapolis	Int.	6	8 2/3	0	0	.000	7	7	3	1.04	0
2009 Pittsburgh d	N.L.	41	47	1	1	.500	42	29	34	3.45	0
2010 Pittsburgh	N.L.	70	80	5	4	.556	70	31	53	2.14	4
Major League Totals	3 Yrs.	120	140	6	6	.500	119	72	98	3.02	4

a Released by Minnesota Twins, June 22, 2005. Signed with San Diego Padres organization, September 17, 2005.
b Traded to Tampa Bay Devil Rays with player to be named later for infielder Russell Branyan, August 24, 2006. Tampa Bay Devil Rays received pitcher Dale Thayer to complete trade, September 15, 2006.
c Selected by Pittsburgh Pirates in Rule V draft, December 6, 2007.
d On disabled list from August 12 to November 17, 2009.

MELANCON, MARK DAVID

Born, Wheat Ridge, Colorado, March 28, 1985.
Bats Right. Throws Right. Height, 6 feet, 2 inches. Weight, 215 pounds.

Year	Club	Lea	G	IP	W	L	Pct	SO	BB	H	ERA	SAVES
2006	Staten Island	N.Y.-Penn.	7	7 2/3	0	1	.000	8	2	9	3.52	2
2007	a		INJURED—Did Not Play									
2008	Trenton	Eastern	19	49 2/3	6	0	1.000	47	12	32	1.81	2
2008	Tampa	Fla.St.	13	25 1/3	1	0	1.000	20	6	26	2.84	0
2008	Scranton/WB	Int.	12	20	1	1	.500	22	4	11	2.70	1
2009	Scranton/WB	Int.	32	53	4	0	1.000	54	11	37	2.89	3
2009	New York	A.L.	13	16 1/3	0	1	.000	10	10	13	3.86	0
2010	Round Rock	P.C.	3	4 1/3	1	0	1.000	2	1	5	0.00	1
2010	Scranton/WB	Int.	40	56 1/3	6	1	.857	58	31	63	3.67	6
2010	New York	A.L.	2	4	0	0	.000	3	0	7	9.00	0
2010	Houston b	N.L.	20	17 1/3	2	0	1.000	19	8	12	3.12	0
Major League Totals		2 Yrs.	35	37 2/3	2	1	.667	32	18	32	4.06	0

a On minor league disabled list from April 5 to September 16, 2007.
b Traded to Houston Astros with infielder Jimmy Parades for infielder Lance Berkman and cash, July 31, 2010.

MIJARES, JOSE MANUEL

Born, Caracas, Venezuela, October 29, 1984.
Bats Left. Throws Left. Height, 6 feet. Weight, 230 pounds.

Year	Club	Lea	G	IP	W	L	Pct	SO	BB	H	ERA	SAVES
2004	Twins	Gulf Coast	19	29 2/3	4	0	1.000	25	15	22	2.43	5
2005	Fort Myers	Fla.St.	5	12	0	0	.000	17	5	5	1.50	0
2005	Beloit	Midwest	20	54 1/3	6	3	.667	78	40	43	4.31	2
2006	Fort Myers	Fla.St.	27	63	3	5	.375	77	27	52	3.57	0
2007	New Britain	Eastern	46	61	5	3	.625	75	48	40	3.54	9
2007	Rochester	Int.	5	8 2/3	0	1	.000	6	5	9	6.23	0
2008	Twins	Gulf Coast	7	11	2	1	.667	16	1	10	2.45	0
2008	Fort Myers	Fla.St.	5	10 1/3	0	0	.000	8	3	7	2.61	0
2008	New Britain	Eastern	11	15 1/3	1	1	.500	17	7	16	2.93	2
2008	Minnesota	A.L.	10	10 1/3	0	1	.000	5	0	3	0.87	0
2009	Rochester	Int.	5	6 1/3	1	0	1.000	4	1	2	0.00	1
2009	Minnesota	A.L.	71	61 2/3	2	2	.500	55	23	50	2.34	0
2010	Rochester	Int.	2	1 2/3	0	0	.000	2	1	6	27.00	0
2010	Minnesota a	A.L.	47	32 2/3	1	1	.500	28	9	34	3.31	0
Major League Totals		3 Yrs.	128	104 2/3	3	4	.429	88	32	87	2.49	0
	Division Series											
2009	Minnesota	A.L.	2	0 2/3	0	1	.000	0	1	1	13.50	0
2010	Minnesota	A.L.	3	1 1/3	0	0	.000	0	1	0	0.00	0
Division Series Totals			5	2	0	1	.000	0	2	1	4.50	0

a On disabled list from April 16 to May 14 and August 12 to September 11, 2010.

MILLER, TREVER DOUGLAS

Born, Louisville, Kentucky, May 29, 1973.
Bats Right. Throws Left. Height, 6 feet, 3 inches. Weight, 200 pounds.

Year	Club	Lea	G	IP	W	L	Pct	SO	BB	H	ERA	SAVES
1991	Bristol	Appal.	13	54	2	7	.222	46	29	60	5.67	0
1992	Bristol	Appal.	12	69 1/3	3	8	.273	64	27	75	4.93	0
1993	Fayettevlle	So.Atl.	28	161	8	13	.381	116	67	151	4.19	0
1994	Trenton	Eastern	26	174 1/3	7	16	.304	73	51	198	4.39	0
1995	Jacksnville	Southern	31	122 1/3	8	2	.800	77	34	122	2.72	0
1996	Toledo	Int.	27	165 1/3	13	6	.684	115	65	167	4.90	0
1996	Detroit a	A.L.	5	16 2/3	0	4	.000	8	9	28	9.18	0
1997	New Orleans	A.A.	29	163 2/3	6	7	.462	99	54	177	3.30	0
1998	Houston	N.L.	37	53 1/3	2	0	1.000	30	20	57	3.04	1
1999	Houston	N.L.	47	49 2/3	3	2	.600	37	29	58	5.07	1
2000	Phil.-Los Angeles b-c	N.L.	16	16 1/3	0	0	.000	11	12	27	10.47	0
2000	Albuquerque	P.C.	12	58	4	2	.667	39	20	60	3.41	0
2001	Sarasota	Fla.St.	3	8	0	0	.000	6	1	3	2.25	0
2001	Pawtucket d-e	Int.	33	116	3	11	.214	93	34	142	5.20	0
2002	Louisville f	Int.	65	82	9	5	.643	80	23	76	3.18	0
2003	Toronto g	A.L.	*79	52 2/3	2	2	.500	44	28	46	4.61	4
2004	Tampa Bay	A.L.	60	49	1	1	.500	43	15	48	3.12	1
2005	Tampa Bay h-i	A.L.	61	44 1/3	2	2	.500	35	29	45	4.06	0
2006	Round Rock	P.C.	2	2	0	0	.000	3	0	0	0.00	0
2006	Houston j	N.L.	70	50 2/3	2	3	.400	56	13	42	3.02	1
2007	Houston k	N.L.	76	46 1/3	0	0	.000	46	23	45	4.86	1

Year	Club	Lea	G	IP	W	L	Pct	SO	BB	H	ERA	SAVES
2008	Tampa Bay l	A.L.	68	43⅓	2	0	1.000	44	20	39	4.15	2
2009	St. Louis	N.L.	70	43⅔	4	1	.800	46	11	31	2.06	0
2010	St. Louis	N.L.	57	36	0	1	.000	22	16	30	4.00	0
Major League Totals		12 Yrs.	646	502	18	16	.529	422	225	496	4.20	10
	Division Series											
1998	Houston	N.L.	1	0	0	0	.000	0	1	0	INF	0
1999	Houston	N.L.	2	1⅓	0	0	.000	2	0	1	0.00	0
2008	Tampa Bay	N.L.	1	0	0	0	.000	0	1	0	INF	0
2009	St. Louis	N.L.	2	0⅔	0	0	.000	1	0	0	0.00	0
Division Series Totals			6	2	0	0	.000	3	2	1	0.00	0
	Championship Series											
2008	Tampa Bay	N.L.	3	0⅔	0	0	.000	1	1	1	0.00	0
	World Series Record											
2008	Tampa Bay	N.L.	2	1	0	0	.000	1	1	1	18.00	0

a Traded to Houston Astros with catcher Brad Ausmus, pitcher C.J. Nitkowski, pitcher Jose Lima and infielder Daryle Ward for outfielder Brian Hunter, infielder Orlando Miller, pitcher Todd Jones and pitcher Doug Brocail, December 10, 1996.
b Traded to Philadelphia Phillies for pitcher Yorkis Perez, March 29, 2000.
c Claimed on waivers by Los Angeles Dodgers, May 19, 2000.
d Filed for free agency, October 15, 2000. Signed with Boston Red Sox organization, January 22, 2001.
e Filed for free agency, October 15, 2001. Signed with Cincinnati Reds organization, November 8, 2001.
f Released by Cincinnati Reds, September 4, 2002. Signed with Toronto Blue Jays, November 13, 2002.
g Not offered contract, December 21, 2003. Signed with Tampa Bay Devil Rays, January 6, 2004.
h On disabled list from June 13 to June 28, 2005.
i Not offered contract, December 21, 2005. Signed with Houston Astros, January 9, 2006.
j On disabled list from April 19 to May 12, 2006.
k Filed for free agency, October 29, 2007. Signed with Tampa Bay Rays, February 6, 2008.
l Not offered contract, November 3, 2008. Signed with St. Louis Cardinals, December 3, 2008.

MILLWOOD, KEVIN AUSTIN

Born, Gastonia, North Carolina, December 24, 1974.
Bats Right. Throws Right. Height, 6 feet, 4 inches. Weight, 230 pounds.

Year	Club	Lea	G	IP	W	L	Pct	SO	BB	H	ERA	SAVES
1993	Braves	Gulf Coast	12	50	3	3	.500	49	28	36	3.06	0
1994	Macon	So. Atl.	12	32⅔	0	5	.000	24	32	31	5.79	1
1994	Danville	Appal.	13	46	3	3	.500	56	34	42	3.72	1
1995	Macon	So. Atl.	29	103	5	6	.455	89	57	86	4.63	0
1996	Durham	Carolina	33	149⅓	6	9	.400	139	58	138	4.28	1
1997	Greenville	Southern	11	61⅓	3	5	.375	61	24	59	4.11	0
1997	Richmond	Int.	9	60⅔	7	0	1.000	46	16	38	1.93	0
1997	Atlanta	N.L.	12	51⅓	5	3	.625	42	21	55	4.03	0
1998	Atlanta	N.L.	31	174⅓	17	8	.680	163	56	175	4.08	0
1999	Atlanta	N.L.	33	228	18	7	.720	205	59	168	2.68	0
2000	Atlanta	N.L.	36	212⅔	10	13	.435	168	62	213	4.66	0
2001	Macon	So.Atl.	1	3	0	0	.000	5	0	0	0.00	0
2001	Greenville	Southern	2	10	0	1	.000	10	3	9	4.50	0
2001	Atlanta a	N.L.	21	121	7	7	.500	84	40	121	4.31	0
2002	Atlanta b	N.L.	35	217	18	8	.692	178	65	186	3.24	0
2003	Philadelphia c-d	N.L.	35	222	14	12	.538	169	68	210	4.01	0
2004	Philadelphia e-f	N.L.	25	141	9	6	.600	125	51	155	4.85	0
2005	Cleveland g-h	A.L.	30	192	9	11	.450	146	52	182	*2.86	0
2006	Texas	A.L.	34	215	16	12	.571	157	53	228	4.52	0
2007	Frisco	Texas	1	5	0	0	.000	3	1	1	0.00	0
2007	Texas i	A.L.	31	172⅔	10	14	.417	123	67	213	5.16	0
2008	Frisco	Texas	1	4	0	1	.000	6	2	5	2.25	0
2008	Texas j	A.L.	29	168⅔	9	10	.474	125	49	220	5.07	0
2009	Texas k	A.L.	31	198⅔	13	10	.565	123	71	195	3.67	0
2010	Baltimore l-m	A.L.	31	190⅔	4	*16	.200	132	65	223	5.10	0
Major League Totals		14 Yrs.	414	2505	159	137	.537	1940	779	2544	4.11	0
	Division Series											
1999	Atlanta	N.L.	2	10	1	0	1.000	9	0	1	0.90	1
2000	Atlanta	N.L.	1	4⅔	0	1	.000	3	3	4	7.71	0
2002	Atlanta	N.L.	2	11	1	1	.500	14	0	7	3.27	0
Division Series Totals			5	25⅔	2	2	.500	26	3	12	3.16	1
	Championship Series											
1999	Atlanta	N.L.	2	12⅔	1	0	1.000	9	1	13	3.55	0
2001	Atlanta	N.L.	1	1	0	0	.000	1	0	0	0.00	0
Championship Series Totals			3	13⅔	1	0	1.000	10	1	13	3.29	0

Year	Club	Lea	G	IP	W	L	Pct	SO	BB	H	ERA	SAVES
	World Series											
1999	Atlanta	N.L.	1	2	0	1	.000	2	2	8	18.00	0

a On disabled list from May 7 to July 20, 2001.
b Traded to Philadelphia Phillies for catcher Johnny Estrada, December 20, 2002.
c Pitched no-hit, no-run game against San Francisco Giants, April 27, 2003.
d Filed for free agency, October 29, 2003, re-signed with Philadelphia Phillies, December 19, 2003.
e On disabled list from August 6 to September 12, 2004.
f Filed for free agency, October 28, 2004. Signed with Cleveland Indians, January 7, 2005.
g On disabled list from May 26 to June 16, 2005.
h Filed for free agency, October 28, 2005. Signed with Texas Rangers, December 29, 2005.
i On disabled list from April 29 to May 14 and May 15 to June 1, 2007.
j On disabled list from May 11 to May 28 and July 24 to August 15, 2008.
k Traded to Baltimore Orioles with cash for pitcher Chris Ray and pitcher Ben Snyder, December 9, 2009.
l On disabled list from July 6 to July 22, 2010.
m Filed for free agency, November 1, 2010.

MISCH, PATRICK THEODORE JOSEPH (PAT)

Born, Northbrook, Illinois, August 18, 1981.
Bats Right. Throws Left. Height, 6 feet, 2 inches. Weight, 195 pounds.

Year	Club	Lea	G	IP	W	L	Pct	SO	BB	H	ERA	SAVES
2003	Salem-Keizer	Northwest	14	86⅔	7	5	.583	61	20	78	2.18	0
2004	Norwich	Eastern	26	159	7	6	.538	123	35	138	3.06	0
2005	Norwich	Eastern	9	61⅓	4	2	.667	43	7	63	3.52	0
2005	Fresno	P.C.	19	102	3	9	.250	69	40	135	6.35	0
2006	Connecticut	Eastern	18	103⅔	5	4	.556	79	24	95	2.26	0
2006	Fresno	P.C.	10	65	4	2	.667	57	11	74	4.02	0
2006	San Francisco	N.L.	1	1	0	0	.000	1	0	2	0.00	0
2007	Fresno	P.C.	34	66⅔	2	5	.286	74	19	54	2.30	1
2007	San Francisco	N.L.	18	40⅓	0	4	.000	26	12	47	4.24	0
2008	Fresno	P.C.	20	87	6	5	.545	56	27	101	5.38	0
2008	San Francisco	N.L.	15	52⅓	0	3	.000	38	15	56	5.68	0
2009	Fresno	P.C.	12	27	3	0	1.000	12	4	24	2.00	1
2009	Buffalo	Int.	6	25⅓	1	2	.333	21	4	27	4.26	0
2009	San Francisco-New York a	N.L.	26	62⅓	3	4	.429	23	22	68	4.48	0
2010	Buffalo	Int.	23	150⅔	11	4	.733	99	24	150	3.23	0
2010	New York	N.L.	12	37⅔	0	4	.000	23	4	43	3.82	0
Major League Totals		5 Yrs.	72	193⅔	3	15	.167	111	53	216	4.60	0

a Claimed on waivers by New York Mets, June 3, 2009.

MOEHLER, BRIAN MERRITT

Born, Rockingham, North Carolina, December 31, 1971.
Bats Right. Throws Right. Height, 6 feet, 3 inches. Weight, 235 pounds.

Year	Club	Lea	G	IP	W	L	Pct	SO	BB	H	ERA	SAVES
1993	Niagara Fls	N.Y.-Penn.	12	58⅔	6	5	.545	38	27	51	3.22	0
1994	Lakeland	Fla.St.	26	164⅔	12	12	.500	92	65	153	3.01	0
1995	Jacksnville	Southern	28	162⅓	8	10	.444	89	52	176	4.82	0
1996	Jacksnville	Southern	28	173⅓	15	6	.714	120	50	186	3.48	0
1996	Detroit	A.L.	2	10⅓	0	1	.000	2	8	11	4.35	0
1997	Detroit a	A.L.	31	175⅓	11	12	.478	97	61	198	4.67	0
1998	Detroit	A.L.	33	221⅓	14	13	.519	123	56	220	3.90	0
1999	Detroit	A.L.	32	196⅓	10	*16	.385	106	59	229	5.04	0
2000	Detroit	A.L.	29	178	12	9	.571	103	40	222	4.50	0
2000	West Michigan b	Midwest	1	6⅓	0	1	.000	4	1	5	4.26	0
2001	Detroit	A.L.	1	8	0	0	.000	2	1	6	3.38	0
2001	Toledo c	Int.	2	10⅓	0	2	.000	6	2	12	4.35	0
2002	Lakeland	Fla.St.	2	12⅓	1	1	.500	7	1	10	2.92	0
2002	Toledo	Int.	4	24	2	1	.667	7	3	28	4.88	0
2002	Detroit	A.L.	3	19⅔	1	1	.500	13	2	17	2.29	0
2002	Cincinnati d-e-f	N.L.	10	43⅓	2	4	.333	18	11	61	6.02	0
2003	Houston	N.L.	3	13⅔	0	0	.000	5	6	22	7.90	0
2003	New Orleans g-h	P.C.	1	2	0	0	.000	3	0	3	4.50	0
2004	Greenville i-j	Southern	20	108	3	9	.250	57	27	113	4.17	0
2005	Florida k	N.L.	37	158⅓	6	12	.333	95	42	198	4.55	0
2006	Marlins	Gulf Coast	1	5	0	1	.000	4	0	8	3.60	0
2006	Florida l-m	N.L.	29	122	7	11	.389	58	38	164	6.57	0
2007	Houston n-o	N.L.	42	59⅔	1	4	.200	36	17	67	4.07	1
2008	Houston	N.L.	31	150	11	8	.579	82	36	166	4.56	0
2009	Corpus Christi	Texas	1	5	0	0	.000	2	0	11	14.40	0
2009	Round Rock	P.C.	1	4	0	0	.000	0	3	3	2.25	0

Year	Club	Lea	G	IP	W	L	Pct	SO	BB	H	ERA	SAVES
2009	Houston p	N.L.	29	154⅔	8	12	.400	91	51	187	5.47	0
2010	Round Rock	P.C.	1	3	0	0	.000	1	0	1	0.00	0
2010	Houston q-r	N.L.	20	56⅔	1	4	.200	28	26	66	4.92	0
Major League Totals		14 Yrs.	332	1567⅓	84	107	.440	859	454	1834	4.81	1

a On disabled list from August 7 to August 22, 1997.
b On disabled list from April 17 to May 18, 2000.
c On disabled list from April 6 to November 14, 2001.
d On disabled list from March 22 to July 3, 2002.
e Traded to Cincinnati Reds with infielder Matt Boone for infielder David Espinosa, two players to be named later, July 23, 2002. Detroit Tigers received outfielder Gary Varner to complete trade, August 30, 2002.
f On disabled list from August 28 to September 13, 2002.
g Filed for free agency, October 28, 2002. Signed with Houston Astros, January 17, 2003.
h On disabled list from April 17 to September 29, 2003.
i Filed for free agency, October 27, 2003. Signed with Atlanta Braves organization, February 17, 2004.
j Filed for free agency, October 15, 2004. Signed with Florida Marlins organization, December 14, 2004.
k Filed for free agency, October 27, 2005, re-signed with Florida Marlins, December 7, 2005.
l On disabled list from July 2 to July 30, 2006.
m Filed for free agency, October 28, 2006. Signed with Houston Astros organization, January 19, 2007.
n Filed for free agency, October 29, 2007.
o Signed with Houston Astros organization, January 29, 2008.
p On disabled list from April 14 to May 4, 2009.
q On disabled list from July 8 to November 1, 2010.
r Filed for free agency, November 1, 2010.

MONASTERIOS (HERNANDEZ), CARLOS

Born, Higuerote, Venezuela, March 21, 1986.
Bats Right. Throws Right. Height, 6 feet, 2 inches. Weight, 175 pounds.

Year	Club	Lea	G	IP	W	L	Pct	SO	BB	H	ERA	SAVES
2006	Phillies	Gulf Coast	4	14⅔	0	2	.000	11	3	18	3.68	0
2006	Yankees a	Gulf Coast	7	30⅓	1	2	.333	24	3	23	2.97	0
2007	Lakewood	So.Atl.	26	156	11	11	.500	114	55	155	4.62	0
2008	Clearwater	Fla.St.	17	94⅓	5	8	.385	66	33	109	5.63	0
2009	Reading	Eastern	2	7⅓	0	0	.000	4	2	8	3.68	0
2009	Clearwater b-c	Fla.St.	35	82	5	6	.455	71	27	71	3.73	2
2010	Albuquerque	P.C.	2	6⅔	0	0	.000	5	3	7	5.40	0
2010	Los Angeles d	N.L.	32	88⅓	3	5	.375	52	29	99	4.38	0

a Traded by New York Yankees to Philadelphia Phillies with infielder C.J. Henry, pitcher Matt Smith and catcher Jesus Sanchez for outfielder Bobby Abreu and pitcher Cory Lidle, July 30, 2006.
b Selected by New York Mets in Rule V draft, December 10, 2009.
c Sold to Los Angeles Dodgers, December 10, 2009.
d On disabled list from June 19 to July 7, 2010.
a On disabled list from April 22 to June 12, 2009.

MORROW, BRANDON JOHN

Born, Santa Rosa, California, July 26, 1984.
Bats Right. Throws Right. Height, 6 feet, 3 inches. Weight, 190 pounds.

Year	Club	Lea	G	IP	W	L	Pct	SO	BB	H	ERA	SAVES
2006	Mariners	Arizona	7	13	0	2	.000	13	9	10	2.77	0
2006	Inland Empire	Calif.	1	3	0	0	.000	4	0	0	0.00	0
2007	Seattle	A.L.	60	63⅓	3	4	.429	66	50	56	4.12	0
2008	West Tenn	Southern	6	7⅓	0	0	.000	8	6	3	0.00	0
2008	Tacoma	P.C.	6	23⅓	1	2	.333	26	11	17	5.01	0
2008	Seattle	A.L.	45	64⅔	3	4	.429	75	34	40	3.34	10
2009	Tacoma	P.C.	10	55	5	3	.625	40	23	50	3.60	0
2009	Seattle a-b	A.L.	26	69⅔	2	4	.333	63	44	66	4.39	6
2010	Toronto	A.L.	26	146⅓	10	7	.588	178	66	136	4.49	0
Major League Totals		4 Yrs.	157	344	18	19	.486	382	194	298	4.19	16

a On disabled list from April 24 to May 9, 2009.
b Traded to Toronto Blue Jays for pitcher Brandon League and outfielder Johermyn Chavez, December 23, 2009.

MORTON, CHARLES A. (CHARLIE)

Born, Flemington, New Jersey, October 12, 1983.
Bats Right. Throws Right. Height, 6 feet, 4 inches. Weight, 190 pounds.

Year	Club	Lea	G	IP	W	L	Pct	SO	BB	H	ERA	SAVES
2002	Braves	Gulf Coast	11	39⅔	1	7	.125	32	30	37	4.54	0
2003	Danville	Appal.	14	54	2	5	.286	46	25	65	4.67	0
2004	Rome	So.Atl.	27	116⅔	7	9	.438	102	67	140	4.86	2

Year	Club	Lea	G	IP	W	L	Pct	SO	BB	H	ERA	SAVES
2005	Rome	So.Atl.	26	$124\frac{2}{3}$	5	9	.357	86	62	124	5.20	1
2006	Myrtle Beach	Carolina	30	100	6	7	.462	75	54	116	5.40	2
2007	Mississippi	Southern	41	$79\frac{2}{3}$	4	6	.400	67	37	80	4.29	0
2008	Richmond	Int.	13	79	5	2	.714	72	27	51	2.05	0
2008	Atlanta	N.L.	16	$74\frac{2}{3}$	4	8	.333	48	41	80	6.15	0
2009	Gwinnett	Int.	10	$64\frac{2}{3}$	7	2	.778	55	16	52	2.51	0
2009	Indianapolis	Int.	1	7	0	0	.000	7	1	4	0.00	0
2009	Pittsburgh a-b	N.L.	18	97	5	9	.357	62	40	102	4.55	0
2010	Indianapolis	Int.	14	80	4	4	.500	53	30	83	3.83	0
2010	Pittsburgh c	N.L.	17	$79\frac{2}{3}$	2	12	.143	59	26	112	7.57	0
Major League Totals		3 Yrs.	51	$251\frac{1}{3}$	11	29	.275	169	107	294	5.98	0

a On disabled list from March 27 to April 11, 2009.
b Traded to Pittsburgh Pirates with outfielder Gorkys Hernandez and pitcher Jeff Locke for outfielder Nate McLouth, June 3, 2009.
c On disabled list from May 28 to July 2, 2010.

MOTA, GUILLERMO

Born, San Pedro de Macoris, Dominican Republic, July 25, 1973.
Bats Right. Throws Right. Height, 6 feet, 6 inches. Weight, 210 pounds.

Year	Club	Lea	G	IP	W	L	Pct	SO	BB	H	ERA	SAVES
1997	Cape Fear a-b	So.Atl.	25	126	5	10	.333	112	33	135	4.36	0
1998	Jupiter	Fla.St.	20	41	3	2	.600	27	6	18	0.66	2
1998	Harrisburg	Eastern	12	17	2	0	1.000	19	2	10	1.06	4
1999	Ottawa	Int.	14	19	2	0	1.000	17	5	16	1.89	5
1999	Montreal	N.L.	51	$55\frac{1}{3}$	2	4	.333	27	25	54	2.93	0
2000	Ottawa	Int.	35	63	4	5	.444	35	31	49	2.29	7
2000	Montreal	N.L.	29	30	1	1	.500	24	12	27	6.00	0
2001	Ottawa	Int.	4	4	0	0	.000	4	0	1	2.25	0
2001	Montreal c	N.L.	53	$49\frac{2}{3}$	1	3	.250	31	18	51	5.26	0
2002	Las Vegas	P.C.	20	$36\frac{2}{3}$	1	3	.250	38	8	34	2.95	1
2002	Los Angeles d	N.L.	43	$60\frac{2}{3}$	1	3	.250	49	27	45	4.15	0
2003	Los Angeles	N.L.	76	105	6	3	.667	99	26	78	1.97	1
2004	Los Angeles-Florida e	N.L.	78	$96\frac{2}{3}$	9	8	.529	85	37	75	3.07	4
2005	Jupiter	Fla.St.	2	$2\frac{2}{3}$	0	0	.000	4	0	3	0.00	0
2005	Florida f-g	N.L.	56	67	2	2	.500	60	32	65	4.70	2
2006	Cleveland h	A.L.	34	$37\frac{2}{3}$	1	3	.250	27	19	45	6.21	0
2006	New York i-j	N.L.	18	18	3	0	1.000	19	5	10	1.00	0
2007	New Orleans	P.C.	7	$7\frac{2}{3}$	0	1	.000	7	5	11	7.04	0
2007	New York k	N.L.	52	$59\frac{1}{3}$	2	2	.500	47	18	63	5.76	0
2008	Milwaukee l	N.L.	58	57	5	6	.455	50	28	52	4.11	1
2009	Los Angeles m-n	N.L.	61	$65\frac{1}{3}$	3	4	.429	39	24	53	3.44	0
2010	San Francisco o-p	N.L.	56	54	1	3	.250	38	22	49	4.33	1
Major League Totals		12 Yrs.	665	$755\frac{2}{3}$	37	42	.468	595	293	667	3.92	9
	Division Series											
2006	New York	N.L.	2	4	1	0	1.000	5	0	6	6.75	0
2008	Milwaukee	N.L.	2	$1\frac{2}{3}$	0	0	.000	0	0	2	5.40	0
Division Series Totals			4	$5\frac{2}{3}$	1	0	1.000	5	0	8	6.35	0
	Championship Series											
2006	New York	N.L.	5	$4\frac{1}{3}$	0	0	.000	2	2	4	4.15	0
	World Series Record											
2010	San Francisco	N.L.	2	$2\frac{1}{3}$	0	0	.000	0	2	1	0.00	0

a Played infield, starting in the Dominican Summer League and finishing in the Florida State League, from 1991 to 1996.
b Selected by Montreal Expos from New York Mets in Rule V draft, December 9, 1996.
c On disabled list from July 13 to September 1, 2001.
d Traded to Los Angeles Dodgers with outfielder Wilkin Ruan for pitcher Matt Herges and infielder Jorge Nunez, March 23, 2002.
e Traded to Florida Marlins with catcher Paul LoDuca and outfielder Juan Encarnacion for pitcher Brad Penny, pitcher Bill Murphy and infielder Hee Seop Choi, July 30, 2004.
f On disabled list from May 1 to May 27, 2005.
g Traded to Boston Red Sox with pitcher Josh Beckett and infielder Mike Lowell for infielder Hanley Ramirez, pitcher Anibal Sanchez and pitcher Jesus Delgado, November 24, 2005.
h Traded to Cleveland Indians with infielder Andy Marte and catcher Kelly Shoppach for outfielder Coco Crisp, pitcher David Riske and catcher Josh Bard, January 27, 2006.
i Traded to New York Mets for player to be named later, August 20, 2006.
j Filed for free agency, October 30, 2006, re-signed with New York Mets, December 7, 2006.
k Traded to Milwaukee Brewers for catcher Johnny Estrada, November 20, 2007.
l Filed for free agency, November 3, 2008. Signed with Los Angeles Dodgers, January 14, 2009.
m On disabled list from August 30 to September 14, 2009.

n Filed for free agency, November 6, 2009. Signed with San Francisco Giants organization, February 21, 2010.
o On disabled list from August 23 to September 7, 2010.
p Filed for free agency, November 1, 2010, re-signed with San Francisco Giants organization, December 20, 2010.

MOTTE, JASON LOUIS

Born, Port Huron, Michigan, June 22, 1982.
Bats Right. Throws Right. Height, 6 feet. Weight, 195 pounds.

Year Club	Lea	G	IP	W	L	Pct	SO	BB	H	ERA	SAVES
2006 Quad Cities..........	Midwest	8	12⅔	1	1	.500	13	3	16	4.97	0
2006 State College a....	N.Y.-Penn.	21	26⅓	1	2	.333	25	4	30	3.08	8
2007 Palm Beach	Fla.St.	9	10	1	0	1.000	6	1	7	0.90	3
2007 Springfield............	Texas	44	49	3	3	.500	63	22	36	2.20	8
2008 Memphis	P.C.	63	66⅔	4	3	.571	110	26	64	3.24	9
2008 St. Louis...............	N.L.	12	11	0	0	.000	16	3	5	0.82	1
2009 St. Louis...............	N.L.	69	56⅔	4	4	.500	54	23	57	4.76	0
2010 Memphis	P.C.	2	2⅔	0	0	.000	2	1	2	3.38	0
2010 St. Louis b	N.L.	56	52⅓	4	2	.667	54	18	41	2.24	2
Major League Totals	3 Yrs.	137	120	8	6	.571	124	44	103	3.30	3
Division Series											
2009 St. Louis...............	N.L.	1	1	0	0	.000	0	0	0	0.00	0

a Played catcher 2003-2006.
b On disabled list from August 3 to August 30, 2010.

MOYER, JAMIE

Born, Sellersville, Pennsylvania, November 18, 1962.
Bats Left. Throws Left. Height, 6 feet. Weight, 180 pounds.

Year Club	Lea	G	IP	W	L	Pct	SO	BB	H	ERA	SAVES
1984 Geneva..........	N.Y.-Penn.	14	*104⅔	*9	3	.750	*120	31	59	1.89	0
1985 Winston-Salem	Carolina	12	94	8	2	.800	94	22	82	2.30	0
1985 Pittsfield...........	Eastern	15	96⅔	7	6	.538	51	32	99	3.72	0
1986 Pittsfield...........	Eastern	6	41	3	1	.750	42	16	27	0.88	0
1986 Iowa.................	A.A.	6	42⅓	3	2	.600	25	11	25	2.55	0
1986 Chicago	N.L.	16	87⅓	7	4	.636	45	42	107	5.05	0
1987 Chicago	N.L.	35	201	12	15	.444	147	97	210	5.10	0
1988 Chicago a.............	N.L.	34	202	9	15	.375	121	55	212	3.48	0
1989 Charlotte Rangers	Gulf C.	3	11	1	0	1.000	18	1	8	1.64	0
1989 Tulsa	Texas	2	12⅓	1	1	.500	9	3	16	5.11	0
1989 Texas b..............	A.L.	15	76	4	9	.308	44	33	84	4.86	0
1990 Texas c..............	A.L.	33	102⅓	2	6	.250	58	39	115	4.66	0
1991 Louisville	A.A.	20	125⅔	5	10	.333	69	43	125	3.80	0
1991 St. Louis d-e	N.L.	8	31⅓	0	5	.000	20	16	38	5.74	0
1992 Toledo f	Int.	21	138⅔	10	8	.556	80	37	128	2.86	0
1993 Rochester.............	Int.	8	54	6	0	1.000	41	13	42	1.67	0
1993 Baltimore	A.L.	25	152	12	9	.571	90	38	154	3.43	0
1994 Baltimore.............	A.L.	23	149	5	7	.417	87	38	158	4.77	0
1995 Baltimore g-h.........	A.L.	27	115⅔	8	6	.571	65	30	117	5.21	0
1996 Boston-Seattle i-j-k	A.L.	34	160⅔	13	3	*.813	79	46	177	3.98	0
1997 Tacoma	P.C.	1	5	1	0	1.000	6	0	1	0.00	0
1997 Seattle l	A.L.	30	188⅔	17	5	.773	113	43	187	3.86	0
1998 Seattle	A.L.	34	234⅓	15	9	.625	158	42	234	3.53	0
1999 Seattle	A.L.	32	228	14	8	.636	137	48	235	3.87	0
2000 Seattle m	A.L.	26	154	13	10	.565	98	53	173	5.49	0
2001 Seattle	A.L.	33	209⅔	20	6	.769	119	44	187	3.43	0
2002 Seattle n.............	A.L.	34	230⅔	13	8	.619	147	50	198	3.32	0
2003 Seattle	A.L.	33	215	21	7	.750	129	66	199	3.27	0
2004 Seattle	A.L.	34	202	7	13	.350	125	63	217	5.21	0
2005 Seattle o.............	A.L.	32	200	13	7	.650	102	52	225	4.28	0
2006 Seattle	A.L.	25	160	6	12	.333	82	44	179	4.39	0
2006 Philadelphia p	N.L.	8	51⅓	5	2	.714	26	7	49	4.03	0
2007 Philadelphia..........	N.L.	33	199⅓	14	12	.538	133	66	222	5.01	0
2008 Philadelphia q	N.L.	33	196⅓	16	7	.696	123	62	199	3.71	0
2009 Philadelphia...........	N.L.	30	162	12	10	.545	94	43	177	4.94	0
2010 Philadelphia r-s	N.L.	19	111⅔	9	9	.500	63	20	103	4.84	0
Major League Totals	24 Yrs.	686	4020⅓	267	204	.567	2405	1137	4156	4.24	0
Divisional Series											
1997 Seattle	A.L.	1	4⅔	0	1	.000	2	1	5	5.79	0
2001 Seattle	A.L.	2	12	2	0	1.000	10	2	8	1.50	0
2007 Philadelphia..........	N.L.	1	6	0	0	.000	2	2	5	1.50	0
2008 Philadelphia..........	N.L.	1	4	0	1	.000	3	3	4	4.50	0
Division Series Totals		5	26⅔	2	2	.500	17	8	22	2.70	0

Year	Club	Lea	G	IP	W	L	Pct	SO	BB	H	ERA	SAVES
	Championship Series											
2001	Seattle	A.L.	1	7	1	0	1.000	5	1	4	2.57	0
2008	Philadelphia	N.L.	1	1 1/3	0	1	.000	2	0	6	40.50	0
Championship Series Totals			2	8 1/3	1	1	.500	7	1	10	8.64	0
	World Series Record											
2008	Philadelphia	N.L.	1	6 1/3	0	0	.000	5	1	5	4.26	0

a Traded to Texas Rangers with outfielder Rafael Palmeiro and pitcher Drew Hall for infielders Curtis Wilkerson and Luis Benitez, pitchers Mitch Williams, Paul Kilgus and Steve Wilson, and outfielder Pablo Delgado, December 5, 1988.
b On disabled list from May 31 to September 1, 1989.
c Released, November 13, 1990. Signed with St. Louis Cardinals organization, January 10, 1991.
d Became free agent, October 15, 1991. Signed with Chicago Cubs organization, January 8, 1992.
e Released by Chicago Cubs, March 30, 1992. Signed with Detroit Tigers organization, March 30, 1992.
f Became free agent, October 15, 1992. Signed with Baltimore Orioles organization, December 19, 1992.
g Filed for free agency, November 12, 1995.
h Signed with Boston Red Sox, January 2, 1996.
i Traded to Seattle Mariners for outfielder Darren Bragg, July 30, 1996.
j Filed for free agency, October 29, 1996.
k Re-signed with Seattle Mariners, November 20, 1996.
l On disabled list from April 1 to April 29, 1997.
m On disabled list from April 15 to June 1, 2000.
n Filed for free agency, October 28, 2002, re-signed with Seattle Mariners, December 7, 2002.
o Filed for free agency, November 7, 2005, re-signed with Seattle Mariners, December 7, 2005.
p Traded to Philadelphia Phillies for pitcher Andrew Baldwin and pitcher Andrew Barb, August 19, 2006.
q Filed for free agency, November 6, 2008, re-signed with Philadelphia Phillies, December 15, 2008.
r On disabled list from July 21 to October 28, 2010.
s Filed for free agency, October 28, 2010.

MOYLAN, PETER MICHAEL

Born, Attadale, Western Australia,Australia, December 2, 1978.
Bats Right. Throws Right. Height, 6 feet, 2 inches. Weight, 200 pounds.

Year	Club	Lea	G	IP	W	L	Pct	SO	BB	H	ERA	SAVES
1996	Twins	Gulf Coast	13	28 2/3	1	1	.500	16	9	34	4.08	1
1997	Twins	Gulf Coast	12	40	4	2	.667	40	10	46	4.05	0
2006	Richmond	Int.	35	56 2/3	1	7	.125	54	38	61	6.35	1
2006	Atlanta	N.L.	15	15	0	0	.000	14	5	18	4.80	0
2007	Richmond a	Int.	2	2	0	0	.000	3	1	0	0.00	1
2007	Atlanta	N.L.	80	90	5	3	.625	63	31	65	1.80	1
2008	Atlanta b	N.L.	7	5 2/3	0	1	.000	5	1	5	1.59	1
2009	Atlanta	N.L.	87	73	6	2	.750	61	35	65	2.84	0
2010	Atlanta	N.L.	85	63 2/3	6	2	.750	52	37	53	2.97	1
Major League Totals		5 Yrs.	274	247 1/3	17	8	.680	195	109	206	2.58	3
	Division Series											
2010	Atlanta	N.L.	4	1	0	0	.000	1	0	1	0.00	0

a Released by Minnesota Twins, April 1, 1998. Joined the Australian World Baseball team in 2006. Signed with Atlanta Braves organization, March 10, 2006.
b On disabled list from April 12 to November 3, 2008.

MUJICA, EDWARD JOSE

Born, Valencia, Venezuela, May 10, 1984.
Bats Right. Throws Right. Height, 6 feet, 2 inches. Weight, 215 pounds.

Year	Club	Lea	G	IP	W	L	Pct	SO	BB	H	ERA	SAVES
2003	Burlington	Appal.	14	55 2/3	2	6	.250	41	20	57	4.37	0
2004	Lake County	So.Atl.	26	124	7	7	.500	89	32	130	4.65	2
2005	Kinston	Carolina	25	26	1	0	1.000	32	2	17	2.08	14
2005	Akron	Eastern	27	34 1/3	2	1	.667	33	5	36	2.88	10
2006	Akron	Eastern	12	19	1	0	1.000	17	9	11	0.00	8
2006	Buffalo	Int.	22	32 2/3	3	1	.750	29	5	31	2.48	5
2006	Cleveland	A.L.	10	18 1/3	0	1	.000	12	0	25	2.95	0
2007	Buffalo	Int.	34	37 2/3	2	1	.667	44	9	35	5.02	14
2007	Cleveland	A.L.	10	13	0	0	.000	7	2	19	8.31	0
2008	Buffalo	Int.	18	26	0	2	.000	27	10	29	4.15	4
2008	Cleveland	A.L.	33	38 2/3	3	2	.600	27	10	46	6.75	0
2009	San Diego a	N.L.	67	93 2/3	3	5	.375	76	19	101	3.94	2
2010	San Diego b	N.L.	59	69 2/3	2	1	.667	72	6	59	3.62	0
Major League Totals		5 Yrs.	179	233 1/3	8	9	.471	194	37	250	4.47	2

a Sold to San Diego Padres, April 1, 2009.
b Traded to Florida Marlins with pitcher Ryan Webb for outfielder Cameron Maybin, November 13, 2010.

MYERS, BRETT ALLEN

Born, Jacksonville, Florida, August 17, 1980.
Bats Right. Throws Right. Height, 6 feet, 4 inches. Weight, 240 pounds.

Year Club	Lea	G	IP	W	L	Pct	SO	BB	H	ERA	SAVES
1999 Phillies	Gulf Coast	7	27	2	1	.667	30	7	17	2.33	0
2000 Piedmont	So.Atl.	27	$175\frac{1}{3}$	13	7	.650	140	69	165	3.18	0
2001 Reading	Eastern	26	156	13	4	.765	130	43	156	3.87	0
2002 Scranton-WB	Int.	19	128	9	6	.600	97	20	121	3.59	0
2002 Philadelphia	N.L.	12	72	4	5	.444	34	29	73	4.25	0
2003 Philadelphia	N.L.	32	193	14	9	.609	143	76	205	4.43	0
2004 Philadelphia	N.L.	32	176	11	11	.500	116	62	196	5.52	0
2005 Philadelphia	N.L.	34	$215\frac{1}{3}$	13	8	.619	208	68	193	3.72	0
2006 Philadelphia	N.L.	31	198	12	7	.632	189	63	194	3.91	0
2007 Clearwater	Fla.St.	3	$3\frac{1}{3}$	0	0	.000	4	1	2	0.00	0
2007 Philadelphia a	N.L.	51	$68\frac{2}{3}$	5	7	.417	83	27	61	4.33	21
2008 Clearwater	Fla.St.	1	$6\frac{2}{3}$	0	1	.000	6	1	7	2.70	0
2008 Reading	Eastern	1	8	0	1	.000	10	2	5	2.25	0
2008 Lehigh	Int.	2	$12\frac{1}{3}$	1	1	.500	12	4	12	3.65	0
2008 Philadelphia	N.L.	30	190	10	13	.435	163	65	197	4.55	0
2009 Lakewood	So.Atl.	1	1	0	0	.000	1	1	0	0.00	0
2009 Clearwater	Fla.St.	1	1	0	0	.000	3	0	2	0.00	0
2009 Reading	Eastern	2	4	0	1	.000	7	1	2	2.25	0
2009 Lehigh Valley	Int.	2	2	0	0	.000	3	0	0	0.00	1
2009 Philadelphia b-c	N.L.	18	$70\frac{2}{3}$	4	3	.571	50	23	74	4.84	0
2010 Houston	N.L.	33	$223\frac{2}{3}$	14	8	.636	180	66	212	3.14	0
Major League Totals	9 Yrs.	273	$1407\frac{1}{3}$	87	71	.551	1166	479	1405	4.20	21
Division Series											
2007 Philadelphia	N.L.	2	$1\frac{1}{3}$	0	0	.000	3	0	2	0.00	0
2008 Philadelphia	N.L.	1	7	1	0	1.000	4	3	2	2.57	0
2009 Philadelphia	N.L.	1	$0\frac{2}{3}$	0	0	.000	0	2	0	0.00	0
Division Series Totals		4	9	1	0	1.000	7	5	4	2.00	0
Championship Series											
2008 Philadelphia	N.L.	1	5	1	0	1.000	6	4	6	9.00	0
World Series Record											
2008 Philadelphia	N.L.	1	7	0	1	.000	2	3	7	3.86	0
2009 Philadelphia	N.L.	1	1	0	0	.000	2	0	1	9.00	0
World Series Totals		2	8	0	1	.000	4	3	8	4.50	0

a On disabled list from May 24 to July 27, 2007.
b On disabled list from May 28 to September 4, 2009.
c Filed for free agency, November 6, 2009. Signed with Houston Astros, January 9, 2010.

NARVESON, CHRISTOPHER GREGG (CHRIS)

Born, Englewood, Colorado, December 20, 1981.
Bats Left. Throws Left. Height, 6 feet, 3 inches. Weight, 205 pounds.

Year Club	Lea	G	IP	W	L	Pct	SO	BB	H	ERA	SAVES
2000 Johnson City	Appal.	12	55	2	4	.333	63	25	57	3.27	0
2001 Potomac	Carolina	11	$66\frac{2}{3}$	4	3	.571	53	13	52	2.57	0
2001 Peoria	Midwest	8	50	3	3	.500	53	11	32	1.98	0
2002 Johnson City	Appal.	6	$18\frac{1}{3}$	0	2	.000	16	6	23	4.91	0
2002 Peoria	Midwest	9	$42\frac{1}{3}$	2	1	.667	36	8	49	4.46	0
2003 Palm Beach	Fla.St.	15	$91\frac{1}{3}$	7	7	.500	65	19	83	2.86	0
2003 Tennessee	Southern	10	57	4	3	.571	34	26	56	3.00	0
2004 Tennessee	Southern	23	$127\frac{2}{3}$	5	10	.333	121	51	114	4.16	0
2004 Tulsa a	Texas	4	20	0	3	.000	14	13	16	3.15	0
2005 Pawtucket	Int.	21	$111\frac{1}{3}$	4	5	.444	66	46	109	4.77	0
2005 Memphis b-c	P.C.	2	$6\frac{2}{3}$	0	1	.000	8	7	11	12.15	0
2006 Palm Beach	Fla.St.	3	17	0	0	.000	13	1	9	2.12	0
2006 Memphis	P.C.	15	80	8	5	.615	58	33	70	2.81	0
2006 St. Louis	N.L.	5	$9\frac{1}{3}$	0	0	.000	12	5	6	4.82	0
2007 Palm Beach	Fla.St.	3	10	0	0	.000	6	3	10	2.70	0
2007 Memphis d	P.C.	9	$45\frac{2}{3}$	3	2	.600	35	21	41	5.72	0
2008 Nashville	P.C.	28	136	6	13	.316	125	57	140	5.43	0
2009 Nashville	P.C.	26	$75\frac{1}{3}$	4	4	.500	76	26	59	3.70	5
2009 Milwaukee	N.L.	21	47	2	0	1.000	46	16	45	3.83	0
2010 Milwaukee	N.L.	37	$167\frac{2}{3}$	12	9	.571	137	59	172	4.99	0
Major League Totals	3 Yrs.	63	224	14	9	.609	195	80	223	4.74	0

a Sent by St. Louis Cardinals to Colorado Rockies as player to be named later for outfielder Larry Walker, August 11, 2004.

b Traded to Boston Red Sox with catcher Charles Johnson and cash for pitcher Byung-Hyun Kim, March 30, 2005.
c Claimed on waivers by St. Louis Cardinals, August 9, 2005.
d Filed for free agency, October 29, 2007. Signed with Milwaukee Brewers organization, December 4, 2007.

NATHAN, JOSEPH MICHAEL (JOE)

Born, Houston, Texas, November 22, 1974.
Bats Right. Throws Right. Height, 6 feet, 4 inches. Weight, 220 pounds.

Year	Club	Lea	G	IP	W	L	Pct	SO	BB	H	ERA	SAVES
1995	San Francisco a	N.L.					Did Not Pitch					
1996							Did Not Play					
1997	Salem-Keizer	Northwest	18	62	2	1	.667	44	26	53	2.47	2
1998	Shreveport	Texas	4	15⅓	1	3	.250	10	9	20	8.80	0
1998	San Jose	California	22	122	8	6	.571	118	48	100	3.32	0
1999	Shreveport	Texas	2	8⅔	0	1	.000	7	7	5	3.12	0
1999	San Francisco	N.L.	19	90⅓	7	4	.636	54	46	84	4.18	1
1999	Fresno	P.C.	13	74⅔	6	4	.600	82	36	68	4.46	0
2000	San Francisco	N.L.	20	93⅓	5	2	.714	61	63	89	5.21	0
2000	San Jose	California	1	5	0	1	.000	2	1	4	3.60	0
2000	Bakersfield	California	1	5⅓	1	0	1.000	6	7	2	5.06	0
2000	Fresno b	P.C.	3	14⅓	0	2	.000	9	7	15	4.40	0
2001	Fresno	P.C.	10	46⅓	0	5	.000	21	33	63	7.77	0
2001	Shreveport	Texas	21	62⅓	3	6	.333	33	37	73	6.93	0
2002	Fresno	P.C.	31	146⅓	6	12	.333	117	74	167	5.60	0
2002	San Francisco	N.L.	4	3⅔	0	0	.000	2	0	1	0.00	0
2003	San Francisco c	N.L.	78	79	12	4	.750	83	33	51	2.96	0
2004	Minnesota	A.L.	73	72⅓	1	2	.333	89	23	48	1.62	44
2005	Minnesota	A.L.	69	70	7	4	.636	94	22	46	2.70	43
2006	Minnesota	A.L.	64	68⅓	7	0	1.000	95	16	38	1.58	36
2007	Minnesota	A.L.	68	71⅔	4	2	.667	77	19	54	1.88	37
2008	Minnesota	A.L.	68	67⅔	1	2	.333	74	18	43	1.33	39
2009	Minnesota	A.L.	70	68⅔	2	2	.500	89	22	42	2.10	47
2010	Minnesota d	A.L.					INJURED—Did Not Play					
Major League Totals		10 Yrs.	533	685	46	22	.676	718	262	496	2.75	247
	Division Series											
2003	San Francisco	N.L.	2	0⅓	0	1	.000	1	1	4	81.00	0
2004	Minnesota	A.L.	3	5	0	1	.000	6	5	2	3.60	1
2006	Minnesota	A.L.	1	0⅔	0	0	.000	1	0	1	0.00	0
2009	Minnesota	A.L.	2	2	0	0	.000	2	1	5	9.00	0
Division Series Totals			8	8	0	2	.000	10	7	12	7.88	1

a Played shortstop in 1995.
b On disabled list from May 13 to June 5 and July 14 to August 18, 2000.
c Traded to Minnesota Twins with pitcher Boof Bonser and pitcher Francisco Liriano for catcher A.J. Pierzynski, November 14, 2003.
d On disabled list from March 26 to November 3, 2010.

NIEMANN, JEFFREY WARREN (JEFF)

Born, Houston, Texas, February 28, 1983.
Bats Right. Throws Right. Height, 6 feet, 9 inches. Weight, 260 pounds.

Year	Club	Lea	G	IP	W	L	Pct	SO	BB	H	ERA	SAVES
2005	Visalia	Calif.	5	20⅓	0	1	.000	28	10	12	3.98	0
2005	Montgomery	Southern	6	10⅓	0	1	.000	14	5	7	4.35	0
2006	Montgomery	Southern	14	77⅓	5	5	.500	84	29	56	2.68	0
2007	Durham	Int.	25	131	12	6	.667	123	46	144	3.98	0
2008	Durham	Int.	24	133	9	5	.643	128	50	101	3.59	0
2008	Tampa Bay	A.L.	5	16	2	2	.500	14	8	18	5.06	0
2009	Tampa Bay	A.L.	31	180⅔	13	6	.684	125	59	185	3.94	0
2010	Tampa Bay a	A.L.	30	174⅓	12	8	.600	131	61	159	4.39	0
Major League Totals		3 Yrs.	66	371	27	16	.628	270	128	362	4.20	0
	Division Series											
2010	Tampa Bay	N.L.	1	3	0	0	.000	4	1	1	0.00	0

a On disabled list from August 4 to August 25, 2010.

NIESE, JONATHON JOSEPH

Born, Lima, Ohio, October 27, 1986.
Bats Left. Throws Left. Height, 6 feet, 4 inches. Weight, 215 pounds.

Year	Club	Lea	G	IP	W	L	Pct	SO	BB	H	ERA	SAVES
2005	Mets	Gulf Coast	7	24⅔	1	0	1.000	24	10	23	3.65	0
2006	St. Lucie	Fla.St.	2	10	0	2	.000	10	5	8	4.50	0
2006	Hagerstown	So.Atl.	25	123⅔	11	9	.550	132	62	121	3.93	0

Year	Club	Lea	G	IP	W	L	Pct	SO	BB	H	ERA	SAVES
2007	St. Lucie	Fla.St.	27	$134\frac{1}{3}$	11	7	.611	110	31	151	4.29	0
2008	Binghamton	Eastern	22	$124\frac{1}{3}$	6	7	.462	112	44	118	3.04	0
2008	New Orleans	P.C.	7	$39\frac{2}{3}$	5	1	.833	32	14	34	3.40	0
2008	New York	N.L.	3	14	1	1	.500	11	8	20	7.07	0
2009	Buffalo	Int.	16	$94\frac{1}{3}$	5	6	.455	82	26	95	3.82	0
2009	New York a	N.L.	5	$25\frac{2}{3}$	1	1	.500	18	9	27	4.21	0
2010	Buffalo	Int.	1	6	0	0	.000	3	0	8	3.00	0
2010	New York b	N.L.	30	$173\frac{2}{3}$	9	10	.474	148	62	192	4.20	0
Major League Totals		3 Yrs.	38	$213\frac{1}{3}$	11	12	.478	177	79	239	4.39	0

a On disabled list from August 6 to November 12, 2009.
b On disabled list from May 17 to June 5, 2010.

NIPPERT, DUSTIN DAVID

Born, Wheeling, West Virginia, May 6, 1981.
Bats Right. Throws Right. Height, 6 feet, 7 inches. Weight, 225 pounds.

Year	Club	Lea	G	IP	W	L	Pct	SO	BB	H	ERA	SAVES
2002	Missoula	Pioneer	17	$54\frac{2}{3}$	4	2	.667	77	9	42	1.65	0
2003	South Bend	Midwest	17	$95\frac{2}{3}$	6	4	.600	96	32	66	2.82	0
2004	El Paso	Texas	14	$71\frac{2}{3}$	2	5	.286	73	40	77	3.64	0
2005	Tennessee	Southern	18	$117\frac{1}{3}$	8	3	.727	97	42	95	2.38	0
2005	Arizona	N.L.	3	$14\frac{2}{3}$	1	0	1.000	11	13	10	5.52	0
2006	Arizona	N.L.	2	10	0	2	.000	9	7	15	11.70	0
2006	Tucson	P.C.	25	$140\frac{1}{3}$	13	8	.619	130	52	161	4.87	0
2007	Tucson	P.C.	10	36	0	3	.000	46	23	23	4.75	0
2007	Arizona	N.L.	36	$45\frac{1}{3}$	1	1	.500	38	16	48	5.56	0
2008	Oklahoma	P.C.	12	$63\frac{1}{3}$	6	2	.750	43	16	65	3.98	0
2008	Texas a-b	A.L.	20	$71\frac{2}{3}$	3	5	.375	55	37	92	6.40	0
2009	Frisco	Texas	4	$12\frac{2}{3}$	0	1	.000	8	6	8	2.84	0
2009	Okla.	P.C.	1	5	1	0	1.000	6	2	2	1.80	0
2009	Texas c	A.L.	20	$69\frac{2}{3}$	5	3	.625	54	29	64	3.88	0
2010	Frisco	Texas	2	$3\frac{1}{3}$	0	0	.000	7	1	1	0.00	0
2010	Oklahoma	P.C.	1	3	0	0	.000	3	0	1	0.00	0
2010	Texas d-e	A.L.	38	$56\frac{2}{3}$	4	5	.444	47	34	61	4.29	0
Major League Totals		6 Yrs.	119	268	14	16	.467	214	136	290	5.31	0
	Division Series											
2010	Texas	A.L.	1	1	0	0	.000	0	0	2	18.00	0
	Championship Series											
2007	Arizona	N.L.	2	$2\frac{1}{3}$	0	0	.000	2	0	1	0.00	0

a Traded to Texas Rangers for pitcher Jose Marte, March 28, 2008.
b On disabled list from April 22 to May 30, 2008.
c On disabled list from March 27 to July 7, 2009.
d On disabled list from July 20 to September 3, 2010.
e Not offered contract, December 2, 2010.

NOLASCO, CARLOS ENRIQUE (RICKY)

Born, Corona, California, December 13, 1982.
Bats Right. Throws Right. Height, 6 feet, 2 inches. Weight, 220 pounds.

Year	Club	Lea	G	IP	W	L	Pct	SO	BB	H	ERA	SAVES
2001	Cubs	Arizona	5	18	1	0	1.000	23	5	11	1.50	0
2002	Boise	Northwest	15	$90\frac{2}{3}$	7	2	.778	92	25	72	2.48	0
2003	Daytona	Fla.St.	26	149	11	5	.688	136	48	129	2.96	0
2004	Iowa	P.C.	9	$40\frac{2}{3}$	2	3	.400	28	16	68	9.30	0
2004	West Tenn	Southern	19	107	6	4	.600	115	37	104	3.70	0
2005	West Tenn a	Southern	27	$161\frac{2}{3}$	14	3	.824	173	46	151	2.89	0
2006	Florida	N.L.	35	140	11	11	.500	99	41	157	4.82	0
2007	Florida	N.L.	5	$21\frac{1}{3}$	1	2	.333	11	9	26	5.48	0
2007	Marlins	Gulf Coast	2	$3\frac{1}{3}$	0	0	.000	8	0	4	2.70	0
2007	Jupiter	Fla.St.	5	12	1	1	.500	9	1	10	0.75	0
2007	Carolina	Southern	1	3	0	1	.000	2	1	2	6.00	0
2007	Albuquerque b	P.C.	4	$15\frac{1}{3}$	0	2	.000	15	4	29	14.09	0
2008	Florida	N.L.	34	$212\frac{1}{3}$	15	8	.652	186	42	192	3.52	0
2009	New Orleans	P.C.	2	15	1	1	.500	12	3	12	2.40	0
2009	Florida	N.L.	31	185	13	9	.591	195	44	188	5.06	0
2010	Florida c	N.L.	26	$157\frac{2}{3}$	14	9	.609	147	33	169	4.51	0
Major League Totals		5 Yrs.	131	$716\frac{1}{3}$	54	39	.581	638	169	732	4.45	0

a Traded by Chicago Cubs to Florida Marlins with pitcher Sergio Mitre and pitcher Renyel Pinto for outfielder Juan Pierre, December 7, 2005.
b On disabled list from April 7 to May 1 and May 18 to August 20, 2007.
c On disabled list from September 1 to November 5, 2010.

NORRIS, DAVID STEFAN (BUD)

Born, Greenbrae, California, March 2, 1985.
Bats Right. Throws Right. Height, 6 feet. Weight, 225 pounds.

Year	Club	Lea	G	IP	W	L	Pct	SO	BB	H	ERA	SAVES
2006	Tri-City	N.Y.-Penn.	15	38	2	0	1.000	46	13	28	3.79	2
2007	Salem	Carolina	1	6	1	0	1.000	2	1	4	1.50	0
2007	Lexington	So.Atl.	22	$96\frac{2}{3}$	2	8	.200	117	41	85	4.75	0
2008	Corpus Christi	Texas	19	80	3	8	.273	84	31	89	4.05	0
2009	Round Rock	P.C.	19	120	4	9	.308	112	53	104	2.63	0
2009	Houston	N.L.	11	$55\frac{2}{3}$	6	3	.667	54	25	59	4.53	0
2010	Round Rock	P.C.	3	$14\frac{2}{3}$	1	0	1.000	14	6	16	3.07	0
2010	Houston a	N.L.	27	$153\frac{2}{3}$	9	10	.474	158	77	151	4.92	0
Major League Totals		2 Yrs.	38	$209\frac{1}{3}$	15	13	.536	212	102	210	4.82	0

a On disabled list from May 24 to June 27, 2010.

NUNEZ (MORALES), LEONEL (LEO)

Born, Jamao Norte, Dominican Republic, August 14, 1983.
Bats Right. Throws Right. Height, 6 feet, 1 inch. Weight, 165 pounds.

Year	Club	Lea	G	IP	W	L	Pct	SO	BB	H	ERA	SAVES
2001	Pirates	Gulf Coast	10	$53\frac{1}{3}$	2	2	.500	34	9	62	4.39	0
2002	Pirates	Gulf Coast	11	$60\frac{1}{3}$	4	2	.667	52	5	54	3.43	0
2002	Hickory	So.Atl.	1	4	0	0	.000	1	3	5	0.00	0
2003	Williamsport	N.Y.-Penn.	8	$38\frac{1}{3}$	4	3	.571	41	12	31	3.05	0
2003	Hickory	So.Atl.	13	$48\frac{1}{3}$	2	1	.667	37	14	59	5.59	0
2004	Hickory a	So.Atl.	27	144	10	4	.714	140	46	121	3.13	1
2005	High Desert	Calif.	8	13	0	0	.000	15	3	23	9.00	0
2005	Wichita	Texas	12	13	1	0	1.000	14	2	8	0.69	4
2005	Kansas City	A.L.	41	$53\frac{2}{3}$	3	2	.600	32	18	73	7.55	0
2006	Wichita	Texas	15	21	1	2	.333	22	12	18	4.29	3
2006	Kansas City	A.L.	7	$13\frac{1}{3}$	0	0	.000	7	5	15	4.72	0
2006	Omaha	P.C.	23	38	2	2	.500	33	13	37	2.13	5
2007	Wichita	Texas	6	$20\frac{2}{3}$	1	0	1.000	13	6	10	0.87	0
2007	Omaha	P.C.	5	23	1	2	.333	19	4	16	2.74	0
2007	Kansas City b	A.L.	13	$43\frac{2}{3}$	2	4	.333	37	10	44	3.92	0
2008	NW Arkansas	Texas	1	2	0	0	.000	2	0	0	0.00	0
2008	Omaha	P.C.	4	4	0	0	.000	3	1	7	6.75	0
2008	Kansas City c-d	A.L.	45	$48\frac{1}{3}$	4	1	.800	26	15	45	2.98	0
2009	Florida	N.L.	75	$68\frac{2}{3}$	4	6	.400	60	27	59	4.06	26
2010	Florida	N.L.	68	65	4	3	.571	71	21	62	3.46	30
Major League Totals		6 Yrs.	249	$292\frac{2}{3}$	17	16	.515	233	96	298	4.40	56

a Traded to Kansas City Royals by Pittsburgh Pirates for catcher Benito Santiago, December 16, 2004.
b On disabled list from April 1 to June 10, 2007.
c On disabled list from May 28 to July 21, 2008.
d Traded to Florida Marlins for infielder Mike Jacobs, October 30, 2008.

O'DAY, DARREN CHRISTOPHER

Born, Jacksonville, Florida, October 22, 1982.
Bats Right. Throws Right. Height, 6 feet, 4 inches. Weight, 225 pounds.

Year	Club	Lea	G	IP	W	L	Pct	SO	BB	H	ERA	SAVES
2006	Cedar Rapids	Midwest	17	$23\frac{1}{3}$	3	1	.750	14	2	20	2.70	1
2006	Orem	Pioneer	14	$14\frac{1}{3}$	0	1	.000	15	5	11	2.51	7
2007	Rancho Cucamonga	Calif.	24	24	4	0	1.000	26	6	10	0.75	11
2007	Arkansas	Texas	29	$29\frac{1}{3}$	3	4	.429	22	14	27	3.99	10
2008	Salt Lake	P.C.	21	33	2	2	.500	30	7	29	3.27	7
2008	Los Angeles a	A.L.	30	$43\frac{1}{3}$	0	1	.000	29	14	49	4.57	0
2009	New York	N.L.	4	3	0	0	.000	2	1	5	0.00	0
2009	Texas b	A.L.	64	$55\frac{2}{3}$	2	1	.667	54	17	36	1.94	2
2010	Texas	A.L.	72	62	6	2	.750	45	12	43	2.03	0
Major League Totals		3 Yrs.	170	164	8	4	.667	130	44	133	2.63	2
	Division Series											
2010	Texas	A.L.	4	2	0	0	.000	4	0	2	0.00	0
	Championship Series											
2010	Texas	A.L.	3	$0\frac{2}{3}$	0	1	.000	1	1	1	13.50	0
	World Series Record											
2010	Texas	A.L.	4	2	0	0	.000	3	0	3	13.50	0

a Selected by New York Mets in Rule V draft, December 11, 2008.
b Claimed on waivers by Texas Rangers, April 22, 2009.

O'FLAHERTY, ERIC GEORGE

Born, Walla Walla, Washington, February 5, 1985.
Bats Left. Throws Left. Height, 6 feet, 2 inches. Weight, 220 pounds.

Year	Club	Lea	G	IP	W	L	Pct	SO	BB	H	ERA	SAVES
2003	Mariners	Arizona	13	27 2/3	3	0	1.000	20	7	17	1.95	0
2003	Everett	Northwest	3	10 2/3	1	0	1.000	7	3	8	3.38	0
2004	Wisconsin	Midwest	12	57 1/3	3	3	.500	38	23	83	6.12	0
2005	Wisconsin	Midwest	45	69 2/3	4	4	.500	51	30	73	3.75	13
2006	Inland Empire	Calif.	16	28 2/3	0	1	.000	33	6	31	3.45	1
2006	San Antonio	Texas	25	39 1/3	2	2	.500	36	15	45	1.14	7
2006	Tacoma	P.C.	2	3 2/3	1	0	1.000	4	1	3	0.00	0
2006	Seattle	A.L.	15	11	0	0	.000	6	6	18	4.09	0
2007	Tacoma	P.C.	6	8	0	0	.000	8	4	5	1.13	3
2007	Seattle	A.L.	56	52 1/3	7	1	.875	36	20	45	4.47	0
2008	Seattle	A.L.	7	6 2/3	0	1	.000	4	4	16	20.25	0
2008	West Tenn	Southern	1	2	0	0	.000	2	0	1	0.00	0
2008	Tacoma a	P.C.	14	16 1/3	1	0	1.000	19	9	23	4.96	2
2009	Atlanta	N.L.	78	56 1/3	2	1	.667	39	18	52	3.04	0
2010	Gwinnett	Int.	3	4	0	0	.000	5	1	1	0.00	0
2010	Atlanta b	N.L.	56	44	3	2	.600	36	18	37	2.45	0
Major League Totals		5 Yrs.	212	170 1/3	12	5	.706	121	66	168	4.07	0

a Claimed on waivers by Atlanta Braves, November 20, 2008.
b On disabled list from July 10 to August 20, 2010.

OGANDO, ALEXI

Born, San Pedro de Macoris, Dominican Republic, October 5, 1983.
Bats Right. Throws Right. Height, 6 feet, 4 inches. Weight, 185 pounds.

Year	Club	Lea	G	IP	W	L	Pct	SO	BB	H	ERA	SAVES
2010	Texas a-b-c	A.L.	44	41 2/3	4	1	.800	39	16	31	1.30	0
	Division Series											
2010	Texas	A.L.	1	0 1/3	0	0	.000	0	0	1	0.00	0
	Championship Series											
2010	Texas	A.L.	2	2	0	0	.000	2	1	3	4.50	0
	World Series Record											
2010	Texas	A.L.	2	3 2/3	0	0	.000	6	0	1	0.00	0

a Played as an outfielder in the Arizona and Northern Leagues in 2003-2004.
b Confined to the Dominican Republic with visa problems 2005-2009.
c Selected by Texas Rangers from Oakland Athletics in Rule V draft. December 8, 2005.

OHLENDORF, CURTIS ROSS (ROSS)

Born, Austin, Texas, August 8, 1982.
Bats Right. Throws Right. Height, 6 feet, 4 inches. Weight, 235 pounds.

Year	Club	Lea	G	IP	W	L	Pct	SO	BB	H	ERA	SAVES
2004	Yakima	Northwest	7	29	2	3	.400	28	19	22	2.79	0
2005	South Bend	Midwest	27	157	11	10	.524	144	48	181	4.53	0
2006	Tucson	P.C.	1	5	0	0	.000	4	0	6	1.80	0
2006	Tennessee	Southern	27	177 2/3	10	8	.556	125	29	180	3.29	0
2007	Yankees	Gulf Coast	4	16	1	1	.500	17	1	13	3.94	0
2007	Scranton-WB	Int.	21	66 1/3	3	3	.500	48	24	86	5.02	0
2007	New York a	A.L.	6	6 1/3	0	0	.000	9	2	5	2.84	0
2008	Indianapolis	Int.	7	46 2/3	4	3	.571	40	8	46	3.47	0
2008	Scranton-WB	Int.	5	22 1/3	1	1	.500	25	5	28	4.03	0
2008	New York	A.L.	25	40	1	1	.500	36	19	50	6.52	0
2008	Pittsburgh b	N.L.	5	22 2/3	0	3	.000	13	12	36	6.35	0
2009	Pittsburgh	N.L.	29	176 2/3	11	10	.524	109	53	165	3.92	0
2010	Altoona	Eastern	1	4	0	0	.000	6	1	3	0.00	0
2010	Pittsburgh c	N.L.	21	108 1/3	1	11	.083	79	44	106	4.07	0
Major League Totals		4 Yrs.	86	354	13	25	.342	246	130	362	4.40	0
	Division Series											
2007	New York	A.L.	1	1	0	0	.000	0	1	4	27.00	0

a Traded by Arizona Diamondbacks to New York Yankees with pitcher Steven Jackson, pitcher Luis Vizcaino and infielder Alberto Gonzalez for pitcher Randy Johnson and cash, January 9, 2007.
b Traded to Pittsburgh Pirates with outfielder Jose Tabata, pitcher Jeff Karstens and pitcher Dan McCutchen for outfielder Xavier Nady and pitcher Damaso Marte, July 26, 2008.
c On disabled list from April 12 to May 10 and August 24 to November 3, 2010.

OHMAN, WILLIAM MC DANIEL (WILL)

Born, Frankfurt, West Germany, August 13, 1977.
Bats Left. Throws Left. Height, 6 feet, 2 inches. Weight, 190 pounds.

Year Club	Lea	G	IP	W	L	Pct	SO	BB	H	ERA	SAVES
1998 Williamsprt.	N.Y.-Penn.	10	39	4	4	.500	35	13	39	6.46	0
1998 Rockford	Midwest	4	24 1/3	1	1	.500	21	7	25	4.44	0
1999 Daytona	Fla.St.	31	106 2/3	4	7	.364	97	41	102	3.46	5
2000 West Tenn	Southern	59	71 1/3	6	4	.600	85	36	53	1.89	3
2000 Chicago	N.L.	6	3 1/3	1	0	1.000	2	4	4	8.10	0
2001 Iowa	P.C.	40	51	5	2	.714	66	18	51	4.06	4
2001 Chicago	N.L.	11	11 2/3	0	1	.000	12	6	14	7.71	0
2002 Chicago a	N.L.			INJURED—Did Not Play							
2003 Chicago b	N.L.			INJURED—Did Not Play							
2004 Iowa c	P.C.	45	52 1/3	3	3	.500	75	29	53	4.30	0
2005 Iowa	P.C.	8	8 2/3	1	0	1.000	12	2	4	4.15	1
2005 Chicago	N.L.	69	43 1/3	2	2	.500	45	24	32	2.91	0
2006 Chicago	N.L.	78	65 1/3	1	1	.500	74	34	51	4.13	0
2007 Iowa	P.C.	9	6 2/3	0	0	.000	9	5	7	2.70	0
2007 Chicago d	N.L.	56	36 1/3	2	4	.333	33	16	42	4.95	1
2008 Atlanta	N.L.	83	58 2/3	4	1	.800	53	22	51	3.68	1
2009 Los Angeles	N.L.	21	12 1/3	1	0	1.000	7	8	12	5.84	1
2009 Inland Empire	Calif.	3	2 2/3	0	0	.000	2	1	5	13.50	0
2009 Albuquerque e-f-g	P.C.	8	7 2/3	0	0	.000	9	3	3	1.17	0
2010 Baltimore	A.L.	51	30	0	0	.000	29	18	30	3.30	0
2010 Florida h-i-j	N.L.	17	12	0	2	.000	14	5	10	3.00	0
Major League Totals	8 Yrs.	392	273	11	11	.500	269	137	246	4.09	3

a On disabled list from March 15 to October 9, 2002.
b On disabled list from March 28 to September 29, 2003.
c Released by Chicago Cubs, October 20, 2003, re-signed with Chicago Cubs organization, February 11, 2004.
d Traded to Atlanta Braves with infielder Omar Infante for pitcher Jose Ascanio, December 4, 2007.
e Filed for free agency, October 30, 2008. Signed with Los Angeles Dodgers, March 30, 2009.
f On disabled list from May 28 to November 9, 2009.
g Filed for free agency, November 9, 2009.
h Signed with Baltimore Orioles organization, February 9, 2010.
i Traded to Florida Marlins for pitcher Rick Vanden Hurk, July 31, 2010.
j Filed for free agency, November 1, 2010. Signed with Chicago White Sox, January 10, 2011

OKAJIMA, HIDEKI

Born, Kyoto, Japan, December 25, 1975.
Bats Left. Throws Left. Height, 6 feet, 1 inch. Weight, 195 pounds.

Year Club	Lea	G	IP	W	L	Pct	SO	BB	H	ERA	SAVES
1995 Yomiuri	Japan Cent.	1	5	0	0	.000	9	2	5	1.80	0
1996 Yomiuri	Japan Cent.	5	12 2/3	1	0	1.000	8	9	13	0.71	0
1997 Yomiuri	Japan Cent.	25	109 1/3	4	9	.308	102	59	92	3.46	0
1998 Yomiuri	Japan Cent.	14	62 1/3	3	6	.333	54	32	61	4.33	0
1999 Yomiuri	Japan Cent.	37	69 2/3	4	1	.800	77	28	42	2.97	0
2000 Yomiuri	Japan Cent.	56	72 1/3	5	4	.556	102	31	53	3.11	7
2001 Yomiuri	Japan Cent.	58	62	2	1	.667	70	39	62	2.76	25
2002 Yomiuri	Japan Cent.	52	55 2/3	6	3	.667	58	33	42	3.40	0
2003 Yomiuri	Japan Cent.	41	38 2/3	2	3	.400	29	20	45	4.89	0
2004 Yomiuri	Japan Cent.	53	46 2/3	4	3	.571	53	20	33	3.09	5
2005 Yomiuri	Japan Cent.	42	53	1	0	1.000	56	19	55	4.75	0
2006 Hokkaido a	Japan Pac.	55	54 2/3	2	2	.500	63	14	46	2.14	4
2007 Boston	A.L.	66	69	3	2	.600	63	17	50	2.22	5
2008 Boston	A.L.	64	62	3	2	.600	60	23	49	2.61	1
2009 Boston	A.L.	68	61	6	0	1.000	53	21	56	3.39	0
2010 Pawtucket	Int.	3	2 1/3	0	0	.000	0	0	6	19.29	0
2010 Boston b-c	A.L.	56	46	4	4	.500	33	20	59	4.50	0
Major League Totals	4 Yrs.	254	238	16	8	.667	209	81	214	3.06	6
Division Series											
2007 Boston	A.L.	2	2 1/3	0	0	.000	2	1	1	0.00	0
2008 Boston	A.L.	3	2 2/3	0	0	.000	0	1	3	6.75	0
2009 Boston	A.L.	1	0 1/3	0	0	.000	0	0	0	0.00	0
Division Series Totals		6	5 1/3	0	0	.000	2	2	4	3.38	0
Championship Series											
2007 Boston	A.L.	3	5	0	0	.000	3	2	4	0.00	0
2008 Boston	A.L.	5	7 1/3	0	0	.000	5	1	1	0.00	0
Championship Series Totals		8	12 1/3	0	0	.000	8	3	5	0.00	0

Year	Club	Lea	G	IP	W	L	Pct	SO	BB	H	ERA	SAVES
	World Series Record											
2007	Boston	A.L.	3	$3\frac{2}{3}$	0	0	.000	6	0	4	7.36	0

a Signed with Boston Red Sox, November 30, 2006.
b On disabled list from August 6 to August 28, 2010.
c Not offered contract, December 2, 2010. re-signed with Boston Red Sox, January 10, 2011.

OLIVER, DARREN CHRISTOPHER

Born, Rio Linda, California, October 6, 1970.
Bats Right. Throws Left. Height, 6 feet, 2 inches. Weight, 200 pounds.

Year	Club	Lea	G	IP	W	L	Pct	SO	BB	H	ERA	SAVES
1988	Rangers	Gulf Coast	12	$54\frac{1}{3}$	5	1	.833	59	18	39	2.15	0
1989	Gastonia	So.Atl.	24	$122\frac{1}{3}$	8	7	.533	108	82	86	3.16	0
1990	Rangers	Gulf Coast	3	6	0	0	.000	7	1	1	0.00	0
1990	Gastonia	So.Atl.	1	2	0	0	.000	2	4	1	13.50	0
1991	Charlotte	Fla.St.	2	8	0	1	.000	12	3	6	4.50	0
1992	Charlotte	Fla.St.	8	25	1	0	1.000	33	10	11	0.72	2
1992	Tulsa	Texas	3	$14\frac{1}{3}$	0	1	.000	14	4	15	3.14	0
1993	Tulsa	Texas	46	$73\frac{1}{3}$	7	5	.583	77	41	51	1.96	6
1993	Texas	A.L.	2	$3\frac{1}{3}$	0	0	.000	4	1	2	2.70	0
1994	Okla City	A.A.	6	$7\frac{1}{3}$	0	0	.000	6	3	1	0.00	0
1994	Texas	A.L.	43	50	4	0	1.000	50	35	40	3.42	2
1995	Texas	A.L.	17	49	4	2	.667	39	32	47	4.22	0
1996	Charlotte	Fla.St.	2	12	0	1	.000	9	3	8	3.00	0
1996	Texas	A.L.	30	$173\frac{2}{3}$	14	6	.700	112	76	190	4.66	0
1997	Texas	A.L.	32	$201\frac{1}{3}$	13	12	.520	104	82	213	4.20	0
1998	Oklahoma	P.C.	1	5	0	0	.000	1	1	2	0.00	0
1998	Texas a	A.L.	19	$103\frac{1}{3}$	6	7	.462	58	43	140	6.53	0
1998	St. Louis b-c	N.L.	10	57	4	4	.500	29	23	64	4.26	0
1999	St. Louis	N.L.	30	$196\frac{1}{3}$	9	9	.500	119	74	197	4.26	0
2000	Texas	A.L.	21	108	2	9	.182	49	42	151	7.42	0
2000	Oklahoma	P.C.	7	32	2	1	.667	28	14	22	1.97	0
2000	Tulsa d-e	Texas	1	$4\frac{2}{3}$	0	1	.000	5	2	10	11.57	0
2001	Texas	A.L.	28	154	11	11	.500	104	65	189	6.02	0
2001	Oklahoma	P.C.	1	3	0	0	.000	3	0	3	0.00	0
2001	Tulsa f-g	Texas	1	5	0	1	.000	5	2	4	5.40	0
2002	Memphis	P.C.	5	16	0	2	.000	9	17	17	7.87	0
2002	Boston h	A.L.	14	58	4	5	.444	32	27	70	4.66	0
2003	Colorado i	N.L.	33	$180\frac{1}{3}$	13	11	.542	88	61	201	5.04	0
2004	Florida-Houston j-k-l	N.L.	27	$72\frac{2}{3}$	3	3	.500	46	21	87	5.94	0
2005	Iowa	P.C.	3	$13\frac{1}{3}$	0	3	.000	10	5	28	13.50	0
2005	Tucson m-n-o-p	P.C.	4	$18\frac{1}{3}$	1	0	1.000	8	3	33	6.38	0
2006	New York q	N.L.	45	81	4	1	.800	60	21	70	3.44	0
2007	Los Angeles	A.L.	61	$64\frac{1}{3}$	3	1	.750	51	23	58	3.78	0
2008	Los Angeles r	A.L.	54	72	7	1	.875	48	16	67	2.88	0
2009	Los Angeles s-t	A.L.	63	73	5	1	.833	65	22	61	2.71	0
2010	Texas	A.L.	64	$61\frac{2}{3}$	1	2	.333	65	15	53	2.48	1
Major League Totals		17 Yrs.	593	1759	107	85	.557	1123	679	1900	4.67	3
	Division Series											
1996	Texas	A.L.	1	8	0	1	.000	3	2	6	3.38	0
2006	New York	N.L.	1	$1\frac{1}{3}$	0	0	.000	0	0	3	20.25	0
2007	Los Angeles	A.L.	1	$0\frac{2}{3}$	0	0	.000	0	0	2	27.00	0
2008	Los Angeles	A.L.	2	$1\frac{1}{3}$	0	0	.000	1	1	0	0.00	0
2009	Los Angeles	A.L.	3	$2\frac{1}{3}$	1	0	1.000	2	0	1	0.00	0
2010	Texas	A.L.	3	$4\frac{1}{3}$	0	1	.000	5	1	3	4.15	0
Division Series Totals			11	18	1	2	.333	11	4	15	5.00	0
	Championship Series											
2006	New York	N.L.	1	6	0	0	.000	3	1	3	0.00	0
2009	Los Angeles	A.L.	5	$6\frac{1}{3}$	0	0	.000	6	4	6	4.26	0
2010	Texas	A.L.	3	$2\frac{1}{3}$	0	0	.000	1	3	1	7.71	1
Championship Series Totals			9	$14\frac{2}{3}$	0	0	.000	10	8	10	3.07	1
	World Series Record											
2010	Texas	A.L.	2	$2\frac{2}{3}$	0	0	.000	4	0	3	3.38	0

a On disabled list from June 11 to June 26, 1998.
b Traded to St. Louis Cardinals with infielder Fernando Tatis and player to be named later for infielder Royce Clayton and pitcher Todd Stottlemyre, July 31, 1998.
c St. Louis Cardinals received infielder Mark Little to complete trade, August 9, 1998.
d Filed for free agency, October 29, 1999. Signed with Texas Rangers, January 27, 2000.
e On disabled list from June 17 to July 19 and July 31 to August 31, 2000.
f On disabled list from May 8 to June 6, 2001.

g Traded to Boston Red Sox for outfielder Carl Everett, December 12, 2001.
h Released by Boston Red Sox, July 2, 2002. Signed with St. Louis Cardinals organization, July 20, 2002.
i Released by St. Louis Cardinals, August 13, 2002. Signed with Colorado Rockies organization, January 29, 2003.
j Filed for free agency, October 26, 2003. Signed with Florida Marlins, January 28, 2004.
k Sold to Houston Astros, July 22, 2004.
l On disabled list from August 6 to September 6, 2004.
m Filed for free agency, November 8, 2004. Signed with Colorado Rockies organization, January 22, 2005.
n Released by Colorado Rockies, March 31, 2005. Signed with Arizona Diamondbacks organization, April 12, 2005.
o Released by Arizona Diamondbacks, May 3, 2005. Signed with Chicago Cubs organization, May 7, 2005.
p Released by Chicago Cubs, May 20, 2005. Signed with New York Mets organization, December 16, 2005.
q Filed for free agency, October 31, 2006. Signed with Los Angeles Angels, December 11, 2006.
r Filed for free agency, October 31, 2008, re-signed with Los Angeles Angels, January 17, 2009.
s On disabled list from April 19 to May 4, 2009.
t Filed for free agency, November 5, 2009. Signed with Texas Rangers, December 22, 2009.

OLSEN, SCOTT MATTHEW

Born, Kalamazoo, Michigan, January 12, 1984.
Bats Left. Throws Left. Height, 6 feet, 4 inches. Weight, 215 pounds.

Year	Club	Lea	G	IP	W	L	Pct	SO	BB	H	ERA	SAVES
2002	Marlins	Gulf Coast	13	$51^{2}/_{3}$	2	3	.400	50	17	39	2.96	0
2003	Greensboro	So.Atl.	25	$128^{1}/_{3}$	7	9	.438	129	59	101	2.81	0
2004	Jupiter	Fla.St.	25	$136^{1}/_{3}$	7	6	.538	158	53	127	2.97	0
2005	Carolina	Southern	14	$80^{1}/_{3}$	6	4	.600	94	27	75	3.92	0
2005	Florida	N.L.	5	$20^{1}/_{3}$	1	1	.500	21	10	21	3.98	0
2006	Albuquerque	P.C.	1	$6^{1}/_{3}$	0	0	.000	5	3	5	0.00	0
2006	Florida	N.L.	31	$180^{2}/_{3}$	12	10	.545	166	75	160	4.04	0
2007	Florida	N.L.	33	$176^{2}/_{3}$	10	15	.400	133	85	226	5.81	0
2008	Florida a	N.L.	33	$201^{2}/_{3}$	8	11	.421	113	69	195	4.20	0
2009	Potomac	Carolina	1	3	0	0	.000	4	0	3	0.00	0
2009	Syracuse	Int.	3	$12^{2}/_{3}$	1	0	1.000	9	6	19	5.68	0
2009	Washington b-c	N.L.	11	$62^{2}/_{3}$	2	4	.333	42	25	83	6.03	0
2010	Nationals	Gulf Coast	2	5	0	0	.000	3	1	3	1.80	0
2010	Hagerstown	So.Atl.	1	4	0	0	.000	4	0	2	2.25	0
2010	Potomac	Carolina	1	5	0	0	.000	4	0	6	5.40	0
2010	Syracuse	Int.	1	$6^{1}/_{3}$	0	0	.000	4	1	8	5.68	0
2010	Washington d-e	N.L.	17	81	4	8	.333	53	27	93	5.56	0
Major League Totals		6 Yrs.	130	723	37	49	.430	528	291	778	4.85	0

a Traded to Washington Nationals with outfielder Josh Willingham for infielder Emilio Bonifacio, pitcher P.J. Dean and infielder Jake Smolinski, November 11, 2008.
b On disabled list from May 17 to June 29 and July 11 to November 8, 2009.
c Not offered contract, December 12, 2009, re-signed with Washington Nationals, December 14, 2009.
d On disabled list from May 22 to July 29, 2010.
e Waived by Washington Nationals, November 6, 2010. Signed with Pittsburgh Pirates, December 10, 2010.

ONDRUSEK, LOGAN JARED

Born, Hallettsville, Texas, February 13, 1985.
Bats Right. Throws Right. Height, 6 feet, 8 inches. Weight, 225 pounds.

Year	Club	Lea	G	IP	W	L	Pct	SO	BB	H	ERA	SAVES
2005	Billings	Pioneer	15	$55^{1}/_{3}$	1	6	.143	46	19	72	6.02	0
2006	Dayton	Midwest	27	$52^{2}/_{3}$	4	5	.444	47	19	48	3.42	0
2006	Billings	Pioneer	1	1	0	1	.000	3	1	4	27.00	0
2006	Chattanooga	Southern	1	4	0	0	.000	7	3	0	0.00	0
2007	Sarasota	Fla.St.	31	124	7	10	.412	86	48	131	4.43	1
2008	Sarasota	Fla.St.	40	$79^{2}/_{3}$	1	7	.125	58	32	93	4.97	1
2008	Louisville	Int.	1	$1^{1}/_{3}$	0	0	.000	1	2	1	0.00	0
2009	Sarasota	Fla.St.	13	$18^{2}/_{3}$	2	0	1.000	12	7	7	0.96	0
2009	Louisville	Int.	19	$20^{2}/_{3}$	0	0	.000	11	2	16	1.74	12
2009	Carolina	Southern	24	$32^{2}/_{3}$	2	1	.667	24	12	21	1.65	7
2010	Louisville	Int.	14	$19^{2}/_{3}$	0	1	.000	14	3	21	4.12	1
2010	Cincinnati	N.L.	60	$58^{2}/_{3}$	5	0	1.000	39	20	49	3.68	0
	Division Series											
2010	Cincinnati	N.L.	2	2	0	0	.000	0	1	0	0.00	0

O'SULLIVAN, SEAN DANIEL

Born, San Diego, California, September 1, 1987.
Bats Right. Throws Right. Height, 6 feet, 2 inches. Weight, 230 pounds.

Year	Club	Lea	G	IP	W	L	Pct	SO	BB	H	ERA	SAVES
2006	Orem	Pioneer	14	$71^{1}/_{3}$	4	0	1.000	55	7	65	2.14	0
2007	Cedar Rapids	Midwest	25	$158^{1}/_{3}$	10	7	.588	125	40	136	2.22	0

Year	Club	Lea	G	IP	W	L	Pct	SO	BB	H	ERA	SAVES
2008	Rancho Cucamonga	Calif.	28	158	16	8	.667	111	50	167	4.73	0
2009	Arkansas	Texas	3	$18^{2}/_{3}$	1	2	.333	14	0	21	5.30	0
2009	Salt Lake	P.C.	14	69	6	4	.600	48	20	74	5.48	0
2009	Los Angeles	A.L.	12	$51^{2}/_{3}$	4	2	.667	29	16	60	5.92	0
2010	Salt Lake	P.C.	15	85	5	5	.500	58	31	95	4.76	0
2010	Los Angeles-Kansas City a	A.L.	19	$83^{2}/_{3}$	4	6	.400	43	31	90	5.49	0
Major League Totals		2 Yrs.	31	$135^{1}/_{3}$	8	8	.500	72	47	150	5.65	0

a Traded to Kansas City Royals with pitcher Will Smith for infielder Alberto Callaspo, July 22, 2010.

OSWALT, ROY EDWARD

Born, Kosciusko, Mississippi, August 29, 1977.
Bats Right. Throws Right. Height, 6 feet. Weight, 185 pounds.

Year	Club	Lea	G	IP	W	L	Pct	SO	BB	H	ERA	SAVES
1997	Astros	Gulf Coast	5	$28^{1}/_{3}$	1	1	.500	28	7	25	0.64	0
1997	Auburn	N.Y.-Penn.	9	$51^{2}/_{3}$	2	4	.333	44	15	50	4.53	0
1998	Astros	Gulf Coast	4	16	1	1	.500	27	1	10	2.25	0
1998	Auburn	N.Y.-Penn.	11	$70^{1}/_{3}$	4	5	.444	67	31	49	2.18	0
1999	Michigan	Midwest	22	$151^{1}/_{3}$	13	4	.765	143	54	144	4.46	0
2000	Kissimmee	Fla.St.	8	$45^{1}/_{3}$	4	3	.571	47	11	52	2.98	0
2000	Round Rock	Texas	19	$129^{2}/_{3}$	11	4	.733	141	22	106	1.94	2
2001	New Orleans	P.C.	5	31	2	3	.400	34	6	32	4.35	0
2001	Houston	N.L.	28	$141^{2}/_{3}$	14	3	.824	144	24	126	2.73	0
2002	Houston	N.L.	35	233	19	9	.679	208	62	215	3.01	0
2003	New Orleans	P.C.	1	3	0	0	.000	2	0	3	3.00	0
2003	Houston a	N.L.	21	$127^{1}/_{3}$	10	5	.667	108	29	116	2.97	0
2004	Houston	N.L.	36	237	*20	10	.667	206	62	233	3.49	0
2005	Houston	N.L.	35	$241^{2}/_{3}$	20	12	.625	184	48	243	2.94	0
2006	Houston b	N.L.	33	$220^{2}/_{3}$	15	8	.652	166	38	220	*2.98	0
2007	Houston	N.L.	33	212	14	7	.667	154	60	221	3.18	0
2008	Houston c	N.L.	32	$208^{2}/_{3}$	17	10	.630	165	47	199	3.54	0
2009	Houston d	N.L.	30	$181^{1}/_{3}$	8	6	.571	138	42	183	4.12	0
2010	Houston-Philadelphia e	N.L.	33	$211^{2}/_{3}$	13	13	.500	193	55	162	2.76	0
Major League Totals		10 Yrs.	316	2015	150	83	.644	1666	467	1918	3.18	0
	Division Series											
2004	Houston	N.L.	2	$11^{1}/_{3}$	1	0	1.000	8	4	15	2.38	0
2005	Houston	N.L.	1	$7^{1}/_{3}$	1	0	1.000	7	2	6	3.68	0
2010	Philadelphia	N.L.	1	5	0	0	.000	5	1	5	5.40	0
Division Series Totals			4	$23^{2}/_{3}$	2	0	1.000	20	7	26	3.42	0
	Championship Series											
2004	Houston	N.L.	2	8	0	0	.000	2	4	11	6.75	0
2005	Houston	N.L.	2	14	2	0	1.000	12	4	8	1.29	0
2010	Philadelphia	N.L.	3	$14^{2}/_{3}$	1	1	.500	14	3	14	1.84	0
Championship Series Totals			7	$36^{2}/_{3}$	3	1	.750	28	11	33	2.70	0
	World Series Record											
2005	Houston	N.L.	1	6	0	0	.000	3	5	8	7.50	0

a On disabled list from May 16 to May 31 and June 19 to July 7 and July 30 to September 8, 2003.
b On disabled list from May 30 to June 14, 2006.
c On disabled list from July 12 to July 28, 2008.
d On disabled list from September 16 to October 13, 2009.
e Traded to Philadelphia Phillies with cash for pitcher J.A.Happ, outfielder Anthony Gose and infielder Jonathan Villar, July 29, 2010.

PADILLA, VICENTE DE LA CRUZ

Born, Chinandega, Nicaragua, September 27, 1977.
Bats Right. Throws Right. Height, 6 feet, 2 inches. Weight, 220 pounds.

Year	Club	Lea	G	IP	W	L	Pct	SO	BB	H	ERA	SAVES
1999	High Desert	California	9	$50^{2}/_{3}$	4	1	.800	55	17	50	3.73	0
1999	Tucson	P.C.	18	$93^{2}/_{3}$	7	4	.636	58	24	107	3.75	0
1999	Arizona	N.L.	5	$2^{2}/_{3}$	0	1	.000	0	3	7	16.88	0
2000	Tucson	P.C.	12	$18^{1}/_{3}$	0	1	.000	22	8	22	4.42	1
2000	Arizona-Philadelphia a	N.L.	55	$65^{1}/_{3}$	4	7	.364	51	28	72	3.72	2
2001	Scranton-WB	Int.	16	$81^{2}/_{3}$	7	0	1.000	75	11	64	2.42	0
2001	Philadelphia b	N.L.	23	34	3	1	.750	29	12	36	4.24	0
2002	Philadelphia	N.L.	32	206	14	11	.560	128	53	198	3.28	0
2003	Philadelphia	N.L.	32	$208^{2}/_{3}$	14	12	.538	133	62	196	3.62	0
2004	Clearwater	Fla.St.	1	2	0	1	.000	1	1	3	9.00	0
2004	Scranton/WB	Int.	2	$4^{2}/_{3}$	0	0	.000	6	5	6	13.50	0

Year	Club	Lea	G	IP	W	L	Pct	SO	BB	H	ERA	SAVES
2004	Philadelphia c	N.L.	20	$115\frac{1}{3}$	7	7	.500	82	36	119	4.53	0
2005	Clearwater	Fla.St.	1	5	0	1	.000	3	1	4	1.80	0
2005	Scranton/WB	Int.	1	5	1	0	1.000	4	2	6	3.60	0
2005	Philadelphia d-e	N.L.	27	147	9	12	.429	103	74	146	4.71	0
2006	Texas f	A.L.	33	200	15	10	.600	156	70	206	4.50	0
2007	Frisco	Texas	6	12	0	1	.000	12	9	14	8.25	0
2007	Texas g	A.L.	23	$120\frac{1}{3}$	6	10	.375	71	50	146	5.76	0
2008	Texas h	A.L.	29	171	14	8	.636	127	65	185	4.74	0
2009	Albuquerque	P.C.	1	5	1	0	1.000	5	3	3	3.60	0
2009	Texas	A.L.	18	108	8	6	.571	59	42	120	4.92	0
2009	Los Angeles i-j-k	N.L.	8	$39\frac{1}{3}$	4	0	1.000	38	12	36	3.20	0
2010	Inland Empire	Calif.	3	$10\frac{2}{3}$	0	0	.000	10	1	6	0.84	0
2010	Albuquerque	P.C.	1	$5\frac{2}{3}$	0	1	.000	5	0	8	6.35	0
2010	Los Angeles l-m	N.L.	16	95	6	5	.545	84	24	79	4.07	0
Major League Totals		12 Yrs.	321	$1512\frac{2}{3}$	104	90	.536	1061	531	1546	4.31	2
	Division Series											
2009	Los Angeles	N.L.	1	7	1	0	1.000	4	1	4	0.00	0
	Championship Series											
2009	Los Angeles	N.L.	2	$10\frac{1}{3}$	0	1	.000	9	3	8	6.10	0

a Traded to Philadelphia Phillies with infielder Travis Lee, pitcher Omar Daal and pitcher Nelson Figueroa for pitcher Curt Schilling, July 26, 2000.
b On disabled list from May 4 to May 30, 2001.
c On disabled list from May 30 to August 10, 2004.
d On disabled list from March 25 to April 19, 2005.
e Traded to Texas Rangers for player to be named later, December 12, 2005. Philadelphia Phillies received pitcher Ricardo Rodriguez to complete trade, December 19, 2005.
f Filed for free agency, October 30, 2006, re-signed with Texas Rangers, December 9, 2006.
g On disabled list from June 22 to August 15, 2007.
h On disabled list from July 5 to July 20 and August 25 to September 9, 2008.
i On disabled list from May 17 to June 2, 2009.
j Released by Texas Rangers, August 17, 2009. Signed with Los Angeles Dodgers organization, August 19, 2009.
k Filed for free agency, November 6, 2009, Re-signed with Los Angeles Dodgers, January 21, 2010.
l On disabled list from April 23 to June 19 and August 16 to September 3, 2010.
m Filed for free agency, November 1, 2010, re-signed with Los Angeles Dodgers, December 9, 2010.

PALMER, JONATHAN MATT (MATT)

Born, Memphis, Tennessee, March 21, 1979.
Bats Right. Throws Right. Height, 6 feet, 2 inches. Weight, 225 pounds.

Year	Club	Lea	G	IP	W	L	Pct	SO	BB	H	ERA	SAVES
2002	Salem-Keizer	Northwest	16	$53\frac{2}{3}$	3	2	.600	49	23	44	1.84	0
2003	Norwich	Eastern	5	$6\frac{2}{3}$	0	0	.000	5	5	12	13.50	0
2003	Hagerstown	So.Atl.	44	$52\frac{1}{3}$	5	0	1.000	56	15	21	1.20	25
2004	Norwich	Eastern	42	$79\frac{1}{3}$	4	7	.364	81	51	66	3.06	8
2005	Norwich	Eastern	11	27	0	1	.000	20	9	22	2.67	1
2006	Connecticut	Eastern	15	$62\frac{1}{3}$	5	3	.625	51	10	50	1.30	0
2006	Fresno	P.C.	15	91	6	4	.600	64	30	91	4.05	0
2007	Connecticut	Eastern	1	5	0	0	.000	3	2	8	10.80	0
2007	Fresno	P.C.	29	150	11	8	.579	98	51	155	4.32	0
2008	San Francisco	N.L.	3	$12\frac{2}{3}$	0	2	.000	3	13	17	8.53	0
2008	Fresno	P.C.	26	142	6	10	.375	143	72	138	4.18	0
2009	Salt Lake	P.C.	2	$7\frac{2}{3}$	1	1	.500	5	3	13	11.74	0
2009	Los Angeles a	A.L.	40	$121\frac{1}{3}$	11	2	.846	69	55	105	3.93	0
2010	Angels	Arizona	2	4	0	0	.000	2	1	2	0.00	0
2010	Salt Lake	P.C.	13	$46\frac{1}{3}$	2	3	.400	36	19	32	2.72	2
2010	Los Angeles b	A.L.	14	$33\frac{2}{3}$	1	2	.333	17	20	38	4.54	0
Major League Totals		3 Yrs.	57	$167\frac{2}{3}$	12	6	.667	89	88	160	4.40	0
	Championship Series											
2009	Los Angeles	A.L.	2	$2\frac{2}{3}$	0	0	.000	2	1	5	13.50	0

a Filed for free agency, November 3, 2008. Signed with Los Angeles Angels organization, January 13, 2009.
b On disabled list from May 7 to July 26, 2010.

PAPELBON, JONATHAN ROBERT

Born, Baton Rouge, Louisiana, November 23, 1980.
Bats Right. Throws Right. Height, 6 feet, 4 inches. Weight, 230 pounds.

Year	Club	Lea	G	IP	W	L	Pct	SO	BB	H	ERA	SAVES
2003	Lowell	N.Y.-Penn.	13	$32\frac{2}{3}$	1	2	.333	36	9	43	6.34	0
2004	Sarasota	Fla.St.	24	$129\frac{2}{3}$	12	7	.632	153	43	97	2.64	0
2005	Portland	Eastern	14	87	5	2	.714	83	23	59	2.48	0

Year	Club	Lea	G	IP	W	L	Pct	SO	BB	H	ERA	SAVES
2005	Pawtucket	Int.	7	27 2/3	1	2	.333	27	3	21	2.93	1
2005	Boston	A.L.	17	34	3	1	.750	34	17	33	2.65	0
2006	Boston	A.L.	59	68 1/3	4	2	.667	75	13	40	0.92	35
2007	Boston	A.L.	59	58 1/3	1	3	.250	84	15	30	1.85	37
2008	Boston	A.L.	67	69 1/3	5	4	.556	77	8	58	2.34	41
2009	Boston	A.L.	66	68	1	1	.500	76	24	54	1.85	38
2010	Boston	A.L.	65	67	5	7	.417	76	28	57	3.90	37
Major League Totals		6 Yrs.	333	365	19	18	.514	422	105	272	2.22	188
	Division Series											
2005	Boston	A.L.	2	4	0	0	.000	2	0	2	0.00	0
2007	Boston	A.L.	1	1 1/3	1	0	1.000	1	2	0	0.00	0
2008	Boston	A.L.	3	5	1	0	1.000	7	1	2	0.00	1
2009	Boston	A.L.	2	2	0	1	.000	1	2	4	13.50	0
Division Series Totals			8	12 1/3	2	1	.667	11	5	8	2.19	1
	Championship Series											
2007	Boston	A.L.	3	5	0	0	.000	3	2	3	0.00	1
2008	Boston	A.L.	4	5 1/3	0	0	.000	6	1	1	0.00	2
Championship Series Totals			7	10 1/3	0	0	.000	9	3	4	0.00	3
	World Series Record											
2007	Boston	A.L.	3	4 1/3	0	0	.000	3	0	2	0.00	3

PARK, CHAN HO

Born, Kongju, South Korea, June 30, 1973.
Bats Right. Throws Right. Height, 6 feet, 2 inches. Weight, 210 pounds.

Year	Club	Lea	G	IP	W	L	Pct	SO	BB	H	ERA	SAVES
1994	Los Angeles	N.L.	2	4	0	0	.000	6	5	5	11.25	0
1994	San Antonio	Texas	20	101 1/3	5	7	.417	100	57	91	3.55	0
1995	Albuquerque	P.C.	23	110	6	7	.462	101	76	93	4.91	0
1995	Los Angeles	N.L.	2	4	0	0	.000	7	2	2	4.50	0
1996	Los Angeles	N.L.	48	108 2/3	5	5	.500	119	71	82	3.64	0
1997	Los Angeles	N.L.	32	192	14	8	.636	166	70	149	3.38	0
1998	Los Angeles	N.L.	34	220 2/3	15	9	.625	191	97	199	3.71	0
1999	Los Angeles	N.L.	33	194 1/3	13	11	.542	174	100	208	5.23	0
2000	Los Angeles	N.L.	34	226	18	10	.643	217	124	173	3.27	0
2001	Los Angeles	N.L.	36	234	15	11	.577	218	91	183	3.50	0
2002	Oklahoma	P.C.	1	3	0	1	.000	3	3	9	27.00	0
2002	Texas a-b	A.L.	25	145 2/3	9	8	.529	121	78	154	5.75	0
2003	Texas	A.L.	7	29 2/3	1	3	.250	16	25	34	7.58	0
2003	Frisco	Texas	2	11	1	0	1.000	6	4	10	2.45	0
2003	Oklahoma c	P.C.	3	18 1/3	1	0	1.000	12	8	27	5.89	0
2004	Rangers	Arizona	4	21	1	1	.500	20	6	15	1.71	0
2004	Frisco	Texas	2	11 1/3	0	2	.000	5	5	16	8.74	0
2004	Oklahoma	P.C.	4	19 1/3	0	2	.000	19	3	21	3.72	0
2004	Texas d	A.L.	16	95 2/3	4	7	.364	63	33	105	5.46	0
2005	Texas	A.L.	20	109 2/3	8	5	.615	80	54	130	5.66	0
2005	San Diego e	N.L.	10	45 2/3	4	3	.571	33	26	50	5.91	0
2006	San Diego f	N.L.	24	136 2/3	7	7	.500	96	44	146	4.81	0
2007	New York	N.L.	1	4	0	1	.000	4	2	6	15.75	0
2007	New Orleans	P.C.	9	51 2/3	4	4	.500	49	16	64	5.57	0
2007	Round Rock g-h-i	P.C.	15	84	2	10	.167	70	24	100	6.21	0
2008	Los Angeles j	N.L.	54	95 1/3	4	4	.500	79	36	97	3.40	2
2009	Philadelphia k	N.L.	45	83 1/3	3	3	.500	73	33	84	4.43	0
2010	Scranton/WB	Int.	1	1	0	0	.000	2	0	1	0.00	0
2010	New York	A.L.	27	35 1/3	2	1	.667	29	12	40	5.60	0
2010	Pittsburgh l-m-n	N.L.	26	28 1/3	2	2	.500	23	7	25	3.49	0
Major League Totals		17 Yrs.	476	1993	124	98	.559	1715	910	1872	4.36	2
	Division Series											
2006	San Diego	N.L.	1	2	0	0	.000	0	0	1	0.00	0
	Championship Series											
2008	Los Angeles	N.L.	4	1 2/3	0	0	.000	1	1	1	0.00	0
2009	Philadelphia	N.L.	4	3 1/3	0	1	.000	3	1	4	8.10	0
Championship Series Totals			8	5	0	1	.000	4	2	5	5.40	0
	World Series Record											
2009	Philadelphia	N.L.	4	3 1/3	0	0	.000	3	1	2	0.00	0

a Filed for free agency, November 5, 2001. Signed with Texas Rangers, January 16, 2002.
b On disabled list from April 2 to May 12 and August 7 to August 23, 2002.
c On disabled list from April 28 to June 7 and June 8 to November 14, 2003.
d On disabled list from May 20 to August 26, 2004.

e Traded to San Diego Padres for infielder Phil Nevin and cash, July 30, 2005.
f On disabled list from July 26 to August 11 and August 21 to September 22, 2006.
g Filed for free agency, October 31, 2006. Signed with New York Mets, February 9, 2007.
h Released by New York Mets, June 3, 2007. Signed with Houston Astros organization, June 12, 2007.
i Filed for free agency, October 29, 2007. Signed with Los Angeles Dodgers organization, November 8, 2007.
j Filed for free agency, November 1, 2008. Signed with Philadelphia Phillies, January 6, 2009.
k Filed for free agency, November 9, 2009. Signed with New York Yankees, February 28, 2010.
l On disabled list from April 14 to May 17, 2010.
m Claimed on waivers by Pittsburgh Pirates, August 4, 2010.
n Filed for free agency, November 1, 2010. Signed with Orix Buffaloes (Japan), December 20, 2010.

PARNELL, ROBERT ALLEN (BOBBY)

Born, Salisbury, North Carolina, September 8, 1984.
Bats Right. Throws Right. Height, 6 feet, 4 inches. Weight, 200 pounds.

Year Club	Lea	G	IP	W	L	Pct	SO	BB	H	ERA	SAVES
2005 Brooklyn	N.Y.-Penn.	15	73	2	3	.400	67	29	48	1.73	0
2006 St. Lucie	Fla.St.	3	$11\frac{2}{3}$	0	1	.000	13	9	16	9.26	0
2006 Hagerstown	So.Atl.	18	$93\frac{2}{3}$	5	10	.333	84	40	84	4.04	0
2007 Binghamton	Eastern	17	$88\frac{2}{3}$	5	5	.500	74	38	98	4.77	0
2007 St. Lucie	Fla.St.	12	$55\frac{1}{3}$	3	3	.500	62	22	56	3.25	0
2008 Binghamton	Eastern	24	$127\frac{2}{3}$	10	6	.625	91	57	126	4.30	0
2008 New Orleans	P.C.	5	$20\frac{1}{3}$	2	2	.500	23	9	25	6.64	0
2008 New York	N.L.	6	5	0	0	.000	3	2	3	5.40	0
2009 New York	N.L.	68	$88\frac{1}{3}$	4	8	.333	74	46	101	5.30	1
2010 Buffalo	Int.	24	$41\frac{1}{3}$	1	1	.500	42	17	36	4.14	4
2010 New York	N.L.	41	35	0	1	.000	33	8	41	2.83	0
Major League Totals	3 Yrs.	115	$128\frac{1}{3}$	4	9	.308	110	56	145	4.63	1

PARRA, MANUEL ALEX (MANNY)

Born, Carmichael, California, October 30, 1982.
Bats Left. Throws Left. Height, 6 feet, 3 inches. Weight, 210 pounds.

Year Club	Lea	G	IP	W	L	Pct	SO	BB	H	ERA	SAVES
2002 Brewers	Arizona	1	2	0	0	.000	4	0	1	4.50	0
2002 Ogden	Pioneer	11	$47\frac{2}{3}$	3	1	.750	51	10	59	3.21	0
2003 Beloit	Midwest	23	$138\frac{2}{3}$	11	2	.846	117	24	127	2.73	0
2004 High Desert	Calif.	13	$67\frac{1}{3}$	5	2	.714	64	19	76	3.48	0
2004 Huntsville	Southern	3	6	0	1	.000	10	0	5	3.00	0
2005 Huntsville	Southern	16	91	5	6	.455	86	21	111	3.96	0
2006 Brevard County	Fla.St.	15	$54\frac{2}{3}$	1	3	.250	61	32	47	2.96	0
2006 Huntsville	Southern	6	$31\frac{1}{3}$	3	0	1.000	29	8	26	2.87	0
2007 Huntsville	Southern	13	$80\frac{2}{3}$	7	3	.700	81	26	70	2.68	0
2007 Nashville	P.C.	4	26	3	1	.750	25	7	15	1.73	0
2007 Milwaukee a	N.L.	9	$26\frac{1}{3}$	0	1	.000	26	12	25	3.76	0
2008 Milwaukee	N.L.	32	166	10	8	.556	147	75	181	4.39	0
2009 Nashville	P.C.	4	$24\frac{2}{3}$	1	2	.333	19	13	16	2.92	0
2009 Milwaukee	N.L.	27	140	11	11	.500	116	77	179	6.36	0
2010 Milwaukee	N.L.	42	122	3	10	.231	129	63	135	5.02	0
Major League Totals	4 Yrs.	110	$454\frac{1}{3}$	24	30	.444	418	227	520	5.13	0
Division Series											
2008 Milwaukee	N.L.	2	$2\frac{1}{3}$	0	0	.000	3	1	2	0.00	0

a On disabled list from August 31 to September 21, 2007.

PAULEY, DAVID WAYNE

Born, Longmont, Colorado, June 17, 1983.
Bats Right. Throws Right. Height, 6 feet, 2 inches. Weight, 210 pounds.

Year Club	Lea	G	IP	W	L	Pct	SO	BB	H	ERA	SAVES
2001 Idaho Falls	Pioneer	15	$68\frac{2}{3}$	4	9	.308	53	24	88	6.03	0
2002 Eugene	Northwest	15	80	6	1	.857	62	18	81	2.81	0
2003 Fort Wayne	Midwest	22	$117\frac{2}{3}$	7	7	.500	117	38	109	3.29	1
2004 Lake Elsinore a	Calif.	27	$153\frac{1}{3}$	7	12	.368	128	60	155	4.17	0
2005 Portland	Eastern	27	156	9	7	.563	104	34	169	3.81	0
2006 Portland	Eastern	10	$60\frac{1}{3}$	2	3	.400	47	17	54	2.39	0
2006 Boston	A.L.	3	16	0	2	.000	10	6	31	7.87	0
2006 Pawtucket b	Int.	9	$50\frac{1}{3}$	1	3	.250	25	18	60	5.54	0
2007 Pawtucket	Int.	27	$153\frac{2}{3}$	6	6	.500	110	49	164	4.33	0
2008 Pawtucket	Int.	25	147	14	4	.778	103	41	147	3.55	0
2008 Boston	A.L.	6	$12\frac{1}{3}$	0	1	.000	11	5	23	11.68	0

Year	Club	Lea	G	IP	W	L	Pct	SO	BB	H	ERA	SAVES
2009	Norfolk c-d	Int.	27	152 1/3	9	12	.429	108	45	171	4.37	0
2010	Tacoma	P.C.	15	85 2/3	1	6	.143	56	26	82	3.68	0
2010	Seattle	A.L.	19	90 2/3	4	9	.308	51	30	89	4.07	0
Major League Totals		3 Yrs.	28	119	4	12	.250	72	41	143	5.37	0

a Traded by San Diego Padres to Boston Red Sox with outfielder Jay Payton, infielder Ramon Vazquez and cash for outfielder Dave Roberts, December 20, 2004.
b On disabled list from August 29 to November 6, 2006.
c Traded to Baltimore Orioles for pitcher Randor Bierd, January 19, 2009.
d Filed for free agency, November 9, 2009. Signed with Seattle Mariners organization, December 14, 2009.

PAULINO (DEL GUIDICE), FELIPE ADOLFO

Born, Santo Domingo, Dominican Republic, October 5, 1983.
Bats Right. Throws Right. Height, 6 feet, 2 inches. Weight, 260 pounds.

Year	Club	Lea	G	IP	W	L	Pct	SO	BB	H	ERA	SAVES
2003	Martinsville	Appal.	16	25 2/3	2	2	.500	27	19	23	5.61	1
2004	Greenville	Appal.	10	32	1	3	.250	37	22	30	7.59	0
2005	Tri-City	N.Y.-Penn.	13	30 2/3	2	2	.500	34	11	21	3.82	1
2005	Lexington	So.Atl.	7	24 1/3	1	1	.500	30	6	21	1.85	0
2006	Salem	Carolina	27	126 1/3	9	7	.563	91	59	119	4.35	0
2007	Corpus Christi	Texas	22	112	6	9	.400	110	49	103	3.62	0
2007	Houston	N.L.	5	19	2	1	.667	11	7	22	7.11	0
2008	Round Rock a	P.C.	1	0 2/3	0	0	.000	1	1	1	0.00	0
2009	Round Rock	P.C.	7	34 2/3	2	1	.667	29	23	30	3.12	0
2009	Houston b	N.L.	23	97 2/3	3	11	.214	93	37	126	6.27	0
2010	Corpus Christi	Texas	1	4	0	0	.000	3	1	2	0.00	0
2010	Houston c-d	N.L.	19	91 2/3	1	9	.100	83	46	95	5.11	0
Major League Totals		3 Yrs.	47	208 1/3	6	21	.222	187	90	243	5.83	0

a On disabled list from March 21 to September 30, 2008.
b On disabled list from June 8 to June 27, 2009.
c On disabled list from June 21 to September 12, 2010.
d Traded to Colorado Rockies for infielder Clint Barmes, November 18, 2010.

PAVANO, CARL ANTHONY

Born, New Britain, Connecticut, January 8, 1976.
Bats Right. Throws Right. Height, 6 feet, 5 inches. Weight, 240 pounds.

Year	Club	Lea	G	IP	W	L	Pct	SO	BB	H	ERA	SAVES
1994	Red Sox	Gulf Coast	9	44	4	3	.571	47	7	31	1.84	0
1995	Michigan	Midwest	22	141 1/3	6	6	.500	138	52	118	3.44	0
1996	Trenton	Eastern	27	185	16	5	.762	146	47	154	2.63	0
1997	Pawtucket a	Int.	23	161 2/3	11	6	.647	147	34	148	3.12	0
1998	Jupiter	Fla.St.	4	15	0	0	.000	14	3	20	6.60	0
1998	Ottawa	Int.	3	18 2/3	1	0	1.000	14	7	12	2.41	0
1998	Montreal	N.L.	24	134 2/3	6	9	.400	83	43	130	4.21	0
1999	Montreal	N.L.	19	104	6	8	.429	70	35	117	5.63	0
1999	Ottawa b	Int.	2	5	0	1	.000	3	0	7	9.00	0
2000	Montreal c	N.L.	15	97	8	4	.667	64	34	89	3.06	0
2001	Jupiter	Fla.St.	3	12 1/3	1	1	.500	11	2	10	2.19	0
2001	Ottawa	Int.	4	27 2/3	2	1	.667	19	5	27	3.58	0
2001	Montreal d	N.L.	8	42 2/3	1	6	.143	36	16	59	6.33	0
2002	Ottawa	Int.	3	20 1/3	3	0	1.000	9	2	23	3.10	0
2002	Montreal-Florida e	N.L.	37	136	6	10	.375	92	45	174	5.16	0
2003	Florida	N.L.	33	201	12	13	.480	133	49	204	4.30	0
2004	Florida f	N.L.	31	222 1/3	18	8	.692	139	49	212	3.00	0
2005	Yankees	Gulf Coast	1	5	0	0	.000	5	0	2	1.80	0
2005	Tampa	Fla.St.	1	6	0	1	.000	3	0	6	4.50	0
2005	New York g	A.L.	17	100	4	6	.400	56	18	129	4.77	0
2006	Trenton	Eastern	3	11	1	0	1.000	12	0	6	1.64	0
2006	Tampa	Fla.St.	3	11 2/3	0	2	.000	10	3	10	2.31	0
2006	Columbus h	Int.	1	6	1	0	1.000	5	1	8	3.00	0
2007	New York i	A.L.	2	11 1/3	1	0	1.000	4	2	12	4.76	0
2008	Charleston	So.Atl.	2	5	0	0	.000	6	1	6	1.80	0
2008	Trenton	Eastern	3	14	1	1	.500	13	3	14	3.86	0
2008	New York j-k	A.L.	7	34 1/3	4	2	.667	15	10	41	5.77	0
2009	Cleveland-Minnesota l-m	A.L.	33	199 1/3	14	12	.538	147	39	235	5.10	0
2010	Minnesota n	A.L.	32	221	17	11	.607	117	37	227	3.75	0
Major League Totals		12 Yrs.	258	1503 2/3	97	89	.522	956	377	1629	4.34	0

Year	Club	Lea	G	IP	W	L	Pct	SO	BB	H	ERA	SAVES
	Division Series											
2003	Florida	N.L.	3	2 2/3	2	0	1.000	1	1	1	0.00	0
2009	Minnesota	A.L.	1	7	0	1	.000	9	0	5	2.57	0
2010	Minnesota	A.L.	1	6	0	1	.000	3	1	10	6.00	0
Division Series Totals			5	15 2/3	2	2	.500	13	2	16	3.45	0
	Championship Series											
2003	Florida	N.L.	3	7 2/3	0	0	.000	8	1	8	2.35	0
	World Series Record											
2003	Florida	N.L.	2	9	0	0	.000	6	1	8	1.00	0

a Traded by Boston Red Sox to Montreal Expos with player to be named later for pitcher Pedro Martinez, November 18, 1997. Montreal Expos received pitcher Tony Armas to complete trade, December 18, 1997.
b On disabled list from July 12 to September 11, 1999.
c On disabled list from June 25 to November 13, 2000.
d On disabled list from March 23 to August 15, 2001.
e Traded to Florida Marlins with pitcher Graeme Lloyd, infielder Mike Mordecai and pitcher Justin Wayne for outfielder Cliff Floyd, infielder Wilton Guerrero and cash, July 11, 2002.
f Filed for free agency, November 3, 2004. Signed with New York Yankees, December 22, 2004.
g On disabled list from June 28 to October 31, 2005.
h On disabled list from March 29 to October 31, 2006.
i On disabled list from April 10 to October 31, 2007.
j On disabled list from March 21 to August 23, 2008.
k Filed for free agency, November 5, 2008. Signed with Cleveland Indians, January 6, 2009.
l Traded to Minnesota Twins for player to be named later, August 7, 2009. Cleveland Indians received pitcher Yohan Pinto to complete trade, August 28, 2009.
m Filed for free agency, November 7, 2009. Accepted arbitration, December 7, 2009.
n Filed for free agency, November 1, 2010, re-signed with Minnesota Twins, January 19, 2011.

PEAVY, JACOB EDWARD (JAKE)

Born, Mobile, Alabama, May 3, 1981.
Bats Right. Throws Right. Height, 6 feet, 1 inch. Weight, 195 pounds.

Year	Club	Lea	G	IP	W	L	Pct	SO	BB	H	ERA	SAVES
1999	Padres	Arizona	13	73 2/3	7	1	.875	90	23	52	1.34	0
1999	Idaho Falls	Pioneer	2	11	2	0	1.000	13	1	5	0.00	0
2000	Fort Wayne	Midwest	26	133 2/3	13	8	.619	164	53	107	2.90	0
2001	Mobile	Southern	5	28	2	1	.667	44	12	19	2.57	0
2002	Mobile	Southern	14	80 1/3	4	5	.444	89	30	65	2.80	0
2002	San Diego	N.L.	17	97 2/3	6	7	.462	90	33	106	4.52	0
2003	San Diego	N.L.	32	194 2/3	12	11	.522	156	82	173	4.11	0
2004	Mobile	Southern	1	4 2/3	0	1	.000	4	2	7	5.79	0
2004	San Diego a	N.L.	27	166 1/3	15	6	.714	173	53	146	*2.27	0
2005	San Diego	N.L.	30	203	13	7	.650	*216	50	162	2.88	0
2006	San Diego	N.L.	32	202 1/3	11	14	.440	215	62	187	4.09	0
2007	San Diego b	N.L.	34	223 1/3	*19	6	.760	*240	68	169	*2.54	0
2008	San Diego c	N.L.	27	173 2/3	10	11	.476	166	59	146	2.85	0
2009	Charlotte	Int.	4	15 1/3	1	1	.500	17	4	14	2.93	0
2009	San Diego	N.L.	13	81 2/3	6	6	.500	92	28	69	3.97	0
2009	Chicago d-e	A.L.	3	20	3	0	1.000	18	6	11	1.35	0
2010	Chicago f	A.L.	17	107	7	6	.538	93	34	98	4.63	0
Major League Totals		9 Yrs.	232	1469 2/3	102	74	.580	1459	475	1267	3.36	0
	Division Series											
2005	San Diego	N.L.	1	4 1/3	0	1	.000	3	3	8	16.62	0
2006	San Diego	N.L.	1	5 1/3	0	1	.000	2	1	11	8.44	0
Division Series Totals			2	9 2/3	0	2	.000	5	4	19	12.10	0

a On disabled list from May 20 to July 2, 2004.
b Selected Cy Young Award Winner in National League for 2007.
c On disabled list from May 15 to June 12, 2008.
d Traded to Chicago White Sox for pitcher Aaron Poreda, pitcher Clayton Richard, pitcher Adam Russell and pitcher Dexter Carter, July 31, 2009.
e On disabled list from June 9 to September 19, 2009.
f On disabled list from July 7 to November 2, 2010.

PELFREY, MICHAEL ALAN (MIKE)

Born, Wright-Patterson AFB, Ohio, January 14, 1984.
Bats Right. Throws Right. Height, 6 feet, 7 inches. Weight, 230 pounds.

Year	Club	Lea	G	IP	W	L	Pct	SO	BB	H	ERA	SAVES
2006	St. Lucie	Fla.St.	4	22	2	1	.667	26	2	17	1.64	0
2006	Binghamton	Eastern	12	66 1/3	4	2	.667	77	26	60	2.71	0
2006	New York	N.L.	4	21 1/3	2	1	.667	13	12	25	5.48	0

Year	Club	Lea	G	IP	W	L	Pct	SO	BB	H	ERA	SAVES
2006	Norfolk	Int.	2	8	1	0	1.000	6	5	4	2.25	0
2007	St. Lucie	Fla.St.	1	6	0	0	.000	2	3	5	3.00	0
2007	New Orleans	P.C.	14	74	3	6	.333	56	26	74	4.01	0
2007	New York	N.L.	15	$72^{2}/_{3}$	3	8	.273	45	39	85	5.57	0
2008	New York	N.L.	32	$200^{2}/_{3}$	13	11	.542	110	64	209	3.72	0
2009	New York	N.L.	31	$184^{1}/_{3}$	10	12	.455	107	66	213	5.03	0
2010	New York	N.L.	34	204	15	9	.625	113	68	213	3.66	1
Major League Totals		5 Yrs.	116	683	43	41	.512	388	249	745	4.31	1

PENA, RAMON ANTONIO (TONY)

Born, Santo Domingo, Dominican Republic, January 9, 1982.
Bats Right. Throws Right. Height, 6 feet, 1 inch. Weight, 220 pounds.

Year	Club	Lea	G	IP	W	L	Pct	SO	BB	H	ERA	SAVES
2002	Missoula a	Pioneer	4	20	1	2	.333	14	3	26	6.30	0
2003	South Bend	Midwest	27	$160^{1}/_{3}$	9	5	.643	119	30	149	2.86	0
2004	El Paso	Texas	7	43	3	3	.500	36	5	47	5.44	0
2005	Tennessee	Southern	25	$148^{1}/_{3}$	7	13	.350	95	40	165	4.43	0
2006	Tennessee	Southern	17	$20^{1}/_{3}$	2	0	1.000	17	5	18	0.89	6
2006	Tucson	P.C.	24	$26^{1}/_{3}$	3	1	.750	21	2	17	1.71	7
2006	Arizona	N.L.	25	$30^{2}/_{3}$	3	4	.429	21	8	36	5.58	1
2007	Arizona	N.L.	75	$85^{1}/_{3}$	5	4	.556	63	31	63	3.27	2
2008	Arizona	N.L.	72	$72^{2}/_{3}$	3	2	.600	52	17	80	4.33	3
2009	Arizona	N.L.	37	34	5	3	.625	26	11	41	4.24	1
2009	Chicago b	A.L.	35	36	1	2	.333	29	9	40	3.75	1
2010	Chicago	A.L.	52	$100^{2}/_{3}$	5	3	.625	56	45	108	5.10	0
Major League Totals		5 Yrs.	296	$359^{1}/_{3}$	22	18	.550	247	121	368	4.33	8
	Division Series											
2007	Arizona	N.L.	2	2	0	0	.000	0	0	2	0.00	0
	Championship Series											
2007	Arizona	N.L.	3	$3^{1}/_{3}$	0	0	.000	7	0	1	0.00	0

a Played under name of Adriano Rosario 2002-2004
b Traded to Chicago White Sox for infielder Brandon Allen, July 7, 2009.

PENNY, BRADLEY WAYNE (BRAD)

Born, Broken Arrow, Oklahoma, May 24, 1978.
Bats Right. Throws Right. Height, 6 feet, 4 inches. Weight, 260 pounds.

Year	Club	Lea	G	IP	W	L	Pct	SO	BB	H	ERA	SAVES
1996	Diamondbcks	Arizona	11	$49^{2}/_{3}$	2	2	.500	52	14	36	2.36	0
1997	South Bend	Midwest	25	$118^{2}/_{3}$	10	5	.667	116	43	91	2.73	0
1998	High Desert	California	28	164	14	5	.737	207	35	138	2.96	0
1999	El Paso a-b-c	Texas	17	90	2	7	.222	100	25	109	4.80	0
1999	Portland	Eastern	6	$32^{1}/_{3}$	1	0	1.000	35	14	28	3.90	0
2000	Brevard County	Fla.St.	2	8	0	1	.000	11	4	5	1.13	0
2000	Calgary	P.C.	3	15	2	0	1.000	16	10	8	1.80	0
2000	Florida d	N.L.	23	$119^{2}/_{3}$	8	7	.533	80	60	120	4.81	0
2001	Florida	N.L.	31	205	10	10	.500	154	54	183	3.69	0
2002	Jupiter	Fla.St.	2	$7^{2}/_{3}$	0	0	.000	9	0	5	0.00	0
2002	Florida e	N.L.	24	$129^{1}/_{3}$	8	7	.533	93	50	148	4.66	0
2003	Florida	N.L.	32	$196^{1}/_{3}$	14	10	.583	138	56	195	4.13	0
2004	Florida-Los Angeles f-g	N.L.	24	143	9	10	.474	111	45	130	3.15	0
2005	Vero Beach	Fla.St.	1	5	1	0	1.000	3	1	2	1.80	0
2005	Las Vegas	P.C.	1	6	1	0	1.000	9	2	5	3.00	0
2005	Los Angeles h	N.L.	29	$175^{1}/_{3}$	7	9	.438	122	41	185	3.90	0
2006	Los Angeles	N.L.	34	189	*16	9	.640	148	54	206	4.33	0
2007	Los Angeles	N.L.	33	208	16	4	*.800	135	73	199	3.03	0
2008	Las Vegas	P.C.	1	4	0	0	.000	4	1	6	4.50	0
2008	Los Angeles i-j	N.L.	19	$94^{2}/_{3}$	6	9	.400	51	42	112	6.27	0
2009	Boston	A.L.	24	$131^{2}/_{3}$	7	8	.467	89	42	160	5.61	0
2009	San Francisco k-l	N.L.	6	$41^{2}/_{3}$	4	1	.800	20	9	31	2.59	0
2010	St. Louis m-n	N.L.	9	$55^{2}/_{3}$	3	4	.429	35	9	63	3.23	0
Major League Totals		11 Yrs.	288	$1689^{1}/_{3}$	108	88	.551	1176	535	1732	4.11	0
	Division Series											
2003	Florida	N.L.	2	$5^{2}/_{3}$	0	0	.000	6	1	5	6.35	0
2006	Los Angeles	N.L.	1	1	0	1	.000	1	2	2	18.00	0
Division Series Totals			3	$6^{2}/_{3}$	0	1	.000	7	3	7	8.10	0
	Championship Series											
2003	Florida	N.L.	3	4	1	1	.500	0	3	9	15.75	0

Year	Club	Lea	G	IP	W	L	Pct	SO	BB	H	ERA	SAVES
	World Series Record											
2003	Florida	N.L.	2	12⅓	2	0	1.000	7	5	15	2.19	0

a On disabled list from April 20 to 30, 1999.
b Traded by Arizona Diamondbacks to Florida Marlins with pitcher Vladimir Nunez and player to be named later for pitcher Matt Mantei, July 9, 1999.
c Florida Marlins received outfielder Abraham Nunez to complete trade, December 13, 1999.
d On disabled list from July 20 to September 1, 2000.
e On disabled list from May 19 to July 2, 2002.
f Traded to Los Angeles Dodgers with pitcher Bill Murphy and infielder Hee Seop Choi for catcher Paul LoDuca, outfielder Juan Encarnacion and pitcher Guillermo Mota, July 30, 2004.
g On disabled list from August 9 to September 22, 2004.
h On disabled list from March 25 to April 24, 2005.
i On disabled list from June 15 to August 8 and August 14 to September 10 and September 24 to November 4, 2008.
j Not offered contract, November 5, 2008. Signed with Boston Red Sox, January 9, 2009.
k Released by Boston Red Sox, August 27, 2009. Signed with San Francisco Giants organization, August 31, 2009.
l Filed for free agency, November 5, 2009. Signed with St. Louis Cardinals, December 9, 2009.
m On disabled list from May 22 to November 1, 2010.
n Filed for free agency, November 1, 2010. Signed with Detroit Tigers, January 18, 2011.

PERALTA (GUTIERREZ), JOEL

Born, Bonao, Dominican Republic, March 23, 1976.
Bats Right. Throws Right. Height, 5 feet, 11 inches. Weight, 195 pounds.

Year	Club	Lea	G	IP	W	L	Pct	SO	BB	H	ERA	SAVES
2000	Boise	Northwest	4	8⅓	0	0	.000	9	5	12	6.48	0
2000	Butte a	Pioneer	10	19	2	1	.667	17	10	24	6.63	1
2001	Cedar Rapids	Midwest	41	42⅓	0	0	.000	53	5	27	2.13	23
2001	Arkansas	Texas	9	10	0	1	.000	14	5	15	6.30	2
2002	Cedar Rapids	Midwest	41	47⅓	5	0	1.000	53	11	28	0.95	21
2002	Arkansas	Texas	12	17⅔	0	0	.000	11	10	25	6.62	0
2003	Salt Lake	P.C.	1	0	0	0	.000	0	1	0	0.00	0
2003	Arkansas	Texas	47	52⅓	5	4	.556	48	12	39	2.24	20
2004	Angels	Arizona	2	4⅓	0	0	.000	9	0	1	2.08	0
2004	Rancho Cucamonga	Calif.	1	2	0	0	.000	1	1	5	9.00	0
2004	Salt Lake	P.C.	39	56	4	2	.667	68	18	64	4.98	1
2005	Los Angeles	A.L.	28	34⅔	1	0	1.000	30	14	28	3.89	0
2005	Salt Lake b	P.C.	19	20	4	1	.800	18	6	11	2.70	10
2006	Omaha	P.C.	6	7⅔	1	0	1.000	8	3	8	2.35	2
2006	Kansas City	A.L.	64	73⅔	1	3	.250	57	17	74	4.40	1
2007	Kansas City	A.L.	62	87⅔	1	3	.250	66	19	93	3.80	1
2008	Omaha	P.C.	10	18⅔	1	0	1.000	19	6	9	0.00	2
2008	Kansas City	A.L.	40	52⅔	1	2	.333	38	14	56	5.98	0
2009	Colorado Springs	P.C.	31	36⅔	6	0	1.000	32	11	31	2.45	4
2009	Colorado c-d	N.L.	27	24⅔	0	3	.000	22	12	27	6.20	0
2010	Syracuse	Int.	28	33⅓	2	0	1.000	38	7	24	1.08	20
2010	Washington e	N.L.	39	49	1	0	1.000	49	9	30	2.02	0
Major League Totals		6 Yrs.	260	322⅓	5	11	.313	262	85	308	4.22	2

a Released by Oakland Athletics, July 4, 1998. Signed with Anaheim Angels organization, February 25, 1999.
b Claimed on waivers by Kansas City Royals, October 7, 2005.
c Released by Kansas City Royals, March 31, 2009. Signed with Colorado Rockies organization, April 8, 2009.
d Filed for free agency, October 26, 2009. Signed with Washington Nationals organization, December 15, 2009.
e Not offered contract, December 2, 2010. Signed with Tampa Bay Rays, December 17, 2010.

PEREZ, CHRISTOPHER RALPH (CHRIS)

Born, Bradenton, Florida, July 1, 1985.
Bats Right. Throws Right. Height, 6 feet, 4 inches. Weight, 225 pounds.

Year	Club	Lea	G	IP	W	L	Pct	SO	BB	H	ERA	SAVES
2006	Quad Cities	Midwest	25	29⅓	2	0	1.000	32	19	20	1.84	12
2007	Memphis	P.C.	15	14	0	1	.000	15	13	6	4.50	8
2007	Springfield	Texas	39	40⅔	2	0	1.000	62	28	17	2.43	27
2008	Memphis	P.C.	26	25⅓	1	1	.500	38	12	18	3.20	11
2008	St. Louis	N.L.	41	41⅔	3	3	.500	42	22	34	3.46	7
2009	Memphis	P.C.	3	4	1	0	1.000	4	3	0	0.00	2
2009	St. Louis	N.L.	29	23⅔	1	1	.500	30	15	17	4.18	1
2009	Cleveland a	A.L.	32	33⅓	0	1	.000	38	12	24	4.32	1
2010	Cleveland	A.L.	63	63	2	2	.500	61	28	40	1.71	23
Major League Totals		3 Yrs.	165	161⅔	6	7	.462	171	77	115	3.06	32

a Traded to Cleveland Indians with player to be named later for infielder Mark DeRosa, June 27, 2009. Cleveland Indians received pitcher Jess Todd to complete trade, July 26, 2009.

PEREZ, RAFAEL JEROME

Born, Santo Domingo, Dominican Republic, May 15, 1982.
Bats Left. Throws Left. Height, 6 feet, 3 inches. Weight, 185 pounds.

Year	Club	Lea	G	IP	W	L	Pct	SO	BB	H	ERA	SAVES
2003	Burlington	Appal.	13	69	9	3	.750	63	16	56	1.70	0
2004	Kinston	Carolina	1	4 2/3	0	0	.000	3	2	10	11.57	0
2004	Lake County	So.Atl.	23	115	7	6	.538	99	47	121	4.85	0
2005	Kinston	Carolina	14	77 2/3	8	5	.615	48	32	54	3.36	0
2005	Akron	Eastern	15	66 2/3	4	3	.571	46	12	53	1.75	1
2006	Akron	Eastern	12	67 1/3	4	5	.444	53	22	53	2.81	0
2006	Buffalo	Int.	13	27 1/3	0	3	.000	33	8	20	2.63	0
2006	Cleveland	A.L.	18	12 1/3	0	0	.000	15	6	10	4.38	0
2007	Buffalo	Int.	8	46 2/3	3	3	.500	31	11	53	3.66	0
2007	Cleveland	A.L.	44	60 2/3	1	2	.333	62	15	41	1.78	1
2008	Cleveland	A.L.	73	76 1/3	4	4	.500	86	23	67	3.54	2
2009	Columbus	Int.	16	21 2/3	1	0	1.000	23	5	23	0.83	3
2009	Cleveland	A.L.	54	48	4	3	.571	32	25	66	7.31	0
2010	Cleveland	A.L.	70	61	6	1	.857	36	25	72	3.25	0
Major League Totals		5 Yrs.	259	258 1/3	15	10	.600	231	94	256	3.80	3
	Division Series											
2007	Cleveland	A.L.	3	6	1	0	1.000	6	1	3	1.50	0
	Championship Series											
2007	Cleveland	A.L.	3	1	0	0	.000	0	2	7	45.00	0

PERRY, RYAN KEITH

Born, Pomona, California, February 13, 1987.
Bats Right. Throws Right. Height, 6 feet, 4 inches. Weight, 200 pounds.

Year	Club	Lea	G	IP	W	L	Pct	SO	BB	H	ERA	SAVES
2008	Lakeland	Fla.St.	12	11 2/3	1	2	.333	12	7	15	3.86	4
2008	Tigers	Gulf Coast	2	2	0	0	.000	4	0	0	0.00	0
2009	Toledo	Int.	8	13 2/3	1	0	1.000	12	4	13	2.63	3
2009	Detroit	A.L.	53	61 2/3	0	1	.000	60	38	56	3.79	0
2010	Toledo	Int.	3	3 2/3	0	0	.000	4	4	1	0.00	0
2010	Detroit a	A.L.	60	62 2/3	3	5	.375	45	23	55	3.59	2
Major League Totals		2 Yrs.	113	124 1/3	3	6	.333	105	61	111	3.69	2

a On disabled list from June 7 to July 3, 2010.

PETTITTE, ANDREW EUGENE (ANDY)

Born, Baton Rouge, Louisiana, June 15, 1972.
Bats Left. Throws Left. Height, 6 feet, 5 inches. Weight, 225 pounds.

Year	Club	Lea	G	IP	W	L	Pct	SO	BB	H	ERA	SAVES
1991	Yankees	Gulf Coast	6	36 2/3	4	1	.800	51	8	16	0.98	0
1991	Oneonta	N.Y.-Penn.	6	33	2	2	.500	32	16	33	2.18	0
1992	Greensboro	So. Atl.	27	168	10	4	.714	130	55	141	2.20	0
1993	Prince William	Carolina	26	159 2/3	11	9	.550	129	47	146	3.04	0
1993	Albany	Eastern	1	5	1	0	1.000	6	2	5	3.60	0
1994	Albany	Eastern	11	73	7	2	.778	50	18	60	2.71	0
1994	Columbus	Int.	16	96 2/3	7	2	.778	61	21	101	2.98	0
1995	Columbus	Int.	2	11 2/3	0	0	.000	8	0	7	0.00	0
1995	New York	A.L.	31	175	12	9	.571	114	63	183	4.17	0
1996	New York	A.L.	35	221	*21	8	.724	162	72	229	3.87	0
1997	New York	A.L.	35	240 1/3	18	7	.720	166	65	233	2.88	0
1998	New York	A.L.	33	216 1/3	16	11	.593	146	87	226	4.24	0
1999	Tampa	Fla.St.	1	5	1	0	1.000	8	2	4	0.00	0
1999	New York a	A.L.	31	191 2/3	14	11	.560	121	89	216	4.70	0
2000	New York b	A.L.	32	204 2/3	19	9	.679	125	80	219	4.35	0
2001	New York c	A.L.	31	200 2/3	15	10	.600	164	41	224	3.99	0
2002	Tampa	Fla.St.	2	5	0	0	.000	4	0	3	0.00	0
2002	Norwich	Eastern	1	6 1/3	0	0	.000	5	0	2	1.42	0
2002	New York d	A.L.	22	134 2/3	13	5	.722	97	32	144	3.27	0
2003	New York e	A.L.	33	208 1/3	21	8	.724	180	50	227	4.02	0
2004	Round Rock	Texas	2	8	0	0	.000	9	2	4	2.25	0
2004	Houston f	N.L.	15	83	6	4	.600	79	31	71	3.90	0
2005	Houston	N.L.	33	222 1/3	17	9	.654	171	41	188	2.39	0
2006	Houston g	N.L.	36	214 1/3	14	13	.519	178	70	238	4.20	0
2007	New York h	A.L.	36	215 1/3	15	9	.625	141	69	238	4.05	0
2008	New York i-j	A.L.	33	204	14	14	.500	158	55	233	4.54	0
2009	New York k	A.L.	32	194 2/3	14	8	.636	148	76	193	4.16	0

Year Club	Lea	G	IP	W	L	Pct	SO	BB	H	ERA	SAVES
2010 New York l-m..........	A.L.	21	129	11	3	.786	101	41	123	3.28	0
Major League Totals	16 Yrs.	489	3055⅓	240	138	.635	2251	962	3185	3.88	0
Division Series											
1995 New York	A.L.	1	7	0	0	.000	0	3	9	5.14	0
1996 New York	A.L.	1	6⅓	0	0	.000	3	6	4	5.68	0
1997 New York	A.L.	2	11⅔	0	2	.000	5	1	15	8.49	0
1998 New York	A.L.	1	7	1	0	1.000	8	0	3	1.29	0
1999 New York	A.L.	1	7⅓	1	0	1.000	5	0	7	1.23	0
2000 New York	A.L.	2	11⅓	1	0	1.000	7	3	15	3.97	0
2001 New York	A.L.	1	6⅓	0	1	.000	4	2	7	1.42	0
2002 New York	A.L.	1	3	0	0	.000	1	0	8	12.00	0
2003 New York	A.L.	1	7	1	0	1.000	10	3	4	1.29	0
2005 Houston	N.L.	1	7	1	0	1.000	6	2	4	3.86	0
2007 New York	A.L.	1	6⅓	0	0	.000	5	2	7	0.00	0
2009 New York	A.L.	1	6⅓	1	0	1.000	7	1	3	1.42	0
2010 New York	A.L.	1	7	1	0	1.000	4	1	5	2.57	0
Division Series Totals		15	93⅔	7	3	.700	65	24	91	3.65	0
Championship Series											
1996 New York	A.L.	2	15	1	0	1.000	7	5	10	3.60	0
1998 New York	A.L.	1	4⅔	0	1	.000	1	3	8	11.57	0
1999 New York	A.L.	1	7⅓	1	0	1.000	5	1	8	2.45	0
2000 New York	A.L.	1	6⅔	1	0	1.000	2	1	9	2.70	0
2001 New York	A.L.	2	14⅓	2	0	1.000	8	2	11	2.51	0
2003 New York	A.L.	2	11⅔	1	0	1.000	10	4	17	4.63	0
2005 Houston	N.L.	2	12⅓	0	1	.000	6	4	15	5.11	0
2009 New York	A.L.	2	12⅔	1	0	1.000	8	2	14	2.84	0
2010 New York	A.L.	1	7	0	1	.000	5	0	5	2.57	0
Championship Series Totals		14	91⅔	7	3	.700	52	22	97	3.83	0
World Series Record											
1996 New York	A.L.	2	10⅔	1	1	.500	5	4	11	5.91	0
1998 New York	A.L.	1	7⅓	1	0	1.000	4	3	5	0.00	0
1999 New York	A.L.	1	3⅔	0	0	.000	1	1	10	12.27	0
2000 New York	A.L.	2	13⅔	0	0	.000	9	4	16	1.98	0
2001 New York	A.L.	2	9	0	2	.000	9	2	12	10.00	0
2003 New York	A.L.	2	15⅔	1	1	.500	14	4	12	0.57	0
2005 Houston	N.L.	1	6	0	0	.000	4	0	8	3.00	0
2009 New York	A.L.	2	11⅔	2	0	1.000	10	8	9	5.40	0
World Series Totals............		13	77⅔	5	4	.556	56	26	83	4.06	0

a On disabled list from March 26 to April 17, 1999.
b On disabled list from April 8 to April 25, 2000.
c On disabled list from June 16 to July 1, 2001.
d On disabled list from April 16 to June 14, 2002.
e Filed for free agency, November 6, 2003. Signed with Houston Astros, December 11, 2003.
f On disabled list from April 7 to April 29 and from May 27 to June 29 and from August 18 to October 28, 2004.
g Filed for free agency, November 6, 2006. Signed with New York Yankees, December 8, 2006.
h Filed for free agency, November 12, 2007, re-signed with New York Yankees, December 12, 2007.
i On disabled list from March 21 to April 5, 2008.
j Filed for free agency, November 9, 2008, re-signed with New York Yankees, January 26, 2009.
k Filed for free agency, November 19, 2009, re-signed with New York Yankees, December 9, 2009.
l On disabled list from July 19 to September 17, 2010.
m Filed for free agency, November 1, 2010.

PINEIRO, JOEL ALBERTO

Born, Rio Piedras, Puerto Rico, September 25, 1978.
Bats Right. Throws Right. Height, 6 feet, 1 inch. Weight, 200 pounds.

Year Club	Lea	G	IP	W	L	Pct	SO	BB	H	ERA	SAVES
1997 Mariners...........	Arizona	1	3	1	0	1.000	4	0	1	0.00	0
1997 Everett	Northwest	18	49	4	2	.667	59	18	54	5.33	2
1998 Wisconsin	Midwest	16	96	8	4	.667	84	28	92	3.19	0
1998 Lancaster.........	California	9	45	2	0	1.000	48	22	58	7.80	0
1998 Orlando	Southern	1	5	1	0	1.000	2	2	7	5.40	0
1999 New Haven.........	Eastern	28	166	10	15	.400	116	52	190	4.72	0
2000 New Haven.........	Eastern	9	52⅓	2	1	.667	43	12	42	4.13	0
2000 Tacoma	P.C.	10	61	7	1	.875	41	22	53	2.80	0
2000 Seattle	A.L.	8	19⅓	1	0	1.000	10	13	25	5.59	0
2001 Tacoma	P.C.	18	77	6	3	.667	64	33	68	3.62	0
2001 Seattle	A.L.	17	75⅓	6	2	.750	56	21	50	2.03	0
2002 Seattle	A.L.	37	194⅓	14	7	.667	136	54	189	3.24	0

Year	Club	Lea	G	IP	W	L	Pct	SO	BB	H	ERA	SAVES
2003	Seattle	A.L.	32	$211\frac{2}{3}$	16	11	.593	151	76	192	3.78	0
2004	Seattle a	A.L.	21	$140\frac{2}{3}$	6	11	.353	111	43	144	4.67	0
2005	Tacoma	P.C.	1	7	0	0	.000	6	0	5	1.29	0
2005	Seattle b	A.L.	30	189	7	11	.389	107	56	224	5.62	0
2006	Seattle c	A.L.	40	$165\frac{2}{3}$	8	13	.381	87	64	209	6.36	1
2007	Lowell	N.Y.-Penn.	1	1	0	0	.000	2	0	0	0.00	0
2007	Pawtucket	Int.	2	8	0	0	.000	3	4	3	2.25	0
2007	Boston	A.L.	31	34	1	1	.500	20	14	41	5.03	0
2007	St. Louis d-e-f	N.L.	11	$63\frac{2}{3}$	6	4	.600	40	12	69	3.96	0
2008	Memphis	P.C.	1	6	0	0	.000	5	1	6	3.00	0
2008	St. Louis g	N.L.	26	$148\frac{2}{3}$	7	7	.500	81	35	180	5.15	1
2009	St. Louis h	N.L.	32	214	15	12	.556	105	27	218	3.49	0
2010	Los Angeles i	A.L.	23	$152\frac{1}{3}$	10	7	.588	92	34	155	3.84	0
Major League Totals		11 Yrs.	308	$1608\frac{2}{3}$	97	86	.530	996	449	1696	4.34	2
	Division Series											
2009	St. Louis	N.L.	1	4	0	1	.000	3	0	7	9.00	0
	Championship Series											
2001	Seattle	A.L.	1	2	0	0	.000	5	2	4	4.50	0

a On disabled list from July 26 to November 1, 2004.
b On disabled list from March 27 to April 15, 2005.
c Not offered contract, December 12, 2006. Signed with Boston Red Sox, January 4, 2007.
d On disabled list from June 28 to July 13, 2007.
e Traded to St. Louis Cardinals for player to be named later, July 31, 2007.
f Boston Red Sox received outfielder Sean Danielson to complete trade, November 2, 2007.
g On disabled list from March 21 to April 13 and May 21 to June 12, 2008.
h Filed for free agency, November 6, 2009. Signed with Los Angeles Angels, February 4, 2010.
i On disabled list from July 30 to September 14, 2010.

PORCELLO, FREDERICK ALFRED (RICK)

Born, Morristown, New Jersey, December 27, 1988.
Bats Right. Throws Right. Height, 6 feet, 5 inches. Weight, 200 pounds.

Year	Club	Lea	G	IP	W	L	Pct	SO	BB	H	ERA	SAVES
2008	Lakeland	Fla.St.	24	125	8	6	.571	72	33	116	2.66	0
2009	Detroit	A.L.	31	$170\frac{2}{3}$	14	9	.609	89	52	176	3.96	0
2010	Toledo	Int.	4	28	1	2	.333	19	10	24	3.21	0
2010	Detroit	A.L.	27	$162\frac{2}{3}$	10	12	.455	84	38	188	4.92	0
Major League Totals		2 Yrs.	58	$333\frac{1}{3}$	24	21	.533	173	90	364	4.43	0

PRICE, DAVID TAYLOR

Born, Murfreesboro, Tennessee, August 26, 1985.
Bats Left. Throws Left. Height, 6 feet, 6 inches. Weight, 225 pounds.

Year	Club	Lea	G	IP	W	L	Pct	SO	BB	H	ERA	SAVES
2008	Vero Beach	Fla.St.	6	$34\frac{2}{3}$	4	0	1.000	37	7	28	1.82	0
2008	Montgomery	Southern	9	57	7	0	1.000	55	16	42	1.89	0
2008	Durham	Int.	4	18	1	1	.500	17	9	22	4.50	0
2008	Tampa Bay	A.L.	5	14	0	0	.000	12	4	9	1.93	0
2009	Durham	Int.	8	$34\frac{1}{3}$	1	4	.200	35	18	28	3.93	0
2009	Tampa Bay	A.L.	23	$128\frac{1}{3}$	10	7	.588	102	54	119	4.42	0
2010	Tampa Bay	A.L.	32	$208\frac{2}{3}$	19	6	*.760	188	79	170	2.72	0
Major League Totals		3 Yrs.	60	351	29	13	.690	302	137	298	3.31	0
	Division Series											
2010	Tampa Bay	N.L.	2	$12\frac{2}{3}$	0	2	.000	14	0	17	4.97	0
	Championship Series											
2008	Tampa Bay	N.L.	3	$2\frac{1}{3}$	1	0	1.000	4	2	0	0.00	1
	World Series Record											
2008	Tampa Bay	N.L.	2	$3\frac{1}{3}$	0	0	.000	4	2	2	2.70	0

PUTZ, JOSEPH JASON (J.J.)

Born, Trenton, Michigan, February 2, 1977.
Bats Right. Throws Right. Height, 6 feet, 5 inches. Weight, 250 pounds.

Year	Club	Lea	G	IP	W	L	Pct	SO	BB	H	ERA	SAVES
1999	Everett	Northwest	10	$22\frac{1}{3}$	0	0	.000	17	11	23	4.84	2
2000	Wisconsin	Midwest	26	$142\frac{2}{3}$	12	6	.667	105	63	130	3.15	0
2001	San Antonio	Texas	27	148	7	9	.438	135	59	145	3.83	0
2002	San Antonio	Texas	15	84	3	10	.231	60	28	84	3.64	0
2002	Tacoma	P.C.	9	54	2	4	.333	39	21	51	3.83	0

Year	Club	Lea	G	IP	W	L	Pct	SO	BB	H	ERA	SAVES
2003	Tacoma	P.C.	41	86	0	3	.000	60	34	69	2.51	11
2003	Seattle	A.L.	3	$3\frac{2}{3}$	0	0	.000	3	3	4	4.91	0
2004	Tacoma	P.C.	7	$8\frac{1}{3}$	0	0	.000	13	3	10	4.32	3
2004	Seattle	A.L.	54	63	0	3	.000	47	24	66	4.71	9
2005	Seattle	A.L.	64	60	6	5	.545	45	23	58	3.60	1
2006	Seattle	A.L.	72	$78\frac{1}{3}$	4	1	.800	104	13	59	2.30	36
2007	Seattle	A.L.	68	$71\frac{2}{3}$	6	1	.857	82	13	37	1.38	40
2008	Azl Mariners	Arizona	2	3	0	0	.000	4	0	2	0.00	0
2008	Tacoma	P.C.	1	$1\frac{2}{3}$	0	0	.000	1	0	0	0.00	0
2008	Seattle a-b	A.L.	47	$46\frac{1}{3}$	6	5	.545	56	28	46	3.88	15
2009	New York c-d	N.L.	29	$29\frac{1}{3}$	1	4	.200	19	19	29	5.22	2
2010	Chicago e-f	A.L.	60	54	7	5	.583	65	15	41	2.83	3
Major League Totals		8 Yrs.	397	$406\frac{1}{3}$	30	24	.556	421	138	340	3.19	106

a On disabled list from April 2 to April 22 and June 12 to July 20, 2008.

b Traded to New York Mets with pitcher Sean Green and outfielder Jeremy Reed for pitcher Aaron Heilman, outfielder Endy Chavez, pitcher Jason Vargas, infielder Mike Carp, outfielder Ezequiel Carrera and pitcher Maikel Cleto, December 10, 2008.

c On disabled list from June 5 to November 7, 2009.

d Filed for free agency, November 7, 2009. Signed with Chicago White Sox, December 11, 2009.

e On disabled list from August 25 to September 9, 2010.

f Filed for free agency, November 1, 2010. Signed with Arizona Diamondbacks, December 7, 2010.

QUALLS, CHAD MICHAEL

Born, Lomita, California, August 17, 1978.

Bats Right. Throws Right. Height, 6 feet, 5 inches. Weight, 220 pounds.

Year	Club	Lea	G	IP	W	L	Pct	SO	BB	H	ERA	SAVES
2001	Michigan	Midwest	26	162	15	6	.714	125	31	149	3.72	0
2002	Round Rock	Texas	29	163	6	13	.316	142	67	174	4.36	0
2003	Round Rock	Texas	28	$175\frac{1}{3}$	8	11	.421	132	61	174	3.85	0
2004	New Orleans	P.C.	32	$106\frac{2}{3}$	3	6	.333	72	30	134	5.57	1
2004	Houston	N.L.	25	33	4	0	1.000	24	8	34	3.55	1
2005	Houston	N.L.	77	$79\frac{2}{3}$	6	4	.600	60	23	73	3.28	0
2006	Houston	N.L.	81	$88\frac{2}{3}$	7	3	.700	56	28	76	3.76	0
2007	Houston a	N.L.	79	$82\frac{2}{3}$	6	5	.545	78	25	84	3.05	5
2008	Arizona	N.L.	77	$73\frac{2}{3}$	4	8	.333	71	18	61	2.81	9
2009	Arizona b	N.L.	51	52	2	2	.500	45	7	53	3.63	24
2010	Arizona	N.L.	43	38	1	4	.200	34	15	61	8.29	12
2010	Tampa Bay c-d-e	A.L.	27	21	2	0	1.000	15	6	24	5.57	0
Major League Totals		7 Yrs.	460	$468\frac{2}{3}$	32	26	.552	383	130	466	3.82	51
	Division Series											
2004	Houston	N.L.	4	4	0	0	.000	3	1	4	6.75	0
2005	Houston	N.L.	2	3	0	0	.000	1	2	5	6.00	0
2010	Tampa Bay	N.L.	2	$1\frac{2}{3}$	0	0	.000	0	0	4	10.80	0
Division Series Totals			8	$8\frac{2}{3}$	0	0	.000	4	3	13	7.27	0
	Championship Series											
2004	Houston	N.L.	2	4	0	1	.000	4	2	8	11.25	0
2005	Houston	N.L.	4	$4\frac{2}{3}$	1	0	1.000	4	0	0	0.00	0
Championship Series Totals			6	$8\frac{2}{3}$	1	1	.500	8	2	8	5.19	0
	World Series Record											
2005	Houston	N.L.	3	$5\frac{1}{3}$	0	0	.000	5	2	3	1.69	0

a Traded to Arizona Diamondbacks with pitcher Juan Gutierrez and outfielder Chris Burke for pitcher Jose Valverde, December 14, 2007.

b On disabled list from August 31 to November 20, 2009.

c Traded to Tampa Bay Rays for player to be named later, July 31, 2010.

d Arizona Diamondbacks received pitcher Matt Gorgen to complete trade, September 9, 2010.

e Filed for free agency, November 1, 2010. Signed with San Diego Padres, January 19, 2011.

RAMIREZ, RAMON SANTO

Born, Puerto Plata, Dominican Republic, August 31, 1981.

Bats Right. Throws Right. Height, 5 feet, 11 inches. Weight, 190 pounds.

Year	Club	Lea	G	IP	W	L	Pct	SO	BB	H	ERA	SAVES
2002	Hiroshima a-b	Japan Cent.	2	3	0	0	.000	3	2	3	3.00	0
2003	Tampa	Fla.St.	14	$74\frac{1}{3}$	2	8	.200	70	20	88	5.21	0
2003	Trenton	Eastern	4	$21\frac{1}{3}$	1	1	.500	21	8	18	1.69	0
2003	Columbus c	Int.	2	6	0	1	.000	5	1	5	4.50	0
2004	Trenton	Eastern	18	114	4	6	.400	128	32	116	4.66	0
2004	Columbus	Int.	4	18	0	3	.000	17	8	25	8.50	0

Year	Club	Lea	G	IP	W	L	Pct	SO	BB	H	ERA	SAVES
2005	Columbus	Int.	6	27	1	3	.250	26	9	32	5.33	0
2005	Trenton	Eastern	15	89	6	5	.545	82	35	79	3.84	0
2005	Tulsa d	Texas	9	25 1/3	2	1	.667	23	8	27	5.33	0
2006	Colorado Springs	P.C.	1	1	0	0	.000	1	0	0	0.00	0
2006	Colorado	N.L.	61	67 2/3	4	3	.571	61	27	58	3.46	0
2007	Colorado Springs	P.C.	25	27 2/3	4	0	1.000	35	16	18	2.28	0
2007	Colorado e	N.L.	22	17 1/3	2	2	.500	15	6	21	8.31	0
2008	Kansas City f-g	A.L.	71	71 2/3	3	2	.600	70	31	57	2.64	1
2009	Boston	A.L.	70	69 2/3	7	4	.636	52	32	61	2.84	0
2010	Boston	A.L.	44	42 1/3	0	3	.000	31	16	39	4.46	2
2010	San Francisco h	N.L.	25	27	1	0	1.000	15	11	13	0.67	1
Major League Totals		5 Yrs.	293	295 2/3	17	14	.548	244	123	249	3.29	4
	Division Series											
2009	Boston	A.L.	1	0	0	0	.000	0	1	1	INF	0
2010	San Francisco	N.L.	1	2	0	1	.000	1	0	1	4.50	0
Division Series Totals			2	2	0	1	.000	1	1	2	13.50	0
	Championship Series											
2010	San Francisco	N.L.	2	1	0	0	.000	0	1	3	27.00	0
	World Series Record											
2010	San Francisco	N.L.	2	1	0	0	.000	1	1	1	18.00	0

a Played for Texas Rangers in the Dominican Summer League as an infielder 1997. Did not play 1998 through 2001.
b Released by Texas Rangers, June 4, 1998. Signed with Hiroshima (Japan) 2002.
c Signed with New York Yankees organization, March 5, 2003.
d Traded to Colorado Rockies with pitcher Eduardo Sierra for pitcher Shawn Chacon, July 28, 2005.
e On disabled list from April 18 to May 15 and September 8 to October 31, 2007.
f Traded to Kansas City Royals for player to be named later, March 26, 2008. Colorado Rockies received pitcher Jorge De La Rosa to complete trade, April 30, 2008.
g Traded to Boston Red Sox for outfielder Coco Crisp, November 19, 2008.
h Traded to San Francisco Giants for pitcher Daniel Turpen, July 31, 2010.

RAUCH, JON ERICH

Born, Louisville, Kentucky, September 27, 1978.
Bats Right. Throws Right. Height, 6 feet, 11 inches. Weight, 290 pounds.

Year	Club	Lea	G	IP	W	L	Pct	SO	BB	H	ERA	SAVES
1999	Bristol	Appal.	14	56 2/3	4	4	.500	66	16	65	4.45	2
1999	Winston-Salem	Carolina	1	6	0	0	.000	7	3	4	3.00	0
2000	Winston-Salem	Carolina	18	110	11	3	.786	124	33	102	2.86	0
2000	Birmingham	Southern	8	56	5	1	.833	63	16	36	2.25	0
2001	Charlotte	Int.	6	28	1	3	.250	27	7	28	5.79	0
2002	Chicago	A.L.	8	28 2/3	2	1	.667	19	14	28	6.59	0
2002	Charlotte	Int.	19	109 1/3	7	8	.467	97	42	91	4.28	0
2003	Charlotte	Int.	24	124 2/3	7	1	.875	94	35	121	4.11	0
2004	Charlotte	Int.	14	72 1/3	6	3	.667	61	25	57	3.11	0
2004	Chicago	A.L.	2	8 2/3	1	1	.500	4	4	16	6.23	0
2004	Edmonton	P.C.	3	18	1	1	.500	13	2	17	4.50	0
2004	Montreal a-b	N.L.	9	23 1/3	3	0	1.000	18	7	14	1.54	0
2005	New Orleans	P.C.	7	21 1/3	1	1	.500	25	2	19	2.53	0
2005	Washington c	N.L.	15	30	2	4	.333	23	11	24	3.60	0
2006	Washington	N.L.	85	91 1/3	4	5	.444	86	36	78	3.35	2
2007	Washington	N.L.	*88	87 1/3	8	4	.667	71	21	75	3.61	4
2008	Washington-Arizona d	N.L.	74	71 2/3	4	8	.333	66	16	69	4.14	18
2009	Arizona	N.L.	58	54 1/3	2	2	.500	35	17	57	4.14	2
2009	Minnesota e	A.L.	17	15 2/3	5	1	.833	14	6	13	1.72	0
2010	Minnesota f	A.L.	59	57 2/3	3	1	.750	46	14	61	3.12	21
Major League Totals		8 Yrs.	415	468 2/3	34	27	.557	382	146	435	3.71	47
	Division Series											
2009	Minnesota	A.L.	3	1 1/3	0	0	.000	0	2	1	6.75	0
2010	Minnesota	A.L.	2	1 2/3	0	0	.000	1	0	0	0.00	0
Division Series Totals			5	3	0	0	.000	1	2	1	3.00	0

a Traded to Montreal Expos with pitcher Gary Majewski for outfielder Carl Everett, July 18, 2004.
b On disabled list from August 14 to September 14, 2004.
c On disabled list from May 26 to September 6, 2005.
d Traded to Arizona Diamondbacks for infielder Emilio Bonifacio, July 22, 2008.
e Traded to Minnesota Twins for player to be named later, August 28, 2009. Arizona Diamondbacks received pitcher Kevin Mulvey to complete trade, September 1, 2009.
f Filed for free agency, November 1, 2010. Signed with Toronto Blue Jays, January 17, 2011.

RAY, CHRISTOPHER THOMAS (CHRIS)

Born, Tampa, Florida, January 12, 1982.
Bats Right. Throws Right. Height, 6 feet, 3 inches. Weight, 225 pounds.

Year	Club	Lea	G	IP	W	L	Pct	SO	BB	H	ERA	SAVES
2003	Aberdeen	N.Y.-Penn.	9	38⅓	2	0	1.000	44	10	32	2.82	0
2004	Frederick	Carolina	14	73⅓	6	3	.667	74	20	82	3.80	0
2004	Delmarva	So.Atl.	10	50	2	3	.400	46	17	43	3.42	0
2005	Bowie	Eastern	31	37⅓	1	2	.333	40	7	17	0.96	18
2005	Baltimore	A.L.	41	40⅔	1	3	.250	43	18	34	2.66	0
2006	Baltimore	A.L.	61	66	4	4	.500	51	27	45	2.73	33
2007	Baltimore a	A.L.	43	42⅔	5	6	.455	44	18	35	4.43	16
2008	Frederick	Carolina	1	1	0	0	.000	1	0	3	18.00	0
2008	Bowie	Eastern	1	1	0	0	.000	2	0	0	0.00	0
2008	Orioles	Gulf Coast	3	3	0	0	.000	3	0	3	0.00	0
2008	Aberdeen	N.Y.-Penn.	3	3	0	0	.000	5	0	4	0.00	0
2008	Delmarva b	So.Atl.	1	1	0	0	.000	2	0	1	0.00	0
2009	Bowie	Eastern	3	3	0	0	.000	2	2	0	0.00	0
2009	Norfolk	Int.	8	12	0	1	.000	13	4	5	2.25	1
2009	Baltimore c-d	A.L.	46	43⅓	0	4	.000	39	23	64	7.27	0
2010	San Jose	Calif.	1	1⅔	0	1	.000	1	0	7	10.80	0
2010	Texas	A.L.	35	31⅔	2	0	1.000	16	16	24	3.41	1
2010	San Francisco e-f-g	N.L.	28	24	3	0	1.000	15	9	24	4.13	1
Major League Totals		5 Yrs.	254	248⅓	15	17	.469	208	111	226	4.02	51

a On disabled list from July 21 to October 23, 2007.
b On disabled list from March 21 to October 21, 2008.
c On disabled list from July 6 to July 31, 2009.
d Traded to Texas Rangers with pitcher Ben Snyder for pitcher Kevin Millwood and cash, December 9, 2009.
e Traded to San Francisco Giants with pitcher Michael Main for catcher Bengie Molina and cash, July 1, 2010.
f On disabled list from August 18 to September 2, 2010.
g Not offered contract, December 2, 2010.

REYES (VALARDE), DENNYS

Born, Higuera de Zaragoza, Mexico, April 19, 1977.
Bats Left. Throws Left. Height, 6 feet, 3 inches. Weight, 246 pounds.

Year	Club	Lea	G	IP	W	L	Pct	SO	BB	H	ERA	SAVES
1993	Mexico City Reds a	Mexican	7	5⅓	0	1	.000	5	9	4	5.06	0
1994	Vero Beach	Fla.St.	9	41⅔	2	4	.333	25	18	58	6.70	0
1994	Great Falls	Pioneer	14	66⅔	7	1	.875	70	25	71	3.78	0
1995	Mexico	Mexican	17	58⅔	5	5	.500	44	41	76	6.60	0
1995	Vero Beach	Fla.St.	3	10	1	0	1.000	9	6	8	1.80	0
1996	San Bernardino	Calif.	29	166	11	12	.478	176	77	166	4.17	0
1997	San Antonio	Texas	12	80⅓	8	1	.889	66	28	79	3.02	0
1997	Albuquerque	P.C.	10	57⅓	6	3	.667	45	33	70	5.65	0
1997	Los Angeles	N.L.	14	47	2	3	.400	36	18	51	3.83	0
1998	Albuquerque	P.C.	7	43⅔	1	4	.200	58	18	31	1.44	0
1998	Indianapolis	Int.	4	24	2	0	1.000	27	14	20	3.00	0
1998	Los Angeles-Cincinnati b	N.L.	19	67⅓	3	5	.375	77	47	62	4.54	0
1999	Cincinnati	N.L.	65	61⅔	2	2	.500	72	39	53	3.79	2
2000	Cincinnati	N.L.	62	43⅔	2	1	.667	36	29	43	4.53	0
2001	Cincinnati	N.L.	35	53	2	6	.250	52	35	51	4.92	0
2001	Louisville c-d	Int.	7	34⅓	4	2	.667	34	16	34	3.67	0
2002	Colorado	N.L.	43	40⅓	0	1	.000	30	24	43	4.24	0
2002	Texas e	A.L.	15	42⅓	4	3	.571	29	21	55	6.38	0
2003	Tucson	P.C.	33	31⅔	2	1	.667	30	22	24	2.84	2
2003	Pittsburgh-Arizona f-g-h	N.L.	15	12⅔	0	0	.000	16	10	15	10.66	0
2004	Kansas City i	A.L.	40	108	4	8	.333	91	50	114	4.75	0
2005	San Diego j	N.L.	36	43⅔	3	2	.600	35	32	57	5.15	0
2006	Rochester	Int.	4	18	1	0	1.000	13	3	11	0.50	0
2006	Minnesota	A.L.	66	50⅔	5	0	1.000	49	15	35	0.89	0
2007	Minnesota k	A.L.	50	29⅓	2	1	.667	21	21	34	3.99	0
2008	Minnesota l	A.L.	75	46⅓	3	0	1.000	39	15	40	2.33	0
2009	St. Louis	N.L.	75	41	0	2	.000	33	21	35	3.29	1
2010	St. Louis m-n	N.L.	59	38	3	1	.750	25	21	34	3.55	1
Major League Totals		14 Yrs.	669	725	35	35	.500	641	398	722	4.18	4
	Division Series											
2006	Minnesota	A.L.	2	1	0	0	.000	0	2	1	9.00	0
2009	St. Louis	N.L.	2	1	0	0	.000	2	0	1	9.00	0
Division Series Totals			4	2	0	0	.000	2	2	2	9.00	0

a Sold to Los Angeles Dodgers, July 5, 1993.

b Traded to Cincinnati Reds with infielder Paul Konerko for pitcher Jeff Shaw, July 4, 1998.
c On disabled list from May 30 to July 2, 2001.
d Traded to Colorado Rockies with infielder Pokey Reese for pitcher Gabe White and pitcher Luke Hudson, December 18, 2001.
e Traded to Texas Rangers with outfielder Todd Hollandsworth for outfielder Gabe Kapler, outfielder Jason Romano and cash, July 31, 2002.
f Not offered contract, December 20, 2002. Signed with Pittsburgh Pirates organization, February 7, 2003.
g Filed for free agency, May 19, 2003. Signed with Arizona Diamondbacks organization, June 11, 2003.
h Filed for free agency, October 3, 2003. Signed with Kansas City Royals organization, November 6, 2003.
i Filed for free agency, October 29, 2004. Signed with San Diego Padres, November 29, 2004.
j Released by San Diego Padres, July 18, 2005. Signed with Minnesota Twins organization, December 23, 2005.
k On disabled list from May 21 to June 14 and August 22 to October 10, 2007.
l Filed for free agency, October 30, 2008. Signed with St. Louis Cardinals, March 5, 2009.
m On disabled list from August 16 to September 2, 2010.
n Filed for free agency, November 1, 2010. Signed with Philadelphia Phillies, December 9, 2010.

RHODES, ARTHUR LEE

Born, Waco, Texas, October 24, 1969.
Bats Left. Throws Left. Height, 6 feet, 2 inches. Weight, 210 pounds.

Year Club	Lea	G	IP	W	L	Pct	SO	BB	H	ERA	SAVES
1988 Bluefield	Appal.	11	35⅓	3	4	.429	44	15	29	3.31	0
1989 Erie	N.Y.-Penn.	5	31	2	0	1.000	45	10	13	1.16	0
1989 Frederick	Carolina	7	24⅓	2	2	.500	28	19	19	5.18	0
1990 Frederick	Carolina	13	80⅔	4	6	.400	103	21	62	2.12	0
1990 Hagerstown	Eastern	12	72⅓	3	4	.429	60	39	62	3.73	0
1991 Hagerstown	Eastern	19	106⅔	7	4	.636	115	47	73	2.70	0
1991 Baltimore	A.L.	8	36	0	3	.000	23	23	47	8.00	0
1992 Rochester	Int.	17	101⅔	6	6	.500	115	46	84	3.72	0
1992 Baltimore	A.L.	15	94⅓	7	5	.583	77	38	87	3.63	0
1993 Rochester	Int.	6	26⅔	1	1	.500	33	15	26	4.05	0
1993 Baltimore	A.L.	17	85⅔	5	6	.455	49	49	91	6.51	0
1994 Frederick	Carolina	1	5	0	0	.000	7	0	3	0.00	0
1994 Baltimore	A.L.	10	52⅔	3	5	.375	47	30	51	5.81	0
1994 Rochester	Int.	15	90⅓	7	5	.583	86	34	70	2.79	0
1995 Rochester	Int.	4	30	2	1	.667	33	8	27	2.70	0
1995 Baltimore	A.L.	19	75⅓	2	5	.286	77	48	68	6.21	0
1996 Baltimore	A.L.	28	53	9	1	.900	62	23	48	4.08	1
1997 Baltimore	A.L.	53	95⅓	10	3	.769	102	26	75	3.02	1
1998 Rochester	Int.	1	2	0	0	.000	1	1	3	4.50	0
1998 Baltimore a	A.L.	45	77	4	4	.500	83	34	65	3.51	4
1999 Baltimore b	A.L.	43	53	3	4	.429	59	45	43	5.43	3
2000 Seattle	A.L.	72	69⅓	5	8	.385	77	29	51	4.28	0
2001 Seattle	A.L.	71	68	8	0	1.000	83	12	46	1.72	3
2002 Seattle	A.L.	66	69⅔	10	4	.714	81	13	45	2.33	2
2003 Seattle c	A.L.	67	54	3	3	.500	48	18	53	4.17	3
2004 Sacramento	P.C.	2	2	0	0	.000	3	1	0	0.00	0
2004 Oakland d-e-f	A.L.	37	38⅔	3	3	.500	34	21	46	5.12	9
2005 Akron	Eastern	1	1	0	0	.000	0	0	0	0.00	0
2005 Cleveland g	A.L.	47	43⅓	3	1	.750	43	12	33	2.08	0
2006 Philadelphia h	N.L.	55	45⅔	0	5	.000	48	30	47	5.32	4
2007 Seattle i-j	A.L.			INJURED—Did Not Play							
2008 West Tenn	Southern	1	0⅓	0	1	.000	1	1	2	27.00	0
2008 Seattle	A.L.	36	22	2	1	.667	26	13	17	2.86	1
2008 Florida k-l	N.L.	25	13⅓	2	0	1.000	14	3	11	0.68	1
2009 Cincinnati	N.L.	66	53⅓	1	1	.500	48	20	37	2.53	0
2010 Cincinnati m	N.L.	69	55	4	4	.500	50	18	38	2.29	0
Major League Totals	19 Yrs.	849	1154⅔	84	66	.560	1131	505	999	4.06	32
Division Series											
1996 Baltimore	A.L.	2	1	0	0	.000	1	1	1	9.00	0
1997 Baltimore	A.L.	1	2⅓	0	0	.000	4	0	0	0.00	0
2000 Seattle	A.L.	3	2⅔	0	0	.000	2	2	0	0.00	0
2001 Seattle	A.L.	3	2⅔	0	0	.000	1	0	1	0.00	0
2010 Cincinnati	N.L.	1	0⅓	0	0	.000	1	0	0	0.00	0
Division Series Totals		10	9	0	0	.000	9	3	2	1.00	0
Championship Series											
1996 Baltimore	A.L.	3	2	0	0	.000	2	0	2	0.00	0
1997 Baltimore	A.L.	2	2⅓	0	0	.000	2	3	2	0.00	0
2000 Seattle	A.L.	4	2	0	1	.000	5	4	8	31.50	0
2001 Seattle	A.L.	2	2	0	0	.000	2	0	2	4.50	0
Championship Series Totals		11	8⅓	0	1	.000	11	7	14	8.64	0

a On disabled list from July 5 to August 17, 1998.
b Filed for free agency, November 1, 1999. Signed with Seattle Mariners, December 21, 1999.
c Filed for free agency, October 27, 2003. Signed with Oakland Athletics, December 22, 2003.
d On disabled list from June 28 to August 18, 2004.
e Traded to Pittsburgh Pirates with pitcher Mark Redman for catcher Jason Kendall and cash, November 25, 2004.
f Traded to Cleveland Indians for outfielder Matt Lawton, December 11, 2004.
g On disabled list from August 12 to September 2, 2005.
h Traded to Philadelphia Phillies for outfielder Jason Michaels, January 27, 2006.
i Filed for free agency, October 28, 2006. Signed with Seattle Mariners, January 25, 2007.
j On disabled list from April 2 to October 24, 2007.
k Traded to Florida Marlins for pitcher Gaby Hernandez, July 31, 2008.
l Filed for free agency, November 1, 2008. Signed with Cincinnati Reds, December 12, 2008.
m Filed for free agency, November 1, 2010. Signed with Texas Rangers, January 3, 2011.

RICHARD, CLAYTON COLBY

Born, Lafayette, Indiana, September 12, 1983.
Bats Left. Throws Left. Height, 6 feet, 5 inches. Weight, 240 pounds.

Year	Club	Lea	G	IP	W	L	Pct	SO	BB	H	ERA	SAVES
2005	Great Falls	Pioneer	10	41	2	1	.667	39	12	37	2.85	0
2005	Kannapolis	So.Atl.	3	$10\frac{1}{3}$	0	1	.000	8	1	14	5.23	0
2006	Winston-Salem	Carolina	4	$23\frac{2}{3}$	1	3	.250	12	6	29	4.56	0
2006	Kannapolis	So.Atl.	18	$95\frac{2}{3}$	6	6	.500	54	28	117	3.67	0
2007	Winston-Salem	Carolina	28	$161\frac{1}{3}$	8	12	.400	99	59	159	3.63	0
2008	Birmingham	Southern	13	$83\frac{2}{3}$	6	6	.500	53	16	66	2.47	0
2008	Charlotte	Int.	7	44	6	0	1.000	33	4	33	2.45	0
2008	Chicago a	A.L.	13	$47\frac{2}{3}$	2	5	.286	29	13	61	6.04	0
2009	Chicago	A.L.	26	89	4	3	.571	66	37	94	4.65	0
2009	San Diego b	N.L.	12	64	5	2	.714	48	34	60	4.08	0
2010	San Diego	N.L.	33	$201\frac{2}{3}$	14	9	.609	153	78	206	3.75	0
Major League Totals		3 Yrs.	84	$402\frac{1}{3}$	25	19	.568	296	162	421	4.27	0
Division Series												
2008	Chicago	A.L.	2	$6\frac{1}{3}$	0	0	.000	6	3	5	1.42	0

a On disabled list from March 22 to May 29, 2008.
b Traded to San Diego Padres with pitcher Aaron Poreda, pitcher Adam Russell and pitcher Dexter Carter for pitcher Jake Peavy, July 31, 2009.

RIVERA, MARIANO

Born, Panama City, Panama, November 29, 1969.
Bats Right. Throws Right. Height, 6 feet, 2 inches. Weight, 195 pounds.

Year	Club	Lea	G	IP	W	L	Pct	SO	BB	H	ERA	SAVES
1990	Yankees	Gulf Coast	22	52	5	1	.833	58	7	17	0.17	1
1991	Greensboro	So. Atl.	29	$114\frac{2}{3}$	4	9	.308	123	36	103	2.75	0
1992	Ft. Lauderdale	Fla. St.	10	$59\frac{1}{3}$	5	3	.625	42	5	40	2.28	0
1993	Yankees	Gulf Coast	2	4	0	1	.000	6	1	2	2.25	0
1993	Greensboro	So. Atl.	10	$39\frac{1}{3}$	1	0	1.000	32	15	31	2.06	0
1994	Tampa	Fla. St.	7	$36\frac{2}{3}$	3	0	1.000	27	12	34	2.21	0
1994	Albany	Eastern	9	$63\frac{1}{3}$	3	0	1.000	39	8	58	2.27	0
1994	Columbus	Int.	6	31	4	2	.667	23	10	34	5.81	0
1995	Columbus	Int.	7	30	2	2	.500	30	3	25	2.10	0
1995	New York	A.L.	19	67	5	3	.625	51	30	71	5.51	0
1996	New York	A.L.	61	$107\frac{2}{3}$	8	3	.727	130	34	73	2.09	5
1997	New York	A.L.	66	$71\frac{2}{3}$	6	4	.600	68	20	65	1.88	43
1998	New York a	A.L.	54	$61\frac{1}{3}$	3	0	1.000	36	17	48	1.91	36
1999	New York	A.L.	66	69	4	3	.571	52	18	43	1.83	*45
2000	New York	A.L.	66	$75\frac{2}{3}$	7	4	.636	58	25	58	2.85	36
2001	New York	A.L.	71	$80\frac{2}{3}$	4	6	.400	83	12	61	2.34	*50
2002	Yankees	Gulf Coast	1	2	0	0	.000	2	1	2	0.00	0
2002	New York b	A.L.	45	46	1	4	.200	41	11	35	2.74	28
2003	New York c	A.L.	64	$70\frac{2}{3}$	5	2	.714	63	10	61	1.66	40
2004	New York	A.L.	74	$78\frac{2}{3}$	4	2	.667	66	20	65	1.94	*53
2005	New York	A.L.	71	$78\frac{1}{3}$	7	4	.636	80	18	50	1.38	43
2006	New York	A.L.	63	75	5	5	.500	55	11	61	1.80	34
2007	New York d	A.L.	67	$71\frac{1}{3}$	3	4	.429	74	12	68	3.15	30
2008	New York	A.L.	64	$70\frac{2}{3}$	6	5	.545	77	6	41	1.40	39
2009	New York	A.L.	66	$66\frac{1}{3}$	3	3	.500	72	12	48	1.76	44
2010	New York e	A.L.	61	60	3	3	.500	45	11	39	1.80	33
Major League Totals		16 Yrs.	978	1150	74	55	.574	1051	267	887	2.23	559
Division Series												
1995	New York	A.L.	3	$5\frac{1}{3}$	1	0	1.000	8	1	3	0.00	0

Year	Club	Lea	G	IP	W	L	Pct	SO	BB	H	ERA	SAVES
1996	New York	A.L.	2	4 2/3	0	0	.000	1	1	0	0.00	0
1997	New York	A.L.	2	2	0	0	.000	1	0	2	4.50	1
1998	New York	A.L.	3	3 1/3	0	0	.000	2	1	1	0.00	2
1999	New York	A.L.	2	3	0	0	.000	3	0	1	0.00	2
2000	New York	A.L.	3	5	0	0	.000	2	0	2	0.00	3
2001	New York	A.L.	3	5	0	0	.000	4	0	4	0.00	2
2002	New York	A.L.	1	1	0	0	.000	0	0	1	0.00	1
2003	New York	A.L.	2	4	0	0	.000	4	0	0	0.00	2
2004	New York	A.L.	4	5 2/3	1	0	1.000	2	0	2	0.00	0
2005	New York	A.L.	2	3	0	0	.000	2	1	1	3.00	2
2006	New York	A.L.	1	1	0	0	.000	0	0	1	0.00	0
2007	New York	A.L.	3	4 2/3	0	0	.000	6	1	2	0.00	0
2009	New York	A.L.	3	3 2/3	0	0	.000	7	1	4	0.00	1
2010	New York	A.L.	3	3 1/3	0	0	.000	1	0	2	0.00	2
Division Series Totals			37	54 2/3	2	0	1.000	43	6	26	0.33	18
	Championship Series											
1996	New York	A.L.	2	4	1	0	1.000	5	1	6	0.00	0
1998	New York	A.L.	4	5 2/3	0	0	.000	5	1	0	0.00	1
1999	New York	A.L.	3	4 2/3	1	0	1.000	3	0	5	0.00	2
2000	New York	A.L.	3	4 2/3	0	0	.000	1	0	4	1.93	1
2001	New York	A.L.	4	4 2/3	1	0	1.000	3	1	2	1.93	2
2003	New York	A.L.	4	8	1	0	1.000	6	0	5	1.13	2
2004	New York	A.L.	5	7	0	0	.000	6	2	6	1.29	2
2009	New York	A.L.	5	7	0	0	.000	4	2	3	1.29	2
2010	New York	A.L.	3	3	0	0	.000	1	0	2	0.00	1
Championship Series Totals			33	48 2/3	4	0	1.000	34	7	33	0.92	13
	World Series Record											
1996	New York	A.L.	4	5 2/3	0	0	.000	4	3	4	1.59	0
1998	New York	A.L.	3	4 1/3	0	0	.000	4	0	5	0.00	3
1999	New York	A.L.	3	4 2/3	1	0	1.000	3	1	3	0.00	2
2000	New York	A.L.	4	6	0	0	.000	7	1	4	3.00	2
2001	New York	A.L.	4	6 1/3	1	1	.500	7	1	6	1.42	0
2003	New York	A.L.	2	4	0	0	.000	4	0	2	0.00	1
2009	New York	A.L.	4	5 1/3	0	0	.000	3	2	3	0.00	2
World Series Totals			24	36 1/3	2	1	.667	32	8	27	0.99	11

a On disabled list from April 6 to April 24, 1998.

b On disabled list from June 9 to June 25 and July 21 to August 8 and August 18 to September 20, 2002.

c On disabled list from March 25 to April 29, 2003.

d Filed for free agency, October 30, 2007, re-signed with New York Yankees, December 17, 2007.

e Filed for free agency, November 1, 2010, re-signed with New York Yankees, December 14, 2010.

ROBERTSON, DAVID

Born, Birmingham, Alabama, April 9, 1985.

Bats Right. Throws Right. Height, 5 feet, 11 inches. Weight, 190 pounds.

Year	Club	Lea	G	IP	W	L	Pct	SO	BB	H	ERA	SAVES
2007	Trenton	Eastern	2	4	0	0	.000	9	2	2	2.25	0
2007	Tampa	Fla.St.	18	33 1/3	3	1	.750	37	15	18	1.08	1
2007	Charleston	So.Atl.	24	47	5	2	.714	67	15	25	0.77	3
2008	Trenton	Eastern	9	18 2/3	0	0	.000	26	6	8	0.96	2
2008	Scranton/WB	Int.	21	35	4	0	1.000	51	17	20	2.06	1
2008	New York	A.L.	25	30 1/3	4	0	1.000	36	15	29	5.34	0
2009	Scranton/WB	Int.	8	14 2/3	0	3	.000	25	6	10	1.84	2
2009	New York	A.L.	45	43 2/3	2	1	.667	63	23	36	3.30	1
2010	New York	A.L.	64	61 1/3	4	5	.444	71	33	59	3.82	1
Major League Totals		3 Yrs.	134	135 1/3	10	6	.625	170	71	124	3.99	2
	Division Series											
2009	New York	A.L.	1	1	1	0	1.000	0	0	1	0.00	0
2010	New York	A.L.	2	0 2/3	0	0	.000	1	1	0	0.00	0
Division Series Totals			3	1 2/3	1	0	1.000	1	1	1	0.00	0
	Championship Series											
2009	New York	A.L.	2	2	1	0	1.000	1	2	1	0.00	0
2010	New York	A.L.	4	2 2/3	0	0	.000	4	1	8	20.25	0
Championship Series Totals			6	4 2/3	1	0	1.000	5	3	9	11.57	0
	World Series Record											
2009	New York	A.L.	2	2 1/3	0	0	.000	2	1	2	0.00	0

ROBERTSON, NATHAN DANIEL (NATE)

Born, Wichita, Kansas, September 3, 1977.
Bats Right. Throws Left. Height, 6 feet, 2 inches. Weight, 225 pounds.

Year	Club	Lea	G	IP	W	L	Pct	SO	BB	H	ERA	SAVES
1999	Utica	N.Y.-Penn.	5	26	2	0	1.000	26	8	22	2.77	0
1999	Kane County	Midwest	8	51	6	1	.857	33	12	42	2.29	0
2000	Kane County	Midwest	6	$17\frac{2}{3}$	0	2	.000	15	6	24	5.09	0
2001	Brevard County	Fla.St.	19	$106\frac{1}{3}$	11	4	.733	67	43	95	2.88	0
2002	Portland	Eastern	27	163	10	9	.526	109	50	156	3.42	0
2002	Florida	N.L.	6	$8\frac{1}{3}$	0	1	.000	3	4	15	11.88	0
2003	Toledo	Int.	24	155	9	7	.563	102	47	145	3.14	0
2003	Detroit a	A.L.	8	$44\frac{2}{3}$	1	2	.333	33	23	55	5.44	0
2004	Detroit	A.L.	34	$196\frac{2}{3}$	12	10	.545	155	66	210	4.90	1
2005	Detroit	A.L.	32	$196\frac{2}{3}$	7	16	.304	122	65	202	4.48	0
2006	Detroit	A.L.	32	$208\frac{2}{3}$	13	13	.500	137	67	206	3.84	0
2007	Erie	Eastern	1	6	1	0	1.000	6	1	0	0.00	0
2007	Detroit b	A.L.	30	$177\frac{2}{3}$	9	13	.409	119	63	199	4.76	0
2008	Detroit	A.L.	32	$168\frac{2}{3}$	7	11	.389	108	62	218	6.35	0
2009	Toledo	Int.	5	19	1	1	.500	21	4	19	1.89	0
2009	Detroit c	A.L.	28	$49\frac{2}{3}$	2	3	.400	35	28	59	5.44	0
2010	Memphis	P.C.	6	20	2	1	.667	12	6	32	9.45	0
2010	Lehigh Valley	Int.	2	$10\frac{2}{3}$	1	1	.500	6	2	10	3.38	0
2010	Florida-Philadelphia d-e-f-g	N.L.	21	$101\frac{1}{3}$	6	8	.429	63	42	115	5.95	0
Major League Totals		9 Yrs.	223	$1152\frac{1}{3}$	57	77	.425	775	420	1279	5.01	1
	Division Series											
2006	Detroit	A.L.	1	$5\frac{2}{3}$	0	1	.000	1	0	12	11.12	0
	Championship Series											
2006	Detroit	A.L.	1	5	1	0	1.000	4	3	6	0.00	0
	World Series Record											
2006	Detroit	A.L.	1	5	0	1	.000	3	3	5	3.60	0

a Traded to Detroit Tigers with pitcher Gary Knotts and pitcher Rob Henkel for pitcher Mark Redman and pitcher Jerrod Fuell, January 11, 2003.
b On disabled list from June 6 to June 26, 2007.
c On disabled list from May 6 to May 21 and June 27 to August 28, 2009.
d Traded to Florida Marlins for pitcher Jay Voss, March 30, 2010.
e Released by Florida Marlins, July 27, 2010. Signed with St. Louis Cardinals organization, August 2, 2010.
f Filed for free agency, August 23, 2010. Signed with Philadelphia Phillies organization, August 24, 2010.
g Released by Philadelphia Phillies, September 10, 2010.

RODNEY, FERNANDO

Born, Samana, Dominican Republic, March 17, 1977.
Bats Right. Throws Right. Height, 5 feet, 11 inches. Weight, 220 pounds.

Year	Club	Lea	G	IP	W	L	Pct	SO	BB	H	ERA	SAVES
1998	Detroit	Dominican	11	32	1	3	.250	37	19	25	3.38	1
1999	Lakeland	Fla.St.	4	$6\frac{1}{3}$	1	0	1.000	5	1	7	1.42	2
1999	Tigers	Gulf Coast	22	30	3	3	.500	39	21	20	2.40	9
2000	West Michigan	Midwest	22	$82\frac{2}{3}$	6	4	.600	56	35	74	2.94	0
2001	Erie	Eastern	4	$6\frac{1}{3}$	0	0	.000	8	3	7	4.26	1
2001	Lakeland	Fla.St.	16	$55\frac{1}{3}$	4	2	.667	44	19	53	3.42	0
2001	Tigers	Gulf Coast	1	1	0	0	.000	1	1	0	0.00	0
2002	Erie	Eastern	21	$20\frac{1}{3}$	1	0	1.000	18	5	14	1.33	11
2002	Detroit	A.L.	20	18	1	3	.250	10	10	25	6.00	0
2002	Toledo	Int.	20	$22\frac{1}{3}$	1	1	.500	25	9	13	0.81	4
2003	Toledo	Int.	38	$40\frac{2}{3}$	1	1	.500	58	13	22	1.33	23
2003	Detroit	A.L.	27	$29\frac{2}{3}$	1	3	.250	33	17	35	6.07	3
2004	Detroit a	A.L.	INJURED—Did Not Play									
2005	Toledo	Int.	3	3	0	0	.000	4	1	2	3.00	0
2005	Detroit b	A.L.	39	44	2	3	.400	42	17	39	2.86	9
2006	Detroit	A.L.	63	$71\frac{2}{3}$	7	4	.636	65	34	51	3.52	7
2007	Toledo	Int.	4	3	0	0	.000	4	2	4	0.00	0
2007	Detroit c	A.L.	48	$50\frac{2}{3}$	2	6	.250	54	21	46	4.26	1
2008	Toledo	Int.	4	$5\frac{1}{3}$	1	0	1.000	8	5	3	6.75	0
2008	Detroit d	A.L.	38	$40\frac{1}{3}$	0	6	.000	49	30	34	4.91	13
2009	Detroit e	A.L.	73	$75\frac{2}{3}$	2	5	.286	61	41	70	4.40	37
2010	Los Angeles	A.L.	72	68	4	3	.571	53	35	70	4.24	14
Major League Totals		8 Yrs.	380	398	19	33	.365	367	205	370	4.27	84
	Championship Series											
2006	Detroit	A.L.	3	$3\frac{2}{3}$	0	0	.000	4	1	1	0.00	0
	World Series Record											
2006	Detroit	A.L.	4	4	0	0	.000	5	4	5	4.50	0

a On disabled list from March 26 to October 4, 2004.
b On disabled list from March 29 to June 9, 2005.
c On disabled list from May 21 to June 5 and June 24 to August 4, 2007.
d On disabled list from March 30 to June 16, 2008.
e Filed for free agency, November 5, 2009. Signed with Los Angeles Angels, December 24, 2009.

RODRIGUEZ (MURILLO), FRANCISCO

Born, Mexicali, Mexico, February 26, 1983.
Bats Right. Throws Right. Height, 6 feet, 1 inch. Weight, 195 pounds.

Year Club	Lea	G	IP	W	L	Pct	SO	BB	H	ERA	SAVES
2005 Puebla a	Mexican	33	85	4	4	.500	36	45	94	5.61	0
2006 Rancho Cucamonga	Calif.	26	133 1/3	5	13	.278	83	68	158	5.47	0
2007 Rancho Cucamonga	Calif.	39	105 2/3	4	8	.333	70	53	117	5.96	2
2008 Arkansas	Texas	50	75 1/3	5	5	.500	69	33	76	3.82	2
2009 Salt Lake	P.C.	44	77 1/3	5	4	.556	60	40	67	3.96	0
2010 Salt Lake	P.C.	13	22 1/3	2	1	.667	19	6	19	3.63	0
2010 Los Angeles	A.L.	43	47 1/3	1	3	.250	36	26	46	4.37	0

a Signed with Anaheim Angels, December 26, 2005.

RODRIGUEZ, FRANCISCO JOSE

Born, Caracas, Venezuela, January 7, 1982.
Bats Right. Throws Right. Height, 6 feet. Weight, 195 pounds.

Year Club	Lea	G	IP	W	L	Pct	SO	BB	H	ERA	SAVES
1999 Boise	Northwest	1	5	1	0	1.000	6	1	3	5.40	0
1999 Butte	Pioneer	12	51 2/3	1	1	.500	69	21	33	3.31	0
2000 Lake Elsinore	California	13	64	4	4	.500	79	32	43	2.81	0
2001 Rancho Cucamonga	California	20	113 2/3	5	7	.417	147	55	127	5.38	0
2002 Arkansas	Texas	23	41 1/3	3	3	.500	61	15	32	1.96	9
2002 Salt Lake	P.C.	27	42	2	3	.400	59	13	30	2.57	6
2002 Anaheim	A.L.	5	5 2/3	0	0	.000	13	2	3	0.00	0
2003 Anaheim	A.L.	59	86	8	3	.727	95	35	50	3.03	2
2004 Anaheim	A.L.	69	84	4	1	.800	123	33	51	1.82	12
2005 Los Angeles a	A.L.	66	67 1/3	2	5	.286	91	32	45	2.67	*45
2006 Los Angeles	A.L.	69	73	2	3	.400	98	28	52	1.73	*47
2007 Los Angeles	A.L.	64	67 1/3	5	2	.714	90	34	50	2.81	40
2008 Los Angeles b	A.L.	*76	68 1/3	2	3	.400	77	34	54	2.24	*62
2009 New York	N.L.	70	68	3	6	.333	73	38	51	3.71	35
2010 New York	N.L.	53	57 1/3	4	2	.667	67	21	45	2.20	25
Major League Totals	9 Yrs.	531	577	30	25	.545	727	257	401	2.50	268
Division Series											
2002 Anaheim	A.L.	3	5 2/3	2	0	1.000	8	2	2	3.18	0
2004 Anaheim	A.L.	2	4 2/3	0	2	.000	5	3	4	3.86	0
2005 Los Angeles	A.L.	3	3 1/3	0	0	.000	2	0	5	2.70	2
2007 Los Angeles	A.L.	1	0 1/3	0	0	.000	1	1	1	54.00	0
2008 Los Angeles	A.L.	2	2 1/3	0	1	.000	2	2	5	7.71	0
Division Series Totals		11	16 1/3	2	3	.400	18	8	17	4.96	2
Championship Series											
2002 Anaheim	A.L.	4	4 1/3	2	0	1.000	7	2	2	0.00	0
2005 Los Angeles	A.L.	2	2 1/3	0	0	.000	3	3	2	0.00	1
Championship Series Totals		6	6 2/3	2	0	1.000	10	5	4	0.00	1
World Series Record											
2002 Anaheim	A.L.	4	8 2/3	1	1	.500	13	1	6	2.08	0

a On disabled list from May 15 to June 1, 2005.
b Filed for free agency, November 3, 2008. Signed with New York Mets, December 10, 2008.

RODRIGUEZ, WANDY FULTON

Born, Santiago Rodriguez, Dominican Republic, January 18, 1979.
Bats Both. Throws Left. Height, 5 feet, 11 inches. Weight, 160 pounds.

Year Club	Lea	G	IP	W	L	Pct	SO	BB	H	ERA	SAVES
2001 Martinsville	Appal.	12	74	4	3	.571	67	20	54	1.58	0
2002 Lexington	So.Atl.	28	159 1/3	11	4	.733	137	44	167	3.78	0
2003 Salem	Carolina	20	111	8	7	.533	72	41	102	3.49	0
2004 Round Rock	Texas	26	142 2/3	11	6	.647	115	57	159	4.48	0
2005 Corpus Christi	Texas	1	3 1/3	0	0	.000	3	2	3	2.70	0
2005 Round Rock	P.C.	8	46 1/3	4	2	.667	48	16	43	3.69	0
2005 Houston	N.L.	25	128 2/3	10	10	.500	80	53	135	5.53	0
2006 Round Rock	P.C.	5	26	2	2	.500	13	13	32	6.92	0
2006 Houston	N.L.	30	135 2/3	9	10	.474	98	63	154	5.64	0

Year	Club	Lea	G	IP	W	L	Pct	SO	BB	H	ERA	SAVES
2007	Houston	N.L.	31	$182\frac{2}{3}$	9	13	.409	158	62	179	4.58	0
2008	Corpus Christi	Texas	1	6	0	0	.000	0	1	4	1.50	0
2008	Houston a	N.L.	25	$137\frac{1}{3}$	9	7	.563	131	44	136	3.54	0
2009	Houston	N.L.	33	$205\frac{2}{3}$	14	12	.538	193	63	192	3.02	0
2010	Houston	N.L.	32	195	11	12	.478	178	68	183	3.60	0
Major League Totals		6 Yrs.	176	985	62	64	.492	838	353	979	4.18	0
	Division Series											
2005	Houston	N.L.	1	1	0	0	.000	2	0	1	9.00	0
	World Series Record											
2005	Houston	N.L.	2	$3\frac{2}{3}$	0	1	.000	2	5	4	2.45	0

a On disabled list from April 20 to May 28, 2008.

ROGERS, ESMIL A.

Born, Santo Domingo, Dominican Republic, August 14, 1985.
Bats Right. Throws Right. Height, 6 feet, 1 inch. Weight, 190 pounds.

Year	Club	Lea	G	IP	W	L	Pct	SO	BB	H	ERA	SAVES
2006	Casper	Pioneer	15	$63\frac{1}{3}$	3	6	.333	40	24	78	6.96	0
2007	Asheville	So.Atl.	19	$117\frac{2}{3}$	7	4	.636	90	42	125	3.75	0
2008	Modesto	Calif.	25	$143\frac{2}{3}$	9	7	.563	116	45	146	3.95	0
2009	Tulsa	Texas	15	$94\frac{1}{3}$	8	2	.800	83	19	87	2.48	0
2009	Colorado Springs	P.C.	12	$60\frac{2}{3}$	3	5	.375	46	35	77	7.42	0
2009	Colorado	N.L.	1	4	0	0	.000	3	2	3	4.50	0
2010	Colorado Springs	P.C.	12	61	3	3	.500	53	19	62	5.75	0
2010	Colorado	N.L.	28	72	2	3	.400	66	26	94	6.13	0
Major League Totals		2 Yrs.	29	76	2	3	.400	69	28	97	6.04	0

ROMERO, JUAN CARLOS (J.C.)

Born, Rio Piedras, Puerto Rico, June 4, 1976.
Bats Both. Throws Left. Height, 5 feet, 11 inches. Weight, 205 pounds.

Year	Club	Lea	G	IP	W	L	Pct	SO	BB	H	ERA	SAVES
1997	Elizabethtown	Appal.	18	24	3	2	.600	29	7	27	4.88	3
1997	Ft. Myers	Fla.St.	7	$12\frac{1}{3}$	1	1	.500	9	4	11	4.38	0
1998	New Britain	Eastern	51	78	6	3	.667	79	43	48	2.19	2
1999	New Britain	Eastern	36	53	4	4	.500	53	34	51	3.40	7
1999	Salt Lake	P.C.	15	$19\frac{2}{3}$	4	1	.800	20	14	18	3.20	1
1999	Minnesota	A.L.	5	$9\frac{2}{3}$	0	0	.000	4	0	13	3.72	0
2000	Fort Myers	Fla.St.	2	$4\frac{2}{3}$	0	0	.000	3	1	4	1.93	0
2000	Salt Lake	P.C.	17	$65\frac{1}{3}$	4	2	.667	38	25	60	3.44	4
2000	Minnesota a	A.L.	12	$57\frac{2}{3}$	2	7	.222	50	30	72	7.02	0
2001	Edmonton	P.C.	12	$63\frac{2}{3}$	3	3	.500	55	24	67	3.68	0
2001	Minnesota	A.L.	14	65	1	4	.200	39	24	71	6.23	0
2002	Minnesota	A.L.	81	81	9	2	.818	76	36	62	1.89	1
2003	Minnesota	A.L.	73	63	2	0	1.000	50	42	66	5.00	0
2004	Rochester	Int.	3	8	0	0	.000	11	5	4	2.25	0
2004	Minnesota	A.L.	74	$74\frac{1}{3}$	7	4	.636	69	38	61	3.51	1
2005	Minnesota b	A.L.	68	57	4	3	.571	48	39	50	3.47	0
2006	Los Angeles c	A.L.	65	$48\frac{1}{3}$	1	2	.333	31	28	57	6.70	0
2007	Boston	A.L.	23	20	1	0	1.000	11	15	24	3.15	1
2007	Philadelphia d-e	N.L.	51	$36\frac{1}{3}$	1	2	.333	31	25	15	1.24	0
2008	Philadelphia	N.L.	81	59	4	4	.500	52	38	41	2.75	1
2009	Lakewood	So.Atl.	1	2	0	0	.000	2	0	0	0.00	0
2009	Clearwater	Fla.St.	1	$0\frac{1}{3}$	0	0	.000	1	1	0	0.00	0
2009	Reading	Eastern	1	1	0	0	.000	0	0	0	0.00	0
2009	Lehigh Valley	Int.	5	$4\frac{2}{3}$	0	1	.000	5	2	5	3.86	0
2009	Philadelphia f	N.L.	21	$16\frac{2}{3}$	0	0	.000	12	13	13	2.70	0
2010	Clearwater	Fla.St.	3	4	0	0	.000	5	1	3	2.25	0
2010	Lehigh Valley	Int.	3	$2\frac{1}{3}$	0	1	.000	4	4	2	0.00	0
2010	Philadelphia g-h	N.L.	60	$36\frac{2}{3}$	1	0	1.000	28	29	30	3.68	3
Major League Totals		12 Yrs.	628	$624\frac{2}{3}$	33	28	.541	501	357	575	4.08	7
	Division Series											
2002	Minnesota	A.L.	3	$3\frac{1}{3}$	0	0	.000	2	1	3	0.00	0
2003	Minnesota	A.L.	3	$3\frac{1}{3}$	0	0	.000	1	2	3	0.00	0
2004	Minnesota	A.L.	2	1	0	0	.000	1	1	0	9.00	0
2007	Philadelphia	N.L.	3	2	0	1	.000	1	0	3	4.50	0
2008	Philadelphia	N.L.	1	$0\frac{1}{3}$	0	0	.000	0	0	0	0.00	0
2010	Philadelphia	N.L.	1	$0\frac{2}{3}$	0	0	.000	0	0	0	0.00	0
Division Series Totals			13	$10\frac{2}{3}$	0	1	.000	5	4	9	1.69	0

Year	Club	Lea	G	IP	W	L	Pct	SO	BB	H	ERA	SAVES
	Championship Series											
2002	Minnesota	A.L.	4	2	0	1	.000	3	2	4	22.50	0
2008	Philadelphia	N.L.	3	2⅓	0	0	.000	3	3	0	0.00	0
2010	Philadelphia	N.L.	1	0⅓	0	0	.000	0	0	0	0.00	0
Championship Series Totals			8	4⅔	0	1	.000	6	5	4	9.64	0
	World Series Record											
2008	Philadelphia	N.L.	4	4⅔	2	0	1.000	4	0	2	0.00	0

a On disabled list from March 25 to May 9, 2000.
b Traded to Los Angeles Angels for infielder Alexi Casilla, December 9, 2005.
c Filed for free agency, October 28, 2006. Signed with Boston Red Sox, December 15, 2006.
d Released by Boston Red Sox, June 18, 2007. Signed with Philadelphia Phillies organization, June 22, 2007.
e Filed for free agency, October 30, 2007, re-signed with Philadelphia Phillies, November 10, 2007.
f On disabled list from July 20 to September 28, 2009.
g On disabled list from March 26 to April 22, 2010.
h Filed for free agency, November 4, 2010, re-signed with Philadelphia Phillies, January 6, 2011.

ROMERO, RICARDO (RICKY)

Born, Los Angeles, California, November 6, 1984.
Bats Right. Throws Left. Height, 6 feet. Weight, 215 pounds.

Year	Club	Lea	G	IP	W	L	Pct	SO	BB	H	ERA	SAVES
2005	Dunedin	Fla.St.	8	30⅔	1	0	1.000	22	7	36	3.82	0
2005	Auburn	N.Y.-Penn.	1	2	0	0	.000	2	1	2	0.00	0
2006	New Hampshire	Eastern	12	67⅓	2	7	.222	41	26	65	5.08	0
2006	Dunedin	Fla.St.	10	58⅓	2	1	.667	61	14	48	2.47	0
2007	New Hampshire	Eastern	18	88⅓	3	6	.333	80	51	98	4.89	0
2007	Dunedin	Fla.St.	1	4⅔	0	0	.000	2	1	4	3.86	0
2008	New Hampshire	Eastern	21	121⅔	5	5	.500	78	55	139	4.96	0
2008	Syracuse	Int.	7	42⅔	3	3	.500	38	20	42	3.38	0
2009	Dunedin	Fla.St.	1	4	0	1	.000	5	1	6	13.50	0
2009	New Hampshire	Eastern	1	5⅓	0	0	.000	4	5	3	1.69	0
2009	Las Vegas	P.C.	1	5	0	0	.000	3	2	8	7.20	0
2009	Toronto a	A.L.	29	178	13	9	.591	141	79	192	4.30	0
2010	Toronto	A.L.	32	210	14	9	.609	174	82	189	3.73	0
Major League Totals		2 Yrs.	61	388	27	18	.600	315	161	381	3.99	0

a On disabled list from April 20 to May 15, 2009.

ROMO, SERGIO FRANCISCO

Born, Brawley, California, March 4, 1983.
Bats Right. Throws Right. Height, 5 feet, 11 inches. Weight, 190 pounds.

Year	Club	Lea	G	IP	W	L	Pct	SO	BB	H	ERA	SAVES
2005	Salem-Keizer	Northwest	15	68⅔	7	1	.875	65	9	70	2.75	0
2006	Augusta	So.Atl.	31	103⅓	10	2	.833	95	19	78	2.53	4
2007	San Jose	Calif.	41	66⅓	6	2	.750	106	15	35	1.36	9
2008	Connecticut	Eastern	24	27	1	3	.250	30	7	22	4.00	11
2008	Fresno	P.C.	3	6	0	0	.000	7	2	3	0.00	0
2008	San Francisco	N.L.	29	34	3	1	.750	33	8	16	2.12	0
2009	San Jose	Calif.	3	4⅔	0	0	.000	6	2	2	0.00	0
2009	Fresno	P.C.	3	3	0	0	.000	3	0	2	0.00	0
2009	San Francisco a	N.L.	45	34	5	2	.714	41	11	30	3.97	2
2010	San Francisco	N.L.	68	62	5	3	.625	70	14	46	2.18	0
Major League Totals		3 Yrs.	142	130	13	6	.684	144	33	92	2.63	2
	Division Series											
2010	San Francisco	N.L.	2	0⅔	1	0	1.000	0	0	3	40.50	0
	Championship Series											
2010	San Francisco	N.L.	3	2⅓	0	0	.000	3	1	2	0.00	0
	World Series Record											
2010	San Francisco	N.L.	1	0⅔	0	0	.000	1	0	1	0.00	0

a On disabled list from March 26 to May 30, 2009.

ROWLAND-SMITH, RYAN BENJAMIN

Born, Sydney, Australia, January 26, 1983.
Bats Left. Throws Left. Height, 6 feet, 3 inches. Weight, 240 pounds.

Year	Club	Lea	G	IP	W	L	Pct	SO	BB	H	ERA	SAVES
2001	Mariners	Arizona	17	33⅓	1	1	.500	39	9	25	2.97	5
2002	Wisconsin	Midwest	12	41⅓	1	2	.333	38	19	50	6.75	0
2002	Everett	Northwest	18	61⅔	4	1	.800	58	22	58	2.77	2

Year	Club	Lea	G	IP	W	L	Pct	SO	BB	H	ERA	SAVES
2003	Inland Empire	Calif.	15	19⅔	0	1	.000	15	8	12	3.20	0
2003	Wisconsin	Midwest	13	32⅓	3	0	1.000	37	14	22	1.11	1
2004	Inland Empire	Calif.	29	99⅔	5	3	.625	119	30	107	3.79	3
2005	San Antonio a	Texas	33	122	6	7	.462	102	51	133	4.35	0
2006	Inland Empire	Calif.	7	6⅓	0	1	.000	9	2	8	5.68	0
2006	San Antonio	Texas	23	41⅓	1	3	.250	48	18	38	2.83	4
2007	Tacoma	P.C.	25	41⅔	3	4	.429	50	22	35	3.67	1
2007	Seattle	A.L.	26	38⅔	1	0	1.000	42	15	39	3.96	0
2008	Tacoma	P.C.	3	18⅔	2	0	1.000	12	7	12	2.89	0
2008	Seattle	A.L.	47	118⅓	5	3	.625	77	48	114	3.42	2
2009	Tacoma	P.C.	10	56⅓	5	3	.625	38	10	61	4.31	0
2009	Seattle b	A.L.	15	96⅓	5	4	.556	52	27	87	3.74	0
2010	Tacoma	P.C.	6	37	2	4	.333	24	5	45	5.11	0
2010	Seattle c-d	A.L.	27	109⅓	1	10	.091	49	44	141	6.75	0
Major League Totals		4 Yrs.	115	362⅔	12	17	.414	220	134	381	4.57	2

a Selected by Minnesota Twins in Rule V draft, December 13, 2004. Returned to Seattle Mariners, March 25, 2005.
b On disabled list from April 11 to June 23, 2009.
c On disabled list from July 28 to September 3, 2010.
d Not offered contract, December 2, 2010. Signed with Houston Astros, December 10, 2010.

RUSSELL, JAMES CLAYTON

Born, Cincinnati, Ohio, January 8, 1986.
Bats Left. Throws Left. Height, 6 feet, 4 inches. Weight, 205 pounds.

Year	Club	Lea	G	IP	W	L	Pct	SO	BB	H	ERA	SAVES
2007	Cubs	Arizona	1	2	0	0	.000	2	0	0	0.00	0
2007	Peoria	Midwest	2	7	0	0	.000	9	4	3	0.00	0
2008	Daytona	Fla.St.	8	41	2	2	.500	24	13	36	3.51	0
2008	Tennessee	Southern	18	86⅓	4	8	.333	62	25	111	6.36	0
2009	Iowa	P.C.	26	65⅔	3	3	.500	46	19	71	3.43	0
2009	Tennessee	Southern	11	37	2	3	.400	26	9	45	5.11	0
2010	Iowa	P.C.	5	11	0	0	.000	10	4	11	5.73	0
2010	Chicago	N.L.	57	49	1	1	.500	42	11	55	4.96	0

RZEPCZYNSKI, MARC WALTER

Born, Yorba Linda, California, August 29, 1985.
Bats Left. Throws Left. Height, 6 feet, 1 inch. Weight, 205 pounds.

Year	Club	Lea	G	IP	W	L	Pct	SO	BB	H	ERA	SAVES
2007	Auburn	N.Y.-Penn.	11	45⅔	5	0	1.000	49	17	33	2.76	0
2008	Lansing	Midwest	22	121	7	6	.538	124	42	100	2.83	0
2009	New Hampshire	Eastern	14	76⅔	7	5	.583	88	36	80	2.93	0
2009	Las Vegas	P.C.	2	11⅓	2	0	1.000	16	4	7	0.79	0
2009	Toronto	A.L.	11	61⅓	2	4	.333	60	30	51	3.67	0
2010	Las Vegas	P.C.	12	67	5	5	.500	61	27	81	6.04	0
2010	Toronto a	A.L.	14	63⅔	4	4	.500	57	30	72	4.95	0
Major League Totals		2 Yrs.	25	125	6	8	.429	117	60	123	4.32	0

a On disabled list from March 31 to May 19, 2010.

SABATHIA, CARSTEN CHARLES (C.C.)

Born, Vallejo, California, July 21, 1980.
Bats Left. Throws Left. Height, 6 feet, 7 inches. Weight, 290 pounds.

Year	Club	Lea	G	IP	W	L	Pct	SO	BB	H	ERA	SAVES
1998	Burlington	Appal.	5	18	1	0	1.000	35	8	20	4.50	0
1999	Kinston	Carolina	7	32	3	3	.500	29	19	30	5.34	0
1999	Mahoning Valley	N.Y.-Penn.	6	19⅔	0	0	.000	27	12	9	1.83	0
1999	Columbus a	So.Atl.	3	16⅔	2	0	1.000	20	5	8	1.08	0
2000	Kinston	Carolina	10	56	3	2	.600	69	24	48	3.54	0
2000	Akron	Eastern	17	90⅓	3	7	.300	90	48	75	3.59	0
2001	Cleveland	A.L.	33	180⅓	17	5	.773	171	95	149	4.39	0
2002	Cleveland	A.L.	33	210	13	11	.542	149	88	198	4.37	0
2003	Cleveland	A.L.	30	197⅔	13	9	.591	141	66	190	3.60	0
2004	Cleveland	A.L.	30	188	11	10	.524	139	72	176	4.12	0
2005	Akron	Eastern	2	9	0	1	.000	9	2	4	1.00	0
2005	Cleveland b	A.L.	31	196⅔	15	10	.600	161	62	185	4.03	0
2006	Buffalo	Int.	1	5	1	0	1.000	5	1	6	1.80	0
2006	Cleveland c	A.L.	28	192⅔	12	11	.522	172	44	182	3.22	0

Year	Club	Lea	G	IP	W	L	Pct	SO	BB	H	ERA	SAVES
2007	Cleveland d	A.L.	34	*241	19	7	.731	209	37	238	3.21	0
2008	Cleveland	A.L.	18	122 1/3	6	8	.429	123	34	117	3.83	0
2008	Milwaukee e-f	N.L.	17	130 2/3	11	2	.846	128	25	106	1.65	0
2009	New York	A.L.	34	230	*19	8	.704	197	67	197	3.37	0
2010	New York	A.L.	34	237 2/3	*21	7	.750	197	74	209	3.18	0
Major League Totals		10 Yrs.	322	2127	157	88	.641	1787	664	1947	3.57	0
	Division Series											
2001	Cleveland	A.L.	1	6	1	0	1.000	5	5	6	3.00	0
2007	Cleveland	A.L.	1	5	1	0	1.000	5	6	4	5.40	0
2008	Milwaukee	N.L.	1	3 2/3	0	1	.000	5	4	6	12.27	0
2009	New York	A.L.	1	6 2/3	1	0	1.000	8	0	8	1.35	0
2010	New York	A.L.	1	6	1	0	1.000	5	3	5	4.50	0
Division Series Totals			5	27 1/3	4	1	.800	28	18	29	4.61	0
	Championship Series											
2007	Cleveland	A.L.	2	10 1/3	0	2	.000	9	7	17	10.45	0
2009	New York	A.L.	2	16	2	0	1.000	12	3	9	1.13	0
2010	New York	A.L.	2	10	1	0	1.000	10	4	17	6.30	0
Championship Series Totals			6	36 1/3	3	2	.600	31	14	43	5.20	0
	World Series Record											
2009	New York	A.L.	2	13 2/3	0	1	.000	12	6	11	3.29	0

a On disabled list from April 1 through June 20, 1999.
b On disabled list from March 25 to April 17, 2005.
c On disabled list from April 3 to May 2, 2006.
d Selected Cy Young Award Winner in American League for 2007.
e Traded to Milwaukee Brewers for outfielder Matt LaPorta, pitcher Zach Jackson, pitcher Rob Bryson and player to be named later, July 7, 2008. Cleveland Indians received outfielder Michael Brantley to complete trade, October 3, 2008.
f Filed for free agency, November 1, 2008. Signed with New York Yankees, December 18, 2008.

SAITO, TAKASHI

Born, Miyagi, Japan, February 14, 1970.
Bats Left. Throws Right. Height, 6 feet, 2 inch. Weight, 215 pounds.

Year	Club	Lea	G	IP	W	L	Pct	SO	BB	H	ERA	SAVES
1992	Yokohama	Japan Cent.	6	16	0	2	.000	21	10	18	8.44	0
1993	Yokohama	Japan Cent.	29	149	8	10	.444	125	61	127	3.81	0
1994	Yokohama	Japan Cent.	28	181	9	12	.429	169	69	175	3.13	0
1995	Yokohama	Japan Cent.	26	162	8	9	.471	132	45	166	3.94	0
1996	Yokohama	Japan Cent.	28	196 2/3	10	10	.500	206	63	157	3.29	0
1997							INJURED—Did Not Play					
1998	Yokohama	Japan Cent.	34	143 2/3	13	5	.722	101	23	131	2.94	1
1999	Yokohama	Japan Cent.	26	184 2/3	14	3	.824	125	31	178	3.95	0
2000	Yokohama	Japan Cent.	19	115 2/3	6	10	.375	97	36	123	5.52	0
2001	Yokohama	Japan Cent.	50	64 2/3	7	1	.857	60	14	51	1.67	27
2002	Yokohama	Japan Cent.	39	47 2/3	1	2	.333	46	15	37	2.45	20
2003	Yokohama	Japan Cent.	17	103 1/3	6	7	.462	72	22	103	4.18	0
2004	Yokohama	Japan Cent.	16	44	2	5	.286	37	13	64	7.71	0
2005	Yokohama	Japan Cent.	21	106	3	4	.429	93	29	111	3.82	0
2006	Los Angeles a	N.L.	72	78 1/3	6	2	.750	107	23	48	2.07	24
2007	Los Angeles	N.L.	63	64 1/3	2	1	.667	78	13	33	1.40	39
2008	Los Angeles b-c	N.L.	45	47	4	4	.500	60	16	40	2.49	18
2009	Boston d	A.L.	56	55 2/3	3	3	.500	52	25	50	2.43	2
2010	Gwinnett	Int.	1	1	0	0	.000	1	0	1	0.00	0
2010	Atlanta e-f	N.L.	56	54	2	3	.400	69	17	41	2.83	1
Major League Totals		5 Yrs.	292	299 1/3	17	13	.567	366	94	212	2.19	84
	Division Series											
2006	Los Angeles	N.L.	2	2 2/3	0	0	.000	4	0	0	0.00	0
2008	Los Angeles	N.L.	1	0	0	0	.000	0	0	3	INF	0
2009	Boston	A.L.	1	1	0	0	.000	0	0	2	0.00	0
Division Series Totals			4	3 2/3	0	0	.000	4	0	5	4.91	0

a Signed with Los Angeles Dodgers organization, February 7, 2006.
b On disabled list from July 13 to September 13, 2008.
c Not offered contract, December 12, 2008. Signed with Boston Red Sox, January 10, 2009.
d Filed for free agency, October 19, 2009. Signed with Atlanta Braves, December 3, 2009.
e On disabled list from June 4 to June 22, 2010.
f Released by Atlanta Braves, October 18, 2010. Signed with Milwaukee Brewers, January 5, 2011.

SALE, CHRISTOPHER (CHRIS)

Born, Lakeland, Florida, March 30, 1989.
Bats Left. Throws Left. Height, 6 feet, 5 inches. Weight, 170 pounds.

Year	Club	Lea	G	IP	W	L	Pct	SO	BB	H	ERA	SAVES
2010	Winston-Salem	Carolina	4	4	0	0	.000	4	2	3	2.25	0
2010	Charlotte	Int.	7	6⅓	0	0	.000	15	4	3	2.84	0
2010	Chicago	A.L.	21	23⅓	2	1	.667	32	10	15	1.93	4

SANABIA, ALEJANDRO

Born, San Diego, California, September 8, 1988.
Bats Right. Throws Right. Height, 6 feet, 1 inch. Weight, 165 pounds.

Year	Club	Lea	G	IP	W	L	Pct	SO	BB	H	ERA	SAVES
2006	Marlins	Gulf Coast	11	16⅔	3	1	.750	16	7	10	3.24	0
2007	Jamestown	N.Y.-Penn.	15	66⅔	2	6	.250	69	17	73	5.13	0
2008	Greensboro	So.Atl.	19	96⅔	5	5	.500	75	25	106	4.93	0
2009	Jupiter	Fla.St.	19	104⅓	9	5	.643	68	36	89	3.45	0
2010	Jacksonville	Southern	14	84⅓	5	1	.833	65	16	59	2.03	0
2010	New Orleans	P.C.	2	14	1	0	1.000	5	3	9	1.29	0
2010	Florida	N.L.	15	72⅓	5	3	.625	47	16	74	3.73	0

SANCHES, BRIAN LEE

Born, Beaumont, Texas, August 8, 1978.
Bats Right. Throws Right. Height, 6 feet. Weight, 195 pounds.

Year	Club	Lea	G	IP	W	L	Pct	SO	BB	H	ERA	SAVES
1999	Spokane	Northwest	9	34	1	1	.500	51	12	32	4.76	0
2000	Wilmington	Carolina	28	158	6	12	.333	122	69	132	3.53	0
2001	Wichita	Texas	29	134	7	9	.438	95	61	152	5.98	0
2002	Wichita	Texas	33	116⅔	10	6	.625	101	43	111	4.40	0
2003	Wichita a	Texas	38	85⅓	1	5	.167	73	17	84	3.16	2
2004	Reading	Eastern	41	69⅔	4	2	.667	60	25	55	2.71	3
2004	Scranton/WB b	Int.	4	6	0	0	.000	4	3	9	7.50	0
2005	Scranton/WB	Int.	51	83	5	3	.625	75	27	81	3.69	1
2006	Scranton/WB	Int.	36	43⅔	3	2	.600	52	13	24	1.85	19
2006	Philadelphia	N.L.	18	21⅓	0	0	.000	22	13	23	5.91	0
2007	Ottawa	Int.	36	47⅓	2	3	.400	52	8	57	4.75	16
2007	Philadelphia c	N.L.	12	14⅔	1	1	.500	9	12	13	5.52	0
2008	Washington	N.L.	12	11	2	0	1.000	10	5	16	7.36	0
2008	Columbus d	Int.	32	33⅔	2	1	.667	45	9	24	2.41	13
2009	New Orleans	P.C.	16	17⅔	1	1	.500	22	4	13	2.04	4
2009	Florida	N.L.	47	56⅓	4	2	.667	51	26	50	2.56	0
2010	Jupiter	Fla.St.	3	4	0	1	.000	6	0	2	2.25	0
2010	Florida e	N.L.	61	63⅔	2	2	.500	54	27	43	2.26	0
Major League Totals		5 Yrs.	150	167	9	5	.643	146	83	145	3.45	0

a Traded by Kansas City Royals to San Diego Padres with pitcher Chris Tierney for outfielder Rondell White, August 26, 2003.
b Traded to Philadelphia Phillies for player named later, April 1, 2004. San Diego Padres received catcher Mauber Lopez to complete trade, August 2, 2004.
c Filed for free agency, October 29, 2007. Signed with Washington Nationals organization, December 21, 2007.
d Filed for free agency, September 29, 2008. Signed with Florida Marlins organization, November 17, 2008.
e On disabled list from April 3 to April 26, 2010.

SANCHEZ, ANIBAL ALEJANDRO

Born, Maracay, Venezuela, February 27, 1984.
Bats Right. Throws Right. Height, 6 feet. Weight, 180 pounds.

Year	Club	Lea	G	IP	W	L	Pct	SO	BB	H	ERA	SAVES
2004	Lowell a	N.Y.-Penn.	15	76⅓	4	4	.500	101	29	43	1.77	0
2005	Wilmington	Carolina	14	78⅔	6	1	.857	95	24	53	2.40	0
2005	Portland b	Eastern	11	57⅓	3	5	.375	63	16	53	3.45	0
2006	Carolina	Southern	15	85⅔	3	6	.333	92	27	82	3.15	0
2006	Florida	N.L.	18	114⅓	10	3	.769	72	46	90	2.83	0
2007	Florida c	N.L.	6	30	2	1	.667	14	19	43	4.80	0
2008	Marlins	Gulf Coast	1	5	1	0	1.000	4	1	4	3.60	0
2008	Jupiter	Fla.St.	2	10	0	0	.000	9	4	7	1.80	0
2008	Carolina	Southern	2	13	1	0	1.000	12	5	12	3.46	0
2008	Florida d	N.L.	10	51⅔	2	5	.286	50	27	54	5.57	0
2009	Marlins	Gulf Coast	1	2⅔	0	0	.000	0	2	3	3.38	0
2009	Jupiter	Fla.St.	3	13⅓	1	0	1.000	12	3	7	0.68	0
2009	Jacksonville	Southern	2	10⅓	1	0	1.000	8	3	5	2.61	0

Year	Club	Lea	G	IP	W	L	Pct	SO	BB	H	ERA	SAVES
2009	Florida e	N.L.	16	86	4	8	.333	71	46	84	3.87	0
2010	Florida	N.L.	32	195	13	12	.520	157	70	192	3.55	0
Major League Totals		5 Yrs.	82	477	31	29	.517	364	208	463	3.74	0

a On minor league disabled list July 1 to September 16, 2003.
b Traded by Boston Red Sox to Florida Marlins with infielder Hanley Ramirez and pitcher Jesus Delgado for pitcher Josh Beckett, infielder Mike Lowell and pitcher Guillermo Mota, November 24, 2005.
c On minor league disabled list May 7 to September 30, 2007.
d On disabled list from March 21 to July 31, 2008.
e On disabled list from May 8 to June 2 and June 3 to August 21, 2009.

SANCHEZ, JONATHAN O.

Born, Mayaguez, Puerto Rico, November 19, 1982.
Bats Left. Throws Left. Height, 6 feet, 2 inches. Weight, 190 pounds.

Year	Club	Lea	G	IP	W	L	Pct	SO	BB	H	ERA	SAVES
2004	Giants	Arizona	9	26	5	0	1.000	27	9	22	2.77	1
2004	Salem-Keizer	Northwest	6	22 1/3	2	1	.667	34	19	16	4.84	0
2005	Augusta	So.Atl.	25	125 2/3	5	7	.417	166	39	122	4.08	0
2006	Connecticut	Eastern	13	31 1/3	2	1	.667	46	9	14	1.15	2
2006	Fresno	P.C.	6	23 2/3	2	2	.500	28	13	13	3.80	0
2006	San Francisco	N.L.	27	40	3	1	.750	33	23	39	4.95	0
2007	San Jose	Calif.	2	3	0	0	.000	5	1	0	0.00	0
2007	Fresno	P.C.	6	20 2/3	0	0	.000	27	8	15	2.18	0
2007	San Francisco a	N.L.	33	52	1	5	.167	62	28	57	5.88	0
2008	San Francisco b	N.L.	29	158	9	12	.429	157	75	154	5.01	0
2009	San Francisco c	N.L.	32	163 1/3	8	12	.400	177	88	135	4.24	0
2010	San Francisco	N.L.	34	193 1/3	13	9	.591	205	*96	142	3.07	0
Major League Totals		5 Yrs.	155	606 2/3	34	39	.466	634	310	527	4.26	0
	Division Series											
2010	San Francisco	N.L.	1	7 1/3	0	0	.000	11	1	2	1.23	0
	Championship Series											
2010	San Francisco	N.L.	2	8	0	1	.000	8	5	8	4.50	0
	World Series Record											
2010	San Francisco	N.L.	1	4 2/3	0	1	.000	3	3	6	7.71	0

a On disabled list from June 25 to July 19, 2007.
b On disabled list from August 12 to September 1, 2008.
c Pitched no-hit, no-run game against San Diego Padres, July 10, 2009.

SANTANA, ERVIN RAMON

Born, La Romana, Dominican Republic, January 10, 1983.
Bats Right. Throws Right. Height, 6 feet, 2 inches. Weight, 185 pounds.

Year	Club	Lea	G	IP	W	L	Pct	SO	BB	H	ERA	SAVES
2001	Angels	Arizona	10	58 2/3	3	2	.600	69	35	40	3.22	0
2001	Provo	Pioneer	4	18 2/3	2	1	.667	22	12	19	7.71	0
2002	Cedar Rapids	Midwest	27	147	14	8	.636	146	48	133	4.16	0
2003	Rancho Cucamonga	California	20	124 2/3	10	2	.833	130	36	98	2.53	0
2003	Arkansas	Texas	6	29 2/3	1	1	.500	23	12	23	3.94	0
2004	Arkansas	Texas	8	43 2/3	2	1	.667	48	18	41	3.30	0
2005	Arkansas	Texas	7	39	5	1	.833	32	15	34	2.31	0
2005	Salt Lake	P.C.	3	19 1/3	1	0	1.000	17	2	19	4.19	0
2005	Los Angeles	A.L.	23	133 2/3	12	8	.600	99	47	139	4.65	0
2006	Los Angeles	A.L.	33	204	16	8	.667	141	70	181	4.28	0
2007	Salt Lake	P.C.	5	32 1/3	2	1	.667	32	10	39	5.01	0
2007	Los Angeles	A.L.	28	150	7	14	.333	126	58	174	5.76	0
2008	Los Angeles	A.L.	32	219	16	7	.696	214	47	198	3.49	0
2009	Azl Angels	Arizona	1	3 1/3	0	0	.000	7	0	3	0.00	0
2009	Rancho Cucamonga	Calif.	1	4 2/3	0	0	.000	3	0	4	5.79	0
2009	Salt Lake	P.C.	1	5	1	0	1.000	4	1	3	3.60	0
2009	Los Angeles a	A.L.	24	139 2/3	8	8	.500	107	47	159	5.03	0
2010	Los Angeles	A.L.	33	222 2/3	17	10	.630	169	73	221	3.92	0
Major League Totals		6 Yrs.	173	1069	76	55	.580	856	342	1072	4.39	0
	Division Series											
2005	Los Angeles	A.L.	1	5 1/3	1	0	1.000	2	3	5	5.06	0
2007	Los Angeles	A.L.	1	2	0	0	.000	2	0	0	0.00	0
2008	Los Angeles	A.L.	1	5 1/3	0	0	.000	3	0	8	8.44	0
Division Series Totals			3	12 2/3	1	0	1.000	7	3	13	5.68	0
	Championship Series											
2005	Los Angeles	A.L.	1	4 1/3	0	1	.000	2	3	3	10.38	0

Year	Club	Lea	G	IP	W	L	Pct	SO	BB	H	ERA	SAVES
2009	Los Angeles	A.L.	4	5⅔	1	1	.500	5	4	5	1.59	0
Championship Series Totals			5	10	1	2	.333	7	7	8	5.40	0

a On disabled list from March 27 to May 14 and June 17 to July 3, 2009.

SANTANA, JOHAN ALEXANDER

Born, Tovar, Venezuela, March 13, 1979.
Bats Left. Throws Left. Height, 6 feet. Weight, 210 pounds.

Year	Club	Lea	G	IP	W	L	Pct	SO	BB	H	ERA	SAVES
1996	Houston/Bos	Dominican	23	40	4	3	.571	51	22	26	2.70	3
1997	Auburn	N.Y.-Penn.	1	4	0	0	.000	5	6	1	2.25	0
1997	Astros	Gulf Coast	9	36⅓	0	4	.000	25	18	49	7.93	0
1998	Quad City	Midwest	2	6⅔	0	1	.000	6	3	14	9.45	0
1998	Auburn	N.Y.-Penn.	15	86⅔	7	5	.583	88	21	81	4.36	0
1999	Michigan a-b	Midwest	27	160⅓	8	8	.500	150	55	162	4.66	0
2000	Minnesota	A.L.	30	86	2	3	.400	64	54	102	6.49	0
2001	Minnesota	A.L.	15	43⅔	1	0	1.000	28	16	50	4.74	0
2002	Edmonton	P.C.	11	48⅔	5	2	.714	75	27	37	3.14	0
2002	Minnesota	A.L.	27	108⅓	8	6	.571	137	49	84	2.99	1
2003	Minnesota	A.L.	45	158⅓	12	3	.800	169	47	127	3.07	0
2004	Minnesota c	A.L.	34	228	20	6	.769	*265	54	156	*2.61	0
2005	Minnesota	A.L.	33	231⅔	16	7	.696	*238	45	180	2.87	0
2006	Minnesota d	A.L.	34	*233⅔	*19	6	.760	*245	47	186	*2.77	0
2007	Minnesota	A.L.	33	219	15	13	.536	235	52	183	3.33	0
2008	New York e	N.L.	34	*234⅓	16	7	.696	206	63	206	*2.53	0
2009	New York f	N.L.	25	166⅔	13	9	.591	146	46	156	3.13	0
2010	New York	N.L.	29	199	11	9	.550	144	55	179	2.98	0
Major League Totals		11 Yrs.	339	1908⅔	133	69	.658	1877	528	1609	3.10	1
	Division Series											
2002	Minnesota	A.L.	2	3	0	0	.000	2	2	3	6.00	0
2003	Minnesota	A.L.	2	7⅔	0	1	.000	6	3	9	7.04	0
2004	Minnesota	A.L.	2	12	1	0	1.000	12	4	14	0.75	0
2006	Minnesota	A.L.	1	8	0	1	.000	8	1	5	2.25	0
Division Series Totals			7	30⅔	1	2	.333	28	10	31	3.23	0
	Championship Series											
2002	Minnesota	A.L.	4	3⅓	0	1	.000	4	0	4	10.80	0

a Selected by Florida Marlins from Houston Astros in Rule V draft, December 13, 1999.
b Traded to Minnesota Twins with cash for pitcher Jared Camp, December 13, 1999.
c Selected Cy Young Award Winner in American League for 2004.
d Selected Cy Young Award Winner in American League for 2006.
e Traded to New York Mets for outfielder Carlos Gomez, pitcher Philip Humber, pitcher Kevin Mulvey and pitcher Deolis Garcia, February 2, 2008.
f On disabled list from August 25 to October 14, 2009.

SANTOS, SERGIO JOSE

Born, Bellflower, California, July 4, 1983.
Bats Right. Throws Right. Height, 6 feet, 3 inches. Weight, 240 pounds.

Year	Club	Lea	G	IP	W	L	Pct	SO	BB	H	ERA	SAVES
2009	Winston-Salem a-b-c-d-e	Carolina	8	7⅔	0	0	.000	7	3	9	5.87	0
2009	Charlotte	Int.	3	5	0	1	.000	7	7	5	9.00	0
2009	Kannapolis	So.Atl.	8	7⅓	0	1	.000	10	3	8	7.36	0
2009	Birmingham	Southern	7	8⅔	0	1	.000	6	7	15	10.38	0
2010	Chicago	A.L.	56	51⅔	2	2	.500	56	26	53	2.96	1

a Played infield in the minors for 2003 through 2008.
b Traded by Arizona Diamondbacks to Toronto Blue Jays with infielder Troy Glaus for infielder Orlando Hudson and pitcher Miguel Batista, December 27, 2005.
c Claimed on waivers by Minnesota Twins, May 16, 2008.
d Filed for free agency, November 3, 2008. Signed with Chicago White Sox organization, January 12, 2009.
e Sold to San Francisco Giants, March 20, 2009. Sold to Chicago White Sox, April 1, 2009.

SAUNDERS, JOSEPH FRANCIS (JOE)

Born, Falls Church, Virginia, June 16, 1981.
Bats Left. Throws Left. Height, 6 feet, 3 inches. Weight, 210 pounds.

Year	Club	Lea	G	IP	W	L	Pct	SO	BB	H	ERA	SAVES
2002	Cedar Rapids	Midwest	5	28⅔	3	1	.750	27	9	16	1.88	0
2002	Provo	Pioneer	8	32⅓	2	1	.667	21	11	40	3.62	0
2003	Provo a	Pioneer	INJURED—Did Not Play									

Year	Club	Lea	G	IP	W	L	Pct	SO	BB	H	ERA	SAVES
2004	Rancho Cucamonga....	Calif.	19	105⅔	9	7	.563	76	23	106	3.41	0
2004	Arkansas	Texas	8	39	4	3	.571	25	14	51	5.77	0
2005	Arkansas	Texas	18	105⅔	7	4	.636	80	32	107	3.49	0
2005	Salt Lake	P.C.	9	55	3	3	.500	29	21	65	4.58	0
2005	Los Angeles...........	A.L.	2	9⅓	0	0	.000	4	4	10	7.71	0
2006	Salt Lake	P.C.	21	135	10	4	.714	97	38	117	2.67	0
2006	Los Angeles...........	A.L.	13	70⅔	7	3	.700	51	29	71	4.71	0
2007	Salt Lake	P.C.	14	86⅓	4	7	.364	84	20	89	5.11	0
2007	Los Angeles...........	A.L.	18	107⅓	8	5	.615	69	34	129	4.44	0
2008	Los Angeles...........	A.L.	31	198	17	7	.708	103	53	187	3.41	0
2009	Los Angeles b	A.L.	31	186	16	7	.696	101	64	202	4.60	0
2010	Los Angeles...........	A.L.	20	120⅔	6	10	.375	64	45	135	4.62	0
2010	Arizona c	N.L.	13	82⅔	3	7	.300	50	19	97	4.25	0
Major League Totals		6 Yrs.	128	774⅔	57	39	.594	442	248	831	4.29	0
	Division Series											
2008	Los Angeles...........	A.L.	1	4⅔	0	0	.000	2	4	5	7.71	0
	Championship Series											
2009	Los Angeles...........	A.L.	2	10⅓	0	1	.000	5	6	13	4.35	0

a On minor league disabled list from April 3 to September 18, 2003.
b On disabled list from August 8 to August 26, 2009.
c Traded to Arizona Diamondbacks with pitcher Rafael Rodriguez, pitcher Patrick Corbin and player to be named later for pitcher Danny Haren, July 25, 2010. Arizona Diamondbacks received pitcher Tyler Skaggs to complete trade, August 7, 2010.

SCHERZER, MAXWELL M. (MAX)

Born, St. Louis, Missouri, July 27, 1984.
Bats Right. Throws Right. Height, 6 feet, 3 inches. Weight, 215 pounds.

Year	Club	Lea	G	IP	W	L	Pct	SO	BB	H	ERA	SAVES
2007	Fort Worth	Amer.Assoc.	3	16	1	0	1.000	25	4	9	0.56	0
2007	Visalia	Calif.	3	17	2	0	1.000	30	2	5	0.53	0
2007	Mobile a-b	Southern	14	73⅔	4	4	.500	76	40	64	3.91	0
2008	Tucson	P.C.	13	53	1	1	.500	79	22	35	2.72	0
2008	Arizona..............	N.L.	16	56	0	4	.000	66	21	48	3.05	0
2009	Visalia	Calif.	1	4⅔	0	0	.000	5	4	1	1.93	0
2009	Arizona a-b...........	N.L.	30	170⅓	9	11	.450	174	63	166	4.12	0
2010	Toledo	Int.	2	15	2	0	1.000	17	2	4	0.60	0
2010	Detroit	A.L.	31	195⅔	12	11	.522	184	70	174	3.50	0
Major League Totals		3 Yrs.	77	422	21	26	.447	424	154	388	3.69	0

a Signed by independent Fort Worth (American Association), 2007.
b Signed by Arizona Diamondbacks, May 31, 2007.
a On disabled list from March 29 to April 14, 2009.
b Traded to Detroit Tigers with pitcher Daniel Schlereth for pitcher Edwin Jackson and pitcher Ian Kennedy, December 9, 2009.

SCHLERETH, DANIEL ROBERT

Born, Anchorage, Alaska, May 9, 1986.
Bats Left. Throws Left. Height, 6 feet. Weight, 210 pounds.

Year	Club	Lea	G	IP	W	L	Pct	SO	BB	H	ERA	SAVES
2008	South Bend	Midwest	7	9	1	0	1.000	14	4	3	2.00	0
2008	Missoula	Pioneer	3	3	0	0	.000	6	2	3	0.00	0
2009	Mobile	Southern	21	26⅔	0	0	.000	39	16	14	1.01	4
2009	Reno	P.C.	1	1	0	0	.000	1	1	1	0.00	0
2009	Arizona a	N.L.	21	18⅓	1	4	.200	22	15	15	5.89	0
2010	Toledo	Int.	38	49⅓	1	3	.250	60	34	40	2.37	0
2010	Detroit	A.L.	18	18⅔	2	0	1.000	19	10	20	2.89	1
Major League Totals		2 Yrs.	39	37	3	4	.429	41	25	35	4.38	1

a Traded to Detroit Tigers with pitcher Max Scherzer for pitcher Edwin Jackson and pitcher Ian Kennedy, December 9, 2009.

SHEETS, BEN M.

Born, Baton Rouge, Louisiana, July 18, 1978.
Bats Right. Throws Right. Height, 6 feet, 1 inch. Weight, 220 pounds.

Year	Club	Lea	G	IP	W	L	Pct	SO	BB	H	ERA	SAVES
1999	Stockton.............	Calif.	5	27⅔	1	0	1.000	28	14	23	3.58	0
1999	Ogden	Pioneer	2	8	0	1	.000	12	2	8	5.63	0
2000	Indianapolis	Int.	14	81⅔	3	5	.375	59	31	77	2.87	0

Year	Club	Lea	G	IP	W	L	Pct	SO	BB	H	ERA	SAVES
2000	Huntsville	Southern	13	72	5	3	.625	60	25	55	1.88	0
2001	Indianapolis	Int.	2	$10\frac{2}{3}$	1	1	.500	6	3	14	3.38	0
2001	Milwaukee a	N.L.	25	$151\frac{1}{3}$	11	10	.524	94	48	166	4.76	0
2002	Milwaukee	N.L.	34	$216\frac{2}{3}$	11	16	.407	170	70	237	4.15	0
2003	Milwaukee	N.L.	34	$220\frac{2}{3}$	11	13	.458	157	43	232	4.45	0
2004	Milwaukee	N.L.	34	237	12	14	.462	264	32	201	2.70	0
2005	Milwaukee b	N.L.	22	$156\frac{2}{3}$	10	9	.526	141	25	142	3.33	0
2006	Huntsville	Southern	1	$2\frac{2}{3}$	0	0	.000	5	0	4	3.38	0
2006	Brewers	Arizona	1	$4\frac{1}{3}$	0	0	.000	8	2	5	10.38	0
2006	Nashville	P.C.	3	15	2	1	.667	15	5	9	2.40	0
2006	Milwaukee c	N.L.	17	106	6	7	.462	116	11	105	3.82	0
2007	Milwaukee d	N.L.	24	$141\frac{1}{3}$	12	5	.706	106	37	138	3.82	0
2008	Milwaukee	N.L.	31	$198\frac{1}{3}$	13	9	.591	158	47	181	3.09	0
2009					INJURED—Did Not Play							
2010	Oakland e-f-g	A.L.	20	$119\frac{1}{3}$	4	9	.308	84	43	123	4.53	0
Major League Totals		9 Yrs.	241	$1547\frac{1}{3}$	90	92	.495	1290	356	1525	3.79	0

a On disabled list from August 6 to September 21, 2001.
b On disabled list from April 21 to May 28 and August 27 to October 10, 2005.
c On disabled list from March 24 to April 16 and May 3 to July 25, 2006.
d On disabled list from July 15 to August 29, 2007.
e Filed for free agency, October 30, 2008. Signed with Oakland Athletics, January 26, 2010.
f On disabled list from July 21 to November 1, 2010.
g Filed for free agency, November 1, 2010.

SHERRILL, GEORGE FRIEDERICH

Born, Memphis, Tennessee, April 19, 1977.
Bats Left. Throws Left. Height, 6 feet. Weight, 225 pounds.

Year	Club	Lea	G	IP	W	L	Pct	SO	BB	H	ERA	SAVES
1999	Evansville (Ind)	Frontier	22	40	2	4	.333	33	18	40	3.15	2
2000	Evansville (Ind)	Frontier	13	$75\frac{1}{3}$	3	5	.375	61	35	71	4.66	2
2001	Sioux Falls (Ind)	Northern	48	$58\frac{2}{3}$	4	4	.500	45	14	53	2.45	2
2002	Winnipeg (Ind)	Northern	38	41	3	5	.375	61	13	35	3.07	2
2003	Winnipeg (Ind)	Northern	16	16	1	0	1.000	30	4	8	1.13	2
2003	San Antonio a	Texas	16	$27\frac{1}{3}$	3	0	1.000	31	12	19	0.33	0
2004	Tacoma	P.C.	36	$50\frac{1}{3}$	4	2	.667	62	9	42	2.32	13
2004	Seattle	A.L.	21	$23\frac{2}{3}$	2	1	.667	16	9	24	3.80	0
2005	Mariners	Arizona	3	4	0	0	.000	5	0	0	0.00	0
2005	Tacoma	P.C.	22	$23\frac{2}{3}$	1	3	.250	38	6	19	2.28	7
2005	Seattle	A.L.	29	19	4	3	.571	24	7	13	5.21	0
2006	Seattle	A.L.	72	40	2	4	.333	42	27	30	4.28	1
2007	Seattle	A.L.	73	$45\frac{2}{3}$	2	0	1.000	56	17	28	2.36	3
2008	Baltimore b-c	A.L.	57	$53\frac{1}{3}$	3	5	.375	58	33	47	4.72	31
2009	Baltimore	A.L.	42	$41\frac{1}{3}$	0	1	.000	39	13	34	2.40	20
2009	Los Angeles d	N.L.	30	$27\frac{2}{3}$	1	0	1.000	22	11	19	0.65	1
2010	Inland Empire	Calif.	2	2	0	0	.000	2	0	3	4.50	0
2010	Albuquerque	P.C.	2	$1\frac{2}{3}$	0	0	.000	3	0	2	0.00	0
2010	Los Angeles e-f	N.L.	65	$36\frac{1}{3}$	2	2	.500	25	24	46	6.69	0
Major League Totals		7 Yrs.	389	287	16	16	.500	282	141	241	3.76	56
	Division Series											
2009	Los Angeles	N.L.	3	$2\frac{1}{3}$	1	0	1.000	0	1	1	3.86	0
	Championship Series											
2009	Los Angeles	N.L.	3	2	0	0	.000	2	3	2	13.50	0

a Signed with Seattle Mariners, July 2, 2003.
b Traded to Baltimore Orioles with pitcher Tony Butler, outfielder Adam Jones, pitcher Kam Mickolio and pitcher Chris Tillman for pitcher Erik Bedard, February 8, 2008.
c On disabled list from August 16 to September 11, 2008.
d Traded to Los Angeles Dodgers for infielder Joshua Bell and pitcher Steve Johnson, July 30, 2009.
e On disabled list from May 24 to June 8, 2010.
f Not offered contract, December 2, 2010. Signed with Atlanta Braves, December 10, 2010.

SHIELDS, JAMES ANTHONY (JAMIE)

Born, Newhall, California, December 20, 1981.
Bats Right. Throws Right. Height, 6 feet, 4 inches. Weight, 215 pounds.

Year	Club	Lea	G	IP	W	L	Pct	SO	BB	H	ERA	SAVES
2001	Hudson Valley	N.Y.-Penn.	5	$27\frac{1}{3}$	2	1	.667	25	5	27	2.30	0
2001	Charleston-SC	So.Atl.	10	$71\frac{1}{3}$	4	5	.444	60	10	63	2.65	0
2002	Charleston-SC a				INJURED—Did Not Play							
2003	Bakersfield	Calif.	26	$143\frac{2}{3}$	10	10	.500	119	38	161	4.45	1

Year	Club	Lea	G	IP	W	L	Pct	SO	BB	H	ERA	SAVES
2004	Bakersfield	Calif.	20	117	8	5	.615	92	33	119	4.23	0
2004	Montgomery	Southern	4	18⅓	0	3	.000	14	8	24	7.85	0
2005	Durham	Int.	1	6	1	0	1.000	6	3	9	6.00	0
2005	Montgomery	Southern	17	109⅓	7	5	.583	104	31	95	2.80	0
2006	Durham	Int.	10	61⅓	3	2	.600	64	6	60	2.64	0
2006	Tampa Bay	A.L.	21	124⅔	6	8	.429	104	38	141	4.84	0
2007	Tampa Bay	A.L.	31	215	12	8	.600	184	36	202	3.85	0
2008	Tampa Bay	A.L.	33	215	14	8	.636	160	40	208	3.56	0
2009	Tampa Bay	A.L.	33	219⅔	11	12	.478	167	52	239	4.14	0
2010	Tampa Bay	A.L.	34	203⅓	13	15	.464	187	51	*246	5.18	0
Major League Totals		5 Yrs.	152	977⅔	56	51	.523	802	217	1036	4.25	0
	Division Series											
2008	Tampa Bay	N.L.	1	6⅓	1	0	1.000	4	1	6	4.26	0
2010	Tampa Bay	N.L.	1	4⅓	0	1	.000	2	0	4	8.31	0
Division Series Totals			2	10⅔	1	1	.500	6	1	10	5.91	0
	Championship Series											
2008	Tampa Bay	N.L.	2	13	0	2	.000	9	5	15	3.46	0
	World Series Record											
2008	Tampa Bay	N.L.	1	5⅔	1	0	1.000	4	2	7	0.00	0

a On minor league disabled list April 4 to September 10, 2002.

SHIELDS, ROBERT SCOT (SCOT)

Born, Fort Lauderdale, Florida, July 22, 1975.
Bats Right. Throws Right. Height, 6 feet, 1 inch. Weight, 170 pounds.

Year	Club	Lea	G	IP	W	L	Pct	SO	BB	H	ERA	SAVES
1997	Boise	Northwest	30	52	7	2	.778	61	24	45	2.94	2
1998	Cedar Rapids	Midwest	58	74	6	5	.545	81	29	62	3.65	7
1999	Lake Elsinore	California	24	107⅓	10	3	.769	113	39	91	2.52	1
1999	Erie	Eastern	10	74⅔	4	4	.500	81	26	57	2.89	0
2000	Edmonton	P.C.	27	163	7	13	.350	156	82	158	5.41	0
2001	Salt Lake	P.C.	21	137⅔	6	11	.353	104	31	141	4.97	0
2001	Anaheim	A.L.	8	11	0	0	.000	7	7	8	0.00	0
2002	Salt Lake	P.C.	28	47	2	2	.500	50	6	39	3.06	1
2002	Anaheim	A.L.	29	49	5	3	.625	30	21	31	2.20	0
2003	Anaheim	A.L.	44	148⅓	5	6	.455	111	38	138	2.85	1
2004	Anaheim	A.L.	60	105⅓	8	2	.800	109	40	97	3.33	4
2005	Los Angeles	A.L.	78	91⅔	10	11	.476	98	37	66	2.75	7
2006	Los Angeles	A.L.	74	87⅔	7	7	.500	84	24	70	2.87	2
2007	Los Angeles	A.L.	71	77	4	5	.444	77	33	62	3.86	2
2008	Salt Lake	P.C.	1	1	0	0	.000	3	0	2	0.00	0
2008	Los Angeles a	A.L.	64	63⅓	6	4	.600	64	29	56	2.70	4
2009	Los Angeles b	A.L.	20	17⅔	1	3	.250	12	15	16	6.62	1
2010	Los Angeles c	A.L.	43	46	0	3	.000	39	34	45	5.28	0
Major League Totals		10 Yrs.	491	697	46	44	.511	631	278	589	3.18	21
	Division Series											
2004	Anaheim	A.L.	2	3	0	0	.000	3	2	5	6.00	0
2005	Los Angeles	A.L.	4	5	1	1	.500	5	3	4	3.60	0
2007	Los Angeles	A.L.	2	4	0	0	.000	4	4	0	2.25	0
2008	Los Angeles	A.L.	4	5⅔	0	1	.000	7	1	6	4.76	0
Division Series Totals			12	17⅔	1	2	.333	19	10	15	4.08	0
	Championship Series											
2005	Los Angeles	A.L.	4	6	0	0	.000	5	1	4	0.00	0
	World Series Record											
2002	Anaheim	A.L.	1	1⅔	0	0	.000	1	0	5	5.40	0

a On disabled list from March 21 to April 5, 2008.
b On disabled list from May 27 to November 12, 2009.
c Filed for free agency, November 1, 2010.

SILVA, CARLOS

Born, Bolivar, Venezuela, April 23, 1979.
Bats Right. Throws Right. Height, 6 feet, 4 inches. Weight, 250 pounds.

Year	Club	Lea	G	IP	W	L	Pct	SO	BB	H	ERA	SAVES
1996	Martinsvlle	Appal.	7	18	0	0	.000	16	5	20	4.00	0
1997	Martinsvlle	Appal.	11	57⅔	2	2	.500	31	14	66	5.15	0
1998	Martinsvlle	Appal.	7	41	1	4	.200	21	4	48	5.05	0
1998	Batavia	N.Y.-Penn.	9	45⅓	2	3	.400	27	9	61	6.35	0
1999	Piedmont	So.Atl.	26	164⅓	11	8	.579	99	41	176	3.12	0

Year	Club	Lea	G	IP	W	L	Pct	SO	BB	H	ERA	SAVES
2000	Clearwater	Fla.St.	26	176 1/3	8	13	.381	82	26	229	3.57	0
2001	Reading	Eastern	28	180	15	8	.652	100	27	197	3.90	0
2002	Reading	Eastern	2	3	0	0	.000	1	0	0	0.00	1
2002	Philadelphia a	N.L.	68	84	5	0	1.000	41	22	88	3.21	1
2003	Philadelphia b	N.L.	62	87 1/3	3	1	.750	48	37	92	4.43	1
2004	Minnesota	A.L.	33	203	14	8	.636	76	35	255	4.21	0
2005	Beloit	Midwest	1	5	0	0	.000	3	0	5	1.80	0
2005	Minnesota c	A.L.	27	188 1/3	9	8	.529	71	9	212	3.44	0
2006	Minnesota	A.L.	36	180 1/3	11	15	.423	70	32	246	5.94	0
2007	Minnesota d	A.L.	33	202	13	14	.481	89	36	229	4.19	0
2008	Seattle e	A.L.	28	153 1/3	4	15	.211	69	32	213	6.46	0
2009	Everett	Northwest	1	1	0	0	.000	3	0	3	9.00	0
2009	Tacoma	P.C.	2	3	0	0	.000	2	0	3	3.00	0
2009	Seattle f-g	A.L.	8	30 1/3	1	3	.250	10	11	41	8.60	0
2010	Peoria	Midwest	2	7 1/3	0	1	.000	5	2	8	6.14	0
2010	Chicago h	N.L.	21	113	10	6	.625	80	24	120	4.22	0
Major League Totals		9 Yrs.	316	1241 2/3	70	70	.500	554	238	1496	4.68	2
	Division Series											
2004	Minnesota	A.L.	1	5	0	1	.000	1	0	10	10.80	0

a On disabled list from May 27 to June 14, 2002.
b Traded to Minnesota Twins with infielder Nick Punto and player to be named later for pitcher Eric Milton, December 3, 2003. Minnesota Twins received pitcher Bobby Korecky to complete trade, December 17, 2003.
c On disabled list from April 7 to April 22, 2005.
d Filed for free agency, October 29, 2007. Signed with Seattle Mariners, December 20, 2007.
e On disabled list from August 16 to September 1, 2008.
f On disabled list from May 7 to September 15, 2009.
g Traded to Chicago Cubs for outfielder Milton Bradley, December 18, 2009.
h On disabled list from August 2 to September 7, 2010.

SIMON (CABRERA), ALFREDO

Born, Santiago, Dominican Republic, May 8, 1981.
Bats Right. Throws Right. Height, 6 feet, 4 inches. Weight, 230 pounds.

Year	Club	Lea	G	IP	W	L	Pct	SO	BB	H	ERA	SAVES
2001	Phillies	Gulf Coast	10	43 1/3	2	2	.500	40	23	35	2.91	0
2002	Batavia	N.Y.-Penn.	15	90 1/3	9	2	.818	77	46	79	3.59	0
2003	Lakewood	So.Atl.	14	71 1/3	5	0	1.000	66	25	59	3.79	2
2004	San Jose	Calif.	6	31 2/3	1	2	.333	21	12	44	5.68	0
2004	Clearwater a	Fla.St.	22	134 2/3	7	9	.438	107	38	121	3.27	0
2005	Norwich	Eastern	43	91 1/3	3	8	.273	60	24	104	5.03	19
2006	San Jose	Calif.	18	36 1/3	2	4	.333	35	14	43	6.44	0
2006	Fresno b-c-d	P.C.	10	52	0	6	.000	35	19	76	6.75	0
2007	Oklahoma e	P.C.	22	119	5	10	.333	73	46	152	6.43	0
2008	Monterrey	Mexican	15	81	7	2	.778	61	20	66	2.67	0
2008	Norfolk f-g-h	Int.	1	4 2/3	0	1	.000	5	2	9	7.71	0
2008	Baltimore	A.L.	4	13	0	0	.000	8	2	16	6.23	0
2009	Baltimore i-j	A.L.	2	6 1/3	0	1	.000	3	2	8	9.95	0
2010	Norfolk	Int.	4	17	1	1	.500	14	5	15	1.59	0
2010	Baltimore k	A.L.	49	49 1/3	4	2	.667	37	22	54	4.93	17
Major League Totals		3 Yrs.	55	68 2/3	4	3	.571	48	26	78	5.64	17

a Traded by Philadelphia Phillies to San Francisco Giants with outfielder Ricky Ledee for pitcher Felix Rodriguez, July 30, 2004.
b Filed for free agency, October 15,2006. Signed with Texas Rangers organization, November 3, 2006.
c Selected by Baltimore Orioles in Rule V draft, December 7, 2006.
d Traded to Philadelphia Phillies for catcher Adam Domachie and cash, December 7, 2006.
e Returned to Texas Rangers, March 17, 2007.
f Filed for free agency, October 29, 2007. Signed with Los Angeles Dodgers organization, January 20, 2008.
g Released by Los Angeles Dodgers, March 30, 2008. Signed with Monterrey (Mexican) for 2008.
h Signed with Baltimore Orioles organization, September 5, 2008.
i On disabled list from April 15 to October 30, 2009.
j Filed for free agency, November 9, 2009, re-signed with Baltimore Orioles, December 2, 2009.
k On disabled list from May 25 to June 14, 2010.

SIPP, TONY MARCEL

Born, Pascagoula, Mississippi, July 12, 1983.
Bats Left. Throws Left. Height, 6 feet. Weight, 190 pounds.

Year	Club	Lea	G	IP	W	L	Pct	SO	BB	H	ERA	SAVES
2004	Mahoning Valley	N.Y.-Penn.	10	42 2/3	3	1	.750	74	13	33	3.16	0
2005	Kinston	Carolina	22	47 1/3	2	2	.500	59	23	34	2.66	2

Year	Club	Lea	G	IP	W	L	Pct	SO	BB	H	ERA	SAVES
2005	Lake County	So.Atl.	13	69	4	1	.800	71	19	47	2.22	0
2006	Akron	Eastern	29	60⅓	4	2	.667	80	21	44	3.13	3
2007	a		INJURED—Did Not Play									
2008	Kinston	Carolina	5	8	0	0	.000	10	3	4	1.13	0
2008	Akron	Eastern	16	21⅔	0	3	.000	32	7	19	3.74	1
2008	Indians	Gulf Coast	3	4	0	0	.000	4	1	0	0.00	0
2009	Columbus	Int.	12	17	1	0	1.000	22	6	17	3.71	1
2009	Cleveland	A.L.	46	40	2	0	1.000	48	25	27	2.93	0
2010	Cleveland	A.L.	70	63	2	2	.500	69	39	48	4.14	1
Major League Totals		2 Yrs.	116	103	4	2	.667	117	64	75	3.67	1

a On minor league disabled list from April 5 to September 21, 2007.

SLATEN, DOUGLAS (DOUG)

Born, Venice, California, February 4, 1980.
Bats Left. Throws Left. Height, 6 feet, 5 inches. Weight, 215 pounds.

Year	Club	Lea	G	IP	W	L	Pct	SO	BB	H	ERA	SAVES
2000	Diamondbacks	Arizona	9	9⅓	0	0	.000	7	3	7	0.96	0
2001	Lancaster	Calif.	28	157⅔	9	8	.529	110	45	207	4.79	0
2002	Lancaster	Calif.	8	35	1	6	.143	23	12	59	9.00	0
2002	South Bend	Midwest	7	14⅓	0	0	.000	5	4	18	4.40	0
2003	Lancaster	Calif.	32	119⅓	6	7	.462	78	47	156	6.03	0
2004	South Bend	Midwest	36	44	5	2	.714	40	13	44	2.25	5
2004	El Paso	Texas	11	9	0	1	.000	6	10	16	10.00	0
2005	Tennessee	Southern	58	61⅓	2	2	.500	72	26	61	4.26	1
2006	Tennessee	Southern	40	43	2	3	.400	59	15	31	1.88	8
2006	Tucson	P.C.	18	20	2	1	.667	21	7	10	0.45	2
2006	Arizona	N.L.	9	5⅔	0	0	.000	3	2	3	0.00	0
2007	Arizona	N.L.	61	36⅓	3	2	.600	28	14	41	2.72	0
2008	Tucson	P.C.	6	6⅔	0	0	.000	9	4	6	4.05	0
2008	Arizona a	N.L.	45	32⅓	0	3	.000	20	14	33	4.73	0
2009	Arizona	N.L.	11	6⅓	0	0	.000	4	1	10	7.11	0
2009	Reno b	P.C.	39	43⅔	3	2	.600	40	15	41	3.09	9
2010	Syracuse	Int.	11	17	1	0	1.000	17	1	12	0.00	0
2010	Washington	N.L.	49	40⅔	4	1	.800	36	19	34	3.10	0
Major League Totals		5 Yrs.	175	121⅓	7	6	.538	91	50	121	3.49	0
	Championship Series											
2007	Arizona	N.L.	3	1⅓	0	0	.000	1	2	1	0.00	0

a On disabled list from July 19 to August 13, 2008.
b Claimed on waivers by Washington Nationals, November 5, 2009.

SLOWEY, KEVIN MICHAEL

Born, Conroe, Texas, May 4, 1984.
Bats Right. Throws Right. Height, 6 feet, 3 inches. Weight, 195 pounds.

Year	Club	Lea	G	IP	W	L	Pct	SO	BB	H	ERA	SAVES
2005	Elizabethton	Appal.	4	7⅔	0	0	.000	15	0	2	1.17	1
2006	New Britain	Eastern	9	59⅓	4	3	.571	52	13	50	3.19	0
2006	Fort Myers	Fla.St.	14	89⅓	4	2	.667	99	9	52	1.01	0
2007	Rochester	Int.	20	133⅔	10	5	.667	107	18	110	1.89	0
2007	Minnesota	A.L.	13	66⅔	4	1	.800	47	11	82	4.72	0
2008	Fort Myers	Fla.St.	2	8	0	0	.000	10	2	1	1.13	0
2008	Rochester	Int.	1	5	0	1	.000	9	2	3	3.60	0
2008	Minnesota a	A.L.	27	160⅓	12	11	.522	123	24	161	3.99	0
2009	Minnesota b	A.L.	16	90⅔	10	3	.769	75	15	113	4.86	0
2010	Minnesota c	A.L.	30	155⅔	13	6	.684	116	29	172	4.45	0
Major League Totals		4 Yrs.	86	473⅓	39	21	.650	361	79	528	4.41	0

a On disabled list from April 4 to May 7, 2008.
b On disabled list from July 4 to November 10, 2009.
c On disabled list from August 22 to September 6, 2010.

SMITH, JOSEPH MICHAEL (JOE)

Born, Cincinnati, Ohio, March 22, 1984.
Bats Right. Throws Right. Height, 6 feet, 2 inches. Weight, 205 pounds.

Year	Club	Lea	G	IP	W	L	Pct	SO	BB	H	ERA	SAVES
2006	Binghamton	Eastern	10	12⅔	0	2	.000	12	11	12	5.68	0
2006	Brooklyn	N.Y.-Penn.	17	20	0	1	.000	28	3	10	0.45	9
2007	New Orleans	P.C.	8	9	0	0	.000	5	4	7	2.00	2

Year	Club	Lea	G	IP	W	L	Pct	SO	BB	H	ERA	SAVES
2007	New York	N.L.	54	44⅓	3	2	.600	45	21	48	3.45	0
2008	New York a-b	N.L.	82	63⅓	6	3	.667	52	31	51	3.55	0
2009	Columbus	Int.	5	5	0	0	.000	6	1	4	0.00	0
2009	Cleveland c	A.L.	37	34	0	0	.000	30	13	30	3.44	0
2010	Columbus	Int.	20	23	2	1	.667	19	10	17	1.96	2
2010	Cleveland	A.L.	53	40	2	2	.500	32	24	30	3.83	0
Major League Totals		4 Yrs.	226	181⅔	11	7	.611	159	89	159	3.57	0

a Traded to Seattle Mariners with pitcher Aaron Heilman, outfielder Endy Chavez, pitcher Jason Vargas, infielder Mike Carp, outfielder Ezequiel Carrera and pitcher Maikel Cleto for pitcher J.J. Putz, pitcher Sean Green and outfielder Jeremy Reed, December 10, 2008.

b Traded to Cleveland Indians with pitcher Luis Valbuena for outfielder Franklin Gutierrez, December 10, 2008.

c On disabled list from April 29 to June 9 and September 1 to October 14, 2009.

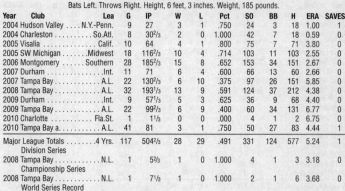

SONNANSTINE, ANDREW MICHAEL (ANDY)

Born, Barberton, Ohio, March 18, 1983.

Bats Left. Throws Right. Height, 6 feet, 3 inches. Weight, 185 pounds.

Year	Club	Lea	G	IP	W	L	Pct	SO	BB	H	ERA	SAVES
2004	Hudson Valley	N.Y.-Penn.	9	27	3	1	.750	24	3	18	1.00	1
2004	Charleston	So.Atl.	8	30⅔	2	0	1.000	42	7	18	0.59	0
2005	Visalia	Calif.	10	64	4	1	.800	75	7	71	3.80	0
2005	SW Michigan	Midwest	18	116⅔	10	4	.714	103	11	103	2.55	0
2006	Montgomery	Southern	28	185⅔	15	8	.652	153	34	151	2.67	0
2007	Durham	Int.	11	71	6	4	.600	66	13	60	2.66	0
2007	Tampa Bay	A.L.	22	130⅔	6	10	.375	97	26	151	5.85	0
2008	Tampa Bay	A.L.	32	193⅓	13	9	.591	124	37	212	4.38	0
2009	Durham	Int.	9	57⅓	5	3	.625	36	9	68	4.40	0
2009	Tampa Bay	A.L.	22	99⅔	6	9	.400	60	34	131	6.77	0
2010	Charlotte	Fla.St.	1	1⅓	0	0	.000	4	1	2	6.75	0
2010	Tampa Bay a	A.L.	41	81	3	1	.750	50	27	83	4.44	1
Major League Totals		4 Yrs.	117	504⅔	28	29	.491	331	124	577	5.24	1
	Division Series											
2008	Tampa Bay	N.L.	1	5⅔	1	0	1.000	4	1	3	3.18	0
	Championship Series											
2008	Tampa Bay	N.L.	1	7⅓	1	0	1.000	2	1	6	3.68	0
	World Series Record											
2008	Tampa Bay	N.L.	1	4	0	1	.000	2	3	6	6.75	0

a On disabled list from July 23 to August 8, 2010.

SORIA, JOAKIM AGUSTIN (RAMOS)

Born, Monclova, Mexico, May 18, 1984.

Bats Right. Throws Right. Height, 6 feet, 3 inches. Weight, 185 pounds.

Year	Club	Lea	G	IP	W	L	Pct	SO	BB	H	ERA	SAVES
2002	Dodgers	Gulf Coast	4	5	0	0	.000	6	0	6	3.60	0
2003						INJURED—Did Not Play						
2004	Dodgers	Dominican	4	5⅓	0	0	.000	4	5	3	1.69	1
2005	Mexico City a	Mexican	30	66⅓	5	0	1.000	60	31	75	4.48	0
2006	Mexico City	Mexican	39	37	0	0	.000	30	11	37	3.89	15
2006	Fort Wayne b	Midwest	7	11⅔	1	0	1.000	11	2	5	2.31	0
2007	Kansas City c	A.L.	62	69	2	3	.400	75	19	46	2.48	17
2008	Kansas City	A.L.	63	67⅓	2	3	.400	66	19	39	1.60	42
2009	Kansas City d	A.L.	47	53	3	2	.600	69	16	44	2.21	30
2010	Kansas City	A.L.	66	65⅔	1	2	.333	71	16	53	1.78	43
Major League Totals		4 Yrs.	238	255	8	10	.444	281	70	182	2.01	132

a Released by Los Angeles Dodgers, October 12, 2004. Signed with San Diego Padres, December 20, 2005.

b Selected by Kansas City Royals from San Diego Padres in Rule V draft, December 7, 2006.

c On disabled list from May 23 to June 7, 2007.

d On disabled list from May 8 to June 2, 2009.

SORIANO, RAFAEL

Born, San Jose, Dominican Republic, December 19, 1979.

Bats Right. Throws Right. Height, 6 feet, 1 inch. Weight, 220 pounds.

Year	Club	Lea	G	IP	W	L	Pct	SO	BB	H	ERA	SAVES
1999	Everett	Northwest	14	75⅓	5	4	.556	83	49	56	3.11	0
2000	Wisconsin	Midwest	21	122⅓	8	4	.667	90	50	97	2.87	0
2001	San Bernardino	Calif.	15	89	6	3	.667	98	39	49	2.53	0

Year	Club	Lea	G	IP	W	L	Pct	SO	BB	H	ERA	SAVES
2001	San Antonio	Texas	8	48⅓	2	2	.500	53	14	34	3.35	0
2002	San Antonio	Texas	10	46⅔	2	3	.400	52	15	32	2.31	0
2002	Seattle a	A.L.	10	47⅓	0	3	.000	32	16	45	4.56	1
2003	Tacoma	P.C.	11	62	4	3	.571	63	12	43	3.19	0
2003	Seattle	A.L.	40	53	3	0	1.000	68	12	30	1.53	1
2004	Seattle	A.L.	6	3⅓	0	3	.000	3	3	9	13.50	0
2004	Inland Empire	Calif.	2	8	0	0	.000	9	1	7	2.25	0
2004	San Antonio	Texas	2	8	1	0	1.000	10	0	4	1.13	0
2004	Tacoma b	P.C.	3	3⅔	0	0	.000	5	2	2	2.45	0
2005	Inland Empire	Calif.	3	4	0	0	.000	5	0	2	0.00	0
2005	San Antonio	Texas	1	1	0	0	.000	0	0	0	0.00	0
2005	Everett	Northwest	4	6	0	0	.000	8	2	6	3.00	0
2005	Tacoma	P.C.	5	5⅓	1	0	1.000	11	1	3	0.00	0
2005	Seattle c	A.L.	7	7⅓	0	0	.000	9	1	6	2.45	0
2006	Seattle d-e	A.L.	53	60	1	2	.333	65	21	44	2.25	2
2007	Atlanta	N.L.	71	72	3	3	.500	70	15	47	3.00	9
2008	Mississippi	Southern	2	2	0	0	.000	2	1	1	0.00	0
2008	Atlanta f	N.L.	14	14	0	1	.000	16	9	7	2.57	3
2009	Atlanta g	N.L.	77	75⅔	1	6	.143	102	27	53	2.97	27
2010	Tampa Bay h	A.L.	64	62⅓	3	2	.600	57	14	36	1.73	*45
Major League Totals		9 Yrs.	342	395	11	20	.355	422	118	277	2.73	88
	Division Series											
2010	Tampa Bay	N.L.	3	3	0	0	.000	1	0	4	9.00	1

a On disabled list from July 3 to August 2, 2002.
b On disabled list from May 10 to November 1, 2004.
c On disabled list from April 1 to September 5, 2005.
d On disabled list from July 20 to August 4, 2006.
e Traded to Atlanta Braves for pitcher Horacio Ramirez, December 7, 2006.
f On disabled list from April 7 to May 28 and June 6 to July 21 and August 3 to November 3, 2008.
g Traded to Tampa Bay Rays for pitcher Jesse Chavez, December 11, 2009.
h Filed for free agency, November 1, 2010. Signed with New York Yankees, January 18, 2011.

STAMMEN, CRAIG N.

Born, Coldwater, Ohio, March 9, 1984.
Bats Right. Throws Right. Height, 6 feet, 3 inches. Weight, 210 pounds.

Year	Club	Lea	G	IP	W	L	Pct	SO	BB	H	ERA	SAVES
2005	Vermont	N.Y.-Penn.	13	51	4	5	.444	32	12	62	4.06	0
2006	Potomac	Carolina	7	29⅔	0	2	.000	16	7	34	5.76	0
2006	Savannah	So.Atl.	21	113	6	9	.400	93	29	110	3.58	0
2007	Potomac	Carolina	28	125	8	6	.571	96	54	156	4.18	0
2007	Columbus	Int.	1	3⅔	0	1	.000	2	3	4	12.27	0
2008	Potomac	Carolina	15	69⅓	4	2	.667	62	17	59	2.21	1
2008	Harrisburg	Eastern	6	38⅓	3	1	.750	31	11	22	1.64	0
2008	Columbus	Int.	9	43	1	4	.200	35	16	62	7.33	0
2009	Syracuse	Int.	7	40	4	2	.667	14	8	33	1.80	0
2009	Washington	N.L.	19	105⅔	4	7	.364	48	24	112	5.11	0
2010	Syracuse	Int.	3	20	2	0	1.000	10	3	18	2.25	0
2010	Washington	N.L.	35	128	4	4	.500	85	41	151	5.13	0
Major League Totals		2 Yrs.	54	233⅔	8	11	.421	133	65	263	5.12	0

STAUFFER, TIMOTHY JAMES (TIM)

Born, Portland, Maine, June 2, 1982.
Bats Right. Throws Right. Height, 6 feet, 1 inch. Weight, 205 pounds.

Year	Club	Lea	G	IP	W	L	Pct	SO	BB	H	ERA	SAVES
2004	Lake Elsinore	Calif.	6	35⅓	2	0	1.000	30	9	28	1.78	0
2004	Portland	P.C.	14	81⅓	6	3	.667	50	26	83	3.54	0
2004	Mobile	Southern	8	51⅓	3	2	.600	33	13	56	2.63	0
2005	San Diego	N.L.	15	81	3	6	.333	49	29	92	5.33	0
2005	Portland	P.C.	13	75⅓	3	5	.375	64	17	90	5.14	0
2006	San Diego	N.L.	1	6	1	0	1.000	2	1	3	1.50	0
2006	Portland	P.C.	28	153	7	12	.368	89	52	199	5.53	0
2007	San Diego	N.L.	2	7⅔	0	1	.000	6	6	15	21.13	0
2007	Portland	P.C.	25	130⅔	8	5	.615	96	36	147	4.34	0
2008	San Diego a	N.L.				INJURED—Did Not Play						
2009	San Antonio	Texas	12	19	1	0	1.000	12	4	13	1.89	1
2009	Portland	P.C.	4	23	2	1	.667	16	4	16	2.35	0
2009	San Diego	N.L.	14	73	4	7	.364	53	34	71	3.58	0

Year	Club	Lea	G	IP	W	L	Pct	SO	BB	H	ERA	SAVES
2010	Portland	P.C.	6	17 2/3	0	0	.000	8	7	24	4.58	0
2010	San Diego b	N.L.	32	82 2/3	6	5	.545	61	24	65	1.85	0
Major League Totals		5 Yrs.	64	250 1/3	14	19	.424	171	94	246	4.06	0

a On disabled list from March 26 to October 8, 2008.
b On disabled list from May 11 to July 1, 2010.

STOREN, DREW PATRICK

Born, Brownsburg, Indiana, August 11, 1987.
Bats Both. Throws Right. Height, 6 feet, 2 inches. Weight, 180 pounds.

Year	Club	Lea	G	IP	W	L	Pct	SO	BB	H	ERA	SAVES
2009	Potomac	Carolina	7	10	1	0	1.000	11	2	7	1.80	2
2009	Harrisburg	Eastern	10	12 1/3	1	0	1.000	12	6	3	0.00	9
2009	Hagerstown	So.Atl.	11	14 2/3	0	1	.000	26	0	11	3.68	0
2010	Harrisburg	Eastern	7	9 1/3	0	0	.000	11	1	5	0.96	4
2010	Syracuse	Int.	6	7 1/3	0	0	.000	4	2	7	1.23	0
2010	Washington	N.L.	54	55 1/3	4	4	.500	52	22	48	3.58	5

STRASBURG, STEPHEN JAMES

Born, San Diego, California, July 20, 1988.
Bats Right. Throws Right. Height, 6 feet, 4 inches. Weight, 220 pounds.

Year	Club	Lea	G	IP	W	L	Pct	SO	BB	H	ERA	SAVES
2010	Harrisburg	Eastern	5	22	3	1	.750	27	6	13	1.64	0
2010	Syracuse	Int.	6	33 1/3	4	1	.800	38	7	18	1.08	0
2010	Washington a	N.L.	12	68	5	3	.625	92	17	56	2.91	0

a On disabled list from July 22 to November 10, 2010.

STREET, HUSTON LOWELL

Born, Austin, Texas, August 2, 1983.
Bats Right. Throws Right. Height, 6 feet. Weight, 190 pounds.

Year	Club	Lea	G	IP	W	L	Pct	SO	BB	H	ERA	SAVES
2004	Kane County	Midwest	9	10 2/3	0	1	.000	14	5	9	1.69	4
2004	Sacramento	P.C.	2	2	0	0	.000	2	0	2	0.00	1
2004	Midland	Texas	10	13 1/3	1	0	1.000	14	3	10	1.35	3
2005	Oakland a	A.L.	67	78 1/3	5	1	.833	72	26	53	1.72	23
2006	Oakland b	A.L.	69	70 2/3	4	4	.500	67	13	64	3.31	37
2007	Sacramento	P.C.	1	1	0	0	.000	2	0	1	0.00	0
2007	Oakland c	A.L.	48	50	5	2	.714	63	12	35	2.88	16
2008	Oakland d	A.L.	63	70	7	5	.583	69	27	58	3.73	18
2009	Colorado	N.L.	64	61 2/3	4	1	.800	70	13	43	3.06	35
2010	Tulsa	Texas	2	1 1/3	0	0	.000	2	1	1	0.00	0
2010	Colorado Springs	P.C.	7	7	1	1	.500	9	2	11	10.29	0
2010	Colorado e	N.L.	44	47 1/3	4	4	.500	45	11	39	3.61	20
Major League Totals		6 Yrs.	355	378	29	17	.630	386	102	292	3.00	149
	Division Series											
2006	Oakland	A.L.	3	3	0	0	.000	1	1	4	3.00	2
2009	Colorado	N.L.	3	2 2/3	0	2	.000	1	3	6	13.50	1
Division Series Totals			6	5 2/3	0	2	.000	2	4	10	7.94	3
	Championship Series											
2006	Oakland	A.L.	2	3 1/3	0	1	.000	3	0	4	10.80	0

a Selected Rookie of the Year in American League for 2005.
b On disabled list from August 19 to September 8, 2006.
c On disabled list from May 13 to July 23, 2007.
d Traded to Colorado Rockies with outfielder Carlos Gonzalez and pitcher Greg Smith for outfielder Matt Holliday, November 12, 2008.
e On disabled list from March 26 to June 22, 2010.

SUPPAN, JEFFREY SCOT (JEFF)

Born, Oklahoma City, Oklahoma, January 2, 1975.
Bats Right. Throws Right. Height, 6 feet, 2 inch. Weight, 235 pounds.

Year	Club	Lea	G	IP	W	L	Pct	SO	BB	H	ERA	SAVES
1993	Red Sox	Gulf Coast	10	57 2/3	4	3	.571	64	16	52	2.18	0
1994	Sarasota	Fla. St.	27	174	13	7	.650	173	50	153	3.26	0
1995	Trenton	Eastern	15	99	6	2	.750	88	26	86	2.36	0

Year	Club	Lea	G	IP	W	L	Pct	SO	BB	H	ERA	SAVES
1995	Pawtucket	Int.	7	45⅔	2	3	.400	32	9	50	5.32	0
1995	Boston	A.L.	8	22⅔	1	2	.333	19	5	29	5.96	0
1996	Pawtucket	Int.	22	145⅓	10	6	.625	142	25	130	3.22	0
1996	Boston a	A.L.	8	22⅔	1	1	.500	13	13	29	7.54	0
1997	Pawtucket	Int.	9	60⅔	5	1	.833	40	15	51	3.71	0
1997	Boston b	A.L.	23	112⅓	7	3	.700	67	36	140	5.69	0
1998	Arizona	N.L.	13	66	1	7	.125	39	21	82	6.68	0
1998	Tucson c	P.C.	13	67	4	3	.571	62	17	75	3.63	0
1998	Kansas City	A.L.	4	12⅔	0	0	.000	12	1	9	0.71	0
1999	Kansas City	A.L.	32	208⅔	10	12	.455	103	62	222	4.53	0
2000	Kansas City	A.L.	35	217	10	9	.526	128	84	240	4.94	0
2001	Kansas City	A.L.	34	218⅓	10	14	.417	120	74	227	4.37	0
2002	Kansas City d	A.L.	33	208	9	16	.360	109	68	229	5.32	0
2003	Pittsburgh	N.L.	21	141	10	7	.588	78	31	147	3.57	0
2003	Boston e-f	A.L.	11	63	3	4	.429	32	20	70	5.57	0
2004	St. Louis	N.L.	31	188	16	9	.640	110	65	192	4.16	0
2005	St. Louis	N.L.	32	194⅓	16	10	.615	114	63	206	3.57	0
2006	St. Louis g	N.L.	32	190	12	7	.632	104	69	207	4.12	0
2007	Milwaukee	N.L.	34	206⅔	12	12	.500	114	68	243	4.62	0
2008	Milwaukee h	N.L.	31	177⅔	10	10	.500	90	67	207	4.96	0
2009	Wisconsin	Midwest	1	3⅓	0	1	.000	1	0	5	10.80	0
2009	Nashville	P.C.	1	3⅔	0	1	.000	3	0	8	12.27	0
2009	Milwaukee i	N.L.	30	161⅔	7	12	.368	80	74	200	5.29	0
2010	Wisconsin	Midwest	1	4⅓	0	0	.000	4	3	7	2.08	0
2010	Milwaukee-St. Louis j-k-l-m	N.L.	30	101⅓	3	8	.273	51	37	130	5.06	0
Major League Totals		16 Yrs.	442	2512	138	143	.491	1383	858	2809	4.69	0
Division Series												
2004	St. Louis	N.L.	1	7	1	0	1.000	2	3	2	2.57	0
2006	St. Louis	N.L.	1	4⅓	0	1	.000	3	3	6	6.23	0
2008	Milwaukee	N.L.	1	3	0	1	.000	3	2	6	15.00	0
Division Series Totals			3	14⅓	1	2	.333	8	8	14	6.28	0
Championship Series												
2004	St. Louis	N.L.	2	12	1	1	.500	9	4	8	3.00	0
2005	St. Louis	N.L.	1	5	0	0	.000	5	3	3	1.80	0
2006	St. Louis	N.L.	2	15	1	0	1.000	6	6	5	0.60	0
Championship Series Totals			5	32	2	1	.667	20	13	16	1.69	0
World Series Record												
2004	St. Louis	N.L.	1	4⅔	0	1	.000	4	1	8	7.71	0
2006	St. Louis	N.L.	1	6	0	0	.000	4	2	8	4.50	0
World Series Totals			2	10⅔	0	1	.000	8	3	16	5.91	0

a On disabled list from August 25 to September 30, 1996.
b Selected in expansion draft by Arizona Diamondbacks, November 18, 1997.
c Sold to Kansas City Royals, September 3, 1998.
d Not offered contract, December 20, 2002. Signed with Pittsburgh Pirates, January 29, 2003.
e Traded to Boston Red Sox with pitcher Brandon Lyon and pitcher Anastacio Martinez for infielder Freddy Sanchez, pitcher Mike Gonzalez and cash, July 31, 2003.
f Filed for free agency, October 27, 2003. Signed with St. Louis Cardinals, December 16, 2003.
g Filed for free agency, November 1, 2006. Signed with Milwaukee Brewers, December 24, 2006.
h On disabled list from July 7 to July 22, 2008.
i On disabled list from July 28 to August 25, 2009.
j On disabled list from March 26 to April 15, 2010.
k Released by Milwaukee Brewers, June 7, 2010. Signed with St. Louis Cardinals, June 14, 2010.
l On disabled list from August 1 to September 1, 2010.
m Filed for free agency, November 1, 2010.

TAKAHASHI, HISANORI

Born, Tokyo, Japan, April 2, 1975.
Bats Left. Throws Left. Height, 5 feet, 10 inches. Weight, 170 pounds.

Year	Club	Lea	G	IP	W	L	Pct	SO	BB	H	ERA	SAVES
2000	Yomirui	Japan Cent.	24	135⅔	9	6	.600	102	36	133	3.18	0
2001	Yomirui	Japan Cent.	30	134⅔	9	9	.500	99	52	126	3.94	0
2002	Yomirui	Japan Cent.	24	163⅓	10	4	.714	145	39	143	3.09	0
2003	Yomirui	Japan Cent.	13	86⅔	4	4	.500	78	27	79	3.84	0
2004	Yomirui	Japan Cent.	16	91	5	10	.333	61	26	107	5.44	0
2005	Yomirui	Japan Cent.	27	163	8	12	.400	135	48	171	4.47	0
2006	Yomirui	Japan Cent.	35	62	2	6	.250	51	15	70	4.94	15
2007	Yomirui	Japan Cent.	28	186⅔	14	4	.778	141	50	168	2.75	0
2008	Yomirui	Japan Cent.	23	122	8	5	.615	94	30	127	4.13	0
2009	Yomirui	Japan Cent.	25	144	10	6	.625	126	36	147	2.94	0

Year	Club	Lea	G	IP	W	L	Pct	SO	BB	H	ERA	SAVES
2010	New York a-b	N.L.	53	122	10	6	.625	114	43	116	3.61	8

a Signed with New York Mets organization, February 11, 2010.
b Waived by New York Mets, November 5, 2010. Signed with Los Angeles Angels, December 2, 2010.

TALBOT, MITCHELL R. (MITCH)

Born, Cedar City, Utah, October 17, 1983.
Bats Right. Throws Right. Height, 6 feet, 2 inches. Weight, 200 pounds.

Year	Club	Lea	G	IP	W	L	Pct	SO	BB	H	ERA	SAVES
2003	Martinsville	Appal.	12	54	4	4	.500	46	11	45	2.83	0
2004	Lexington	So.Atl.	27	152⅔	10	10	.500	115	49	145	3.83	0
2005	Salem	Carolina	27	151⅓	8	11	.421	100	46	169	4.34	0
2006	Montgomery	Southern	10	66⅓	4	3	.571	59	18	51	1.90	0
2006	Corpus Christi a	Texas	18	90⅓	6	4	.600	96	29	94	3.39	1
2007	Durham	Int.	29	161	13	9	.591	124	59	169	4.53	0
2008	Durham	Int.	28	161	13	9	.591	141	35	165	3.86	0
2008	Tampa Bay	A.L.	3	9⅔	0	0	.000	5	11	16	11.17	0
2009	Charlotte	Fla.St.	1	3	0	0	.000	6	0	1	0.00	0
2009	Rays	Gulf Coast	4	11	0	0	.000	21	0	5	0.82	0
2009	Durham b	Int.	10	54⅓	4	4	.500	40	18	67	4.47	0
2010	Mahoning Valley	N.Y.-Penn.	1	3	0	0	.000	0	1	2	3.00	0
2010	Cleveland c	A.L.	28	159⅓	10	13	.435	88	69	169	4.41	0
Major League Totals		2 Yrs.	31	169	10	13	.435	93	80	185	4.79	0

a Traded by Houston Astros to Tampa Bay Devil Rays with infielder Ben Zobrist for infielder Aubrey Huff and cash, July 12, 2006.
b Sent to Cleveland Indians to complete trade for Kelly Shoppach, December 21, 2009.
c On disabled list from July 30 to August 14, 2010.

TALLET, BRIAN CURTIS

Born, Midwest City, Oklahoma, September 21, 1977.
Bats Left. Throws Left. Height, 6 feet, 7 inches. Weight, 220 pounds.

Year	Club	Lea	G	IP	W	L	Pct	SO	BB	H	ERA	SAVES
2000	Mahoning Valley	N.Y.-Penn.	6	15⅔	0	0	.000	20	3	10	1.15	0
2001	Kinston	Carolina	27	160	9	7	.563	164	38	134	3.04	0
2002	Akron	Eastern	18	102⅓	10	1	.909	73	32	93	3.08	0
2002	Buffalo	Int.	8	44	2	3	.400	25	16	47	3.07	0
2002	Cleveland	A.L.	2	12	1	0	1.000	5	4	9	1.50	0
2003	Buffalo	Int.	15	84	4	4	.500	67	34	89	5.14	0
2003	Cleveland	A.L.	5	19	0	2	.000	9	8	23	4.74	0
2004	Akron	Eastern	14	22⅔	1	1	.500	24	13	26	5.56	1
2004	Buffalo	Int.	5	8⅔	0	0	.000	7	3	7	4.15	0
2004	Mahoning Valley	N.Y.-Penn.	2	2⅔	0	0	.000	2	0	3	0.00	0
2004	Lake County a	So.Atl.	2	2	0	0	.000	1	0	1	0.00	0
2005	Cleveland	A.L.	2	4⅔	0	0	.000	2	3	6	7.71	0
2005	Buffalo	Int.	22	97⅔	6	5	.545	61	25	98	4.05	0
2006	Syracuse	Int.	20	25⅓	1	2	.333	21	10	32	5.68	3
2006	Toronto b	A.L.	44	54⅓	3	0	1.000	37	31	45	3.81	0
2007	Syracuse	Int.	7	6⅔	0	0	.000	11	3	4	1.35	0
2007	Toronto	A.L.	48	62⅓	2	4	.333	54	28	49	3.47	0
2008	Syracuse	Int.	2	2	0	0	.000	1	1	2	4.50	0
2008	Toronto c	A.L.	51	56⅓	1	2	.333	47	22	52	2.88	0
2009	Toronto	A.L.	37	160⅔	7	9	.438	120	72	169	5.32	0
2010	Dunedin	Fla.St.	1	4	0	0	.000	3	1	2	0.00	0
2010	Las Vegas	P.C.	1	1⅓	0	1	.000	1	1	9	54.00	0
2010	Toronto d-e	A.L.	34	77⅓	2	6	.250	53	38	84	6.40	0
Major League Totals		8 Yrs.	223	446⅔	16	23	.410	327	206	437	4.65	0

a On disabled list from April 1 to July 26, 2004.
b Traded to Toronto Blue Jays for pitcher Bubbie Buzachero, January 17, 2006.
c On disabled list from July 26 to August 16, 2008.
d On disabled list from April 18 to June 1, 2010.
e Filed for free agency, November 12, 2010. Signed with St. Louis Cardinals, November 30, 2010.

TEJEDA, ROBINSON GARCIA

Born, Bani, Dominican Republic, March 24, 1982.
Bats Right. Throws Right. Height, 6 feet, 3 inches. Weight, 250 pounds.

Year	Club	Lea	G	IP	W	L	Pct	SO	BB	H	ERA	SAVES
1999	Phillies	Gulf Coast	12	46⅓	1	3	.250	39	27	47	4.27	0
2000	Phillies	Gulf Coast	10	39	2	5	.286	22	12	44	5.54	0

Year	Club	Lea	G	IP	W	L	Pct	SO	BB	H	ERA	SAVES
2001	Lakewood	So.Atl.	26	150⅔	8	9	.471	152	58	128	3.40	0
2002	Clearwater	Fla.St.	17	99⅔	4	8	.333	87	48	73	3.97	0
2003	Clearwater	Fla.St.	11	64⅔	2	4	.333	42	23	53	3.20	0
2003	Lakewood	So.Atl.	5	18⅔	0	3	.000	20	16	17	5.30	0
2004	Reading	Eastern	27	150⅓	8	14	.364	133	59	148	5.15	0
2005	Scranton/WB	Int.	5	28⅓	2	0	1.000	28	13	21	2.22	0
2005	Philadelphia	N.L.	26	85⅔	4	3	.571	72	51	67	3.57	0
2006	Rangers	Arizona	2	4	0	0	.000	6	0	4	6.75	0
2006	Oklahoma	P.C.	15	80	6	2	.750	79	42	61	3.15	0
2006	Texas a	A.L.	14	73⅔	5	5	.500	40	32	83	4.28	0
2007	Texas	A.L.	19	95⅓	5	9	.357	69	60	110	6.61	0
2007	Oklahoma	P.C.	5	18⅔	1	3	.250	20	15	27	8.20	0
2008	Oklahoma	P.C.	10	33	1	1	.500	39	10	20	2.18	1
2008	Texas-Kansas City b	A.L.	29	45⅓	2	2	.500	45	24	27	3.97	0
2009	NW Arkansas	Texas	2	3⅔	0	1	.000	5	2	3	4.91	0
2009	Omaha	P.C.	1	2	0	1	.000	1	3	1	0.00	0
2009	Kansas City c	A.L.	35	73⅔	4	2	.667	87	50	43	3.54	0
2010	Kansas City d	A.L.	54	61	3	5	.375	56	26	55	3.54	0
Major League Totals		6 Yrs.	177	434⅔	23	26	.469	369	243	385	4.39	0

a Traded to Texas Rangers with outfielder Jake Blalock for outfielder David Dellucci, April 1, 2006.
b Claimed on waivers by Kansas City Royals, June 24, 2008.
c On disabled list from May 21 to June 20, 2009.
d On disabled list from July 30 to August 29, 2010.

TEXEIRA, KANEKOA JACOB

Born, Maui, Hawaii, February 6, 1986.
Bats Right. Throws Right. Height, 6 feet, 2 inches. Weight, 190 pounds.

Year	Club	Lea	G	IP	W	L	Pct	SO	BB	H	ERA	SAVES
2006	Bristol	Appal.	19	23⅔	1	2	.333	29	5	15	0.76	3
2006	Kannapolis	So.Atl.	4	6	0	0	.000	2	1	8	4.50	0
2007	Kannapolis	So.Atl.	39	53⅔	5	2	.714	58	22	49	3.69	16
2008	Winston-Salem	Carolina	36	38⅔	3	1	.750	36	14	28	0.93	20
2008	Birmingham a	Southern	15	22⅓	3	2	.600	24	7	18	2.01	1
2009	Trenton b	Eastern	41	101⅓	9	6	.600	88	43	90	2.84	2
2010	Seattle-Kansas City c-d	A.L.	43	61⅓	1	1	.500	33	25	73	4.84	0
Major League Totals		1 Yrs.	43	61⅓	1	1	.500	33	25	73	4.84	0

a Traded by Chicago White Sox to New York Yankees with infielder Nick Swisher for infielder Wilson Betemit, pitcher Jeff Marquez and pitcher Jhonny Nunez, November 13, 2008.
b Selected by Seattle Mariners in Rule V draft, December 10, 2009.
c Claimed on waivers by Kansas City Royals, June 3, 2010.
d On disabled list from August 28 to September 24, 2010.

THATCHER, JOSEPH (JOE)

Born, Indianapolis, Indiana, October 4, 1981.
Bats Left. Throws Left. Height, 6 feet, 2 inches. Weight, 230 pounds.

Year	Club	Lea	G	IP	W	L	Pct	SO	BB	H	ERA	SAVES
2004	River City	Frontier	29	41⅓	2	3	.400	55	15	38	2.98	5
2005	River City	Frontier	18	21⅓	4	2	.667	27	4	18	1.27	5
2005	Brevard County a	Fla.St.	7	9	0	0	.000	14	0	6	0.00	2
2005	Helena	Pioneer	6	7⅔	2	0	1.000	10	1	8	3.52	2
2006	Brevard County	Fla.St.	16	30⅔	3	1	.750	32	9	12	0.29	2
2006	West Virginia	So.Atl.	26	29⅔	1	3	.250	42	6	28	2.43	10
2006	Huntsville	Southern	4	5⅓	1	0	1.000	6	2	2	1.69	0
2007	Huntsville	Southern	14	16⅓	1	0	1.000	20	2	11	0.55	0
2007	Nashville	P.C.	24	21⅔	2	1	.667	33	7	19	2.08	1
2007	Portland	P.C.	8	8⅔	1	0	1.000	11	1	10	1.04	0
2007	San Diego b	N.L.	22	21	2	2	.500	16	6	13	1.29	0
2008	San Diego	N.L.	25	25⅔	0	4	.000	17	13	42	8.42	0
2008	Portland	P.C.	37	39	5	2	.714	44	11	38	2.77	3
2009	Portland	P.C.	19	19	1	2	.333	22	5	18	1.89	1
2009	San Diego	N.L.	52	45	1	0	1.000	55	18	37	2.80	0
2010	Portland	P.C.	6	5	0	1	.000	3	3	6	3.60	0
2010	San Diego c	N.L.	65	35	1	0	1.000	45	7	23	1.29	0
Major League Totals		4 Yrs.	164	126⅔	4	6	.400	133	44	115	3.27	0

a Signed by Milwaukee Brewers, July 19, 2005.
b Traded to San Diego Padres with pitcher Will Inman and pitcher Steve Garrison for pitcher Scott Linebrink, July 25, 2007.
c On disabled list from March 26 to April 22, 2010.

THOMAS, BRADLEY RICHARD (BRAD)

Born, Sydney, New South Wales, Australia, October 12, 1977.
Bats Left. Throws Left. Height, 6 feet, 4 inches. Weight, 235 pounds.

Year	Club	Lea	G	IP	W	L	Pct	SO	BB	H	ERA	SAVES
1996	Great Falls	Pioneer	11	$35^2/_3$	3	2	.600	28	11	48	6.31	0
1997	Elizabethtn a	Appal.	14	$70^1/_3$	3	4	.429	53	21	78	4.48	0
1998	Fort Wayne	Midwest	27	$152^1/_3$	11	8	.579	126	45	146	2.95	0
1999	Fort Myers	Fla.St.	27	$152^2/_3$	8	11	.421	108	46	182	4.78	0
2000	New Britain	Eastern	14	$75^1/_3$	6	6	.500	66	46	80	4.06	0
2000	Fort Myers	Fla.St.	12	65	6	2	.750	57	16	62	1.66	0
2001	New Britain	Eastern	19	$119^1/_3$	10	3	.769	97	26	91	1.96	0
2001	Minnesota	A.L.	5	$16^1/_3$	0	2	.000	6	14	20	9.37	0
2002	Edmonton	P.C.	28	152	6	12	.333	97	54	175	5.74	0
2003	Rochester	Int.	15	$58^2/_3$	0	3	.000	50	10	68	3.53	0
2003	Twins	Gulf Coast	2	10	0	0	.000	12	1	6	0.00	0
2003	Minnesota	A.L.	3	$4^2/_3$	0	1	.000	2	3	6	7.71	0
2004	Minnesota	A.L.	3	$2^2/_3$	0	0	.000	0	1	7	16.88	0
2004	Pawtucket b-c	Int.	4	$4^1/_3$	0	1	.000	1	6	6	10.38	0
2005	Nippon d	Japan Pac.	38	$48^1/_3$	1	5	.167	51	39	54	4.66	1
2006	Nippon	Japan Pac.	40	$45^2/_3$	4	1	.800	43	23	50	3.74	1
2007	Tacoma e	P.C.	34	$116^1/_3$	8	6	.571	100	42	138	4.87	2
2008	Hanwha	Korea	59	$63^1/_3$	3	6	.333	63	23	52	2.84	31
2009	Hanwha	Korea	45	50	2	5	.286	56	20	43	2.88	13
2010	Detroit g	A.L.	49	$69^1/_3$	6	2	.750	30	29	77	3.89	0
Major League Totals		4 Yrs.	60	93	6	5	.545	38	47	110	5.42	0

a Released by Los Angeles Dodgers, May 9, 1997. Signed with Minnesota Twins organization, May 12, 1997.
b On disabled list from April 23 to October 12, 2004.
c Sold to Boston Red Sox, April 21, 2004.
d Filed for free agency, October 15, 2004. Signed with Nippon (Japan) for 2005.
e Signed with Seattle Mariners organization, March 1, 2007.
f Filed for free agency, October 29. 2007. Signed with Hanwa (Korea) for 2008.
g Signed with Detroit Tigers, December 7, 2009.

THORNTON, MATTHEW J. (MATT)

Born, Three Rivers, Michigan, September 15, 1976.
Bats Left. Throws Left. Height, 6 feet, 6 inches. Weight, 235 pounds.

Year	Club	Lea	G	IP	W	L	Pct	SO	BB	H	ERA	SAVES
1998	Everett	Northwest	2	$1^1/_3$	0	0	.000	0	3	1	27.00	0
1999	Wisconsin	Midwest	25	$29^1/_3$	0	0	.000	34	25	39	4.91	1
2000	Wisconsin	Midwest	26	$103^1/_3$	6	9	.400	88	72	94	4.01	0
2001	San Bernardino	California	27	157	14	7	.667	192	60	126	2.52	0
2002	San Antonio	Texas	12	62	1	5	.167	44	29	52	3.63	0
2003	Inland Empire	California	2	9	0	0	.000	14	4	9	4.00	0
2003	Tacoma	P.C.	2	9	0	2	.000	5	3	14	8.00	0
2003	San Antonio	Texas	4	$25^1/_3$	3	0	1.000	18	9	8	0.36	0
2004	Tacoma	P.C.	16	83	7	5	.583	74	63	85	5.20	0
2004	Seattle	A.L.	19	$32^2/_3$	1	2	.333	30	25	30	4.13	0
2005	Seattle	A.L.	55	57	0	4	.000	57	42	54	5.21	0
2006	Chicago a	A.L.	63	54	5	3	.625	49	21	46	3.33	2
2007	Chicago	A.L.	68	$56^1/_3$	4	4	.500	55	26	59	4.79	2
2008	Chicago	A.L.	74	$67^1/_3$	5	3	.625	77	19	48	2.67	1
2009	Chicago	A.L.	70	$72^1/_3$	6	3	.667	87	20	58	2.74	4
2010	Chicago b	A.L.	61	$60^2/_3$	5	4	.556	81	20	41	2.67	8
Major League Totals		7 Yrs.	410	$400^1/_3$	26	23	.531	436	173	336	3.55	17
Division Series												
2008	Chicago	A.L.	3	$3^1/_3$	0	0	.000	2	2	2	0.00	0

a Traded to Chicago White Sox for outfielder Joe Borchard, March 20, 2006.
b On disabled list from August 18 to September 3, 2010.

TILLMAN, CHRISTOPHER S. (CHRIS)

Born, Anaheim, California, April 15, 1988.
Bats Right. Throws Right. Height, 6 feet, 5 inches. Weight, 195 pounds.

Year	Club	Lea	G	IP	W	L	Pct	SO	BB	H	ERA	SAVES
2006	Mariners	Arizona	5	11	2	0	1.000	16	5	9	0.82	1
2006	Everett	Northwest	5	$19^2/_3$	1	3	.250	29	15	25	7.78	0
2007	High Desert	Calif.	20	$102^2/_3$	6	7	.462	105	48	107	5.26	0
2007	Wisconsin	Midwest	8	33	1	4	.200	34	13	31	3.55	0
2008	Bowie a	Eastern	28	$135^2/_3$	11	4	.733	154	65	115	3.18	0

Year	Club	Lea	G	IP	W	L	Pct	SO	BB	H	ERA	SAVES
2009	Norfolk	Int.	18	$96\frac{2}{3}$	8	6	.571	99	26	85	2.70	0
2009	Baltimore	A.L.	12	65	2	5	.286	39	24	77	5.40	0
2010	Norfolk	Int.	21	$121\frac{1}{3}$	11	7	.611	94	30	120	3.34	0
2010	Baltimore	A.L.	11	$53\frac{2}{3}$	2	5	.286	31	31	51	5.87	0
Major League Totals		2 Yrs.	23	$118\frac{2}{3}$	4	10	.286	70	55	128	5.61	0

a Traded by Seattle Mariners to Baltimore Orioles with pitcher Tony Butler, outfielder Adam Jones, pitcher Kam Mickolio and pitcher George Sherrill for pitcher Erik Bedard, February 8, 2008.

TOMLIN, JOSHUA A. (JOSH)

Born, Tyler, Texas, October 19, 1984.
Bats Right. Throws Right. Height, 6 feet, 1 inch. Weight, 195 pounds.

Year	Club	Lea	G	IP	W	L	Pct	SO	BB	H	ERA	SAVES
2006	Mahoning Valley	N.Y.-Penn.	15	$77\frac{1}{3}$	8	2	.800	69	15	56	2.09	0
2007	Kinston	Carolina	6	$27\frac{2}{3}$	1	1	.500	20	12	24	3.58	0
2007	Lake County	So.Atl.	26	$103\frac{2}{3}$	10	3	.769	89	19	103	3.30	0
2008	Kinston	Carolina	40	$102\frac{2}{3}$	9	5	.643	109	16	82	2.98	3
2008	Buffalo	Int.	1	7	1	0	1.000	3	1	6	3.86	0
2009	Akron	Eastern	26	145	14	9	.609	125	27	149	4.16	0
2010	Columbus	Int.	20	$107\frac{1}{3}$	8	4	.667	80	33	83	2.68	0
2010	Cleveland	A.L.	12	73	6	4	.600	43	19	72	4.56	0

TRONCOSO, RAMON JOSE

Born, San Jose de Ocoa, Dominican Republic, February 16, 1983.
Bats Right. Throws Right. Height, 6 feet, 2 inches. Weight, 220 pounds.

Year	Club	Lea	G	IP	W	L	Pct	SO	BB	H	ERA	SAVES
2005	Ogden	Pioneer	29	$36\frac{2}{3}$	6	2	.750	30	12	40	3.68	13
2005	Columbus	So.Atl.	13	$37\frac{2}{3}$	2	3	.400	27	13	58	6.69	1
2006	Vero Beach	Fla.St.	18	$29\frac{1}{3}$	1	3	.250	31	14	43	6.75	0
2006	Columbus	So.Atl.	23	$33\frac{2}{3}$	4	0	1.000	22	7	28	2.41	15
2007	Inland Empire	Calif.	16	26	3	1	.750	30	3	18	1.04	7
2007	Jacksonville	Southern	35	52	7	3	.700	39	18	52	3.12	7
2008	Las Vegas	P.C.	22	$30\frac{2}{3}$	4	0	1.000	18	16	43	4.99	0
2008	Los Angeles	N.L.	32	38	1	1	.500	38	12	37	4.26	0
2009	Los Angeles	N.L.	73	$82\frac{2}{3}$	5	4	.556	55	34	83	2.72	6
2010	Albuquerque	P.C.	15	22	0	2	.000	19	11	23	5.73	1
2010	Los Angeles	N.L.	52	54	2	3	.400	34	18	55	4.33	0
Major League Totals		3 Yrs.	157	$174\frac{2}{3}$	8	8	.500	127	64	175	3.56	6
	Championship Series											
2009	Los Angeles	N.L.	3	3	0	0	.000	3	3	0	0.00	0

UEHARA, KOJI

Born, Osaka, Japan, April 3, 1975.
Bats Right. Throws Right. Height, 6 feet, 1 inch. Weight, 190 pounds.

Year	Club	Lea	G	IP	W	L	Pct	SO	BB	H	ERA	SAVES
1999	Yomiuri	Japan Cent.	25	$197\frac{2}{3}$	20	4	.833	179	24	153	2.09	0
2000	Yomiuri	Japan Cent.	20	131	9	7	.562	126	22	112	3.57	0
2001	Yomiuri	Japan Cent.	24	$138\frac{2}{3}$	10	7	.588	108	28	133	4.02	0
2002	Yomiuri	Japan Cent.	26	204	17	5	.773	182	23	173	2.60	0
2003	Yomiuri	Japan Cent.	27	$207\frac{1}{3}$	16	5	.762	194	28	190	3.17	0
2004	Yomiuri	Japan Cent.	22	163	13	5	.722	153	23	135	2.60	0
2005	Yomiuri	Japan Cent.	27	$187\frac{1}{3}$	9	12	.429	145	22	164	3.31	0
2006	Yomiuri	Japan Cent.	24	$168\frac{1}{3}$	8	9	.471	151	21	157	3.21	0
2007	Yomiuri	Japan Cent.	55	62	4	3	.571	66	4	47	1.74	32
2008	Yomiuri	Japan Cent.	26	$89\frac{2}{3}$	6	5	.545	72	16	90	3.81	1
2009	Baltimore a-b	A.L.	12	$66\frac{2}{3}$	2	4	.333	48	12	71	4.05	0
2010	Baltimore c-d	A.L.	43	44	1	2	.333	55	5	37	2.86	13
Major League Totals		2 Yrs.	55	$110\frac{2}{3}$	3	6	.333	103	17	108	3.58	13

a Signed with Baltimore Orioles, January 13, 2009.
b On disabled list from May 24 to June 11 and June 24 to November 6, 2009.
c On disabled list from March 26 to May 6 and May 20 to June 27, 2010.
d Filed for free agency, November 1, 2010, re-signed with Baltimore Orioles, December 9, 2010.

VALDES, RAUL

Born, Havana, Cuba, November 27, 1977.
Bats Left. Throws Left. Height, 5 feet, 11 inches. Weight, 190 pounds.

Year	Club	Lea	G	IP	W	L	Pct	SO	BB	H	ERA	SAVES
2005	Iowa	P.C.	25	98 2/3	6	7	.462	73	39	135	5.93	1
2005	West Tenn	Southern	5	23	2	0	1.000	18	3	28	5.09	0
2006	Iowa	P.C.	7	32	1	3	.250	20	11	44	7.59	0
2006	Nashua	Can.-Am	4	23	2	1	.667	17	11	30	5.09	0
2006	New Jersey a	Can.-Am	17	83 1/3	7	3	.700	62	22	82	2.81	0
2007	Binghamton	Eastern	20	29 1/3	0	1	.000	28	9	35	3.68	1
2007	St. Lucie	Fla.St.	3	7 1/3	0	1	.000	5	6	8	6.14	0
2008-09					Did Not Play							
2010	Buffalo	Int.	9	36	2	1	.667	36	9	34	3.00	0
2010	New York b-c	N.L.	38	58 2/3	3	3	.500	56	27	59	4.91	1

a Released by Chicago Cubs, May 17, 2006. Signed with New York Mets organization. November 10, 2006.
b Confined to the Dominican Republic with visa problems 2008-2009.
c Filed for free agency, November 5, 2010. Signed with St. Louis Cardinals organization, November 19, 2010.

VALVERDE, JOSE RAFAEL

Born, San Pedro de Macoris, Dominican Republic, July 24, 1979.
Bats Right. Throws Right. Height, 6 feet, 4 inches. Weight, 255 pounds.

Year	Club	Lea	G	IP	W	L	Pct	SO	BB	H	ERA	SAVES
1997	Arizona	Dominican	14	18 2/3	0	0	.000	19	13	20	5.30	0
1998	Arizona	Dominican	23	51 1/3	1	3	.250	56	22	31	1.75	7
1999	Diamondbacks	Arizona	20	28 2/3	1	2	.333	47	10	34	4.08	8
1999	South Bend	Midwest	2	2 2/3	0	0	.000	3	2	2	0.00	0
2000	South Bend	Midwest	31	31 2/3	0	5	.000	39	25	31	5.40	14
2000	Missoula	Pioneer	12	11 2/3	1	0	1.000	24	4	3	0.00	4
2001	El Paso	Texas	39	41 1/3	2	2	.500	72	27	36	3.92	13
2002	Tucson	P.C.	49	47 2/3	2	4	.333	65	23	45	5.85	5
2003	Tucson	P.C.	22	29	1	1	.500	26	14	26	3.10	5
2003	Arizona	N.L.	54	50 1/3	2	1	.667	71	26	24	2.15	10
2004	Arizona	N.L.	29	29 2/3	1	2	.333	38	17	23	4.25	8
2004	Tucson a	P.C.	10	10 2/3	1	1	.500	5	5	9	4.22	3
2005	Tucson	P.C.	2	2	0	0	.000	3	1	1	0.00	0
2005	Arizona b	N.L.	61	66 1/3	3	4	.429	75	20	51	2.44	15
2006	Tucson	P.C.	15	17 2/3	1	0	1.000	18	10	13	3.06	3
2006	Arizona	N.L.	44	49 1/3	2	3	.400	69	22	50	5.84	18
2007	Arizona c	N.L.	65	64 1/3	1	4	.200	78	26	46	2.66	*47
2008	Houston	N.L.	74	72	6	3	.667	83	23	62	3.38	*44
2009	Corpus Christi	Texas	2	2	0	0	.000	2	2	0	0.00	0
2009	Houston d-e	N.L.	52	54	4	2	.667	56	21	40	2.33	25
2010	Detroit	A.L.	60	63	2	4	.333	63	32	41	3.00	26
Major League Totals		8 Yrs.	439	449	21	23	.477	533	187	337	3.15	193
	Division Series											
2007	Arizona	N.L.	3	3	0	0	.000	6	1	1	0.00	1
	Championship Series											
2007	Arizona	N.L.	1	1 2/3	0	1	.000	2	3	1	5.40	0

a On disabled list from June 14 to October 4, 2004.
b On disabled list from March 25 to May 2, 2005.
c Traded to Houston Astros for pitcher Chad Qualls, pitcher Juan Gutierrez and outfielder Chris Burke, December 14, 2007.
d On disabled list from April 27 to June 13, 2009.
e Filed for free agency, November 9, 2009. Signed with Detroit Tigers, January 19, 2010.

VARGAS, JASON MATTHEW

Born, Apple Valley, California, February 2, 1983.
Bats Left. Throws Left. Height, 6 feet. Weight, 215 pounds.

Year	Club	Lea	G	IP	W	L	Pct	SO	BB	H	ERA	SAVES
2004	Jamestown	N.Y.-Penn.	8	41 1/3	3	1	.750	41	13	35	1.96	0
2004	Greensboro	So.Atl.	3	19	2	1	.667	17	2	9	2.37	0
2005	Greensboro	So.Atl.	5	33 2/3	4	1	.800	33	10	16	0.80	0
2005	Jupiter	Fla.St.	9	55 1/3	2	3	.400	60	14	47	3.42	0
2005	Carolina	Southern	3	19	1	0	1.000	25	7	13	2.84	0
2005	Florida	N.L.	17	73 2/3	5	5	.500	59	31	71	4.03	0
2006	Florida	N.L.	12	43	1	2	.333	25	30	50	7.33	0
2006	Albuquerque a	P.C.	13	69	3	6	.333	51	28	98	7.43	0
2007	New York	N.L.	2	10 1/3	0	1	.000	4	2	17	12.19	0
2007	New Orleans b	P.C.	24	125	9	7	.563	108	44	141	4.97	0

Year	Club	Lea	G	IP	W	L	Pct	SO	BB	H	ERA	SAVES
2008	New York c-d	N.L.			INJURED—Did Not Play							
2009	Tacoma	P.C.	9	$51\frac{2}{3}$	4	3	.571	46	15	48	3.14	0
2009	Seattle	A.L.	23	$91\frac{2}{3}$	3	6	.333	54	24	98	4.91	0
2010	Seattle	A.L.	31	$192\frac{2}{3}$	9	12	.429	116	54	187	3.78	0
Major League Totals		5 Yrs.	85	$411\frac{1}{3}$	18	26	.409	258	141	423	4.66	0

a Traded to New York Mets with pitcher Adam Bostick for pitcher Matt Lindstrom and pitcher Henry Owens, November 20, 2006.

b On disabled list from September 21 to November 6, 2007.

c On disabled list from March 21 to November 3, 2008.

d Traded to Seattle Mariners with pitcher Aaron Heilman, outfielder Endy Chavez, infielder Mike Carp, outfielder Ezequiel Carrera, pitcher Maikel Cleto and pitcher Joe Smith for pitcher J.J. Putz, pitcher Sean Green and outfielder Jeremy Reed, December 10, 2008.

VASQUEZ, ESMERLING

Born, Tenares, Dominican Republic, November 7, 1983.
Bats Right. Throws Right. Height, 6 feet, 1 inch. Weight, 175 pounds.

Year	Club	Lea	G	IP	W	L	Pct	SO	BB	H	ERA	SAVES
2004	Yakima	Northwest	5	$5\frac{2}{3}$	0	0	.000	7	0	10	6.35	1
2004	Missoula	Pioneer	19	$30\frac{2}{3}$	3	2	.600	33	21	22	3.52	5
2005	South Bend	Midwest	53	$71\frac{2}{3}$	6	4	.600	79	47	63	3.64	3
2006	Lancaster	Calif.	34	$117\frac{2}{3}$	4	9	.308	115	51	129	5.89	0
2007	Mobile	Southern	29	$165\frac{1}{3}$	10	6	.625	151	60	125	2.99	0
2008	Tucson	P.C.	24	83	3	6	.333	57	73	79	6.72	0
2009	Reno	P.C.	6	$9\frac{2}{3}$	0	0	.000	9	3	7	0.93	1
2009	Arizona	N.L.	53	53	3	3	.500	45	29	52	4.42	0
2010	Reno	P.C.	1	1	0	0	.000	1	0	1	0.00	0
2010	Arizona	N.L.	57	$53\frac{2}{3}$	1	6	.143	55	38	46	5.20	0
Major League Totals		2 Yrs.	110	$106\frac{2}{3}$	4	9	.308	100	67	98	4.81	0

VAZQUEZ, JAVIER CARLOS

Born, Ponce, Puerto Rico, June 25, 1976.
Bats Right. Throws Right. Height, 6 feet, 2 inches. Weight, 215 pounds.

Year	Club	Lea	G	IP	W	L	Pct	SO	BB	H	ERA	SAVES
1994	Expos	Gulf Coast	15	$67\frac{2}{3}$	5	2	.714	56	15	37	2.53	0
1995	Albany	So.Atl.	21	$102\frac{2}{3}$	6	6	.500	87	47	109	5.08	0
1996	Delmarva	So.Atl.	27	$164\frac{1}{3}$	14	3	.824	173	57	138	2.68	0
1997	Wst Plm Bch	Fla.St.	19	$112\frac{2}{3}$	6	3	.667	100	28	98	2.16	0
1997	Harrisburg	Eastern	6	42	4	0	1.000	47	12	15	1.07	0
1998	Montreal	N.L.	33	$172\frac{1}{3}$	5	15	.250	139	68	196	6.06	0
1999	Ottawa	Int.	7	$42\frac{2}{3}$	4	2	.667	46	16	45	4.85	0
1999	Montreal	N.L.	26	$154\frac{2}{3}$	9	8	.529	113	52	154	5.00	0
2000	Montreal	N.L.	33	$217\frac{2}{3}$	11	9	.550	196	61	247	4.05	0
2001	Montreal	N.L.	32	$223\frac{2}{3}$	16	11	.593	208	44	197	3.42	0
2002	Montreal	N.L.	34	$230\frac{1}{3}$	10	13	.435	179	49	*243	3.91	0
2003	Montreal a	N.L.	34	$230\frac{2}{3}$	13	12	.520	241	57	198	3.24	0
2004	New York b	A.L.	32	198	14	10	.583	150	60	195	4.91	0
2005	Arizona c	N.L.	33	$215\frac{2}{3}$	11	15	.423	192	46	223	4.42	0
2006	Chicago	A.L.	33	$202\frac{2}{3}$	11	12	.478	184	56	206	4.84	0
2007	Chicago	A.L.	32	$216\frac{2}{3}$	15	8	.652	213	50	197	3.74	0
2008	Chicago d	A.L.	33	$208\frac{1}{3}$	12	16	.429	200	61	214	4.67	0
2009	Atlanta e	N.L.	32	$219\frac{1}{3}$	15	10	.600	238	44	181	2.87	0
2010	New York f	A.L.	31	$157\frac{1}{3}$	10	10	.500	121	65	155	5.32	0
Major League Totals		13 Yrs.	418	$2647\frac{1}{3}$	152	149	.505	2374	713	2606	4.26	0
	Division Series											
2004	New York	A.L.	1	5	0	0	.000	6	2	7	9.00	0
2008	Chicago	A.L.	1	$4\frac{1}{3}$	0	1	.000	6	1	8	12.46	0
Division Series Totals			2	$9\frac{1}{3}$	0	1	.000	12	3	15	10.61	0
	Championship Series											
2004	New York	A.L.	2	$6\frac{1}{3}$	1	0	1.000	6	7	9	9.95	0

a Traded to New York Yankees for infielder Nick Johnson, outfielder Juan Rivera and pitcher Randy Choate, December 4, 2003.

b Traded to Arizona Diamondbacks with pitcher Brad Halsey, catcher Dioner Navarro and cash for pitcher Randy Johnson, January 11, 2005.

c Traded to Chicago White Sox for pitcher Orlando Hernandez, pitcher Luis Vizcaino and outfielder Chris Young, December 20, 2005.

d Traded to Atlanta Braves with pitcher Boone Logan for catcher Tyler Flowers, infielder Jonathan Gilmore, infielder Brent Lillibridge and pitcher Santos Rodriguez, December 4, 2008.

e Traded to New York Yankees with pitcher Boone Logan for outfielder Melky Cabrera, pitcher Arodys Vizcaino, pitcher Michael Dunn and cash, December 22, 2009.

f Filed for free agency, November 1, 2010. Signed with Florida Marlins, December 2, 2010.

VENTERS, JONATHAN WILLIAM (JONNY)

Born, Pikeville, Kentucky, March 20, 1985.
Bats Left. Throws Left. Height, 6 feet, 3 inches. Weight, 195 pounds.

Year	Club	Lea	G	IP	W	L	Pct	SO	BB	H	ERA	SAVES
2004	Braves	Gulf Coast	11	42⅓	1	6	.143	54	12	53	5.74	0
2005	Rome	So.Atl.	23	103	8	6	.571	66	52	100	3.93	3
2006	a		INJURED—Did Not Play									
2007	Myrtle Beach	Carolina	17	79⅔	3	3	.500	64	38	60	3.39	1
2008	Myrtle Beach	Carolina	5	17⅔	1	2	.333	7	7	21	4.08	1
2008	Braves	Gulf Coast	4	7⅔	0	0	.000	10	2	10	4.70	0
2008	Mississippi	Southern	3	9	1	0	1.000	7	5	10	1.00	0
2009	Gwinnett	Int.	17	91⅓	4	7	.364	58	42	103	5.62	0
2009	Mississippi	Southern	12	65⅓	4	4	.500	40	35	60	2.76	0
2010	Gwinnett	Int.	2	6⅔	1	0	1.000	6	1	4	1.35	0
2010	Atlanta	N.L.	79	83	4	4	.500	93	39	61	1.95	1
	Division Series											
2010	Atlanta	N.L.	4	5⅓	0	0	.000	8	0	7	0.00	0

a On minor league disabled list from April 6 to September 9, 2006.

VERAS, JOSE ENGER

Born, Santo Domingo, Dominican Republic, October 20, 1980.
Bats Right. Throws Right. Height, 6 feet, 5 inches. Weight, 235 pounds.

Year	Club	Lea	G	IP	W	L	Pct	SO	BB	H	ERA	SAVES
1998	Devil Rays	Gulf Coast	5	16	1	1	.500	19	12	19	6.75	0
1999	Princeton	Appal.	14	60⅔	3	5	.375	48	50	74	7.12	0
2000	Charleston-SC	So.Atl.	20	106⅔	8	8	.500	102	41	125	4.81	0
2001	Bakersfield	Calif.	27	153	9	8	.529	138	55	163	4.53	0
2002	Bakersfield	Calif.	11	59	3	4	.429	57	30	77	5.34	0
2002	Hudson Valley	N.Y.-Penn.	2	7	0	0	.000	7	5	2	0.00	0
2003	Durham	Int.	3	5⅓	0	0	.000	3	1	9	8.44	0
2003	Orlando	Southern	27	130⅓	6	9	.400	118	53	108	3.45	0
2004	Durham	Int.	30	84⅓	6	5	.545	63	33	101	5.23	0
2004	Montgomery a	Southern	3	10	1	0	1.000	6	7	10	6.30	0
2005	Oklahoma b	P.C.	57	61⅔	3	5	.375	72	33	63	3.79	24
2006	Columbus	Int.	50	59⅔	5	3	.625	68	19	49	2.41	21
2006	New York	A.L.	12	11	0	0	.000	6	5	8	4.09	1
2007	Yankees	Gulf Coast	2	2	0	0	.000	1	0	2	0.00	0
2007	Tampa	Fla.St.	2	3	0	0	.000	5	2	0	0.00	0
2007	Scranton-WB	Int.	12	16	2	0	1.000	17	7	17	4.50	4
2007	New York c	A.L.	9	9⅓	0	0	.000	7	7	6	5.79	2
2008	Scranton-WB	Int.	13	13	0	0	.000	21	4	8	1.38	9
2008	New York	A.L.	60	57⅔	5	3	.625	63	29	52	3.59	0
2009	Columbus	Int.	7	7	0	1	.000	9	2	3	1.29	0
2009	New York-Cleveland d-e	A.L.	47	50⅓	4	3	.571	40	28	42	5.19	0
2010	New Orleans	P.C.	24	29⅓	1	1	.500	37	15	34	4.60	2
2010	Florida f	N.L.	48	48	3	3	.500	54	29	32	3.75	0
Major League Totals		5 Yrs.	176	176⅓	12	9	.571	170	98	140	4.24	3
	Division Series											
2007	New York	A.L.	2	0⅔	0	0	.000	1	1	1	0.00	0

a Filed for free agency from Tampa Bay Devil Rays, October 15, 2004. Signed with Texas Rangers organization, November 15, 2004.

b Filed for free agency, October 15, 2005. Signed with New York Yankees organization, December 12, 2005.

c On disabled list from March 23 to August 14, 2007.

d Sold to Cleveland Indians, June 24, 2009.

e Not offered contract, December 12, 2009. Signed with Florida Marlins organization, January 29, 2010.

f Not offered contract, December 2, 2010. Signed with Pittsburgh Pirates organization, January 18, 2011.

VERLANDER, JUSTIN BROOKS

Born, Manakin Sabot, Virginia, February 20, 1983.
Bats Right. Throws Right. Height, 6 feet, 5 inches. Weight, 200 pounds.

Year	Club	Lea	G	IP	W	L	Pct	SO	BB	H	ERA	SAVES
2005	Lakeland	Fla.St.	13	86	9	2	.818	104	19	70	1.67	0
2005	Erie	Eastern	7	32⅔	2	0	1.000	32	7	11	0.28	0
2005	Detroit	A.L.	2	11⅓	0	2	.000	7	5	15	7.15	0
2006	Detroit a	A.L.	30	186	17	9	.654	124	60	187	3.63	0

Year	Club	Lea	G	IP	W	L	Pct	SO	BB	H	ERA	SAVES
2007	Detroit b	A.L.	32	201⅔	18	6	*.750	183	67	181	3.66	0
2008	Detroit	A.L.	33	201	11	*17	.393	163	87	195	4.84	0
2009	Detroit	A.L.	35	*240	*19	9	.679	*269	63	219	3.45	0
2010	Detroit	A.L.	33	224⅓	18	9	.667	219	71	190	3.37	0
Major League Totals		6 Yrs.	165	1064⅓	83	52	.615	965	353	987	3.81	0
	Division Series											
2006	Detroit	A.L.	1	5⅓	0	0	.000	5	4	7	5.06	0
	Championship Series											
2006	Detroit	A.L.	1	5⅓	1	0	1.000	6	1	7	6.75	0
	World Series Record											
2006	Detroit	A.L.	2	11	0	2	.000	12	5	12	5.73	0

a Selected Rookie of the Year in American League for 2006.
b Pitched no-hit, no-run game against Milwaukee Brewers, June 12, 2007.

VILLANUEVA, CARLOS MANUEL

Born, Santiago, Dominican Republic, November 28, 1983.
Bats Right. Throws Right. Height, 6 feet, 2 inches. Weight, 215 pounds.

Year	Club	Lea	G	IP	W	L	Pct	SO	BB	H	ERA	SAVES
2002	Giants	Arizona	19	30⅓	4	0	1.000	23	3	24	0.59	3
2003	Giants	Arizona	12	59	3	6	.333	67	13	64	3.97	0
2004	Beloit a	Midwest	25	114⅔	8	8	.500	113	30	102	3.77	1
2005	Brevard County	Fla.St.	21	112⅓	8	1	.889	124	32	78	2.32	0
2005	Huntsville	Southern	4	20⅔	1	3	.250	14	9	21	7.40	0
2006	Huntsville	Southern	11	62⅓	4	5	.444	59	14	60	3.75	0
2006	Nashville	P.C.	11	66⅓	7	1	.875	61	26	42	2.71	0
2006	Milwaukee	N.L.	10	53⅔	2	2	.500	39	11	43	3.69	0
2007	Nashville	P.C.	2	8⅓	0	0	.000	9	1	3	3.24	0
2007	Milwaukee	N.L.	59	114⅓	8	5	.615	99	53	101	3.94	1
2008	Milwaukee	N.L.	47	108⅓	4	7	.364	93	30	112	4.07	1
2009	Milwaukee	N.L.	64	96	4	10	.286	83	35	102	5.34	3
2010	Nashville	P.C.	11	14⅓	0	0	.000	14	7	13	3.77	1
2010	Milwaukee b	N.L.	50	52⅔	2	0	1.000	67	22	48	4.61	1
Major League Totals		5 Yrs.	230	425	20	24	.455	381	151	406	4.34	6
	Division Series											
2008	Milwaukee	N.L.	2	3⅔	0	0	.000	3	0	0	0.00	0

a Traded to Milwaukee Brewers by San Francisco Giants with pitcher Glenn Woolard for pitcher Wayne Franklin and pitcher Leo Estrella, March 30, 2004.
b Traded to Toronto Blue Jays for player to be named later, December 3, 2010.

VOLQUEZ, EDINSON

Born, Santo Domingo, Dominican Republic, July 3, 1983.
Bats Right. Throws Right. Height, 6 feet, 1 inch. Weight, 200 pounds.

Year	Club	Lea	G	IP	W	L	Pct	SO	BB	H	ERA	SAVES
2003	Rangers	Arizona	10	27	2	1	.667	28	11	24	4.00	1
2004	Stockton	Calif.	8	39⅔	4	1	.800	34	14	31	2.95	0
2004	Clinton	Midwest	22	91	4	4	.500	77	30	83	4.05	3
2005	Bakersfield	Calif.	11	66⅔	5	4	.556	77	12	64	4.18	0
2005	Rangers	Arizona	1	2	0	0	.000	2	0	2	0.00	0
2005	Frisco	Texas	10	58⅔	1	5	.167	49	17	58	4.14	0
2005	Texas	A.L.	6	12⅔	0	4	.000	11	10	25	14.21	0
2006	Oklahoma	P.C.	21	120⅔	6	6	.500	130	72	86	3.21	0
2006	Texas	A.L.	8	33⅓	1	6	.143	15	17	52	7.29	0
2007	Bakersfield	Calif.	7	35⅓	0	4	.000	38	20	27	7.13	0
2007	Frisco	Texas	11	58⅓	8	1	.889	62	19	46	3.55	0
2007	Oklahoma	P.C.	8	51	6	1	.857	66	21	25	1.41	0
2007	Texas a	A.L.	6	34	2	1	.667	29	15	34	4.50	0
2008	Cincinnati	N.L.	33	196	17	6	.739	206	93	167	3.21	0
2009	Cincinnati b	N.L.	9	49⅔	4	2	.667	47	32	34	4.35	0
2010	Dayton	Midwest	2	13	0	0	.000	19	4	11	1.38	0
2010	Lynchburg	Carolina	2	8	1	0	1.000	7	0	3	0.00	0
2010	Louisville	Int.	4	23	3	0	1.000	21	8	11	1.96	0
2010	Cincinnati c	N.L.	12	62⅔	4	3	.571	67	35	59	4.31	0
Major League Totals		6 Yrs.	74	388⅓	28	22	.560	375	202	371	4.36	0
	Division Series											
2010	Cincinnati	N.L.	1	1⅔	0	1	.000	0	2	4	21.60	0

a Traded to Cincinnati Reds with pitcher Danny Herrera for outfielder Josh Hamilton, December 21, 2007.
b On disabled list from May 17 to June 1 and June 2 to November 16, 2009.
c On disabled list from February 24 to July 17, 2010.

VOLSTAD, CHRISTOPHER KENNETH (CHRIS)

Born, Palm Beach Gardens, Florida, September 23, 1986.
Bats Right. Throws Right. Height, 6 feet, 8 inches. Weight, 225 pounds.

Year	Club	Lea	G	IP	W	L	Pct	SO	BB	H	ERA	SAVES
2005	Marlins	Gulf Coast	6	27	1	1	.500	26	4	25	2.33	0
2005	Jamestown	N.Y.-Penn.	7	38	3	2	.600	29	11	43	2.13	0
2006	Greensboro	So.Atl.	26	152	11	8	.579	99	36	161	3.08	0
2007	Jupiter	Fla.St.	21	126	8	9	.471	93	37	152	4.50	0
2007	Carolina	Southern	7	42 2/3	4	2	.667	25	10	41	3.16	0
2008	Carolina	Southern	15	91	4	4	.500	56	30	86	3.36	0
2008	Florida	N.L.	15	84 1/3	6	4	.600	52	36	76	2.88	0
2009	New Orleans	P.C.	1	4	0	1	.000	7	2	5	6.75	0
2009	Florida	N.L.	29	159	9	13	.409	107	59	169	5.21	0
2010	New Orleans	P.C.	3	17	1	0	1.000	13	9	13	3.18	0
2010	Florida	N.L.	30	175	12	9	.571	102	60	187	4.58	0
Major League Totals		3 Yrs.	74	418 1/3	27	26	.509	261	155	432	4.47	0

WAGNER, WILLIAM EDWARD (BILLY)

Born, Tannersville, Virginia, July 25, 1971.
Bats Left. Throws Left. Height, 5 feet, 11 inches. Weight, 205 pounds.

Year	Club	Lea	G	IP	W	L	Pct	SO	BB	H	ERA	SAVES
1993	Auburn	N.Y.-Penn.	7	28 2/3	1	3	.250	31	25	25	4.08	0
1994	Quad City	Midwest	26	153	8	9	.471	204	91	99	3.29	0
1995	Jackson	Texas	12	70	2	2	.500	77	36	49	2.57	0
1995	Tucson	P.C.	13	76 1/3	5	3	.625	80	32	70	3.18	0
1995	Houston	N.L.	1	0 1/3	0	0	.000	0	0	0	0.00	0
1996	Tucson	P.C.	12	74	6	2	.750	86	33	62	3.28	0
1996	Houston a	N.L.	37	51 2/3	2	2	.500	67	30	28	2.44	9
1997	Houston	N.L.	62	66 1/3	7	8	.467	106	30	49	2.85	23
1998	Jackson	Texas	3	3	0	0	.000	7	0	1	0.00	0
1998	Houston b	N.L.	58	60	4	3	.571	97	25	46	2.70	30
1999	Houston	N.L.	66	74 2/3	4	1	.800	124	23	35	1.57	39
2000	Houston c	N.L.	28	27 2/3	2	4	.333	28	18	28	6.18	6
2001	Round Rock	Texas	1	1	0	0	.000	2	0	0	0.00	0
2001	Houston d	N.L.	64	62 2/3	2	5	.286	79	20	44	2.73	39
2002	Houston	N.L.	70	75	4	2	.667	88	22	51	2.52	35
2003	Houston e	N.L.	78	86	1	4	.200	105	23	52	1.78	44
2004	Reading	Eastern	1	1	0	0	.000	2	0	1	0.00	0
2004	Philadelphia f	N.L.	45	48 1/3	4	0	1.000	59	6	31	2.42	21
2005	Philadelphia g	N.L.	75	77 2/3	4	3	.571	87	20	45	1.51	38
2006	New York	N.L.	70	72 1/3	3	2	.600	94	21	59	2.24	40
2007	New York	N.L.	66	68 1/3	2	2	.500	80	22	55	2.63	34
2008	Binghamton	Eastern	1	1	0	0	.000	2	0	0	0.00	0
2008	New York h	N.L.	45	47	0	1	.000	52	10	32	2.30	27
2009	Mets	Gulf Coast	2	2	0	0	.000	2	0	0	0.00	0
2009	St. Lucie	Fla.St.	5	5	0	0	.000	8	0	3	0.00	0
2009	New York	N.L.	2	2	0	0	.000	4	1	0	0.00	0
2009	Boston i-j-k	A.L.	15	13 2/3	1	1	.500	22	7	8	1.98	0
2010	Atlanta l	N.L.	71	69 1/3	7	2	.778	104	22	38	1.43	37
Major League Totals		16 Yrs.	853	903	47	40	.540	1196	300	601	2.31	422
	Division Series											
1997	Houston	N.L.	1	1	0	0	.000	2	0	3	18.00	0
1998	Houston	N.L.	1	1	1	0	1.000	1	0	4	18.00	0
1999	Houston	N.L.	1	1	0	0	.000	1	0	0	0.00	0
2001	Houston	N.L.	2	1 2/3	0	0	.000	3	0	1	5.40	0
2006	New York	N.L.	3	3	0	0	.000	4	0	3	3.00	2
2009	Boston	A.L.	2	1	0	0	.000	2	1	2	18.00	0
2010	Atlanta	N.L.	1	0 1/3	0	0	.000	0	0	1	0.00	0
Division Series Totals			11	9	1	0	1.000	13	1	14	8.00	2
	Championship Series											
2006	New York	N.L.	3	2 2/3	0	1	.000	0	1	7	16.88	1

a On disabled list from August 23 to September 7, 1996.
b On disabled list from July 16 to August 7, 1998.
c On disabled list from June 18 to November 5, 2000.
d On disabled list from June 4 to June 19, 2001.
e Traded to Philadelphia Phillies for pitcher Brandon Duckworth, pitcher Taylor Buchholz and pitcher Ezequiel Astacio, November 3, 2003.
f On disabled list from May 8 to June 8 and from July 22 to September 4, 2004.
g Filed for free agency, October 27, 2005. Signed with New York Mets, November 29, 2005.

h On disabled list from August 3 to October 9, 2008.
i On disabled list from March 27 to August 20, 2009.
j Traded to Boston Red Sox for two players to be named later, August 25, 2009. New York Mets received outfielder Chris Carter and infielder Eddie Lora to complete trade, October 7, 2009.
k Filed for free agency, November 5, 2009. Signed with Atlanta Braves, December 2, 2009.
l Announced retirement, October 12, 2010.

WAINWRIGHT, ADAM PARRISH

Born, Brunswick, Georgia, August 30, 1981.
Bats Right. Throws Right. Height, 6 feet, 7 inches. Weight, 205 pounds.

Year Club	Lea	G	IP	W	L	Pct	SO	BB	H	ERA	SAVES
2000 Danville	Appal.	6	29⅓	2	2	.500	39	2	28	3.68	0
2000 Braves	Gulf Coast	7	32	4	0	1.000	42	10	15	1.13	0
2001 Macon	So.Atl.	28	164⅔	10	10	.500	184	48	144	3.77	0
2002 Myrtle Beach	Carolina	28	163⅓	9	6	.600	167	66	149	3.31	0
2003 Greenville a	Southern	27	149⅔	10	8	.556	128	37	133	3.37	0
2004 Memphis	P.C.	12	63⅔	4	4	.500	64	28	68	5.37	0
2005 Memphis	P.C.	29	182	10	10	.500	147	51	204	4.40	0
2005 St. Louis	N.L.	2	2	0	0	.000	0	1	2	13.50	0
2006 St. Louis	N.L.	61	75	2	1	.667	72	22	64	3.12	3
2007 St. Louis	N.L.	32	202	14	12	.538	136	70	212	3.70	0
2008 Springfield	Texas	1	4⅔	0	0	.000	7	0	4	0.00	0
2008 Memphis	P.C.	2	3⅔	0	1	.000	3	2	8	12.27	0
2008 St. Louis b	N.L.	20	132	11	3	.786	91	34	122	3.20	0
2009 St. Louis	N.L.	34	*233	*19	8	.704	212	66	216	2.63	0
2010 St. Louis	N.L.	33	230⅓	20	11	.645	213	56	186	2.42	0
Major League Totals	6 Yrs.	182	874⅓	66	35	.653	724	249	802	2.97	3
Division Series											
2006 St. Louis	N.L.	3	3⅔	0	0	.000	6	0	3	0.00	1
2009 St. Louis	N.L.	1	8	0	0	.000	7	1	3	1.13	0
Division Series Totals		4	11⅔	0	0	.000	13	1	6	0.77	1
Championship Series											
2006 St. Louis	N.L.	3	3	0	0	.000	4	1	2	0.00	2
World Series Record											
2006 St. Louis	N.L.	3	3	1	0	1.000	5	1	2	0.00	1

a Traded by Atlanta Braves to St. Louis Cardinals with pitcher Jason Marquis and pitcher Ray King for catcher Eli Marrero and outfielder J.D. Drew, December 13, 2003.
b On disabled list from June 8 to August 22, 2008.

WAKEFIELD, TIMOTHY STEPHEN (TIM)

Born, Melborne, Florida, August 2, 1966.
Bats Right. Throws Right. Height, 6 feet, 2 inches. Weight, 230 pounds.

Year Club	Lea	G	IP	W	L	Pct	SO	BB	H	ERA	SAVES
1989 Welland	N.Y.-Penn.	18	39⅔	1	1	.500	42	21	30	3.40	2
1990 Salem	Carolina	28	190⅓	10	14	.417	127	85	187	4.73	0
1991 Buffalo	A.A.	1	4⅔	0	1	.000	4	1	8	11.57	0
1991 Carolina	Southern	26	183	15	8	.652	123	51	155	2.90	0
1992 Buffalo	A.A.	20	135⅓	10	3	.769	71	51	122	3.06	0
1992 Pittsburgh	N.L.	13	92	8	1	.889	51	35	76	2.15	0
1993 Carolina	Southern	9	56⅔	3	5	.375	36	22	68	6.99	0
1993 Pittsburgh	N.L.	24	128⅓	6	11	.353	59	75	145	5.61	0
1994 Buffalo	A.A.	30	175⅔	5	15	.250	83	98	197	5.84	0
1995 Pawtucket	Int.	4	25	2	1	.667	14	9	23	2.52	0
1995 Boston a-b	A.L.	27	195⅓	16	8	.667	119	68	163	2.95	0
1996 Boston	A.L.	32	211⅔	14	13	.519	140	90	238	5.14	0
1997 Boston c	A.L.	35	201⅓	12	*15	.444	151	87	193	4.25	0
1998 Boston	A.L.	36	216	17	8	.680	146	79	211	4.58	0
1999 Boston	A.L.	49	140	6	11	.353	104	72	146	5.08	15
2000 Boston d	A.L.	51	159⅓	6	10	.375	102	65	170	5.48	0
2001 Boston	A.L.	45	168⅔	9	12	.429	148	73	156	3.90	3
2002 Boston	A.L.	45	163⅓	11	5	.688	134	51	121	2.81	3
2003 Boston	A.L.	35	202⅓	11	7	.611	169	71	193	4.09	1
2004 Boston	A.L.	32	188⅓	12	10	.545	116	63	197	4.87	0
2005 Boston	A.L.	33	225⅓	16	12	.571	151	68	210	4.15	0
2006 Boston e	A.L.	23	140	7	11	.389	90	51	135	4.63	0
2007 Boston	A.L.	31	189	17	12	.586	110	64	191	4.76	0
2008 Boston f	A.L.	30	181	10	11	.476	117	60	154	4.13	0
2009 Pawtucket	Int.	2	9⅓	1	1	.500	7	2	5	2.89	0

Year	Club	Lea	G	IP	W	L	Pct	SO	BB	H	ERA	SAVES
2009	Boston g	A.L.	21	129⅔	11	5	.688	72	50	137	4.58	0
2010	Boston	A.L.	32	140	4	10	.286	84	36	153	5.34	0
Major League Totals		18 Yrs.	594	3071⅔	193	172	.529	2063	1158	2989	4.38	22
	Division Series											
1995	Boston	A.L.	1	5⅓	0	1	.000	4	5	5	11.81	0
1998	Boston	A.L.	1	1⅓	0	1	.000	1	2	3	33.75	0
1999	Boston	A.L.	2	2	0	0	.000	4	4	3	13.50	0
2003	Boston	A.L.	2	7⅔	0	1	.000	7	3	6	3.52	0
2005	Boston	A.L.	1	5⅓	0	1	.000	4	1	6	6.75	0
Division Series Totals			7	21⅔	0	4	.000	20	15	23	9.14	0
	Championship Series											
1992	Pittsburgh	N.L.	2	18	2	0	1.000	7	5	14	3.00	0
2003	Boston	A.L.	3	14	2	1	.667	10	6	8	2.57	0
2004	Boston	A.L.	3	7⅓	1	0	1.000	6	3	9	8.59	0
2007	Boston	A.L.	1	4⅔	0	1	.000	7	2	5	9.64	0
2008	Boston	A.L.	1	2⅔	0	1	.000	2	2	6	16.88	0
Championship Series Totals			10	46⅔	5	3	.625	32	18	42	5.21	0
	World Series Record											
2004	Boston	A.L.	1	3⅔	0	0	.000	2	5	3	12.27	0

a Released by Pittsburgh Pirates, April 20, 1995.
b Signed by Boston Red Sox, April 27, 1995.
c On disabled list from April 15 to May 6, 1997.
d Filed for free agency, October 31, 2000, re-signed with Boston Red Sox, December 7, 2000.
e On disabled list from July 18 to September 13, 2006.
f On disabled list from August 7 to August 26, 2008.
g On disabled list from July 18 to August 26, 2009.

WEAVER, JEFFREY CHARLES (JEFF)

Born, Northridge, California, August 22, 1976.
Bats Right. Throws Right. Height, 6 feet, 5 inches. Weight, 200 pounds.

Year	Club	Lea	G	IP	W	L	Pct	SO	BB	H	ERA	SAVES
1998	Jamestown	N.Y.-Penn.	3	12	1	0	1.000	12	1	6	1.50	0
1998	W Michigan	Midwest	2	13	1	0	1.000	21	0	8	1.38	0
1999	Jacksonville	Southern	1	6	0	0	.000	6	0	5	3.00	0
1999	Detroit	A.L.	30	163⅔	9	12	.429	114	56	176	5.55	0
2000	Toledo	Int.	1	5⅓	0	1	.000	10	1	5	3.38	0
2000	Detroit	A.L.	31	200	11	15	.423	136	52	205	4.32	0
2001	Detroit	A.L.	33	229⅓	13	16	.448	152	68	235	4.08	0
2002	Detroit-New York a-b	A.L.	32	199⅔	11	11	.500	132	48	193	3.52	2
2003	New York c	A.L.	32	159⅓	7	9	.438	93	47	211	5.99	0
2004	Los Angeles	N.L.	34	220	13	13	.500	153	67	219	4.01	0
2005	Los Angeles	N.L.	34	224	14	11	.560	157	43	220	4.22	0
2006	Los Angeles	A.L.	16	88⅔	3	10	.231	62	21	114	6.29	0
2006	St. Louis d-e	N.L.	15	83⅓	5	4	.556	45	26	99	5.18	0
2007	Seattle f-g	A.L.	27	146⅔	7	13	.350	80	35	190	6.20	0
2008	Nashville h-i	P.C.	9	55	2	4	.333	37	20	64	6.22	0
2008	Buffalo	Int.	13	29⅔	2	2	.500	22	10	38	6.07	0
2009	Albuquerque	P.C.	5	12⅔	1	0	1.000	12	2	11	3.55	1
2009	Los Angeles j-k	N.L.	28	79	6	4	.600	64	33	87	3.65	0
2010	Los Angeles l-m	N.L.	43	44⅓	5	1	.833	26	20	48	6.09	0
Major League Totals		11 Yrs.	355	1838	104	119	.466	1214	516	1997	4.71	2
	Division Series											
2002	New York	A.L.	2	2⅔	0	0	.000	1	3	4	6.75	0
2004	Los Angeles	N.L.	1	4⅔	0	1	.000	4	2	8	11.57	0
2006	St. Louis	N.L.	1	5	1	0	1.000	3	3	2	0.00	0
2009	Los Angeles	N.L.	1	1⅓	1	0	1.000	1	0	1	0.00	0
Division Series Totals			5	13⅔	2	1	.667	9	8	15	5.27	0
	Championship Series											
2006	St. Louis	N.L.	2	11⅔	1	1	.500	2	4	10	3.09	0
	World Series Record											
2003	New York	A.L.	1	1	0	1	.000	0	0	1	9.00	0
2006	St. Louis	N.L.	2	13	1	1	.500	14	2	13	2.77	0
World Series Totals			3	14	1	2	.333	14	2	14	3.21	0

a Traded to Oakland Athletics for infielder Carlos Pena, pitcher Franklyn German and player to be named later, July 5, 2002. Detroit Tigers received pitcher Jeremy Bonderman to complete trade, August 22, 2002.
b Traded to New York Yankees for pitcher Ted Lilly, pitcher Jason Arnold and outfielder John-Ford Griffin, July 5, 2002.

c Traded to Los Angeles Dodgers with pitcher Yhency Brazoban, player to be named later and cash for pitcher Kevin Brown, December 13, 2003.
d Filed for free agency, October 28, 2005. Signed with Los Angeles Angels, February 15, 2006.
e Traded to St. Louis Cardinals for outfielder Terry Evans, July 5, 2006.
f Filed for free agency, October 31, 2006. Signed with Seattle Mariners, January 29, 2007.
g On disabled list from May 11 to June 9, 2007.
h Filed for free agency, October 31, 2007. Signed with Milwaukee Brewers organization, April 15, 2008.
i Released by Milwaukee Brewers, June 12, 2008. Signed with Cleveland Indians organization, July 5, 2008.
j Filed for free agency, November 3, 2008. Signed with Los Angeles Dodgers organization, February 9, 2009.
k Filed for free agency, November 6, 2009, re-signed with Los Angeles Dodgers organization, February 8, 2010.
l On disabled list from April 22 to May 7 and August 3 to August 22, 2010.
m Filed for free agency, November 1, 2010.

WEAVER, JERED DAVID

Born, Northridge, California, October 4, 1982.
Bats Right. Throws Right. Height, 6 feet, 7 inches. Weight, 205 pounds.

Year Club	Lea	G	IP	W	L	Pct	SO	BB	H	ERA	SAVES
2005 Arkansas	Texas	8	43	3	3	.500	46	19	43	3.98	0
2006 Salt Lake	P.C.	12	77	6	1	.857	93	10	63	2.10	0
2006 Los Angeles	A.L.	19	123	11	2	.846	105	33	94	2.56	0
2007 Rancho Cucamonga	Calif.	2	11	1	0	1.000	12	3	5	0.82	0
2007 Los Angeles a	A.L.	28	161	13	7	.650	115	45	178	3.91	0
2008 Los Angeles	A.L.	30	$176\frac{2}{3}$	11	10	.524	152	54	173	4.33	0
2009 Los Angeles	A.L.	33	211	16	8	.667	174	66	196	3.75	0
2010 Inland Empire	Calif.	1	3	0	0	.000	3	1	2	0.00	0
2010 Los Angeles	A.L.	34	$224\frac{1}{3}$	13	12	.520	*233	54	187	3.01	0
Major League Totals	5 Yrs.	144	896	64	39	.621	779	252	828	3.55	0
Division Series											
2007 Los Angeles	A.L.	1	5	0	1	.000	5	3	4	3.60	0
2008 Los Angeles	A.L.	1	2	1	0	1.000	3	1	1	0.00	0
2009 Los Angeles	A.L.	1	$7\frac{1}{3}$	1	0	1.000	7	2	2	1.23	0
Division Series Totals		3	$14\frac{1}{3}$	2	1	.667	15	6	7	1.88	0
Championship Series											
2009 Los Angeles	A.L.	3	$6\frac{1}{3}$	0	0	.000	7	4	5	4.26	0

a On disabled list from March 23 to April 17, 2007.

WEBB, BRANDON TYLER

Born, Ashland, Kentucky, May 9, 1979.
Bats Right. Throws Right. Height, 6 feet, 3 inches. Weight, 230 pounds.

Year Club	Lea	G	IP	W	L	Pct	SO	BB	H	ERA	SAVES
2000 Diamondbacks	Arizona	1	1	0	0	.000	3	0	2	9.00	0
2000 South Bend	Midwest	12	$16\frac{2}{3}$	0	0	.000	18	9	10	3.24	2
2001 Lancaster	California	29	$162\frac{1}{3}$	6	10	.375	158	44	174	3.99	0
2002 El Paso	Texas	26	152	10	6	.625	122	59	141	3.14	0
2002 Tucson	P.C.	1	7	0	1	.000	5	4	5	3.86	0
2003 Tucson	P.C.	3	18	1	1	.500	17	9	18	6.00	0
2003 Arizona a	N.L.	29	$180\frac{2}{3}$	10	9	.526	172	68	140	2.84	0
2004 Arizona	N.L.	35	208	7	*16	.304	164	*119	194	3.59	0
2005 Arizona	N.L.	33	229	14	12	.538	172	59	229	3.54	0
2006 Arizona b	N.L.	33	235	*16	8	.667	178	50	216	3.10	0
2007 Arizona	N.L.	34	*$236\frac{1}{3}$	18	10	.643	194	72	209	3.01	0
2008 Arizona	N.L.	34	$226\frac{2}{3}$	*22	7	.759	183	65	206	3.30	0
2009 Arizona c	N.L.	1	4	0	0	.000	2	2	6	13.50	0
2010 Arizona d-e	N.L.				INJURED—Did Not Play						
Major League Totals	7 Yrs.	199	$1319\frac{2}{3}$	87	62	.584	1065	435	1200	3.27	0
Division Series											
2007 Arizona	N.L.	1	7	1	0	1.000	9	3	4	1.29	0
Championship Series											
2007 Arizona	N.L.	1	6	0	1	.000	4	2	7	6.00	0

a On disabled list from May 24 to June 8, 2003.
b Selected Cy Young Award Winner in National League for 2006.
c On disabled list from April 7 to November 20, 2009.
d On disabled list from March 26 to November 1, 2010.
e Filed for free agency, November 1, 2010. Signed with Texas Rangers, January 3, 2011.

WEBB, RYAN CHRISTOPHER

Born, Clearwater, Florida, February 5, 1986.
Bats Right. Throws Right. Height, 6 feet, 6 inches. Weight, 215 pounds.

Year	Club	Lea	G	IP	W	L	Pct	SO	BB	H	ERA	SAVES
2004	Athletics	Arizona	8	20 1/3	1	1	.500	23	1	18	4.87	0
2005	Kane County	Midwest	24	128 2/3	5	11	.313	84	41	139	4.76	0
2006	Stockton	Calif.	23	117 2/3	8	9	.471	96	37	160	5.28	0
2007	Stockton	Calif.	15	83	4	7	.364	71	22	83	5.75	0
2007	Midland	Texas	5	25 2/3	0	4	.000	16	10	34	9.12	0
2008	Midland	Texas	25	130	9	8	.529	94	44	165	5.19	0
2009	Sacramento	P.C.	31	45 2/3	7	1	.875	39	15	57	4.34	2
2009	Portland	P.C.	3	3	0	0	.000	0	1	3	3.00	0
2009	San Diego a	N.L.	28	25 2/3	2	1	.667	19	11	27	3.86	0
2010	Portland	P.C.	17	20 2/3	1	0	1.000	23	5	12	0.87	1
2010	San Diego b	N.L.	54	59	3	1	.750	44	19	64	2.90	0
Major League Totals		2 Yrs.	82	84 2/3	5	2	.714	63	30	91	3.19	0

a Traded by Oakland Athletics to San Diego Padres with pitcher Craig Italiano and player to be named later for outfielder Scott Hairston, July 5, 2009. San Diego Padres received pitcher Sean Gallagher to complete trade, July 28, 2009.

b Traded to Florida Marlins with pitcher Edward Mujica for outfielder Cameron Maybin, November 13, 2010.

WELLS, RANDY DAVID

Born, Belleville, Illinois, August 28, 1982.
Bats Right. Throws Right. Height, 6 feet, 3 inches. Weight, 230 pounds.

Year	Club	Lea	G	IP	W	L	Pct	SO	BB	H	ERA	SAVES
2003	Cubs	Arizona	3	5	0	0	.000	4	4	5	3.60	0
2003	Lansing	Midwest	1	1	0	0	.000	0	0	1	0.00	0
2004	Lansing	Midwest	36	107 2/3	6	6	.500	121	40	112	4.43	1
2005	Daytona	Fla.St.	41	98 2/3	10	2	.833	106	22	93	2.74	2
2005	West Tenn	Southern	6	9 1/3	0	1	.000	4	7	13	3.86	1
2006	Iowa	P.C.	13	69	5	5	.500	59	23	87	4.96	0
2006	West Tenn	Southern	12	62 1/3	4	2	.667	54	13	45	1.59	0
2007	Iowa	P.C.	40	95 2/3	5	6	.455	101	41	100	4.52	2
2008	Toronto	A.L.	1	1	0	0	.000	0	1	0	0.00	0
2008	Iowa	P.C.	27	118 2/3	10	4	.714	102	34	127	4.02	0
2008	Chicago a	N.L.	3	4 1/3	0	0	.000	1	2	0	0.00	0
2009	Iowa	P.C.	5	26	3	0	1.000	21	7	19	2.77	0
2009	Chicago	N.L.	27	165 1/3	12	10	.545	104	46	165	3.05	0
2010	Chicago	N.L.	32	194 1/3	8	14	.364	144	63	209	4.26	0
Major League Totals		3 Yrs.	63	365	20	24	.455	249	112	374	3.65	0

a Selected by Toronto Blue Jays from Chicago Cubs in Rule V draft, December 6, 2007. Returned to Chicago Cubs, April 16, 2008.

WESTBROOK, JACOB CAUTHEN (JAKE)

Born, Athens, Georgia, September 29, 1977.
Bats Right. Throws Right. Height, 6 feet, 3 inches. Weight, 215 pounds.

Year	Club	Lea	G	IP	W	L	Pct	SO	BB	H	ERA	SAVES
1996	Rockies	Arizona	11	62 2/3	4	2	.667	57	14	66	2.87	0
1996	Portland	Northwest	4	24 2/3	1	1	.500	19	5	22	2.55	0
1997	Asheville a	So.Atl.	28	170	14	11	.560	92	55	176	4.29	0
1998	Jupiter	Fla.St.	27	171	11	6	.647	79	60	169	3.26	0
1999	Harrisburg b	Eastern	27	174 2/3	11	5	.688	90	63	180	3.92	0
2000	Columbus	Int.	16	89	5	7	.417	61	38	94	4.65	0
2000	New York c-d-e-f	A.L.	3	6 2/3	0	2	.000	1	4	15	13.50	0
2001	Buffalo	Int.	12	64 2/3	8	1	.889	45	23	60	3.20	0
2001	Cleveland	A.L.	23	64 2/3	4	4	.500	48	22	79	5.85	0
2002	Akron	Eastern	3	15	0	1	.000	8	1	13	4.80	0
2002	Buffalo	Int.	1	6	1	0	1.000	2	0	8	6.00	0
2002	Cleveland g	A.L.	11	41 2/3	1	3	.250	20	12	50	5.83	0
2003	Buffalo	Int.	2	10	1	0	1.000	7	4	0	0.00	0
2003	Cleveland	A.L.	34	133	7	10	.412	58	56	142	4.33	0
2004	Cleveland	A.L.	33	215 2/3	14	9	.609	116	61	208	3.38	0
2005	Cleveland	A.L.	34	210 2/3	15	15	.500	119	56	218	4.49	0
2006	Cleveland	A.L.	32	211 1/3	15	10	.600	109	55	*247	4.17	0
2007	Lake County	So.Atl.	1	5	0	1	.000	5	0	6	7.20	0
2007	Akron	Eastern	1	2 1/3	0	1	.000	1	3	5	15.43	0
2007	Buffalo	Int.	2	5 1/3	0	1	.000	5	5	9	8.44	0
2007	Cleveland h	A.L.	25	152	6	9	.400	93	55	159	4.32	0

Year	Club	Lea	G	IP	W	L	Pct	SO	BB	H	ERA	SAVES
2008	Lake County	So.Atl.	1	$3\frac{2}{3}$	0	0	.000	4	1	3	2.45	0
2008	Akron	Eastern	1	6	0	0	.000	2	4	3	0.00	0
2008	Cleveland i	A.L.	5	$34\frac{2}{3}$	1	2	.333	19	7	33	3.12	0
2009	Akron	Eastern	3	9	0	1	.000	8	6	1	2.00	0
2009	Cleveland j	A.L.			INJURED—Did Not Play							
2010	Cleveland	A.L.	21	$127\frac{2}{3}$	6	7	.462	73	44	133	4.65	0
2010	St. Louis k-l	N.L.	12	75	4	4	.500	55	24	70	3.48	0
Major League Totals		10 Yrs.	233	1273	73	75	.493	711	396	1354	4.29	0
	Division Series											
2007	Cleveland	A.L.	1	5	0	1	.000	1	0	9	10.80	0
	Championship Series											
2007	Cleveland	A.L.	2	$12\frac{2}{3}$	1	1	.500	7	4	16	3.55	0

a Traded to Montreal Expos by Colorado Rockies with pitcher John Nicholson and outfielder Mike Hamlin for infielder Mike Lansing, November 18, 1997.
b Traded to New York Yankees with two players to be named later for pitcher Hideki Irabu, December 22, 1999. Pitchers Ted Lilly and Christian Parker were sent to New York Yankees to complete trade, March 17 and March 22, 2000.
c On disabled list from May 5 to 23, 2000.
d Sent to Cleveland Indians by New York Yankees with pitcher Zach Day to complete trade for outfielder David Justice, July 24, 2000.
e On disabled list from July 25 to September 1, 2000.
f On disabled list from September 1 to October 31, 2000.
g On disabled list from March 30 to July 11 and August 26 to November 4, 2002.
h On disabled list from May 3 to June 24, 2007.
i On disabled list from April 20 to May 28 and May 29 to November 13, 2008.
j On disabled list from March 26 to November 18, 2009.
k Traded to St. Louis Cardinals with cash for pitcher Corey Kluber, July 31, 2010.
l File for free agency, November 1, 2010, re-signed with St. Louis Cardinals, November 16, 2010.

WHEELER, DANIEL MICHAEL (DAN)

Born, Providence, Rhode Island, December 10, 1977.
Bats Right. Throws Right. Height, 6 feet, 3 inches. Weight, 220 pounds.

Year	Club	Lea	G	IP	W	L	Pct	SO	BB	H	ERA	SAVES
1997	Hudson Valley	N.Y.-Penn.	15	84	6	7	.462	81	17	75	3.00	0
1998	Chston-SC	So.Atl.	29	181	12	14	.462	136	29	206	4.43	0
1999	Orlando	Southern	9	58	3	0	1.000	53	8	56	3.26	0
1999	Durham	Int.	14	$82\frac{1}{3}$	7	5	.583	58	25	103	4.92	0
1999	Tampa Bay	A.L.	6	$30\frac{2}{3}$	0	4	.000	32	13	35	5.87	0
2000	Tampa Bay	A.L.	11	23	1	1	.500	17	11	29	5.48	0
2000	Durham	Int.	26	$150\frac{1}{3}$	5	11	.313	91	42	183	5.63	0
2001	Durham	Int.	18	$65\frac{1}{3}$	3	5	.375	39	11	72	5.23	0
2001	Tampa Bay	A.L.	13	$17\frac{2}{3}$	1	0	1.000	12	5	30	8.66	0
2001	Orlando	Southern	3	16	0	2	.000	12	6	15	2.81	0
2002	Richmond a	Int.	27	155	9	6	.600	110	42	163	4.65	0
2003	Norfolk b	Int.	22	$45\frac{2}{3}$	4	2	.667	44	16	48	3.94	4
2003	New York	N.L.	35	51	1	3	.250	35	17	49	3.71	2
2004	Norfolk	Int.	5	$7\frac{1}{3}$	1	0	1.000	10	2	8	2.45	0
2004	New York-Houston c	N.L.	46	65	3	1	.750	55	20	76	4.29	0
2005	Houston	N.L.	71	$73\frac{1}{3}$	2	3	.400	69	19	53	2.21	3
2006	Houston	N.L.	75	$71\frac{1}{3}$	3	5	.375	68	24	58	2.52	9
2007	Houston	N.L.	45	$49\frac{2}{3}$	1	4	.200	56	13	46	5.07	11
2007	Tampa Bay d	A.L.	25	25	0	5	.000	26	10	28	5.76	0
2008	Tampa Bay	A.L.	70	$66\frac{1}{3}$	5	6	.455	53	22	44	3.12	13
2009	Tampa Bay	A.L.	69	$57\frac{2}{3}$	4	5	.444	45	9	41	3.28	2
2010	Tampa Bay e	A.L.	64	$48\frac{1}{3}$	2	4	.333	46	16	36	3.35	3
Major League Totals		11 Yrs.	530	579	23	41	.359	514	179	525	3.84	43
	Division Series											
2004	Houston	N.L.	1	1	0	0	.000	0	0	0	0.00	0
2005	Houston	N.L.	3	$4\frac{1}{3}$	0	0	.000	5	3	4	2.08	0
2008	Tampa Bay	N.L.	1	1	0	0	.000	1	0	1	9.00	1
2010	Tampa Bay	N.L.	1	1	0	0	.000	2	0	0	0.00	0
Division Series Totals			6	$7\frac{1}{3}$	0	0	.000	8	3	5	2.45	1
	Championship Series											
2004	Houston	N.L.	4	7	1	0	1.000	9	0	4	0.00	0
2005	Houston	N.L.	3	$2\frac{2}{3}$	0	0	.000	2	0	2	0.00	0
2008	Tampa Bay	N.L.	3	5	0	0	.000	5	3	5	5.40	0
Championship Series Totals			10	$14\frac{2}{3}$	1	0	1.000	16	3	11	1.84	0
	World Series Record											
2005	Houston	N.L.	2	2	0	0	.000	1	1	2	13.50	0

Year	Club	Lea	G	IP	W	L	Pct	SO	BB	H	ERA	SAVES
2008	Tampa Bay	N.L.	3	2⅔	0	0	.000	3	1	3	6.75	0
World Series Totals			5	4⅔	0	0	.000	4	2	5	9.64	0

a Released by Tampa Bay Devil Rays, December 13, 2001. Signed with Atlanta Braves organization, January 20, 2002.

b Filed for free agency, October 15, 2002. Signed with New York Mets organization, January 27, 2003.

c Traded to Houston Astros for outfielder Adam Seuss, August 27, 2004.

d Traded to Tampa Bay Devil Rays for infielder Ty Wigginton, July 28, 2007.

e Filed for free agency, November 3, 2010. Signed with Boston Red Sox, December 18, 2010.

WILLIS, DONTRELLE WAYNE

Born, Oakland, California, January 12, 1982.
Bats Left. Throws Left. Height, 6 feet, 4 inches. Weight, 225 pounds.

Year	Club	Lea	G	IP	W	L	Pct	SO	BB	H	ERA	SAVES
2000	Cubs	Arizona	9	28	3	1	.750	22	8	26	3.86	0
2001	Boise	Northwest	15	93⅔	8	2	.800	77	19	76	2.98	0
2002	Kane County	Midwest	19	127⅔	10	2	.833	101	21	91	1.83	0
2002	Jupiter a	Fla.St.	5	30	2	0	1.000	27	3	24	1.80	0
2003	Carolina	Southern	6	36⅓	4	0	1.000	32	9	24	1.49	0
2003	Florida b	N.L.	27	160⅔	14	6	.700	142	58	148	3.30	0
2004	Florida	N.L.	32	197	10	11	.476	139	61	210	4.02	0
2005	Florida	N.L.	34	236⅓	*22	10	.688	170	55	213	2.63	0
2006	Florida	N.L.	34	223⅓	12	12	.500	160	83	234	3.87	0
2007	Florida c	N.L.	35	205⅓	10	15	.400	146	87	241	5.17	0
2008	Lakeland	Fla.St.	6	28	0	3	.000	18	11	30	4.50	0
2008	Toledo	Int.	6	28⅓	3	1	.750	20	14	34	4.45	0
2008	Detroit d	A.L.	8	24	0	2	.000	18	35	18	9.38	0
2009	Lakeland	Fla.St.	1	7	0	1	.000	2	0	8	5.14	0
2009	Erie	Eastern	1	6	1	0	1.000	6	3	3	3.00	0
2009	Toledo	Int.	5	24⅓	1	2	.333	15	17	22	4.81	0
2009	Detroit e	A.L.	7	33⅔	1	4	.200	17	28	37	7.49	0
2010	Giants	Arizona	3	2	0	1	.000	1	1	4	9.00	0
2010	Fresno	P.C.	5	5⅓	0	0	.000	6	4	2	5.06	0
2010	Detroit	A.L.	9	43⅓	1	2	.333	33	29	48	4.98	0
2010	Arizona f-g-h	N.L.	6	22⅓	1	1	.500	14	27	24	6.85	0
Major League Totals		8 Yrs.	192	1146	71	63	.530	839	463	1173	4.12	0
	Division Series											
2003	Florida	N.L.	2	5⅔	0	0	.000	3	2	7	7.94	0
	Championship Series											
2003	Florida	N.L.	2	3⅓	0	1	.000	4	6	4	18.90	0
	World Series Record											
2003	Florida	N.L.	3	3⅔	0	0	.000	3	2	4	0.00	0

a Traded by Chicago Cubs to Florida Marlins with pitcher Julian Tavarez, pitcher Jose Cueto and catcher Ryan Jorgensen for pitcher Antonio Alfonseca and pitcher Matt Clement, March 27, 2002.

b Selected Rookie of the Year in National League for 2003.

c Traded to Detroit Tigers with infielder Miguel Cabrera for pitcher Burke Badenhop, pitcher Eulogio De La Cruz, pitcher Andrew Miller, catcher Mike Rabelo and outfielder Cameron Maybin, December 5, 2007.

d On disabled list from April 12 to May 21, 2008.

e On disabled list from March 29 to May 13 and June 15 to October 15, 2009.

f Traded to Arizona Diamondbacks with cash for pitcher Billy Buckner, June 1, 2010.

g Released by Arizona Diamondbacks, July 6, 2010. Signed with San Francisco Giants organization, July 15, 2010.

h Filed for free agency, November 6, 2010. Signed with Cincinnati Reds organization, November 23, 2010.

WILSON, BRIAN PATRICK

Born, Londonderry, New Hampshire, March 16, 1982.
Bats Right. Throws Right. Height, 6 feet, 1 inch. Weight, 205 pounds.

Year	Club	Lea	G	IP	W	L	Pct	SO	BB	H	ERA	SAVES
2004	Hagerstown	So.Atl.	23	57⅓	2	5	.286	41	22	63	5.34	3
2005	Norwich	Eastern	15	15⅔	0	0	.000	22	5	6	0.57	8
2005	Fresno	P.C.	9	11⅓	1	1	.500	13	8	8	3.97	0
2005	Augusta	So.Atl.	26	33	5	1	.833	30	7	23	0.82	13
2006	San Jose	Calif.	1	1	0	0	.000	1	1	1	9.00	0
2006	Fresno	P.C.	24	28	1	3	.250	30	14	20	2.89	7
2006	San Francisco	N.L.	31	30	2	3	.400	23	21	32	5.40	1
2007	San Jose	Calif.	3	3	0	0	.000	6	0	1	0.00	2
2007	Fresno	P.C.	31	34⅓	1	2	.333	37	24	24	2.10	11
2007	San Francisco	N.L.	24	23⅔	1	2	.333	18	7	16	2.28	6
2008	San Francisco	N.L.	63	62⅓	3	2	.600	67	28	62	4.62	41

Year	Club	Lea	G	IP	W	L	Pct	SO	BB	H	ERA	SAVES
2009	San Francisco	N.L.	68	72⅓	5	6	.455	83	27	60	2.74	38
2010	San Francisco	N.L.	70	74⅔	3	3	.500	93	26	62	1.81	*48
Major League Totals		5 Yrs.	256	263	14	16	.467	284	109	232	3.18	134
	Division Series											
2010	San Francisco	N.L.	3	4	0	0	.000	5	2	2	0.00	2
	Championship Series											
2010	San Francisco	N.L.	4	5	1	0	1.000	7	2	2	0.00	3
	World Series Record											
2010	San Francisco	N.L.	3	2⅔	0	0	.000	4	0	1	0.00	1

WILSON, CHRISTOPHER JOHN (C.J.)

Born, Newport Beach, California, November 18, 1980.
Bats Left. Throws Left. Height, 6 feet, 2 inches. Weight, 215 pounds.

Year	Club	Lea	G	IP	W	L	Pct	SO	BB	H	ERA	SAVES
2001	Pulaski	Appal.	8	37⅔	1	0	1.000	49	9	24	0.96	0
2001	Savannah	So.Atl.	5	34	1	2	.333	26	9	30	3.18	0
2002	Charlotte	Fla.St.	26	106	10	2	.833	76	41	86	3.06	1
2002	Tulsa	Texas	5	30	1	0	1.000	17	12	23	1.80	0
2003	Frisco	Texas	22	123	6	9	.400	89	38	135	5.05	0
2004					INJURED—Did Not Play							
2005	Bakersfield	Calif.	4	13⅔	0	1	.000	14	4	10	3.29	0
2005	Frisco	Texas	12	44⅔	0	4	.000	43	14	51	4.43	0
2005	Texas	A.L.	24	48	1	7	.125	30	18	63	6.94	1
2006	Frisco	Texas	4	3⅓	0	0	.000	6	2	3	2.70	0
2006	Oklahoma	P.C.	9	11	1	0	1.000	17	5	10	2.45	2
2006	Texas a	A.L.	44	44⅓	2	4	.333	43	18	39	4.06	1
2007	Texas	A.L.	66	68⅓	2	1	.667	63	33	50	3.03	12
2008	Texas b	A.L.	50	46⅓	2	2	.500	41	27	49	6.02	24
2009	Texas	A.L.	74	73⅔	5	6	.455	84	32	66	2.81	14
2010	Texas	A.L.	33	204	15	8	.652	170	*93	161	3.35	0
Major League Totals		6 Yrs.	291	484⅔	27	28	.491	431	221	428	3.90	52
	Division Series											
2010	Texas	A.L.	1	6⅓	1	0	1.000	7	2	2	0.00	0
	Championship Series											
2010	Texas	A.L.	2	12	0	1	.000	6	6	12	6.00	0
	World Series Record											
2010	Texas	A.L.	1	6	0	1	.000	4	2	3	3.00	0

a On disabled list from March 24 to April 14, 2006.
b On disabled list from August 6 to October 2, 2008.

WOLF, RANDALL CHRISTOPHER (RANDY)

Born, Canoga Park, California, August 22, 1976.
Bats Left. Throws Left. Height, 6 feet. Weight, 205 pounds.

Year	Club	Lea	G	IP	W	L	Pct	SO	BB	H	ERA	SAVES
1997	Batavia	N.Y.-Penn.	7	40	4	0	1.000	53	8	29	1.58	0
1998	Reading	Eastern	4	25	2	0	1.000	33	4	15	1.44	0
1998	Scranton-WB	Int.	24	148	9	7	.563	118	48	167	4.62	0
1999	Scranton-WB	Int.	12	77⅓	4	5	.444	72	29	73	3.61	0
1999	Philadelphia	N.L.	22	121⅔	6	9	.400	116	67	126	5.55	0
2000	Philadelphia	N.L.	32	206⅓	11	9	.550	160	83	210	4.36	0
2001	Scranton-WB	Int.	2	9	0	1	.000	7	5	10	5.00	0
2001	Reading	Eastern	1	6	0	0	.000	7	2	5	4.50	0
2001	Philadelphia a	N.L.	28	163	10	11	.476	152	51	150	3.70	0
2002	Clearwater	Fla.St.	1	5	0	0	.000	8	1	1	0.00	0
2002	Philadelphia b	N.L.	31	210⅔	11	9	.550	172	63	172	3.20	0
2003	Philadelphia	N.L.	33	200	16	10	.615	177	78	176	4.23	0
2004	Reading	Eastern	1	4	0	0	.000	4	0	5	2.25	0
2004	Philadelphia c	N.L.	23	136⅔	5	8	.385	89	36	145	4.28	0
2005	Philadelphia d	N.L.	13	80	6	4	.600	61	26	87	4.39	0
2006	Clearwater	Fla.St.	2	5⅔	0	0	.000	4	4	6	0.00	0
2006	Reading	Eastern	3	12	1	1	.500	11	7	15	6.75	0
2006	Lakewood	So.Atl.	2	8	0	0	.000	7	3	2	1.13	0
2006	Philadelphia e-f	N.L.	12	56⅔	4	0	1.000	44	33	63	5.56	0
2007	Inland Empire	Calif.	1	4	0	0	.000	4	1	6	6.75	0
2007	Los Angeles g-h	N.L.	18	102⅔	9	6	.600	94	39	110	4.73	0
2008	San Diego-Houston i-j	N.L.	33	190⅓	12	12	.500	162	71	191	4.30	0
2009	Los Angeles k	N.L.	34	214⅓	11	7	.611	160	58	178	3.23	0

Year	Club	Lea	G	IP	W	L	Pct	SO	BB	H	ERA	SAVES
2010	Milwaukee	N.L.	34	$215\frac{2}{3}$	13	12	.520	142	87	213	4.17	0
Major League Totals		12 Yrs.	313	1898	114	97	.540	1529	692	1821	4.13	0
	Division Series											
2009	Los Angeles	N.L.	1	$3\frac{2}{3}$	0	0	.000	2	5	6	4.91	0
	Championship Series											
2009	Los Angeles	N.L.	1	$5\frac{1}{3}$	0	0	.000	2	2	4	5.06	0

a On disabled list from August 2 to September 1, 2001.
b On disabled list from March 25 to April 12, 2002.
c On disabled list from June 3 to June 26 and August 29 to October 8, 2004.
d On disabled list from June 12 to November 1, 2005.
e On disabled list from March 24 to July 30, 2006.
f Filed for free agency, October 28, 2006. Signed with Los Angeles Dodgers, November 28, 2006.
g On disabled list from July 4 to October 31, 2007.
h Filed for free agency, November 9, 2007. Signed with San Diego Padres, December 10, 2007.
i Traded to Houston Astros for pitcher Chad Reineke, July 22, 2008.
j Filed for free agency, October 31, 2008. Signed with Los Angeles Dodgers, February 6, 2009.
k Filed for free agency, November 5, 2009. Signed with Milwaukee Brewers, December 14, 2009.

WOOD, BLAKE DANIEL

Born, Atlanta, Georgia, August 8, 1985.
Bats Right. Throws Right. Height, 6 feet, 5 inches. Weight, 230 pounds.

Year	Club	Lea	G	IP	W	L	Pct	SO	BB	H	ERA	SAVES
2006	Idaho Falls	Pioneer	12	52	3	1	.750	46	15	50	4.50	0
2007	Royals	Arizona	4	$9\frac{2}{3}$	0	0	.000	15	0	9	0.00	0
2007	Wilmington	Carolina	2	$9\frac{2}{3}$	0	1	.000	11	3	9	4.66	0
2007	Burlington	Midwest	7	$35\frac{2}{3}$	2	1	.667	26	14	32	3.03	0
2008	Wilmington	Carolina	10	$57\frac{1}{3}$	3	2	.600	63	15	32	2.67	0
2008	NW Arkansas	Texas	18	$86\frac{2}{3}$	5	7	.417	76	32	96	5.30	0
2009	Royals	Arizona	3	4	0	1	.000	4	1	4	0.00	0
2009	NW Arkansas	Texas	17	$78\frac{2}{3}$	2	8	.200	49	28	92	5.83	0
2010	Omaha	P.C.	12	$16\frac{2}{3}$	2	1	.667	12	7	12	2.16	5
2010	Kansas City	A.L.	51	$49\frac{2}{3}$	1	3	.250	31	22	54	5.07	0

WOOD, KERRY LEE

Born, Irving, Texas, June 16, 1977.
Bats Right. Throws Right. Height, 6 feet, 5 inches. Weight, 210 pounds.

Year	Club	Lea	G	IP	W	L	Pct	SO	BB	H	ERA	SAVES
1995	Cubs	Gulf Coast	1	3	0	0	.000	2	1	0	0.00	0
1995	Williamsport	N.Y.-Penn.	2	$4\frac{1}{3}$	0	0	.000	5	5	5	10.38	0
1996	Daytona a	Fla.St.	22	$114\frac{1}{3}$	10	2	.833	136	70	72	2.91	0
1997	Orlando	Southern	19	94	6	7	.462	106	79	58	4.50	0
1997	Iowa	A.A.	10	$57\frac{2}{3}$	4	2	.667	80	52	35	4.68	0
1998	Iowa	P.C.	1	5	1	0	1.000	11	2	1	0.00	0
1998	Chicago b	N.L.	26	$166\frac{2}{3}$	13	6	.684	233	85	117	3.40	0
1999	Chicago c	N.L.	INJURED—Did Not Play									
2000	Daytona	Fla.St.	2	12	2	0	1.000	17	5	3	1.50	0
2000	Iowa	P.C.	1	7	0	0	.000	7	4	4	2.57	0
2000	Chicago d	N.L.	23	137	8	7	.533	132	87	112	4.80	0
2001	Chicago e	N.L.	28	$174\frac{1}{3}$	12	6	.667	217	92	127	3.36	0
2002	Chicago	N.L.	33	$213\frac{2}{3}$	12	11	.522	217	97	169	3.66	0
2003	Chicago	N.L.	32	211	14	11	.560	*266	100	152	3.20	0
2004	Iowa	P.C.	1	5	1	0	1.000	4	1	2	0.00	0
2004	Chicago f	N.L.	22	$140\frac{1}{3}$	8	9	.471	144	51	127	3.72	0
2005	Peoria	Midwest	2	$2\frac{1}{3}$	0	0	.000	5	0	1	0.00	0
2005	Iowa	P.C.	3	$12\frac{2}{3}$	0	0	.000	18	6	11	2.84	0
2005	Chicago g	N.L.	21	66	3	4	.429	77	26	52	4.23	0
2006	Peoria	Midwest	1	5	0	0	.000	12	1	1	0.00	0
2006	Iowa	P.C.	1	5	0	1	.000	3	2	5	1.80	0
2006	Chicago h-i	N.L.	4	$19\frac{2}{3}$	1	2	.333	13	8	19	4.12	0
2007	Azl Cubs	Arizona	4	4	0	1	.000	5	1	4	2.25	0
2007	Peoria	Midwest	3	3	1	0	1.000	3	1	1	0.00	0
2007	Tennessee	Southern	1	$1\frac{2}{3}$	0	0	.000	1	1	0	0.00	0
2007	Chicago j-k	N.L.	22	$24\frac{1}{3}$	1	1	.500	24	13	18	3.33	0
2008	Chicago l-m	N.L.	65	$66\frac{1}{3}$	5	4	.556	84	18	54	3.26	34
2009	Cleveland	A.L.	58	55	3	3	.500	63	28	48	4.25	20
2010	Akron	Eastern	3	$2\frac{2}{3}$	0	1	.000	2	3	4	20.25	0
2010	Cleveland-New York n-o-p	A.L.	47	46	3	4	.429	49	29	35	3.13	8
Major League Totals		12 Yrs.	381	$1320\frac{1}{3}$	83	68	.550	1519	634	1030	3.65	62

Year	Club	Lea	G	IP	W	L	Pct	SO	BB	H	ERA	SAVES
	Division Series											
1998	Chicago	N.L.	1	5	0	1	.000	5	4	3	1.80	0
2003	Chicago	N.L.	2	15 1/3	2	0	1.000	18	7	7	1.76	0
2007	Chicago	N.L.	2	3	0	0	.000	2	0	3	3.00	0
2008	Chicago	N.L.	1	1	0	0	.000	0	0	2	0.00	0
2010	New York	A.L.	3	2	0	0	.000	3	2	4	4.50	0
Division Series Totals			9	26 1/3	2	1	.667	28	13	19	2.05	0
	Championship Series											
2003	Chicago	N.L.	2	12 1/3	0	1	.000	13	7	14	7.30	0
2010	New York	A.L.	4	6	0	0	.000	4	3	2	1.50	0
Championship Series Totals			6	18 1/3	0	1	.000	17	10	16	5.40	0

a On disabled list from May 24 to June 19, 1996.
b Selected Rookie of the Year in National League for 1998.
c On disabled list from March 31 to November 2, 1999.
d On disabled list from March 25 to May 1 and July 30 to August 21, 2000.
e On disabled list from August 4 to September 7, 2001.
f On disabled list from May 12 to July 11, 2004.
g On disabled list from May 1 to June 29 and July 21 to August 5 and August 30 to October 31, 2005.
h On disabled list from March 27 to May 18 and June 7 to October 29, 2006.
i Filed for free agency, October 29, 2006, re-signed with Chicago Cubs, November 15, 2006.
j On disabled list from March 29 to August 3, 2007.
k Filed for free agency, October 29, 2007, re-signed with Chicago Cubs, November 28, 2007.
l On disabled list from July 14 to August 5, 2008.
m Filed for free agency, October 31, 2008. Signed with Cleveland Indians, December 13, 2008.
n On disabled list from March 26 to May 7 and July 12 to July 31, 2010.
o Traded to New York Yankees with cash for two players to be named later, July 31, 2010. Cleveland Indians received infielder Matthew Cusick and pitcher Andrew Shive to complete trade, October 21, 2010.
p Filed for free agency, November 1, 2010. Signed with Chicago Cubs, December 17, 2010.

WOOD, TRAVIS A.

Born, Little Rock, Arkansas, February 6, 1987.
Bats Right. Throws Left. Height, 5 feet, 11 inches. Weight, 165 pounds.

Year	Club	Lea	G	IP	W	L	Pct	SO	BB	H	ERA	SAVES
2005	Reds	Gulf Coast	8	24	0	0	.000	45	7	13	0.75	0
2005	Billings	Pioneer	6	24 2/3	2	0	1.000	22	13	15	1.82	0
2006	Dayton	Midwest	27	140	10	5	.667	133	56	108	3.66	0
2007	Sarasota	Fla.St.	12	46 1/3	3	2	.600	54	27	49	4.86	0
2008	Sarasota	Fla.St.	9	46 2/3	3	4	.429	41	21	39	2.70	0
2008	Chattanooga	Southern	17	80	4	9	.308	58	48	91	7.09	0
2009	Louisville	Int.	8	48 2/3	4	2	.667	32	16	43	3.14	0
2009	Carolina	Southern	19	119	9	3	.750	103	37	78	1.21	0
2010	Louisville	Int.	16	100	5	6	.455	99	24	86	3.06	0
2010	Cincinnati	N.L.	17	102 2/3	5	4	.556	86	26	85	3.51	0
	Division Series											
2010	Cincinnati	N.L.	1	3 1/3	0	0	.000	3	1	1	0.00	0

WRIGHT, JAMEY ALAN

Born, Oklahoma City, Oklahoma, December 24, 1974.
Bats Right. Throws Right. Height, 6 feet, 6 inches. Weight, 235 pounds.

Year	Club	Lea	G	IP	W	L	Pct	SO	BB	H	ERA	SAVES
1993	Rockies	Arizona	8	36	1	3	.250	26	9	35	4.00	0
1994	Asheville	So.Atl.	28	143 1/3	7	14	.333	103	59	188	5.97	0
1995	Salem	Carolina	26	171	10	8	.556	95	72	160	2.47	0
1995	New Haven	Eastern	1	3	0	1	.000	0	3	6	9.00	0
1996	New Haven	Eastern	7	44 2/3	5	1	.833	54	12	27	0.81	0
1996	Colorado Springs	P.C.	9	59 2/3	4	2	.667	40	22	53	2.72	0
1996	Colorado	N.L.	16	91 1/3	4	4	.500	45	41	105	4.93	0
1997	Salem	Carolina	1	1	0	1	.000	1	1	1	9.00	0
1997	Colorado Springs	P.C.	2	11	1	0	1.000	11	5	9	1.64	0
1997	Colorado a	N.L.	26	149 2/3	8	12	.400	59	71	198	6.25	0
1998	Colorado	N.L.	34	206 1/3	9	14	.391	86	95	235	5.67	0
1999	Colorado	N.L.	16	94 1/3	4	3	.571	49	54	110	4.87	0
1999	Colorado Springs b	P.C.	17	100 1/3	5	7	.417	75	38	133	6.46	0
2000	Huntsville	Southern	2	12 1/3	2	0	1.000	10	5	7	0.00	0
2000	Indianapolis	Int.	1	5	0	0	.000	7	3	8	1.80	0
2000	Milwaukee c	N.L.	26	164 2/3	7	9	.438	96	88	157	4.10	0
2001	Milwaukee d	N.L.	33	194 2/3	11	12	.478	129	98	201	4.90	0
2002	Indianapolis	Int.	3	15 1/3	1	1	.500	13	5	16	4.11	0

Year	Club	Lea	G	IP	W	L	Pct	SO	BB	H	ERA	SAVES
2002	Milwaukee-St. Louis e-f-g	N.L.	23	129 1/3	7	13	.350	77	75	130	5.29	0
2003	Indianapolis	Int.	7	22	1	3	.250	17	10	32	7.36	0
2003	Oklahoma	P.C.	7	39 1/3	2	1	.667	40	21	38	4.12	0
2003	Omaha	P.C.	13	76 2/3	3	5	.375	65	38	70	3.64	0
2003	Kansas City h-i-j-k	A.L.	4	25 1/3	1	2	.333	19	11	23	4.26	0
2004	Omaha	P.C.	18	104 2/3	8	6	.571	70	35	111	4.21	0
2004	Colorado l-m	N.L.	14	78 2/3	2	3	.400	41	45	82	4.12	0
2005	Colorado n	N.L.	34	171 1/3	8	16	.333	101	81	201	5.46	0
2006	San Francisco o	N.L.	34	156	6	10	.375	79	64	167	5.19	0
2007	Frisco	Texas	1	4	0	0	.000	2	0	6	4.50	0
2007	Oklahoma	P.C.	3	16 1/3	2	1	.667	11	3	21	4.41	0
2007	Texas p-q	A.L.	20	77	4	5	.444	39	41	72	3.62	0
2008	Texas r	A.L.	75	84 1/3	8	7	.533	60	35	93	5.12	0
2009	Kansas City s	A.L.	65	79	3	5	.375	60	44	73	4.33	0
2010	Sacramento	P.C.	10	14	1	0	1.000	16	9	23	9.00	1
2010	Cleveland-Seattle t-u	A.L.	46	58 1/3	1	3	.250	28	25	55	4.17	0
Major League Totals		15 Yrs.	466	1760 1/3	83	118	.413	968	868	1902	5.00	0

a On disabled list from May 15 to June 8, 1997.
b Traded to Milwaukee Brewers with catcher Henry Blanco and pitcher Justin Miller for infielder Jeff Cirillo and pitcher Scott Karl, December 13, 1999.
c On disabled list from March 28 to May 22, 2000.
d On disabled list from May 21 to June 10, 2001.
e On disabled list from April 5 to May 24, 2002.
f Traded to St. Louis Cardinals with cash for outfielder Chris Morris and player to be named later, August 29, 2002. Milwaukee Brewers received pitcher Mike Matthews to complete trade, September 11, 2002.
g Filed for free agency, November 1, 2002. Signed with Seattle Mariners organization, January 24, 2003.
h Released by Seattle Mariners, March 18, 2003. Signed with Milwaukee Brewers organization, March 23, 2003.
i Released by Milwaukee Brewers, April 28, 2003. Signed with Texas Rangers organization, May 5, 2003.
j Released by Texas Rangers, June 16, 2003. Signed with Kansas City Royals organization, June 24, 2003.
k Filed for free agency, October 30, 2003, re-signed with Kansas City Royals organization, March 29, 2004.
l Released by Kansas City Royals, July 21, 2004. Signed with Colorado Rockies organization, July 22, 2004.
m Filed for free agency, November 1, 2004, re-signed with Colorado Rockies, December 21, 2004.
n Filed for free agency, November 2, 2005. Signed with San Francisco Giants organization, January 17, 2006.
o Filed for free agency, November 2, 2006. Signed with Texas Rangers organization, January 25, 2007.
p On disabled list from April 11 to June 16, 2007.
q Filed for free agency, November 12, 2007, re-signed with Texas Rangers organization, January 11, 2008.
r Filed for free agency, October 30, 2008. Signed with Kansas City Royals organization, February 10, 2009.
s Filed for free agency, November 5, 2009. Signed with Cleveland Indians organization, February 9, 2010.
t Released by Cleveland Indians, June 10, 2010. Signed with Seattle Mariners, July 15, 2010.
u Filed for free agency, November 1, 2010.

WUERTZ, MICHAEL JAMES

Born, Austin, Minnesota, December 15, 1978.
Bats Right. Throws Right. Height, 6 feet, 3 inches. Weight, 205 pounds.

Year	Club	Lea	G	IP	W	L	Pct	SO	BB	H	ERA	SAVES
1998	Williamsport	N.Y.-Penn.	14	86 1/3	7	5	.583	59	19	79	3.44	0
1999	Lansing	Midwest	28	161 1/3	11	12	.478	127	44	191	4.80	0
2000	Daytona	Fla.St.	28	171 1/3	12	7	.632	142	64	166	3.78	0
2001	West Tenn	Southern	27	160	4	9	.308	135	58	160	3.99	0
2002	Iowa	P.C.	28	154	9	5	.643	131	69	185	5.55	0
2003	Iowa	P.C.	43	124	3	9	.250	92	35	140	4.57	1
2004	Chicago	N.L.	31	29	1	0	1.000	30	17	22	4.34	1
2004	Iowa	P.C.	37	44 2/3	1	1	.500	59	15	30	2.42	19
2005	Chicago	N.L.	75	75 2/3	6	2	.750	89	40	60	3.81	0
2006	Iowa	P.C.	30	41 2/3	6	0	1.000	67	9	30	1.73	10
2006	Chicago	N.L.	41	40 2/3	3	1	.750	42	16	35	2.66	0
2007	Chicago	N.L.	73	72 1/3	2	3	.400	79	35	64	3.48	0
2008	Iowa	P.C.	17	20	0	1	.000	29	14	13	3.60	4
2008	Chicago	N.L.	45	44 2/3	1	1	.500	30	20	44	3.63	0
2009	Oakland a	A.L.	74	78 2/3	6	1	.857	102	23	52	2.63	4
2010	Stockton	Calif.	2	3	0	0	.000	3	0	3	0.00	0
2010	Sacramento	P.C.	4	4 2/3	0	0	.000	3	3	4	0.00	0
2010	Oakland b	A.L.	48	39 2/3	2	3	.400	40	21	35	4.31	6
Major League Totals		7 Yrs.	387	380 2/3	21	11	.656	412	172	312	3.45	11
	Division Series											
2007	Chicago	N.L.	2	1 2/3	0	0	.000	2	1	0	0.00	0

a Traded to Oakland Athletics for outfielder Richie Robnett and infielder Justin Sellers, February 2, 2009.
b On disabled list from March 26 to May 3, 2010.

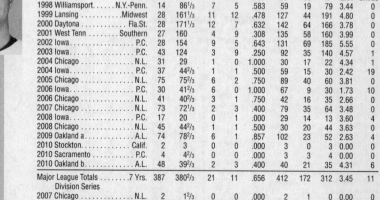

YOUNG, CHRISTOPHER RYAN (CHRIS)

Born, Dallas, Texas, May 25, 1979.
Bats Right. Throws Right. Height, 6 feet, 10 inches. Weight, 280 pounds.

Year	Club	Lea	G	IP	W	L	Pct	SO	BB	H	ERA	SAVES
2001	Hickory	So.Atl.	12	74 1/3	5	3	.625	72	20	79	4.12	0
2002	Hickory a	So.Atl.	26	144 2/3	11	9	.550	136	34	127	3.11	0
2003	Harrisburg	Eastern	15	83	4	4	.500	64	22	83	4.01	0
2003	Brevard County	Fla.St.	8	50	5	2	.714	39	5	26	1.62	0
2004	Frisco	Texas	18	88 1/3	6	5	.545	75	31	94	4.48	0
2004	Oklahoma	P.C.	5	30 1/3	3	0	1.000	34	9	20	1.48	0
2004	Texas b	A.L.	7	36 1/3	3	2	.600	27	10	36	4.71	0
2005	Lynchburg	Carolina	10	15	0	1	.000	14	5	9	3.00	2
2005	Tulsa	Texas	35	53	3	2	.600	35	17	53	4.75	1
2005	Texas c-d	A.L.	31	164 2/3	12	7	.632	137	45	162	4.26	0
2006	San Diego	N.L.	31	179 1/3	11	5	.688	164	69	134	3.46	0
2007	San Diego e	N.L.	30	173	9	8	.529	167	72	118	3.12	0
2008	Lake Elsinore	Calif.	2	8 2/3	0	1	.000	7	1	5	3.12	0
2008	San Diego f	N.L.	18	102 1/3	7	6	.538	93	48	84	3.96	0
2009	San Diego g	N.L.	14	76	4	6	.400	50	40	70	5.21	0
2010	San Antonio	Texas	1	0 2/3	0	1	.000	1	4	2	67.50	0
2010	Portland	P.C.	2	6 1/3	0	0	.000	4	2	2	1.42	0
2010	San Diego h-i	N.L.	4	20	2	0	1.000	15	11	10	0.90	0
Major League Totals		7 Yrs.	135	751 2/3	48	34	.585	653	295	614	3.80	0
	Division Series											
2006	San Diego	N.L.	1	6 2/3	1	0	1.000	9	2	4	0.00	0

a Traded by Pittsburgh Pirates to Montreal Expos with pitcher Jon Searles for pitcher Matt Herges, December 20, 2002.
b Traded to Texas Rangers with catcher Josh McKinley for catcher Einar Diaz, April 3, 2004.
c Traded to Arizona Diamondbacks with pitcher Orlando Hernandez and pitcher Luis Vizcaino for pitcher Javier Vazquez, December 20, 2005.
d Traded to San Diego Padres with infielder Adrian Gonzalez and outfielder Terrmel Sledge for pitcher Adam Eaton, pitcher Akinori Otsuka and catcher Billy Killian, January 4, 2006.
e On disabled list from July 25 to August 9, 2007.
f On disabled list from May 22 to July 29 and August 11 to September 1, 2008.
g On disabled list from June 15 to October 28, 2009.
h On disabled list from April 7 to September 18, 2010.
i Filed for free agency, November 3, 2010.

ZAMBRANO, CARLOS ALBERTO

Born, Puerto Cabello, Venezuela, June 1, 1981.
Bats Both. Throws Right. Height, 6 feet, 5 inches. Weight, 255 pounds.

Year	Club	Lea	G	IP	W	L	Pct	SO	BB	H	ERA	SAVES
1998	Cubs	Arizona	14	40	0	1	.000	36	25	39	3.15	1
1999	Lansing	Midwest	27	153 1/3	13	7	.650	98	62	150	4.17	0
2000	Iowa	P.C.	34	56 2/3	2	5	.286	46	40	54	3.97	6
2000	West Tenn	Southern	9	60 1/3	3	1	.750	43	21	39	1.34	0
2001	Iowa	P.C.	26	150 2/3	10	5	.667	155	68	124	3.88	0
2001	Chicago	N.L.	6	7 2/3	1	2	.333	4	8	11	15.26	0
2002	Iowa	P.C.	3	9	0	0	.000	11	6	2	0.00	0
2002	Chicago a	N.L.	32	108 1/3	4	8	.333	93	63	94	3.66	0
2003	Chicago	N.L.	32	214	13	11	.542	168	94	188	3.11	0
2004	Chicago	N.L.	31	209 2/3	16	8	.667	188	81	174	2.75	0
2005	Chicago	N.L.	33	223 1/3	14	6	.700	202	86	170	3.26	0
2006	Chicago	N.L.	33	214	*16	7	*.696	210	*115	162	3.41	0
2007	Chicago	N.L.	34	216 1/3	18	13	.581	177	*101	187	3.95	0
2008	Chicago b-c	N.L.	30	188 2/3	14	6	.700	130	72	172	3.91	0
2009	Peoria	Midwest	1	5	0	0	.000	5	0	4	0.00	0
2009	Daytona	Fla.St.	1	3 2/3	0	1	.000	1	3	5	9.82	0
2009	Chicago d	N.L.	28	169 1/3	9	7	.563	152	78	155	3.77	0
2010	Cubs	Arizona	1	1	0	0	.000	1	0	0	0.00	0
2010	Iowa	P.C.	3	4	0	0	.000	4	1	6	6.75	0
2010	Chicago	N.L.	36	129 2/3	11	6	.647	117	69	119	3.33	0
Major League Totals		10 Yrs.	295	1681	116	74	.611	1441	767	1432	3.50	0
	Division Series											
2003	Chicago	N.L.	1	5 2/3	0	0	.000	4	0	11	4.76	0
2007	Chicago	N.L.	1	6	0	0	.000	8	1	4	1.50	0
2008	Chicago	N.L.	1	6 1/3	0	1	.000	7	2	6	4.26	0
Division Series Totals			3	18	0	1	.000	19	3	21	3.50	0
	Championship Series											
2003	Chicago	N.L.	2	11	0	1	.000	8	5	14	5.73	0

a On disabled list from May 10 to June 7, 2002.
b On disabled list from June 19 to July 4, 2008.
c Pitched no-hit, no-run game against Houston Astros, September 14, 2008.
d On disabled list from May 4 to May 22 and August 6 to August 25, 2009.

ZIEGLER, BRAD GREGORY

Born, Pratt, Kansas, October 10, 1979.
Bats Right. Throws Right. Height, 6 feet, 4 inches. Weight, 200 pounds.

Year	Club	Lea	G	IP	W	L	Pct	SO	BB	H	ERA	SAVES
2003	Batavia	N.Y.-Penn.	3	6	1	0	1.000	6	1	5	1.50	0
2004	Schaumburg	Northern	4	24	3	0	1.000	26	1	12	1.50	0
2004	Modesto a-b	Calif.	16	92 1/3	9	2	.818	77	22	94	3.90	0
2005	Stockton	Calif.	24	141	9	7	.563	144	20	166	4.66	0
2005	Midland	Texas	4	21	2	1	.667	20	4	27	6.86	0
2006	Sacramento	P.C.	4	21	0	1	.000	11	5	32	6.00	0
2006	Midland	Texas	23	141 2/3	9	6	.600	88	37	151	3.37	0
2007	Sacramento	P.C.	35	54 2/3	8	3	.727	44	14	46	2.96	1
2007	Midland	Texas	15	23 2/3	4	0	1.000	18	4	19	1.14	1
2008	Sacramento	P.C.	19	24 1/3	2	0	1.000	20	4	15	0.37	8
2008	Oakland	A.L.	47	59 2/3	3	0	1.000	30	22	47	1.06	11
2009	Oakland	A.L.	69	73 1/3	2	4	.333	54	28	82	3.07	7
2010	Oakland	A.L.	64	60 2/3	3	7	.300	41	28	54	3.26	0
Major League Totals		3 Yrs.	180	193 2/3	8	11	.421	125	78	183	2.51	18

a Released by Philadelphia Phillies, March 28, 2004. Signed with independent Schaumburg (Northern), April 18, 2004.
b Sold to Oakland Athletics organization, June 16, 2004.

ZIMMERMANN, JORDAN M.

Born, Auburndale, Wisconsin, May 23, 1986.
Bats Right. Throws Right. Height, 6 feet, 2 inches. Weight, 220 pounds.

Year	Club	Lea	G	IP	W	L	Pct	SO	BB	H	ERA	SAVES
2007	Vermont	N.Y.-Penn.	13	53	5	2	.714	71	18	45	2.38	0
2008	Potomac	Carolina	5	27 1/3	3	1	.750	31	8	15	1.65	1
2008	Harrisburg	Eastern	20	106 2/3	7	2	.778	103	39	89	3.21	0
2009	Potomac	Carolina	1	3 1/3	0	0	.000	6	1	2	2.70	0
2009	Syracuse	Int.	1	5 1/3	0	0	.000	4	1	4	5.06	0
2009	Washington a	N.L.	16	91 1/3	3	5	.375	92	29	95	4.63	0
2010	Hagerstown	So.Atl.	1	5	0	1	.000	3	1	7	10.80	0
2010	Potomac	Carolina	4	13	0	1	.000	13	0	11	0.00	0
2010	Harrisburg	Eastern	1	4 2/3	0	0	.000	3	2	1	0.00	0
2010	Syracuse	Int.	4	17	1	0	1.000	12	3	8	0.53	0
2010	Washington b	N.L.	7	31	1	2	.333	27	10	31	4.94	0
Major League Totals		2 Yrs.	23	122 1/3	4	7	.364	119	39	126	4.71	0

a On disabled list from July 19 to November 8, 2009.
b On disabled list from February 19 to July 31, 2010.

ZITO, BARRY WILLIAM

Born, Las Vegas, Nevada, May 13, 1978.
Bats Left. Throws Left. Height, 6 feet, 4 inches. Weight, 210 pounds.

Year	Club	Lea	G	IP	W	L	Pct	SO	BB	H	ERA	SAVES
1999	Vancouver	P.C.	1	6	1	0	1.000	6	2	5	1.50	0
1999	Midland	Texas	4	22	2	1	.667	29	11	22	4.91	0
1999	Visalia	California	8	40 1/3	3	0	1.000	62	22	21	2.45	0
2000	Sacramento	P.C.	18	101 2/3	8	5	.615	91	45	88	3.19	0
2000	Oakland	A.L.	14	92 2/3	7	4	.636	78	45	64	2.72	0
2001	Oakland	A.L.	35	214 1/3	17	8	.680	205	80	184	3.49	0
2002	Oakland a	A.L.	35	229 1/3	*23	5	.821	182	78	182	2.75	0
2003	Oakland	A.L.	35	231 2/3	14	12	.538	146	88	186	3.30	0
2004	Oakland	A.L.	34	213	11	11	.500	163	81	216	4.48	0
2005	Oakland	A.L.	35	228 1/3	14	13	.519	171	89	185	3.86	0
2006	Oakland b	A.L.	34	221	16	10	.615	151	99	211	3.83	0
2007	San Francisco	N.L.	34	196 2/3	11	13	.458	131	83	182	4.53	0
2008	San Francisco	N.L.	32	180	10	*17	.370	120	102	186	5.15	0
2009	San Francisco	N.L.	33	192	10	13	.435	154	81	179	4.03	0
2010	San Francisco	N.L.	34	199 1/3	9	14	.391	150	84	184	4.15	0
Major League Totals		11 Yrs.	355	2198 1/3	142	120	.542	1651	910	1959	3.86	0

Year Club	Lea	G	IP	W	L	Pct	SO	BB	H	ERA	SAVES
Division Series											
2000 Oakland	A.L.	1	5 2/3	1	0	1.000	5	2	7	1.59	0
2001 Oakland	A.L.	1	8	0	1	.000	6	1	2	1.13	0
2002 Oakland	A.L.	1	6	1	0	1.000	8	4	5	4.50	0
2003 Oakland	A.L.	2	13	1	1	.500	13	4	9	3.46	0
2006 Oakland	A.L.	1	8	1	0	1.000	1	3	4	1.13	0
Division Series Totals		6	40 2/3	4	2	.667	33	14	27	2.43	0
Championship Series											
2006 Oakland	A.L.	1	3 2/3	0	1	.000	0	3	7	12.27	0

a Selected Cy Young Award Winner in American League for 2002.
b Filed for free agency, October 31, 2006. Signed with San Francisco Giants, December 29, 2006.

ZUMAYA, JOEL MARTIN

Born, Chula Vista, California, November 9, 1984.
Bats Right. Throws Right. Height, 6 feet, 3 inches. Weight, 210 pounds.

Year Club	Lea	G	IP	W	L	Pct	SO	BB	H	ERA	SAVES
2002 Tigers	Gulf Coast	9	37 1/3	2	1	.667	46	11	21	1.93	0
2003 West Michigan	Midwest	19	90 1/3	7	5	.583	126	38	69	2.79	0
2004 Erie	Eastern	4	20	2	2	.500	29	10	19	6.30	0
2004 Lakeland	Fla.St.	16	94	6	4	.600	92	43	65	3.54	0
2005 Erie	Eastern	18	107 1/3	8	3	.727	143	52	71	2.77	0
2005 Toledo	Int.	8	44	1	2	.333	56	24	30	2.66	0
2006 Detroit	A.L.	62	83 1/3	6	3	.667	97	42	56	1.94	1
2007 Toledo	Int.	3	2 2/3	0	0	.000	2	2	3	6.75	0
2007 Detroit a	A.L.	28	33 2/3	2	3	.400	27	17	23	4.28	1
2008 Lakeland	Fla.St.	2	3	0	0	.000	2	1	1	0.00	0
2008 Toledo	Int.	4	4	0	0	.000	4	2	5	2.25	0
2008 Detroit b	A.L.	21	23 1/3	0	2	.000	22	22	24	3.47	1
2009 Lakeland	Fla.St.	2	2 1/3	0	1	.000	4	5	3	11.57	0
2009 Toledo	Int.	3	4	0	0	.000	5	0	3	0.00	0
2009 Detroit c	A.L.	29	31	3	3	.500	30	22	34	4.94	1
2010 Detroit d	A.L.	31	38 1/3	2	1	.667	34	11	32	2.58	1
Major League Totals	5 Yrs.	171	209 2/3	13	12	.520	210	114	169	3.05	5
Division Series											
2006 Detroit	A.L.	2	2	0	0	.000	3	0	0	0.00	0
Championship Series											
2006 Detroit	A.L.	1	1	0	0	.000	0	0	1	9.00	0
World Series Record											
2006 Detroit	A.L.	3	3	0	1	.000	3	3	1	3.00	0

a On disabled list from May 3 to August 21, 2007.
b On disabled list from March 30 to June 20 and August 13 to September 30, 2008.
c On disabled list from March 27 to April 25 and July 18 to November 6, 2009.
d On disabled list from June 29 to November 2, 2010.

Photo Courtesy of the Seattle Mariners

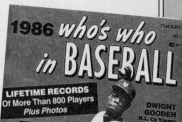